Philosophy, Politics, and Economics

An Anthology

By

Jonathan Anomaly
Duke University, University of North Carolina

Geoffrey Brennan
Duke University, University of North Carolina

Michael C. Munger
Duke University

Geoffrey Sayre-McCord
University of North Carolina

New York Oxford
OXFORD UNIVERSITY PRESS

It furthers the University's objective of excellence in research, scholarship, and education by publishing worldwide.

Oxford New York
Auckland Cape Town Dar es Salaam Hong Kong Karachi
Kuala Lumpur Madrid Melbourne Mexico City Nairobi
New Delhi Shanghai Taipei Toronto

With offices in
Argentina Austria Brazil Chile Czech Republic France Greece
Guatemala Hungary Italy Japan Poland Portugal Singapore
South Korea Switzerland Thailand Turkey Ukraine Vietnam

For titles covered by Section 112 of the US Higher Education Opportunity Act please visit www.oup.com/us/he for the latest information about pricing and alternate formats.

Published by Oxford University Press
198 Madison Avenue, New York, New York 10016
http://www.oup.com

Library of Congress Cataloging-in-Publication Data
Anomaly, Jonathan.
Philosophy, politics, and economics : an anthology / by Jonathan Anomaly, Duke University, UNC Chapel Hill, Geoffrey Brennan, Duke University, UNC Chapel Hill, Michael C. Munger, Duke University, Geoffrey Sayre-McCord, UNC Chapel Hill.
pages cm
Includes bibliographical references.
ISBN 978-0-19-020731-1
1. Political science--Philosophy. 2. Economics--Philosophy. 3. Social sciences--Philosophy.
I. Brennan, Geoffrey, 1944- II. Munger, Michael C. III. Sayre-McCord, Geoffrey, 1956- IV. Title.
JA71.A586 2015
320.1--dc23

2014044469

Printing number: 9 8 7 6 5 4 3 2

Printed in the United States of America
on acid-free paper

Contents

Preface

Philosophy, politics, and economics (PPE) began as an interdisciplinary degree program at Oxford in 1924. Nearly a century later it has spread to over one hundred universities around the world as a significant area of study. Although research at the intersection of the three disciplines has flourished for decades, no anthology has attempted to map the terrain of PPE as a research program.

This book is intended as a primer for PPE students, and a reference for those interested in the core topics that comprise PPE. Although we briefly introduce each topic and review some key concepts at the beginning of each chapter, we do not pretend to cover the entire field. Instead, we end each chapter introduction with a list of further readings, and refer readers to introductory textbooks like Daniel Hausman's *Economic Analysis, Moral Philosophy, and Public Policy*, and Jerry Gaus's *On Philosophy, Politics and Economics.* Professor Gaus has had a profound influence on each of us, and we take great pleasure in dedicating this book to him.

Like the PPE program at Duke and the University of North Carolina, this book was a collaborative effort. Anomaly spearheaded the project and wrote the chapter introductions, but all of us contributed to the content and organization of the book. In many ways, the finished product embodies Adam Smith's lesson that the division of labor and exchange of ideas can produce surprising and salutary results. We would especially like to thank Alyssa Palazzo and Robert Miller at Oxford University Press, our copy editor, Elizabeth Bortka, and Lauren Katz at Duke University. We would also like to thank Elizabeth Anderson, Erik Angner, Jack Barlow, Colin Bird, Jason Brennan, Paul Hurley, David Lefkowitz, Loren Lomasky, David Schmidtz, and Kevin Vallier for their helpful comments on an earlier draft.

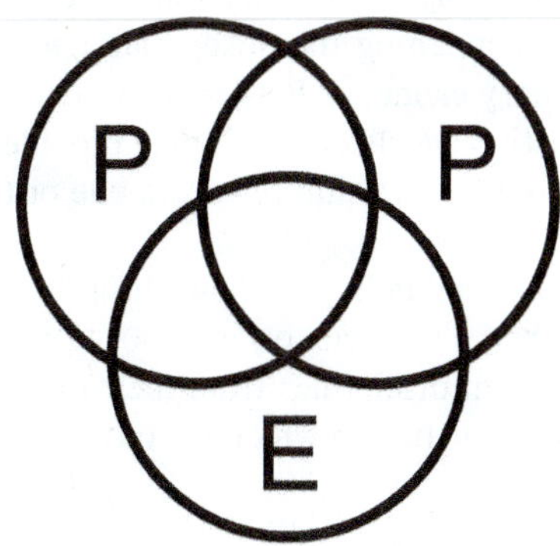

Introduction

Any PPE Program, whatever its distinctiveness in other ways, is committed to the idea that there is value in doing philosophy, political science, and economics in juxtaposition.

That value reflects two facts:

1. Many important issues—from environmental pollution to vaccination policy, from global poverty to the proliferation of nuclear weapons—have moral, political, and economic dimensions.
2. The three disciplines, having developed in isolation and largely independently, lead us to think about their overlapping subject matter in rather different ways—ways that often sit uncomfortably together and can be difficult to reconcile.

This second fact is worth emphasizing. Disciplines are distinguished not just by their different subject matter but also by their different ways of thinking. A good PPE student can simultaneously look at the world through different windows, and be aware in each case of the characteristic features of the disciplinary perspective she is using. She can recognize where there are conflicts between disciplinary visions and what reconciliations might be on offer. She derives from this capacity a perspective—something that is both broad and deep—that is an important intellectual accomplishment.[1]

In this sense, PPE takes the component disciplines as having presumptive authority. The object of PPE is not to do philosophy, political science, or economics *better.* It is to bring a perspective to issues all three take within their purview in a different, and revealing, way. It is true that each discipline will be somewhat critical of its fellows—each will think that the others get something important wrong. PPE is not some overarching grand synthesis that will resolve these differences—something like a separate approach, more or less rival to each of the component disciplinary elements. Rather, as we understand it, PPE offers a distinctive perspective—not a distinctive discipline—that provides insight not available to those who consider social and political institutions from one or the other disciplines to the exclusion of the others.

The PPE student gains an understanding of how the primary disciplines fit together with—or break from—each other. The focus on juxtaposition is meant to distinguish the *intersection* of the three component disciplines from their *union.* In our view, a PPE program is not well constituted by a structure in which the only requirement is that students do courses in each discipline separately. Students rapidly become adept at putting on their respective disciplinary hats and doing what their various courses require. But PPE demands, we think, the exercise of exploring the contrasts and complementarities between different "hats"—something most effectively done in an organized context rather than left to students to do, unaided, if they happen to decide to pursue it for themselves.

The selection of readings in this anthology is designed to facilitate precisely this kind of exploration. We have chosen selections by philosophers, political scientists, and economists that we hope will make salient the different approaches to issues where each discipline sees itself (we think rightly) as having something distinctive to say. We hope that students might ask questions, in each case, about what each discipline brings to the topic.

The readings are deliberately heterogeneous in other ways. Some of them are directed at substantive topics, like the operation of markets both in general and in specific cases (such as sex and drugs and human organs). Some are directed at broadly methodological questions, like how to understand "rationality" or "paternalism." And we have aimed for a mix of classical and contemporary authors.

Of course, all of the classical works (written by Hobbes, Rousseau, Hume, Smith, Marx, and Mill) were written at a time when the division of intellectual labor was much less finely grained than it now is—where the separation of economics from philosophy, and of philosophy from politics, had simply not occurred. These classical writers by necessity speak in a PPE voice; engaging with their ideas invites the student to focus on the intersection between Ph, PS, and E. But it remains an interesting question as to what each discipline, as it has developed, is likely to take from each reading—and why.

In making the selection, there were many options. A strong case can be made for including topics that we have omitted (such as social choice or invisible hand mechanisms or feasibility considerations in ethics, all of which we would have included had we the space) and for different readings than the ones we finally chose. Although we managed in the end to come to a consensus, there were, predictably enough, some differences that had to be negotiated among us. As economics insists, life is full of hard choices! And of course, PPE tends to be differently viewed depending on the base discipline from which one approaches it.

Each section is prefaced by short explanatory introductions and followed with suggestions for further reading, should a course designer want to focus more attention on particular topics or pursue them at a more advanced level. Our aim has been to choose readings that are student-friendly. But we do not think the readings are easy. Almost all of them deal with ideas that deserve a lot of thought. Our own experience in teaching PPE is that it is a bad idea to overload students with reading. They need to complement detailed textual study with serious reflection: they ought to be encouraged to engage with the ideas rather than simply describe what some author says. Put another way, a clear understanding of the message in the texts should be seen as a prerequisite to, and instrumental for, engagement with the arguments. We do not see PPE as simply describing what the different disciplines do. We want students to get down into the fray—to work out for themselves what approaches are useful, which arguments are coherent, and what claims can be defended by them as true.

NOTE

1. This second aspect is one of the features that distinguishes PPE from the related interdisciplinary exercises of "policy studies." For example, a course in policy studies will tend to select policy issues for their immediate relevance or their practical import, whereas PPE tends to select issues to be addressed with an eye to their conceptual value: issues should illuminate the differences between the economic and philosophical approaches, or between optimization with and without political constraints. The object ought to be to make salient the differences in disciplinary perspectives, as well as to show how a sense of those differences can have important policy upshots. Moreover, whereas "policy studies" by definition tends to focus on issues of policy, PPE might well range over comparisons of political *institutions*—democracy (under various descriptions) or federalism or the normative authority of national boundaries, matters that a policy focus tends to take as given.

1 Political Authority

To what extent, and under what conditions, is the state morally justified in coercing citizens? Is there a corresponding moral obligation to obey the state's directives apart from the threat of punishment for disobedience, or the moral content of the directive itself? These are the central questions of political authority. Plato is among the first philosophers to address these questions—most fully in his dialogue, "Crito." Socrates, having been convicted by a jury of his peers for corrupting the youth, and denying the existence of the officially recognized gods, finds himself in jail facing a penalty of death. The dialogue begins with a visit by Crito, who arranges for Socrates's escape. Socrates is willing to go along with Crito's plan if he can be convinced that he does not have an obligation to obey the authorities who have sentenced him. He tells Crito that the political society in which he finds himself helped raise and nurture him, like a surrogate parent, and has given him the opportunity to leave when he came of age. Consequently, by remaining in the country he seems to have tacitly consented to the authority of the government. Can he complain when the verdict of its court system convicts him of violating its laws?

In a frequently cited passage in Plato's *Republic* Socrates's interlocutor, Glaucon, suggests a different—contractarian—foundation for the state's authority.

> They say that to do injustice is, by nature, good; to suffer injustice, evil; but that the evil is greater than the good. And so when men have both done and suffered injustice and have had experience of both, not being able to avoid the one and obtain the other, they think that they had better agree among themselves to have neither; hence there arise laws and mutual covenants; and that which is ordained by law is termed by them lawful and just. This they affirm to be the origin and nature of justice; it is a mean or compromise, between the best of all, which is to do injustice and not be punished, and the worst of all, which is to suffer injustice without the power of retaliation; and justice, being at a middle point between the two, is tolerated not as a good, but as the lesser evil, and honored by reason of the inability of men to do injustice. For no man who is worthy to be called a man would ever submit to such an agreement if he were able to resist; he would be mad if he did. Such is the received account, Socrates, of the nature and origin of justice.

Glaucon suggests that the authority of the state's laws derives from their being mutually advantageous. In doing so, he anticipates Hobbes's theory of political authority by first describing why people's desires are frustrated in conditions of anarchy, and then suggesting that our goals are likely to be better achieved by submitting to a common set of rules or conventions.

Hobbes's theory of political authority is striking in its attempt to derive a powerful conclusion from parsimonious premises. Hobbes assumes that people have a diversity of desires—desires that vary across people and change throughout each person's life. But there is at least one overriding desire that we all have in common: the desire to live, and to satisfy future desires.

Because our ends conflict, and resources are scarce, we are ensnared in conflict that can be modeled along the lines of prisoner's dilemmas and assurance games (see chapter 3 for more on this). Although it may be anachronistic to graft concepts from game theory onto Hobbes's argument for the authority of government, they nicely capture the logic of his argument. The only way to avoid perpetual war in a state of nature, Hobbes suggests, is to cede our unlimited right to pursue our ends without constraint to a third party with the power to establish and enforce a common set of rules. It is the unique ability of a powerful third party—a "Leviathan," or sovereign—to force people to behave themselves that is, on Hobbes's view, the foundation of political authority.

Hobbes seems to think *actual* consent is not necessary for generating political obligation. Instead, he suggests that if a government makes us better off than we would be in a state of nature, this fact suffices to establish that people would have reason to consent (given the grim alternatives), and that is enough to create political authority.

Locke takes a different view, claiming that even in a state of nature people possess moral rights. Government does not create our moral rights, as Hobbes supposes, but is merely a fair and efficient way to secure our rights. Government acquires authority based on consent, and retains authority only so long as it acts as an impartial umpire in adjudicating rights disputes. Locke suggests that political authority can be based on express consent to a set of political institutions, or tacit consent, implied by enjoying the government's protections and declining to emigrate.

Hume seizes on this aspect of Locke's theory and argues that tacit consent cannot justify political authority unless emigration is a viable option. If leaving a state is costly or dangerous, the choice to remain is deeply constrained rather than freely chosen. But then political authority cannot be justified on tacit consent grounds, undermining the force of any theory of political obligation that rests on consent.

Like Hobbes and Locke, Rousseau works within the social contract tradition, which grounds political authority in consent. Like Hobbes and Locke, Rousseau assumes people have more liberty but less security in the state of nature. Resource scarcity induces people to form a political society through which they can arrive at a set of mutually advantageous rules. But not just any rules will do. For Rousseau, unlike Locke and Hobbes, a state only has authority over its citizens if its institutions are democratic (and each citizen has consented to its institutions). Rousseau suggests that only a democratic process can transform each individual's will into a "general will" that has moral authority over all citizens, including those who oppose any particular law that emerges from the democratic process. Some degree of democracy is, then, a necessary but not sufficient condition for authority.

Recent philosophers like John Simmons and Michael Huemer have considered traditional arguments from Plato to the present and found none of them compelling. They conclude that we should take seriously the position that most states simply do not have moral authority over their citizens, since most citizens have not had an opportunity to consent to the state's putative authority. On this view, often called philosophical anarchism (as distinct from political anarchism), we are obligated to submit to the state's decrees only if those decrees coincide with moral obligations we already have.

FURTHER READING

Hampton, Jean. 1988. *Hobbes and the Social Contract Tradition*. Cambridge University Press.

Hardin, Russell. 1989. "Rationally Justifying Political Coercion." *Journal of Philosophical Research* 15: 79–92.

Huemer, Michael. 2012. *The Problem of Political Authority*. Palgrave MacMillan.

Kavka, Gregory. 1986. *Hobbesian Moral and Political Theory*. Princeton University Press.

Klosko, George. 2005. *Political Obligations*. Oxford University Press.

Simmons, John. 2002. "Political Obligation and Authority." In Robert Simon, ed. *The Blackwell Guide to Social and Political Philosophy*. Wiley-Blackwell Press.

PLATO

Crito

360 BCE

About the time of Socrates' trial, a state galley had set out on an annual religious mission to Delos and while it was away no execution was allowed to take place. So it was that Socrates was kept in prison for a month after the trial. The ship has now arrived at Cape Sunium in Attica and is thus expected at the Piraeus momentarily. So Socrates' old and faithful friend, Crito, makes one last effort to persuade him to escape into exile, and all arrangements for this plan have been made. It is this conversation between the two old friends that Plato professes to report in this dialogue. It is, as Crito plainly tells him, his last chance, but Socrates will not take it, and he gives his reasons for his refusal. Whether this conversation took place at this particular time is not important, for there is every reason to believe that Socrates' friends tried to plan his escape, and that he refused. Plato more than hints that the authorities would not have minded much, as long as he left the country.

43 SOCRATES: Why have you come so early, Crito? Or is it not still early?

CRITO: It certainly is.

S: How early?

C: Early dawn.

S: I am surprised that the warder was willing to listen to you.

C: He is quite friendly to me by now, Socrates. I have been here often and I have given him something.

S: Have you just come, or have you been here for some time?

C: A fair time.

S: Then why did you not wake me right away but b
sit there in silence?

From Plato and G. M. A. Grube, *Five Dialogues*. Indianapolis: Hackett Pub. Co., 2002.

C: By Zeus no, Socrates. I would not myself want to be in distress and awake so long. I have been surprised to see you so peacefully asleep. It was on purpose that I did not wake you, so that you should spend your time most agreeably. Often in the past throughout my life, I have considered the way you live happy, and especially so now that you bear your present misfortune so easily and lightly.

S: It would not be fitting at my age to resent the fact that I must die now.

c C: Other men of your age are caught in such misfortunes, but their age does not prevent them resenting their fate.

S: That is so. Why have you come so early?

C: I bring bad news, Socrates, not for you, apparently, but for me and all your friends the news is bad and hard to bear. Indeed, I would count it among the hardest.

d S: What is it? Or has the ship arrived from Delos, at the arrival of which I must die?

C: It has not arrived yet, but it will, I believe, arrive today, according to a message brought by some men from Sunium, where they left it. This makes it obvious that it will come today, and that your life must end tomorrow.

S: May it be for the best. If it so please the gods, so be it. However, I do not think it will arrive today.

C: What indication have you of this?

44 S: I will tell you. I must die the day after the ship arrives.

C: That is what those in authority say.

S: Then I do not think it will arrive on this coming day, but on the next. I take to witness of this a dream I had a little earlier during this night. It looks as if it was the right time for you not to wake me.

C: What was your dream?

S: I thought that a beautiful and comely woman
b dressed in white approached me. She called me and said: "Socrates, may you arrive at fertile Phthia[1] on the third day."

C: A strange dream, Socrates.

S: But it seems clear enough to me, Crito.

C: Too clear it seems, my dear Socrates, but listen to me even now and be saved. If you die, it will not be a single misfortune for me. Not only will I be deprived of a friend, the like of whom I shall never find again, but many people who do not know you or me very well will think that I could have saved you if I
were willing to spend money, but that I did not care c
to do so. Surely there can be no worse reputation than to be thought to value money more highly than one's friends, for the majority will not believe that you yourself were not willing to leave prison while we were eager for you to do so.

S: My good Crito, why should we care so much for what the majority think? The most reasonable people, to whom one should pay more attention, will believe that things were done as they were done.

C: You see, Socrates, that one must also pay atten- d
tion to the opinion of the majority. Your present situation makes clear that the majority can inflict not the least but pretty well the greatest evils if one is slandered among them.

S: Would that the majority could inflict the greatest evils, for they would then be capable of the greatest good, and that would be fine, but now they cannot do either. They cannot make a man either wise or foolish, but they inflict things haphazardly.

C: That may be so. But tell me this, Socrates, are e
you anticipating that I and your other friends would have trouble with the informers if you escape from here, as having stolen you away, and that we should be compelled to lose all our property or pay heavy fines and suffer other punishment besides? If you
have any such fear, forget it. We would be justified in 45
running this risk to save you, and worse, if necessary. Do follow my advice, and do not act differently.

S: I do have these things in mind, Crito, and also many others.

C: Have no such fear. It is not much money that some people require to save you and get you out of here. Further, do you not see that those informers are cheap, and that not much money would be needed to deal with them? My money is available and is, I think, sufficient. If, because of your affection for me,
you feel you should not spend any of mine, there are b
those strangers here ready to spend money. One of them, Simmias the Theban, has brought enough for this very purpose. Cebes, too, and a good many others. So, as I say, do not let this fear make you hesitate to save yourself, nor let what you said in court trouble you, that you would not know what to do with

yourself if you left Athens, for you would be wel-
c comed in many places to which you might go. If you want to go to Thessaly, I have friends there who will greatly appreciate you and keep you safe, so that no one in Thessaly will harm you.

Besides, Socrates, I do not think that what you are doing is right, to give up your life when you can save it, and to hasten your fate as your enemies would hasten it, and indeed have hastened it in their wish to destroy you. Moreover, I think you are betraying
d your sons by going away and leaving them, when you could bring them up and educate them. You thus show no concern for what their fate may be. They will probably have the usual fate of orphans. Either one should not have children, or one should share with them to the end the toil of upbringing and education. You seem to me to choose the easiest path, whereas one should choose the path a good and courageous man would choose, particularly when one claims throughout one's life to care for virtue.

e I feel ashamed on your behalf and on behalf of us, your friends, lest all that has happened to you be thought due to cowardice on our part: the fact that your trial came to court when it need not have done so, the handling of the trial itself, and now this absurd ending which will be thought to have got beyond our control through some cowardice and
46 unmanliness on our part, since we did not save you, or you save yourself, when it was possible and could be done if we had been of the slightest use. Consider, Socrates, whether this is not only evil, but shameful, both for you and for us. Take counsel with yourself, or rather the time for counsel is past and the decision should have been taken, and there is no further opportunity, for this whole business must be ended tonight. If we delay now, then it will no longer be possible, it will be too late. Let me persuade you on every count, Socrates, and do not act otherwise.

b S: My dear Crito, your eagerness is worth much if it should have some right aim; if not, then the greater your keenness the more difficult it is to deal with. We must therefore examine whether we should act in this way or not, as not only now but at all times I am the kind of man who listens only to the argument that on reflection seems best to me. I cannot, now that this fate has come upon me, discard the arguments I used; they seem to me much the same. I value and respect the same principles as before, and if we have no c
better arguments to bring up at this moment, be sure that I shall not agree with you, not even if the power of the majority were to frighten us with more bogeys, as if we were children, with threats of incarcerations and executions and confiscation of property. How should we examine this matter most reasonably? Would it be by taking up first your argument about the opinions of men, whether it is sound in every case that one should pay attention to some opinions, but d
not to others? Or was that well-spoken before the necessity to die came upon me, but now it is clear that this was said in vain for the sake of argument, that it was in truth play and nonsense?

I am eager to examine together with you, Crito, whether this argument will appear in any way different to me in my present circumstances, or whether it remains the same, whether we are to abandon it or believe it. It was said on every occasion by those who thought they were speaking sensibly, as I have just now been speaking, that one should greatly value e
some people's opinions, but not others. Does that seem to you a sound statement?

You, as far as a human being can tell, are exempt from the likelihood of dying tomorrow, so the present misfortune is not likely to lead you astray. Con- 47
sider then, do you not think it a sound statement that one must not value all the opinions of men, but some and not others, nor the opinions of all men, but those of some and not of others? What do you say? Is this not well said?

C: It is.

S: One should value the good opinions, and not the bad ones?

C: Yes.

S: The good opinions are those of wise men, the bad ones those of foolish men?

C: Of course.

S: Come then, what of statements such as this: Should a man professionally engaged in physical b
training pay attention to the praise and blame and opinion of any man, or to those of one man only, namely a doctor or trainer?

C: To those of one only.

S: He should therefore fear the blame and welcome the praise of that one man, and not those of the many?

C: Obviously.

S: He must then act and exercise, eat and drink in the way the one, the trainer and the one who knows, thinks right, not all the others?

C: That is so.

c S: Very well. And if he disobeys the one, disregards his opinion and his praises while valuing those
of the many who have no knowledge, will he not
suffer harm?

C: Of course.

S: What is that harm, where does it tend, and what part of the man who disobeys does it affect?

C: Obviously the harm is to his body, which it ruins.

S: Well said. So with other matters, not to enumerate them all, and certainly with actions just and
unjust, shameful and beautiful, good and bad, about
which we are now deliberating, should we follow the
d opinion of the many and fear it, or that of the one, if
there is one who has knowledge of these things and
before whom we feel fear and shame more than
before all the others. If we do not follow his directions, we shall harm and corrupt that part of ourselves that is improved by just actions and destroyed
by unjust actions. Or is there nothing in this?

C: I think there certainly is, Socrates.

S: Come now, if we ruin that which is improved
by health and corrupted by disease by not following
the opinions of those who know, is life worth living
e for us when that is ruined? And that is the body, is
it not?

C: Yes.

S: And is life worth living with a body that is corrupted and in bad condition?

C: In no way.

S: And is life worth living for us with that part of
us corrupted that unjust action harms and just action
benefits? Or do we think that part of us, whatever it
is, that is concerned with justice and injustice, is in-
48 ferior to the body?

C: Not at all.

S: It is more valuable?

C: Much more.

S: We should not then think so much of what the majority will say about us, but what he will say who understands justice and injustice, the one, that is, and the truth itself. So that, in the first place, you were wrong to believe that we should care for the opinion of the many about what is just, beautiful, good, and their opposites. "But," someone might say "the many are able to put us to death."

C: That too is obvious, Socrates, and someone b
might well say so.

S: And, my admirable friend, that argument that we have gone through remains, I think, as before. Examine the following statement in turn as to whether it stays the same or not, that the most important thing is not life, but the good life.

C: It stays the same.

S: And that the good life, the beautiful life, and the just life are the same; does that still hold, or not?

C: It does hold.

S: As we have agreed so far, we must examine
next whether it is right for me to try to get out of here c
when the Athenians have not acquitted me. If it is
seen to be right, we will try to do so; if it is not, we
will abandon the idea. As for those questions you
raise about money, reputation, the upbringing of
children, Crito, those considerations in truth belong
to those people who easily put men to death and
would bring them to life again if they could, without
thinking; I mean the majority of men. For us, however, since our argument leads to this, the only valid
consideration, as we were saying just now, is whether
we should be acting rightly in giving money and
gratitude to those who will lead me out of here, and
ourselves helping with the escape, or whether in d
truth we shall do wrong in doing all this. If it appears
that we shall be acting unjustly, then we have no need
at all to take into account whether we shall have to
die if we stay here and keep quiet, or suffer in another way, rather than do wrong.

C: I think you put that beautifully, Socrates, but see what we should do.

S: Let us examine the question together, my dear e
friend, and if you can make any objection while I am
speaking, make it and I will listen to you, but if you
have no objection to make, my dear Crito, then stop
now from saying the same thing so often, that I must

leave here against the will of the Athenians. I think it
important to persuade you before I act, and not to act
against your wishes. See whether the start of our en-
49 quiry is adequately stated, and try to answer what I
ask you in the way you think best.

C: I shall try.

S: Do we say that one must never in any way do
wrong willingly, or must one do wrong in one way
and not in another? Is to do wrong never good or admirable, as we have agreed in the past, or have all
these former agreements been washed out during the
last few days? Have we at our age failed to notice for
b some time that in our serious discussions we were no
different from children? Above all, is the truth such
as we used to say it was, whether the majority agree
or not, and whether we must still suffer worse things
than we do now, or will be treated more gently, that
nonetheless, wrongdoing is in every way harmful
and shameful to the wrongdoer? Do we say so or not?

C: We do.

S: So one must never do wrong.

C: Certainly not.

S: Nor must one, when wronged, inflict wrong in return, as the majority believe, since one must never do wrong.

c C: That seems to be the case.

S: Come now, should one injure anyone or not, Crito?

C: One must never do so.

S: Well then, if one is oneself injured, is it right, as the majority say, to inflict an injury in return, or is it not?

C: It is never right.

S: Injuring people is no different from wrongdoing.

C: That is true.

S: One should never do wrong in return, nor injure
d any man, whatever injury one has suffered at his
hands. And Crito, see that you do not agree to this,
contrary to your belief. For I know that only a few
people hold this view or will hold it, and there is no
common ground between those who hold this view
and those who do not, but they inevitably despise
each other's views. So then consider very carefully
whether we have this view in common, and whether
you agree, and let this be the basis of our deliberation, that neither to do wrong or to return a wrong is
ever right, not even to injure in return for an injury
received. Or do you disagree and do not share this
view as a basis for discussion? I have held it for a long e
time and still hold it now, but if you think otherwise,
tell me now. If, however, you stick to our former
opinion, then listen to the next point.

C: I stick to it and agree with you. So say on.

S: Then I state the next point, or rather I ask you: when one has come to an agreement that is just with someone, should one fulfill it or cheat on it?

C: One should fulfill it.

S: See what follows from this: if we leave here
without the city's permission, are we injuring people 50
whom we should least injure? And are we sticking to
a just agreement, or not?

C: I cannot answer your question, Socrates. I do not know.

S: Look at it this way. If, as we were planning to
run away from here, or whatever one should call it,
the laws and the state came and confronted us and
asked: "Tell me, Socrates, what are you intending to
do? Do you not by this action you are attempting
intend to destroy us, the laws, and indeed the whole b
city, as far as you are concerned? Or do you think it
possible for a city not to be destroyed if the verdicts
of its courts have no force but are nullified and set at
naught by private individuals?" What shall we answer
to this and other such arguments? For many things
could be said, especially by an orator on behalf of
this law we are destroying, which orders that the
judgments of the courts shall be carried out. Shall we
say in answer, "The city wronged me, and its deci- c
sion was not right." Shall we say that, or what?

C: Yes, by Zeus, Socrates, that is our answer.

S: Then what if the laws said: "Was that the agreement between us, Socrates, or was it to respect the
judgments that the city came to?" And if we won-
dered at their words, they would perhaps add:
"Socrates, do not wonder at what we say but answer,
since you are accustomed to proceed by question and
answer. Come now, what accusation do you bring d
against us and the city, that you should try to destroy
us? Did we not, first, bring you to birth, and was it not
through us that your father married your mother and
begat you? Tell us, do you find anything to criticize
in those of us who are concerned with marriage?"

And I would say that I do not criticize them. "Or in
those of us concerned with the nurture of babies and
the education that you too received? Were those assigned to that subject not right to instruct your father
to educate you in the arts and in physical culture?"
e And I would say that they were right. "Very well,"
they would continue, "and after you were born and
nurtured and educated, could you, in the first place,
deny that you are our offspring and servant, both you
and your forefathers? If that is so, do you think that
we are on an equal footing as regards the right, and
that whatever we do to you it is right for you to do to
us? You were not on an equal footing with your father
as regards the right, nor with your master if you had
one, so as to retaliate for anything they did to you, to
51 revile them if they reviled you, to beat them if they
beat you, and so with many other things. Do you
think you have this right to retaliation against your
country and its laws? That if we undertake to destroy
you and think it right to do so, you can undertake to
destroy us, as far as you can, in return? And will you
say that you are right to do so, you who truly care for
virtue? Is your wisdom such as not to realize that
your country is to be honoured more than your
mother, your father and all your ancestors, that it is
more to be revered and more sacred, and that it
b counts for more among the gods and sensible men,
that you must worship it, yield to it and placate its
anger more than your father's? You must either persuade it or obey its orders, and endure in silence
whatever it instructs you to endure, whether blows or
bonds, and if it leads you into war to be wounded or
killed, you must obey. To do so is right, and one must
not give way or retreat or leave one's post, but both in
war and in courts and everywhere else, one must
obey the commands of one's city and country, or per-
c suade it as to the nature of justice. It is impious to
bring violence to bear against your mother or father,
it is much more so to use it against your country."
What shall we say in reply, Crito, that the laws speak
the truth, or not?

C: I think they do.

S: "Reflect now, Socrates," the laws might say
"that if what we say is true, you are not treating us
rightly by planning to do what you are planning. We
have given you birth, nurtured you, educated you, we
have given you and all other citizens a share of all d
the good things we could. Even so, by giving every
Athenian the opportunity, after he has reached manhood and observed the affairs of the city and us the
laws, we proclaim that if we do not please him, he
can take his possessions and go wherever he pleases.
Not one of our laws raises any obstacle or forbids
him, if he is not satisfied with us or the city, if one of
you wants to go and live in a colony or wants to go
anywhere else, and keep his property. We say, how- e
ever, that whoever of you remains, when he sees how
we conduct our trials and manage the city in other
ways, has in fact come to an agreement with us to
obey our instructions. We say that the one who disobeys does wrong in three ways, first because in us 52
he disobeys his parents, also those who brought him
up, and because, in spite of his agreement, he neither
obeys us nor, if we do something wrong, does he try
to persuade us to do better. Yet we only propose
things, we do not issue savage commands to do
whatever we order; we give two alternatives, either to
persuade us or to do what we say. He does neither.
We do say that you too, Socrates, are open to those
charges if you do what you have in mind; you would
be among, not the least, but the most guilty of the
Athenians." And if I should say "Why so?" they
might well be right to upbraid me and say that I am
among the Athenians who most definitely came to
that agreement with them. They might well say: b
"Socrates, we have convincing proofs that we and
the city were congenial to you. You would not have
dwelt here most consistently of all the Athenians if
the city had not been exceedingly pleasing to you.
You have never left the city, even to see a festival, nor
for any other reason except military service; you
have never gone to stay in any other city, as people
do; you have had no desire to know another city or c
other laws; we and our city satisfied you.

"So decisively did you choose us and agree to be
a citizen under us. Also, you have had children in
this city, thus showing that it was congenial to you.
Then at your trial you could have assessed your penalty at exile if you wished, and you are now attempting to do against the city's wishes what you could
then have done with her consent. Then you prided
yourself that you did not resent death, but you chose,

as you said, death in preference to exile. Now, however, those words do not make you ashamed, and you pay no heed to us, the laws, as you plan to destroy us,
d and you act like the meanest type of slave by trying to run away, contrary to your undertakings and your agreement to live as a citizen under us. First then, answer us on this very point, whether we speak the truth when we say that you agreed, not only in words but by your deeds, to live in accordance with us." What are we to say to that, Crito? Must we not agree?

C: We must, Socrates.

S: "Surely," they might say, "you are breaking the undertakings and agreements that you made with us
e without compulsion or deceit, and under no pressure of time for deliberation. You have had seventy years during which you could have gone away if you did not like us, and if you thought our agreements unjust. You did not choose to go to Sparta or to Crete, which
53 you are always saying are well governed, nor to any other city, Greek or foreign. You have been away from Athens less than the lame or the blind or other handicapped people. It is clear that the city has been outstandingly more congenial to you than to other Athenians, and so have we, the laws, for what city can please without laws? Will you then not now stick to our agreements? You will, Socrates, if we can persuade you, and not make yourself a laughingstock by leaving the city.

"For consider what good you will do yourself or your friends by breaking our agreements and committing such a wrong? It is pretty obvious that your friends will themselves be in danger of exile, dis-
b franchisement and loss of property. As for yourself, if you go to one of the nearby cities—Thebes or Megara, both are well governed—you will arrive as an enemy to their government; all who care for their city will look on you with suspicion, as a destroyer of the laws. You will also strengthen the conviction of the jury that they passed the right sentence on you, for anyone who destroys the laws could easily be
c thought to corrupt the young and the ignorant. Or will you avoid cities that are well governed and men who are civilized? If you do this, will your life be worth living? Will you have social intercourse with them and not be ashamed to talk to them? And what will you say? The same as you did here, that virtue and justice are man's most precious possession, along with lawful behaviour and the laws? Do you not think that Socrates would appear to be an un- d
seemly kind of person? One must think so. Or will you leave those places and go to Crito's friends in Thessaly? There you will find the greatest license and disorder, and they may enjoy hearing from you how absurdly you escaped from prison in some disguise, in a leather jerkin or some other things in which escapees wrap themselves, thus altering your appearance. Will there be no one to say that you, likely to live but a short time more, were so greedy for life that you transgressed the most important laws? Possibly, Socrates, if you do not annoy anyone, e
but if you do, many disgraceful things will be said about you.

"You will spend your time ingratiating yourself with all men, and be at their beck and call. What will you do in Thessaly but feast, as if you had gone to a banquet in Thessaly? As for those conversations of yours about justice and the rest of virtue, where will they be? You say you want to live for the sake of your 54
children, that you may bring them up and educate them. How so? Will you bring them up and educate them by taking them to Thessaly and making strangers of them, that they may enjoy that too? Or not so, but they will be better brought up and educated here, while you are alive, though absent? Yes, your friends will look after them. Will they look after them if you go and live in Thessaly, but not if you go away to the underworld? If those who profess themselves your friends are any good at all, one must assume b
that they will.

"Be persuaded by us who have brought you up, Socrates. Do not value either your children or your life or anything else more than goodness, in order that when you arrive in Hades you may have all this as your defence before the rulers there. If you do this deed, you will not think it better or more just or more pious here, nor will any one of your friends, nor will it be better for you when you arrive yonder. As it is, you depart, if you depart, after being wronged not by us, the laws, but by men; but if you depart after shame- c
fully returning wrong for wrong and injury for injury, after breaking your agreement and contract with us, after injuring those you should injure least—yourself,

your friends, your country and us—we shall be angry with you while you are still alive, and our brothers, the laws of the underworld, will not receive you kindly, knowing that you tried to destroy us as far as you could. Do not let Crito persuade you, rather than
d us, to do what he says."

Crito, my dear friend, be assured that these are the words I seem to hear, as the Corybants seem to hear the music of their flutes, and the echo of these words resounds in me, and makes it impossible for me to hear anything else. As far as my present beliefs go, if you speak in opposition to them, you will speak in vain. However, if you think you can accomplish anything, speak.

C: I have nothing to say, Socrates.

S: Let it be then, Crito, and let us act in this way,
since this is the way the god is leading us. e

NOTE

1. A quotation from the ninth book of the Iliad (363). Achilles has rejected all the presents of Agamemnon for him to return to the battle, and threatens to go home. He says his ships will sail in the morning, and with good weather he might arrive on the third day "in fertile Phthia" (which is his home). The dream means, obviously, that on the third day Socrates' soul, after death, will find its home. As always, counting the first member of a series, the third day is the day after tomorrow.

THOMAS HOBBES

Leviathan

1651

OF THE NATURAL CONDITION OF MANKIND AS CONCERNING THEIR FELICITY AND MISERY

NATURE hath made men so equal in the faculties of body and mind as that, though there be found one man sometimes manifestly stronger in body or of quicker mind than another, yet when all is reckoned together the difference between man and man is not so considerable as that one man can thereupon claim to himself any benefit to which another may not pretend as well as he. For as to the strength of body, the weakest has strength enough to kill the strongest, either by secret machination or by confederacy with others that are in the same danger with himself.

And as to the faculties of the mind, setting aside the arts grounded upon words, and especially that skill of proceeding upon general and infallible rules, called science, which very few have and but in few things, as being not a native faculty born with us, nor attained, as prudence, while we look after somewhat else, I find yet a greater equality amongst men than that of strength. For prudence is but experience, which equal time equally bestows on all men in those things they equally apply themselves unto. That which may perhaps make such equality incredible is but a vain conceit of one's own wisdom, which almost all men think they have in a greater degree

From Thomas Hobbes and A. R. Waller, *Leviathan*. Oxford: Clarendon Press, 1909.

than the vulgar; that is, than all men but themselves, and a few others, whom by fame, or for concurring with themselves, they approve. For such is the nature of men that howsoever they may acknowledge many others to be more witty, or more eloquent or more learned, yet they will hardly believe there be many so wise as themselves; for they see their own wit at hand, and other men's at a distance. But this proveth rather that men are in that point equal, than unequal. For there is not ordinarily a greater sign of the equal distribution of anything than that every man is contented with his share.

From this equality of ability ariseth equality of hope in the attaining of our ends. And therefore if any two men desire the same thing, which nevertheless they cannot both enjoy, they become enemies; and in the way to their end (which is principally their own conservation, and sometimes their delectation only) endeavour to destroy or subdue one another. And from hence it comes to pass that where an invader hath no more to fear than another man's single power, if one plant, sow, build, or possess a convenient seat, others may probably be expected to come prepared with forces united to dispossess and deprive him, not only of the fruit of his labour, but also of his life or liberty. And the invader again is in the like danger of another.

And from this diffidence of one another, there is no way for any man to secure himself so reasonable as anticipation; that is, by force, or wiles, to master the persons of all men he can so long till he see no other power great enough to endanger him: and this is no more than his own conservation requireth, and is generally allowed. Also, because there be some that, taking pleasure in contemplating their own power in the acts of conquest, which they pursue farther than their security requires, if others, that otherwise would be glad to be at ease within modest bounds, should not by invasion increase their power, they would not be able, long time, by standing only on their defence, to subsist. And by consequence, such augmentation of dominion over men being necessary to a man's conservation, it ought to be allowed him.

Again, men have no pleasure (but on the contrary a great deal of grief) in keeping company where there is no power able to overawe them all. For every man looketh that his companion should value him at the same rate he sets upon himself, and upon all signs of contempt or undervaluing naturally endeavours, as far as he dares (which amongst them that have no common power to keep them in quiet is far enough to make them destroy each other), to extort a greater value from his contemners, by damage; and from others, by the example.

So that in the nature of man, we find three principal causes of quarrel. First, competition; secondly, diffidence; thirdly, glory.

The first maketh men invade for gain; the second, for safety; and the third, for reputation. The first use violence, to make themselves masters of other men's persons, wives, children, and cattle; the second, to defend them; the third, for trifles, as a word, a smile, a different opinion, and any other sign of undervalue, either direct in their persons or by reflection in their kindred, their friends, their nation, their profession, or their name.

Hereby it is manifest that during the time men live without a common power to keep them all in awe, they are in that condition which is called war; and such a war as is of every man against every man. For WAR consisteth not in battle only, or the act of fighting, but in a tract of time, wherein the will to contend by battle is sufficiently known: and therefore the notion of time is to be considered in the nature of war, as it is in the nature of weather. For as the nature of foul weather lieth not in a shower or two of rain, but in an inclination thereto of many days together: so the nature of war consisteth not in actual fighting, but in the known disposition thereto during all the time there is no assurance to the contrary. All other time is PEACE.

Whatsoever therefore is consequent to a time of war, where every man is enemy to every man, the same consequent to the time wherein men live without other security than what their own strength and their own invention shall furnish them withal. In such condition there is no place for industry, because the fruit thereof is uncertain: and consequently no culture of the earth; no navigation, nor use of the commodities that may be imported by sea; no commodious building; no instruments of moving and removing such things as require much force; no knowledge of the face of the earth; no account of time; no arts; no letters; no society; and which is worst of all, continual fear, and danger of violent death; and the life of man, solitary, poor, nasty, brutish, and short.

It may seem strange to some man that has not well weighed these things that Nature should thus dissociate and render men apt to invade and destroy one another: and he may therefore, not trusting to this inference, made from the passions, desire perhaps to have the same confirmed by experience. Let him therefore consider with himself: when taking a journey, he arms himself and seeks to go well accompanied; when going to sleep, he locks his doors; when even in his house he locks his chests; and this when he knows there be laws and public officers, armed, to revenge all injuries shall be done him; what opinion he has of his fellow subjects, when he rides armed; of his fellow citizens, when he locks his doors; and of his children, and servants, when he locks his chests. Does he not there as much accuse mankind by his actions as I do by my words? But neither of us accuse man's nature in it. The desires, and other passions of man, are in themselves no sin. No more are the actions that proceed from those passions till they know a law that forbids them; which till laws be made they cannot know, nor can any law be made till they have agreed upon the person that shall make it.

It may peradventure be thought there was never such a time nor condition of war as this; and I believe it was never generally so, over all the world: but there are many places where they live so now. For the savage people in many places of America, except the government of small families, the concord whereof dependeth on natural lust, have no government at all, and live at this day in that brutish manner, as I said before. Howsoever, it may be perceived what manner of life there would be, where there were no common power to fear, by the manner of life which men that have formerly lived under a peaceful government use to degenerate into a civil war.

But though there had never been any time wherein particular men were in a condition of war one against another, yet in all times kings and persons of sovereign authority, because of their independency, are in continual jealousies, and in the state and posture of gladiators, having their weapons pointing, and their eyes fixed on one another; that is, their forts, garrisons, and guns upon the frontiers of their kingdoms, and continual spies upon their neighbours, which is a posture of war. But because they uphold thereby the industry of their subjects, there does not follow from it that misery which accompanies the liberty of particular men.

To this war of every man against every man, this also is consequent; that nothing can be unjust. The notions of right and wrong, justice and injustice, have there no place. Where there is no common power, there is no law; where no law, no injustice. Force and fraud are in war the two cardinal virtues. Justice and injustice are none of the faculties neither of the body nor mind. If they were, they might be in a man that were alone in the world, as well as his senses and passions. They are qualities that relate to men in society, not in solitude. It is consequent also to the same condition that there be no propriety, no dominion, no mine and thine distinct; but only that to be every man's that he can get, and for so long as he can keep it. And thus much for the ill condition which man by mere nature is actually placed in; though with a possibility to come out of it, consisting partly in the passions, partly in his reason.

The passions that incline men to peace are: fear of death; desire of such things as are necessary to commodious living; and a hope by their industry to obtain them. And reason suggesteth convenient articles of peace upon which men may be drawn to agreement. These articles are they which otherwise are called the laws of nature, whereof I shall speak more particularly in the two following chapters.

OF THE FIRST AND SECOND NATURAL LAWS, AND OF CONTRACTS

THE right of nature, which writers commonly call *jus naturale,* is the liberty each man hath to use his own power as he will himself for the preservation of his own nature; that is to say, of his own life; and consequently, of doing anything which, in his own judgement and reason, he shall conceive to be the aptest means thereunto.

By LIBERTY is understood, according to the proper signification of the word, the absence of external impediments; which impediments may oft take away part of a man's power to do what he would, but cannot hinder him from using the power left him according as his judgement and reason shall dictate to him.

A LAW OF NATURE, *lex naturalis,* is a precept, or general rule, found out by reason, by which a man is forbidden to do that which is destructive of his life, or taketh away the means of preserving the same, and to omit that by which he thinketh it may be best preserved. For though they that speak of this subject use to confound *jus* and *lex,* right and law, yet they ought to be distinguished, because RIGHT consisteth in liberty to do, or to forbear; whereas LAW determineth and bindeth to one of them: so that law and right differ as much as obligation and liberty, which in one and the same matter are inconsistent.

And because the condition of man (as hath been declared in the precedent chapter) is a condition of war of every one against every one, in which case every one is governed by his own reason, and there is nothing he can make use of that may not be a help unto him in preserving his life against his enemies; it followeth that in such a condition every man has a right to every thing, even to one another's body. And therefore, as long as this natural right of every man to every thing endureth, there can be no security to any man, how strong or wise soever he be, of living out the time which nature ordinarily alloweth men to live. And consequently it is a precept, or general rule of reason: that every man ought to endeavour peace, as far as he has hope of obtaining it; and when he cannot obtain it, that he may seek and use all helps and advantages of war. The first branch of which rule containeth the first and fundamental law of nature, which is: *to seek peace and follow it.* The second, the sum of the right of nature, which is: *by all means we can to defend ourselves.*

From this fundamental law of nature, by which men are commanded to endeavour peace, is derived this second law: *that a man be willing, when others are so too, as far forth as for peace and defence of himself he shall think it necessary, to lay down this right to all things; and be contented with so much liberty against other men as he would allow other men against himself.* For as long as every man holdeth this right, of doing anything he liketh; so long are all men in the condition of war. But if other men will not lay down their right, as well as he, then there is no reason for anyone to divest himself of his: for that were to expose himself to prey, which no man is bound to, rather than to dispose himself to peace. This is that law of the gospel: *Whatsoever you require that others should do to you, that do ye to them.* And that law of all men, *quod tibi fieri non vis, alteri ne feceris* [Do not do to others what you would not have them do to you].

To lay down a man's right to anything is to divest himself of the liberty of hindering another of the benefit of his own right to the same. For he that renounceth or passeth away his right giveth not to any other man a right which he had not before, because there is nothing to which every man had not right by nature, but only standeth out of his way that he may enjoy his own original right without hindrance from him, not without hindrance from another. So that the effect which redoundeth to one man by another man's defect of right is but so much diminution of impediments to the use of his own right original.

Right is laid aside, either by simply renouncing it, or by transferring it to another. By simply RENOUNCING, when he cares not to whom the benefit thereof redoundeth. By TRANSFERRING, when he intendeth the benefit thereof to some certain person or persons. And when a man hath in either manner abandoned or granted away his right, then is he said to be OBLIGED, or BOUND, not to hinder those to whom such right is granted, or abandoned, from the benefit of it: and that he ought, and it is DUTY, not to make void that voluntary act of his own: and that such hindrance is INJUSTICE, and INJURY, as being *sine jure;* the right being before renounced or transferred. So that injury or injustice, in the controversies of the world, is somewhat like to that which in the disputations of scholars is called absurdity. For as it is there called an absurdity to contradict what one maintained in the beginning; so in the world it is called injustice, and injury voluntarily to undo that which from the beginning he had voluntarily done. The way by which a man either simply renounceth or transferreth his right is a declaration, or signification, by some voluntary and sufficient sign, or signs, that he doth so renounce or transfer, or hath so renounced or transferred the same, to him that accepteth it. And these signs are either words only, or actions only; or, as it happeneth most often, both words and actions. And the same are the BONDS, by which men are bound and obliged: bonds that have their strength, not from their own nature (for nothing is more easily broken than a man's word), but from fear of some evil consequence upon the rupture.

Whensoever a man transferreth his right, or renounceth it, it is either in consideration of some right reciprocally transferred to himself, or for some other good he hopeth for thereby. For it is a voluntary act: and of the voluntary acts of every man, the object is some good to himself. And therefore there be some rights which no man can be understood by any words, or other signs, to have abandoned or transferred. As first a man cannot lay down the right of resisting them that assault him by force to take away his life, because he cannot be understood to aim thereby at any good to himself. The same may be said of wounds, and chains, and imprisonment, both because there is no benefit consequent to such patience, as there is to the patience of suffering another to be wounded or imprisoned, as also because a man cannot tell when he seeth men proceed against him by violence whether they intend his death or not. And lastly the motive and end for which this renouncing and transferring of right is introduced is nothing else but the security of a man's person, in his life, and in the means of so preserving life as not to be weary of it. And therefore if a man by words, or other signs, seem to despoil himself of the end for which those signs were intended, he is not to be understood as if he meant it, or that it was his will, but that he was ignorant of how such words and actions were to be interpreted.

The mutual transferring of right is that which men call CONTRACT. [. . .]

If a covenant be made wherein neither of the parties perform presently, but trust one another, in the condition of mere nature (which is a condition of war of every man against every man) upon any reasonable suspicion, it is void: but if there be a common power set over them both, with right and force sufficient to compel performance, it is not void. For he that performeth first has no assurance the other will perform after, because the bonds of words are too weak to bridle men's ambition, avarice, anger, and other passions, without the fear of some coercive power; which in the condition of mere nature, where all men are equal, and judges of the justness of their own fears, cannot possibly be supposed. And therefore he which performeth first does but betray himself to his enemy, contrary to the right he can never abandon of defending his life and means of living.

But in a civil estate, where there be a power set up to constrain those that would otherwise violate their faith, that fear is no more reasonable; and for that cause, he which by the covenant is to perform first is obliged so to do.

The cause of fear, which maketh such a covenant invalid, must be always something arising after the covenant made, as some new fact or other sign of the will not to perform, else it cannot make the covenant void. For that which could not hinder a man from promising ought not to be admitted as a hindrance of performing. [. . .]

Covenants entered into by fear, in the condition of mere nature, are obligatory. For example, if I covenant to pay a ransom, or service for my life, to an enemy, I am bound by it. For it is a contract, wherein one receiveth the benefit of life; the other is to receive money, or service for it, and consequently, where no other law (as in the condition of mere nature) forbiddeth the performance, the covenant is valid. Therefore prisoners of war, if trusted with the payment of their ransom, are obliged to pay it: and if a weaker prince make a disadvantageous peace with a stronger, for fear, he is bound to keep it; unless (as hath been said before) there ariseth some new and just cause of fear to renew the war. And even in Commonwealths, if I be forced to redeem myself from a thief by promising him money, I am bound to pay it, till the civil law discharge me. For whatsoever I may lawfully do without obligation, the same I may lawfully covenant to do through fear: and what I lawfully covenant, I cannot lawfully break. [. . .]

A covenant not to defend myself from force, by force, is always void. For (as I have shown before) no man can transfer or lay down his right to save himself from death, wounds, and imprisonment, the avoiding whereof is the only end of laying down any right; and therefore the promise of not resisting force, in no covenant transferreth any right, nor is obliging. For though a man may covenant thus, unless I do so, or so, kill me; he cannot covenant thus, unless I do so, or so, I will not resist you when you come to kill me. For man by nature chooseth the lesser evil, which is danger of death in resisting, rather than the greater, which is certain and present death in not resisting. And this is granted to be true by all men, in that they lead criminals to execution, and prison, with armed men, notwithstanding that such criminals have consented to the law by which they are condemned.

A covenant to accuse oneself, without assurance of pardon, is likewise invalid. For in the condition of nature where every man is judge, there is no place for accusation: and in the civil state the accusation is followed with punishment, which, being force, a man is not obliged not to resist. The same is also true of the accusation of those by whose condemnation a man falls into misery; as of a father, wife, or benefactor. For the testimony of such an accuser, if it be not willingly given, is presumed to be corrupted by nature, and therefore not to be received: and where a man's testimony is not to be credited, he is not bound to give it. Also accusations upon torture are not to be reputed as testimonies. For torture is to be used but as means of conjecture, and light, in the further examination and search of truth: and what is in that case confessed tendeth to the ease of him that is tortured, not to the informing of the torturers, and therefore ought not to have the credit of a sufficient testimony: for whether he deliver himself by true or false accusation, he does it by the right of preserving his own life.

The force of words being (as I have formerly noted) too weak to hold men to the performance of their covenants, there are in man's nature but two imaginable helps to strengthen it. And those are either a fear of the consequence of breaking their word, or a glory or pride in appearing not to need to break it. This latter is a generosity too rarely found to be presumed on, especially in the pursuers of wealth, command, or sensual pleasure, which are the greatest part of mankind. The passion to be reckoned upon is fear; whereof there be two very general objects: one, the power of spirits invisible; the other, the power of those men they shall therein offend. Of these two, though the former be the greater power, yet the fear of the latter is commonly the greater fear. [. . .]

OF OTHER LAWS OF NATURE

FROM that law of nature by which we are obliged to transfer to another such rights as, being retained, hinder the peace of mankind, there followeth a third; which is this: that men perform their covenants made; without which covenants are in vain, and but empty words; and the right of all men to all things remaining, we are still in the condition of war.

And in this law of nature consisteth the fountain and original of JUSTICE. For where no covenant hath preceded, there hath no right been transferred, and every man has right to everything and consequently, no action can be unjust. But when a covenant is made, then to break it is unjust and the definition of INJUSTICE is no other than the not performance of covenant. And whatsoever is not unjust is just.

But because covenants of mutual trust, where there is a fear of not performance on either part (as hath been said in the former chapter), are invalid, though the original of justice be the making of covenants, yet injustice actually there can be none till the cause of such fear be taken away; which, while men are in the natural condition of war, cannot be done. Therefore before the names of just and unjust can have place, there must be some coercive power to compel men equally to the performance of their covenants, by the terror of some punishment greater than the benefit they expect by the breach of their covenant, and to make good that propriety which by mutual contract men acquire in recompense of the universal right they abandon: and such power there is none before the erection of a Commonwealth.

And this is also to be gathered out of the ordinary definition of justice in the Schools, for they say that justice is the constant will of giving to every man his own. And therefore where there is no own, that is, no propriety, there is no injustice; and where there is no coercive power erected, that is, where there is no Commonwealth, there is no propriety, all men having right to all things: therefore where there is no Commonwealth, there nothing is unjust. So that the nature of justice consisteth in keeping of valid covenants, but the validity of covenants begins not but with the constitution of a civil power sufficient to compel men to keep them: and then it is also that propriety begins.

The foole hath said in his heart, there is no such thing as justice, and sometimes also with his tongue, seriously alleging that every man's conservation and contentment being committed to his own care, there could be no reason why every man might not do what he thought conduced thereunto: and therefore also to make, or not make; keep, or not keep, covenants was not against reason when it conduced to one's benefit. He does not therein deny that there be covenants; and that they are sometimes broken, sometimes kept; and that such breach of them may be called injustice, and the observance of them justice: but he questioneth whether injustice, taking away the fear of God (for the same foole hath said in his heart there is no God), may not sometimes stand with that reason which dictateth to every man his own good; and particularly then, when it conduceth to such a benefit as shall put a man in a condition to neglect not only the dispraise and revilings, but also the power of other men. The kingdom of God is gotten by violence: but what if it could be gotten by unjust violence? Were it against reason so to get it, when it is impossible to receive hurt by it? And if it be not against reason, it is not against justice: or else justice is not to be approved for good. From such reasoning as this, successful wickedness hath obtained the name of virtue. . . . This specious reasoning is nevertheless false.

For the question is not of promises mutual, where there is no security of performance on either side, as when there is no civil power erected over the parties promising; for such promises are no covenants: but either where one of the parties has performed already, or where there is a power to make him perform, there is the question whether it be against reason; that is, against the benefit of the other to perform, or not. And I say it is not against reason. For the manifestation whereof we are to consider; first, that when a man doth a thing, which notwithstanding anything can be foreseen and reckoned on tendeth to his own destruction, howsoever some accident, which he could not expect, arriving may turn it to his benefit; yet such events do not make it reasonably or wisely done. Secondly, that in a condition of war, wherein every man to every man, for want of a common power to keep them all in awe, is an enemy, there is no man can hope by his own strength, or wit, to defend himself from destruction without the help of confederates; where every one expects the same defence by the confederation that anyone else does: and therefore he which declares he thinks it reason to deceive those that help him can in reason expect no other means of safety than what can be had from his own single power. He, therefore, that breaketh his covenant, and consequently declareth that he thinks he may with reason do so, cannot be received into any society that unite themselves for peace and defence but by the error of them that receive him; nor when he is received be retained in it without seeing the danger of their error; which errors a man cannot reasonably reckon upon as the means of his security: and therefore if he be left, or cast out of society, he perisheth; and if he live in society, it is by the errors of other men, which he could not foresee nor reckon upon, and consequently against the reason of his preservation; and so, as all men that contribute not to his destruction forbear him only out of ignorance of what is good for themselves.

As for the instance of gaining the secure and perpetual felicity of heaven by any way, it is frivolous; there being but one way imaginable, and that is not breaking, but keeping of covenant.

And for the other instance of attaining sovereignty by rebellion; it is manifest that, though the event follow, yet because it cannot reasonably be expected, but rather the contrary, and because by gaining it so, others are taught to gain the same in like manner, the attempt thereof is against reason. Justice therefore, that is to say, keeping of covenant, is a rule of reason by which we are forbidden to do anything destructive to our life, and consequently a law of nature.

There be some that proceed further and will not have the law of nature to be those rules which conduce to the preservation of man's life on earth, but to the attaining of an eternal felicity after death; to which they think the breach of covenant may conduce, and consequently be just and reasonable; such are they that think it a work of merit to kill, or depose, or rebel against the sovereign power constituted over them by their own consent. But because there is no natural knowledge of man's estate after death, much less of the reward that is then to be given to breach of faith, but only a belief grounded upon other men's saying that they know it supernaturally or that they know those that knew them that knew others that knew it supernaturally, breach of faith cannot be called a precept of reason or nature.

OF THE CAUSES, GENERATION, AND DEFINITION OF A COMMONWEALTH

[T]he laws of nature, as justice, equity, modesty, mercy, and, in sum, doing to others as we would be done to, of themselves, without the terror of some power to cause them to be observed, are contrary to our natural passions, that carry us to partiality, pride, revenge, and the like. And covenants, without the sword, are but words and of no strength to secure a man at all. Therefore, notwithstanding the laws of nature (which every one hath then kept, when he has the will to keep them, when he can do it safely), if there be no power erected, or not great enough for our security, every man will and may lawfully rely on his own strength and art for caution against all other men. And in all places, where men have lived by small families, to rob and spoil one another has been a trade, and so far from being reputed against the law of nature that the greater spoils they gained, the greater was their honour; and men observed no other laws therein but the laws of honour; that is, to abstain from cruelty, leaving to men their lives and instruments of husbandry. And as small families did then; so now do cities and kingdoms, which are but greater families (for their own security), enlarge their dominions upon all pretences of danger, and fear of invasion, or assistance that may be given to invaders; endeavour as much as they can to subdue or weaken their neighbours by open force, and secret arts, for want of other caution, justly; and are remembered for it in after ages with honour. [. . .]

The only way to erect such a common power, as may be able to defend them from the invasion of foreigners, and the injuries of one another, and thereby to secure them in such sort as that by their own industry and by the fruits of the earth they may nourish themselves and live contentedly, is to confer all their power and strength upon one man, or upon one assembly of men, that may reduce all their wills, by plurality of voices, unto one will: which is as much as to say, to appoint one man, or assembly of men, to bear their person; and every one to own and acknowledge himself to be author of whatsoever he that so beareth their person shall act, or cause to be acted, in those things which concern the common peace and safety; and therein to submit their wills, every one to his will, and their judgements to his judgement. This is more than consent, or concord; it is a real unity of them all in one and the same person, made by covenant of every man with every man, in such manner as if every man should say to every man: I authorise and give up my right of governing myself to this man, or to this assembly of men, on this condition; that thou give up, thy right to him, and authorise all his actions in like manner. This done, the multitude so united in one person is called a COMMONWEALTH; in Latin, CIVITAS. This is the generation of that great LEVIATHAN, or rather, to speak more reverently, of that mortal god to which we owe, under the immortal God, our peace and defence. For by this authority, given him by every particular man in the Commonwealth, he hath the use of so much power and strength conferred on him that, by terror thereof, he is enabled to form the wills of them all, to peace at home, and mutual aid against their enemies abroad. And in him consisteth the essence of the Commonwealth; which, to define it, is: one person, of whose acts a great multitude, by mutual covenants one with another, have made themselves every one the author, to the end he may use the strength and means of them all as he shall think expedient for their peace and common defence.

And he that carryeth this person is called SOVEREIGN, and said to have sovereign power; and every one besides, his SUBJECT. [. . .]

John Locke

Popular Basis of Political Authority

1689

4. To understand Political Power right, and derive it from its Original, we must consider what State all Men are naturally in, and that is, a *State of perfect Freedom* to order their Actions, and dispose of their Possessions, and Persons as they think fit, within the bounds of the Law of Nature, without asking leave, or depending upon the Will of any other Man. A *State* also *of Equality,* wherein all the Power and Jurisdiction is reciprocal, no one having more than another: there being nothing more evident, than that Creatures of the same species and rank promiscuously born to all the same advantages of Nature, and the use of the same faculties, should also be equal one amongst another without Subordination or Subjection, unless the Lord and Master of them all, should by any manifest Declaration of his Will set one above another, and confer on him by an evident and clear appointment an undoubted Right to Dominion and Sovereignty.

6. But though this be a *State of Liberty,* yet it is *not a State of Licence,* though Man in that State have an uncontroleable Liberty, to dispose of his Person or Possessions, yet he has not Liberty to destroy himself, or so much as any Creature in his Possession, but where some nobler use, than its bare Preservation calls for it. The *State of Nature* has a Law of Nature to govern it, which obliges every one: And Reason, which is that Law, teaches all Mankind, who will but consult it, that being all equal and independent, no one ought to harm another in his Life, Health, Liberty, or Possessions. For Men being all the Workmanship of one Omnipotent, and infinitely wise Maker; All the Servants of one Sovereign Master, sent into the World by his order and about his business, they are his Property, whose Workmanship they are, made to last during his, not one another's Pleasure. And being furnished with like Faculties, sharing all in one Community of Nature, there cannot be supposed any such *Subordination* among us, that may Authorize us to destroy one another, as if we were made for one another's uses, as the inferior ranks of Creatures are for ours. Every one as he is *bound to preserve himself,* and not to quit his Station wilfully; so by the like reason when his own Preservation comes not in competition, ought he, as much as he can, *to preserve the rest of Mankind,* and

From John Locke, "Popular Basis of Political Authority," from *Two Treatises of Government*, Book II, ed. Thomas Hollis. London: A. Millar et al., 1764.

may not unless it be to do Justice on an Offender, take away, or impair the life, or what tends to the Preservation of the Life, Liberty, Health, Limb or Goods of another.

7. And that all Men may be restrained from invading others' Rights, and from doing hurt to one another, and the Law of Nature be observed, which willeth the Peace and *Preservation of all Mankind,* the *Execution* of the Law of Nature is in that State, put into every Man's hands, whereby everyone has a right to punish the transgressors of that Law to such a Degree, as may hinder its Violation. For the *Law of Nature* would, as all other Laws that concern Men in this World, be in vain, if there were no body that in the State of Nature, had a *Power to Execute* that Law, and thereby preserve the innocent and restrain offenders, and if any one in the State of Nature may punish another, for any evil he has done, every one may do so. For in that *State of perfect Equality,* where naturally there is no superiority or jurisdiction of one, over another, what any may do in Prosecution of that Law, every one must needs have a Right to do.

8. And thus in the State of Nature, *one Man comes by a Power over another;* but yet no Absolute or Arbitrary Power, to use a Criminal when he has got him in his hands, according to the passionate heats, or boundless extravagancy of his own Will, but only to retribute to him, so far as calm reason and conscience dictates, what is proportionate to his Transgression, which is so much as may serve for *Reparation* and *Restraint.* For these two are the only reasons, why one Man may lawfully do harm to another, which is that we call *punishment.* In transgressing the Law of Nature, the Offender declares himself to live by another Rule, than that of *reason* and common Equity, which is that measure God has set to the actions of Men, for their mutual security: and so he becomes dangerous to Mankind, the tye, which is to secure them from injury and violence, being slighted and broken by him. Which being a trespass against the whole Species, and the Peace and Safety of it, provided for by the Law of Nature, every man upon this score, by the Right he hath to preserve Mankind in general, may restrain, or where it is necessary, destroy things noxious to them, and so may bring such evil on any one, who hath transgressed that Law, as may make him repent the doing of it, and thereby deter him, and by his Example others, from doing the like mischief. And in this case, and upon this ground, every *Man hath a Right to punish the Offender, and be Executioner of the Law of Nature.*

9. I doubt not but this will seem a very strange Doctrine to some Men: but before they condemn it, I desire them to resolve me, by what Right any Prince or State can put to death, or *punish an Alien,* for any Crime he commits in their Country. 'Tis certain their Laws by vertue of any Sanction they receive from the promulgated Will of the Legislative, reach not a Stranger. They speak not to him, nor if they did, is he bound to hearken to them. The Legislative Authority, by which they are in Force over the Subjects of that Common-wealth, hath no Power over him. Those who have the Supream Power of making Laws in *England, France* or *Holland,* are to an *Indian,* but like the rest of the World, Men without Authority: And therefore if by the Law of Nature, every Man hath not a Power to punish Offences against it, as he soberly judges the Case to require, I see not how the Magistrates of any Community, can *punish an Alien* of another Country, since in reference to him, they can have no more Power, than what every Man naturally may have over another.

10. Besides the Crime which consists in violating the Law, and varying from the right Rule of Reason, whereby a Man so far becomes degenerate, and declares himself to quit the Principles of Human Nature, and to be a noxious Creature, there is commonly *injury* done to some Person or other, and some other Man receives damage by his Transgression, in which Case he who hath received any damage, has besides the right of punishment common to him with other Men, a particular Right to seek *Reparation* from him that has done it. And any other Person who finds it just, may also joyn with him that is injur'd, and assist him in recovering from the Offender, so much as may make satisfaction for the harm he has suffer'd.

11. From these *two distinct Rights,* the one of *Punishing* the Crime *for restraint,* and preventing the like Offence, which right of punishing is in every body; the other of taking *reparation,* which belongs only to the injured party, comes it to pass that the

Magistrate, who by being Magistrate, hath the common right of punishing put into his hands, can often, where the publick good demands not the execution of the Law, *remit* the punishment of Criminal Offences by his own Authority, but yet cannot *remit* the satisfaction due to any private Man, for the damage he has received. That, he who has suffered the damage has a Right to demand in his own name, and he alone can *remit:* The damnified Person has this Power of appropriating to himself, the Goods or Service of the Offender, by *Right of Self-preservation,* as every Man has a Power to punish the Crime, to prevent its being committed again, *by the Right he has of Preserving all Mankind,* and doing all reasonable things he can in order to that end: and thus it is, that every Man in the State of Nature, has a Power to kill a Murderer, both to deter others from doing the like Injury, which no Reparation can compensate, by the Example of the punishment that attends it from every body, and also *to secure* Men from the attempts of a Criminal, who having renounced Reason, the common Rule and Measure, God hath given to Mankind, hath by the unjust Violence and Slaughter he hath committed upon one, declared War against all Mankind, and therefore may be destroyed as a *Lyon* or a *Tyger,* one of those wild Savage Beasts, with whom Men can have no Society nor Security: And upon this is grounded the great Law of Nature, *Who so sheddeth Man's Blood, by Man shall his Blood be shed.* And *Cain* was so fully convinced, that every one had a Right to destroy such a Criminal, that after the Murther of his Brother, he cries out, *Every one that findeth me, shall slay me;* so plain was it writ in the Hearts of all Mankind.

12. By the same reason, may a Man in the State of Nature *punish the lesser breaches* of that Law. It will perhaps be demanded, with death? I answer, Each Transgression may be *punished* to that *degree,* and with so much *Severity* as will suffice to make it an ill bargain to the Offender, give him cause to repent, and terrifie others from doing the like. Every Offence that can be committed in the State of Nature, may in the State of Nature be also punished, equally, and as far forth as it may, in a Common-wealth; for though it would be besides my present purpose, to enter here into the particulars of the Law of Nature, or its *measures of punishment;* yet, it is certain there is such a Law, and that too, as intelligible and plain to a rational Creature, and a Studier of that Law, as the positive Laws of Common-wealths, nay possibly plainer; As much as Reason is easier to be understood, than the Phansies and intricate Contrivances of Men, following contrary and hidden interests put into Words; For so truly are a great part of the *Municipal Laws* of Countries, which are only so far right, as they are founded on the Law of Nature, by which they are to be regulated and interpreted.

13. To this strange Doctrine, *viz.* That *in the State of Nature, every one has the Executive Power* of the Law of Nature, I doubt not but it will be objected, That it is unreasonable for Men to be Judges in their own Cases, that Self-love will make Men partial to themselves and their Friends. And on the other side, that Ill Nature, Passion and Revenge will carry them too far in punishing others. And hence nothing but Confusion and Disorder will follow, and that therefore God hath certainly appointed Government to restrain the partiality and violence of Men. I easily grant, that *Civil Government* is the proper Remedy for the Inconveniences of the State of Nature, which must certainly be Great, where Men may be Judges in their own Case, since 'tis easily to be imagined, that he who was so unjust as to do his Brother an Injury, will scarce be so just as to condemn himself for it: But I shall desire those who make this Objection, to remember that *Absolute Monarchs* are but Men, and if Government is to be the Remedy of those Evils, which necessarily follow from Men's being Judges in their own Cases, and the State of Nature is therefore not to be endured, I desire to know what kind of Government that is, and how much better it is than the State of Nature, where one Man commanding a multitude, has the Liberty to be Judge in his own Case, and may do to all his Subjects whatever he pleases, without the least liberty to any one to question or controle those who Execute his Pleasure? And in whatsoever he doth, whether led by Reason, Mistake or Passion, must be submitted to? Much better it is in the State of Nature wherein Men are not bound to submit to the unjust will of another: And if he that judges, judges amiss in his own, or any other Case, he is answerable for it to the rest of Mankind.

119. *Every Man* being, as has been shewed, *naturally free,* and nothing being able to put him into subjection to any Earthly Power, but only his own Consent; it is to be considered, what shall be understood to be *a sufficient Declaration of* a Man's *Consent, to make him subject* to the Laws of any Government. There is a common distinction of an express and a tacit consent, which will concern our present Case. No body doubts but an *express Consent,* of any Man, entring into any Society, makes him a perfect Member of that Society, a Subject of that Government. The difficulty is, what ought to be look'd upon as a *tacit Consent,* and how far it binds, *i.e.* how far any one shall be looked on to have consented, and thereby submitted to any Government, where he has made no Expressions of it at all. And to this I say, that every Man, that hath any Possession, or Enjoyment, of any part of the Dominions of any Government, doth thereby give his *tacit Consent,* and is as far forth obliged to Obedience to the Laws of that Government, during such Enjoyment, as any one under it; whether this his Possession be of Land, to him and his Heirs for ever, or a Lodging only for a Week; or whether it be barely travelling freely on the Highway; and in Effect, it reaches as far as the very being of any one within the Territories of that Government.

120. To understand this the better, it is fit to consider, that every Man, when he, at first, incorporates himself into any Commonwealth, he, by his uniting himself thereunto, annexed also, and submits to the Community those Possessions, which he has, or shall acquire, that do not already belong to any other Government. For it would be a direct Contradiction, for any one, to enter into Society with others for the securing and regulating of Property: And yet to suppose his Land, whose Property is to be regulated by the Laws of the Society, should be exempt from the Jurisdiction of that Government, to which he himself the Proprietor of the Land, is a Subject. By the same Act therefore, whereby any one unites his person, which was before free, to any Commonwealth; by the same he unites his Possessions, which were before free, to it also; and they become, both of them, Person and Possession, subject to the Government and Dominion of that Commonwealth, as long as it hath a being. *Whoever* therefore, from thenceforth, by Inheritance, Purchase, Permission, or other ways *enjoys any part of the Land,* so annext to, and under the Government *of that Commonwealth, must take it with the Condition* it is under; that is, *of submitting to the Government of the Commonwealth,* under whose Jurisdiction it is, as far forth, as any Subject of it.

121. But since the Government has a direct Jurisdiction only over the Land, and reaches the Possessor of it, (before he has actually incorporated himself in the Society) only as he dwells upon, and enjoys that: *The Obligation* any one is under, by Virtue of such Enjoyment, *to submit to the Government, begins and ends with the Enjoyment;* so that whenever the Owner, who has given nothing but such a *tacit Consent* to the Government, will, by Donation, Sale, or otherwise, quit the said Possession, he is at liberty to go and incorporate himself into any other Commonwealth, or to agree with others to begin a new one, *in vacuis locis,* in any part of the World, they can find free and unpossessed: Whereas he, that has once, by actual Agreement, and any *express* Declaration, given his *Consent* to be of any Commonweal, is perpetually and indispensably obliged to be and remain unalterably a Subject to it, and can never be again in the liberty of the state of Nature; unless by any Calamity, the Government, he was under, comes to be dissolved; or else by some publick Act cuts him off from being any longer a Member of it.

122. But submitting to the Laws of any Country, living quietly, and enjoying Priviledges and Protection under them, *makes not a Man a Member of that Society:* This is only a local Protection and Homage due to, and from all those, who, not being in a state of War, come within the Territories belonging to any Government, to all parts whereof the force of its Law extends. But this no more *makes a Man a Member of that Society,* a perpetual Subject of that Commonwealth, than it would make a Man a Subject to another in whose Family he found it convenient to abide for some time; though, whilst he continued in it, he were obliged to comply with the Laws, and submit to the Government he found there. And thus we see, that *Foreigners,* by living all their Lives under another Government, and enjoying the Priviledges and Protection of it, though they are bound, even in Conscience, to submit to its Administration,

as far forth as any Denison; yet do not thereby come to be *Subjects or Members of that Commonwealth.* Nothing can make any Man so, but his actually entering into it by positive Engagement, and express Promise and Compact. This is that, which I think, concerning the beginning of Political Societies, and that *Consent which makes any one a Member* of any Commonwealth.

DAVID HUME

Of the Original Contract

1748

As no party, in the present age, can well support itself without a philosophical or speculative system of principles annexed to its political or practical one, we accordingly find, that each of the factions into which this nation is divided has reared up a fabric of the former kind, in order to protect and cover that scheme of actions which it pursues. The people being commonly very rude builders, especially in this speculative way, and more especially still when actuated by party-zeal, it is natural to imagine that their workmanship must be a little unshapely, and discover evident marks of that violence and hurry in which it was raised. The one party, by tracing up government to the Deity, endeavoured to render it so sacred and inviolate, that it must be little less than sacrilege, however, tyrannical it may become, to touch or invade it in the smallest article. The other party, by founding government altogether on the consent of the people, suppose that there is a kind of *original contract,* by which the subjects have tacitly reserved the power of resisting their sovereign, whenever they find themselves aggrieved by that authority, with which they have, for certain purposes, voluntarily intrusted him. These are the speculative principles of the two parties, and these, too, are the practical consequences deduced from them.

I shall venture to affirm, *That both these* systems *of speculative principles are just; though not in the sense intended by the parties:* and, *That both the* schemes *of practical consequences are prudent; though not in the extremes to which each party, in opposition to the other, has commonly endeavoured to carry them . . .*

When we consider how nearly equal all men are in their bodily force, and even in their mental powers and faculties, till cultivated by education, we must necessarily allow, that nothing but their own consent could, at first, associate them together, and subject them to any authority. The people, if we trace government to its first origin in the woods and deserts, are the source of all power and jurisdiction, and voluntarily, for the sake of peace and order, abandoned their native liberty, and received laws from their equal and companion. The conditions upon which they were willing to submit, were either expressed, or were so clear and obvious, that it might well be esteemed superfluous to express them. If this, then, be meant by the *original contract,* it cannot be denied, that all government is, at first, founded on a contract, and that the most ancient rude combinations of mankind were formed chiefly by that principle. In vain are we asked in what records this

From David Hume, *Essays and Treatises on Several Subjects*. London: A. Millar, 1764.

charter of our liberties is registered. It was not written on parchment, nor yet on leaves or barks of trees. It preceded the use of writing, and all the other civilized arts of life. But we trace it plainly in the nature of man, and in the equality, or something approaching equality, which we find in all the individuals of that species. The force, which now prevails, and which is founded on fleets and armies, is plainly political, and derived from authority, the effect of established government. A man's natural force consists only in the vigour of his limbs, and the firmness of his courage; which could never subject multitudes to the command of one. Nothing but their own consent, and their sense of the advantages resulting from peace and order, could have had that influence.

Yet even this consent was long very imperfect, and could not be the basis of a regular administration. The chieftain, who had probably acquired his influence during the continuance of war, ruled more by persuasion than command; and till he could employ force to reduce the refractory and disobedient, the society could scarcely be said to have attained a state of civil government. No compact or agreement, it is evident, was expressly formed for general submission; an idea far beyond the comprehension of savages: each exertion of authority in the chieftain must have been particular, and called forth by the present exigencies of the case: the sensible utility, resulting from his interposition, made these exertions become daily more frequent; and their frequency gradually produced an habitual, and, if you please to call it so, a voluntary, and therefore precarious, acquiescence in the people.

But philosophers, who have embraced a party (if that be not a contradiction in terms), are not contented with these concessions. They assert, not only that government in its earliest infancy arose from consent, or rather the voluntary acquiescence of the people; but also that, even at present, when it has attained its full maturity, it rests on no other foundation. They affirm, that all men are still born equal, and owe allegiance to no prince or government, unless bound by the obligation and sanction of a *promise*. And as no man, without some equivalent, would forego the advantages of his native liberty, and subject himself to the will of another, this promise is always understood to be conditional, and imposes on him no obligation, unless he meet with justice and protection from his sovereign. These advantages the sovereign promises him in return; and if he fail in the execution, he has broken, on his part, the articles of engagement, and has thereby freed his subject from all obligations to allegiance. Such, according to these philosophers, is the foundation of authority in every government, and such the right of resistance possessed by every subject.

But would these reasoners look abroad into the world, they would meet with nothing that, in the least, corresponds to their ideas, or can warrant so refined and philosophical a system. On the contrary, we find everywhere princes who claim their subjects as their property, and assert their independent right of sovereignty, from conquest or succession. We find also everywhere subjects who acknowledge this right in their prince, and suppose themselves born under obligations of obedience to a certain sovereign, as much as under the ties of reverence and duty to certain parents. These connexions are always conceived to be equally independent of our consent, in Persia and China; in France and Spain; and even in Holland and England, wherever the doctrines above-mentioned have not been carefully inculcated. Obedience or subjection becomes so familiar, that most men never make any inquiry about its origin or cause, more than about the principle of gravity, resistance, or the most universal laws of nature. Or if curiosity ever move them; as soon as they learn that they themselves and their ancestors have, for several ages, or from time immemorial, been subject to such a form of government or such a family, they immediately acquiesce, and acknowledge their obligation to allegiance. Were you to preach, in most parts of the world, that political connexions are founded altogether on voluntary consent or a mutual promise, the magistrate would soon imprison you as seditious for loosening the ties of obedience; if your friends did not before shut you up as delirious, for advancing such absurdities. It is strange that an act of the mind, which every individual is supposed to have formed, and after he came to the use of reason too, otherwise it could have no authority; that this act, I say, should be so much unknown to all of them, that over the face of the whole earth, there scarcely remain any traces or memory of it.

But the contract, on which government is founded, is said to be the *original contract;* and consequently may be supposed too old to fall under the knowledge of the present generation. If the agreement, by which savage men first associated and conjoined their force, be here meant, this is acknowledged to be real; but being so ancient, and being obliterated by a thousand changes of government and princes, it cannot now be supposed to retain any authority. If we would say anything to the purpose, we must assert that every particular government which is lawful, and which imposes any duty of allegiance on the subject, was, at first, founded on consent and a voluntary compact. But, besides that this supposes the consent of the fathers to bind the children, even to the most remote generations (which republican writers will never allow), besides this, I say, it is not justified by history or experience in any age or country of the world.

Almost all the governments which exist at present, or of which there remains any record in story, have been founded originally, either on usurpation or conquest, or both, without any presence of a fair consent or voluntary subjection of the people. When an artful and bold man is placed at the head of an army or faction, it is often easy for him, by employing, sometimes violence, sometimes false presences, to establish his dominion over a people a hundred times more numerous than his partisans. He allows no such open communication, that his enemies can know, with certainty, their number or force. He gives them no leisure to assemble together in a body to oppose him. Even all those who are the instruments of his usurpation may wish his fall; but their ignorance of each other's intention keeps them in awe, and is the sole cause of his security. By such arts as these many governments have been established; and this is all the *original contract* which they have to boast of.

The face of the earth is continually changing, by the increase of small kingdoms into great empires, by the dissolution of great empires into smaller kingdoms, by the planting of colonies, by the migration of tribes. Is there anything discoverable in all these events but force and violence? Where is the mutual agreement or voluntary association so much talked of?

Even the smoothest way by which a nation may receive a foreign master, by marriage or a will, is not extremely honourable for the people; but supposes them to be disposed of, like a dowry or a legacy, according to the pleasure or interest of their rulers.

But where no force interposes, and election takes place; what is this election so highly vaunted? It is either the combination of a few great men, who decide for the whole, and will allow of no opposition; or it is the fury of a multitude, that follow a seditious ringleader, who is not known, perhaps, to a dozen among them, and who owes his advancement merely to his own impudence, or to the momentary caprice of his fellows.

Are these disorderly elections, which are rare too, of such mighty authority as to be the only lawful foundation of all government and allegiance?

In reality, there is not a more terrible event than a total dissolution of government, which gives liberty to the multitude, and makes the determination or choice of a new establishment depend upon a number, which nearly approaches to that of the body of the people: for it never comes entirely to the whole body of them. Every wise man then wishes to see, at the head of a powerful and obedient army, a general who may speedily seize the prize, and give to the people a master which they are so unfit to choose for themselves. So little correspondent is fact and reality to those philosophical notions.

Let not the establishment at the *Revolution* deceive us, or make us so much in love with a philosophical origin to government, as to imagine all others monstrous and irregular. Even that event was far from corresponding to these refined ideas. It was only the succession, and that only in the regal part of the government, which was then changed: and it was only the majority of seven hundred, who determined that change for near ten millions. I doubt not, indeed, but the bulk of those ten millions acquiesced willingly in the determination: but was the matter left, in the least, to their choice? Was it not justly supposed to be, from that moment, decided, and every man punished, who refused to submit to the new sovereign? How otherwise could the matter have ever been brought to any issue or conclusion?

The republic of Athens was, I believe, the most extensive democracy that we read of in history: yet if we make the requisite allowances for the women, the slaves, and the strangers, we shall find, that that establishment was not at first made, nor any law ever voted, by a tenth part of those who were bound to pay obedience to it; not to mention the islands and foreign dominions, which the Athenians claimed as theirs by right of conquest. And as it is well known that popular assemblies in that city were always full of license and disorder, notwithstanding the institutions and laws by which they were checked; how much more disorderly must they prove, where they form not the established constitution, but meet tumultuously on the dissolution of the ancient government, in order to give rise to a new one? How chimerical must it be to talk of a choice in such circumstances?

The Achæans enjoyed the freest and most perfect democracy of all antiquity; yet they employed force to oblige some cities to enter into their league, as we learn from Polybius.

Harry the IVth and Harry the VIIth of England, had really no title to the throne but a parliamentary election; yet they never would acknowledge it, lest they should thereby weaken their authority. Strange, if the only real foundation of all authority be consent and promise?

It is in vain to say, that all governments are, or should be, at first, founded on popular consent, as much as the necessity of human affairs will admit. This favours entirely my pretension. I maintain, that human affairs will never admit of this consent, seldom of the appearance of it; but that conquest or usurpation, that is, in plain terms, force, by dissolving the ancient governments, is the origin of almost all the new ones which were ever established in the world. And that in the few cases where consent may seem to have taken place, it was commonly so irregular, so confined, or so much intermixed either with fraud or violence, that it cannot have any great authority.

My intention here is not to exclude the consent of the people from being one just foundation of government where it has place. It is surely the best and most sacred of any. I only pretend, that it has very seldom had place in any degree, and never almost in its full extent; and that, therefore, some other foundation of government must also be admitted.

Were all men possessed of so inflexible a regard to justice, that, of themselves, they would totally abstain from the properties of others; they had for ever remained in a state of absolute liberty, without subjection to any magistrate or political society: but this is a state of perfection, of which human nature is justly deemed incapable. Again, were all men possessed of so perfect an understanding as always to know their own interests, no form of government had ever been submitted to but what was established on consent, and was fully canvassed by every member of the society: but this state of perfection is likewise much superior to human nature. Reason, history, and experience shew us, that all political societies have had an origin much less accurate and regular; and were one to choose a period of time when the people's consent was the least regarded in public transactions, it would be precisely on the establishment of a new government. In a settled constitution their inclinations are often consulted; but during the fury of revolutions, conquests, and public convulsions, military force or political craft usually decides the controversy.

When a new government is established, by whatever means, the people are commonly dissatisfied with it, and pay obedience more from fear and necessity, than from any idea of allegiance or of moral obligation. The prince is watchful and jealous, and must carefully guard against every beginning or appearance of insurrection. Time, by degrees, removes all these difficulties, and accustoms the nation to regard, as their lawful or native princes, that family which at first they considered as usurpers or foreign conquerors. In order to found this opinion, they have no recourse to any notion of voluntary consent or promise, which, they know, never was, in this case, either expected or demanded. The original establishment was formed by violence, and submitted to from necessity. The subsequent administration is also supported by power, and acquiesced in by the people, not as a matter of choice, but of obligation. They imagine not that their consent gives their prince a title: but they willingly consent, because they think, that, from long possession, he has acquired a title, independent of their choice or inclination.

Should it be said, that, by living under the dominion of a prince which one might leave, every individual has given a *tacit* consent to his authority, and promised him obedience; it may be answered, that such an implied consent can only have place where a man imagines that the matter depends on his choice. But where he thinks (as all mankind do who are born under established governments) that, by his birth, he owes allegiance to a certain prince or certain form of government; it would be absurd to infer a consent or choice, which he expressly, in this case, renounces and disclaims.

Can we seriously say, that a poor peasant or artisan has a free choice to leave his country, when he knows no foreign language or manners, and lives, from day to day, by the small wages which he acquires? We may as well assert that a man, by remaining in a vessel, freely consents to the dominion of the master; though he was carried on board while asleep, and must leap into the ocean and perish, the moment he leaves her.

What if the prince forbid his subjects to quit his dominions; as in Tiberius's time, it was regarded as a crime in a Roman knight that he had attempted to fly to the Parthians, in order to escape the tyranny of that emperor? Or as the ancient Muscovites prohibited all travelling under pain of death? And did a prince observe, that many of his subjects were seized with the frenzy of migrating to foreign countries, he would, doubtless, with great reason and justice, restrain them, in order to prevent the depopulation of his own kingdom. Would he forfeit the allegiance of all his subjects by so wise and reasonable a law? Yet the freedom of their choice is surely, in that case, ravished from them.

A company of men, who should leave their native country, in order to people some uninhabited region, might dream of recovering their native freedom; but they would soon find, that their prince still laid claim to them, and called them his subjects, even in their new settlement. And in this he would but act conformably to the common ideas of mankind.

The truest *tacit* consent of this kind that is ever observed, is when a foreigner settles in any country, and is beforehand acquainted with the prince, and government, and laws, to which he must submit: yet is his allegiance, though more voluntary, much less expected or depended on, than that of a natural born subject. On the contrary, his native prince still asserts a claim to him. And if he punish not the renegade, where he seizes him in war with his new prince's commission; this clemency is not founded on the municipal law, which in all countries condemns the prisoner; but on the consent of princes, who have agreed to this indulgence, in order to prevent reprisals. . . .

JEAN-JACQUES ROUSSEAU

The Social Contract

1762

1. SUBJECT OF THE FIRST BOOK

Man is born free; and everywhere he is in chains. One thinks himself the master of others, and still remains a greater slave than they. How did this change come about? I do not know. What can make it legitimate? That question I think I can answer.

If I took into account only force, and the effects derived from it, I should say: "As long as a people is compelled to obey, and obeys, it does well; as soon as it can shake off the yoke, and shakes it off, it does still

From Jean-Jacques Rousseau and G. D. H. Cole, *The Social Contract & Discourses*. London: Dent, 1923.

better; for, regaining its liberty by the same right as took it away, either it is justified in resuming it, or there was no justification for those who took it away." But the social order is a sacred right which is the basis of all other rights. Nevertheless, this right does not come from nature, and must therefore be founded on conventions. Before coming to that, I have to prove what I have just asserted.

2. THE FIRST SOCIETIES

The most ancient of all societies, and the only one that is natural, is the family: and even so the children remain attached to the father only so long as they need him for their preservation. As soon as this need ceases, the natural bond is dissolved. The children, released from the obedience they owed to the father, and the father, released from the care he owed his children, return equally to independence. If they remain united, they continue so no longer naturally, but voluntarily; and the family itself is then maintained only by convention.

This common liberty results from the nature of man. His first law is to provide for his own preservation, his first cares are those which he owes to himself; and, as soon as he reaches years of discretion, he is the sole judge of the proper means of preserving himself, and consequently becomes his own master.

The family then may be called the first model of political societies: the ruler corresponds to the father, and the people to the children; and all, being born free and equal, alienate their liberty only for their own advantage. The whole difference is that, in the family, the love of the father for his children repays him for the care he takes of them, while, in the State, the pleasure of commanding takes the place of the love which the chief cannot have for the peoples under him.

Grotius denies that all human power is established in favour of the governed, and quotes slavery as an example. His usual method of reasoning is constantly to establish right by fact. It would be possible to employ a more logical method, but none could be more favourable to tyrants.

It is then, according to Grotius, doubtful whether the human race belongs to a hundred men, or that hundred men to the human race: and, throughout his book, he seems to incline to the former alternative, which is also the view of Hobbes. On this showing, the human species is divided into so many herds of cattle, each with its ruler, who keeps guard over them for the purpose of devouring them.

As a shepherd is of a nature superior to that of his flock, the shepherds of men, i.e., their rulers, are of a nature superior to that of the peoples under them. Thus, Philo tells us, the Emperor Caligula reasoned, concluding equally well either that kings were gods, or that men were beasts.

The reasoning of Caligula agrees with that of Hobbes and Grotius. Aristotle, before any of them, had said that men are by no means equal naturally, but that some are born for slavery, and others for dominion.

Aristotle was right; but he took the effect for the cause. Nothing can be more certain than that every man born in slavery is born for slavery. Slaves lose everything in their chains, even the desire of escaping from them: they love their servitude, as the comrades of Ulysses loved their brutish condition. If then there are slaves by nature, it is because there have been slaves against nature. Force made the first slaves, and their cowardice perpetuated the condition.

I have said nothing of King Adam, or Emperor Noah, father of the three great monarchs who shared out the universe, like the children of Saturn, whom some scholars have recognised in them. I trust to getting due thanks for my moderation; for, being a direct descendant of one of these princes, perhaps of the eldest branch, how do I know that a verification of titles might not leave me the legitimate king of the human race? In any case, there can be no doubt that Adam was sovereign of the world, as Robinson Crusoe was of his island, as long as he was its only inhabitant; and this empire had the advantage that the monarch, safe on his throne, had no rebellions, wars, or conspirators to fear.

3. THE RIGHT OF THE STRONGEST

The strongest is never strong enough to be always the master, unless he transforms strength into right, and obedience into duty. Hence the right of the strongest, which, though to all seeming meant ironically, is really laid down as a fundamental principle. But are we never to have an explanation of this phrase? Force is a physical power, and I fail to see what moral effect it can have. To yield to force is an act of necessity, not of will—at the most, an act of prudence. In what sense can it be a duty?

Suppose for a moment that this so-called "right" exists. I maintain that the sole result is a mass of inexplicable nonsense. For, if force creates right, the effect changes with the cause: every force that is greater than the first succeeds to its right. As soon as it is possible to disobey with impunity, disobedience is legitimate; and, the strongest being always in the right, the only thing that matters is to act so as to become the strongest. But what kind of right is that which perishes when force fails? If we must obey perforce, there is no need to obey because we ought; and if we are not forced to obey, we are under no obligation to do so. Clearly, the word "right" adds nothing to force: in this connection, it means absolutely nothing.

Obey the powers that be. If this means yield to force, it is a good precept, but superfluous: I can answer for its never being violated. All power comes from God, I admit; but so does all sickness: does that mean that we are forbidden to call in the doctor? A brigand surprises me at the edge of a wood: must I not merely surrender my purse on compulsion; but, even if I could withhold it, am I in conscience bound to give it up? For certainly the pistol he holds is also a power.

Let us then admit that force does not create right, and that we are obliged to obey only legitimate powers. In that case, my original question recurs.

4. SLAVERY

Since no man has a natural authority over his fellow, and force creates no right, we must conclude that conventions form the basis of all legitimate authority among men.

If an individual, says Grotius, can alienate his liberty and make himself the slave of a master, why could not a whole people do the same and make itself subject to a king? There are in this passage plenty of ambiguous words which would need explaining; but let us confine ourselves to the word *alienate.* To alienate is to give or to sell. Now, a man who becomes the slave of another does not give himself; he sells himself, at the least for his subsistence: but for what does a people sell itself? A king is so far from furnishing his subjects with their subsistence that he gets his own only from them; and, according to Rabelais, kings do not live on nothing. Do subjects then give their persons on condition that the king takes their goods also? I fail to see what they have left to preserve.

It will be said that the despot assures his subjects civil tranquillity. Granted; but what do they gain, if the wars his ambition brings down upon them, his insatiable avidity, and the vexatious conduct of his ministers press harder on them than their own dissensions would have done? What do they gain, if the very tranquillity they enjoy is one of their miseries? Tranquillity is found also in dungeons; but is that enough to make them desirable places to live in? The Greeks imprisoned in the cave of the Cyclops lived there very tranquilly, while they were awaiting their turn to be devoured.

To say that a man gives himself gratuitously, is to say what is absurd and inconceivable; such an act is null and illegitimate, from the mere fact that he who does it is out of his mind. To say the same of a whole people is to suppose a people of madmen; and madness creates no right.

Even if each man could alienate himself, he could not alienate his children: they are born men and free; their liberty belongs to them, and no one but they has the right to dispose of it. Before they come to years of discretion, the father can, in their name, lay down conditions for their preservation and well-being, but he cannot give them irrevocably and without conditions: such a gift is contrary to the ends of nature, and exceeds the rights of paternity. It would therefore be necessary, in order to legitimise an arbitrary government, that in every generation the people should be in a position to accept or reject it; but, were this so, the government would be no longer arbitrary.

To renounce liberty is to renounce being a man, to surrender the rights of humanity and even its duties. For him who renounces everything no indemnity is possible. Such a renunciation is incompatible with man's nature; to remove all liberty from his will is to remove all morality from his acts. Finally, it is an empty and contradictory convention that sets up, on the one side, absolute authority, and, on the other, unlimited obedience. Is it not clear that we can be under no obligation to a person from whom we have the right to exact everything? Does not this condition alone, in the absence of equivalence or exchange, in itself involve the nullity of the act? For what right can my slave have against me, when all that he has belongs to me, and, his right being mine, this right of mine against myself is a phrase devoid of meaning?

Grotius and the rest find in war another origin for the so-called right of slavery. The victor having, as they hold, the right of killing the vanquished, the latter can buy back his life at the price of his liberty; and this convention is the more legitimate because it is to the advantage of both parties.

But it is clear that this supposed right to kill the conquered is by no means deducible from the state of war. Men, from the mere fact that, while they are living in their primitive independence, they have no mutual relations stable enough to constitute either the state of peace or the state of war, cannot be naturally enemies. War is constituted by a relation between things, and not between persons; and, as the state of war cannot arise out of simple personal relations, but only out of real relations, private war, or war of man with man, can exist neither in the state of nature, where there is no constant property, nor in the social state, where everything is under the authority of the laws.

Individual combats, duels and encounters, are acts which cannot constitute a state; while the private wars, authorised by the Establishments of Louis IX, King of France, and suspended by the Peace of God, are abuses of feudalism, in itself an absurd system if ever there was one, and contrary to the principles of natural right and to all good polity.

War then is a relation, not between man and man, but between State and State, and individuals are enemies only accidentally, not as men, nor even as citizens, but as soldiers; not as members of their country, but as its defenders. Finally, each State can have for enemies only other States, and not men; for between things disparate in nature there can be no real relation.

Furthermore, this principle is in conformity with the established rules of all times and the constant practice of all civilised peoples. Declarations of war are intimations less to powers than to their subjects. The foreigner, whether king, individual, or people, who robs, kills or detains the subjects, without declaring war on the prince, is not an enemy, but a brigand. Even in real war, a just prince, while laying hands, in the enemy's country, on all that belongs to the public, respects the lives and goods of individuals: he respects rights on which his own are founded. The object of the war being the destruction of the hostile State, the other side has a right to kill its defenders, while they are bearing arms; but as soon as they lay them down and surrender, they cease to be enemies or instruments of the enemy, and become once more merely men, whose life no one has any right to take. Sometimes it is possible to kill the State without killing a single one of its members; and war gives no right which is not necessary to the gaining of its object. These principles are not those of Grotius: they are not based on the authority of poets, but derived from the nature of reality and based on reason.

The right of conquest has no foundation other than the right of the strongest. If war does not give the conqueror the right to massacre the conquered peoples, the right to enslave them cannot be based upon a right which does not exist. No one has a right to kill an enemy except when he cannot make him a slave, and the right to enslave him cannot therefore be derived from the right to kill him. It is accordingly an unfair exchange to make him buy at the price of his liberty his life, over which the victor holds no right. Is it not clear that there is a vicious circle in founding the right of life and death on the right of slavery, and the right of slavery on the right of life and death?

Even if we assume this terrible right to kill everybody, I maintain that a slave made in war, or a conquered people, is under no obligation to a master, except to obey him as far as he is compelled to do so. By taking an equivalent for his life, the victor has not done him a favour; instead of killing him without profit, he has killed him usefully. So far then is he from acquiring over him any authority in addition to that of force, that the state of war continues to subsist between them: their mutual relation is the effect of it, and the usage of the right of war does not imply a treaty of peace. A convention has indeed been made; but this convention, so far from destroying the state of war, presupposes its continuance.

So, from whatever aspect we regard the question, the right of slavery is null and void, not only as being illegitimate, but also because it is absurd and meaningless. The words *slave* and *right* contradict each other, and are mutually exclusive. It will always be equally foolish for a man to say to a man or to a people: "I make with you a convention wholly at your expense and wholly to my advantage; I shall keep it as long as I like, and you will keep it as long as I like."

5. THAT WE MUST ALWAYS GO BACK TO A FIRST CONVENTION

Even if I granted all that I have been refuting, the friends of despotism would be no better off. There will always be a great difference between subduing a multitude and ruling a society. Even if scattered individuals were successively enslaved by one man, however numerous they might be, I still see no more than a master and his slaves, and certainly not a people and its ruler; I see what may be termed an aggregation, but not an association; there is as yet neither public good nor body politic. The man in question, even if he has enslaved half the world, is still only an individual; his interest, apart from that of others, is still a purely private interest. If this same man comes to die, his empire, after him, remains scattered and without unity, as an oak falls and dissolves into a heap of ashes when the fire has consumed it.

A people, says Grotius, can give itself to a king. Then, according to Grotius, a people is a people before it gives itself. The gift is itself a civil act, and implies public deliberation. It would be better, before examining the act by which a people gives itself to a king, to examine that by which it has become a people; for this act, being necessarily prior to the other, is the true foundation of society.

Indeed, if there were no prior convention, where, unless the election were unanimous, would be the obligation on the minority to submit to the choice of the majority? How have a hundred men who wish for a master the right to vote on behalf of ten who do not? The law of majority voting is itself something established by convention, and presupposes unanimity, on one occasion at least.

6. THE SOCIAL COMPACT

I suppose men to have reached the point at which the obstacles in the way of their preservation in the state of nature show their power of resistance to be greater than the resources at the disposal of each individual for his maintenance in that state. That primitive condition can then subsist no longer; and the human race would perish unless it changed its manner of existence.

But, as men cannot engender new forces, but only unite and direct existing ones, they have no other means of preserving themselves than the formation, by aggregation, of a sum of forces great enough to overcome the resistance. These they have to bring into play by means of a single motive power, and cause to act in concert.

This sum of forces can arise only where several persons come together: but, as the force and liberty of each man are the chief instruments of his self-preservation, how can he pledge them without harming his own interests, and neglecting the care he owes to himself? This difficulty, in its bearing on my present subject, may be stated in the following terms:

> *"The problem is to find a form of association which will defend and protect with the whole common force the person and goods of each associate, and in which each, while uniting himself with all, may*

still obey himself alone, and remain as free as before." This is the fundamental problem of which the *Social Contract* provides the solution.

The clauses of this contract are so determined by the nature of the act that the slightest modification would make them vain and ineffective; so that, although they have perhaps never been formally set forth, they are everywhere the same and everywhere tacitly admitted and recognised, until, on the violation of the social compact, each regains his original rights and resumes his natural liberty, while losing the conventional liberty in favour of which he renounced it.

These clauses, properly understood, may be reduced to one—the total alienation of each associate, together with all his rights, to the whole community; for, in the first place, as each gives himself absolutely, the conditions are the same for all; and, this being so, no one has any interest in making them burdensome to others.

Moreover, the alienation being without reserve, the union is as perfect as it can be, and no associate has anything more to demand: for, if the individuals retained certain rights, as there would be no common superior to decide between them and the public, each, being on one point his own judge, would ask to be so on all; the state of nature would thus continue, and the association would necessarily become inoperative or tyrannical.

Finally, each man, in giving himself to all, gives himself to nobody; and as there is no associate over whom he does not acquire the same right as he yields others over himself, he gains an equivalent for everything he loses, and an increase of force for the preservation of what he has.

If then we discard from the social compact what is not of its essence, we shall find that it reduces itself to the following terms:

"Each of us puts his person and all his power in common under the supreme direction of the general will, and, in our corporate capacity, we receive each member as an indivisible part of the whole."

At once, in place of the individual personality of each contracting party, this act of association creates a moral and collective body, composed of as many members as the assembly contains votes, and receiving from this act its unity, its common identity, its life and its will. This public person, so formed by the union of all other persons formerly took the name of *city,* and now takes that of *Republic* or *body politic*; it is called by its members *State* when passive, *Sovereign* when active, and *Power* when compared with others like itself. Those who are associated in it take collectively the name of *people,* and severally are called *citizens,* as sharing in the sovereign power, and *subjects,* as being under the laws of the State. But these terms are often confused and taken one for another: it is enough to know how to distinguish them when they are being used with precision.

7. THE SOVEREIGN

This formula shows us that the act of association comprises a mutual undertaking between the public and the individuals, and that each individual, in making a contract, as we may say, with himself, is bound in a double capacity; as a member of the Sovereign he is bound to the individuals, and as a member of the State to the Sovereign. But the maxim of civil right, that no one is bound by undertakings made to himself, does not apply in this case; for there is a great difference between incurring an obligation to yourself and incurring one to a whole of which you form a part.

Attention must further be called to the fact that public deliberation, while competent to bind all the subjects to the Sovereign, because of the two different capacities in which each of them may be regarded, cannot, for the opposite reason, bind the Sovereign to itself; and that it is consequently against the nature of the body politic for the Sovereign to impose on itself a law which it cannot infringe. Being able to regard itself in only one capacity, it is in the position of an individual who makes a contract with himself; and this makes it clear that there neither is nor can be any kind of fundamental law binding on the body of the people—not even the social contract itself. This does not mean that the body politic cannot enter into undertakings with others, provided the contract is not infringed by them; for in relation to what is external to it, it becomes a simple being, an individual.

But the body politic or the Sovereign, drawing its being wholly from the sanctity of the contract, can never bind itself, even to an outsider, to do anything derogatory to the original act, for instance, to alienate any part of itself, or to submit to another Sovereign. Violation of the act by which it exists would be self-annihilation; and that which is itself nothing can create nothing.

As soon as this multitude is so united in one body, it is impossible to offend against one of the members without attacking the body, and still more to offend against the body without the members resenting it. Duty and interest therefore equally oblige the two contracting parties to give each other help; and the same men should seek to combine, in their double capacity, all the advantages dependent upon that capacity.

Again, the Sovereign, being formed wholly of the individuals who compose it, neither has nor can have any interest contrary to theirs; and consequently the sovereign power need give no guarantee to its subjects, because it is impossible for the body to wish to hurt all its members. We shall also see later on that it cannot hurt any in particular. The Sovereign, merely by virtue of what it is, is always what it should be.

This, however, is not the case with the relation of the subjects to the Sovereign, which, despite the common interest, would have no security that they would fulfil their undertakings, unless it found means to assure itself of their fidelity.

In fact, each individual, as a man, may have a particular will contrary or dissimilar to the general will which he has as a citizen. His particular interest may speak to him quite differently from the common interest: his absolute and naturally independent existence may make him look upon what he owes to the common cause as a gratuitous contribution, the loss of which will do less harm to others than the payment of it is burdensome to himself; and, regarding the moral person which constitutes the State as a *persona ficta,* because not a man, he may wish to enjoy the rights of citizenship without being ready to fulfil the duties of a subject. The continuance of such an injustice could not but prove the undoing of the body politic.

In order then that the social compact may not be an empty formula, it tacitly includes the undertaking, which alone can give force to the rest, that whoever refuses to obey the general will shall be compelled to do so by the whole body. This means nothing less than that he will be forced to be free; for this is the condition which, by giving each citizen to his country, secures him against all personal dependence. In this lies the key to the working of the political machine; this alone legitimises civil undertakings, which, without it, would be absurd, tyrannical, and liable to the most frightful abuses.

8. THE CIVIL STATE

The passage from the state of nature to the civil state produces a very remarkable change in man, by substituting justice for instinct in his conduct, and giving his actions the morality they had formerly lacked. Then only, when the voice of duty takes the place of physical impulses and right of appetite, does man, who so far had considered only himself, find that he is forced to act on different principles, and to consult his reason before listening to his inclinations. Although, in this state, he deprives himself of some advantages which he got from nature, he gains in return others so great, his faculties are so stimulated and developed, his ideas so extended, his feelings so ennobled, and his whole soul so uplifted, that, did not the abuses of this new condition often degrade him below that which he left, he would be bound to bless continually the happy moment which took him from it for ever, and, instead of a stupid and unimaginative animal, made him an intelligent being and a man.

Let us draw up the whole account in terms easily commensurable. What man loses by the social contract is his natural liberty and an unlimited right to everything he tries to get and succeeds in getting; what he gains is civil liberty and the proprietorship of all he possesses. If we are to avoid mistake in weighing one against the other, we must clearly distinguish natural liberty, which is bounded only by the strength of the individual, from civil liberty, which is limited by the general will; and possession, which is merely the effect of force or the right of the first occupier, from property, which can be founded only on a positive title.

We might, over and above all this, add, to what man acquires in the civil state, moral liberty, which alone makes him truly master of himself; for the mere impulse of appetite is slavery, while obedience to a law which we prescribe to ourselves is liberty. But I have already said too much on this head, and the philosophical meaning of the word liberty does not now concern us.

9. REAL PROPERTY

Each member of the community gives himself to it, at the moment of its foundation, just as he is, with all the resources at his command, including the goods he possesses. This act does not make possession, in changing hands, change its nature, and become property in the hands of the Sovereign; but, as the forces of the city are incomparably greater than those of an individual, public possession is also, in fact, stronger and more irrevocable, without being any more legitimate, at any rate from the point of view of foreigners. For the State, in relation to its members, is master of all their goods by the social contract, which, within the State, is the basis of all rights; but, in relation to other powers, it is so only by the right of the first occupier, which it holds from its members.

The right of the first occupier, though more real than the right of the strongest, becomes a real right only when the right of property has already been established. Every man has naturally a right to everything he needs; but the positive act which makes him proprietor of one thing excludes him from everything else. Having his share, he ought to keep to it, and can have no further right against the community. This is why the right of the first occupier, which in the state of nature is so weak, claims the respect of every man in civil society. In this right we are respecting not so much what belongs to another as what does not belong to ourselves.

In general, to establish the right of the first occupier over a plot of ground, the following conditions are necessary: first, the land must not yet be inhabited; secondly, a man must occupy only the amount he needs for his subsistence; and, in the third place, possession must be taken, not by an empty ceremony, but by labour and cultivation, the only sign of proprietorship that should be respected by others, in default of a legal title.

In granting the right of first occupancy to necessity and labour, are we not really stretching it as far as it can go? Is it possible to leave such a right unlimited? Is it to be enough to set foot on a plot of common ground, in order to be able to call yourself at once the master of it? Is it to be enough that a man has the strength to expel others for a moment, in order to establish his right to prevent them from ever returning? How can a man or a people seize an immense territory and keep it from the rest of the world except by a punishable usurpation, since all others are being robbed, by such an act, of the place of habitation and the means of subsistence which nature gave them in common? When Núñez Balboa, standing on the seashore, took possession of the South Seas and the whole of South America in the name of the crown of Castile, was that enough to dispossess all their actual inhabitants, and to shut out from them all the princes of the world? On such a showing, these ceremonies are idly multiplied, and the Catholic King need only take possession all at once, from his apartment, of the whole universe, merely making a subsequent reservation about what was already in the possession of other princes.

We can imagine how the lands of individuals, where they were contiguous and came to be united, became the public territory, and how the right of Sovereignty, extending from the subjects over the lands they held, became at once real and personal. The possessors were thus made more dependent, and the forces at their command used to guarantee their fidelity. The advantage of this does not seem to have been felt by ancient monarchs, who called themselves

Kings of the Persians, Scythians, or Macedonians, and seemed to regard themselves more as rulers of men than as masters of a country. Those of the present day more cleverly call themselves Kings of France, Spain, England, etc.: thus holding the land, they are quite confident of holding the inhabitants.

The peculiar fact about this alienation is that, in taking over the goods of individuals, the community, so far from despoiling them, only assures them legitimate possession, and changes usurpation into a true right and enjoyment into proprietorship. Thus the possessors, being regarded as depositaries of the public good, and having their rights respected by all the members of the State and maintained against foreign aggression by all its forces, have, by a cession which benefits both the public and still more themselves, acquired, so to speak, all that they gave up. This paradox may easily be explained by the distinction between the rights which the Sovereign and the proprietor have over the same estate, as we shall see later on.

It may also happen that men begin to unite one with another before they possess anything, and that, subsequently occupying a tract of country which is enough for all, they enjoy it in common, or share it out among themselves, either equally or according to a scale fixed by the Sovereign. However the acquisition be made, the right which each individual has to his own estate is always subordinate to the right which the community has over all: without this, there would be neither stability in the social tie, nor real force in the exercise of Sovereignty.

I shall end this chapter and this book by remarking on a fact on which the whole social system should rest: i.e., that, instead of destroying natural inequality, the fundamental compact substitutes, for such physical inequality as nature may have set up between men, an equality that is moral and legitimate, and that men, who may be unequal in strength or intelligence, become every one equal by convention and legal right.

2 Rational Choice

Within the social sciences, the dominant view is that a person counts as rational as long as she chooses what, as it seems to her, will most likely satisfy her preferences. Much of economics works with the assumption that people are rational (in this sense) and uses that assumption to create models that can generate powerful predictions of how people will behave. In this sense, "rationality" is not a normative concept used to evaluate people or their actions, but an analytic tool used to explain and predict behavior. Often, though, "rationality" is a term of evaluation that reflects a standard that people, their beliefs, their preferences, and their choices might live up to, but regularly do not. Thinking of rationality in this second (normative) sense fits with the common observation that people are regularly less than rational, preferring and believing and choosing things that they should not.

To count as rational in the non-normative sense an agent's preference ordering must be "complete" (the preferences cover all relevant alternatives, allowing each to be compared to the others) and "transitive" (if the agent prefers A to B, and B to C, she also prefers A to C but not C to A). But apart from formal conditions requiring consistency between preferences, rational agency places no constraints on the content of preferences. As Gary Becker puts it, agents who are rational in the economic sense "maximize welfare *as they conceive it*, whether they be selfish, altruistic, loyal, spiteful, or masochistic." Since resources are scarce and information is costly to consume, rational agents will not be perfectly informed. Far from it. Rational agents try to maximize their welfare subject to constraints like time and money, the cost of gathering and processing information, and the opportunity cost of spending scarce energy on one endeavor rather than another.

Becker thinks the assumption of rationality helps illuminate otherwise puzzling behavior. For example, if we assume people are rational, Becker argues, we can predict that crime rates will be determined by the quality and quantity of employment opportunities, the likelihood and magnitude of punishment, and the efficacy of non-legal punishments like ostracism for violating social norms. Similar arguments can be applied to people's willingness to indulge racist attitudes in the marketplace, the amount they invest in human capital (his term for education), and their choice of whether (and when) to get married and have children. All of these decisions, Becker suggests, are made by rational individuals against the backdrop of different incentives, constraints, and preferences.

David Schmidtz challenges the centrality of self-interest in the *homo economicus* (or "economic man") model of human behavior, which is the version of rational choice theory that emerged to explain consumer behavior. Schmidtz points out that we need not assume people are selfish wealth maximizers to model them as rational. All we need to do is understand their goals or preferences, which may include a concern with other people's welfare. Altruistic reasons for action are perfectly explicable and even commonplace. Thus, Schmidtz thinks, models that fail to account for altruistic goals or preferences are impoverished descriptions of human behavior.

In attempting to efficiently achieve their goals, or maximize the satisfaction of their preferences, rational agents sometimes face situations in which there are joint gains to be had over the long run by forging cooperative agreements, but potential gains to be had in the short run by breaking such agreements once the other person has performed her part. David Gauthier thinks that such cases challenge the idea that a rational person will always directly attempt to maximize the satisfaction of her preferences. Gauthier distinguishes between *straightforward* and *constrained* maximizers. Straightforward maximizers assess the expected utility of forming a plan or signing a contract (at t_1) and then separately assess the utility of executing a plan or complying with a contract (at t_2). By contrast, *constrained maximizers* assess the expected utility of forming and executing a plan or contract as a bundle. In situations of interdependence, and under the right conditions, constrained maximizers can better achieve their goals than straightforward maximizers because they can be trusted to follow through on their plans or comply with their contracts.

Gauthier's principle of constrained maximization is akin to Hobbes's third law of nature, "that men perform their Covenants made; without which, covenants are in vain. . . ." Gauthier follows Hobbes in thinking that, if it is rational to make a mutually beneficial contract, it may be rational to follow through on it, even when there are real and immediate benefits to be gained by breaking it. The key point here is that trust transforms interactions and makes possible opportunities for mutual advantage that are otherwise beyond reach. But those who are worthy of trust reason in ways that differ from those who are untrustworthy.

One problem with Gauthier's theory, illustrated in Gregory Kavka's brilliant "toxin puzzle" thought experiment, is that our ability to reason in a constrained or unconstrained way may not be fully under our control. Another problem is that Gauthier's argument suggests that the best course of action—if it is available—is to pretend to be a constrained maximizer while being a straightforward maximizer. Anyone who has ever been to a singles bar will recognize that this problem is not simply hypothetical.

FURTHER READING

Angner, Erik. 2012. *A Course in Behavioral Economics*. Palgrave MacMillan.

Dawes, Robyn and Reid Hastie. 2009. *Rational Choice in an Uncertain World*, 2nd ed. Sage Publications.

Gaus, Gerald. 2010. "The Limits of *Homo Economicus*." In *Essays on Philosophy, Politics, and Economics*, edited by Favor, Gaus, and LaMont. Stanford University Press.

Gauthier, David. 1994. "Assure and Threaten." *Ethics* 104(4): 690–721.

Gintis, Herbert. 2000. "Beyond *Homo Economicus*: Evidence from Experimental Economics." Ecological Economics, 35: 311–322.

Mele, Alfred and Piers Rawling. 2004. The Oxford Handbook of Rationality. Oxford University Press.

Moser, Paul. 1990. *Rationality in Action: Contemporary Approaches*. Cambridge University Press.

Nozick, Robert. 1993. *The Nature of Rationality*. Princeton University Press.

Parfit, Derek. 1986. *Reasons and Persons*. Oxford University Press.

Smith, Vernon. 2009. *Rationality in Economics: Constructivist and Ecological Forms*. Cambridge University Press.

GARY BECKER

The Economic Way of Looking at Behavior

1993

THE ECONOMIC APPROACH

My research uses the economic approach to analyze social issues that range beyond those usually considered by economists. This paper will describe the approach and illustrate it with examples drawn from past and current work.

Unlike Marxian analysis, the economic approach I refer to does not assume that individuals are motivated solely by selfishness or material gain. It is a *method* of analysis, not an assumption about particular motivations. Along with others, I have tried to pry economists away from narrow assumptions about self-interest. Behavior is driven by a much richer set of values and preferences.

The analysis assumes that individuals maximize welfare *as they conceive it,* whether they be selfish, altruistic, loyal, spiteful, or masochistic. Their behavior is forward-looking, and it is also assumed to be consistent over time. In particular, they try as best they can to anticipate the uncertain consequences of their actions. Forward-looking behavior, however, may still be rooted in the past, for the past can exert a long shadow on attitudes and values.

Actions are constrained by income, time, imperfect memory and calculating capacities, and other limited resources, and also by the opportunities available in the economy and elsewhere. These opportunities are largely determined by the private and collective actions of other individuals and organizations.

Different constraints are decisive for different situations, but the most fundamental constraint is limited time. Economic and medical progress have greatly increased length of life, but not the physical flow of time itself, which always restricts everyone to twenty-four hours per day. So while goods and services have expanded enormously in rich countries, the total time available to consume has not. . . .

CRIME AND PUNISHMENT

I began to think about crime in the 1960s after driving to Columbia University for an oral examination of a student in economic theory. I was late and had to decide quickly whether to put the car in a parking lot or risk getting a ticket for parking illegally on the street. I calculated the likelihood of getting a ticket, the size of the penalty, and the cost of putting the car in a lot. I decided it paid to take the risk and park on the street. (I did not get a ticket.)

As I walked the few blocks to the examination room, it occurred to me that the city authorities had probably gone through a similar analysis. The frequency of their inspection of parked vehicles and the size of the penalty imposed on violators should depend on their estimates of the type of calculations potential violators like me would make. Of course, the first question I put to the hapless student was to work out the optimal behavior of both the offenders and the police, something I had not yet done.

In the 1950s and 1960s, intellectual discussions of crime were dominated by the opinion that criminal behavior was caused by mental illness and social oppression, and that criminals were helpless "victims." A book by a well-known psychiatrist was entitled *The Crime of Punishment* (see Menninger 1966).

Gary becker, "The Economic Way of Looking at Behavior". *Journal of Political Economy,* 1993, vol. 101, no. 3.

Such attitudes began to exert a major influence on social policy, as laws changed to expand criminals' rights. These changes reduced the apprehension and conviction of criminals and provided less protection to the law-abiding population.

I was not sympathetic to the assumption that criminals had radically different motivations from everyone else. I explored instead the theoretical and empirical implications of the assumption that criminal behavior is rational, but again "rationality" did not imply narrow materialism. It recognized that many people were constrained by moral and ethical considerations, and they did not commit crimes even when these were profitable and there was no danger of detection. However, police and jails would be unnecessary if such attitudes always prevailed. Rationality implied that some individuals become criminals because of the financial and other rewards from crime compared to legal work, taking account of the likelihood of apprehension and conviction, and the severity of punishment.

The amount of crime is determined not only by the rationality and preferences of would-be criminals but also by the economic and social environment created by public policies, including expenditures on police, punishments for different crimes, and opportunities for employment, schooling, and training programs. Clearly, the types of legal jobs available as well as law, order, and punishment are an integral part of the economic approach to crime.

Total public spending on fighting crime can be reduced, while keeping the mathematically expected punishment unchanged, by offsetting a cut in expenditures on catching criminals with a sufficient increase in the punishment to those convicted. However, risk-preferring individuals are more deterred from crime by a higher probability of conviction than by severe punishments. Therefore, optimal behavior by the state would balance the reduced spending on police and courts from lowering the probability of conviction against the preference of risk-preferring criminals for a lesser certainty of punishment. The state should also consider the likelihood of punishing innocent persons.

In the early stages of my work on crime, I was puzzled by why theft is socially harmful since it appears merely to redistribute resources, usually from wealthier to poorer individuals. I resolved the puzzle by pointing out that criminals spend on weapons and on the value of the time in planning and carrying out their crimes, and that such spending is socially unproductive—it is what is now called "rent seeking"—because it does not create wealth, only forcibly redistributes it. I approximated the social cost of theft by the dollars stolen since rational criminals would be willing to spend up to that amount on their crimes. I should have added the resources spent by potential victims protecting themselves against crime.

One reason why the economic approach to crime became so influential is that the same analytic apparatus can be used to study enforcement of all laws, including minimum wage legislation, clean air acts, insider trader and other violations of security laws, and income tax evasions. Since few laws are self-enforcing, they require expenditures on conviction and punishment to deter violators. The U.S. Sentencing Commission (1992) has explicitly used the economic analysis of crime to develop rules to be followed by judges in punishing violators of federal statutes.

Studies of crime that use the economic approach have become common during the past quarter century. These include analysis of the optimal marginal punishments to deter increases in the severity of crimes—for example, to deter a kidnapper from killing his victim—and the relation between private and public enforcement of laws.

Fines are preferable to imprisonment and other types of punishment because they can deter crimes effectively if criminals have sufficient financial resources—if they are not "judgment proof," to use legal jargon. Moreover, fines are more efficient than other methods because the cost to offenders is also revenue to the state.

Empirical assessments of the effects on crime rates of prison terms, conviction rates, unemployment levels, income inequality, and other variables have become more numerous and more accurate. The greatest controversies surround the question of whether capital punishment deters murders, a controversy that arouses much emotion but is far from being resolved.

HUMAN CAPITAL

Until the 1950s economists generally assumed that labor power was given and not augmentable. The sophisticated analyses of investments in education and other training by Adam Smith, Alfred Marshall, and Milton Friedman were not integrated into discussions of productivity. Then Theodore W. Schultz and others began to pioneer the exploration of the implications of human capital investments for economic growth and related economic questions.

Human capital analysis starts with the assumption that individuals decide on their education, training, medical care, and other additions to knowledge and health by weighing the benefits and costs. Benefits include cultural and other nonmonetary gains along with improvement in earnings and occupations, whereas costs usually depend mainly on the forgone value of the time spent on these investments. The concept of human capital also covers accumulated work and other habits, even including harmful addictions such as smoking and drug use. Human capital in the form of good work habits or addictions to heavy drinking has major positive or negative effects on productivity in both market and nonmarket sectors.

The various kinds of behavior included under the rubric of human capital help explain why the concept is so powerful and useful. It also means that the process of investing or disinvesting in human capital often alters the very nature of a person: training may change a lifestyle from one with perennial unemployment to one with stable and good earnings, or accumulated drinking may destroy a career, health, and even the capacity to think straight.

Human capital is so uncontroversial nowadays that it may be difficult to appreciate the hostility in the 1950s and 1960s toward the approach that went with the term. The very concept of *human* capital was alleged to be demeaning because it treated people as machines. To approach schooling as an investment rather than a cultural experience was considered unfeeling and extremely narrow. As a result, I hesitated a long time before deciding to call my book *Human Capital* (1964) and hedged the risk by using a long subtitle that I no longer remember. Only gradually did economists, let alone others, accept the concept of human capital as a valuable tool in the analysis of various economic and social issues.

My work on human capital began with an effort to calculate both private and social rates of return to men, women, blacks, and other groups from investments in different levels of education. After a while it became clear that the analysis of human capital can help explain many regularities in labor markets and the economy at large. It seemed possible to develop a more general theory of human capital that includes firms as well as individuals and that could consider its macroeconomic implications. . . .

One of the most influential theoretical concepts in human capital analysis is the distinction between general and specific training or knowledge. By definition, firm-specific knowledge is useful only in the firms providing it, whereas general knowledge is useful also in other firms. Teaching someone to operate an IBM-compatible personal computer is general training, whereas learning the authority structure and the talents of employees in a particular company is specific knowledge. This distinction helps explain why workers with highly specific skills are less likely to quit their jobs and are the last to be laid off during business downturns. It also explains why most promotions are made from within a firm rather than through hiring—workers need time to learn about a firm's structure and "culture"—and why better accounting methods would include the specific human capital of employees among the principal asset of most companies. . . .

Human capital theory gives a provocative interpretation of the so-called gender gap in earnings. Traditionally, women have been far more likely than men to work part-time and intermittently partly because they usually withdrew from the labor force for a while after having children. As a result, they had fewer incentives to invest in education and training that improved earnings and job skills.

During the past twenty-five years all this changed. The decline in family size, the growth in divorce rates, the rapid expansion of the service sector (where most women are employed), the continuing economic development that raised the earnings of women along with those of men, and civil rights legislation encouraged greater labor force participation by women and, hence, greater investment in market-oriented skills. In practically all rich countries, these forces significantly improved both the occupations and relative earnings of women.

The United States' experience is especially well documented. The gender gap in earnings among full-time men and women remained at about 35 percent from the mid-fifties to the mid-seventies. Then women began a steady economic advance, which is still continuing; it narrowed the gap to under 25 percent. Women are flocking to business, law, and medical schools, and they are working at skilled jobs that they formerly shunned or were excluded from.

Schultz and others early on emphasized that investments in human capital are a major contributor to economic growth. But after a while the relation of human capital to growth was neglected, as economists became discouraged about whether the available growth theory gave many insights into the progress of different countries. The revival of more formal models of endogenous growth has brought human capital once again to the forefront of the discussions.

FORMATION, DISSOLUTION, AND STRUCTURE OF FAMILIES

The rational choice analysis of family behavior builds on maximizing behavior, investments in human capital, the allocation of time, and discrimination against women and other groups. The rest of the lecture focuses on this analysis since it is still quite controversial, and I can discuss some of my current research.

Writing *A Treatise on the Family* (1981) is the most difficult sustained intellectual effort I have undertaken. The family is arguably the most fundamental and oldest of institutions: some authors trace its origin to more than 40,000 years ago. The *Treatise* tries to analyze not only modern Western families but those in other cultures and changes in family structure during the past several centuries.

Trying to cover this broad subject required a degree of mental commitment over more than 6 years, during many nighttime as well as daytime hours, that left me intellectually and emotionally exhausted. In his autobiography, Bertrand Russell says that writing the *Principia Mathematica* used up so much of his mental powers that he was never again fit for really hard intellectual work. It took about 2 years after finishing the *Treatise* to regain my intellectual zest.

The analysis of fertility has a long and honorable history in economics, but until recent years marriage and divorce, and the relations between husbands, wives, parents, and children, had been largely neglected by economists. The point of departure of my work on the family is the assumption that when men and women decide to marry, or have children, or divorce, they attempt to raise their welfare by comparing benefits and costs. So they marry when they expect to be better off than if they remained single, and they divorce if that is expected to increase their welfare.

People who are not intellectuals are often surprised when told that this approach is controversial since it seems obvious to them that individuals try to improve their welfare by marriage and divorce. The rational choice approach to marriage and other behavior is in fact often consistent with the instinctive economics "of the common person".

Still, intuitive assumptions about behavior are only the *starting point* of systematic analysis, for alone they do not yield many interesting implications. Marquis of Deffand said, when commenting on the story that St. Denis walked two leagues while carrying his head in his hands, that "the distance is nothing; it is only the first step that is difficult." The first one in new research is also important, but it is of little value without second, third, and several additional steps (I owe this reference to the marquis and the comparison with research to Richard Posner). The rational choice approach takes further steps by using a framework that combines maximizing behavior with the analysis of marriage and divorce markets, specialization and the division of labor, old-age support, investments in children, and legislation that affects families. The implications of the full model are often not so obvious and sometimes run sharply counter to received opinion.

For example, contrary to a common belief about divorce among the rich, the economic analysis of family decisions shows that wealthier couples are *less* likely to divorce than poorer couples. According to this theory, richer couples tend to gain a lot from remaining married, whereas many poorer couples do not. A poor woman may well doubt whether it is worth staying married to someone who is chronically unemployed. Empirical studies for many countries do indicate that marriages of richer couples are much more stable.

Efficient bargaining between husbands and wives implies that the trend in Europe and the United States toward no-fault divorce during the past two decades did not raise divorce rates and, therefore, contrary to many claims, that it could not be responsible for the rapid rise in these rates. However, the theory does indicate that no-fault divorce hurts women with children whose marriages are broken up by their husbands. Feminists initially supported no-fault divorce, but some now have second thoughts about whether it has favorable effects on divorced women.

Economic models of behavior have been used to study fertility ever since Thomas Malthus's classic essay; the great Swedish economist, Knut Wicksell, was attracted to economics by his belief in the Malthusian predictions of overpopulation. But Malthus's conclusion that fertility would rise and fall as incomes increased and decreased was contradicted by the large decline in birth rates after some countries became industrialized during the latter part of the nineteenth century and the early part of this century.

The failure of Malthus's simple model of fertility persuaded economists that family size decisions lay beyond economic calculus. The neoclassical growth model reflects this belief, for in most versions it takes population growth as exogenous and given.

However, the trouble with the Malthusian approach is not its use of economics per se, but an economics inappropriate for modern life. It neglects that the time spent on child care becomes more expensive when countries are more productive. The higher value of time raises the cost of children and thereby reduces the demand for large families. It also fails to consider that the greater importance of education and training in industrialized economies encourages parents to invest more in the skills of their children, which also raises the cost of large families. The growing value of time and the increased emphasis on schooling and other human capital explain the decline in fertility as countries develop, and many other features of birth rates in modern economies.

In almost all societies, married women have specialized in bearing and rearing children and in certain agricultural activities, whereas married men have done most of the fighting and market work. It should not be controversial to recognize that the explanation is a combination of biological differences between men and women—especially differences in their innate capacities to bear and rear children—and legal and other discrimination against women in market activities, partly through cultural conditioning. However, large and highly emotional differences of opinion exist over the relative importance of biology and discrimination in generating the traditional division of labor in marriages.

Contrary to allegations in many attacks on the economic approach to the gender division of labor, this analysis does not try to weight the relative importance of biology and discrimination. Its main contribution is to show how sensitive the division of labor is to *small* differences in either. Since the return from investing in a skill is greater when more time is spent utilizing the skill, a married couple could gain much from a sharp division of labor because the husband would specialize in some types of human capital and the wife in others. Given such a large gain from specialization within a marriage, only a *little* discrimination against women or *small* biological differences in child-rearing skills would cause the division of labor between household and market tasks to be strongly and systematically related to gender. The sensitivity to small differences explains why the empirical evidence cannot readily choose between biological and "cultural" interpretations. This theory also explains why many women entered the labor force as families became smaller, divorce became more common, and earning opportunities for women improved.

Relations among family members differ radically from those among employees of firms and members of other organizations. The interactions among husbands, wives, parents, and children are more likely to be motivated by love, obligation, guilt, and a sense of duty than by self-interest narrowly interpreted.

It was demonstrated about 20 years ago that altruism within families enormously alters how they respond to shocks and public policies that redistribute resources among members. It was shown that exogenous redistributions of resources from an altruist to her beneficiaries (or vice versa) may not affect the welfare of anyone because the altruist would try to reduce her gifts by the amount redistributed (Becker 1974). Barro (1974) derived this result in an intergenerational context, which cast doubt on the common assumption that government deficits and related fiscal policies have real effects on the economy.

The "Rotten Kid Theorem"—the name is very popular even when critics disagree with the analysis—carries the discussion of altruism further, for it shows how the behavior of selfish individuals is affected by altruism. Under some conditions, even selfish persons (of course, most parents believe that the best example of selfish beneficiaries and altruistic benefactors is selfish children with altruistic parents) are induced to act *as though* they are altruistic toward their benefactors because that raises their own selfish welfare. They act this way because otherwise gifts from their benefactors would be reduced enough to make them worse off.

The Bible, Plato's *Republic,* and other early writings discussed the treatment of young children by their parents and of elderly parents by adult children. Both the elderly and children need care: in one case because of declining health and energy, and in the other because of biological growth and dependency. A powerful implication of the economic analysis of relations within families is that these two issues are closely related.

Parents who leave sizable bequests do not need old-age support because instead they help out their children. I mentioned earlier one well-known implication of this: under certain conditions, budget deficits and social security payments to the elderly have no real effects because parents simply offset the bigger taxes in the future on their children through larger bequests.

It is much less appreciated that altruistic parents who leave bequests also tend to invest more in their children's skills, habits, and values. For they gain from financing all investments in the education and skills of children that yield a higher rate of return than the return on savings. They can indirectly save for old age by investing in children, and then reducing bequests when elderly. Both parents and children would be better off when parents make all investments in children that yield a higher return than that on savings, and then adjust bequests to the efficient level of investment.

However, even in rich countries, many parents do not plan on leaving bequests. These parents want old-age support, and they "underinvest" in their children's education and other care. They underinvest because they cannot compensate themselves for greater spending on children by reducing bequests since they do not plan on leaving any.

Both the children and parents would be better off if the parents agreed to invest more in the children in return for a commitment by the children to care for them when they need help. But how can such a commitment be enforced? Economists and lawyers usually recommend a written contract to ensure commitment, but can you imagine a society that will enforce contracts between adults and 10-year-olds or teenagers? . . .

CONCLUDING COMMENTS

An important step in extending the traditional analysis of individual rational choice is to incorporate into the theory a much richer class of attitudes, preferences, and calculations. This step is prominent in all the examples I consider. The analysis of discrimination includes in preferences a dislike of—prejudice against—members of particular groups, such as blacks or women. In deciding whether to engage in illegal activities, potential criminals are assumed to act as though they consider both the gains and the risks, including the likelihood they will be caught and severity of punishments. In human capital theory, people rationally evaluate the benefits and costs of activities, such as education, training, expenditures on health, migration, and formation of habits that radically alter the way they are. The economic approach to the family assumes that even intimate decisions such as marriage, divorce, and family size are reached through weighing the advantages and disadvantages of alternative actions. The weights are determined by preferences that critically depend on the altruism and feelings of duty and obligation toward family members.

Since the economic, or rational choice, approach to behavior builds on a theory of individual decisions, criticisms of this theory usually concentrate on particular assumptions about how these decisions are made. Among other things, critics deny that individuals act consistently over time, and question whether behavior is forward-looking, particularly in situations that differ significantly from those usually considered by economists—such as those involving criminal, addictive, family, or political behavior. This is not the place to go into a detailed response to the criticisms, so I simply assert that no approach of comparable generality has yet been developed that offers serious competition to rational choice theory.

I have intentionally chosen certain topics for my research—such as addiction—to probe the boundaries of rational choice theory. William Blake said that you never know what is enough until you see what is more than enough. My work may have sometimes assumed too much rationality, but I believe it has been an antidote to the extensive research that does not credit people with enough rationality.

While the economic approach to behavior builds on a theory of individual choice, it is not mainly concerned with individuals. It uses theory at the micro level as a powerful tool to derive implications at the group or macro level. Rational individual choice is combined with assumptions about technologies and other determinants of opportunities, equilibrium in market and nonmarket situations, and laws, norms, and traditions to obtain results concerning the behavior of groups. It is mainly because the theory derives implications at the macro level that it is of interest to policymakers and those studying differences among countries and cultures.

None of the theories considered in this lecture aims for the greatest generality; instead, each tries to derive concrete implications about behavior that can be tested with survey and other data. Disputes over whether punishments deter crime, whether the lower earnings of women compared to those of men are mainly due to discrimination or lesser human capital, or whether no-fault divorce laws increase divorce rates—all raise questions about the empirical relevance of predictions derived from a theory based on individual rationality.

A close relation between theory and empirical testing helps prevent both the theoretical analysis and the empirical research from becoming sterile. Empirically oriented theories encourage the development of new sources and types of data, the way human capital theory stimulated the use of survey data, especially panels. At the same time, puzzling empirical results force changes in theory, as models of altruism and family preferences have been enriched to cope with the finding that parents in Western countries tend to bequeath equal amounts to different children.

I have been impressed by how many economists want to work on social issues rather than those forming the traditional core of economics. At the same time, specialists from fields that do consider social questions are often attracted to the economic way of modeling behavior because of the analytical power provided by the assumption of individual rationality. Thriving schools of rational choice theorists and empirical researchers are active in sociology, law, political science, and history and, to a lesser extent, in anthropology and psychology. The rational choice model provides the most promising basis presently available for a unified approach to the analysis of the social world by scholars from different social sciences.

David Schmidtz

Reasons for Altruism

1993

According to a well-known version of the instrumental model, rational choice consists of maximizing one's utility, or more precisely, maximizing one's utility subject to a budget constraint. We seek the point of highest utility lying within our limited means. The term "utility" could mean a lot of different things, but in recent times theorists have often taken it to mean something related to or even identical to preference satisfaction (and thus utility functions are sometimes called preference functions). To have a preference is to *care,* to want one alternative more than another.

People are self-regarding insofar as they care about their own welfare.[1] People are *purely* self-regarding if they care about no one's welfare other than their own and recognize no constraints on how they treat others beyond those constraints imposed by circumstances: their limited time and income, legal restrictions, and so on. The question is, is it rational—is it *uniquely* rational—to be purely self-regarding? The instrumentalist model does not say. For that matter, neither does the instrumentalist model assume people care about welfare (their own or others'). The instrumentalist model allows that Hume could "prefer the destruction of the whole world to the scratching of my finger."[2]

1. AN ANALYSIS OF OTHER-REGARD

The departures from pure self-regard that concern us here come in two varieties. First, we might care about other people, which is to say their welfare enters the picture through our preference functions. Indeed, a desire to help other people often is among our strongest desires. Second, the welfare of others can enter the picture in the form of self-imposed constraints we acknowledge when pursuing our goals. In different words, an otherwise optional course of action may be seen as either forbidden or required, depending on how it would affect others. There may be limits to what we are willing to do to others in the course of pursuing our goals.[3]

Insofar as one's other-regard takes the form of caring about other people's welfare, one exhibits *concern.* Insofar as it takes the form of adherence to constraints on what one may do to others, one exhibits *respect.* As I use the terms, we have concern for people when we care about how life is treating them (so to speak), whereas we respect people when we care about how *we* are treating them, and constrain ourselves accordingly. Note that what motivates one kind of other-regard need not motivate the other. Joe may find it out of the question to violate other people's rights but at the same time be unconcerned about other people's welfare.[4] Jane may care about feeding the poor and have no qualms about taking other people's money to buy the food. In short, unconcerned people can be principled, and concerned people can be ruthless.

I use the term *altruism* to characterize a kind of action. In particular, an action is altruistic only if it is motivated by regard for others. Expressing concern or respect as a mere means to some other end is not altruistic. The expression is altruistic only if concern or respect for others is what motivates it. (People can act from mixed motives. Robin Hood may undertake a course of action in order to help the poor, make

David Schmidtz, "Reasons for Altruism." *Social Philosophy and Policy* 10 (1993): 52–68. By permission of Cambridge University Press.

himself look good, and hurt the rich. His action is at once altruistic, self-serving, and vicious.) Whether altruistic action is coextensive with other-regarding action is a terminological matter. Some classify respect for others as altruistic; others would say that to respect others is merely to give them their due, to do what justice requires, and thus cannot count as altruistic.

This definition of altruism leaves open questions about how altruism relates to justice and other essentially moral concepts. There is good reason not to try to settle these questions with definitions. For example, if we elect to stipulate that an act cannot be altruistic unless it goes beyond requirements of justice, then we cannot count ourselves as observing instances of altruism until we settle what justice requires. Someone might wish to define altruism as other-regarding action that goes beyond requirements of justice, but identifying acts as altruistic would then be fraught with difficulties, and pointlessly so. The difficulties would be mere artifacts of a bad definition.

Terminological issues aside, the issue of substance is twofold. We have both concern and respect for others, which raises a question about whether these departures from pure self-regard are rational. This chapter explores reasons for both departures, while acknowledging that some people consider one or the other to be the canonical form of altruism.[5]

Of course, one account of our reasons for altruism is built into altruism's definition. As it happens, we are not purely self-regarding. We have other-regarding preferences that can weigh against our self-regarding preferences. If we prefer on balance to act on our concern for others, then by that very fact we have reasons for altruism. The reasons are not purely self-regarding reasons, to be sure, but they are still reasons, and reasons from our points of view. Therefore, given that we are as we are, altruism sometimes is rational.

It hardly needs to be said, though, that no one would be satisfied with an argument that stopped here. A satisfying account of our reasons for altruism will not take our other-regarding preferences as given. Neither is it enough to offer a purely descriptive account of concern and respect—a biological or psychological or sociological account of what causes us to develop concern and respect for others. Biology and psychology are relevant, but they are not enough. We want an account according to which it is rational for us to have other-regarding preferences in the first place.

The interesting question, then, is this: if we were to abstract from our other-regarding interests and consider the matter from a purely self-regarding perspective, would we have reason from that perspective to affirm our other-regarding interests? This section has characterized altruism as action motivated either by respect or concern for others. The task now is to explain how self-regarding concerns could give people reasons to cultivate concern and respect for others.[6]

Since this essay aims to rationally ground respect and concern for others, readers may expect me to take for granted that self-regard is the fixed point around which all else must revolve if altruism is to have a place in rational choice theory's normative universe. That is not the plan. To be sure, self-regard enters the argument as an explanatory tool rather than as the thing to be explained, but that does not mean we can take it for granted. On the contrary, my conclusion is this: human self-regard is a fragile thing. *Self-regard's fragility is one source of its explanatory power.* Although we have a certain amount of respect and concern for ourselves, this amount is not unlimited and is not fixed. It varies. It is influenced by our choices, and this fact has a direct bearing on how regard for others fits into the lives of self-regarding human agents. The following sections elaborate.

2. *HOMO ECONOMICUS*

As already mentioned, to be instrumentally rational is to be committed to serving preferences *of* oneself, but one may or may not be committed to serving preferences *regarding* oneself. When we combine the instrumental model of rationality with a stipulation that rational agents are purely self-regarding, the result is the *Homo economicus* model of rational agency. I want to stress that the reasons given here to nurture other-regard are reasons for beings like us, not for beings like *Homo economicus.* The *Homo economicus* model leaves no room for altruism. The fact that the *Homo economicus* model assumes pure self-regard, however, is only part of the reason why it leaves no room for altruism. The real problem lies in how the assumption of pure self-regard works when combined with the underlying instrumental model of rationality.

The instrumental model of rationality is static, in the sense that it does not provide for rational choice among ends. The instrumental model can (and for my purposes should) be enriched by allowing for the possibility of endogenous preferences (that is, preferences that change in response to choices). This enriched model might explain how we develop our preferences. Even so, something is missing, because a person could have endogenous preferences and still think preference satisfaction is all that matters. For *Homo economicus,* there remains only one question: how much can I get? We go beyond *Homo economicus* and develop a truly reflective rationality as we come to see that the quality of our lives is a function not only of what we get but also of what we are.[7] And what we are, no less than what we get, depends on what we choose.

This section's main point is that whether or not we intend to do so, we develop new preferences as we go, which creates the possibility that beings like ourselves might come to be other-regarding. The next section argues that the same fluidity and capacity for reflecting on our ends that makes possible the cultivation of other-regarding concern also makes it important. There are reasons to embrace and nurture our concern for others, reasons that have to do with what is conducive to our own health, survival, and growth.

3. REASONS FOR CONCERN

As Nagel sees it, "altruistic reasons are parasitic upon self-interested ones; the circumstances in the lives of others which altruism requires us to consider are circumstances which those others already have reason to consider from a self-interested point of view."[8] Altruistic reasons could be parasitic on self-regarding reasons in a second way, insofar as reflective self-regard is the seed from which our regard for others must grow. Or perhaps the last claim is too strong. Respect and concern for others might, for all we know, be the phenotypic expression of a recessive gene. Even so, it remains the case that we do not really give a rationale for other-regarding concerns until we explain how people could abstract from their other-regarding concerns and still find reason from a purely self-regarding perspective to embrace concern for others. Thus, for those who seek to explain how other-regard could be rational, it seems obvious that our other concerns, that is, our self-regarding concerns, must inevitably have explanatory primacy. If we take this approach, it seems we are committed to viewing other-regard as parasitic on self-regard for its rational reconstruction even if not for its literal origin.

However, this is only half of the picture. On closer inspection, the apparently parasitic relationship between other-regard and self-regard turns out to be symbiotic. Insofar as other-regard has to be nurtured, we need self-regarding reasons to initiate the nurturing process. But self-regard is not automatic either. (It may be standard equipment, so to speak, but even standard equipment requires maintenance.) Our interests are not static. They wax and wane and change shape over time, and self-regarding interests are not exempt. An enduring self-regard requires maintenance.

How, then, do we maintain self-regard? Consider that our preference functions are, in effect, a representation of what we have to live for. To enrich the function by cultivating new concerns is to have more to live for. As we increase our potential for happiness, it may become harder to attain our maximum possible happiness, but that is no reason not to expand our potential. New concerns leave us open to the possibility of new frustrations and disappointments, but also to the possibility of deeper and broader satisfaction. And one crucial way to nurture self-regard is to nurture concerns that give us more to live for than we have if we care only about ourselves.

It is rational for beings like us to be peaceful and productive, to try to earn a sense of genuinely belonging in our community. Not many things are more important to us than being able to honestly consider ourselves important parts of a community. When evaluating our goals, we have to ask whether pursuing them is an appropriate way to use our talents, given our circumstances and tastes. We also have to ask how valuable our services would be to others in the various ways we could employ our talents.

The latter consideration is not decisive, of course, for if you are bored by computers and feel alive only when philosophizing about morality, then devoting yourself to computer programming might be irrational, even though your programming services are in greater demand. (What might make it irrational is that you would be responding to others at the cost of becoming unresponsive to yourself.) Nevertheless, to create a place for ourselves in society as peaceful and productive members, we must have regard for the interests of others, for serving the interests of others develops and gives value to our own latent productivity. For many of us, being honest and productive members of a community we respect is an end in itself. Even when it is not, it remains that much of what we want from life (and from our communities) comes to us in virtue of our importance to others.[9]

This is not to deny that when personal survival is an urgent concern, it can be quite sufficient to capture our attention. In such cases, we may have no need for other-regarding concerns. Indeed, we may view ourselves as not being able to afford other-regarding concerns. To cultivate additional preferences when our hands are already full is to cultivate frustration. But when circumstances leave us with free time, a more reflective kind of rationality will weigh in favor of trying to develop broader interests. We may begin with a goal of survival, but because we are reflective, we need to cultivate concerns other than survival. If there were nothing for the sake of which we were surviving, reflection on this fact would tend to undermine our commitment to survival.

Because we are reflective, it is conducive to survival to have a variety of preferences in addition to a preference for survival, preferences whose satisfaction gives significance and value to our survival it otherwise would not have. Paradoxically, it can be healthy to cultivate preferences that can cut against the pursuit of health. Other ends compete with the end of health for our attention, but also reinforce our concern for our health by giving it instrumental value. Developing concerns beyond the interest we take in ourselves is one way (even if not the only way) of making ourselves and our projects important enough to be worth caring about.

I conclude that we have self-regarding reasons to incorporate (so far as we are able to do so) other-regarding preferences into our utility functions, or in other words, to internalize other-regarding concerns. As these new preferences become part of the function, they acquire a certain autonomy, becoming more than mere means to previously given ends. The element of autonomy is crucial. The new preferences must take on lives of their own; we must come to care about them independently of how seeking to satisfy them bears on ends we already had. If they fail to become ends in themselves, then we fail to achieve our purpose in cultivating them, which is to have more to live for. We cultivate a richer set of concerns as a means to a further end, but we cultivate so as to reap new *ends*, not merely new means of serving ends we already have.

That we nurture our emerging ends for the sake of preexisting ends does not stop them from becoming ends we pursue for their own sake. The cultivation *process* is an effective means to existing ends only if the *things being cultivated* are more than that. Our ultimate interest is in having something to live for, being able to devote ourselves to the satisfaction of preferences we judge worthy of satisfaction. Not having other-regarding preferences is costly, for it drastically limits what one has to live for. A person may have no concern for others, but her lack of concern is nothing to envy.[10] Concern for ourselves gives us something to live for. Concern for others as well as ourselves gives us more.

This section has argued that, to the extent that we are reflectively rather than instrumentally rational, we cannot afford the poverty of ends that pure self-regard would saddle us with. Under conditions that leave us time for reflection, we need to have a variety of ongoing concerns with respect to which our survival—our selves—can take on value as a means. When these further ends are in place, survival comes to be more than a biological given; an agent who has further ends not only happens to have the goal of survival but can give reasons why survival is important. As a biologically given end, survival can confer value on our pursuits insofar as they take on value as means to the end of survival, but survival can also come to possess its own value insofar as it comes to be a means to our emerging further ends. Survival thus becomes an end we have reasons to pursue, quite apart from the fact that the end of survival is biologically given. The next three sections turn to the topic of other-regarding respect, and the more general phenomenon of commitment and counter-preferential choice. Section 4 discusses how our self-imposed constraints (along with our preferences) change over time, and sections 5 and 6 discuss why we might want them to change.

4. THE MECHANISM OF COMMITMENT

My distinction between concern and respect for others is like Amartya Sen's distinction between sympathy and commitment. Sen says that when a person's sense of well-being is psychologically tied to someone else's welfare in the right sort of way, it is a case of sympathy, whereas commitment involves counterpreferential choice. "If the knowledge of torture of others makes you sick, it is a case of sympathy; if it does not make you feel personally worse off, but if you think it is wrong and you are ready to do something to stop it, it is a case of commitment."[11] Whether or not it is best to follow Sen in describing commitment as counterpreferential choice, at very least we can say that commitment involves a different kind of preference than does sympathy.

What I call concern for others seems essentially identical to what Sen calls sympathy.[12] What Sen calls commitment, however, is broader than what I call respect for others. Commitment involves adherence to principles, whereas respect for others involves adherence to principles of a more specific kind, namely those that specify constraints on what we may do to others in the course of pursuing our goals. This section describes a process by which we can become committed (in Sen's broad sense). Section 5 considers why it can be rational to cultivate commitments (in the broad sense), and section 6 explores reasons why commitment typically seems to involve the more particular kind of commitment that I call respect for others.

Of course, not everyone sees a need to argue that there are processes by which people develop genuine commitments. Indeed, some people believe we become committed by choosing to be committed and that is all there is to it. Nothing said here is meant to deny that we can simply choose to be committed, but because some people do deny it, this section offers an account of a process by which a person can internalize commitments, thereby making them genuine. This section is addressed mainly to those who are skeptical about whether human commitment is really possible.

Geoffrey Sayre-McCord once proposed a thought experiment in which we imagine we have an opportunity to choose whether we will have a disposition to be moral. "With one hand, say, we might pull a lever that frees us of moral compunction and clears our minds of morality; with the other, we might pull a lever that gives us the will to do what we believe morality demands."[13] Which lever do we have reason to pull, all things considered?

The idea that we could choose a disposition is by no means merely a thought experiment. To borrow Sayre-McCord's metaphor, our actions pull the levers that form our characters. We would not want to pull a lever that would make us act as automatons. Nor can we, for we have no such lever. We would not want to pull a lever that would make us subject to absolute constraints. Nor can we. Again, we have no such lever. But many of us would pull a lever that would strengthen our disposition to be honest, for example, if only we had such a lever.

And in fact, we do. One of the consequences of action is habituation. Because we are creatures of habit, there is a sense in which pulling the lever is possible and a sense in which doing so can be rational. With every action, we have a marginal effect on our own character and on our self-conception. Character is a variable. It is not, however, subject to direct control. Actions that shape character are under our control. Character itself is not. It is neither fixed nor straightforwardly determined by choice. Rather, character is a function of choice. It is shaped by patterns of choice.[14]

Because people are creatures of habit, time eventually leaves a person with the accumulation of dispositions that we think of as a character. We do not face new situations as blank slates. Yet our accumulation of psychological baggage can seem obtrusive at times, leaving us to wonder why we are not blank slates. Why are we creatures of habit to begin with? We evolved as creatures of habit presumably because having routines for coping with repeatedly encountered situations helps us to conserve our cognitive capacities for circumstances that are novel. As Broadie says, "habits of doing what is usually desirable are important, not least because at any level they free the agent to reach for special achievement on a higher level."[15] In any event, if the advantage in developing routine responses is real, we need not regret being creatures of habit. However, the price is that, if we are creatures of habit, shaping our characters as we go, then making sure we can live with the changing shape of our accumulation of dispositions will be an ongoing project.

Habituation, then, is a mechanism of commitment. Of course, this is not to say that habits and commitments are the same thing. Kate can be in the habit of checking her mailbox twice a day without being committed to doing so. Likewise, Kate can be committed to standing by her husband even if he is arrested for drunk driving, although she has not yet had occasion to make a habit of it. But the fact that habits and commitments are not the same thing does not stop habituation from being one kind of process by which Kate can internalize a general commitment to her husband and thereby make it genuine. (Her general commitment will then be operative in all kinds of circumstances, even the unprecedented circumstance of his being arrested for drunk driving.)

We might wonder why we pay relatively little conscious attention to the ongoing process of habituation by which we internalize commitments. Why are we so often oblivious to the importance of cultivating good habits? Natural selection builds in a bias—a sometimes unhealthy bias—for the concrete. We have a potential for reflective rationality, but its flowering has not been a precondition of genetic fitness. People are built to worry about things that can draw blood, not about the decay of their characters. The cost of damaging our characters is easily overlooked, because it is not reflected in some obvious frustration of our preferences. Rather, it is reflected in something more subtle, in changes to the preferences themselves.[16] And so it turns out that when it comes to sorting out what is in our self-interest, we are relatively inept in situations where what is at stake is our character. Our ineptness notwithstanding, however, it remains possible for us to develop and reinforce our commitments, including commitments that embody respect for others. The next two sections offer reasons why we might want to do so.

5. REASONS FOR COMMITMENT

Section 3 undertook to show that we have reason to try to enrich our preference functions, for if we develop preferences that go beyond pure self-regard, we will have more to live for. Section 4 explored habituation as a mechanism by which we might internalize self-imposed constraints. This section explains why we might consider some self-imposed constraints worth the price.

There is an important place in our lives for strategic behavior, that is, for seeking effective means to current goals, given how we expect others to act and react. But this important place is not without limits. We want to achieve our goals, to be sure, but we also want to deserve to achieve our goals, and this is not at all like our other goals. (We care about what we are, not only about what we get.) We seek not merely to earn the respect and concern of others; more fundamentally, we seek to earn our own respect and concern. For whatever reason, it is a simple fact that a person of principle inspires more respect than a person driven by mere expedience. Kate may duly note that the object of her attention is herself, but that fact is not enough to guarantee that the object will hold her attention. The motivating power of Kate's self-interest is not without limit, and it is not fixed. The more worthy her self is of her interest, the better off she is. Consequently, there is this advantage in having a principled character: we become selves worth struggling for.

Plato took justice to consist of giving each citizen his due, interpreted not as harming enemies and helping friends (Polemarchus's proposal in *Republic,* bk. 1) but rather as possessing what is properly one's own and performing what is properly one's own task (Socrates' proposal in bk. 4). Plato tried to argue that, like unjust cities that degenerate into tyranny and civil war, souls whose parts fail to possess what is properly theirs and do the job that is properly theirs will be at war with themselves. The ultimate point of the argument was to connect justice to rationality (without reducing it to rationality). Few people accept Plato's argument at face value, of course, but even if Plato failed to connect rationality to justice, he did in the course of the argument connect rationality to integrity.

Integrity and justice are analogous, insofar as both are species of the genus "giving each part of the whole its due." To have integrity is to be true to oneself, to give each part of oneself its due. To be just is to give each person, each part of the whole society, its due. Plato's argument went awry when he mistook this analogy for a case of identity, which might be one reason why his conclusion about the rationality of being just rings false.[17] But what rings true is that having integrity is rational.

Having integrity is not merely good strategy, a matter of prudence. On the contrary, it is far more important than that. Being a person of integrity may on occasion be wildly imprudent, but that likelihood is not decisive even on prudential grounds. Indeed, the point here is that people who have no commitment to integrity have less to live for, which in the long run tends to undermine their commitment to prudence as well. Although integrity may be incompatible with prudence in exceptional cases, it also rationally justifies prudence in ordinary cases. Integrity rationally justifies prudence because it involves committing oneself to having a self worth caring about.

A person who does not have commitments has little with which to identify himself. What we are is in large part what we stand for. We think of having to make a stand on behalf of our ideals or on behalf of our loved ones as frightening and painful, and it often is. Yet, to make a stand for what we think is right is one of the most self-defining things we can do.

6. RESPECT FOR OTHERS

The reasons offered in section 3 for cultivating other-regarding concern had to do with the value of enriching our set of goals. Our goals are what we have to live for, and enriching our set of goals gives us more to live for. We do not live for our constraints. Nor would enriching our set of constraints give us more to live for in any direct way, but it does help define *who* we are living for. In effect, our constraints help define what we are living with, what means we can employ while still remaining persons worth living for. Defining our constraints is prior to the strategy we formulate and execute within those constraints. It is a prerequisite of prudence.

Why, then, does having a principled character involve respect for others? There is an alternative, namely that we might accept a suitably demanding set of commitments to ourselves. We might, for example, commit ourselves to achieving excellence in particular endeavors. This means that reasons for commitment per se do not automatically translate into reasons for commitments embodying respect for others. What then leads us to develop commitments of an other-regarding nature? Something like this, perhaps: we want more than to be at peace with ourselves. We also want more than to be liked and respected by others. We want to deserve to be liked and respected. Being a liar can hurt one not only by disrupting our purely internal integrity but also by precluding the kind of honest rapport one wants to have with others, precluding one's integration into the larger wholes that would otherwise give one more to live for. As Gerald Postema wisely observes,

> to cut oneself off from others is to cut oneself off from oneself, for it is only in the mirror of the souls of others that one finds one's own self, one's character. The pleasures and satisfactions of conversation and intercourse are essential to human life, because they are essential to a sense of one's continuity through a constantly changing external and internal world. . . . Thus, a truly successful strategy of deception effectively cuts oneself off from the community in which alone one can find the confirmation essential to one's own sense of self.[18]

The point is that, human psychology being what it is, respect for others turns out to be part and parcel of having integrity, because integrity has external as well as internal components. Being true to ourselves ordinarily involves presenting ourselves truly to others, but integrity involves not only honestly presenting ourselves to the world but also *integrating* ourselves into the world, achieving a certain fit. We give ourselves more to live for by becoming important parts of something bigger than ourselves. A principled character lets one pursue this wider integration without losing one's own identity. People of principled character—those with nothing to hide—can seek integration on their own terms.

We may never quite swallow the conclusion that it is rational to be just, in the sense of giving each person what he or she is due. Yet, it surely is rational to give our own interests their due, and (human psychology being what it is) we have a strong interest in being able to think of ourselves as decent human beings. We identify ourselves largely in terms of what we do, and therefore individual rationality behooves us to do things that can support the kind of self-conception we would like to have. Thus, being a person of integrity rather than an opportunist is rational not only as a prospective policy (i.e., as something that is advantageous in a long-run probabilistic sense); there is also something to be said for it on a case-by-case basis, even when we see in retrospect that we could have lied or cheated without being caught. We desire integrity not only in an internal sense but also in the sense of being integrated into a social structure—functioning well within structures that make up our environment. We seek real rapport with others, not merely a sham. We want to feel that we belong, and it is our real selves for which we want a sense of belonging, not merely our false facades.

So, how does that give us reasons to fall on grenades for the sake of our comrades? It may not. Considerations weighing in favor of having a principled character in ordinary cases need not do so in extraordinary cases. Nevertheless, ordinary cases are the crucibles within which characters take shape. It is in the ordinary course of events that we create the characters we carry into emergencies. Conversely, in emergencies, we learn something about what we have created. We find out what we are made of, so to speak, and the knowledge can have a lasting effect, for good or ill, as we resume our normal lives. There is a precious dignity in knowing one has a character that does not wither away under pressure.

Insofar as we maintain a critical perspective on our ends, it is conceivable that, in an emergency, we will question the concerns and commitments that call on us to fall on a grenade for the sake of our comrades. Depending on how well we have internalized our concerns and commitments, we may find ourselves able to reject them. If we reject our concerns and commitments, though, we cheapen our past as well as our possible future. We reveal ourselves to have been only superficially concerned and committed. Upon being convicted of corrupting the youth, Socrates willingly went to his death, so the legend goes, because his other alternatives were inconsistent with principles by which he had lived to that point. He was seventy years old, and his life as a whole would not have been improved by running away to spend his remaining years as an escaped convict.

Our reasons for acting as we do in a given situation stem from concerns we bring with us to that situation. Thus the rationality of internalizing a given concern does not turn on the consequences of acting on it in a single case. The relevant consequences are those that follow from a certain concern being part of one's life.[19] This is why the task of providing reasons for altruism is first and foremost the task of providing reasons for altruism of the more mundane variety. It is fine to consider whether it can be rational to die for one's comrades, but in truth, the central cases are cases of simply lending a hand in the ordinary course of events. We stop to give people directions. We push their cars out of snowbanks. We hold doors open for people whose hands are full. And we walk away from these mundane encounters feeling grateful for the chance to be helpful.[20]

In nurturing concerns that give us more to live for, we develop concerns that can become more important to us than life itself. In the ordinary course of events, this is a splendid result, but in extraordinary situations, concerns worth living for can become concerns worth dying for. One may some day find oneself in a situation where one's other-regarding concerns dictate a course of action that will seriously jeopardize one's purely self-regarding interests. The consequences might lead an observer to avoid developing similar commitments and concerns; the observer has not yet internalized those concerns and commitments, and after witnessing their worst-case results, internalizing them may seem unwise, if not downright impossible. But for us, already having those concerns and commitments (not merely observing them), failing to act on them is what would be irrational. When the emergency comes that calls on one to pay the price of having one's commitments, one no longer has the option of acting as if one's slate of commitments were blank. One got the benefits of integrity by accepting the risks associated with becoming actually committed, and when the emergency comes, one is actually committed.

Gregory Kavka points out that it can be rational to accept a *risk* of death even when it would not be rational to accept *certain* death.[21] And when one develops concerns so deep and genuine that they may some day lead one to willingly give one's life for one's comrades or one's children, one is accepting a risk, not a certainty. Meanwhile, those concerns give one more to live for. One has no intention of actually dying for one's comrades or children, but if one gets unlucky, one may some day find oneself in a situation in which dying for them is one's preferred alternative.

Altruism will involve self-sacrifice in exceptional cases, but not as a matter of routine. Altruism involves costs, of course, as does any action, but that an action is costly is not enough to make it a self-sacrifice. Cost-bearing becomes self-sacrificial only when agents deliberately give up something they prefer more for the sake of something they prefer less. Thus, only purely self-regarding agents will view altruism as necessarily self-sacrificial. For agents who have other-regarding concerns, acting on those concerns will be self-sacrificial if it costs too much, and only if it costs too much.

Needless to say, we may regret sacrificing one goal for the sake of another, even when both goals are of a self-regarding nature, and even when we have no doubt that what we give up is less important than what we gain. I may feel anguish when I give up coaching Little League football in order to pursue my career in a different city, but the regret I feel when I sacrifice one part of my life for the sake of another is neither necessary nor sufficient to indicate that my choice is a self-sacrifice. However painful it feels, I am not sacrificing myself when I sacrifice a less important goal for the sake of a more important goal. On the contrary, in a world that sometimes requires painful trade-offs, we affirm ourselves and our commitments and our values when we act for the sake of what we consider most important. This is what altruism can amount to for other-regarding agents.[22]

That also reveals the limits of rational altruism. For beings who begin with self-regarding ends, it would be irrational to nurture commitments that lead to self-sacrifice as a matter of course. The point is to have more to live for, and to meet the prerequisites of prudence. We accomplish this by nurturing respect and concern for family, friends, neighbors, the strangers we meet, and so on. There are forms of respect that, under normal conditions, we can easily afford to extend to the whole world, but we have only so much capacity for genuine concern. If we tried to care about everyone, our lives would be impoverished rather than enriched.

This has implications for morality as well as for rationality. Although I think morality requires us to respect everyone, I do not believe it requires us to care about everyone.[23] I have not argued for that conclusion here, but in any event, if morality did require us to care about everyone, then that would be one place where morality and rationality part company.

7. THE FRAGILITY OF SELF-REGARD

The model of reflective rational choice is, I have shown, rich enough not only to allow for but even to justify the development of other-regarding concern and respect. In particular, the fragility of self-regard can give us reason to develop concerns and commitments that go beyond self-regard. In the process, one acquires a rationale for one's fragile self-regard and thereby makes it more robust.

The emergence of these new reasons for action is driven by instrumental reasons, but this does not imply that the new reasons are themselves instrumental reasons. The concern and respect for others that is rationally grounded in reflective self-regard may be of an entirely wholehearted and uncalculating kind. Indeed, that is what we are striving for, for those are the most rewarding concerns a person can have.

Does this mean that concern for others is rationally *required?* I would say not. That concern for others is rationally justifiable does not imply that a lack of concern is unjustifiable. To be sure, most of us are rationally required to nurture other-regarding concerns and commitments, but we are rationally required in virtue of social and psychological circumstances that are not quite universal. People whose survival is immediately secure will be driven to cultivate concerns beyond mere survival.[24]

However, being driven to develop concerns beyond survival is not the same as being driven to develop concern for others. Some people have the option of fashioning more ambitious sets of concerns that would be fulfilling yet would still count as purely self-regarding. Even for such people, caring for others remains reasonable, because caring for others remains a particularly effective way of giving oneself more to live for. But it is not uniquely reasonable. Many kinds of commitments and concerns can be motivated by our need to have something to live for; not all of them are other-regarding, and some of them are evil. People commit acts of vandalism for the sake of having something to do. They go to war for the sake of having something to live for.

Be that as it may, the project of showing that altruism is reasonable does not require us to show that altruism is uniquely reasonable. We do not need to prove that failing to care about others would be unreasonable. For most of us, failing to care about others really would be unreasonable, because for most of us, there are no self-concerns that could give us as much to live for as we have in virtue of caring for others. Section 3 argued that we cannot afford to be purely self-regarding, but that may not be true of everyone. There are reasons for altruism, but there also are people for whom those reasons are not compelling. Is the existence of such people a problem? It surely is a practical problem, insofar as the rest of us need to deal with such people. Some readers might feel that the existence of such people is also a problem for my argument; that is, a person might reply to my reasons for altruism by insisting that not everyone has the kind of reasons discussed here. There are people, sociopaths perhaps, who have no reasons to care about others.

My response is that looking for reasons for everyone is a mistake. If we presume at the outset that our reasons to care about others must be reasons for everyone, the reasons we produce are likely to be reasons for no one. Such reasons likely will be mere philosophical sleight of hand, a distraction from our real-world concerns. Let us face the fact that our reasons for altruism can be real without being reasons for everyone. We must look for the real reasons, and accept that human societies need to deal with the fact that not everyone has real reasons.

In closing, a word on the larger project of identifying connections between rationality and morality. There is a limit to how much other-regard is rational, but whether that opens a gap between rationality and morality is an open question, for there is also a limit to how much other-regard is morally required. This is in part a point about morality leaving room for people to pursue their own projects, but it is also a reminder that the consequences of other-regard are only so good. Whether other-regarding action has better consequences than self-regarding action in a given case is an empirical matter.

Other-regarding action can sometimes seem morally dubious, even apart from its immediate consequences in a given case. *Paternalism,* for example, is a form of altruism, an expression of concern for others (i.e., for their welfare) that overrides one's respect for others (i.e., for their preferences). Altruistic though it might be, paternalism often is objectionable. To give another example, teachers should grade term papers on the basis of what they believe the papers deserve, not what they believe the authors need. Anyone who has ever graded term papers knows how difficult it can be to ignore one's concern for others, but there are cases in which one is morally required to make the effort. From the viewpoints both of the agent and of those persons the agent might affect, neither self-regard nor other-regard is intrinsically exalted. A great deal depends on how a concern plays itself out.

In *The Republic,* Socrates concluded that individuals need justice within themselves for more or less the same reasons and with more or less the same urgency as society needs justice within itself. But this did not answer Glaucon's question. Glaucon did not ask whether the individual needs to give each part of himself its due. He did not ask whether society needs to give each part of itself its due. What he asked was whether the individual needs to give each part of society its due. If Thrasymachus neglects to give other people their due, must he at the same time be neglecting to give a part of himself its due?

He might be.[25] Characters like Thrasymachus have reason to act only when doing so satisfies their purely self-regarding ends. Because almost nothing counts as a reason for Thrasymachus to act (in particular, regard for others does not), his life is impoverished in a certain way. He has fewer reasons to live than the rest of us. (To have *fewer* reasons to live is not necessarily to have less reason to live, but that will be the tendency.) Thrasymachus lacks a kind of respect and concern for others that could have given him reason to pursue a range of goals. I realize that if Thrasymachus were here, he would laugh at me for saying this, for the range of goals I am talking about would mean nothing to him, but the bottom line remains: those goals could have enriched his life.

NOTES

1. Insofar as we can distinguish between interests and preferences, welfare is a matter of serving interests rather than satisfying preferences. There is a perfectly natural sense in which many people have preferences the satisfaction of which is not in their interest.

2. Hume (1978) Part 3, sec. 3.

3. People have tried to distinguish between self-regarding and other-regarding actions, separating actions affecting only the agent from actions affecting others as well. (See Mill's *On Liberty,* for example.) The distinction is supposed to define a sphere of self-regarding activity with which society may not interfere, but the line has proven notoriously difficult to draw, because a person seeking to justify interference with activities she dislikes can always claim she is being *affected* in some way, and thus that the activity is not purely self-regarding. By contrast, the distinction between self-regarding and other-regarding concerns is unproblematic. However hard it is to find important examples of actions that affect only oneself, the distinction between caring about others and caring only about oneself remains sharp.

4. The distinction between respect and concern does not correspond to a distinction between duties of noninterference and duties to provide positive aid. Expressions of concern typically will involve lending aid; yet, out of concern, one might resist one's urge to help a child, knowing that children need to learn to take care of themselves. And expressions of respect typically will involve noninterference; yet, out of respect, one might lend aid to a war veteran.

5. The people I have polled usually agree that one of the two is the canonical form, but it turns out that they are evenly split on which one it is.

6. It may seem that if the original motivation is self-regarding, then we cannot be talking about genuine altruism. Not so. The point of the discussion is to consider whether we can be motivated by reason A to endorse a disposition to be motivated by reason B. (Can one be led by concern for one's health to try to cultivate a liking for vegetables?) Whether the acts motivated by reason B are altruistic depends on the nature of reason B, not reason A. If reason B consists of respect or concern for others, then acts motivated by it are altruistic. It makes no difference whether reason A consists of something else.

7. I thank Jean Hampton for suggesting this way of describing the contrast.

8. Nagel (1970) 16.

9. As Bricker (1980, 401) says, "to be prudent is to effect a reconciliation between oneself and one's world." And, we might add, our world consists in large part of other people.

10. Similarly, Kavka says "an immoralist's gloating that it does not pay him to be moral because the satisfactions of morality are not for him [is] like the pathetic boast of a deaf person that he saves money because it does not pay him to buy opera records" (1984, 307).

11. Sen (1990) 31.

12. Sen (1990, 31) considers sympathy to be egoistic, however, on the grounds that sympathetic action is still action done to satisfy one's own preferences. For what it is worth, I disagree. Whether my preferences are egoistic depends on their content, not on the bare fact that I happen to have them.

13. Sayre-McCord (1989) 115.

14. Thus, when we interpret Sayre-McCord's thought experiment as a metaphor for habituation, we reproduce a core insight of book 2 of Aristotle's *Nicomachean Ethics*. On the choice of character, see also Long (1992).

15. Broadie (1991) 109.

16. Allan Gibbard (1990, 276) notes that feelings can induce beliefs whose acceptance has the effect of making the feelings seem reasonable. The beliefs induced, we might add, can amplify our original feelings in the course of giving them a rationale. Some of us, when angry at our spouses, are tempted to dredge up a history of slights suffered at the hands of that person so as to justify our present feelings, and our new beliefs about that person's general inhumanity amplify our original anger to the point where our final blow-up is spectacular, and barely intelligible to observers. We need to be careful about our negative feelings, for the beliefs they induce can do lasting damage.

17. Unlike the analogy between integrity and justice, the often-discussed connection between the soul of the state and the soul of the citizen is much more than a matter of analogy. Lear (1992) argues that Plato believed not only that the souls of citizens and the soul of the state are like each other but also that the reason they are like each other is because they are outgrowths of each other. The state is the milieu within which children grow up, and so the characters of its adult citizens reflect that milieu. At the same time, the state's ongoing evolution or devolution lies in the hands of its adult citizens, and so reflects the characters of its adult citizens.

18. Postema (1988) 35.

19. McClennen (1988) argues that one can be better off as a resolute chooser, i.e., a person who can adopt plans and stick to them. For example, suppose Kate wants to buy a television set, but if she does, she will then need to decide whether to watch game shows. Kate's most-preferred option is to buy the television, resolving never to watch game shows. However, she is not sure she can trust herself never to watch game shows, and would rather not have a television set at all than to end up watching game shows. Subsequently, having bought a television set, how can Kate eschew game shows, if watching them is now her most preferred option? What difference does it make that she resolved last week when she bought her television never to watch game shows? My theory is that genuine resolve is the sort of thing we build over time. Kate is *rational* to build up her capacity for resolve because, as she proves to herself that she can carry out plans calling for resolve, she becomes able to trust herself to make choices that will be optimal if and only if she ignores temptations associated with those choices.

20. It would be a mistake to say something cannot be altruistic if you really enjoy doing it. This would put the cart before the horse. If you help other people for their sake, you are altruistic whether or not you like having the concern for others that your action expresses. In the *Grounding of the Metaphysics of Morals,* Kant said getting joy out of an action can rob it of moral worth, which seems wrong, but even if he had been right, enjoying an action can affect its moral worth without changing the fact that the action is altruistic.

21. Kavka (1984) 307–10.

22. I thank Lainie Ross for helping me work out the connection between altruism and sacrifice. See also Aristotle's discussion of friendship and sacrifice in *Nicomachean Ethics* (1169a).

23. Galston (1993) distinguishes between progressively more expansive forms of altruism, and draws attention to the moral cost of altruism in its more expansive incarnations. For example, Galston says, the concern expressed by rescuers of Jewish refugees in Nazi-occupied Europe was an expansive, cosmopolitan form of altruism. Commendable though it was on its face, this cosmopolitan form of altruism often went hand in hand with a failure to express concern for family members whom the rescue effort put at risk. The more cosmopolitan form of altruism came at the expense of the more parochial form. More parochial forms of altruism sometimes are not consistent with expressing concern for everyone.

24. See chapter 3.

25. Griswold (1994) finds a close connection between justice as an excellence of self and justice as a kind of respect we owe to others, because it is in treating others with concern and respect that we perfect ourselves.

David Gauthier

Rationality: Maximization Constrained

1986

> *The Foole hath said in his heart, there is no such thing as justice, and sometimes also with his tongue, seriously alleging, that every man's conservation and contentment, being committed to his own care, there could be no reason why every man might not do what he thought conduced thereunto: and therefore also to make, or not make; keep, or not keep Covenants, was not against Reason, when it conduced to one's benefit.*
>
> *Thomas Hobbes,* Leviathan, *1651, chapter 15*

2.1

The Foole rejects what would seem to be the ordinary view that, given neither unforeseen circumstances nor misrepresentation of terms, it is rational to comply with an agreement if it is rational to make it. He insists that holders of this view have failed to think out the full implications of the maximizing conception of practical rationality. In choosing one takes one's stand in the present, and looks to the expected utility that will result from each possible action. What has happened may affect this utility; that one has agreed may affect the utility one expects from doing, or not doing, what would keep the agreement. But what has happened provides in itself no reason for choice. That one had reason for making an agreement can give one reason for keeping it only by affecting the utility of compliance. To think otherwise is to reject utility-maximization.

Let us begin our answer to the Foole by distinguishing between an individual strategy and a joint strategy.[1] An individual strategy is a lottery over the possible actions of a single actor. A joint strategy is a lottery over possible outcomes. Co-operators have joint strategies available to them.

We may think of participation in a co-operative activity, such as a hunt, in which each huntsman has his particular role co-ordinated with that of the others, as the implementation of a single joint strategy. We may also extend the notion to include participation in a practice, such as the making and keeping of promises, where each person's behaviour is predicated on the conformity of others to the practice.

An individual is not able to ensure that he acts on a joint strategy, since whether he does depends, not only on what he intends, but on what those with whom he interacts intend. But we may say that an individual bases his action on a joint strategy in so far as he intentionally chooses what the strategy requires of him. Normally, of course, one bases one's action on a joint strategy only if one expects those with whom one interacts to do so as well, so that one expects actually to act on that strategy. But we need not import such an expectation into the conception of basing one's action on a joint strategy.

A person co-operates with his fellows only if he bases his actions on a joint strategy; to agree to co-operate is to agree to employ a joint rather than an individual strategy. The Foole insists that it is rational to co-operate only if the utility one expects from acting on the co-operative joint strategy is at least

From David Gauthier, "Compliance: Maximization Constrained," chapter 6 of *Morals By Agreement*. New York: Oxford University Press, 1986. By permission of Oxford University Press.

equal to the utility one would expect were one to act instead on one's best individual strategy. This defeats the end of co-operation, which is in effect to substitute a joint strategy for individual strategies in situations in which this substitution is to everyone's benefit.

A joint strategy is fully rational only if it yields an optimal outcome, or in other words, only if it affords each person who acts on it the maximum utility compatible in the situation with the utility afforded each other person who acts on the strategy. Thus we may say that a person acting on a rational joint strategy maximizes his utility, subject to the constraint set by the utilities it affords to every other person. An individual strategy is rational if and only if it maximizes one's utility given the *strategies* adopted by the other persons; a joint strategy is rational only if (but not if and only if) it maximizes one's utility given the *utilities* afforded to the other persons.

Let us say that a *straightforward* maximizer is a person who seeks to maximize his utility given the strategies of those with whom he interacts. A *constrained* maximizer, on the other hand, is a person who seeks in some situations to maximize her utility, given not the strategies but the utilities of those with whom she interacts. The Foole accepts the rationality of straightforward maximization. We accept the rationality of constrained maximization.

A constrained maximizer has a conditional disposition to base her actions on a joint strategy, without considering whether some individual strategy would yield her greater expected utility. But not all constraint could be rational; we must specify the characteristics of the conditional disposition. We shall therefore identify a constrained maximizer thus: (i) someone who is conditionally disposed to base her actions on a joint strategy or practice should the utility she expects were everyone so to base his action be no less than what she would expect were everyone to employ individual strategies, and approach what she would expect from the co-operative outcome determined by minimax relative concession; (ii) someone who actually acts on this conditional disposition should her expected utility be greater than what she would expect were everyone to employ individual strategies. Or in other words, a constrained maximizer is ready to co-operate in ways that, if followed by all, would yield outcomes that she would find beneficial and not unfair, and she does co-operate should she expect an actual practice or activity to be beneficial. In determining the latter she must take into account the possibility that some persons will fail, or refuse, to act co-operatively. Henceforth, unless we specifically state otherwise, we shall understand by a constrained maximizer one with this particular disposition.

There are three points in our characterization of constrained maximization that should be noted. The first is that a constrained maximizer is conditionally disposed to act, not only on the unique joint strategy that would be prescribed by a rational bargain, but on any joint strategy that affords her a utility approaching what she would expect from fully rational co-operation. The range of acceptable joint strategies is, and must be left, unspecified. The idea is that in real interaction it is reasonable to accept co-operative arrangements that fall short of the ideal of full rationality and fairness, provided they do not fall too far short. At some point, of course, one decides to ignore a joint strategy, even if acting on it would afford one an expected utility greater than one would expect were everyone to employ an individual strategy, because one hopes thereby to obtain agreement on, or acquiescence in, another joint strategy which in being fairer is also more favourable to oneself. At precisely what point one decides this we make no attempt to say. We simply defend a conception of constrained maximization that does not require that all acceptable joint strategies be ideal.

Constrained maximization thus links the idea of morals by agreement to actual moral practice. We suppose that some moral principles may be understood as representing joint strategies prescribed to each person as part of the ongoing co-operative arrangements that constitute society. These principles require each person to refrain from the direct pursuit of her maximum utility, in order to achieve mutually advantageous and reasonably fair outcomes. Actual moral principles are not in general those to which we should have agreed in a fully rational bargain, but it is reasonable to adhere to them in so far as they offer a reasonable approximation to ideal principles. We may defend actual moral principles by reference to ideal co-operative arrangements, and the closer the principles fit, the stronger the defence. We do not of course suppose that our actual moral principles derive historically from a bargain, but in so far as the constraints they impose are acceptable to a rational constrained maximizer, we may fit them into the framework of a morality rationalized by the idea of agreement.

The second point is that a constrained maximizer does not base her actions on a joint strategy whenever a nearly fair and optimal outcome would result were everyone to do likewise. Her disposition to co-operate is conditional on her expectation that she will benefit in comparison with the utility she could expect were no one to cooperate. Thus she must estimate the likelihood that others involved in the prospective practice or interaction will act co-operatively, and calculate, not the utility she would expect were all to co-operate, but the utility she would expect if she co-operates, given her estimate of the degree to which others will co-operate. Only if this exceeds what she would expect from universal non-co-operation, does her conditional disposition to constraint actually manifest itself in a decision to base her actions on the co-operative joint strategy.

Thus, faced with persons whom she believes to be straightforward maximizers, a constrained maximizer does not play into their hands by basing her actions on the joint strategy she would like everyone to accept, but rather, to avoid being exploited, she behaves as a straightforward maximizer, acting on the individual strategy that maximizes her utility given the strategies she expects the others to employ. A constrained maximizer makes reasonably certain that she is among like-disposed persons before she actually constrains her direct pursuit of maximum utility.

But note that a constrained maximizer may find herself required to act in such a way that she would have been better off had she not entered into co-operation. She may be engaged in a co-operative activity that, given the willingness of her fellows to do their part, she expects to be fair and beneficial, but that, should chance so befall, requires her to act so that she incurs some loss greater than had she never engaged herself in the endeavour. Here she would still be disposed to comply, acting in a way that results in real disadvantage to herself, because given her *ex ante* beliefs about the dispositions of her fellows and the prospects of benefit, participation in the activity affords her greater expected utility than non-participation.

And this brings us to the third point, that constrained maximization is not straightforward maximization in its most effective disguise. The constrained maximizer is not merely the person who, taking a larger view than her fellows, serves her overall interest by sacrificing the immediate benefits of ignoring joint strategies and violating co-operative arrangements in order to obtain the long-run benefits of being trusted by others.[2] Such a person exhibits no real constraint. The constrained maximizer does not reason more effectively about how to maximize her utility, but reasons in a different way. We may see this most clearly by considering how each faces the decision whether to base her action on a joint strategy. The constrained maximizer considers (i) whether the outcome, should everyone do so, be nearly fair and optimal, and (ii) whether the outcome she realistically expects should she do so affords her greater utility than universal non-co-operation. If both of these conditions are satisfied she bases her action on the joint strategy. The straight-forward maximizer considers simply whether the outcome he realistically expects should he base his action on the joint strategy affords him greater utility than the outcome he would expect were he to act on any alternative strategy—taking into account, of course, long-term as well as short-term effects. Only if this condition is satisfied does he base his action on the joint strategy.

Consider a purely isolated interaction, in which both parties know that how each chooses will have no bearing on how each fares in other interactions. Suppose that the situation has the familiar Prisoner's Dilemma structure; each benefits from mutual co-operation in relation to mutual non-co-operation, but each benefits from non-co-operation whatever the other does. In such a situation, a straightforward maximizer chooses not to co-operate. A constrained maximizer chooses to co-operate if, given her estimate of whether or not her partner will choose to co-operate, her own expected utility is greater than the utility she would expect from the non-co-operative outcome.

Constrained maximizers can thus obtain co-operative benefits that are unavailable to straightforward maximizers, however farsighted the latter may be. But straightforward maximizers can, on occasion, exploit unwary constrained maximizers. Each supposes her disposition to be rational. But who is right?

2.2

To demonstrate the rationality of suitably constrained maximization we solve a problem of rational choice. We consider what a rational individual would choose, given the alternatives of adopting straightforward maximization, and of adopting constrained maximization, as his disposition for strategic behaviour. Although this choice is about interaction, to make it is not to engage in interaction. Taking others' dispositions as fixed, the individual reasons parametrically to his own best disposition. Thus he compares the expected utility of disposing himself to maximize utility given others' expected strategy choices, with the utility of disposing himself to co-operate with others in bringing about nearly fair and optimal outcomes.

To choose between these dispositions, a person needs to consider only those situations in which they would yield different behaviour. If both would be expressed in a maximizing individual strategy, or if both would lead one to base action on the joint strategy one expects from others, then their utility expectations are identical. But if the disposition to constraint would be expressed in basing action on a joint strategy, whereas the disposition to maximize straightforwardly would be expressed in defecting from the joint strategy, then their utility expectations differ. Only situations giving rise to such differences need be considered. These situations must satisfy two conditions. First, they must afford the prospect of mutually beneficial and fair co-operation, since otherwise constraint would be pointless. And second, they must afford some prospect for individually beneficial defection, since otherwise no constraint would be needed to realize the mutual benefits.

We suppose, then, an individual, considering what disposition to adopt, for situations in which his expected utility is u should each person act on an individual strategy, u' should all act on a co-operative joint strategy, and u'' should he act on an individual strategy and the others base their actions on a co-operative joint strategy, and u is less than u' (so that he benefits from co-operation as required by the first condition) and u' in turn is less than u'' (so that he benefits from defection as required by the second condition).

Consider these two arguments which this person might put to himself:

> Argument (1): Suppose I adopt straightforward maximization. Then if I expect the others to base their actions on a joint strategy, I defect to my best individual strategy, and expect a utility, u''. If I expect the others to act on individual strategies, then so do I, and expect a utility, u. If the probability that others will base their actions on a joint strategy is p, then my overall expected utility is $[pu'' + (1 - p)u]$.

Suppose I adopt constrained maximization. Then if I expect the others to base their actions on a joint strategy, so do I, and expect a utility u'. If I expect the others to act on individual strategies, then so do I, and expect a utility, u. Thus my overall expected utility is $[pu' + (1 - p)u]$.

Since u'' is greater than u', $[pu'' + (1 - p)u]$ is greater than $[pu' + (1 - p)u]$, for any value of p other than 0 (and for $p = 0$, the two are equal). Therefore, to maximize my overall expectation of utility, I should adopt straightforward maximization.

> Argument (2): Suppose I adopt straightforward maximization. Then I must expect the others to employ maximizing individual strategies in interacting with me; so do I, and expect a utility, u.

Suppose I adopt constrained maximization. Then if the others are conditionally disposed to constrained maximization, I may expect them to base their actions on a co-operative joint strategy in interacting with me; so do I, and expect a utility u'. If they are not so disposed, I employ a maximizing strategy and expect u as before. If the probability that others are disposed to constrained maximization is p, then my overall expected utility is $[pu' + (1 - p)u]$.

Since u' is greater than u, $[pu' + (1 - p)u]$ is greater than u for any value of p other than 0 (and for $p = 0$, the two are equal). Therefore, to maximize my overall expectation of utility, I should adopt constrained maximization.

Since these arguments yield opposed conclusions, they cannot both be sound. The first has the form of a dominance argument. In any situation in which others act non-co-operatively, one may expect the same utility whether one is disposed to straightforward or to constrained maximization. In any situation in which others act co-operatively, one may expect a greater utility if one is disposed to straightforward maximization. Therefore one should adopt straightforward maximization. But this argument would be valid only if the probability of others acting co-operatively were, as the argument assumes, independent of one's own disposition. And this is not the case. Since persons disposed to co-operation only act co-operatively with those whom they suppose to be similarly disposed, a straightforward maximizer does not have the opportunities to benefit which present themselves to the constrained maximizer. Thus argument (1) fails.

Argument (2) takes into account what argument (1) ignores—the difference between the way in which constrained maximizers interact with those similarly disposed, and the way in which they interact with straightforward maximizers. Only those disposed to keep their agreements are rationally acceptable as parties to agreements. Constrained maximizers are able to make beneficial agreements with their fellows that the straightforward cannot, not because the latter would be unwilling to agree, but because they would not be admitted as parties to agreement given their disposition to violation. Straightforward maximizers are disposed to take advantage of their fellows should the opportunity arise; knowing this, their fellows would prevent such opportunity arising. With the same opportunities, straightforward maximizers would necessarily obtain greater benefits. A dominance argument establishes this. But because they differ in their dispositions, straightforward and constrained maximizers differ also in their opportunities, to the benefit of the latter.

But argument (2) unfortunately contains an undefended assumption. A person's expectations about how others will interact with him depend strictly on his own choice of disposition only if that choice is known by the others. What we have shown is that, if the straightforward maximizer and the constrained maximizer appear in their true colours, then the constrained maximizer must do better. But need each so appear? The Foole may agree, under the pressure of our argument and its parallel in the second argument we ascribed to Hobbes, that the question to be asked is not whether it is or is not rational to keep (particular) covenants, but whether it is or is not rational to be (generally) disposed to the keeping of covenants, and he may recognize that he cannot win by pleading the cause of straightforward maximization in a direct way. But may he not win by linking straightforward maximization to the appearance of constraint? Is not the Foole's ultimate argument that the truly prudent person, the fully rational utility-maximizer, must seek to appear trustworthy, an upholder of his agreements? For then he will not be excluded from the co-operative arrangements of his fellows, but will be welcomed as a partner, while he awaits opportunities to benefit at their expense—and, preferably, without their knowledge, so that he may retain the guise of constraint and trustworthiness.

There is a short way to defeat this manoeuvre. Since our argument is to be applied to ideally rational persons, we may simply add another idealizing assumption, and take our persons to be *transparent*.[3] Each is directly aware of the disposition of his fellows, and so aware whether he is interacting with straightforward or constrained maximizers. Deception is impossible; the Foole must appear as he is.

But to assume transparency may seem to rob our argument of much of its interest. We want to relate our idealizing assumptions to the real world. If constrained maximization defeats straightforward maximization only if all persons are transparent, then we shall have failed to show that under actual, or realistically possible, conditions, moral constraints are rational. We shall have refuted the Foole but at the price of robbing our refutation of all practical import.

However, transparency proves to be a stronger assumption than our argument requires. We may appeal instead to a more realistic *translucency,* supposing that persons are neither transparent nor opaque, so that their disposition to co-operate or not may be ascertained by others, not with certainty, but as more than mere guesswork. Opaque beings would be condemned to seek political solutions for those problems of natural interaction that could not be met by the market. But we shall show that for beings as translucent as we may reasonably consider ourselves to be, moral solutions are rationally available.

2.3

If persons are translucent, then constrained maximizers (CMs) will sometimes fail to recognize each other, and will then interact non-co-operatively even if co-operation would have been mutually beneficial. CMs will sometimes fail to identify straightforward maximizers (SMs) and will then act co-operatively; if the SMs correctly identify the CMs they will be able to take advantage of them. Translucent CMs must expect to do less well in interaction than would transparent CMs; translucent SMs must expect to do better than would transparent SMs. Although it would be rational to choose to be a CM were one transparent, it need not be rational if one is only translucent. Let us examine the conditions under which the decision to dispose oneself to constrained maximization is rational for translucent persons, and ask if these are (or may be) the conditions in which we find ourselves.

As in the preceding subsection, we need consider only situations in which CMs and SMs may fare differently. These are situations that afford both the prospect of mutually beneficial co-operation (in relation to non-co-operation) and individually beneficial defection (in relation to co-operation). Let us simplify by supposing that the non-cooperative outcome results unless (i) those interacting are CMs who achieve mutual recognition, in which case the co-operative outcome results, or (ii) those interacting include CMs who fail to recognize SMs but are themselves recognized, in which case the outcome affords the SMs the benefits of individual defection and the CMs the costs of having advantage taken of mistakenly basing their actions on a co-operative strategy. We ignore the inadvertent taking of advantage when CMs mistake their fellows for SMs.

There are then four possible pay-offs—non-co-operation, co-operation, defection, and exploitation (as we may call the outcome for the person whose supposed partner defects from the joint strategy on which he bases his action). For the typical situation, we assign defection the value 1, co-operation u'' (less than 1), non-co-operation u' (less than u''), and exploitation 0 (less than u'). We now introduce three probabilities. The first, p, is the probability that CMs will achieve mutual recognition and so successfully co-operate. The second, q, is the probability that CMs will fail to recognize SMs but will themselves be recognized, so that defection and exploitation will result. The third, r, is the probability that a randomly selected member of the population is a CM. (We assume that everyone is a CM or an SM, so the probability that a randomly selected person is an SM is $(1 - r)$.) The values of p, q, and r must of course fall between 0 and 1.

Let us now calculate expected utilities for CMs and SMs in situations affording both the prospect of mutually beneficial co-operation and individually beneficial defection. A CM expects the utility u' unless (i) she succeeds in co-operating with other CMs or (ii) she is exploited by an SM. The probability of (i) is the combined probability that she interacts with a CM, r, and that they achieve mutual recognition, p, or rp. In this case she gains $(u'' - u')$ over her non-co-operative expectation u'. Thus the effect of (i) is to increase her utility expectation by a value $[rp(u'' - u')]$. The probability of (ii) is the combined probability that she interacts with an SM, $1 - r$, and that she fails to recognize him but is recognized, q, or $(1 - r)q$. In this case she receives 0, so she loses her non-co-operative expectation u'. Thus the effect of (ii) is to reduce her utility expectation by a value $[(1 - r)qu']$. Taking both (i) and (ii) into account, a CM expects the utility $\{u' + [rp(u'' - u')] - (1 - r) qu'\}$.

An SM expects the utility u' unless he exploits a CM. The probability of this is the combined probability that he interacts with a CM, r, and that he recognizes her but is not recognized by her, q, or rq. In this case he gains $(1 - u')$ over his non-co-operative expectation u'. Thus the effect is to increase his utility expectation by a value $[rq(1 - u')]$. An SM thus expects the utility $\{u' + [rq(1 - u')]\}$.

It is rational to dispose oneself to constrained maximization if and only if the utility expected by a CM is greater than the utility expected by an SM, which obtains if and only if p/q is *greater* than $\{(1 - u')/(u'' - u') + [(1 - r)u']/[r(u'' - u')]\}$.

The first term of this expression, $[(1 - u')/(u'' - u')]$, relates the gain from defection to the gain through co-operation. The value of defection is of course greater than that of cooperation, so this term is greater than 1. The second term, $\{[(1 - r)u']/[r(u'' - u')]\}$, depends for its value on r. If $r = 0$ (i.e., if there are no CMs in the population), then its value is infinite. As r increases, the value of the expression decreases, until if $r = 1$ (i.e. if there are only CMs in the population) its value is 0.

We may now draw two important conclusions. First, it is rational to dispose oneself to constrained maximization only if the ratio of p to q, i.e. the ratio between the probability that an interaction involving CMs will result in co-operation and the probability that an interaction involving CMs and SMs will involve exploitation and defection, is greater than the ratio between the gain from defection and the gain through co-operation. If everyone in the population is a CM, then we may replace "only if" by "if and only if" in this statement, but in general it is only a necessary condition of the rationality of the disposition to constrained maximization.

Second, as the proportion of CMs in the population increases (so that the value of r increases), the value of the ratio of p to q that is required for it to be rational to dispose oneself to constrained maximization decreases. The more constrained maximizers there are, the greater the risks a constrained maximizer may rationally accept of failed cooperation and exploitation. However, these risks, and particularly the latter, must remain relatively small.

We may illustrate these conclusions by introducing typical numerical values for cooperation and non-co-operation, and then considering different values for r. One may suppose that on the whole, there is no reason that the typical gain from defection over co-operation would be either greater or smaller than the typical gain from cooperation over non-co-operation, and in turn no reason that the latter gain would be greater or smaller than the typical loss from non-co-operation to exploitation. And so, since defection has the value 1 and exploitation 0, let us assign co-operation the value 2/3 and non-co-operation 1/3.

The gain from defection, $(1 - u')$, thus is 2/3; the gain through co-operation, $(u'' - u')$, is 1/3. Since p/q must exceed $\{(1 - u')/(u'' - u') + [(1 - r)u']/[r(u'' - u')]\}$ for constrained maximization to be rational, in our typical case the probability p that CMs successfully cooperate must be more than twice the probability q that CMs are exploited by SMs, however great the probability r that a randomly selected person is a CM. If three persons out of four are CMs, so that $r = 3/4$, then p/q must be greater than 7/3; if one person out of two is a CM, then p/q must be greater than 3; if one person in four is a CM, then p/q must be greater than 5. In general, p/q must be greater than $2 + (1 - r)/r$, or $(r + 1)/r$.

Suppose a population evenly divided between constrained and straightforward maximizers. If the constrained maximizers are able to co-operate successfully in two-thirds of their encounters, and to avoid being exploited by straightforward maximizers in four-fifths of their encounters, then constrained maximizers may expect to do better than their fellows. Of course, the even distribution will not be stable; it will be rational for the straightforward maximizers to change their disposition. These persons are sufficiently translucent for them to find morality rational.

2.4

A constrained maximizer is conditionally disposed to co-operate in ways that, followed by all, would yield nearly optimal and fair outcomes, and does co-operate in such ways when she may actually expect to benefit. In the two preceding subsections, we have argued that one is rationally so disposed if persons are transparent, or if persons are sufficiently translucent and enough are like-minded. But our argument has not appealed explicitly to the particular requirement that co-operative practices and activities be nearly optimal and fair. We have insisted that the co-operative outcome afford one a utility greater than non-co-operation, but this is much weaker than the insistence that it approach the outcome required by minimax relative concession.

But note that the larger the gain from co-operation, $(u'' - u')$, the smaller the minimum value of p/q that makes the disposition to constrained maximization rational. We may take p/q to be a measure of translucency; the more translucent constrained maximizers are, the better they are at achieving co-operation among themselves (increasing p) and avoiding exploitation by straightforward maximizers (decreasing q). Thus as practices and activities fall short of optimality, the expected value of co-operation, u'', decreases, and so the degree of translucency required to make co-operation rational increases. And as practices and activities fall short of fairness, the expected value of cooperation for those with less than fair shares decreases, and so the degree of translucency to make co-operation rational for them increases. Thus our argument does appeal implicitly to the requirement that co-operation yield nearly fair and optimal outcomes.

But there is a further argument in support of our insistence that the conditional disposition to co-operate be restricted to practices and activities yielding nearly optimal and fair outcomes. And this argument turns, as does our general argument for constraint, on how one's dispositions affect the characteristics of the situations in which one may reasonably expect to find oneself. Let us call a person who is disposed to cooperate in ways that, followed by all, yield nearly optimal and fair outcomes, *narrowly compliant.* And let us call a person who is disposed to co-operate in ways that, followed by all, merely yield her some benefit in relation to universal non-co-operation, *broadly compliant.* We need not deny that a broadly compliant person would expect to benefit in some situations in which a narrowly compliant person could not. But in many other situations a broadly compliant person must expect to lose by her disposition. For in so far as she is known to be broadly compliant, others will have every reason to maximize their utilities at her expense, by offering "co-operation" on terms that offer her but little more than she could expect from non-co-operation. Since a broadly compliant person is disposed to seize whatever benefit a joint strategy may afford her, she finds herself with opportunities for but little benefit.

Since the narrowly compliant person is always prepared to accept co-operative arrangements based on the principle of minimax relative concession, she is prepared to be co-operative whenever co-operation can be mutually beneficial on terms equally rational and fair to all. In refusing other terms she does not diminish her prospects for co-operation with other rational persons, and she ensures that those not disposed to fair co-operation do not enjoy the benefits of any co-operation, thus making their unfairness costly to themselves, and so irrational.

In the next chapter we shall extend the conception of narrow compliance, so that it includes taking into account not only satisfaction of minimax relative concession, but also satisfaction of a standard of fairness for the initial bargaining position. We shall then find that for some circumstances, narrow compliance sets too high a standard. If the institutions of society fail to be both rational and impartial, then the narrowly compliant person may be unable to effect any significant reform of them, while depriving herself of what benefits an imperfect society nevertheless affords. Then—we must admit—rationality and impartiality can fail to coincide in individual choice.

But we suppose that among fully rational persons, institutions, practices, and agreements that do not satisfy the requirements of minimax relative concession must prove unstable. There would, of course, be some persons with an interest in maintaining the unfairness inherent in such structures. But among the members of a society each of whom is, and knows her fellows to be, rational and adequately informed, those who find themselves with less than they could expect from fair and optimal co-operation can, by disposing themselves to narrow compliance, effect the reform of their society so that it satisfies the requirements of justice. Reflection on how partiality sustains itself shows that, however important coercive measures may be, their effectiveness depends finally on an uncoerced support for norms that directly or indirectly sustain this partiality, a support which would be insufficiently forthcoming from clear-headed constrained maximizers of individual utility.

2.5

To conclude this long section, let us supplement our argument for the rationality of disposing ourselves to constrained maximization with three reflections on its implications—for conventional morality, for the treatment of straightforward maximizers, and for the cultivation of translucency.

First, we should not suppose that the argument upholds all of conventional morality, or all of those institutions and practices that purport to realize fair and optimal outcomes. If society is, in Rawls's words, "a cooperative venture for mutual advantage," then it is rational to pay one's share of social costs—one's taxes. But it need not be rational to pay one's taxes, at least unless one is effectively coerced into payment, if one sees one's tax dollars used (as one may believe) to increase the chances of nuclear warfare and to encourage both corporate and individual parasitism. If tax evasion seems to many a rational practice, this does not show that it is irrational to comply with fair and optimal arrangements, but only, perhaps, that it is irrational to acquiesce willingly in being exploited.

Second, we should not suppose it is rational to dispose oneself to constrained maximization, if one does not also dispose oneself to exclude straightforward maximizers from the benefits realizable by co-operation. Hobbes notes that those who think they may with reason violate their covenants, may not be received into society except by the error of their fellows. If their fellows fall into that error, then they will soon find that it pays no one to keep covenants. Failing to exclude straightforward maximizers from the benefits of co-operative arrangements does not, and cannot, enable them to share in the long-run benefits of co-operation; instead, it ensures that the arrangements will prove ineffective, so that there are no benefits to share. And then there is nothing to be gained by constrained maximization; one might as well join the straightforward maximizers in their descent to the natural condition of humankind.

A third consideration relates more closely to the conceptions introduced in 2.3. Consider once again the probabilities p and q, the probability that CMs will achieve mutual recognition and co-operate, and the probability that CMs will fail to recognize SMs but will be recognized by them and so be exploited. It is obvious that CMs benefit from increasing p and decreasing q. And this is reflected in our calculation of expected utility for CMs; the value of $\{u' + [rp(u'' - u')] - (1 - r)qu'\}$ increases as p increases and as q decreases.

What determines the values of p and q? p depends on the ability of CMs to detect the sincerity of other CMs and to reveal their own sincerity to them. q depends on the ability of CMs to detect the insincerity of SMs and conceal their own sincerity from them, and the ability of SMs to detect the sincerity of CMs and conceal their own insincerity from them. Since any increase in the ability to reveal one's sincerity to other CMs is apt to be offset by a decrease in the ability to conceal one's sincerity from SMs, a CM is likely to rely primarily on her ability to detect the dispositions of others, rather than on her ability to reveal or conceal her own.

The ability to detect the dispositions of others must be well developed in a rational CM. Failure to develop this ability, or neglect of its exercise, will preclude one from benefiting from constrained maximization. And it can then appear that constraint is irrational. But what is actually irrational is the failure to cultivate or exercise the ability to detect others' sincerity or insincerity.

Both CMs and SMs must expect to benefit from increasing their ability to detect the dispositions of others. But if both endeavour to maximize their abilities (or the expected utility, net of costs, of so doing), then CMs may expect to improve their position in relation to SMs. For the benefits gained by SMs, by being better able to detect their potential victims, must be on the whole offset by the losses they suffer as the CMs become better able to detect them as potential exploiters. On the other hand, although the CMs may not enjoy any net gain in their interactions with SMs, the benefits they gain by being better able to detect other CMs as potential co-operators are not offset by corresponding losses, but rather increased as other CMs become better able to detect them in return.

Thus as persons rationally improve their ability to detect the dispositions of those with whom they interact, the value of p may be expected to increase, while the value of q remains relatively constant. But then p/q increases, and the greater it is, the less favourable need be other circumstances for it to be rational to dispose oneself to constrained maximization. Those who believe rationality and morality to be at loggerheads may have failed to recognize the importance of cultivating their ability to distinguish sincere co-operators from insincere ones.

David Hume points out that if "it should be a virtuous man's fate to fall into the society of ruffians," then "his particular regard to justice being no longer of use to his own safety or that of others, he must consult the dictates of self-preservation alone."[4] If we fall into a society—or rather into a state of nature—of straightforward maximizers, then constrained maximization, which disposes us to justice, will indeed be of no use to us, and we must then consult only the direct dictates of our own utilities. In a world of Fooles, it would not pay to be a constrained maximizer, and to comply with one's agreements. In such circumstances it would not be rational to be moral.

But if we find ourselves in the company of reasonably just persons, then we too have reason to dispose ourselves to justice. A community in which most individuals are disposed to comply with fair and optimal agreements and practices, and so to base their actions on joint co-operative strategies, will be self-sustaining. And such a world offers benefits to all which the Fooles can never enjoy.

Hume finds himself opposed by "a sensible knave" who claimed that "*honesty is the best policy*, may be a good general rule, but is liable to many exceptions; and he . . . conducts himself with most wisdom, who observes the general rule, and takes advantage of all the exceptions."[5] Hume confesses candidly that "if a man think that this reasoning much requires an answer, it would be a little difficult to find any which will to him appear satisfactory and convincing."[6] A little difficult, but not, if we are right, impossible. For the answer is found in treating honesty, not as a policy, but as a disposition. Only the person truly disposed to honesty and justice may expect fully to realize their benefits, for only such a person may rationally be admitted to those mutually beneficial arrangements—whether actual agreements or implicitly agreed practices—that rest on honesty and justice, on voluntary compliance. But such a person is not able, given her disposition, to take advantage of the "exceptions; she rightly judges such conduct irrational. The Foole and the sensible knave, seeing the benefits to be gained from the exceptions, from the advantageous breaches in honesty and compliance, but not seeing beyond these benefits, do not acquire the disposition. Among knaves they are indeed held for sensible, but among us, if we be not corrupted by their smooth words, they are only fools.

3.1

In defending constrained maximization we have implicitly reinterpreted the utility-maximizing conception of practical rationality. The received interpretation, commonly accepted by economists and elaborated in Bayesian decision theory and the Von Neumann-Morgenstern theory of games, identifies rationality with utility-maximization at the level of particular choices. A choice is rational if and only if it maximizes the actor's expected utility. We identify rationality with utility-maximization at the level of dispositions to choose. A disposition is rational if and only if an actor holding it can expect his choices to yield no less utility than the choices he would make were he to hold any alternative disposition. We shall consider whether particular choices are rational if and only if they express a rational disposition to choose.

It might seem that a maximizing disposition to choose would express itself in maximizing choices. But we have shown that this is not so. The essential point in our argument is that one's disposition to choose affects the situations in which one may expect to find oneself. A straightforward maximizer, who is disposed to make maximizing choices, must expect to be excluded from co-operative arrangements which he would find advantageous. A constrained maximizer may expect to be included in such arrangements. She benefits from her disposition, not in the choices she makes, but in her opportunities to choose.

We have defended the rationality of constrained maximization as a disposition to choose by showing that it would be rationally chosen. Now this argument is not circular; constrained maximization is a disposition for strategic choice that would be parametrically chosen. But the idea of a choice among dispositions to choose is a heuristic device to express the underlying requirement, that a rational disposition to choose be utility-maximizing. In parametric contexts, the disposition to make straightforwardly maximizing choices is uncontroversially utility-maximizing. We may therefore employ the device of a parametric choice among dispositions to choose to show that in strategic contexts, the disposition to make constrained choices, rather than straightforwardly maximizing choices, is utility-maximizing. We must however emphasize that it is not the choice itself, but the maximizing character of the disposition in virtue of which it is choiceworthy, that is the key to our argument.

But there is a further significance in our appeal to a choice among dispositions to choose. For we suppose that the capacity to make such choices is itself an essential part of human rationality. We could imagine beings so wired that only straightforward maximization would be a psychologically possible mode of choice in strategic contexts. Hobbes may have thought that human beings were so wired, that we were straightforwardly-maximizing machines. But if he thought this, then he was surely mistaken. At the core of our rational capacity is the ability to engage in self-critical reflection. The fully rational being is able to reflect on his standard of deliberation, and to change that standard in the light of reflection. Thus we suppose it possible for persons, who may initially assume that it is rational to extend straightforward maximization from parametric to strategic contexts, to reflect on the implications of this extension, and to reject it in favour of constrained maximization. Such persons would be making the very choice, of a disposition to choose, that we have been discussing in this chapter.

And in making that choice, they would be expressing their nature not only as rational beings, but also as moral beings. If the disposition to make straightforwardly maximizing choices were wired in to us, we could not constrain our actions in the way required for morality. Moral philosophers have rightly been unwilling to accept the received interpretation of the relation between practical rationality and utility-maximization because they have recognized that it left no place for a rational constraint on directly utility-maximizing behaviour, and so no place for morality as ordinarily understood. But they have then turned to a neo-Kantian account of rationality which has led them to dismiss the idea that those considerations that constitute a person's reasons for acting must bear some particular relationship to the person.[7] They have failed to relate our nature as moral beings to our everyday concern with the fulfilment of our individual preferences. But we have shown how morality issues from that concern. When we correctly understand how utility-maximization is identified with practical rationality, we see that morality is an essential part of maximization.

3.2

An objector might grant that it may be rational to dispose oneself to constrained maximization, but deny that the choices one is then disposed to make are rational.[8] The objector claims that we have merely exhibited another instance of the rationality of not behaving rationally. And before we can accuse the objector of paradox, he brings further instances before us.

Consider, he says, the costs of decision-making. Maximizing may be the most reliable procedure, but it need not be the most cost-effective. In many circumstances, the rational person will not maximize but satisfice—set a threshold level of fulfilment and choose the first course of action of those coming to mind that one expects to meet this level. Indeed, our objector may suggest, human beings, like other higher animals, are natural satisficers. What distinguishes us is that we are not hard-wired, so that we can choose differently, but the costs are such that it is not generally advantageous to exercise our option, even though we know that most of our choices are not maximizing.

Consider also, he says, the tendency to wishful thinking. If we set ourselves to calculate the best or maximizing course of action, we are likely to confuse true expectations with hopes. Knowing this, we protect ourselves by choosing on the basis of fixed principles, and we adhere to these principles even when it appears to us that we could do better to ignore them, for we know that in such matters appearances often deceive. Indeed, our objector may suggest, much of morality may be understood, not as constraints on maximization to ensure fair mutual benefit, but as constraints on wish-fulfilling behaviour to ensure closer approximation to maximization.

Consider again, he says, the benefits of threat behaviour. I may induce you to perform an action advantageous to me if I can convince you that, should you not do so, I shall then perform an action very costly to you, even though it would not be my utility maximizing choice. Hijackers seize aircraft, and threaten the destruction of everyone aboard, themselves included, if they are not transported to Havana. Nations threaten nuclear retaliation should their enemies attack them. Although carrying out a threat would be costly, if it works the cost need not be borne, and the benefit, not otherwise obtainable, is forthcoming.

But, our objector continues, a threat can be effective only if credible. It may be that to maximize one's credibility, and one's prospect of advantage, one must dispose oneself to carry out one's threats if one's demands are not met. And so it may be rational to dispose oneself to threat enforcement. But then, by parity of reasoning with our claims about constrained maximization, we must suppose it to be rational actually to carry out one's threats. Surely we should suppose instead that, although it is clearly irrational to carry out a failed threat, yet it may be rational to dispose oneself to just this sort of irrationality. And so similarly we should suppose that although it is clearly irrational to constrain one's maximizing behaviour, yet it may be rational to dispose oneself to this irrationality.

We are unmoved. We agree that an actor who is subject to certain weaknesses or imperfections may find it rational to dispose himself to make choices that are not themselves rational. Such dispositions may be the most effective way of compensating for the weakness or imperfection. They constitute a second-best rationality, as it were. But although it may be rational for us to satisfice, it would not be rational for us to perform the action so chosen if, cost free, the maximizing action were to be revealed to us. And although it may be rational for us to adhere to principles as a guard against wish-fulfilment, it would not be rational for us to do so if, beyond all doubt, the maximizing action were to be revealed to us.

Contrast these with constrained maximization. The rationale for disposing oneself to constraint does not appeal to any weakness or imperfection in the reasoning of the actor; indeed, the rationale is most evident for perfect reasoners who cannot be deceived. The disposition to constrained maximization overcomes externalities; it is directed to the core problem arising from the structure of interaction. And the entire point of disposing oneself to constraint is to adhere to it in the face of one's knowledge that one is not choosing the maximizing action.

Imperfect actors find it rational to dispose themselves to make less than rational choices. No lesson can be drawn from this about the dispositions and choices of the perfect actor. If her dispositions to choose are rational, then surely her choices are also rational.

But what of the threat enforcer? Here we disagree with our objector; it may be rational for a perfect actor to dispose herself to threat enforcement, and if it is, then it is rational for her to carry out a failed threat. Equally, it may be rational for a perfect actor to dispose herself to threat resistance, and if it is, then it is rational for her to resist despite the cost to herself. Deterrence, we have argued elsewhere, may be a rational policy, and non-maximizing deterrent choices are then rational.[9]

In a community of rational persons, however, threat behaviour will be proscribed. Unlike co-operation, threat behaviour does not promote mutual advantage. A successful threat simply redistributes benefits in favour of the threatener; successful threat resistance maintains the status quo. Unsuccessful threat behaviour, resulting in costly acts of enforcement or resistance, is necessarily non-optimal; its very *raison d'être* is to make everyone worse off. Any person who is not exceptionally placed must then have the *ex ante* expectation that threat behaviour will be overall disadvantageous. Its proscription must be part of a fair and optimal agreement among rational persons; one of the constraints imposed by minimax relative concession is abstinence from the making of threats. Our argument thus shows threat behaviour to be both irrational and immoral.

Constrained maximizers will not dispose themselves to enforce or to resist threats among themselves. But there are circumstances, beyond the moral pale, in which a constrained maximizer might find it rational to dispose herself to threat enforcement. If she found herself fallen among straightforward maximizers, and especially if they were too stupid to become threat resisters, disposing herself to threat enforcement might be the best thing she could do. And for her, carrying out failed threats would be rational, though not utility-maximizing.

Our objector has not made good his case. The dispositions of a fully rational actor issue in rational choices. Our argument identifies practical rationality with utility-maximization at the level of dispositions to choose, and carries through the implications of that identification in assessing the rationality of particular choices.

3.3

To conclude this chapter, let us note an interesting parallel to our theory of constrained maximization—Robert Trivers' evolutionary theory of reciprocal altruism.[10] We have claimed that a population of constrained maximizers would be rationally stable; no one would have reason to dispose herself to straightforward maximization. Similarly, if we think of constrained and straightforward maximization as parallel to genetic tendencies to reciprocal altruism and egoism, a population of reciprocal altruists would be genetically stable; a mutant egoist would be at an evolutionary disadvantage. Since she would not reciprocate, she would find herself excluded from co-operative relationships.

Trivers argues that natural selection will favour the development of the capacity to detect merely simulated altruism. This of course corresponds to our claim that constrained maximizers, to be successful, must be able to detect straightforward maximizers whose offers to co-operation are insincere. Exploitative interactions between CMs and SMs must be avoided.

Trivers also argues that natural selection will favour the development of guilt, as a device motivating those who fail to reciprocate to change their ways in future.[11] In our argument, we have not appealed to any affective disposition; we do not want to weaken the position we must defeat, straightforward maximization, by supposing that persons are emotionally indisposed to follow it. But we may expect that in the process of socialization, efforts will be made to develop and cultivate each person's feelings so that, should she behave as an SM, she will experience guilt. We may expect our affective capacities to be shaped by social practices in support of co-operative interaction.

If a population of reciprocal altruists is genetically stable, surely a population of egoists is also stable. As we have seen, the argument for the rationality of constrained maximization turns on the proportion of CMs in the population. A small proportion of CMs might well suffer more from exploitation by undetected SMs than by co-operation among themselves unless their capacities for detecting the dispositions of others were extraordinarily effective. Similarly, a mutant reciprocal altruist would be at a disadvantage among egoists; her attempts at co-operation would be rebuffed and she would lose by her efforts in making them.

Does it then follow that we should expect both groups of reciprocal altruists and groups of egoists to exist stably in the world? Not necessarily. The benefits of co-operation ensure that, in any given set of circumstances, each member of a group of reciprocal altruists should do better than a corresponding member of a group of egoists. Each reciprocal altruist should have a reproductive advantage. Groups of reciprocal altruists should therefore increase relative to groups of egoists in environments in which the two come into contact. The altruists must prevail—not in direct combat between the two (although the co-operation possible among reciprocal altruists may bring victory there), but in the indirect combat for evolutionary survival in a world of limited resources.

In his discussion of Trivers's argument, Jon Elster notes two points of great importance which we may relate to our own account of constrained maximization. The first is, "The altruism is the more efficient because it is *not* derived from calculated self-interest."[12] This is exactly our point at the end of 2.1—constrained maximization is not straightforward maximization in its most effective guise. The constrained maximizer genuinely ignores the call of utility-maximization in following the co-operative practices required by minimax relative concession. There is no simulation; if there were, the benefits of co-operation would not be fully realized.

The second is that Trivers's account "does not purport to explain specific instances of altruistic behaviour, such as, say, the tendency to save a drowning person. Rescue attempts are explained by a general tendency to perform acts of altruism, and this tendency is then made the object of the evolutionary explanation."[13] In precisely the same way, we do not purport to give a utility-maximizing justification for specific choices of adherence to a joint strategy. Rather we explain those choices by a general disposition to choose fair, optimizing actions whenever possible, and this tendency is then given a utility-maximizing justification.

We do not, of course, have the competence to discuss whether or not human beings are genetically disposed to utility-maximizing behaviour. But if human beings are so disposed, then we may conclude that the disposition to constrained maximization increases genetic fitness.

NOTES

1. Our answer to the Foole builds on, but supersedes, my discussion in "Reason and Maximization," *Canadian Journal of Philosophy* 4 (1975), pp. 424–33.

2. Thus constrained maximization is not parallel to such strategies as "tit-for-tat" that have been advocated for so-called iterated Prisoner's Dilemmas. Constrained maximizers may co-operate even if neither expects her choice to affect future situations. Thus our treatment of co-operation does not make the appeal to reciprocity necessary to Robert Axelrod's account; see "The Emergence of Co-operation among Egoists," *American Political Science Review* 75 (1981), pp. 306–18.

3. That the discussion in "Reason and Maximization" assumes transparency was pointed out to me by Derek Parfit. See his discussion of "the self-interest theory" in *Reasons and Persons* (Oxford, 1984), esp. pp. 18–19. See also the discussion of "Reason and Maximization" in S. L. Darwall, *Impartial Reason* (Ithaca, NY, 1983), esp, pp. 197–8.

4. Hume, *Enquiry,* iii. i, p. 187.

5. Ibid., ix. ii, pp. 282–3.

6. Ibid., ix. ii, p. 283.

7. See, for example, T. Nagel, *The Possibility of Altruism* (Oxford, 1970), pp. 90–124.

8. The objector might be Derek Parfit; see *Reasons and Persons,* pp. 19–23. His book appeared too recently to permit discussion of his arguments here.

9. See "Deterrence, Maximization, and Rationality," *Ethics* 94 (1984), pp. 474–95; also in D. MacLean (ed.), *The Security Gamble: Deterrence Dilemmas in the Nuclear Age* (Totowa, NJ, 1984), pp. 101–22.

10. See R. L. Trivers, "The Evolution of Reciprocal Altruism," *Quarterly Review of Biology* 46 (1971), pp. 35–57.

11. Ibid., p. 50.

12. J. Elster, *Ulysses and the Sirens: Studies in Rationality and Irrationality* (Cambridge, 1979), p. 145.

13. Ibid., pp. 145–6.

Gregory Kavka

The Toxin Puzzle

1983

You are feeling extremely lucky. You have just been approached by an eccentric billionaire who has offered you the following deal. He places before you a vial of toxin that, if you drink it, will make you painfully ill for a day, but will not threaten your life or have any lasting effects. (Your spouse, a crack biochemist, confirms the properties of the toxin.) The billionaire will pay you one million dollars tomorrow morning if, at midnight tonight, you *intend* to drink the toxin tomorrow afternoon. He emphasizes that you need not drink the toxin to receive the money; in fact, the money will already be in your bank account hours before the time for drinking it arrives, if you succeed. (This is confirmed by your daughter, a lawyer, after she examines the legal and financial documents that the billionaire has signed.) All you have to do is sign the agreement and then intend at midnight tonight to drink the stuff tomorrow afternoon. You are perfectly free to change your mind after receiving the money and not drink the toxin. (The presence or absence of the intention is to be determined by the latest "mind-reading" brain scanner and computing device designed by the great Doctor X. As a cognitive scientist, materialist, and faithful former student of Doctor X, you have no doubt that the machine will correctly detect the presence or absence of the relevant intention.)

Confronted with this offer, you gleefully sign the contract, thinking "what an easy way to become a millionaire." Not long afterwards, however, you begin to worry. You had been thinking that you could avoid drinking the toxin and just pocket the million. But you realize that if you are thinking in those terms when midnight rolls around, you will not be intending to drink the toxin tomorrow. So maybe you will actually have to drink the stuff to collect the money. It will not be pleasant, but it is sure worth a day of suffering to become a millionaire.

However, as occurs to you immediately, it cannot really be necessary to drink the toxin to pocket the money. That money will either be or not be in your bank account by 10 a.m. tomorrow, you will know then whether it is there or not, and your drinking or not drinking the toxin hours later cannot affect the completed financial transaction. So instead of planning to drink the toxin, you decide to intend today to drink it and then change your mind after midnight. But if that is your plan, then it is obvious that you do not intend to drink the toxin. (At most you intend to intend to drink it.) For having such an intention is incompatible with planning to change your mind tomorrow morning.

At this point, your son, a strategist for the Pentagon, makes a useful suggestion. Why not bind yourself to drink the stuff tomorrow, by today making irreversible arrangements that will give you sufficient independent incentive to drink it? You might promise someone who would not later release you from the promise that you will drink the toxin tomorrow afternoon. Or you could sign a legal agreement obligating you to donate all your financial assets (including the million if you win it) to your least favourite political party, if you do not drink it. You might even hire a hitman to kill you if you do not swallow the toxin. This would assure you of a day of misery, but also of becoming rich.

Unfortunately, your daughter the lawyer, who has read the contract carefully, points out that arrangement of such external incentives is ruled out, as are such alternative gimmicks as hiring a hypnotist to implant the intention, forgetting the main relevant facts of the situation, and so forth. (Promising *yourself* that

Gregory Kavka, "The Toxin Puzzle." *Analysis* 43 (1983): 33–36. By permission of Oxford University Press.

you will drink the toxin could help if you were one of those strange people who take pride in never releasing oneself from a promise to oneself, no matter what the circumstances. Alas, you are not.)

Thrown back on your own resources, you desperately try to convince yourself that, despite the temporal sequence, drinking the toxin tomorrow afternoon is a necessary condition of pocketing the million that morning. Remembering Newcomb's Problem, you seek inductive evidence that this is so, hoping that previous recipients of the billionaire's offer won the million when and only when they drank the toxin. But, alas, your nephew, a private investigator, discovers that you are the first one to receive the offer (or that past winners drank less often than past losers). By now midnight is fast approaching and in a panic you try to summon up an act of will, gritting your teeth and muttering "I will drink that toxin" over and over again.

We need not complete this tale of high hopes disappointed (or fulfilled) to make the point that there is a puzzle lurking here. You are asked to form a simple intention to perform an act that is well within your power. This is the kind of thing we all do many times every day. You are provided with an overwhelming incentive for doing so. Yet you cannot do so (or have extreme difficulty doing so) without resorting to exotic tricks involving hypnosis, hired killers, etc. Nor are your difficulties traceable to an uncontrollable fear of the negative consequences of the act in question—you would be perfectly willing to undergo the after-effects of the toxin to earn the million.

Two points underlie our puzzle. The first concerns the nature of intentions. If intentions were inner performances or self-directed commands, you would have no trouble earning your million. You would only need to keep your eye on the clock, and then perform or command to yourself at midnight. Similarly, if intentions were simply decisions, and decisions were volitions fully under the agent's control, there would be no problem. But intentions are better viewed as dispositions to act which are based on *reasons to act*—features of the act itself or its (possible) consequences that are valued by the agent. (Specifying the exact nature of the relationship between intentions and the reasons that they are based on is a difficult and worthy task, but one that need not detain us. For an account that is generally congenial to the views presented here, see Davidson's "Intending," in his *Essays on Actions and Events*.) Thus, we can explain your difficulty in earning a fortune: you cannot intend to act as you have no reason to act, at least when you have substantial reasons not to act. And you have (or will have when the time comes) no reason to drink the toxin, and a very good reason not to, for it will make you quite sick for a day.

This brings us to our second point. While you have no reasons to drink the toxin, you have every reason (or at least a million reasons) to *intend* to drink it. Now when reasons for intending and reasons for acting diverge, as they do here, confusion often reigns. For we are inclined to evaluate the rationality of the intention both in terms of its consequences and in terms of the rationality of the intended action. As a result, when we have good reasons to intend but not to act, conflicting standards of evaluation come into play and something has to give way: either rational action, rational intention, or aspects of the agent's own rationality (e.g., his correct belief that drinking the toxin is not necessary for winning the million).

I made some similar points in an earlier article ("Some Paradoxes of Deterrence," *Journal of Philosophy*, June 1978), but there I was discussing an example involving conditional intentions. The toxin puzzle broadens the application of that discussion, by showing that its conclusions may apply to cases involving unconditional intentions as well. It also reveals that intentions are only partly volitional. One cannot intend whatever one wants to intend any more than one can believe whatever one wants to believe. As our beliefs are constrained by our evidence, so our intentions are constrained by our reasons for action.

***

Editor's Note: Kavka's essay was written largely as a rebuttal to Gauthier's revisionary theory of rational choice. Gauthier later responded to Kavka's challenge by arguing that a Constrained Maximizer may be a toxin drinker, since the kind of person who is disposed to drink toxin in Kavka's scenario is the kind of person who enjoys more opportunities for fruitful interaction. As Gauthier puts it, "The rational outcome of your deliberation tomorrow morning is the action that will be part of your life going as well as possible, subject to the constraint that it be compatible with your commitment—in this case, compatible with the sincere intention that you form today to drink the toxin. And so the rational action is to drink the toxin." David Gauthier, "Assure and Threaten," *Ethics*, 104(4): 690–721.

3 Game Theory

The basic concepts of game theory are indispensable for illuminating the structure and consequences of strategic situations. Indeed, Herbert Gintis and Samuel Bowles have described game theory as a set of tools that unify the behavioral sciences. To assist the reader encountering game theory for the first time, we end this chapter with an appendix of simple games and essential definitions, as well as a list of recommended introductory readings.

Game theory is the study of interdependence, or strategic choice, which occurs when the outcome of an interaction depends on the choices each party makes. In most strategic settings, all people can do is select a *course of action*, but the actual *outcome* depends on what other people do. Consider the classic prisoner's dilemma story:

> You and I are arrested for robbing a bank and interrogated separately. The ambitious district attorney wants at least one prosecution (to show that he's tough on crime), and so offers each of us the following deal: "You have a choice—snitch on your accomplice or stay silent. If you snitch and your accomplice doesn't, I will drop all charges against you and use your testimony to ensure that your accomplice serves a life sentence. Likewise, if he snitches on you and you stay silent, he will go free while you do the time. If you both snitch I get two convictions, but I'll see to it that you both get early parole after a five-year sentence. If you both stay silent, I'll have to settle for token sentences on firearms possession charges, and each of you will get a five-month sentence."

The prisoner's dilemma is interesting because each accomplice's attempt to minimize his own sentence produces a result that is worse for both than it would be if the two accomplices could find a reliable way to cooperate. Each is best off snitching because it will yield either his 1st or 3rd best outcome, rather than his 2nd or 4th best. Each thinks: no matter what the other person does, I'm better off snitching—if he stays silent and I snitch, I go free (rather than getting five months); if he snitches and I snitch, I get five years (rather than a life sentence). The accomplices can see that mutual silence is a better joint outcome than mutual snitching, yet snitching is the predictable result of causally independent choices. In more technical terms, snitching is the **Nash Equilibrium**, which is defined as any position in a payoff matrix from which neither player can unilaterally improve his outcome. The Nash Equilibrium is **Pareto-dominated** by mutual silence, meaning that both would be better off with mutual silence, even if they cannot achieve this end.

In describing games like the prisoner's dilemma, Simon Blackburn crucially distinguishes *empirical* games from *interpreted* games. An empirical game describes the objective features and possible outcomes of a strategic interaction. For example, in the prisoner's dilemma, we are presented with 1) accomplices who only care about themselves, 2) prison terms associated with different combinations of choices, and 3) an ambitious district attorney who wants to prosecute the detainees and give them extended sentences. An interpreted game is how the players think about the outcomes (or how theorists think that players think about the outcomes).

To see the distinction, suppose the accomplices are Romeo and Juliet. If we describe the game again with the same structure of payoffs, but the accomplices are in love, we might observe both staying silent, contrary to the prediction of the model. A naïve observer who doesn't know the players' feelings for each other might conclude that by staying silent they are behaving irrationally. But a more accurate conclusion is that they care about each other and wish to minimize their joint time in prison, or that each wants to minimize the time the *other* spends in prison. If this were true, the "interpreted" game may not fit the prisoner's dilemma model even if the "empirical" game superficially resembles a prisoner's dilemma. Another way of putting the point is that when we construct a payoff matrix, we can use objective outcomes like prison sentences, or we can use subjective preferences over outcomes which reflect everything the players care about (including, potentially, one another). Each approach can be useful under different conditions. For example, if we assume each player cares only about himself, we can predict what rational players will do simply by looking at the objective outcomes. But if we assume the players have complex motivations, including altruistic concerns, we may wish to translate objective payoffs into subjective preferences over outcomes. Doing so will lead us to a more precise prediction if we have reliable access to the players' motivations.

As the Romeo and Juliet example suggests, prisoner's dilemmas do not require narrowly self-interested preferences. Indeed, Romeo and Juliet can still be in a prisoner's dilemma if their goal is to minimize the sentence of the other player. If we replace the district attorney with the prince of Verona, and leave the structure of prison sentences the same as described above, what happens? The prince tells Romeo he gets to choose Juliet's move, and Juliet gets to choose for Romeo. Here it is evident that they are still in a prisoner's dilemma, since the rational choice is a unique, Pareto-dominated Nash equilibrium (we invite you to fill out a payoff matrix and see for yourself).

We begin our game theory applications with a classic from Thomas Schelling. Schelling was awarded the Nobel Prize in 2006 for applying abstract models to everyday phenomena like traffic congestion and racial segregation in neighborhoods and prisons. Schelling's analysis of neighborhood segregation (or aggregation, as he prefers to call it), reveals the backside of Adam Smith's invisible hand: individually innocent choices can produce patterns that are generally harmful. Everyone is worse off than they would be if they could coordinate their efforts to produce an alternative pattern. This argument casts doubt on two common assumptions: 1) that an observer can infer the intentions of agents from looking at the aggregate results of their behavior; 2) that when a group faces a collective action problem, there will be an obvious solution to it. Game theory reveals that, as a general matter, neither of these claims is true.

An important illustration is Gerry Mackie's modern classic on foot binding and female genital mutilation. Mackie suggests that people—in this case, women in traditional societies—can be trapped at suboptimal equilibria even when it is clear to them that all would be better off if each behaved differently. Game theory provides us with an explanation of why, under these circumstances, people may not be able to achieve their collective aims.

The paper by Brennan and Tullock unpacks the collective notion of an army as a unitary actor. The problem is universal: a military unit is much stronger if all of its members stand and fight, but each individual may be tempted to flee to save his own life. Military units have generally called this "the morale problem." Good morale is simply the name we give to units that cohere, while units that disintegrate have bad morale. Brennan and Tullock note that the problem might be conceived as psychological—inducing individuals to subsume their own identities to the group. But often the solutions actual armies have used to improve unit cohesion are *institutional.*

In particular, there are three types of solutions to the problem of morale for military units: positive incentives, punishments, and institutional structure. The so-called British square, a formation that invited an enemy to surround the group and which prevented any effective mobile operations, was never broken in a combat situation. This happy result (for the British) is often attributed to the bulldog character of the British people. Of course, if that were true, the formation would have been irrelevant; the culture itself was indomitable. What Brennan and Tullock point out is that the British square effectively undermined the rationale for desertion, because the only way to run away was to charge directly into an enemy line. Bravery required less courage than cowardice, and so the British were brave. This explanation may be only part of the story. Still, this is one of the attractions of game theory: it can offer overlooked explanations for conventions or rules that turn out to serve deeper purposes.

FURTHER READING

Camerer, Colin. 2003. *Behavioral Game Theory: Experiments in Strategic Interaction*. Princeton University Press.

Binmore, Ken. 1994. *Game Theory and the Social Contract: Playing Fair*, vol. 1. MIT Press.

Binmore, Ken. 1998. *Game Theory and the Social Contract: Just Playing*, vol. 2. MIT Press.

Gintis, Herbert. 2009. *Game Theory Evolving*, 2nd edition. Princeton University Press.

Gintis, Herbert. 2014. *The Bounds of Reason: Game Theory and the Unification of the Behavioral Sciences*, revised edition. Princeton University Press.

Lewis, David. 2002. *Convention: A Philosophical Study*. Blackwell Publishing.

Ross, Don. "Game Theory." *The Stanford Encyclopedia of Philosophy*. http://plato.stanford.edu/entries/game-theory/

Sugden, Robert. 2000. "Credible Worlds: The Status of Theoretical Models in Economics." *Journal of Economic Methodology*, 7(1): 1–31.

Appendix

Five Games

Definitions

An **equilibrium point**, or "Nash equilibrium," is any cell in a payoff matrix from which neither player can improve his outcome by unilaterally changing his choice.

A strategy **dominates** another strategy if regardless of what the other person does, you are better off playing it.

A distribution of payoffs **Pareto-dominates** another (or is "Pareto superior to" it) if it would make at least one player better off without hurting any other player.

Advice to students

When looking at games it is important to think about what is in the payoff matrix. Are we looking at years in prison, where—people with unusual utility functions notwithstanding—the agents wish to have lower numbers rather than higher numbers? Or are we looking at ordinal or cardinal utilities in which higher numbers are better than lower numbers? In order to avoid confusion, the following diagrams use ordered preferences over outcomes, so that 1st best ranks above 2nd best, 2nd above 3rd, and 3rd above 4th. Finally, when a payoff matrix features utilities or ranked preferences rather than, say, years in prison, the utility assignments should include everything the relevant parties care about, including utility they get from keeping promises, being (or being seen as) a cooperative person, and so on.

The following are commonly used two-person games of simultaneous choice. The games are defined by the orderings of preferences, so the specific examples should be taken as illustrations of a kind of structure rather than integral to the games they represent.

Prisoners' Dilemma

Suppose you play baseball in the 1990s and your trainer informs you that you can inject synthetic testosterone and significantly increase your lean muscle mass. You consider your options: if few other people choose to use it, you can dominate the sport; if lots of others use it, you'd better follow suit if you want to keep your job. Suppose, however, that injecting increases your chance of infertility and testicular cancer. In the absence of penalties, injecting is the only equilibrium. *The PD has a unique, Pareto-dominated equilibrium point.*

		Canseco	
		Abstain	Inject
Clemens	Abstain	2nd, 2nd	4th, 1st
	Inject	1st, 4th	3rd, 3rd NE

Assurance Game

In 1967 Israel fought a preemptive war to defend itself against an impending invasion by its neighbors. In the process it captured the Golan Heights from Syria—land which most Israelis didn't particularly want, but which allowed their military to monitor Syria's military. Ever since, Syria has sent suicide bombers into Israel, and Israel has retained the Golan Heights. Both would benefit from a land for peace deal, but Israel is not sure that if they return the land Syria will leave them alone, while Syria is not sure that if they leave Israelis alone they will return the land. *The assurance game has two equilibria: one risk-dominant, one payoff-dominant.* The payoff-dominant equilibrium Pareto dominates the risk-dominant equilibrium.

Israel

		Return land	Retain land
Syria	Stop killing	1st, 1st NE	4th, 2nd
	Keep killing	2nd, 4th	3rd, 3rd NE

Pure Coordination Game

Suppose surfers and swimmers prefer to ride waves in separate groups so that swimmers don't get run over by surfers, and surfers don't get slowed down by swimmers. If each side of the Manhattan Beach pier has equally good waves, then swimmers will choose one side, and surfers will move to the other. There are two equilibria, surfers on the North side and swimmers on the South side, and vice-versa. Once a recognizable pattern is established, nobody has a reason to deviate from the pattern. The result is a self-enforcing convention.

Kelly Slater

		North	South
Michael Phelps	South	1st, 1st NE	2nd, 2nd
	North	2nd, 2nd	1st, 1st NE

Impure Coordination Game

Suppose Lindsay and Paris want to show off their new lap dogs at a trendy night club on the Sunset Strip. Both prefer to go out together, but each prefers a different scene. Lindsay prefers the Roxy to the Whiskey, while Paris prefers the Whiskey to the Roxy. Once a club is selected neither has a reason to unilaterally change her move.

Lindsay

		Whiskey	Roxy
Paris	Whiskey	1st, 2nd NE	3rd, 3rd
	Roxy	3rd, 3rd	2nd, 1st NE

Chicken

After supporting a communist revolution in Cuba the Soviet Union's premier, Khrushchev, seeks to install nuclear warheads in Cuba capable of striking the United States. The CIA captures photographs of the missiles and gets word that the USSR is shipping warheads to Cuba tomorrow. Kennedy must decide whether to intercept the Russian ship in the open ocean, and risk a nuclear confrontation, or to let it pass through to Cuba. If the US blocks the USSR, and the USSR retreats, the US gets its best outcome and the USSR loses face (and vice versa). If both retreat, war is averted, but neither gains a tactical advantage. If both charge ahead, nuclear war ensues—the worst outcome for both.

Khrushchev

		Retreat	Charge
Kennedy	Retreat	2nd, 2nd	3rd, 1st NE
	Charge	1st, 3rd NE	4th, 4th

SIMON BLACKBURN

Game Theory and Rational Choice

1998

There is, I admit, the obligation of the Treaty . . . but I am not able to subscribe to the doctrine of those who have held in this House what plainly amounts to an assertion, that the simple fact of the existence of a guarantee is binding on every party to it, irrespectively altogether of the particular position in which it may find itself at the time when the occasion for acting on the guarantee arises.

W. E. Gladstone[1]

1. UTILITIES, PREFERENCES, AND CHOICES[2]

Bishop Butler showed convincingly that it is not at all true that people act so as to maximize the intensity or duration of some psychological state.[3] They do not even always act with their own interests in mind, where these interests are construed as states of themselves. Nor would we want them to do so. So we could conclude that the principle of acting to maximize expected utility has been exploded as empirically and normatively bogus. But suppose instead we interpret utility and interests differently. Suppose we interpret people as having an interest in some object when that object figures in their decision-making. We are here talking of what Bishop Butler called "particular appetites," which are directed to a whole variety of things, so objects, interests, and concerns here include states that are not states of the subject: the survival of the whales, or the relief of the famine, or the death of the blasphemer. It is this kind of interest that is to matter. In the apt phrase of David Gauthier, "It is not interests in the self, that take oneself as object, but interests of the self, held by oneself as subject, that provide the basis for rational choice and action."[4]

Now this does not by itself give us any conception of the "sum" of an agent's concerns, for you cannot add, for instance, the fate of the whales and the death of the infidel. Yet someone may be concerned about each of these. So no conception of an agent's overall utility seems to arise. But what we do have are agents who are concerned about various things, and who prefer various outcomes to others. An agent may care more about the fate of the whales than about the death of the infidel, and this asymmetry could show itself in her choices and actions. The brilliant idea on which the theory of rational choice rests (officially) is that we can *reverse* our reading of the principle that rational agents act so as to maximize utility. Instead of this being a specific principle, with "utility" a particular kind of goal, we see utility itself as a construct from mathematically tractable ways of handling their concerns. We see where peoples' utilities lie by seeing what they care about.

Ramsey saw that, given very weak assumptions, an agent with an ordering of preferences over each of some set of options can be represented as if she had attached measurable "values," called utilities, to those options.[5] The provision of a scale is just like that of providing numerical measures for weights, given only the results from a balance. A balance is simply an empirical determination of when one object

From Simon Blackburn, *Ruling Passions: A Theory of Practical Reasoning*. New York: Oxford University Press, 1998. pp. 161–179. By permission of Oxford University Press.

weighs at least as much as another. An element has at least as great a weight as another if and only if the other does not outweigh it, which is to tip the balance against it. So the results of tests for whether one object is at least as heavy as another can be presented numerically, with the numbers representing weights of the objects in the set. Similarly, then we can say that if *a* is preferred to *b,* and *b* to *c, a* has (arbitrarily) three units of utility to the agent, *b* has 2, and *c* has 1. More accurately, the value of an option is equated with its *expected* utility, since an option's actual utility to an agent may be discounted by a probability factor. Ramsey provided the basic way of solving for both expectations and utilities, given an agent disposed to make sufficient choices amongst options. In the standard development, for instance, an agent might be offered choices between one outcome and only the chance of another, and behaviour over a series of such choices can give a measure of how much one outcome is preferred to another. An agent might just prefer a 50 percent chance of *b* to certain *a,* but also prefer a 10 percent chance of *c* to certain *b,* in which case she prefers *c* to *b* more than she prefers *b* to *a.* For she jumps at even a faint chance of *c* instead of *b,* whereas it takes a good chance of *b* for her to prefer the gamble to certain *a.* The numbers to be attached to her utilities for *a, b,* and *c* will represent that difference.

So if we have preferences across choices in a set, we can represent their utilities numerically. But what corresponds to the empirical results from the balance, telling us when *a* is preferred to *b*? The obvious answer is that you see what an agent prefers by seeing what she chooses, or what she would choose under conditions designed to minimize interfering factors or "noise."[6] True preferences are those that are revealed by decisions. It is, after all, a truism that to know what you or anyone else wants, see what you or anyone else chooses, or would choose given suitable options. To know that you prefer oil to butter, you see whether you choose it, at least when nothing further hangs on the decision. It is, however, quite a long road from simple choice behaviour, as it might be witnessed by a camera, to an interpretation of an agent's preferences. We need to know how the agent thinks of the situation, that is, the beliefs they have about what they are doing and causing. In particular we will need to distinguish between what an agent *chooses* and what she *prefers* when preference relates to aspects of a situation beyond her control. She may prefer some upshot to others, but choose differently because she does not expect that upshot to be realized. This distinction becomes important in strategic problems and games, where an agent conforms her move to safeguard her situation in the light of what she expects others to do, and this may be very different from aiming at the outcome she would actually regard as best.

Meanwhile, putting the two foundation stones of the theory of rational choice together, we have:

> (*Util*) A utility function is defined such that the expected utility of *a* is at least as great as that of *b* if and only if *a* is weakly preferred to *b* (i.e., preferred to *b*, or at least as much as *b*). Such a function can be defined over a set of options if preference satisfies two consistency conditions: for all outcomes *a, b* either *a* is weakly preferred to *b*, or *b* to *a* (totality), and if *a* is weakly preferred to *b*, and *b* to *c*, then *a* is weakly preferred to *c* (transitivity).

> (*Revpref*) Choice behaviour is primitive. If a player makes choices, then he or she is making choices as though he were equipped with a preference relation which has that choice preferred to others, in the light of what else he believes about the situation. An eligible agent is always interpretable as though he were seeking to further a preference.

The first part of the approach makes utilities "logical constructions" out of preferences, while the second makes preferences logical constructions out choices, given beliefs.

Util and *Revpref* apply to anyone with consistent, transitive preferences over a set of options. We can call such persons eligible persons. It is extremely important not to confuse the issue by calling them rational, as is frequently done, because this perpetuates the illusion that we are talking about special sorts of person, or giving *recommendations* in the name of reason. Whereas all we can say so far is that an ineligible person would simply be someone who cannot be interpreted in terms of utilities, so far as the set of options in play is concerned. Similarly, if a balance cannot weigh some element in a set of objects, or if it weighs $a > b$, and $b > c$, but $c > a$, then it cannot deliver a set of weights defined over the set. This makes it a bad balance, but it may be useful for other purposes, such as introducing philosophy of science to students, or confusing an enemy.

Putting *Util* and *Revpref* together means that we can always interpret any eligible agent as if they were seeking to maximize expected utility. . . . *Util* and *Revpref* deliver what is wanted, and we shall see that it is very doubtful whether any other approach could do so.

Do the principles make it analytic that anybody can be interpreted as pursuing their own utility? Not quite, because you can forfeit eligibility. It is appropriate to compare the methodology of interpretation to determine the content of propositions from the inferential habits of agents. Logic imposes a similar grid, in the sense that it is only if agent's inferential patterns are isomorphic with the deductive relationships amongst propositions that we can interpret them as thinking in terms of those propositions. It might sound as though this makes it impossible for anybody to hold a contradiction, or flout any sufficiently elementary logical law. But the interpretational strategy is not quite as charitable as that. If enough else is true of an agent to suggest that she must by one statement mean "*p*" and must by another statement mean "not-*p*" and she is sincere in asserting both, then we do not automatically reinterpret to preserve her logicality. Similarly, given enough chaos in an agent's dispositions to choose, then Ramsey's grid becomes inapplicable. But, the case is necessarily exceptional. Even chaos can be interpreted: perhaps one of the agent's concerns, and hence a source of their utility, is to display a charming unpredictability.

We should now pause to disarm two possible objections to *Util* and *Revpref.* One thing that disturbs some economists is that utility, as here defined, need have nothing to do with an agent's welfare, nor with their personal economic gain. We need only remember Butler's man who runs upon certain ruin in order to revenge himself on his enemy. He prefers revenge, hence revenge has a higher expected utility. But his welfare is predictably diminished. Amartya Sen, for example, finds this troubling.[7] Sen believes that this undermines the authority of an approach based on *Util.* But it should not do so. "Welfare" implies a specific empirical aim, and we will get no authoritative conception of a rational or even an admirable agent as one who is wrapped up in her own welfare. Choice by contrast is truly the upshot of whatever the player cares about, and all we have is a conception of utility derived entirely from choice. We certainly cannot criticize either axiom by reminding ourselves of the heterogeneous nature of desire, for they are designed precisely in order to cope with that nature. An agent, for instance, who prefers revenge to life or liberty attaches a higher expected utility to revenge. This is now definition, not doctrine.

The same caveats apply if we start to contrast preference with principle or with conscience, as Sen also does. There is certainly a vernacular distinction here, for we talk of being obliged to do what we do not prefer to do. But preference, revealed by choice, may include the preference for acting on any specific principle: the preference to keep a promise, or keep a vow to God, or to avoid the gaze of the man within, or the preference to do one's bit, or the preference for being the man who bought the Brooklyn Bridge, rather than the man who sold it. The better way to describe the "conflict" between a narrow sense of preference and what happens when principle is introduced is to say that sometimes we are obliged to do what we would not otherwise have preferred to do; but this leaves it open that now, in the presence of the obligation, our preference is actually that we conform to the requirements of obligation or duty. The counterfactual preference that we would have had, had we not made the promise, or felt obliged to cooperate, or whatever it is, is not our all-things-considered preference: our strongest concern. There is an element of regimentation here. We sometimes choose things because we think of ourselves as having to do so, rather than wanting to do so. The view that preferences are revealed by decisions accommodates such cases by saying that your choice then reveals that you prefer to fulfil your role, or do your duty, or follow your principles. If a choice is apparently unmotivated, like the destructive behaviour of a child in a tantrum, then we say that it reveals that the agent prefers to be a nuisance, or make a scene. If the agent's behaviour is sufficiently random to defy interpretation then he is ineligible, and cannot be understood in terms of preferences and beliefs.

Still, the word "preference" disguises where we are. It tempts us towards thinking of desires with narrow and perhaps hedonistic objects. By contrast, it is common to think of values as things of greater weight and dignity. Values come in the region of what we are set on preferring, or prefer to prefer, or what we fail to prefer only at some cost. If this bothers us, it would be better to substitute a word like "concerns" or "aims." In a decision-theoretic situation, a higher number attached to the utility of a choice represents the extent to which the agent is concerned about it, or the strength of purpose with which she aims at it. And by *Revpref* this in turn is measured simply by the extent to which she inclines towards it. Principles and keeping promises, or telling the truth, or stoning the unfaithful. We could substitute for *Revpref* a principle *Revconc*:

> (*Revconc*) Choice behaviour is primitive. If a player makes choices, then he or she is making choices as though he were equipped with a concern relation which has his concerns better met by that choice than others, in the light of what else he believes about the situation. An eligible agent is always interpretable as though he were seeking to do what most concerns him.

I shall continue to talk of preference since it is entrenched in the literature. But *Revconc* represents the true situation better.

We now have all the ingredients for the tautologous or mathematically imposed way of reading the principle of maximizing expected utility. *Homo economicus* is now not a special kind of agent, but *any agent at all* described in terms of concerns and utility. Ramsey's approach gives us a kind of grid within which to place our understanding of agents. In fulfiling this role it does not issue recommendations or norms, or give advice in the name of "reason." The framework by itself issues no empirical predictions, nor any normative recommendations. Why not? No empirical predictions, because nothing an agent does is inconsistent with it. The agent who ignores his own welfare is as much "maximizing utility" when he indulges his revenge as the one who swallows his vengeful feelings and goes about cultivating his bank balance. If you did it, that just shows where your concerns lay, and, perhaps in retrospect, that you attached more expected utility to doing it than doing the other thing. More surprisingly, it seems that the approach issues no recommendations, because a recommendation is something you can succeed in following, or in disobeying. But under the present suggestions, nothing you do would count as acting not to maximize expected utility. As Wittgenstein might have said, anything you do would equally accord with the advice, and that means that no advice was given.

This last claim may look to be a little too strong.[8] We can return to the question of whether logic has any normative bite, given its similar status as an interpretative grid.[9] We want to say both that interpretation must represent its subjects as obedient to logic, and that this obedience should play a role in their system of normative governance: should dictate their inferential habits from within. Can we similarly say that obedience to the norms of expected utility theory is an interpretative grid, but also something to which a subject should conform his or her deliberations? Up to a point. A subject may, from within the deliberative perspective, be fairly clear about his concerns. And a decision theorist may be able to say that with those concerns, in such-and-such an environment, such-and-such a policy is the correct one to follow. What is not thereby given is what to say if the agent does something else: whether this illustrates "irrationality," or mere lack of awareness of the totality of operating concerns. We shall see more of this in what follows.

2. BLACKMAILERS AND CENTIPEDES

So what goes on when we apply the mathematical apparatus to the kind of decision problems that arise? For game theorists certainly give advice, indeed conflicting advice, yet we just came close to suggesting that any such pretension must be based on confusion.

To sort this out, and indeed to bring us back to ethics, we need to distinguish between what I shall call an empirical situation or an empirical game, and the theoretical situation, or *interpreted* game. The empirical situation is described in empirical terms: if someone makes such-and-such a choice, then they will receive so many dollars, or so many years in prison, for example, according to the move the other player makes. But describing a problem in these terms is not describing it in the terms in which an agent necessarily sees his or her situation. They may not care about dollars, they may even not care about years in prison. They may also care about such things as how the dollars were gained, or how the years in prison were avoided. In fact, if we think of an "option" in a concrete situation, then there is no limit to the number of features that, potentially, might engage someone's concerns. Imagine someone choosing to stay at home, rather than go to the Alps. What attracted or repelled him? Was it: staying at home, being in London when it is relatively empty, staying-at-home-with-Aunt-Mary, staying-near-Jane-and-not-having-to-face-the-channel-crossing . . . or whatever, for an indefinitely large number of possible qualifications and riders?

It is now widely recognized that in the application of decision theory, interpretation is critical. For example, John Broome presented a plausible case in which, when offered pairwise options, someone shows intransitivity, and hence is apparently bound to seem ineligible.[10] Offered a choice between going to Rome and hiking in the Alps, Maurice prefers Rome ($R > A$). Offered a choice between going to Rome and staying at home, he would stay at home ($H > R$). Transitivity requires that $H > A$. But, alas, offered a choice between staying at home and going to the Alps, Maurice would go to the Alps. This is classic intransitivity of preferences, and would equally classically be a hallmark of irrationality (in our terms, we would say that Maurice is ineligible, or has no defined preferences over this set of options). But suppose we can interpret Maurice as follows. Rome beats the Alps in a straight choice, because the Alps are frightening, and the alternative is interesting enough. Home beats Rome in a straight choice, because although Rome is interesting, home is comfortable. But if the options are home or the Alps, it would be cowardly to avoid the challenge: to allow comfort to overcome the frisson of danger is unmanly (note that there was nothing cowardly about preferring Rome to the Alps: the interest of museums defends against any incipient charge of cowardice). In other words, different contexts of choice must be taken into account. A sufficiently fine-grained description of Maurice's practical thinking reveals nothing irrational at all. Home-when-the-alternative-is-the-Alps represents one object of concern, and one that does not appeal to Maurice as much as Home-when-the-alternative-is-Rome. "Outcomes" as objects of concern are more finegrained than outcomes thought of as identified empirical states, and they come identified by particular complexes of potentially important properties.

But what is right is that Maurice as so far described has no answer to the question of which of the three he prefers when *all three* are on the table. We have only given him pairwise preferences. If we sought to infer his "all three" preferences from that, there would be inconsistent ways of doing it. But that would be our fault (for trying to do such a thing) rather than Maurice's (for being in a state from which it cannot be done). Maurice would need to confront the question only if and when it comes up, and then indeed he has to change in some way before selecting one option as best overall. But there is nothing irrational or defective about a Maurice who simply puts aside the question of what he would do if all three came up. Perhaps, indeed, he knows that they will not, for instance because his climbing and museum-going partner will have already limited the options before him.

Obviously we need to know something about the agent's pattern of concerns to select one conceptualization of the situation, and say that he preferred this to the other decision, also conceptualized in terms of features that mattered. There can arise here a kind of circularity in the theory of interpretation. If we start with raw behaviour, as registered by a camera or a choreographer, we do not know which features of the situation are part of the agent's decision-making representation of it. We don't know what he understood or believed about the situation, and the consequences of different actions. But fortunately the problem of interpretation is not impenetrable. We guess at which features of situations matter by seeing the agent's raw dispositions to move and avoid; we feed back our interpretation, and learn how he sees his situation by applying our theory of which features are significant to him. In other words, there is a to-and-fro between our understanding of which features of situations in general matter to the agent, and our understanding of how he thought about the options in front of him on any concrete occasion.

To illustrate the distinction between the theoretical and the empirical situation further, consider Adam and Eve. They each face a simple choice, *X* or *Y*. If they choose *X* then they gain $1 and the other gets $0; vice versa if they choose *Y*. This describes the empirical situation, and it is identical for each of them. Now suppose Adam chooses *X*. This choice shows what he prefers, and this shows what was his expected utility: higher if he gets $1 than if Eve does. Suppose Eve chooses *Y*. This shows what she prefers, and shows that her expected utility is higher if Adam gets a dollar than if she does. Maybe she is altruistic, or expects benefits from Adam in return, or hates money, or wants to score off the experimenter, or whatever.

This means that Adam and Eve were in different theoretical games or choice situations. We can write the same empirical choice for each of them:

X $1 for me, $0 for the other;
Y $0 for me, $1 for the other.

But we cannot write the same theoretical choice for each of them:

X n units of utility for me, $(n - m)$ for the other;
Y $(n - m)$ units of utility for me, m for the other.

For only Adam is in this choice situation, with positive n and positive smaller m. We *must* (by *Util* and *Revpref*) write a different matrix for Eve: one in which she gets more units of utility by choosing *Y* than by choosing *X*, since that is what she actually does. We can sum this up by saying that Adam is correctly modelled by the second, theoretical, description, but Eve is not.

Can anyone recommend Adam's choice over Eve's, or vice versa? One might like or dislike someone whose preferences go with their own monetary gain. But as it stands, Eve is just someone with one set of preferences, and Adam is someone with another, and that is all there is to it.

With the distinction between the empirical and the theoretical to hand, we can now consider more interesting decisions. Consider first the situation of Blackmail. The story is that before the situation arises Eve has committed an indiscretion. If Adam does nothing, he has $1, and Eve has $2. If he blackmails Eve and she submits, he takes one of Eve's dollars. But if she does not submit, she blows the gaff on him, revealing him as a blackmailer, but also revealing her own indiscretion: a cost of everything they have, so leaving them $0 each. It is common to describe the different options as "hawkish" or "doveish," the idea being that one option in each case is more aggressive, and the other less so (this is preferable to saying that one option involves "ratting" or "cheating," as is sometimes done, since the hawkish option need involve no defection from any previous agreement or any previous convention of behaviour).

ADAM: Dove: the status quo: he has $1, Eve enjoys $2

HAWK: he makes his threat: it moves to Eve's turn . . .

EVE: Dove: she submits, and is left with $1, Adam has $2

HAWK: she blows the gaff, and they are each left with $0.

We can draw the choices in the diagram:

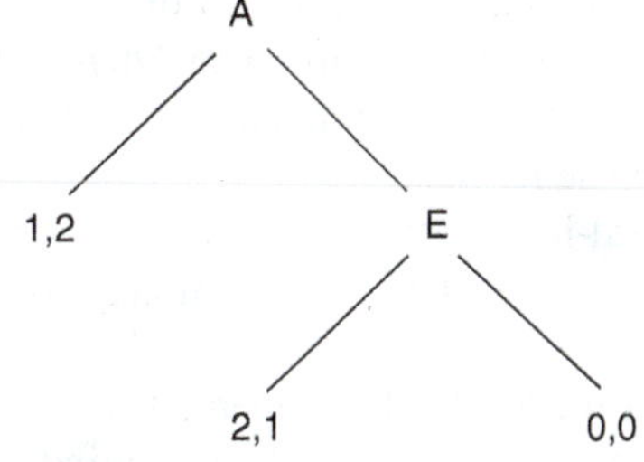

Hawkish options are to the right, doveish ones to the left. Adam's holdings are described first, Eve's second. This is the empirical situation. What should Adam do? What should Eve do?

As we should by now expect, there is no unique answer. For it depends on the theoretical game.

Suppose, first, that for each of them, expected utility (measured, remember, by what they are inclined to choose) simply goes along with their own dollars. This means that they care about nothing except their own dollar holdings. Suppose, too, that each knows this about the other. Then Adam knows what will happen if it comes to Eve's turn: she will play dove, to keep $1, instead of playing hawk and moving to $0. And knowing this, Adam will play hawk, for, given that all he cares about is dollars, it would be a contradiction (by *Util* and *Revconc*) for him to stick with less utility, i.e. fewer dollars, when by a simple choice he can have more. So he will play hawk, Eve will submit, and Adam takes one of Eve's dollars.

Poor Eve. But now suppose Eve has been to a good school, which has taught her to be proud and vengeful. And suppose Adam knows this. Then Adam knows that Eve's *theoretical* situation is not represented by the dollar payoffs. Submitting and leaving Adam better off might be unthinkable to this Eve. Her preference, and hence her utility, would be to blow the gaff, even if this means running upon her own financial ruin. In terms of utilities, her play might look like this:

Eve: Dove: she submits and is left with −20 units of utility overall, Adam with +5

Hawk: she blows the gaff, and is left overall with −10, Adam with −5.

Each loses dollars in the gaff-blowing finale and the (arbitrary) negative figures simply represent that it is worse for each of them than the status quo. But Eve prefers it to losing only $1 to Adam, and having to live with the fact of having been blackmailed. That is worse for her.

In a real-life situation, Adam may know the empirical game. But he is very unlikely to know the theoretical game: in fact nobody is likely to know it until after the actions have been taken, and revealed the agents' concerns. If Adam is minded to be a blackmailer, he had better look out not to pick on vengeful and proud subjects. And if Eve is going to be a possible target for blackmail, she had better develop and even publicize a nice vengeful streak. In other words, we can reflect on the social situations in which people may find themselves, and recognize which characters will succeed and which will not in those situations. The game theorist can *only* say: be someone, or don't be someone, who is modelled as being in this or that theoretical game. What she *cannot* say is: once you are in this or that empirical game, play this or that way.

Now consider more interesting situations. One that has attracted some attention is Centipede. In this game, we imagine a known sequence of actions, either co-operative or not, taken by each player in turn. At any point a non-co-operative move breaks the sequence, and each player stops with the payoff so far. Each combined sequence of (co-operation + reciprocation) ratchets up the payoffs. But at any stage a player's co-operation is an *immediate* loss; it only recoups when the other player reciprocates.

	1a	1e	2a	2e		98a	98e	99a	99e	
	A>	E>	A>	E	. . .	A>	E>	A>	E>	End
A	1	0	2	1		98	97	99	98	100
E	1	3	2	4		98	100	99	101	100

So in the diagram Adam's move at 1a takes him from 1 to 0; Eve's move at 1e takes her from 3 to 2, and so on. The classic example of this kind of structure is Hume's case where I help you get your corn in, expecting you to help me when my field, which ripens later, is ready. If we each co-operate we each do better, and we suppose that each passing season increases our wealth. But if I co-operate and you don't reciprocate I am worse off than if I hadn't bothered. Maybe I am too tired to get much of my own harvest in, and in any event your harvest being on the market depresses prices. But you are better off than if you reciprocate in return: reciprocating means hard work, and in turn you get a better price for your corn, if less of mine is harvested.[11]

If the figures measure something we care about, such as money, it seems obvious that we ought to co-operate. Each co-operative round racks up our holdings. But the classical analysis has problems with this. Under that analysis we suppose that each player knows the other is rational, each player knows the other's payoffs, and each knows that the other knows this (and so on: the structure of the game is "common knowledge" between them). But in particular, each of them knows when the game ends (perhaps their leases have a definite term). Now consider the last round. Each knows it will be the last round. Eve's reciprocity leads her to loss: she substitutes 100 for her 101. So, she won't reciprocate. But knowing this, Adam won't co-operate on round 99. But knowing that, Eve won't co-operate just before, and so on back. The backwards induction means that truly rational players, knowing their situation and knowing that the other knows it, never start on cooperation, but would stay with their miserable holding of 1 each.[12]

This seems very odd: if you're so smart, how come you ain't rich? Again, the first step to a solution is to distinguish the empirical game from the theoretical game. Empirically, the set-up may be as given, if the units represent dollar holdings, for example. But what inclinations might each player plausibly have? Among other things: not being idiotic enough not to try co-operation; feeling a bit of a bounder for not reciprocating; feeling that once the pattern is established, it would be wrong to break it, and trusting the partner to feel the same. If Eve has such inclinations, and Adam can reasonably expect her to have them, and vice versa, then the pattern of reciprocation is established, and they do well.

The theoretical game need not at all share the empirical game's feature that Eve's final co-operation represents pure loss. As a real, multifaceted person, she may be proud of the pattern and loyal to it; she may not want to be the first and last to break it; she may have formed an affection for Adam as the seasons unwound; she may be going to take up a new lease and foresees that she will need co-operation either from Adam or from other people in the future. She may feel unease at the real or imagined verdict of others. Hence Adam cannot predict that she will defect even on the final round. Hence Eve cannot predict on any previous round that Adam will defect because he will expect her to defect immediately afterwards. And in fact, even if Adam does suspect that Eve will defect on the final round, he in turn might be loyal to the pattern for similar reasons, and prefer to leave with an intact sense of having done his bit.

Of course Eve may be tempted to cheat at the end, and Adam may fear this; one can well imagine them becoming uneasy as the last seasons draw on. Eve might be a bounder, and Adam may indeed wake to find that she has decamped leaving him tired out and with his harvest still to gather. But it would be strange for him to fear that outcome so much that he never risks co-operation.

At this a game theorist may well complain that we have illegitimately introduced concerns that are not represented in the game's payoff structure. In other words, we are (arbitrarily from his point of view) specifying that the theoretical game is not like the empirical game. But if he stringently insists that the numbers do represent expected utilities, then there is nothing paradoxical or surprising in the result that the sequence never gets started. Adam expects to lose by his first action of helping Eve, for $0 < 1$. So he won't do it, period. Remember that by *Revpref* and *Util* nobody ever chooses in such a way that their expected utility is diminished by the choice. It is a matter of definition that people act so as to maximize expected utility (if they can be interpreted as acting at all in terms of the choices we are describing). If you know some agent's expected utilities, you know what they will do. If they expect loss from a choice, then they won't make it (definition, again). So indeed we don't here have a coherent description of a theoretical game that gets off the runway at all, but this is no longer surprising. Rather, if Adam really expects loss through making a first co-operative move, then this must be because he expects Eve not to co-operate back, and then he will not essay the move himself. It would be as if Eve had already posted a notice saying that under no circumstances will she ever help with Adam's harvest. And then, of course, they stay impoverished at the baseline. People might post such notices, just as real neighbours do, but not because they are especially "rational." They post them because they are jealous and fearful, or too shortsighted to see beyond this year's possibility of loss, too bound up with the immediate future to let the prospect of increasing prosperity in the distant future lure them.

In Blackmail, we saw that Eve needed to have gone to a good school to flourish in the world of people like Adam. Assuming that he has not been educated to find blackmail repellent, then her public nastiness alone protects her. In Centipede, the farmers need to be people with some reason for expecting each other to co-operate. They need to have and hope for a little bit of ethics. Hume was the first to recognize that the prevalence of such interdependencies is sufficient to explain the evolution of many of our social concerns. In a famous passage (talking not about mutual aid, but about abstaining from predating upon one another's property), he says:

I observe, that it will be for my interest to leave another in the possession of his goods, *provided* he will act in the same manner with regard to me. He is sensible of a like interest in the regulation of his conduct. When this common sense of interest is mutually expressed, and is known to both, it produces a suitable resolution and behaviour. And this may properly enough be called a convention or agreement betwixt us, though without the interposition of a promise; since the actions of each of us have a reference to those of the other, and are performed upon the supposition that something is to be performed on the other part. Two men who pull the oars of a boat, do it by an agreement or convention, though they have never given promises to each other. Nor is the rule concerning the stability of possession the less derived from human conventions, that it arises gradually, and acquires force by a slow progression, and by our repeated experience of the inconveniences of transgressing it. On the contrary, this experience assures us still more, that the sense of interest has become common to all our fellows, and gives us a confidence of the future regularity of their conduct: And 'tis only on the expectation of this, that our moderation and abstinence are founded. In like manner are languages gradually established by human conventions, without any promise. In like manner do gold and silver become the common measures of exchange, and are esteemed sufficient payment for what is of a hundred times their value.[13]

He was sufficiently proud of discovering this mechanism to return to it later:

Thus two men pull the oars of a boat by common convention, for common interest, without any promise or contract: thus gold and silver are made the measures of exchange: Thus speech and words and language are fixed by human convention and agreement. Whatever is advantageous to two or more persons, if all perform their part; but what loses all advantage, if only one perform, can arise from no other principle. There would otherwise be no motive for any one of them to enter into that scheme of conduct.[14]

One of Hume's major concerns in these passages is to show that the origin of this kind of co-operation does not lie in the giving of any explicit promise or the formation of a contract. The convention is a natural growth, founded originally on the hope or expectation of benefit in return. Just as various mammals go in for "reciprocal altruism," scratching another's back if they get theirs scratched in return, without any kind of contract, so do we.

3. THE PRISONERS' DILEMMA

And so to the most discussed decision problem of all, the celebrated prisoner's dilemma.[15] Here again we have an empirical game and a theoretical game. But to analyse it I shall reverse the order so far adopted, and present the theoretical game first. Each player plays at the same time, knowing that the ordering of the other is the same as his or her own.

In the diagram below we are told only Adam's preferences. Adam's first preference is that he play hawk, and Eve dove. His second is that both play dove, his third is that both play hawk, and fourth that Eve plays hawk while he plays dove. We suppose that Eve is a mirror-image of Adam. Her preferences are the same as applied to her, that is, she prefers most her playing hawk and Adam playing dove, and so on down. So Adam's best outcome is her worst, and vice versa. They each rank <H, H> 3rd, and <D, D> 2nd. I shall call this ordering of preference, the prisoners' dilemma ordering. I shall call <H, H> War (short for the war of all against all); <H, D> Victory (for whoever plays H); <D, D> Co-operation, and <D, H> Ruin. So their ranking is Victory, Cooperation, War, Ruin: <V, C, W, R>. We are, of course, not told by how much Adam prefers one option to another.

Maybe the fourth option is truly terrible, and the first truly wonderful, but maybe not.

		Adam	
		H	D
Eve	H	3rd	4th
	D	1st	2nd

What will Adam do, understanding this to be the situation? Choices are thought of at this stage as made independently, and in ignorance of the other's choice. So it seems as though Adam must play hawk. Here is the famous proof: the "dominance" argument. Adam knows that either Eve plays hawk, or she plays dove, and which she plays is independent of anything he does. Suppose she plays hawk. Then Adam is better off playing hawk: he gets his War instead of Ruin. Suppose she plays dove. Then Adam is better off playing hawk: he gets his Victory instead of Co-operation. Playing hawk therefore has greater utility than playing dove for Adam. Mathematically its greater expected utility than playing dove is the sum:

(W − R)(Prob. Eve plays hawk) + (V − C)(Prob. Eve plays dove)

where "W" represents the utility Adam attaches to the War outcome, and so on for the others. The increased utility of War over Ruin is multiplied by the probability of Eve playing hawk, and the increased utility of Victory over Co-operation is multiplied by the probability of Eve playing dove. We know this expression is positive, since otherwise we would have got the rankings wrong. Knowing it is positive, we can only interpret Adam as being in this theoretical situation if he chooses the hawk option. If he were to choose the other, then by *Revconc* and *Util* dove is outranking hawk in terms of utilities, in which case the sum total of his concerns is not as described in the diagram.

The same reasoning applies to Eve, and so she also plays hawk. If each knows that the other is truly described by the matrix, then there is no probability of either of them playing dove. Knowing this, the sum for Adam reduces to (W − R)(1 + 0), which is just (W − R).

There are empirical situations that are artificial examples of this structure, and there are social situations that are plausibly modelled by means of it.

1. Artificial games: I put Adam and Eve in separate rooms in a laboratory, and tell them to press the red button (hawkish) or green (doveish). I make sure they know that the dollar payout is as follows, where subscripts indicate who gets what.

		Adam	
		Hawk	Dove
Eve	Hawk	1e,1a	3e,0a
	Dove	0e,3a	2e,2a

Each might prefer most of all that they get the three, and the other zero. Each has as second best that they get two each and as third best that they get one each. If this is the sum total of their concerns, each plays hawk, and gets one.

2. In the original example of the structure, two prisoners were supposed kept apart from each other. To each of them the prosecutor offers the same option: they can confess the crime, or not. If A confesses, and E confesses, then each suffer the penalty for their crime. If A confesses and E does not, then A goes free, and E suffers an extended sentence (punished both for the crime, and for being a hard case). If each refuses to confess, then all that can happen is that each suffers a reduced sentence, say on the lesser charge of wasting police time.

3. There are social situations in which we do not have two persons, but in which each person is similarly situated, and can be thought of as acting in the light of what "the rest" are doing. Consider gun control. It may be best for me if I am armed and nobody else is, for I can then exert power over the others, since they are unarmed. It is worst for me if the rest are armed, and I am not, for then they can (collectively or individually) exercise power over me. If this means that I am described by the <V, C, W, R> ordering, then I will arm. If we are all like that, we all arm, even although we recognize that a world in which nobody is armed is preferable to the one we bring about in which everyone is armed.

Other social cases show essentially the same structure. Each does best of all by having more than the socially optimal number of cows on the common grazing while the others restrain themselves; each does worst if they show restraint while the others do not. The result is an overstocked and underproductive common. Each fisherman may wish that fish stocks were kept at a sustainable level. But, if he expects the others to fish for as much as they can, he cannot survive by exercising restraint himself, and if in turn the others exercise restraint, it makes it better still for him to get as much as he likes. Or, in wage bargaining, each group may do best if they get all they can while others exercise restraint; each does worst if they exercise restraint while the others get what they can; and the result is unrestrained competition which, we may realistically suppose, is economically much less good than the solution produced by general restraint.

Further situations of the same general pattern go under the heading of "collective actions." Here we consider a good which is "joint in supply," meaning that consumption by one does not diminish the amount available to others, and non-excludable, meaning that nobody can be excluded from participating in it. A good defence system is the standard example. The collective action problem is that of motivating people to contribute to such goods. Everyone has a motive for "free-riding": it goes best for them if other people contribute to providing the good, and they do not, although they then benefit from it. And even if they are loath to free-ride, they may believe that too many others will do so, so any contribution they might feel inclined to make will be wasted ("the assurance problem"). This is in fact the problem that Hume thought motivated the origins of government: in a large community it is a problem insoluble except by an external authority able to insist on contribution and attach penalties to free-riding.[16]

NOTES

1. Hansard, 10 August 1870. I owe the reference to Keith Wilson, ed., *Decisions for War 1914* (New York: St. Martin's Press, 1995), 189. Gladstone cites as like-minded authorities Lords Aberdeen and Palmerston.

2. This essay recapitulates chapter 6 of *Ruling Passions* and also elaborates some of the dialogue from my "Practical Tortoise Raising."

3. Joseph Butler, *Fifteen Sermons Preached at the Rolls Chapel*, ed. Rev. D. Matthews, Sermon XI.

4. David Gauthier, *Morals by Agreement* (Oxford: Oxford University Press, 1986), 7.

5. For other presentations see J. von Neumann and O. Morgenstern, *The Theory of Games and Economic Behavior* (Princeton, N.J.: Princeton University Press, 1944); David Gauthier, *Morals by Agreement,* chs. 1 and 2; Ken Binmore, *Game Theory and the Social Contract,* vol. i (Cambridge, Mass.: MIT Press, 1994); David M. Kreps, *Game Theory and Economic Modelling* (Oxford: Oxford University Press, 1990); Robyn M. Dawes, *Rational Choice in an Uncertain World* (Orlando, Fla.: Harcourt, Brace, 1988), 154 ff.

6. This answer was initially defended in the work of the economist P. A. Samuelson, *Foundations of Economic Analysis* (Cambridge, Mass.: Harvard University Press, 1947).

7. Amartya Sen, *Choice, Welfare and Measurement* (Cambridge, Mass.: MIT Press, 1982), esp. the essays collected in Pt. I.

8. I am indebted here to discussions with Eric Cave.

9. See, for instance, W. V. Quine, *Philosophy of Logic* (Englewood Cliffs, N.J.: Prentice-Hall 1970). 80–5.

10. John Broome, *Weighing Goods* (Oxford: Blackwell, 1991), 100–2.

11. Hume, *Treatise,* III. ii. 5, p. 519.

12. Philip Pettit and Robert Sugden, "The Backward Induction Paradox," *Journal of Philosophy* 86 (1989), 169–82. See also J. Sobel, "Backward Induction Arguments: A Paradox Regained," *Philosophy of Science* 60 (1993), 114–33; Luc Bovens, "The Backward Induction Argument etc.," *Analysis* 57 (1997), 179–86.

13. *Treatise,* III. ii. 2, p. 490.

14. *Enquiry Concerning the Principles of Morals,* App. III, p. 306.

15. The name is due to A. W. Tucker, although the structure appears to have been discovered previously by Merrill Flood and Melvin Dresher. See Russell Hardin, *Collective Action* (Baltimore, Md.: Johns Hopkins University Press, 1982), 24.

16. *Treatise,* III. ii. 7, p. 538.

THOMAS SCHELLING

Dynamic Models of Segregation

1978

People get separated along many lines and in many ways. There is segregation by sex, age, income, language, religion, color, personal taste, and the accidents of historical location. Some segregation results from the practices of organizations. Some is deliberately organized. Some results from the interplay of individual choices that discriminate. Some of it results from specialized communication systems, like languages. And some segregation is a corollary of other modes of segregation: residence is correlated with job location and transport.

If blacks exclude whites from their church, or whites exclude blacks, the segregation is organized; and it may be reciprocal or one-sided. If blacks just happen to be Baptists and whites Methodists, the two colors will be segregated Sunday morning whether they intend to be or not. If blacks join a black church because they are more comfortable among their own color, and whites a white church for the same reason, undirected individual choice can lead to segregation. And if the church bulletin board is where people advertise rooms for rent, blacks will rent rooms from blacks and whites from whites because of a communication system that is connected with churches that are correlated with color.

Some of the same mechanisms segregate college professors. The college may own some housing, from which all but college staff are excluded. Professors choose housing commensurate with their incomes, and houses are clustered by price while professors are clustered by income. Some professors prefer an academic neighborhood; any differential in professorial density will cause them to converge and increase the local density, and attract more professors. And house-hunting professors learn about available housing from colleagues and their spouses, and the houses they learn about are naturally the ones in neighborhood where professors already live.

The similarity ends there, and nobody is about to propose a commission to desegregate academics. Professors are not much missed by those they escape from in their residential choices. They are not much noticed by those they live among, and, though proportionately concentrated, are usually a minority in their neighborhood. While indeed they escape classes of people they would not care to live among, they are more conscious of where they do live than of where they don't, and the active choice is more like congregation than segregation, though the result may not be so different.

This chapter is about the kind of segregation—or separation, or sorting—that can result from discriminatory individual behavior. By "discriminatory" I mean reflecting an awareness, conscious or unconscious, of sex or age or religion or color or whatever the basis of segregation is, an awareness that influences decisions on where to live, whom to sit by, what occupation to join or to avoid, whom to play with, or whom to talk to. It examines some of the *individual* incentives and individual perceptions of difference that can lead *collectively* to segregation. It also examines the extent to which inferences can be drawn from actual collective segregation about the preferences of individuals, the strengths of those preferences, and the facilities for exercising them.

The main concern is segregation by "color" in the United States. The analysis, though, is so abstract that any twofold distinction could constitute an interpretation—whites and blacks, boys and girls, officers and enlisted men, students and faculty.

From Thomas C. Schelling, *Micromotives and Macrobehavior.* New York: Norton, 2006. By permission of W. W. Norton and Company.

The only requirement of the analysis is that the distinction be twofold, exhaustive, and recognizable. (Skin color, of course, is neither dichotomous nor even unidimensional, but by convention the distinction is nearly twofold, even in the United States census.)

At least two main processes of segregation are outside this analysis. One is organized action—legal or illegal, coercive or merely exclusionary, subtle or flagrant, open or covert, kindly or malicious, moralistic or pragmatic. The other is the process, largely but not entirely economic, by which the poor get separated from the rich, the less educated from the more educated, the unskilled from the skilled, the poorly dressed from the well dressed—in where they work and live and eat and play, in whom they know and whom they date and whom they go to school with. Evidently color is correlated with income, and income with residence; so even if residential choices were color-blind and unconstrained by organized discrimination, whites and blacks would not be randomly distributed among residences.

It is not easy to draw the lines separating "individually motivated" segregation from the more organized kind or from the economically induced kind. Habit and tradition are substitutes for organization. Fear of sanctions can coerce behavior whether or not the fear is justified, and whether the sanctions are consensual, conspiratorial, or dictated. Common expectations can lead to concerted behavior.

The economically induced separation is also intermixed with discrimination. To choose a neighborhood is to choose neighbors. To pick a neighborhood with good schools, for example, is to pick a neighborhood of *people* who want good schools. People may furthermore rely, even in making economic choices, on information that is color-discriminating; believing that darker-skinned people are on the average poorer than lighter-skinned, one may consciously or unconsciously rely on color as an index of poverty or, believing that others rely on color as an index, adopt their signals and indices accordingly.

For all these reasons, the lines dividing the individually motivated, the collectively enforced, and the economically induced segregation are not clear lines at all. They are furthermore not the only mechanisms of segregation. Separate or specialized communication systems—especially distinct languages—can have a strong segregating influence that, though interacting with the three processes mentioned, is nevertheless a different one.

INDIVIDUAL INCENTIVES AND COLLECTIVE RESULTS

Economists are familiar with systems that lead to aggregate results that the individual neither intends nor needs to be aware of, results that sometimes have no recognizable counterpart at the level of the individual. The creation of money by a commercial banking system is one; the way savings decisions cause depressions or inflations is another.

Biological evolution is responsible for a lot of sorting and separating, but the little creatures that mate and reproduce and forage for food would be amazed to know that they were bringing about separation of species, territorial sorting, or the extinction of species. Among social examples, the coexistence or extinction of second languages is a phenomenon that, though affected by decrees and school curricula, corresponds to no conscious collective choice.

Romance and marriage are exceedingly individual and private activities, at least in this country, but their genetic consequences are altogether aggregate. The law and the church may constrain us in our choices, and some traditions of segregation are enormously coercive; but, outside of royal families, there are few marriages that are part of a genetic plan. When a short boy marries a tall girl, or a blonde a brunette, it is no part of the individual's purpose to increase genetic randomness or to change some frequency distribution within the population.

Some of the phenomena of segregation may be similarly complex in relation to the dynamics of individual choice. One might even be tempted to suppose that some "unseen hand" separates people in a manner that, though foreseen and intended by no one, corresponds to some consensus or collective preference or popular will. But in economics we know a great many macro-phenomena, like depression and inflation, that do not reflect any universal desire for lower incomes or higher prices. The same applies to bank failures and market crashes. What goes on in the "hearts and minds" of small savers has little to do with whether or not they cause a depression. The hearts and minds and motives and habits of millions of people who participate in a segregated society may or may not bear close correspondence with the massive results that collectively they can generate.

A special reason for doubting any social efficiency in aggregate segregation is that the range of choice is often so meager. The demographic map of almost any American metropolitan area suggests that it is easy to find residential areas that are all white or nearly so and areas that are all black or nearly so but hard to find localities in which neither whites nor nonwhites are more than, say, three-quarters of the total. And, comparing decennial maps, it is nearly impossible to find an area that, if integrated within that range, will remain integrated long enough for a couple to get their house paid for or their children through school.

SOME QUANTITATIVE CONSTRAINTS

Counting blacks and whites in a residential block or on a baseball team will not tell how they get along. But it tells something, especially if numbers and ratios matter to the people who are moving in or out of the block or being recruited for the team. With quantitative analysis there are a few logical constraints, analogous to the balance-sheet identities in economics. (Being logical constraints, they contain no news unless one just never thought of them before.)

The simplest constraint on dichotomous mixing is that, within a given set of boundaries, not both groups can enjoy numerical superiority. For the whole population the numerical ratio is determined at any given time; but locally, in a city or a neighborhood, a church or a school or a restaurant, either blacks or whites can be a majority. But if each insists on being a local majority, there is only one mixture that will satisfy them—complete segregation.

Relaxing the condition, if whites want to be at least three-fourths and blacks at least one-third, it won't work. If whites want to be at least two-thirds and blacks no fewer than one-fifth, there is a small range of mixtures that meet the conditions. And not everybody can be in the mixtures if the overall ratio is outside the range.

In spatial arrangements, like a neighborhood or a hospital ward, everybody is next to somebody. A neighborhood may be 10 percent black or white; but if you have a neighbor on either side, the minimum nonzero percentage of opposite color is 50. If people draw their boundaries differently we can have everybody in a minority: at dinner, with men and women seated alternately, everyone is outnumbered two to one locally by the opposite sex but can join a three-fifths majority if he extends his horizon to the next person on either side.

SEPARATING MECHANISMS

The simple mathematics of ratios and mixtures tells us something about what outcomes are logically possible, but tells us little about the behavior that leads to, or that leads away from, particular outcomes. To understand what kinds of segregation or integration may result from individual choice, we have to look at the processes by which various mixtures and separations are brought about. We have to look at the incentives and the behavior that the incentives motivate, and particularly the way that different individuals comprising the society impinge on each other's choices and react to each other's presence.

There are many different incentives or criteria by which blacks and whites, or boys and girls, become separated. Whites may simply prefer to be among whites and blacks among blacks. Alternatively, whites may merely avoid or escape blacks and blacks avoid or escape whites. Whites may prefer the company of whites, while the blacks don't care. Whites may prefer to be among whites and blacks also prefer to be among whites, but if the whites can afford to live or to eat or to belong where the blacks cannot afford to follow, separation can occur.

Whites and blacks may not mind each other's presence, may even prefer integration, but may nevertheless wish to avoid minority status. Except for a mixture at exactly 50:50, no mixture will then be self-sustaining because there is none without a minority, and if the minority evacuates, complete segregation occurs. If both blacks and whites can tolerate minority status but place a limit on how small the minority is—for example, a 25 percent minority—initial mixtures ranging from 25 percent to 75 percent will survive but initial mixtures more extreme than that will lose their minority members and become all of one color. And if those who leave move to where they constitute a majority, they will increase the majority there and may cause the other color to evacuate.

Evidently if there are lower limits to the minority status that either color can tolerate, and if complete segregation obtains initially, no individual will move to an area dominated by the other color. Complete segregation is then a stable equilibrium.

SORTING AND SCRAMBLING

Minor-league players at Dodgertown—the place where Dodger-affiliated clubs train in the spring—are served cafeteria style. "A boy takes the first seat available," according to the general manager. "This has been done deliberately. If a white boy doesn't want to eat with a colored boy, he can go out and buy his own food. We haven't had any trouble."

Major-league players are not assigned seats in their dining hall; and though mixed tables are not rare, they are not the rule either. If we suppose that major- and minor-league racial attitudes are not strikingly different, we may conclude that racial preference in the dining hall is positive but less than the price of the nearest meal.

Actually, though, there is an alternative: whites and blacks in like-colored clusters can enter the line together and, once they have their trays, innocently take the next seats alongside each other. Evidently they don't. If they did, some scrambling system would have had to be invented. Maybe we conclude, then, that the racial preferences, though enough to make separate eating the general rule, are not strong enough to induce the slight trouble of picking partners before getting food. Or perhaps we conclude that players lack the strategic foresight to beat the cafeteria line as a seat-scrambling device.

But even a minor-league player knows how to think ahead a couple of outs in deciding whether a sacrifice fly will advance the ball team. It is hard to believe that if a couple of players wanted to sit together it would not occur to them to meet at the beginning of the line; and the principle extends easily to segregation by color.

We are left with some alternative hypotheses. One is that players are relieved to have an excuse to sit without regard to color, and cafeteria-line-scrambling eliminates an embarrassing choice. Another is that players can ignore, accept, or even prefer mixed tables but become uncomfortable or self-conscious, or think that others are uncomfortable or self-conscious, when the mixture is lopsided. Joining a table with blacks and whites is a casual thing, but being the seventh at a table with six players of opposite color imposes a threshold of self-consciousness that spoils the easy atmosphere and can lead to complete and sustained separation.

Hostesses are familiar with the problem. Men and women mix nicely at stand-up parties until, partly at random and partly because a few men or women get stuck in a specialized conversation, some clusters form that are nearly all male or all female; selective migration then leads to the cocktail-party equivalent of the Dodgertown major-league dining hall. Hostesses, too, have their equivalent of the cafeteria-line rule: they alternate sexes at the dinner table, grasp people by the elbows and move them around the living room, or bring in coffee and make people serve themselves to disturb the pattern.

Sometimes the problem is the other way around. It is usually good to segregate smokers from non-smokers in planes and other enclosed public places; swimmers and surfers should be segregated in the interest of safety; and an attempt is made to keep slow-moving vehicles in the right-hand lane of traffic. Many of these dichotomous groupings are asymmetrical: cigar smokers are rarely bothered by people who merely breathe; the surfer dislikes having his board hit anybody in the head but there is somebody else who dislikes it much more; and the driver of a slow truck passing a slower one on a long grade is less conscious of who is behind him than the driver behind is of the truck in front. Styles of behavior differ: surfers like to be together and cluster somewhat in the absence of regulation; water-skiers prefer dispersal and are engaged in a mobile sport, and rarely reach accommodation with swimmers on how to share the water.

These several processes of separation, segregation, sharing, mixing, dispersal—sometimes even pursuit—have a feature in common. The consequences are aggregate but the decisions are exceedingly individual. The swimmer who avoids the part of the beach where the surfers are clustered, and the surfer who congregates where the surfboards are, are reacting individually to an environment that consists mainly of other individuals who are reacting likewise. The results can be unintended, even unnoticed. Non-smokers may concentrate in the least smoky railroad car; as that car becomes crowded, smokers, choosing less crowded cars, find themselves among smokers, whether they notice it or not, and less densely crowded, whether they appreciate it or not.

The more crucial phenomena are of course residential decisions and others, like occupational choice, inter-city migration, school- and church-population, where the separating and mixing involve lasting associations that matter. The minor-league players who eat lunch at Dodgertown have no cafeteria-line mechanism to scramble their home addresses; and even if they were located at random, they would usually not be casually integrated, because mixed residential areas are few and the choice, for a black or for a white, is between living among blacks or living among whites—unless even that choice is restricted.

It is not easy to tell from the aggregate phenomenon just what the motives are behind the individual decisions, or how strong they are. The smoker on an airplane may not know that the person in front of him is sensitive to tobacco smoke; the water-skier might be willing to stay four hundred yards offshore if doing so didn't just leave a preferred strip to other skiers. The clustered men and women at that cocktail party may be bored and wish the hostess could shake things up, but without organization no one can do any good by himself. And people who are happy to work where English and French are both spoken may find it uncomfortable if their own language falls to extreme minority status; and by withdrawing they only aggravate the situation that induced them to withdraw.

People who have to choose between polarized extremes—a white neighborhood or a black, a French-speaking club or one where English alone is spoken, a school with few whites or one with few blacks—will often choose in the way that reinforces the polarization. Doing so is no evidence that they prefer segregation, only that, if segregation exists and they have to choose between exclusive association, people elect like rather than unlike environments.

The dynamics are not always transparent. There are chain reactions, exaggerated perceptions, lagged responses, speculation on the future, and organized efforts that may succeed or fail. Three people of a particular group may break leases and move out of an apartment without being noticed, but if they do it the same week somebody will notice and comment. Other residents are then alerted to whether the whites or the blacks or the elderly, or the families with children or the families without, are moving away, thereby generating the situation of minority status they thought they foresaw.

Some of the processes may be passive, systemic, unmotivated but nevertheless biased. If job vacancies are filled by word of mouth or apartments go to people who have acquaintances in the building, or if boys can marry only girls they know and can know only girls who speak their language, a biased communication system will preserve and enhance the prevailing homogeneities.

A SELF-FORMING NEIGHBORHOOD MODEL

Some vivid dynamics can be generated by any reader with a half-hour to spare, a roll of pennies and a roll of dimes, a tabletop, a large sheet of paper, a spirit of scientific inquiry, or, lacking that spirit, a fondness for games.

Get a roll of pennies, a roll of dimes, a ruled sheet of paper divided into one-inch squares, preferably at least the size of a checkerboard (sixty-four squares in eight rows and eight columns) and find some device for selecting squares at random. We place dimes and pennies on some of the squares, and suppose them to represent the members of two homogeneous groups—men and women, blacks and whites, French-speaking and English-speaking, officers and enlisted men, students and faculty, surfers and swimmers, the well dressed and the poorly dressed, or any other dichotomy that is exhaustive and recognizable. We can spread them at random or put them in contrived patterns. We can use equal numbers of dimes and pennies or let one be a minority. And we can stipulate various rules for individual decision.

For example, we can postulate that every dime wants at least half its neighbors to be dimes, every penny wants a third of its neighbors to be pennies, and any dime or penny whose immediate neighborhood does not meet these conditions gets up and moves. Then by inspection we locate the ones that are due to move, move them, keep on moving them if necessary and, when everybody on the board has settled down, look to see what pattern has emerged. (If the situation never "settles down," we look to see what kind of endless turbulence or cyclical activity our postulates have generated.)

Define each individual's neighborhood as the eight squares surrounding him; he is the center of a 3-by-3 neighborhood. He is content or discontent with his neighborhood according to the colors of the occupants of those eight surrounding squares, some of which may be empty. We furthermore suppose that, if he is discontent with the color of his own neighborhood, he moves to the nearest empty square that meets his demands.

As to the order of moves, we can begin with the discontents nearest the center of the board and let them move first, or start in the upper left and sweep downward to the right, or let the dimes move first and then the pennies; it usually turns out that the precise order is not crucial to the outcome.

Then we choose an overall ratio of pennies to dimes, the two colors being about equal or one of them being a "minority." There are two different ways we can distribute the dimes and the pennies. We can put them in some prescribed pattern that we want to test, or we can spread them at random.

Start with equal numbers of dimes and pennies and suppose that the demands of both are "moderate"—each wants something more than one-third of his neighbors to be like himself. The number of neighbors that a coin can have will be anywhere from zero to eight. We make the following specifications. If a person has one neighbor, he must be the same color; of two neighbors, one must be his color; of three, four, or five neighbors, two must be his color; and of six, seven, or eight neighbors, he wants at least three.

It is possible to form a pattern that is regularly "integrated" that satisfies everybody. An alternating pattern does it (Figure 1), on condition that we take care of the corners.

No one can move, except to a corner, because there are no other vacant cells; but no one wants to move. We now mix them up a little, and in the process empty some cells to make movement feasible.

There are 60 coins on the board. We remove 20, using a table of random digits; we then pick 5 empty squares at random and replace a dime or a penny with a 50-50 chance. The result is a board with 64 cells, 45 occupied and 19 blank. Forty individuals are just where they were before we removed 20 neighbors and added 5 new ones. The left side of Figure 2 shows one such result, generated by exactly this process. The #'s are dimes and the *O*'s are pennies; alternatively, the #'s speak French and the *O*'s speak English, the #'s are black and the *O*'s are white, the #'s are boys and the *O*'s are girls, or whatever you please.

The right side of Figure 2 identifies the individuals who are not content with their neighborhoods given the rules. Six #'s and three *O*'s want to move; the rest are content as things stand. The pattern is still "integrated"; even the discontent are not without some

```
□ # O # O # O □
# O # O # O # O
O # O # O # O #
# O # O # O # O
O # O # O # O #
# O # O # O # O
O # O # O # O #
□ O # O # O # □
```

FIGURE 1

```
– # – # O # – O      – – – # – # – –
# # # O – O # O      – – – – – – – –
– # O – – # O #      – – – – – – – –
– O # O # O # O      – – # – # – # –
O O O # O O O –      – – – – – – – –
# – # # # – – O      # – – – – – – –
– # O # O # O –      – – O – O – O –
– O – O – – # –      – – – – – – – –
```

FIGURE 2

neighbors like themselves, and few among the content are without neighbors of opposite color. The general pattern is not strongly segregated in appearance. One is hard-put to block out #-neighborhoods or *O*-neighborhoods at this stage. The problem is to satisfy a fraction, 9 of 45, among the #'s and *O*'s by letting them move somewhere among the 19 blank cells.

Anybody who moves leaves a blank cell that somebody can move into. Also, anybody who moves leaves behind a neighbor or two of his own color; and when he leaves a neighbor, his neighbor loses a neighbor and may become discontent. Anyone who moves gains neighbors like himself, adding a neighbor like them to their neighborhood but also adding one of opposite color to the unlike neighbors he acquires.

I cannot too strongly urge you to get the dimes and pennies and do it yourself. I can show you an outcome or two. A computer can do it for you a hundred times, testing variations in neighborhood demands, overall ratios, sizes of neighborhoods, and so forth. But there is nothing like tracing it through for yourself and seeing the thing work itself out. In an hour you can do it several times and experiment with different rules of behavior, sizes and shapes of boards, and (if you turn some of the coins heads and some tails) subgroups of dimes and pennies that make different demands (trucks) on the color compositions of their neighborhoods.

CHAIN REACTION

What is instructive about the experiment is the "unraveling" process. Everybody who selects a new environment affects the environments of those he leaves and those he moves among. There is a chain reaction. It may be quickly damped, with little motion, or it may go on and on and on with striking results. (The results of course are only suggestive, because few of us live in square cells on a checkerboard.)

One outcome for the situation depicted in Figure 2 is shown in Figure 3. It is "one outcome" because I have not explained exactly the order in which individuals moved. If the reader reproduces the experiment himself, he will get a slightly different configuration, but the general pattern will not be much different. Figure 4 is a replay from Figure 2, the only difference from Figure 3 being in the order of moves. It takes a few minutes to do the experiment again, and one quickly gets an impression of the kind of outcome to expect. Changing the neighborhood demands, or using twice as many dimes as pennies, will drastically affect the results; but for any given set of numbers and demands, the results are fairly stable.

All the people are content in Figures 3 and 4. And they are more segregated. This is more than just a visual impression: we can make a few comparisons. In Figure 2 the *O*'s altogether had as many *O*'s for neighbors as they had #'s; some had more or less than the average, and 3 were discontent. For the #'s the ratio of #-neighbors to *O*-neighbors was 1:1, with a little colony of #'s in the upper left corner and 6 widely distributed discontents. After sorting themselves out in Figure 3, the average ratio of like to unlike neighbors for #'s and *O*'s together was 2.3:1, more than double the original ratio. And it is about triple the ratio that any individual demanded! Figure 4 is even more extreme. The ratio of like to unlike neighbors is 2.8:1, nearly triple the starting ratio and four times the minimum demanded.

Another comparison is the number who had no opposite neighbors in Figure 2. Three were in that

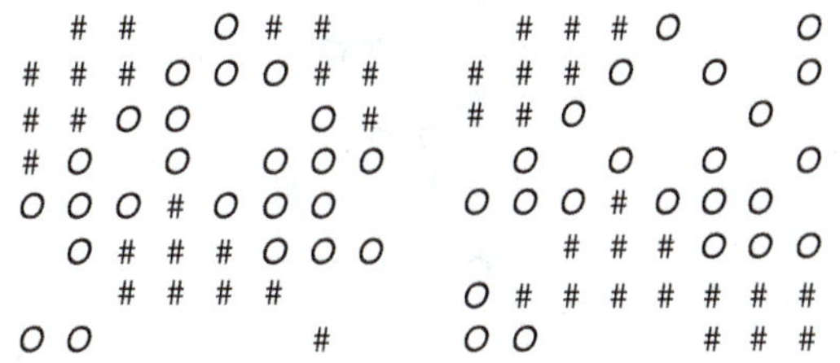

FIGURE 3 **FIGURE 4**

condition before people started moving; in Figure 3 there are 8 without neighbors of opposite color, and in Figure 4 there are 14.

What can we conclude from an exercise like this? We may at least be able to disprove a few notions that are themselves based on reasoning no more complicated than the checkerboard. Propositions beginning with "It stands to reason that . . ." can sometimes be discredited by exceedingly simple demonstrations that, though perhaps true, they do not exactly "stand to reason." We can at least persuade ourselves that certain mechanisms could work, and that observable aggregate phenomena could be compatible with types of "molecular movement" that do not closely resemble the aggregate outcomes that they determine.

There may be a few surprises. What happens if we raise the demands of one color and lower the demands of the other? Figure 5 shows typical results. Here we increased by one the number of like neighbors that a # demanded and decreased by one the number that an *O* demanded, as compared with Figures 3 and 4. By most measures, "segregation" is about the same as in Figures 3 and 4. The difference is in population densities: the *O*'s are spread out all over their territory, while the #'s are packed in tight. The reader will discover, if he actually gets those pennies and dimes and tries it for himself, that something similar would happen if the demands of the two colors were equal but one color outnumbered the other by two or three to one. The minority then tends to be noticeably more tightly packed. Perhaps from Figure 5 we could conclude that if surfers mind the presence of swimmers less than swimmers mind the presence of surfers, they will become almost completely separated, but the surfers will enjoy a greater expanse of water.

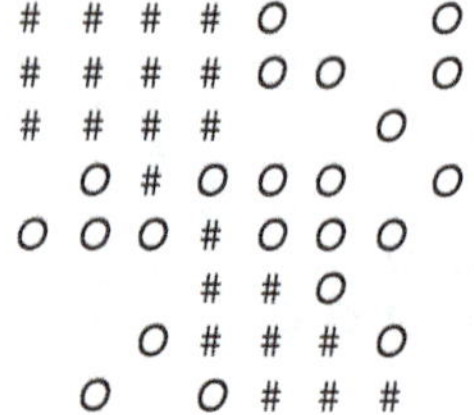

FIGURE 5

IS IT "SEGREGATED"?

The reader might try guessing what set of individual preferences led from Figure 2 to the pattern in Figure 6.

The ratio of like to unlike neighbors for all the #'s and *O*'s together is slightly more than three to one; and there are 6 *O*'s and 8 #'s that have no neighbors of opposite color. The result is evidently segregation; but, following a suggestion of my dictionary, we might say that the process is one of *aggregation,* because the rules of behavior ascribed both to #'s and to *O*'s in Figure 6 were simply that each would move to acquire three neighbors of like color irrespective of the presence or absence of neighbors of opposite color. As an individual motivation, this is quite different from the one that formed the patterns in Figures 3 and 4. But in the aggregate it may be hard to discern which motivation underlies the pattern, and the process, of segregated residence. And it matters!

The first impact of a display like this on a reader may be—unless he finds it irrelevant—discouragement. A moderate urge to avoid small-minority status may cause a nearly integrated pattern to unravel, and highly segregated neighborhoods to form. Even a deliberately arranged viable pattern, as in Figure 1, when buffeted by a little random motion, proves unstable and gives way to the separate neighborhoods of Figures 3 through 8. These then prove to be fairly immune to continued random turnover.

For those who deplore segregation, however, and especially for those who deplore more segregation than people were seeking when they collectively segregated themselves, there may be a note of hope. The underlying motivation can be far less extreme than the observable patterns of separation. What it takes to keep things

```
  # #     # #
# # #   # # #
# # O O O # O
  O O O O O O O
O O O # O O O
  O # # # O O O
  # # #   O O
  # #
```

FIGURE 6

from unraveling is to be learned from Figure 2; the later figures indicate only how hard it may be to restore such "integration" as would satisfy the individuals, once the process of separation has stabilized. In Figure 2 only 9 of the 45 individuals are motivated to move, and if we could persuade them to stay everybody else would be all right. Indeed, the reader might exercise his own ingenuity to discover how few individuals would need to be invited into Figure 2 from outside, or how few individuals would need to be relocated in Figure 2, to keep anybody from wanting to move. If two lonely #'s join a third lonely #, none of them is lonely anymore, but the first will not move to the second unless assured that the third will arrive, and without some concert or regulation, each will go join some larger cluster, perhaps abandoning some nearby lonely neighbor in the process and surely helping to outnumber the opposite color at their points of arrival.

THE BOUNDED-NEIGHBORHOOD MODEL

Turn now to a different model, and change the definition of "neighborhood." Instead of everyone's defining his neighborhood by reference to his own location, there is a common definition of the neighborhood and its boundaries. A person is either inside it or outside. Everyone is concerned about the color *ratio* within the neighborhood but not with the arrangement of colors within the neighborhood. "Residence" can therefore just as well be interpreted as membership or participation in a job, office, university, church, voting bloc, restaurant, or hospital.

In this model there is one particular area that everybody, black or white, prefers to its alternatives. He will live in it unless the percentage of residents of opposite color exceeds some limit. Each person, black or white, has his own limit. ("Tolerance," I shall occasionally call it.) If a person's limit is exceeded in this area he will go someplace else—a place, presumably, where his own color predominates or where color does not matter.

"Tolerance," it should be noticed, is a *comparative* measure. And it is specific to this location. Whites who appear, in this location, to be less tolerant of *blacks* than other whites may be merely more tolerant of the alternative *locations*.

Evidently the limiting ratios must be compatible for some blacks and some whites—as percentages they must add to at least 100—or no contented mixture of any whites and blacks is possible. Evidently, too, if nobody can tolerate extreme ratios, an area initially occupied by one color alone would remain so.

Gerry Mackie

Ending Foot Binding and Infibulation: A Convention Account

1996

Female genital mutilation in Africa persists despite modernization, public education, and legal prohibition. Female footbinding in China lasted for 1,000 years but ended in a single generation. I show that each practice is a self-enforcing convention, in Schelling's (1960) sense,

Gerry Mackie, "Ending Foot Binding and Infibulation: A Convention Account." *American Sociological Review* 61 (6) (1996): 999–1017. By permission of *American Sociological Review.*

maintained by inter-dependent expectations on the marriage market. Each practice originated under conditions of extreme resource polygyny as a means of enforcing the imperial male's exclusive sexual access to his female consorts. Extreme polygyny also caused a competitive upward flow of women and a downward flow of conjugal practices, accounting for diffusion of the practices. A Schelling coordination diagram explains how the three methods of the Chinese campaign to abolish footbinding succeeded in bringing it to a quick end. The pivotal innovation was to form associations of parents who pledged not to footbind their daughters nor let their sons marry footbound women. The "convention" hypothesis predicts that promotion of such pledge associations would help bring female genital mutilation to an end.

Female genital mutilation (clitoridectomy and infibulation; hereafter FGM), a painful and dangerous practice, is one of the major human rights and public health problems in the world today. It affects perhaps as many as 100 million women across some two dozen countries in Africa. Opposition to FGM is now part of American human rights policy (U.S. Department of State 1994:*xvi*), and the U.S. Agency for International Development is assisting the African organizations working to eradicate it (Mann 1994).

Rather than diminishing with modernization, the practice is spreading. Many observers, especially those indigenous, predict that ending infibulation will be slow—taking up to 300 years, according to one educated Sudanese (Lightfoot-Klein 1989:135). Painful and dangerous footbinding afflicted most Chinese women for a thousand years, and reform-minded Chinese women at one time "agreed that footbinding was of no use, but could only be given up by degrees" (Little 1899:152). Yet footbinding ended, for the most part, in a single generation. I will show that footbinding and infibulation are closely equivalent practices, and thus that the successful campaign to end footbinding in China has lessons for the efforts to end infibulation in Africa.

Footbinding and infibulation correspond as follows: Both customs are nearly universal where practiced; they are persistent and are practiced even by those who oppose them. Both control sexual access to females and ensure female chastity and fidelity. Both are necessary for proper marriage and family honor. Both are believed to be sanctioned by tradition. Both are said to be ethnic markers, and distinct ethnic minorities may lack the practices. Both seem to have a past of contagious diffusion. Both are exaggerated over time and both increase with status. Both are supported and transmitted by women, are performed on girls about six to eight years old, and are generally not initiation rites. Both are believed to promote health and fertility. Both are defined as aesthetically pleasing compared with the natural alternative. Both are said to properly exaggerate the complementarity of the sexes, and both are claimed to make intercourse more pleasurable for the male. Important general differences between Imperial China and Sudanic Africa are elite concubinage in China versus commonplace polygyny in Africa, exogamy versus endogamy, and agrarian and commercial versus pastoral and horticultural production.[1] Important similarities between Imperial China and Sudanic Africa are their histories of imperial female slavery and their rules of emancipation for the children of concubines.

As far as I know, Ortner (1978) was the first on record with a theory relating the complex of female purity, family honor, seclusion, chastity, and fidelity (with reference to footbinding and female genital mutilation) to a past of highly stratified empires. Extreme resource polygyny and consequent hypergynous competition in an imperial past elicited the complex of honor and modesty, which persists beyond the originating conditions.[2] Stacey (1983:40–43) applied Ortner's theory to the case of footbinding. Dickemann (1979, 1981) presented a similar theory of paternity confidence in much greater detail, but with a strongly sociobiological bent. I borrow and modify the paternity-confidence hypothesis and, with the help of simple game theory, supplement it with an explicit theory of the endurance and demise of mutilating practices. I use Schelling's (1960, 1978) account of conventions as solutions to recurrent coordination problems to explain the local universality and persistence of footbinding and infibulation, which originated as paternity-confidence mechanisms under conditions of imperial female slavery. The strongest alternative theory—ascribing female mutilation to patriarchy—does not explain the nonuniversality of the practices under universal patriarchy, maintenance beyond originating conditions, or the end of footbinding. I use a Schelling coordination diagram to show that the end of footbinding was a convention shift in direct response to the three methods of the abolition campaigns. The major alternative theory of cessation—generalized modernization—does not seem to apply to footbinding or infibulation. Therefore the methods used to end footbinding in China might well work to end FGM in Africa.

FOOTBINDING

Beginning at about age six to eight, the female child's four smaller toes were bent under the foot, the sole was forced to the heel, and then the foot was wrapped in a tight bandage day and night in order to mold a bowed and pointed four-inch-long appendage. Footbinding was extremely painful in the first 6 to 10 years of formative treatment. Complications included ulceration, paralysis, gangrene, and mortification of the lower limbs (Drucker 1981); perhaps 10 percent of girls did not survive the treatment (Fairbank 1992). The saying was: A mother can't love both her daughter and her daughter's feet at the same time (Blake 1994:682). Bound feet were malodorous, and treated women were crippled and largely housebound. The custom was defended even by women and was transmitted by them.

Footbinding appeared in the Sung Dynasty (960–1279), a time of strong urbanization, expanding bureaucracy, commercialization of agriculture, monetization, and thriving trade. The respective imperial capitals at the opposite ends of the Grand Canal were the largest and richest cities in the world (Fairbank and Reischauer 1978:116–51). The status of women declined in the Sung: Concubinage expanded, upper-class dowries increased, and a neo-Confucian ideology including tenets of female chastity, seclusion, and subordination, emerged and came to reign (Ebrey 1991). The first unequivocal record of footbinding is praise by an eleventh-century poet of a dancer in "the palace style." A late fourteenth-century document quotes an early twelfth-century discussion of the recent origin of footbinding. Citing a source otherwise unknown to China scholars, the same discussion also states that footbinding was invented by a favorite dancer in the palace of Southern T'ang emperor and love poet Li Yu (937–978) and then spread by imitation until people were ashamed not to practice it. Casual references become more common from the late twelfth century on (Ebrey 1990; Levy 1966).

The practice effloresced along three dimensions over several centuries. First, it spread from the imperial palace, to court circles, to the larger upper classes, and then to the middle and lower classes; eventually the higher the social status, the smaller the foot. Second, it became more exaggerated over time; a practice supposedly originating among dancers eventually made dance a forgotten art. Third, it radiated from the imperial capitals to the rest of the empire. Footbinding was clearly the normal practice by the Ming Dynasty (1368–1644). As measured in 1835, it prevailed in the whole empire among the Chinese, affecting 50 to 80 percent of women depending on the locale, the disgraceful exceptions only among the lowest classes, wherever woman's work was needed in the field or workshop (Levy 1966:23–106). The missionary Justus Doolittle (1865:201) reported that bound feet were a sign of "gentility," that "many poor families prefer to struggle along for a precarious living, bringing up their daughters with small feet . . . in order to attain a more competent support," and that some Chinese opposed footbinding as useless but felt obliged to conform for the sake of proper marriage.

The Manchu conquerors opposed footbinding, but their efforts to abolish it in 1665 failed entirely, despite intimidating penalties. An 1847 Manchu edict against footbinding also failed. Throughout the nineteenth century the practice was condemned by influential liberal literati, but with no apparent effect (Levy 1966:68–74). Some of the Protestant missionaries, particularly the women, denounced the custom.

The first antifootbinding society was founded in 1874 by local missionaries for their converts. Inspired by the American prohibitionist pledge to abstain from alcohol, the society introduced the effective technique of pledging members not to bind daughters nor let sons marry bound women. Western women organized the national Natural Foot Society, aimed at the non-Christian elite, in Shanghai in 1895. An indigenous Anti-Footbinding Society established headquarters in Shanghai in 1897 and eventually acquired 300,000 members. The societies propagandized the disadvantages of footbinding in Chinese cultural terms, promoted pledge associations, and subtly conveyed international disapproval of the custom. By 1908, leading Chinese public opinion was opposed to footbinding, and the leadership of the Natural Foot Society was transferred to a committee of Chinese women. The Nationalist Revolution banned footbinding in 1912, and the decree succeeded in many locales (Drucker 1981).

Footbinding started to end in China between the Boxer Rebellion of 1900 and the Revolution of 1911, certainly among the upper strata of the larger cities. Although there was local variability in onset of cessation, available evidence is that whenever binding did end, it ended rapidly. As measured by a sociologist's data, for example, the population of Tinghsien, a conservative rural area 125 miles south of Peking, went from 99 percent bound in 1889 to 94 percent bound in 1899 to zero bound in 1919 (Gamble 1943).

The Chinese offered various explanations for footbinding. It was said to distinguish the Chinese from the invading Mongols and other barbarians and to enhance the difference between men and women. It was believed to promote good health and fertility (Blake 1994:686). For Chinese men, bound feet were universally associated with higher-status love and sex, and so carried strong connotations of both modesty and lasciviousness. Bound feet became a sexual fetish; they were said to be conducive to better intercourse, but this claim was medically false (Van Gulik 1961:219). The leading neo-Confucian philosopher Chu Hsi imposed footbinding on a southern province in the twelfth century so as to enforce female chastity (an apocryphal tale, according to Ebrey 1990). The historical record contains several explicit statements over the centuries that the purpose of footbinding was to hobble women and thereby promote their seclusion and fidelity. Finally, the record is abundantly clear that the immediate explanation always given for footbinding in its heyday was to secure a proper marriage (Levy 1966).

Levy (1966) believes that footbinding originated in aesthetic appreciation of the small foot and was maintained by male erotic interest. Veblen (1934) regards it as an ostentatious display of the practicing family's wealth. Freud (1961) concludes that footbinding appeased male castration anxieties. Ebrey (1990) proposes that the practice arose in the Sung as a way of ethnically differentiating civilized Chinese from invading northern barbarians and of maintaining gender distinctions as refined Chinese males became more effeminate. Blake's "mindful-body" theory interprets footbinding as a voluntary ordeal by which mothers taught their daughters to succeed in the male-controlled neo-Confucian world, related to the intensification of agricultural labor in the period of duration (all cited in Blake 1994). Gates (1989) points to the commodification of agriculture and textile production in the Sung. Some missionaries blame flawed national character (Greenhalgh 1977). Fairbank and Feuerwerker (1986:29) attribute footbinding's generality and maintenance to homogeneous culture and peasant subservience to elite norms.

Daly (1978:130–33) links footbinding, genital mutilation, and other misogynistic practices in a patriarchal sado-ritual syndrome that is obsessed with purity, is sanctioned by tradition, and has "an inherent tendency to 'catch on' and spread, since [the rituals] appeal to imaginations conditioned by the omnipresent ideology of male domination," uses women as scapegoats and token torturers, ritualizes and "normativizes" atrocities, and is legitimated by male scholars despite appearances of disapproval. Greenhalgh (1977) ties the custom to the patriarchal Chinese family, arguing that footbinding consolidates and perpetuates the kinship system. She takes note of upward marriage, of downwardly migrating custom, of footbinding as the "essential criterion for any girl's marriageability," of the self-perpetuating character of the practice, and of the shock delivered by Western imperialism. Greenhalgh also offers an explicit theory of footbinding's end: Expanding employment and education opportunities, improving transportation, and capitalist individualism were attracting women away from the weakened patriarchal family and to the labor market.

INFIBULATION

FGM occurs in Egypt and in what was formerly called the Sudanic Belt in Africa (the savanna lands between the desert to the north and the jungle to the south, or between the Tropic of Cancer to the north and the Equator to the south); from the Atlantic Coast of western Africa to Egypt in the northeast and Kenya in the southeast. Infibulation, the harshest practice, occurs contiguously in Egyptian Nubia, the Sudan, Eritrea, Djibouti, and Somalia, also known as Islamic Northeast Africa.

The following classification of female genital operations is paraphrased from Kouba and Muasher (1985:96):

1. Mild *sunna:* The pricking of the prepuce of the clitoris with a sharp instrument such as a pin, which leaves little or no damage. (*Sunna* means "tradition" in Arabic.)
2. Clitoridectomy/excision: The removal of part or all of the clitoris as well as part or all of the labia minora. The resulting scar tissue may be so extensive as to cover the vaginal opening.
3. Infibulation/Pharaonic circumcision: Clitoridectomy and the excision of the labia minora as well as the inner walls of the labia majora. The raw edges of the vulva are then sewn together with catgut or held against each other with thorns. The raw edges of the labia majora are sutured together or approximated so that the opposite sides will heal together and form a wall over the vaginal opening. A small sliver of wood is inserted into the vagina to stop coalescence of the labia majora in front of the vaginal orifice and to allow for the passage of urine and menstrual flow.

For the sake of brevity, I concentrate on infibulation.

The operation takes place from a few days after birth to before the birth of the first child (depending on local custom), but mostly seems to be performed on girls around age eight, safely before puberty. It is usually done among women, in private, with little ceremony; only rarely does it have the trappings of an initiation rite. The girl is held down amid singing and shouting, which drown out her screams. Except recently among the affluent, the operation is inflicted without painkiller or antiseptic precaution. Then the girl lies with her legs tied together for several weeks. Urination and (later) menstruation are difficult because of the pencil-point opening left by the operation. After marriage, penetration takes two weeks to two years to accomplish, or is facilitated by knife; it is traumatically painful for the female, and some men feel guilt and revulsion at the cruelty involved. Childbirth requires introcision and resewing of the genital area. Virtually every ethnography and report states that FGM is defended and transmitted by the women. The mothers who have this done to their daughters love their children and want the best for them (Assaad 1980).

Health consequences are severe. Immediate: Pain, hemorrhage, shock, acute urinary retention, urinary infection, blood poisoning (septicemia), fever, tetanus, and death. Intermediate: Delay in wound healing, pelvic infection, dysmenorrhea, cysts and abscesses, keloid scar, and painful intercourse. Late: Haematocolpos (vaginal closure and accumulation of menstrual fluid), infertility and miscarriage, recurrent urinary tract infection, difficulty in urinating, calculus and stone formation, hypersensitivity, and anal incontinence and fissure. Intercourse: Difficulty in penetration, painful intercourse, and use of misplaced deinfibulation wound as false vagina. Delivery: Prolonged and obstructed labor, hemorrhage leading to shock and death, perineal laceration, uterine inertia, and stillborn or brain-damaged infants. Postnatal: Urinary and rectal fistula causing odor and miscarriages, and prolapse of uterus and adjacent organs. Sexual problems: Lack of orgasm, anxiety, depression, and frustration (summarized from headings in Koso-Thomas 1987:25–28).

The origins of FGM are obscure. Widstrand (1964:116) traces several classical references to the second century B.C.E. geographer Agatharchides of Cnidus, who, reporting on tribes residing on the western coast of the Red Sea, wrote that one group excised their women in the manner of the Egyptians, and that another group "cut off in infancy with razors the whole portion that others circumcise" (Agatharchides 1989:111–12).[3] The geographic distribution of FGM suggests that it originated on the western coast of the Red Sea, where infibulation is most intense, diminishing to clitoridectomy in westward and southward radiation. Whatever the earliest origins of FGM, there is certainly an association between infibulation and slavery. The Egyptians raided and traded the Black south for slaves from dynastic to Byzantine times, and Sudanic slaves were exported through the Red Sea to the Persian Gulf before the rise of Islam (Beachey 1976: 2–4). The Islamic slave trade delivered many Sudanic concubines and maids to Egypt and Arabia.

In 1609 Dos Santos reported that inland from Mogadishu (Somalia) a group has "a custome to sew up their Females, specially their slaves being young to make them unable for conception, which makes these Slaves sell dearer, both for their chastitie, and for better confidence which their Masters put in them" (Fr. Joao dos Santos, *Ethiopia Oriental,* in Freeman-Grenville 1962). Browne, reporting in 1799 on his African travels, wrote that the Egyptians practice female excision, and that infibulation to prevent pregnancy is general among female slaves, who come from the Black south. Other early travelers to Egypt—Larrey in 1803 and Burckhardt in 1819—confirm Browne and claim that slave traders infibulated young female captives (Widstrand 1964:102).[4] Curiously, infibulation is called "Sudanese circumcision" by the Egyptians, but "Pharaonic circumcision" (i.e., Egyptian) by the Sudanese (Kouba and Muasher 1985).

Infibulation is not only nearly universal and persistent where practiced, but is expanding its territory. It is spreading from Arabized northern Sudan further into indigenously populated areas of southern and western Sudan; as Arabized traders enter or as indigenes urbanize, the less advantaged adopt infibulation to make their daughters more marriageable to the high-status outsiders. For example, infibulation was unknown in Nyala in west Sudan 50 years ago, but it now saturates the area and is universal in Nyertete merely 20 years after introduction. Where practiced in the Sudan, FGM affects 99 percent of women; 83 percent are infibulated. Moreover, infibulation has been further exaggerated in the Sudan, beginning among educated urban dwellers and spreading to the uneducated in the villages, with the new practice of reinfibulation to pinhole size after each birth; this is quite damaging to the woman's physical integrity over time (reinfibulation is reported among 2 percent of women over age 64 and among 54 percent ages 25 to 34; among 70 percent of urban women and 28 percent of rural women) (Dareer 1982:57; Lightfoot-Klein 1989:48–49, 31, 98–99).

In Somalia, 99 percent of women are mutilated (76 percent of those are infibulated), and the infibulation rate nears 95 percent among the noble northern clans (Grassivaro-Gallo and Abdisamed 1985). Infibulation was not reported among the southern Sab at the beginning of the century, but has commenced among them. Reportedly they want to gain higher social status by emulating the noble northerners (Grassivaro-Gallo and Viviani 1992). Grassivaro-Gallo and Abdisamed (1985) conducted a large but nonrandom survey of women in the capital. According to their analysis of a subsample (parental origin and place of operation in the same region), infibulation is attenuating to clitoridectomy. However, disaggregating these data into high-infibulation regional origin and low-infibulation regional origin shows that the apparent attenuation is due simply to the inclusion of the southern Sab in the sample. Other than among respondents originating from the capital or the atypical south, the infibulation rate of subject women was 95 percent, the same as for their mothers.[5]

The most common explanation given by participants is that infibulation is required for marriage and honor. Infibulation prepares for marriage, is a prerequisite for marriage, makes for better marriage prospects, makes possible the security available through marriage, and so on. It fosters virginity, first, because the physical barrier prevents rape, and second, because the physical barrier and the attenuation of sexual desire protect the supposedly oversexed and promiscuous woman from temptation. It is proof of virginity and secures fidelity by reduction of female desire and by reinfibulation upon the prolonged absence of the husband. Infibulation is closely associated with the modesty code.

One common explanation, sometimes neglected due to the inquisitive bias of intellectuals, is simply that "such is the custom or tradition here." A variation on the custom explanation is that "this is a practice that distinguishes us from neighboring groups." A related explanation of FGM that is conventional among some European-educated Africanists is that the practice functions to promote the solidarity of the group. That explanation originated with Kenyatta, the functionalist Malinowski's pupil, who used British attempts to prohibit clitoridectomy among his Kikuyu as a theme of ethnic unification and nationalist agitation. Religious command is another common explanation: For many of the practitioners, tradition and religion mean one and the same thing (Boddy 1991).

FGM is found only in or adjacent to Islamic groups (some neighboring Christians practice it to avoid damnation). This is curious because FGM, beyond the mild *sunna* supposedly akin to male circumcision, is not found in most Islamic countries nor is it required by Islam. Mutilation is not practiced in Mecca or Medina, and Saudis reportedly find the custom pagan. The Koran is silent on FGM, but several *hadith* (sayings attributed to Mohammed) recommend attenuating the practice for the woman's sake, praise it as noble but not commanded, or advise that female converts refrain from mutilation because even if pleasing to the husband it is painful to the wife. In Egypt, the Christian Copts follow the same practice of clitoridectomy as their Islamic neighbors; in the Sudan the tiny Coptic minority follows the same practice of infibulation as their Islamic neighbors (Cloudsley 1983). Catholic missionaries among the Egyptian Copts in the seventeenth century initially forbade clitoral excision as an allegedly Jewish practice, but male converts to Catholicism refused to marry intact women and so would return to the Coptic Church. Then a special investigation by the Vatican decreed that the oversized clitoris alleged among Egyptian women justified excision as conducive to marriage (Meinardus 1967).

The remaining explanations seem to be post hoc. Infibulation is sometimes justified as clean and aesthetic. It is said to prevent malodorous discharge; however, the prolongation of urination and menstruation and other complications make that a false belief. The judgment that natural genitals are ugly is like the old Chinese judgment that natural feet are ugly. Infibulation is also said to promote health and fertility, and to make child-bearing easier; obviously these are false beliefs. Infibulation is said to enhance male intercourse, but reports from Nubia and the Sudan indicate that men aware of the difference prefer intact or excised women to infibulated women (Boddy 1982; Lightfoot-Klein 1989:97). The story of enlarged genitals accepted by Catholic worthies with respect to the Egyptians, and by Arabs with respect to excising Africans, is medically false.

Freud (as related by Bonaparte 1953:191–92) hypothesized that FGM assists the transition from clitoral orgasm to vaginal orgasm, in other words, that FGM is a realization of his theoretical clitoridectomy. The most ambitious study to date, comparative-ethnographic in approach, agrees with the indigenous interpretation that infibulation is related to guaranteeing virginity and chastity, and with academic interpretations relating infibulation to "the requirement of virginity and chastity in societies where the honor of the family is contingent on the honor of its women; a precaution against rape . . . ; a necessary preliminary to adult status and marriage" (Hicks 1993:181).

Infibulation seems to have attenuated to clitoridectomy in Egyptian Nubia (Kennedy 1970). Kennedy explains this change with a modernization hypothesis. As Nubians lost their land to the flooding of the Aswan dam, took up wage labor, and came into contact with urban values, along with increased education and communication, then dependence on the patrilineage decreased, the nuclear family thrived, modern egalitarian ideas were adopted, and so on. Hayes (1975:630–31) finds that the manifest function of infibulation "is to regulate female sexuality in order to safeguard virginity, thus protecting the honor of a woman's and her husband's patrilineages." Latent functions include contributing to the village economy, maintaining the status and role of midwives, and limiting population. Building on Kennedy, Hayes predicts that industrialization and urbanization weaken the corporate nature of the lineage and that FGM then becomes less severe.

Some explanations fail the comparative test. Boddy (1982) relates Sudanese infibulation to a complex of symbols for pure, clean, and smooth (she is correct, I believe, that infibulation emphasizes female fertility by de-emphasizing female sexuality). Grassivaro-Gallo and Viviani (1992) claim that Somali infibulation is an evolutionary adaptation to make female shepherds and goatherds odorless and safe from prey. The symbolic associations of Boddy's riverine agriculturists, however, do not explain infibulation on the pastoral plains of Somalia; nor does Grassivaro-Gallo's hypothesis apply to infibulation along the Sudanese Nile. Neither theory accounts for the maintenance of infibulation among urban dwellers and educated elites.

THE CONVENTION HYPOTHESIS

Conventions

This is an account of conventions as solutions to coordination problems, as developed by Schelling (1960) and Lewis (1969). (This game-theoretic account of coordination problems assumes strategic rationality: "Rationality" means choosing what one wants more over what one wants less, whether self-regarding or other-regarding, given beliefs and constraints; a "strategic" situation is one characterized by the interdependence of decisions; see Elster 1986.) Schelling said that the coordination game lies behind the stability of institutions and traditions, yet can also explain rapid change. How can the same mechanism explain both stability and change? Look at the sample coordination game in Figure 1B. (Generally for the games in Figure 1, there are two players; each player has two strategies; the lower left payoff in any box is that of player Row-Chooser, and the upper right payoff in any box is that of player Column-Chooser. Assume that the players can't talk to each other and that they play pure strategies, not a probabilistic mixture of strategies.) In Figure 1B, Row-Chooser chooses Row 1 (R1) and Column-Chooser chooses Column 1 (C1), then they coordinate on R1C1 and carry home a payoff of 2 each; the same is true if they coordinate on R2C2. If coordination fails—say they choose R1C2, or R2C1—then each gets nothing. The usual illustration of this is whether to drive on the left side of the road or the right. It doesn't matter which side I drive on, so long as everyone else does the same.

Consider now the game in Figure 1A. Here, only R1C1 is an equilibrium choice. Figure 1A does not represent a coordination problem; for that, there must be at least two proper coordination equilibria, according to Lewis (1969). Figure 1B does represent a coordination problem. So does Figure 1C. In Figure 1C, R1C1 is better for each player than R2C2, and R2C2 is better for each player than the miscoordination at R1C2 or R2C1. If people are stuck at inferior equilibrium R2C2, they may lack a concerted way to move to superior equilibrium R1C1. In this paper, I concentrate on that type of problem. Figure 1D also represents a coordination problem, but now with a bargaining aspect. Here, Column-Chooser does best at R1C1, while Row-Chooser does best at R2C2, and each likes either of these coordination equilibria better than miscoordination at R1C2 or R2C1. This game has all the ingredients of power and tragedy (Knight 1992 is the definitive treatment). *Any* game with two or more proper coordination equilibria represents a coordination problem.

Singling out a coordination equilibrium is a matter of concordant mutual expectations. If there are two of us and we can talk, then we can each promise to choose either right or left, and the promise is self-enforcing. If there are hundreds of us, however, express agreement is difficult. Many conventions suggesting a single choice of equilibrium in a coordination problem are not expressly agreed to; rather, they are tacit. Schelling (1960) urges that there is no logical solution to the tacit coordination problem; rather, solutions are suggested by their psychological salience. The salient choice is not uniquely *good,* just noticeably *unique*. It all depends on what the players believe about each other. In novel play of Game 1C, absent credible communication, superior R1C1 stands out as the salient choice for most people. But in a recurring game, precedent is strongly salient.

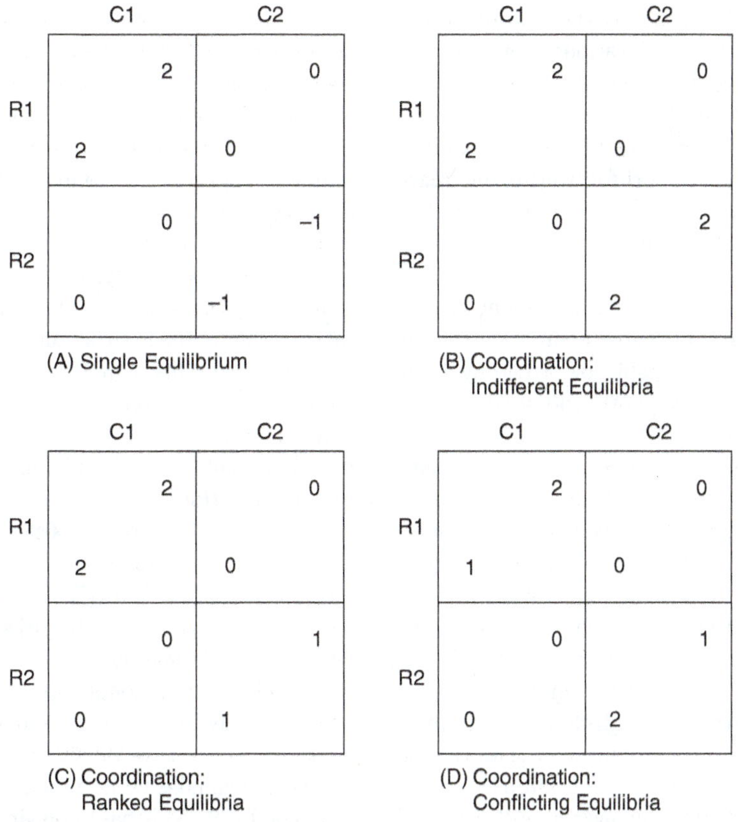

FIGURE 1 Game Matrices

If we played the same Game 1C yesterday at R1C1, then R1C1 is the salient choice today. If the choice made yesterday was the inferior R2C2, R2C2 is weakly salient today; and if R2C2 was the choice in our last 10 games, it is strongly salient in our next. Coordination by precedent is convention.

At 5:00 A.M., Sunday, September 22, 1967, Sweden switched from driving on the left side of the road to driving on the right (Hardin 1988; Ullman-Margalit 1977). Sweden, or at least its authorities, saw driving on the left as more like the game in 1C than the game in 1B. The rest of continental Europe drove on the right, so as international traffic increased, visitors to Sweden caused accidents by driving in the wrong lane as did nonchalant Swedes abroad. Thus Swedes would be better off driving on the right, moving from R2C2 to R1C1 in something like Game 1C. Even if the millions of Swedes were each convinced that driving on the right would be better, they could never spontaneously, by some invisible hand, get to the better coordination equilibrium. Convention is self-enforcing: Any one person driving to the right to demonstrate its advantages would end up dead. For example, in left-driving Pakistan a local religious party decreed that the pious must drive on the right. The decree was rescinded in two weeks after a number of serious accidents (Bedi 1994).

Paternity Confidence

How do the practices of footbinding and infibulation fit the convention model just described? For the explanation to succeed, one assumption must be true:

that humans strongly desire to successfully raise their biological children.[6] The various forms of marriage and family serve this end. Females are certain of maternity, but males are not certain of paternity. In the standard premodern case, the female requires assurances of resource support for bearing and rearing children, and the male requires assurances that the children are his offspring. Because of the desire for children, each party prefers marriage to nonmarriage. Marriage is a deeply interdependent choice and is a coordination equilibrium. Families advertise their male offspring as capable of providing both generous and sustained support, and their female offspring as both fertile and faithful.[7]

Under conditions of resource equality, humans compete in conveying the many signs of trustworthiness to possible marriage partners. Under conditions of resource inequality, conventions of wealth and honor emerge as signs of higher rank. When the inequality of resource control reaches a certain extreme, polygyny and hypergyny appear because a female is then more likely to raise children successfully as the second wife of a high-ranking man than as the first wife of a low-ranking man. The richest families will also then prefer male children to female children because each polygynous son will generate more grandchildren than the equivalent daughter. The higher the male's rank, the greater the resource support he offers, the greater number of consorts he attracts, the greater his costs of fidelity control, and thus the greater the competition among female families to guarantee paternity confidence. Therefore, families will advertise the honor of their lines, the purity of their females, and their members' commitment to the values of chastity and fidelity, the so-called modesty code.

A highly polygynous apex induces an upward flow of women (hypergyny) and a downward flow of conjugal practices. If humans want to have their own children, then an emperor will take costly measures to ensure that the several thousand women he supports are sexually reserved for him, while the interests of his wives and concubines will be to seek clandestine insemination from men more available than he. It is then in the emperor's interest to inflict costly methods of fidelity control. The next lower stratum, competing to provide wives and concubines to the apex, will imitate and exaggerate the fidelity-control practice so as to gain economic, social, and reproductive access to the palace. The vacuum of women in the first lower stratum will be filled by women moving up from the second lower stratum, who in turn will adopt the fidelity-control convention, and so on, all the way down.

Local conventions of modesty emerge; footbinding in one place, infibulation in another. Under extreme polygyny and hypergyny, the conventions are most intense at the highest rank but domino down to the lowest rank that can afford the practice. Female modesty in these circumstances is a positional good (valued not for attaining a standard, but for its rank; not "excellent," but "best") and thus is driven to maximum affordable values on the conventions: "One wrong word about his sister and he'll kill you"; "The errant daughter shall die"; "The smaller the foot, the better the family"; "The smaller the infibulation opening, the better the girl's reputation." Naive observation of runaway modesty practices gives rise to the folk belief, in honor cultures, that women must be excessively lustful to necessitate such scrupulous guarding—the "two-Marys" or "madonna-whore" complex. The false belief in enlarged genitals as the rationale for FGM is based on similar reasoning.

Mutilation is a conventional prerequisite of marriage, *originating* as a sign of paternity confidence in a game of coordination with conflict like that shown in Figure 1D. Mutilation is a superior equilibrium for the originating male emperor in terms of maximizing the number of his own children; it is an inferior equilibrium for the females under his control. A convention signifying paternity confidence was imposed at the social apex, and then hypertrophied and diffused in positional competition. Mutilation is *maintained* as the inferior equilibrium in a game of coordination with ranked equilibria like the one in Figure 1C. It is an inferior convention for the ordinary male and for his one female mate: The monogamous male has trivial fidelity-assurance costs, and both male and female could better afford children if the female's fertility, productivity, and longevity were not damaged by mutilation. For the purposes of reform it is important to realize that the ordinary male, when fully informed, may be motivated to support convention shift.

Men and women prefer marriage to nonmarriage. Both men and women would be better off marrying without the mutilating practice (R1C1), but they are trapped by the inferior convention (R2C2). However the custom originated, as soon as women believed that men would not marry an unmutilated woman, and men believed that an unmutilated woman would not be a faithful partner in marriage, and so forth, expectations were mutually concordant and a self-enforcing convention was locked in. A woman would not choose nonmarriage and not to have her own children; a man would not choose an unfaithful partner and not to have his own children.

Imperial Female Slavery

FGM is pre-Islamic but was exaggerated by its intersection with the Islamic modesty code of family honor, female purity, virginity, chastity, fidelity, and seclusion. I propose that imperial polygyny in Arabia and Egypt, and indirectly in Istanbul, induced an eastward flow of female slaves through the mainly polygynous Sudanic Belt into infibulating slave centers in Sudan and a westward flow of Islamization and FGM. Arabized pastoralists raided northeastern Africa for slaves, and, because Islam forbade the enslavement of Moslems, ventured further as closer sources converted. The Sudanic slaves were shipped down Nile Valley routes or through the Red Sea to Egyptian or Arabian markets. The distribution of infibulation in Sudan in the nineteenth century, by far the peak period of slaving (almost one-half million were exported by way of the Red Sea [Clarence-Smith 1989:5]), follows the caravan routes (Hicks 1993:21–23). Slave raiding and slave concubinage continue in today's Sudan (U.S. Department of State 1994:285). The further radiation of clitoridectomy follows the channel of raiding and trading west to the Atlantic and southeast to Kenya. A practice associated with shameful female slavery came to stand for honor. Since defenders of infibulation regard the uninfibulated as no better than contemptible slaves, demonstrating its origin in the slave trade might contribute to its eradication.

Hereditary stratification decreased in "egalitarian" Sung China (Ebrey 1991), but wealth stratification increased with strong urbanization (Ma 1971:144). Commercialization probably decreased the relative price of female labor in agriculture, outdoor work, and increased its price in indoor work, such as commodity textile production, household services, and male entertainment. In the China of female infanticide, poor and middle-range families in the southern Sung capital preferred female children because of their bright prospects as concubines and maids for rich families (Ma 1971:143). Perhaps footbinding arose as a slave traders' restraint on girl children; its obvious purpose was to keep them from running away. Then, nubile courtesans adapted dance performance to the restraint. The eleventh-century poet wrote, "Anointed with fragrance, she takes lotus steps;/ Though often sad, she steps with swift lightness" (Levy 1966:47). Why is she sad? Because, she remembers her impoverished freedom in her prosperous imprisonment? The imperial capitals contained not only the thousands of concubines, dancers, and servants of the emperor, but also an upper class serviced by additional legions of concubines, courtesans, and housemaids as well as government-owned brothels for low-ranking officers and soldiers (Van Gulik 1961:212–35). The many women of the emperor and of other officials no doubt needed guarding against escape, trysts, rape, and bastardy. Initial adoption of footbinding by the imperial seraglio may have had a secondary aesthetic aspect, but the fidelity-control aspect must have been primary. Notice as well that footbinding made it harder for barbarian raiders to steal the palace women because they would have had to be carried rather than driven.

Belief Traps

The women who practice infibulation are caught in a belief trap. The Bambara of Mali believe that the clitoris will kill a man if it comes in contact with the penis during intercourse. In Nigeria, some groups believe that a baby will die if its head touches the clitoris during delivery (Lightfoot-Klein 1989:38–9). I call these self-enforcing beliefs: a belief that cannot be revised because the believed costs of testing the belief are too high. Koso-Thomas (1987) interviewed

50 women in Sierra Leone who had known sexual experience before clitoridectomy. All reported decreased sexual satisfaction after the operation, but they were unaware of the causal relationship until informed by the interviewer. Ironically, some of these women had become promiscuous in their search for lost satisfaction. Lightfoot-Klein's (1989:22, 59) initial interviews with Sudanese women elicited the response, for example, that urination was "normal." She then switched to more descriptive questions such as "How long does it take you to urinate?" The answer then was "Normal—about 15 minutes."

The painful surgery, prolonged urination and menstruation, traumatic penetration, and unbearable childbirth accompanying infibulation are all accepted as normal. Because it is inflicted on all girls before puberty they have no basis of comparison; the connection between cause and effect is remote; and the cost of testing pertinent beliefs is prohibitive to any one individual. Once in place, conventions regulating access to reproduction are deeply entrenched, in part because dissenters fail to have descendants. Adult-to-child transmission augments persistence. One consequence of a culturally insulated group's becoming stuck in an inferior convention is that as the period of origination passes, knowledge of the superior coordination equilibrium disappears, as if the northwest quadrant of the matrix in Figure 1C were to fade away. Exposure to an alternative convention is a necessary but not sufficient condition for convention shift. Such exposure may have contributed to the abandonment of Chinese footbinding.

Evaluation

By making three assumptions—that people are strategically rational, that people desire to successfully raise their own children, and in each case that there was an originating condition of imperial female slavery—I have been able to show why female mutilation is a self-enforcing convention, nearly universal where practiced, persistent, and practiced even by those who oppose it; why it is necessary for a proper marriage; and why it is such an obviously compelling tradition to practitioners. That the convention is universal within overlapping marriage markets explains why distinct ethnic minorities may not conform and why practitioners later come to regard it as an ethnic marker. The fact that overlapping marriage markets are initially hypergynous, and the consequent positional competition, explain contagious diffusion, exaggeration over time, and status grading. The men who perpetrate female enslavements and mutilations are not absolved under this hypothesis; but, as Ortner (1978:32) discerns, the resulting hypergynous competition explains why women as well as men actively perpetuate the honor and modesty code, and resolves a major puzzle. Moreover, the convention hypothesis explains how incentives to conform linger after originating conditions have faded. The belief that mutilation is excellent for health and fertility is self-enforcing, a trap. Similarly, the tales of aesthetic appreciation, sexual pleasure, and gender complementarity are associationist folk explanations.

Freudian theory offers two disparate mechanisms that explain nothing about the details or correspondences of infibulation and foot-binding. The missionaries' flawed-national-character explanation (still alive in some of the denunciations of FGM) neglects references to honor and modesty, practice by opposing families, and especially the end of footbinding. Otherwise, alternative theories are not so much conflicting as incomplete. The aesthetic interest, erotic interest, and ostentation theories each explain only a few of the observations, and especially fail at accounting for local universality, persistence, and practice by opposing families. The ethnic differentiation theory is consistent with the observations except for references to controlling sexual access to females, practice by opposing families, and the end of footbinding. Fairbank and Feuerwerker's (1986) appeal to cultural homogeneity and compliance with elite norms explains contagion, local universality, and stubborn persistence as well as references to tradition, ethnicity and status; but the convention hypothesis explains their homogeneity and norm compliance, and explains sudden change.

Blake (1994) carefully recounts the observed facts on footbinding, and his complicated theory that (among other things) it functioned to obscure the labor power of women accounts for the major observations. Blake detects a puzzling conflict between the strict Confucian norm against mutilation of the body and the widespread norm of mutilating women's feet. Those norms are consistent under the convention account, however, because each was justified in terms of promoting fertility. He surveys the relation between the duration of the patrilineal family and hobbling, on the one hand, and the changing demand for female labor, on the other, but characterizes that relation equivocally. With one exception, the convention hypothesis is the only theory that shows how mutilation could be practiced by those who oppose it and that explains and predicts change. The exception is the theory that the patrilineage rises and falls with economic conditions. The patrilineage theory, however, does not explain the absence of mutilation under similar economic and family conditions elsewhere. Functionalism explains everything but change, which may be why this theory is found linked with the patrilineage theory; functional stability disrupted by modernization covers the observations but is vague on origins and on variations.

Daly's (1978) inductively constructed patriarchal sado-ritual syndrome accounts for most observations, but not for variations in the presence and type of mutilation under a universal patriarchy. The sudden end of footbinding before the end of male domination she assigns to the similarly malicious category of patriarchal "reversal." Dickemann's (1981) paternity confidence theory is comprehensive but does not, as does the convention hypothesis, explain endurance beyond originating conditions or the rapid demise of such practices. The strength of the convention hypothesis is in explaining the end of footbinding, thereby disclosing tactics for the eradication of FGM.

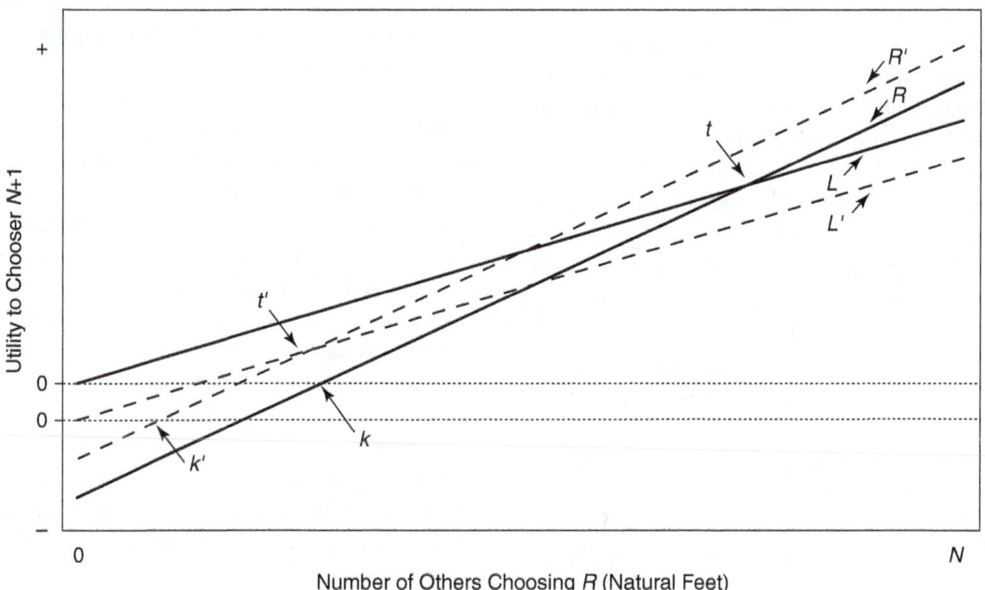

FIGURE 2 Schelling Coordination Diagram for Chinese Footbinding

Note: L = utility of choice resulting in an inferior equilibrium (footbinding); R = utility of choice resulting in a superior equilibrium (natural feet); L' = utility of footbinding after hearing of its disadvantages; R' = utility of natural feet after hearing of its advantages; k = minimum number of people required to be better off together choosing natural feet; k' = new smaller k resulting from a successful propaganda campaign; t = Point at which marriage market tips to either footbinding or to natural feet; t' = new tipping point resulting from a successful propaganda campaign; 0 = arbitrary zero value of inferior equilibrium (footbinfing); 0' = arbitrary zero value of footbinding after hearing of its disadvantage.

ESCAPING INFERIOR CONVENTIONS

The work of the antifootbinding reformers had three aspects (Drucker 1981; Levy 1966: 74–88). First, they carried out a modern education campaign, which explained that the rest of the world did not bind women's feet—that China was losing face in the world and was subject to international ridicule. Second, their education campaign explained the advantages of natural feet and the disadvantages of bound feet. Third, they formed natural-foot societies, whose members pledged not to bind their daughters' feet nor to let their sons marry women with bound feet. These three tactics are appropriate for escaping an inferior convention. I will illustrate with a Schelling diagram (see Figure 2).

The Schelling coordination diagram is a way of visualizing a many-person version of the two-person coordination game in Figure 1C. Suppose a reference population of *n+1* homogeneous individuals in a marriage market. The vertical axis represents higher or lower value to the typical chooser. The horizontal axis runs from zero other people on the left to *n* other people on the right. In this particular application, one curve, *L*, represents the choice resulting in an inferior equilibrium (footbinding); it starts at an arbitrary zero value on the left and rises to the right. *L* slopes down to the left because the greater the proportion of people who footbind, the less is footbinding a positional advantage in securing marriage. A second curve, *R*, represents the choice resulting in a superior equilibrium (natural feet); it starts below *L* on the left, intersects *L*, and ends above *L* on the right. *R* slopes up to the right because the greater the number of potential marriage partners, the better the individual's marriage match.[8] The point *n/3* along the horizontal axis would represent the value to individual *n+1* of choosing *L* or *R* when one-third of the others choose *R* and two-thirds of them choose *L*. There are two equilibria: the inferior, where everyone chooses *L* (where *L* meets the left vertical axis), and the superior, where everyone chooses *R* (where *R* meets the right vertical axis). If we are stuck at *L*, the footbinding equilibrium, how can we get to *R*, the natural feet equilibrium? Schelling (1978, chap. 7) calls the process "getting over the hump" and "beyond the intersection."

The reformers' campaign stressed that China was alone in the world in binding female feet. This provides an escape from the belief trap, a realization that the superior convention *R* (right) is available. Next, if everybody is choosing *L* (left), footbinding, then notice in the diagram that there is some number *k* of us who would be better off choosing natural feet. The critical number *k* is reached where the rising *R* curve attains the elevation of the left extremity of the *L* curve (an arbitrary zero in the diagram). Thus, if *k* or more of us can organize into an antifootbinding association, pledging not to footbind daughters nor let sons marry footbound women, we are better off; beyond this threshold, the advantages of natural feet outweigh the disadvantages of a smaller mate-selection pool. The initial *k* formations were enforced by public pledge within church fellowships, and the proven technique then was borrowed and spread by nonchurch reformers. Reneging on a public pledge is damaging to family honor, and any temptation to renege disappears upon reaching *k:* Getting to *k* is getting over the hump.

Next, notice where *L* intersects *R*, labeled *t*. This is the tipping point. Any number of choosers to the left of this point drives the marriage market (with the exception of any *organized k*) to the equilibrium of all footbinding. Any number of choosers to the right of this point drives individuals to the equilibrium of all natural feet. If we get just to the right of the intersection *t*, we will tip all the way to the superior equilibrium on the right vertical axis.

There is some minimum number *k* of us who benefit from getting together on the practice of natural feet, even at the cost of fewer potential marriage partners to choose from. Suppose that it's fairly easy to get the requisite *k* together, but much harder to organize the *t* people we need to tip the equilibrium (the situation is such that *k* is small and *t* is large). What else can we do? We should recruit more members to our antifootbinding association because each new member above *k* benefits every individual member of the association. Also, we should conduct an education and propaganda campaign on the disadvantages of footbinding and on the advantages of natural feet. To the extent our campaign is successful, people come to value footbinding less and natural feet more, even though they are still stuck at the inferior equilibrium: The L curve shifts down and right to L', the R curve shifts up and left to R'. One result of our information campaign is a new k', smaller than the old k, so fewer people are needed for an effective antifootbinding association. Another result is a new t', smaller than the old k, so fewer people are needed to tip the marriage market into the superior equilibrium. The way I have constructed the diagram, t' is less than k; thus, we are beyond the intersection and so achieve the superior equilibrium. To reiterate: First, k organizes; second, k propagandizes; third, if the propaganda is successful the tipping point t' becomes less than the k already organized; thus, fourth, the entire marriage market tips to the superior equilibrium.

I have given a temporal interpretation to Figure 2. The diagram can also be interpreted to represent heterogeneity. R' and L' could represent the preferences of those who have come to believe that footbinding is worse than the average person thinks it is, while R and L represent the beliefs of the average person. A small cadre of fanatics, who think that footbinding is extremely evil, can organize at the smaller k', and their successful proselytization can then accrete k' and erode t. Also, marriage markets tend to be local but overlapping. Suppose that some local marriage markets complete their tipping to natural feet. Their overlapping membership in other untipped local marriage markets may then compose sufficient k and t to tip some of those other markets, and so on. The global collection of overlapping local marriage markets will follow a logic of change similar to that of a local marriage market.

An analogy may ease comprehension of the model. For originating circumstances, imagine a seated audience where the tallest people have grabbed the front row. The view of the tallest (extreme polygynists) in the front row is obscured by being too close to the elevated stage, so they stand (footbind). Thus the second, third, and all the rest of the rows must stand to regain their views of the stage. The front row is better off, but everyone else is worse off because their view is no better than before, but now they incur the cost of standing. (Behind the first row the advantage of tallness is accentuated by standing, but the tall still would rather sit if enough other people would do so). For maintaining circumstances represented in Figure 2, imagine that over time the tallest drift away from the audience and that the ease of sitting (natural feet) is forgotten. Standing is now entrenched as the convention. Visitors tell people that elsewhere audiences sit. People begin to think that sitting might be better, but only if enough other people sit; any one person sitting alone gets no view of the stage (reproductive death). If a column (k) can be organized to sit, its members suffer a poor view of the stage but are compensated by the ease of sitting. The members of k then have two incentives, to recruit the contiguous columns and to inform everyone that sitting is better and that standing is worse than people thought.

As I have drawn it, both the reforming association and the education campaign were necessary for the reform. In an easier situation, education alone might suffice. New information shows that L is extremely disadvantageous and that R is extremely advantageous; the L curve shifts down and right and the R curve up and left so that now the left beginning of the R' curve is above the left beginning of the L' curve. After effective education the population spontaneously chooses all R. This is an optimistic analysis, however. It is like an outsider coming along and saying, "Don't you people know that sitting is better than standing?" To which the insiders can reply, "Maybe, maybe not, but we're all standers around here, and sitting wouldn't work." To the extent that people depend on others for the evaluation of information, a sort of suboptimal belief equilibrium might persist. Practically, reforming associations might still be recommended because of their frequency and demonstration effects (whereby a noticeable number of people make the change without suffering harm).

The natural-foot movement was identified with liberal modernizers and women's rights advocates and proceeded in the years of change culminating in the Revolution of 1911. It would be reasonable to consider the reform as part of a wave of modernization. Urban economic development encourages migration from the countryside and provides alternative opportunities of support for women (and young men). Each effect weakens the traditional family, but strengthens the independence and bargaining power of women, and so on.[9] But marriage modernization is standardly supposed to have occurred after 1949, while even dissidents from the standard view trace it no further back than the 1930s (Zang 1993). Zang's 1982–1983 urban survey data demonstrate modernization phenomena: 54 percent parental arrangement of mate choice for those married in 1900–1938, 31 percent in 1946–1949, 20 percent in 1950–1953, and 1 percent in 1977–1982; and median bride age increased, proportion of nuclear families increased slightly, and proportion of stem families and joint families decreased slightly from 1900–1938 to 1977–1982.

Contrast the relative lateness, gradualness, and incompleteness of those urban family modernization trends with the earliness, suddenness, and completeness of the end of footbinding in urban China (1895–1912). I believe that exposure to a specific superior alien convention and the specific innovation of the 1895 organization and education campaign, rather than any generalized modernizing trend, were responsible for the reform.[10] Doolittle (1865) reported that early modernization was intensifying the practice: "It is believed that, were it not for the poverty of the people, all the females would in a generation or two have small feet" (p. 201). Why would footbinding come to an end just as it became more affordable?

Kennedy (1970) and Hayes (1975) predict that infibulation will come to an end with increasing modernization. I have two objections to the modernization hypothesis. First, Kennedy's infibulating Nubians who began to circulate in Egyptian society did not abandon FGM but merely adopted the clitoridectomy of the more numerous and more prosperous Egyptians around them, just as immigrant Egyptian Copts adopted infibulation in urban Sudan (Cloudsley 1983). Second, as we have seen, in the Sudan modernization is accompanied by an increase in both the demographic expanse and the physical intensity of infibulation; similarly, in Somalia infibulation has increased with development.

The success of the tactics of the antifootbinding societies supports the hypothesis that footbinding was a self-enforcing convention. What evidence is there that infibulation is as well? Educated Sudanese men and women interviewed by Lightfoot-Klein (1989:99) blamed the other sex for perpetuating reinfibulation. Similarly, educated respondents in Somalia told Grassivaro-Gallo and Abdisamed (1985:317) that their spouses were responsible for inflicting infibulation on their daughters. Their data also show that the type and frequency of FGM are predicted by region of present residence, not by the birthplace of the mother or father; this finding suggests that local marriage-market calculations prevail over simple conformist transmission. In the northern Sudan village on the Nile studied by Boddy (1982:685), the local marriage convention had shifted from infibulation to excision around 1969. This was disclosed by the existence of a cohort of unmarried infibulated women whose younger, excised sisters and cousins had married. Abdalla's (1982) survey in 1980 of 70 Somali female and 40 male university students revealed that 60 percent of the women and 58 percent of the men believed that FGM should be abolished, although 66 percent of women and 50 percent of men planned to mutilate their daughters. Thus a majority (acting collectively) would abolish the practice, while a majority (acting individually) would inflict it on their daughters. This is a sure sign of being trapped in an inferior convention. As Abdalla (1982:94–95) puts it, "No one dares to be the first to abandon it."

CONCLUSIONS AND RECOMMENDATIONS

Colonial efforts to outlaw FGM in the Sudan and Kenya sparked political reaction. More recent international and national efforts to discourage or prohibit it have had no apparent effect. Only two instances of recession are known, according to Lightfoot-Klein (1989:50–51); both are doubtful on closer examination (see Brooks 1995; Megafu 1983). Lightfoot-Klein reports that infibulation is being *introduced* in parts of Uganda as an imagined return to African traditions. Legal prohibition has not worked. The consensus approach to eradication is to publicize the objectively bad consequences of female mutilation (initiatives are summarized in Hosken 1993:390–418).

Infibulation is an absolutely necessary precondition to marriage in the Sudan, according to Gruenbaum (1982), who continues that policy recommendations "have seldom recognized the significance of linkage between the operations and the social goal of maintaining the reputations and marriageability of daughters in a strongly patriarchal society" (p. 5). Testimony of an Islamic scholar that infibulation is not religiously commanded, or promoting greater awareness of medical hazards, "would not be sufficient for a mother to risk her daughter's marriageability" (p. 7) because of the importance of marriage and children. Gruenbaum recommends increased employment and educational opportunities to promote the independence of women.

The convention hypothesis predicts that if a convention ends, it will end quickly. The sudden end of footbinding in response to abolition campaigns supports the convention hypothesis and predicts that equivalent African campaigns could help end FGM. The convention hypothesis recommends three types of action. First, let people know the physiological facts, explaining to women and men the advantages of natural genitals and the disadvantages of mutilation. An education campaign is a banally obvious measure. What is not so obvious is that an ultimately successful education campaign may not have any behavioral effects until the moment of convention shift. Knowing that we are at an inferior coordination equilibrium is necessary but not sufficient for change. We may each come to believe that sitting is better than standing, but only if enough others make the change at the same time. Reformers and their funders should therefore measure progress by attitudinal rather than behavioral change.

Second, international public opinion should deplore the bad health consequences of FGM, and such judgment should be conveyed tactfully to practicing populations. Some African nationalists and cultural relativists claim that FGM is a matter to be worked out by African women.[11] This is so, but in the Chinese case, indigenous reformers were more helped by the exposure to an alternative convention and by international condemnation of footbinding as wrong than they were hindered by the obtuse xenophobia of some of the Western reformers. The followers of mutilation are good people who love their children; any campaign that insinuates otherwise is doomed to provoke defensive reaction. Because these parents love their children, they will be motivated to change, once they learn of the bad health consequences of FGM, and once a way to change is found. FGM will end sooner or later; better that it ends sooner than later.[12] Outside opposition to mutilation, whether from various feminist groups or now by American human rights policy, will have an eventual effect, and thus is worthwhile.

Third, associations of parents who pledge not to infibulate their daughters nor let their sons marry infibulated women may, as in China, decisively lead to change. Tribal facial scarring is common in the Sudan, but is in disrepute among westernized youths in the capital. Why then is infibulation not in disrepute? One of Lightfoot-Klein's (1989: 49, 116) respondents explained that if you give up scarring you lose your beauty, but to give up infibulation is to become shameful. Losing your beauty is sad, but losing your honor is unthinkable. Scarring is on the wane, I think, because it is part of an "average opinion game" (Van Huyck, Battalio, and Beil 1991): Faces are visible, and international images enlarge the reference group. Infibulation is invisible, however, and is also a matter of honor, a positional good unamenable to compromise. Honor depends on local marriage markets, not on international images.

Pledge associations might be even more important in Africa than in China because the public invisibility of FGM makes it harder for people to judge any change in the expectations of others; they are less sure of where they are on the Schelling diagram (Figure 2) I drew to describe the end of footbinding. The technique of pledge associations is not reported in the FGM literature, and explaining its potential is intended as the central contribution of this article.

REFERENCES

Abdalla, Raqiya Haji Dualeh. 1982. *Sisters in Affliction: Circumcision and Infibulation of Women in Africa.* London, England: Zed Press.

Agatharchides. 1989. *On the Erythraean Sea.* Translated by S.M. Burstein. London, England: The Hakluyt Society.

Assaad, Marie Bassili. 1980. "Female Circumcision in Egypt: Social Implications, Current Research, and Prospects for Change." *Studies in Family Planning* 11:3–16.

Beachey, R. W. 1976. *The Slave Trade of Eastern Africa.* New York: Barnes and Noble.

Bedi, Rahul. 1994. "Pakistan: Religious Right Puts Bhutto in a Spot." InterPress Service, May 27.

Blake, C. Fred. 1994. "Footbinding in Neo-Confucian China and the Appropriation of Female Labor." *Signs* 19:676–712.

Boddy, Janice. 1982. "Womb as Oasis: Pharaonic Circumcision in Rural Northern Sudan." *American Ethnologist* 9:682–98.

———. 1991. "Body Politics: Continuing the Anti-Circumcision Crusade." *Medical Anthropology Quarterly* n.s.5:15–17.

Bonaparte, Marie. 1953. *Female Sexuality.* New York: International Universities Press.

Brooks, Geraldine. 1995. *Nine Parts of Desire.* New York: Anchor Books.

Clarence-Smith, William Gervase, ed. 1989. *The Economics of the Indian Ocean Slave Trade in the Nineteenth Century.* London, England: Frank Cass.

Cloudsley, Anne. 1983. *Women of Omdurman: Life, Love and the Cult of Virginity.* New York: St. Martin's.

Croll, Elisabeth. 1981. *The Politics of Marriage in Contemporary China.* Cambridge, England: Cambridge University Press.

Daly, Mary. 1978. *Gyn/Ecology.* Boston, MA: Beacon Press.

Dareer, Asma El. 1982. *Woman, Why do You Weep?: Circumcision and Its Consequences.* London, England: Zed Press.

Dawit, Seble and Salem Mekuria. 1993. "The West Just Doesn't Get It." *The New York Times,* December 7, p. A27.

Dickemann, Mildred. 1979. "The Ecology of Mating Systems in Hypergynous Dowry Societies." *Social Science Information* 18:163–95.

———. 1981. "Paternal Confidence and Dowry Competition: A Biocultural Analysis of Purdah." Pp. 417–38 in *Natural Selection and Social Behavior,* edited by R.D. Alexander and D. W. Tinkle. New York: Chiron Press.

Doolittle, Justus. 1865. *Social Life of the Chinese.* New York: Harper and Brothers.

Drucker, Alison R. 1981. "The Influence of Western Women on the Anti-Footbinding Movement 1840–1911." *Historical Reflections* 8: 179–99.

Ebrey, Patricia. 1990. "Women, Marriage, and the Family in Chinese History." Pp. 197–223 in *Heritage of China,* edited by P.S. Ropp. Berkeley, CA: University of California Press.

———. 1991. "Shifts in Marriage Finance from the Sixth to the Thirteenth Century." Pp. 97–132 in *Marriage and Inequality in Chinese Society,* edited by R.S. Watson and P.B. Ebrey. Berkeley, CA: University of California Press.

Elster, Jon. 1986. "Introduction." Pp. 1–33 in *Rational Choice,* edited by J. Elster. New York: New York University Press.

Fairbank, John. 1992. *China: A New History.* Cambridge, MA: Harvard University Press.

Fairbank, John and Albert Feuerwerker, eds. 1986. *The Cambridge History of China,* vol. 13. Cambridge, England: Cambridge University Press.

Fairbank, John and Edwin O. Reischauer. 1978. *China.* Boston, MA: Houghton-Mifflin.

Freeman-Grenville, G.S.P., ed. 1962. *The East African Coast: Select Documents from the First to the Earlier Nineteenth Century.* Oxford, England: Clarendon Press.

Freud, Sigmund. 1961. "Fetishism." Pp. 149–57 in *The Standard Edition of the Complete Psychological Works of S. Freud,* vol. 21, edited and translated by J. Strachey. London, England: Hogarth.

Gamble, Sidney D. 1943. "The Disappearance of Foot-Binding in Tinghsien." *The American Journal of Sociology* 49:181–83.

Gates, Hill. 1989. "The Commoditization of Chinese Women." *Signs* 14:799–832.

———. Forthcoming. "Footbinding and Handspinning." In *Economy and Culture in China,* edited by E. Young. Ann Arbor, MI: Houghton-Mifflin.

Grassivaro-Gallo, Pia and Marian Abdisamed. 1985. "Female Circumcision in Somalia: Anthropological Traits." *Anthropoligischer Anzeiger* 43:311–26.

Grassivaro-Gallo, Pia and Franco Viviani. 1992. "The Origin of Infibulation in Somalia: An Ethological Hypothesis." *Ethology and Sociobiology* 13:253–65.

Greenhalgh, Susan. 1977. "Bound Feet, Hobbled Lives: Women in Old China." *Frontiers* 2:7–21.

Gruenbaum, Ellen. 1982. "The Movement against Clitoridectomy and Infibulation in Sudan." *Medical Anthropology Quarterly* 13(2):4–11.

Hardin, Russell. 1988. *Morality within the Limits of Reason.* Chicago, IL: University of Chicago Press.

Hayes, Rose Oldfield. 1975. "Female Genital Mutilation, Women's Roles, and the Patrilineage in Modern Sudan: A Functional Analysis." *American Ethnologist* 2:617–33.

Hicks, Esther K. 1993. *Infibulation.* New Brunswick, NJ: Transaction Publishers.

Hosken, Fran P. 1993. *The Hosken Report: Genital and Sexual Mutilation of Females,* 4th ed. Lexington, MA: WIN News.

Kennedy, John G. 1970. "Circumcision and Excision in Egyptian Nubia." *Man* n.s.5:175–91.

Knight, Jack. 1992. *Institutions and Social Conflict.* Cambridge, England: Cambridge University Press.

Koso-Thomas, Olayinka. 1987. *The Circumcision of Women: A Strategy for Eradication.* London, England: Zed Books.

Kouba, Leonard J. and Judith Muasher. 1985. "Female Circumcision in Africa." *African Studies Review* 28:95–110.

Levy, Howard S. 1966. *Chinese Footbinding.* New York: Walton Rawls.

Lewis, David. 1969. *Convention: A Philosophical Study.* Cambridge, MA: Harvard University Press.

Lightfoot-Klein, Hanny. 1989. *Prisoners of Ritual: An Odyssey into Female Genital Circumcision.* Binghamton, NY: Haworth Press.

Little, Mrs. Archibald. 1899. *Intimate China.* London, England: Hutchinson and Co.

Ma, Laurence J.C. 1971. *Commercial Development and Urban Change in Sung China.* Ann Arbor, MI: University of Michigan.

Mann, Judy. 1994. "From Victims to Agents of Change," *The Washington Post,* April 29, p. E3.

Megafu, U. 1983. "Female Ritual Circumcision in Africa." *East African Medical Journal* 60: 793–800.

Meinardus, Otto. 1967. "Mythological, Historical and Sociological Aspects of the Practice of Female Circumcision among the Egyptians." *Acta Ethnographica Academiae Scientiarum Hungaricae* 16:387–97.

Ortner, Sherry B. 1978. "The Virgin and the State." *Feminist Studies* 4(3): 19–36.

Ross, Alvin E. and Marilda A. Oliveira Sotomayor. 1990. *Two-Sided Matching.* Cambridge, England: Cambridge University Press.

Schelling, Thomas C. 1960. *The Strategy of Conflict.* Cambridge, MA: Harvard University Press.

———. 1978. *Micromotives and Macrobehavior.* New York: W.W. Norton.

Stacey, Judith. 1983. *Patriarchy and Socialist Revolution in China.* Berkeley, CA: University of California Press.

Ullmann-Margalit, Edna. 1977. *The Emergence of Norms.* Oxford, England: Clarendon Press.

U.S. Department of State. 1994. *Country Reports on Human Rights Practices for 1993.* Joint Committee Print, Committee on Foreign Affairs, U.S. House of Representatives, and the Committee on Foreign Relations, U.S. Senate, 103d Cong. 2d sess., February.

Van Gulik, R.H. 1961. *Sexual Life in Ancient China.* Leiden, Netherlands: E. J. Brill.

Van Huyck, John B., Raymond C. Battalio, and Richard O. Beil. 1991. "Strategic Uncertainty, Equilibrium Selection, and Coordination Failure in Average Opinion Games." *The Quarterly Journal of Economics* 106:885–910.

Veblen, Thorstein. 1934. *The Theory of the Leisure Class.* New York: Modern Library.

Widstrand, Carl. 1964. "Female Infibulation." *Studia Ethnographica Upsaliensia* 20:95–122.

Zang, Xiaowei. 1993. "Household Structure and Marriage in Urban China: 1900–1982." *Journal of Comparative Family Studies* 24:35–44.

NOTES

1. In this article, *Sudanic* refers to the region across Africa, and *Sudan* refers to the country in Northeast Africa.

2. For the periods under discussion, a man in China could have one wife and additional concubines, in non-Islamic Sudanic Africa many wives and concubines, and under Islam four wives and additional slave concubines: All are termed *polygyny* for the purposes of this article. *Hypergyny* is when women marry up—that is, a pattern of females marrying into higher ranking families.

3. Today's Beja, pastoralists and recent slaveholders inhabiting the same territory, are almost certainly their direct descendants. According to Hicks (1993:215), some Beja populations excise; others infibulate.

4. Widstrand speculates that the travelers were misinformed, and that instead slave traders paid a higher price for women already infibulated in their home territory. This may be true, but Browne and Burckhardt each visited the Sudan. Hicks (1993:22), relying on Cloudsley's (1983:112) misinterpretation of Widstrand's speculation, mistakenly denies that an association between slavery and infibulation is established.

5. Of the capital residents originating from high-infibulation regions, 49 percent expect that their daughters will not be infibulated (but will be mutilated); from low-infibulation areas, 65 percent. I doubt, however, that Somali hopes will be realized short of a convention shift.

6. I simplify and purge of sociobiological assumptions Dickemann's (1979, 1981) brilliant argument.

7. Consider, for example, the Ming Dynasty (1368–1644) saying quoted by Levy (1966): "If you care for a son, you don't go easy on his studies; if you care for a daughter, you don't go easy on her footbinding" (p. 49).

8. Ross and Sotomayor (1990) demonstrate that, for any individual, a larger marriage pool is never worse and may (often) be better than a smaller marriage pool.

9. On Chinese marriage modernization generally, see Croll (1981, chap.7).

10. Shortly before this article went to press, Gates (forthcoming) provided me with some of her work in progress: Original survey data and a theory on the differential distribution and disappearance of footbinding in China. Some of her observations support parts of my argument, for example, that footbinding was necessary to a proper marriage and that wherever footbinding ended, it ended rapidly. Gates's respondents almost never report having received any direct antifootbinding propaganda, however, and thus she believes it is unlikely that the reforming associations had much to do with cessation. Gates argues, therefore, that the convention hypothesis is unsupported, except perhaps among elite or urban populations. Gates shows that the local proportion of women bound was higher where the work available to females could be done with bound feet (e.g., household textile production). Footbinding declined, according to Gates, as the cheaper products of modern industry displaced the products of female household labor.

My view is that Gates's data and parts of her theory complement rather than contradict the convention hypothesis. There is evidence in her work for indirect influence of reforming associations and elite practices on the rural masses. The convention hypothesis recognizes the tradeoff between higher marital status and family need for heavy labor that Gates confirms was explicitly discussed in families. Gates takes note of the peculiarity of the permanent disappearance of footbinding as compared to uneven changes in other gender customs. Finally, the fact that FGM is less of a hindrance to female labor than was footbinding may have implications for reform policy. Full discussion of these intriguing issues must await another occasion.

11. See, for example, Dawit and ekuria (1993): "A media campaign in the West will not stop genital mutilation" (p. A27).

12. One self-fulfilling reform tactic might be to warn parents to wait because future convention shifts may make their irreversibly mutilated daughters unmarriageable. The failure of such a tactic would deepen the convention trap, however.

Geoffrey Brennan and Gordon Tullock

An Economic Theory of Military Tactics: Methodological Individualism at War

1982

1. INTRODUCTION

The theory of military tactics that is presented here is not economic in any obvious sense. We are not concerned with the role of the productive economy as a strategic element in the conduct of total warfare. Nor are we concerned with what might be termed "economic" aspects of logistics. Our discussion is, rather, economic in terms of the method of analysis.

Two aspects of economic method are relevant here. The first is the individualistic perspective. Although

Geoffrey Brennan and Gordon Tullock, "An Economic Theory of Military Tactics." *Journal of Economic Behavior and Organization* 3 (1982): 225–242. By permission of *Journal of Economic Behavior and Organization.*

in modern economics, collections of individuals are sometimes treated as "entities" for analytic purposes (examples of "the household," "the firm," and even occasionally "the state" spring to mind) the *ultimate* unit of analysis is always the individual; more aggregative analysis must be regarded as only provisionally legitimate. In other words, the economist is always sensitive to the possibility that the holistic treatment of groups of individuals may mislead greatly, or involve overlooking dimensions of reality that are extremely important. This paper reflects such a sensitivity.

The second aspect of economic method relevant here is that much of economics deals with the problem of how to structure the institutional order that governs the ways in which individual agents interact with one another, so as to achieve certain well-defined objectives. The prime example of such an institutional order is the freely operating market. The market is widely recognized among professional economists to possess the attractive property that under certain circumstances all the scope for mutual benefits is exhausted. The operation of the market in such settings is often contrasted with the operation of other social co-ordinating/decision-making mechanisms such as majoritarian politics which do not have this property. More generally, the properties of alternative institutional structures represents a major line of enquiry in modern economic analysis.

That these aspects of economics bear particularly on the question of military tactics is perhaps not entirely obvious, and certainly does not appear to have been explicitly recognized in much of the relevant literature. More conventional analysis of military tactics seems to involve an approach in which opposing *armies* are conceived as the units of analysis. Battle can then be analyzed in much the same way as a game of chess may be. The role of the general is seen to be the deployment of his forces in the most effective way: discussion of good "generalship" focuses naturally on such matters as intelligent use of terrain, rapid mobility, concentration of strength at crucial points and so on. Disaggregation to the level of the individual soldier is seen as an unnecessary refinement, and to present only the danger of losing sight of the wood for the trees.

However, as the initial quotation from du Picq cogently reminds us, the forces available to the general are not chess pieces, but men—men whose actions are governed by their individual states of mind and not necessarily by the wills of their generals. We must at least allow the logical possibility that at times the interests of any one individual may be at odds with the interests of the general or of the army "as a whole." Indeed, the central element of our thesis in this paper is that this is characteristically the case, and that an essential ingredient in the analysis of military engagements is missed if this fact is not recognized. Armies must be analyzed as collections of independent individuals who are, in some senses, as much at war with one another and their own leaders as they are with enemy forces.

There are, of course, some aspects of the problem here that have been widely discussed in orthodox military literature. The importance of "morale" in unifying the perceived interests of individual soldiers has, for example, been emphasized as a crucial ingredient in ensuring success in battle. "Morale is to the physical," remarks Napoleon "as three is to one." And it is not for nothing that much of our referenced material comes from the (largely ignored) writings of du Picq, for whom morale is the sine qua non of tactical strength. Where our treatment differs from du Picq's, and a fortiori from other writers in the area, is that the economist's perspective encourages an examination of technical or "institutional" rather than purely psychological aspects of what might broadly be termed the "morale problem."

Our argument develops as follows. In section 2 we lay out the theory in terms of some simple examples. In section 3, we discuss the relevance of this general theory for military contexts. Section 4 discusses incentives and monitoring as aspects of a theory of military science, and section 5 spells out some implications of the argument. Section 6 draws the relevant conclusions.

2. The central analytic element in our discussion is a variant of the familiar prisoners' dilemma problem. This particular form of interaction in its many guises underlies a large part of the more interesting areas of economics—the theory of market failure in the provision of public goods; the modern theory of the firm; much of the economic theory of politics; and the theory of labor unions; to mention some of the more conspicuous examples. In one sense, the prisoners' dilemma is so familiar a tool of modern social analysis that to rehearse it yet again may seem entirely unnecessary. On the other hand, the military application is probably of sufficient intrinsic interest to justify spelling out the details. Moreover, there are some major wrinkles in this application that merit its being viewed as an analytically distinct and independently interesting case.

We shall begin our discussion with the simplest possible example, and complicate the analysis where necessary as we proceed. Accordingly, let us consider the following example.

Two individuals, A and B, are walking a deserted street. Suddenly they see a man, C, running towards them. The man is waving a meat-cleaver about his head, and has a wild eye: he yells abuse at them, and shouts out his intent to kill them both. What is rational for A and B to do?

It is clear that if A and B jointly tackle C, the probability that they will overcome him is quite large: the probability that either A or B will be seriously hurt is not zero but is fairly small (say one in five). Hence, the expectation for each of A and B of being seriously hurt *if both stay* is low, in this case one in ten.

Suppose, however, that A runs away and B stays. Then A will be perfectly safe; but B will face a significant chance, say one in two, of being seriously hurt. Likewise, if A says to fight while B runs. There are then, in this example significant "economics of scale" in fighting: the chance of C killing either is much smaller when both remain than when only one does. In other words, there are strong *technical* advantages to numerical superiority.

But what if both run away? In this case, it is fairly likely that C will catch up with one of them—a probability of two in three, say. But since there is no way of knowing ex ante who will be the unlucky one, the probability that each faces of being hurt if both run is only one in three.

We can depict this situation as a non-zero sum game matrix as in Table 1. The first entry in each pay-off pair is the probability that A will be seriously hurt—the second entry, the probability that B will be seriously hurt. If we can presume that A and B are indifferent to one another's fate, and that being seriously hurt is something each would prefer to avoid, then we can depict this matrix in more familiar pay-off terms, as illustrated in Table 2. The pay-off pair (a, b) for each outcome indicates the pay-off a to A and the pay-off b to B respectively.

Table 1

		B's actions	
		Stay and fight	Run
A's actions	Stay and fight	$\left[\frac{1}{10}, \frac{1}{10}\right]$	$\left[\frac{1}{2}, 0\right]$
	Run	$\left[0, \frac{1}{2}\right]$	$\left[\frac{1}{3}, \frac{1}{3}\right]$

Table 2

		B's actions	
		Stay and fight	Run
A's actions	Stay and fight	[−10, −10]	[−60, 0]
	Run	[0, −50]	[−33, −33]

The characteristic feature of this interaction is that the rational course of action for each individual is to *run*; that is, the strategy "run" maximizes the pay-off (minimizes the loss) to each individual irrespective of what the other does. Consider B's calculus, for example. If A chooses to stay and fight, B will endure an expected cost of 10 if he also stays, but zero if he runs—it is therefore rational to run. If A runs, however, B faces an expected cost of 50 if he stays to fight, but faces an expected cost of only 33 if he runs—it is again rational to run. B finds that it is rational to run whatever A does. And since the interaction is totally symmetric, A will find it rational to run whatever B does. Yet clearly, for the two of them, considered as a group, the worst possible outcome is for both to run; what is collectively rational is individually irrational and vice versa.

This simple example is an entirely standard version of the prisoners' dilemma problem. It captures, in our view, the essential element in the relation between members of an army under attack: the *collectively* rational thing to do is to stay and fight, the individually rational thing to do is to run (or attempt to avoid conflict in some other manner). It also exposes the *essential* tactical problem—how to organize one's forces in such a way as to induce each individual to behave in the collective interest. It fails, however, to capture one crucial feature of the strategic element in military engagement because it assumes that the attacking force, C, is going to attack independently of what A and B do.

To depict the essential nature of military confrontation, we need to be able to reflect in our analytics, simultaneously, the prisoners' dilemma interaction that connects each individual with his fellow-soldiers on his own side *and* the overall strategic interaction between the opposing "collectivities." We expand our example modestly. We suppose the "attacker" to be not one determined madman, C, but two ordinary "soldiers," C and D. We thus have two armies, each composed of two persons[1]—and for simplicity of treatment, we shall suppose that each individual is exactly like all the others. This total symmetry assumption means that the pay-off matrix and the consequent calculus can be set out simply for a single representative individual. This matrix is, however, complicated by the fact that, in deciding his course of action, the individual must consider not just the possible actions of his comrades but also the possible actions of his enemies. And we must be careful to motivate the individuals in such a way that it is in some manner "rational" for them to be involved in the military confrontation at all.

In setting out our example, several pieces of background data are necessary. In particular, we need to specify: the pay-off to each if his army is victorious; the probability of victory; the probability of being injured; and the costs of being injured. Where applicable, we shall follow the terms of the earlier, simpler case.

Accordingly, suppose that two armies, I and II, are disputing the ownership of some territory, which has a value to each army of 20 units (10 units to each soldier) if the army proves victorious.[2] The probability of victory is, of course, a function of the relative actual fighting strengths, and is assumed to be as indicated in Table 3.

The probability of being seriously injured in the course of battle depends crucially on what other individuals choose to do. We show the relevant probabilities for the typical soldier in Table 4. They correspond as far as possible to the earlier example—specifically, the structure of probabilities in the third and fourth rows exactly mirrors that in Table 1. As before, we suppose that cost of injury to be 100 to each.

Finally, we include, as an additional potentially relevant consideration, the psychic cost of running away. "Cowardice" may be personally demeaning. We therefore indicate a cost of, say, two units sustained by anyone who adopts that strategy. On this basis, we can collect together the information in Tables 3 and 4 and the various values of injury and victory to the individual soldier and depict it all in the form of a pay-off matrix, shown as Table 5. The structure of the matrix is identical to that of Table 4, but here we show the returns to the soldier from running and from fighting, for all the relevant possible actions by others.

Several aspects of this interaction are worth emphasizing. First and most important for our purposes, is that the "rational" strategy for the individual is

Table 3

Probability of victory

Army I	2	2	2	1	1	1	0	0	0
Army II	2	1	0	2	1	0	2	1	0
Probability that I beats									
II	50%	80%	100%	20%	50%	100%	0	0	no outcome

Table 4

Probability of serious injury

Enemy's actions	Own actions: Fight	Own actions: Run	Comrade's actions
Both run	$\frac{1}{100}$	0	fights
	$\frac{1}{50}$	0	runs
One runs,	$\frac{1}{10}$	0	fights
One fights	$\frac{1}{2}$	$\frac{1}{3}$	runs
Both fight	$\frac{1}{2}$	$\frac{1}{20}$	fights
	$\frac{4}{5}$	$\frac{2}{3}$	runs

Table 5

Enemy's actions	Own actions: Fight	Own actions: Run	Comrade's actions
Both run	9	8	fights
	8	−2	runs
One runs,	−2	3	fights
One fights	−45	−36	runs
Both fight	−45	−5	fights
	−78	−68	runs

always to run unless both the enemy run away first. If the enemy both run away, then it is rational for the individual to "stay and fight" *whatever* his comrade does. If there is to be battle, however, then it is rational for the individual to run, and to do so whatever his comrade does. It follows that the soldier's behavior is independent of the behavior of his *comrade*: it depends solely on the behavior of the *enemy*. For this reason, each individual soldier has to predict what the enemy will do before he can choose the action that is best for himself. In this sense, the individual soldier is engaged in a complex multi-person game of "chicken," which has the structure indicated in Table 6. Clearly, the best outcome for each soldier is that where the enemy runs. However, since this is also true for opposing soldiers the essential feature of this game becomes one of *bluff*, because if

Table 6

		Opposing army	
		Fight	Run
Individual soldier	Fight	(−40, −40)	(9, 9)
	Run	(−30, −30)	(−2, −2)

the opposing army chooses to fight, it is individually rational to run away. If the soldier believes the opposing army will indeed engage in actual combat, then the prisoners' dilemma interaction depicted in Table 2 will apply, and it is rational for him to break ranks and flee. If, on the other hand, he believes that the opposing army will break ranks before his own does, it is rational for him to stand.

Suppose, however, that we collapse the interaction in Table 5 into an aggregate interaction between opposing *armies*. To do so, we note that:

i. since if the opposing army flees, it is rational for each soldier to stay, the return to each is 9 units in the top left-hand corner of the pay-off matrix,
ii. since if the opposing army fights, it is rational for every individual to flee the return to each is −68 units in the bottom right-hand corner of the pay-off matrix.

The return to each *army* becomes the simple sum of the returns to the individual soldiers who compose that army; accordingly we can represent the interaction between opposing armies as in Table 7.

This aggregative interaction clearly has an "equilibrium" outcome: that in which both armies *fight*.[3] This interaction too is of the prisoners' dilemma form—the outcome generates a pay-off (or −90 units) to each army, which is less than the pay-off (of −4) to each that might have emerged if both had

Table 7

		Army II	
		Fight	Run
Army I	Fight	(−90, −90)	(18, −136)
	Run	(−136, 18)	(−4, −4)

agreed not to fight. This fact simply reflects our belief that battle is not in toto a positive sum activity. The object of conflict is simply the distribution of a given prize between warring parties; the prize is not *created* by the conflict itself. And since conflict uses up resources, the result is necessarily negative sum.[4]

Our interest here is not, however, in whether warfare is a globally rational activity. It is rather in the proper understanding of warfare for purposes of developing a theory of military tactics. What we have tried to expose by our simple example here is the following set of propositions:

1. that, considering the pay-offs to the *collection* of individuals who make up an army, it will in general be *collectively* rational to stand and fight (rather than run),
2. that, notwithstanding this fact, it will typically be in the interests of individual soldiers *not* to stand and fight, unless the enemy runs,
3. that, therefore, there is a divergence between the individual and collective interests of those who make up an army, which is a crucial ingredient in successful conduct of war to overcome.

On this reckoning, the central element in the conduct of battle is *not* an actual engagement of opposing forces, but rather a confrontation of two opposing *networks* of agents, in which it is that *network* rather than the agents themselves which is the object of destruction. In other words, victory is not so much a matter of killing one's opponents as it is of breaking apart the intrinsically delicate basis for co-operation among the separate elements that compose the opposing force.

3. This account may well appear totally obvious as a theoretical construct, and yet have virtually nothing to do with the actual conduct of battle. In order to establish at least a presumptive connection between our simple theory and what actually occurs in the field, it may be useful to offer a few appropriate quotations from Armand du Picq's *Battle Studies.*

Consider, for example, in the light of our claim of the relavance of the general prisoners' dilemma interaction, du Picq's description of "the advance";

> We rush forward, but . . . generally we rush with prudence, with a tendency to let the most urgent ones, the most intrepid ones, pass on. It is strange but true that the nearer we approach the enemy, the less we are closed up. (du Picq [1946, p. 145])

Shirking on a minor scale perhaps? We get a feel for du Picq's assessment of the magnitude of the problem in his account of Napoleon's attack on Wagram:

> Out of the twenty-two thousand men (that made up Napoleon's mass) three thousand to fifteen hundred reached the position. Clearly the position was not carried by them, but by the material and moral effect of a battery of one-hundred pieces, cavalry, etc. etc. Were the other nineteen thousand men disabled? No! Seven out of twenty-two, a third—an enormous proportion—may have been hit. What became of the twelve thousand unaccounted for? They had lain down on the road, had played dummy in order not to go on to the end. In the confused mass of a column of deployed battalions, surveillance—difficult enough in a column at normal distances—is impossible. Nothing is easier than dropping out through inertia; nothing more common. (du Picq [1946, p. 150])

du Picq (1946, 127) also clearly recognized the implications of all this for incentives to cut and run:

> He who calm and strong of heart awaits his enemy has all the advantages of fire. But the moral impulse of the assailant demoralizes the assailed. He is frightened; he sets his sight no longer; he does not even aim his piece. His lines are broken without defense, unless indeed his cavalry waiting halted, horsemen a meter apart and in two ranks, does not break first and destroy all formation.

On this basis, he further saw that the chief element in victory was to convince the opponent of one's determination to fight. Once so convinced, the opposition would flee. As du Picq saw it, this gave a considerable intrinsic advantage to offense—but whether or not he was correct in this, he clearly interpreted battle as a "moral" rather than "physical" engagement.

> Indeed, the physical impulse is nothing. The moral impulse is everything. The moral impulse lies in the perception by the enemy of the resolution that animates you. They say that the battle of Amstetten was the *only one* in which a line actually waited for the shock of another line charging with the bayonets. Even then the Russians gave way before the moral and not before the

> physical impulse . . . They waited long enough to receive bayonet thrusts, even blows with the rifle (in the back . . .). This done, they fled." (du Picq [1946, p. 126])

Or again on the psychological dimensions of aggression:

> . . . but the enemy does not stand; the moral pressure of the danger that precedes you is too strong for him. Otherwise, those who stood and aimed even with empty rifles, would never see a charge come up to them. The first line of the assailant would be sensible of death and no one would wish to be in the first rank. Therefore, the enemy never merely stands; because if he does, it is you that flee. This always does away with the shock. The enemy entertains no smaller anxiety than yours. When he sees you near, the question for him also is whether to flee or to advance. Two moral impulses are in conflict. (du Picq [1946, p. 146])

4. In this view of things, a crucial ingredient in the whole military enterprise is to circumvent the natural predilection towards breaking formation and fleeing or towards not engaging the enemy in the first place—a predilection which is endemic to the basic nature of collective conflict. There are, in fact, three distinct ways in which this might be done:

i. we might seek to change the individual's valuation of alternative actions *directly* by psychological means,
ii. we might adopt a system of "side-payments" (rewards and/or punishments) which alter the relative costs and benefits so as to redirect self-interest to the desired ends,
iii. we might adopt an "institutional arrangement"—in this case some means of deploying men, organizing forces or some such—which changes the costs and benefits of alternative courses of action, without any direct "side-payments" within the group.

The distinction between (ii) and (iii) can possibly be clarified by examples as the discussion proceeds. What should at this point be emphasized is that the three options are not in any sense mutually exclusive. In general, we should expect all three to be used—that optimization would occur at all (three) margins, to use the economist's jargon.

Let us briefly examine the options in turn.

4.1. Psychological "Morale Building"

The means of morale-building through changing individuals' preferences directly has been widely discussed in military contexts and requires no additional commentary from us. Building affection among comrades, developing hatred for the enemy, establishing and augmenting a sense of military honor are all part of what is at stake here. Likewise, presumably, uniforms and military music and parades—indeed, all the panoply of chocolate-box soldiery—can be accounted for along such lines.[5] The point to be made here is the simple one that changing individuals' preferences—overcoming the natural predilection towards self-concern—is not a costless operation by any means. One would therefore not expect it to be the only, or necessarily the most important, instrument used to solve the prisoners' dilemma problem in its military variant.

4.2. Positive Incentives

Economists typically focus on "side-payments" or "bribes" as the primary means of changing individuals' behavior. The market is, after all, the prime institution through which this is done in social life. In the military context, positive incentives (like profits and incomes in markets) are an important element in structuring individual behavior, though such effects are not widely discussed in the military literature (at least to our knowledge).

Some examples are obvious. Military decoration for acts of "bravery" is one such.[6] A system of promotion, based on acts of bravery, is another, particularly when promotion involves being shifted out of the "firing line." At one level, it might seem that moving a courageous and effective soldier out of the direct line of battle and into some "safe," behind-lines, job for which he may be relatively ill-equipped is a mammoth violation of the principle of comparative advantage. It does, however, have the virtue of establishing incentives for courageous behavior among persons whose natural instincts are not towards bravery at all, and can in principle be entirely justified on such grounds.

In some ways the most conspicuous example of positive incentives in military history has been the "spoils" system. To take a specific case, consider the British navy in the days of sail. Any enemy merchant ship captured by a British ship was auctioned with its cargo and resultant proceeds divided: one quarter to the admiral of the relevant British fleet; and one quarter to the captain, one quarter shared among the officers and one quarter among the enlisted men of the successful British vessel. If an enemy naval vessel was captured, the British Admiralty would pay its assessed value to be divided in the same proportions. Interestingly enough, the Admiralty would also do this for enemy naval vessels *sunk*. This structure of incentives obviously provided the admiral with some cash incentive to dispose his ships in such a way that they were more likely to make captures, and the captain and men of each ship to be anxious to engage. Free-rider problems were not necessarily entirely overcome, but were substantially moderated by this means.

4.3. Negative Incentives

Negative incentive structures have always been extensively used in military settings. Traditionally, anyone who was detected displayed cowardice in battle—anything from running away to shirking—became the victim of the stringent system of military discipline, enforced by execution and/or torture (flogging was the standard form). Indeed, in some cases, offenders would be dispatched instantly by an officer's pistol.

Again the example of the British navy is instructive. All non-commissioned officers carried truncheons which they were free to use in dealing with men who were too slow, clumsy or reluctant in battle. The hatches of the naval vessel during engagement were guarded by marines whose orders were to prevent anyone going below deck who had no business there. Marine guards enforced these positions rigorously: superior officers were perfectly capable of enforcing orders, and would have no doubt executed an entire ship's crew if necessary (or clapped them in irons for future attention). In fact, this marine assignment was, as warship assignments go, somewhat less dangerous than most on a wooden ship being fired at by cannon at close range. No location was safe, but the hatch guard was less dangerous than most.

For the record, the navy was by no means alone in extensive use of negative incentives. The British army of the day also had a strict disciplinary system, and punishment was hardly less severe than in the navy.[7] And such systems long predate the period of British ascendancy. Frederick the Great, for example, is reported to have remarked that a soldier should be more frightened of his officers than of the enemy!

Since, from the point of view of the military establishment negative incentives are cheaper than positive ones, one would perhaps expect them to be used more extensively. There are, however, obvious natural limits: enforcement of negative incentives requires some agent, whose actions are enforced by some other agent higher up the hierarchy. Not all of these agents can be motivated by negative incentives. A system that applies negative incentives at the lower end and moves gradually to positive incentives at the top seems like a natural equilibrium arrangement. Likewise, in the use of positive incentives, one would expect the structure of rewards to be strongly regressive: higher officers must be given a strong incentive to enforce negative incentives imposed more extensively at lower levels of the institutional hierarchy. In this connection, recall the characteristically regressive structure of the British navy's distribution of spoils.

Now one might suppose that limits are also placed on the use of negative incentives by the requirement to obtain recruits for the rank and file. Beyond some point, this is clearly a valid conjecture. But it must be emphasized that the incentive structure itself—even if implemented by severe punishment—is in the positive interests of potential recruits. Within the prisoners dilemma interaction that connects individual members of the army, each individual has a preference for an institutional structure in which *no-one* runs away: strong enforcement procedures ensure the *collectively preferred* outcome where everyone stays to fight, as opposed to the individually rational equilibrium where both run. Consider again the interaction depicted in Table 2. The effective choice is between the [– 10, – 10] outcome, under effective enforcement, and the [–33, –33] outcome in its absence. Clearly, the former is to be preferred. In that sense, recruitment is *easier,* not more difficult, in a context where the expected costs associated with "free-riding" on one's comrades-in-arms are *larger* rather than smaller. It was not for nothing that England maintained an entirely volunteer army throughout a period in which discipline was strict and punishment for violation extremely severe: this is *precisely* what the theory predicts.

4.4. Strategic Solutions

There is a further form of solution to the free-rider problem in he military context—one that depends not on internally arranged side-payments, but on purely strategic considerations. The characteristic feature of these solutions is that forces are so organized that the *enemy* effectively enforces the appropriate incentive structure. Essentially, the group is able to precommit itself in such a way that it is no longer individually rational for any soldier to cut and run.

A simple example may illustrate. The British square was, on the face of it, a slightly absurd military formation. It exposed the British force to attack from all sides at once, was relatively immobile, and relinquished all possible protection that the terrain might have afforded. Yet from Fontenoy to Abu Clea in the Sudan, no British square was ever broken. Why? Given the focus on "incentive" questions, the answer seems simple. No soldier could effectively break ranks without running towards the enemy. This fact entirely altered the strategic interaction between individual British soldiers: it was now in each soldier's self-interest to stay and fight, and hence the collectively desired outcome required virtually no enforcement. The situation facing each individual soldier in the square formation can be depicted in Table 8. The equilibrium outcome in this interaction is to stay and fight: this is the best course of action for A *whatever* D does, and vice versa.[8] Presumably, highly mobile heavy artillery rendered the square entirely obsolete as a strategic device—but its success for over a century illustrates the central analytic point nicely.

Table 8

		B's actions	
		Stay and fight	Run
A's actions	Stay and fight	[−10, −10]	[−20, −30]
	Run	[−30, −20]	[−30, −30]

A somewhat similar example seems to be provided by late nineteenth and twentieth century trench warfare. One of the strategic advantages of "digging in" was that the individual soldier in many cases took greater risks by "running" than by staying to fight, since in order to run away he had to leap out of his trench and expose himself to enemy fire. No such analogous incentive structure was relevant for *attacking* forces who necessarily had to expose themselves in "going over the top"—a fact which in itself substantially altered the relative advantages of attack and defense.

The basic point here is that there may exist means of deploying forces, using terrain and so on—all standard parts of military strategy as conventionally conceived—that serve not so much to increase *physical* strength vis-a-vis one's enemy as they do to circumvent the "free rider" incentives within one's one forces.

4.5. Monitoring and Strategy

Even where this is not so, and one must rely on the various forms of incentives earlier discussed, strategic considerations remain relevant to the "morale" problems we are dealing with here. This is so because *any* form of incentives requires a strict monitoring system: individual soldiers who are encouraged to undertake acts of bravery because of the prospects of reward must believe that those acts will be observed; those who are discouraged from shirking (in its various forms) because of the prospects of punishment must believe that such shirking is likely to be detected.

It seems clear that the ease with which behavior can be monitored is partly dependent on such considerations as the deployment of forces, the use of terrain, the width of the front, the formation of units and so on. Napoleon, it is said, always kept his crack troops in reserve—doubtless to maintain flexibility in his battle strategy. But the monitoring advantages are also not negligible. Crack troops are much less likely to drift quietly away from the scene of battle when unobserved. And front lines will be much more reluctant to break ranks if they suspect that they will be observed in doing so, and possibly run directly into the line of fire of their own rear lines.

Of course, the precise monitoring arrangements that are optimal cannot be specified in abstraction from the nature of the weaponry, the magnitude of the forces involved, the range of "visibility" and so on. What seems clear, however, is that, while wars continue to be fought by man (and not machines), "morale" will remain a major element of military theory and the implications of alternative military tactics for the feasibility of monitoring will remain central to the whole strategic question.

5. It may be useful at this point to spell out some implications of the foregoing discussion for some particular issues in military theory. We do so briefly and suggestively in what follows for a couple of matters on which our approach sheds, we believe, interesting light.

5.1. The Role of Relative Numbers

One interesting question in military theory is why numerical superiority has not generally proven a better predictor of success than it appears to have been. Examples abound in war history of cases in which forces have overcome opposing armies that had *overwhelming* numerical superiority. To mention some specific famous cases: at the battle of Arbela in 331 B.C., Alexander overcame a Persian army *five* times larger than his own; Hannibal at the famous battle of Cannae totally destroyed a Roman army of 85,000 men with a force scarcely more than half that; in the American Civil War, Lee consistently defeated Union forces in spite of their significant numerical superiority.

Or, to put what is the same question a slightly different way, why is it that it is usually necessary to inflict only modest losses on one's enemy to secure victory? Losses of, say, thirty percent killed or wounded are exceptionally large—normally too large for an army to sustain, *even when despite its losses it remains numerically superior to its foe.*

This is perhaps difficult to explain if war is conceived as a battle to the death by opposing generals: but once the prisoners' dilemma interaction among members of each army is recognized, and elevated to its proper place in the understanding of actual warfare, there is little to explain. In fact, there is considerable literature on the effects of increased numbers of "players" on likely outcomes under the prisoners dilemma interaction. As the number of players increases, the incentives for each player to free ride increases—the "collectively rational" outcome becomes less and less likely. The role that any single individual plays in whether his army wins or loses becomes increasingly insignificant. To be sure, there are important threshold effects here: being one of an army of one hundred thousand, is not perhaps so different from being one in an army of three hundred thousand, in terms of perceived contribution. On the other hand, being one of ten colonels in command of ten thousand men may be rather different in incentive implications from being one of thirty. In any case, we do not claim that numerical superiority is a military *disadvantage*—only that the advantages of numbers are rather less striking than a holistic approach would indicate.

5.2. On Guerilla Warfare

The cases in which guerilla tactics have proven successful as the major means of conducting a war are surprisingly few. It could no doubt be argued that the Boers did much better (given their resources) by pursuing guerilla tactics than they would have done in open battle against the British, though the record is not entirely clear. And in the other often-cited case of the Vietnam war it is by no means obvious that, absent political crisis at home, the U.S. forces could not have ultimately secured victory in the field relatively easily.

The rarity of successful guerilla tactics is "surprising" because one would have thought that with the advantages of consistent surprise and rapid mobility that guerilla operations make possible, a force might over the long haul be able to inflict much greater losses on its opponent than in direct conflict between entire armies.

But guerilla operations clearly greatly increase monitoring costs. Scope for shirking on the part of entire units, of lying low unobserved by individual soldiers and leaving everything to the "intrepid few," is much greater than in conventional warfare. Accordingly, the theory here would predict that guerilla operations would inflict much less damage on the enemy than its apparent tactical advantages would suggest.[9]

The case of guerilla tactics that seems to have come closest to success is that of German submarine operations in the two World Wars. We have not seen any relevant figures on this, but we conjecture that the extent of shirking was considerable—that many U-boats more or less quietly sat out the war on the ocean floor, participating minimally in naval conflict.

5.3. The Role of Individual Heroism

Can a single act of heroism by a single individual or small group exercise any sort of influence on the course of a battle, in which the number of participants is enormous? Certainly, the romantic mythology of military history would have us believe so. But are such possibilities purely mythical? It is surely tempting to think so; we would predict that conventional "morale-building" would involve assuring individual soldiers that they exercise a major influence on the course of battle even when in fact they only do so *collectively*. But there seem to be many examples where small numbers of individuals (sometimes a single person) have had a major effect on battle outcomes. The attack by American torpedo planes, for example, at Midway was spectacularly dangerous, and led to a much higher casualty rate than, say, the famous charge of the Light Brigade. But because it distracted Japanese fighter planes from the approaching dive-bombers, it made the U.S. victory at Midway decisive and thereby ultimate victory in the Pacific war possible. A somewhat similar circumstance arose at the battle of Chancellorsville when Stonewall Jackson was rolling up the flank of the Union army. The commander of the troop of cavalry who was guarding the Union headquarters suddenly observed Jackson's army corps coming down the road towards him. He instantly charged directly into the front of Jackson's corp. This was a totally suicidal act. But it threw Jackson into sufficient confusion that he stopped the advance to straighten things out. By the time he was reorganized, sufficient union forces were available to stop him. Without this suicidal charge the Confederate forces might have wiped out the Union army at Chancellorsville.

In the account of military engagement that we have given, the possibility that a single "suicidal" act may turn the course of battle is not too remote. In the initial example depicted in Table 2 above, A and B will individually have an incentive to flee if they are convinced that C will in fact attack. As the number of individuals subject to attack increases, the strength of the incentive to run increases—again, given the conviction that C will attack. If an apparently suicidal feat is undertaken by C (or by C and a relatively small number of his comrades) and if A, B and comrades see this as evidence that C's force *will* attack *whatever* the cost, the tide of battle can be decisively turned in C's favor—the *moral* strength (in du Picq's terms) passes to C. In this sense, "impossible" feats of daring, victory against "insuperable" odds, become entirely possible.

Our account acknowledges room for the hero. It is difficult to see how a more holistic account can coherently do so.

6. In this paper, we have attempted to provide a perspective on military engagement that focuses attention on the relation between individuals who *compose* an army, rather than on the relation between opposing armies. That former relation can be characterized as a "prisoners' dilemma." That is, each individual soldier has an incentive to act in a way that is disastrous for the army as a whole. Accordingly, a central problem in military tactics is to establish a set of private incentives that will induce each individual soldier to act in the collective interest. Such an incentive structure requires enforcement, and such enforcement requires monitoring. For this reason, differential monitoring costs become a crucial ingredient in such tactical decisions as how to deploy forces, what military technology to use, what use to make of terrain—indeed how to conduct the entire war. We do not claim, of course, that monitoring costs are the *only* issues in tactical choices. We do claim that they are much more important than most military literature allows. We also claim that recognition of the intrinsic prisoners' dilemma problem in the military context is central to a proper military theory.

The economist may, of course, reply that all this is obvious—that anyone familiar with the modern theory of the firm is entirely aware of the importance of monitoring "worker performance" and that the incentive to shirk is no different in the military setting than it is in other sorts of labor markets. It seems to us, however, that this claim ignores the peculiar role that free-riding plays in the context of military theory. When firm competes against firm the central object in that competition is to outsell one's competitor: it is *not,* specifically, to "prise apart" the individuals who compose the competing firms. But that "prising apart" is precisely the central object in military confrontation. An army is not a single mass, but rather a collection of individuals connected to one another and their common purpose by an inherently fragile web. The aim of battle is not to annihilate the opposing mass, but to sever that web within it. This particular understanding is not, we think, a conventional one in military literature, where holistic methods of analysis are common. Nor, perhaps, is it entirely obvious. Yet it is an understanding that springs naturally from an individualistic approach to military science. And in our view, that individualistic approach is, here as elsewhere, the uniquely appropriate one for the study of human conduct.

REFERENCES

Buchanan, James, Robert Tollison and Gordon Tullock (eds.). 1980. *Toward a Theory of the Rent-Seeking Society.* College Station, TX: Texas A&M Press.

Du Picq, Armand. 1946. *Battle Studies.* Harrisburg, PA: Military Service Publishing Company.

Tullock, Gordon. 1973. *The Social Dilemma: The Economics of War and Revolution.* Blacksburg: University Publications.

Tullock, Gordon. 1980. *Trials on Trial.* New York: Columbia University Press.

NOTES

1. It may be complained that the two-person case is too small a scale to represent any interesting model of military reality. Two responses are possible. First, that military units are typically composed of sub-units and that the incentive structure here outlined is applicable to the decision makers for those sub-units, as well as for individuals *within* those sub-units. Second, that the relevant dimensions of the problem are *under*stated not overstated by focusing on the small numbers case. With larger numbers, the influence that any one individual so dier exercises on the outcome of battle tends to correspondingly lower, and hence the incentive to "free ride" correspondingly greater.

2. The territory can be assumed to be currently owned by other parties who cannot or will not defend themselves.

3. The case in which all soldiers on both sides run away is set aside. Presumably if this happened, the battle game would be replayed, until some outcome emerged.

4. There is a clear analogy here between battle and the general problem of "rent-seeking." See Buchanan et al. (1980) and Tullock (1980).

5. Interestingly enough, these psychological techniques of minimizing "shirking" seem relatively less significant in most market contexts—although international experience differs somewhat in this respect. In Japan, for example, there seems to be more attention to "morale" in this sense than in the U.S. or Europe.

6. Military decoration clearly has an intrinsic prestige value. It probably also has some financial value in addition (improvement future employment prospects, for example).

7. The British army was entirely a volunteer force: the lower ranks of the navy at this time were filled by conscription.

8. Du Picq's (1946, p. 169) diagnosis of this is beautifully to the point: "Moral reasons and no others make the soldier in a square feel himself stronger than when in a

line. He feels himself watched from behind and has nowhere to go."

9. We should note in this connection that, in modern times the night attack has rarely been used although it apparently represents an easy method of avoiding the aimed fire from rifles and machine guns. It is likely that the reason it has rarely been used is the impossibility of enforcing the advance by a dispersed body of men at night. In the 19th century when night attacks were more common, the formations were very dense and depended on very straight lines, frequently made straight by carrying a rope stretched between the two ends.

4 Property

At first blush the idea of property rights is puzzling. Although many people think that we are born with a moral right to the use of our body and our labor, very few people think that we are born with a right to exclusive ownership of external objects or resources. So an important question is how we might justify the right, moral or otherwise, to acquire exclusive ownership of external things.

John Locke begins with the assumption that people initially own the world's resources in common. He then suggests at least two justifications for why we should allow private ownership of what began as common resources. The first appeals to the idea that we own our bodies and our labor, and maintains that by "mixing our labor" with things we can come to own them as well. Locke's second justification is that without ownership we would be unlikely to cultivate natural resources, and improve them by creating things that people value. The same argument can be applied to the ideas created through intellectual labor. Without the ability to exclude people from freely adopting new ideas, there would likely be fewer incentives to create and package them in forms that other people can use. To varying degrees, this may be as true for works of art like literature and music as it is for physical objects like boats and spears. Locke famously attaches two provisos to the legitimate acquisition of property. The first is that when taking a natural resource from the commons we must leave "enough and as good for others," and the second is that we must make use of a resource "before it spoils." These appear to be fairness constraints on the legitimate acquisition of property. But they also raise new problems.

David Schmidtz asks how, in a world of scarcity, any original acquisition of property could satisfy Locke's "enough and as good" proviso. After all, in making something exclusively mine, haven't you been left with less, and in a way that makes you worse off than you were before my appropriation? Schmidtz thinks the question is only puzzling if we see the acquisition of property as a zero sum game: a situation in which gains for some entail losses for others, so that the gains and losses sum to zero. But the world is not always like that. Indeed, Locke's second argument for private property explains why: allowing people to have private property provides incentives to conserve or cultivate resources in ways that end up making nearly everyone better off.

Schmidtz introduces the "tragedy of the commons," a term coined by Garrett Hardin, to make his point. Commons tragedies occur when resources are commonly held, and when the benefits of use go to each person, but the costs are shared by everyone. Suppose twenty people hunt buffalo on a common prairie. Each buffalo gives each hunter 10 utility points, but as the buffalo edge toward extinction all hunters lose 100 utility points every time another buffalo bites the dust. If by killing a buffalo each hunter gains 10 points and loses only 5 points, it is individually rational to continue hunting at a rate that leaves everyone in the group worse off (notice that commons tragedies can often be modeled as *n*-person prisoner's dilemmas). According to Schmidtz, leaving resources as a commons rather than allowing people to take exclusive control of them can lead people violate the spirit of Locke's proviso—that is, it can lead people to use resources in ways that make others worse off than they would be under a system of private property.

David Hume argues that property rights can be fully explained and justified as mutually advantageous conventions, without the need to appeal (as Locke does) to pre-existing rights and moral provisos. The fact that we are all better off with property rights, than we would be without, is enough to make sense of why we would establish a convention of recognizing private property and enough to show that recognizing such rights is morally justified. Hume thinks of *justice* as the virtue of distributing property in a way that tends to maximize social welfare,[1] and sums up his view as follows:

> *What is a man's property?* Anything, which it is lawful for him, and for him alone, to use. *But what rule have we, by which we can distinguish these objects?* Here we must have recourse to statutes, customs, precedents, analogies, and a hundred other circumstances. . . . But the ultimate point, in which they all professedly terminate, is the interest and happiness of human society. Where this enters not into consideration, nothing can appear more whimsical, unnatural, and even superstitious, than...the laws of justice and of property.

Locke's notion of property rights as basic moral entitlements to use our bodies, labor and land in specified ways inspired classical liberal and libertarian philosophers who see property rights as protecting important spheres of liberty. Hume's idea of property rights as conventions for increasing social welfare anticipated many economists who see property rights as mechanisms for solving commons tragedies and incentivizing the preservation and development of valuable resources.

Not everybody follows Locke and Hume in emphasizing the virtues of property rights. Marx, for instance, thinks of the "benefits" of private property as depending on the owners of capital exploiting their workers and alienating them from their labor. Anticipating Marx's view, Rousseau says, provocatively, "The first person who, having enclosed a plot of land, took it into his head to say this is mine and found people simple enough to believe him was the true founder of civil society. What crimes, wars, murders, what miseries and horrors would the human race have been spared, had someone pulled up the stakes or filled in the ditch and cried out to his fellow men: 'Do not listen to this imposter. You are lost if you forget that the fruits of the earth belong to all and the earth to no one!'"

Needless to say, Marx and Rousseau's view of private property as an instrument for the powerful to dominate the powerless contrasts sharply with the views of Hume and Locke. Still, followers of Locke and Hume, no less than Marx and Rousseau, might well think that property rights have disproportionately benefited some, and failed to offer others compensating benefits. Beginning with Locke's assumption that the earth is, initially, the common property of all, and that property is justified by its ability to increase aggregate welfare, Thomas Paine argued that those who have been made worse off by the institution of property (and he thinks the poorest in civil society fall into that category) have a right to compensating benefits paid for by a tax on the use of natural resources.

NOTE

1. One can see why many utilitarians claim Hume as a forerunner, and why Jeremy Bentham said upon reading Hume, "I felt as if the scales had fallen from my eyes."

FURTHER READING

Demsetz, Harold. 1967. "Toward a Theory of Property Rights." *The American Economic Review* 57 (2): 347–359

Gaus, Gerald. 2012. "Property." *The Oxford Handbook of Political Philosophy*, edited by David Estlund. Oxford University Press.

Mack, Eric. 2013. "John Locke on Property." Online Library of Liberty. Liberty Fund, Inc. http://oll.libertyfund.org/pages/eric-mack-on-john-locke-on-property-january-2013

Narveson, Jan. 2010. "Property and Rights." *Social Philosophy and Policy* 27 (1): 101–134.

Railton, Peter. 1985. "Locke, Stock, and Peril: Natural Property Rights, Pollution, and Risk." In *Facts, Values and Norms*. Cambridge University Press, 2003 187–225.

Rose, Carol. 2009. "Liberty, Property, Environmentalism." *Social Philosophy and Policy* 26 (2): 1–25.

Sreenivasan, Gopal. 1995. *The Limits of Lockean Rights in Property*. Oxford University Press.

Van der Vossen, Bas. 2009. "What Counts as Original Appropriation?" *Politics, Philosophy, & Economics* 8 (4): 355–373.

Waldron, Jeremy. 1991. *The Right to Private Property*. Oxford University Press.

Wilson, James. 2012. "On the Value of the Intellectual Commons." In *New Frontiers in the Philosophy of Intellectual Property*, edited by Annabelle Lever. Cambridge University Press.

JOHN LOCKE

Of Property

1689

Sec. 26. God, who hath given the world to men in common, hath also given them reason to make use of it to the best advantage of life, and convenience. The earth, and all that is therein, is given to men for the support and comfort of their being. And tho' all the fruits it naturally produces, and beasts it feeds, belong to mankind in common, as they are produced by the spontaneous hand of nature; and no body has originally a private dominion, exclusive of the rest of mankind, in any of them, as they are thus in their natural state: yet being given for the use of men, there must of necessity be a means to appropriate them some way or other, before they can be of any use, or at all beneficial to any particular man. The fruit, or venison, which nourishes the wild Indian, who knows no enclosure, and is still a tenant in common, must be his, and so his, i.e. a part of him, that another can no longer have any right to it, before it can do him any good for the support of his life.

Sec. 27. Though the earth, and all inferior creatures, be common to all men, yet every man has a property in his own person: this no body has any

From John Locke, "Of Property," from *Two Treatises of Government*, Book II, ed. Thomas Hollis. London: A. Millar et al., 1764.

right to but himself. The labour of his body, and the work of his hands, we may say, are properly his. Whatsoever then he removes out of the state that nature hath provided, and left it in, he hath mixed his labour with, and joined to it something that is his own, and thereby makes it his property. It being by him removed from the common state nature hath placed it in, it hath by this labour something annexed to it, that excludes the common right of other men: for this labour being the unquestionable property of the labourer, no man but he can have a right to what that is once joined to, at least where there is enough, and as good, left in common for others.

Sec. 28. He that is nourished by the acorns he picked up under an oak, or the apples he gathered from the trees in the wood, has certainly appropriated them to himself. No body can deny but the nourishment is his. I ask then, when did they begin to be his? when he digested? or when he eat? or when he boiled? or when he brought them home? or when he picked them up? and it is plain, if the first gathering made them not his, nothing else could. That labour put a distinction between them and common: that added something to them more than nature, the common mother of all, had done; and so they became his private right. And will any one say, he had no right to those acorns or apples, he thus appropriated, because he had not the consent of all mankind to make them his? Was it a robbery thus to assume to himself what belonged to all in common? If such a consent as that was necessary, man had starved, notwithstanding the plenty God had given him. We see in commons, which remain so by compact, that it is the taking any part of what is common, and removing it out of the state nature leaves it in, which begins the property; without which the common is of no use. And the taking of this or that part, does not depend on the express consent of all the commoners. Thus the grass my horse has bit; the turfs my servant has cut; and the ore I have digged in any place, where I have a right to them in common with others, become my property, without the assignation or consent of any body. The labour that was mine, removing them out of that common state they were in, hath fixed my property in them.

Sec. 29. By making an explicit consent of every commoner, necessary to any one's appropriating to himself any part of what is given in common, children or servants could not cut the meat, which their father or master had provided for them in common, without assigning to every one his peculiar part. Though the water running in the fountain be every one's, yet who can doubt, but that in the pitcher is his only who drew it out? His labour hath taken it out of the hands of nature, where it was common, and belonged equally to all her children, and hath thereby appropriated it to himself.

Sec. 30. Thus this law of reason makes the deer that Indian's who hath killed it; it is allowed to be his goods, who hath bestowed his labour upon it, though before it was the common right of every one. And amongst those who are counted the civilized part of mankind, who have made and multiplied positive laws to determine property, this original law of nature, for the beginning of property, in what was before common, still takes place; and by virtue thereof, what fish any one catches in the ocean, that great and still remaining common of mankind; or what ambergrise[1] any one takes up here, is by the labour that removes it out of that common state nature left it in, made his property, who takes that pains about it. And even amongst us, the hare that any one is hunting, is thought his who pursues her during the chase: for being a beast that is still looked upon as common, and no man's private possession; whoever has employed so much labour about any of that kind, as to find and pursue her, has thereby removed her from the state of nature, wherein she was common, and hath begun a property.

Sec. 31. It will perhaps be objected to this, that if gathering the acorns, or other fruits of the earth, &c. makes a right to them, then any one may ingross as much as he will. To which I answer, Not so. The same law of nature, that does by this means give us property, does also bound that property too. God has given us all things richly, 1 Tim. vi. 12. is the voice of reason confirmed by inspiration. But how far has he given it us? To enjoy. As much as any one can make use of to any advantage of life before it spoils, so much he may by his labour fix a property in: whatever is beyond this, is more than his share, and belongs to others. Nothing was made by God for man to spoil or destroy. And thus, considering the plenty of natural provisions there was a long time in the world, and the few spenders; and to how small a part of that provision the industry of one man could extend itself, and ingross it to the prejudice of others; especially keeping within the bounds, set by reason, of what might serve for his use; there could be then little room for quarrels or contentions about property so established.

Sec. 32. But the chief matter of property being now not the fruits of the earth, and the beasts that subsist on it, but the earth itself; as that which takes in and carries with it all the rest; I think it is plain, that property in that too is acquired as the former. As much land as a man tills, plants, improves, cultivates, and can use the product of, so much is his property. He by his labour does, as it were, inclose it from the common. Nor will it invalidate his right, to say every body else has an equal title to it; and therefore he cannot appropriate, he cannot inclose, without the consent of all his fellow-commoners, all mankind. God, when he gave the world in common to all mankind, commanded man also to labour, and the penury of his condition required it of him. God and his reason commanded him to subdue the earth, i.e. improve it for the benefit of life, and therein lay out something upon it that was his own, his labour. He that in obedience to this command of God, subdued, tilled and sowed any part of it, thereby annexed to it something that was his property, which another had no title to, nor could without injury take from him.

NOTE

1. Ambergrise is a substance extracted from animals and used as perfume.

DAVID HUME

Of Justice and Property

1751

PART 1

That justice is useful to society, and consequently that *part* of its merit, at least, must arise from that consideration, it would be a superfluous undertaking to prove. That public utility is the *sole* origin of justice, and that reflections on the beneficial consequences of this virtue are the *sole* foundation of its merit; this proposition, being more curious and important, will better deserve our examination and enquiry.

Let us suppose, that nature has bestowed on the human race such profuse *abundance* of all *external* conveniencies, that, without any uncertainty in the event, without any care or industry on our part, every individual finds himself fully provided with whatever his most voracious appetites can want, or luxurious imagination wish or desire. His natural beauty, we shall suppose, surpasses all acquired ornaments: The perpetual clemency of the seasons renders useless all cloaths or covering: The raw herbage affords him the most delicious fare; the clear fountain, the richest beverage. No laborious occupation required: No tillage: No navigation. Music, poetry, and contemplation form his sole business: Conversation, mirth, and friendship his sole amusement.

From David Hume and L. A. Selby-Bigge, *Enquiries Concerning the Human Understanding and Concerning the Principles of Morals*. Oxford: Clarendon Press, 1902.

It seems evident, that, in such a happy state, every other social virtue would flourish, and receive tenfold encrease; but the cautious, jealous virtue of justice would never once have been dreamed of. For what purpose make a partition of goods, where every one has already more than enough? Why give rise to property, where there cannot possibly be any injury? Why call this object *mine,* when, upon the seizing of it by another, I need but stretch out my hand to possess myself of what is equally valuable? Justice, in that case, being totally USELESS, would be an idle ceremonial, and could never possibly have place in the catalogue of virtues.

We see, even in the present necessitous condition of mankind, that, wherever any benefit is bestowed by nature in an unlimited abundance, we leave it always in common among the whole human race, and make no subdivisions of right and property. Water and air, though the most necessary of all objects, are not challenged as the property of individuals; nor can any man commit injustice by the most lavish use and enjoyment of these blessings. In fertile extensive countries, with few inhabitants, land is regarded on the same footing. And no topic is so much insisted on by those, who defend the liberty of the seas, as the unexhausted use of them in navigation. Were the advantages, procured by navigation, as inexhaustible, these reasoners had never had any adversaries to refute; nor had any claims ever been advanced of a separate, exclusive dominion over the ocean.

It may happen, in some countries, at some periods, that there be established a property in water, none in land; if the latter be in greater abundance than can be used by the inhabitants, and the former be found, with difficulty, and in very small quantities.

Again; suppose, that, though the necessities of human race continue the same as at present, yet the mind is so enlarged, and so replete with friendship and generosity, that every man has the utmost tenderness for every man, and feels no more concern for his own interest than for that of his fellows: It seems evident, that the USE of justice would, in this case, be suspended by such an extensive benevolence, nor would the divisions and barriers of property and obligation have ever been thought of. Why should I bind another, by a deed or promise, to do me any good office, when I know that he is already prompted, by the strongest inclination, to seek my happiness, and would, of himself, perform the desired service; except the hurt, he thereby receives, be greater than the benefit accruing to me? In which case, he knows, that, from my innate humanity and friendship, I should be the first to oppose myself to his imprudent generosity. Why raise land-marks between my neighbour's field and mine, when my heart has made no division between our interests; but shares all his joys and sorrows with the same force and vivacity as if originally my own? Every man, upon this supposition, being a second self to another, would trust all his interests to the discretion of every man; without jealousy, without partition, without distinction. And the whole human race would form only one family; where all would lie in common, and be used freely, without regard to property; but cautiously too, with as entire regard to the necessities of each individual, as if our own interests were most intimately concerned.

In the present disposition of the human heart, it would, perhaps, be difficult to find compleat instances of such enlarged affections; but still we may observe, that the case of families approaches towards it; and the stronger the mutual benevolence is among the individuals, the nearer it approaches; till all distinction of property be, in a great measure, lost and confounded among them. Between married persons, the cement of friendship is by the laws supposed so strong as to abolish all division of possessions; and has often, in reality, the force ascribed to it. And it is observable, that, during the ardour of new enthusiasms, when every principle is enflamed into extravagance, the community of goods has frequently been attempted; and nothing but experience of its inconveniencies, from the returning or disguised selfishness of men, could make the imprudent fanatics adopt anew the ideas of justice and of separate property. So true is it, that this virtue derives its existence entirely from its necessary *use* to the intercourse and social state of mankind.

To make this truth more evident, let us reverse the foregoing suppositions; and carrying every thing to the opposite extreme, consider what would be the effect of these new situations. Suppose a society to fall into such want of all common necessaries, that the utmost frugality and industry cannot preserve the greater number from perishing, and the whole from extreme misery: It will readily, I believe, be admitted, that the strict laws of justice are suspended, in such a pressing emergence, and give place to the stronger motives of necessity and self-preservation. Is it any crime, after a shipwreck, to seize whatever means or instrument of safety one can lay hold of, without regard to former limitations of property? Or if a city besieged were perishing with hunger; can we imagine, that men will see any means of preservation before them, and lose their lives, from a scrupulous regard to what, in other situations, would be the rules of equity and justice? The USE and TENDENCY of that virtue is to procure happiness and security, by preserving order in society: But where the society is ready to perish from extreme necessity, no greater evil can be dreaded from violence and injustice; and every man may now provide for himself by all the means, which prudence can dictate, or humanity permit. The public, even in less urgent necessities, opens granaries, without the consent of proprietors; as justly supposing, that the authority of magistracy may, consistent with equity, extend so far: But were any number of men to assemble, without the tye of laws or civil jurisdiction; would an equal partition of bread in a famine, though effected by power and even violence, be regarded as criminal or injurious?

Suppose likewise, that it should be a virtuous man's fate to fall into the society of ruffians, remote from the protection of laws and government; what conduct must he embrace in that melancholy situation? He sees such a desperate rapaciousness prevail; such a disregard to equity, such contempt of order, such stupid blindness to future consequences, as must immediately have the most tragical conclusion, and must terminate in destruction to the greater number, and in a total dissolution of society to the rest. He, mean while, can have no other expedient than to arm himself, to whomever the sword he seizes, or the buckler, may belong: To make provision of all means of defence and security: And his particular regard to justice being no longer of USE to his own safety or that of others, he must consult the dictates of self-preservation alone, without concern for those who no longer merit his care and attention.

When any man, even in political society, renders himself, by his crimes, obnoxious to the public, he is punished by the laws in his goods and person; that is, the ordinary rules of justice are, with regard to him, suspended for a moment, and it becomes equitable to inflict on him, for the *benefit* of society, what, otherwise, he could not suffer without wrong or injury.

The rage and violence of public war; what is it but a suspension of justice among the warring parties, who perceive, that this virtue is now no longer of any *use* or advantage to them? The laws of war, which then succeed to those of equity and justice, are rules calculated for the *advantage* and *utility* of that, particular state, in which men axe now placed. And were a civilized nation engaged with barbarians, who observed no rules even of war; the former must also suspend their observance of them, where they no longer serve to any purpose; and must render every action or rencounter as bloody and pernicious as possible to the first aggressors.

Thus, the rules of equity or justice depend entirely on the particular state and condition, in which men are placed, and owe their origin and existence to that UTILITY, which results to the public from their strict and regular observance. Reverse, in any considerable circumstance, the condition of men: Produce extreme abundance or extreme necessity: Implant in the human breast perfect moderation and humanity, or perfect rapaciousness and malice: By rendering justice totally *useless,* you thereby totally destroy its essence, and suspend its obligation upon mankind.

The common situation of society is a medium amidst all these extremes. We are naturally partial to ourselves, and to our friends; but are capable of learning the advantage resulting from a more equitable conduct. Few enjoyments are given us from the open and liberal hand of nature; but by art, labour, and industry, we can extract them in great abundance. Hence the ideas of property become necessary in all civil society: Hence justice derives its usefulness to the public: And hence alone arises its merit and moral obligation.

These conclusions are so natural and obvious, that they have not escaped even the poets, in their descriptions of the felicity, attending the golden age or the reign of SATURN. The seasons, in that first period of nature, were so temperate, if we credit these agreeable fictions, that there was no necessity for men to provide themselves with cloaths and houses, as a security against the violence of heat and cold: The rivers flowed with wine and milk: The oaks yielded honey; and nature spontaneously produced her greatest delicacies. Nor were these the chief advantages of that happy age. Tempests were not alone removed from nature; but those more furious tempests were unknown to human breasts, which now cause such uproar, and engender such confusion. Avarice, ambition, cruelty, selfishness, were never heard of: Cordial affection, compassion, sympathy, were the only movements with which the mind was yet acquainted. Even the punctilious distinction of *mine* and *thine* was banished from among that happy race of mortals, and carried with it the very notion of property and obligation, justice and injustice.

This *poetical* fiction of the *golden age* is, in some respects, of a piece with the *philosophical* fiction of the *state of nature;* only that the former is represented as the most charming and most peaceable condition, which can possibly be imagined; whereas the latter is painted out as a state of mutual war and violence, attended with the most extreme necessity. On the first origin of mankind, we are told, their ignorance and savage nature were so prevalent, that they could give no mutual trust, but must each depend upon himself, and his own force or cunning for protection and security. No law was heard of: No rule of justice known: No distinction of property regarded: Power was the only measure of right; and a perpetual war of all against all was the result of men's untamed selfishness and barbarity.

Whether such a condition of human nature could ever exist, or if it did, could continue so long as to merit the appellation of a *state,* may justly be doubted. Men are necessarily born in a family-society, at least; and are trained up by their parents to some rule of conduct and behaviour. But this must be admitted, that, if such a state of mutual war and violence was ever real, the suspension of all laws of justice, from their absolute inutility, is a necessary and infallible consequence.

The more we vary our views of human life, and the newer and more unusual the lights are, in which we survey it, the more shall we be convinced, that the origin here assigned for the virtue of justice is real and satisfactory.

Were there a species of creatures, intermingled with men, which, though rational, were possessed of such inferior strength, both of body and mind, that they were incapable of all resistance, and could never, upon the highest provocation, make us feel the effects of their resentment; the necessary consequence, I think, is, that we should be bound, by the laws of humanity, to give gentle usage to these creatures, but should not, properly speaking, lie under any restraint of justice with regard to them, nor could they possess any right or property, exclusive of such arbitrary lords. Our intercourse with them could not be called society, which supposes a degree of equality; but absolute command on the one side, and servile obedience on the other. Whatever we covet, they must instantly resign: Our permission is the only tenure, by which they hold their possessions: Our compassion and kindness the only check, by which they curb our lawless will: And as no inconvenience ever results from the exercise of a power, so firmly established in nature, the restraints of justice and property, being totally *useless,* would never have place in so unequal a confederacy.

This is plainly the situation of men, with regard to animals; and how far these may be said to possess reason, I leave it to others to determine. The great superiority of civilized EUROPEANS above barbarous INDIANS, tempted us to imagine ourselves on the same footing with regard to them, and made us throw off all restraints of justice, and even of humanity, in our treatment of them. In many nations, the female sex are reduced to like slavery, and are rendered incapable of all property, in opposition to their lordly masters. But though the males, when united, have, in all countries, bodily force sufficient to maintain this severe tyranny; yet such are the insinuation, address, and charms of their fair companions, that women are commonly able to break the confederacy, and share with the other sex in all the rights and privileges of society.

Were the human species so framed by nature as that each individual possessed within himself every faculty, requisite both for his own preservation and for the propagation of his kind: Were all society and intercourse cut off between man and man, by the primary intention of the Supreme Creator: It seems evident, that so solitary a being would be as much incapable of justice, as of social discourse and conversation. Where mutual regards and forbearance serve to no manner of purpose, they would never direct the conduct of any reasonable man. The headlong course of the passions would be checked by no reflection on future consequences. And as each man is here supposed to love himself alone, and to depend only on himself and his own activity for safety and happiness, he would, on every occasion, to the utmost of his power, challenge the preference above every other being, to none of which he is bound by any ties, either of nature or of interest.

But suppose the conjunction of the sexes to be established in nature, a family immediately arises; and particular rules being found requisite for its subsistence, these are immediately embraced; though without comprehending the rest of mankind within their prescriptions. Suppose, that several families unite together into one society, which is totally disjoined from all others, the rules, which preserve peace and order, enlarge themselves to the utmost extent of that society; but becoming then entirely useless, lose their force when carried one step farther. But again suppose, that several distinct societies maintain a kind of intercourse for mutual convenience and advantage, the boundaries of justice still grow larger, in proportion to the largeness of men's views, and the force of their mutual connexions. History, experience, reason sufficiently instruct us in this natural progress of human sentiments, and in the gradual enlargement of our regards to justice, in proportion as we become acquainted with the extensive utility of that virtue.

PART 2

If we examine the *particular* laws, by which justice is directed, and property determined; we shall still be presented with the same conclusion. The good of mankind is the only object of all these laws and regulations. Not only it is requisite, for the peace and interest of society, that men's possessions should be separated; but the rules, which we follow, in making the separation, are such as can best be contrived to serve farther the interests of society.

We shall suppose, that a creature, possessed of reason, but unacquainted with human nature, deliberates with himself what RULES of justice or property would best promote public interest, and establish peace and security among mankind: His most obvious thought would be, to assign the largest possessions to the most extensive virtue, and give every one the power of doing good, proportioned to his inclination. In a perfect theocracy, where a being, infinitely intelligent, governs by particular volitions, this rule would certainly have place, and might serve to the wisest purposes: But were mankind to execute such a law; so great is the uncertainty of merit, both from its natural obscurity, and from the self-conceit of each individual, that no determinate rule of conduct would ever result from it; and the total dissolution of society must be the immediate consequence. Fanatics may suppose, *that dominion is founded on grace*, and *that saints alone inherit the earth*; but the civil magistrate very justly puts these sublime theorists on the same footing with common robbers, and teaches them by the severest discipline, that a rule, which, in speculation, may seem the most advantageous to society, may yet be found, in practice, totally pernicious and destructive.

That there were *religious* fanatics of this kind in ENGLAND, during the civil wars, we learn from history; though it is probable, that the obvious *tendency* of these principles excited such horror in mankind, as soon obliged the dangerous enthusiasts to renounce, or at least conceal their tenets. Perhaps, the *levellers,* who claimed an equal distribution of property, were a kind of *political* fanatics, which arose from the religious species, and more openly avowed their pretensions; as carrying a more plausible appearance, of being practicable in themselves, as well as useful to human society.

It must, indeed, be confessed, that nature is so liberal to mankind, that, were all her presents equally divided among the species, and improved by art and industry, every individual would enjoy all the necessaries, and even most of the comforts of life; nor would ever be liable to any ills, but such as might accidentally arise from the sickly frame and constitution of his body. It must also be confessed, that, wherever we depart from this equality, we rob the poor of more satisfaction than we add to the rich, and that the slight gratification of a frivolous vanity, in one individual, frequently costs more than bread to many families, and even provinces. It may appear withal, that the rule of equality, as it would be highly *useful*, is not altogether *impracticable*; but has taken place, at least in an imperfect degree, in some republics; particularly that of SPARTA; where it was attended, it is said, with the most beneficial consequences. Not to mention, that the AGRARIAN laws, so frequently claimed in ROME, and carried into execution in many GREEK cities, proceeded, all of them, from a general idea of the utility of this principle.

But historians, and even common sense, may inform us, that, however specious these ideas of *perfect* equality may seem, they are really, at bottom, *impracticable*; and were they not so, would be extremely *pernicious* to human society. Render possessions ever so equal, men's different degrees of art, care, and industry will immediately break that equality. Or if you check these virtues, you reduce society to the most extreme indigence; and instead of preventing want and beggary in a few, render it unavoidable to the whole community. The most rigorous inquisition too is requisite to watch every inequality on its first appearance; and the most severe jurisdiction, to punish and redress it. But besides, that so much authority must soon degenerate into tyranny, and be exerted with great partialities; who can possibly be possessed of it, in such a situation as is here supposed? Perfect equality of possessions, destroying all subordination, weakens extremely the authority of magistracy, and must reduce all power nearly to a level, as well as property.

We may conclude, therefore, that, in order to establish laws for the regulation of property, we must be acquainted with the nature and situation of man; must reject appearances, which may be false, though specious; and must search for those rules, which are, on the whole, most *useful* and *beneficial*. Vulgar sense and slight experience are sufficient for this purpose; where men give not way to too selfish avidity, or too extensive enthusiasm.

Who sees not, for instance, that whatever is produced or improved by a man's art or industry ought, for ever, to be secured to him, in order to give encouragement to such *useful* habits and accomplishments? That the property ought also to descend to children and relations, for the same *useful* purpose? That it may be alienated by consent, in order to beget that commerce and intercourse, which is so *beneficial* to human society? And that all contracts and promises ought carefully to be fulfilled, in order to secure mutual trust and confidence, by which the general *interest* of mankind is so much promoted?

Examine the writers on the laws of nature; and you will always find, that, whatever principles they set out with, they are sure to terminate here at last, and to assign, as the ultimate reason for every rule which they establish, the convenience and necessities of mankind. A concession thus extorted, in opposition to systems, has more authority, than if it had been made in prosecution of them.

What other reason, indeed, could writers ever give, why this must be *mine* and that *yours*; since uninstructed nature, surely, never made any such distinction? The objects, which receive those appellations, are, of themselves, foreign to us; they are totally disjoined and separated from us; and nothing but the general interests of society can form the connexion.

Sometimes, the interests of society may require a rule of justice in a particular case; but may not determine any particular rule, among several, which are all equally beneficial. In that case, the slightest *analogies* are laid hold of, in order to prevent that indifference and ambiguity, which would be the source of perpetual dissention. Thus possession alone, and first possession, is supposed to convey property, where no body else has any preceding claim and pretension. Many of the reasonings of lawyers are of this analogical nature, and depend on very slight connexions of the imagination.

Does any one scruple, in extraordinary cases, to violate all regard to the private property of individuals, and sacrifice to public interest a distinction, which had been established for the sake of that interest? The safety of the people is the supreme law: All other particular laws are subordinate to it, and dependent on it: And if, in the *common* course of things, they be followed and regarded; it is only because the public safety and interest *commonly* demand so equal and impartial an administration.

Sometimes both *utility* and *analogy* fail, and leave the laws of justice in total uncertainty. Thus, it is highly requisite, that prescription or long possession should convey property; but what number of days or months or years should be sufficient for that purpose, it is impossible for reason alone to determine. *Civil laws* here supply the place of the natural *code,* and assign different terms for prescription, according to the different *utilities,* proposed by the legislator. Bills of exchange and promissory notes, by the laws of most countries, prescribe sooner than bonds, and mortgages, and contracts of a more formal nature.

In general, we may observe, that all questions of property are subordinate to the authority of civil laws, which extend, restrain, modify, and alter the rules of natural justice, according to the particular *convenience* of each community. The laws have, or ought to have, a constant reference to the constitution of government, the manners, the climate, the religion, the commerce, the situation of each society. A late author of genius, as well as learning, has prosecuted this subject at large, and has established, from these principles, a system of political knowledge, which abounds in ingenious and brilliant thoughts, and is not wanting in solidity.

What is a man's property? Any thing, which it is lawful for him, and for him alone, to use. *But what rule have we, by which we can distinguish these objects?* Here we must have recourse to statutes, customs, precedents, analogies, and a hundred other circumstances; some of which are constant and inflexible, some variable and arbitrary. But the ultimate point, in which they all professedly terminate, is, the interest and happiness of human society. Where this enters not into consideration, nothing can appear more whimsical, unnatural, and even superstitious, than all or most of the laws of justice and of property.

Those, who ridicule vulgar superstitions, and expose the folly of particular regards to meats, days, places, postures, apparel, have an easy task; while they consider all the qualities and relations of the objects, and discover no adequate cause for that affection or antipathy, veneration or horror, which have so mighty an influence over a considerable part of mankind. A SYRIAN would have starved rather than taste pigeon; an EGYPTIAN would not have approached bacon: But if these species of food be examined by the senses of sight, smell, or taste, or scrutinized by the sciences of chymistry, medicine, or physics; no difference is ever found between them and any other species, nor can that precise circumstance be pitched on, which may afford a just foundation for the religious passion. A fowl on Thursday is lawful food; on Friday abominable: Eggs, in this house, and in this diocese, are permitted during lent; a hundred paces farther, to eat them is a damnable sin. This earth or building, yesterday was profane; to-day, by the muttering of certain words, it has become holy and sacred. Such reflections as these, in the mouth of a philosopher, one may safely say, are too obvious to have any influence; because they must always, to every man, occur at first sight; and where they prevail not, of themselves, they are surely obstructed by education, prejudice, and passion, not by ignorance or mistake.

It may appear to a careless view, or rather, a too abstracted reflection, that there enters a like superstition into all the sentiments of justice; and that, if a man expose its object, or what we call property, to the same scrutiny of sense and science, he will not, by the most accurate enquiry, find any foundation for the difference made by moral sentiment. I may lawfully nourish myself from this tree; but the fruit of another of the same species, ten paces off, it is criminal for me to touch. Had I worne this apparel an hour ago, I had merited the severest punishment; but a man, by pronouncing a few magical syllables, has now rendered it fit for my use and service. Were this house placed in the neighbouring territory, it had been immoral for me to dwell in it; but being built on this side the river, it is subject to a different municipal law, and, by its becoming mine, I incur no blame or censure. The same species of reasoning, it may be thought, which so successfully exposes superstition, is also applicable to justice; nor is it possible, in the one case more than in the other, to point out, in the object, that precise quality or circumstance, which is the foundation of the sentiment.

But there is this material difference between *superstition* and *justice,* that the former is frivolous, useless, and burdensome; the latter is absolutely requisite to the well-being of mankind and existence of society. When we abstract from this circumstance (for it is too apparent ever to be overlooked) it must be confessed, that all regards to right and property, seem entirely without foundation, as much as the grossest and most vulgar superstition. Were the interests of society nowise concerned, it is as unintelligible, why another's articulating certain sounds, implying consent, should change the nature of my actions with regard to a particular object, as why the reciting of a liturgy by a priest, in a certain habit and posture, should dedicate a heap of brick and timber, and render it, thenceforth and for ever, sacred.

These reflections are far from weakening the obligations of justice, or diminishing any thing from the most sacred attention to property. On the contrary, such sentiments must acquire new force from the present reasoning. For what stronger foundation can be desired or conceived for any duty, than to observe, that human society, or even human nature could not subsist, without the establishment of it; and will still arrive at greater degrees of happiness and perfection, the more inviolable the regard is, which is paid to that duty?

The dilemma seems obvious: As justice evidently tends to promote public utility and to support civil society, the sentiment of justice is either derived from our reflecting on that tendency, or like hunger, thirst, and other appetites, resentment, love of life, attachment to offspring, and other passions, arises from a simple original instinct in the human breast, which nature has implanted for like salutary purposes. If the latter be the case, it follows, that property, which is the object of justice, is also distinguished by a simple, original instinct, and is not ascertained by any argument or reflection. But who is there that ever heard of such an instinct? Or is this a subject, in which new discoveries can be made? We may as well expect to discover, in the body, new senses, which had before escaped the observation of all mankind.

But farther, though it seems a very simple proposition to say, that nature, by an instinctive sentiment, distinguishes property, yet in reality we shall find, that there are required for that purpose ten thousand different instincts, and these employed about objects of the greatest intricacy and nicest discernment. For when a definition of *property* is required, that relation is found to resolve itself into any possession acquired by occupation, by industry, by prescription, by inheritance, by contract, &c. Can we think, that nature, by an original instinct, instructs us in all these methods of acquisition?

These words too, *inheritance* and *contract,* stand for ideas infinitely complicated; and to define them exactly, a hundred volumes of laws, and a thousand volumes of commentators, have not been found sufficient. Does nature, whose instincts in men are all simple, embrace such complicated and artificial objects, and create a rational creature, without trusting any thing to the operation of his reason?

But even though all this were admitted, it would not be satisfactory. Positive laws can certainly transfer property. Is it by another original instinct, that we recognize the authority of kings and senates, and mark all the boundaries of their jurisdiction? Judges too, even though their sentence be erroneous and illegal, must be allowed, for the sake of peace and order, to have decisive authority, and ultimately to determine property. Have we original, innate ideas of prætors and chancellors and juries? Who sees not, that all these institutions arise merely from the necessities of human society?

All birds of the same species, in every age and country, build their nests alike: In this we see the force of instinct. Men, in different times and places, frame their houses differently: Here we perceive the influence of reason and custom. A like inference may be drawn from comparing the instinct of generation and the institution of property.

How great soever the variety of municipal laws, it must be confessed, that their chief outlines pretty regularly concur; because the purposes, to which they tend, are every where exactly similar. In like manner, all houses have a roof and walls, windows and chimneys; though diversified in their shape, figure, and materials. The purposes of the latter, directed to the conveniencies of human life, discover not more plainly their origin from reason and reflection, than do those of the former, which point all to a like end.

I need not mention the variations, which all the rules of property receive from the finer turns and connexions of the imagination, and from the subtilties and abstractions of law-topics and reasonings. There is no possibility of reconciling this observation to the notion of original instincts.

What alone will beget a doubt concerning the theory, on which I insist, is the influence of education and acquired habits, by which we are so accustomed to blame injustice, that we are not, in every instance, conscious of any immediate reflection on the pernicious consequences of it. The views the most familiar to us are apt, for that very reason, to escape us; and what we have very frequently performed from certain motives, we are apt likewise to continue mechanically, without recalling, on every occasion, the reflections, which first determined us. The convenience, or rather necessity, which leads to justice, is so universal, and every where points so much to the same rules, that the habit takes place in all societies; and it is not without some scrutiny, that we are able to ascertain its true origin. The matter, however, is not so obscure, but that, even in common life, we have, every moment, recourse to the principle of public utility, and ask, *What must become of the world, if such practices prevail? How could society subsist under such disorders?* Were the distinction or separation of possessions entirely useless, can any one conceive, that it ever should have obtained in society?

Thus we seem, upon the whole, to have attained a knowledge of the force of that principle here insisted on, and can determine what degree of esteem or moral approbation may result from reflections on public interest and utility. The necessity of justice to the support of society is the SOLE foundation of that virtue; and since no moral excellence is more highly esteemed, we may conclude, that this circumstance of usefulness has, in general, the strongest energy, and most entire command over our sentiments. It must, therefore, be the source of a considerable part of the merit ascribed to humanity, benevolence, friendship, public spirit, and other social virtues of that stamp; as it is the SOLE source of the moral approbation paid to fidelity, justice, veracity, integrity, and those other estimable and useful qualities and principles. It is entirely agreeable to the rules of philosophy, and even of common reason; where any principle has been found to have a great force and energy in one instance, to ascribe to it a like energy in all similar instances. This indeed is NEWTON's chief rule of philosophizing.

KARL MARX

Capital: "Primitive Accumulation"

1867

We have seen how money is changed into capital; how through capital surplus-value is made, and from surplus-value more capital. But the accumulation of capital presupposes surplus-value; surplus-value presupposes capitalistic production; capitalistic production presupposes the preexistence of considerable masses of capital and of labour-power in the hands of producers of commodities. The whole movement,

Karl Marx, "The Secret of Primitive Accumulation," from *Capital: A Critique of Political Economy. Volume I: The Process of Capitalist Production*, translated from the 3rd German edition by Samuel Moore and Edward Aveling, ed. Frederick Engels. Revised and amplified according to the 4th German edition by Ernest Untermann. Chicago: Charles H. Kerr and Co., 1909.

therefore, seems to turn in a vicious circle, out of which we can only get by supposing a primitive accumulation (previous accumulation of Adam Smith) preceding capitalistic accumulation; an accumulation not the result of the capitalist mode of production, but its starting point.

This primitive accumulation plays in Political Economy about the same part as original sin in theology. Adam bit the apple, and thereupon sin fell on the human race. Its origin is supposed to be explained when it is told as an anecdote of the past. In times long gone by there were two sorts of people; one, the diligent, intelligent, and, above all, frugal élite; the other, lazy rascals, spending their substance, and more, in riotous living. The legend of the logical original sin tells us certainly how man came to be condemned to eat his bread in the sweat of his brow; but the history of economic original sin reveals to us that there are people to whom this is by no means essential. Never mind! Thus it came to pass that the former sort accumulated wealth, and the latter sort had at last nothing to sell except their own skins. And from this original sin dates the poverty of the great majority that, despite all its labour, has up to now nothing to sell but itself, and the wealth of the few that increases constantly although they have long ceased to work. Such insipid childishness is every day preached to us in the defence of property . . . But as soon as the question of property crops up, it becomes a sacred duty to proclaim the intellectual food of the infant as the one thing fit for all ages and for all stages of development. In actual history it is notorious that conquest, enslavement, robbery, murder, briefly force, play the great part. In the tender annals of Political Economy, the idyllic reigns from all time immemorial. Right and "labour" were from all time the sole means of enrichment, the present year of course always excepted. As a matter of fact, the methods of primitive accumulation are anything but idyllic.

In themselves, money and commodities are no more capital than are the means of production and of subsistence. They want transforming into capital. But this transformation itself can only take place under certain circumstances that centre in this, *viz.*, that two very different kinds of commodity-possessors must come face to face and into contact; on the one hand, the owners of money, means of production, means of subsistence, who are eager to increase the sum of values they possess, by buying other people's labour-power; on the other hand, free labourers, the sellers of their own labour-power, and therefore the sellers of labour. Free labourers, in the double sense that neither they themselves form part and parcel of the means of production, as in the case of slaves, bondsmen, &c., nor do the means of production belong to them, as in the case of peasant-proprietors; they are, therefore, free from, unencumbered by, any means of production of their own. With this polarisation of the market for commodities, the fundamental conditions of capitalist production are given. The capitalist system presupposes the complete separation of the labourers from all property in the means by which they can realise their labour. As soon as capitalist production is once on its own legs, it not only maintains this separation, but reproduces it on a continually extending scale. The process, therefore, that clears the way for the capitalist system, can be none other than the process which takes away from the labourer the possession of his means of production; a process that transforms, on the one hand, the social means of subsistence and of production into capital, on the other, the immediate producers into wage-labourers. The so-called primitive accumulation, therefore, is nothing else than the historical process of divorcing the producer from the means of production. It appears as primitive, because it forms the pre-historic stage of capital and of the mode of production corresponding with it.

The economic structure of capitalistic society has grown out of the economic structure of feudal society. The dissolution of the latter set free the elements of the former.

The immediate producer, the labourer, could only dispose of his own person after he had ceased to be attached to the soil and ceased to be the slave, serf, or bondman of another. To become a free seller of labour-power, who carries his commodity wherever he finds a market, he must further have escaped from the regime of the guilds, their rules for apprentices and journeymen, and the impediments of their labour regulations. Hence, the historical movement which changes the producers into wage-workers, appears, on the one hand, as their emancipation from serfdom and from the fetters of the guilds, and this side alone exists for our bourgeois historians. But, on the other hand, these new freedmen became sellers of themselves only after they had been robbed of all their own means of production, and of all the guarantees of existence afforded by the old feudal arrangements. And the history of this, their expropriation, is written in the annals of mankind in letters of blood and fire.

The industrial capitalists, these new potentates, had on their part not only to displace the guild masters of handicrafts, but also the feudal lords, the possessors of the sources of wealth. In this respect their conquest of social power appears as the fruit of a victorious struggle both against feudal lordship and its revolting prerogatives, and against the guilds and the fetters they laid on the free development of production and the free exploitation of man by man. The chevaliers d'industrie, however, only succeed in supplanting the chevaliers of the sword by making use of events of which they themselves were wholly innocent. They have risen by means as vile as those by which the Roman freed-man once on a time made himself the master of his *patronus*.

The starting-point of the development that gave rise to the wage-labourer as well as to the capitalist, was the servitude of the labourer. The advance consisted in a change of form of this servitude, in the transformation of feudal exploitation into capitalist exploitation. To understand its march, we need not go back very far. Although we come across the first beginnings of capitalist production as early as the 14th or 15th century, sporadically, in certain towns of the Mediterranean, the capitalistic era dates from the 16th century. Wherever it appears, the abolition of serfdom has been long effected, and the highest development of the middle ages, the existence of sovereign towns, has been long on the wane.

In the history of primitive accumulation, all revolutions are epoch-making that act as levers for the capitalist class in course of formation; but, above all, those moments when great masses of men are suddenly and forcibly torn from their means of subsistence, and hurled as free and "unattached" proletarians on the labour market. The expropriation of the agricultural producer, of the peasant, from the soil, is the basis of the whole process . . .

THOMAS PAINE

Agrarian Justice

1797

To preserve the benefits of what is called civilized life, and to remedy at the same time the evil which it has produced, ought to be considered as one of the first objects of reformed legislation.

Whether that state that is proudly, perhaps erroneously, called civilization, has most promoted or most injured the general happiness of man is a question that may be strongly contested. On one side, the spectator is dazzled by splendid appearances; on the other, he is shocked by extremes of wretchedness; both of which it has erected. The most affluent and the most miserable of the human

Thomas Paine, "Agrarian Justice," from *The Writings of Thomas Paine*, collected and edited by Moncure Daniel Conway. New York: G. P. Putnam's Sons, 1894.

race are to be found in the countries that are called civilized.

To understand what the state of society ought to be, it is necessary to have some idea of the natural and primitive state of man; such as it is at this day among the Indians of North America. There is not, in that state, any of those spectacles of human misery which poverty and want present to our eyes in all the towns and streets in Europe.

Poverty, therefore, is a thing created by that which is called civilized life. It exists not in the natural state. On the other hand, the natural state is without those advantages which flow from agriculture, arts, science and manufactures. The life of an Indian is a continual holiday, compared with the poor of Europe; and, on the other hand it appears to be abject when compared to the rich.

Civilization, therefore, or that which is so-called, has operated two ways: to make one part of society more affluent, and the other more wretched, than would have been the lot of either in a natural state.

It is always possible to go from the natural to the civilized state, but it is never possible to go from the civilized to the natural state. The reason is that man in a natural state, subsisting by hunting, requires ten times the quantity of land to range over to procure himself sustenance, than would support him in a civilized state, where the earth is cultivated. When, therefore, a country becomes populous by the additional aids of cultivation, art and science, there is a necessity of preserving things in that state; because without it there cannot be sustenance for more, perhaps, than a tenth part of its inhabitants. The thing, therefore, now to be done is to remedy the evils and preserve the benefits that have arisen to society by passing from the natural to that which is called the civilized state.

In taking the matter upon this ground, the first principle of civilization ought to have been, and ought still to be, that the condition of every person born into the world, after a state of civilization commences, ought not to be worse than if he had been born before that period.

But the fact is that the condition of millions, in every country in Europe, is far worse than if they had been born before civilization began, had been born among the Indians of North America at the present. I will show how this fact has happened.

It is a position not to be controverted that the earth, in its natural, cultivated state was, and ever would have continued to be, *the common property of the human race*. In that state every man would have been born to property. He would have been a joint life proprietor with rest in the property of the soil, and in all its natural productions, vegetable and animal.

But the earth in its natural state, as before said, is capable of supporting but a small number of inhabitants compared with what it is capable of doing in a cultivated state. And as it is impossible to separate the improvement made by cultivation from the earth itself, upon which that improvement is made, the idea of landed property arose from that parable connection; but it is nevertheless true, that it is the value of the improvement, only, and not the earth itself, that is individual property.

Every proprietor, therefore, of cultivated lands, owes to the community *ground-rent* (for I know of no better term to express the idea) for the land which he holds; and it is from this ground-rent that the fund proposed in this plan is to issue.

It is deducible, as well from the nature of the thing as from all the stories transmitted to us, that the idea of landed property commenced with cultivation, and that there was no such thing, as landed property before that time. It could not exist in the first state of man, that of hunters. It did not exist in the second state, that of shepherds: neither Abraham, Isaac, Jacob, nor Job, so far as the history of the Bible may credited in probable things, were owners of land.

Their property consisted, as is always enumerated in flocks and herds, they traveled with them from place to place. The frequent contentions at that time about the use of a well in the dry country of Arabia, where those people lived, also show that there was no landed property. It was not admitted that land could be claimed as property.

There could be no such thing as landed property originally. Man did not make the earth, and, though he had a natural right to *occupy* it, he had no right to *locate as his property* in perpetuity any part of it; neither did the Creator of the earth open a land-office, from whence the first title-deeds should issue. Whence then, arose the idea of landed property? I answer as before, that when cultivation began the idea of landed property began with it, from the impossibility of separating the improvement made by cultivation from the earth itself, upon which that improvement was made.

The value of the improvement so far exceeded the value of the natural earth, at that time, as to absorb it; till, in the end, the common right of all became confounded into the cultivated right of the individual. But there are, nevertheless, distinct species of rights, and will continue to be, so long as the earth endures.

It is only by tracing things to their origin that we can gain rightful ideas of them, and it is by gaining such ideas that we, discover the boundary that divides right from wrong, and teaches every man to know his own. I have entitled this tract "Agrarian Justice" to distinguish it from "Agrarian Law."

Nothing could be more unjust than agrarian law in a country improved by cultivation; for though every man, as an inhabitant of the earth, is a joint proprietor of it in its natural state, it does not follow that he is a joint proprietor of cultivated earth. The additional value made by cultivation, after the system was admitted, became the property of those who did it, or who inherited it from them, or who purchased it. It had originally no owner. While, therefore, I advocate the right, and interest myself in the hard case of all those who have been thrown out of their natural inheritance by the introduction of the system of landed property, I equally defend the right of the possessor to the part which is his.

Cultivation is at least one of the greatest natural improvements ever made by human invention. It has given to created earth a tenfold value. But the landed monopoly that began with it has produced the greatest evil. It has dispossessed more than half the inhabitants of every nation of their natural inheritance, without providing for them, as ought to have been done, an indemnification for that loss, and has thereby created a species of poverty and wretchedness that did not exist before.

In advocating the case of the persons thus dispossessed, it is a right, and not a charity, that I am pleading for. But it is that kind of right which, being neglected at first, could not be brought forward afterwards till heaven had opened the way by a revolution in the system of government. Let us then do honor to revolutions by justice, and give currency to their principles by blessings.

Having thus in a few words, opened the merits of the case, I shall now proceed to the plan I have to propose, which is, To create a national fund, out of which there shall be paid to every person, when arrived at the age of twenty-one years, the sum of fifteen pounds sterling, as a compensation in part, for the loss of his or her natural inheritance, by the introduction of the system of landed property:

And also, the sum of ten pounds per annum, during life, to every person now living, of the age of fifty years, and to all others as they shall arrive at that age.

MEANS BY WHICH THE FUND IS TO BE CREATED

I have already established the principle, namely, that the earth, in its natural uncultivated state was, and ever would have continued to be, the *common property of the human race;* that in that state, every person would have been born to property; and that the system of landed property, by its inseparable connection with cultivation, and with what is called civilized life, has absorbed the property of all those whom it dispossessed, without providing, as ought to have been done, an indemnification for that loss.

The fault, however, is not in the present possessors. No complaint is tended, or ought to be alleged against them, unless they adopt the crime by opposing justice. The fault is in the system, and it has stolen perceptibly upon the world, aided afterwards by the agrarian law of the sword.

But the fault can be made to reform itself by successive generations; and without diminishing or deranging the property of any of present possessors, the operation of the fund can yet commence, and in full activity, the first year of its establishment, or soon after, as I shall show.

It is proposed that the payments, as already stated, be made to every person, rich or poor. It is best to make it so, to prevent invidious distinctions. It is also right it should be so, because it is in lieu of the natural inheritance, which, as a right, belongs to every man, over and above property he may have created, or inherited from those who did. Such persons as do not choose to receive it can throw it into the common fund.

Taking it then for granted that no person ought to be in a worse condition when born under what is called a state of civilization, than he would have been had he been born in a state of nature, and that civilization ought to have made, and ought still to make, provision for that purpose, it can only be done by subtracting from property a portion equal in value to the natural inheritance it has absorbed.

Various methods may be proposed for this purpose, but that which appears to be the best (not only because it will operate without deranging any present possessors, or without interfering with the collection of taxes or *emprunts* necessary for the purposes of government and the Revolution, but because it will be the least troublesome and the most effectual, and also because the subtraction will be made at a time that best admits it) is at the moment that property is passing by the death of one person to the possession of another. In this case, the bequeather gives nothing: the receiver pays nothing. The only matter to him is that the monopoly of natural inheritance, to which there never was a right, begins to cease in his person. A generous man would not wish it to continue, and a just man will rejoice to see it abolished. . .

I care not how affluent some may be, provided that none be miserable in consequence of it. But it is impossible to enjoy affluence with the felicity it is capable of being enjoyed, while so much misery is mingled in the scene. The sight of the misery, and the unpleasant sensations it suggests, which, though they may be suffocated cannot be extinguished, are a greater drawback upon the felicity of affluence than the proposed ten percent upon property is worth. He that would not give the one to get rid of the other has no charity, even for himself.

There are, in every country, some magnificent charities established by individuals. It is, however, but little that any individual can do, when the whole extent of the misery to be relieved is considered. He may satisfy his conscience, but not his heart. He may give all that he has, and that all will relieve but little. It is only by organizing civilization upon such principles as to act like a system of pulleys, that the whole weight of misery can be removed.

The plan here proposed will reach the whole. It will immediately relieve and take out of view three classes of wretchedness—the blind, the lame, and the aged poor; and it will furnish the rising generation with means to prevent their becoming poor; and it will do this without deranging or interfering with any national measures.

To show that this will be the case, it is sufficient to observe that the operation and effect of the plan will, in all cases, be the same as if every individual were *voluntarily* to make his will and dispose of his property in the manner here proposed.

But it is justice, and not charity, that is the principle of the plan. . . .

Land, as before said, is the free gift of the Creator in common to the human race. Personal property is the *effect of society*; and it is as impossible for an individual to acquire personal property without the aid of society, as it is for him to make land originally.

Separate an individual from society, and give him an island or a continent to possess, and he cannot acquire personal property. He cannot be rich. So inseparably are the means connected with the end, in all cases, that where the former do not exist the latter cannot be obtained. All accumulation, therefore, of personal property, beyond what a man's own hands produce, is derived to him by living in society; and he owes on every principle of justice, of gratitude, and of civilization, a part of that accumulation back again to society from whence the whole came.

This is putting the matter on a general principle, and perhaps it is best to do so; for if we examine the case minutely it will be found that the accumulation of personal property is, in many instances, the effect of paying too little for the labor that produced it; the consequence of which is that the working hand perishes in old age, and the employer abounds in affluence.

It is, perhaps, impossible to proportion exactly the price of labor to the profits it produces; and it will also be said, as an apology for the injustice, that were a workman to receive an increase of wages daily he would not save it against old age, nor be much better for it in the interim. Make, then, society the treasurer to guard it for him in a common fund; for it is no reason that, because he might not make a good use of it for himself, another should take it.

DAVID SCHMIDTZ

The Institution of Property

1994

The evolution of property law is driven by an ongoing search for ways to internalize externalities: positive externalities associated with productive effort and negative externalities associated with misuse of commonly held resources. In theory, and sometimes in practice, costs are internalized over time. Increasingly, people pay for their own mistakes and misfortunes, and not for mistakes and misfortunes of others.

If all goes well, property law enables would-be producers to capture the benefits of productive effort. It also enables people to insulate themselves from negative externalities associated with activities around the neighborhood. Property law is not perfect. To minimize negative externalities that neighbors might otherwise impose on each other, people resort to nuisance and zoning laws. People turn to institutions like the Environmental Protection Agency for the same reasons they turn to central planners in other parts of the world; they think decentralized decision making is chaos, and that with chaos comes a burgeoning of negative externalities.

What is the reality? The reality is that decentralization may or may not be chaos. It depends on institutional structure. An open-access commons decentralizes decision making in one way; private property decentralizes it in another way, with systematically different results.

Philosophers speak of the ideal of society as a cooperative venture for mutual advantage. To be a cooperative venture for mutual advantage, though, society must first be a setting in which mutually advantageous interaction is possible. In the parlance of game theorists, society must be a positive sum game. What determines the extent to which society is a positive sum game? This essay explains how property institutions convert negative-sum or zero-sum games into positive-sum games, setting the stage for society's flourishing as a cooperative venture.

The term "property rights" is used to refer to a bundle of rights that could include rights to sell, lend, bequeath, and so on. In what follows, I use the phrase

David Schmidtz and Elizabeth Willott, *Environmental Ethics: What Really Matters, What Really Works.* New York: Oxford University Press. Reprinted by permission of Oxford University Press, 2011.

to refer primarily to the right of owners to exclude non-owners. Private owners have the right to exclude non-owners, but the right to exclude is a feature of property rights in general rather than the defining feature of private ownership in particular. The National Park Service claims a right to exclude. Communes claim a right to exclude nonmembers. This essay does not settle which kind or which mix of public and private property institutions is best. Instead, it asks how we could justify *any* institution that recognizes a right to exclude.

ORIGINAL APPROPRIATION: THE PROBLEM

The right to exclude presents a philosophical problem, though. Consider how full-blooded rights differ from mere liberties. If I am at liberty to plant a garden that means my planting a garden is permitted. That leaves open the possibility of you being at liberty to interfere with my gardening as you see fit. Thus, mere liberties are not full-blooded rights. When I stake a claim to a piece of land, though, I claim to be changing other people's liberties—canceling them somehow—so that other people no longer are at liberty to use the land without my permission. To say I have a right to the land is to say I have a right to exclude.

From where could such rights have come? There must have been a time when no one had a right to exclude. Everyone had liberties regarding the land, but not rights. (Perhaps this does not seem obvious, but if no one owns the land, no one has a right to exclude. If no one has a right to exclude, everyone has liberties.) How, then, did we get from each person having a liberty to someone having an exclusive right to the land? What justifies original appropriation, that is, staking a claim to previously unowned resources?

To justify a claim to unowned land, people need not make as strong a case as would be needed to justify confiscating land already owned by someone else. Specifically, since there is no prior owner in original appropriation cases, there is no one from whom one can or needs to get consent. What, then, must a person do? Locke's idea seems to have been that any residual (perhaps need-based) communal claim to the land could be met if a person could appropriate it without prejudice to other people, in other words, if a person could leave "enough and as good" for others. This so-called Lockean Proviso can be interpreted in many ways, but an adequate interpretation will note that this is its point: to license claims that can be made without making other people worse off. In the language of modern environmental economics, we might read it as a call for sustainable use.

We also should consider whether the "others" who are to be left with enough and as good include not just people currently on the scene but latecomers as well, including people not yet born. John Sanders asks, "What possible argument could at the same time require that the present generation have scruples about leaving enough and as good for one another, while shrugging off such concern for future generations?" (Sanders 1987, p. 377). Most theorists accept the more demanding interpretation. It fits better with Locke's idea that the preservation of humankind (which includes future generations) is the ultimate criterion by which any use of resources is assessed. Aside from that, we have a more compelling defense of an appropriation (especially in environmental terms) when we can argue that there was enough left over not just for contemporaries but also for generations to come.

Of course, when we justify original appropriation, we do not in the process justify expropriation. Some say institutions that license expropriation make people better off; I think our histories of violent expropriation are ongoing tragedies for us all. Capitalist regimes have tainted histories. Communist regimes have tainted histories. Indigenous peoples have tainted histories. Europeans took land from native American tribes, and before that, those tribes took the same land from other tribes. We may regard those expropriations as the history of markets or governments or Christianity or tribalism or simply as the history of the human race. It makes little difference. This essay discusses the history of property institutions, not because their history can justify them, but rather because their history shows how some of them enable people to make themselves and the people around them better off without destroying their environment. Among such institutions are those that license original appropriation (and not expropriation).

ORIGINAL APPROPRIATION: A SOLUTION

Private property's philosophical critics often have claimed that justifying original appropriation is the key to justifying private property, frequently offering a version of Locke's Proviso as the standard of justification. Part of the Proviso's attraction for such critics was that it seemingly could not be met. Even today, philosophers generally conclude that the Proviso is, at least in the case of land appropriation, logically impossible to satisfy, and thus that (private) property in land cannot possibly be justified along Lockean lines.

The way Judith Thomson puts it, if "the first labor-mixer must literally leave as much and as good for others who come along later, then no one can come to own anything, for there are only finitely many things in the world so that every taking leaves less for others" (Thomson 1990, p. 330). To say the least, Thomson is not alone:

"We leave enough and as good for others only when what we take is not scarce" (Fried 1995, p. 230n).

"The Lockean Proviso, in the contemporary world of overpopulation and scarce resources, can almost never be met" (Held 1980, p. 6).

"Every acquisition worsens the lot of others—and worsens their lot in relevant ways" (Bogart 1985, p. 834).

"The condition that there be enough and as good left for others could not of course be literally satisfied by any system of private property rights" (Sartorius 1984, p. 210).

"If the 'enough and as good' clause were a necessary condition on appropriation, it would follow that, in these circumstances, the only legitimate course for the inhabitants would be death by starvation . . . since *no* appropriation would leave enough and as good in common for others" (Waldron 1976, p. 325).

And so on. If we take something out of the cookie jar, we *must* be leaving less for others. This appears self-evident. It has to be right.

Appropriation Is Not a Zero-Sum Game

But it is not right. First, it is by no means impossible—certainly not logically impossible—for a taking to leave as much for others. Surely we can at least imagine a logically possible world of magic cookie jars in which, every time you take out one cookie, more and better cookies take its place.

Second, the logically possible world I just imagined is the sort of world we actually live in. Philosophers writing about original appropriation tend to speak as if people who arrive first are luckier than those who come later. The truth is, first appropriators begin the process of resource creation; latecomers get most of the benefits. Consider America's first permanent English settlement, the Jamestown colony of 1607. (Or, if you prefer, imagine the lifestyles of people crossing the Bering Strait from Asia twelve thousand years ago.) Was their situation better than ours? How so? Was it that they never worried about being overcharged for car repairs? They never awoke in the middle of the night to the sound of noisy refrigerators, leaky faucets, or flushing toilets? They never had to change a light bulb? They never agonized over the choice of long distance telephone companies?

Philosophers are taught to say, in effect, that original appropriators got the good stuff for free. We have to pay for ugly leftovers. But in truth, original appropriation benefits latecomers far more than it benefits original appropriators. Original appropriation is a cornucopia of wealth, but mainly for latecomers. The people who got here first never dreamt of things we latecomers take for granted. The poorest among us have life expectancies exceeding theirs by several decades. This is not political theory. It is not economic rhetoric. It is fact.

Original appropriation diminishes the stock of what can be originally appropriated, at least in the case of land, but that is not the same thing as diminishing the stock of what can be owned.[1] On the contrary, in taking control of resources and thereby removing those particular resources from the stock of goods that can be acquired by originally appropriation, people typically generate massive increases in the stock of goods that can be acquired by trade. The lesson is that appropriation typically is not a zero-sum game. It normally is a positive sum game. As Locke himself stressed, it creates the possibility of mutual benefit on a massive scale. It creates the possibility of society as a cooperative venture.

The argument is not merely that enough is produced in appropriation's aftermath to compensate latecomers who lost out in the race to appropriate. The argument is that the bare fact of being an original appropriator is not the prize. The prize is prosperity, and latecomers win big, courtesy of those who got here first. If anyone had a right to be compensated, it would be the first appropriators.

The Commons Before Appropriation Is Not Zero-Sum Either

The second point is that the commons before appropriation is not a zero-sum game either. Typically it is a negative sum game. Let me tell two stories. The first comes from the coral reefs of the Philippine and Tongan Islands (Chesher 1985; Gomez, Alcala, and San Diego, 1981). People once fished those reefs with lures and traps, but have recently caught on to a technique called bleach-fishing, which involves dumping bleach into the reefs. Fish cannot breathe sodium hypochlorite. Suffocated, they float to the surface where they are easy to collect.[2]

The problem is, the coral itself is composed of living animals. The coral suffocates along with the fish, and the dead reef is no longer a viable habitat. (Another technique, blast-fishing, involves dynamiting the reefs. The concussion produces an easy harvest of stunned fish and dead coral.) You may say people ought to be more responsible. They ought to preserve the reefs for their children.

That would miss the point, which is that individual fishermen lack the option of saving the coral for their children. Individual fishermen obviously have the option of not destroying it themselves, but what happens if they elect not to destroy it? What they want is for the reef to be left for their children; what is actually happening is that the reef is left for the next blast-fisher down the line. If a fisherman wants to have anything at all to give his children, he must act quickly, destroying the reef and grabbing the fish himself. It does no good to tell fishermen to take responsibility. They are taking responsibility—for their children. Existing institutional arrangements do not empower them to take responsibility in a way that would save the reef.

Under the circumstances, they are at liberty to not destroy the reef themselves, but they are not at liberty to do what is necessary to save the reef for their children. To save the reef for their children, fishermen must have the power to restrict access to the reef. They must claim a right to exclude blast-fishers. Whether they stake that claim as individuals or as a group is secondary, so long as they actually succeed in restricting access. But one way or another, they must claim and effectively exercise a right to restrict access.

The second story comes from the Cayman Islands.[3] The Atlantic Green Turtle has long been prized as a source of meat and eggs. The turtles were a commonly held resource and were being harvested in an unsustainable way. In 1968, when by some estimates there were as few as three to five thousand left in the wild, a group of entrepreneurs and concerned scientists created Cayman Turtle Farm and began raising and selling captive-bred sea turtles. In the wild, as few as one tenth of one percent of wild hatchlings survive to adulthood. Most are seized by predators before they can crawl from nest to sea. Cayman Farm, though, boosted the survival rate of captive-bred animals to well over fifty percent. At the peak of operations, they were rearing in excess of a hundred thousand turtles. They were releasing one percent of their hatchlings into the wild at the age of ten months, an age at which hatchlings had a decent chance of surviving to maturity.

In 1973, commerce in Atlantic Green Turtles was restricted by CITES (the Convention on International

Trade in Endangered Species) and, in the United States, by the Fish and Wildlife Service, the Department of Commerce, and the Department of the Interior. Under the newly created Endangered Species Act, the U.S. classified the Atlantic Green Turtle as an endangered species, but Cayman Farm's business was unaffected, at first, because regulations pertaining to commerce in Atlantic Green Turtles exempted commerce in captive-bred animals. In 1978, however, the regulations were published in their final form, and although exemptions were granted for trade in captive-bred animals of other species, no exemption was made for trade in turtles. The company could no longer do business in the U.S. Even worse, the company no longer could ship its products through American ports, so it no longer had access via Miami to world markets. The Farm exists today only to serve the population of the Cayman Islands themselves.

What do these stories tell us? The first tells us we do not need to justify failing to preserve the commons in its pristine, original, unappropriated form, because preserving the commons in pristine original form is not an option. The commons is not a time capsule. Leaving our environment in the commons is not like putting our environment in a time capsule as a legacy for future generations. In some cases, putting resources in a time capsule might be a good idea. However, the second story reminds us: there are ways to take what we find in the commons and preserve it—to put it in a time capsule—but before we can put something in a time capsule, we have to appropriate it.[4]

Justifying the Game

Note a difference between justifying institutions that regulate appropriation and justifying particular acts of appropriation. Think of original appropriation as a game and of particular acts of appropriation as moves within the game. Even if the game is justified, a given move within the game may have nothing to recommend it. Indeed, we could say (for argument's sake) that any act of appropriation will seem arbitrary when viewed in isolation, and some will seem unconscionable. Even so, there can be compelling reasons to have an institutional framework that recognizes property claims on the basis of moves that would carry no weight in an institutional vacuum. Common law implicitly acknowledges morally weighty reasons for not requiring original appropriators to supply morally weighty reasons for their appropriations. Carol Rose (1985) argues that a rule of first possession, when the world is notified in an unambiguous way, induces discovery (and future productive activity) and minimizes disputes over discovered objects. Particular acts of appropriation are justified not because they carry moral weight but because they are permitted moves within a game that carries moral weight.

Needless to say, the cornucopia of wealth generated by the appropriation and subsequent mobilization of resources is not an unambiguous benefit. The commerce made possible by original appropriation creates pollution, and other negative externalities as well. (I will return to this point.) Further, there may be people who attach no value to the increases in life expectancy and other benefits that accompany the appropriation of resources for productive use. Some people may prefer a steady-state system that indefinitely supports their lifestyles as hunter-gatherers, untainted by the shoes and tents and safety matches of Western culture. If original appropriation forces such people to participate in a culture they want no part of, then from their viewpoint, the game does more harm than good.

Here are two things to keep in mind, though. First, as I said, the commons is not a time capsule. It does not preserve the status quo. For all kinds of reasons, quality of life could drop after appropriation. However, pressures that drive waves of people to appropriate are a lot more likely to compromise quality of life when those waves wash over an unregulated commons. In an unregulated commons, those who conserve pay the costs but do not get the benefits of conservation, while overusers get the benefits but do not pay the costs of overuse. Therefore, an unregulated commons is a prescription for overuse, not for conservation.

Second, the option of living the life of a hunter-gatherer has not entirely disappeared. It is not a comfortable life. It never was. But it remains an option.

There are places in northern Canada and elsewhere where people can and do live that way. As a bonus, those who opt to live as hunter-gatherers retain the option of participating in Western culture on a drop-in basis during medical emergencies, to trade for supplies, and so on. Obviously, someone might respond, "Even if the hunter-gatherer life is an option now, that option is disappearing as expanding populations equipped with advancing technologies claim the land for other purposes." Well, probably so. What does that prove? It proves that, in the world as it is, if hunter-gatherers want their children to have the option of living as hunter-gatherers, then they need to stake a claim to the territory on which they intend to preserve that option. They need to argue that they, as rightful owners, have a right to regulate access to it. If they want a steady-state civilization, they need to be aware that they will not find it in an unregulated commons. They need to argue that they have a right to exclude oil companies, for example, which would love to be able to treat northern Canada as an unregulated commons.

When someone says appropriation does not leave enough and as good for others, the reply should be "compared to what?" Compared to the commons as it was? As it is? As it will be? Often, in fact, leaving resources *in the commons* does not leave enough and as good for others. The Lockean Proviso, far from forbidding appropriation of resources from the commons, actually requires appropriation under conditions of scarcity. Moreover, the more scarce a resource is, the more urgently the Proviso requires that it be removed from the negative sum game that is the unregulated commons. Again, when the burden of common use exceeds the resource's ability to renew itself, the Proviso comes to require, not merely permit, people to appropriate and regulate access to the resource. Even in an unregulated commons, some fishermen will practice self-restraint, but something has to happen to incline the group to practice self-restraint in cases where it already has shown it has no such inclination in an unregulated commons.

Removing goods from the commons stimulates increases in the stock of what can be owned and limits losses that occur in tragic commons. Appropriation replaces a negative sum with a positive sum game. Therein lies a justification for social structures enshrining a right to remove resources from the unregulated commons: when resources become scarce, we need to remove them if we want them to be there for our children. Or anyone else's.

WHAT KIND OF PROPERTY INSTITUTION IS IMPLIED?

I have defended appropriation of, and subsequent regulation of access to, scarce resources as a way of preserving (and creating) resources for the future. When resources are abundant, the Lockean Proviso permits appropriation; when resources are scarce, the Proviso requires appropriation. It is possible to appropriate without prejudice to future generations. Indeed, when resources are scarce, it is leaving them in the commons that is prejudicial to future generations.

Private property enables people (and gives them an incentive) to take responsibility for conserving scarce resources. It preserves resources under a wide variety of circumstances. It is the preeminent vehicle for turning negative sum commons into positive sum property regimes. However, it is not the only way. Evidently, it is not always the best way, either. Public property is ubiquitous, and it is not only rapacious governments and mad ideologues who create it. Sometimes it evolves spontaneously as a response to real problems, enabling people to remove a resource from an unregulated commons and collectively take responsibility for its management. The following sections discuss research by Martin Bailey, Harold Demsetz, Robert Ellickson, and Carol Rose, showing how various property institutions help to ensure that enough and as good is left for future generations.

The Unregulated Commons

An unregulated commons need not be a disaster. An unregulated commons will work well enough so long as the level of use remains within the land's carrying capacity. However, as use nears carrying capacity, there will be pressure to shift to a more exclusive regime. As an example of an unregulated commons evolving into something else as increasing traffic begins to exceed carrying capacity, consider Harold Demsetz's account of how property institutions evolved among indigenous tribes of the Labrador peninsula. As Demsetz tells the story, the region's people had, for generations, treated the land as an open-access commons. The human population was small. There was plenty to eat. Thus, the pattern of exploitation was within the land's carrying capacity. The resource maintained itself. In that situation, the Proviso, as interpreted above, was satisfied. Original appropriation would have been permissible, other things equal, but it was not required.

With the advent of the fur trade, though, the scale of hunting and trapping activity increased sharply. The population of game animals began to dwindle. The unregulated commons had worked for a while, but now the tribes were facing a classic tragedy. The benefits of exploiting the resource were internalized but the costs were not, and the arrangement was no longer viable. Clans began to mark out family plots. The game animals in question were small animals like beaver and otter that tend not to migrate from one plot to another. Thus, marking out plots of land effectively privatized small game as well as the land itself. In sum, the tribes converted the commons in non-migratory fur-bearing game to family parcels when the fur trade began to spur a rising demand that exceeded the land's carrying capacity. When demand began to exceed carrying capacity, that was when the Proviso came not only to permit but to require original appropriation.

One other nuance of the privatization of fur-bearing game: although the fur was privatized, the meat was not. There was still plenty of meat to go around, so tribal law allowed trespass on another clan's land to hunt for meat. Trespassers could kill a beaver and take the meat, but had to leave the pelt displayed in a prominent place to signal that they had eaten and had respected the clan's right to the pelt. The new customs went to the heart of the matter, privatizing what had to be privatized, leaving intact liberties that people had always enjoyed with respect to other resources where unrestricted access had not yet become a problem.

The Communal Alternative[5]

We can contrast the unregulated or open-access commons with communes. A commune is a restricted-access commons. In a commune, property is owned by the group rather than by individual members. People as a group claim and exercise a right to exclude. Typically, communes draw a sharp distinction between members and nonmembers, and regulate access accordingly. Public property tends to restrict access by time of day or year. Some activities are permitted; others are prohibited.

Ellickson believes a broad campaign to abolish either private property or public and communal property would be ludicrous. Each kind of property serves social welfare in its own way. Likewise, every ownership regime has its own externality problems. Communal management leads to overconsumption and to shirking on maintenance and improvements, because people receive only a fraction of the value of their labor, and bear only a fraction of the costs of their consumption. To minimize these disincentives, a commune must intensively monitor people's production and consumption activities.

In practice, communal regimes can lead to indiscriminate dumping of wastes, ranging from piles of unwashed dishes to ecological disasters that threaten whole continents. Privately managed parcels also can lead to indiscriminate dumping of wastes and to various other uses that ignore spillover effects on neighbors. One advantage of private property is that owners can buy each other out and reshuffle their holdings in such a way as to minimize the extent to which their activities bother each other. But it does not always work out so nicely, and the reshuffling itself can be a waste. There are transaction costs. Thus, one plausible social goal would be to have a system that combines private and public property in a way that reduces the sum of transaction costs and the cost of externalities.

LOCAL VERSUS REMOTE EXTERNALITIES

Is it generally best to convert an unregulated commons to smaller private parcels or to manage it as a commune with power to exclude non-members? It depends on what kind of activities people tend to engage in. Ellickson separates activities into three categories: small (like cultivating a tomato plant), medium (like damming part of a river to create a pond for ducks), and large (like using an industrial smokestack to disperse noxious fumes). The distinction is not meant to be sharp. As one might expect, it is a matter of degree. It concerns the relative size of the area over which externalities are worth worrying about. The effects of small events are confined to one's own property. Medium events affect people in the immediate neighborhood. Their external effects are localized. Large events affect people who are more remote.

Ellickson says private regimes are clearly superior as methods for minimizing the costs of small and medium events. Small events are not much of a problem for private regimes. When land is parceled out, the effects of small events are internalized. Neighbors do not care much when we pick tomatoes on our own land; they care a great deal when we pick tomatoes on the communal plot. In the former case, we are minding our own business; in the latter, we are minding theirs.

In contrast, the effects of medium events tend to spill over onto one's neighbors, and thus can be a source of friction. Nevertheless, privatization has the advantage of limiting the number of people having to be consulted about how to deal with the externality, which reduces transaction costs. Instead of consulting the entire community of communal owners, each at liberty with respect to the affected area, one consults a handful of people who own parcels in the immediate area of the medium event. A further virtue of privatization is that disputes arising from medium events tend to be left in the hands of people in the immediate vicinity, who tend to have a better understanding of local conditions and thus are in a better position to devise resolutions without harmful unintended consequences. They are in a better position to foresee the costs and benefits of a medium event.

When it comes to large events, though, there is no easy way to say which mix of private and public property is best. Large events involve far-flung externalities among people who do not have face-to-face relationships. The difficulties in detecting such externalities, tracing them to their source, and holding people accountable for them are difficulties for any kind of property regime. It is no easy task to devise institutions that encourage pulp mills to take responsibility for their actions while simultaneously encouraging people downstream to take responsibility for their welfare, and thus to avoid being harmed by large-scale negative externalities. Ellickson says there is no general answer to the question of which regime best deals with them.

A large event will fall into one of two categories. Releasing toxic wastes into the atmosphere, for example, may violate existing legal rights or community norms. Or, such laws or norms may not yet be in place. Most of the problems arise when existing customs or laws fail to settle who (in effect) has the right of way. That is not a problem with parceling land per se but rather with the fact that key resources like air and waterways remain in a largely unregulated commons.

So, privatization exists in different degrees and takes different forms. Different forms have different incentive properties. Simply parceling out land or sea is not always enough to stabilize possession of resources that make land or sea valuable in the first place. Suppose, for example, that fish are known to migrate from one parcel to another. In that case, owners have an incentive to grab as many fish as they can whenever the school passes through their own territory. Thus, simply dividing fishing grounds into parcels may not be enough to put fishermen in a position collectively to avoid exceeding sustainable yields. It depends on the extent to which the sought-after fish migrate from one parcel to another, and on conventions that are continuously evolving to help neighbors deal with the inadequacy of their fences (or other ways of marking off territory). Clearly, then, not all forms of privatization are equally good at internalizing externalities. Privatization per se is not a panacea, and not all forms of privatization are equal. There are obvious difficulties with how private property regimes handle large events. The nature and extent of the difficulties depends on details. So, for purposes of comparison, Ellickson looked at how communal regimes handle large events.

JAMESTOWN AND OTHER COMMUNES

The Jamestown Colony is North America's first permanent English settlement. It begins in 1607 as a commune, sponsored by London-based Virginia Company. Land is held and managed collectively. The colony's charter guarantees to each settler an equal share of the collective product regardless of the amount of work personally contributed. Of the original group of one hundred and four settlers, two thirds die of starvation and disease before their first winter. New shiploads replenish the population, but the winter of 1609 cuts the population from five hundred to sixty. In 1611, visiting Governor Thomas Dale finds living skeletons bowling in the streets, waiting for someone else to plant the crops. Their main food source consists of wild animals such as turtles and raccoons, which settlers hunt and eat by dark of night before neighbors can demand equal shares. In 1614, Governor Dale has seen enough. He assigns three-acre plots to individual settlers, which reportedly increases productivity seven-fold. The colony converts the rest of its land holdings to private parcels in 1619.

Why go communal in the first place? Are there advantages to communal regimes? One advantage is obvious. Communal regimes can help people spread risks under conditions where risks are substantial and where alternative risk-spreading mechanisms, like insurance, are unavailable. But as communities build up capital reserves to the point where they can offer insurance, they tend to privatize, for insurance lets them secure a measure of risk-spreading without having to endure the externalities that afflict a communal regime.

A communal regime might also be an effective response to economies of scale in large scale public works that are crucial in getting a community started. To build a fort, man its walls, dig wells, and so on, a communal economy is an obvious choice as a way of mobilizing the teams of workers needed to execute these urgent tasks. But again, as these tasks are completed and community welfare increasingly comes to depend on small events, the communal regime gives way to private parcels. At Jamestown, Plymouth, the Amana colonies, and Salt Lake, formerly communal settlers "understandably would switch to private land tenure, the system that most cheaply induces individuals to undertake small and medium events that are socially useful" (Ellickson 1993, p. 1,342). (The legend of Salt Lake says the sudden improvement in the fortunes of once-starving Mormons occurred in 1848 when God sent sea gulls to save them from plagues of locusts, at the same time as they coincidentally were switching to private plots. Similarly, the Jamestown tragedy sometimes is attributed to harsh natural conditions, as if those conditions suddenly changed in 1614, multiplying productivity seven-fold while Governor Dale coincidentally was cutting the land into parcels.)

Of course, the tendency toward decentralized and individualized forms of management is only a (strong) tendency and, in any case, there are tradeoffs. For example, what would be a small event on a larger parcel becomes a medium event under more crowded conditions. Loud music is an innocuous small event on a ranch but an irritating medium event in an apartment complex. Changes in technology or population density affect the scope or incidence of externalities. The historical trend, though, is that as people become aware of and concerned about a medium or large event, they seek ways of reducing the extent to which the event's cost is externalized. Social evolution is partly a process of perceiving new externalities and devising institutions to internalize them.

Historically, the benefits of communal management have not been enough to keep communes together indefinitely. Perhaps the most enduring and successful communes in human memory are the agricultural settlements of the Hutterites, dating in Europe back to the sixteenth century. There are now around twenty-eight thousand people living in such communities. Hutterites believe in a fairly strict sharing of assets. They forbid the possession of radio or television sets, to give one example of how strictly they control contact with the outside world.

Ellickson says Hutterite communities have three special things going for them: 1. A population cap: when a settlement reaches a population of one hundred and twenty, a portion of the community must leave to start a new community. The cap helps them retain a close-knit society; 2. Communal dining and worship: people congregate several times a day, which facilitates a rapid exchange of information about individual behavior and a ready avenue for supplying feedback to those whose behavior deviates from the norm; 3. A ban on birth control: the average woman bears nine children, which more than offsets the trickle of emigration. We might add that Hutterite culture and education leave people ill-prepared to live in anything other than a Hutterite society, which surely accounts in part for the low emigration rate.

Ellickson discusses other examples of communal property regimes. But the most pervasive example of communal ownership in America, Ellickson says, is the family household. American suburbia consists of family communes nested within a network of open-access roadways. Family homes tacitly recognize limits to how far we can go in converting common holdings to individual parcels. Consider your living room. You could fully privatize, having one household member own it while others pay user fees. The fees could be used to pay family members or outside help to keep it clean. In some respects, it would be better that way. The average communal living room today, for example, is notably subject to overgrazing and shirking on maintenance. Yet we put up with it. No one charges user fees to household members. Seeing the living room degraded by communal use may be irritating, but it is better than treating it as one person's private domain.

Some institutions succeed while embodying a form of ownership that is essentially collective. History indicates, though, that members of successful communes internalize the rewards that come with that collective responsibility. In particular, they reserve the right to exclude nonmembers. A successful commune does not run itself as an open-access commons.

GOVERNANCE BY CUSTOM

Many commons (such as our living rooms) are regulated by custom rather than by government, so saying there is a role for common property and saying there is a role for government management of common property are two different things. As Ellickson notes, "Group ownership does not necessarily imply government ownership, of course. The sorry environmental records of federal land agencies and Communist regimes are a sharp reminder that governments are often particularly inept managers of large tracts." Carol Rose tells of how, in the nineteenth century, public property was thought to be owned by society at large. The idea of public property often was taken to imply no particular role for government beyond whatever enforcement role is implied by private property. Society's right to such property was held to precede and supersede any claim by government. Rose says, "Implicit in these older doctrines is the notion that, even if a property should be open to the public, it does not follow that public rights should necessarily vest in an active governmental manager" (Rose 1986, p. 720). Sometimes, rights were understood to be held by an "unorganized public" rather than by a "governmentally organized public" (Rose 1986, p. 736).

Along the same lines, open-field agricultural practices of medieval times gave peasants exclusive cropping rights to scattered thin strips of arable land in each of the village fields. The strips were private only during the growing season, after which the land reverted to the commons for the duration of the grazing season. Thus, ownership of parcels was usufructuary in the sense that once the harvest was in, ownership reverted to the common herdsmen without negotiation or formal transfer. The farmer had an exclusive claim to the land only so long as he was using it for the purpose of bringing in a harvest. The scattering of strips was a means of diversification, reducing the risk of being ruined by small or medium events: small fires, pest infestations, etc. The post-harvest commons in grazing land exploited economies of scale in fencing and tending a herd.

According to Martin Bailey, the pattern observed by Rose and Ellickson also was common among aboriginal tribes. That is, tribes that practiced agriculture treated the land as private during the growing season, and often treated it as a commons after the crops were in. Hunter-gatherer societies did not practice agriculture, but they too tended to leave the land in the commons during the summer when game was plentiful. It was during the winter, when food was most scarce, that they privatized. The rule among hunter-gatherers is that where group hunting's advantages are considerable, that factor dominates. But in the winter, small game is relatively more abundant, less migratory, and evenly spread. There was no "feast or famine" pattern of the sort one expects to see with big-game hunting. Rather, families tended to gather enough during the course of the day to get themselves through the day, day after day, with little to spare.

Even though this pattern corroborates my own general thesis, I confess to being a bit surprised. I might have predicted that it would be during the harshest part of the year that families would band together and throw everything into the common pot in order to pull through. Not so. It was when the land was nearest its carrying capacity that they recognized the imperative to privatize.

Customary use of medieval commons was hedged with restrictions limiting depletion of resources. Custom prohibited activities inconsistent with the land's ability to recover (Rose 1986, p. 743). In particular, the custom of "stinting" allowed the villagers to own livestock only in proportion to the relative size of their (growing season) land holdings. Governance by custom enabled people to avoid commons tragedies.[6]

Custom is a form of management unlike exclusive ownership by either individuals or governments. Custom is a self-managing system for according property rights (Rose 1986, p. 742). For example, custom governs the kind of rights-claims you establish by taking a place in line at a supermarket checkout counter. Rose believes common concerns often are best handled by decentralized, piecemeal, and self-managing customs that tend to arise as needed at the local level. So, to the previous section's conclusion that a successful commune does not run itself as an open-access commons, we can add that a successful commune does not entrust its governance to a distant bureaucracy.

THE HUTTERITE SECRET

I argued that the original appropriation of (and subsequent regulation of access to) scarce resources is justifiable as a mechanism for preserving opportunities for future generations. There are various means of exclusive control, though. Some internalize externalities better than others, and how well they do so depends on the context. My argument does not presume there is one form of exclusive control that uniquely serves this purpose. Which form is best depends on what kind of activities are most prevalent in a community at any given time. It also depends on the extent to which public ownership implies control by a distant bureaucracy rather than by local custom.

As mentioned earlier, I have heard people say Jamestown failed because it faced harsh natural conditions. But communal (and non-communal) settlements typically face harsh natural conditions. Jamestown had to deal with summer in Virginia. Hutterites dealt with winter on the Canadian prairie. It is revealing, not misleading, to compare Jamestown to settlements that faced harsher conditions more successfully. It also is fair to compare the two Jamestowns: the one before and the one immediately following Governor Dale's mandated privatization. What distinguished the first Jamestown from the second was not the harshness of its natural setting but rather the thoroughness with which it prevented people from internalizing externalities.

Sociologist Michael Hechter considers group solidarity to be a function of (a) the extent to which members depend on the group and (b) the extent to which the group can monitor and enforce compliance with expectations that members will contribute to the group rather than free ride upon it (Hechter 1983, p. 21). On this analysis, it is unsurprising that Hutterite communal society has been successful. Members are extremely dependent, for their upbringing leaves them unprepared to live in a non-Hutterite culture. Monitoring is intense. Feedback is immediate. But if that is the secret of Hutterite success, why did Jamestown fail? They too were extremely dependent on each other. They too had nowhere else to go. Monitoring was equally unproblematic. Everyone knew who was planting crops (no one) and who was bowling (everyone). What was the problem?

The problem lay in the guarantee embedded in the Jamestown colony's charter. Jamestown's charter entitled people to an equal share regardless of personal contribution, which is to say it took steps to ensure that individual workers would be maximally alienated from the fruits of their labors. The charter ensured that workers would think of their work as disappearing into an open-access commons.

Robert Goodin says, "Working within the constraints set by natural scarcity, the greatest practical obstacle to achieving as much justice as resources permit is, and always has been, the supposition that each of us should cultivate his own garden" (Goodin 1985, p. 1). However, Jamestown's charter did not suppose each of us should cultivate his own garden. It supposed the opposite. Colonists abided by the charter, and even while they suffered, people in other colonies were tending their own gardens, and thriving.

We should applaud institutions that encourage people to care for each other. But telling people they are required to tend someone else's garden rather than their own does not encourage people to care for each other. It does the opposite. It encourages spite. The people of Jamestown reached the point where they would rather die, bowling in the street, than tend the gardens of their free-riding neighbors, and die they did.

REFERENCES

Martin J. Bailey, "Approximate Optimality of Aboriginal Property Rights." *Journal of Law and Economics* 35 (1992): 183–98.

J. H. Bogart, "Lockean Provisos and State of Nature Theories." *Ethics* 95 (1985): 828–36.

R. Chesher, "Practical Problems in Coral Reef Utilization and Management: a Tongan Case Study." *Proceedings of the Fifth International Coral Reef Congress* 4 (1985): 213–24.

Harold Demsetz, "Toward a Theory of Property Rights." *American Economic Review* (Papers & Proceedings) 57 (1967): 347–59.

Robert C. Ellickson, "Property in Land." *Yale Law Journal* 102 (1993): 1315–1400.

Peggy Fosdick and Sam Fosdick, *Last Chance Lost?* (York, PA: Irvin S. Naylor Publishing, 1994).

Barbara Fried, "Wilt Chamberlain Revisited: Nozick's 'Justice in Transfer' and the Problem of Market-Based Distribution." *Philosophy and Public Affairs* 24 (1995): 226–45.

E. Gomez, A. Alcala, and A. San Diego. "Status of Philippine Coral Reefs—1981." *Proceedings of the Fourth International Coral Reef Symposium* 1 (1981): 275–85.

Robert E. Goodin, *Protecting the Vulnerable: Toward a Reanalysis of Our Social Responsibilities.* (Chicago: University of Chicago Press, 1985).

Michael Hechter, "A Theory of Group Solidarity." In Hechter, ed., *Microfoundations of Macrosociology* (Philadelphia: Temple University Press, 1983) pp. 16–57.

Virginia Held, "Introduction." In Held, ed., *Property, Profits, & Economic Justice* (Belmont: Wadsworth, 1980).

John Locke, *Second Treatise of Government,* ed. P. Laslett. (Cambridge: Cambridge University Press, 1690 [reprinted 1960]).

J. Madeleine Nash, "Wrecking the Reefs." *Time* (September 30, 1996): 60–2.

Carol Rose, "Possession as the Origin of Property." *University of Chicago Law Review* 52 (1985) 73–88.

Carol Rose, "The Comedy of the Commons: Custom, Commerce, and Inherently Public Property." *University of Chicago Law Review* 53 (1986) 711–87.

John T. Sanders, "Justice and the Initial Acquisition of Private Property." *Harvard Journal of Law and Public Policy* 10 (1987) 367–99.

Rolf Sartorius, "Persons and Property." In Ray Frey, ed., *Utility and Rights* (Minneapolis: University of Minnesota Press, 1984)

Judith Jarvis Thomson, *The Realm of Rights* (Cambridge: Harvard University Press, 1990).

Jeremy Waldron, "Enough and As Good Left For Others." *Philosophical Quarterly* 29 (1976): 319–28.

NOTES

1. Is it fair for latecomers to be excluded from acquiring property by rules allowing original appropriation? Sanders (1987, p. 385) notes that latecomers "are *not* excluded from acquiring property by these rules. They are, instead, excluded from being the first to own what has not been owned previously. Is *that* unfair?"

2. Nash (1996) says fishermen currently pump 330,000 pounds of cyanide per year into Philippine reefs.

3. I thank Peggy Fosdick at the National Aquarium in Baltimore for correspondence and documents. See also Fosdick and Fosdick (1994).

4. A private nonprofit organization, the Nature Conservancy, is pursuing such a strategy. Although not itself an original appropriator, it has acquired over a billion dollars' worth of land in an effort to preserve natural ecosystems. Note that this includes habitat for endangered species that have no market value.

5. This essay discusses Ellickson's article in some detail. While I take little credit for the ideas in the next few sections, any errors are presumably mine.

6. Of course, no one thinks governance by custom automatically solves commons problems. Custom works when local users can restrict outsider access and monitor insider behavior, but those conditions are not always met, and tragedies like those discussed earlier continue to occur.

7. One can see why many utilitarians claim Hume as a forerunner, and why Jeremy Bentham said upon reading Hume, "I felt as if the scales had fallen from my eyes."

8. *Two Treatises of Government*, Second Treatise, Chapter Five.

5 Markets

Discussions about markets are often unproductive because of their association with various political ideologies. Some proclaim their allegiance to free markets, while others see markets as a way for the powerful to promote class interests. But a market is merely an arena of exchange, a place in time or space in which goods are traded. Goods come in many different forms—tables and chairs, labor, books, ideas—and markets exist whenever goods are exchanged for other goods, or for money. The reader should be suspicious, then, about arguments for or against markets in general, since a lot depends on what is being traded, on the circumstances under which the trade is being made, and on what the relevant alternatives are.

MARKET ADVANTAGES

The classic explanation of how markets produce an abundance of wealth and a profusion of ideas comes from the first few chapters of Adam Smith's *Wealth of Nations*. Here Smith maintains that most productivity gains occasioned by market exchange come from the division of labor, or specialization. When the size of a market increases, Smith argues, producers have strong incentives to hire increasingly specialized workers whose labor, when brought together, produces exponential productivity gains. Since market exchange incentivizes specialization, and specialization is limited only by the extent of the market, Smith's argument suggests that trade is an increasingly positive sum game, and that more trading partners tends to make people across the globe better off than they would be with protectionist policies that insulate us from foreigners.

Smith introduces the idea of an invisible hand in the second chapter, when he says "[i]t is not from the benevolence of the butcher, the brewer, or the baker that we expect our dinner, but from their regard to their own interest." Smith's insight is that the benefits of the market do not depend on the beneficence of those within it. Self-interested action in the marketplace tends to make all parties better off (provided background rules defining property rights are clear, and rules against force and fraud are enforced), as if the process were guided by the invisible hand of someone concerned with social welfare. The invisible hand doesn't get explicitly mentioned until book IV of *Wealth,* but the idea pervades Smith's explanation of the advantage of market exchange from the beginning:

> [When a person directs his labor] in such a manner as its produce may be of the greatest value, he intends only his own gain, and he is in this, as in many other cases, led by an invisible hand to promote an end which was no part of his intention. Nor is it always the worse for the society that it was not part of it. By pursuing his own interest he frequently promotes that of the society more effectually than when he really intends to promote it (Book IV, ch. 2).

Smith often speaks of *cooperation* rather than *competition* as a central feature of market exchange, but he thinks of cooperation in an unusual way. As markets grow, people specialize and develop skills that allow them to make increasingly narrow but valuable contributions toward products consumed by people around the world. They are cooperating, in a sense, with people they may never know to create products of higher quality and lower price than would be possible if each person acted in isolation. Exchange then allows us to bring together resources from faraway places, and draw upon the ideas and labor of people distant in time and space.

Hayek argues that markets have another advantage: the prices that emerge within a market embody information about people's preferences and the relative scarcity and value placed on the alternative use of resources. If the price of coffee goes up, nobody needs to know *why* in order to respond in a socially beneficial way: consumers respond by economizing on coffee and searching for substitutes like tea; producers search for ways to increase the supply of coffee, or invent substitutes. Government planners, Hayek thinks, could not possibly have the kind of information that prices embody, and even if they did, they would lack the incentive to use the information to allocate scarce resources effectively. In some ways, Hayek thinks, we are better off not knowing why prices change, or how to make things as simple as shoes or pencils from scratch. Being able to use products without knowing how they were created frees up time to devote to other valuable pursuits, and it frees up cognitive space so that we can consume information that we care about.

Leonard Read's classic essay *I, Pencil* links Smith's point about specialization with Hayek's insight about how prices in a well-functioning market inadvertently lead people to behave in ways that are socially beneficial. Very few people, if any, know how to make a simple pencil from scratch, and yet each person, responding to signals sent by the relative prices of different inputs, does his part to produce pencils so cheap that most people can afford to ignore the store price and throw them into their shopping cart without thinking twice.

MARKET FAIRNESS

The history of analyzing the conditions under which the market price is the "just price," and the conditions under which exchange is voluntary, passes from Aristotle to Aquinas to Locke. Aquinas asks whether it can ever be just to "charge more than a thing is worth"? He gives a nuanced answer, noting that fraud, misrepresentation, or force all disqualify exchanges as sinful.

John Locke's short 1670 essay, "Venditio," takes up the question in a surprisingly modern way. He argues that the market price is always just, but that the prices actually observed in asymmetric bargains where one side has much greater power are not market prices. Market prices, Locke holds, require that both sides have good alternatives to striking a bargain, a conclusion that is quite close to the modern microeconomic conception of perfect competition. Michael Munger (2011) has tried to formalize notions of voluntary bargains and just prices in his conception of truly voluntary, or "euvoluntary," exchange. Munger argues that we should take the requirement of good alternatives seriously, maintaining that many actual exchanges are less than fully voluntary because of the lack of good alternatives. Nonetheless, one should be careful: the peasant who believes he must sell his kidney to feed his starving family will not be helped if the only thing the state does is to outlaw the sale of kidneys. The underlying cause of the desperate situation, the lack of alternatives, is made even worse by denying the peasant access to the one avenue available to him to mitigate the problem.

Adam Smith worries that although specialization and exchange generate social wealth and protect an important sphere of liberty, specialization can create jobs that dull the senses and stultify the mind. For some workers, Smith fears, "his dexterity at his own particular trade seems . . . to be acquired at the expence of his intellectual, social, and martial virtues" (V.1.178). For this reason, Smith sees a role for the state to promote the education of adults as well as children.

Smith also recognizes that markets might fail to supply what economists now call "public goods." In particular, Smith argues that governments should provide a military and court system, as well as "those public institutions and those public works, which, though they may be in the highest degree advantageous to a great society, are, however, of such a nature that the profit could never repay the expence to any individual or small number of individuals. . . ." (*Wealth*, V.1.69). Funding education (without monopolizing its delivery) and facilitating commerce by maintaining transportation infrastructure are among the central public goods Smith thinks the state should provide.

MARKET FAILURES

Public goods are widely considered a central source of market failure. As Tyler Cowen explains, goods are "public" when they have two features: *nonrivalry* and *nonexcludability.* Nonrivalry occurs when one person's consumption of a good doesn't diminish the amount available for others to consume, and nonexcludability means that nobody can be excluded from enjoying a good once it is produced. Most public goods are impure (they are either partly rival or partly excludable). For example, when car manufacturers were required to install catalytic converters in cars sold in California, the air in Los Angeles improved considerably, and residents could breathe cleaner air. But for those who live near the beach the benefits were minimal, since the breeze already blew smog particles toward Eastern Los Angeles. Clean air—and the policy that produced it—is still a paradigm public good, but one that is partly *rival.* Usually rivalry and excludability are a function of cost rather than an unchanging fact about the universe. Thus, we might sing a beautiful new song in public and then tell our listeners to swear never to repeat it. It is not impossible to prevent them from singing the song, but the cost of doing so might be prohibitive: we might bribe them to sign a contract, chain them to a fence and monitor them, or spend hours convincing them that the song simply isn't worth singing. Many goods are public because it is too costly to exclude those who benefit from them but don't contribute to their production.

It is worth emphasizing that public goods need not be "good for the public" in any sense. Publishing the genetic code of a virus with the power to kill millions of people is a clear case of a public good, though it may only be perceived as beneficial by scientists who study it, or dictators who wish to use it to kill innocent people. When thinking about which public goods governments ought to provide, we need to make a number of normative assumptions about the value of the good, the relative cost of market and government provision (or some combination of public and private provision), the opportunity costs of money spent on either directly providing or indirectly facilitating the provision of public goods, and which members of the public matter (e.g. one's constituents, citizens, or everyone who might be affected). Anomaly argues that the case for government provision of public goods requires us to answer normative questions that are often ignored by economists and policymakers.

Externalities occur whenever one person's actions impact another person's welfare, though the term comes from situations in which there are benefits or costs borne by people who are "external" to an exchange. Voluntary exchange generally promotes economically efficient outcomes in which net benefits are maximized. But uncompensated externalities can result in either too much of a socially harmful activity (such as pollution) or too little of a socially beneficial activity (such as basic science research, which cannot be patented). As Cowen suggests, public goods can often be thought of as nonexcludable positive externalities—benefits that generally don't get factored into private economic decisions. Friedman focuses on the challenge public goods and externalities pose to market efficiency, and discusses the many ingenious ways in which social norms and private contracts can facilitate the provision of public goods without government intervention. But there is no magic formula. Friedman, Cowen, and Anomaly emphasize that for any case of market failure—the failure of markets to efficiently allocate resources—created by externalities or public goods, we should compare the expected moral and economic consequences of free markets with the expected consequences of various kinds of government intervention. In other words, we need to compare the prospect of market failure with that of government failure.

FURTHER READING

Akerlof, George. 1970. "The Market for Lemons: Quality, Uncertainty, and the Market Mechanism." *The Quarterly Journal of Economics* 84 (3): 488–500.

Bastiat, Frédéric. 1850. "What Is Seen and What Is Not Seen." In *Selected Essays on Political Economy*, translated by Seymour Cain. The Foundation for Economic Education.

Brennan, Jason. 2014. *Why Not Capitalism?* Routledge Press.

Cohen, Gerald. 2009. *Why Not Socialism?* Princeton University Press.

Friedman, Milton. 2002 (40th anniversary edition). *Capitalism and Freedom.* University of Chicago Press.

Leeson, Peter. 2011. *The Invisible Hook: The Hidden Economics of Pirates.* Princeton University Press.

Otteson, James. 2014. *The End of Socialism*. Cambridge University Press.
Munger, Michael. 2011. "Euvoluntary or Not, Exchange is Just." *Social Philosophy and Policy* 28 (2): 192–211.
Radford, R.A. 1945. "The Economic Organization of a POW Camp." *Economica* 12 (48): 189–201.
Ridley, Matt. 2011. *The Rational Optimist: How Prosperity Evolves*. Harper Perennial.
Seabright, Paul. 2010. *The Company of Strangers: A Natural History of Economic Life*. Revised edition. Princeton University Press.

Market Advantages

Adam Smith

Wealth of Nations, "Of the Division of Labor"

1776

The greatest improvement in the productive powers of labour, and the greater part of the skill, dexterity, and judgment with which it is any where directed, or applied, seem to have been the effects of the division of labour.

The effects of the division of labour, in the general business of society, will be more easily understood, by considering in what manner it operates in some particular manufactures. It is commonly supposed to be carried furthest in some very trifling ones; not perhaps that it really is carried further in them than in others of more importance: but in those trifling manufactures which are destined to supply the small wants of but a small number of people, the whole number of workmen must necessarily be small; and those employed in every different branch of the work can often be collected into the same workhouse, and placed at once under the view of the spectator. In those great manufactures, on the contrary, which are destined to supply the great wants of the great body of the people, every different branch of the work employs so great a number of workmen, that it is impossible to collect them all into the same workhouse. We can seldom see more, at one time, than those employed in one single branch. Though in such manufactures, therefore, the work may really be divided into a much greater number of parts, than in those of a more trifling nature, the division is not near so obvious, and has accordingly been much less observed.

To take an example, therefore, from a very trifling manufacture; but one in which the division of labour has been very often taken notice of, the trade of the pin-maker; a workman not educated to this business

From Adam Smith and Edwin Cannan, *An Inquiry into the Nature and Causes of the Wealth of Nations*, Book 1. London: Methuen, 1904.

(which the division of labour has rendered a distinct trade), nor acquainted with the use of the machinery employed in it (to the invention of which the same division of labour has probably given occasion), could scarce, perhaps, with his utmost industry, make one pin in a day, and certainly could not make twenty. But in the way in which this business is now carried on, not only the whole work is a peculiar trade, but it is divided into a number of branches, of which the greater part are likewise peculiar trades. One man draws out the wire, another straights it, a third cuts it, a fourth points it, a fifth grinds it at the top for receiving the head; to make the head requires two or three distinct operations; to put it on, is a peculiar business, to whiten the pins is another; it is even a trade by itself to put them into the paper; and the important business of making a pin is, in this manner, divided into about eighteen distinct operations, which, in some manufactories, are all performed by distinct hands, though in others the same man will sometimes perform two or three of them. I have seen a small manufactory of this kind where ten men only were employed, and where some of them consequently performed two or three distinct operations. But though they were very poor, and therefore but indifferently accommodated with the necessary machinery, they could, when they exerted themselves, make among them about twelve pounds of pins in a day. There are in a pound upwards of four thousand pins of a middling size. Those ten persons, therefore, could make among them upwards of forty-eight thousand pins in a day. Each person, therefore, making a tenth part of forty-eight thousand pins, might be considered as making four thousand eight hundred pins in a day. But if they had all wrought separately and independently, and without any of them having been educated to this peculiar business, they certainly could not each of them have made twenty, perhaps not one pin in a day; that is, certainly, not the two hundred and fortieth, perhaps not the four thousand eight hundredth part of what they are at present capable of performing, in consequence of a proper division and combination of their different operations.

In every other art and manufacture, the effects of the division of labour are similar to what they are in this very trifling one; though, in many of them, the labour can neither be so much subdivided, nor reduced to so great a simplicity of operation. The division of labour, however, so far as it can be introduced, occasions, in every art, a proportionable increase of the productive powers of labour. The separation of different trades and employments from one another, seems to have taken place, in consequence of this advantage. This separation too is generally carried furthest in those countries which enjoy the highest degree of industry and improvement; what is the work of one man in a rude state of society, being generally that of several in an improved one. In every improved society, the farmer is generally nothing but a farmer; the manufacturer, nothing but a manufacturer. The labour too which is necessary to produce any one complete manufacture, is almost always divided among a great number of hands. How many different trades are employed in each branch of the linen and woollen manufactures, from the growers of the flax and the wool, to the bleachers and smoothers of the linen, or to the dyers and dressers of the cloth! The nature of agriculture, indeed, does not admit of so many subdivisions of labour, nor of so complete a separation of one business from another, as manufactures. It is impossible to separate so entirely, the business of the grazier from that of the corn-farmer, as the trade of the carpenter is commonly separated from that of the smith. The spinner is almost always a distinct person from the weaver; but the ploughman, the harrower, the sower of the seed, and the reaper of the corn, are often the same. The occasions for those different sorts of labour returning with the different seasons of the year, it is impossible that one man should be constantly employed in any one of them. This impossibility of making so complete and entire a separation of all the different branches of labour employed in agriculture, is perhaps the reason why the improvement of the productive powers of labour in this art, does not always keep pace with their improvement in manufactures. The most opulent nations, indeed, generally excel all their neighbours in agriculture as well as in manufactures; but they are commonly more distinguished by their superiority in the latter than in the former. Their lands are in general better cultivated, and having more labour and expence bestowed upon them, produce more in proportion to the extent and natural fertility of the ground. But this superiority of produce is seldom much more than in proportion to the superiority of labour and expence. In agriculture, the labour of the rich country is not always much more productive than that of the poor; or, at least, it is never so much more productive, as it commonly is in manufactures. The corn of the rich country, therefore, will not always, in the same degree of goodness, come cheaper to market than that of the poor. The corn of Poland, in the same degree of goodness, is as cheap as that of France, notwithstanding the superior opulence and improvement of the latter country. The corn of France is, in the corn provinces, fully as good, and in most years nearly about the same price with the corn of England, though, in opulence and improvement, France is perhaps inferior to England. The corn-lands of England, however, are better cultivated than those of France, and the corn-lands of France are said to be much better cultivated than those of Poland. But though the poor country, notwithstanding the inferiority of its cultivation, can, in some measure, rival the rich in the cheapness and goodness of its corn, it can pretend to no such competition in its manufactures; at least if those manufactures suit the soil, climate, and situation of the rich country. The silks of France are better and cheaper than those of England, because the silk manufacture, at least under the present high duties upon the importation of raw silk, does not so well suit the climate of England as that of France. But the hard-ware and the coarse woollens of England are beyond all comparison superior to those of France, and much cheaper too in the same degree of goodness. In Poland there are said to be scarce any manufactures of any kind, a few of those coarser household manufactures excepted, without which no country can well subsist.

This great increase of the quantity of work which, in consequence of the division of labour, the same number of people are capable of performing, is owing to three different circumstances; first to the increase of dexterity in every particular workman; secondly, to the saving of the time which is commonly lost in passing from one species of work to another; and lastly, to the invention of a great number of machines which facilitate and abridge labour, and enable one man to do the work of many.

First, the improvement of the dexterity of the workman necessarily increases the quantity of the work he can perform; and the division of labour, by reducing every man's business to some one simple operation, and by making this operation the sole employment of his life, necessarily increases very much the dexterity of the workman. A common smith, who, though accustomed to handle the hammer, has never been used to make nails, if upon some particular occasion he is obliged to attempt it, will scarce, I am assured, be able to make above two or three hundred nails in a day, and those too very bad ones. A smith who has been accustomed to make nails, but whose sole or principal business has not been that of a nailer, can seldom with his utmost diligence make more than eight hundred or a thousand nails in a day. I have seen several boys under twenty years of age who had never exercised any other trade but that of making nails, and who, when they exerted themselves, could make, each of them, upwards of two thousand three hundred nails in a day. The making of a nail, however, is by no means one of the simplest operations. The same person blows the bellows, stirs or mends the fire as there is occasion, heats the iron, and forges every part of the nail: In forging the head too he is obliged to change his tools. The different operations into which the making of a pin, or of a metal button, is subdivided, are all of them much more simple, and the dexterity of the person, of whose life it has been the sole business to perform them, is usually much greater. The rapidity with which some of the operations of those manufactures are performed, exceeds what the human hand could, by those who had never seen them, be supposed capable of acquiring.

Secondly, the advantage which is gained by saving the time commonly lost in passing from one sort of work to another, is much greater than we should at first view be apt to imagine it. It is impossible to pass very quickly from one kind of work to another; that is carried on in a different place, and with quite different tools. A country weaver, who cultivates a small farm, must lose a good deal of time in passing from his loom to the field, and from the field to his loom. When the two trades can be carried on in the same workhouse, the loss of time is no doubt much less. It is even in this case, however, very considerable. A man commonly saunters a little in turning his hand from one sort of employment to another. When he first begins the new work he is seldom very keen and hearty; his mind, as they say, does not go to it, and for some time he rather trifles than applies to good purpose. The habit of sauntering and of indolent careless application, which is naturally, or rather necessarily acquired by every country workman who is obliged to change his work and his tools every half hour, and to apply his hand in twenty different ways almost every day of his life; renders him almost always slothful and lazy, and incapable of any vigorous application even on the most pressing occasions. Independent, therefore, of his deficiency in point of dexterity, this cause alone must always reduce considerably the quantity of work which he is capable of performing.

Thirdly, and lastly, every body must be sensible how much labour is facilitated and abridged by the application of proper machinery. It is unnecessary to give any example. I shall only observe, therefore, that the invention of all those machines by which labour is so much facilitated and abridged, seems to have been originally owing to the division of labour. Men are much more likely to discover easier and readier methods of attaining any object, when the whole attention of their minds is directed towards that single object, than when it is dissipated among a great variety of things. But in consequence of the division of labour, the whole of every man's attention comes naturally to be directed towards some one very simple object. It is naturally to be expected, therefore, that some one or other of those who are employed in each particular branch of labour should soon find out easier and readier methods of performing their own particular work, wherever the nature of it admits of such improvement. A great part of the machines made use of in those manufactures in which labour is most subdivided, were originally the inventions of common workmen, who, being each of them employed in some very simple operation, naturally turned their thoughts towards finding out easier and readier methods of performing it. Whoever has been much accustomed to visit such manufactures, must frequently have been shewn very pretty machines, which were the inventions of such workmen, in order to facilitate and quicken their own particular part of the work. In the first fire-engines, a boy was constantly employed to open and shut alternately the communication between the boiler and the cylinder, according as the piston either ascended or descended. One of those boys, who loved to play with his companions, observed that, by tying a string from the handle of the valve which opened this communication, to another part of the machine, the valve would open and shut without his assistance, and leave him at liberty to divert himself with his play-fellows. One of the greatest improvements that has been made upon this machine, since it was first invented, was in this manner the discovery of a boy who wanted to save his own labour.

All the improvements in machinery, however, have by no means been the inventions of those who had occasion to use the machines. Many improvements have been made by the ingenuity of the makers of the machines, when to make them became the business of a peculiar trade; and some by that of those who are called philosophers or men of speculation, whose trade it is not to do anything, but to observe everything; and who, upon that account, are often capable of combining together the powers of the most distant and dissimilar objects. In the progress of society, philosophy or speculation becomes, like every other employment, the principal or sole trade and occupation of a particular class of citizens. Like every other employment too, it is subdivided into a great number of different branches, each of which affords occupation to a peculiar tribe or class of philosophers; and this subdivision of employment in philosophy, as well as in every other business, improves dexterity, and saves time. Each individual becomes more expert in his own peculiar branch, more work is done upon the whole, and the quantity of science is considerably increased by it.

It is the great multiplication of the productions of all the different arts, in consequence of the division of labour, which occasions, in a well-governed society, that universal opulence which extends itself to the lowest ranks of the people. Every workman has a great quantity of his own work to dispose of beyond what he himself has occasion for; and every other workman being exactly in the same situation, he is enabled to exchange a great quantity of his own goods for a great quantity, or, what comes to the same thing, for the price of a great quantity of theirs. He supplies them abundantly with what they have occasion for, and they accommodate him as amply with what he has occasion for, and a general plenty diffuses itself through all the different ranks of the society.

Observe the accommodation of the most common artificer or day-labourer in a civilized and thriving country, and you will perceive that the number of people of whose industry a part, though but a small part, has been employed in procuring him this accommodation, exceeds all computation. The woollen coat, for example, which covers the day-labourer, as coarse and rough as it may appear, is the produce of the joint labour of a great multitude of workmen. The shepherd, the sorter of the wool, the wool-comber or carder, the dyer, the scribbler, the spinner, the weaver, the fuller, the dresser, with many others, must all join their different arts in order to complete even this homely production. How many merchants and carriers, besides, must have been employed in transporting the materials from some of those workmen to others who often live in a very distant part of the country! how much commerce and navigation in particular, how many ship-builders, sailors, sail-makers, rope-makers, must have been employed in order to bring together the different drugs made use of by the dyer, which often come from the remotest corners of the world! What a variety of labour too is necessary in order to produce the tools of the meanest of those workmen! To say nothing of such complicated machines as the ship of the sailor, the mill of the fuller, or even the loom of the weaver, let us consider only what a variety of labour is requisite in order to form that very simple machine, the shears with which the shepherd clips the wool. The miner, the builder of the furnace for smelting the ore, the feller of the timber, the burner of the charcoal to be made use of in the smelting-house, the brick-maker, the brick-layer, the workmen who attend the furnace, the mill-wright, the forger, the smith, must all of them join their different arts in order to produce them. Were we to examine, in the same manner, all the different parts of his dress and household furniture, the coarse linen shirt which he wears next his skin, the shoes which cover his feet, the bed which he lies on, and all the different parts which compose it, the kitchen-grate at which he prepares his victuals, the coals which he makes use of for that purpose, dug from the bowels of the earth, and brought to him perhaps by a long sea and a long land carriage, all the other utensils of his kitchen, all the furniture of his table, the knives and forks, the earthen or pewter plates upon which he serves up and divides his victuals, the different hands employed in preparing his bread and his beer, the glass window which lets in the heat and the light, and keeps out the wind and the rain, with all the knowledge and art requisite for preparing that beautiful and happy invention, without which these northern parts of the world could scarce have afforded a very comfortable habitation, together with the tools of all the different workmen employed in producing those different conveniencies; if we examine, I say, all these things, and consider what a variety of labour is employed about each of them, we shall be sensible that without the assistance and co-operation of many thousands, the very meanest person in a civilized country could not be provided, even according to what we very falsely imagine, the easy and simple manner in which he is commonly accommodated. Compared, indeed, with the more extravagant luxury of the great, his accommodation must no doubt appear extremely simple and easy; and yet it may be true, perhaps, that the accommodation of an European prince does not always so much exceed that of an industrious and frugal peasant, as the accommodation of the latter exceeds that of many an African king, the absolute master of the lives and liberties of ten thousand naked savages.

OF THE PRINCIPLE WHICH GIVES OCCASION TO THE DIVISION OF LABOUR

This division of labour, from which so many advantages are derived, is not originally the effect of any human wisdom, which foresees and intends that general opulence to which it gives occasion. It is the necessary, though very slow and gradual, consequence of a certain propensity in human nature which has in view no such extensive utility; the propensity to truck, barter, and exchange one thing for another.

Whether this propensity be one of those original principles in human nature, of which no further account can be given; or whether, as seems more probable, it be the necessary consequence of the faculties of reason and speech, it belongs not to our present subject to enquire. It is common to all men, and to be found in no other race of animals, which seem to know neither this nor any other species of contracts. Two greyhounds, in running down the same hare, have sometimes the appearance of acting in some sort of concert. Each turns her towards his companion, or endeavours to intercept her when his companion turns her towards himself. This, however, is not the effect of any contract, but of the accidental concurrence of their passions in the same object at that particular time. Nobody ever saw a dog make a fair and deliberate exchange of one bone for another with another dog. Nobody ever saw one animal by its gestures and natural cries signify to another, this is mine, that yours; I am willing to give this for that. When an animal wants to obtain something either of a man or of another animal, it has no other means of persuasion but to gain the favour of those whose service it requires. A puppy fawns upon its dam, and a spaniel endeavours by a thousand attractions to engage the attention of its master who is at dinner, when it wants to be fed by him. Man sometimes uses the same arts with his brethren, and when he has no other means of engaging them to act according to his inclinations, endeavours by every servile and fawning attention to obtain their good will. He has not time, however, to do this upon every occasion. In civilized society he stands at all times in need of the cooperation and assistance of great multitudes, while his whole life is scarce sufficient to gain the friendship of a few persons. In almost every other race of animals each individual, when it is grown up to maturity, is entirely independent, and in its natural state has occasion for the assistance of no other living creature. But man has almost constant occasion for the help of his brethren, and it is in vain for him to expect it from their benevolence only. He will be more likely to prevail if he can interest their self-love in his favour, and show them that it is for their own advantage to do for him what he requires of them. Whoever offers to another a bargain of any kind, proposes to do this. Give me that which I want, and you shall have this which you want, is the meaning of every such offer; and it is in this manner that we obtain from one another the far greater part of those good offices which we stand in need of. It is not from the benevolence of the butcher, the brewer, or the baker, that we expect our dinner, but from their regard to their own interest. We address ourselves, not to their humanity but to their self-love, and never talk to them of our own necessities but of their advantages. Nobody but a beggar chuses to depend chiefly upon the benevolence of his fellow-citizens. Even a beggar does not depend upon it entirely. The charity of well-disposed people, indeed, supplies him with the whole fund of his subsistence. But though this principle ultimately provides him with all the necessaries of life which he has occasion for, it neither does nor can provide him with them as he has occasion for them. The greater part of his occasional wants are supplied in the same manner as those of other people, by treaty, by barter, and by purchase. With the money which one man gives him he purchases food. The old cloaths which another bestows upon him he exchanges for other old cloaths which suit him better, or for lodging, or for food, or for money, with which he can buy either food, cloaths, or lodging, as he has occasion.

As it is by treaty, by barter, and by purchase, that we obtain from one another the greater part of those mutual good offices which we stand in need of, so it is this same trucking disposition which originally gives occasion to the division of labour. In a tribe of hunters or shepherds a particular person makes bows and arrows, for example, with more readiness and dexterity than any other. He frequently exchanges them for cattle or for venison with his companions; and he finds at last that he can in this manner get more cattle and venison, than if he himself went to the field to catch them. From a regard to his own interest, therefore, the making of bows and arrows grows to be his chief business, and he becomes a sort of armourer. Another excels in making the frames and covers of their little huts or moveable houses. He is accustomed to be of use in this way to his neighbours, who reward him in the same manner with cattle and with venison, till at last he finds it his interest to dedicate himself entirely to this employment, and to become a sort of house-carpenter. In the same manner a third becomes a smith or a brazier; a fourth a tanner or dresser of hides or skins, the principal part of the clothing of savages. And thus the certainty of being able to exchange all that surplus part of the produce of his own labour, which is over and above his own consumption, for such parts of the produce of other men's labour as he may have occasion for, encourages every man to apply himself to a particular occupation, and to cultivate and bring to perfection whatever talent or genius he may possess for that particular species of business.

The difference of natural talents in different men is, in reality, much less than we are aware of; and the very different genius which appears to distinguish men of different professions, when grown up to maturity, is not upon many occasions so much the cause, as the effect of the division of labour. The difference between the most dissimilar characters, between a philosopher and a common street porter, for example, seems to arise not so much from nature, as from habit, custom, and education. When they came into the world, and for the first six or eight years of their existence, they were perhaps, very much alike, and neither their parents nor playfellows could perceive any remarkable difference. About that age, or soon after, they come to be employed in very different occupations. The difference of talents comes then to be taken notice of, and widens by degrees, till at last the vanity of the philosopher is willing to acknowledge scarce any resemblance. But without the disposition to truck, barter, and exchange, every man must have procured to himself every necessary and conveniency of life which he wanted. All must have had the same duties to perform, and the same work to do, and there could have been no such difference of employment as could alone give occasion to any great difference of talents.

As it is this disposition which forms that difference of talents, so remarkable among men of different professions, so it is this same disposition which renders that difference useful. Many tribes of animals acknowledged to be all of the same species, derive from nature a much more remarkable distinction of genius, than what, antecedent to custom and education, appears to take place among men. By nature a philosopher is not in genius and disposition half so different from a street porter, as a mastiff is from a greyhound, or a greyhound from a spaniel, or this last from a shepherd's dog. Those different tribes of animals, however, though all of the same species, are of scarce any use to one another. The strength of the mastiff is not in the least supported either by the swiftness of the greyhound, or by the sagacity of the spaniel, or by the docility of the shepherd's dog. The effects of those different geniuses and talents, for want of the power or disposition to barter and exchange, cannot be brought into a common stock, and do not in the least contribute to the better accommodation and conveniency of the species. Each animal is still obliged to support and defend itself, separately and independently, and derives no sort of advantage from that variety of talents with which nature has distinguished its fellows. Among men, on the contrary, the most dissimilar geniuses are of use to one another; the different produces of their respective talents, by the general disposition to truck, barter, and exchange, being brought, as it were, into a common stock, where every man may purchase whatever part of the produce of other men's talents he has occasion for.

THAT THE DIVISION OF LABOUR IS LIMITED BY THE EXTENT OF THE MARKET

As it is the power of exchanging that gives occasion to the division of labour, so the extent of this division must always be limited by the extent of that power, or, in other words, by the extent of the market. When the market is very small, no person can have any encouragement to dedicate himself entirely to one employment, for want of the power to exchange all that surplus part of the produce of his own labour, which is over and above his own consumption, for such parts of the produce of other men's labour as he has occasion for.

There are some sorts of industry, even of the lowest kind, which can be carried on nowhere but in a great town. A porter, for example, can find employment and subsistence in no other place. A village is by much too narrow a sphere for him; even an ordinary market town is scarce large enough to afford him constant occupation. In the lone houses and very small villages which are scattered about in so desert a country as the Highlands of Scotland, every farmer must be butcher, baker and brewer for his own family. In such situations we can scarce expect to find even a smith, a carpenter, or a mason, within less than twenty miles of another of the same trade. The scattered families that live at eight or ten miles distance from the nearest of them, must learn to perform themselves a great number of little pieces of work, for which, in more populous countries, they would call in the assistance of those workmen. Country workmen are almost everywhere obliged to apply themselves to all the different branches of industry that have so much affinity to one another as to be employed about the same sort of materials. A country carpenter deals in every sort of work that is made of wood: a country smith in every sort of work that is made of iron. The former is not only a carpenter, but a joiner, a cabinet maker, and even a carver in wood, as well as a wheelwright, a ploughwright, a cart and wagon maker. The employments of the latter are still more various. It is impossible there should be such a trade as even that of a nailer in the remote and inland parts of the Highlands of Scotland. Such a workman at the rate of a thousand nails a day, and three hundred working days in the year, will make three hundred thousand nails in the year. But in such a situation it would be impossible to dispose of one thousand, that is, of one day's work in the year.

As by means of water-carriage a more extensive market is opened to every sort of industry than what land-carriage alone can afford it, so it is upon the sea-coast, and along the banks of navigable rivers, that industry of every kind naturally begins to subdivide and improve itself, and it is frequently not till a long time after that those improvements extend themselves to the inland parts of the country. A broad-wheeled wagon, attended by two men, and drawn by eight horses, in about six weeks time carries and brings back between London and Edinburgh near four ton weight of goods. In about the same time a ship navigated by six or eight men, and sailing between the ports of London and Leith, frequently carries and brings back two hundred ton weight of goods. Six or eight men, therefore, by the help of water-carriage, can carry and bring back in the same time the same quantity of goods between London and Edinburgh, as fifty broad-wheeled wagons, attended by a hundred men, and drawn by four hundred horses. Upon two hundred tons of goods, therefore, carried by the cheapest land-carriage from London to Edinburgh, there must be charged the maintenance of a hundred men for three weeks, and both the maintenance, and, what is nearly equal to the maintenance, the wear and tear of four hundred horses as well as of fifty great wagons. Whereas, upon the same quantity of goods carried by water, there is to be charged only the maintenance of six or eight men, and the wear and tear of a ship of two hundred tons burthen, together with the value of the superior risk, or the difference of the insurance between land and water-carriage. Were there no other communication between those two places, therefore, but by land-carriage, as no goods could be transported from the one to the other, except such whose price was very considerable in proportion to their weight, they could carry on but a small part of that commerce which at present subsists between them, and consequently could give but a small part of that encouragement which they at present mutually afford to each other's industry. There could be little or no commerce of any kind between the distant parts of the world. What goods could bear the expence of land-carriage between London and Calcutta? Or if there were any so precious as to be able to support this expence, with what safety could they be transported through the territories of so many barbarous nations? Those two cities, however, at present carry on a very considerable commerce with each other, and by mutually affording a market, give a good deal of encouragement to each other's industry.

Since such, therefore, are the advantages of water-carriage, it is natural that the first improvements of art and industry should be made where this conveniency opens the whole world for a market to the produce of every sort of labour, and that they should always be much later in extending themselves into the inland parts of the country. The inland parts of the country can for a long time have no other market for the greater part of their goods, but the country which lies round about them, and separates them from the sea-coast, and the great navigable rivers. The extent of their market, therefore, must for a long time be in proportion to the riches and populousness of that country, and consequently their improvement must always be posterior to the improvement of that country. In our North American colonies the plantations have constantly followed either the sea-coast or the banks of the navigable rivers, and have scarce anywhere extended themselves to any considerable distance from both.

FRIEDRICH HAYEK

The Use of Knowledge in Society

1945

What is the problem we wish to solve when we try to construct a rational economic order? On certain familiar assumptions the answer is simple enough. If we possess all the relevant information, if we can start out from a given system of preferences, and if we command complete knowledge of available means, the problem which remains is purely one of logic. That is, the answer to the question of what is the best use of the available means is implicit in our assumptions. The conditions which the solution of this optimum problem must satisfy have been fully worked out and can be stated best in mathematical form: put at their briefest, they are that the marginal rates of substitution between any two commodities or factors must be the same in all their different uses.

This, however, is emphatically *not* the economic problem which society faces. And the economic calculus which we have developed to solve this logical problem, though an important step toward the solution of the economic problem of society, does not yet provide an answer to it. The reason for this is that the "data" from which the economic calculus starts are never for the whole society "given" to a single mind which could work out the implications, and can never be so given.

The peculiar character of the problem of a rational economic order is determined precisely by the fact that the knowledge of the circumstances of which we must make use never exists in concentrated or integrated form but solely as the dispersed bits of incomplete and frequently contradictory knowledge which all the separate individuals possess. The economic problem of society is thus not merely a problem of how to allocate "given" resources—if "given" is taken to mean given to a single mind which deliberately solves the problem set by these "data." It is

Friedrich Hayek, "The Use of Knowledge in Society." *American Economic Review* 35 (4) (1945): 519–30. By permission of *American Economic Review.*

rather a problem of how to secure the best use of resources known to any of the members of society, for ends whose relative importance only these individuals know. Or, to put it briefly, it is a problem of the utilization of knowledge which is not given to anyone in its totality.

This character of the fundamental problem has, I am afraid, been obscured rather than illuminated by many of the recent refinements of economic theory, particularly by many of the uses made of mathematics. Though the problem with which I want primarily to deal in this paper is the problem of a rational economic organization, I shall in its course be led again and again to point to its close connections with certain methodological questions. Many of the points I wish to make are indeed conclusions toward which diverse paths of reasoning have unexpectedly converged. But, as I now see these problems, this is no accident. It seems to me that many of the current disputes with regard to both economic theory and economic policy have their common origin in a misconception about the nature of the economic problem of society. This misconception in turn is due to an erroneous transfer to social phenomena of the habits of thought we have developed in dealing with the phenomena of nature.

In ordinary language we describe by the word "planning" the complex of interrelated decisions about the allocation of our available resources. All economic activity is in this sense planning; and in any society in which many people collaborate, this planning, whoever does it, will in some measure have to be based on knowledge which, in the first instance, is not given to the planner but to somebody else, which somehow will have to be conveyed to the planner. The various ways in which the knowledge on which people base their plans is communicated to them is the crucial problem for any theory explaining the economic process, and the problem of what is the best way of utilizing knowledge initially dispersed among all the people is at least one of the main problems of economic policy, or of designing an efficient economic system.

The answer to this question is closely connected with that other question which arises here, that of who is to do the planning. It is around this question that all the dispute about "economic planning" centers. This is not a dispute about whether planning is to be done or not. It is a dispute as to whether planning is to be done centrally, by one authority for the whole economic system, or is to be divided among many individuals. Planning in the specific sense in which the term is used in contemporary controversy necessarily means central planning—direction of the whole economic system according to one unified plan. Competition, on the other hand, means decentralized planning by many separate persons. The halfway house between the two, about which many people talk but which few like when they see it, is the delegation of planning to organized industries, or, in other words, monopolies.

Which of these systems is likely to be more efficient depends mainly on the question under which of them we can expect that fuller use will be made of the existing knowledge. This, in turn, depends on whether we are more likely to succeed putting at the disposal of a single central authority all the knowledge which ought to be used but which is initially dispersed among many different individuals, or in conveying to the individuals such additional knowledge as they need in order to enable them to dovetail their plans with those of others.

It will at once be evident that on this point the position will be different with respect to different kinds of knowledge. The answer to our question will therefore largely turn on the relative importance of the different kinds of knowledge: those more likely to be at the disposal of particular individuals and those which we should with greater confidence expect to find in the possession of an authority made up of suitably chosen experts. If it is today so widely assumed that the latter will be in a better position, this is because one kind of knowledge, namely, scientific knowledge, occupies now so prominent a place in public imagination that we tend to forget that it is not the only kind that is relevant. It may be admitted that, as far as scientific knowledge is concerned, a body of suitably chosen experts may be in the best position to command all the best knowledge available—though this is of course merely shifting the difficulty to the problem of selecting the experts. What I wish to point out is that, even assuming that this problem can be readily solved, it is only a small part of the wider problem.

Today it is almost heresy to suggest that scientific knowledge is not the sum of all knowledge. But a little reflection will show that there is beyond question a body of very important but unorganized knowledge which cannot possibly be called scientific in the sense of knowledge of general rules: the knowledge of the particular circumstances of time and place. It is with respect to this that practically every individual has some advantage over all others because he possesses unique information of which beneficial use might be made, but of which use can be made only if the decisions depending on it are left to him or are made with his active co-operation. We need to remember only how much we have to learn in any occupation after we have completed our theoretical training, how big a part of our working life we spend learning particular jobs, and how valuable an asset in all walks of life is knowledge of people, of local conditions, and of special circumstances. To know of and put to use a machine not fully employed, or somebody's skill which could be better utilized, or to be aware of a surplus stock which can be drawn upon during an interruption of supplies, is socially quite as useful as the knowledge of better alternative techniques. The shipper who earns his living from using otherwise empty or half-filled journeys of tramp-steamers, or the estate agent whose whole knowledge is almost exclusively one of temporary opportunities, or the arbitrageur who gains from local differences of commodity prices—are all performing eminently useful functions based on special knowledge of circumstances of the fleeting moment not known to others.

It is a curious fact that this sort of knowledge should today be generally regarded with a kind of contempt and that anyone who by such knowledge gains an advantage over somebody better equipped with theoretical or technical knowledge is thought to have acted almost disreputably. To gain an advantage from better knowledge of facilities of communication or transport is sometimes regarded as almost dishonest, although it is quite as important that society make use of the best opportunities in this respect as in using the latest scientific discoveries. This prejudice has in a considerable measure affected the attitude toward commerce in general compared with that toward production. Even economists who regard themselves as definitely immune to the crude materialist fallacies of the past constantly commit the same mistake where activities directed toward the acquisition of such practical knowledge are concerned—apparently because in their scheme of things all such knowledge is supposed to be "given." The common idea now seems to be that all such knowledge should as a matter of course be readily at the command of everybody, and the reproach of irrationality leveled against the existing economic order is frequently based on the fact that it is not so available. This view disregards the fact that the method by which such knowledge can be made as widely available as possible is precisely the problem to which we have to find an answer.

If it is fashionable today to minimize the importance of the knowledge of the particular circumstances of time and place, this is closely connected with the smaller importance which is now attached to change as such. Indeed, there are few points on which the assumptions made (usually only implicitly) by the "planners" differ from those of their opponents as much as with regard to the significance and frequency of changes which will make substantial alterations of production plans necessary. Of course, if detailed economic plans could be laid down for fairly long periods in advance and then closely adhered to, so that no further economic decisions of importance would be required, the task of drawing up a comprehensive plan governing all economic activity would be much less formidable.

It is, perhaps, worth stressing that economic problems arise always and only in consequence of change. As long as things continue as before, or at least as they were expected to, there arise no new problems requiring a decision, no need to form a new plan. The belief that changes have become less important in modern times implies the contention that economic problems also have become less important. This belief in the decreasing importance of change is, for that reason, usually held by the same people who argue that the importance of economic considerations has been driven into the background by the growing importance of technological knowledge.

Is it true that, with the elaborate apparatus of modern production, economic decisions are required only at long intervals, as when a new factory is to be erected or a new process to be introduced? Is it true that, once a plant has been built, the rest is all more or less mechanical, determined by the character of the plant, and leaving little to be changed in adapting to the ever changing circumstances of the moment?

The fairly widespread belief in the affirmative is not, as far as I can ascertain, borne out by the practical experience of the businessman. In a competitive industry at any rate—and such an industry alone can serve as a test—the task of keeping cost from rising requires constant struggle, absorbing a great part of the energy of the manager. How easy it is for an inefficient manager to dissipate the differentials on which profitability rests and that it is possible, with the same technical facilities, to produce with a great variety of costs are among the commonplaces of business experience which do not seem to be equally familiar in the study of the economist. The very strength of the desire, constantly voiced by producers and engineers, to be allowed to proceed untrammeled by considerations of money costs, is eloquent testimony to the extent to which these factors enter into their daily work.

One reason why economists are increasingly apt to forget about the constant small changes which make up the whole economic picture is probably their growing preoccupation with statistical aggregates, which show a very much greater stability than the movements of the detail. The comparative stability of the aggregates cannot, however, be accounted for—as the statisticians occasionally seem to be inclined to do—by the "law of large numbers" or the mutual compensation of random changes. The number of elements with which we have to deal is not large enough for such accidental forces to produce stability. The continuous flow of goods and services is maintained by constant deliberate adjustments, by new dispositions made every day in the light of circumstances not known the day before, by B stepping in at once when A fails to deliver. Even the large and highly mechanized plant keeps going largely because of an environment upon which it can draw for all sorts of unexpected needs: tiles for its roof, stationery or its forms, and all the thousand and one kinds of equipment in which it cannot be self-contained and which the plans for the operation of the plant require to be readily available in the market.

This is, perhaps, also the point where I should briefly mention the fact that the sort of knowledge with which I have been concerned is knowledge of the kind which by its nature cannot enter into statistics and therefore cannot be conveyed to any central authority in statistical form. The statistics which such a central authority would have to use would have to be arrived at precisely by abstracting from minor differences between the things, by lumping together, as resources of one kind, items which differ as regards location, quality, and other particulars, in a way which may be very significant for the specific decision. It follows from this that central planning based on statistical information by its nature cannot take direct account of these circumstances of time and place and that the central planner will have to find some way or other in which the decisions depending on them can be left to the "man on the spot."

If we can agree that the economic problem of society is mainly one of rapid adaptation to changes in the particular circumstances of time and place, it would seem to follow that the ultimate decisions must be left to the people who are familiar with these circumstances, who know directly of the relevant changes and of the resources immediately available to meet them. We cannot expect that this problem will be solved by first communicating all this knowledge to a central board which, after integrating all knowledge, issues its orders. We must solve it by some form of decentralization. But this answers only part of our problem. We need decentralization because only thus can we insure that the knowledge of the particular circumstances of time and place will be promptly used. But the "man on the spot" cannot decide solely on the basis of his limited but intimate knowledge of the facts of his immediate surroundings. There still remains the problem of communicating to him such further information as he needs to fit his decisions into the whole pattern of changes of the larger economic system.

How much knowledge does he need to do so successfully? Which of the events which happen beyond the horizon of his immediate knowledge are of relevance to his immediate decision, and how much of them need he know?

There is hardly anything that happens anywhere in the world that *might* not have an effect on the decision he ought to make. But he need not know of these events as such, nor of *all* their effects. It does not matter for him *why* at the particular moment more screws of one size than of another are wanted, *why* paper bags are more readily available than canvas bags, or *why* skilled labor, or particular machine tools, have for the moment become more difficult to obtain. All that is significant for him *is how much more or less* difficult to procure they have become compared with other things with which he is also concerned, or how much more or less urgently wanted are the alternative things he produces or uses. It is always a question of the relative importance of the particular things with which he is concerned, and the causes which alter their relative importance are of no interest to him beyond the effect on those concrete things of his own environment. . . .

Fundamentally, in a system in which the knowledge of the relevant facts is dispersed among many people, prices can act to coordinate the separate actions of different people in the same way as subjective values help the individual to coordinate the parts of his plan. It is worth contemplating for a moment a very simple and commonplace instance of the action of the price system to see what precisely it accomplishes. Assume that somewhere in the world a new opportunity for the use of some raw material, say, tin, has arisen, or that one of the sources of supply of tin has been eliminated. It does not matter for our purpose—and it is significant that it does not matter—which of these two causes has made tin more scarce. All that the users of tin need to know is that some of the tin they used to consume is now more profitably employed elsewhere and that, in consequence, they must economize tin. There is no need for the great majority of them even to know where the more urgent need has arisen, or in favor of what other needs they ought to husband the supply. If only some of them know directly of the new demand, and switch resources over to it, and if the people who are aware of the new gap thus created in turn fill it from still other sources, the effect will rapidly spread throughout the whole economic system and influence not only all the uses of tin but also those of its substitutes and the substitutes of these substitutes, the supply of all the things made of tin, and their substitutes, and so on; and all this without the great majority of those instrumental in bringing about these substitutions knowing anything at all about the original cause of these changes. The whole acts as one market, not because any of its members survey the whole field, but because their limited individual fields of vision sufficiently overlap so that through many intermediaries the relevant information is communicated to all. The mere fact that there is one price for any commodity—or rather that local prices are connected in a manner determined by the cost of transport, etc.—brings about the solution which (it is just conceptually possible) might have been arrived at by one single mind possessing all the information which is in fact dispersed among all the people involved in the process.

We must look at the price system as such a mechanism for communicating information if we want to understand its real function—a function which, of course, it fulfils less perfectly as prices grow more rigid. (Even when quoted prices have become quite rigid, however, the forces which would operate through changes in price still operate to a considerable extent through changes in the other terms of the contract.) The most significant fact about this system is the economy of knowledge with which it operates, or how little the individual participants need to know in order to be able to take the right action. In abbreviated form, by a kind of symbol, only the most essential information is passed on and passed on only to those concerned. It is more than a metaphor to describe the price system as a kind of machinery for registering change, or a system of telecommunications which enables individual producers to watch merely the movement of a few pointers, as an engineer might watch the hands of a few dials, in order to adjust their activities to changes of which they may never know more than is reflected in the price movement.

Of course, these adjustments are probably never "perfect" in the sense in which the economist conceives of them in his equilibrium analysis. But I fear that our theoretical habits of approaching the problem with the assumption of more or less perfect knowledge on the part of almost everyone has made us somewhat blind to the true function of the price mechanism and led us to apply rather misleading standards in judging its efficiency. The marvel is that in a case like that of a scarcity of one raw material, without an order being issued, without more than perhaps a handful of people knowing the cause, tens of thousands of people whose identity could not be ascertained by months of investigation, are made to use the material or its products more sparingly; that is, they move in the right direction. This is enough of a marvel even if, in a constantly changing world, not all will hit it off so perfectly that their profit rates will always be maintained at the same even or "normal" level.

I have deliberately used the word "marvel" to shock the reader out of the complacency with which we often take the working of this mechanism for granted. I am convinced that if it were the result of deliberate human design, and if the people guided by the price changes understood that their decisions have significance far beyond their immediate aim, this mechanism would have been acclaimed as one of the greatest triumphs of the human mind. Its misfortune is the double one that it is not the product of human design and that the people guided by it usually do not know why they are made to do what they do. But those who clamor for "conscious direction"—and who cannot believe that anything which has evolved without design (and even without our understanding it) should solve problems which we should not be able to solve consciously—should remember this: The problem is precisely how to extend the span of our utilization of resources beyond the span of the control of any one mind; and therefore, how to dispense with the need of conscious control, and how to provide inducements which will make the individuals do the desirable things without anyone having to tell them what to do.

The problem which we meet here is by no means peculiar to economics but arises in connection with nearly all truly social phenomena, with language and with most of our cultural inheritance, and constitutes really the central theoretical problem of all social science. As Alfred Whitehead has said in another connection, "It is a profoundly erroneous truism, repeated by all copy-books and by eminent people when they are making speeches, that we should cultivate the habit of thinking what we are doing. The precise opposite is the case. Civilization advances by extending the number of important operations which we can perform without thinking about them."

This is of profound significance in the social field. We make constant use of formulas, symbols, and rules whose meaning we do not understand and through the use of which we avail ourselves of the assistance of knowledge which individually we do not possess. We have developed these practices and institutions by building upon habits and institutions which have proved successful in their own sphere and which have in turn become the foundation of the civilization we have built up.

The price system is just one of those formations which man has learned to use (though he is still very far from having learned to make the best use of it) after he had stumbled upon it without understanding it. Through it not only a division of labor but also a coordinated utilization of resources based on an equally divided knowledge has become possible. The people who like to deride any suggestion that this may be so usually distort the argument by insinuating that it asserts that by some miracle just that sort of system has spontaneously grown up which is best suited to modern civilization. It is the other way round: man has been able to develop that division of labor on which our civilization is based because he happened to stumble upon a method which made it possible. Had he not done so, he might still have developed some other, altogether different, type of civilization, something like the "state" of the termite ants, or some other altogether unimaginable type. All that we can say is that nobody has yet succeeded in designing an alternative system in which certain features of the existing one can be preserved which are dear even to those who most violently assail it—such as particularly the extent to which the individual can choose his pursuits and consequently freely use his own knowledge and skill.

LEONARD READ

I, Pencil

1958

I am a lead pencil—the ordinary wooden pencil familiar to all boys and girls and adults who can read and write.

Writing is both my vocation and my avocation; that's all I do.

You may wonder why I should write a genealogy. Well, to begin with, my story is interesting. And, next, I am a mystery—more so than a tree or a sunset or even a flash of lightning. But, sadly, I am taken for granted by those who use me, as if I were a mere incident and without background. This supercilious attitude relegates me to the level of the commonplace. This is a species of the grievous error in which mankind cannot too long persist without peril. For, the wise G. K. Chesterton observed, "We are perishing for want of wonder, not for want of wonders."

I, Pencil, simple though I appear to be, merit your wonder and awe, a claim I shall attempt to prove. In fact, if you can understand me—no, that's too much to ask of anyone—if you can become aware of the miraculousness which I symbolize, you can help save the freedom mankind is so unhappily losing. I have a profound lesson to teach. And I can teach this lesson better than can an automobile or an airplane or a mechanical dishwasher because—well, because I am seemingly so simple.

Simple? Yet, *not a single person on the face of this earth knows how to make me.* This sounds fantastic, doesn't it? Especially when it is realized that there are about one and one-half billion of my kind produced in the U.S.A. each year.

Pick me up and look me over. What do you see? Not much meets the eye—there's some wood, lacquer, the printed labeling, graphite lead, a bit of metal, and an eraser.

INNUMERABLE ANTECEDENTS

Just as you cannot trace your family tree back very far, so is it impossible for me to name and explain all my antecedents. But I would like to suggest enough of them to impress upon you the richness and complexity of my background.

My family tree begins with what in fact is a tree, a cedar of straight grain that grows in Northern California and Oregon. Now contemplate all the saws and trucks and rope and the countless other gear used in harvesting and carting the cedar logs to the railroad siding. Think of all the persons and the numberless skills that went into their fabrication: the mining of ore, the making of steel and its refinement into saws, axes, motors; the growing of hemp and bringing it through all the stages to heavy and strong rope; the logging camps with their beds and mess halls, the cookery and the raising of all the foods. Why, untold thousands of persons had a hand in every cup of coffee the loggers drink!

The logs are shipped to a mill in San Leandro, California. Can you imagine the individuals who make flat cars and rails and railroad engines and who construct and install the communication systems incidental thereto? These legions are among my antecedents.

Consider the millwork in San Leandro. The cedar logs are cut into small, pencil-length slats less than one-fourth of an inch in thickness. These are kiln dried and then tinted for the same reason women put rouge on their faces. People prefer that I look pretty, not a pallid white. The slats are waxed and kiln dried again. How many skills went into the making of the tint and the kilns, into supplying the heat, the light

Leonard Read, "I, Pencil." *The Freeman*, December 1958. Permission by Foundation for Economic Education (www.FEE.org).

and power, the belts, motors, and all the other things a mill requires? Sweepers in the mill among my ancestors? Yes, and included are the men who poured the concrete for the dam of a Pacific Gas & Electric Company hydroplant which supplies the mill's power!

Don't overlook the ancestors present and distant who have a hand in transporting sixty carloads of slats across the nation.

Once in the pencil factory—$4,000,000 in machinery and building, all capital accumulated by thrifty and saving parents of mine—each slat is given eight grooves by a complex machine, after which another machine lays leads in every other slat, applies glue, and places another slat atop— a lead sandwich, so to speak. Seven brothers and I are mechanically carved from this "wood-clinched" sandwich.

My "lead" itself—it contains no lead at all—is complex. The graphite is mined in Ceylon. Consider these miners and those who make their many tools and the makers of the paper sacks in which the graphite is shipped and those who make the string that ties the sacks and those who put them aboard ships and those who make the ships. Even the lighthouse keepers along the way assisted in my birth—and the harbor pilots.

The graphite is mixed with clay from Mississippi in which ammonium hydroxide is used in the refining process. Then wetting agents are added such as sulfonated tallow—animal fats chemically reacted with sulfuric acid. After passing through numerous machines, the mixture finally appears as endless extrusions—as from a sausage grinder-cut to size, dried, and baked for several hours at 1,850 degrees Fahrenheit. To increase their strength and smoothness the leads are then treated with a hot mixture which includes candelilla wax from Mexico, paraffin wax, and hydrogenated natural fats.

My cedar receives six coats of lacquer. Do you know all the ingredients of lacquer? Who would think that the growers of castor beans and the refiners of castor oil are a part of it? They are. Why, even the processes by which the lacquer is made a beautiful yellow involve the skills of more persons than one can enumerate!

Observe the labeling. That's a film formed by applying heat to carbon black mixed with resins. How do you make resins and what, pray, is carbon black?

My bit of metal—the ferrule—is brass. Think of all the persons who mine zinc and copper and those who have the skills to make shiny sheet brass from these products of nature. Those black rings on my ferrule are black nickel. What is black nickel and how is it applied? The complete story of why the center of my ferrule has no black nickel on it would take pages to explain.

Then there's my crowning glory, inelegantly referred to in the trade as "the plug," the part man uses to erase the errors he makes with me. An ingredient called "factice" is what does the erasing. It is a rubber-like product made by reacting rape-seed oil from the Dutch East Indies with sulfur chloride. Rubber, contrary to the common notion, is only for binding purposes. Then, too, there are numerous vulcanizing and accelerating agents. The pumice comes from Italy; and the pigment which gives "the plug" its color is cadmium sulfide.

NO ONE KNOWS

Does anyone wish to challenge my earlier assertion that no single person on the face of this earth knows how to make me?

Actually, millions of human beings have had a hand in my creation, no one of whom even knows more than a very few of the others. Now, you may say that I go too far in relating the picker of a coffee berry in far off Brazil and food growers elsewhere to my creation; that this is an extreme position. I shall stand by my claim. There isn't a single person in all these millions, including the president of the pencil company, who contributes more than a tiny, infinitesimal bit of knowhow. From the standpoint of know-how the only difference between the miner of graphite in Ceylon and the logger in Oregon is in the *type* of know-how. Neither the miner nor the logger can be dispensed with, any more than can the chemist at the factory or the worker in the oil field—paraffin being a by-product of petroleum.

Here is an astounding fact: Neither the worker in the oil field nor the chemist nor the digger of graphite or clay nor any who mans or makes the ships or trains or trucks nor the one who runs the machine that does the knurling on my bit of metal nor the president of the company performs his singular task because he wants me. Each one wants me less, perhaps, than does a child in the first grade. Indeed, there are some among this vast multitude who never saw a pencil nor would they know how to use one. Their motivation is other than me. Perhaps it is something like this: Each of these millions sees that he can thus exchange his tiny know-how for the goods and services he needs or wants. I may or may not be among these items.

NO MASTER MIND

There is a fact still more astounding: the absence of a master mind, of anyone dictating or forcibly directing these countless actions which bring me into being. No trace of such a person can be found. Instead, we find the Invisible Hand at work. This is the mystery to which I earlier referred.

It has been said that "only God can make a tree." Why do we agree with this? Isn't it because we realize that we ourselves could not make one? Indeed, can we even describe a tree? We cannot, except in superficial terms. We can say, for instance, that a certain molecular configuration manifests itself as a tree. But what mind is there among men that could even record, let alone direct, the constant changes in molecules that transpire in the life span of a tree? Such a feat is utterly unthinkable!

I, Pencil, am a complex combination of miracles: a tree, zinc, copper, graphite, and so on. But to these miracles which manifest themselves in Nature an even more extraordinary miracle has been added: the configuration of creative human energies—millions of tiny know-hows configurating naturally and spontaneously in response to human necessity and desire and *in the absence of any human master-minding!* Since only God can make a tree, I insist that only God could make me. Man can no more direct these millions of know-hows to bring me into being than he can put molecules together to create a tree.

The above is what I meant when writing, "If you can become aware of the miraculousness which I symbolize, you can help save the freedom mankind is so unhappily losing." For, if one is aware that these know-hows will naturally, yes, automatically, arrange themselves into creative and productive patterns in response to human necessity and demand—that is, in the absence of governmental or any other coercive masterminding—then one will possess an absolutely essential ingredient for freedom: *a faith in free people.* Freedom is impossible without this faith.

Once government has had a monopoly of a creative activity such, for instance, as the delivery of the mails, most individuals will believe that the mails could not be efficiently delivered by men acting freely. And here is the reason: Each one acknowledges that he himself doesn't know how to do all the things incident to mail delivery. He also recognizes that no other individual could do it. These assumptions are correct. No individual possesses enough know-how to perform a nation's mail delivery any more than any individual possesses enough know-how to make a pencil. Now, in the absence of faith in free people—in the unawareness that millions of tiny know-hows would naturally and miraculously form and cooperate to satisfy this necessity—the individual cannot help but reach the erroneous conclusion that mail can be delivered only by governmental "master-minding."

TESTIMONY GALORE

If I, Pencil, were the only item that could offer testimony on what men and women can accomplish when free to try, then those with little faith would have a fair case. However, there is testimony galore; it's all about us and on every hand. Mail delivery is exceedingly simple when compared, for instance, to the making of an automobile or a calculating machine or a grain combine or a milling machine or to tens of thousands of other things. Delivery? Why, in this area where men have been left free to try, they deliver the human voice around the world in less than one second; they deliver an event visually and in motion to any person's home when it is happening; they deliver 150 passengers from Seattle to Baltimore in less than four hours; they deliver gas from

Texas to one's range or furnace in New York at unbelievably low rates and without subsidy; they deliver each four pounds of oil from the Persian Gulf to our Eastern Seaboard—halfway around the world—for less money than the government charges for delivering a one-ounce letter across the street!

The lesson I have to teach is this: *Leave all creative energies uninhibited.* Merely organize society to act in harmony with this lesson. Let society's legal apparatus remove all obstacles the best it can. Permit these creative know-hows freely to flow. Have faith that free men and women will respond to the Invisible Hand. This faith will be confirmed. I, Pencil, seemingly simple though I am, offer the miracle of my creation as testimony that this is a practical faith, as practical as the sun, the rain, a cedar tree, the good earth.

Market Fairness

St. Thomas Aquinas

Sins Committed in Buying and Selling

1265

OF CHEATING, WHICH IS COMMITTED IN BUYING AND SELLING (FOUR ARTICLES)

We must now consider those sins which relate to voluntary commutations. First, we shall consider cheating, which is committed in buying and selling: secondly, we shall consider usury, which occurs in loans. In connection with the other voluntary commutations no special kind of sin is to be found distinct from rapine and theft.

Under the first head there are four points of inquiry:

1. Of unjust sales as regards the price; namely, whether it is lawful to sell a thing for more than its worth?
2. Of unjust sales on the part of the thing sold;
3. Whether the seller is bound to reveal a fault in the thing sold?
4. Whether it is lawful in trading to sell a thing at a higher price than was paid for it?

WHETHER IT IS LAWFUL TO SELL A THING FOR MORE THAN ITS WORTH?

Objection 1: It would seem that it is lawful to sell a thing for more than its worth. In the commutations of human life, civil laws determine that which is just. Now according to these laws it is just for buyer and

From Thomas Aquinas *Summa Theologica*. XXVI, XLV, XXVI, XLV. London: Burns Oates & Washbourne, 1920.

seller to deceive one another (Cod. IV, xliv, De Rescind. Vend. 8,15): and this occurs by the seller selling a thing for more than its worth, and the buyer buying a thing for less than its worth. Therefore it is lawful to sell a thing for more than its worth.

Objection 2: Further, that which is common to all would seem to be natural and not sinful. Now Augustine relates that the saying of a certain jester was accepted by all, "You wish to buy for a song and to sell at a premium," which agrees with the saying of Prov. 20:14. "It is naught, it is naught, saith every buyer: and when he is gone away, then he will boast." Therefore it is lawful to sell a thing for more than its worth.

Objection 3: Further, it does not seem unlawful if that which honesty demands be done by mutual agreement. Now, according to the Philosopher (Ethic. viii, 13), in the friendship which is based on utility, the amount of the recompense for a favor received should depend on the utility accruing to the receiver: and this utility sometimes is worth more than the thing given, for instance if the receiver be in great need of that thing, whether for the purpose of avoiding a danger, or of deriving some particular benefit. Therefore, in contracts of buying and selling, it is lawful to give a thing in return for more than its worth.

On the contrary, It is written (Mat. 7:12): "All things . . . whatsoever you would that men should do to you, do you also to them." But no man wishes to buy a thing for more than its worth. Therefore no man should sell a thing to another man for more than its worth.

I answer that, It is altogether sinful to have recourse to deceit in order to sell a thing for more than its just price, because this is to deceive one's neighbor so as to injure him. Hence Tully says (De Offic. iii, 15): "Contracts should be entirely free from double-dealing: the seller must not impose upon the bidder, nor the buyer upon one that bids against him."

But, apart from fraud, we may speak of buying and selling in two ways. First, as considered in themselves, and from this point of view, buying and selling seem to be established for the common advantage of both parties, one of whom requires that which belongs to the other, and vice versa, as the Philosopher states (Polit. i, 3). Now whatever is established for the common advantage, should not be more of a burden to one party than to another, and consequently all contracts between them should observe equality of thing and thing. Again, the quality of a thing that comes into human use is measured by the price given for it, for which purpose money was invented, as stated in Ethic. v, 5. Therefore if either the price exceed the quantity of the thing's worth, or, conversely, the thing exceed the price, there is no longer the equality of justice: and consequently, to sell a thing for more than its worth, or to buy it for less than its worth, is in itself unjust and unlawful.

Secondly we may speak of buying and selling, considered as accidentally tending to the advantage of one party, and to the disadvantage of the other: for instance, when a man has great need of a certain thing, while another man will suffer if he be without it. In such a case the just price will depend not only on the thing sold, but on the loss which the sale brings on the seller. And thus it will be lawful to sell a thing for more than it is worth in itself, though the price paid be not more than it is worth to the owner. Yet if the one man derive a great advantage by becoming possessed of the other man's property, and the seller be not at a loss through being without that thing, the latter ought not to raise the price, because the advantage accruing to the buyer, is not due to the seller, but to a circumstance affecting the buyer. Now no man should sell what is not his, though he may charge for the loss he suffers.

On the other hand if a man find that he derives great advantage from something he has bought, he may, of his own accord, pay the seller something over and above: and this pertains to his honesty.

Reply to Objection 1: As stated above human law is given to the people among whom there are many lacking virtue, and it is not given to the virtuous alone. Hence human law was unable to forbid all that is contrary to virtue; and it suffices for it to prohibit whatever is destructive of human intercourse, while it treats other matters as though they were lawful, not by approving of them, but by not punishing them. Accordingly, if without employing deceit the seller disposes of his goods for more than their worth, or the buyer obtain them for less than their worth, the law looks upon this as licit, and provides no punishment for so doing, unless the excess be too great, because then even human law demands restitution to be made, for instance if a man be deceived in regard to more than half the amount of the just price of a thing.

On the other hand the Divine law leaves nothing unpunished that is contrary to virtue. Hence, according to the Divine law, it is reckoned unlawful if the equality of justice be not observed in buying and selling: and he who has received more than he ought must make compensation to him that has suffered loss, if the loss be considerable. I add this condition, because the just price of things is not fixed with mathematical precision, but depends on a kind of estimate, so that a slight addition or subtraction would not seem to destroy the equality of justice.

Reply to Objection 2: As Augustine says "this jester, either by looking into himself or by his experience of others, thought that all men are inclined to wish to buy for a song and sell at a premium. But since in reality this is wicked, it is in every man's power to acquire that justice whereby he may resist and overcome this inclination." And then he gives the example of a man who gave the just price for a book to a man who through ignorance asked a low price for it. Hence it is evident that this common desire is not from nature but from vice, wherefore it is common to many who walk along the broad road of sin.

Reply to Objection 3: In commutative justice we consider chiefly real equality. On the other hand, in friendship based on utility we consider equality of usefulness, so that the recompense should depend on the usefulness accruing, whereas in buying it should be equal to the thing bought.

WHETHER A SALE IS RENDERED UNLAWFUL THROUGH A FAULT IN THE THING SOLD?

Objection 1: It would seem that a sale is not rendered unjust and unlawful through a fault in the thing sold. For less account should be taken of the other parts of a thing than of what belongs to its substance. Yet the sale of a thing does not seem to be rendered unlawful through a fault in its substance: for instance, if a man sell instead of the real metal, silver or gold produced by some chemical process, which is adapted to all the human uses for which silver and gold are necessary, for instance in the making of vessels and the like. Much less therefore will it be an unlawful sale if the thing be defective in other ways.

Objection 2: Further, any fault in the thing, affecting the quantity, would seem chiefly to be opposed to justice which consists in equality. Now quantity is known by being measured: and the measures of things that come into human use are not fixed, but in some places are greater, in others less, as the Philosopher states (Ethic. v, 7). Therefore just as it is impossible to avoid defects on the part of the thing sold, it seems that a sale is not rendered unlawful through the thing sold being defective.

Objection 3: Further, the thing sold is rendered defective by lacking a fitting quality. But in order to know the quality of a thing, much knowledge is required that is lacking in most buyers. Therefore a sale is not rendered unlawful by a fault (in the thing sold).

On the contrary, Ambrose says (De Offic. iii, 11): "It is manifestly a rule of justice that a good man should not depart from the truth, nor inflict an unjust injury on anyone, nor have any connection with fraud."

I answer that, A threefold fault may be found pertaining to the thing which is sold. One, in respect of the thing's substance: and if the seller be aware of a fault in the thing he is selling, he is guilty of a fraudulent sale, so that the sale is rendered unlawful. Hence we find it written against certain people (Is. 1:22), "Thy silver is turned into dross, thy wine is mingled with water": because that which is mixed is defective in its substance.

Another defect is in respect of quantity which is known by being measured: wherefore if anyone knowingly make use of a faulty measure in selling, he is guilty of fraud, and the sale is illicit. Hence it is written (Deut. 25:13, 14): "Thou shalt not have divers weights in thy bag, a greater and a less: neither shall there be in thy house a greater bushel and a less," and further on (Dt. 25:16): "For the Lord . . . abhorreth him that doth these things, and He hateth all injustice."

A third defect is on the part of the quality, for instance, if a man sell an unhealthy animal as being a healthy one: and if anyone do this knowingly he is guilty of a fraudulent sale, and the sale, in consequence, is illicit.

In all these cases not only is the man guilty of a fraudulent sale, but he is also bound to restitution. But if any of the foregoing defects be in the thing sold, and he knows nothing about this, the seller does not sin, because he does that which is unjust materially, nor is his deed unjust, as shown above. Nevertheless he is bound to compensate the buyer, when the defect comes to his knowledge. Moreover what has been said of the seller applies equally to the buyer. For sometimes it happens that the seller thinks his goods to be specifically of lower value, as when a man sells gold instead of copper, and then if the buyer be aware of this, he buys it unjustly and is bound to restitution: and the same applies to a defect in quantity as to a defect in quality.

Reply to Objection 1: Gold and silver are costly not only on account of the usefulness of the vessels and other like things made from them, but also on account of the excellence and purity of their substance. Hence if the gold or silver produced by alchemists has not the true specific nature of gold and silver, the sale thereof is fraudulent and unjust, especially as real gold and silver can produce certain results by their natural action, which the counterfeit gold and silver of alchemists cannot produce. Thus the true metal has the property of making people joyful, and is helpful medicinally against certain maladies. Moreover real gold can be employed more frequently, and lasts longer in its condition of purity than counterfeit gold. If however real gold were to be produced by alchemy, it would not be unlawful to sell it for the genuine article, for nothing prevents art from employing certain natural causes for the production of natural and true effects, as Augustine says (De Trin. iii, 8) of things produced by the art of the demons.

Reply to Objection 2: The measures of salable commodities must needs be different in different places, on account of the difference of supply: because where there is greater abundance, the measures are wont to be larger. However in each place those who govern the state must determine the just measures of things salable, with due consideration for the conditions of place and time. Hence it is not lawful to disregard such measures as are established by public authority or custom.

Reply to Objection 3: As Augustine says (De Civ. Dei xi, 16) the price of things salable does not depend on their degree of nature, since at times a horse fetches a higher price than a slave; but it depends on their usefulness to man. Hence it is not necessary for the seller or buyer to be cognizant of the hidden qualities of the thing sold, but only of such as render the thing adapted to man's use, for instance, that the horse be strong, run well and so forth. Such qualities the seller and buyer can easily discover.

WHETHER THE SELLER IS BOUND TO STATE THE DEFECTS OF THE THING SOLD?

Objection 1: It would seem that the seller is not bound to state the defects of the thing sold. Since the seller does not bind the buyer to buy, he would seem to leave it to him to judge of the goods offered for sale. Now judgment about a thing and knowledge of that thing belong to the same person. Therefore it does not seem imputable to the seller if the buyer be deceived in his judgment, and be hurried into buying a thing without carefully inquiring into its condition.

Objection 2: Further, it seems foolish for anyone to do what prevents him carrying out his work. But if a man states the defects of the goods he has for sale, he prevents their sale: wherefore Tully (De Offic. iii, 13) pictures a man as saying: "Could anything be more absurd than for a public crier, instructed by the owner, to cry: 'I offer this unhealthy horse for sale?'" Therefore the seller is not bound to state the defects of the thing sold.

Objection 3: Further, man needs more to know the road of virtue than to know the faults of things offered for sale. Now one is not bound to offer advice to all or to tell them the truth about matters pertaining to virtue, though one should not tell anyone what is false. Much less therefore is a seller bound to tell the faults of what he offers for sale, as though he were counseling the buyer.

Objection 4: Further, if one were bound to tell the faults of what one offers for sale, this would only be in order to lower the price. Now sometimes the price would be lowered for some other reason, without any defect in the thing sold: for instance, if the seller carry wheat to a place where wheat fetches a high price, knowing that many will come after him carrying wheat; because if the buyers knew this they would give a lower price. But apparently the seller need not give the buyer this information. Therefore, in like manner, neither need he tell him the faults of the goods he is selling.

On the contrary, Ambrose says (De Offic. iii, 10): "In all contracts the defects of the salable commodity must be stated; and unless the seller make them known, although the buyer has already acquired a right to them, the contract is voided on account of the fraudulent action."

I answer that, It is always unlawful to give anyone an occasion of danger or loss, although a man need not always give another the help or counsel which would be for his advantage in any way; but only in certain fixed cases, for instance when someone is subject to him, or when he is the only one who can assist him. Now the seller who offers goods for sale, gives the buyer an occasion of loss or danger, by the very fact that he offers him defective goods, if such defect may occasion loss or danger to the buyer—loss, if, by reason of this defect, the goods are of less value, and he takes nothing off the price on that account—danger, if this defect either hinder the use of the goods or render it hurtful, for instance, if a man sells a lame for a fleet horse, a tottering house for a safe one, rotten or poisonous food for wholesome. Wherefore if such like defects be hidden, and the seller does not make them known, the sale will be illicit and fraudulent, and the seller will be bound to compensation for the loss incurred.

On the other hand, if the defect be manifest, for instance if a horse have but one eye, or if the goods though useless to the buyer, be useful to someone else, provided the seller take as much as he ought from the price, he is not bound to state the defect of the goods, since perhaps on account of that defect the buyer might want him to allow a greater rebate than he need. Wherefore the seller may look to his own indemnity, by withholding the defect of the goods.

Reply to Objection 1: Judgment cannot be pronounced save on what is manifest: for "a man judges of what he knows" (Ethic. i, 3). Hence if the defects of the goods offered for sale be hidden, judgment of them is not sufficiently left with the buyer unless such defects be made known to him. The case would be different if the defects were manifest.

Reply to Objection 2: There is no need to publish beforehand by the public crier the defects of the goods one is offering for sale, because if he were to begin by announcing its defects, the bidders would be frightened to buy, through ignorance of other qualities that might render the thing good and serviceable. Such defect ought to be stated to each individual that offers to buy: and then he will be able to compare the various points one with the other, the good with the bad: for nothing prevents that which is defective in one respect being useful in many others.

Reply to Objection 3: Although a man is not bound strictly speaking to tell everyone the truth about matters pertaining to virtue, yet he is so bound in a case when, unless he tells the truth, his conduct would endanger another man in detriment to virtue: and so it is in this case.

Reply to Objection 4: The defect in a thing makes it of less value now than it seems to be: but in the case cited, the goods are expected to be of less value at a future time, on account of the arrival of other merchants, which was not foreseen by the buyers. Wherefore the seller, since he sells his goods at the price actually offered him, does not seem to act contrary to justice through not stating what is going to happen. If however he were to do so, or if he lowered his price, it would be exceedingly virtuous on his part: although he does not seem to be bound to do this as a debt of justice.

WHETHER, IN TRADING, IT IS LAWFUL TO SELL A THING AT A HIGHER PRICE THAN WHAT WAS PAID FOR IT

Objection 1: It would seem that it is not lawful, in trading, to sell a thing for a higher price than we paid for it. For Chrysostom says on Mat. 21:12: "He that buys a thing in order that he may sell it, entire and unchanged, at a profit, is the trader who is cast out of God's temple." Cassiodorus speaks in the same sense in his commentary on Ps. 70:15, "Because I have not known learning, or trading" according to another version: "What is trade," says he, "but buying at a cheap price with the purpose of retailing at a higher price?" and he adds: "Such were the tradesmen whom Our Lord cast out of the temple." Now no man is cast out of the temple except for a sin. Therefore such like trading is sinful.

Objection 2: Further, it is contrary to justice to sell goods at a higher price than their worth, or to buy them for less than their value, as shown above (A[1]). Now if you sell a thing for a higher price than you paid for it, you must either have bought it for less than its value, or sell it for more than its value. Therefore this cannot be done without sin.

Objection 3: Further, Jerome says (Ep. ad Nepot. lii): "Shun, as you would the plague, a cleric who from being poor has become wealthy, or who, from being a nobody has become a celebrity." Now trading would net seem to be forbidden to clerics except on account of its sinfulness. Therefore it is a sin in trading, to buy at a low price and to sell at a higher price.

On the contrary, Augustine commenting on Ps. 70:15, "Because I have not known learning," says: "The greedy tradesman blasphemes over his losses; he lies and perjures himself over the price of his wares. But these are vices of the man, not of the craft, which can be exercised without these vices." Therefore trading is not in itself unlawful.

I answer that, A tradesman is one whose business consists in the exchange of things. According to the Philosopher (Polit. i, 3), exchange of things is twofold; one, natural as it were, and necessary, whereby one commodity is exchanged for another, or money taken in exchange for a commodity, in order to satisfy the needs of life. Such like trading, properly speaking, does not belong to tradesmen, but rather to housekeepers or civil servants who have to provide the household or the state with the necessaries of life. The other kind of exchange is either that of money for money, or of any commodity for money, not on account of the necessities of life, but for profit, and this kind of exchange, properly speaking, regards tradesmen, according to the Philosopher (Polit. i, 3). The former kind of exchange is commendable because it supplies a natural need: but the latter is justly deserving of blame, because, considered in itself, it satisfies the greed for gain, which knows no limit and tends to infinity. Hence trading, considered in itself, has a certain debasement attaching thereto, in so far as, by its very nature, it does not imply a virtuous or necessary end. Nevertheless gain which is the end of trading, though not implying, by its nature, anything virtuous or necessary, does not, in itself, connote anything sinful or contrary to virtue: wherefore nothing prevents gain from being directed to some necessary or even virtuous end, and thus trading becomes lawful. Thus, for instance, a man may intend the moderate gain which he seeks to acquire by trading for the upkeep of his household, or for the assistance of the needy: or again, a man may take to trade for some public advantage, for instance, lest his country lack the necessaries of life, and seek gain, not as an end, but as payment for his labor.

Reply to Objection 1: The saying of Chrysostom refers to the trading which seeks gain as a last end. This is especially the case where a man sells something at a higher price without its undergoing any change. For if he sells at a higher price something that has changed for the better, he would seem to receive the reward of his labor. Nevertheless the gain itself may be lawfully intended, not as a last end, but for the sake of some other end which is necessary or virtuous, as stated above.

Reply to Objection 2: Not everyone that sells at a higher price than he bought is a tradesman, but only he who buys that he may sell at a profit. If, on the contrary, he buys not for sale but for possession, and afterwards, for some reason wishes to sell, it is not a trade transaction even if he sell at a profit. For he may lawfully do this, either because he has bettered the thing, or because the value of the thing has changed with the change of place or time, or on account of the danger he incurs in transferring the thing from one place to another, or again in having it carried by another. In this sense neither buying nor selling is unjust.

Reply to Objection 3: Clerics should abstain not only from things that are evil in themselves, but even from those that have an appearance of evil. This happens in trading, both because it is directed to worldly gain, which clerics should despise, and because trading is open to so many vices, since "a merchant is hardly free from sins of the lips" (Ecclus. 26:28). There is also another reason, because trading engages the mind too much with worldly cares, and consequently withdraws it from spiritual cares; wherefore the Apostle says (2 Tim. 2:4): "No man being a soldier to God entangleth himself with secular businesses." Nevertheless it is lawful for clerics to engage in the first mentioned kind of exchange, which is directed to supply the necessaries of life, either by buying or by selling.

JOHN LOCKE

What is a Fair Price?

1695

"VENDITIO" (1695)

Upon demand what is the measure that ought to regulate the price for which anyone sells so as to keep it within the bounds of equity and justice, I suppose it in short to be this: the market price at the place where he sells. Whosoever keeps to that in whatever he sells I think is free from cheat, extortion and oppression, or any guilt in whatever he sells, supposing no fallacy in his wares.

To explain this a little: A man will not sell the same wheat this year under 10s[hillings] per bushel which the last year he sold for 5s. This is no extortion by the above said rule, because it is this year the market price, and if he should sell under that rate he would not do a beneficial thing to the consumers, because others then would buy up his corn at his low rate and sell it again to others at the market rate, and so they make profit of his weakness and share a part of his money. If to prevent this he will sell his wheat only to the poor at this under rate, this indeed is charity, but not what strict justice requires. For that only requires that we should sell to all buyers at the market rate, for if it be unjust to sell it to a poor man at 10s per bushel it is also unjust to sell it to the rich for 10s, for justice has but one measure for all men. If you think him bound to sell it to the rich too, who is the consumer, under the market rate, but not to a jobber or engrosser, to this I answer he cannot know whether the rich buyer will not sell it again and so gain the money which he loses. But if it be said 'tis unlawful to sell the same corn for 10s this week which I sold the last year or week for 5s because it is worth no more now than it was then, having no new qualities put into it to make it better, I answer it is worth no more, 'tis

From John Locke and David Wootton, *Political Writings*. Indianapolis: Hackett Publishing, 2003.

true, in its natural value, because it will not feed more men nor better feed them than it did last year, but yet it is worth more in its political or marchand value, as I may so call it, which lies in the proportion of the quantity of wheat to the proportion of money in that place and the need of one and the other. This same market rate governs too in things sold in shops or private houses, and is known by this, that a man sells not dearer to one than he would to another. He that makes use of another's ignorance, fancy, or necessity to sell ribbon or cloth, etc. dearer to him than to another man at the same time, cheats him.

But in things that a man does not set to sale, this market price is not regulated by that of the next market, but by the value that the owner puts on it himself: e.g. x has an horse that pleases him and is for his turn; this *y* would buy of him; *x* tells him he has no mind to sell; *y* presses him to set him a price, and thereupon *x* demands and takes £40 for his horse, which in a market or fair would not yield above twenty. But supposing *y* refusing to give £40, *z* comes the next day and desires to buy this horse, having such a necessity to have it that if he should fail of it, it would make him lose a business of much greater consequence, and this necessity *x* knows. If in this case he make *z* pay £50 for the horse which he would have sold to *y* for £40, he oppresses him and is guilty of extortion whereby he robs him of £10, because he does not sell the horse to him, as he would to another, at his own market rate, which was £40, but makes use of *z*'s necessity to extort £10 from him above what in his own account was the just value, the one man's money being as good as the other's. But yet he had done no injury to *y* in taking his £40 for an horse which at the next market would not have yielded above £20 because he sold it at the market rate of the place where the horse was sold, viz. his own house, where he would not have sold it to any other at a cheaper rate than he did to *y*. For if by any artifice he had raised *y*'s longing for that horse, or because of his great fancy sold it dearer to him than he would to another man, he had cheated him too. But what anyone has he may value at what rate he will, and transgresses not against justice if he sells it at any price, provided he makes no distinction of buyers, but parts with it as cheap to this as he would to any other buyer. I say he transgresses not against justice. What he may do against charity is another case.

To have a fuller view of this matter, let us suppose a merchant of Danzig sends two ships laden with corn, whereof the one puts into Dunkirk, where there is almost a famine for want of corn, and there he sells his wheat for 20s a bushel, whilst the other ship sells his at Ostend just by for 5s. Here it will be demanded whether it be not oppression and injustice to make such an advantage of their necessity at Dunkirk as to sell to them the same commodity at 20s per bushel which he sells for a quarter the price but twenty miles off? I answer no, because he sells at the market rate at the place where he is, but sells there no dearer to Thomas than he would to Richard. And if there he should sell for less than his corn would yield, he would only throw his profit into other men's hands, who buying of him under the market rate would sell it again to others at the full rate it would yield. Besides, as there can be no other measure set to a merchant's gain but the market price where he comes, so if there were any other measure, as 5 or 10 per cent as the utmost justifiable profit, there would be no commerce in the world, and mankind would be deprived of the supply of foreign mutual conveniences of life. For the buyer, not knowing what the commodity cost the merchant to purchase and bring thither, could be under no tic of giving him the profit of 5 or 10 per cent, and so can have no other rule but of buying as cheap as he can, which turning often to the merchant's downright loss when he comes to a bad market, if he has not the liberty on his side to sell as dear as he can when he comes to a good market. This obligation to certain loss often, without any certainty of reparation, will quickly put an end to merchandizing. The measure that is common to buyer and seller is just that if one should buy as cheap as he could in the market, the other should sell as dear as he could there, everyone running his venture and taking his chance, which by the mutual and perpetually changing wants of money and commodities in buyer and seller comes to a pretty equal and fair account.

But though he that sells his corn in a town pressed with famine at the utmost rate he can get for it does no injustice against the common rule of traffic, yet if he carry it away unless they will give him more than they are able, or extorts so much from their present necessity as not to leave them the means of subsistence afterwards, he offends against the common rule of charity as a man, and if they perish any of them by reason of his extortion is no doubt guilty of murder. For though all the selling merchant's gain arises only from the advantage he makes of the buyer's want, whether it be a want of necessity or fancy that's all one, yet he must not make use of his necessity to his destruction, and enrich himself so as to make another perish. He is so far from being permitted to gain to that degree, that he is bound to be at some loss, and impart of his own to save another from perishing.

Dunkirk is the market to which the English merchant has carried his corn, and by reason of their necessity it proves a good one, and there he may sell his corn as it will yield at the market rate, for 20s per bushel. But if a Dunkirker should at the same time come to England to buy corn, not to sell to him at the market rate, but to make him, because of the necessity of his country, pay 10s per bushel when you sold to others for five, would be extortion.

A ship at sea that has an anchor to spare meets another which has lost all her anchors. What here shall be the just price that she shall sell her anchor to the distressed ship? To this I answer the same price that she would sell the same anchor to a ship that was not in that distress. For that still is the market rate for which one would part with anything to anybody who was not in distress and absolute want of it. And in this case the master of the vessel must make his estimate by the length of his voyage, the season and seas he sails in, and so what risk he shall run himself by parting with his anchor, which all put together perhaps he would not part with it at any rate, but if he would, he must then take no more for it from a ship in distress than he would from any other. And here we see, the price which the anchor cost him, which is the market price at another place, makes no part of the measure of the price which he fairly sells it for at sea. And therefore I put in "the place where the thing is sold": i.e. the measure of rating anything in selling is the market price where the thing is sold. Whereby it is evident that a thing may be lawfully sold for 10, 20, nay cent [100] per cent, and ten times more in one place than is the market price in another place perhaps not far off. These are my extemporary thought[s] concerning this matter.

Adam Smith

Wealth of Nations, "Of the Expences of the Sovereign"

1776

BOOK V, PART I

Of the Expence of Defence

The first duty of the sovereign, that of protecting the society from the violence and invasion of other independent societies, can be performed only by means of a military force. But the expence both of preparing this military force in time of peace, and of employing it in time of war, is very different in the different states of society, in the different periods of improvement.

The number of those who can go to war, in proportion to the whole number of the people, is necessarily much smaller in a civilized than in a rude state

From Adam Smith and Edwin Cannan, *An Inquiry into the Nature and Causes of the Wealth of Nations*, Book V. London: Methuen, 1904.

of society. In a civilized society, as the soldiers are maintained altogether by the labour of those who are not soldiers, the number of the former can never exceed what the latter can maintain, over and above maintaining, in a manner suitable to their respective stations, both themselves and the other officers of government and law whom they are obliged to maintain. In the little agrarian states of ancient Greece, a fourth or a fifth part of the whole body of the people considered themselves as soldiers, and would sometimes, it is said, take a field. Among the civilized nations of modern Europe, it is commonly computed that not more than one-hundredth part of the inhabitants in any country can be employed as soldiers without ruin to the country which pays the expences of their service.

A shepherd has a great deal of leisure; a husbandman, in the rude state of husbandry, has some; an artificer or manufacturer has none at all. The first may, without any loss, employ a great deal of his time in martial exercises; the second may employ some part of it; but the last cannot employ a single hour in them without some loss, and his attention to his own interest naturally leads him to neglect them altogether. These improvements in husbandry too, which the progress of arts and manufactures necessarily introduces, leave the husbandman as little leisure as the artificer. Military exercises come to be as much neglected by the inhabitants of the country as by those of the town, and the great body of the people becomes altogether unwarlike. That wealth, at the same time, which always follows the improvements of agriculture and manufactures, and which in reality is no more than the accumulated produce of those improvements, provokes the invasion of all their neighbours. An industrious, and upon that account a wealthy nation, is of all nations the most likely to be attacked; and unless the state takes some new measures for the public defence, the natural habits of the people render them altogether incapable of defending themselves.

In these circumstances there seem to be but two methods by which the state can make any tolerable provision for the public defence.

It may either, first, by means of a very rigorous police, and in spite of the whole bent of the interest, genius, and inclinations of the people, enforce the practice of military exercises, and oblige either all the citizens of the military age, or a certain number of them, to join in some measure the trade of a soldier to whatever other trade or profession they may happen to carry on.

Or, secondly, by maintaining and employing a certain number of citizens in the constant practice of military exercises, it may render the trade of a soldier a particular trade, separate and distinct from all others.

PART II

Of the Expence of Justice

The second duty of the sovereign, that of protecting, as far as possible, every member of the society from the injustice or oppression of every other member of it, or the duty of establishing an exact administration of justice, requires, too, very different degrees of expence in the different periods of society.

The office of judge is in itself so very honourable that men are willing to accept of it, though accompanied with very small emoluments. The inferior office of justice of peace, though attended with a good deal of trouble, and in most cases with no emoluments at all, is an object of ambition to the greater part of our country gentlemen. The salaries of all the different judges, high and low, together with the whole expence of the administration and execution of justice, even where it is not managed with very good economy, makes, in any civilized country, but a very inconsiderable part of the whole expence of government.

The whole expence of justice, too, might easily be defrayed by the fees of court; and, without exposing the administration of justice to any real hazard of corruption, the public revenue might thus be discharged from a certain, though, perhaps, but a small incumbrance. It is difficult to regulate the fees of court effectually where a person so powerful as the sovereign is to share in them, and to derive any considerable part of his revenue from them. It is very easy where the judge is the principal person who can reap any benefit from them. The law can very easily oblige the judge to respect the regulation, though it might not always be able to make the sovereign respect it. Where the fees of court are precisely regulated and ascertained, where they are paid all at once, at a certain period of every process, into the hands of a cashier or receiver, to be by him distributed in certain known proportions among the different judges after the process is decided, and not till it is decided, there seems to be no more danger of corruption than where such fees are prohibited altogether. Those fees, without occasioning any considerable increase in the expence of a lawsuit, might be rendered fully sufficient for defraying the whole expence of justice. . . .

When the judicial is united to the executive power, it is scarce possible that justice should not frequently be sacrificed to what is vulgarly called politics. The persons entrusted with the great interests of the state may, even without any corrupt views, sometimes imagine it necessary to sacrifice to those interests the rights of a private man. But upon the impartial administration of justice depends the liberty of every individual, the sense which he has of his own security. In order to make every individual feel himself perfectly secure in the possession of every right which belongs to him, it is not only necessary that the judicial should be separated from the executive power, but that it should be rendered as much as possible independent of that power. The judge should not be liable to be removed from his office according to the caprice of that power. The regular payment of his salary should not depend upon the good-will, or even upon the good economy, of that power.

PART III

Of the Expence of Public Works and Public Institutions

The third and last duty of the sovereign or commonwealth is that of erecting and maintaining those public institutions and those public works, which, though they may be in the highest degree advantageous to a great society, are, however, of such a nature that the profit could never repay the expence to any individual or small number of individuals, and which it therefore cannot be expected that any individual or small number of individuals should erect or maintain. The performance of this duty requires, too, very different degrees of expence in the different periods of society.

After the public institutions and public works necessary for the defence of the society, and for the administration of justice, both of which have already been mentioned, the other works and institutions of this kind are chiefly those for facilitating the commerce of the society, and those for promoting the instruction of the people. The institutions for instruction are of two kinds: those for the education of youth, and those for the instruction of people of all ages. The consideration of the manner in which the expence of those different sorts of public works and institutions may be most properly defrayed, will divide this third part of the present chapter into three different articles.

Article I

Of the Public Works and Institutions for Facilitating the Commerce of the Society

That the erection and maintenance of the public works which facilitate the commerce of any country, such as good roads, bridges, navigable canals, harbours, &c. must require very different degrees of expence in the different periods of society is evident without any proof. The expence of making and maintaining the public roads of any country must evidently increase with the annual produce of the land and labour of that country, or with the quantity and weight of the goods which it becomes necessary to fetch and carry upon those roads. The strength of a bridge must be suited to the number and weight of the carriages which are likely to pass over it. The depth and the supply of water for a navigable canal must be proportioned to the number and tonnage of the lighters which are likely to carry goods upon it; the extent of a harbour to the number of the shipping which are likely to take shelter in it.

It does not seem necessary that the expence of those public works should be defrayed from that public revenue, as it is commonly called, of which the collection and application are in most countries assigned to the executive power. The greater part of such public works may easily be so managed as to afford a particular revenue sufficient for defraying their own expence, without bringing any burden upon the general revenue of the society.

A highway, a bridge, a navigable canal, for example, may in most cases be both made and maintained by a small toll upon the carriages which make use of them: a harbour, by a moderate port-duty upon the tonnage of the shipping which load or unload in it. The coinage, another institution for facilitating commerce, in many countries, not only defrays its own expence, but affords a small revenue or seignorage to the sovereign. The post-office, another institution for the same purpose, over and above defraying its own expence, affords in almost all countries a very considerable revenue to the sovereign.

When the carriages which pass over a highway or a bridge, and the lighters which sail upon a navigable canal, pay toll in proportion to their weight or their tonnage, they pay for the maintenance of those public works exactly in proportion to the wear and tear which they occasion of them. It seems scarce possible to invent a more equitable way of maintaining such works. This tax or toll too, though it is advanced by the carrier, is finally paid by the consumer, to whom it must always be charged in the price of the goods. As the expence of carriage, however, is very much reduced by means of such public works, the goods, notwithstanding the toll, come cheaper to the consumer than they could otherwise have done; their price not being so much raised by the toll, as it is lowered by the cheapness of the carriage. The person who finally pays this tax, therefore, gains by the application more than he loses by the payment of it. His payment is exactly in proportion to his gain. It is in reality no more than a part of that gain which he is obliged to give up in order to get the rest. It seems impossible to imagine a more equitable method of raising a tax.

When the toll upon carriages of luxury, upon coaches, post-chaises, &c. is made somewhat higher in proportion to their weight, than upon carriages of necessary use, such as carts, waggons, &c. the indolence and vanity of the rich is made to contribute in a very easy manner to the relief of the poor, by rendering cheaper the transportation of heavy goods to all the different parts of the country.

Even those public works which are of such a nature that they cannot afford any revenue for maintaining themselves, but of which the conveniency is nearly confined to some particular place or district, are always better maintained by a local or provincial revenue, under the management of a local or provincial administration, than by the general revenue of the state, of which the executive power must always have the management. Were the streets of London to be lighted and paved at the expence of the treasury, is there any probability that they would be so well lighted and paved as they are at present, or even at so small an expence? The expence, besides, instead of being raised by a local tax upon the inhabitants of each particular street, parish, or district in London, would, in this case, be defrayed out of the general revenue of the state, and would consequently be raised by a tax upon all the inhabitants of the kingdom, of whom the greater part derive no sort of benefit from the lighting and paving of the streets of London.

Article II

Of the Expence of the Institutions for the Education of Youth

The institutions for the education of the youth may, in the same manner, furnish a revenue sufficient for defraying their own expence. The fee or honorary which the scholar pays to the master naturally constitutes a revenue of this kind.

Ought the public, therefore, to give no attention, it may be asked, to the education of the people? Or if it ought to give any, what are the different parts of education which it ought to attend to in the different orders of the people? and in what manner ought it to attend to them?

In some cases the state of the society necessarily places the greater part of individuals in such situations as naturally form in them, without any attention of government, almost all the abilities and virtues which that state requires, or perhaps can admit of. In other cases the state of the society does not place the part of individuals in such situations, and some attention of government is necessary in order to prevent the almost entire corruption and degeneracy of the great body of the people.

In the progress of the division of labour, the employment of the far greater part of those who live by labour, that is, of the great body of the people, comes to be confined to a few very simple operations, frequently to one or two. But the understandings of the greater part of men are necessarily formed by their ordinary employments. The man whose whole life is spent in performing a few simple operations, of which the effects are perhaps always the same, or very nearly the same, has no occasion to exert his understanding or to exercise his invention in finding out expedients for removing difficulties which never occur. He naturally loses, therefore, the habit of such exertion, and generally becomes as stupid and ignorant as it is possible for a human creature to become. The torpor of his mind renders him not only incapable of relishing or bearing a part in any rational conversation, but of conceiving any generous, noble, or tender sentiment, and consequently of forming any just judgment concerning many even of the ordinary duties of private life. Of the great and extensive interests of his country he is altogether incapable of judging, and unless very particular pains have been taken to render him otherwise, he is equally incapable of defending his country in war. The uniformity of his stationary life naturally corrupts the courage of his mind, and makes him regard with abhorrence the irregular, uncertain, and adventurous life of a soldier. It corrupts even the activity of his body, and renders him incapable of exerting his strength with vigour and perseverance in any other employment than that to which he has been bred. His dexterity at his own particular trade seems, in this manner, to be acquired at the expence of his intellectual, social, and martial virtues. But in every improved and civilized society this is the state into which the labouring poor, that is, the great body of the people, must necessarily fall, unless government takes some pains to prevent it.

It is otherwise in the barbarous societies, as they are commonly called, of hunters, of shepherds, and even of husbandmen in that rude state of husbandry which precedes the improvement of manufactures and the extension of foreign commerce. In such societies the varied occupations of every man oblige every man to exert his capacity and to invent expedients for removing difficulties which are continually occurring. Invention is kept alive, and the mind is not suffered to fall into that drowsy stupidity which, in a civilized society, seems to benumb the understanding of almost all the inferior ranks of people. In those barbarous societies, as they are called, every man, it has already been observed, is a warrior. Every man, too, is in some measure a statesman, and can form a tolerable judgment concerning the interest of the society and the conduct of those who govern it. How far their chiefs are good judges in peace, or good leaders in war, is obvious to the observation of almost every single man among them. In such a society, indeed, no man can well acquire that improved and refined understanding which a few men sometimes possess in a more civilized state. Though in a rude society there is a good deal of variety in the occupations of every individual, there is not a great deal in those of the whole society. Every man does, or is capable of doing, almost everything which any other man does, or is capable of doing. Every man has a considerable degree of knowledge, ingenuity, and invention: but scarce any man has a great degree. The degree, however, which is commonly possessed, is generally sufficient for conducting the whole simple business of the society. In a civilized state, on the contrary, though there is little variety in the occupations of the greater part of individuals, there is an almost infinite variety in those of the whole society. These varied occupations present an almost infinite variety of objects to the contemplation of those few, who, being attached to no particular occupation themselves, have leisure and inclination to examine the occupations of other people. The contemplation of so great a variety of objects necessarily exercises their minds in endless comparisons and combinations, and renders their understandings, in an extraordinary degree, both acute and comprehensive. Unless those few, however, happen to be placed in some very particular situations, their great abilities, though honourable to themselves, may contribute very little to the good government or happiness of their society. Notwithstanding the great abilities of those few, all the nobler parts of the human character may be, in a great measure, obliterated and extinguished in the great body of the people.

The education of the common people requires, perhaps, in a civilized and commercial society, the attention of the public more than that of people of some rank and fortune. People of some rank and fortune are generally eighteen or nineteen years of age before they enter upon that particular business, profession, or trade, by which they propose to distinguish themselves in the world. They have before that full time to acquire, or at least to fit themselves for afterwards acquiring, every accomplishment which can recommend them to the public esteem, or render them worthy of it. Their parents or guardians are generally sufficiently anxious that they should be so accomplished, and are, in most cases, willing enough to lay out the expence which is necessary for that purpose. If they are not always properly educated, it is seldom from the want of expence laid out upon their education, but from the improper application of that expence. It is seldom from the want of masters, but from the negligence and incapacity of the masters who are to be had, and from the difficulty, or rather from the impossibility, which there is in the present state of things of finding any better. The employments, too, in which people of some rank or fortune spend the greater part of their lives are not, like those of the common people, simple and uniform. They are almost all of them extremely complicated, and such as exercise the head more than the hands. The understandings of those who are engaged in such employments can seldom grow torpid for want of exercise. The employments of people of some rank and fortune, besides, are seldom such as harass them from morning to night. They generally have a good deal of leisure, during which they may perfect themselves in every branch either of useful or ornamental knowledge of which they may have laid the foundation, or for which they may have acquired some taste in the earlier part of life.

It is otherwise with the common people. They have little time to spare for education. Their parents can scarce afford to maintain them even in infancy. As soon as they are able to work they must apply to some trade by which they can earn their subsistence. That trade, too, is generally so simple and uniform as to give little exercise to the understanding, while, at the same time, their labour is both so constant and so severe, that it leaves them little leisure and less inclination to apply to, or even to think of, anything else.

But though the common people cannot, in any civilized society, be so well instructed as people of some rank and fortune, the most essential parts of education, however, to read, write, and account, can be acquired at so early a period of life that the greater part even of those who are to be bred to the lowest occupations have time to acquire them before they can be employed in those occupations. For a very small expence the public can facilitate, can encourage, and can even impose upon almost the whole body of the people the necessity of acquiring those most essential parts of education.

The public can facilitate this acquisition by establishing in every parish or district a little school, where children may be taught for a reward so moderate that even a common labourer may afford it; the master being partly, but not wholly, paid by the public, because, if he was wholly, or even principally, paid by it, he would soon learn to neglect his business. In Scotland the establishment of such parish schools has taught almost the whole common people to read, and a very great proportion of them to write and account. In England the establishment of charity schools has had an effect of the same kind, though not so universally, because the establishment is not so universal. If in those little schools the books, by which the children are taught to read, were a little more instructive than they commonly are, and if, instead of a little smattering of Latin, which the children of the common people are sometimes taught there, and which can scarce ever be of any use to them, they were instructed in the elementary parts of geometry and mechanics, the literary education of this rank of people would perhaps be as complete as it can be. There is scarce a common trade which does not afford some opportunities of applying to it the principles of geometry and mechanics, and which would not therefore gradually exercise and improve the common people in those principles, the necessary introduction to the most sublime as well as to the most useful sciences.

The public can encourage the acquisition of those most essential parts of education by giving small premiums, and little badges of distinction, to the children of the common people who excel in them.

The public can impose upon almost the whole body of the people the necessity of acquiring those most essential parts of education, by obliging every man to undergo an examination or probation in them before he can obtain the freedom in any corporation, or be allowed to set up any trade either in a village or town corporate.

It was in this manner, by facilitating the acquisition of their military and gymnastic exercises, by encouraging it, and even by imposing upon the whole body of the people the necessity of learning those exercises, that the Greek and Roman republics maintained the martial spirit of their respective citizens. They facilitated the acquisition of those exercises by appointing a certain place for learning and practising them, and by granting to certain masters the privilege of teaching in that place. Those masters do not appear to have had either salaries or exclusive privileges of any kind. Their reward consisted altogether in what they got from their scholars; and a citizen who had learnt his exercises in the public Gymnasia had no sort of legal advantage over one who had learnt them privately, provided the latter had learnt them equally well. Those republics encouraged the acquisition of those exercises by bestowing little premiums and badges of distinction upon those who excelled in them. To have gained a prize in the Olympic games, gave illustration, not only to the person who gained it, but to his whole family and kindred. The obligation which every citizen was under to serve a certain number of years, if called upon, in the armies of the republic, sufficiently imposed the necessity of learning those exercises, without which he could not be fit for that service.

That in the progress of improvement the practice of military exercises, unless government takes proper pains to support it, goes gradually to decay, and, together with it, the martial spirit of the great body of the people, the example of modern Europe sufficiently demonstrates. But the security of every society must always depend, more or less, upon the martial spirit of the great body of the people. In the present times, indeed, that martial spirit alone, and unsupported by a well-disciplined standing army, would not perhaps be sufficient for the defence and security of any society. But where every citizen had the spirit of a soldier, a smaller standing army would surely be requisite. That spirit, besides, would necessarily diminish very much the dangers to liberty, whether real or imaginary, which are commonly apprehended from a standing army. As it would very much facilitate the operations of that army against a foreign invader, so it would obstruct them as much if, unfortunately, they should ever be directed against the constitution of the state.

The ancient institutions of Greece and Rome seem to have been much more effectual for maintaining the martial spirit of the great body of the people than the establishment of what are called the militias of modern times. They were much more simple. When they were once established they executed themselves, and it required little or no attention from government to maintain them in the most perfect vigour. Whereas to maintain, even in tolerable execution, the complex regulations of any modern militia, requires the continual and painful attention of government, without which they are constantly falling into total neglect and disuse. The influence, besides, of the ancient institutions was much more universal. By means of them the whole body of the people was completely instructed in the use of arms. Whereas it is but a very small part of them who can ever be so instructed by the regulations of any modern militia, except, perhaps, that of Switzerland. But a coward, a man incapable either of defending or of revenging himself, evidently wants one of the most essential parts of the character of a man. He is as much mutilated and deformed in his mind as another is in his body, who is either deprived of some of its most essential members, or has lost the use of them. He is evidently the more wretched and miserable of the two; because happiness and misery, which reside altogether in the mind, must necessarily depend more upon the healthful or unhealthful, the mutilated or entire state of the mind, than upon that of the body. Even though the martial spirit of the people were of no use towards the defence of the society, yet to prevent that sort of mental mutilation, deformity, and wretchedness, which cowardice necessarily involves in it, from spreading themselves through the great body of the people, would still deserve the most serious attention of government, in the same manner as it would deserve its most serious attention to prevent a leprosy or any other loathsome and offensive disease, though neither mortal nor dangerous, from spreading itself among them, though perhaps no other public good might result from such attention besides the prevention of so great a public evil.

The same thing may be said of the gross ignorance and stupidity which, in a civilized society, seem so frequently to benumb the understandings of all the inferior ranks of people. A man without the proper use of the intellectual faculties of a man, is, if possible, more contemptible than even a coward, and seems to be mutilated and deformed in a still more essential part of the character of human nature. Though the state was to derive no advantage from the instruction of the inferior ranks of people, it would still deserve its attention that they should not be altogether uninstructed. The state, however, derives no inconsiderable advantage from their instruction. The more they are instructed the less liable they are to the delusions of enthusiasm and superstition, which, among ignorant nations, frequently occasion the most dreadful disorders. An instructed and intelligent people, besides, are always more decent and orderly than an ignorant and stupid one. They feel themselves, each individually, more respectable and more likely to obtain the respect of their lawful superiors, and they are therefore more disposed to respect those superiors. They are more disposed to examine, and more capable of seeing through, the interested complaints of faction and sedition, and they are, upon that account, less apt to be misled into any wanton or unnecessary opposition to the measures of government. In free countries, where the safety of government depends very much upon the favourable judgment which the people may form of its conduct, it must surely be of the highest importance that they should not be disposed to judge rashly or capriciously concerning it.

CONCLUSION

The expence of defending the society, and that of supporting the dignity of the chief magistrate, are both laid out for the general benefit of the whole society. It is reasonable, therefore, that they should be defrayed by the general contribution of the whole society, all the different members contributing, as nearly as possible, in proportion to their respective abilities.

The expence of the administration of justice, too, may, no doubt, be considered as laid out for the benefit of the whole society. There is no impropriety, therefore, in its being defrayed by the general contribution of the whole society. The persons, however, who gave occasion to this expence are those who, by their injustice in one way or another, make it necessary to seek redress or protection from the courts of justice. The persons again most immediately benefited by this expence are those whom the courts of justice either restore to their rights or maintain in their rights. The expence of the administration of justice, therefore, may very properly be defrayed by the particular contribution of one or other, or both, of those two different sets of persons, according as different occasions may require, that is, by the fees of court. It cannot be necessary to have recourse to the general contribution of the whole society, except for the conviction of those criminals who have not themselves any estate or fund sufficient for paying those fees.

Those local or provincial expences of which the benefit is local or provincial (what is laid out, for example, upon the police of a particular town or district) ought to be defrayed by a local or provincial revenue, and ought to be no burden upon the general revenue of the society. It is unjust that the whole society should contribute towards an expence of which the benefit is confined to a part of the society.

The expence of maintaining good roads and communications is, no doubt, beneficial to the whole society, and may, therefore, without any injustice be defrayed by the general contribution of the whole society. This expence, however, is most immediately and directly beneficial to those who travel or carry goods from one place to another, and to those who consume such goods. The turnpike tolls in England, and the duties called peages in other countries, lay it altogether upon those two different sets of people, and thereby discharge the general revenue of the society from a very considerable burden.

The expence of the institutions for education and religious instruction is likewise, no doubt, beneficial to the whole society, and may, therefore, without injustice, be defrayed by the general contribution of the whole society. This expence, however, might perhaps with equal propriety, and even with some advantage, be defrayed altogether by those who receive the immediate benefit of such education and instruction, or by the voluntary contribution of those who think they have occasion for either the one or the other.

Market Failures

Tyler Cowen

Public Goods

2008

Public goods have two distinct aspects: nonexcludability and nonrivalrous consumption. "Nonexcludability" means that the cost of keeping nonpayers from enjoying the benefits of the good or service is prohibitive. If an entrepreneur stages a fireworks show, for example, people can watch the show from their windows or backyards. Because the entrepreneur cannot charge a fee for consumption, the fireworks show may go unproduced, even if **DEMAND** for the show is strong.

The fireworks example illustrates the related free-rider problem. Even if the fireworks show is worth ten dollars to each person, arguably few people will pay ten dollars to the entrepreneur. Each person will seek to "free ride" by allowing others to pay for the show, and then watch for free from his or her backyard. If the free-rider problem cannot be solved, valuable goods and services—ones people otherwise would be willing to pay for—will remain unproduced.

The second aspect of public goods is what economists call "nonrivalrous consumption." Assume the entrepreneur manages to exclude noncontributors from watching the show (perhaps one can see the show only from a private field). A price will be

Reprinted with permission from David R. Henderson, ed., *The Concise Encyclopedia of Economics*. Indianapolis: Liberty Fund, 2008.

charged for entrance to the field, and people who are unwilling to pay this price will be excluded. If the field is large enough, however, exclusion is inefficient. Even nonpayers could watch the show without increasing the show's cost or diminishing anyone else's enjoyment. In other words, the relevant consumption is nonrivalrous. Nonetheless, nonexcludability is usually considered the more important of the two aspects of public goods. If the good is excludable, private entrepreneurs will try to serve as many fee-paying customers as possible, charging lower prices to some customers if need be.

One of the best examples of a public good is national **DEFENSE**. To the extent one person in a geographic area is defended from foreign attack or invasion, other people in that same area are likely defended also. This makes it hard to charge people for defense, which means that defense faces the classic free-rider problem. Indeed, almost all economists are convinced that the only way to provide a sufficient level of defense is to have government do it and fund defense with taxes.

Many other problems, though, that are often perceived as public-goods problems are not really, and markets handle them reasonably well. For instance, although many people think a television signal is a public good, cable television services scramble their transmissions so that nonsubscribers cannot receive broadcasts easily. In other words, the producers have figured out how to exclude nonpayers. Both throughout history and today, private roads have been financed by tolls charged to road users. Other goods often seen as public goods, such as private protection and fire services, are frequently sold through the private sector on a fee basis. Excluding nonpayers is possible. In other cases, potentially public goods are funded by advertisements, as happens with television and radio.

Partially public goods also can be tied to purchases of private goods, thereby making the entire package more like a private good. Shopping malls, for instance, provide shoppers with a variety of services that are traditionally considered public goods: lighting, protection services, benches, and restrooms are examples. Charging directly for each of these services would be impractical. Therefore, the shopping mall finances the services through receipts from the sale of private goods in the mall. The public and private goods are "tied" together. Private condominiums and retirement communities also are market institutions that tie public goods to private services. They use monthly membership dues to provide a variety of public services.

Some public goods are provided through fame incentives or through personal motives to do a good job. The World Wide Web offers many millions of home pages and informational sites, and most of their constructors have not received any payment. The writers either want recognition or seek to reach other people for their own pleasure or to influence their thinking.

The "reciprocity motive" is another possible solution, especially in small groups. I may contribute to a collective endeavor as part of a broader strategy to signal that I am a public-minded, cooperative individual. You may then contribute in return, hoping that we develop an ongoing agreement—often implicit—to both contribute over time. The agreement can be self-sustaining if I know that my withdrawal will cause the withdrawal of others as well. A large body of anecdotal and experimental evidence suggests that such arrangements, while imperfect, are often effective. Roommates, for instance, often have implicit or explicit agreements about who will take out the trash or do the dishes. These arrangements are enforced not by contract but rather by the hope of continuing cooperation.

Other problems can be solved by defining individual **PROPERTY RIGHTS** in the appropriate economic resource. Cleaning up a polluted lake, for instance, involves a free-rider problem if no one owns the lake. If there is an owner, however, that person can charge higher prices to fishermen, boaters, recreational users, and others who benefit from the lake. Privately owned bodies of water are common in the British Isles, where, not surprisingly, lake owners maintain quality.

Well-defined property rights can solve apparent public-goods problems in other environmental areas, such as land use and species preservation. The buffalo neared extinction and the cow did not because cows could be privately owned and husbanded for profit. It is harder to imagine easily enforceable private property rights in schools of fish. For this reason we see a mix of government **REGULATION** and privately determined quotas in that area. The depletion of fish stocks nonetheless looms as a problem, as does the more general loss of biodiversity.

For environmental problems involving the air, it is difficult to imagine how property rights could be defined and enforced effectively. Market mechanisms alone probably cannot prevent depletion of the Earth's ozone layer. In such cases economists recognize the likely necessity of a governmental regulatory solution.

Contractual arrangements can sometimes be used to overcome what otherwise would be public goods and **EXTERNALITIES** problems. If the research and development activities of one firm benefit other firms in the same industry, these firms may pool their resources and agree to a joint project (**ANTITRUST** regulations permitting). Each firm will pay part of the cost, and the contributing firms will share the benefits. Contractual arrangements sometimes fail. The costs of bargaining and striking an agreement may be very high. Some parties to the agreement may seek to hold out for a better deal, and the agreement may collapse. In other cases it is simply too costly to contact and deal with all the potential beneficiaries of an agreement. A factory, for instance, might find it impossible to negotiate directly with each affected citizen to decrease pollution.

The imperfections of market solutions to public-goods problems must be weighed against the imperfections of government solutions. Governments rely on bureaucracy, respond to poorly informed voters, and have weak incentives to serve consumers. Therefore they produce inefficiently. Furthermore, politicians may supply public "goods" in a manner to serve their own interests rather than the interests of the public; examples of wasteful government spending and pork barrel projects are legion. Government often creates a problem of "forced riders" by compelling persons to support projects they do not desire. Private means of avoiding or transforming public-goods problems, when available, are usually more efficient than governmental solutions.

JONATHAN ANOMALY

Public Goods and Government Action

2015

WHY PUBLIC GOODS MATTER

Markets are miraculous mechanisms for enhancing human welfare. In the absence of externalities, the free exchange of private goods leads to (presumptive) Pareto improvements. Even when externalities occur, market exchange tends to produce net gains by promoting specialization (Smith, 1776). But when confronted with public goods like the preservation of our atmosphere's ozone layer, uncoordinated exchange can leave everyone worse off than they might otherwise be if they could find a way to coordinate.

Jonathan Anomaly, "Public Goods and Government Action." *Politics, Philosophy, and Economics*. By permission of Sage Publishing, 2015.

Goods are public if they exhibit *nonrivalry* and *nonexcludability*.[1] Of the two characteristics, nonexcludability arguably poses the main challenge for producing public goods privately.[2] This is because—in textbook cases—when a good is available to all and is costly to produce, some people will be tempted to free ride on the efforts of others. Other people, recognizing the existence of free riders, will decline to contribute because they lack the assurance that enough others will pitch in to make their effort worthwhile.

As a general rule, when the number of people needed to produce a public good increases, the feasibility of market provision declines and welfare gains are accordingly difficult to produce through private exchange. In other words, public goods pose a problem—for welfare economics, at least—to the extent that they induce market failure. Thus, many have argued, government can potentially improve the situation by directly supplying or indirectly encouraging the provision of public goods.

Indeed, Adam Smith argued that governments should be tasked with three main roles, all of which can be aptly described as the provision of public goods. The first two are to supply a military to defend against external invasion, and to maintain an impartial legal and judicial system. "The third and last duty of the sovereign or commonwealth," Smith says,

> is that of erecting or maintaining those public institutions and those public works, which, although they may be in the highest degree advantageous to a great society, are, however, of such a nature, that the profit could not repay the expense to any individual or small number of individuals, and which it therefore cannot be expected that any individual or small number of individuals should erect or maintain (1776: Bk 5, ch. 1).

As it turns out, the problem of producing public goods is primarily about how the number of contributors needed to produce them affects transaction costs (Coase, 1960) and strategic behavior (Buchanan, 1999).[3] When a public good is local, like a neighborhood playground, its potential beneficiaries can usually find a way to coordinate and forge a contract that facilitates private provision. They can also develop mechanisms to exclude free riders and solve the assurance problem through conditionally binding contracts (Schmidtz, 1987). When a public good is global in scope, like the reduction of ozone-depleting chemical emissions, it often becomes more difficult—sometimes impossible—for the relevant parties to find one another, for negotiators to distinguish free riders from honest holdouts, and for private provision to occur.

Economists consider public goods problematic because they represent situations in which free markets can lead to unexploited gains from trade. But they also pose a problem for political philosophy if, following Rawls, we think of political society as a "cooperative venture for mutual advantage" (Rawls, 1971: 4). Voluntary exchange is a key source of mutual advantage, but when the costs of producing a collective good are borne by individuals, while the benefits are dispersed, mutual gains may require government action. In a sense, coercively enforced government mandates (such as laws regulating pollution) can be considered a kind of cooperation for mutual advantage if each person whose liberty is limited sees this as the only feasible way to achieve a goal that makes everyone better off. The question for political philosophy, then, is how we should think about the vast range of public goods that markets and governments might provide.

My concern in this article is to develop the rudiments of a normative theory of public goods. I'll begin with a brief discussion of why many philosophers think public goods provision should form the core of government action, and then develop a set of questions that theorists and policy makers should ask when confronted with prospective public goods. The objective is not to provide definitive answers to these questions, but rather to frame the issue without settling it in favor of any particular view about the proper scope of government action.

FORERUNNERS

In different ways, Thomas Hobbes and David Hume anticipated Adam Smith's view that the fundamental function of government is to provide public goods. Hobbes argued that the creation and enforcement of rules of conduct, including moral and legal rules, allows us to rise above the state of nature and enjoy the fruits of our labor: without enforceable laws, unrestrained competition for scarce resources threatens our security and undermines our ability to trust people with whom we would otherwise interact. In a state of nature, Hobbes tells us:

> [T]here is no place for industry, because the fruit thereof is uncertain: and consequently no culture of the earth; no navigation, nor use of the commodities that may be imported by sea; no commodious building; no instruments of moving and removing such things as require much force; no knowledge of the face of the earth; no account of time; no arts; no letters; no society; and which is worst of all, continual fear, and danger of violent death. . . . (1651: Bk 1, ch. 13).

The only way to avoid this disaster, Hobbes thinks, is for people "to confer all their power and strength upon one man, or upon one assembly of men, that may reduce all their wills, by plurality of voices, unto one will" (1651: Bk 1, ch. 17). As many commentators have suggested (Hampton, 1986; Kavka, 1986) Hobbes's argument for despotism is less interesting than his argument that life in a political society typically makes all of us better off than we would be in a state of nature, and thus that government itself is a public good, as well as a potential supplier of public goods. Eighty years after Hobbes published *Leviathan* and 200 years before Paul Samuelson coined the term "public good" (Samuelson, 1954), Hume clearly anticipated the public-goods argument for government action:

> Two neighbours may agree to drain a meadow, which they possess in common; because it is easy for them to know each other's mind; and each must perceive, that the immediate consequence of his failing in his part, is, the abandoning the whole project. But it is very difficult, and indeed impossible, that a thousand persons should agree in any such action; it being difficult for them to concert so complicated a design, and still more difficult for them to execute it; while each seeks a pretext to free himself of the trouble and expence, and would lay the whole burden on others. Political society easily remedies both these inconveniences. Magistrates find an immediate interest in the interest of any considerable part of their subjects. They need consult no body but themselves to form any scheme for the promoting of that interest. And as the failure of any one piece in the execution is connected, though not immediately, with the failure of the whole, they prevent that failure, because they find no interest in it, either immediate or remote. Thus bridges are built; harbours opened; ramparts raised; canals formed; fleets equipped; and armies disciplined every where, by the care of government, which, though composed of men subject to all human infirmities, becomes, by one of the finest and most subtle inventions imaginable, a composition, which is, in some measure, exempted from all these infirmities (Hume, 1739: Bk 3, Pt 2, ch. 7).

In the purest cases—like those mentioned by Hobbes, Hume, and Smith—governments can provide benefits that would be difficult or impossible to attain if individuals were left to their own devices. For this reason, nearly all plausible political theories endorse some government provision of public goods, though each will support a different bundle, and for different reasons.[4] According to David Schmidtz, "one of the most attractive features of the public goods argument [for government intervention] is the minimal nature of the normative assumptions it must make in order to ground a justification of the state" (1991: 82). The minimal normative assumption Schmidtz has in mind is that government action is occasionally the only feasible or cost-effective way of bringing about an outcome which each person sees as beneficial—or would see as beneficial under idealized epistemic conditions—but which they lack the power to bring about unilaterally.

One problem with goods that are accessible to a large number of people is that there will usually be some people who consider the good harmful rather than beneficial. After all, a "good" in the economic sense is any product that can be used to satisfy a desire, not a product that is desirable, or even widely desired.[5] For example, a public park is a local public good that is considered beneficial by those who use it and those who enjoy seeing trees in their neighborhood. But for those who suffer pollen allergies, or who prefer urban to rural landscapes, parks are a nuisance. When this is true, government provision of public goods begins to look more like redistribution than mutual benefit.[6]

Still, most political philosophers will agree that providing relatively pure public goods should be government's core function. The problem is how to determine which public goods governments should supply.

PUBLIC GOODS AND PUBLIC POLICY

When confronted with policies that produce public goods, we should consider the following questions:

1. What is current demand for the good?
2. What would demand be if people had reasonably stable and well-formed preferences?
3. Do the benefits of providing the good exceed the costs of provision?
4. Are the costs and benefits of provision fairly distributed?
5. Would the good be more efficiently provided by government or markets?
6. If a public good is an artifact of public policy, should governments supply it anyway, or should they alter the policies or incentive structures that make the good public to begin with?
7. Is government provision of public goods paternalistic, or otherwise morally objectionable?

In each of the following subsections I will attempt to show why these questions matter, and how difficult it is to answer them.

Gauging Demand

One problem with deciding which public goods governments should supply is that there is no obvious way of measuring demand. In ordinary markets, goods are produced and sold in discrete units, and firms competing for customers have a powerful incentive to figure out how much of a given good to produce. But public goods cannot be packaged and sold in an obvious way, since suppliers can't attach prices to units of an indivisible good. For example, some people value saving an endangered species or eradicating a disease. But these are not goods that are easy to sell in a market, or to quantify the value of, especially because most of the benefits will go to future people who do not yet exist.

Contingent valuation (CV) surveys try to gauge demand for public goods by asking people how much they would be willing to pay for the production or preservation of public goods. CV surveys seem like a scientifically sound and morally neutral way of using *hypothetical* markets to calculate how much people want a good that *actual* markets are unlikely to produce. But CV surveys suffer serious problems, and it is unclear whether they are capable of accurately revealing demand for public goods.

A familiar problem with contingent valuation stems from biases embedded in survey questions and in the psychology of survey subjects. For example, in surveys with lists of different public goods, people's willingness to pay seems to vary greatly with the ordering of items on the list (Samples and Hollyer, 1990; Tolley et al., 1983). When people are asked how much they would pay to save an endangered elephant, say, or to clean up a polluted lake, their answer is partly determined by which question is posed first. In one survey, respondents were asked how much they would pay to preserve *each of three* different wilderness areas, and then asked how much they would be willing to pay to preserve *all three*. In some cases, people were willing to pay more to preserve each of three wilderness areas than they would to preserve all three together (Diamond et al., 1993).

In addition to CV surveys eliciting apparently inconsistent responses, some researchers question whether survey subjects are attempting to state their true demand for public goods. The worry is not that survey takers will strategically disguise their preferences (since little can be gained by giving false answers to questions about nonbinding projects), but rather that they may be doing something else altogether. For example, Diamond and Hausman (1994) suggest that respondents may be expressing an attitude that gives them a warm glow, even if they wouldn't be willing to support their response to a hypothetical question with actual money; or they may be describing what they think good citizens are supposed to say, rather than calculating how much benefit they would derive, all things considered, from allocating a specific amount to a particular public good.

Limited information further complicates the use of CV surveys to gauge demand for public goods. Because information is costly to gather, and even costlier to process and organize, economists emphasize the role of rational ignorance in decision making—especially in the realm of science and politics (Downs, 1957; Hayek, 1945). Learning how your microwave oven works will not make it work better, but it will mean you have less time to spend on other valuable pursuits. Learning how price controls on agricultural commodities impact consumers will not repay investment, unless you're a farmer, politician, lobbyist, or an unusually concerned and curious citizen. Generalizing this point, consumers of public goods will have little incentive or ability to inform themselves about all possible public goods that might be provided or preserved.

In markets for private goods, consumers internalize the benefits and costs of their purchases. If you don't like your new car or the cup of coffee you've purchased, you have an incentive to spend more time comparing alternative brands of cars and coffee, and adjust your behavior accordingly. But if a new kind of pollutant is thought by scientists to deplete the earth's ozone layer, to warm the planet, or to threaten the ecosystem of an endangered species, there is little reason for most people to study the issue carefully, since each person's consumption choices have a negligible impact on whether the atmosphere is altered, or another species goes extinct. This line of reasoning suggests that ignorance by respondents to CV surveys is not anomalous; it is a predictable fact explained by the incentive structure of public goods problems.

Finally, many argue that since willingness to pay for a public good is constrained by ability to pay, how much of a public good people want changes over time, and depends precariously on budget constraints. Poorer people, for example, are usually willing to pay less for environmental goods than wealthier people. The relationship between ability to pay and willingness to pay is further complicated by the fact that questions on CV surveys are usually hypothetical and answers are nonbinding. People's stated willingness to pay may be exaggerated by the fact that in answering hypothetical questions they don't need to pay close attention to how much money they actually have, or expect to make (Cornes and Sandler, 1996: 507; Schmidtz, 2001: 169).

To sum up, when people are asked how much they currently value a public good, like the preservation of the endangered California Condor, their answers may be affected in different ways by their budget constraints, by the order of the questions asked, by the context in which questions are asked, by how much (or little) they know about the California Condor and its relationship to its ecosystem, and many other variables. This suggests that CV surveys are flawed tools for gauging demand for public goods. Suppose, however, that we could find a more accurate way of measuring demand. Would this imply that governments should supply public goods when demand is strong? Although this may be a prima facie argument for state provision of public goods, other considerations must be addressed first.

Evaluating Demand

As we have seen, one of the most intractable problems with using surveys to gauge demand for public goods is that many people lack the information or expertise to register preferences over important policy issues. Demand can be based on ill-informed, inconsistent, or otherwise poorly formed preferences. It can also be tainted by *irrational* (in addition to *rationally ignorant*) political and economic beliefs (Caplan, 2008; Huemer, 2015).[7] Ultimately, this is not just a problem with the use of surveys, but one that stems from limited information and the incentives surrounding public goods.

This suggests that even if we could measure demand for public goods with a high degree of accuracy, it may not have normative significance or public policy implications. Some economic theories of welfare imply that we are better off—that our welfare is increased—when more of our desires are satisfied. But this is a substantive value claim, and it is clearly false in some cases.

First, some desires are part of an inconsistent set, so the satisfaction of one implies the frustration of another. Consider a drug addict with a desire for another fix of heroin and a desire to be the kind of person who doesn't want heroin. In this case, a first order desire (for drugs) conflicts with a second order desire (to not be an addict), and the second order desire seems to have normative authority. This is not to say that all desires for drugs are irrational, or involve internal conflict, but rather that some desires are rooted in impulses we would prefer not to have. It is hard to argue that satisfying such desires makes our lives go better.

Second, some of our desires are based on poorly formed or unjustified beliefs. Consider a recent example. In the early 21st century, many people in the US and UK declined to vaccinate their children because they believed the measles, mumps and rubella (MMR) vaccine causes autism. The belief can be traced in part to skepticism about the efficacy of vaccines in general, but also to a study conducted in the UK that specifically alleged a causal link between the MMR vaccine and autism. The study was never replicated, the sample on which its conclusions were based was far too small to draw statistically significant conclusions, the lead author of the study had numerous conflicts of interest, and eventually the study was retracted by the journal in which it was published—though not before the British media had managed to convince many citizens of the study's soundness.[8] In the decade that followed, thousands of parents declined to vaccinate their children because they believed in a bogus causal connection between MMR and autism. Some children died as a consequence; many others acted as vectors for preventable diseases. Beliefs about MMR causing autism were clearly unjustified, but to those who held these beliefs, overturning government requirements or incentives for parents to vaccinate their children constituted a public good for which there was significant demand. This is a paradigm case, however, in which we should not encourage government provision of public goods simply because demand is high.[9]

One way of dealing with this problem is to consider which public goods people would be willing to pay for if they had reasonably well-formed preferences.[10] Instead of using the satisfaction of actual desires as an automatic index of welfare, or using existing demand to determine which public goods governments ought to supply, we should also consider counterfactual desires, suitably informed. Generally speaking, the satisfaction of desires is more likely to increase a person's welfare if desires are consistent, stable, and based on beliefs that survive critical reflection.[11] Some argue that we should abandon the connection between desire satisfaction and welfare in favor of a more substantive or objective theory of well-being.[12] But this is a controversial move because it requires an objective account of value about which there is little consensus. Although such theories should be part of the public discussion, we should avoid defending policies by appealing to controversial theories of value.

A theory of welfare that prioritizes higher order and informed desires captures the intuition that not all desires are equally worth satisfying—that satisfying some desires can diminish rather than enhance welfare. But it allows us to avoid contentious appeals to objective value. For our purposes, it also implies that policy makers should consider providing public goods for which there is widespread demand only if demand is rooted in minimally well-formed preferences.[13]

Benefits and Costs

Suppose we agree that policy makers should focus their attention on public goods for which there is (or would be) widespread demand among reasonably reflective and informed citizens. Before concluding that public goods ought to be publicly supplied, we should also consider the magnitude of the costs and benefits associated with government provision.

For example, basic science research is one of the most important public goods human beings can produce, but discoveries about the basic structure of the universe are not patentable. Markets, therefore, may provide a relatively low level of basic science research.[14] Of course, some people will study science simply to satisfy their curiosity (Galileo and Einstein made many important discoveries in their spare time), and private firms may have some reason to fund basic science research in the hope that it will eventually reward investment. But most firms are run by people whose security and salary depend on short-term profitability rather than the long-term financial health of the firm they work for. And most people have little time to pursue science as a hobby after a long day at work. So there is good reason to believe that individual people and profit-seeking firms will produce less basic science research than they would under a system in which public funding for such research is available.[15] Up to a point, the benefits produced by publicly funded basic science research almost certainly exceed the cost of provision, as long as the funds find their way to capable scientists. But *how much* funding for public goods like basic science research should governments supply?

Welfare economists suggest that governments should attempt to supply an "efficient" level of public goods. The efficiency criterion is a consequentialist moral standard which I will discuss in a little more detail in the next section. But it is worth emphasizing that requiring government agencies to perform a cost-benefit analysis (CBA) before providing public goods does not commit us to the efficiency criterion of welfare economics, or to any other consequentialist moral theory (Schmidtz, 2001). Instead, tallying up costs and benefits can help us evaluate whether a particular political intervention is justified by highlighting the values at stake, as well as the welfare effects on the relevant parties. CBA can—in principle, at least—help policy makers think through complex issues, and help citizens keep track of how policy makers make decisions.

In the case of basic science research, for instance, we might think about how much money should be spent trying to find out how the influenza virus evolves, and how much (if any) should be allocated to study the chemical composition of Jupiter. If a CBA shows that research into the evolution of flu viruses yields greater returns on investment—returns that include welfare effects on future people—than research into the composition of planets like Jupiter, policy makers may have reason to prioritize funding for microbiology over planetary astronomy. But this does not imply that we should consider CBA the sole determinant of public goods provision. CBA is bound to be imperfect, and it may fail to capture all of the relevant values at stake (Kelman, 1981), even if it helps policy makers and theorists think through the relevant trade-offs (Schmidtz, 2001). If government provision of a public good fails a CBA, this gives us a strong reason to think government should not provide it. If government provision of a public good passes a CBA, this provides a defeasible reason for the state to provide it. However, we should also consider how the benefits and costs of provision are distributed, and whether there are private alternatives to public provision.

Fairness

Many publicly financed public goods shower benefits on some people and impose costs on others. In some cases, this seems fair: it may be worth spending money now on polio eradication or pollution abatement, even if the primary beneficiaries are future people who don't incur any of the costs. But it is often unfair, as when a US congressman uses federal tax revenue to finance pet projects in his district in order to curry favor with his constituents. When each congressman does this, both congressman and constituents are better off, since the constituents pay only a fraction of the cost of the relevant public good, and the congressman (who often attaches his name to the road or bridge that is built) is more likely to get reelected. But when all congressmen do this, all constituents (though not all congressmen) are arguably worse off. The overall game is a multi-player prisoner's dilemma, and the aggregate results are evidently unfair.

The subject of distributive justice is a contentious one, and I do not wish to defend any particular view. But it is worth mentioning some prominent distributive principles that policy makers should consider before deciding to use state power to provide public goods. According to the Pareto principle, a public good should be provided if it makes some people better off without leaving others worse off. If the initial distribution is fair, Pareto improvements are among the least controversial distributive moves, even when they require government coercion to produce (Gaus, 2007: ch. 3). Imagine, counterfactually, that everyone considers the current distribution of resources fair, and a proposed program to reduce pollution will cost everyone the equivalent of US$5 in resources but will benefit everyone by at least US$5. It looks like this move is both fair and mutually beneficial. The problem is that there are few policies that make some people better off and *none* worse off.

The Pareto principle, then, appears to be overly restrictive: it prevents states from making almost any policy change, since at least one person is likely to be unhappy with any new policy. One response by proponents of Pareto is to move from the evaluation of specific policies to that of constitutional design (Buchanan and Tullock, 1962; Sugden, 1990). The idea is that if each person must consent to (or be made better off by) any particular policy, no policy change will ever occur. But carefully crafted constitutional rules for policy making could lead to Pareto improvements in the ex ante sense. Not everybody will be happy with *any particular policy,* but everyone can expect to be better off with whatever *set of policies* emerges from the decision procedure specified by the constitution. Examples of such constitutional rules include taxing people—to the extent possible—in proportion to the benefit they receive from any particular public good (Buchanan and Brennan, 1999), minimizing the use of taxation as a means of redistribution (Sugden, 1990), and requiring that rules be general, impartial, and universally applicable (Buchanan, 1993).

Whatever general rules constrain the creation of policy, the restrictiveness of the Pareto standard has led many welfare economists and utilitarians to endorse the Kaldor-Hicks principle, according to which the provision of a public good is justified up to the point at which net social benefits are maximized, even if this entails a loss for some people. The principle requires that those who gain from a policy can, in principle, compensate the losers. If the losers are compensated, Kaldor-Hicks becomes a more flexible version of the Pareto principle. There are obvious objections to principles that allow policy makers to impose losses on some people so that others may benefit, and my object is not to defend any particular distributive principle.

Instead, I want to emphasize that most real-world public goods do not benefit everyone, and when they do, they do not benefit everyone equally. Even for a pure public good for which there is almost universal demand, such as saving African lions from extinction, there will be some people who consider the outcome deleterious rather than beneficial (tribal people who are occasionally eaten by lions, for example, and people who would rather save elephants, say, than lions). When this is true—when some people bear the costs, and others get the benefits—we should carefully consider whether a public good should be produced at all, who should shoulder the costs, and how it should be produced, given the range of public and private alternatives.

Public and Private Provision

Those who write about public goods theory often correctly complain that non-specialists confuse public goods with public policy. People tend to assume that public goods exist whenever government agents attempt to do what is "good for the public" in some vague sense. This is an understandable mistake. But, in a less excusable mistake, some scholars have accused pioneers of public goods theory of assuming that the failure of markets to provide public goods automatically implies that governments should step in to supply them. For example, Randall Holcombe argues that

> public goods theory is part of the government-produced propaganda designed to enhance the appearance of legitimacy of the state. . . . People who believe the theory are more likely to support government intervention into the economy, and are more likely to view government production as a legitimate activity of the state. (Holcombe, 2000: 137)

This is a conceptual mistake and a dubious empirical claim.

None of the academic economists who first described public goods made the assumption that the failure of markets to provide public goods always merits government action. In fact, AC Pigou, who is often caricatured as assuming that governments should always correct market failures by taxing negative externalities and subsidizing public goods, warns against this assumption:

> It is not sufficient to contrast the imperfect adjustments of unfettered private enterprise with the best adjustment that economists in their studies can imagine. For we cannot expect that any public authority will attain, or will even whole-heartedly seek, that ideal. Such authorities are liable alike to ignorance, to sectional pressure and to personal corruption by private interest. (Pigou, 1932: 332)

Similarly, Samuelson says "the term 'public good' . . . cannot be interpreted to imply that private goods should be produced by private enterprise and public goods should be produced by government directly." Instead, Samuelson suggests,

> where the consumption externalities intrinsic to a nonprivate good occur, all that I would insist on is that *laissez faire* cannot be counted on to lead to an optimum. There is a *prima facie* case, so to speak, for social concern and scrutiny of the outcome. . . . [But] the exact form in which the social concern ought to manifest itself depends on a host of considerations that have to be added to the model. (Samuelson, 1972: 52)

More recently, Hal Varian emphasizes that

> [t]he standard theory of public goods doesn't call for government intervention—it just says that when public goods are present, simple markets won't achieve efficient outcomes. Conventional economic theory is mute on the question of whether there is any other mechanism that will improve upon the market (Varian, 1993: 545).[16]

Indeed, there are two common ways of privately producing public goods: charity and assurance contracts. It is a familiar fact that private charities can produce public goods. For example, the Nature Conservancy buys land from foreign governments and farmers to preserve endangered forests and animals, and Planned Parenthood provides information and contraception services that promote public health by decreasing sexually transmitted diseases and unwanted pregnancies. Most contributors, presumably, have altruistic motivations—they care about improving the lot of other people and animals. But it is also possible to produce public goods for fun or for profit. For example, some people paint murals in public spaces or plant trees in parks in order to beautify a city or restore a native plant habitat. Others produce public goods for less altruistic reasons, including fame, fortune, or necessity. Members of a tribe might pool their labor in order to build a bridge or wage war against their neighbors. Of course, these goods might be described as less than fully public if those who don't contribute are excluded from using the goods, or from other social benefits. In this case people produce collective goods by creating exclusion mechanisms. This suggests that many goods that appear to be public can be transformed into private goods or impure public goods through the invention of subtle exclusion mechanisms. When this is true, there is no reason to assume government is necessary to produce public goods (whether state provision or private provision is more *efficient* is a separate empirical question).

Another way public goods can be produced privately is that profit-seeking firms may be able to find people who are willing to contribute to a collective endeavor, but who lack the assurance that like-minded people will do their part. Firms can then charge a fee for helping people coordinate their efforts by creating a contract between willing cooperators. It is worth remembering that public goods create two separate problems: the *free rider problem* (people who want the good, but who try to avoid paying for it), and the *assurance problem* (people who want a good, and are willing to pay for it, but who fear that others will not contribute enough to produce it). For local public goods that aren't consumed by many people, conditionally binding assurance contracts can solve both problems reasonably well (Schmidtz, 1987). Conditionally binding contracts solve the assurance problem by charging people (in money or labor) for a public good only if enough others pledge to contribute to produce the public good. Since most public goods are not binary—they are not all-or-nothing[17]—we can imagine a range of such contracts producing different kinds and quantities of public goods. Firms that profit by underwriting such contracts have an incentive to pay careful attention to how much different people are willing to pay for public goods. However, as the number of people needed to produce a public good increases, strategic behavior is likely to emerge, and transaction costs may become prohibitive. This suggests that many large-scale public goods, especially global and inter-generational goods like the reduction of ozone-depleting chemicals, are unlikely to be produced through assurance contracts. Moreover, since contracts must be enforceable to be effective, governments will almost always play some role in the provision of public goods, even if their role is simply to establish the rules of contract and provide judicial arbitration for contract disputes.

The crucial role of government in creating and enforcing the basic rules of the game suggests that the dichotomy between private and public production of public goods is a bit artificial. In addition to enforcing contracts and adjudicating disputes, governments can also facilitate the production of public goods by altering property rights or reducing transaction costs (Coase, 1960; Hampton, 1987). For example, by exempting private charities from taxation, government might facilitate the emergence of public goods without directly producing them (Cowen, 2006). This may be preferable in cases where people with local knowledge are better able to determine which public goods would benefit those around them. Still, there is a useful conceptual distinction between government directly producing public goods, and providing them indirectly by creating a legal environment or incentive structure that makes it easier for individuals to do so. For example, to the extent that education creates the public good of skilled citizens and competent voters, governments might produce the good *directly* through government-run schools, or *indirectly* by funding a voucher program in which education is competitively produced by privately run schools.

The distinction between direct and indirect provision is especially useful to make when thinking about the efficiency of markets and governments at producing public goods.[18] As a rule of thumb, markets tend to under-produce public goods, while governments tend to over-produce them. This is true in part because politicians are imperfectly informed, and because they spend other people's money (Schmidtz, 1993; Tullock, 1971). They also have an incentive to deliver gifts to the most politically powerful of their constituents, and impose the costs on less powerful people. Before we conclude that governments should (directly or indirectly) produce public goods, we should keep in mind that state action can create new externalities and novel public goods problems.

Primary and Secondary Public Goods

When governments produce public goods, they can simultaneously solve old problems and create new ones. For example, in the USA many state governments require citizens to purchase automobile insurance. In theory this is done to pool risk, and to protect people from damage others may impose on them but lack the ability to pay for.[19] The idea seems to be that there is a public good associated with bringing everyone into an insurance pool so that each can share the risks of driving and protect themselves against large losses imposed by those who are both uninsured and cannot afford to pay for the accidents they cause. But a predictable consequence of forced risk-sharing is that people have less incentive to take precautions to protect their own cars from minor accidents and theft. Insurance mandates transform time and money spent on protecting one's car into a public good since all members of the pool bear the cost of damaged property. The only way to encourage people to spend more resources protecting their car is to permit insurance companies to charge co-payments, to change the insurance mandate, or to create another policy that encourages each person to take more precaution against theft and damage. Thus, new mandates can both solve and create public goods problems (or, more generally, externalities); they can also create additional enforcement and compliance costs.

When a public good is an artifact of public policy, it is an open question whether governments should supply it, or whether they should alter the policies that make the good public to begin with. Consider a more controversial example. Many argue that reducing obesity is a public good because it will save money for all people in an insurance pool (in states with private health insurance) or all taxpayers (in states with government-financed health care). Similar arguments are often applied to smokers. Public goods arguments are frequently invoked to justify taxing cigarettes, and regulating what kinds of food and drink people consume. One problem with these arguments is that some evidence indicates that, on average, adults who choose to smoke (or allow themselves to become obese) do *not* impose net medical costs on other people over their lifetimes, since they die younger but live long enough to contribute nearly as much money in taxes and insurance premiums as healthier people (Barendregt et al., 1997; van Ball et al., 2008). If so, the public goods argument evaporates. However, even if smokers and obese people do impose significant costs on other people, so that there's a public good associated with reducing smoking and obesity, these costs are largely a function of public policy (Anomaly, 2012). This is true partly because insurance companies and other firms are often not allowed to price discriminate by charging more for services rendered to people who engage in risky behavior, and because social welfare programs typically cover people's costs regardless of the choices they make.

When public policy creates new kinds of public goods problems, we should think about whether further policies that attempt to provide the relevant public good should be passed, or whether those that create the problem should be repealed or altered.

Paternalism and Self-Subversion

The use of government coercion always raises deep moral questions.[20] Since compulsion is sometimes the only way for governments to produce public goods, we should be cautious about how much discretionary power we give to policy makers to decide which public goods should be produced.

I argued above that not all desires are worth satisfying. If demand for public goods stems from poorly formed desires, people will not necessarily be made better off when their desires are satisfied. The converse is also true: people can be made better off when their desires are frustrated. Indeed, many public goods are supplied despite popular opposition, and benefit people in ways they fail to understand. Consider free trade agreements, which are mutually beneficial but often unpopular; or treaties that reduce pollution by restricting trade in certain chemicals, such as ozone-depleting chlorofluorocarbons. Few people have an incentive to take economics and environmental science courses, or to inform themselves about the details of international treaties. So it is not surprising that many people are poorly informed about policies that provide global public goods.[21] When this is true, it may be legitimate for policy makers to provide public goods for which there *would be* widespread demand if desires were adequately informed.

One of the practical problems with a theory that says some desires count more than others is that it seems to empower policy makers to pass repressive laws by invoking the counterfactual desires their constituents would have if they were more thoughtful or informed. David Schmidtz worries that one problem with using government power to supply public goods is that it is paternalistic: "compelling us to contribute is paternalistic insofar as it does something for each of us that is good for us but that we cannot do for ourselves because we lack the collective will." He goes on to say that "[t]his paternalism is benign in the sense that the end it helps us attain is not only good for us but is also an end we actually desire" (Schmidtz, 1991: 2). Although I agree that paternalism is a real worry, Schmidtz uses the term "paternalism" in a way that I think we should reject. Gerald Dworkin suggests instead that for compulsion to count as paternalistic, it must override our judgment about purely self-regarding conduct (Dworkin, 1972). On Dworkin's influential account (in contrast to Schmidtz), if each of us recognizes an end as beneficial, but we lack the power to bring it about without the force of law, a law that compels us to do our part to achieve the end is not paternalistic since it does not override our judgment. Moreover, even when some people do not consider the coercive provision of a particular public good beneficial, if the reason for government provision is to prevent people from harming others, coercion is not paternalistic (whether any particular use of coercion is objectionable for other reasons is a separate question). For example, if the Center for Disease Control advocates a policy that requires most people to get vaccinated against smallpox, this is not paternalistic if the reason for requiring vaccination is to prevent people from spreading the smallpox virus to others.[22]

Paternalism aside, we might worry that if policy makers believe the theory that some public goods should be publicly provided because people *would* endorse their provision if they were adequately informed, they might be tempted to use this rationale to defend morally objectionable policies by appealing to the counterfactual desires of their constituents. While it is true that policy makers can misuse arguments, this does not show that the theory from which their arguments are drawn is false. For example, Henry Sidgwick famously argued that utilitarianism may be self-effacing (which implies that nobody should use it as a decision procedure) without being self-undermining (which implies that it is false). According to Sidgwick,

> a Utilitarian may reasonably desire, on Utilitarian principles, that some of his conclusions should be rejected by mankind generally; or even that the vulgar should keep aloof from his system as a whole, in so far as the inevitable indefiniteness and complexity of its calculations render it likely to lead to bad results in their hands (Sidgwick, 1874: 490).

The worry I want to raise is a natural extension of Sidgwick's. If policy makers tend to misuse arguments to justify policies that are not consistent with the arguments they appeal to, it may be desirable that they stop appealing to such arguments.

While it is conceivable that we would be better off if the theory of public goods had never been invented, or never been propagated to policy makers, this seems overly pessimistic. It is always possible for policy makers to appeal to arguments and principles that are either self-serving or unintentionally harmful. But this gives us a reason to constrain their discretionary power and pay attention to political incentives, not a reason to change our view about the complex connection between desire satisfaction, welfare, and public goods.

CONCLUSION

I have argued that although public goods are sources of market failure, and that governments can sometimes intervene to improve the outcome, widespread demand for public goods is, at best, a necessary condition for government intervention. There is no automatic link between demand and welfare, and the link is especially tenuous in the case of public goods because people have less incentive to become informed about goods which they lack the power to unilaterally produce or consume. In markets, poorly formed preferences are punished because buyers bear the costs of bad choices. In the political realm, this is rarely true since individual citizens have little power to decide through consumption or voting which public goods will be provided. This suggests that before policy makers decide to address a public goods problem with the machinery of government, they should consider whether demand for public goods stems from well-formed desires, whether the costs of public provision exceed the benefits, and whether markets will, all things considered, produce a better or worse outcome than government action.

NOTES

1. Nonrivalry in consumption means that one person's consumption doesn't change the amount available for others to consume; nonexcludability means that nobody can be excluded from enjoying the good once its available. Many *apparent* public goods are easily provided by creating exclusion mechanisms (thus converting them into club goods) or by charging people as they use more of a good.

2. Head (1962) argues that the inability to separate public goods into discrete units with prices creates the main provision problem.

3. James Buchanan explains it as follows:

> The individual, as a member of a large group characterized by general interdependence among all of its members, will not expect to influence the behavior of other individuals through his own actions. He will not behave strategically; he will not bargain; he will not "game." Instead, he will simply adjust his own behavior to the behavior of others, taken as a composite unit. . . . He accepts the totality of others' action as a parameter for

> his own decisions, as a part of the environment, a part of nature, so to speak. . . . The small number case provides the individual with motivation both to initiate trade and to bargain over terms. The effective large number case . . . tends to eliminate both trading and bargaining behavior" (1999: 82).

4. Scholars who explore how public goods can be supplied through non-governmental means (Ostrom, 1990) usually focus on local public goods with some degree of rivalry or excludability. Indeed, when cultural norms emerge among a small community of people, and norm violators are penalized—usually in the form of social stigma (in mild cases) or expulsion (in serious cases)—members of the community can transform public goods into private goods by excluding rule breakers from a variety of social benefits to which rule followers have access. In these cases cultural norms essentially serve the same function as enforceable property rights in large, liberal societies. Although adhering to norms and punishing norm violators is itself a public goods problem in the absence of state institutions, natural selection seems to have partly solved the problem by equipping most of us with moral emotions like shame and indignation, along with a powerful desire to punish those who undermine mutually-beneficial social norms (Gintis and Bowles, 2008; Ostrom, 2000).

5. For this reason, it can be misleading to describe public goods in terms of *benefits* that are non-rival and non-excludable. Technically, a good can be public even if it benefits nobody at all. The essential feature of public goods is that they must be available to everyone (and in equal amounts) if they are available to anyone. Thus, some public goods—even pure public goods—may not be desired by anybody, and may be despised by nearly everybody. For example, a museum in Tel Aviv that glamorizes Nazism, but which doesn't charge admission fees, is a public good in the technical sense, but one for which there is little demand.

6. Mancur Olson's (1965) influential treatment of public goods problems as prisoners' dilemmas must be modified. First, since almost no public good is pure, we cannot represent all rational players as choosing a Pareto-dominated Nash equilibrium, as they would if the game were a true prisoner's dilemma. Second, while public goods are defined by generic features—*nonrivalry* and *nonexcludability*—prisoners' dilemmas, like all games, are defined by the preferences over outcomes of the particular people playing the game. If players are relatively altruistic, for example, the Pareto optimal action may be identical with the Nash equilibrium, in which case it's not a prisoner's dilemma. If the utilities in a game reflect everything the players care about, and some players care how an outcome is reached, or about the other people with whom they are playing, they may be modeled by a different game than other players in the same situation with different motivations.

7. Some take this to show that we should rely more on expert opinion than on citizens' sentiments on complex issues that require a high degree of scientific competence. Others take it to suggest skepticism about empowering experts who will also be subject to bias if not ignorance.

8. For more on the scandal, see Paul Offit (2010). For more on the moral significance of the controversy, see Tom Sorrel (2007).

9. Other recent cases that are structurally similar include unfounded skepticism among many Americans about the connection between carbon emissions and climate change, and an unfounded belief among many Europeans that genetically modified foods cause various medical disorders.

10. Preferences differ from desires only in the sense that preferences are rankings over alternative bundles of goods or states of affairs, while desires can be aimed at a single good or state of affairs.

11. See especially Richard Brandt (1979), David Gauthier (1986: ch. 2), and Hausman and McPherson (2006: ch. 8) for attempts to distinguish which satisfied preferences should count as welfare-enhancing rather than welfare-diminishing.

12. See Parfit (1984: ch. 6).

13. This criterion is admittedly vague. But, as Aristotle reminds us, we shouldn't expect more precision than a subject matter admits of:

> We must be content in speaking of such subjects and with such premises to indicate the truth roughly and in outline, and in speaking about things which are only for the most part true and with premises of the same kind to reach conclusions that are no better. In the same spirit, therefore, should each type of statement be received; for it is the mark of an educated man to look for precision in each class of things just so far as the nature of the subject admits (350 BCE, Bk 1, Section 3).

14. Stiglitz (1999).

15. This is a clear case in which the dichotomy between market versus government or public versus private provision is artificially stark. Much basic science research is funded by state governments, but distributed to private, public, and non-profit institutions—including firms and universities—on a competitive basis.

16. Mill and Sidgwick also anticipated arguments that (what we now call) market failures should always be

compared with governmental policies that might make the problem worse, given the incentive and information problems faced by bureaucrats. See Steven Medema (2007).

17. See Harold Demsetz (1993: 564).

18. Although I am tempted to distinguish between public *production* and public *provision* of public goods, since most authors who write about public goods equate "provision" and "production," I will stick with *direct* versus *indirect* provision, and use "provision" and "production" interchangeably.

19. Insurance mandates can also be a way for legislators to redistribute risk and wealth without the state getting directly involved in taxing and spending. More cynically, they are sometimes simply a legally-sanctioned transfer of wealth from citizens to insurance companies. I do not take a stand on whether insurance mandates are justified, or whether the argument from risk sharing or adverse selection is plausible.

20. Although some use "coercion" to refer to the use or threat of force by one party against another in such a way that the coerced party's rights are violated, I use "coercion" in a morally neutral way. "Coercion" *does* imply that the coerced party's viable options are diminished (due in part to a fear of punishment), but it *does not* imply that his rights are violated or that his welfare is reduced. Indeed, Hobbes argues that coercively enforced laws can promote welfare by increasing trust, coordination, and exchange (Hobbes, 1651: ch. 15).

21. For example, most people have never heard of the Montreal Protocol on ozone depletion, and among those who have, many believe that climate change and ozone depletion are the same problem. According to a recent survey on American attitudes about climate change,

> large majorities incorrectly think that the hole in the ozone layer and aerosol spray cans contribute to global warming, leading many to incorrectly believe that banning aerosol spray cans or stopping rockets from punching holes in the ozone layer are viable solutions (Leiserowitz et al., 2010: 4).

22. Public goods that are justified not as mechanisms to prevent people from harming others, but rather as a way of promoting a preference we would have if better informed *would* count as paternalistic on Dworkin's view, and potentially as justified paternalism.

REFERENCES

Anomaly J (2012). Is obesity a public health problem? *Public Health Ethics* 5(3): 216–221.

Aristotle (350 BCE). *Nichomachean Ethics.* Available at: http://classics.mit.edu/Aristotle/nicomachaen.html (accessed 9 January 2013).

Barendregt J, Bonneux L, and van der Mass P (1997). The health care costs of smoking. *New England Journal of Medicine* 337: 1052–1057.

Brandt R (1979). *A Theory of the Good and the Right.* Oxford, UK: Clarendon Press.

Buchanan J (1993). How can constitutions be designed so that politicians who seek to serve the public interest can survive and prosper? *Constitutional Political Economy* 4(1): 1–6.

Buchanan J (1999). The demand and supply of public goods. In: *The Collected Works of James M. Buchanan.* Indianapolis, IN: Liberty Fund. First published 1968.

Buchanan J and Brennan G (1999). The reason of rules: constitutional political economy. Indianapolis, IN: Liberty Fund. First published 1985.

Buchanan J and Tullock G (1962). *The Calculus of Consent.* Ann Arbor, MI: University of Michigan Press.

Caplan B (2008). *The Myth of the Rational Voter.* Princeton, NJ: Princeton University Press.

Coase R (1960). The problem of social cost. *The Journal of Law and Economics* 3: 1–44.

Cornes R and Sandler T (1996). The theory of externalities, public goods, and club goods. Cambridge, UK: Cambridge University Press.

Cowen T (2006). *Good and Plenty.* Princeton, NJ: Princeton University Press.

Demsetz H (1993). The private production of public goods, once again. *Critical Review* 7(4): 559–566.

Diamond P and Hausman J (1994). Contingent valuation: Is some number better than no number? *Journal of Economic Perspectives* 8(4): 45–64.

Diamond P, Hausman J, Leonard GK, et al. (1993). Does contingent valuation measure preferences? Experimental evidence. In: Jerry Hausman (ed.) *Contingent Valuation: A Critical Assessment.* Amsterdam: North Holland Press.

Downs A (1957). An economic theory of political action in a democracy. *The Journal of Political Economy* 65(2): 135–160.

Dworkin G (1972). Paternalism. *The Monist* 56: 64–84.

Gaus G (2007). *On Philosophy, Politics and Economics.* Belmont, CA: Thomson Wadsworth.

Gauthier D (1986). *Morals by Agreement.* Oxford, UK: Oxford University Press.

Gintis H and Bowles S (2008). The evolutionary basis of collective action. In: *The Oxford Handbook of Political Economy.* Oxford, UK: Oxford University Press.

Hampton J (1986). *Hobbes and the Social Contract Tradition.* Cambridge, UK: Cambridge University Press.

Hampton J (1987). Free rider problems in the production of collective goods. *Economics and Philosophy* 3: 245–273.

Hausman D and McPherson M (2006). *Economic Analysis, Moral Philosophy and Public Policy,* 2nd ed. Cambridge, UK: Cambridge University Press.

Hayek F (1945). The use of knowledge in society. *American Economic Review* 35(4): 519–530.

Head JG (1962). Public goods and public policy. *Public Finance* 17(3): 197–219.

Hobbes T (1651). *Leviathan.* Available at: http://oll.libertyfund.org/?option=com_staticxt&static file=show.php%3Ftitle=869 (accessed 9 January 2013).

Holcombe R (2000). Public goods theory and public policy. *The Journal of Value Inquiry* 34: 273–286.

Huemer M (2015). Why people are irrational about politics. Present volume.

Hume D (1739). A Treatise of Human Nature. Available at: http://oll.libertyfund.org/index.php? option=com_staticxt&staticfile=show.php%3Ftitle=342&Itemid=27#toc_list (accessed 9 January 2013).

Kavka G (1986). *Hobbesian Moral and Political Theory.* Princeton, NJ: Princeton University Press.

Kelman S (1981). Cost-benefit analysis: An ethical critique. *Regulation* 5: 33–40.

Leiserowitz A, Smith N, and Marlon JR (2010). *Americans' Knowledge of Climate Change.* New Haven, CT: Yale Project on Climate Change Communication. Available at: http://environment. yale.edu/climate/files/Climate ChangeKnowledge2010.pdf (accessed 9 January 2013).

Medema S (2007). The hesitant hand: Mill, Sidgwick and the evolution of the theory of market failure. *History of Political Economy* 39(3): 331–358.

Offit P (2010). *Autism's False Prophets.* New York, NY: Columbia University Press.

Olson M (1965). *The Logic of Collective Action.* Cambridge, MA: Harvard University Press.

Ostrom E (1990). *Governing the Commons: The Evolution of Institutions for Collective Action.* Cambridge, UK: Cambridge University Press.

Ostrom E (2000). Collective action and the evolution of social norms. *Journal of Economic Perspectives* 14(3): 137–158.

Parfit D (1984). *Reasons and Persons.* Oxford, UK: Oxford University Press.

Pigou AC (1932). *The Economics of Welfare,* 4th ed. London, UK: Macmillan Press.

Rawls J (1971). *A Theory of Justice.* Cambridge, MA: Harvard University Press.

Samples K and Hollyer J (1990). *Contingent Valuation of Wildlife Resources in the Presence of Substitutes and Complements.* Boulder, CO: Westview Press.

Samuelson P (1954). The pure theory of public expenditure. *The Review of Economics and Statistics* 37(4): 350–356.

Samuelson P (1972). Indeterminacy of government role in public-good theory. In: RC Merton (ed.) *The Collected Scientific Papers of Paul A. Samuelson, volume 3.* Cambridge, MA: MIT Press.

Schmidtz D (1987). Contracts and public goods. *Harvard Journal of Law and Public Policy* 10: 475–503.

Schmidtz D (1991). *The Limits of Government: An Essay on the Public Goods Argument.* Boulder, CO: Westview Press.

Schmidtz D (1993). Market failure. *Critical Review* 7(4): 525–537.

Schmidtz D (2001). A place for cost-benefit analysis. *Philosophical Issues* 35: 148–170.

Sidgwick H (1981). *The Methods of Ethics,* 7th ed. Indianapolis, IN: Hackett Publishing. First published 1874.

Smith A (1776). *An Inquiry into the Nature and Causes of the Wealth of Nations.* Available at: Econlib.org/library/smithsmWN.html (accessed 9 January 2013).

Sorrel T (2007). Parental knowledge and expert choice in the debate about MMR and autism. In: *Ethics, Prevention and Public Health.* Oxford, UK: Oxford University Press.

Stiglitz J (1999). Knowledge as a global public good. In: Inge Kaul (ed.) *Global Public Goods.* Oxford, UK: Oxford University Press.

Sugden R (1990). Rules for choosing among public goods: A contractarian approach. *Constitutional Political Economy* 1(2): 63–82.

Tolley G, Randall A, Blomquist G, et al. (1983). Establishing and valuing the effects of improved visibility in the Eastern United States. Report to the US Environmental Protection Agency, Washington, DC.

Tullock G (1971). Public decisions as public goods. *Journal of Political Economy* 79(4): 913–918.

van Ball P, Polder J, de Wit G, et al. (2008). Lifetime medical costs of obesity. *PLOS Medicine* 5: 242–249.

Varian H (1993). Markets for public goods? *Critical Review* 7(4): 539–557.

DAVID FRIEDMAN

Market Failures

1990

TRANSACTION COSTS: BARTER, MARRIAGE, AND MONEY

Barter vs. Money

The simplest form of trade is barter; I trade goods that I have and you want for goods that you have and I want. This raises a problem. I must find a trading partner who has what I want and wants what I have: what economists call a *double coincidence of wants.* In a simple society in which there are only a few goods being traded, this may not be a serious problem; but in a complicated society such as ours, it is. If I want to buy a car, I first look in the classified ads to find someone who is selling the kind of car I want, then call him up and ask him if he wants to be taught economics in exchange for his car. This drastically reduces the number of potential trading partners.

The solution is the development of money—some good that almost everyone is willing to accept in exchange. Money usually starts out as some good (gold, cloth, cattle—the word "pecuniary" comes from the Latin word for cattle) valued for its own uses; people are willing to accept it even if they do not intend to consume it, because they know they can later exchange it for something else. In a money economy, I find one person who wants what I have, sell it to him, and then use the money to buy what I want from someone else.

The advantage of money is obvious; the disadvantage is that you cannot eat it or wear it (exception: *wadmal,* wool cloth used as money in medieval Iceland). If markets are *thin*—if there are few people buying or selling—the individual who chooses to hold a stock of money may find that he cannot easily exchange it for what he needs when he needs it.

Thin markets cause two different problems for someone who wants to buy or sell. The first is that there may be nobody who wants what he is selling today or is selling what he wants to buy; the mere process of locating a trading partner may be expensive and time consuming. The second is that if he does find a trading partner, he becomes part of a bilateral monopoly—one buyer, one seller. Bilateral monopoly, for reasons discussed in an earlier chapter, can lead to substantial *transaction costs:* time and energy spent haggling over the price, and deals that do not get made because of a breakdown in bargaining.

In a society in which markets are thin and the number of traded commodities is small enough so that the double coincidence problem is not too serious, individuals may find it more convenient to hold wealth in the form of goods rather than money. This was probably the situation in early medieval Europe. Coins existed and were used in exchange; but barter was, for several centuries, more common.

A Market We All Know and Love

In order to understand the difficulties of barter, it is useful to consider the large-scale barter market of which you are all part—the marriage/dating/sex market. The reason this is a barter market is that if I am going out with or married to you, you are necessarily going out with or married to me. I must find a woman whom I want and who wants me—the double coincidence of wants.

David Friedman, "Market Failures," from *Price Theory: An Intermediate Text.* Cincinnati, OH: South-Western Pub. Co., 1990. Permission by South-Western Publishing Company.

We observe, in this market, large search costs, long search times, lots of frustrated and/or lonely people of both sexes—in other words, a market where traders have a hard time getting together, due largely to the high transaction costs of barter.

PUBLIC GOODS AND EXTERNALITIES

If every individual in a group behaves rationally, the result may be undesirable—for every individual. This happens when one person's actions impose costs or benefits on others. Examples include students cutting across the lawn and fighters running away in battle, shooting their weapons without aiming them, or not shooting at all. In such situations, the rationality of the individual does not imply that the group acts as if it were rational.

The rest of this chapter will be devoted to a discussion of situations of this sort. I will start with a number of specific examples and then go on to explain the two general categories under which many such problems are usually classed in economics: public goods and externalities. I will end by discussing the special problems associated with imperfect information.

Good for Each May Not Be Good for All: Some Examples

I will give three examples of conflicts between the individual rationality of the members of a group and their welfare. Two—the first and the last—are situations that should be familiar to every reader over the age of 17. The other is a widely discussed public policy issue with which I hope most of you have had no personal experience.

To Vote or Not to Vote? In deciding whether to vote in the next election, one should consider both costs and benefits. The costs are fairly obvious: a certain amount of time standing in line and additional time spent studying issues and candidates in order to decide how to vote. The benefits are of two sorts: those that do not depend on the effect of your vote on the election, and those that do. An example of the first sort might be your feeling of having done your civic duty or your pleasure at voting against a candidate you particularly dislike.

The second sort of benefit comes from the effect of your vote on the outcome of the election. In evaluating such benefits, you should consider two questions: how important it is that the right candidate win and how likely it is that your vote will affect the outcome. In most large elections, the probability that your vote will affect the outcome is very small; in a presidential election, it is well under one in a million. Unless getting the right person elected is immensely valuable to you—so valuable that you are willing to bear the costs of voting in exchange for one chance in a million of influencing the outcome—the effect of your vote on the election is not a good reason for voting unless you expect the election to be extraordinarily close. If you vote anyway—because you enjoy voting or because you believe that good citizens vote or because you like being part of a history-making event reported on nationwide television—the minuscule effect of your vote on the election gives you very little incentive to be sure you are voting for the best candidate.

The usual response to arguments of this sort is either "You are saying people should be selfish" or "What if everyone did that?" The answer to the first is that I have not assumed that you are selfish in any conventional sense of the word. I assume you are concerned with costs and benefits, but I include as a benefit the achieving of whatever objectives you happen to have. Obviously individuals have objectives that are not selfish in any narrow sense—they value the welfare of their children, their friends, and (to a lesser degree) people they do not even know. One reason you might put a high value on electing the right candidate is the belief that doing so will benefit not only yourself but hundreds of millions of other people. If you were so altruistic as to give the same weight to the welfare of every other person as to your own, then the benefit of electing the right candidate would be hundreds of millions of times as great as the direct benefit to you. That might be a sufficient reason to spend an hour or two voting, even if you realized that all you were buying was one chance in a million of influencing the outcome of the election. Casual observation suggests that few people are that altruistic.

The question "What if everybody acted like that?" can be answered in two ways. The first is to point out that if enough people refrained from voting, the remaining voters would each have a substantial chance of influencing the outcome of the election, and it would then pay them to vote. The equilibrium would be a situation in which the (say) ten thousand most concerned citizens voted.

The second answer to the question "What if everybody acted like that?" is to point out that the question implicitly assumes that true beliefs must have desirable consequences—and therefore that beliefs with undesirable consequences must be false. There is no reason why this must always be so. Perhaps it is true both that sensible people will not vote and that if everyone acts on that principle the consequences will be bad. If so, it might be wise for me not to tell you that sensible people do not vote, but that does not make it untrue. A statement may be both true and dangerous. The previous sentence is such a statement—since it provides ammunition for those who wish to argue against free speech.

The apparent paradox—that if everyone correctly perceives how to act in his own interest and does so, everyone may be worse off as a result—comes from the fact that different people have different objectives. Suppose there are a hundred of us, each of whom can individually choose action A or action B. My taking action A gives me $10 and costs the rest of you a total of $20. Your taking action A gives you $10 and costs the rest of us, including me, a total of $20. As long as we act separately, it is in the interest of each of us to take action A—making us all worse off than if we had all taken action B. The problem is that I only control my action—and I am better off taking A than B. This, of course, is the problem we encountered long ago in the discussion of why soldiers run away.

A simple and striking example of such a situation is the prisoner's dilemma. Joe and Mike, the two accused criminals, would both be better off if they both kept silent. But if Mike confesses, the D.A. will have the evidence needed to convict Joe—and will punish him for his silence with a stiff sentence. So if Mike is going to confess, Joe had better confess too. If Mike stays silent and Joe confesses, the D.A. will express his gratitude by letting Joe off with a token sentence. So if Mike is not going to confess, Joe is better off confessing. Whatever Mike does, Joe is better off confessing, and similarly for Mike. They both confess, and both get worse sentences than if they had both kept silent.

Plea Bargaining: A Real-World Prisoner's Dilemma. A plea bargain is an arrangement by which a prosecutor, instead of trying a defendant on a charge of, say, first-degree murder, allows the defendant to plead guilty to a lesser charge, such as second-degree murder or manslaughter. It is widely criticized as a way of letting criminals off lightly. In fact, it seems likely that the existence of plea bargaining results in criminals being punished more severely rather than less. If plea bargaining were abolished—as some people suggest it should be—the result might well be to reduce the sentence received by the average criminal.

How can this be? Surely a criminal will only plead guilty to the lesser charge if doing so is in his interest—which means that a certain conviction on the less serious charge is preferable, for him, to whatever he believes the chance is of being convicted on the more serious charge. True. But the chance of a conviction depends on what resources, of money and time, the prosecution spends on that particular case—which in turn depends on how many other cases had to go to trial and how many were settled by plea bargaining.

Suppose there are 100 cases per year, and the district attorney has a budget of $100,000. He can only spend $1,000 on each case, with the result that 50 percent of the criminals are acquitted. With plea bargaining, the D.A. concentrates his resources on the ten criminals who refuse to accept the bargain he offers. He spends $10,000 prosecuting each of them and gets a conviction rate of 90 percent. Each criminal deciding whether to accept the D.A.'s offer knows that, if he refuses, he has about a 90 percent chance of being convicted—so he accepts any offer that he prefers to a 90 percent chance of conviction.

On average, all the criminals, both the ones who accept the bargain and the ones who do not, are worse off—more severely punished—than if the D.A. prosecuted all of them on the more severe charge and convicted half. Each individual criminal benefits by accepting the D.A.'s offer—but by doing so, he frees resources that the D.A. can then use against another criminal, raising the average conviction rate. The higher conviction rate makes criminals willing to accept worse bargains. All of the criminals would be better off if none of them accepted the D.A.'s offer, but each is better off accepting. This is the prisoner's dilemma in real life.

Why Traffic Jams. This is a situation in which each individual takes the action that is in his individual interest; they are all, as a result, worse off than if they had acted differently. A more familiar example of such a situation occurs twice a day, five days a week, about two blocks from where I used to live. The time is rush hour; the scene is the intersection of Wilshire Boulevard and Westwood Avenue in Los Angeles, said to be the busiest intersection in the world. As the light on Wilshire goes green, ten lanes of traffic surge forward. As it turns yellow, a last few cars try to make it across. Since Wilshire is packed with cars, they fail and end up in the intersection, blocking the cars on Westwood, which now have a green light. Gradually the cars in the intersection make it across, allowing the traffic on Westwood to surge forward—just as the light changes, trapping another batch of cars in the intersection.

If drivers on both streets refrained from entering the intersection until there was clearly enough room for them on the far side, the jam would not occur. Traffic would flow faster, and they would all get where they are going sooner. Yet each individual driver is behaving rationally. My aggressive driving on Wilshire benefits me (I may make it across before the light changes, and at worst I will get far enough into the intersection not to be blocked by cars going the other way at the next stage of the jam) and harms drivers on Westwood. Your aggressive driving on Westwood benefits you and harms drivers (possibly including me) on Wilshire. The harm is much larger than the benefit, so on net we are all worse off. But I receive all of the benefit and none of the harm from the particular decision that I control. I am correctly choosing the action that best achieves my objectives—but if we each made a mistake and drove less aggressively, we would all be better off.

My point, in this and the previous examples, is not that rationality implies selfishness. That is a parody of economics. Drivers may value other people's time as well as (although probably not as much as) their own.

The point—which to some readers may seem paradoxical—is that rational behavior by every individual in a group may sometimes lead to an outcome that is undesirable in terms of precisely the same objectives (getting home earlier in this case or getting a light sentence or surviving a battle in some of the other cases we have discussed) that each individual's rational behavior is correctly calculated to achieve. Such situations often involve what economists call public goods or externalities, two concepts that we will now discuss.

Public Goods

There are a number of different, closely related definitions of a *public good.* I prefer to define it as "*a good such that, if it is produced at all, the producer cannot control who gets it.*" The public-good *problem* arises because the producer of a public good cannot, like the producer of an ordinary ("private") good, tell the consumer that he can only have it if he pays for it; the consumer knows that if it is produced at all, the producer has no control over who gets it.

One example of a public good is a radio broadcast; if it is made at all, anyone who owns a radio and lives in the right area can receive it. This example demonstrates several important things about public goods. The first is that whether or not a good is public depends on the nature of the good. It is not that the producer *should* not control who gets it but that he *cannot;* or, at least, he can control who gets it, if at all, only at a prohibitively high cost (hiring detectives to creep around people's houses and arrest them if they are listening to the broadcast without having paid for it). While the publicness of a good may be affected by the legal system (whether it is legal to listen to a broadcast without the broadcaster's permission), it is mostly just a fact of nature; even if it were legal to forbid unauthorized listening, the law would be prohibitively expensive to enforce.

A second important thing to note about a public good is that it is *not* defined as a good produced by the government. In this country, radio broadcasts are mostly private; they are still public goods. Many of the things government does produce, such as mail delivery, are private goods; the government can and does refuse to deliver your letter if it does not have a stamp on it. The fact that a good is public presents a problem to a private producer—the problem of how to get paid for producing it—but the problem is not necessarily an insoluble one, as the example of a radio broadcast illustrates.

Private Production of Public Goods. There are a number of ways in which the problem of producing public goods privately may be solved. One, which works best if the size of the public (the group of people who will receive the good if it is produced) is small, is a unanimous contract. The producer gets all the members of the public together, tells them how much he wants each to pay toward the cost of producing the good, and announces that unless each agrees to chip in if everyone else does, the good will not be produced.

Assume that they believe him. Consider the logic of the situation from the standpoint of a single member of the group deciding whether he should agree to chip in. He reasons as follows:

Either someone else is going to refuse, in which case the deal falls through, I get my money back, and my agreement costs me nothing, or else everyone else is going to agree. If everyone else agrees and I refuse, I do not have to pay for the public good, but I also do not get it. So as long as the good is worth more to me than my share of the cost, I ought to agree.

The same argument applies to everyone, so if the public good is worth more to the consumers than it costs to produce, the entrepreneur should be able to divide up the cost in such a way that each individual finds it in his interest to agree.

One difficulty with this is that if the public is large, it may be hard to organize a unanimous contract. One solution is to find a *privileged minority:* a subgroup of the public that is small enough so that its members can form their own unanimous contract and that receives enough benefit from the public good so that its members can be persuaded to bear the whole cost. When I mow my front lawn, I am acting as a privileged minority (of one); the mowed lawn makes the neighborhood more attractive, benefiting everyone, but I receive enough of the benefit to be willing to pay the whole cost.

Consider how this might work in the case of one of the largest public goods in our society and one of the most difficult to produce privately: national defense. Suppose the inhabitants of Hawaii believe that there is a 10 percent chance of a nuclear strike against their island next year. If the strike occurs, the island will be wiped out. The inhabitants can flee the island before the attack, so the cost will be distributed roughly in proportion to the value of the land they own. Table 1 is an (entirely imaginary) listing of how land ownership is divided on the island and how much each owner would pay, if necessary, to prevent the attack.

Table 1

Landowner	Value of Land	Value of Defense
Dole Pineapple	$400,000,000	$40,000,000
Hilton Hotels	$400,000,000	$40,000,000
United Fruit Co.	$300,000,000	$30,000,000
Maxwell House Coffee	$250,000,000	$25,000,000
Howard Johnson's	$200,000,000	$10,000,000
Everyone Else	$900,000,000	$90,000,000

Suppose an entrepreneur comes up with a system for defending Hawaii from nuclear attack at a cost of $100 million. He goes to Dole, Hilton, United Fruit, and Maxwell House and tells them that if they pay him $110 million, he will defend the island. Since the value to them of the defense is more than that and since there are only a few firms that have to agree, they raise the money.

In this case, the story has a happy ending. Suppose, however, that the total cost of the defense is $149 million. It is still worth having—the top five landowners alone value it at more than its cost—but it will be very hard to get. If the entrepreneur asks the Big 5 to each put up the same proportion of the value of their land (just under 10 percent), Howard Johnson will refuse. Unfortunately for Hawaii, the Howard Johnson firm is run by an optimist who believes the chance of an attack is only 5 percent and therefore is willing to pay only 5 percent of his land value to protect against the attack.

If the information on Table 1 were a matter of public knowledge, agreement could still be reached, with Howard Johnson contributing at half the rate of the other four. The problem is that the other contributors are likely to view Howard Johnson's optimism as a bargaining ploy, a way to get them to pay more than their share of the cost. If there is no simple rule for dividing up the cost of defense, agreement on who pays what may well be impossible.

The larger the number of people whose agreement is needed and the less obvious it is how much each values what he is getting, the harder it will be to get agreement. If the public good is cheap—if defense costs only $40 million—the problem is soluble; the entrepreneur can either leave Howard Johnson out of the contract or else charge everyone 5 percent of land value and still raise enough money. But if the cost of the public good is a large fraction of the benefit it produces and if the benefit is spread among many people, raising the money is a serious and perhaps insoluble problem.

In the example discussed, the concentration of land ownership in Hawaii greatly simplified the situation. The Big 5 were a privileged minority; they received a large fraction of the total benefit, so the entrepreneur could, with luck, raise the money he needed from them while ignoring the large number of small holders. The term "privileged minority," which is commonly used in this way, has always struck me as somewhat strange, since the minority has the "privilege" of paying for what all the other members of the public get for free.

Unanimous contracts are one solution to the problem of producing a public good. Another solution is to convert the public good temporarily into a private good. Suppose the public good is flood control; building a dam will reduce floods in the valley below, increasing the value of farm land there. One way to pay for the dam is for the entrepreneur to buy up as much as possible of the land in the valley (or buy options on the land at its current price), build the dam, then sell the land back (or sell the options back to the owners). Since the new flood protection makes the land worth more than when he bought it, he should be able to get a higher price than he paid, for either the land or the options.

Another ingenious solution, which would never have occurred to me if I had not seen it in operation, is to combine two public goods and give away the package. The first public good has a positive cost of production and a positive value to the customer; the second has a negative cost of production and a negative value to the customer. The package has zero or negative cost of production and positive value to the consumer.

This is how radio and television broadcasts are produced; the first good is the program and the second the commercial. Commercials have a negative cost of production from the standpoint of the broadcaster; he gets paid by the sponsor to broadcast them. Since there is usually no convenient way to listen to the program without hearing the commercials, the listener must choose to accept or reject a package deal—program plus commercial. If the net value of the package is positive to him, he will accept it. If the net cost (cost of operating the station minus payment from the sponsor) is negative, if advertising revenues more than cover operating expenses, the broadcaster can and will stay in business.

An interesting example of the public-good problem, and several interesting solutions, occur in the computer industry. A $300 computer program can be copied onto a $3 floppy disk. Programs can be protected against copying, but this is inconvenient for the user, who would like at least one backup copy in case his original gets damaged and who may also find it convenient to copy several of the programs he has purchased onto one disk. Even if programs are protected, someone with a reasonable amount of expertise can frequently "break" the protection—figure out how to copy them. There are even programs on the market designed to copy copy-protected programs. In one case, a program capable of copying other copy-protected programs was copy-protected against itself; a second company sold a program to copy it!

If you cannot effectively copy-protect a program, selling it to one person means, in effect, giving it to everyone. The program is then a public good and figuring out how to make money producing it is a public-good problem. Firms that produce and sell software have come up with a number of ingenious solutions. One of them is *bundling.* You sell a computer along with a bundle of programs designed to run on that particular computer; in effect you charge for the programs in the price of the computer. Anyone can copy the programs—but to use them, he has to buy the computer. Another kind of bundling is to sell a package consisting of a program plus service: a voice on the other end of a telephone to answer questions about how to make the program work. The seller keeps track of who bought the program and only gives help to registered owners. A third kind of bundling is exemplified by the way in which I "sell" the computer programs that go with this book. A professor who adopts the book is given a free copy of the programs and permission to make copies for his students. I get paid for my work writing the programs in increased sales of the book. I hope.

As these examples suggest, there are a variety of ways in which public goods can be privately produced. Each of these may succeed, under some circumstances, in producing some quantity of a public good. None of them can be relied on to lead to an efficient level of production in the strong sense in which we have been using the term—an outcome so good that it could not be improved by a bureaucrat-god. Typically, the private producer of a public good succeeds in collecting only part of the additional value of each unit of the good produced. He produces up to the point where what he gets for an additional unit (an additional hour of broadcasting, or an additional dollar spent making the program better) is equal to what it costs him. That is a lower level of output than the efficient point where marginal cost to the producer equals marginal value to the consumer.

To see more clearly the sense in which private production of public goods is inefficient, consider some of our examples. In the Hawaiian defense case, Hawaii was worth defending as long as the cost was less than $245 million, since that was the total value of the defense to all the inhabitants put together. If the cost of the defense happened to be only $40 million, private arrangements might produce it, which is the efficient outcome. If the cost were $235 million, it is unlikely that the defense would be produced; since it still costs less than its value, a bureaucrat-god who ordered Hawaii defended would be producing a net benefit. So if the cost of defending Hawaii is $235 million, private production results in an inefficient outcome. Hawaii is worth defending—and is undefended. The private production of public goods is inefficient in the sense of sometimes leading to an inefficient outcome—failing to produce a good that is worth producing.

We have assumed that there are only two possible amounts of defense: none or enough. Whether or not that is plausible in the case of defense, the equivalent assumption is obviously wrong for radio broadcasts or computer programs; in each case, the manufacturer decides how much he will spend and what quality of product he will produce. The efficient outcome is one in which he makes all quality improvements that are worth more to the consumers than they cost him to make. But from his standpoint, improvements are worth making only if they increase his revenue by at least as much as they cost. Since he will be able to collect only part of the value he produces, there may be improvements worth making that he does not find it in his interest to make; so here again the outcome could be improved by a bureaucrat-god. The good may be produced, but it is generally underproduced: An increase in quality, number of hours of broadcasting, or some other dimension would result in net benefits. So private production of public goods is generally inefficient in the technical sense in which I have been using the word.

The Efficient Quantity of a Public Good. While we have talked about producing the efficient outcome, we have not yet discussed how, in principle, one would find out what it is. Figure 1 shows the answer to that question, for a very small public. D_1, D_2, D_3 are the demand curves for radio broadcasting of three listeners. Each shows how much broadcasting a listener would buy if it were an ordinary private good—how many hours per day he would pay for as a function of the price per hour. The figure assumes that number of hours per day of broadcasting is the only relevant quality variable, the only way in which the broadcaster can affect the value to his "customers" of what he produces. MC shows the marginal cost curve faced by the broadcaster-how much each additional hour per day of broadcasting costs him.

As usual, the efficient solution is to produce where MV=MC—to keep increasing the number of hours as long as the value of an additional hour to the listeners is at least as great as its cost of production. Each extra hour of broadcasting benefits all three customers; its marginal value is the sum of its marginal value to Customer 1, its marginal value to Customer 2, and its marginal value to Customer 3. So the total MV curve is the vertical sum of the MV curves for the customers, each of which equals the corresponding demand curve. The result is shown on the figure. Q* is the efficient quantity.

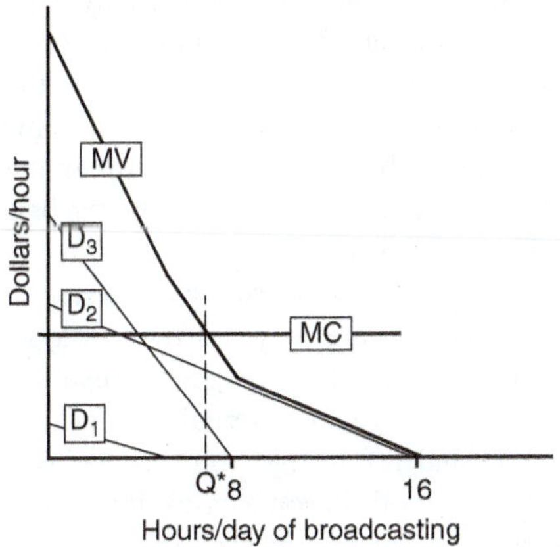

FIGURE 1 *Calculating the efficient quantity of a public good.* MV shows the total marginal value to the three customers—the vertical sum of their demand curves. The efficient quantity Q* is where MV=MC.

Public Production of Public Goods. One obvious solution to the public-good problem is to have the government produce the good and pay for it out of taxes. This may or may not be an improvement on imperfect private production. The problem is that the mechanism by which we try to make the government act in our interest—voting—itself involves the private production of a public good. As I pointed out earlier in this chapter, when you spend time and energy deciding which candidate best serves the general interest and then voting accordingly, most of the benefit of your expenditure goes to other people. You are producing a public good: a vote for the better candidate. That is a very hard public good to produce privately, since the public is a very large one: the whole population of the country. Hence it is underproduced—very much underproduced. The underproduction of that public good means that people do not find it in their interest to spend much effort deciding who is the best candidate—which in turn means that democracy does not work very well, so we cannot rely on the government to act in our interest.

If we cannot rely on the government to act in our interest, we cannot rely on it to produce the efficient quantity of public goods. Just as with a government agency regulating a natural monopoly, the administrators controlling the public production of a public good may find that their own private interest, or the political interest of the administration that appointed them, does not lead them to maximize economic welfare.

Even if the government wishes to produce the efficient amount of a public good, it faces problems similar to the problems of regulators trying to satisfy the second efficiency condition. In order to decide how much to produce, the government must know how much potential consumers value the good. In an ordinary market, the producer measures the demand curve by offering his product at some price and seeing how many he sells. The producer of a public good cannot do that, since he cannot control who gets the good, so the government must find some indirect way of estimating demand. Individuals who want the public good have an incentive, if asked, to overstate how much they want it—which means that a public opinion poll may produce a very poor estimate of demand.

In dealing with the public-good problem, just as in dealing with the closely related problem of natural monopoly, we are faced with a choice among different imperfect ways of solving the problem, some private and some governmental. None of the alternatives can be expected to generate an efficient result. As I pointed out earlier, the fact that something is inefficient means that it could be improved by a bureaucrat-god. That does not necessarily mean that it can be improved by us, since we do not have any bureaucrat-gods available.

As you may have realized by now, public-good problems of one sort or another are very common—indeed many common problems, both public and private, can be viewed as public-good problems. One example is the problem of getting anything accomplished in a meeting. Most of us like attention: When we are in a meeting and happen to have the floor, we take the opportunity not only to say what we have to say about the issue on hand but also to show how clever, witty, and wise we are. This imposes a cost on other people (unless we really are witty and wise); if there are sixty people in the room, every minute I speak costs a person-hour of listener time. Brevity, in this case, is a public good—and underproduced.

At the beginning of this section, I mentioned that different economists use slightly different definitions of a public good. The definition I have used emphasizes *non-excludability:* the inability of the producer to control which consumers get the good. The other characteristic usually associated with a public good is that one person's use does not reduce the amount available for someone else. A different way of stating this is to say that the marginal cost of producing the good is zero on the margin of how many people get it, although there may still be a cost to producing more on the margin of how much of it they get. Something that is a public good in only this sense (it has zero marginal cost, but the producer can control who gets it) is simply a natural monopoly with MC = 0. Since the problems associated with natural monopoly have already been discussed, I prefer to concentrate on the inability of the producer to control who consumes the good, which seems to me to be the essential characteristic of public goods responsible for the special problems associated with them.

Externalities

The long-winded speaker is underproducing the public good of brevity. Another, and equivalent, way of describing the situation is to say that he is overproducing his speech. The problem can be described either as underproduction due to the public-good problem or as overproduction due to the existence of an externality.

An *externality* is a net cost or benefit that my action imposes on you. Familiar examples—in addition to the cost of listening to me talk too long in a meeting—are pollution (a negative externality—a cost) and scientific progress as a result of theoretical research (a positive externality—a benefit). Externalities are all around us: When I paint my house or mow my lawn, I confer positive externalities on my neighbors; when you smoke in a restaurant or play loud music in the dorm at 1:00 a.m., you confer negative externalities on yours.

The problem with externalities is that since you, rationally enough, do not take them into account in deciding whether or not to smoke or play the music, you may do so even when the total cost (including the cost to your neighbors) is greater than the total benefit. Similarly, I may fail to mow my lawn this week because the benefit to me is less than the cost, even though the total benefit (including the benefit to my neighbors) is more.

As you can see by these examples, "externalities" and "public goods" are really different ways of describing the same problems. A positive externality is a public good; a negative externality is a "negative" public good and refraining from producing it is a positive public good. In some cases, it may be easier to look at the problem one way, in some cases the other—but it is the same problem.

Figure 2 is a graphical analysis of the inefficiency due to an externality. D is the demand curve for steel. S is the industry supply curve for the competitive industry that produces steel. The industry produces a quantity Q_s at a price P_s.

In addition to the costs that the industry pays for its inputs, there is another cost to producing steel: pollution. For every ton of steel it produces, the industry also produces a negative externality of $10. So the true marginal cost of a ton of steel is $10 above the marginal private cost, the cost to the industry, which is what determines the industry's supply curve. S' is what the supply curve would be if the industry included in its calculations the cost of the pollution it produced. The efficient level of output is where marginal cost equals marginal value—where S' intersects D at a quantity of Q_s'. From the standpoint of efficiency, the situation is exactly as if the supply curve were S' but the industry, for some reason, produced Q_s. The resulting inefficiency is the colored area A on the figure. The society as a whole—producers, consumers, and victims of pollution—is that much worse off than if the firms produced the efficient quantity Q_s'.

So far we have assumed that the only way of reducing pollution is to reduce the amount of steel produced. There may be other alternatives. By filtering its smokestacks or using low sulfur coal, the firm may be able to eliminate a dollar's worth of pollution at a cost of less than a dollar.

Figure 3 shows that possibility. For simplicity, I assume that the cost for a given reduction of pollution per ton is proportional to the amount of steel the firm is producing. TC is the total cost function for producing pollution control. It shows how many dollars must be spent on pollution control per ton of steel produced in order to reduce pollution per ton to any particular level. MC is the corresponding marginal cost function, showing the cost of the additional pollution control required to eliminate an additional dollar's worth of pollution.

As we already know, the efficient quantity of output occurs where marginal cost equals marginal value. The value of eliminating $5 worth of pollution is $5; marginal value is $1 per dollar. The steel firm should keep increasing its expenditure on pollution

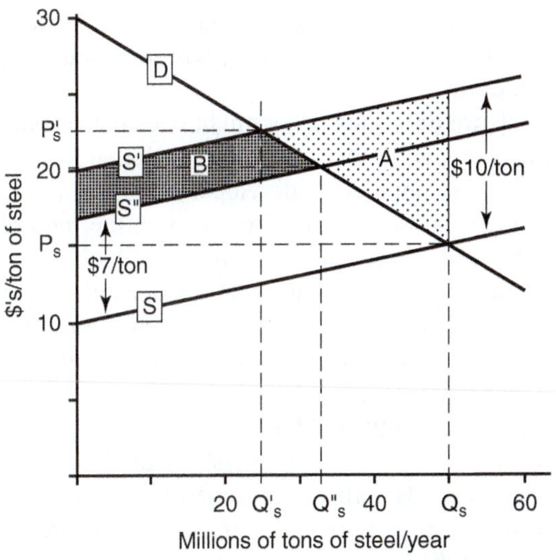

FIGURE 2 *Supply and demand for steel.* (Q_s, P_s) is the uncontrolled equilibrium. S' is what the supply curve would be if the steel firms included in their cost calculations the cost ($10/ton) that their pollution imposes on others. S" is what it would be if the firms included pollution cost, but reduced it by purchasing the efficient level of pollution control, as shown on Figure 3.

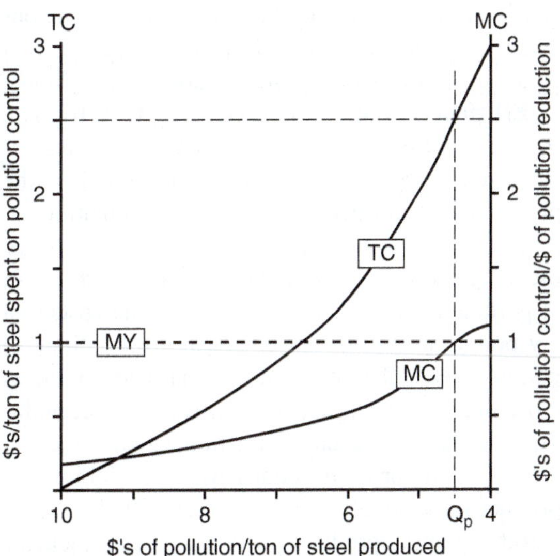

FIGURE 3 *Cost curves for controlling pollution.* TC shows total cost/ton of steel for reducing pollution as a function of the amount of pollution produced. MC is the corresponding marginal cost, MV the marginal value of pollution control.

control until the last dollar buys exactly a dollar's worth of pollution control. The efficient amount of pollution per ton is at Q_p, where MC crosses MV.

If steel firms install the efficient level of pollution control, they will spend $2.50/ton on pollution control and produce $4.50/ton worth of pollution. The cost of producing steel, including the cost to the producers of controlling pollution and the cost to everyone else of the pollution they do not control, is $7/ton higher than the cost to the firms of producing steel with no pollution control. The corresponding supply curve is S" on Figure 2. The efficient quantity of steel is Q_s".

What is the efficiency loss from producing Q_s without pollution control instead of Q_s" with pollution control? Producing Q_s without pollution control instead of Q_s' without pollution control costs area A. Producing Q_s' without pollution control instead of Q_s" with pollution control raises the supply curve from S" to S' and moves quantity from Q_s" to Q_s', so it costs the shaded area B, the resulting change in total surplus. Going from S' and Q_s to S' and Q_s' saves area A; going from there to S" and Q_s" saves an additional area B; so the net savings in moving from the initial inefficient outcome to the final efficient one is A+B. That is the inefficiency of the uncontrolled outcome, compared to the outcome that would be chosen by a bureaucrat-god.

Efficient Pollution and How to Get It: The Public Solution. The textbook solution to externalities is to impose the cost on, or give the benefit to, the producer. If I am benefiting others by scientific research, subsidize me; if I am polluting the air, charge me an *effluent fee* of so many dollars per cubic foot of pollution emitted, corresponding to the costs that my pollution imposes on others. I will continue to pollute only if the net value of what I am doing is more than the damage done—in which case, pollution is efficient. If each steel firm must pay an effluent fee of $1 for each dollar's worth of pollution it produces, the supply curve for steel will shift to S" and the quantity produced will be Q_s". The industry will produce an efficient amount of steel—and an efficient amount of pollution.

"Pollution" is a loaded word. To be in favor of pollution sounds like being in favor of evil; the phrase "an efficient level of pollution," lifted from a book like this one, would be fine ammunition for a speech on the inhumanity of economics—and economists.

If you find the idea that some amount of pollution is desirable a shocking one, consider that carbon dioxide is commonly regarded as a pollutant, and the only way you can stop producing it is to stop breathing. This is an extreme case, but it makes an important point—that the real issue is whether, in any particular case, the costs of pollution are greater than the costs of not polluting.

While there is, in this sense, an efficient level of pollution, it is not clear how to get that level. The problem with using effluent fees to control externalities is the same as the problem with government provision of public goods; it depends on the government finding it in its interest to act in the interest of the public and knowing how to do so. Just as in previous cases, "knowing how" includes somehow estimating the value of something to people by some method other than offering it at a price and seeing whether they take it. The result of the governmental solution may be better or worse than the alternatives of either accepting the overproduction of negative externalities and the underproduction of positive ones, or dealing with the problem in some imperfect private way.

Private Solutions. How might one control externalities privately? One (real-world) solution is a proprietary community. A developer builds a housing development and sells the houses with the requirement that the buyer must join the neighborhood association. The neighborhood association either takes care of lawns, painting, and other things that affect the general appearance of the community or requires the owners to do so. A friend of mine who lived in such a community could not change the color of his front door without his neighbors' permission.

This sounds rather like government regulation masquerading as a private contract, but there are two important differences. It is in the private interest of the developer to set up the best possible rules, in order to maximize the price for which he can sell the houses. And nobody is forced to purchase a house and membership from that developer; if the package is not at least as attractive as any alternative, the customer can and will go elsewhere.

There is another private solution that applies to the case where "You" and "I" are not two people but two firms—*merger.* If a factory and a resort are both on the same lake and the factory's pollution is ruining the resort's business, one solution is for the two firms to join. After the resort buys out the factory, or vice versa, the combined firm will be trying to maximize the combined income. If controlling the factory's effluent increases the resort's income by more than it costs the factory, it will pay the merged firm to control the effluent. The externality is no longer external.

One way of looking at firms is precisely as ways of controlling such problems. One could imagine an economy of tiny firms, perhaps with only one person in each, coordinating their activities through the market. One reason we do not do things that way is that, when many firms are jointly producing a single product, decisions by each one affect all the others. If I am doing a crucial part of the job and make a mistake that delays it for six months, I am imposing large costs on the other firms—which I may not be able to compensate them for. By combining all of us into one firm, that sort of externality is internalized.

The disadvantage of doing it that way is that we introduce a new kind of externality. Now that I am an employee instead of an independent business, the cost of my sleeping on the job is borne by everyone else. So a firm must monitor its employees in ways in which it does not have to monitor other firms. The efficient size of firm is then determined by the balance between problems associated with coordinating a lot of small firms and problems associated with running one large firm.

Another solution to externality problems is the definition and enforcement of property rights in whatever is affected by the externality. It is in one sense a governmental solution, since property rights are defined by courts and legislatures, and in another sense a private solution, since once property rights are defined it is the market and not the government that decides what happens. An example is the case of British trout streams. Trout streams in Britain are private property. Each stream is owned by someone—frequently the local fishing club. An industrial polluter dumping effluent into such a stream is guilty of trespass, just as if he dumped it on someone's lawn. If he believes the stream is more valuable as a place to dump his effluent than as a trout stream, it is up to him to buy it. If he believes (and the fishing club does not) that his effluent will not hurt the trout, he can buy the stream and then—if he is right—rent the fishing rights back to the previous owners.

As this example suggests, what is or is not an externality depends in part on how property rights are defined. When I produce an automobile, I am producing something of value to you. It is not an externality because I can control whether you get it and will refuse to give it to you unless you pay me for it. Some externality problems arise because property rights are not defined when they should be: If land were not property, my fertilizing it or planting a crop would confer positive externalities on whoever later came by and harvested my crop. Under those circumstances, crops would not be planted. Other problems arise because there is no way of defining property rights that does not lead to externalities in one direction or another. If I have to get your permission to play my stereo when you want to sleep, I can no longer impose an externality on you—but your decision to go to sleep when I want to play my stereo imposes an externality on me! If only two people are involved, they may be able to work out an efficient arrangement by mutual negotiation—but air pollution in Los Angeles affects several million people. Just as in the case of producing a public good, the problems of negotiating a unanimous contract become larger the larger the number of people involved.

One way of looking at this is to say that all public-good/externality problems are really transaction-cost problems. If bargaining were costless, then the problems leading to inefficiency could always be solved. As long as there was some change that would produce net benefits, someone could put together a deal that would divide up the gain in such a way as to benefit all concerned. This argument has a name—it is called the *Coase Theorem* (after economist Ronald Coase). Looked at in this way, the interesting question is always "What are the transaction costs that prevent the efficient outcome from being reached?"

Joint Causation, or Why Not Evacuate Los Angeles?

Half of Coase's contribution to understanding externalities was the observation that the problem would vanish if bargaining between the affected parties were costless; the problem could thus be seen as the result not of externalities but of transaction costs. The other half was the observation that the traditional analysis of externalities contained a fundamental error.

So far we have followed the pre-Coasian analysis in treating an externality as a cost imposed by one person on another. That is not quite right. As Coase pointed out, the typical externality is a cost jointly produced by the actions of both parties. There would be no pollution problem in Los Angeles if there were no pollution, but there would also be no problem, even if there were lots of pollution, if nobody tried to live and breathe in Los Angeles.

If evacuating Los Angeles does not strike you as a very satisfactory solution to the problem of smog, consider some more plausible examples. The military owns bomb ranges: pieces of land used to test bombs, artillery shells, and the like. If you happen to be camping in one, the dropping of a three hundred pound bomb next to your tent imposes serious externalities. It seems more natural to solve the problem by removing the campers than by removing the bombs.

Another example is airplane noise, which can be a considerable problem for people who live near large airports. One approach to the problem is to modify planes to make them quieter, close the airport when people are asleep, and instruct pilots to begin their descent as near the airport as possible. An alternative is to soundproof the houses near the airport. Another alternative is not to have anyone living near the airport: keep the land empty, use it for a water reservoir, or fill it with noisy factories where no one will notice the minor disturbance produced by a 747 two hundred feet over the roof.

It is not immediately obvious which of these alternatives provides the most efficient way of dealing with airport noise. If we try to solve the problem by the equivalent of an effluent fee (more generally described as a *Pigouvian tax,* after A.C. Pigou, the inventor of the traditional analysis of externalities), we may never find out. Charging the airlines for the cost of the noise they produce give them an incentive to reduce noise, but that may be the wrong solution—it might be less costly to soundproof the houses or pay their occupants to move out.

The problem is that the cost is jointly produced by the actions of both parties. If we do nothing, the cost is entirely borne by one party (the homeowners in our example) so the other has no incentive to reduce it—even if he can do so at the lower cost. If we impose a Pigouvian tax on the "polluter," the "victim" may find that his best tactic is to do nothing—even if he is the one who can solve the problem at the lower cost. If, as a third alternative, we let the victim sue the polluter, the victim has no incentive at all to avoid (or reduce) the cost—whatever he loses he gets back in damage payments. Any of the alternatives might or might not give the efficient outcome, depending on whether it happens to impose the externality on the party who can avoid it at the lowest cost. If the efficient solution requires actions by both parties—soundproofing plus some noise reduction, for example—none of the alternatives may be able to produce it.

What lessons can we learn from this depressing tangle? The first is that the traditional analysis of externalities, and the associated solution of Pigouvian taxes, applies only to the special case where we already know which party is the least cost avoider of the problem—that emission controls for automobiles in Southern California cost less than evacuating that end of the state. The second is that in the more general situation, where we do not know who can solve the problem at lowest cost, the best solution may be to fall back on Coase's other idea: negotiations between the parties. If the airlines are liable for damage produced by noise pollution, they may choose to pay people living near the airport to soundproof their houses. They may even choose to buy the houses, tear them down, and rent out the land to people who want to build noisy factories. If the airlines are not liable for damages, it may be in the interest of the local homeowners to offer to pay the cost of noise reduction if that is cheaper than soundproofing. So the best solution to such problems may be for the legal system to clearly define who has the right to do what and then permit the affected individuals to bargain among themselves.

In defining the initial rights—in deciding, for instance, whether the airlines have the right to make noise or must buy that right from the homeowners—one should consider the transaction costs of getting from each possible definition to each possible solution. If there are 10,000 homeowners living near the airport, raising money to pay the airlines to keep down their noise will be a public good for a public of 10,000; so it will almost certainly not be produced, even if it is worth producing. If the airlines have the right to make noise and not pay damages, they will continue producing noise whether or not it is efficient—homeowners will put up with the sound, soundproof, or sell out. If the airline is permitted to make the noise but must pay damages to affected homeowners, the airline can negotiate separately with each homeowner, buying or soundproofing some houses and paying damages on the rest if that is cheaper than modifying the planes—which should ultimately lead to the efficient solution.

Suppose, as another alternative, that each homeowner has an absolute right to be free from noise. In that case it does the airline no good to soundproof houses or buy them unless all 10,000 are included. The result is a *holdout problem.* Any one homeowner can try to get the airline to pay him the entire savings from soundproofing the houses instead of the planes, by threatening to withhold his consent. With 10,000 homeowners, every one of whom must agree, the deal is unlikely to go through—even if it is the lowest cost solution to the problem.

In this particular case, the best solution may be a legal rule permitting homeowners to collect damages but not to forbid the noise. That allows whichever of the three solutions turns out to be most efficient to occur with either no transaction (the airline reduces its noise) or a relatively simple and inexpensive one (the airline deals separately with the homeowners who are willing, and pays damages to the holdouts). This solution depends, however, on the damage done by the noise being something a court can measure. One can imagine many cases where that would not be the case, and where a different rule might be more likely to lead to an efficient outcome.

Voluntary Externalities: Sharecropping

Externalities can be eliminated by a contractual arrangement, as when two firms merge or when I agree, in exchange for a payment, not to do something that injures you. Externalities can also be created by contract. One example that I will discuss a little later is the case of insurance. By purchasing fire insurance, I create an externality: If I am careless with matches, part of the cost will be borne by the insurance company instead of by me. A second example is the case of *sharecropping.*

Sharecropping means that a farmer pays, instead of rent, a fixed percentage of his crop to the owner of the land he farms. It seems an odd and inefficient arrangement. If I must pay half of my crop to my landlord, it only pays me to make investments of labor or capital if the payoff is at least twice the cost. I have, by contract, created an externality of 50 percent.

This raises an obvious puzzle. Sharecropping is a common arrangement, appearing in many different societies at different times in history. If it is inefficient, why does it exist?

One way of answering the question is to consider the alternatives. There are two obvious ones. The landlord could hire the farmer to work his land, paying him a fixed wage, or the farmer could pay a fixed rent to the landlord and keep all of the crop.

Converting the sharecropper into an employee is hardly a solution; instead of collecting half the return from additional inputs of labor he collects none of it. Switching from sharecropping to renting may be a solution, but it has some problems. For one thing, farm output may vary unpredictably from year to year. If the farmer has agreed to pay a fixed rent, he does very well in good years but may starve to death in bad ones—the rent may be more than the full value of his crop.

Seen from this standpoint, sharecropping is, like insurance, a device for spreading risk. The landlord and the farmer divide the risk, instead of the farmer taking all of it. If the random factors affect different pieces of land differently, a landlord who owns several pieces of land can expect random effects to average out, just as they do for an insurance company. When there is lots of rain he gets very little from tenants farming low-lying areas, which flood, but lots from tenants farming hilltops that are usually too dry to grow much. Just as with insurance, the two parties pay a price in inefficiency due to externalities in order to get a benefit in risk spreading.

One way of reducing that price is for the landlord to monitor the farmer—just as he would do if the farmer were an employee. If he concludes that the farmer is not working hard enough there is nothing the landlord can do this year, but he can find another sharecropper next year. Sharecroppers require more monitoring than tenants but less than employees, since they get at least part of the output they produce.

Another explanation for sharecropping, at least in some societies, may be that the landlord is also contributing inputs: experience, administration, perhaps capital. If so, giving him a fraction of the output reduces the farmer's incentive but increases the landlord's. In this case as in many others, there may be no efficient contract—no contract that does as well as rule by a bureaucrat-god. Just as in choosing firm size, or controlling externalities that are jointly caused, or picking a rule for product liability, choosing the optimal contract involves tradeoffs among different imperfect ways of coordinating individuals whose actions are interdependent.

Pecuniary Externalities

Suppose something I do imposes both positive and negative externalities, and by some coincidence they are exactly equal. I will, as always, treat the external costs and benefits as if they were zero—and in this case, I will be right. Since on net all of the costs and benefits caused by my action are borne by me, I will make the efficient decision as to whether or not to do it.

One would think it an unlikely coincidence for positive and negative externalities to precisely cancel; but there is an important situation, called a *pecuniary externality,* in which that is exactly what happens. Whenever I decide to produce more or less of some good, to enter or leave some profession, to change my consumption pattern, or in almost any other way to alter my market behavior, one result is to slightly shift some supply or demand curve and so to change some price; this affects all other buyers and sellers of the good whose price has changed. In a competitive market, the change in price due to one person's actions is tiny—but in calculating the size of the effect, one must multiply the small change in price by the large quantity of goods for which the price has changed—the entire market. When, for example, I decide to become the million and first physician, the effect of my decision in driving down the wages of each existing physician is tiny, but it must be multiplied by a million physicians. The product is not necessarily negligible.

It appears that there can be no economic action without important externalities. But these are precisely the sort of externality that can be ignored. When price falls by a penny, what is lost by a seller is gained by a buyer; the loss to the physicians is a gain to their patients. The result is a pecuniary externality. My decision to enter a profession, to buy or to sell goods, may have more than a negligible effect on others through its effect on the price of goods or services they buy or sell, but that effect imposes neither net costs nor net benefits, so ignoring it does not produce an inefficient outcome.

Religious Radio: An Application of Public-Good Theory

Whenever I spend much time listening to a variety of stations on the radio, I am struck by how many of them are religious. One could take this as evidence that America is a very religious country—except that the popularity of religion on the airwaves does not seem to be matched elsewhere. If I go to a newsstand or a bookstore, I see relatively few religious newspapers, magazines, or books—far fewer, as a percentage of the total, than radio programs.

There is a simple explanation for this discrepancy. Publishers can control who gets their publications; broadcasters cannot control who listens to their broadcasts. Broadcasters, unlike publishers, are producing a public good and depend on some solution to the problem of producing a public good privately in order to stay in business.

Commercials are one solution to that problem; religion is another. The people who listen to religious broadcasters presumably believe in the religion. For most of them, that means that they believe in the existence of a god who rewards virtue and punishes vice. If, as many radio preachers claim, donating money to their programs is a virtuous act, then the program is no longer a pure public good. The preacher may not know which listeners help pay for the show and which do not, but God knows. One of the benefits produced by the program is an increased chance of a heavenly reward; you are more likely to get that benefit if you pay for it. Thus religion provides a solution to the public-good problem.

Nothing in the analysis depends on whether the particular religion is or is not true; what matters is only that the listeners believe it is true and act accordingly. The result is that religious broadcasters have an advantage over secular broadcasters. Both produce programs that their listeners value, but the religious broadcaster is better able to get the listener to pay for them. The religious publisher has no corresponding advantage over the secular publisher. So religion is more common on the air than in print.

INFORMATION PROBLEMS

There is an ambiguity in the definition of "rational." In some contexts a rational individual is one who makes the right decision, the decision he would have made if he knew all of the relevant facts, in other contexts a rational individual is one who makes the right decision about what facts to learn and then the best possible decision in the context of what he knows. I suggested that the latter definition is appropriate in situations where an essential part of the problem is the cost of getting and using information.

It is tempting to argue that information costs are simply one of the costs of producing and consuming goods, and so can be included in our analysis just like any other costs. In some situations that argument is correct. But, as we will see in this part of the chapter, information costs are frequently associated with problems that lead to market failure.

Information as a Public Good

One cost of buying goods is the cost of acquiring information about what to buy. This may be one reason firms are as large as they are; brand names represent a sort of informational capital. There may be a better deal available from an unknown producer, but the cost of determining that it is a better deal may be greater than the savings. Not only do you know that the brand-name product has been of good quality in the past, you also believe that the producer has an incentive to maintain the quality so as not to destroy the value of his brand name.

Why do we rely on brand names instead of buying information about the quality of goods from someone who specializes in producing such information? To some extent, we do buy information: by reading *Consumer Reports, Car and Driver,* or *Handgun Tests* and by taking economics courses. Yet much of the information we use we produce for ourselves—probably a much larger fraction than of most other things we consume. Since we do not have the time to become experts on everything we buy, we end up depending on brand names and other indirect (and very imperfect) ways of evaluating quality.

Why do we produce so much information for ourselves? Why is information a particularly hard good to produce and sell on the market?

The problem is that it is hard to protect the property rights of a producer of information. If I sell you a car, you can resell it only by giving up its use yourself. If I sell you a fact, you can both use that fact and make it available to all your friends and neighbors. This makes it difficult for those who produce facts to sell them for their full value. It is the same problem that I earlier discussed in the case of computer programs—which can be thought of as a kind of information. Information is in large part a public good; because it is a public good, it is under-produced.

One solution to this problem is provided by large brand-name retailers such as Sears. Sears does not produce what it sells, but it does select it. You may buy any particular product only once every year or two, which makes it hard to judge which producer is best. But you buy something from Sears much more often, so it is easier for you to judge that Sears (or one of its competitors) "on average" gives you good value for your money. Sears is in the business of learning which brands of the products it buys represent good value for the money and selling them to you under its brand name, thus implicitly selling you the information. By not telling you who really makes the product, it prevents you from reselling the information—to a friend who would then buy the same brand at a discount store. All you can tell your friend is to buy from Sears—which is fine with Sears.

Information Asymmetry—The Market for Lemons

Consider a situation where information is not merely imperfect but asymmetrical. The market for used cars may be a good example. The best way of finding out whether a car is a lemon is to drive it for a year or two. The seller of a used car has done so; potential buyers have not. While they can, at some cost, have the car examined by a mechanic, that may or may not be sufficient.

Suppose, to simplify our analysis, that there are only two kinds of cars: good cars and lemons. There are also two kinds of people: sellers and buyers. Each seller has a car, which he is interested in selling if he can get a reasonable price. Half have good cars; half have lemons. Each buyer would like to buy a car—if he can get it for a reasonable price. Sellers know what kind of car they have; buyers do not.

Both buyers and sellers prefer good cars to lemons. Sellers value lemons at \$2,000 and good cars at \$4,000—at any price above that they are willing to sell. Buyers value lemons at \$2,500 and good cars at \$5,000—at any lower price they are willing to buy. It appears that all of the cars should sell—lemons for between \$2,000 and \$2,500, good cars between \$4,000 and \$5,000.

There is a problem. Buyers cannot, at a reasonable cost, tell whether a car is a lemon. The sellers know, but have no way of conveying the information, since it is obviously in the interest of every seller to claim that his car is a good one. So each buyer is buying a gamble—some probability of getting a good car and some probability of getting a lemon.

It looks as though the probabilities are 50-50, since half the cars are lemons. If so, and if the buyers are risk-neutral, they will offer no more than the average of the values of the two kinds of cars, which is \$3,750. At that price, owners of lemons will be glad to sell, but owners of good cars will not.

The buyers can work out the logic of the preceding paragraph for themselves. While a car offered for sale has a 50 percent chance of being good, a car that is actually sold is certain to be a lemon, since owners of good cars will refuse the best offer buyers are willing to make. Buyers take that fact into account, and reduce their offers accordingly. All of the cars are worth more to the buyers than the sellers, but only the lemons get sold. That is an inefficient outcome. In more complicated situations, with a range of qualities of cars, the result may be even worse; in some cases only the single worst car gets sold.

One obvious solution is for sellers with good cars to offer a guarantee—perhaps a guarantee to buy it back a year later for purchase price minus a year's rental if the buyer decides the car is a lemon. One problem with this solution is that the condition of the car a year hence depends on a lot of things other than its condition today, including how it is treated by its new owner.

Adverse Selection

The problem I have just been describing is known, in the context of insurance markets, as *adverse selection*. Consider health or life insurance. The customer has information about himself that the insurance company cannot easily obtain: how carefully he drives, what medical problems he has had in the past, whether he is planning to take up hang gliding, skydiving, or motorcycle racing in the near future. The more likely a potential customer is to collect on his insurance the greater its value to him—and its cost to the insurance company. If the customer knows he is a bad risk and the insurance company does not, insurance is a good deal—for the customer.

The good risk would be happy to buy insurance at a price reflecting the low probability that he will get sick or die next year, but the insurance company will not offer it to him at that price, since the insurance company does not know he is a good risk. The result is that bad risks are more likely to buy insurance than good risks. Insurance companies, knowing that, must adjust their rates accordingly—the very fact that someone buys insurance is evidence that he is a bad risk and should therefore be charged a high price. The higher price results in even fewer good risks buying insurance—resulting in an even higher price. The equilibrium result may well be that many good risks are priced out of the market, even though there is a price at which they would be willing to buy insurance and the insurance companies would gain by selling it to them. Just as with automobiles, one can even construct a situation where only the worst risks end up insured, everyone else having been driven out of the market. Again we have an inefficient outcome.

Insurance companies try to control this problem in a variety of ways, including medical checkups for new customers and provisions in insurance contracts denying payment to people who say they have no dangerous hobbies and then die when their parachutes fail to open two miles up. A less obvious solution is selling insurance to groups. If all employees of a factory are covered by the same insurance, the insurance company is getting a random assortment of good and bad risks. The good risks get a worse deal than the bad, but since they still get insured the insurance rates reflect the risk of insuring an average employee rather than an average bad risk. If insuring everyone is the efficient outcome, the group policy produces an efficient allocation of insurance, plus a redistribution of income from the good risks, who are paying more than their insurance costs to produce, to the bad risks who are paying less.

One argument in favor of universal, governmentally provided health insurance is that it is a group policy carried to its ultimate extreme—everyone is in the group. It thus eliminates the problem of adverse selection (except, perhaps, for people with health problems who decide to immigrate in order to take advantage of the program). Whether the net effect is an improvement depends on how well the government can and does deal with other problems of providing insurance.

Moral Hazard

It may have occurred to you that there is another potential inefficiency associated with insurance. Most of the things we insure against are at least partly under our own control. That is true not only of my health and the chance of my house burning down, but even of losses from "acts of God" such as floods or tornadoes. I cannot control the flood, but I can control the loss—by deciding where to live and what precautions to take.

Whether or not I am insured, I take those precautions, and only those precautions, that save me more than they cost me. Once I have bought fire insurance, part of the cost of being careless with matches and part of the benefit of installing a sprinkler system have been transferred to the insurance company; the cost to me is no longer the entire cost, so the result is no longer efficient. If a sprinkler system costs $1,000 and produces a benefit of $800 to me in reduced risk of being burned alive and another $600 to the insurance company in reduced probability of having to replace my house, it is worth buying—but not to me.

So people who are insured will take less than the efficient level of precaution. This problem is known as *moral hazard.* It is an inefficiency resulting from an externality; once I am insured someone else bears some of the cost of my actions.

Insurance companies try to control moral hazard just as they try to control adverse selection. One way is by specifying, so far as possible, the precautions that the insured will take—requiring a factory to install and maintain a sprinkler system as a condition of providing fire insurance. Another is *co-insurance*—insuring for only part of the value, in order to make sure that the customer has at least a substantial stake in preventing the risk that is insured against. If, in my previous example, the house was insured for only half its value, the sprinkler system would be worth more to me than it cost, so I would buy it. If, at the opposite extreme, the insurance company makes the mistake of insuring a building for more than it is worth, the probability of a fire may become very high indeed.

Warning

In thinking about market failure, it is often tempting to interpret the problem in terms of fairness rather than efficiency. Externalities are then seen as wrong because they are unfair, because one person is suffering and another gaining, and public goods as a problem because some consumers get what others pay for.

That is a mistake. Consider the situation of a hundred identical individuals polluting and breathing the same air. On net there is no unfairness—everyone gains by being able to pollute and loses by being polluted. Yet because each person bears only 1 percent of his pollution, each pollutes at far above the efficient level and all are, as a result, worse off.

The same is true for the other kinds of market failure. The ultimate problem with public goods is not that one person pays for what someone else gets but that nobody pays and nobody gets, even though the good is worth more than it would cost to produce. The major cost of adverse selection is not that some people buy lemons or write life insurance policies on skydivers. The major cost is that cars are not sold, even though they are worth selling, and people do not get insured, even though they are worth insuring.

PROBLEMS

1. Describe two public-good problems that you have yourself observed and in some way been involved with in the past year and discuss how they might be dealt with.
2. In ordinary markets, supply and demand are balanced by price. Given that our customs prohibit, in most social contexts, cash payments as part of a date (or a marriage), what sorts of "prices" balance those markets in the United States at present? If supply and demand on the dating/sex/marriage market are not balanced (quantity supplied is not equal to quantity demanded: more men want to go out or have sex or get married than women, or vice versa), what mechanisms ration out the insufficient supply (decide which men get women, or vice versa)? What prices balance supply and demand for similar markets in other countries or have done so at other times?
3. How would the style of dating and marriage change if a war substantially reduced the ratio of men to women? How would it change if a lot of men migrated to the United States, substantially raising the ratio of men to women?
4. "Heterosexual men are traditionally hostile to homosexual men. If they correctly considered their own interests, their attitude would be just the opposite." Discuss.
5. "The public-good problem is both an argument for government intervention in the market and an argument against government intervention in the market." Explain.
6. Students frequently argue that grades should be deemphasized or abolished. The same students start the first class of the quarter by asking me about my grading policy—and continue throughout the course to exhibit a keen interest in what will or will not be on the final exam. Is their behavior inconsistent?
7. A tape recorder can copy a recording of a concert onto a cassette just as a computer can copy a program onto a disk. Why is the problem of pirating (making copies without paying royalties) less serious in the case of tapes than in the case of programs?
8. In my experience, FM radio is less religious than AM; you may wish to check that conclusion for yourself. Can you suggest any reasons why? (I am not sure I know the answer to this one.)
9. Last year Bryan and Brian occupied separate apartments; each consumed 400 gallons per month of hot water. This year they are sharing a larger apartment. To their surprise, they find they are consuming 1,000 gallons per month. Explain.
10. One of my students cannot possibly take the midterm at the scheduled time. I am afraid that if I give it to him early, he might talk about it to other students, giving them an unfair advantage, and that if I give it to him late, other students might talk to him about it, giving him an unfair advantage. Given the problems associated with property in information, which problem do you think is more likely to arise? Discuss. Does it depend on whether the students believe that I grade on a curve?

6 Collective Action

Collective action occurs when members of a group coordinate their actions to achieve a common goal. A collective action *problem* arises when people acting independently will predictably produce a worse outcome than they would if they could find a way to coordinate their actions. We saw in the previous chapter how markets can underprovide public goods because of incentive and information problems faced by people who are given the option of voluntarily contributing to produce or preserve a good that is freely available to everyone. Public goods problems are ultimately one kind of collective action problem.

We begin this chapter with Mancur Olson's paradoxical argument that in politics small groups are able to exploit large groups. It would appear that democracy would favor larger groups, but that conclusion rests on the fallacious assumption that members of large groups will always act in a concerted way to advance their interests. On Olson's view, it is often the case that members of large groups fail to achieve their objectives because, as the numbers in a group increase, each member of the group is more likely to see his own contribution as unlikely to make a difference. Smaller groups are often able to organize effectively, Olson thinks, because members of small groups understand that they are more likely to make a difference in achieving a shared objective, and are more likely to get a bigger share of the benefits if the objective is achieved.

This is why, according to Olson, small groups with *concentrated benefits* (often, producers) can organize effectively in lobbying government for subsidies, price supports, and special provisions that reduce competition and raise prices. Consumers pay slightly more, but consumers are so numerous and the costs so dispersed that counter-organization is difficult. So these subsidies and policies persist, even though the number of consumers whose interests are hurt substantially exceeds the number of producers who benefit.

This argument was first used by Anthony Downs (1957) to explain why democracies often exhibit an anti-consumer bias. For example, if each consumer pays an extra $10 per year for milk because of government price supports, and each producer gets an additional $10,000 in benefits from price supports, it is unlikely that any individual consumer will be angry enough to protest the special treatment of dairy farmers; meanwhile, dairy farmers will have a substantial interest in lobbying to maintain price supports. Similar arguments may apply to trade unions and other groups that lobby to restrict competition and impose licensing schemes that benefit their members but drive prices up and quality down for consumers of their products.

One of the apparent implications of Olson's reasoning in *The Logic of Collective Action* is that for public goods with widely diffuse benefits, we can expect that potential consumers of these goods will often contribute nothing at all toward their production. This so-called "zero contribution thesis" is not explicitly endorsed by Olson. In fact, he points out that public goods are occasionally produced when large, well-organized groups give contributors various fringe benefits, or *selective incentives,* to induce contribution. Yet it does seem to follow from some of what he says.

Many scholars have experimentally tested the zero contribution thesis, and have found it inadequate. Consider the following game, which can be played in a classroom full of students: allocate a handful of tokens to each member of a group, and ask whether they'd like to invest some or all of their tokens in a group exchange. Any amount "invested" is immediately doubled and redistributed evenly to the entire group, regardless of who invests it, and how much they invest. Investment choices are made anonymously, so that nobody knows how much others have invested in the group exchange.

One might suspect that people would decide not to invest themselves, or not to invest much, hoping to reap the benefits of the doubling of others' investment without the costs, at least when they are in large groups where anonymity is maintained and their individual contribution (even when doubled) will yield less than was invested. Yet most studies find that subjects generally invest about half of their initial endowment, at least in single play games. Although contributions tend to decline when the game is repeated, they rarely fall to zero, and one of the reasons people give for investing about half of their initial endowment is that they think this is *fair.* (Exactly why investing half is thought to be fair is unclear). This suggests that public goods might sometimes be produced, despite incentives not to contribute, if people believe fairness requires them to contribute. Of course a concern for fairness is not sufficient to produce many public goods, especially at an optimal level, but it may help explain why people often voluntarily edit Wikipedia articles, for example, or donate to environmental charities.

Perhaps more interestingly, when asked why they don't contribute their entire endowment in public goods games, many people say they would contribute more if they had some assurance that others would too.

Some economists hold that many subjects in experimental public goods games do not know what they are doing, and learn over time to play the individually optimal strategy, which explains why contributions tend to fall in repeated games.

Others, like Elinor Ostrom, argue that ignorance of the structure of public goods problems does not explain positive contributions, or decreasing contributions in repeated rounds. In fact, she thinks, people who understand the game better tend to make *larger* rather than smaller contributions. Further, Ostrom notes that contributions increase when there is face-to-face communication which, she suggests, increases trust. Finally, she thinks that people will often defect in subsequent rounds not out of selfishness, but in order to punish free riders in previous rounds. Herbert Gintis and Samuel Bowles call this "altruistic punishment," whereby people withhold contributions out of a sense of moral indignation toward others who they believe have unfairly withheld contributions in previous rounds.

Gintis and Bowles give a similar explanation for behavior in what are called ultimatum games. In such games an experimenter offers to give a Proposer and Responder $10 to split, provided the Proposer offers a split that the Responder accepts. One might think that as long as a Proposer offers the Responder at least a penny, the Responder will accept the offer, since if Responder vetoes the split Responder gets nothing.

There is abundant evidence that Responders treat very low offers as unfair, and consequently reject them. They thereby pay a personal price to see "justice" meted out to the miserly Proposer. Although different cultures and conditions determine what is considered an unacceptably low or unfair offer, the rejection of offers that are considered unfair seems to be universal.

Gintis and Bowles try to account for the nature and evolution of the pro-social emotions that they think explain behavior in Public Goods and Ultimatum games. Strikingly, individuals with such emotions are worse off in isolation, but (small) groups of individuals endowed with pro-social emotions are actually better off. This observation is consistent with a hypothesis first entertained by Charles Darwin in *The Descent of Man.* Darwin argued that "although a high standard of morality gives but a slight or no advantage to each individual man and his children over the other men of the same tribe . . . an increase in the number of well-endowed men and an advancement in the standard of morality will certainly give an immense advantage to one tribe over another." More specifically, "A tribe including many members who, from possessing in a high degree the spirit of patriotism, fidelity, obedience, courage, and sympathy, were always ready to aid one another, and to sacrifice themselves for the common good, would be victorious over most other tribes; and this would be natural selection." If Darwin is right, and if genes and culture have co-evolved in the ways he suggests, as Gintis and Bowles maintain, this give us reason to think some public goods can be produced through voluntary cooperation rather than political coercion. For whatever reason, many people are more willing to cooperate, and more willing to punish noncooperators, than simple models of *homo economicus* predict.

Jean Hampton carefully distinguishes collective action problems from prisoner's dilemmas. Although many collective action problems look like *n*-person prisoner's dilemmas, Hampton argues that this superficial similarity can be deceiving: often collective action (and public goods) problems are better represented by coordination games, assurance games, or nested games. This may help explain why in some contexts people make significant contributions in public goods games, and why varying the size of the group and initial conditions (including their ability to communicate before playing) can elicit different contribution rates.

FURTHER READING

Explaining Collective Action

Binmore, Ken. 2006. "Why Do People Cooperate?" *Politics, Philosophy and Economics* 5 (1): 81–96.

Bowles, Samuel and Herbert Gintis. 2011. *A Cooperative Species: Human Reciprocity and its Evolution.* Princeton University Press.

Frank, Robert, Thomas Gilovich, and Dennis Regan. 1993. "Does Studying Economics Inhibit Cooperation?" *The Journal of Economic Perspectives* 7 (2): 159–171.

Gintis, Herbert, Samuel Bowles, Robert Boyd, and Ernst Fehr. 2003. "Explaining Altruistic Behavior in Humans." *Evolution and Human Behavior* 24: 153–72.

Marwell, Gerald and Ruth Ames. 1981. "Economists Free Ride, Does Anyone Else?" *Journal of Public Economics* 15: 295–310.

Olson, Mancur. 1971. *The Logic of Collective Action: Public Goods and the Theory of Groups.* Harvard University Press.

Ostrom, Elinor and James Walker. 2004. *Trust and Reciprocity: Interdisciplinary Lessons from Experimental Research.* Russell Sage Foundation.

Sandler, Todd. 2004. *Global Collective Action.* Cambridge University Press.

Sources of Collective Action

Anomaly, Jonny and Geoffrey Brennan. 2014. "Social Norms, the Invisible Hand, and the Law." *University of Queensland Law Journal*, 33(2): 263–283.

Bicchieri, Cristina. 2015. *Norms in the Wild: How to Diagnose, Measure, and Change Social Norms*. Cambridge University Press.

Ellickson, Robert. 2001. "The Market for Social Norms." *American Law and Economics Review*, 3: 1–49.

Ferguson, William. 2013. *Collective Action and Exchange: A Game Theoretic Approach to Contemporary Political Economy*. Stanford Economics and Finance.

McAdams, Richard. 1997. "The Origin, Development, and Regulation of Norms." *Michigan Law Review*, 96(2): 338–433.

Posner, Eric. 2002. *Law and Social Norms*. Harvard University Press.

MANCUR OLSON

The Logic of Collective Action

1965

It is often taken for granted, at least where economic objectives are involved, that groups of individuals with common interests usually attempt to further those common interests. Groups of individuals with common interests are expected to act on behalf of their common interests much as single individuals are often expected to act on behalf of their personal interests. This opinion about group behavior is frequently found not only in popular discussions but also in scholarly writings. Many economists of diverse methodological and ideological traditions have implicitly or explicitly accepted it. This view has, for example, been important in many theories of labor unions, in Marxian theories of class action, in concepts of "countervailing power," and in various discussions of economic institutions. It has, in addition, occupied a prominent place in political science, at least in the United States, where the study of pressure groups has been dominated by a celebrated "group theory" based on the idea that groups will act when necessary to further their common or group goals. Finally, it has played a significant role in many well-known sociological studies.

The view that groups act to serve their interests presumably is based upon the assumption that the individuals in groups act out of self-interest. If the individuals in a group altruistically disregarded their personal welfare, it would not be very likely that collectively they would seek some selfish common or group objective. Such altruism, is, however, considered exceptional, and self-interested behavior is usually thought to be the rule, at least when economic issues are at stake; no one is surprised when individual businessmen seek higher profits, when individual workers seek higher wages, or when individual consumers seek lower prices. The idea that groups tend

From Mancur Olson, *The Logic of Collective Action: Public Goods and the Theory of Groups*. Cambridge, MA: Harvard University Press. By permission of Harvard University Press, 1971.

to act in support of their group interests is supposed to follow logically from this widely accepted premise of rational, self-interested behavior. In other words, if the members of some group have a common interest or objective, and if they would all be better off if that objective were achieved, it has been thought to follow logically that the individuals in that group would, if they were rational and self-interested, act to achieve that objective.

But it is *not* in fact true that the idea that groups will act in their self-interest follows logically from the premise of rational and self-interested behavior. It does *not* follow, because all of the individuals in a group would gain if they achieved their group objective, that they would act to achieve that objective, even if they were all rational and self-interested. Indeed, unless the number of individuals in a group is quite small, or unless there is coercion or some other special device to make individuals act in their common interest, *rational, self-interested individuals will not act to achieve their common or group interests.* In other words, even if all of the individuals in a large group are rational and self-interested, and would gain if, as a group, they acted to achieve their common interest or objective, they will still not voluntarily act to achieve that common or group interest. The notion that groups of individuals will act to achieve their common or group interests, far from being a logical implication of the assumption that the individuals in a group will rationally further their individual interests, is in fact inconsistent with that assumption. This inconsistency will be explained in the following chapter.

If the members of a large group rationally seek to maximize their personal welfare, they will *not* act to advance their common or group objectives unless there is coercion to force them to do so, or unless some separate incentive, distinct from the achievement of the common or group interest, is offered to the members of the group individually on the condition that they help bear the costs or burdens involved in the achievement of the group objectives. Nor will such large groups form organizations to further their common goals in the absence of the coercion or the separate incentives just mentioned. These points hold true even when there is unanimous agreement in a group about the common good and the methods of achieving it.

The widespread view, common throughout the social sciences, that groups tend to further their interests, is accordingly unjustified, at least when it is based, as it usually is, on the (sometimes implicit) assumption that groups act in their self-interest because individuals do. There is paradoxically the logical possibility that groups composed of either altruistic individuals or irrational individuals may sometimes act in their common or group interests. But, as later, empirical parts of this study will attempt to show, this logical possibility is usually of no practical importance. Thus the customary view that groups of individuals with common interests tend to further those common interests appears to have little if any merit.

None of the statements made above fully applies to small groups, for the situation in small groups is much more complicated. In small groups there may very well be some voluntary action in support of the common purposes of the individuals in the group, but in most cases this action will cease before it reaches the optimal level for the members of the group as a whole. In the sharing of the costs of efforts to achieve a common goal in small groups, there is however a surprising tendency for the "exploitation" of the *great* by the *small.*

The combination of individual interests and common interests in an organization suggests an analogy with a competitive market. The firms in a perfectly competitive industry, for example, have a common interest in a higher price for the industry's product. Since a uniform price must prevail in such a market, a firm cannot expect a higher price for itself unless all of the other firms in the industry also have this higher price. But a firm in a competitive market also has an interest in selling as much as it can, until the cost of producing another unit exceeds the price of that unit. In this there is no common interest; each firm's interest is directly opposed to that of every other firm, for the more other firms sell, the lower the price and income for any given firm. In short, while all firms have a common interest in a higher price, they have antagonistic interests where output is concerned. This can be illustrated with a simple supply-and-demand model. For the sake of a simple argument, assume that a perfectly competitive industry is momentarily in a disequilibrium position, with price exceeding marginal cost for all firms at their present output. Suppose, too, that all of the adjustments will be made by the firms already in the industry rather than by new entrants, and that the industry is on an inelastic portion of its demand curve. Since price exceeds marginal cost for all firms, output will increase. But as all firms increase production, the price falls; indeed, since the industry demand curve is by assumption inelastic, the total revenue of the industry will decline. Apparently each firm finds that with price exceeding marginal cost, it pays to increase its output, but the result is that each firm gets a smaller profit. Some economists in an earlier day may have questioned this result, but the fact that profit-maximizing firms in a perfectly competitive industry can act contrary to their interests as a group is now widely understood and accepted. A group of profit-maximizing firms can act to reduce their aggregate profits because in perfect competition each firm is, by definition, so small that it can ignore the effect of its output on price. Each firm finds it to its advantage to increase output to the point where marginal cost equals price and to ignore the effects of its extra output on the position of the industry. It is true that the net result is that all firms are worse off, but this does not mean that every firm has not maximized its profits. If a firm, foreseeing the fall in price resulting from the increase in industry output, were to restrict its own output, it would lose more than ever, for its price would fall quite as much in any case and it would have a smaller output as well. A firm in a perfectly competitive market gets only a small part of the benefit (or a small share of the industry's extra revenue) resulting from a reduction in that firm's output.

For these reasons it is now generally understood that if the firms in an industry are maximizing profits, the profits for the industry as a whole will be less than they might otherwise be. And almost everyone would agree that this theoretical conclusion fits the facts for markets characterized by pure competition. The important point is that this is true because, though all the firms have a common interest in a higher price for the industry's product, it is in the interest of each firm that the other firms pay the cost—in terms of the necessary reduction in output—needed to obtain a higher price.

About the only thing that keeps prices from falling in accordance with the process just described in perfectly competitive markets is outside intervention. Government price supports, tariffs, cartel agreements, and the like may keep the firms in a competitive market from acting contrary to their interests. Such aid or intervention is quite common. It is then important to ask how it comes about. How does a competitive industry obtain government assistance in maintaining the price of its product?

Consider a hypothetical, competitive industry, and suppose that most of the producers in that industry desire a tariff, a price-support program, or some other government intervention to increase the price for their product. To obtain any such assistance from the government, the producers in this industry will presumably have to organize a lobbying organization; they will have to become an active pressure group. This lobbying organization may have to conduct a considerable campaign. If significant resistance is encountered, a great amount of money will be required. Public relations experts will be needed to influence the newspapers, and some advertising may be necessary. Professional organizers will probably be needed to organize "spontaneous grassroots" meetings among the distressed producers in the industry, and to get those in the industry to write letters to their congressmen. The campaign for the government assistance will take the time of some of the producers in the industry, as well as their money.

There is a striking parallel between the problem the perfectly competitive industry faces as it strives to obtain government assistance, and the problem it faces in the marketplace when the firms increase output and bring about a fall in price. *Just as it was not rational for a particular producer to restrict his output in order that there might be a higher price for the product of his industry, so it would not be rational for him to sacrifice his time and money to support a lobbying organization to obtain government assistance for the industry. In neither case would it be in the interest of the individual producer to assume any of the costs himself. A lobbying organization, or indeed a labor union or any other organization, working in the interest of a large group of firms or workers in some industry, would get no assistance from the rational, self-interested individuals in that industry.* This would be true even if everyone in the industry were absolutely convinced that the proposed program was in their interest (though in fact some might think otherwise and make the organization's task yet more difficult).

Although the lobbying organization is only one example of the logical analogy between the organization and the market, it is of some practical importance. There are many powerful and well-financed lobbies with mass support in existence now, but these lobbying organizations do not get that support because of their legislative achievements. The most powerful lobbying organizations now obtain their funds and their following for other reasons, as later parts of this study will show.

Some critics may argue that the rational person will, indeed, support a large organization, like a lobbying organization, that works in his interest, because he knows that if he does not, others will not do so either, and then the organization will fail, and he will be without the benefit that the organization could have provided. This argument shows the need for the analogy with the perfectly competitive market. For it would be quite as reasonable to argue that prices will never fall below the levels a monopoly would have charged in a perfectly competitive market, because if one firm increased its output, other firms would also, and the price would fall; but each firm could foresee this, so it would not start a chain of price-destroying increases in output. In fact, it does not work out this way in a competitive market; nor in a large organization. When the number of firms involved is large, no one will notice the effect on price if one firm increases its output, and so no one will change his plans because of it. Similarly, in a large organization, the loss of one dues payer will not noticeably increase the burden for any other one dues payer, and so a rational person would not believe that if he were to withdraw from an organization he would drive others to do so.

The foregoing argument must at the least have some relevance to economic organizations that are mainly means through which individuals attempt to obtain the same things they obtain through their activities in the market. Labor unions, for example, are organizations through which workers strive to get the same things they get with their individual efforts in the market—higher wages, better working conditions, and the like. It would be strange indeed if the workers did not confront some of the same problems in the union that they meet in the market, since their efforts in both places have some of the same purposes.

However similar the purposes may be, critics may object that attitudes in organizations are not at all like those in markets. In organizations, an emotional or ideological element is often also involved. Does this make the argument offered here practically irrelevant?

A most important type of organization—the national state—will serve to test this objection. Patriotism is probably the strongest non-economic motive for organizational allegiance in modern times. This age is sometimes called the age of nationalism. Many nations draw additional strength and unity from some powerful ideology, such as democracy or communism, as well as from a common religion, language, or cultural inheritance. The state not only has many such powerful sources of support; it also is very important economically. Almost any government is economically beneficial to its citizens, in that the law and order it provides is a prerequisite of all civilized economic activity. But despite the force of patriotism, the appeal of the national ideology, the bond of a common culture, and the indispensability of the system of law and order, no major state in modern history has been able to support itself through voluntary dues or contributions. Philanthropic contributions are not even a significant source of revenue for most countries. Taxes, *compulsory* payments by definition, are needed. Indeed, as the old saying indicates, their necessity is as certain as death itself.

If the state, with all of the emotional resources at its command, cannot finance its most basic and vital activities without resort to compulsion, it would seem that large private organizations might also have difficulty in getting the individuals in the groups whose interests they attempt to advance to make the necessary contributions voluntarily.

The reason the state cannot survive on voluntary dues or payments, but must rely on taxation, is that the most fundamental services a nation-state provides are, in one important respect, like the higher price in a competitive market: they must be available to everyone if they are available to anyone. The basic and most elementary goods or services provided by government, like defense and police protection, and the system of law and order generally, are such that they go to everyone or practically everyone in the nation. It would obviously not be feasible, if indeed it were possible, to deny the protection provided by the military services, the police, and the courts to those who did not voluntarily pay their share of the costs of government, and taxation is accordingly necessary. The common or collective benefits provided by governments are usually called "public goods" by economists, and the concept of public goods is one of the oldest and most important ideas in the study of public finance. A common, collective, or public good is here defined as any good such that, if any person X_i in a group $X_1, \ldots, X_i, \ldots, X_n$ consumes it, it cannot feasibly be withheld from the others in that group. In other words, those who do not purchase or pay for any of the public or collective good cannot be excluded or kept from sharing in the consumption of the good, as they can where noncollective goods are concerned.

Students of public finance have, however, neglected the fact that *the achievement of any common goal or the satisfaction of any common interest means that a public or collective good has been provided for that group.*[1] The very fact that a goal or purpose is *common* to a group means that no one in the group is excluded from the benefit or satisfaction brought about by its achievement. As the opening paragraphs of this chapter indicated, almost all groups and organizations have the purpose of serving the common interests of their members. As R. M. MacIver puts it, "Persons . . . have common interests in the degree to which they participate in a cause . . . which indivisibly embraces them all." It is of the essence of an organization that it provides an inseparable, generalized benefit. It follows that the provision of public or collective goods is the fundamental function of organizations generally. A state is first of all an organization that provides public goods for its members, the citizens; and other types of organizations similarly provide collective goods for their members.

And just as a state cannot support itself by voluntary contributions, or by selling its basic services on the market, neither can other large organizations support themselves without providing some sanction, or some attraction distinct from the public good itself, that will lead individuals to help bear the burdens of maintaining the organization. The individual member of the typical large organization is in a position analogous to that of the firm in a perfectly competitive market, or the taxpayer in the state: his own efforts will not have a noticeable effect on the situation of his organization, and he can enjoy any improvements brought about by others whether or not he has worked in support of his organization.

There is no suggestion here that states or other organizations provide *only* public or collective goods. Governments often provide noncollective goods like electric power, for example, and they usually sell such goods on the market much as private firms would do. Moreover, as later parts of this study will argue, large organizations that are not able to make membership compulsory *must also* provide some noncollective goods in order to give potential members an incentive to join. Still, collective goods are the characteristic organizational goods, for ordinary noncollective goods can always be provided by individual action, and only where common purposes or collective goods are concerned is organization or group action ever indispensable.

NOTE

1. There is no necessity that a public good to one group in a society is necessarily in the interest of the society as a whole. Just as a tariff could be a public good to the industry that sought it, so the removal of the tariff could be a public good to those who consumed the industry's product. This is equally true when the public-good concept is applied only to governments; for a military expenditure, or a tariff, or an immigration restriction that is a public good to one country could be a "public bad" to another country, and harmful to world society as a whole.

Jean Hampton

Free Rider Problems in the Production of Collective Goods

1987

There has been a persistent tendency to identify what is called "the free-rider problem" in the production of collective (or public) goods with the prisoner's dilemma. However, in this article I want to challenge that identification by presenting an analysis of what are in fact *a variety* of collective action problems in the production of collective goods. My strategy is not to consult any intuitions about what the free-rider problem is; rather I will be looking at the problematic game-theoretic structures of various situations associated with the production of different types of collective goods, thereby showing what sorts of difficulties a community concerned with their voluntary production would face. I call all of these dilemmas free-rider problems because in all of them certain individuals find it rational to take advantage of others' willingness to contribute to the good in a way that threatens its production. Some readers may feel that the term "free-rider problem" is so identified with the prisoner's dilemma that my extension of the term in this way "jars"; if so, I invite them to coin another word for the larger phenomenon. My aim is not to engage in linguistic analysis but to attempt at least a partial analysis of the complicated structure of collective good production.

In fact, free-rider problems of this sort are neither purely mathematical nor purely practical difficulties; they are a function of both the mathematical structure of the situation and of human psychology. If we believe that human beings act in ways that are primarily, or even exclusively, self-interested, then producing these goods becomes problematic when the game-theoretic structures underlying their production present to people exploitative opportunities that are individually rational but collectively irrational for them to take. So, once we understand these various mathematical structures, we will see when and how human self-interest can derail the production of these goods.

But it turns out that self-interest is not as much the enemy of their production as traditionally thought. I will argue that many collective action problems are (or can be transformed to become) *coordination* rather than conflict dilemmas, so that the production of collective goods in many situations need not require help in the form of sanctions from the long arm of the state. Hence my analysis should be good news to those who wish to encourage politically uncoerced cooperation.

I. THE "CLASSIC" BUT INCORRECT PD ANALYSIS OF FREE RIDING

Stating the nature of the free-rider problem in English appears easy: any public good which is indivisible but nonexcludable would seem to be one whose benefits an individual can enjoy without paying for them, but if too many people try to take this "free ride," either no amount of the good, or else only a less than socially optimal amount, will be produced.

Jean Hampton, "Free Rider Problems in the Production of Collective Goods." *Economics and Philosophy* 3 (2) (1987): 245–273. By permission of Cambridge University Press.

Nonetheless, this statement of the nature of the problem is blurry. Rawls (1971, p. 267) makes an attempt to get a better statement of it as follows:

> where the public is large and includes many individuals, there is a temptation for each person to try to avoid doing his share. This is because whatever one man does, his action will not significantly affect the amount produced. He regards the collective action of others as already given one way or the other. If the public good is produced his enjoyment of it is not decreased by his not making a contribution. If it is not produced his action would not have changed the situation anyway.[1]

Russell Hardin (1971; 1982, chapter 2, esp. pp. 25ff) has constructed the game-theoretic matrix suggested by Rawls's remarks, and it is reproduced in Figure 1. It depicts a situation in which the collective good will not exist unless at least two people work to produce it; and the more of them who produce it, the less the cost of production to each. In this matrix, the individual's preferences are compared with the preferences of the rest of the group. For our purposes, only the individual's preferences are important, hence they are underlined (1 is most preferred, 4 is least preferred). Note that they match the preferences of any participant of a prisoner's dilemma. In this situation, it is rational for the individual not to pay, no matter what the others do (assuming standard probability assessments). And since every other individual would have the same preferences relative to the rest of the collective, then it seems that it isn't rational for *any* of them to pay the cost of production. Hardin concludes that the voluntary production of collective goods can only succeed when this PD interaction is part of a series of such interactions, or when it is embedded in a wider set of interactions such that the cooperative action dominates (1982, chapters 9–12). (Note that it might also be solved if each player has the rather unusual probability judgment that the others are likely to do what she or he does.[2])

THE INDIVIDUAL	THE COLLECTIVE: Pay	THE COLLECTIVE: Not pay
Pay	2, 1	4, 3
Not Pay	1, 2	3, 3

FIGURE 1

However, a number of theorists, including Hardin himself, have questioned the strict equation of free-rider problems with prisoners' dilemmas.[3] I will now argue that they are right to do so.

II. DEFINING COLLECTIVE GOODS

Collective goods can be defined as goods that benefit a collective and that are "indivisible" or "in joint supply," that is, making them available to one person in the community makes them available to all. Free-rider problems arise in the production of these goods when benefits from them are either difficult or impossible to exclude from people who do not contribute to their production. I will contend in this paper that understanding particular free-rider problems depends upon understanding the *relationship between* the production structure of the collective good in question and the individual group member's expected costs and benefits associated with its production. My strategy for revealing these problems must therefore begin with a "technological" definition of different kinds of collective goods: that is, I will define them not by aggregating individual contributions and benefits, but by aggregating production contributions (regardless of who pays) and amounts of the good thereby generated.[4]

As Hardin (1982, chapter 4) has discussed, some collective goods only exist after a substantial amount has been contributed to their production, and then do not increase in quantity or quality if any further contributions are made. Figure 2 depicts such a good. These goods have been called "pure step goods" (or "lumpy goods") because their creation involves

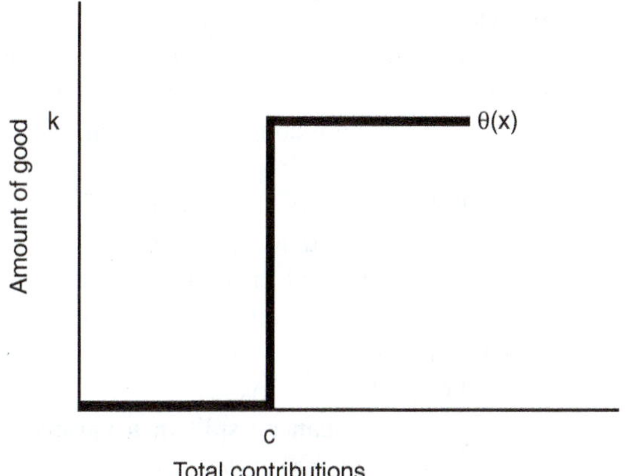

FIGURE 2

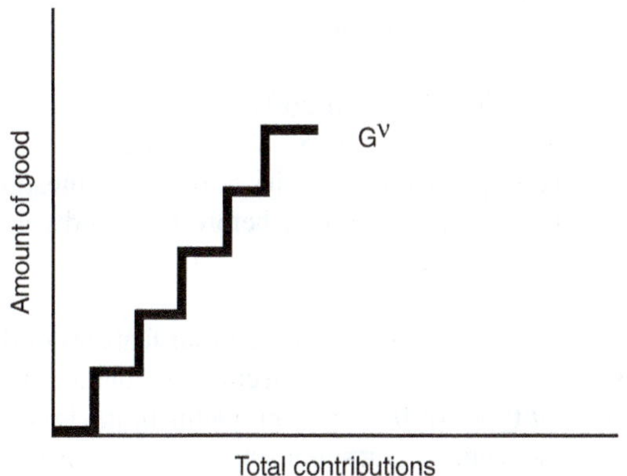

FIGURE 3

taking one big production step and no more. Examples of these goods include the election of a political candidate and objects such as bridges (half a bridge is no bridge at all). We can define this type of good using the following step function: $\theta(x) = 0$ for $x < c$; $= k$ for $x \geq c$.

Other goods come into existence in degrees of quantity or quality, and successive contributions to their production result in further increments of the good (in quantity or quality). I call such goods "incremental collective goods." They can vary from being quite "steppy," as the graph in Figure 3 represents, so that a certain fairly large contribution level must be reached in order for an increment of the good to be produced (for example, the construction of railway lines connecting small towns), to being completely continuous such that *any* contribution, no matter how small, will result in some increase in the good (e.g., clean air or clean water), until some natural boundary is reached. . . .

Finally, collective goods can have a "mixed structure." For example, bringing a collective good into existence can initially require a large production step but increasing this good in quality or quantity thereafter can require only small contributions over a certain range. Hence, although creating a minimally effective bridge over a river is a step good, this bridge's strength and effectiveness might be increased by reinforcing its structure up to a certain point, so that after a certain large step such as the one represented in Figure 2, the good subsequently has the sort of incremental or continuous structure which is represented in Figure 3, and which we could describe using the following step function: $\theta x = 0$ for $x < c$; $= f(x)$ for $x \geq c$ where $f(x)$ is a function with $f(c) = k$ and which monotonically increases (where it may or may not be continuous). Or we might have a "partial step good in reverse," that is, a good which exists naturally at some level and which does not decrease with consumption until some critical consumption point is reached. This good can be defined with the following function: $\theta(x) = k$ for $x \leq c$ and $\theta(x) = f\theta(x)$ for $x \geq c$ where $f\theta$ is a monotonically decreasing function whose maximum value is k. (Again $f\theta$ may or may not be continuous.)

A pure step good is really just a collective good with only a single increment, and a mixed good is just an incremental good whose increments are vastly unequal in size. So we might say that all collective goods are incremental in different ways: some have only one increment (these are step goods); some have more than one increment, where the size of the increments can vary and where there may or may not be some natural bound on how many increments can be produced; and some goods have increments that are infinitesimally small (continuous goods). But for purposes of understanding the problems involved in producing collective goods, there is a significant distinction between what I will call step goods, which have only one increment, and what I will call incremental goods, which have more than one increment (and which include mixed goods and continuous goods). This two-part classification is what I will be primarily relying upon in the rest of this article.

III. THE "BATTLE-OF-THE-SEXES" PROBLEM IN THE SELECTION OF PRODUCERS OF STEP GOODS

We begin by examining free-rider problems involved in step good production. There are two places in which these problems can occur: In this section we will explore problems involved in the *selection* of producers to produce the good; and in the next section we will look at problems involved in the actual *production* of the good by those selected to do so.

To show that what are called "Battle-of-the-Sexes" problems are involved in the selection of producers of a step good, I will use as an example of the production of such a good, Hume's meadow-draining project:

> Two neighbours may agree to drain a meadow, which they possess in common; because 'tis easy for them to know each other's mind; and each must perceive, that the immediate consequence of his failing in his part, is, the abandoning of the whole project. But 'tis very difficult, and indeed impossible, that a thousand persons shou'd agree in any such action; it being difficult for them to concert so complicated a design, and still more difficult for them to execute it; while each seeks a pretext to free himself of the trouble and expense, and wou'd lay the whole burden on others. (III, ii, vii [1978, 538])

I will interpret Hume's remarks so that the situation has the following structure.

1. Draining the meadow is a collective good: i.e., it is indivisible, nonexcludable, and a benefit to the group.
2. It is a step good. It does not make sense to say that the drained meadow can be "incrementally increased" in either quantity or quality after it comes into existence.
3. Individual production costs and benefits from the good are well defined and commonly known, so that individual preferences for producing the good are commonly known.
4. The group involved in producing the good is what Olson (1965, pp. 22–36 and 48–50) calls "latent" as opposed to "privileged" because there is no individual in the group for whom $V_i - C_T > 0$. Here and in the rest of the paper V_i is the amount of benefits to the *i*th individual and C_T is the total cost.
5. Production costs can be split in a variety of ways among the 1,000 group members (that is, the group can define production units in a variety of ways, and assign any number of group members to these units), but the minimum number of people capable of producing the good is two.
6. Finally, individual costs to produce the good are not "retrievable." An individual cannot recoup whatever he pays to drain the meadow (e.g., monetary costs) before the good's production is completed.

We shall vary each of the last four features of the example in this and the next section in order to reveal different types of free-rider problems in the production of step goods. But supposing all six hold, what is the game-theoretic structure of this situation?

Consider that, in order to get the meadow drained, Hume's people must not only decide how many of their number shall participate in the good's production (as we noted, it must be at least two), but they must also decide who these producers will be if they choose a number below 1,000. So they have potentially a two-pronged selection problem here: they must determine the number of producers, and they must define the identity of these producers. Assuming people are largely self-interested, what are their likely preferences in this sort of situation? We would need a 1,000-person matrix to represent them properly, but because I have as little inclination to provide such a matrix as the reader has to see one, I will simplify the situation by supposing there are only three people involved, and then describe their preferences so as to reveal the game-theoretic structure of this type of situation, whether there are three people or 1,000 people involved.[5]

Clearly each player would most prefer the outcome in which the other two players drain the meadow and she languishes at home, eventually enjoying the good produced at no cost to her. Next best is the situation where all of them share the work to be done, which is better than the situation where she and only one other player split the work between them (doing half of the work is worse than doing a third of it). But this option is substantially better than the situation in which the meadow isn't drained because none of them or only one of them is willing to do it, and of course the worst situation for each of them is where she puts in work almost equal to the benefit to be received from the good to be produced, but is never assisted by anyone else, so that the good never gets produced and she loses whatever resources she put into the attempt to produce it.

There is a nice sense in which each player in this sort of game wants to "ride free" on the backs of the other players, insofar as each wants the others to do the work involved in getting the good produced so that he or she can enjoy the benefits of its production for free. Nonetheless, the game is not a prisoner's dilemma. A prisoner's dilemma is one in which noncooperation dominates over cooperation. But in this situation, noncooperation does not dominate. Although you should refuse to cooperate if you think that the other two people will do so, you should *not* refuse—that is, you should volunteer to pay the cost of draining the meadow—if you think that only one, and not the other, is willing to volunteer. It is better for you to do the work to get the meadow drained than to let the meadow go undrained. And of course you know that every other person's preferences are the same as yours. Like you, they want to try to "get out of the work," but like you, they also would rather do the work than see the project abandoned.

This is a three-person, "mixed-motive" or "nonzero sum" game much discussed in game-theoretic literature. Luce and Raiffa (1957, pp. 90–94, and chapter 6) call it "the Battle-of-the-Sexes" game after their unfortunately sexist example of a husband and wife who each prefer different evening activities (he prefers prize fighting and she prefers ballet) but who

		PERSON X	
		ACTION A	ACTION B
PERSON Y	ACTION A	1, 2	3, 3
	ACTION B	3, 3	2, 1

FIGURE 4

would also rather go out with the other to his or her favorite evening activity than to go to his or her own favorite alone. In order to facilitate the discussion of this game, a simplified two-person version of it is given in the matrix in Figure 4.

This type of interaction problem is still on the *coordination side of the game-theoretic spectrum* since coordination of interest predominates and there is more than one coordination equilibrium (represented by the upper left and lower right cells) where this notion is stronger than a Nash equilibrium in that it denotes an outcome in which no one would be better off if any one player, either himself or another, acted differently.[6] In this situation the parties are rational to reach an agreement on their actions so that one of these equilibria will be realized. However, the relative advantages of the different coordination points introduce conflict that might prevent them from coming to an agreement.

I have already hinted that there is another battle-of-the-sexes problem that can be involved in the production of this type of good. In the meadow-draining example there appears to be a variety of ways of splitting costs such that considerably more than two people—maybe even all 1,000 of them—could participate in the good's production. And although everyone will believe it is in his or her interest (as well as in the interest of the group as a whole) to split the cost in *some* way, there might be much disagreement among them about the way to split it. So the group faces a battle-of-the-sexes problem not merely over who will pay the cost to produce the good but also over how to split those costs in the first place. (Note that if they decide to split the costs equally among all the members of the group, there will be no further battle-of-the-sexes problem involved in selecting producers, although this outcome is not a coordination equilibrium and so will not be stable.)

This analysis should illustrate the following point: *free-rider problems have to do with the relationship between the productive units of the good and individual costs in the community.* Battle-of-the-sexes problems occur when there is no one way to link individuals in the group to productive units of the step good: either the units are fixed but the number of individuals who would find it rational to join their fellows in producing these units is greater than the number of units; or the units are not fixed, in which case there are a variety of ways in which individual producers can be linked to the (artificially defined) productive units.[7]

The fact that the battle-of-the-sexes game is a type of coordination game is critical in determining what strategies are effective in solving it. I have discussed the complicated issues involved in the solution of this type of game elsewhere (see Hampton, 1986, chapter 6.5). Suffice it to say here that the task of the players is to effect coordination on one coordination equilibrium, where this can be done via explicit agreement or via the generation of a convention on a "salient" coordination equilibrium by the players. The latter "nonagreement" solution to these dilemmas requires that the players determine the likelihood that the others will pursue any of the possible coordination equilibria, and clearly, any one player's estimation of probabilities here depends in part on what she believes the others believe about which coordination equilibria she will pursue.

This analysis shows that if, in the course of deliberating about being one of the producers of a step good, I reason in the way that Rawls describes, "regard[ing] the collective action of others as already given one way or the other," then I am reasoning fallaciously. Because this is a situation calling for coordination, it is what Elster (1979, pp. 18–19, 117–23) calls a "strategic" situation. Whereas a "parametric" choice situation is one in which the actor's behavior is the sole variable in a fixed environment, a strategic situation is one in which an actor's behavior is but one variable among others, so that his choice must take into account his expectations of these others' choices even as they must take into account their expectations of his and others' choices. The choice situation just described qualifies as strategic because whether others will volunteer to be the good's producers depends in part upon their expectations of whether I or other members of the group are willing to do so. In this, as in any coordination game, each person should make her decisions mindful of her strategic situation, aware that her preferences will have an effect on the other players, whose preferences will have an effect on hers. If she reasons "parametrically" (as Rawls essentially suggests), she is not trying to effect a coordination of all the players' actions; instead she is treating the rest of the group as a single entity unmindful of her, believing that their choices are fixed independently of what she will choose (although she is not sure quite how) such that her choice is the sole variable in the environment. The analysis in this section shows that such reasoning is mistaken.

However, a reader might wonder whether a parametric choice in this situation will be not only justified but also inescapable if the actor does not have adequate information about what others' expectations and preferences are and thus has no easy way to coordinate his actions with them. Whenever such a lack of information exists, feature 3 of Hume's meadow-draining case does not hold: that is, individual costs and benefits involved in the good's production are not commonly known. And if there is no way to persuade someone to provide that information, it is impossible to make one's choice responsive to others' expectations, so that one must choose parametrically, using an expected utility calculation in which one tries to estimate the probability that one is necessary to the production of the collective step good. There are a variety of ways in which this calculation might go, but if one's estimate of the probability is sufficiently low, one will conclude that it is not rational to contribute; and if everyone comes to this conclusion, the collective good will not be produced.

But this lack of information does not make the battle-of-the-sexes structure of the situation disappear, as Pettit (1986, pp. 369–70) has argued; instead, it makes the achievement of coordination in this battle-of-the-sexes situation virtually impossible because there is no way that the players can develop or come to know of a "salient" coordination equilibrium at which to aim. This point is important not merely for the sake of getting the game-theoretic structure of the situation right, but also for the sake of understanding how to solve it. Whereas people fail to cooperate in a prisoner's dilemma because it is individually irrational to do so, in the situation just described people fail to cooperate because there is a dearth of information enabling them to coordinate on a cooperative outcome. If that information is supplied, cooperation is possible. The "economic geometry" of the situation is different, so that the problems preventing cooperation, as well as the remedies that will effect it, differ in the two cases.

Indeed, the fact that we are *not* dealing with a prisoner's dilemma can explain why it is possible to credit the success of (what appear to be) latent groups in providing collective goods to the work of "political entrepreneurs." These are people willing to pay the cost of providing the information necessary to produce public goods because they perceive that this activity will pay off for them *individually* in a big way; e.g., it might enhance their careers or increase their power. But political entrepreneurs couldn't, for example, organize the building of a bridge if people really were in a prisoner's dilemma situation in which noncooperation dominated. That the people face a coordination problem in getting the good produced, only lacking an organizer who can help effect the coordination by obtaining the needed information, is something that his organizational activity presupposes.

Estimates of how often lack of information will attend the production of step goods are hard to make from a philosopher's armchair. Economists and other social scientists are in a better position to make these estimates than I am. But one wonders whether, even if the problem were common, political entrepreneurs would frequently be available (or recruitable, if the group had the resources to pay them in some way)[8] to help resolve it, paving the way for voluntary cooperation.

Feature 3 also does not hold when information about the cost of producing the step good is lacking. In this sort of situation, it would be reasonable for the group to make an estimate of the cost, and then proceed to try to find producers to pay it such that the good will be produced. But if I am deciding whether or not to be a producer, I will note that as long as the other producers pay their share of the estimated cost, my contribution might not be necessary: if the estimate is wrong, then either it is too high, in which case the good will be produced by the others without my contribution, or the estimate is too low, in which case the good will not be produced even if I do contribute. Of course, the better the estimate and the higher my stakes in getting the good produced, the more likely an expected-utility calculation will dictate that I produce. But when the estimate of the good's cost is poor, and/or when one's stakes in getting it produced are low, an expected-utility calculation will likely dictate against production. Perhaps the group might have certain devices available to them that could remedy this situation; for example, they might deliberately overestimate costs but then allow some individuals whose contributions prove to be unnecessary to retrieve them. But if such remedies are not possible, then the group is once again faced with a situation which, *although still a battle-of-the-sexes problem,* is very difficult to solve cooperatively.

Finally, feature 3 doesn't hold if the step goods are *themselves* vague, in the way that, for example, a "heap" of stones is vague. Such vagueness in the definition of these goods encourages people to reason in a way that has been associated with what is called the "Sorites" paradox.[9] Each possible contributor may reason, "My contribution to the heap is unnecessary; either the pile that exists already qualifies as a heap, in which case my stone doesn't contribute anything to the heap's production; or the pile is not a heap, in which case my adding one stone to it won't suddenly cause it to be a heap, meaning that, once again, my stone doesn't contribute anything to the heap's production." Note that this reasoning will be duplicated no matter *what* the estimate of stones needed to produce the heap. In this situation, each member of the group will believe she faces not a single prisoner's dilemma but what I will call an "ordered game set" of prisoner's dilemmas. For any estimate of what is necessary to produce the good by some number $K + 1$ producers where K ranges from 0 to $n - 1$ (assuming there are n members of the group), then Figure 5 shows how an individual will reason when determining whether or not to join with K other producers to pay her share of the estimated cost. Here it appears rational, no matter what the others do, for her not to produce her share of the estimated cost. But Sorites-like reasoning is supposed to be a *mistake,* so that the situation ought to have a battle-of-the-sexes structure. There are, thus far, no uncontroversial proofs showing how it is fallacious, although even were one to be given, it still seems to be the kind of (fallacious) reasoning that people would find tempting, to the detriment of the group.

Let me conclude this discussion of producer-selection problems in step good production by varying features 4 and 5 of Hume's example in order to see how the production of the step good is affected.

Theorists have generally thought that if feature 4 doesn't hold and the group charged with producing a collective good is privileged rather than latent, there is no collective action problem in the production of the good. But this isn't true. Privileged groups can also face a battle-of-the-sexes problem in their attempts to produce a collective good if there is more than one person for whom the value to her as an individual is greater than the total cost. In this case, the group must determine which of these individuals will produce the good, or else work out a way for them to share the production costs. Clearly it is in the interest of these individuals to try to escape paying for the good unless doing so would jeopardize its production. Theorists have tended to overlook the fact that this kind of free-rider problem can exist in privileged groups because they have concentrated only on problems involved in getting people to pay the costs of production, rather than on problems involved in *selecting* people to pay those costs. A privileged group will produce a collective good only if it solves the selection problem.

Finally, suppose we change feature 5 of Hume's meadow draining case—the feature that costs can be split in a variety of ways among more than one individual. If production units of a good are fixed and uniquely assignable to members, then there is no battle-of-the-sexes problem associated with the selection of the good's producers; indeed, *there is no free-rider selection problem at all in this situation.* Assuming that it is common knowledge that only these members can produce the good by paying only these units, they are rational to volunteer to produce it, because they know it will not get produced unless they do so, and they know that they are better off by paying their share of the cost of production and producing the good than they are by not paying the cost

	THE COLLECTIVE	
THE INDIVIDUAL	PRODUCE	NOT PRODUCE
PRODUCE	2	4
NOT PRODUCE	1	3

FIGURE 5

	PERSON A	
PERSON B	PRODUCE	DON'T PRODUCE
PRODUCE	1, 1	2, 2
DON'T PRODUCE	2, 2	2, 2

FIGURE 6

and living without it. Hirshleifer (1983) has suggested that this is actually the way people perceive their situation in times of disaster: each of them believes he or she is the "weakest link" in a fragile chain of producers necessary to prevent a public bad or create a public good.

My analysis in this section has demonstrated that, in general, coordination problems, rather than conflict problems, attend the selection of producers of these goods, so that it is not the individually rational pursuit of collectively irrational outcomes, but paucity of information's preventing successful coordination, that threatens successful production of these goods. However, before we can conclude that there are usually no conflict problems involved in the production of collective goods, we need to analyze the game-theoretic structure of the situation *after* individuals have been chosen to produce the step good.

IV. FREE-RIDER PROBLEMS IN THE PRODUCTION OF STEP GOODS FOLLOWING THE SELECTION OF PRODUCERS

How we answer the question of what sorts of problems are involved in producing goods after their producers have been selected depends upon whether or not production costs are retrievable.[10] In my reconstruction of Hume's meadow case, they were not; this was feature 6 of that case. But if feature 6 does not hold and production costs are retrievable, no further free-rider problem prevents the good's production (see Figure 6).

In this game, the preference for paying is the same as the preference for not paying in the unilateral breach situation because any costs paid can always be retrieved if the other producer fails to contribute. Thus the action of paying dominates weakly over the action of not paying.

However, there are interesting free-rider problems in the production of these goods if feature 6 does not hold and costs are not retrievable. One such

PERSON B \ PERSON A	PRODUCE	DON'T PRODUCE
PRODUCE	1, 1	3, 2
DON'T PRODUCE	2, 3	2, 2

FIGURE 7

problem is a variant of the assurance problem explored by Sen (1973, pp. 96–9; 1967, pp. 112–24), presented in the matrix in Figure 7.

This dilemma is a species of *coordination* problem with two equilibria (the upper left and lower right cells) in which each player is rational to cooperate if the other player cooperates, and each is rational not to do so if the other does not cooperate. Thus, before cooperating each needs to be assured in some way that the other player will also do so. Insofar as the players are the designated producers (and insofar as they know that no one who has not been designated producer will produce the good), they cannot expect the realization of any of the outcomes represented in the battle-of-the-sexes matrix in which they do not do the work but the good is produced anyway. However, each knows that if all of the designated producers do their share of the work, the good will be produced (the situation represented by the upper left cell of the matrix in Figure 7), and each also knows that if some of them don't do their share, then the good will not be produced and those who have worked to produce the good will lose their investment without getting any benefit from the good (because it won't exist—this situation is represented by the lower left and upper right cells of the matrix). Of course, it is rational for everyone to work together to produce the good, but how can each producer be assured that the others will actually do so?

If, as they produce the good, they can watch one another working, then each of them can be completely assured that the others are doing their share. But if such scrutiny is not possible, and if they cannot get information about the extent to which the others are working, should each of them do his/her share of the production work? Elster (1979, p. 20) notes that the maximin rule dictates against doing so. But the maximin rule—if it is ever appropriate—would seem to be inappropriate in those circumstances in which one is able to estimate the probability that the others will do their shares. (And the principle of insufficient reason could be used to estimate probabilities in situations of complete uncertainty.) If the estimate is fairly high, e.g., if there is some way in which the better coordination point is naturally salient, then it is likely that an expected-utility calculation will dictate performance for each of them, and the good will be produced. Moreover, any agreement among them to do the work required would be a way to make doing the work the salient action in the circumstances; each would estimate the probability of the others' doing their tasks as fairly high. (I have argued [Hampton, 1986, chapters 6.2 and 6.5] that this is the most natural way to obtain assurance in any coordination game.) In any case, it seems that the producers in this sort of situation would have a good chance of solving the assurance problem.

However, if there exists what I call a "critical cost point," the producers face a far more difficult problem. Consider Hume's meadow-draining example. Suppose the battle-of-the-sexes problem in the selection of producers were solved, such that you and I are supposed to drain the meadow, where for each of us $V_i > \frac{1}{2}C_T$. Suppose further that each of us will do so by digging irrigation ditches in the meadow that join together and eventually drain into a nearby river. (Thus what we pay, i.e., our labor, is irretrievable.) We both start to work, but after each of us has done a quarter of the total work (so that half the work remains to be done) I run off when you are not looking, leaving you alone to do the rest of the work. Is it rational for you to do it?

Consider that you have paid your contribution, which is equivalent to $\frac{1}{4}C_T$ and this is a "sunk cost," since you cannot retrieve your time and effort. So if you quit now, you are without the good and also without $\frac{1}{4}C_T$, so that your utility is $-\frac{1}{4}C_T$. But remember that half the work remains and that for you $V_i > \frac{1}{2}C_T$. If you continue to work and complete the project, your utility is $V_i - \frac{1}{2}_T - \frac{1}{4}C_T$, which is clearly greater than $-\frac{1}{4}C_T$. So you are rational to complete the job.

Thus, for any producer of the good, whenever the remaining cost of producing a good can be split between all the *other* producers in the group such that, for those other players, their benefit from the good exceeds their share of the remaining cost, then that individual producer is rational to cease work. This calculation dictates nonperformance at what I call the *critical cost point:* that is, the point at which it is rational for only *some* of the selected producers of the good to pay the whole remaining cost.

If this critical cost point has been reached (and note that it might be reached before anyone has paid any cost), what is the structure of the game-theoretic situation faced by the producers? In a two-player game, the matrix in Figure 8 describes the situation (e.g., in the meadow-draining example) and as we see, it depicts the game of chicken.

In this game there is no dominant action, which makes it importantly different from a prisoner's dilemma; nor are there any coordination equilibria, so that unlike the battle-of-the-sexes dilemma, it is not a coordination game. Each player prefers the situation in which he is the person reneged upon by the other, to the situation in which both renege, whereas in a

		PERSON A	
		PRODUCE	DON'T PRODUCE
PERSON B	PRODUCE	2, 2	3, 1
	DON'T PRODUCE	1, 3	4, 4

FIGURE 8

prisoner's dilemma, the latter is preferred to the former. So in this game, if I believe you will pay the remaining share of the cost of production, I am rational to renege, but if I believe you will not do so, I should pay either the entire remaining share or, as long as you continue to put in your original share of the total cost involved, only the remaining cost of my original share of the total cost. Indeed, in this sort of game, if we *each* distrust the other, the result will be that we will both do the work required to get the good produced.

In any case, because there is no dominant action in this sort of game, what is rational for either of us to do can depend upon a wealth of contingencies. And as Taylor and Ward discuss (1982, pp. 354ff), we are certainly well advised to try a precommitment strategy to force the other(s) to cooperate while escaping that fate ourselves. So, in this kind of situation each is trying to be a free rider, not in the sense that he is trying to get out of being selected to be a producer, but in the sense that, as someone who has already been selected, he is trying to get out of doing some (or maybe even all) production work. Moreover, he is not (as in a battle-of-the-sexes game) merely trying to score a "win" over the others in the group, who will still "win" themselves as producers insofar as the benefits they will get from the good exceed the cost to them of their work; instead he is trying to score a win over others in the group who will actually *lose* if he wins, insofar as they will end up by paying *more* for the good produced than the benefit they will receive from it.

Note, however, that an individual's succeeding in being a free rider in this second sense, thereby scoring a win in the chicken game, *is not bad for the collective*. Of course it is bad for the loser, but the collective will still get the good it desires. We have actually discovered a free-rider problem which poses more difficulties for individuals than it does for groups!

Nonetheless, the group will find it difficult to produce this sort of step good if individuals realize *before* the producers are selected, that as producers they run the risk of being exploited in this way. The possibility of exploitation changes the game-theoretic structure of the situation from a battle-of-the-sexes coordination game to a prisoner's dilemma. Each knows that if he contributes to the good's production, he stands a high chance of being exploited by the others and paying more for the good than he will receive from it; and he also knows that if he does not pay anything for the good, either he will get the good for free or he will at least not *lose* anything. Hence, no matter what the others do, it is rational for this individual not to produce, since this action is both the best defensive strategy and the best way to take advantage of an exploitative opportunity. Every other individual's preferences will be symmetric with his, so that no one will find it rational to produce the good.[11]

What can members of a group do to change the structure of the situation so that they can get the good produced?

1. The group can take steps to make production costs retrievable. If, for example, paying the cost involves contributing money, the group can make each producer pay into some kind of escrow account, such that unless all the producers pay, the good will not be produced and the individual's share of the cost will be returned. This strategy makes it impossible for anyone to be an exploiter. (Note also that this strategy solves any assurance problem involved in the good's production; I know that I will pay to produce the good only when all the other producers necessary to its production pay their share.)

2. Where retrievability isn't possible the group can try to destroy the critical cost point. For example, they can use any time deadline for the good's completion in the situation to accomplish this result. If the producers start work at a point where each of them has just enough time to complete his or her individual share of the productive efforts before the deadline for the good's production but *no* time to take on anyone else's share, then no one will be able to exploit the other workers: if one of them ceases work, the others will not be able to take on this work and complete the good's production before the deadline. So, because a reneger can gain nothing by his reneging action (indeed, he suffers a net *loss* equivalent to the work he invested), each producer is rational, as long as he or she can be reasonably assured of the others' performance, to work.

3. Selective incentives can be introduced to make the exploitative option irrational.

However, the fact that the first two strategies can be used in a wide variety of circumstances means that many step goods *can be made to be* (if they are not already) goods whose production poses only coordination problems (assurance and/or battle-of-the-sexes dilemmas) to the group. And these are problems which it is quite possible to solve (if information and mechanisms for coordination exist) without the help of the state.

V. THE GAME-THEORETIC STRUCTURE UNDERLYING THE PRODUCTION OF INCREMENTAL GOODS

What about the production of incremental goods? Surely PD games necessarily attend *their* production, so that the introduction of sanctions will be required to get them produced at optimal levels? . . .

When an individual is determining whether or not to pay the cost of producing an incremental collective good, she must determine whether it is rational for her to produce *any particular increment* of that good by determining whether the cost to her of doing so is greater than or less than the benefit to her *from that increment.* If it is never the case that the cost of supplying any increment of the good is exceeded by the benefit to her from that increment, she is irrational to involve herself in the production of that good, even if she would be better off with the good than without it. But if there are some levels of the good's production in which the benefit to her from an increment exceeds the cost to her of providing it, she is rational to produce it—as long as others find it rational to produce the good up to the level of that increment, and as long as solutions have been found for any of the (previously discussed) game-theoretic problems (e.g., battle-of-the-sexes, assurance, or chicken problems) involved either in selecting producers for the good or in getting them to produce that level of the good. . . .

I suspect that the complicated game-theoretic structure underlying the production of incremental goods has been missed because it is very easy to believe that the appropriate way of reasoning in these situations is: "suppose everyone contributes . . . suppose no one contributes"—assuming, in other words, that the actions of others are given when in fact they are not. In particular, such reasoning will cause one to miss the rationality of contributing to the production of a good in which benefit exceeds cost only at medium levels of the good's production. Sorites-like reasoning may also mislead one about the good's structure: one can believe that the increment one will produce will be "imperceptible" and hence unnecessary. Of course, it would indeed be "imperceptible" in one sense if the benefit one received from that increment was so small that the cost of providing it exceeded one's benefit from it, but it is this *latter* calculation one should be concerned to perform. Unless one does so, dismissing the idea of contributing an increment of the good on the basis of its *smallness alone* is irrational.

Empirical estimates are needed in order to determine how many incremental goods do not pose prisoner's dilemmas at all levels of the good's production. But even if there are a significant number, just because it is utility-maximizing for individuals to pay the cost of producing the incremental good at a certain level, doesn't mean that producing this level of the good is *optimal* for the *group.* Hence, the group might still find it necessary to introduce selective incentives into the situation in order to get an incremental good produced at optimal levels. So haven't we finally discovered the area of collective good production which is, as the traditional analysis suggests, plagued by PD games requiring sanctions for their solution?

Not necessarily; voluntary production at an optimal level of even these goods is still possible *if their increments can be restructured in the right way.* That is, if the group desiring such a good is able to make certain levels of the production of the good impossible, such that it can only be produced in one or more large "steps," the production of the good at an optimal level might pose only a battle-of-the-sexes problem. Suppose, for example, that a security service approached a neighborhood haunted by frequent burglaries and offered to provide patrol service for the neighborhood, with the number of hours of the patrol per week depending upon the number of households paying for the patrol. If the security service offered to make the number of hours strictly dependent upon the number of households contributing (for example, each new contributing household might pay for two more hours of patrol per week), the neighborhood would be asked to produce an incremental collective good and each household might find it individually rational not to pay for its two-hour increment of patrol no matter how many other households did so (i.e., each household might find itself facing a coordinated set of prisoner's dilemmas). But suppose the security service said that it would, at a minimum, provide patrol for half of the hours (50%) of the week as long as it got 40% of the households contributing, but that if less than 40% contributed it would provide no hours of patrol (and any contributions made would be returned to these households). In this second offer, the security service has made an incremental good into a good with at least one large step, and residents of the neighborhood would now have to determine whether they would be better off paying a certain share of the cost of producing this large step than they would be if they refrained from doing so. Suppose that the security service asked each of the households making up the 40% to pay for the equivalent of one hour of the half-week patrol. Each household would then calculate whether or not it was rational to pay for this hour—its share of the cost of this half-week patrol—by determining whether or not the cost of doing so was exceeded by the benefit to it of the *half-week patrol.* In other words, instead of comparing the *cost of providing an increment* of security with *the benefit it would get from that increment,* each household would now compare *its share of the cost of providing 50% of the incremental good,* with *the benefit it would get from 50% of the incremental good.* And while contributing on the basis of the first comparison is likely to be irrational, contributing on the basis of the second comparison could well be rational. So, by transforming the situation into the production of a good that has a very large initial step, the security service has ensured that only the (primarily coordination) problems involved in step good production will be involved here.[12]

Recall at the outset that I said the distinction between incremental goods and step goods was not sharp. The last example illustrates this point. Those collective goods that come in more than one increment can be more or less "steppy"; in particular, the increments involved in their production can be large or small (even infinitesimally small). Moreover, as the example above illustrates, a good that might naturally be thought to come in small increments can be "restructured" such that it can only be produced in increments that have been made (artificially, by the group's reconstruction) quite large. This restructuring is desirable because the larger the increment, the more likely a group can respond to its production in the way they would respond to a pure step good—splitting the cost of producing the (large) increment of the good such that the split cost for a member of the group will be exceeded by the benefit to that member from the entire increment.

VI. CONCLUSION

In this article, I have argued that the production of many collective goods involves only coordination problems, and that the production of other collective goods involves conflict problems that can be transformed—without the use of sanctions—into coordination problems. I have also suggested a variety of strategies for the voluntary solution of these coordination problems by self-interested people. Estimates of how often these strategies are available must be made by others; complicating this task is the fact that I have had to make a number of simplifying assumptions that do not fit with a messier reality. Nonetheless, this analysis should be good news to those who—for practical or theoretical reasons—want to believe that many collective goods can be produced without the help of the state.

REFERENCES

Barry, Brian. 1982. "Political Participation as Rational Action." In *Rational Man and Irrational Society?* edited by Brian Barry and Russell Hardin. Beverly Hills, Cal.: Sage.

Buchanan, James. 1975. *The Limits of Liberty.* Chicago: University of Chicago Press.

Elster, Jon. 1979. *Ulysses and the Sirens.* Cambridge: Cambridge University Press.

Frohlich, Norman, and Oppenheimer, Joe. 1970. "I Get By with a Little Help from My Friends." *World Politics* 23: 104–20.

———. 1978. *Modern Political Economy.* Englewood Cliffs, N.J.: Prentice-Hall.

Frohlich, Norman, Oppenheimer, Joe, and Young, Oran. 1971. *Political Leadership and Collective Goods.* Princeton: Princeton University Press.

Hampton, Jean. 1986. *Hobbes and the Social Contract Tradition.* Cambridge: Cambridge University Press.

Hardin, Russell. 1971. "Collective Action as an Agreeable *n*-Prisoner's Dilemma." *Behavioural Science* 16: 472–79. Reprinted in *Rational Man and Irrational Society?* edited by Brian Barry and Russell Hardin. Beverly Hills, Cal.: Sage, 1982.

———. 1982. *Collective Action.* Baltimore: Johns Hopkins University Press.

Hirshleifer, Jack. 1983. "From Weakest-Link to Best-Shot: The Voluntary Provision of Public Goods." *Public Choice* 41: 371–86.

Hume, David. 1978. *A Treatise of Human Nature.* Edited by L.A. Selby-Bigge, and revised by P. H. Nidditch. Oxford: Oxford University Press.

Jeffrey, Richard. 1965. *The Logic of Decision.* New York: McGraw-Hill. Reprinted 1983.

Lewis, David. 1969. *Convention.* Cambridge: Harvard University Press.

Luce, R., and Raiffa, H. 1957. *Games and Decisions.* New York: Wiley.

Olson, Mancur. 1965. *The Logic of Collective Action.* Cambridge: Harvard University Press. Reprinted 1971.

Pettit, Philip. 1986. "Free Riders and Foul Dealers." *Journal of Philosophy* 83: 361–79.

Sen, Amartya. 1967. "Isolation, Assurance, and the Social Rate of Discount." *Quarterly Journal of Economics* 81: 112–24.

———. 1973. *On Economic Inequality.* Oxford: Clarendon Press.

Schelling, Thomas. 1973. "Hockey Helmets, Concealed Weapons, and Daylight Savings." *Journal of Conflict Resolution* 17: 381–428.

Taylor, Michael, and Ward, Hugh. 1982. "Chickens, Whales, and Lumpy Goods: Alternative Models of Public Goods Provision." *Political Science* 30: 350–70.

Tuck, Richard. 1979. "Is There a Free-Rider Problem, and If So, What Is It?" In *Rational Action,* edited by Ross Harrison. Cambridge: Cambridge University Press.

Wright, Crispin. 1976. "Language-Mastery and the Sorites Paradox." In *Truth and Meaning,* edited by G.E. Evans and J. McDowell. Oxford: Oxford University Press.

NOTES

1. This passage is also cited by Richard Tuck (1979, p. 147).

2. For more on this possible (but controversial) solution to PD games, see Jeffrey (1965).

3. See Hardin (1982, chapter 4, pp. 58–61). Taylor and Ward (1982) want to argue that many free-rider problems are not PDs but chicken games. Frohlich, Oppenheimer, and Young (1971) suggest that the PD is not the correct game-theoretic structure, and Frohlich and Oppenheimer (1970 and 1978) show that there are situations in which voluntary production of these goods is individually rational. This argument is extended and deepened in Frohlich, Hunt, Oppenheimer, and Wagner (1975), which is discussed in footnote 4.

4. I am indebted to Jack Hirschleifer for this characterization of my approach. I developed this approach, as well as the arguments in this paper, in ignorance of the trailblazing paper of Frohlich et al. (1975), who also insisted that free-rider problems have to do with "the shape of [individuals'] utility functions and of the production function governing the supply of the collective good" (p. 328). However, to make this point, they followed Schelling (1973) in employing a graphical representation of *n*-person, binary choice games with externalities in which the number of contributions to the good is represented on the horizontal axis and an individual's benefit from the good is represented on the vertical axis. Although this technique enabled them to show that some free-rider problems are not prisoner's dilemmas, it did not allow them to show that, depending upon the extent to which a collective good is (or can be) produced in larger or smaller increments, a variety of (primarily coordination) problems can arise in connecting possible producers to the good's (naturally or artificially defined) increment(s). In this paper I am experimenting with the use of a different technique in order to make this general point.

5. In Hampton (1986, p. 151) I present a 3-D matrix representing preferences in a battle-of-the-sexes game.

6. This formulation is from David Lewis (1969, p. 14)

7. Without actually presenting this battle-of-the-sexes analysis of free-rider problems in step good production, the discussion of Frohlich et al. (1975) strongly suggests it. Other theorists whose discussion of free-rider problems suggests this game include James Buchanan (1975, p. 37f)

and Brian Barry (1982, p. 56). Taylor and Ward also come close to presenting it, but they mistake the battle-of-the-sexes structure of this situation for the game of chicken, presented later in Figure 8. There is a big difference between the game of chicken, which is a game of *conflict,* and the battle-of-the-sexes dilemma, which is a type of *coordination* game with some conflict of interest. The former has only Nash equilibria, the latter has coordination equilibria; and whereas the former poses the question, "Do we cooperate?," the latter poses the question, "How do we cooperate?" Taylor and Ward mistakenly assimilated the two because they defined (what they called) the "family of chicken games" as games in which it is rational for a player to attempt a "precommitment" strategy, that is, one in which the player binds himself to his favorite outcome, thereby forcing the other player(s) to pursue that outcome (on pain of irrationality) also. However, this strategy is advised not only for players in a chicken game but also for players in a battle-of-the-sexes dilemma, each of whom should try to bind himself irrevocably to his favorite coordination equilibrium, thereby forcing the other player(s) to accept it or else lose all chance of realizing a desirable coordination outcome. It turns out that one cannot define chicken games in terms of a strategy that those who are in a significantly different game-theoretic situation would also be rational to follow. Nonetheless, as we shall discuss later, Taylor and Ward are right to think that *some* free-rider problems are true chicken games. Our analysis will show that these chicken games arise not in the context of getting the producers of a collective good selected, but rather in the context of getting previously selected producers of the collective good to perform.

8. Frohlich et al. (1970, p. 119) suggests that groups may find it rational to subsidize voluntarily the pay of political entrepreneurs.

9. See Tuck (1979, p. 152), who cites Crispin Wright's argument (1976, pp. 223 and 247) that this paradox arises out of the vagueness of our criteria for defining certain entities, such as "heaps."

10. I am told that aspects of the following argument are known in some circles; I do not know of any place where they have been published.

11. In fact, this is what Pettit (1986) calls a "foul dealer" variant of a multiperson PD game, because a lone defector makes one or more cooperators worse off than they would have been had *everyone* defected.

12. Although they do not explicitly pursue this restructuring idea, Frohlich and Oppenheimer (1978) suggest it when they insist that "successful political action based solely on the individual's incentives to obtain the collectively supplied good requires marginal cost sharing" (p. 63).

Elinor Ostrom

Collective Action and the Evolution of Social Norms

2000

With the publication of *The Logic of Collective Action* in 1965, Mancur Olson challenged a cherished foundation of modern democratic thought that groups would tend to form and take collective action whenever members jointly benefitted. Instead, Olson (1965, p. 2) offered the provocative assertion that no self-interested person would contribute to the production of a public good: "[U]nless the number of individuals in a group is quite small, or unless there is coercion or some other special device to make

Elinor Ostrom, "Collective Action and the Evolution of Social Norms." *Journal of Economic Perspectives* 14 (3) (2000): 137–158. Permission by Journal of Economic Perspectives.

individuals act in their common interest, *rational, self-interested individuals will not act to achieve their common or group interests.*" This argument soon became known as the "zero contribution thesis."

The idea that rational agents were not likely to cooperate in certain settings, even when such cooperation would be to their mutual benefit, was also soon shown to have the structure of an *n*-person prisoner's dilemma game (Hardin 1971, 1982). Indeed, the prisoner's dilemma game, along with other social dilemmas, has come to be viewed as the canonical representation of collective action problems (Lichbach, 1996). The zero contribution thesis underpins the presumption in policy textbooks (and many contemporary public policies) that individuals cannot overcome collective action problems and need to have externally enforced rules to achieve their own long-term self-interest.

The zero contribution thesis, however, contradicts observations of everyday life. After all, many people vote, do not cheat on their taxes, and contribute effort to voluntary associations. Extensive fieldwork has by now established that individuals in all walks of life and all parts of the world voluntarily organize themselves so as to gain the benefits of trade, to provide mutual protection against risk, and to create and enforce rules that protect natural resources.[1] Solid empirical evidence is mounting that governmental policy can frustrate, rather than facilitate, the private provision of public goods (Montgomery and Bean, 1999). Field research also confirms that the temptation to free ride on the provision of collective benefits is a universal problem. In all known self-organized resource governance regimes that have survived for multiple generations, participants invest resources in monitoring and sanctioning the actions of each other so as to reduce the probability of free riding (Ostrom, 1990).

While these empirical studies have posed a severe challenge to the zero contribution theory, these findings have not yet been well integrated into an accepted, revised theory of collective action. A substantial gap exists between the theoretical prediction that self-interested individuals will have extreme difficulty in coordinating collective action and the reality that such cooperative behavior is widespread, although far from inevitable.

Both theorists and empirical researchers are trying to bridge this gap. Recent work in game theory—often in a symbiotic relationship with evidence from experimental studies—has set out to provide an alternative micro theory of individual behavior that begins to explain anomalous findings (McCabe, Rassenti and Smith, 1996; Rabin, 1993; Fehr and Schmidt, 1999; Selten, 1991; Bowles, 1998). On the empirical side, considerable effort has gone into trying to identify the key factors that affect the likelihood of successful collective action (Feeny et al., 1990; Baland and Platteau, 1996; Ostrom, forthcoming).

This paper will describe both avenues of research on the underpinnings of collective action, first focusing on the experimental evidence and potential theoretical explanations, and then on the real-world empirical evidence. This two-pronged approach to the problem has been a vibrant area of research that is yielding many insights. A central finding is that the world contains multiple types of individuals, some more willing than others to initiate reciprocity to achieve the benefits of collective action. Thus, a core question is how potential cooperators signal one another and design institutions that reinforce rather than destroy conditional cooperation. While no full-blown theory of collective action yet exists, evolutionary theories appear most able to explain the diverse findings from the lab and the field and to carry the nucleus of an overarching theory.

LABORATORY EVIDENCE ON RATIONAL CHOICE IN COLLECTIVE ACTION SITUATIONS

Most studies by political economists assume a standard model of rational individual action—what I will call a rational egoist. A wide range of economic experiments have found that the rational egoist assumption works well in predicting the outcome in auctions and competitive market situations (Kagel and Roth, 1995). While subjects do not arrive at the predicted equilibrium in the first round of market experiments, behavior closely approximates the predicted equilibrium by the end of the first five rounds in these experiments. One of the major successes of experimental economics is to demonstrate the robustness of microeconomic theory for explaining market behavior.

In regard to collective action situations, on the other hand, the results are entirely different. Linear public good experiments are widely used for examining the willingness of individuals to overcome collective action problems. In a linear public good experiment, each individual is endowed with a fixed set of assets and must decide how many of these assets to contribute to a public good. When an individual makes a contribution of, say, 10 units to the public good, each of the participants in the group, including that individual, receive a benefit of, say, five units apiece. In this setting, the optimal outcome for the group of players as a whole is for everyone to contribute all of their endowments to provide the public good (if a group of 10 people, each individual contribution of 10 will have a social payoff of 50!). However, the unique equilibrium for rational egoists in a single-shot game is that everyone contributes zero, since each individual has access to benefits of the public good funded by the contributions of others, without paying any costs.[2]

If the public goods game is played for a finite number of rounds, zero is also the predicted equilibrium for every round. Rational egoists will reason that zero contribution is the equilibrium in the last round, and because they expect everyone to contribute zero in the last round, they also expect everyone to contribute zero in the second-to-last round, and eventually by backward induction they will work their way to the decision not to contribute to the public good in the present. Of course, these predictions are based on the assumptions that all players are fully rational and interested only in their own immediate financial payoff, that all players understand the structure of the game fully and believe that all other players are fully rational, and that no external actor can enforce agreements between the players.

Since the first public good experiments were undertaken by Dawes, McTavish and Shaklee (1977), a truly huge number of such experiments has been undertaken under various conditions (see Davis and Holt, 1993; Ledyard, 1995; and Offerman, 1997, for an overview). By now seven general findings have been replicated so frequently that these can be considered the core facts that theory needs to explain.

1. Subjects contribute between 40 and 60 percent of their endowments to the public good in a one-shot game as well as in the first round of finitely repeated games.

2. After the first round, contribution levels tend to decay downward, but remain well above zero. A repeated finding is that over 70 percent of subjects contribute nothing in the announced last round of a finitely repeated sequence.

3. Those who believe others will cooperate in social dilemmas are more likely to cooperate themselves. A rational egoist in a public good game, however, should not in any way be affected by a belief regarding the contribution levels of others. The dominant strategy is a zero contribution no matter what others do.

4. In general, learning the game better tends to lead to more cooperation, not less. In a clear test of an earlier speculation that it just took time for subjects to learn the predicted equilibrium strategy in public good games, Isaac, Walker and Williams (1994) repeated the same game for 10 rounds, 40 rounds, and 60 rounds with experienced subjects who were specifically told the end period of each design. They found that the rate of decay is inversely related to the number of decision rounds. In other words, instead of learning *not* to cooperate, subjects learn how to cooperate at a moderate level for ever-longer periods of time!

5. Face-to-face communication in a public good game—as well as in other types of social dilemmas—produces substantial increases in cooperation that are sustained across all periods including the last period (Ostrom and Walker, 1997).[3] The strong effect of communication is not consistent with currently accepted theory, because verbal agreements in these experiments are not enforced. Thus, communication is only "cheap talk" and makes no difference in predicted outcomes in social dilemmas. But instead of using this opportunity to fool others into cooperating, subjects use the time to discuss the

optimal joint strategy, to extract promises from one another, and to give verbal tongue-lashings when aggregate contributions fall below promised levels. Interestingly, when communication is implemented by allowing subjects to signal promises to cooperate through their computer terminals, much less cooperation occurs than in experiments allowing face-to-face communication.

6. When the structure of the game allows it, subjects will expend personal resources to punish those who make below-average contributions to a collective benefit, including the last period of a finitely repeated game. No rational egoist is predicted to spend anything to punish others, since the positive impact of such an action is shared equally with others whether or not they also spend resources on punishing. Indeed, experiments conducted in the United States, Switzerland, and Japan show that individuals who are initially the least trusting are more willing to contribute to sanctioning systems and are likely to be transformed into strong cooperators by the availability of a sanctioning mechanism (Fehr and Gachter, forthcoming). The finding that face-to-face communication is more efficacious than computerized signaling is probably due to the richer language structure available and the added intrinsic costs involved in hearing the intonation and seeing the body language of those who are genuinely angry at free riders (Ostrom, 1998a).

7. The rate of contribution to a public good is affected by various contextual factors including the framing of the situation and the rules used for assigning participants, increasing competition among them, allowing communication, authorizing sanctioning mechanisms, or allocating benefits.

These facts are hard to explain using the standard theory that all individuals who face the same objective game structure evaluate decisions in the same way![4] We cannot simply resort to the easy criticism that undergraduate students are erratic. Increasing the size of the payoffs offered in experiments does not appear to change the broad patterns of empirical results obtained.[5] I believe that one is forced by these well-substantiated facts to adopt a more eclectic (and classical) view of human behavior.

BUILDING A THEORY OF COLLECTIVE ACTION WITH MULTIPLE TYPES OF PLAYERS

From the experimental findings, one can begin to put together some of the key assumptions that need to be included in a revised theory of collective action.

Assuming the existence of two types of "norm-using" players—"conditional cooperators" and "willing punishers"—in addition to rational egoists, enables one to start making more coherent sense out of the findings of the laboratory experiments on contributions to public goods.

Conditional cooperators are individuals who are willing to initiate cooperative action when they estimate others will reciprocate and to repeat these actions as long as a sufficient proportion of the others involved reciprocate. Conditional cooperators are the source of the relatively high levels of contributions in one-shot or initial rounds of prisoner's dilemma and public good games. Their initial contributions may encourage some rational egoists to contribute as well, so as to obtain higher returns in the early rounds of the game (Kreps et al., 1982). Conditional cooperators will tend to trust others and be trustworthy in sequential prisoner's dilemma games as long as the proportion of others who return trust is relatively high. Conditional cooperators tend to vary, however, in their tolerance for free riding. Some are easily disappointed if others do not contribute, so they begin to reduce their own contributions. As they reduce their contributions, they discourage other conditional cooperators from further contributions. Without communication or institutional mechanisms to stop the downward cascade, eventually only the most determined conditional cooperators continue to make positive contributions in the final rounds.

The first four findings are consistent with an assumption that conditional cooperators are involved in most collective action situations. Conditional cooperators are apparently a substantial proportion of the population, given the large number of one-shot and finitely repeated experiments with initial cooperation rates ranging from 40 to 60 percent. Estimating that others are likely to cooperate should increase their willingness to cooperate. Further, knowing the number of repetitions will be relatively long, conditional cooperators can restrain their disappointment with free riders and keep moderate levels of cooperation (and joint payoffs) going for ever-longer periods of time.

The fifth and sixth findings depend on the presence of a third type of player who is willing, if given an opportunity, to punish presumed free riders through verbal rebukes or to use costly material payoffs when available. Willing punishers may also become willing rewarders if the circle of relationships allows them to reward those who have contributed more than the minimal level. Some conditional cooperators may also be willing punishers. Together, conditional cooperators and willing punishers create a more robust opening for collective action and a mechanism for helping it grow. When allowed to communicate on a face-to-face basis, willing punishers convey a considerable level of scorn and anger toward others who have not fully reciprocated their trust and give substantial positive encouragement when cooperation rates are high. Even more important for the long-term sustainability of collective action is the willingness of some to pay a cost to sanction others. The presence of these norm-using types of players is hard to dispute given the empirical evidence. The key question now is: How could these norm-using types of players have emerged and survived in a world of rational egoists?

Emergence and Survival of Multiple Types of Players in Evolutionary Processes

Evolutionary theories provide useful ways of modeling the emergence and survival of multiple types of players in a population. In a strict evolutionary model, individuals inherit strategies and do not change strategies in their lifetime. In this approach, those carrying the more successful strategies for an environment reproduce at a higher rate. After many iterations the more successful strategies come to prominence in the population (Axelrod, 1986). Such models are a useful starting point for thinking about competition and relative survival rates among different strategies.[6]

Human evolution occurred mostly during the long Pleistocene era that lasted for about 3 million years, up to about 10,000 years ago. During this era, humans roamed the earth in small bands of hunter-gatherers who were dependent on each other for mutual protection, sharing food, and providing for the young. Survival was dependent not only on aggressively seeking individual returns but also on solving many day-to-day collective action problems. Those of our ancestors who solved these problems most effectively, and learned how to recognize who was deceitful and who was a trustworthy reciprocator, had a selective advantage over those who did not (Barkow, Cosmides and Tooby, 1992).

Evolutionary psychologists who study the cognitive structure of the human brain conclude that humans do not develop general analytical skills that are then applied to a variety of specific problems. Humans are not terribly skilled at general logical problem solving (as any scholar who has taught probability theory to undergraduates can attest). Rather, the human brain appears to have evolved a domain-specific, human-reasoning architecture (Clark and Karmiloff-Smith, 1991). For example, humans use a different approach to reasoning about deontic relationships—what is forbidden, obligated, or permitted—as contrasted to reasoning about what is true and false. When reasoning about deontic relationships, humans tend to check for violations, or cheaters (Manktelow and Over, 1991). When reasoning about whether empirical relationships are true, they tend to use a confirmation strategy (Oaksford and Chater, 1994). This deontic effect in human reasoning has repeatedly been detected even in children as young as three years old and is not associated with overall intelligence or educational level of the subject (Cummins, 1996).

Thus, recent developments in evolutionary theory and supporting empirical research provide strong support for the assumption that modern humans have inherited a propensity to learn social norms, similar to our inherited propensity to learn grammatical rules (Pinker, 1994). Social norms are shared understandings about actions that are obligatory, permitted, or forbidden (Crawford and Ostrom, 1995).

Which norms are learned, however, varies from one culture to another, across families, and with exposure to diverse social norms expressed within various types of situations. The intrinsic cost or anguish that an individual suffers from failing to use a social norm, such as telling the truth or keeping a promise, is referred to as guilt, if entirely self-inflicted, or as shame, when the knowledge of the failure is known by others (Posner and Rasmusen, 1999).

The Indirect Evolutionary Approach to Adaptation Through Experience

Recent work on an *indirect* evolutionary approach to the study of human behavior offers a rigorous theoretical approach for understanding how preferences—including those associated with social norms—evolve or adapt (Güth and Yaari, 1992; Güth, 1995). In an indirect evolutionary model, players receive objective payoffs, but make decisions based on the transformation of these material rewards into intrinsic preferences. Those who value reciprocity, fairness, and being trustworthy add a subjective change parameter to actions (of themselves or others) that are consistent or not consistent with their norms. This approach allows individuals to start with a predisposition to act in a certain way—thus, they are not rational egoists who only look forward—but it also allows those preferences to adapt in a relatively short number of iterations given the objective payoffs they receive and their intrinsic preferences about those payoffs.

Social dilemmas associated with games of trust, like sequential prisoner's dilemma games, are particularly useful games for discussing the indirect evolutionary approach. In such games, if two players trust each other and cooperate, they can both receive a moderately high payoff. However, if one player cooperates and the other does not, then the one who did not cooperate receives an even higher payoff, while the other receives little or nothing. For a rational egoist playing this game, the choice is not to trust, because the expectation is that the other player will not trust, either. As a result, both players will end up with lower payoffs than if they had been able to trust and cooperate. When considering such games, it is useful to remember that most contractual relationships—whether for private or public goods—have at least an element of this basic structure of trying to assure mutual trust. An indirect evolutionary approach explains how a mixture of norm-users and rational egoists would emerge in settings where standard rational choice theory assumes the presence of rational egoists alone.

In this approach, social norms may lead individuals to behave differently in the same objective situation depending on how strongly they value conformance with (or deviance from) a norm. Rational egoists can be thought of as having intrinsic payoffs that are the same as objective payoffs, since they do not value the social norm of reciprocity. Conditional cooperators (to take only one additional type of player for now) would be modeled as being trustworthy types and would have an additional parameter that adds value to the objective payoffs when reciprocating trust with trustworthiness. By their behavior and resulting interaction, however, different types of players are likely to gain differential objective returns. In a game of trust where players are chosen from a population that initially contains some proportion of rational egoists and conditional cooperators, the level of information about player types affects the relative proportion of rational egoists and conditional cooperators over time. With complete information regarding types, conditional cooperators playing a trustworthy strategy will more frequently receive the higher payoff, while rational egoists will consistently receive a lower payoff, since others will not trust them.

Only the trustworthy type would survive in an evolutionary process with complete information (Güth and Kliemt, 1998, p. 386). Viewed as a cultural evolutionary process, new entrants to the population would be more likely to adopt the preference ordering of those who obtained the higher material payoffs in the immediate past (Boyd and Richerson, 1985). Those who were less successful would tend to learn the values of those who had achieved higher material rewards (Börgers and Sarin, 1997).[7] Where a player's type is common knowledge, rational egoists would not survive. Full and accurate information about all players' types, however, is a very strong assumption and unlikely to be met in most real world settings.

If there is no information about player types for a relatively large population, preferences will evolve so that only rational egoists survive.[8] If information about the proportion of a population that is trustworthy is known, and no information is known about the type of a specific player, Güth and Kliemt (1998) show that first players will trust second players as long as the expected return of meeting trustworthy players and receiving the higher payoff exceeds the payoff obtained when neither player trusts the other. In such a setting, however, the share of the population held by the norm-using types is bound to decline. On the other hand, if there is a noisy signal about a player's type that is at least more accurate than random, trustworthy types will survive as a substantial proportion of the population. Noisy signals may result from seeing one another, face-to-face communication, and various mechanisms that humans have designed to monitor each other's behavior.

Evidence Testing the Indirect Evolutionary Approach

An indirect evolutionary approach is able to explain how a mixture of contingent cooperators and rational egoists would emerge in settings where traditional game theory predicts that only rational egoists should prevail. The first six of the seven core findings summarized above were in part the stimulus for the development of the indirect evolutionary theory and the seventh is not inconsistent (see below for further discussion of it). Given the recent development of this approach, direct tests of this theory are not extensive. From the viewpoint of an indirect evolutionary process, participants in a collective action problem would start with differential, intrinsic preferences over outcomes due to their predispositions toward norms such as reciprocity and trust. Participants would learn about the likely behavior of others and shift their behavior in light of the experience and the objective payoffs they have received. Several recent experiments provide evidence of these kinds of contingent behaviors and behavioral shifts.[9]

In a one-shot, sequential, double-blind prisoner's dilemma experiment, for example, the players were asked to rank their preferences over the final outcomes after they had made their own choice, but before they knew their partner's decision. Forty percent of a pool of 136 subjects ranked the cooperative outcome (C,C) higher than the outcome if they defect while the other cooperates (D,C), and 27 percent were indifferent between these outcomes, even though their individual payoff was substantially higher for them in the latter outcome (Ahn, Ostrom and Walker, 1998).[10] This finding confirms that not all players enter a collective action situation as pure forward-looking rational egoists who make decisions based solely on individual outcomes. Some bring with them a set of norms and values that can support cooperation.

On the other hand, preferences based on these norms can be altered by bad experiences. After 72 subjects had played 12 rounds of a finitely repeated prisoner's dilemma game where partners were randomly matched each round, rates of cooperation were very low and many players had experienced multiple instances where partners had declined to cooperate, only 19 percent of the respondents ranked (C,C) above (D,C), while 17 percent were indifferent (Ahn et al., 1999). In this setting, the norms supporting cooperation and reciprocity were diminished, but not eliminated, by experience.

In another version of the prisoner's dilemma game, Cain (1998) first had players participate in a "dictator game"—in which one player divides a sum of money and the other player must accept the division, whatever it is—and then a prisoner's dilemma game. Stingy players, defined as those who retained at least 70 percent of their endowment in the earlier dictator game, tended to predict that all players would defect in the prisoner's dilemma game. Nice players, defined as those that gave away at least 30 percent of their endowment, tended to predict that other nice players would cooperate and stingy players would defect. Before playing the prisoner's dilemma game, players were told whether their opponent had been "stingy" or "nice" in the dictator game. Nice players chose cooperation in the prisoner's dilemma game 69 percent of the time when they were paired with other nice players and 39 percent of the time when they were paired with stingy players.

Finally, interesting experimental (as well as field) evidence has accumulated that externally imposed rules tend to "crowd out" endogenous cooperative behavior (Frey, 1994). For example, consider some paradoxical findings of Frohlich and Oppenheimer (1996) from a prisoner's dilemma game. One set of groups played a regular prisoner's dilemma game, some with communication and some without. A second set of groups used an externally imposed, incentive-compatible mechanism designed to enhance cooperative choices. In the first phase of the experiment, the second set gained higher monetary returns than the control groups, as expected. In the second phase of the experiment, both groups played a regular prisoner's dilemma game. To the surprise of the experimenters, a higher level of cooperation occurred in the control groups that played the regular prisoner's dilemma in both phases, especially for those who communicated on a face-to-face basis. The greater cooperation that had occurred due to the exogenously created incentive-compatible mechanism appeared to be transient. As the authors put it (p. 180), the removal of the external mechanism "seemed to undermine subsequent cooperation and leave the group worse off than those in the control group who had played a regular prisoner's dilemma."

Several other recent experimental studies have confirmed the notion that external rules and monitoring can crowd out cooperative behavior.[11] These studies typically find that a social norm, especially in a setting where there is communication between the parties, can work as well or nearly as well at generating cooperative behavior as an externally imposed set of rules and system of monitoring and sanctioning. Moreover, norms seem to have a certain staying power in encouraging a growth of the desire for cooperative behavior over time, while cooperation enforced by externally imposed rules can disappear very quickly. Finally, the worst of all worlds may be one where external authorities impose rules but are only able to achieve weak monitoring and sanctioning. In a world of strong external monitoring and sanctioning, cooperation is enforced without any need for internal norms to develop. In a world of no external rules or monitoring, norms can evolve to support cooperation. But in an in-between case, the mild degree of external monitoring discourages the formation of social norms, while also making it attractive for some players to deceive and defect and take the relatively low risk of being caught.

THE EVOLUTION OF RULES AND NORMS IN THE FIELD

Field studies of collective action problems are extensive and generally find that cooperation levels vary from extremely high to extremely low across different settings. (As discussed above, the seventh core finding from experimental research is that contextual factors affect the rate of contribution to public goods.) An immense number of contextual variables are also identified by field researchers as conducive or detrimental to endogenous collective action. Among those proposed are: the type of production and allocation functions; the predictability of resource flows; the relative scarcity of the good; the size of the group involved; the heterogeneity of the group; the dependence of the group on the good; common understanding of the group; the size of the total collective benefit; the marginal contribution by one person to the collective good; the size of the temptation to free ride; the loss to cooperators when others do not cooperate; having a choice of participating or not; the presence of leadership; past experience and level of social capital; the autonomy to make binding rules; and a wide diversity of rules that are used to change the structure of the situation (see literature cited in Ostrom, forthcoming).

Some consistent findings are emerging from empirical field research. A frequent finding is that when the users of a common-pool resource organize themselves to devise and enforce some of their own basic rules, they tend to manage local resources more sustainably than when rules are externally imposed on them (for example, Tang, 1992; Blomquist, 1992; Baland and Platteau, 1996; Wade, 1994). Common-pool resources are natural or humanly created systems that generate a finite flow of benefits where it is costly to exclude beneficiaries and one person's consumption subtracts from the amount of benefits available to others (Ostrom, Gardner and Walker, 1994). The users of a common-pool resource face a first-level dilemma that each individual would prefer that others control their use of the resource while each is able to use the resource freely. An effort to change these rules is a second-level dilemma, since the new rules that they share are a public good. Thus, users face a collective action problem, similar in many respects to the experiments discussed above, of how to cooperate when their immediate best-response strategies lead to suboptimal outcomes for all. A key question now is: How does evolutionary theory help us understand the well-established finding that many groups of individuals overcome both dilemmas? Further, how can we understand how self-organized resource regimes that rarely rely on external third-party enforcement, frequently outperform government-owned resource regimes that rely on externally enforced, formal rules?

The Emergence of Self-Organized Collective Action

From evolutionary theory, we should expect some individuals to have an initial propensity to follow a norm of reciprocity and to be willing to restrict their own use of a common pool resource so long as almost everyone reciprocates. If a small core group of users identify each other, they can begin a process of cooperation without having to devise a full-blown organization with all of the rules that they might eventually need to sustain cooperation over time. The presence of a leader or entrepreneur, who articulates different ways of organizing to improve joint outcomes, is frequently an important initial stimulus (Frohlich, Oppenheimer and Young, 1971; Varughese, 1999).[12]

If a group of users can determine its own membership—including those who agree to use the resource according to their agreed-upon rules and excluding those who do not agree to these rules—the group has made an important first step toward the development of greater trust and reciprocity. Group boundaries are frequently marked by well-understood criteria, like everyone who lives in a particular community or has joined a specific local cooperative. Membership may also be marked by symbolic boundaries and involve complex rituals and beliefs that help solidify individual beliefs about the trustworthiness of others.

Design Principles of Long-Surviving, Self-Organized Resource Regimes

Successful self-organized resource regimes can initially draw upon locally evolved norms of reciprocity and trustworthiness and the likely presence of local leaders in most community settings. More important, however, for explaining their long-term survival and comparative effectiveness, resource regimes that have flourished over multiple generations tend to be characterized by a set of design principles. These design principles are extensively discussed in Ostrom (1990) and have been subjected to extensive empirical testing.[13] Evolutionary theory helps to explain how these design principles work to help groups sustain and build their cooperation over long periods of time.

We have already discussed the first design principle—the presence of clear boundary rules. Using this principle enables participants to know who is in and who is out of a defined set of relationships and thus with whom to cooperate. The second design principle is that the local rules-in-use restrict the amount, timing, and technology of harvesting the resource; allocate benefits proportional to required inputs; and are crafted to take local conditions into account. If a group of users is going to harvest from a resource over the long run, they must devise rules related to how much, when, and how different products are to be harvested, and they need to assess the costs on users of operating a system. Well-tailored rules help to account for the perseverance of the resource itself. How to relate user inputs to the benefits they obtain is a crucial element of establishing a fair system (Trawick, 1999). If some users get all the benefits and pay few of the costs, others become unwilling to follow rules over time.

In long-surviving irrigation systems, for example, subtly different rules are used in each system for assessing water fees used to pay for maintenance activities, but water tends to be allocated proportional to fees or other required inputs (Bardhan, 1999). Sometimes water and responsibilities for resource inputs are distributed on a share basis, sometimes on the order in which water is taken, and sometimes strictly on the amount of land irrigated. No single set of rules defined for all irrigation systems in a region would satisfy the particular problems in managing each of these broadly similar, but distinctly different, systems (Tang, 1992; Lam, 1998).

The third design principle is that most of the individuals affected by a resource regime can participate in making and modifying their rules. Resource regimes that use this principle are both able to tailor better rules to local circumstances and to devise rules that are considered fair by participants. The Chisasibi Cree, for example, have devised a complex set of entry and authority rules related to the fish stocks of James Bay as well as the beaver stock located in their defined hunting territory. Berkes (1987, p. 87) explains that these resource systems and the rules used to regulate them have survived and prospered for so long because effective "social mechanisms ensure adherence to rules which exist by virtue of mutual consent within the community. People who violate these rules suffer not only a loss of favor from the animals (important in the Cree ideology of hunting) but also social disgrace." Fair rules of distribution help to build trusting relationships, since more individuals are willing to abide by these rules because they participated in their design and also because they meet shared concepts of fairness (Bowles, 1998).

In a study of 48 irrigation systems in India, Bardhan (1999) finds that the quality of maintenance of irrigation canals is significantly lower on those systems where farmers perceive the rules to be made by a local elite. On the other hand, those farmers (of the 480 interviewed) who responded that the rules have been crafted by most of the farmers, as contrasted to the elite or the government, have a more positive attitude about the water allocation rules and the rule compliance of other farmers. Further, in all of the villages where a government agency decides how water is to be allocated and distributed, frequent rule violations are reported and farmers tend to contribute less to the local village fund. Consistent with this is the finding by Ray and Williams (1999) that the deadweight loss from upstream farmers stealing water on government-owned irrigation systems in Maharashtra, India, approaches one-fourth of the revenues that could be earned in an efficient water allocation and pricing regime.

Few long-surviving resource regimes rely only on endogenous levels of trust and reciprocity. The fourth design principle is that most long-surviving resource regimes select their own monitors, who are accountable to the users or are users themselves and who keep an eye on resource conditions as well as on user behavior. Further, the fifth design principle points out that these resource regimes use *graduated sanctions* that depend on the seriousness and context of the offense. By creating official positions for local monitors, a resource regime does not have to rely only on willing punishers to impose personal costs on those who break a rule. The community legitimates a position. In some systems, users rotate into this position so everyone has a chance to be a participant as well as a monitor. In other systems, all participants contribute resources and they hire monitors jointly. With local monitors, conditional cooperators are assured that someone is generally checking on the conformance of others to local rules. Thus, they can continue their own cooperation without constant fear that others are taking advantage of them.

On the other hand, the initial sanctions that are imposed are often so low as to have no impact on an expected benefit-cost ratio of breaking local rules (given the substantial temptations frequently involved). Rather, the initial sanction needs to be considered more as information both to the person who is "caught" and to others in the community.

Everyone can make an error or can face difficult problems leading them to break a rule. Rule infractions, however, can generate a downward cascade of cooperation in a group that relies only on conditional cooperation and has no capacity to sanction (for example, Kikuchi et al., 1998). In a regime that uses graduated punishments, however, a person who purposely or by error breaks a rule is notified that others notice the infraction (thereby increasing the individual's confidence that others would also be caught). Further, the individual learns that others basically continue to extend their trust and want only a small token to convey a recognition that the mishap occurred. Self-organized regimes rely more on what Margaret Levi calls "quasi-voluntary" cooperation than either strictly voluntary or coerced cooperation (Levi, 1988). A real threat to the continuance of self-organized regimes occurs, however, if some participants break rules repeatedly. The capability to escalate sanctions enables such a regime to warn members that if they do not conform they will have to pay ever-higher sanctions and may eventually be forced to leave the community.

Let me summarize my argument to this point. When the users of a resource design their own rules (Design Principle 3) that are enforced by local users or accountable to them (Design Principle 4) using graduated sanctions (Design Principle 5) that define who has rights to withdraw from the resource (Design Principle 1) and that effectively assign costs proportionate to benefits (Design Principle 2), collective action and monitoring problems are solved in a reinforcing manner (Agrawal, 1999).

Individuals who think a set of rules will be effective in producing higher joint benefits and that monitoring (including their own) will protect them against being a sucker are willing to undertake conditional cooperation. Once some users have made contingent self-commitments, they are then motivated to monitor other people's behavior, at least from time to time, to assure themselves that others are following the rules most of the time. Conditional cooperation and mutual monitoring reinforce one another, especially in regimes where the rules are designed to reduce monitoring costs. Over time, further adherence to shared norms evolves and high levels of cooperation are achieved without the need to engage in very close and costly monitoring to enforce rule conformance.

The operation of these principles is then bolstered by the sixth design principle that points to the importance of access to rapid, low-cost, local arenas to resolve conflict among users or between users and officials. Rules, unlike physical constraints, have to be understood to be effective. There are always situations in which participants can interpret a rule that they have jointly made in different ways. By devising simple, local mechanisms to get conflicts aired immediately and resolutions that are generally known in the community, the number of conflicts that reduce trust can be reduced. If individuals are going to follow rules over a long period of time, some mechanism for discussing and resolving what constitutes a rule infraction is necessary to the continuance of rule conformance itself.

The capability of local users to develop an evermore effective regime over time is affected by whether they have minimal recognition of the right to organize by a national or local government. This is the seventh design principle. While some resource regimes have operated for relatively long times without such rights (Ghate, 2000), participants have had to rely almost entirely on unanimity as the rule used to change rules. (Otherwise, any temporarily disgruntled participant who voted against a rule change could go to the external authorities to threaten the regime itself!) Unanimity as a decision rule for changing rules imposes high transaction costs and prevents a group from searching for better matched rules at relatively lower costs.

Users frequently devise their own rules without creating formal, governmental jurisdictions for this purpose. In many in-shore fisheries, for example, local fishers devise extensive rules defining who can use a fishing ground and what kind of equipment can be used (Acheson, 1988; Schlager, 1994). As long as external governmental officials give at least minimal recognition to the legitimacy of such rules, the fishers themselves may be able to enforce the rules. But if external governmental officials presume that only they can make authoritative rules, then it is difficult for local users to sustain a self-organized regime (Johnson and Libecap, 1982).

When common pool resources are somewhat larger, an eighth design principle tends to characterize successful systems—the presence of governance activities organized in multiple layers of nested enterprises. The rules appropriate for allocating water among major branches of an irrigation system, for example, may not be appropriate for allocating water among farmers along a single distributory channel. Consequently, among long-enduring self-governed regimes, smaller-scale organizations tend to be nested in ever-larger organizations. It is not unusual to find a large, farmer-governed irrigation system, for example, with five layers of organization each with its own distinct set of rules (Yoder, 1992).

Threats to Sustained Collective Action

All economic and political organizations are vulnerable to threats, and self-organized resource-governance regimes are no exception. Both exogenous and endogenous factors challenge their long-term viability. Here we will concentrate on those factors that affect the distribution of types of participants within a regime and the strength of the norms of trust and reciprocity held by participants. Major migration (out of or into an area) is always a threat that may or may not be countered effectively. Out-migration may change the economic viability of a regime due to loss of those who contribute needed resources. In-migration may bring new participants who do not trust others and do not rapidly learn social norms that have been established over a long period of time. Since collective action is largely based on mutual trust, some self-organized resource regimes that are in areas of rapid settlement have disintegrated within relatively short times (Baland and Platteau, 1996).

In addition to rapid shifts in population due to market changes or land distribution policies, several more exogenous and endogenous threats have been identified in the empirical literature (Sengupta, 1991; Bates, 1987; and literature cited in Ostrom, 1998b; Britt, 2000). These include: 1) efforts by national governments to impose a single set of rules on all governance units in a region; 2) rapid changes in technology, in factor availability, and in reliance on monetary transactions; 3) transmission failures from one generation to the next of the operational principles on which self-organized governance is based; 4) turning to external sources of help too frequently; 5) international aid that does not take account of indigenous knowledge and institutions; 6) growth of corruption and other forms of opportunistic behavior; and 7) a lack of large-scale institutional arrangements that provide fair and low-cost resolution mechanisms for conflicts that arise among local regimes, educational and extension facilities, and insurance mechanisms to help when natural disasters strike at a local level.

Contextual variables are thus essential for understanding the initial growth and sustainability of collective action as well as the challenges that long-surviving, self-organized regimes must try to overcome. Simply saying that context matters is not, however, a satisfactory theoretical approach. Adopting an evolutionary approach is the first step toward a more general theoretical synthesis that addresses the question of how context matters. In particular, we need to address how context affects the presence or absence of conditional cooperators and willing punishers and the likelihood that the norms held by these participants are adopted and strengthened by others in a relevant population.

CONCLUSION

Both laboratory experiments and field studies confirm that a substantial number of collective action situations are resolved successfully, at least in part. The old-style notion, pre-Mancur Olson, that groups would find ways to act in their own collective interest was not entirely misguided. Indeed, recent developments in evolutionary theory—including the study of cultural evolution—have begun to provide genetic and adaptive underpinnings for the propensity to cooperate based on the development and growth of social norms. Given the frequency and diversity of collective action situations in all modern economies, this represents a more optimistic view than the zero contribution hypothesis. Instead of pure pessimism or pure optimism, however, the picture requires further work to explain why some contextual variables enhance cooperation while others discourage it.

Empirical and theoretical work in the future needs to ask how a large array of contextual variables affects the processes of teaching and evoking social norms; of informing participants about the behavior of others and their adherence to social norms; and of rewarding those who use social norms, such as reciprocity, trust, and fairness. We need to understand how institutional, cultural, and biophysical contexts affect the types of individuals who are recruited into and leave particular types of collective action situations, the kind of information that is made available about past actions, and how individuals can themselves change structural variables so as to enhance the probabilities of norm-using types being involved and growing in strength over time.

Further developments along these lines are essential for the development of public policies that enhance socially beneficial, cooperative behavior based in part on social norms. It is possible that past policy initiatives to encourage collective action that were based primarily on externally changing payoff structures for rational egoists may have been misdirected—and perhaps even crowded out the formation of social norms that might have enhanced cooperative behavior in their own way. Increasing the authority of individuals to devise their own rules may well result in processes that allow social norms to evolve and thereby increase the probability of individuals better solving collective action problems.

REFERENCES

Acheson, James M. 1988. *The Lobster Gangs of Maine.* Hanover, NH: University Press of New England.

Agrawal, Arun. 1999. *Greener Pastures: Politics, Markets, and Community among a Migrant Pastoral People.* Durham, NC: Duke University Press.

Ahn, Toh-Kyeong, Elinor Ostrom, David Schmidt and James Walker. 1999. "Dilemma Games: Game Parameters and Matching Protocols." Bloomington: Indiana University, Workshop in Political Theory and Policy Analysis, Working paper.

Ahn, Toh-Kyeong, Elinor Ostrom and James Walker. 1998. "Trust and Reciprocity: Experimental Evidence from PD Games." Bloomington: Indiana University, Workshop in Political Theory and Policy Analysis, Working paper.

Asquith, Nigel M. 1999. *How Should the World Bank Encourage Private Sector Investment in Biodiversity Conservation?* A Report Prepared for Kathy MacKinnon, Biodiversity Specialist, The World Bank, Washington, D.C. Durham, North Carolina: Sanford Institute of Public Policy, Duke University.

Axelrod, Robert. 1986. "An Evolutionary Approach to Norms." *American Political Science Review.* December, 80:4, pp. 1095–1111.

Baland, Jean-Marie and Jean-Philippe Platteau. 1996. *Halting Degradation of Natural Resources: Is There a Role for Rural Communities?* Oxford: Clarendon Press.

Bardhan, Pranab. 1999. "Water Community: An Empirical Analysis of Cooperation on Irrigation in South India." Berkeley: University of California, Department of Economics, Working paper.

Barkow, Jerome H., Leda Cosmides and John Tooby, eds. 1992. *The Adapted Mind: Evolutionary Psychology and the Generation of Culture.* Oxford: Oxford University Press.

Bates, Robert H. 1987. *Essays on the Political Economy of Rural Africa.* Berkeley: University of California Press.

Berkes, Fikret. 1987. "Common Property Resource Management and Cree Indian Fisheries in Subarctic Canada," in *The Question of the Commons: The Culture and Ecology of Communal Resources.* Bonnie J. McCay and James Acheson, eds. Tucson: University of Arizona Press, pp. 66–91.

Blomquist, William. 1992. *Dividing the Waters: Governing Groundwater in Southern California.* San Francisco, CA: ICS Press.

Bohnet, Iris and Bruno S. Frey. 1999. "The Sound of Silence in Prisoner's Dilemma and Dictator Games." *Journal of Economic Behavior and Organization.* January, 38:1, pp. 43–58.

Bohnet, Iris, Bruno S. Frey and Steffen Huck. 1999. "More Order with Less Law: On Contract Enforcement, Trust, and Crowding." Cambridge, MA: Harvard University, Working paper.

Börgers, Tilman and Rajiv Sarin. 1997. "Learning Through Reinforcement and Replicator Dynamics." *Journal of Economic Theory.* 77, pp. 1–14.

Bowles, Samuel. 1998. "Endogenous Preferences: The Cultural Consequences of Markets and Other Economic

Institutions." *Journal of Economic Literature.* March, 36, pp. 75–111.

Boyd, Robert and Peter J. Richerson. 1985. *Culture and the Evolutionary Process.* Chicago: University of Chicago Press.

Britt, Charla. 2000. "Forestry and Forest Policies." Bloomington: Indiana University, Workshop in Political Theory and Policy Analysis, Working paper.

Bromley, Daniel W. et al., eds. 1992. *Making the Commons Work: Theory, Practice, and Policy.* San Francisco, CA: ICS Press.

Cain, Michael. 1998. "An Experimental Investigation of Motives and Information in the Prisoner's Dilemma Game." *Advances in Group Processes.* 15, pp. 133–60.

Cameron, Lisa. 1995. "Raising the Stakes in the Ultimatum Game: Experimental Evidence from Indonesia." Princeton, NJ: Princeton University, Discussion paper.

Cardenas, Juan-Camilo, John K. Stranlund and Cleve E. Willis. 2000. "Local Environmental Control and Institutional Crowding-Out." *World Development.* Autumn, forthcoming.

Chong, Dennis. 1991. *Collective Action and the Civil Rights Movement.* Chicago: University of Chicago Press.

Clark, Andy and Annette Karmiloff-Smith. 1991. "The Cognizer's Innards: A Psychological and Philosophical Perspective on the Development of Thought." *Mind and Language.* Winter, 8:4, pp. 487–519.

Crawford, Sue E. S. and Elinor Ostrom. 1995. "A Grammar of Institutions." *American Political Science Review.* September, 89:3, pp. 582–600.

Cummins, Denise D. 1996. "Evidence of Deontic Reasoning in 3- and 4-Year-Olds." *Memory and Cognition.* 24, pp. 823–29.

Davis, Douglas D. and Charles A. Holt. 1993. *Experimental Economics.* Princeton, NJ: Princeton University Press.

Dawes, Robyn M., Jeanne McTavish and Harriet Shaklee. 1977. "Behavior, Communication, and Assumptions about Other People's Behavior in a Commons Dilemma Situation." *Journal of Personality and Social Psychology.* 35:1, pp. 1–11.

Epstein, Joshua M. and Robert Axtell. 1996. *Growing Artificial Societies: Social Science from the Bottom Up.* Cambridge, MA: MIT Press.

Eshel, Ilan, Larry Samuelson and Avner Shaked. 1998. "Altruists, Egoists, and Hooligans in a Local Interaction Model." *American Economic Review.* March, 88:1, pp. 157–79.

Feeny, David, Fikret Berkes, Bonnie J. McCay and James M. Acheson. 1990. "The Tragedy of the Commons: Twenty-Two Years Later." *Human Ecology.* 18:1, pp. 1–19.

Fehr, Ernst and Simon Gächter. Forthcoming. "Cooperation and Punishment in Public Goods Experiments." *American Economic Review.* 90:1.

Fehr, Ernst and Klaus Schmidt. 1999. "A Theory of Fairness, Competition, and Cooperation." *Quarterly Journal of Economics.* 114:3, pp. 817–68.

Frank, Robert H., Thomas Gilovich and Dennis T. Regan. 1993. "The Evolution of One-Shot Cooperation: An Experiment." *Ethology and Sociobiology.* July, 14, pp. 247–56.

Frey, Bruno S. 1994. "How Intrinsic Motivation is Crowded Out and In." *Rationality and Society.* 6, pp. 334–52.

Frohlich, Norman and Joe A. Oppenheimer. 1996. "Experiencing Impartiality to Invoke Fairness in the N-PD: Some Experimental Results." *Public Choice.* 86, pp. 117–35.

Frohlich, Norman, Joe A. Oppenheimer and Oran Young. 1971. *Political Leadership and Collective Goods.* Princeton, NJ: Princeton University Press.

Ghate, Rucha. 2000. "The Role of Autonomy in Self-Organizing Process: A Case Study of Local Forest Management in India." Bloomington: Indiana University, Workshop in Political Theory and Policy Analysis, Working paper.

Güth, Werner. 1995. "An Evolutionary Approach to Explaining Cooperative Behavior by Reciprocal Incentives." *International Journal of Game Theory.* 24, pp. 323–44.

Güth, Werner and Hartmut Kliemt. 1998. "The Indirect Evolutionary Approach: Bridging the Gap between Rationality and Adaptation." *Rationality and Society.* August, 10:3, pp. 377–99.

Güth, Werner and Menahem Yaari. 1992. "An Evolutionary Approach to Explaining Reciprocal Behavior in a Simple Strategic Game," in *Explaining Process and Change. Approaches to Evolutionary Economics.* Ulrich Witt, ed. Ann Arbor: University of Michigan Press, pp. 23–34.

Hardin, Russell. 1971. "Collective Action as an Agreeable *n*-Prisoners' Dilemma." *Science.* September-October, 16, pp. 472–81.

Hardin, Russell. 1982. *Collective Action.* Baltimore, MD: Johns Hopkins University Press.

Hess, Charlotte. 1999. *A Comprehensive Bibliography of Common Pool Resources.* CD-ROM. Bloomington:

Indiana University, Workshop in Political Theory and Policy Analysis.

Isaac, R. Mark, James Walker and Arlington W. Williams. 1994. "Group Size and the Voluntary Provision of Public Goods: Experimental Evidence Utilizing Large Groups." *Journal of Public Economics.* May, 54:1, pp. 1–36.

Johnson, Ronald N. and Gary D. Libecap. 1982. "Contracting Problems and Regulation: The Case of the Fishery." *American Economic Review.* December, 27:5, pp. 1005–1023.

Kagel, John and Alvin Roth, eds. 1995. *The Handbook of Experimental Economics.* Princeton, NJ: Princeton University Press.

Kikuchi, Masao, Yoriko Watanabe and Toshio Yamagishi. 1996. "Accuracy in the Prediction of Others' Trustworthiness and General Trust: An Experimental Study." *Japanese Journal of Experimental Social Psychology.* 37:1, pp. 23–36.

Kikuchi, Masao, Masako Fujita, Esther Marciano and Yujiro Hayami. 1998. "State and Community in the Deterioration of a National Irrigation System." Paper presented at the World Bank-EDI Conference on "Norms and Evolution in the Grassroots of Asia," Stanford University, February 6–7.

Kreps, David M., Paul Milgrom, John Roberts and Robert Wilson. 1982. "Rational Cooperation in the Finitely Repeated Prisoner's Dilemma." *Journal of Economic Theory.* 27, pp. 245–52.

Lam, Wai Fung. 1998. *Governing Irrigation Systems in Nepal: Institutions, Infrastructure, and Collective Action.* Oakland, CA: ICS Press.

Ledyard, John. 1995. "Public Goods: A Survey of Experimental Research," in *The Handbook of Experimental Economics.* John Kagel and Alvin Roth, eds. Princeton, NJ: Princeton University Press, pp. 111–94.

Levi, Margaret. 1988. *Of Rule and Revenue.* Berkeley: University of California Press.

Lichbach, Mark Irving. 1996. *The Cooperator's Dilemma.* Ann Arbor: University of Michigan Press.

Manktelow, Ken I. and David E. Over. 1991. "Social Roles and Utilities in Reasoning with Deontic Conditionals." *Cognition.* 39, pp. 85–105.

McCabe, Kevin A., Stephen J. Rassenti and Vernon L. Smith. 1996. "Game Theory and Reciprocity in Some Extensive Form Experimental Games." *Proceedings of the National Academy of Sciences.* November, 93, 13,421–13,428.

McCabe, Kevin A. and Vernon L. Smith. 1999. "Strategic Analysis by Players in Games: What Information Do They Use." Tucson: University of Arizona, Economic Research Laboratory, Working paper.

Milgrom, Paul R., Douglass C. North and Barry R. Weingast. 1990. "The Role of Institutions in the Revival of Trade: The Law Merchant, Private Judges, and the Champagne Fairs." *Economics and Politics.* March, 2:1, pp. 1–23.

Montgomery, Michael R. and Richard Bean. 1999. "Market Failure, Government Failure, and the Private Supply of Public Goods: The Case of Climate-Controlled Walkway Networks." *Public Choice.* June, 99:3/4, pp. 403–37.

Morrow, Christopher E. and Rebecca Watts Hull. 1996. "Donor-Initiated Common Pool Resource Institutions: The Case of the Yanesha Forestry Cooperative." *World Development.* 24:10, pp. 1641–1657.

Nowak, Martin A. and Karl Sigmund. 1998. "Evolution of Indirect Reciprocity by Image Scoring." *Nature.* 393:6685, pp. 573–77.

Oaksford, Mike and Nick Chater. 1994. "A Rational Analysis of the Selection Task as Optimal Data Selection." *Psychological Review.* 101:4, pp. 608–31.

Offerman, Theo. 1997. *Beliefs and Decision Rules in Public Goods Games: Theory and Experiments.* Dordrecht, the Netherlands: Kluwer Academic Publishers.

Olson, Mancur. 1965. *The Logic of Collective Action: Public Goods and the Theory of Groups.* Cambridge, MA: Harvard University Press.

Opp, Karl-Dieter, Peter Voss and Christiana Gern. 1995. *Origins of Spontaneous Revolution.* Ann Arbor: University of Michigan Press.

Ostrom, Elinor. 1990. *Governing the Commons: The Evolution of Institutions for Collective Action.* New York: Cambridge University Press.

Ostrom, Elinor. 1998a. "A Behavioral Approach to the Rational Choice Theory of Collective Action." *American Political Science Review.* March, 92:1, pp. 1–22.

Ostrom, Elinor. 1998b. "Institutional Analysis, Design Principles, and Threats to Sustainable Community Governance and Management of Commons," in *Law and the Governance of Renewable Resources: Studies from Northern Europe and Africa.* Erling Berge and Nils Christian Stenseth, eds. Oakland, CA: ICS Press, pp. 27–53.

Ostrom, Elinor. Forthcoming. "Reformulating the Commons," in *The Commons Revisited: An Americas Perspective.* Joanna Burger, Richard Norgaard, Elinor Ostrom, David Policansky, and Bernard Goldstein, eds. Washington, DC: Island Press.

Ostrom, Elinor, Roy Gardner and James Walker. 1994. *Rules, Games, and Common-Pool Resources.* Ann Arbor: University of Michigan Press.

Ostrom, Elinor and James Walker. 1997. "Neither Markets Nor States: Linking Transformation Processes in Collective Action Arenas," in *Perspectives on Public Choice: A Handbook.* Dennis C. Mueller, ed. Cambridge: Cambridge University Press, pp. 35–72.

Pinker, Steven. 1994. *The Language Instinct.* New York: W. Morrow.

Posner, Richard A. and Eric B. Rasmusen. 1999. "Creating and Enforcing Norms, with Special Reference to Sanctions." *International Review of Law and Economics.* September, 19:3, pp. 369–82.

Rabin, Matthew. 1993. "Incorporating Fairness into Game Theory and Economics." *American Economic Review.* 83, pp. 1281–1302.

Ray, Ishar and Jeffrey Williams. 1999. "Evaluation of Price Policy in the Presence of Water Theft." *American Journal of Agricultural Economics.* November, 81, pp. 928–41.

Schlager, Edella. 1994. "Fishers' Institutional Responses to Common-Pool Resource Dilemmas," in *Rules, Games, and Common-Pool Resources.* Elinor Ostrom, Roy Gardner, and James Walker, eds. Ann Arbor: University of Michigan Press, pp. 247–65.

Selten, Reinhard. 1991. "Evolution, Learning, and Economic Behavior." *Games and Economic Behavior.* February, 3:1, pp. 3–24.

Sengupta, Nirmal. 1991. *Managing Common Property: Irrigation in India and the Philippines.* New Delhi: Sage.

Sethi, Rajiv and Eswaran Somanathan. 1996. "The Evolution of Social Norms in Common Property Resource Use." *American Economic Review.* September, 86:4, pp. 766–88.

Tang, Shui Yan. 1992. *Institutions and Collective Action: Self Governance in Irrigation.* San Francisco, CA: ICS Press.

Trawick, Paul. 1999. "The Moral Economy of Water: 'Comedy' and 'Tragedy' in the Andean Commons." Lexington: University of Kentucky, Department of Anthropology, Working paper.

Varughese, George. 1999. "Villagers, Bureaucrats, and Forests in Nepal: Designing Governance for a Complex Resource." Ph.D. dissertation, Indiana University.

Wade, Robert. 1994. *Village Republics: Economic Conditions for Collective Action in South India.* San Francisco, CA: ICS Press.

Yoder, Robert D. 1992. *Performance of the Chhattis Mauja Irrigation System, a Thirty-five Hundred Hectare System Built and Managed by Farmers in Nepal.* Colombo, Sri Lanka: International Irrigation Management Institute.

NOTES

1. See Milgrom, North and Weingast (1990) and Bromley et al. (1992). An extensive bibliography by Hess (1999) on diverse institutions for dealing with common pool resources can be searched on the web at <http://www.indiana.edu/~workshop/wsl/wsl.html>.

2. In a linear public good game, utility is a linear function of individual earnings,

$$U_i = U_i\left[\left(E - x_i\right) + A \cdot P\left(\sum x_i\right)\right],$$

where E is an individual endowment of assets, x_i is the amount of this endowment contributed to provide the good, A is the allocation formula used to distribute the group benefit to individual players, and P is the production function. In a linear public good game, A is specified as $1/N$ and $0 < 1/N < P < 1$ (but both of these functions vary in other types of collective action). So long as $P < 1$, contributing to the collective good is never an optimal strategy for a fully self-interested player.

3. Even more startling, Bohnet and Frey (1999) find that simply allowing subjects to see the other persons with whom they are playing greatly increases cooperation as contrasted to completely anonymous situations. Further, Frank, Gilovich and Regan (1993) find that allowing subjects to have a face-to-face discussion enables them to predict who will play cooperatively at a rate significantly better than chance.

4. Although the discussion here focuses on collective action and public good games in particular, a broader range of experiments exists in which the rational egoist's prediction pans out badly. These include the ultimatum game, the dictator game, the trust game, and common-pool resources games with communication.

5. Most of these experiments involve ultimatum games but the findings are quite relevant. Cameron (1995), for example, conducted ultimatum experiments in Indonesia and thereby was able to use sums that amounted to three months' wages. In this extremely tempting situation, she still found that 56 percent of the Proposers allocated between 40 and 50 percent of this very substantial sum to the Responder.

6. For examples of strict evolutionary models involving collective action, see Nowak and Sigmund (1998), Sethi and Somanathan (1996) and Epstein and Axtell (1996).

7. Eshel, Samuelson and Shaked (1998) develop a learning model where a population of Altruists who adopt a strategy of providing a local public good interacts in a local neighborhood with a population of Egoists who free ride. In this local interaction setting, Altruists' strategies are imitated sufficiently often in a Markovian learning process to become one of the absorbing states. Altruists

interacting with Egoists outside a circular local neighborhood are not so likely to survive.

8. This implies that, in a game where players know only their own payoffs and not the payoffs of others, they are more likely to behave like rational egoists. McCabe and Smith (1999) show that players tend to evolve toward the predicted, subgame perfect outcomes in experiments where they have only private information of their own payoffs and to cooperative outcomes when they have information about payoffs and the moves made by other players (see also McCabe, Rassenti and Smith, 1996).

9. Further, Kikuchi, Watanabe and Yamagishi (1996) have found that those who express a high degree of trust are able to predict others' behavior more accurately than those with low levels of trust.

10. To examine the frequency of nonrational egoist preferences, a group of 181 undergraduates was given a questionnaire containing a similar payoff structure on the first day of classes at Indiana University in January 1999. They were asked to rank their preferences. In this nondecision setting, 52 percent reflected preferences that were not consistent with being rational egoists; specifically, 27 percent ranked the outcome (C,C) over (D,C) and 25 percent were indifferent.

11. Bohnet, Frey and Huck (1999) set up a sequential prisoner's dilemma, but add a regulatory regime where a "litigation process" is initiated if there is a breach of performance. Cardenas, Stranlund and Willis (2000) describe an experiment based on harvesting from a common-pool resource conducted in three rural villages in Columbia where exogenous but imperfect rule enforcement generated less cooperation than allowing face-to-face communication.

12. Empirical studies of civil rights movements, where contributions can be very costly, find that organizers search for ways to assure potential participants of the importance of shared internal norms and that many others will also participate (Chong, 1991). Membership in churches and other groups that jointly commit themselves to protests and other forms of collective action is also an important factor (Opp, Voss and Gern, 1995).

13. The design principles that characterize long-standing common-pool resource regimes have now been subject to considerable further empirical studies since they were first articulated (Ostrom, 1990). While minor modifications have been offered to express the design principles somewhat differently, no empirical study has challenged their validity, to my knowledge (Morrow and Hull, 1996; Asquith, 1999; Bardhan, 1999; Lam, 1998).

Samuel Bowles and Herbert Gintis

The Evolutionary Basis of Collective Action

2006

1 INTRODUCTION

Many aspects of political behavior have been illuminated by standard models in which political actors maximize self-interested preferences. The works of Downs (1957), Buchanan and Tullock (1962), Buchanan, Tollison, and Tullock (1980), and Becker (1983), as well as those inspired by these seminal contributions, have contributed to our understanding of voter, party, and policy preferences, interest group politics, rent-seeking, coalition formation, bargaining, and other aspects of political behavior. Using this framework, works on electoral

Samuel Bowles and Herbert Gintis, "The Evolutionary Basis of Collective Action," from Barry R. Weingast and Donald A. Wittman, eds., *The Oxford Handbook of Political Economy*. Oxford: Oxford University Press, 2006. By permission of Oxford University Press.

support for the welfare state (Benabou and Ok 2001; Moene and Wallerstein 2002), informal enforcement of contracts (Greif 1994; Greif, Milgrom, and Weingast 1994), the efficiency of democratic governance (Wittman 1989), nationalism (Breton et al. 1995), and ethnic conflict (Varshney 2003) have produced important and sometimes surprising insights.

Yet as Ostrom (1998) and others have pointed out, a number of critical aspects of political behavior remain difficult to explain within this framework. These include the fact that people bother to vote at all, and electoral support for costly redistributive programs from which the voter concerned is unlikely to benefit and for which he will certainly pay additional taxes (Luttmer 2001; Fong 2001; Fong, Bowles, and Gintis 2004), and many forms of political violence (Stern 2003). Among the more striking examples of the shortcomings of the standard model is the large class of political behavior that takes the form of voluntary contribution to public goods. Included is participation in joint political activities and other forms of collective action (Moore 1978; Wood 2003; Scott 1976), the adherence to social norms (Young and Burke 2001; Andreoni, Erard, and Feinstein 1998), and the punishment of those violating social norms (Mahdi 1986; Harding 1978; Boehm 1993; Wiessner 2003).

When one is motivated to bear personal costs to help or to hurt others we say that one has *other-regarding* preferences, meaning that affecting the states experienced by someone other than oneself is part of one's motivations. Unlike the conventional self-regarding preferences of *Homo economicus,* social preferences are other-regarding. Generosity towards others and punishing those who violate norms are commonly motivated by other-regarding preferences.

We use the term self-regarding rather than "selfish" to describe the standard assumptions about preferences to avoid the circularity arising from the fact that all uncoerced actions are motivated by preferences and hence might confusingly be termed selfish, leaving only those actions that violate one's preference ordering to be called unselfish (but which would better be called non-rational). To explain behavior, both other-regarding and self-regarding preferences must be transitive, and when they are (as we assume) the actions they motivate are rational in the strict sense typically adopted in economics and decision theory. The common designation of generous behavior as "irrational" is based on a gratuitous conflation of rationality and self-regarding preferences.

We explore two problems in the study of the political behaviors supporting collective action. The first concerns the view frequently advanced by economists and biologists that cooperative behaviors can be fully explained on the basis of self-interested motivations, once one takes account of the repeated nature of interactions and the degree of genetic relatedness among members of a cooperating group. We show that repeated interactions and kin-based altruism, while strong influences on behavior in many settings, do not provide an adequate account of the forms of cooperation observed in natural and experimental settings.

These and other types of political behavior are based on preferences that include a concern for the well-being of others and a taste not only for fairness but also for retribution. We review recent behavioral experiments documenting the variety and extent of these so called social preferences and the manner in which the existence of even a minority of individuals with social preferences can dramatically affect group behavior (see Bowles and Gintis 2005*b*; Gintis et al. 2005; and Henrich et al. 2004 for a more extensive review of this evidence).

The second is the puzzle of how these social preferences could have evolved by means of genetic transmission and natural selection, or cultural learning and socialization, or both. The puzzle arises because the political behaviors motivated by social preferences are often altruistic in the biological sense—of conferring gains on others in one's group while entailing costs—and altruistic behaviors will be disadvantaged in most evolutionary processes that favor higher payoff types. Our treatment of these topics is necessarily cursory, drawing extensively on work presented more fully in Bowles and Gintis (2007), Gintis et al. (2005), and Henrich et al. (2004).

2 THE COOPERATIVE SPECIES

Cooperation among humans is unique in nature, extending to a large number of unrelated individuals and taking a vast array of forms. By cooperation we mean engaging with others in a mutually beneficial activity. Cooperative behavior may confer benefits net of costs on the individual cooperator, and thus may be motivated by entirely self-regarding preferences. In this case, cooperation is a form of what biologists call *mutualism,* namely an activity that confers net benefits both on the actor and on others.

But, cooperation may also incur net costs to the individual. In this case cooperative behavior constitutes a form of *altruism.* In contrast to mutualistic cooperation, altruistic cooperation would not be undertaken by an individual whose motives were entirely self-regarding and thus did not take account of the effects of one's actions on others.

While the high frequency of altruistic cooperation in humans relative to other species could be an evolutionary accident, a more plausible explanation is that altruistic cooperation among humans is the result of capacities that are unique to our species and that strongly promote our relative reproductive fitness. Thus we seek an explanation of cooperation that works for humans, but which, because it involves capacities that are unique to humans, does not work for other species, or works substantially less well.

Central to our explanation will be human cognitive, linguistic, and physical capacities that allow the formulation of general norms of social conduct, the emergence of social institutions regulating this conduct, the psychological capacity to internalize norms, and the capacity to base group membership on such non-kin characteristics as ethnicity and linguistic differences, which in turn facilitates costly conflicts among groups. Also important is the unique human capacity to use projectile weapons, a consequence of which is to lower the cost of punishing norm violators within a group, and to render intergroup conflicts more lethal.

Thus, our account of human sociality and its evolution hinges critically on a reconsideration of the canonical economic model of self-interested behavior. But more than individual motivation is involved. The extraordinary levels of cooperation observed in human society cannot be attributed simply to our generosity towards those with whom we interact or our capacity to favor the advancement of our nation or ethnic group over our individual well-being. The regulation of social interactions by group-level norms and institutions plays no less a role than altruistic individual motives in understanding how the cooperative species came to be. The institutions that regulate behaviors among non-kin affect the rewards and penalties associated with particular behaviors, often favoring the adoption of cooperative actions over others. In the social environments common to human interactions, the self-regarding are often induced to act in the interest of the group. Of course it will not do to posit these rules and institutions a priori. Rather, we show that these could have co-evolved with other human traits in a plausible representation of the relevant ecologies and social environments.

Cooperation is not an end to be valued in its own right, but rather is a means that under some conditions may contribute to human well-being. In other settings, competition plays no less essential a role. Similarly, the individual motives and group-level institutions that account for cooperation among humans include not only the most elevated—a concern for others, fair-mindedness, and democratic accountability of leaders, for example—but also the most venal: vengeance, exclusion of "outsiders," and frequent warfare among groups, for example.

Our reasoning is disciplined in three ways. First, the forms of cooperation we seek to explain are confirmed by natural observation, historical accounts, and behavioral experiments. Second, our account is based on a plausible evolutionary dynamic involving some combination of genetic and cultural transmission, the consistency of which can be demonstrated through formal modeling. Third, agent-based simulations show that our models can account for human cooperation under parameter values consistent with what can be reasonably inferred about the environments in which humans evolved.

3 MUTUALISTIC COOPERATION

Because mutualistic cooperation will be sustained by individuals with entirely self-regarding preferences, it is treated in standard biological and economic models as an expression of self-interest. "Natural selection favors these . . . behaviors," wrote Robert Trivers in his "The evolution of reciprocal altruism" (1971), "because in the long run they benefit the organism performing them. . . . two individuals who risk their lives to save each other will be selected over those who face drowning on their own" (pp. 34–5). Cooperation, in Trivers's interpretation, is simply symbiosis with a time lag. Trivers's explanation initially found favor among biologists and economists because it is consistent with both the common biological reasoning that natural selection will not favor altruistic behaviors and with the canonical economic assumption of self-interest.

Trivers identified the conditions under which assisting another would be reciprocated in the future with a likelihood sufficient to make mutual assistance a form of mutualism. These conditions favoring reciprocal altruism included an extended lifetime, mutual dependence, and other reasons for limited dispersal so that groups remain together, extended periods of parental care, attenuated dominance hierarchies, and frequent combat with conspecifics and predators. Foraging bands of humans, he pointed out, exhibit all of these conditions. Michael Taylor (1976) and Robert Axelrod and William Hamilton (1981) subsequently formalized Trivers's argument using the theory of repeated games. In economics, analogous reasoning is summarized in the folk theorem, which shows that cooperation among self-regarding individuals can be sustained as long as interactions are expected to be repeated with sufficient frequency and individuals are not too impatient (Fudenberg and Maskin 1986; Fudenberg, Levine, and Maskin 1994).

But, in many important human social environments, Trivers's conditions favoring reciprocal altruism do not hold, yet cooperation among non-kin is commonly observed. These include contributing to common projects when community survival is threatened, and cooperation among very large numbers of people who do not share common knowledge of one another's actions. In fact, the scope of application of the folk theorem is quite restricted, especially in groups of any significant size, once the problem of cooperation is posed in an evolutionary setting and account is taken of "noise" arising from mistaken behaviors and misinformation about the behaviors of others.

A plausible model of cooperation must satisfy the following five conditions. First, it must be *incentive compatible.* In particular, those who provide the rewards and inflict punishments dictated by the rules for cooperation must have the motivation to do so. Second, a model must be *dynamically stable,* in the sense that random fluctuations, errors, and mutations (the emergence of novel strategies) do not disrupt cooperation or entail excessive efficiency losses. Third, the organizational forms and incentive mechanisms deployed in the model must reflect the types of strategic interaction and incentives widely observed in human groups. In particular, the model should work well with group sizes on the order of ten to twenty, and the incentive to punish defectors should reflect those deployed in real-world public goods game settings. Fourth, the model should not require extraordinary *informational requirements.* Finally the model should work with *plausible discount factors.* It is reasonable to suppose that within a group faced by a public goods game, there will be a distribution of discount factors among members, and average discount factors can be high in some periods and low in others, as the probability of group dissolution rises and falls.

A careful analysis shows that all models of cooperation based on tit-for-tat and related repeated game strategies, when played among self-interested individuals violate at least one of these conditions, and hence fail to solve the problem of cooperation among unrelated agents.[1] First, reciprocal altruism fails when a social group is threatened with dissolution, since members who sacrifice now on behalf of group members do not have a high probability of being repaid in the (highly uncertain) future.

Second, many human interactions in the relevant evolutionary context took the form of n-person public goods games—food sharing and other co-insurance, upholding social norms among group members, information sharing, and common defense—rather than dyadic interactions. The difficulty in sustaining cooperation in public goods games by means of the standard tit-for-tat and related repeated game strategies increases exponentially with group size (Bowles and Gintis 2007), even if interactions are repeated with high probability. The reason is that in groups larger than two, withdrawing cooperation in response to a single defection imposes a blanket punishment on all, defectors and cooperators alike. But, targeting punishment on defectors alone does not work in large groups unless members have unrealistically accurate information about the actions taken by others.

Third, the contemporary study of human behavior has documented a large class of social behaviors inexplicable in terms of reciprocal altruism. For instance, there is extensive support for income redistribution in advanced industrial economies, even among those who cannot expect to be net beneficiaries (Fong, Bowles, and Gintis, 2005). Under some circumstances group incentives for large work teams are effective motivators even when the opportunity for reciprocation is absent and the benefits of cooperation are so widely shared that a self-interested group member would gain from free riding on the effort of others (Ghemawat 1995; Hansen 1997; Knez and Simester 2001). Finally, laboratory and field experiments show that other-regarding motives are frequently robust causes of cooperative behavior, even in one-shot, anonymous settings.

4 STRONG RECIPROCITY: EVIDENCE FROM BEHAVIORAL EXPERIMENTS

A more direct reason for doubting the interpretation that most cooperation is mutualistic is given by the compelling evidence that many (perhaps most) people behave in ways inconsistent with the assumption that they are motivated by self-regarding preferences. A suggestive body of evidence points to the importance of a suite of behaviors that we call *strong reciprocity.* A strong reciprocator comes to a new social situation with a predisposition to cooperate, is predisposed to respond to cooperative behavior on the part of others by maintaining or increasing his level of cooperation, and responds to antisocial behavior on the part of others by retaliating against the offenders, even at a cost to himself, and even when he cannot not reasonably expect future personal gains from such retaliation. The strong reciprocator is thus both a *conditionally altruistic cooperator* and a *conditionally altruistic punisher* whose actions benefit other group members at a personal cost. We call this "strong reciprocity" to distinguish it from "weak" (i.e. self-regarding) forms of reciprocity, such as Trivers's reciprocal altruism.

Strong reciprocity is an example of a larger class of so-called *social preferences* which describe the motivations of people who care (one way or the other) about the well-being of others, and not only have preferences over the states they and others experience but also care about how the states came about.

In the ultimatum game, under conditions of anonymity, two players are shown a sum of money, say \$10. One of the players, called the "proposer," is instructed to offer any number of dollars, from \$1 to \$10, to the second player, who is called the "responder." The proposer can make only one offer. The responder, again under conditions of anonymity, can either accept or reject this offer. If the responder accepts the offer, the money is shared accordingly. If the responder rejects the offer, both players receive nothing.

Since the game is played only once and the players do not know each other's identity, a self-interested responder will accept any positive amount of money. Knowing this, a self-interested proposer will offer the minimum possible amount, \$1, and this will be accepted. However, when actually played, *the self-interested outcome is never attained and never even approximated.* In fact, as many replications of this experiment have documented, under varying conditions and with varying amounts of money, proposers routinely offer respondents very substantial amounts (50 per cent of the total generally being the modal offer), and respondents frequently reject offers below

30 per cent (Camerer and Thaler 1995; Güth and Tietz 1990; Roth et al. 1991).

Strong reciprocity emerges in many other experimental games, some of which are described in Table 1 (from Camerer and Fehr 2004). In all cases, given the one-shot, anonymous nature of the game, self-regarding agents would neither contribute to the common good, nor reward others for so contributing. Nor would they punish others for failing to contribute. Yet, in each game, under many different conditions and in different cultures, a considerable fraction of agents contributes, and enough agents punish free riding that even the self-regarding agent often contributes simply to avoid punishment.

5 THE EVOLUTION OF STRONG RECIPROCITY

If preferences were entirely self-regarding, the extent of human cooperation would indeed be puzzling. But if social preferences are common, the puzzle takes a somewhat different form: how might strong reciprocity and other altruistic preferences that support cooperation have evolved over the course of human history? The puzzle is posed especially clearly if the processes of cultural and genetic evolution favor behavioral traits that on average are associated with higher levels of material success. We think that this assumption of what is called a *payoff monotonic dynamic* is not entirely adequate. But Gintis (2000) and Bowles and Gintis (2004) adopt just such an evolutionary model to show that individuals behaving as strong reciprocators can proliferate in a population in which they were initially rare, and that their presence in a population could sustain high levels of cooperation among group members.

One intuition behind these models is that in groups with strong reciprocators present, group members whose self-regarding preferences lead them to shirk on contributing to common projects will be punished by being ostracized from the group. Strong reciprocators bear the cost not only of contributing to common projects, but also of punishing the shirking of the self-interested members. If reciprocators are common enough, however, the self-interested members will conform to cooperative norms in order to escape punishment, thereby reducing or eliminating the fitness differences between the reciprocators and the self-interested members. A second argument supporting strong reciprocity is that groups with a sufficient proportion of strong reciprocators will be better able to survive such group crises as war, pestilence, and adverse climatic conditions. In such situations, a group of self-regarding agents would simply disband, since each member will do better to bear the personal costs of abandoning the group rather than bearing the even heavier costs of attempting to preserve the group, most of the gains of which would accrue to other group members. Since strong reciprocators enforce cooperation without regard for the possibility of extinction, a sufficient proportion of strong reciprocators can enhance the possibility of group survival.

Group-level characteristics—such as relatively small group size, limited migration, or frequent intergroup conflicts—have co-evolved with cooperative behaviors. Cooperation is thus based in part on the distinctive capacities of humans to construct institutional environments that limit within-group competition and reduce phenotypic variation within groups, thus heightening the relative importance of between-group competition, and hence allowing individually costly but in-group-beneficial behaviors to coevolve with these supporting environments through a process of interdemic selection.

The idea that the suppression of within-group competition may be a strong influence on evolutionary dynamics has been widely recognized in eusocial insects and other species. Alexander (1979), Boehm (1982), and Eibl-Eibesfeldt (1982) first applied this reasoning to human evolution, exploring the role of culturally transmitted practices that reduce phenotypic variation within groups. Group-level institutions thus are constructed environments capable of imparting distinctive direction and pace to the process of biological evolution and cultural change (Friedman and Singh 2001).

Table 1

Seven experimental games useful for measuring social preferences

Game	Definition of the Game	Real-life Example	Predictions with Selfish Players	Experimental Regularities, References	Interpretation
Prisoner's Dilemma Game	Two players, each of whom can either cooperate or defect. Payoffs are as follows: (payoff matrix: rows Cooperate / Defect; columns Cooperate / Defect) Cooperate, Cooperate: H,H; Cooperate, Defect: S,T Defect, Cooperate: T,S; Defect, Defect: L,L H > L, T > H, L > S	Production of negative externalities (pollution, loud noise), exchange without binding contracts, status competition.	Defect.	50% choose to cooperate. Communication increases frequency of cooperation. Dawes (1980).[a]	Reciprocate expected cooperation.
Public Goods Game	*n* players simultaneously decide about their contribution g_i. ($0 \leq g_i \leq y$) where *y* is players' endowment; each player *i* earns $\pi_i = y - g_i + mG$ where *G* is the sum of all contributions and $m < 1 < mn$.	Team compensation, cooperative production in simple societies, over-use of common resources (e.g. water, fishing grounds).	Each player contributes nothing; that is, $g_i = 0$.	Players contribute 50% of *y* in the one-short game. Contributions unravel over time. Majority chooses $g_i = 0$ in final period. Communication strongly increases cooperation. Individual punishment opportunities greatly increase contributions. Ledyard (1995).[a]	Reciprocate expected cooperation.
Ultimatum Game	Division of a fixed sum of money *S* between a proposer and a responder. Proposer offers *x*. If responder rejects *x* both earn zero; if *x* is accepted the proposer earns $S - x$ and the responder earns *x*.	Monopoly pricing of a perishable good; "11th hour" settlement offers before a time deadline.	Offer $x = \varepsilon$ where ε is the smallest money unit. Any $x > 0$ is accepted.	Most offers are between 0.3 and 0.5S. $x < 0.2S$ rejected half of the time. Competition among proposers has a strong *x*-increasing effect; competition among responders strongly decreases *x*. Güth, Schmittberger, and Schwartze (1982);[b] Camerer (2003).[a]	Responders punish unfair offers; negative reciprocity.
Dictator Game	Like the UG but the responder cannot reject; that is, the "proposer" dictates $(S - x, x)$.	Charitable sharing of a windfall gain (lottery winners giving anonymously to strangers).	No sharing; that is, $x = 0$.	On average "proposers" allocate $x = 0.2S$. Strong variations across experiments and across individuals. Kahneman, Knetsch, and Thaler (1986);[b] Camerer (2003).[a]	Pure altruism.

(*Continued*)

Table 1

Seven experimental games useful for measuring social preferences (Continued)

Game	Definition of the Game	Real-life Example	Predictions with Selfish Players	Experimental Regularities, References	Interpretation
Trust Game	Investor has endowment S and make a transfer y between 0 and S to the trustee. Trustee receives $3y$ and can send back any x between 0 and $3y$. Investor earns $S - y + x$. Trustee earns $3y - x$.	Sequential exchange without binding contracts (buying from sellers on eBay).	Trustee repays nothing: $x = 0$. Investor invests nothing: $y = 0$.	On average $y = 0.5S$ and trustees repay slightly less than $0.5S$. x is increasing in y. Berg, Dickhaut, and McCabe (1995);[b] Camerer (2003).[a]	Trustees show positive reciprocity.
Gift Exchange Game	"Employer" offers a wage w to the "Worker" and announces a desired effort level $\hat{e}$. If Worker rejects $(w, \hat{e})$ both earn nothing. If worker accepts, he can choose *any* e between 1 and 10. Then Employer earns $10e - w$ and Worker earns $w - c(e)$. $c(e)$ is the effort cost which is strictly increasing in e.	Non-contractibility or non-enforceability of the performance (effort, quality of goods) of workers or sellers.	Worker chooses $e = 1$. Employer pays the minimum wage.	Effort increases with the wage w. Employers pay wages that are far above the minimum. Workers accept offers with low wages but respond with $e = 1$. In contrast to the UG, competition among workers (i.e. responders) has no impact on wage offers. Fehr, Kirchsteiger, and Reidl (1993).[b]	Workers reciprocate generous wage offers. Employers appeal to workers' reciprocity by offering generous wages.
Third-party Punishment Game	A and B play a DG. C observes how much of amount S is allocated to B. C can punish A but the punishment is also costly for C.	Social disapproval of unacceptable treatment of others (scolding neighbors).	A allocates nothing to B. C never punishes A.	Punishment of A is higher, the less A allocates to B. Fehr and Fischbacher (2004).[b]	C sanctions violation of a sharing norm.

[a]Denotes survey papers.
[b]Denotes papers that introduced the respective games.
Source: Camerer and Fair 2004.

Bowles, Choi, and Hopfensitz (2003) models an evolutionary dynamic along these lines. They show that intergroup conflicts may explain the evolutionary success of both altruistic forms of human sociality towards non-kin, and group-level institutional structures such as resource-sharing that have emerged and diffused repeatedly in a wide variety of ecologies during the course of human history.

6 PROXIMATE MOTIVES: INTERNALIZED NORMS AND SOCIAL EMOTIONS

An *internal norm* is a pattern of behavior enforced in part by internal sanctions, including shame and guilt. Individuals follow internal norms when they value certain behaviors for their own sake, in addition to, or despite, the effects these behaviors have on personal fitness and/or perceived well-being. The ability to internalize norms is nearly universal among humans. All successful cultures foster internal norms that enhance personal fitness, such as future orientation, good personal hygiene, positive work habits, and control of emotions. Cultures also widely promote altruistic norms that subordinate the individual to group welfare, fostering such behaviors as bravery, honesty, fairness, willingness to cooperate, and empathy with the distress of others (Brown 1991).

If even a fraction of society internalizes the norms of cooperation and punish free riders and other norm violators, a high degree of cooperation can be maintained in the long run. The puzzles are two: why do we internalize norms, and why do cultures promote cooperative behaviors? Gintis (2003) provides an evolutionary model in which the capacity to internalize norms develops because this capacity enhances individual fitness in a world in which social behavior has become too complex to be learned through personal experience alone. It is not difficult to show that if an internal norm is fitness-enhancing, then for plausible patterns of socialization, the allele for internalization of norms is evolutionarily stable. This framework implements the suggestion in Simon (1990) that altruistic norms can "hitchhike" on the general tendency of internal norms to be fitness enhancing.

Pro-social emotions are physiological and psychological reactions that induce agents to engage in cooperative behaviors as we have defined them above. The pro-social emotions include some, such as shame, guilt, empathy, and sensitivity to social sanction, that induce agents to undertake constructive social interactions, and others, such as the desire to punish norm violators, that reduce free riding when the pro-social emotions fail to induce sufficiently cooperative behavior in some fraction of members of the social group (Frank 1987; Hirshleifer 1987). Without the pro-social emotions we would all be sociopaths, and human society would not exist, however strong the institutions of contract, governmental law enforcement, and reputation. Sociopaths have no mental deficit except that their capacity to experience shame, guilt, empathy, and remorse is severely attenuated or absent.

Pro-social emotions function like the basic emotion, "pain," in providing guides for action that bypass the explicit cognitive optimizing process that lies at the core of the standard behavioral model in economics. Antonio Damasio (1994, 173) calls these "somatic markers," that is, a bodily response that "forces attention on the negative outcome to which a given action may lead and functions as an automated alarm signal which says: beware of danger ahead if you choose the option that leads to this outcome. . . . the automated signal protects you against future losses." Emotions thus contribute to the decision-making process, not simply by clouding reason, but in beneficial ways as well. Damasio continues: "suffering puts us on notice. . . . it increases the probability that individuals will heed pain signals and act to avert their source or correct their consequences" (p. 264).

Does shame serve a purpose similar to that of pain? If being socially devalued has fitness costs, and if the amount of shame is closely correlated with the level of these fitness costs, then the answer is affirmative. Shame, like pain, is an aversive stimulus that leads the agent experiencing it to repair the situation that led to the stimulus, and to avoid such situations in the future. Shame, like pain, replaces an involved optimization process with a simple message: whatever you did, undo it if possible, and do not do it again.

Since shame is evolutionarily selected and is costly to use, it very likely confers a selective advantage on those who experience it. Two types of selective advantage are at work here. First, shame may raise the fitness of an agent who has incomplete information (e.g., as to how fitness reducing a particular antisocial action is), limited or imperfect information-processing capacity, and/or a tendency to undervalue costs and benefits that accrue in the future. Probably all three conditions conspire to react suboptimally to social disapprobation in the absence of shame, and shame brings us closer to the optimum. Of course the role of shame in alerting us to negative consequences in the future presupposes that society is organized to impose those costs on rule violators. The emotion of shame may have co-evolved with the emotions motivating punishment of antisocial actions (the reciprocity motive in our model).

The second selective advantage to those experiencing shame arises through the effects of group competition. Where the emotion of shame is common, punishment of antisocial actions will be particularly effective and as a result seldom used. Thus groups in which shame is common can sustain high levels of group cooperation at limited cost and will be more likely to spread through interdemic group selection (Bowles and Gintis 2004; Boyd et al. 2003). Shame thus serves as a means of economizing on costly within-group punishment.

While we think the evidence is strong that pro-social emotions account for important forms of human cooperation, there is no universally accepted model of how emotions combine with more cognitive processes to affect behaviors. Nor is there much agreement on how best to represent the pro-social emotions that support cooperative behaviors.

Bowles and Gintis (2005*b*) considers a public goods game where subjects maximize a utility function that captures five distinct motives: personal material payoffs, one's valuation of the payoffs to others, which depend both on ones' altruism and one's degree of reciprocity, and one's sense of guilt or shame when failing to contribute one's fair share to the collective effort of the group. We have evidence of shame if players who are punished by others respond by behaving more cooperatively than is optimal for a material payoff-maximizing agent. We present indirect empirical evidence suggesting that such emotions play a role in the public goods game.

Direct evidence on the role of emotions in experimental games remains scanty. The forms of arousal associated with emotions are readily measured, but they do not readily allow us to distinguish between, say, fear and anger. Self-reports of emotional states are informative but noisy. Recent advances in brain imaging, however, can identify the areas of the brain that are activated when an experimental subject is confronted with a moral dilemma or unfair treatment by another experimental subject. This use of fMRI and related technology may eventually allow us to distinguish among the emotional responses of subjects in experimental situations.

7 CONCLUSION

The study of collective action and other forms of cooperative behaviors exhibits a curious disparity among social scientists. In the Marxian tradition, and among many historians, sociologists, anthropologists, and political scientists, the fact that people often behave pro-socially in the pursuit of common objectives, even when this involves cooperating in an n-person prisoner's dilemma game, is frequently invoked to explain social structures and their dynamics. Among economists, biologists, and others influenced by their models, by contrast, self-regarding actors will rarely, if ever, cooperate in such a setting.

It may be thought that the key difference accounting for this divergence is the methodological individualism adopted by economists and biologists, in contrast to the more holist or structural approaches adopted by historians and many social scientists outside of economics. According to this view, if anthropologists, sociologists, Marxists, and others were only to ask the obvious question—why would an individual engage in a costly activity to benefit others?—they would agree with the economists. But this is not the case.

The question needs an answer, but in light of what we now know about the nature of social preferences, it is not that altruistic forms of collective action are likely to be an ephemeral and unimportant aspect of political life and that most forms of seemingly altruistic cooperation are just self-interest in disguise. Like adherence to social norms and punishment of those who violate them, collective action is an essential aspect of political behavior and one which is readily explained by the fact that strong reciprocity and other social preferences are sufficiently common in most human populations to support high levels of cooperation in many social settings.

NOTE

1. This analysis is presented in full in Gintis (2004) and Bowles and Gintis (2007), which also shows that recent game-theoretic extensions of these models using repeated game theory (Fudenberg and Maskin 1986; Fudenberg et al. 1994; Sekiguchi 1997; Piccione 2002; Ely and Välimäki 2002; Bhaskar and Obara 2002; Matsushima 2000; Kandori 2002) do not alter this conclusion. These contributions, while important in their own right, either suffer the same problems discussed in the text, or are not stable in a dynamic setting.

REFERENCES

Abreu, D., Pearce, D., and Stacchetti, E. 1990. Toward a theory of discounted repeated games with imperfect monitoring. *Econometrica,* 58: 1041–63.

Alexander, R. D. 1979. *Biology and Human Affairs.* Seattle: University of Washington Press.

Andreoni, J., Erard, B., and Feinstein, J. 1998. Tax compliance. *Journal of Economic Literature,* 36: 818–60.

Aumann, R. J. 1987. Correlated equilibrium and an expression of Bayesian rationality. *Econometrica,* 55: 1–18.

Axelrod, R., and Hamilton, W. D. 1981. The evolution of cooperation. *Science,* 211: 1390–6.

Becker, G. 1983. A theory of competition among pressure groups for political influence. *Quarterly Journal of Economics,* 98: 71–400.

Bénabou, R., and Ok, E. A. 2001. Social mobility and the demand for redistribution: the Poum hypothesis. *Quarterly Journal of Economics,* 116: 47–87.

Berg, J., Dickhaut, J., and McCabe, K. 1995. Trust, reciprocity, and social history. *Games and Economic Behavior,* 10: 122–42.

Bhaskar, V., and Obara, I. 2002. Belief-based equilibria: the repeated prisoner's dilemma with private monitoring. *Journal of Economic Theory,* 102: 40–69.

Boehm, C. 1982. The evolutionary development of morality as an effect of dominance behavior and conflict interference. *Journal of Social and Biological Structures,* 5: 413–21.

Boehm, C.1993. Egalitarian behavior and reverse dominance hierarchy. *Current Anthropology,* 34: 227–54.

Bowles, S., Choi, J. K., and Hopfensitz, A. 2003. The co-evolution of individual behaviors and social institutions. *Journal of Theoretical Biology,* 223: 135–47.

Bowles, S and Gintis, H.2004. The evolution of strong reciprocity: cooperation in heterogeneous populations. *Theoretical Population Biology,* 65: 17–28.

Bowles, S and Gintis, H. 2007. *A Cooperative Species: Human Reciprocity and its Evolution.* Manuscript in preparation.

Bowles, S and Gintis, H. 2005*a*. Social preferences, *Homo economicus,* and *zoon politikon.* In *The Oxford Handbook of Contextual Political Analysis,* ed. R. E. Goodin and C. Tilly. Oxford: Oxford University Press.

Bowles, S and Gintis, H. 2005*b*. Prosocial emotions. In *The Economy as an Evolving Complex System III,* ed. L. E. Blume and S. N. Durlauf. Santa Fe, NM: Santa Fe Institute.

Boyd, R., Gintis, H., Bowles, S., and Richerson, P. J. 2003. Evolution of altruistic punishment. *Proceedings of the National Academy of Sciences,* 100: 3531–5.

Breton, A., Galeotti, G., Salmon, P., and Wintrobe, R. 1995. *Nationalism and Rationality.* Cambridge: Cambridge University Press.

Brown, D. E. 1991. *Human Universal.* New York: McGraw-Hill.

Buchanan, J. and Tullock, G. 1962. *The Calculus of Consent: Logical Foundations of Constitutional Democracy.* Ann Arbor: University of Michigan Press.

Buchanan, J., Tollison, R., and Tullock, G. 1980. *Toward a Theory of the Rent-Seeking Society.* College Station: Texas A&M University Press.

Camerer, C. 2003. *Behavioral Game Theory: Experiments in Strategic Interaction.* Princeton, NJ: Princeton University Press.

Camerer, C. and Fehr, E. 2004. Measuring social norms and preferences using experimental games: a guide for social scientists. pp. 55–95 in *Foundations of Human Sociality: Economic Experiments and Ethnographic Evidence from Fifteen Small-Scale Societies,* ed. J. Henrich, R. Boyd,

S. Bowles, C. F. Camerer, E. Fehr, and H. Gintis. Oxford: Oxford University Press.

Camerer, C. and Thaler, R. 1995. Ultimatums, dictators, and manners. *Journal of Economic Perspectives,* 9: 209–19.

Damasio, A. R. 1994. *Descartes' Error: Emotion, Reason, and the Human Brain.* New York: Avon.

Dawes, R. M. 1980. Social dilemmas. *Annual Review of Psychology,* 31: 169–93.

Downs, A. 1957. *An Economic Theory of Democracy.* Boston: Harper and Row.

Eibl-Eibesfeldt, I. 1982. Warfare, man's indoctrinability and group selection. *Journal of Comparative Ethnology,* 60: 177–98.

Ely, J. C., and Välimäki, J. 2002. A robust folk theorem for the prisoner's dilemma. *Journal of Economic Theory,* 102: 84–105.

Fehr, E., and Fischbacher, U. 2004. Third party punishment and social norms. *Evolution and Human Behavior,* 25: 63–87.

Fehr, E., Kirchsteiger, G., and Riedl, A. 1993. Does fairness prevent market clearing? *Quarterly Journal of Economics,* 108: 437–59.

Fong, C. M. 2001. Social preferences, self-interest, and the demand for redistribution. *Journal of Public Economics,* 82: 225–46.

Fong, C. M., Bowles, S., and Gintis, H. 2004. Reciprocity and the welfare state. In *Moral Sentiments and Material Interests: On the Foundations of Cooperation in Economic Life,* ed. H. Gintis et al. Cambridge, MA: MIT Press.

Frank, R. H. 1987. If *Homo economicus* could choose his own utility function, would he want one with a conscience? *American Economic Review,* 77: 593–604.

Friedman, D., and Singh, N. 2001. Negative reciprocity: the coevolution of memes and genes. *Evolution and Human Behavior,* 25: 155–73.

Fudenberg, D., Levine, D. K., and Maskin, E. 1994. The Folk Theorem with imperfect public information. *Econometrica,* 62: 997–1039.

Fudenberg, D.and Maskin, E. 1986. The folk theorem in repeated games with discounting or with incomplete information. *Econometrica,* 54: 533–54.

Gintis, H. 2000. Strong reciprocity and human sociality. *Journal of Theoretical Biology,* 206: 169–79.

Gintis, H. 2003. The Hitchhiker's Guide to altruism: genes, culture, and the internalization of norms. *Journal of Theoretical Biology,* 220: 407–18.

Gintis, H. 2004. Modeling cooperation among self-interested agents: a critique. Manuscript, Santa Fc Institute.

Gintis, H., Bowles, S., Boyd, R., and Fehr, E. 2005. *Moral Sentiments and Material Interests: On the Foundations of Cooperation in Economic Life.* Cambridge, MA: MIT Press.

Greif, A. 1994. Cultural beliefs and the organization of society: an historical and theoretical reflection on collectivist and individualist societies. *Journal of Political Economy,* 102: 912–50.

Greif, A., Milgrom, P., and Weingast, B. R. 1994. Coordination, commitment, and enforcement: the case of the merchant guild. *Journal of Political Economy,* 104: 745–76.

Güth, W., Schmittberger, R., and Schwat, B. 1982. An experimental analysis of ultimatum bargaining. *Journal of Economic Behavior and Organization,* 3: 367–88.

7 Justice

Market exchange produces far more wealth than would be available to any person living in isolation. But a well-functioning political society is (arguably) necessary to make exchange possible in the first place. Thus it is worth thinking about how a set of political institutions should distribute liberties, rights, opportunities, and wealth. A theory of justice provides us with a normative benchmark against which to measure the justifiability of actual institutions that affect the distribution of goods.

John Stuart Mill offers a refined version of utilitarianism, according to which we ought to act in ways (or follow rules) that maximize aggregate happiness. Mill develops a richer conception of happiness than his teacher, Jeremy Bentham, and argues that an indirect version of utilitarianism is compatible with many traditional principles of justice, including the idea that people should get what they deserve, and that people should be judged by the character virtues they exhibit, rather than how much utility or happiness they produce at any given time. Of particular relevance to distributive justice, Mill suggests that to some extent a utilitarian can separate the production and distribution of goods, so that once we incentivize productivity with markets, governments can distribute income in a way that maximizes social utility. Of course, Mill does not believe that government agents are always well motivated or sufficiently competent to use political institutions to distribute benefits well. But he does suggest that an ideal utilitarian government would try to do so. It is ultimately an empirical question, Mill thinks, precisely which social arrangements—which combination of social and economic liberties—would maximize happiness.

John Rawls offers a systematic vision for how to think about the justice of distributing social and economic goods, one which directly challenges utilitarianism. Rawls calls his approach "justice as fairness." In order to crystallize our intuitions about what a just distribution of goods would look like, Rawls argues that we should adopt a heuristic that reflects our sense of fairness. What he has in mind is that we should choose our social and political institutions assuming we do not know where within a society we find ourselves. Thus we should choose as if we had no knowledge of our particular identities—race, gender, income, religion, or age. If we could choose principles of justice—principles that will inform our political institutions—from behind this "veil of ignorance" we could be reasonably sure that our judgments about principles of distributive justice were not tainted by personal biases or self-interest.

Rawls argues that deliberators behind a veil of ignorance would choose two principles, with the first having absolute priority over the second.

1. Assign equal basic rights and duties to all (including the right to free speech and religious belief, and the duty to pay taxes and comply with laws).
2. Allow social and economic inequalities only when:
    a. they are attached to offices and positions open to all under conditions of fair equality of opportunity.
    b. they are advantageous to the least well off (the difference principle).

Although many find Rawls's two principles, and their relative ranking, plausible, others have argued that Rawls over-emphasizes social liberty, giving economic liberty short shrift, as evidenced by the serial ordering of the principles.

A different sort of objection to Rawls is that deliberators behind a veil of ignorance would choose different principles than the ones Rawls thinks they would. Rawls allows deliberators to have access to any general knowledge—of history, economics, psychology—that might facilitate their decision about which principles to select. The only restriction is that no one has knowledge of facts about *themselves,* or what identity they will have once the (hypothetical) veil is lifted. Armed with this knowledge, they might reason that a relatively free market society with a basic safety net, but very little government intrusion, will maximize their chance of being fairly prosperous, and eliminate the possibility of being in abject poverty. Indeed, under experimental conditions many people seem to reject the second principle—the difference principle—in favor of a principle that maximizes average income, subject to a floor constraint that keeps poverty above some acceptable level. Whatever principles we think deliberators would choose, Rawls suggests that if we are unhappy with the two principles of justice, we might go back and adjust the initial conditions of the thought experiment. The principles that ultimately emerge from this process of adjustment are the result of a "reflective equilibrium," a kind of harmony between our pre-theoretical intuitions and the principles that flow from the thought experiment Rawls runs us through.

Robert Nozick develops his libertarian theory of justice in part as a response to Rawls, and to the collectivist views common to modern political philosophy. In contrast to those who see moral and political philosophy as an attempt to discover the good society, and how best to promote it, Nozick seeks to identify what constraints should bind us in pursuing our individual goals. Nozick argues that rights are moral constraints on action, rather than social or legal conventions for promoting welfare. The question is not what rights a state might allow people to have, as a *means* of constructing the good society. The question instead is how to construct the good society, *given* the rights that the state is morally obligated to respect and protect.

In the selections included, Nozick defends a three part theory of distributive justice, which he calls the Entitlement theory. The first part of the Entitlement theory is a version of Locke's argument: since we own ourselves and our labor, we can claim ownership rights over things we create (using natural resources as inputs) provided we meet certain fairness constraints. These constraints include the proviso that we leave "enough and as good" for others. While Nozick raises deep questions about the workability of Locke's theory, he endorses a modified version of it.

The second part of the Entitlement theory is the principle that we can transfer or sell anything that we rightfully own (presumably having acquired it subject to the first part, above) to other people provided consent is present.

The third part of Nozick's theory of justice is the principle of rectification for past injustice, which permits the state to redistribute resources to the victims of historical injustice, such as theft or slavery.

Nozick sharply contrasts his view from most theories of distributive justice by invoking the distinction between *end-state* and *historical* principles of justice. According to Nozick, an end-state theory assesses the justice of a distribution of resources based on "who ends up with what" rather than *how* the distribution emerged. End-state theories are typically characterized by an attempt to impose a pattern of distribution on members of a society, whereas historical theories come with a commitment to leaving in place whatever distribution happens to emerge.

Most theories of justice, Nozick thinks, attempt to fill in the formula "to each according to X," where X represents some morally salient characteristic like *need* or *merit*. If we replace X with Rawls's difference principle we get "to each equally, except when inequality increases the holdings of the least well-off." Nozick suggests that patterns like this are attractive because they *look* just: they satisfy our desire to fill in formulas or impose patterns.

But Nozick maintains that we should focus not on *who* gets what but *how* they get what they have. Provided the first two principles of justice—justice in acquisition and transfer—were not violated in the process of moving from one distribution to another, there is no further question about whether the new distribution is just. On Nozick's view, it must be.

Perhaps the most memorable illustration of the distinction between end-state and historical principles of justice is Nozick's Wilt Chamberlain example. The idea is to stipulate that we start at a morally desirable (by whatever standard you choose) distribution of resources, D1. We then leave people free to dispose of their resources, and they voluntarily move to a new distribution, D2, when they willingly pay for tickets to watch Wilt Chamberlin. Chamberlain has a lot more money, each of his fans has a little less money, and everyone appears to be happy with the exchange.

Since the morally desirable distribution D1 is unstable if people are allowed to act freely, the society must either coercively re-impose the old pattern, or coercively prevent the new pattern from emerging in the first place. Whatever we think of Nozick's theory, the Chamberlain example seems to point to a deep insight: there is a tradeoff between individual liberty and any attempt to coercively impose a distributive pattern on society.

Nozick's broader critique of Rawls is also influential. In particular, Nozick suggests that once we accept something like Rawls's original position thought experiment, end-state principles must be chosen, since deliberators behind the veil of ignorance will treat all goods, including goods created through labor, as collective assets to be distributed by a central mechanism.

Perhaps the most important move Nozick makes is to say that even if we grant Rawls that people may not *deserve* many of their natural assets, people are nevertheless *entitled* to their natural assets simply as a matter of autonomy and liberty. A genius may be lucky to be a genius, but he is nevertheless entitled to "own" that genius, and to whatever flows from that genius by applying it through work. Nozick grants that the natural distribution of such genetic or natural assets is "arbitrary from a moral point of view." The problem, according to Nozick, is that in Rawls's theory "there is no mention *at all* of how persons have chosen to develop their own natural assets" (ASU, 214).

Gerald Cohen carefully dissects the premises that underlie Robert Nozick's Wilt Chamberlain example. First, Cohen doubts that Nozick's theory of original acquisition bears scrutiny, and questions whether the Lockean foundation even works. The problem, for Nozick, is that if the original acquisition of resources is unjust then no number of later voluntary exchanges will change that fact. Indeed, Nozick's own theory of rectification will likely require redistributions upsetting the results of voluntary exchanges.

Cohen also challenges a central assumption in the Wilt Chamberlain example: that whatever distribution of resources arises from a series of just steps must itself be just. Cohen registers two objections here: (A) If the exchanges are less than fully voluntary—perhaps because the preferences of the parties are induced by propaganda or are otherwise exogenous—it's possible that the participants (in the Wilt Chamberlain case, the fans) will regret the exchange. (B) Even when people do not regret a particular exchange, they may be harmed by the aggregate results of many mutually beneficial exchanges. Each exchange may be morally benign, taken in isolation. But, Cohen argues, many otherwise benign exchanges between people with different abilities or resources can be malign in the aggregate. The differences in accumulated wealth and power may lead to so much inequality that the wealthiest can use their resources to exercise unjust social or political power over others. Worse, some of those harmed by their weakness likely had no part in, and therefore did not benefit from, the transactions that produced the relevant inequalities. Even if Nozick's followers can accommodate such objections, Cohen offers a powerful line of argument through which end-state and collectivist theories might resist the seemingly plausible idea that a series of voluntary exchanges *necessarily* leads to a morally defensible distribution of resources.

FURTHER READING

Frohlich, Norman; Oppenheimer, Joe; Eavey, Cheryl. 1987. "Laboratory Results on Rawls's Distributive Justice." *British Journal of Political Science* 17 (1): 1–21.

Harsanyi, John. "Can the Maximin Principle Serve as the Basis for Morality?" *The American Political Science Review* 69 (2): 594–606.

Hayek, Friedrich. 1976. "The Mirage of Social Justice." In *Law, Legislation and Liberty*, volume 2. University of Chicago Press.

LaMont, Julian and Favor, Christi. 2013. "Distributive Justice." *The Stanford Encyclopedia of Philosophy*. Online at http://plato.stanford.edu/entries/justice-distributive/

Lomasky, Loren and Fernando Teson. 2015. *Justice at a Distance*. Cambridge University Press.

Olsaretti, Serena (editor). 2015. *The Oxford Handbook of Distributive Justice*. Oxford University Press.

Rawls, John. 2001. *Justice as Fairness: A Restatement*. Belknap Press.

Schmidtz, David. 2006. *The Elements of Justice*. Cambridge University Press.

Sen, Amartya. 2009. *The Idea of Justice*. Belknap Press.

Tomasi, John. 2013. *Free Market Fairness*. Princeton University Press.

JOHN STUART MILL

Utilitarianism

1863

The creed which accepts as the foundation of morals, Utility, or the Greatest Happiness Principle, holds that actions are right in proportion as they tend to promote happiness, wrong as they tend to produce the reverse of happiness. By happiness is intended pleasure, and the absence of pain; by unhappiness, pain, and the privation of pleasure. To give a clear view of the moral standard set up by the theory, much more requires to be said; in particular, what things it includes in the ideas of pain and pleasure; and to what extent this is left an open question. But these supplementary explanations do not affect the theory of life on which this theory of morality is grounded—namely, that pleasure, and freedom from pain, are the only things desirable as ends; and that all desirable things (which are as numerous in the utilitarian as in any other scheme) are desirable either for the pleasure inherent in themselves, or as means to the promotion of pleasure and the prevention of pain.

Now, such a theory of life excites in many minds, and among them in some of the most estimable in feeling and purpose, inveterate dislike. To suppose that life has (as they express it) no higher end than pleasure—no better and nobler object of desire and pursuit—they designate as utterly mean and groveling; as a doctrine worthy only of swine, to whom the followers of Epicurus were, at a very early period, contemptuously likened; and modern holders of the doctrine are occasionally made the subject of equally polite comparisons by its German, French, and English assailants.

When thus attacked, the Epicureans have always answered, that it is not they, but their accusers, who represent human nature in a degrading light; since the accusation supposes human beings to be capable of no pleasures except those of which swine are capable. If this supposition were true, the charge could not be gainsaid, but would then be no longer an imputation; for if the sources of pleasure were precisely the same to human beings and to swine, the rule of life which is good enough for the one would be good enough for the other. The comparison of the Epicurean life to that of beasts is felt as degrading, precisely because a beast's pleasures do not satisfy a human being's conceptions of happiness. Human beings have faculties more elevated than the animal appetites, and when once made conscious of them, do not regard anything as happiness which does not include their gratification. I do not, indeed, consider the Epicureans to have been by any means faultless in drawing out their scheme of consequences from the utilitarian principle. To do this in any sufficient manner, many Stoic, as well as Christian elements require to be included. But there is no known Epicurean theory of life which does not assign to the pleasures of the intellect, of the feelings and imagination, and of the moral sentiments, a much higher value as pleasures than to those of mere sensation. It must be admitted, however, that utilitarian writers in general have placed the superiority of mental over bodily pleasures chiefly in the greater permanency, safety, uncostliness, &c., of the former—that is, in their circumstantial advantages rather than in their intrinsic nature. And on all these points utilitarians have fully proved their case; but they might have taken the other, and, as it may be called, higher ground, with entire consistency. It is quite compatible with the principle of utility to recognise the fact, that some kinds of pleasure are more desirable and more

From John Stuart Mill. *Utilitarianism*. Longmans, Green, & Company, 1879.

valuable than others. It would be absurd that while, in estimating all other things, quality is considered as well as quantity, the estimation of pleasures should be supposed to depend on quantity alone.

If I am asked, what I mean by difference of quality in pleasures, or what makes one pleasure more valuable than another, merely as a pleasure, except its being greater in amount, there is but one possible answer. Of two pleasures, if there be one to which all or almost all who have experience of both give a decided preference, irrespective of any feeling of moral obligation to prefer it, that is the more desirable pleasure. If one of the two is, by those who are competently acquainted with both, placed so far above the other that they prefer it, even though knowing it to be attended with a greater amount of discontent, and would not resign it for any quantity of the other pleasure which their nature is capable of, we are justified in ascribing to the preferred enjoyment a superiority in quality, so far outweighing quantity as to render it, in comparison, of small account.

Now it is an unquestionable fact that those who are equally acquainted with, and equally capable of appreciating and enjoying, both, do give a most marked preference to the manner of existence which employs their higher faculties. Few human creatures would consent to be changed into any of the lower animals, for a promise of the fullest allowance of a beast's pleasures; no intelligent human being would consent to be a fool, no instructed person would be an ignoramus, no person of feeling and conscience would be selfish and base, even though they should be persuaded that the fool, the dunce, or the rascal is better satisfied with his lot than they are with theirs. They would not resign what they possess more than he, for the most complete satisfaction of all the desires which they have in common with him. If they ever fancy they would, it is only in cases of unhappiness so extreme, that to escape from it they would exchange their lot for almost any other, however undesirable in their own eyes.

A being of higher faculties requires more to make him happy, is capable probably of more acute suffering, and is certainly accessible to it at more points, than one of an inferior type; but in spite of these liabilities, he can never really wish to sink into what he feels to be a lower grade of existence. We may give what explanation we please of this unwillingness; we may attribute it to pride, a name which is given indiscriminately to some of the most and to some of the least estimable feelings of which mankind are capable; we may refer it to the love of liberty and personal independence, an appeal to which was with the Stoics one of the most effective means for the inculcation of it; to the love of power, or to the love of excitement, both of which do really enter into and contribute to it: but its most appropriate appellation is a sense of dignity, which all human beings possess in one form or other, and in some, though by no means in exact, proportion to their higher faculties, and which is so essential a part of the happiness of those in whom it is strong, that nothing which conflicts with it could be, otherwise than momentarily, an object of desire to them.

Whoever supposes that this preference takes place at a sacrifice of happiness—that the superior being, in anything like equal circumstances, is not happier than the inferior—confounds the two very different ideas, of happiness, and content. It is indisputable that the being whose capacities of enjoyment are low, has the greatest chance of having them fully satisfied; and a highly-endowed being will always feel that any happiness which he can look for, as the world is constituted, is imperfect. But he can learn to bear its imperfections, if they are at all bearable; and they will not make him envy the being who is indeed unconscious of the imperfections, but only because he feels not at all the good which those imperfections qualify. It is better to be a human being dissatisfied than a pig satisfied; better to be Socrates dissatisfied than a fool satisfied. And if the fool, or the pig, is of a different opinion, it is because they only know their own side of the question. The other party to the comparison knows both sides.

It may be objected, that many who are capable of the higher pleasures, occasionally, under the influence of temptation, postpone them to the lower. But this is quite compatible with a full appreciation of the intrinsic superiority of the higher. Men often, from infirmity of character, make their election for the nearer good, though they know it to be the less valuable; and this no less when the choice is between two bodily pleasures, than when it is between bodily and mental. They pursue sensual indulgences to the injury of health, though perfectly aware that health is the greater good. It may be further objected, that many who begin with youthful enthusiasm for everything noble, as they advance in years sink into indolence and selfishness. But I do not believe that those who undergo this very common change, voluntarily choose the lower description of pleasures in preference to the higher. I believe that before they devote themselves exclusively to the one, they have already become incapable of the other. Capacity for the nobler feelings is in most natures a very tender plant, easily killed, not only by hostile influences, but by mere want of sustenance; and in the majority of young persons it speedily dies away if the occupations to which their position in life has devoted them, and the society into which it has thrown them, are not favourable to keeping that higher capacity in exercise. Men lose their high aspirations as they lose their intellectual tastes, because they have not time or opportunity for indulging them; and they addict themselves to inferior pleasures, not because they deliberately prefer them, but because they are either the only ones to which they have access, or the only ones which they are any longer capable of enjoying. It may be questioned whether anyone who has remained equally susceptible to both classes of pleasures, ever knowingly and calmly preferred the lower; though many, in all ages, have broken down in an ineffectual attempt to combine both.

From this verdict of the only competent judges, I apprehend there can be no appeal. On a question which is the best worth having of two pleasures, or which of two modes of existence is the most grateful to the feelings, apart from its moral attributes and from its consequences, the judgment of those who are qualified by knowledge of both, or, if they differ, that of the majority among them, must be admitted as final. And there needs be the less hesitation to accept this judgment respecting the quality of pleasures, since there is no other tribunal to be referred to even on the question of quantity. What means are there of determining which is the acutest of two pains, or the intensest of two pleasurable sensations, except the general suffrage of those who are familiar with both? Neither pains nor pleasures are homogeneous, and pain is always heterogeneous with pleasure. What is there to decide whether a particular pleasure is worth purchasing at the cost of a particular pain, except the feelings and judgment of the experienced? When, therefore, those feelings and judgment declare the pleasures derived from the higher faculties to be preferable *in kind,* apart from the question of intensity, to those of which the animal nature, disjoined from the higher faculties, is susceptible, they are entitled on this subject to the same regard.

I have dwelt on this point, as being a necessary part of a perfectly just conception of Utility or Happiness, considered as the directive rule of human conduct. But it is by no means an indispensable condition to the acceptance of the utilitarian standard; for that standard is not the agent's own greatest happiness, but the greatest amount of happiness altogether; and if it may possibly be doubted whether a noble character is always the happier for its nobleness, there can be no doubt that it makes other people happier, and that the world in general is immensely a gainer by it. Utilitarianism, therefore, could only attain its end by the general cultivation of nobleness of character, even if each individual were only benefited by the nobleness of others, and his own, so far as happiness is concerned, were a sheer deduction from the benefit. But the bare enunciation of such an absurdity as this last renders refutation superfluous.

According to the Greatest Happiness Principle, as above explained, the ultimate end, with reference to and for the sake of which all other things are desirable (whether we are considering our own good or that of other people), is an existence exempt as far as possible from pain, and as rich as possible in enjoyments, both in point of quantity and quality; the test of quality, and the rule for measuring it against quantity, being the preference felt by those who, in their opportunities of experience, to which must be added their habits of self-consciousness and self-observation, are best furnished with the means of comparison. This, being, according to the utilitarian opinion, the end of human action, is necessarily also the standard of morality; which may accordingly be defined, the rules and precepts for human conduct, by the observance of which an existence such as has been described might be, to the greatest extent possible, secured to all mankind; and not to them only, but, so far as the nature of things admits, to the whole sentient creation.

JUSTICE—ON THE CONNECTION BETWEEN JUSTICE AND UTILITY

To have a right . . . is, I conceive, to have something which society ought to defend me in the possession of. If the objector goes on to ask, why it ought? I can give him no other reason than general utility. If that expression does not seem to convey a sufficient feeling of the strength of the obligation, nor to account for the peculiar energy of the feeling, it is because there goes to the composition of the sentiment, not a rational only, but also an animal element, the thirst for retaliation; and this thirst derives its intensity, as well as its moral justification, from the extraordinarily important and impressive kind of utility which is concerned. The interest involved is that of security, to every one's feelings the most vital of all interests. All other earthly benefits are needed by one person, not needed by another; and many of them can, if necessary, be cheerfully foregone, or replaced by something else; but security no human being can possibly do without on it we depend for all our immunity from evil, and for the whole value of all and every good, beyond the passing moment; since nothing but the gratification of the instant could be of any worth to us, if we could be deprived of anything the next instant by whoever was momentarily stronger than ourselves.

Now this most indispensable of all necessaries, after physical nutriment, cannot be had, unless the machinery for providing it is kept unintermittedly in active play. Our notion, therefore, of the claim we have on our fellow-creatures to join in making safe for us the very groundwork of our existence, gathers feelings around it so much more intense than those concerned in any of the more common cases of utility, that the difference in degree (as is often the case in psychology) becomes a real difference in kind. The claim assumes that character of absoluteness, that apparent infinity, and incommensurability with all other considerations, which constitute the distinction between the feeling of right and wrong and that of ordinary expediency and inexpediency. The feelings concerned are so powerful, and we count so positively on finding a responsive feeling in others (all being alike interested), that ought and should grow into must, and recognised indispensability becomes a moral necessity, analogous to physical, and often not inferior to it in binding force exhorted, if the preceding analysis, or something resembling it, be not the correct account of the notion of justice; if justice be totally independent of utility, and be a standard per se, which the mind can recognise by simple introspection of itself; it is hard to understand why that internal oracle is so ambiguous, and why so many things appear either just or unjust, according to the light in which they are regarded.

We are continually informed that Utility is an uncertain standard, which every different person interprets differently, and that there is no safety but in the immutable, ineffaceable, and unmistakable dictates of justice, which carry their evidence in themselves, and are independent of the fluctuations of opinion. One would suppose from this that on questions of justice there could be no controversy; that if we take that for our rule, its application to any given case could leave us in as little doubt as a mathematical demonstration. So far is this from being the fact, that there is as much difference of opinion, and as much discussion, about what is just, as about what is useful to society. Not only have different nations and individuals different notions of justice, but in the mind of one and the same individual, justice is not some one rule, principle, or maxim, but many, which do not always coincide in their dictates, and in choosing between which, he is guided either by some extraneous standard, or by his own personal predilections.

For instance, there are some who say, that it is unjust to punish any one for the sake of example to others; that punishment is just, only when intended for the good of the sufferer himself. Others maintain the extreme reverse, contending that to punish persons who have attained years of discretion, for their own benefit, is despotism and injustice, since if the matter at issue is solely their own good, no one has a right to control their own judgment of it; but that they may justly be punished to prevent evil to others, this being the exercise of the legitimate right of self-defence. . . .

These are difficulties; they have always been felt to be such; and many devices have been invented to turn rather than to overcome them. As a refuge from the last of the three, men imagined what they called the freedom of the will; fancying that they could not justify punishing a man whose will is in a thoroughly hateful state, unless it be supposed to have come into that state through no influence of anterior circumstances. To escape from the other difficulties, a favourite contrivance has been the fiction of a contract, whereby at some unknown period all the members of society engaged to obey the laws, and consented to be punished for any disobedience to them, thereby giving to their legislators the right, which it is assumed they would not otherwise have had, of punishing them, either for their own good or for that of society. This happy thought was considered to get rid of the whole difficulty, and to legitimate the infliction of punishment, in virtue of another received maxim of justice, *Volenti non fit injuria;* that is not unjust which is done with the consent of the person who is supposed to be hurt by it. I need hardly remark, that even if the consent were not a mere fiction, this maxim is not superior in authority to the others which it is brought in to supersede. It is, on the contrary, an instructive specimen of the loose and irregular manner in which supposed principles of justice grow up. This particular one evidently came into use as a help to the coarse exigencies of courts of law, which are sometimes obliged to be content with very uncertain presumptions, on account of the greater evils which would often arise from any attempt on their part to cut finer. But even courts of law are not able to adhere consistently to the maxim, for they allow voluntary engagements to be set aside on the ground of fraud, and sometimes on that of mere mistake or misinformation.

Again, when the legitimacy of inflicting punishment is admitted, how many conflicting conceptions of justice come to light in discussing the proper apportionment of punishments to offences. No rule on the subject recommends itself so strongly to the primitive and spontaneous sentiment of justice, as the *lex talionis,* an eye for an eye and a tooth for a tooth. Though this principle of the Jewish and of the Mahometan law has been generally abandoned in Europe as a practical maxim, there is, I suspect, in most minds, a secret hankering after it; and when retribution accidentally falls on an offender in that precise shape, the general feeling of satisfaction evinced bears witness how natural is the sentiment to which this repayment in kind is acceptable.

With many, the test of justice in penal infliction is that the punishment should be proportioned to the offence; meaning that it should be exactly measured by the moral guilt of the culprit (whatever be their standard for measuring moral guilt): the consideration, what amount of punishment is necessary to deter from the offence, having nothing to do with the question of justice, in their estimation: while there are others to whom that consideration is all in all; who maintain that it is not just, at least for man, to inflict on a fellow creature, whatever may be his offences, any amount of suffering beyond the least that will suffice to prevent him from repeating, and others from imitating, his misconduct.

To take another example from a subject already once referred to. In a co-operative industrial association, **is it just that talent or skill should give a title to superior remuneration?** On the negative side of the question it is argued, that whoever does the best he can, deserves equally well, and ought not in justice to be put in a position of inferiority for no fault of his own; that superior abilities have already advantages more than enough, in the admiration they excite, the personal influence they command, and the internal sources of satisfaction attending them, without adding to these a superior share of the world's goods; and that society is bound in justice rather to make compensation to the less favoured, for this unmerited inequality of advantages, than to aggravate it. On the contrary side it is contended, that society receives more from the more efficient labourer; that his services being more useful, society owes him a larger return for them; that a greater share of the joint result is actually his work, and not to allow his claim to it is a kind of robbery; that if he is only to receive as much as others, he can only be justly required to produce as much, and to give a smaller amount of time and exertion, proportioned to his superior efficiency. Who shall decide between these appeals to conflicting principles of justice? Justice has in this case two sides to it, which it is impossible to bring into harmony, and the two disputants have chosen opposite sides; the one looks to what it is just that the individual should receive, the other to what it is just that the community should give. Each, from his own point of view, is unanswerable; and any choice between them, on grounds of justice, must be perfectly arbitrary. **Social utility alone can decide the preference.**

How many, again, and how irreconcilable, are the standards of justice to which reference is made in discussing the repartition of taxation. One opinion is, that payment to the State should be in numerical proportion to pecuniary means. Others think that justice dictates what they term graduated taxation; taking a higher percentage from those who have more to spare. In point of natural justice a strong case might be made for disregarding means altogether, and taking the same absolute sum (whenever it could be got) from every one: as the subscribers to a mess, or to a club, all pay the same sum for the same privileges, whether they can all equally afford it or not. Since the protection (it might be said) of law and government is afforded to, and is equally required by all, there is no injustice in making all buy it at the same price. It is reckoned justice, not injustice, that a dealer should charge to all customers the same price for the same article, not a price varying according to their means of payment. This doctrine, as applied to taxation, finds no advocates, because it conflicts so strongly with man's feelings of humanity and of social expediency; but the principle of justice which it invokes is as true and as binding as those which can be appealed to against it. Accordingly it exerts a tacit influence on the line of defence employed for other modes of assessing taxation. People feel obliged to argue that the State does more for the rich than for the poor, as a justification for its taking more from them: though this is in reality not true, for the rich would be far better able to protect themselves, in the absence of law or government, than the poor, and indeed would probably be successful in converting the poor into their slaves. Others, again, so far defer to the same conception of justice, as to maintain that all should pay an equal capitation tax for the protection of their persons (these being of equal value to all), and an unequal tax for the protection of their property, which is unequal. To this others reply, that the all of one man is as valuable to him as the all of another. From these confusions there is no other mode of extrication than the utilitarian.

Is then, the difference between the just and the Expedient a merely imaginary distinction? Have mankind been under a delusion in thinking that justice is a more sacred thing than policy, and that the latter ought only to be listened to after the former has been satisfied? By no means. The exposition we have given of the nature and origin of the sentiment, recognises a real distinction; and no one of those who profess the most sublime contempt for the consequences of actions as an element in their morality, attaches more importance to the distinction than I do. While I dispute the pretensions of any theory which sets up an imaginary standard of justice not grounded on utility, I account the justice which is grounded on utility to be the chief part, and incomparably the most sacred and binding part, of all morality. Justice is a name for certain classes of moral rules, which concern the essentials of human well-being more nearly, and are therefore of more absolute obligation, than any other rules for the guidance of life; and the notion which we have found to be of the essence of the idea of justice, that of a right residing in an individual implies and testifies to this more binding obligation. The moral rules which forbid mankind to hurt one another (in which we must never forget to include wrongful interference with each other's freedom) are more vital to human well-being than any maxims, however important, which only point out the best mode of managing some department of human affairs. They have also the peculiarity, that they are the main element in determining the whole of the social feelings of mankind. It is their observance which alone preserves peace among human beings: if obedience to them were not the rule, and disobedience the exception, everyone would see in every one else an enemy, against whom he must be perpetually guarding himself.

Most of the maxims of justice current in the world, and commonly appealed to in its transactions, are simply instrumental to carrying into effect the principles of justice which we have now spoken of. That a person is only responsible for what he has done voluntarily, or could voluntarily have avoided; that it is unjust to condemn any person unheard; that the punishment ought to be proportioned to the offence, and the like, are maxims intended to prevent the just principle of evil for evil from being perverted to the infliction of evil without that justification. The greater part of these common maxims have come into use from the practice of courts of justice, which have been naturally led to a more complete recognition and elaboration than was likely to suggest itself to others, of the rules necessary to enable them to fulfil their double function, of inflicting punishment when due, and of awarding to each person his right.

That first of judicial virtues, impartiality, is an obligation of justice, partly for the reason last mentioned; as being a necessary condition of the fulfilment of the other obligations of justice. But this is not the only source of the exalted rank, among human obligations, of those maxims of equality and impartiality, which, both in popular estimation and in that of the most enlightened, are included among the precepts of justice. In one point of view, they may be considered as corollaries from the principles already laid down. If it is a duty to do to each according to his deserts, returning good for good as well as repressing evil by evil, it necessarily follows that we should treat all equally well (when no higher duty forbids) who have deserved equally well of us, and that society should treat all equally well who have deserved equally well of it, that is, who have deserved equally well absolutely. This is the highest abstract standard of social and distributive justice; towards which all institutions, and the efforts of all virtuous citizens, should be made in the utmost possible degree to converge.

But this great moral duty rests upon a still deeper foundation, being a direct emanation from the first principle of morals, and not a mere logical corollary from secondary or derivative doctrines. It is involved in the very meaning of Utility, or the Greatest Happiness Principle. That principle is a mere form of words without rational signification, unless one person's happiness, supposed equal in degree (with the proper allowance made for kind), is counted for exactly as much as another's. Those conditions being supplied, Bentham's dictum, "everybody to count for one, nobody for more than one," might be written under the principle of utility as an explanatory commentary. The equal claim of everybody to happiness in the estimation of the moralist and the legislator, involves an equal claim to all the means of happiness, except in so far as the inevitable conditions of human life, and the general interest, in which that of every individual is included, set limits to the maxim; and those limits ought to be strictly construed. As every other maxim of justice, so this is by no means applied or held applicable universally; on the contrary, as I have already remarked, it bends to every person's ideas of social expediency. But in whatever case it is deemed applicable at all, it is held to be the dictate of justice. All persons are deemed to have a right to equality of treatment, except when some recognised social expediency requires the reverse. And hence all social inequalities which have ceased to be considered expedient, assume the character not of simple inexpediency, but of injustice, and appear so tyrannical, that people are apt to wonder how they ever could have been tolerated; forgetful that they themselves perhaps tolerate other inequalities under an equally mistaken notion of expediency, the correction of which would make that which they approve seem quite as monstrous as what they have at last learnt to condemn. The entire history of social improvement has been a series of transitions, by which one custom or institution after another, from being a supposed primary necessity of social existence, has passed into the rank of a universally stigmatised injustice and tyranny. So it has been with the distinctions of slaves and freemen, nobles and serfs, patricians and plebeians; and so it will be, and in part already is, with the aristocracies of colour, race, and sex.

It appears from what has been said, that justice is a name for certain moral requirements, which, regarded collectively, stand higher in the scale of social utility, and are therefore of more paramount obligation, than any others; though particular cases may occur in which some other social duty is so important, as to overrule any one of the general maxims of justice. Thus, to save a life, it may not only be allowable, but a duty, to steal, or take by force, the necessary food or medicine, or to kidnap, and compel to officiate, the only qualified medical practitioner. In such cases, as we do not call anything justice which is not a virtue, we usually say, not that justice must give way to some other moral principle, but that what is just in ordinary cases is, by reason of that other principle, not just in the particular case. By this useful accommodation of language, the character of indefeasibility attributed to justice is kept up, and we are saved from the necessity of maintaining that there can be laudable injustice.

The considerations which have now been adduced resolve, I conceive, the only real difficulty in the utilitarian theory of morals. It has always been evident that all cases of justice are also cases of expediency: the difference is in the peculiar sentiment which attaches to the former, as contradistinguished from the latter. If this characteristic sentiment has been sufficiently accounted for; if there is no necessity to assume for it any peculiarity of origin; if it is simply the natural feeling of resentment, moralised by being made coextensive with the demands of social good; and if this feeling not only does but ought to exist in all the classes of cases to which the idea of justice corresponds; that idea no longer presents itself as a stumbling-block to the utilitarian ethics.

Justice remains the appropriate name for certain social utilities which are vastly more important, and therefore more absolute and imperative, than any others are as a class (though not more so than others may be in particular cases); and which, therefore, ought to be, as well as naturally are, guarded by a sentiment not only different in degree, but also in kind; distinguished from the milder feeling which attaches to the mere idea of promoting human pleasure or convenience, at once by the more definite nature of its commands, and by the sterner character of its sanctions.

John Rawls

A Theory of Justice

1971

3. THE MAIN IDEA OF THE THEORY OF JUSTICE

My aim is to present a conception of justice which generalizes and carries to a higher level of abstraction the familiar theory of the social contract as found, say, in Locke, Rousseau, and Kant. In order to do this we are not to think of the original contract as one to enter a particular society or to set up a particular form of government. Rather, the guiding idea is that the principles of justice for the basic structure of society are the object of the original agreement. They are, the principles that free and rational

From John Rawls, *A Theory of Justice*. Cambridge, MA: Belknap Press of Harvard University Press, 1971. By permission of Harvard University Press.

persons concerned to further their own interests would accept in an initial position of equality as defining the fundamental terms of their association. These principles are to regulate all further agreements; they specify the kinds of social cooperation that can be entered into and the forms of government that can be established. This way of regarding the principles of justice I shall call justice as fairness.

Thus we are to imagine that those who engage in social cooperation choose together, in one joint act, the principles which are to assign basic rights and duties and to determine the division of social benefits. Men are to decide in advance how they are to regulate their claims against one another and what is to be the foundation charter of their society. Just as each person must decide by rational reflection what constitutes his good, that is, the system of ends which it is rational for him to pursue, so a group of persons must decide once and for all what is to count among them as just and unjust. The choice which rational men would make in this hypothetical situation of equal liberty, assuming for the present that this choice problem has a solution, determines the principles of justice.

In justice as fairness the original position of equality corresponds to the state of nature in the traditional theory of the social contract. This original position is not, of course, thought of as an actual historical state of affairs, much less as a primitive condition of culture. It is understood as a purely hypothetical situation characterized so as to lead to a certain conception of justice. Among the essential features of this situation is that no one knows his place in society, his class position or social status, nor does any one know his fortune in the distribution of natural assets and abilities, his intelligence, strength, and the like. I shall even assume that the parties do not know their conceptions of the good or their special psychological propensities. The principles of justice are chosen behind a veil of ignorance. This ensures that no one is advantaged or disadvantaged in the choice of principles by the outcome of natural chance or the contingency of social circumstances. Since all are similarly situated and no one is able to design principles to favor his particular condition, the principles of justice are the result of a fair agreement or bargain.

For given the circumstances of the original position, the symmetry of everyone's relations to each other, this initial situation is fair between individuals as moral persons, that is, as rational beings with their own ends and capable, I shall assume, of a sense of justice. The original position is, one might say, the appropriate initial status quo, and thus the fundamental agreements reached in it are fair. This explains the propriety of the name "justice as fairness": it conveys the idea that the principles of justice are agreed to in an initial situation that is fair. The name does not mean that the concepts of justice and fairness are the same, any more than the phrase "poetry as metaphor" means that the concepts of poetry and metaphor are the same.

Justice as fairness begins, as I have said, with one of the most general of all choices which persons might make together, namely, with the choice of the first principles of a conception of justice which is to regulate all subsequent criticism and reform of institutions. Then, having chosen a conception of justice, we can suppose that they are to choose a constitution and a legislature to enact laws, and so on, all in accordance with the principles of justice initially agreed upon. Our social situation is just if it is such that by this sequence of hypothetical agreements we would have contracted into the general system of rules which defines it. Moreover, assuming that the original position does determine a set of principles (that is, that a particular conception of justice would be chosen), it will then be true that whenever social institutions satisfy these principles those engaged in them can say to one another that they are cooperating on terms to which they would agree if they were free and equal persons whose relations with respect to one another were fair. They could all view their arrangements as meeting the stipulations which they would acknowledge in an initial situation that embodies widely accepted and reasonable constraints on the choice of principles. The general recognition of this fact would provide the basis for a public acceptance of the corresponding principles of justice. No society can, of course, be a scheme of cooperation which men enter voluntarily in a literal sense; each person finds himself placed at birth in some particular position in some particular society, and the nature of this position materially affects his life prospects. Yet a society satisfying the principles of justice as fairness comes as close as a society can to being a voluntary scheme, for it meets the principles which free and equal persons would assent to under circumstances that are fair. In this sense its members are autonomous and the obligations they recognize self-imposed.

One feature of justice as fairness is to think of the parties in the initial situation as rational and mutually disinterested. This does not mean that the parties are egoists, that is, individuals with only certain kinds of interests, say in wealth, prestige, and domination. But they are conceived as not taking an interest in one another's interests. They are to presume that even their spiritual aims may be opposed, in the way that the aims of those of different religions may be opposed. Moreover, the concept of rationality must be interpreted as far as possible in the narrow sense, standard in economic theory, of taking the most effective means to given ends. I shall modify this concept to some extent, but one must try to avoid introducing into it any controversial ethical elements. The initial situation must be characterized by stipulations that are widely accepted.

In working out the conception of justice as fairness one main task clearly is to determine which principles of justice would be chosen in the original position. To do this we must describe this situation in some detail and formulate with care the problem of choice which it presents. These matters I shall take up in the immediately succeeding chapters. It may be observed, however, that once the principles of justice are thought of as arising from an original agreement in a situation of equality, it is an open question whether the principle of utility would be acknowledged. Offhand it hardly seems likely that persons who view themselves as equals, entitled to press their claims upon one another, would agree to a principle which may require lesser life prospects for some simply for the sake of a greater sum of advantages enjoyed by others. Since each desires to protect his interests, his capacity to advance his conception of the good, no one has a reason to acquiesce in an enduring loss for himself in order to bring about a greater net balance of satisfaction. In the absence of strong and lasting benevolent impulses, a rational man would not accept a basic structure merely because it maximized the algebraic sum of advantages irrespective of its permanent effects on his own basic rights and interests. Thus it seems that the principle of utility is incompatible with the conception of social cooperation among equals for mutual advantage. It appears to be inconsistent with the idea of reciprocity implicit in the notion of a well-ordered society. Or, at any rate, so I shall argue.

I shall maintain instead that the persons in the initial situation would choose two rather different principles: the first requires equality in the assignment of basic rights and duties, while the second holds that social and economic inequalities, for example inequalities of wealth and authority, are just only if they result in compensating benefits for everyone, and in particular for the least advantaged members of society. These principles rule out justifying institutions on the grounds that the hardships of some are offset by a greater good in the aggregate. It may be expedient but it is not just that some should have less in order that others may prosper. But there is no injustice in the greater benefits earned by a few provided that the situation of persons not so fortunate is thereby improved. The intuitive idea is that since everyone's well-being depends upon a scheme of cooperation without which no one could have a satisfactory life, the division of advantages should be such as to draw forth the willing cooperation of everyone taking part in it, including those less well situated. Yet this can be expected only if reasonable terms are proposed. The two principles mentioned seem to be a fair agreement on the basis of which those better endowed, or more fortunate in their social position, neither of which we can be said to deserve, could expect the willing cooperation of others when some workable scheme is a necessary condition of the welfare of all. Once we decide to look for a conception of justice that nullifies the accidents of natural endowment and the contingencies of social circumstance as counters in quest for political and economic advantage, we are led to these principles. They express the result of leaving aside those aspects of the social world that seem arbitrary from a moral point of view.

The problem of the choice of principles, however, is extremely difficult. I do not expect the answer I shall suggest to be convincing to everyone. It is, therefore, worth noting from the outset that justice as fairness, like other contract views, consists of two parts: (1) an interpretation of the initial situation and of the problem of choice posed there, and (2) a set of principles which, it is argued, would be agreed to. One may accept the first part of the theory (or some variant thereof), but not the other, and conversely. The concept of the initial contractual situation may seem reasonable although the particular principles proposed are rejected. To be sure, I want to maintain that the most appropriate conception of this situation does lead to principles of justice contrary to utilitarianism and perfectionism, and therefore that the contract doctrine provides an alternative to these views. Still, one may dispute this contention even though one grants that the contractarian method is a useful way of studying ethical theories and of setting forth their underlying assumptions.

Justice as fairness is an example of what I have called a contract theory. Now there may be an objection to the term "contract" and related expressions, but I think it will serve reasonably well. Many words have misleading connotations which at first are likely to confuse. The terms "utility" and "utilitarianism" are surely no exception. They too have unfortunate suggestions which hostile critics have been willing to exploit; yet they are clear enough for those prepared to study utilitarian doctrine. The same should be true of the term "contract" applied to moral theories. As I have mentioned, to understand it one has to keep in mind that it implies a certain level of abstraction. In particular, the content of the relevant agreement is not to enter a given society or to adopt a given form of government, but to accept certain moral principles. Moreover, the undertakings referred to are purely hypothetical: a contract view holds that certain principles would be accepted in a well-defined initial situation.

The merit of the contract terminology is that it conveys the idea that principles of justice may be conceived as principles that would be chosen by rational persons, and that in this way conceptions of justice may be explained and justified. The theory of justice is a part, perhaps the most significant part, of the theory of rational choice. Furthermore, principles of justice deal with conflicting claims upon the advantages won by social cooperation; they apply to the relations among several persons or groups. The word "contract" suggests this plurality as well as the condition that the appropriate division of advantages must be in accordance with principles acceptable to all parties. The condition of publicity for principles of justice is also connoted by the contract phraseology. Thus, if these principles are the outcome of an agreement, citizens have a knowledge of the principles that others follow. It is characteristic of contract theories to stress the public nature of political principles. Finally there is the long tradition of the contract doctrine. Expressing the tie with this line of thought helps to define ideas and accords with natural piety. There are then several advantages in the use of the term "contract." With due precautions taken, it should not be misleading.

A final remark. Justice as fairness is not a complete contract theory. For it is clear that the contractarian idea can be extended to the choice of more or less an entire ethical system, that is, to a system including principles for all the virtues and not only for justice. Now for the most part I shall consider only principles of justice and others closely related to them; I make no attempt to discuss the virtues in a systematic way. Obviously if justice as fairness succeeds reasonably well, a next step would be to study the more general view suggested by the name "rightness as fairness." But even this wider theory fails to embrace all moral relationships, since it would seem to include only our relations with other persons and to leave out of account how we are to conduct ourselves toward animals and the rest of nature. I do not contend that the contract notion offers a way to approach these questions which are certainly of the first importance; and I shall have to put them aside. We must recognize the limited scope of justice as fairness and of the general type of view that it exemplifies. How far its conclusions must be revised once these other matters are understood cannot be decided in advance.

4. THE ORIGINAL POSITION AND JUSTIFICATION

I have said that the original position is the appropriate initial status quo which ensures that the fundamental agreements reached in it are fair. This fact yields the name "justice as fairness." It is clear, then, that I want to say that one conception of justice is more reasonable than another, or justifiable with respect to it, if rational persons in the initial situation would choose its principles over those of the other for the role of justice. Conceptions of justice are to be ranked by their acceptability to persons so circumstanced. Understood in this way the question of justification is settled by working out a problem of deliberation: we have to ascertain which principles it would be rational to adopt given the contractual situation. This connects the theory of justice with the theory of rational choice.

If this view of the problem of justification is to succeed, we must, of course, describe in some detail the nature of this choice problem. A problem of rational decision has a definite answer only if we know the beliefs and interests of the parties, their relations with respect to one another, the alternatives between which they are to choose, the procedure whereby they make up their minds, and so on. As the circumstances are presented in different ways, correspondingly different principles are accepted. The concept of the original position, as I shall refer to it, is that of the most philosophically favored interpretation of this initial choice situation for the purposes of a theory of justice.

But how are we to decide what is the most favored interpretation? I assume, for one thing, that there is a broad measure of agreement that principles of justice should be chosen under certain conditions. To justify a particular description of the initial situation one shows that it incorporates these commonly shared presumptions. One argues from widely accepted but weak premises to more specific conclusions. Each of the presumptions should by itself be natural and plausible; some of them may seem innocuous or even trivial. The aim of the contract approach is to establish that taken together they impose significant bounds on acceptable principles of justice. The ideal outcome would be that these conditions determine a unique set of principles: but I shall be satisfied if they suffice to rank the main traditional conceptions of social justice.

One should not be misled, then, by the somewhat unusual conditions which characterize the original position. The idea here is simply to make vivid to ourselves the restrictions that it seems reasonable to impose on arguments for principles of justice, and therefore on these principles themselves. Thus it seems reasonable and generally acceptable that no one should be advantaged or disadvantaged by natural fortune or social circumstances in the choice of principles. It also seems widely agreed that it should be impossible to tailor principles to the circumstances of one's own case. We should ensure further that particular inclinations and aspirations, and persons' conceptions of their good do not affect the principles adopted. The aim is to rule out those principles that it would be rational to propose for acceptance, however little the chance of success, only if one knew certain things that are irrelevant from the standpoint of justice. For example, if a man knew that he was wealthy, he might find it rational to advance the principle that various taxes for welfare measures be counted unjust; if he knew that he was poor, he would most likely propose the contrary principle. To represent the desired restrictions one imagines a situation in which everyone is deprived of this sort of information. One excludes the knowledge of those contingencies which sets men at odds and allows them to be guided by their prejudices. In this manner the veil of ignorance is arrived at in a natural way. This concept should cause no difficulty if we keep in mind the constraints on arguments that it is meant to express. At any time we can enter the original position, so to speak, simply by following a certain procedure, namely, by arguing for principles of justice in accordance with these restrictions.

It seems reasonable to suppose that the parties in the original position are equal. That is, all have the same rights in the procedure for choosing principles; each can make proposals, submit reasons for their acceptance, and so on. Obviously the purpose of these conditions is to represent equality between human beings as moral persons, as creatures having a conception of their good and capable of a sense of justice. The basis of equality is taken to be similarity in these two respects. Systems of ends are not ranked in value; and each man is presumed to have the requisite ability to understand and to act upon whatever principles are adopted. Together with the veil of ignorance, these conditions define the principles of justice as those which rational persons concerned to advance their interests would consent to as equals when none are known to be advantaged or disadvantaged by social and natural contingencies.

There is, however, another side to justifying a particular description of the original position. This is to see if the principles which would be chosen match our considered convictions of justice or extend them in an acceptable way. We can note whether applying these principles would lead us to make the same judgments about the basic structure of society which we now make intuitively and in which we have the greatest confidence; or whether, in cases where our present judgments are in doubt and given with hesitation, these principles offer a resolution which we can affirm on reflection. There are questions which we feel sure must be answered in a certain way. For example, we are confident that religious intolerance and racial discrimination are unjust. We think that we have examined these things with care and have reached what we believe is an impartial judgment not likely to be distorted by an excessive attention to our own interests. These convictions are provisional fixed points which we presume any conception of justice must fit. But we have much less assurance as to what is the correct distribution of wealth and authority. Here we may be looking for a way to remove our doubts. We can check an interpretation of the initial situation, then, by the capacity of its principles to accommodate our firmest convictions and to provide guidance where guidance is needed.

In searching for the most favored description of this situation we work from both ends. We begin by describing it so that it represents generally shared and preferably weak conditions. We then see if these conditions are strong enough to yield a significant set of principles. If not, we look for further premises equally reasonable. But if so, and these principles match our considered convictions of justice, then so far well and good. But presumably there will be discrepancies. In this case we have a choice. We can either modify the account of the initial situation or we can revise our existing judgments, for even the judgments we take provisionally as fixed points are liable to revision. By going back and forth, sometimes altering the conditions of the contractual circumstances, at others withdrawing our judgments and conforming them to principle, I assume that eventually we shall find a description of the initial situation that both expresses reasonable conditions and yields principles which match our considered judgments duly pruned and adjusted. This state of affairs I refer to as reflective equilibrium.[1] It is an equilibrium because at last our principles and judgments coincide; and it is reflective since we know to what principles our judgments conform and the premises of their derivation. At the moment everything is in order. But this equilibrium is not necessarily stable. It is liable to be upset by further examination of the conditions which should be imposed on the contractual situation and by particular cases which may lead us to revise our judgments. Yet for the time being we have done what we can to render coherent and to justify our convictions of social justice. We have reached a conception of the original position.

I shall not, of course, actually work through this process. Still, we may think of the interpretation of the original position that I shall present as the result of such a hypothetical course of reflection. It represents the attempt to accommodate within one scheme both reasonable philosophical conditions on principles as well as our considered judgments of justice. In arriving at the favored interpretation of the initial situation there is no point at which an appeal is made to self-evidence in the traditional sense either of general conceptions or particular convictions. I do not claim for the principles of justice proposed that they are necessary truths or derivable from such truths. A conception of justice cannot be deduced from self-evident premises or conditions on principles; instead, its justification is a matter of the mutual support of many considerations, of everything fitting together into one coherent view.

A final comment. We shall want to say that certain principles of justice are justified because they would be agreed to in an initial situation of equality. I have emphasized that this original position is purely hypothetical. It is natural to ask why, if this agreement is never actually entered into, we should take any interest in these principles, moral or otherwise. The answer is that the conditions embodied in the description of the original position are ones that we do in fact accept. Or if we do not, then perhaps we can be persuaded to do so by philosophical reflection. Each aspect of the contractual situation can be given supporting grounds. Thus what we shall do is to collect together into one conception a number of conditions on principles that we are ready upon due consideration to recognize as reasonable. These constraints express what we are prepared to regard as limits on fair terms of social cooperation. One way to look at the idea of the original position, therefore, is to see it as an expository device which sums up the meaning of these conditions and helps us to extract their consequences. On the other hand, this conception is also an intuitive notion that suggests its own elaboration, so that led on by it we are drawn to define more clearly the standpoint from which we can best interpret moral relationships. We need a conception that enables us to envision our objective from afar: the intuitive notion of the original position is to do this for us.

5. CLASSICAL UTILITARIANISM

There are many forms of utilitarianism, and the development of the theory has continued in recent years. I shall not survey these forms here, nor take account of the numerous refinements found in contemporary discussions. My aim is to work out a theory of justice that represents an alternative to utilitarian thought generally and so to all of these different versions of it. I believe that the contrast between the contract view and utilitarianism remains essentially the same in all these cases. Therefore I shall compare justice as fairness with familiar variants of intuitionism, perfectionism, and utilitarianism in order to bring out the underlying differences in the simplest way. With this end in mind, the kind of utilitarianism I shall describe here is the strict classical doctrine which receives perhaps its clearest and most accessible formulation in Sidgwick. The main idea is that society is rightly ordered, and therefore just, when its major institutions are arranged so as to achieve the greatest net balance of satisfaction summed over all the individuals belonging to it.

We may note first that there is, indeed, a way of thinking of society which makes it easy to suppose that the most rational conception of justice is utilitarian. For consider: each man in realizing his own interests is certainly free to balance his own losses against his own gains. We may impose a sacrifice on ourselves now for the sake of a greater advantage later. A person quite properly acts, at least when others are not affected, to achieve his own greatest good, to advance his rational ends as far as possible. Now why should not a society act on precisely the same principle applied to the group and therefore regard that which is rational for one man as right for an association of men? Just as the well-being of a person is constructed from the series of satisfactions which are experienced at different moments in time and which constitute the life of the individual, so the well-being of society is to be constructed from the fulfillment of the systems of desires of the many individuals who belong to it. Since the principle for an individual is to advance as far as possible his own welfare, his own system of desires, the principle for society is to advance as far as possible the welfare of the group, to realize to the greatest extent the comprehensive system of desire arrived at from the desires of its members. Just as an individual balances present and future gains against present and future losses, so a society may balance satisfactions and dissatisfactions between different individuals. And so by these reflections one reaches the principle of utility in a natural way: a society is properly arranged when its institutions maximize the net balance of satisfaction. The principle of choice for an association of men is interpreted as an extension of the principle of choice for one man. Social justice is the principle of rational prudence applied to an aggregative conception of the welfare of the group.

This idea is made all the more attractive by a further consideration. The two main concepts of ethics are those of the right and the good; the concept of a morally worthy person is, I believe, derived from them. The structure of an ethical theory is, then, largely determined by how it defines and connects these two basic notions. Now it seems that the simplest way of relating them is taken by teleological theories: the good is defined independently from the right, and then the right is defined as that which maximizes the good. More precisely, those institutions and acts are right which of the available alternatives produce the most good, or at least as much good as any of the other institutions and acts open as real possibilities (a rider needed when the maximal class is not a singleton). Teleological theories have a deep intuitive appeal since they seem to embody the idea of rationality. It is natural to think that rationality is maximizing something and that in morals it must be maximizing the good. Indeed, it is tempting to suppose that it is self-evident that things should be arranged so as to lead to the most good.

It is essential to keep in mind that in a teleological theory the good is defined independently from the right. This means two things. First, the theory accounts for our considered judgments as to which things are good (our judgments of value) as a separate class of judgments intuitively distinguishable by common sense, and then proposes the hypothesis that the right is maximizing the good as already specified. Second, the theory enables one to judge the goodness of things without referring to what is right. For example, if pleasure is said to be the sole good, then presumably pleasures can be recognized and ranked in value by criteria that do not presuppose any standards of right, or what we would normally think of as such. Whereas if the distribution of goods is also counted as a good, perhaps a higher order one, and the theory directs us to produce the most good (including the good of distribution among others), we no longer have a teleological view in the classical sense. The problem of distribution falls under the concept of right as one intuitively understands it, and so the theory lacks an independent definition of the good. The clarity and simplicity of classical teleological theories derives largely from the fact that they factor our moral judgments into two classes, the one being characterized separately while the other is then connected with it by a maximizing principle.

Teleological doctrines differ, pretty clearly, according to how the conception of the good is specified. If it is taken as the realization of human excellence in the various forms of culture, we have what may be called perfectionism. This notion is found in Aristotle and Nietzsche, among others. If the good is defined as pleasure, we have hedonism; if as happiness, eudaimonism, and so on. I shall understand the principle of utility in its classical form as defining the good as the satisfaction of desire, or perhaps better, as the satisfaction of rational desire. This accords with the view in all essentials and provides, I believe, a fair interpretation of it. The appropriate terms of social cooperation are settled by whatever in the circumstances will achieve the greatest sum of satisfaction of the rational desires of individuals. It is impossible to deny the initial plausibility and attractiveness of this conception.

The striking feature of the utilitarian view of justice is that it does not matter, except indirectly, how this sum of satisfactions is distributed among individuals any more than it matters, except indirectly, how one man distributes his satisfactions over time. The correct distribution in either case is that which yields the maximum fulfillment. Society must allocate its means of satisfaction whatever these are, rights and duties, opportunities and privileges, and various forms of wealth, so as to achieve this maximum if it can. But in itself no distribution of satisfaction is better than another except that the more equal distribution is to be preferred to break ties.[2] It is true that certain common sense precepts of justice, particularly those which concern the protection of liberties and rights, or which express the claims of desert, seem to contradict this contention. But from a utilitarian standpoint the explanation of these precepts and of their seemingly stringent character is that they are those precepts which experience shows should be strictly respected and departed from only under exceptional circumstances if the sum of advantages is to be maximized.[3] Yet, as with all other precepts, those of justice are derivative from the one end of attaining the greatest balance of satisfaction. Thus there is no reason in principle why the greater gains of some should not compensate for the lesser losses of others; or more importantly, why the violation of the liberty of a few might not be made right by the greater good shared by many. It simply happens that under most conditions, at least in a reasonably advanced stage of civilization, the greatest sum of advantages is not attained in this way. No doubt the strictness of common sense precepts of justice has a certain usefulness in limiting men's propensities to injustice and to socially injurious actions, but the utilitarian believes that to affirm this strictness as a first principle of morals is a mistake. For just as it is rational for one man to maximize the fulfillment of his system of desires, it is right for a society to maximize the net balance of satisfaction taken over all of its members.

The most natural way, then, of arriving at utilitarianism (although not, of course, the only way of doing so) is to adopt for society as a whole the principle of rational choice for one man. Once this is recognized, the place of the impartial spectator and the emphasis on sympathy in the history of utilitarian thought is readily understood. For it is by the conception of the impartial spectator and the use of sympathetic identification in guiding our imagination that the principle for one man is applied to society. It is this spectator who is conceived as carrying out the required organization of the desires of all persons into one coherent system of desire; it is by this construction that many persons are fused into one. Endowed with ideal powers of sympathy and imagination, the impartial spectator is the perfectly rational individual who identifies with and experiences the desires of others as if these desires were his own. In this way he ascertains the intensity of these desires and assigns them their appropriate weight in the one system of desire the satisfaction of which the ideal legislator then tries to maximize by adjusting the rules of the social system. On this conception of society separate individuals are thought of as so many different lines along which rights and duties are to be assigned and scarce means of satisfaction allocated in accordance with rules so as to give the greatest fulfillment of wants. The nature of the decision made by the ideal legislator is not, therefore, materially different from that of an entrepreneur deciding how to maximize his profit by producing this or that commodity, or that of a consumer deciding how to maximize his satisfaction by the purchase of this or that collection of goods. In each case there is a single person whose system of desires determines the best allocation of limited means. The correct decision is essentially a question of efficient administration. This view of social cooperation is the consequence of extending to society the principle of choice for one man, and then, to make this extension work, conflating all persons into one through the imaginative acts of the impartial sympathetic spectator. Utilitarianism does not take seriously the distinction between persons.

6. SOME RELATED CONTRASTS

It has seemed to many philosophers, and it appears to be supported by the convictions of common sense, that we distinguish as a matter of principle between the claims of liberty and right on the one hand and the desirability of increasing aggregate social welfare on the other; and that we give a certain priority, if not absolute weight, to the former. Each member of society is thought to have an inviolability founded on justice or, as some say, on natural right, which even the welfare of every one else cannot override. Justice denies that the loss of freedom for some is made right by a greater good shared by others. The reasoning which balances the gains and losses of different persons as if they were one person is excluded. Therefore in a just society the basic liberties are taken for granted and the rights secured by justice are not subject to political bargaining or to the calculus of social interests.

Justice as fairness attempts to account for these common sense convictions concerning the priority of justice by showing that they are the consequence of principles which would be chosen in the original position. These judgments reflect the rational preferences and the initial equality of the contracting parties. Although the utilitarian recognizes that, strictly speaking, his doctrine conflicts with these sentiments of justice, he maintains that common sense precepts of justice and notions of natural right have but a subordinate validity as secondary rules; they arise from the fact that under the conditions of civilized society there is great social utility in following them for the most part and in permitting violations only under exceptional circumstances. Even the excessive zeal with which we are apt to affirm these precepts and to appeal to these rights is itself granted a certain usefulness, since it counterbalances a natural human tendency to violate them in ways not sanctioned by utility. Once we understand this, the apparent disparity between the utilitarian principle and the strength of these persuasions of justice is no longer a philosophical difficulty. Thus while the contract doctrine accepts our convictions about the priority of justice as on the whole sound, utilitarianism seeks to account for them as a socially useful illusion.

A second contrast is that whereas the utilitarian extends to society the principle of choice for one man, justice as fairness, being a contract view, assumes that the principles of social choice, and so the principles of justice, are themselves the object of an original agreement. There is no reason to suppose that the principles which should regulate an association of men is simply an extension of the principle of choice for one man. On the contrary: if we assume that the correct regulative principle for anything depends on the nature of that thing, and that the plurality of distinct persons with separate systems of ends is an essential feature of human societies, we should not expect the principles of social choice to be utilitarian. To be sure, it has not been shown by anything said so far that the parties in the original position would not choose the principle of utility to define the terms of social cooperation. This is a difficult question which I shall examine later on. It is perfectly possible, from all that one knows at this point, that some form of the principle of utility would be adopted, and therefore that contract theory leads eventually to a deeper and more roundabout justification of utilitarianism. In fact a derivation of this kind is sometimes suggested by Bentham and Edgeworth, although it is not developed by them in any systematic way and to my knowledge it is not found in Sidgwick. For the present I shall simply assume that the persons in the original position would reject the utility principle and that they would adopt instead, for the kinds of reasons previously sketched, the two principles of justice already mentioned. In any case, from the standpoint of contract theory one cannot arrive at a principle of social choice merely by extending the principle of rational prudence to the system of desires constructed by the impartial spectator. To do this is not to take seriously the plurality and distinctness of individuals, nor to recognize as the basis of justice that to which men would consent. Here we may note a curious anomaly. It is customary to think of utilitarianism as individualistic, and certainly there are good reasons for this. The utilitarians were strong defenders of liberty and freedom of thought, and they held that the good of society is constituted by the advantages enjoyed by individuals. Yet utilitarianism is not individualistic, at least when arrived at by the more natural course of reflection, in that, by conflating all systems of desires, it applies to society the principle of choice for one man. And thus we see that the second contrast is related to the first, since it is this conflation, and the principle based upon it, which subjects the rights secured by justice to the calculus of social interests.

The last contrast that I shall mention now is that utilitarianism is a teleological theory whereas justice as fairness is not. By definition, then, the latter is a deontological theory, one that either does not specify the good independently from the right, or does not interpret the right as maximizing the good. (It should be noted that deontological theories are defined as non-teleological ones, not as views that characterize the rightness of institutions and acts independently from their consequences. All ethical doctrines worth our attention take consequences into account in judging rightness. One which did not would simply be irrational, crazy.) Justice as fairness is a deontological theory in the second way. For if it is assumed that the persons in the original position would choose a principle of equal liberty and restrict economic and social inequalities to those in everyone's interests, there is no reason to think that just institutions will maximize the good. (Here I suppose with utilitarianism that the good is defined as the satisfaction of rational desire.) Of course, it is not impossible that the most good is produced but it would be a coincidence. The question of attaining the greatest net balance of satisfaction never arises in justice as fairness; this maximum principle is not used at all.

There is a further point in this connection. In utilitarianism the satisfaction of any desire has some value in itself which must be taken into account in deciding what is right. In calculating the greatest balance of satisfaction it does not matter, except indirectly, what the desires are for. We are to arrange institutions so as to obtain the greatest sum of satisfactions; we ask no questions about their source or quality but only how their satisfaction would affect the total of well-being. Social welfare depends directly and solely upon the levels of satisfaction or dissatisfaction of individuals. Thus if men take a certain pleasure in discriminating against one another, in subjecting others to a lesser liberty as a means of enhancing their self-respect, then the satisfaction of these desires must be weighed in our deliberations according to their intensity, or whatever, along with other desires. If society decides to deny them fulfillment, or to suppress them, it is because they tend to be socially destructive and a greater welfare can be achieved in other ways.

In justice as fairness, on the other hand, persons accept in advance a principle of equal liberty and they do this without a knowledge of their more particular ends. They implicitly agree, therefore, to conform their conceptions of their good to what the principles of justice require, or at least not to press claims which directly violate them. An individual who finds that he enjoys seeing others in positions of lesser liberty understands that he has no claim whatever to this enjoyment. The pleasure he takes in other's deprivations is wrong in itself: it is a satisfaction which requires the violation of a principle to which he would agree in the original position. The principles of right, and so of justice, put limits on which satisfactions have value; they impose restrictions on what are reasonable conceptions of one's good. In drawing up plans and in deciding on aspirations men are to take these constraints into account. Hence in justice as fairness one does not take men's propensities and inclinations as given, whatever they are, and then seek the best way to fulfill them. Rather, their desires and aspirations are restricted from the outset by the principles of justice which specify the boundaries that men's systems of ends must respect. We can express this by saying that in justice as fairness the concept of right is prior to that of the good. A just social system defines the scope within which individuals must develop their aims, and it provides a framework of rights and opportunities and the means of satisfaction within and by the use of which these ends may be equitably pursued. The priority of justice is accounted for, in part, by holding that the interests requiring the violation of justice have no value. Having no merit in the first place, they cannot override its claims.

This priority of the right over the good in justice as fairness turns out to be a central feature of the conception. It imposes certain criteria on the design of the basic structure as a whole; these arrangements must not tend to generate propensities and attitudes contrary to the two principles of justice (that is, to certain principles, which are given from the first a definite content) and they must insure that just institutions are stable. Thus certain initial bounds are placed upon what is good and what forms of character are morally worthy, and so upon what kinds of persons men should be. Now any theory of justice will set up some limits of this kind, namely, those that are required if its first principles are to be satisfied given the circumstances. Utilitarianism excludes those desires and propensities which if encouraged or permitted would, in view of the situation, lead to a lesser net balance of satisfaction. But this restriction is largely formal, and in the absence of fairly detailed knowledge of the circumstances it does not give much indication of what these desires and propensities are. This is not, by itself, an objection to utilitarianism. It is simply a feature of utilitarian doctrine that it relies very heavily upon the natural facts and contingencies of human life in determining what forms of moral character are to be encouraged in a just society. The moral ideal of justice as fairness is more deeply embedded in the first principles of the ethical theory. This is characteristic of natural rights views (the contractarian tradition) in comparison with the theory of utility.

In setting forth these contrasts between justice as fairness and utilitarianism, I have had in mind only the classical doctrine. This is the view of Bentham and Sidgwick and of the utilitarian economists Edgeworth and Pigou. The kind of utilitarianism espoused by Hume would not serve my purpose; indeed, it is not strictly speaking utilitarian. In his well-known arguments against Locke's contract theory, for example, Hume maintains that the principles of fidelity and allegiance both have the same foundation in utility, and therefore that nothing is gained from basing political obligation on an original contract. Locke's doctrine represents, for Hume, an unnecessary shuffle one might as well appeal directly to utility.[4] But all Hume seems to mean by utility is the general interests and necessities of society. The principles of fidelity and allegiance derive from utility in the sense that the maintenance of the social order is impossible unless these principles are generally respected. But then Hume assumes that each man stands to gain, as judged by his long-term advantage, when law and government conform to the precepts founded on utility. No mention is made of the gains of some outweighing the disadvantages of others. For Hume, then, utility seems to be identical with some form of the common good; institutions satisfy its demands when they are to everyone's interests, at least in the long run. Now if this interpretation of Hume is correct, there is offhand no conflict with the priority of justice and no incompatibility with Locke's contract doctrine. For the role of equal rights in Locke is precisely to ensure that the only permissible departures from the state of nature are those which respect these rights and serve the common interest. It is clear that all the transformations from the state of nature which Locke approves of satisfy this condition and are such that rational men concerned to advance their ends could consent to them in a state of equality. Hume nowhere disputes the propriety of these constraints. His critique of Locke's contract doctrine never denies, or even seems to recognize, its fundamental contention.

The merit of the classical view as formulated by Bentham, Edgeworth, and Sidgwick is that it clearly recognizes what is at stake, namely, the relative priority of the principles of justice and the rights which these principles establish. The question is whether the imposition of disadvantages on a few can be outweighed by a greater sum of advantages enjoyed by others; or whether the weight of justice requires an equal liberty for all and permits only those economic and social inequalities which are to each person's interests. Implicit in the contrasts between classical utilitarianism and justice as fairness is a difference in the underlying conceptions of society. In the one we think of a well-ordered society as a scheme of cooperation for reciprocal advantage regulated by principles which persons would choose in an initial situation that is fair, in the other as the efficient administration of social resources to maximize the satisfaction of the system of desire constructed by the impartial spectator from the many individual systems of desires accepted as given. The comparison with classical utilitarianism in its more natural derivation brings out this contrast.

11. TWO PRINCIPLES OF JUSTICE

I shall now state in a provisional form the two principles of justice that I believe would be chosen in the original position. In this section I wish to make only the most general comments, and therefore the first formulation of these principles is tentative. As we go on I shall run through several formulations and approximate step by step the final statement to be given much later. I believe that doing this allows the exposition to proceed in a natural way.

The first statement of the two principles reads as follows.

First: each person is to have an equal right to the most extensive basic liberty compatible with a similar liberty for others.

Second: social and economic inequalities are to be arranged so that they are both (a) reasonably expected to be to everyone's advantage, and (b) attached to positions and offices open to all.

By way of general comment, these principles primarily apply, as I have said, to the basic structure of society. They are to govern the assignment of rights and duties and to regulate the distribution of social and economic advantages. As their formulation suggests, these principles presuppose that the social structure can be divided into two more or less distinct parts, the first principle applying to the one, the second to the other. They distinguish between those aspects of the social system that define and secure the equal liberties of citizenship and those that specify and establish social and economic inequalities. The basic liberties of citizens are roughly speaking political liberty (the right to vote and to be eligible for public office) together with freedom of speech and assembly; liberty of conscience and freedom of thought; freedom of the person along with the right to hold (personal) property; and freedom from arbitrary arrest and seizure as defined by the concept of the rule of law. These liberties are all required to be equal by the first principle, since citizens of a just society are to have the same basic rights.

The second principle applies, in the first approximation, to the distribution of income and wealth and to the design of organizations that make use of differences in authority and responsibility, or chains of command. While the distribution of wealth and income need not be equal, it must be to everyone's advantage, and at the same time, positions of authority and offices of command must be accessible to all. One applies the second principle by holding positions open, and then, subject to this constraint, arranges social and economic inequalities so that everyone benefits.

These principles are to be arranged in a serial order with the first principle prior to the second. This ordering means that a departure from the institutions of equal liberty required by the first principle cannot be justified by, or compensated for, by greater social and economic advantages. The distribution of wealth and income, and the hierarchies of authority, must be consistent with both the liberties of equal citizenship and equality of opportunity.

It is clear that these principles are rather specific in their content, and their acceptance rests on certain assumptions that I must eventually try to explain and justify. A theory of justice depends upon a theory of society in ways that will become evident as we proceed. For the present, it should be observed that the two principles (and this holds for all formulations) are a special case of a more general conception of justice that can be expressed as follows.

> All social values—liberty and opportunity, income and wealth, and the bases of self-respect—are to be distributed equally unless an unequal distribution of any, or all, of these values is to everyone's advantage.

Injustice, then is simply inequalities that are not to the benefit of all. Of course, this conception is extremely vague and requires interpretation.

As a first step, suppose that the basic structure of society distributes tributes certain primary goods, that is, things that every rational man is presumed to want. These goods normally have a use whatever a person's rational plan of life. For simplicity, assume that the chief primary goods at the disposition of society are rights and liberties, powers and opportunities, income and wealth. (Later on in Part Three the primary good of self-respect has a central place.) These are the social primary goods. Other primary goods such as health and vigor, intelligence and imagination, are natural goods; although their possession is influenced by the basic structure, they are not so directly under its control. Imagine, then, a hypothetical initial arrangement in which all the social primary goods are equally distributed: everyone has similar rights and duties, and income and wealth are evenly shared. This state of affairs provides a benchmark for judging improvements. If certain inequalities of wealth and organizational powers would make everyone better off than in this hypothetical starting situation, then they accord with the general conception.

Now it is possible, at least theoretically, that by giving up some of their fundamental liberties men are sufficiently compensated by the resulting social and economic gains. The general conception of justice imposes no restrictions on what sort of inequalities are permissible; it only requires that everyone's position be improved. We need not suppose anything so drastic as consenting to a condition of slavery. Imagine instead that men forego certain political rights when the economic returns are significant and their capacity to influence the course of policy by the exercise of these rights would be marginal in any case. It is this kind of exchange which the two principles as stated rule out; being arranged in serial order they do not permit exchanges between basic liberties and economic and social gains. The serial ordering of principles expresses an underlying preference among primary social goods. When this preference is rational so likewise is the choice of these principles in this order.

In developing justice as fairness I shall, for the most part, leave aside the general conception of justice and examine instead the special case of the two principles in serial order. The advantage of this procedure is that from the first the matter of priorities is recognized and an effort made to find principles to deal with it. One is led to attend throughout to the conditions under which the acknowledgment of the absolute weight of liberty with respect to social and economic advantages, as defined by the lexical order of the two principles, would be reasonable. Offhand, this ranking appears extreme and too special a case to be of much interest; but there is more justification for it than would appear at first sight. Or at any rate, so I shall maintain.Furthermore, the distinction between fundamental rights and liberties and economic and social benefits marks a difference among primary social goods that one should try to exploit. It suggests an important division in the social system. Of course, the distinctions drawn and the ordering proposed are bound to be at best only approximations. There are surely circumstances in which they fail. But it is essential to depict clearly the main lines of a reasonable conception of justice; and under many conditions anyway, the two principles in serial order may serve well enough. When necessary we can fall back on the more general conception.

The fact that the two principles apply to institutions has certain consequences. Several points illustrate this. First of all, the rights and liberties referred to by these principles are those which are defined by the public rules of the basic structure. Whether men are free is determined by the rights and duties established by the major institutions of society. Liberty is a certain pattern of social forms. The first principle simply requires that certain sorts of rules, those defining basic liberties, apply to everyone equally and that they allow the most extensive liberty compatible with a like liberty for all. The only reason for circumscribing the rights defining liberty and making men's freedom less extensive than it might otherwise be is that these equal rights as institutionally defined would interfere with one another.

Another thing to bear in mind is that when principles mention persons, or require that everyone gain from an inequality, the reference is to representative persons holding the various social positions, or offices, or whatever, established by the basic structure. Thus in applying the second principle I assume that it is possible to assign an expectation of well-being to representative individuals holding these positions. This expectation indicates their life prospects as viewed from their social station. In general, the expectations of representative persons depend upon the distribution of rights and duties throughout the basic structure. When this changes, expectations change. I assume, then, that expectations are connected: by raising the prospects of the representative man in one position we presumably increase or decrease the prospects of representative men in other positions. Since it applies to institutional forms, the second principle (or rather the first part of it) refers to the expectations of representative individuals. As I shall discuss below, neither principle applies to distributions of particular goods to particular individuals who may be identified by their proper names. The situation where someone is considering how to allocate certain commodities to needy persons who are known to him is not within the scope of the principles. They are meant to regulate basic institutional arrangements. We must not assume that there is much similarity from the standpoint of justice between an administrative allotment of goods to specific persons and the appropriate design of society. Our common sense intuitions for the former may be a poor guide to the latter.

Now the second principle insists that each person benefit from permissible inequalities in the basic structure. This means that it must be reasonable for each relevant representative man defined by this structure, when he views it as a going concern, to prefer his prospects with the inequality to his prospects without it. One is not allowed to justify differences in income or organizational powers on the ground that the disadvantages of those in one position are out-weighed by the greater advantages of those in another. Much less can infringements of liberty be counterbalanced in this way. Applied to the basic structure, the principle of utility would have us maximize the sum of expectations of representative men (weighted by the number of persons they represent, on the classical view); and this would permit us to compensate for the losses of some by the gains of others. Instead, the two principles require that everyone benefit from economic and social inequalities. It is obvious, however, that there are indefinitely many ways in which all may be advantaged when the initial arrangement of equality is taken as a benchmark. How then are we to choose among these possibilities? The principles must be specified so that they yield a determinate conclusion. I now turn to this problem.

24. THE VEIL OF IGNORANCE

The idea of the original position is to set up a fair procedure so that any principles agreed to will be just. The aim is to use the notion of pure procedural justice as a basis of theory. Somehow we must nullify the effects of specific contingencies which put men at odds and tempt them to exploit social and natural circumstances to their own advantage. Now in order to do this I assume that the parties are situated behind a veil of ignorance. They do not know how the various alternatives will affect their own particular case and they are obliged to evaluate principles solely on the basis of general considerations.[5]

It is assumed, then, that the parties do not know certain kinds of particular facts. First of all, no one knows his place in society, his class position or social status; nor does he know his fortune in the distribution of natural assets and abilities, his intelligence and strength, and the like. Nor, again, does anyone know his conception of the good, the particulars of his rational plan of life, or even the special features of his psychology such as his aversion to risk or liability to optimism or pessimism. More than this, I assume that the parties do not know the particular circumstances of their own society. That is, they do not know its economic or political situation or the level of civilization and culture it has been able to achieve. The persons in the original position have no information as to which generation they belong. These broader restrictions on knowledge are appropriate in part because questions of social justice arise between generations as well as within them, for example, the question of the appropriate rate of capital saving and of the conservation of natural resources and the environment of nature. There is also, theoretically anyway, the question of a reasonable genetic policy. In these cases too, in order to carry through the idea of the original position, the parties must not know the contingencies that set them in opposition. They must choose principles the consequences of which they are prepared to live with whatever generation they turn out to belong to.

As far as possible, then, the only particular facts which the parties know is that their society is subject to the circumstances of justice and whatever this implies. It is taken for granted, however, that they know the general facts about human society. They understand political affairs and the principles of economic theory; they know the basis of social organization and the laws of human psychology. Indeed, the parties are presumed to know whatever general facts affect the choice of the principles of justice. There are no limitations on general information, that is, on general laws and theories, since conceptions of justice must be adjusted to the characteristics of the systems of social cooperation which they are to regulate, and there is no reason to rule out these facts. It is, for example, a consideration against a conception of justice that, in view of the laws of moral psychology, men would not acquire a desire to act upon it even when the institutions of their society satisfied it. For in this case there would be difficulty in securing the stability of social cooperation. It is an important feature of a conception of justice that it should generate its own support. That is, its principles should be such that when they are embodied in the basic structure of society men tend to acquire the corresponding sense of justice. Given the principles of moral learning, men develop a desire to act in accordance with its principles. In this case a conception of justice is stable. This kind of general information is admissible in the original position.

The notion of the veil of ignorance raises several difficulties. Some may object that the exclusion of nearly all particular information makes it difficult to grasp what is meant by the original position. Thus it may be helpful to observe that one or more persons can at any time enter this position, or perhaps, better, simulate the deliberations of this hypothetical situation, simply by reasoning in accordance with the appropriate restrictions. In arguing for a conception of justice we must be sure that it is among the permitted alternatives and satisfies the stipulated formal constraints. No considerations can be advanced in its favor unless they would be rational ones for us to urge were we to lack the kind of knowledge that is excluded. The evaluation of principles must proceed in terms of the general consequences of their public recognition and universal application, it being assumed that they will be complied with by everyone. To say that a certain conception of justice would be chosen in the original position is equivalent to saying that rational deliberation satisfying certain conditions and restriction would reach a certain conclusion. If necessary, the argument to this result could be set out more formally. I shall, however, speak throughout in terms of the notion of the original position. It is more economical and suggestive, and brings out certain essential features that otherwise one might easily overlook.

These remarks show that the original position is not to be thought of as a general assembly which includes at one moment everyone who will live at some time; or, much less, as an assembly of everyone who could live at some time. It is not a gathering of all actual or possible persons. To conceive of the original position in either of these ways is to stretch fantasy too far; the conception would cease to be a natural guide to intuition. In any case, it is important that the original position be interpreted so that one can at any time adopt its perspective. It must make no difference when one takes up this viewpoint, or who does so: the restrictions must be such that the same principles are always chosen. The veil of ignorance is a key condition in meeting this requirement. It insures not only that the information available is relevant, but that it is at all times the same.

It may be protested that the condition of the veil of ignorance is irrational. Surely, some may object, principles should be chosen in the light of all the knowledge available. There are various replies to this contention. Here I shall sketch those which emphasize the simplifications that need to be made if one is to have any theory at all. To begin with, it is clear that since the differences among the parties are unknown to them, and everyone is equally rational and similarly situated, each is convinced by the same arguments. Therefore, we can view the choice in the original position from the standpoint of one person selected at random. If anyone after due reflection prefers a conception of justice to another, then they all do, and a unanimous agreement can be reached. We can, to make the circumstances more vivid, imagine that the parties are required to communicate with each other through a referee as intermediary, and that he is to announce which alternatives have been suggested and the reasons offered in their support. He forbids the attempt to form coalitions, and he informs the parties when they have come to an understanding. But such a referee is actually superfluous, assuming that the deliberations of the parties must be similar.

Thus there follows the very important consequence that the parties have no basis for bargaining in the usual sense. No one knows his situation in society nor his natural assets, and therefore no one is in a position to tailor principles to his advantage. We might imagine that one of the contractees threatens to hold out unless the others agree to principles favorable to him. But how does he know which principles are especially in his interests? The same holds for the formation of coalitions; if a group were to decide to band together to the disadvantage of the others, they would not know how to favor themselves in the choice of principles. Even if they could get everyone to agree to their proposal, they would have no assurance that it was to their advantage, since they cannot identify themselves either by name or description. The one case where this conclusion fails is that of saving. Since the persons in the original position know that they are contemporaries (taking the present time of entry interpretation), they can favor their generation by refusing to make any sacrifices at all for their successors; they simply acknowledge the principle that no one has a duty to save for posterity. Previous generations have saved or they have not there is nothing the parties can now do to affect that. So in this instance the veil of ignorance fails to secure the desired result. Therefore I resolve the question of justice between generations a different way by altering the motivation assumption. But with the adjustment no one is able to formulate principles especially designed to advance his own cause. Whatever his temporal position, each is forced to choose for everyone.[6]

The restrictions on particular information in the original position are, then, of fundamental importance. Without them we would not be able to work out any definite theory of justice at all. We would have to be content with a vague formula stating that justice is what would be agreed to without being able to say much, if anything, about the substance of the agreement itself. The formal constraint of the concept of right, those applying to principles directly, are not sufficient for our purpose. The veil of ignorance makes possible unanimous choice of a particular conception of justice. Without these limitations on knowledge the bargaining problem of the original position would be hopelessly complicated. Even if theoretical a solution were to exist, we would not, at present anyway, be at to determine it.

The notion of the veil of ignorance is implicit, I think, in Kant's ethics. Nevertheless the problem of defining the knowledge of the parties and of characterizing the alternatives open to them has often been passed over, even by contract theories. Sometimes the situation definitive of moral deliberation is presented in such an indeterminate way that one cannot ascertain how it will turn out. Thus Perry's doctrine is essentially contractarian: he holds that social and personal integration must proceed by entirely different principles, the latter by rational prudence the former by the concurrence of persons of good will. He would appear to reject utilitarianism on much the same grounds suggested earlier: namely, that it improperly extends the principle of choice for one person to choices facing society. The right course of action is characterized as that which best advances social aims as these would be formulated by reflective agreement given that the parties have full knowledge of the circumstances and are moved by a benevolent concern for one another's interests. No effort is made, however, to specify in any precise way the possible outcomes of this sort of agreement. Indeed, without a far more elaborate account, no conclusions can be drawn. I do not wish here to criticize others; rather, I want to explain the necessity for what may seem at times like so many irrelevant details.

Now the reasons for the veil of ignorance go beyond mere simplicity. We want to define the original position so that we get the desired solution. If a knowledge of particulars is allowed, then the outcome is biased by arbitrary contingencies. As already observed, to each according to his threat advantage is not a principle of justice. If the original position is to yield agreements that are just, the parties must be fairly situated and treated equally as moral persons. The arbitrariness of the world must be corrected for by adjusting the circumstances of the initial contractual situation. Moreover, if in choosing principles we required unanimity even when there is full information, only a few rather obvious cases could be decided. A conception of justice based on unanimity in these circumstances would indeed be weak and trivial.

But once knowledge is excluded, the requirement of unanimity is not out of place and the fact that it can be satisfied is of great importance. It enables us to say of the preferred conception of justice that it represents a genuine reconciliation of interests.

A final comment. For the most part I shall suppose that the parties possess all general information. No general facts are closed to them. I do this mainly to avoid complications. Nevertheless a conception of justice is to be the public basis of the terms of social cooperation. Since common understanding necessitates certain bounds on the complexity of principles, there may likewise be limits on the use of theoretical knowledge in the original position. Now clearly it would be very difficult to classify and to grade for complexity the various sorts of general facts. I shall make no attempt to do this. We do however recognize an intricate theoretical construction when we meet one. Thus it seems reasonable to say that other things equal one conception of justice is to be preferred to another when it is founded upon markedly simpler general facts, and its choice does not depend upon elaborate calculations in the light of a vast array of theoretically defined possibilities. It is desirable that the grounds for a public conception of justice should be evident to everyone when circumstances permit. This consideration favors, I believe, the two principles of justice over the criterion of utility.

26. THE REASONING LEADING TO THE TWO PRINCIPLES OF JUSTICE

In this and the next two sections I take up the choice between the two principles of justice and the principle of average utility. Determining the rational preference between these two options is perhaps the central problem in developing the conception of justice as fairness as a viable alternative to the utilitarian tradition. I shall begin in this section by presenting some intuitive remarks favoring the two principles. I shall also discuss briefly the qualitative structure of the argument that needs to be made if the case for these principles is to be conclusive.

It will be recalled that the general conception of justice as fairness requires that all primary social goods be distributed equally unless an unequal distribution would be to everyone's advantage. No restrictions are placed on exchanges of these goods and therefore a lesser liberty can be compensated for by greater social and economic benefits. Now looking at the situation from the standpoint of one person selected arbitrarily, there is no way for him to win special advantages for himself. Nor, on the other hand, are there grounds for his acquiescing in special disadvantages. Since it is not reasonable for him to expect more than an equal share in the division of social goods, and since it is not rational for him to agree to less, the sensible thing for him to do is to acknowledge as the first principle of justice one requiring an equal distribution. Indeed, this principle is so obvious that we would expect it to occur to anyone immediately.

Thus, the parties start with a principle establishing equal liberty for all, including equality of opportunity, as well as an equal distribution of income and wealth. But there is no reason why this acknowledgment should be final. If there are inequalities in the basic structure that work to make everyone better off in comparison with the benchmark of initial equality, why not permit them? The immediate gain which a greater equality might allow can be regarded as intelligently invested in view of its future return. If, for example, these inequalities set up various incentives which succeed in eliciting more productive efforts, a person in the original position may look upon them as necessary to cover the costs of training and to encourage effective performance. One might think that ideally individuals should want to serve one another. But since the parties are assumed not to take an interest in one another's interests, their acceptance of these inequalities is only the acceptance of the relations in which men stand in the circumstances of justice. They have no grounds for complaining of one another's motives. A person in the original position would, therefore, concede the justice of these inequalities. Indeed, it would be shortsighted of him not to do so. He would hesitate to agree to these regularities only if he would be dejected by the bare knowledge or perception that others were better situated; and I have assumed that the parties decide as if they are not moved by envy. In order to make the principle regulating inequalities determinate, one looks at the system from the standpoint of the least advantaged representative man. Inequalities are permissible when they maximize, or at least all contribute to, the long-term expectations of the least fortunate group in society.

Now this general conception imposes no constraints on what sorts of inequalities are allowed, whereas the special conception, by putting the two principles in serial order (with the necessary adjustments in meaning) forbids exchanges between basic liberties and economic and social benefits. I shall not try to justify this ordering here. But roughly, the idea underlying this ordering is that if the parties assume that their basic liberties can be effectively exercised, they will not exchange a lesser liberty for an improvement in economic well-being. It is only when social conditions do not allow the effective establishment of these rights that one can concede their limitation; and these restrictions can be granted only to the extent that they are necessary to prepare the way for a free society. The denial of equal liberty can be defended only if it is necessary to raise the level of civilization so that in due course these freedoms can be enjoyed. Thus in adopting a serial order we are in effect making a special assumption in the original position, namely, that the parties know that the conditions of their society, whatever they are, admit the effective realization of the equal liberties. The serial ordering of the two principles of justice eventually comes to be reasonable if the general conception is consistently followed. This lexical ranking is the long-run tendency of the general view. For the most part I shall assume that the requisite circumstances for the serial order obtain.

It seems clear from these remarks that the two principles are at least a plausible conception of justice. The question, though, is how one is to argue for them more systematically. Now there are several things to do. One can work out their consequences for institutions and note their implications for fundamental social policy. In this way they are tested by a comparison with our considered judgments of justice. Part II is devoted to this. But one can also try to find arguments in their favor that are decisive from the standpoint of the original position. In order to see how this might be done, it is useful as a heuristic device to think of the two principles as the maximin solution to the problem of social justice. There is an analogy between the two principles and the maximin rule for choice under uncertainty. This is evident from the fact that the two principles are those a person would choose for the design of a society in which his enemy is to assign him his place. The maximin rule tells us to rank alternatives by their worst possible outcomes: we are to adopt the alternative the worst outcome of which is superior to the worst outcomes of the others. The persons in the original position do not, of course, assume that their initial place in society is decided by a malevolent opponent. As I note below, they should not reason from false premises. The veil of ignorance does not violate this idea, since an absence of information is not misinformation. But that the two principles of justice would be chosen if the parties were forced to protect themselves against such a contingency explains the sense in which this conception is the maximin solution. And this analogy suggests that if the original position has been described so that it is rational for the parties to adopt the conservative attitude expressed by this rule, a conclusive argument can indeed be constructed for these principles. Clearly the maximin rule is not, in general, a suitable guide for choices under uncertainty. But it is attractive in situations marked by certain special features. My aim, then, is to show that a good case can be made for the two principles based on the fact that the original position manifests these features to the fullest possible degree, carrying them to the limit, so to speak.

Consider the gain-and-loss table below. It represents the gains and losses for a situation which is not a game of strategy. There is no one playing against the person making the decision; instead he is faced with several possible circumstances which may or may not obtain. Which circumstances happen to exist does not depend upon what the person choosing decides or whether he announces his moves in advance. The numbers in the table are monetary values (in hundreds of dollars) in comparison with some initial situation. The gain (g) depends upon the individual's decision (d) and the circumstances (c). Thus g = f (d, c). Assuming that there are three possible decisions and three possible circumstances, we might have this gain-and-loss table.

	Circumstances		
Decision	C_1	C_2	C_3
d_1	−7	8	12
d_2	−8	7	14
d_3	5	6	8

The maximin rule requires that we make the third decision. For in this case the worst that can happen is that one gains five hundred dollars, which is better than the worst for the other actions. If we adopt one of these we may lose either eight or seven hundred dollars. Thus, the choice of d_3 maximizes f (d,c) for that value of c, which for a given d, minimizes f. The term "maximin" means the *maximum minimorum.* and the rule directs our attention to the worst that can happen under any proposed course of action, and to decide in the light of that.

Now there appear to be three chief features of situations that give plausibility to this unusual rule. First, since the rule takes no account of the likelihoods of the possible circumstances, there must be some reason for sharply discounting estimates of these probabilities. Offhand, the most natural rule of choice would seem to be to compute the expectation of monetary gain for each decision and then to adopt the course of action with the highest prospect. (This expectation is defined as follows: let g_{ij} represent the numbers in the numbers in the gain-and-loss table, where i is the row index and j is the column index; and let p_j, j = 1, 2, 3, be the likelihoods of the circumstances, with $\Sigma p_s = 1$. Then the expectation for the *i*th decision is equal to $\Sigma\, p_j g_{ij}$.) Thus it must be, for example, that the situation is one in which a knowledge of likelihoods is impossible or at best extremely insecure. In this case it is unreasonable not to be skeptical of probabilistic calculations unless there is no other way out, particularly if the decision is a fundamental one that needs to be justified to others.

The second feature that suggests the maximin rule is the following: the person choosing has a conception of the good such that he cares very little, if anything, for what he might gain above the minimum stipend that he can, in fact, be sure of by following the maximin rule. It is not worthwhile for him to take a chance for the sake of a further advantage, especially when it may turn out that he loses much that is important to him. This last provision bring in the third feature, namely, that the rejected alternatives have outcomes that one can hardly accept. The situation involves grave risks. Of course these features work most effectively in combination. The paradigm situation for following the maximin rule is when all three features are realized to the highest degree. This rule does not, then, generally apply, nor of course is it self-evident. Rather, it is a maxim, a rule of thumb, that comes into its own in special circumstances. Its application depends upon the qualitative structure of the possible gains and losses in relation to one's conception of the good, all this against a background in which it is reasonable to discount conjectural estimates of likelihoods.

It should be noted, as the comments on the gain-and-loss table say, that the entries in the table represent monetary values and not utilities. This difference is significant since for one thing computing expectations on the basis of such objective values is not the same thing as computing expected utility and may lead to different results. The essential point though is that in justice as fairness the parties do not know their conception of the good and cannot estimate their utility in the ordinary sense. In any case, we want to go behind de facto preferences generated by given conditions. Therefore expectations are based upon an index of primary goods and the parties make their choice accordingly. The entries in the example are in terms of money and not utility to indicate this aspect of the contract doctrine.

Now, as I have suggested, the original position has been defined so that it is a situation in which the maximin rule applies. In order to see this, let us review briefly the nature of this situation with these three special features in mind. To begin with, the veil of ignorance excludes all but the vaguest knowledge of likelihoods. The parties have no basis for determining the probable nature of their society, or their place in it. Thus they have strong reasons for being wary of probability calculations if any other course is open to them. They must also take in account the fact that their choice of principles should seem reasonable to others, in particular their descendants, whose rights will be deeply affected by it. There are further grounds for discounting that I shall mention as we go along. For the present it suffices to note that these considerations are strengthened by the fact that the parties know very little about the gain-and-loss table. Not only are they unable to conjecture the likelihoods of the various possible circumstances, they cannot say much about what the possible circumstances are, much less enumerate them and foresee the outcome of each alternative available. Those deciding are much more in the dark than the illustration by a numerical table suggests. It is for this reason that I have spoken of an analogy with the maximin rule.

Several kinds of arguments for the two principles of justice illustrate the second feature. Thus, if we can maintain that these principles provide a workable theory of social justice, and that they are compatible with reasonable demands of efficiency, then this conception guarantees a satisfactory minimum. There may be, on reflection, little reason for trying to do better. Thus much of the argument is to show, by their application to the main questions of social justice, that the two principles are a satisfactory conception. These details have a philosophical purpose. Moreover, this line of thought is practically decisive if we can establish the priority of liberty, the lexical ordering of the two principles. For this priority implies that the persons in the original position have no desire to try for greater gains at the expense of the equal liberties. The minimum assured by the two principles in lexical order is not one that the parties wish to jeopardize for the sake of greater economic and social advantages.

Finally, the third feature holds if we can assume that other conceptions of justice may lead to institutions that the parties would find intolerable. For example, it has sometimes been held that under some conditions the utility principle (in either form) justifies if not slavery or serfdom, at any rate serious infractions of liberty for the sake of greater social benefits. We need not consider here the truth of this claim, or the likelihood that the requisite conditions obtain. For the moment, this contention is only to illustrate the way in which conceptions of justice may allow for outcome which the parties may not be able to accept. And having the ready alternative of the two principles of justice which secure a satisfactory minimum, it seems unwise, if not irrational, for them to take a chance that these outcomes are not realized.

So much, then, for a brief sketch of the features of situations in which the maximin rule comes into its own and of the way in which the arguments for the two principles of justice can be subsumed under them. Thus if the list of traditional views represents the possible decisions, these principles would be selected by the rule. The original position clearly exhibits these special features to a very high degree in view of the fundamental character of the choice of a conception of justice. These remarks about the maximin rule are intended only to clarify the structure of the choice problem in the original position. They depict its qualitative anatomy. The arguments for the two principles will be presented more fully as we proceed. I want to conclude this section by taking up an objection which is likely to be made against the difference principle and which leads into an important question. The objection is that since we are to maximize (subject to the usual constraints) the long-term prospects of the least advantaged, it seems that the justice of large increases or decreases in the expectations of the more advantaged may depend upon small changes in the prospects of those worst off. To illustrate: the most extreme disparities in wealth and income are allowed provided that the expectations of the least fortunate are raised in the slightest degree. But at the same time similar inequalities favoring the more advantaged are forbidden when those in the worst position lose by the least amount. Yet it seems extraordinary that the justice of increasing the expectations of the better placed by a billion dollars, say, should turn on whether the prospects of the least favored increase or decrease by a penny. This objection is analogous to the following difficulty with the maximin rule. Consider the sequence of gain-and-loss tables:

0	N
1/n	1

for all natural numbers n. Even if for some smallish number it is reasonable to select the second row, surely there is another point later in the sequence when it is irrational not to choose the first row contrary to the rule.

Part of the answer is that the difference principle is not intended to apply to such abstract possibilities. As I have said, the problem of social justice is not that of allocating *ad libitum* various amounts of something, whether it be money, or property, or whatever, among given individuals. Nor is there some substance of which expectations are made that can be shuffled from one representative man to another in all possible combinations. The possibilities which the objection envisages cannot arise in real cases; the feasible set is so restricted that they are excluded. The reason for this is that the two principles are tied together as one conception of justice which applies to the basic structure of society as a whole. The operation of the principles of equal liberty and open positions prevents these contingencies from occurring. For as we raise the expectations of the more advantaged the situation of the worst off is continuously improved. Each such increase is in the latter's interest, up to a certain point anyway. For the greater expectations of the more favored presumably cover the costs of training and encourage better performance thereby contributing to the general advantage. While nothing guarantees that inequalities will not be significant, there is a persistent tendency for them to be leveled down by the increasing availability of educated talent and ever widening opportunities. The conditions established by the other principles insure that the disparities likely to result will be much less than the differences that men have often tolerated in the past.

We should also observe that the difference principle not only assumes the operation of other principles, but it presupposes as well a certain theory of social institutions. In particular, as I shall discuss in some detail in Chapter V, it relies on the idea that in a competitive economy (with or without private ownership) with an open class system excessive inequalities will not be the rule. Given the distribution of natural assets and the laws of motivation, great disparities will not long persist. Now the point to stress here is that there is no objection to resting the choice of first principles upon the general facts of economics and psychology. As we have seen the parties in the original position are assumed to know the general facts about human society. Since this knowledge enters into the premises of their deliberations, their choice of principles is relative to these facts. What is essential, of course, is that these premises be true and sufficiently general. It is often objected, for example that utilitarianism may allow for slavery and serfdom, and for other infractions of liberty. Whether these institutions are justified made to depend upon whether actuarial calculations show that they yield a higher balance of happiness. To this the utilitarian replies that the nature of society is such that these calculations are normally against such denials of liberty. Utilitarians seek to account for the claims of liberty and equality by making certain standard assumptions, as I shall refer to them. Thus they suppose that persons have similar utility functions which satisfy the condition of diminishing marginal utility. It follows from these stipulations that, given a fixed amount of income say, the distribution should be equal, once we leave aside affects on future production. For so long as some have more than others, total utility can be increased by transfers to those who have less. The assignment of rights and liberties can be regarded in much the same way. There is nothing wrong with this procedure provided the assumptions are sound.

Contract theory agrees, then, with utilitarianism in holding that the fundamental principles of justice quite properly depend upon the natural facts about men in society. This dependence is made explicit by the description of the original position: the decision of the parties is taken in the light of general knowledge. Moreover, the various elements of the original position presuppose many things about the circumstances of human life. Some philosophers have thought that ethical first principles should be independent of all contingent assumptions, that they should take for granted no truths except those of logic and others that follow from these by an analysis of concepts. Moral conceptions should hold for all possible worlds. Now this view makes moral philosophy the study of the ethics of creation: an examination of the reflections an omnipotent deity might entertain in determining which is the best of all possible worlds. Even the general facts of nature are to be chosen. Certainly we have a natural religious interest in the ethics of creation. But it would appear to outrun human comprehension. From the point of view of contract theory it amounts to supposing that the persons in the original position know nothing at all about themselves or their world. How, then, can they possibly make a decision? A problem of choice is well defined only if the alternatives are suitably restricted by natural laws and other constraints, and those deciding already have certain inclinations to choose among them. Without a definite structure of this kind the question posed is indeterminate. For this reason we need have no hesitation in making the choice of the principles of justice presuppose a certain theory of social institutions. Indeed, one cannot avoid assumptions about general facts any more than one can do without a conception of the good on the basis of which the parties rank alternatives. If these assumptions are true and suitably general, everything is in order, for without these elements the whole scheme would be pointless and empty.

It is evident from these remarks that both general facts as well as moral conditions are needed even in the argument for the first principles of justice. (Of course, it has always been clear that secondary moral rules and particular ethical judgments depend upon factual premises as well as normative principles.) In a contract theory, these moral conditions take the form of a description of the initial contractual situation. It is also clear that there is a division of labor between general facts and moral conditions in arriving at conceptions of justice, and this division can be different from one theory to another. As I have noted before, principles differ in the extent to which they incorporate the desired moral ideal. It is characteristic of utilitarianism that it leaves so much to arguments from general facts. The utilitarian tends to meet objections by holding that the laws of society and of human nature rule out the cases offensive to our considered judgments. Justice as fairness, by contrast, embeds the ideals of justice, as ordinarily understood, more directly into its first principles. This conception relies less on general facts in reaching a match with our judgments of justice. It ensures this fit over a wider range of possible cases.

There are two reasons that justify this embedding of ideals into first principles. First of all, and most obviously, the utilitarian's standard assumptions that lead to the wanted consequences may be only probably true, or even doubtfully so. Moreover, their full meaning and application may be highly conjectural. And the same may hold for all the requisite general suppositions that support the principle of utility. From the standpoint of the original position it may be unreasonable to rely upon these hypotheses and therefore far more sensible to embody the ideal more expressly in the principles chosen. Thus it seems that the parties would prefer to secure their liberties straightway rather than have them depend upon what may be uncertain and speculative actuarial calculations. These remarks are further confirmed by the desirability of avoiding complicated theoretical arguments in arriving at a public conception of justice (§ 24). In comparison with the reasoning for the two principles, the grounds for the utility criterion trespass upon this constraint. But secondly, there is a real advantage in persons announcing to one another once and for all that even though theoretical computations of utility always happen to favor the equal liberties (assuming that this is indeed the case here), they do not wish that things had been different. Since in justice as fairness moral conceptions are public, the choice of the two principles is, in effect, such an announcement. And the benefits of this collective profession favor these principles even though the standard utilitarian assumptions should be true. The relevant point here is that while, in general, an ethical theory can certainly invoke natural facts, there may nevertheless be good reasons for embedding convictions of justice more directly into first principles than a theoretically complete grasp of the contingencies of the world may actually require.

NOTES

1. The process of mutual adjustment of principles and considered judgments is not peculiar to moral philosophy. See Nelson Goodman, *Fact, Fiction, and Forecast* (Cambridge, Mass., Harvard University Press, 1955), pp. 65–68, for parallel remarks concerning the justification of the principles of deductive and inductive inference.

2. On this point see Sidgwick, *The Methods of Ethics,* pp. 416f.

3. See J. S. Mill, *Utilitarianism,* ch. IV, last two pars.

4. "Of the Original Contract," *Essays: Moral, Political, and Literary,* ed. T. H. Green and T. H. Grose, vol. 1 (London, 1875), pp. 454f.

5. The veil of ignorance is so natural a condition that something like it must have occurred to many. The closest express statement of it known to me is found in J. C. Harsanyi, "Cardinal Utility in Welfare Economics and in the Theory of Risk-Taking," *Journal of Political Economy,* vol. 61 (1953). Harsanyi uses it to develop a utilitarian theory, as I discuss below in §§27–28.

6. Rousseau, *The Social Contract,* bk. II, ch. IV, par. 5.

Robert Nozick

Anarchy, State, and Utopia

1974

PREFACE

Individuals have rights, and there are things no person or group may do to them (without violating their rights). So strong and far-reaching are these rights that they raise the question of what, if anything, the state and its officials may do. How much room do individual rights leave for the state? The nature of the state, its legitimate functions and its justifications, if any, is the central concern of this book; a wide and diverse variety of topics intertwine in the course of our investigation.

Our main conclusions about the state are that a minimal state, limited to the narrow functions of protection against force, theft, fraud, enforcement of contracts, and so on, is justified; that any more extensive state will violate persons' rights not to be forced to do certain things, and is unjustified; and that the minimal state is inspiring as well as right. Two noteworthy implications are that the state may not use its coercive apparatus for the purpose of getting some citizens to aid others, or in order to prohibit activities to people for their *own* good or protection. . . .

My emphasis upon the conclusions which diverge from what most readers believe may mislead one into thinking this book is some sort of political tract. It is not; it is a philosophical exploration of issues, many fascinating in their own right, which arise and interconnect when we consider individual rights and the state. The word "exploration" is appropriately chosen. One view about how to write a philosophy book holds that an author should think through all of the details of the view he presents, and its problems, polishing and refining his view to present to the world a finished, complete, and elegant whole. This is not my view. At any rate, I believe that there also is a place and a function in our ongoing intellectual life for a less complete work, containing unfinished presentations, conjectures, open questions and problems, leads, side connections, as well as a main line of argument. There is room for words on subjects other than last words.

Indeed, the usual manner of presenting philosophical work puzzles me. Works of philosophy are written as though their authors believe them to be the absolutely final word on their subject. But it's not, surely, that each philosopher thinks that he finally, thank God, has found the truth and built an impregnable fortress around it. We are all actually much more modest than that. For good reason. Having thought long and hard about the view he proposes, a philosopher has a reasonably good idea about its weak points; the places where great intellectual weight is placed upon something perhaps too fragile to bear it, the places where the unravelling of the view might begin, the unprobed assumptions he feels uneasy about.

One form of philosophical activity feels like pushing and shoving things to fit into some fixed perimeter of specified shape. All those things are lying out there, and they must be fit in. You push and shove the material into the rigid area getting it into the boundary on one side, and it bulges out on another. You run around and press in the protruding bulge, producing yet another in another place. So you push and shove and clip off corners from the things so they'll fit and you press in until finally almost everything sits unstably more or less in there; what doesn't gets heaved *far* away so that it won't be noticed.

From Robert Nozick, *Anarchy, State, and Utopia*. New York: Basic Books, 1974. By permission of Basic Books.

(Of course, it's not all *that* crude. There's also the coaxing and cajoling. And the body English.) *Quickly,* you find an angle from which it looks like an exact fit and take a snapshot; at a fast shutter speed before something else bulges out too noticeably. Then, back to the darkroom to touch up the rents, rips, and tears in the fabric of the perimeter. All that remains is to publish the photograph as a representation of exactly how things are, and to note how nothing fits properly into any other shape.

No philosopher says: "There's where I started, here's where I ended up; the major weakness in my work is that I went from there to here; in particular, here are the most notable distortions, pushings, shovings, maulings, gougings, stretchings, and chippings that I committed during the trip; not to mention the things thrown away and ignored, and all those avertings of gaze."

The reticence of philosophers about the weaknesses they perceive in their own views is not, I think, simply a question of philosophical honesty and integrity, though it *is* that or at least becomes that when brought to consciousness. The reticence is connected with philosophers' purposes in formulating views. Why do they strive to force everything into that one fixed perimeter? Why not another perimeter, or, more radically, why not leave things where they are? What does having everything within a perimeter *do* for us? Why do we want it so? (What does it shield us from?) From these deep (and frightening) questions, I hope not to be able to manage to avert my gaze in future work.

However, my reason for mentioning these issues here is not that I feel they pertain more strongly to this work than to other philosophical writings. What I say in this book is, I think, correct. This is not my way of taking it back. Rather, I propose to give it all to you: the doubts and worries and uncertainties as well as the beliefs, convictions, and arguments.

At those particular points in my arguments, transitions, assumptions, and so forth, where I feel the strain, I try to comment or at least to draw the reader's attention to what makes me uneasy. In advance, it is possible to voice some general theoretical worries. This book does not present a precise theory of the moral basis of individual rights; it does not contain a precise statement and justification of a theory of retributive punishment; or a precise statement of the principles of the tripartite theory of distributive justice it presents. Much of what I say rests upon or uses general features that I believe such theories would have were they worked out. I would like to write on these topics in the future. If I do, no doubt the resulting theory will differ from what I now expect it to be, and this would require some modifications in the superstructure erected here. It would be foolish to expect that I shall complete these fundamental tasks satisfactorily; as it would be to remain silent until they are done. Perhaps this essay will stimulate others to help.

DISTRIBUTIVE JUSTICE

The minimal state is the most extensive state that can be justified. Any state more extensive violates people's rights. Yet many persons have put forth reasons purporting to justify a more extensive state. It is impossible within the compass of this book to examine all the reasons that have been put forth. Therefore, I shall focus upon those generally acknowledged to be most weighty and influential, to see precisely wherein they fail. In this chapter we consider the claim that a more extensive state is justified, because necessary (or the best instrument) to achieve distributive justice; in the next chapter we shall take up diverse other claims.

The term "distributive justice" is not a neutral one. Hearing the term "distribution," most people presume that some thing or mechanism uses some principle or criterion to give out a supply of things. Into this process of distributing shares some error may have crept. So it is an open question, at least, whether *re*distribution should take place; whether we should do again what has already been done once, though poorly. However, we are not in the position of children who have been given portions of pie by someone who now makes last minute adjustments to rectify careless cutting. There is no *central* distribution, no person or group entitled to control all the resources, jointly deciding how they are to be doled out. What each person gets, he gets from others who give to him in exchange for something, or as a gift. In a free society, diverse persons control different resources, and new holdings arise out of the voluntary exchanges and actions of persons. There is no more a distributing or distribution of shares than there is a distributing of mates in a society in which persons choose whom they shall marry. The total result is the product of many individual decisions which the different individuals involved are entitled to make. Some uses of the term "distribution," it is true, do not imply a previous distributing appropriately judged by some criterion (for example, "probability distribution"); nevertheless, despite the title of this chapter, it would be best to use a terminology that clearly is neutral. We shall speak of people's holdings; a principle of justice in holdings describes (part of) what justice tells us (requires) about holdings. I shall state first what I take to be the correct view about justice in holdings, and then turn to the discussion of alternate views.

Section I: The Entitlement Theory

The subject of justice in holdings consists of three major topics. The first is the *original acquisition of holdings,* the appropriation of un-held things. This includes the issues of how unheld things may come to be held, the process, or processes, by which unheld things may come to be held, the things that may come to be held by these processes, the extent of what comes to be held by a particular process, and so on. We shall refer to the complicated truth about this topic, which we shall not formulate here, as the principle of justice in acquisition. The second topic concerns the *transfer of holdings* from one person to another. By what processes may a person transfer holdings to another? How may a person acquire a holding from another who holds it? Under this topic come general descriptions of voluntary exchange, and gift and (on the other hand) fraud, as well as reference to particular conventional details fixed upon in a given society. The complicated truth about this subject (with placeholders for conventional details) we shall call the principle of justice in transfer. (And we shall suppose it also includes principles governing how a person may divest himself of a holding, passing it into an unheld state.)

If the world were wholly just, the following inductive definition would exhaustively cover the subject of justice in holdings.

1. A person who acquires a holding in accordance with the principle of justice in acquisition is entitled to that holding.
2. A person who acquires a holding in accordance with the principle of justice in transfer, from someone else entitled to the holding, is entitled to the holding.
3. No one is entitled to a holding except by (repeated) applications of 1 and 2.

The complete principle of distributive justice would say simply that a distribution is just if everyone is entitled to the holdings they possess under the distribution.

A distribution is just if it arises from another just distribution by legitimate means. The legitimate means of moving from one distribution to another are specified by the principle of justice in transfer. The legitimate first "moves" are specified by the principle of justice in acquisition. Whatever arises from a just situation by just steps is itself just. The means of change specified by the principle of justice in transfer preserve justice. As correct rules of inference are truth-preserving, and any conclusion deduced via repeated application of such rules from only true premises is itself true, so the means of transition from one situation to another specified by the principle of justice in transfer are justice-preserving, and any situation actually arising from repeated transitions in accordance with the principle from a just situation is itself just. The parallel between justice-preserving transformations and truth-preserving transformations illuminates where it fails as well as where it holds. That a conclusion could have been deduced by truth-preserving means from premises that are true suffices to show its truth. That from a just situation a situation *could* have arisen via justice-preserving means does *not* suffice to show its justice. The fact that a thief's victims voluntarily *could* have presented him with gifts does not entitle the thief to his ill-gotten gains. Justice in holdings is historical; it depends upon what actually has happened. We shall return to this point later.

Not all actual situations are generated in accordance with the two principles of justice in holdings: the principle of justice in acquisition and the principle of justice in transfer. Some people steal from others, or defraud them, or enslave them, seizing their product and preventing them from living as they choose, or forcibly exclude others from competing in exchanges. None of these are permissible modes of transition from one situation to another. And some persons acquire holdings by means not sanctioned by the principle of justice in acquisition. The existence of past injustice (previous violations of the first two principles of justice in holdings) raises the third major topic under justice in holdings: the rectification of injustice in holdings. If past injustice has shaped present holdings in various ways, some identifiable and some not, what now, if anything, ought to be done to rectify these injustices? What obligations do the performers of injustice have toward those whose position is worse than it would have been had the injustice not been done? Or, than it would have been had compensation been paid promptly? How, if at all, do things change if the beneficiaries and those made worse off are not the direct parties in the act of injustice, but, for example, their descendants? Is an injustice done to someone whose holding was itself based upon an unrectified injustice? How far back must one go in wiping clean the historical slate of injustices? What may victims of injustice permissibly do in order to rectify the injustices being done to them, including the many injustices done by persons acting through their government? I do not know of a thorough or theoretically sophisticated treatment of such issues. Idealizing greatly, let us suppose theoretical investigation will produce a principle of rectification. This principle uses historical information about previous situations and injustices done in them (as defined by the first two principles of justice and rights against interference), and information about the actual course of events that flowed from these injustices, until the present, and it yields a description (or descriptions) of holdings in the society. The principle of rectification presumably will make use of its best estimate of subjunctive information about what would have occurred (or a probability distribution over what might have occurred, using the expected value) if the injustice had not taken place. If the actual description of holdings turns out not to be one of the descriptions yielded by the principle, then one of the descriptions yielded must be realized.

The general outlines of the theory of justice in holdings are that the holdings of a person are just if he is entitled to them by the principles of justice in acquisition and transfer, or by the principle of rectification of injustice (as specified by the first two principles). If each person's holdings are just, then the total set (distribution) of holdings is just. To turn these general outlines into a specific theory we would have to specify the details of each of the three principles of justice in holdings: the principle of acquisition of holdings, the principle of transfer of holdings, and the principle of rectification of violations of the first two principles. I shall not attempt that task here. (Locke's principle of justice in acquisition is discussed below.)

Historical Principles and End-Result Principles

The general outlines of the entitlement theory illuminate the nature and defects of other conceptions of distributive justice. The entitlement theory of justice in distribution is *historical;* whether a distribution is just depends upon how it came about. In contrast, *current time-slice principles* of justice hold that the justice of a distribution is determined by how things are distributed (who has what) as judged by some *structural* principle(s) of just distribution. A utilitarian who judges between any two distributions by seeing which has the greater sum of utility and, if the sums tie, applies some fixed equality criterion to choose the more equal distribution, would hold a current time-slice principle of justice. As would someone who had a fixed schedule of trade-offs between the sum of happiness and equality. According to a current time-slice principle, all that needs to be looked at, in judging the justice of a distribution, is who ends up with what; in comparing any two distributions one need look only at the matrix presenting the distributions. No further information need be fed into a principle of justice. It is a consequence of such principles of justice that any two structurally identical distributions are equally just. (Two distributions are structurally identical if they present the same profile, but perhaps have different persons occupying the particular slots. My having ten and your having five, and my having five and your having ten are structurally identical distributions.) Welfare economics is the theory of current time-slice principles of justice. The subject is conceived as operating on matrices representing only current information about distribution. This, as well as some of the usual conditions (for example, the choice of distribution is invariant under relabeling of columns), guarantees that welfare economics will be a current time-slice theory, with all of its inadequacies.

Most persons do not accept current time-slice principles as constituting the whole story about distributive shares. They think it relevant in assessing the justice of a situation to consider not only the distribution it embodies, but also how that distribution came about. If some persons are in prison for murder or war crimes, we do not say that to assess the justice of the distribution in the society we must look only at what this person has, and that person has, and that person has, . . . at the current time. We think it relevant to ask whether someone did something so that he *deserved* to be punished, deserved to have a lower share. Most will agree to the relevance of further information with regard to punishments and penalties. Consider also desired things. One traditional socialist view is that workers are entitled to the product and full fruits of their labor; they have earned it; a distribution is unjust if it does not give the workers what they are entitled to. Such entitlements are based upon some past history. No socialist holding this view would find it comforting to be told that because the actual distribution *A* happens to coincide structurally with the one he desires *D, A* therefore is no less just, than *D;* it differs only in that the "parasitic" owners of capital receive under *A* what the workers are entitled to under *D,* and the workers receive under *A* what the owners are entitled to under *D,* namely very little. This socialist rightly, in my view, holds onto the notions of earning, producing, entitlement, desert, and so forth, and he rejects current time-slice principles that look only to the structure of the resulting set of holdings. (The set of holdings resulting from what? Isn't it implausible that how holdings are produced and come to exist has no effect at all on who should hold what?) His mistake lies in his view of what entitlements arise out of what sorts of productive processes.

We construe the position we discuss too narrowly by speaking of *current* time-slice principles. Nothing is changed if structural principles operate upon a time sequence of current time-slice profiles and, for example, give someone more now to counterbalance the less he has had earlier. A utilitarian or an egalitarian or any mixture of the two over time will inherit the difficulties of his more myopic comrades. He is not helped by the fact that *some* of the information others consider relevant in assessing a distribution is reflected, unrecoverably, in past matrices. Henceforth, we shall refer to such unhistorical principles of distributive justice, including the current time-slice principles, as *end-result principles* or *end-state principles.*

In contrast to end-result principles of justice, *historical principles* of justice hold that past circumstances or actions of people can create differential entitlements or differential deserts to things. An injustice can be worked by moving from one distribution to another structurally identical one, for the second, in profile the same, may violate people's entitlements or deserts; it may not fit the actual history.

Patterning

The entitlement principles of justice in holdings that we have sketched are historical principles of justice. To better understand their precise character, we shall distinguish them from another subclass of the historical principles. Consider, as an example, the principle of distribution according to moral merit. This principle requires that total distributive shares vary directly with moral merit; no person should have a greater share than anyone whose moral merit is greater. (If moral merit could be not merely ordered but measured on an interval or ratio scale, stronger principles could be formulated.) Or consider the principle that results by substituting "usefulness to society" for "moral merit" in the previous principle. Or instead of "distribute according to moral merit," or "distribute according to usefulness to society," we might consider "distribute according to the weighted sum of moral merit, usefulness to society, and need," with the weights of the different dimensions equal. Let us call a principle of distribution *patterned* if it specifies that a distribution is to vary along with some natural dimension, weighted sum of natural dimensions, or lexicographic ordering of natural dimensions. And let us say a distribution is patterned if it accords with some patterned principle. (I speak of natural dimensions, admittedly without a general criterion for them, because for any set of holdings some artificial dimensions can be gimmicked up to vary along with the distribution of the set.) The principle of distribution in accordance with moral merit is a patterned historical principle, which specifies a patterned distribution. "Distribute according to I.Q." is a patterned principle that looks to information not contained in distributional matrices. It is not historical, however, in that it does not look to any past actions creating differential entitlements to evaluate a distribution; it requires only distributional matrices whose columns are labeled by I.Q. scores. The distribution in a society, however, may be composed of such simple patterned distributions, without itself being simply patterned. Different sectors may operate different patterns, or some combination of patterns may operate in different proportions across a society. A distribution composed in this manner, from a small number of patterned distributions, we also shall term "patterned." And we extend the use of "pattern" to include the overall designs put forth by combinations of end-state principles.

Almost every suggested principle of distributive justice is patterned: to each according to his moral merit, or needs, or marginal product, or how hard he tries, or the weighted sum of the foregoing, and so on. The principle of entitlement we have sketched is *not* patterned. There is no one natural dimension or weighted sum or combination of a small number of natural dimensions that yields the distributions generated in accordance with the principle of entitlement. The set of holdings that results when some persons receive their marginal products, others win at gambling, others receive a share of their mate's income, others receive gifts from foundations, others receive interest on loans, others receive gifts from admirers, others receive returns on investment, others make for themselves much of what they have, others find things, and so on, will not be patterned. Heavy strands of patterns will run through it; significant portions of the variance in holdings will be accounted for by pattern-variables. If most people most of the time choose to transfer some of their entitlements to others only in exchange for something from them, then a large part of what many people hold will vary with what they held that others wanted. More details are provided by the theory of marginal productivity. But gifts to relatives, charitable donations, bequests to children, and the like, are not best conceived, in the first instance, in this manner. Ignoring the strands of pattern, let us suppose for the moment that a distribution actually arrived at by the operation of the principle of entitlement is random with respect to any pattern. Though the resulting set of holdings will be unpatterned, it will not be incomprehensible, for it can be seen as arising from the operation of a small number of principles. These principles specify how an initial distribution may arise (the principle of acquisition of holdings) and how distributions may be transformed into others (the principle of transfer of holdings). The process whereby the set of holdings is generated will be intelligible, though the set of holdings itself that results from this process will be unpatterned.

The writings of F. A. Hayek focus less than is usually done upon what patterning distributive justice requires. Hayek argues that we cannot know enough about each person's situation to distribute to each according to his moral merit (but would justice demand we do so if we did have this knowledge?); and he goes on to say, "our objection is against all attempts to impress upon society a deliberately chosen pattern of distribution, whether it be an order of equality or of inequality." However, Hayek concludes that in a free society there will be distribution in accordance with value rather than moral merit; that is, in accordance with the perceived value of a person's actions and services to others. Despite his rejection of a patterned conception of distributive justice, Hayek himself suggests a pattern he thinks justifiable: distribution in accordance with the perceived benefits given to others, leaving room for the complaint that a free society does not realize exactly this pattern. Stating this patterned strand of a free capitalist society more precisely, we get "To each according to how much he benefits others who have the resources for benefiting those who benefit them." This will seem arbitrary unless some acceptable initial set of holdings is specified, or unless it is held that the operation of the system over time washes out any significant effects from the initial set of holdings. As an example of the latter, if almost anyone would have bought a car from Henry Ford, the supposition that it was an arbitrary matter who held the money then (and so bought) would not place Henry Ford's earnings under a cloud. In any event, *his* coming to hold it is not arbitrary. Distribution according to benefits to others *is* a major patterned strand in a free capitalist society, as Hayek correctly points out, but it is only a strand and does not constitute the whole pattern of a system of entitlements (namely, inheritance, gifts for arbitrary reasons, charity, and so on) or a standard that one should insist a society fit. Will people tolerate for long a system yielding distributions that they believe are unpatterned? No doubt people will not long accept a distribution they believe is *unjust.* People want their society to be and to look just. But must the look of justice reside in a resulting pattern rather than in the underlying generating principles? We are in no position to conclude that the inhabitants of a society embodying an entitlement conception of justice in holdings will find it unacceptable. Still, it must be granted that were people's reasons for transferring some of their holdings to others always irrational or arbitrary, we would find this disturbing. (Suppose people always determined what holdings they would transfer, and to whom, by using a random device.) We feel more comfortable upholding the justice of an entitlement system if most of the transfers under it are done for reasons. This does not mean necessarily that all deserve what holdings they receive. It means only that there is a purpose or point to someone's transferring a holding to one person rather than to another; that usually we can see what the transferer thinks he's gaining, what cause he thinks he's serving, what goals he thinks he's helping to achieve, and so forth. Since in a capitalist society people often transfer holdings to others in accordance with how much they perceive these others benefiting them, the fabric constituted by the individual transactions and transfers is largely reasonable and intelligible. (Gifts to loved ones, bequests to children, charity to the needy also are nonarbitrary components of the fabric.) In stressing the large strand of distribution in accordance with benefit to others, Hayek shows the point of many transfers, and so shows that the system of transfer of entitlements is not just spinning its gears aimlessly. The system of entitlements is defensible when constituted by the individual aims of individual transactions. No overarching aim is needed, no distributional pattern is required.

To think that the task of a theory of distributive justice is to fill in the blank in "to each according to his _________" is to be predisposed to search for a pattern; and the separate treatment of "from each according to his _________" treats production and distribution as two separate and independent issues. On an entitlement view these are *not* two separate questions. Whoever makes something, having bought or contracted for all other held resources used in the process (transferring some of his holdings for these cooperating factors), is entitled to it. The situation is *not* one of something's getting made, and there being an open question of who is to get it. Things come into the world already attached to people having entitlements over them. From the point of view of the historical entitlement conception of justice in holdings, those who start afresh to complete "to each according to his _________" treat objects as if they appeared from nowhere, out of nothing. A complete theory of justice might cover this limit case as well; perhaps here is a use for the usual conceptions of distributive justice.

So entrenched are maxims of the usual form that perhaps we should present the entitlement conception as a competitor. Ignoring acquisition and rectification, we might say:

> From each according to what he chooses to do, to each according to what he makes for himself (perhaps with the contracted aid of others) and what others choose to

do for him and choose to give him of what they've been given previously (under this maxim) and haven't yet expended or transferred.

This, the discerning reader will have noticed, has its defects as a slogan. So as a summary and great simplification (and not as a maxim with any independent meaning) we have:

From each as they choose, to each as they are chosen.

How Liberty Upsets Patterns

It is not clear how those holding alternative conceptions of distributive justice can reject the entitlement conception of justice in holdings. For suppose a distribution favored by one of these non-entitlement conceptions is realized. Let us suppose it is your favorite one and let us call this distribution D_1; perhaps everyone has an equal share, perhaps shares vary in accordance with some dimension you treasure. Now suppose that Wilt Chamberlain is greatly in demand by basketball teams, being a great gate attraction. (Also suppose contracts run only for a year, with players being free agents.) He signs the following sort of contract with a team: In each home game, twenty-five cents from the price of each ticket of admission goes to him. (We ignore the question of whether he is "gouging" the owners, letting them look out for themselves.) The season starts, and people cheerfully attend his team's games; they buy their tickets, each time dropping a separate twenty-five cents of their admission price into a special box with Chamberlain's name on it. They are excited about seeing him play; it is worth the total admission price to them. Let us suppose that in one season one million persons attend his home games, and Wilt Chamberlain winds up with $250,000, a much larger sum than the average income and larger even than anyone else has. Is he entitled to this income? Is this new distribution D_2, unjust? If so, why? There is *no* question about whether each of the people was entitled to the control over the resources they held in D_1; because that was the distribution (your favorite) that (for the purposes of argument) we assumed was acceptable. Each of these persons *chose* to give twenty-five cents of their money to Chamberlain. They could have spent it on going to the movies, or on candy bars, or on copies of *Dissent* magazine, or of *Monthly Review*. But they all, at least one million of them, converged on giving it to Wilt Chamberlain in exchange for watching him play basketball. If D_1 was a just distribution, and people voluntarily moved from it to D_2, transferring parts of their shares they were given under D_1 (what was it for if not to do something with?), isn't D_2 also just? If the people were entitled to dispose of the resources to which they were entitled (under D_1), didn't this include their being entitled to give it to, or exchange it with, Wilt Chamberlain? Can anyone else complain on grounds of justice? Each other person already has his legitimate share under D_1. Under D_1, there is nothing that anyone has that anyone else has a claim of justice against. After someone transfers something to Wilt Chamberlain, third parties *still* have their legitimate shares; *their* shares are not changed. By what process could such a transfer among two persons give rise to a legitimate claim of distributive justice on a portion of what was transferred, by a third party who had no claim of justice on any holding of the others *before* the transfer?[1] To cut off objections irrelevant here, we might imagine the exchanges occurring in a socialist society, after hours. After playing whatever basketball he does in his daily work, or doing whatever other daily work he does, Wilt Chamberlain decides to put in *overtime* to earn additional money. (First his work quota is set; he works time over that.) Or imagine it is a skilled juggler people like to see, who puts on shows after hours.

Why might someone work overtime in a society in which it is assumed their needs are satisfied? Perhaps because they care about things other than needs. I like to write in books that I read, and to have easy access to books for browsing at odd hours. It would be very pleasant and convenient to have the resources of Widener Library in my back yard. No society, I assume, will provide such resources close to each person who would like them as part of his regular allotment (under D_1). Thus, persons either must do without some extra things that they want, or be allowed to do something extra to get some of these things. On what basis could the inequalities that would eventuate be forbidden? Notice also that small factories would spring up in a socialist society, unless forbidden. I melt down some of my personal possessions (under D_1) and build a machine out of the material. I offer you, and others, a philosophy lecture once a week in exchange for your cranking the handle on my machine, whose products I exchange for yet other things, and so on. (The raw materials used by the machine are given to me by others who possess them under D_1, in exchange for hearing lectures.) Each person might participate to gain things over and above their allotment under D_1. Some persons even might want to leave their job in socialist industry and work full time in this private sector. I shall say something more about these issues in the next chapter. Here I wish merely to note how private property even in means of production would occur in a socialist society that did not forbid people to use as they wished some of the resources they are given under the socialist distribution D_1. The socialist society would have to forbid capitalist acts between consenting adults.

The general point illustrated by the Wilt Chamberlain example and the example of the entrepreneur in a socialist society is that no end-state principle or distributional patterned principle of justice can be continuously realized without continuous interference with people's lives. Any favored pattern would be transformed into one unfavored by the principle, by people choosing to act in various ways; for example, by people exchanging goods and services with other people, or giving things to other people, things the transferers are entitled to under the favored distributional pattern. To maintain a pattern one must either continually interfere to stop people from transferring resources as they wish to, or continually (or periodically) interfere to take from some persons resources that others for some reason chose to transfer to them. (But if some time limit is to be set on how long people may keep resources others voluntarily transfer to them, why let them keep these resources for *any* period of time? Why not have immediate confiscation?) It might be objected that all persons voluntarily will choose to refrain from actions which would upset the pattern. This presupposes unrealistically (1) that all will most want to maintain the pattern (are those who don't, to be "reeducated" or forced to undergo "self-criticism"?), (2) that each can gather enough information about his own actions and the ongoing activities of others to discover which of his actions will upset the pattern, and (3) that diverse and far-flung persons can coordinate their actions to dovetail into the pattern. Compare the manner in which the market is neutral among persons desires, as it reflects and transmits widely scattered information via prices, and coordinates persons' activities.

It puts things perhaps a bit too strongly to say that every patterned (or end-state) principle is liable to be thwarted by the voluntary actions of the individual parties transferring some of their shares they receive under the principle. For perhaps some *very* weak patterns are not so thwarted. Any distributional pattern with any egalitarian component is overturnable by the voluntary actions of individual persons over time; as is every patterned condition with sufficient content so as actually to have been proposed as presenting the central core of distributive justice. Still, given the possibility that some weak conditions or patterns may not be unstable in this way, it would be better to formulate an explicit description of the kind of interesting and contentful patterns under discussion, and to prove a theorem about their instability. Since the weaker the patterning, the more likely it is that the entitlement system itself satisfies it, a plausible conjecture is that any patterning either is unstable or is satisfied by the entitlement system.

Redistribution and Property Rights

Apparently, patterned principles allow people to choose to expend upon themselves, but not upon others, those resources they are entitled to (or rather, receive) under some favored distributional pattern D_1. For if each of several persons chooses to expend some of his D_1 resources upon one other person, then that other person will receive more than his D_1 share, disturbing the favored distributional pattern. Maintaining a distributional pattern is individualism with a vengeance! Patterned distributional principles do not give people what entitlement principles do, only better distributed. For they do not give the right to choose what to do with what one has; they do not give the right to choose to pursue an end involving (intrinsically, or as a means) the enhancement of another's position. To such views, families are disturbing; for within a family occur transfers that upset the favored distributional pattern. Either families themselves become units to which distribution takes place, the column occupiers (on what rationale?), or loving behavior is forbidden. We should note in passing the ambivalent position of radicals toward the family. Its loving relationships are seen as a model to be emulated and extended across the whole society, at the same time that it is denounced as a suffocating institution to be broken and condemned as a focus of parochial concerns that interfere with achieving radical goals. Need we say that it is not appropriate to enforce across the wider society the relationships of love and care appropriate within a family, relationships which are voluntarily undertaken? Incidentally, love is an interesting instance of another relationship that is historical, in that (like justice) it depends upon what actually occurred. An adult may come to love another because of the other's characteristics; but it is the other person, and not the characteristics, that is loved. The love is not transferrable to someone else with the same characteristics, even to one who "scores" higher for these characteristics. And the love endures through changes of the characteristics that gave rise to it. One loves the particular person one actually encountered. Why love is historical, attaching to persons in this way and not to characteristics, is an interesting and puzzling question.

Proponents of patterned principles of distributive justice focus upon criteria for determining who is to receive holdings; they consider the reasons for which someone should have something, and also the total picture of holdings. Whether or not it is better to give than to receive, proponents of patterned principles ignore giving altogether. In considering the distribution of goods, income, and so forth, their theories are theories of recipient justice; they completely ignore any right a person might have to give something to someone. Even in exchanges where each party is simultaneously giver and recipient, patterned principles of justice focus only upon the recipient role and its supposed rights. Thus discussions tend to focus on whether people (should) have a right to inherit, rather than on whether people (should) have a right to bequeath or on whether persons who have a right to hold also have a right to choose that others hold in their place. I lack a good explanation of why the usual theories of distributive justice are so recipient-oriented; ignoring givers and transferers and their rights is of a piece with ignoring producers and their entitlements. But why is it *all* ignored?

Patterned principles of distributive justice necessitate *re*distributive activities. The likelihood is small that any actual freely-arrived-at set of holdings fits a given pattern; and the likelihood is nil that it will continue to fit the pattern as people exchange and give. From the point of view of an entitlement theory, redistribution is a serious matter indeed, involving, as it does, the violation of people's rights. (An exception is those takings that fall under the principle of the rectification of injustices.) From other points of view, also, it is serious.

Taxation of earnings from labor is on a par with forced labor.[2] Some persons find this claim obviously true: taking the earnings of *n* hours labor is like taking *n* hours from the person; it is like forcing the person to work *n* hours for another's purpose. Others find the claim absurd. But even these, *if* they object to forced labor, would oppose forcing unemployed hippies to work for the benefit of the needy. And they would also object to forcing each person to work five extra hours each week for the benefit of the needy. But a system that takes five hours' wages in taxes does not seem to them like one that forces someone to work five hours, since it offers the person forced a wider range of choice in activities than does taxation in kind with the particular labor specified. (But we can imagine a gradation of systems of forced labor, from one that specifies a particular activity, to one that gives a choice among two activities, to . . . ; and so on up.) Furthermore, people envisage a system with something like a proportional tax on everything above the amount necessary for basic needs. Some think this does not force someone to work extra hours, since there is no fixed number of extra hours he is forced to work, and since he can avoid the tax entirely by earning only enough to cover his basic needs. This is a very uncharacteristic view of forcing for those who *also* think people are forced to do something *whenever* the alternatives they face are considerably worse. However, *neither* view is correct. The fact that others intentionally intervene, in violation of a side constraint against aggression, to threaten force to limit the alternatives, in this case to paying taxes or (presumably the worse alternative) bare subsistence, makes the taxation system one of forced labor and distinguishes it from other cases of limited choices which are not forcings.

The man who chooses to work longer to gain an income more than sufficient for his basic needs prefers some extra goods or services to the leisure and activities he could perform during the possible nonworking hours; whereas the man who chooses not to work the extra time prefers the leisure activities to the extra goods or services he could acquire by working more. Given this, if it would be illegitimate for a tax system to seize some of a man's leisure (forced labor) for the purpose of serving the needy, how can it be legitimate for a tax system to seize some of a man's goods for that purpose? Why should we treat the man whose happiness requires certain material goods or services differently from the man whose preferences and desires make such goods unnecessary for his happiness? Why should the man who prefers seeing a movie (and who has to earn money for a ticket) be open to the required call to aid the needy, while the person who prefers looking at a sunset (and hence need earn no extra money) is not? Indeed, isn't it surprising that redistributionists choose to ignore the man whose pleasures are so easily attainable without extra labor, while adding yet another burden to the poor unfortunate who must work for his pleasures? If anything, one would have expected the reverse. Why is the person with the nonmaterial or nonconsumption desire allowed to proceed unimpeded to his most favored feasible alternative, whereas the man whose pleasures or desires involve material things and who must work for extra money (thereby serving whomever considers his activities valuable enough to pay him) is constrained in what he can realize? Perhaps there is no difference in principle. And perhaps some think the answer concerns merely administrative convenience. (These questions and issues will not disturb those who think that forced labor to serve the needy or to realize some favored end-state pattern is acceptable.) In a fuller discussion we would have (and want) to extend our argument to include interest, entrepreneurial profits, and so on. Those who doubt that this extension can be carried through, and who draw the line here at taxation of income from labor, will have to state rather complicated patterned *historical* principles of distributive justice, since end-state principles would not distinguish *sources* of income in any way. It is enough for now to get away from end-state principles and to make clear how various patterned principles are dependent upon particular views about the sources or the illegitimacy or the lesser legitimacy of profits, interest, and so on; which particular views may well be mistaken.

What sort of right over others does a legally institutionalized end-state pattern give one? The central core of the notion of a property right in *X*, relative to which other parts of the notion are to be explained, is the right to determine what shall be done with *X;* the right to choose which of the constrained set of options concerning *X* shall be realized or attempted. The constraints are set by other principles or laws operating in the society; in our theory, by the Lockean rights people possess (under the minimal state). My property rights in my knife allow me to leave it where I will, but not in your chest. I may choose which of the acceptable options involving the knife is to be realized. This notion of property helps us to understand why earlier theorists spoke of people as having property in themselves and their labor. They viewed each person as having a right to decide what would become of himself and what he would do, and as having a right to reap the benefits of what he did.

This right of selecting the alternative to be realized from the constrained set of alternatives may be held by an *individual* or by a *group* with some procedure for reaching a joint decision; or the right may be passed back and forth, so that one year I decide what's to become of *X*, and the next year you do (with the alternative of destruction, perhaps, being excluded). Or, during the same time period, some types of decisions about *X* may be made by me, and others by you. And so on. We lack an adequate, fruitful, analytical apparatus for classifying the *types* of constraints on the set of options among which choices are to be made, and the *types* of ways decision powers can be held, divided, and amalgamated. A *theory* of property would, among other things, contain such a classification of constraints and decision modes, and from a small number of principles would follow a host of interesting statements about the *consequences* and effects of certain combinations of constraints and modes of decision.

When end-result principles of distributive justice are built into the legal structure of a society, they (as do most patterned principles) give each citizen an enforceable claim to some portion of the total social product; that is, to some portion of the sum total of the individually and jointly made products. This total product is produced by individuals laboring, using means of production others have saved to bring into existence, by people organizing production or creating means to produce new things or things in a new way. It is on this batch of individual activities that patterned distributional principles give each individual an enforceable claim. Each person has a claim to the activities and the products of other persons, independently of whether the other persons enter into particular relationships that give rise to these claims, and independently of whether they voluntarily take these claims upon themselves, in charity or in exchange for something.

Whether it is done through taxation on wages or on wages over a certain amount, or through seizure of profits, or through there being a big *social pot* so that it's not clear what's coming from where and what's going where, patterned principles of distributive justice involve appropriating the actions of other persons. Seizing the results of someone's labor is equivalent to seizing hours from him and directing him to carry on various activities. If people force you to do certain work, or unrewarded work, for a certain period of time, they decide what you are to do and what purposes your work is to serve apart from your decisions. This process whereby they take this decision from you makes them a *part-owner* of you; it gives them a property right in you. Just as having such partial control and power of decision, by right, over an animal or inanimate object would be to have a property right in it.

End-state and most patterned principles of distributive justice institute (partial) ownership by others of people and their actions and labor. These principles involve a shift from the classical liberals' notion of self-ownership to a notion of (partial) property rights in *other* people.

Considerations such as these confront end-state and other patterned conceptions of justice with the question of whether the actions necessary to achieve the selected pattern don't themselves violate moral side constraints. Any view holding that there are moral side constraints on actions, that not all moral considerations can be built into end states that are to be achieved, must face the possibility that some of its goals are not achievable by any morally permissible available means. An entitlement theorist will face such conflicts in a society that deviates from the principles of justice for the generation of holdings, if and only if the only actions available to realize the principles themselves violate some moral constraints. Since deviation from the first two principles of justice (in acquisition and transfer) will involve other persons' direct and aggressive intervention to violate rights, and since moral constraints will not exclude defensive or retributive action in such cases, the entitlement theorist's problem rarely will be pressing. And whatever difficulties he has in applying the principle of rectification to persons who did not themselves violate the first two principles are difficulties in balancing the conflicting considerations so as correctly to formulate the complex principle of rectification itself; he will not violate moral side constraints by applying the principle. Proponents of patterned conceptions of justice, however, often will face head-on clashes (and poignant ones if they cherish each party to the clash) between moral side constraints on how individuals may be treated and their patterned conception of justice that presents an end state or other pattern that *must* be realized.

May a person emigrate from a nation that has institutionalized some end-state or patterned distributional principle? For some principles (for example, Hayek's) emigration presents no theoretical problem. But for others it is a tricky matter. Consider a nation having a compulsory scheme of minimal social provision to aid the neediest (or one organized so as to maximize the position of the worst-off group); no one may opt out of participating in it. (None may say,

"Don't compel me to contribute to others and don't provide for me via this compulsory mechanism if I am in need.") Everyone above a certain level is forced to contribute to aid the needy. But if emigration from the country were allowed, anyone could choose to move to another country that did not have compulsory social provision but otherwise was (as much as possible) identical. In such a case, the person's *only* motive for leaving would be to avoid participating in the compulsory scheme of social provision. And if he does leave, the needy in his initial country will receive no (compelled) help from him. What rationale yields the result that the person be permitted to emigrate, yet forbidden to stay and opt out of the compulsory scheme of social provision? If providing for the needy is of overriding importance, this does militate against allowing internal opting out; but it also speaks against allowing external emigration. (Would it also support, to some extent, the kidnapping of persons living in a place without compulsory social provision, who could be forced to make a contribution to the needy in your community?) Perhaps the crucial component of the position that allows emigration solely to avoid certain arrangements, while not allowing anyone internally to opt out of them, is a concern for fraternal feelings within the country. "We don't want anyone here who doesn't contribute, who doesn't care enough about the others to contribute." That concern, in this case, would have to be tied to the view that forced aiding tends to produce fraternal feelings between the aided and the aider (or perhaps merely to the view that the knowledge that someone or other voluntarily is not aiding produces unfraternal feelings).

Locke's Theory of Acquisition

Before we turn to consider other theories of justice in detail, we must introduce an additional bit of complexity into the structure of the entitlement theory. This is best approached by considering Locke's attempt to specify a principle of justice in acquisition. Locke views property rights in an unowned object as originating through someone's mixing his labor with it. This gives rise to many questions. What are the boundaries of what labor is mixed with? If a private astronaut clears a place on Mars, has he mixed his labor with (so that he comes to own) the whole planet, the whole uninhabited universe, or just a particular plot? Which plot does an act bring under ownership? The minimal (possibly disconnected) area such that an act decreases entropy in that area, and not elsewhere? Can virgin land (for the purposes of ecological investigation by high-flying airplane) come under ownership by a Lockean process? Building a fence around a territory presumably would make one the owner of only the fence (and the land immediately underneath it).

Why does mixing one's labor with something make one the owner of it? Perhaps because one owns one's labor, and so one comes to own a previously unowned thing that becomes permeated with what one owns. Ownership seeps over into the rest. But why isn't mixing what I own with what I don't own a way of losing what I own rather than a way of gaining what I don't? If I own a can of tomato juice and spill it in the sea so that its molecules (made radioactive, so I can check this) mingle evenly throughout the sea, do I thereby come to own the sea, or have I foolishly dissipated my tomato juice? Perhaps the idea, instead, is that laboring on something improves it and makes it more valuable, and anyone is entitled to own a thing whose value he has created. (Reinforcing this, perhaps, is the view that laboring is unpleasant. If some people made things effortlessly, as the cartoon characters in *The Yellow Submarine* trail flowers in their wake, would they have lesser claim to their own products whose making didn't *cost* them anything?) Ignore the fact that laboring on something may make it less valuable (spraying pink enamel paint on a piece of driftwood that you have found). Why should one's entitlement extend to the whole object rather than just to the *added value* one's labor has produced? (Such reference to value might also serve to delimit the extent of ownership; for example, substitute "increases the value of" for "decreases entropy in" in the above entropy criterion.) No workable or coherent value-added property scheme has yet been devised, and any such scheme presumably would fall to objections (similar to those) that fell the theory of Henry George.

It will be implausible to view improving an object as giving full ownership to it, if the stock of unowned objects that might be improved is limited. For an object's coming under one person's ownership changes the situation of all others. Whereas previously they were at liberty to use the object, they now no longer are. This change in the situation of others (by removing their liberty to act on a previously unowned object) need not worsen their situation. If I appropriate a grain of sand from Coney Island, no one else may now do as they will with *that* grain of sand. But there are plenty of other grains of sand left for them to do the same with. Or if not grains of sand, then other things. Alternatively, the things I do with the grain of sand I appropriate might improve the position of others, counterbalancing their loss of the liberty to use that grain. The crucial point is whether appropriation of an unowned object worsens the situation of others.

Locke's proviso that there be "enough and as good left in common for others" (sect. 27) is meant to ensure that the situation of others is not worsened. (If this proviso is met is there any motivation for his further condition of nonwaste?) It is often said that this proviso once held but now no longer does. But there appears to be an argument for the conclusion that if the proviso no longer holds, then it cannot ever have held so as to yield permanent and inheritable property rights. Consider the first person *Z* for whom there is not enough and as good left to appropriate. The last person *Y* to appropriate left *Z* without his previous liberty to act on an object, and so worsened *Z*'s situation. So *Y*'s appropriation is not allowed under Locke's proviso. Therefore the next to last person *X* to appropriate left *Y* in a worse position, for *X*'s act ended permissible appropriation. Therefore *X*'s appropriation wasn't permissible. But then the appropriator two from last, *W*, ended permissible appropriation and so, since it worsened *X*'s position, *W*'s appropriation wasn't permissible. And so on back to the first person *A* to appropriate a permanent property right.

This argument, however, proceeds too quickly. Someone may be made worse off by another's appropriation in two ways: first, by losing the opportunity to improve his situation by a particular appropriation or any one; and second, by no longer being able to use freely (without appropriation) what he previously could. A *stringent* requirement that another not be made worse off by an appropriation would exclude the first way if nothing else counterbalances the diminution in opportunity, as well as the second. A *weaker* requirement would exclude the second way, though not the first. With the weaker requirement, we cannot zip back so quickly from *Z* to *A*, as in the above argument; for though person *Z* can no longer *appropriate*, there may remain some for him to *use* as before. In this case *Y*'s appropriation would not violate the weaker Lockean condition. (With less remaining that people are at liberty to use, users might face more inconvenience, crowding, and so on; in that way the situation of others might be worsened, unless appropriation stopped far short of such a point.) It is arguable that no one legitimately can complain if the weaker provision is satisfied. However, since this is less clear than in the case of the more stringent proviso, Locke may have intended this stringent proviso by "enough and as good" remaining, and perhaps he meant the non-waste condition to delay the end point from which the argument zips back.

Is the situation of persons who are unable to appropriate (there being no more accessible and useful unowned objects) worsened by a system allowing appropriation and permanent property? Here enter the various familiar social considerations favoring private property: it increases the social product by putting means of production in the hands of those who can use them most efficiently (profitably); experimentation is encouraged, because with separate persons controlling resources, there is no one person or small group whom someone with a new idea must convince to try it out; private property enables people to decide on the pattern and types of risks they wish to bear, leading to specialized types of risk bearing; private property protects future persons by leading some to hold back resources from current consumption for future markets; it provides alternate sources of employment for unpopular persons who don't have to convince any one person or small group to hire them, and so on. These considerations enter a Lockean theory to support the claim that appropriation of private property satisfies the intent behind the "enough and as good left over" proviso, *not* as a utilitarian justification of property. They enter to rebut the claim that because the proviso is violated no natural right to private property can arise by a Lockean process. The difficulty in working such an argument to show that the proviso is satisfied is in fixing the appropriate base line for comparison. Lockean appropriation makes people no worse off than they would be *how?* This question of fixing the baseline needs more detailed investigation than we are able to give it here. It would be desirable to have an estimate of the general economic importance of original appropriation in order to see how much leeway there is for differing theories of appropriation and of the location of the baseline. Perhaps this importance can be measured by the percentage of all income that is based upon untransformed raw materials and given resources (rather than upon human actions), mainly rental income representing the unimproved value of land, and the price of raw material *in situ,* and by the percentage of current wealth which represents such income in the past.

We should note that it is not only persons favoring *private* property who need a theory of how property rights legitimately originate. Those believing in collective property, for example those believing that a group of persons living in an area jointly own the territory, or its mineral resources, also must provide a theory of how such property rights arise; they must show why the persons living there have rights to determine what is done with the land and resources there that persons living elsewhere don't have (with regard to the same land and resources).

The Proviso

Whether or not Locke's particular theory of appropriation can be spelled out so as to handle various difficulties, I assume that any adequate theory of justice in acquisition will contain a proviso similar to the weaker of the ones we have attributed to Locke. A process normally giving rise to a permanent bequeathable property right in a previously unowned thing will not do so if the position of others no longer at liberty to use the thing is thereby worsened. It is important to specify *this* particular mode of worsening the situation of others, for the proviso does not encompass other modes. It does not include the worsening due to more limited opportunities to appropriate (the first way above, corresponding to the more stringent condition), and it does not include how I "worsen" a seller's position if I appropriate materials to make some of what he is selling, and then enter into competition with him. Someone whose appropriation otherwise would violate the proviso still may appropriate provided he compensates the others so that their situation is not thereby worsened; unless he does compensate these others, his appropriation will violate the proviso of the principle of justice in acquisition and will be an illegitimate one. A theory of appropriation incorporating this Lockean proviso will handle correctly the cases (objections to the theory lacking the proviso) where someone appropriates the total supply of something necessary for life.

A theory which includes this proviso in its principle of justice in acquisition must also contain a more complex principle of justice in transfer. Some reflection of the proviso about appropriation constrains later actions. If my appropriating all of a certain substance violates the Lockean proviso, then so does my appropriating some and purchasing all the rest from others who obtained it without otherwise violating the Lockean proviso. If the proviso excludes someone's appropriating all the drinkable water in the world, it also excludes his purchasing it all. (More weakly, and messily, it may exclude his charging certain prices for some of his supply.) This proviso (almost?) never will come into effect; the more someone acquires of a scarce substance which others want, the higher the price of the rest will go, and the more difficult it will become for him to acquire it all. But still, we can imagine, at least, that something like this occurs: someone makes simultaneous secret bids to the separate owners of a substance, each of whom sells assuming he can easily purchase more from the other owners; or some natural catastrophe destroys all of the supply of something except that in one person's possession. The total supply could not be permissibly appropriated by one person at the beginning. His later acquisition of it all does not show that the original appropriation violated the proviso (even by a reverse argument similar to the one above that tried to zip back from

Z to *A*). Rather, it is the combination of the original appropriation *plus* all the later transfers and actions that violates the Lockean proviso.

Each owner's title to his holding includes the historical shadow of the Lockean proviso on appropriation. This excludes his transferring it into an agglomeration that does violate the Lockean proviso and excludes his using it in a way, in coordination with others or independently of them, so as to violate the proviso by making the situation of others worse than their baseline situation. Once it is known that someone's ownership runs afoul of the Lockean proviso, there are stringent limits on what he may do with (what it is difficult any longer unreservedly to call) "his property." Thus a person may not appropriate the only water hole in a desert and charge what he will. Nor may he charge what he will if he possesses one, and unfortunately it happens that all the water holes in the desert dry up, except for his. This unfortunate circumstance, admittedly no fault of his, brings into operation the Lockean proviso and limits his property rights. Similarly, an owner's property right in the only island in an area does not allow him to order a castaway from a shipwreck off his island as a trespasser, for this would violate the Lockean proviso.

Notice that the theory does not say that owners do have these rights, but that the rights are overridden to avoid some catastrophe. (Overridden rights do not disappear; they leave a trace of a sort absent in the cases under discussion.) There is no such external (and *ad hoc?*) overriding. Considerations internal to the theory of property itself, to its theory of acquisition and appropriation, provide the means for handling such cases. The results, however, may be coextensive with some condition about catastrophe, since the baseline for comparison is so low as compared to the productiveness of a society with private appropriation that the question of the Lockean proviso being violated arises only in the case of catastrophe (or a desert-island situation).

The fact that someone owns the total supply of something necessary for others to stay alive does *not* entail that his (or anyone's) appropriation of anything left some people (immediately or later) in a situation worse than the baseline one. A medical researcher who synthesizes a new substance that effectively treats a certain disease and who refuses to sell except on his terms does not worsen the situation of others by depriving them of whatever he has appropriated. The others easily can possess the same materials he appropriated; the researcher's appropriation or purchase of chemicals didn't make those chemicals scarce in a way so as to violate the Lockean proviso. Nor would someone else's purchasing the total supply of the synthesized substance from the medical researcher. The fact that the medical researcher uses easily available chemicals to synthesize the drug no more violates the Lockean proviso than does the fact that the only surgeon able to perform a particular operation eats easily obtainable food in order to stay alive and to have the energy to work. This shows that the Lockean proviso is not an "end-state principle"; it focuses on a particular way that appropriative actions affect others, and not on the structure of the situation that results.

Intermediate between someone who takes all of the public supply and someone who makes the total supply out of easily obtainable substances is someone who appropriates the total supply of something in a way that does not deprive the others of it. For example, someone finds a new substance in an out-of-the-way place. He discovers that it effectively treats a certain disease and appropriates the total supply. He does not worsen the situation of others; if he did not stumble upon the substance no one else would have, and the others would remain without it. However, as time passes, the likelihood increases that others would have come across the substance; upon this fact might be based a limit to his property right in the substance so that others are not below their baseline position; for example, its bequest might be limited. The theme of someone worsening another's situation by depriving him of something he otherwise would possess may also illuminate the example of patents. An inventor's patent does not deprive others of an object which would not exist if not for the inventor. Yet patents would have this effect on others who independently invent the object. Therefore, these independent inventors, upon whom the burden of proving independent discovery may rest, should not be excluded from utilizing their own invention as they wish (including selling it to others). Furthermore, a known inventor drastically lessens the chances of actual independent invention. For persons who know of an invention usually will not try to reinvent it, and the notion of independent discovery here would be murky at best. Yet we may assume that in the absence of the original invention, sometime later someone else would have come up with it. This suggests placing a time limit on patents, as a rough rule of thumb to approximate how long it would have taken, in the absence of knowledge of the invention, for independent discovery.

I believe that the free operation of a market system will not actually run afoul of the Lockean proviso. (Recall that crucial to our story in Part I of how a protective agency becomes dominant and a *de facto* monopoly is the fact that it wields force in situations of conflict, and is not merely in competition, with other agencies. A similar tale cannot be told about other businesses.) If this is correct, the proviso will not play a very important role in the activities of protective agencies and will not provide a significant opportunity for future state action. Indeed, were it not for the effects of previous *illegitimate* state action, people would not think the possibility of the proviso's being violated as of more interest than any other logical possibility. (Here I make an empirical historical claim; as does someone who disagrees with this.) This completes our indication of the complication in the entitlement theory introduced by the Lockean proviso.

Section II: Rawls' Theory

We can bring our discussion of distributive justice into sharper focus by considering in some detail John Rawls' recent contribution to the subject. *A Theory of Justice* is a powerful, deep, subtle, wide-ranging, systematic work in political and moral philosophy which has not seen its like since the writings of John Stuart Mill, if then. It is a fountain of illuminating ideas, integrated together into a lovely whole. Political philosophers now must either work within Rawls' theory or explain why not. The considerations and distinctions we have developed are illuminated by, and help illuminate, Rawls' masterful presentation of an alternative conception. Even those who remain unconvinced after wrestling with Rawls' systematic vision will learn much from closely studying it. I do not speak only of the Millian sharpening of one's views in combating (what one takes to be) error. It is impossible to read Rawls' book without incorporating much, perhaps transmuted, into one's own deepened view. And it is impossible to finish his book without a new and inspiring vision of what a moral theory may attempt to do and unite; of how *beautiful* a whole theory can be. I permit myself to concentrate here on disagreements with Rawls only because I am confident that my readers will have discovered for themselves its many virtues.

Social Cooperation

> I shall begin by considering the role of the principles of justice. Let us assume, to fix ideas, that a society is a more or less self-sufficient association of persons who in their relations to one another recognize certain rules of conduct as binding and who for the most part act in accordance with them. Suppose further that these rules specify a system of cooperation designed to advance the good of those taking part in it. Then, although a society is a cooperative venture for mutual advantage, it is typically marked by a conflict as well as by an identity of interests. There is an identity of interests since social cooperation makes possible a better life for all than any would have if each were to live solely by his own efforts. There is a conflict of interests since persons are not indifferent as to how the greater benefits produced by their collaboration are distributed, for in order to pursue their ends they each prefer a larger to a lesser share. A set of principles is required for choosing among the various social arrangements which determine this division of advantages and for underwriting an agreement on the proper distributive shares. These principles are the principles of social justice: they provide a way of assigning rights and duties in the basic institutions of society and they define the appropriate distribution of the benefits and burdens of social cooperation. [Rawls, 1971]

Let us imagine *n* individuals who do not cooperate together and who each live solely by their own efforts. Each person i receives a payoff, return, income, and so forth, S_i; the sum total of what each individual gets acting separately is

$$S = \sum_{i=1}^{n} S_i$$

By cooperating together they can obtain a larger sum total T. The problem of distributive social justice, according to Rawls, is how these benefits of cooperation are to be distributed or allocated. This problem might be conceived of in two ways: how is the total T to be allocated? Or, how is the incremental amount due to social cooperation, that is the benefits of social cooperation $T - S$, to be allocated? The latter formulation assumes that each individual i receives from the subtotal S of T, his share S_i. The two statements of the problem differ. When combined with the non-cooperative distribution of S (each i getting S_i), a "fair-looking" distribution of $T - S$ under the second version may not yield a "fair-looking" distribution of T (the first version). Alternatively, a fair-looking distribution of T may give a particular individual i less than his share S_i. (The constraint $T_i \geq S_i$ on the answer to the first formulation of the problem, where T_i is the share in T of the ith individual, would exclude this possibility.) Rawls, without distinguishing these two formulations of the problem, writes as though his concern is the first one, that is, how the total sum T is to be distributed. One might claim, to support a focus on the first issue, that due to the enormous benefits of social cooperation, the noncooperative shares S_i are so small in comparison to any cooperative ones T_i that they may be ignored in setting up the problem of social justice. Though we should note that this certainly is not how people entering into cooperation with one another would agree to conceive of the problem of dividing up cooperation's benefits.

Why does social cooperation *create* the problem of distributive justice? Would there be no problem of justice and no need for a theory of justice, if there was no social cooperation at all, if each person got his share solely by his own efforts? If we suppose, as Rawls seems to, that this situation does *not* raise questions of distributive justice, then in virtue of what facts about social cooperation do these questions of justice emerge? What is it about social cooperation that gives rise to issues of justice? It cannot be said that there will be conflicting claims only where there is social cooperation; that individuals who produce independently and (initially) fend for themselves will not make claims of justice on each other. If there were ten Robinson Crusoes, each working alone for two years on separate islands, who discovered each other and the facts of their different allotments by radio communication via transmitters left twenty years earlier, could they not make claims on each other, supposing it were possible to transfer goods from one island to the next? Wouldn't the one with least make a claim on ground of need, or on the ground that his island was naturally poorest, or on the ground that he was naturally least capable of fending for himself? Mightn't he say that justice demanded he be given some more by the others, claiming it unfair that he should receive so much less and perhaps be destitute, perhaps starving? He might go on to say that the different individual non-cooperative shares stem from differential natural endowments, which are not deserved, and that the task of justice is to rectify these arbitrary facts and inequities. Rather than its being the case that no one *will* make such claims in the situation lacking social cooperation, perhaps the point is that such claims clearly would be without merit. Why would they clearly be without merit? In the social noncooperation situation, it might be said, each individual deserves what he gets unaided by his own efforts; or rather, no one else can make a claim *of justice* against this holding. It is pellucidly clear in this situation who is entitled to what, so no theory of justice is needed. On this view social cooperation introduces a muddying of the waters that makes it unclear or indeterminate who is entitled to what. Rather than saying that no theory of justice applies to this noncooperative case, (wouldn't it be unjust if someone stole another's products in the noncooperative situation?), I would say that it is a clear case of application of the correct theory of justice: the entitlement theory.

How does social cooperation change things so that the same entitlement principles that apply to the noncooperative cases become inapplicable or inappropriate to cooperative ones? It might be said that one cannot disentangle the contributions of distinct individuals who cooperate; everything is everyone's joint product. On this joint product, or on any portion of it, each person plausibly will make claims of equal strength; all have an equally good claim, or at any rate no person has a distinctly better claim than any other. Somehow (this line of thought continues), it must be decided how this total product of joint social cooperation (to which individual entitlements do not apply differentially) is to be divided up: this is the problem of distributive justice.

Don't individual entitlements apply to parts of the cooperatively produced product? First, suppose that social cooperation is based upon division of labor, specialization, comparative advantage, and exchange; each person works singly to transform some input he receives, contracting with others who further transform or transport his product until it reaches its ultimate consumer. People cooperate in making things but they work separately; each person is a miniature firm. The products of each person are easily identifiable, and exchanges are made in open markets with prices set competitively, given informational constraints, and so forth. In such a system of social cooperation, what is the task of a theory of justice? It might be said that whatever holdings result will depend upon the exchange ratios or prices at which exchanges are made, and therefore that the task of a theory of justice is to set criteria for "fair prices." This is hardly the place to trace the serpentine windings of theories of a just price. It is difficult to see why these issues should even arise here. People are choosing to make exchanges with other people and to transfer entitlements, with no restrictions on their freedom to trade with any other party at any mutually acceptable ratio. Why does such sequential social cooperation, linked together by people's voluntary exchanges, raise any special problems about how things are to be distributed? Why isn't the appropriate (a not inappropriate) set of holdings just the one which *actually occurs* via this process of mutually-agreed-to exchanges whereby people choose to give to others what they are entitled to give or hold?

Let us now drop our assumption that people work independently, cooperating only in sequence via voluntary exchanges, and instead consider people who work together jointly to produce something. Is it now impossible to disentangle people's respective contributions? The question here is not whether marginal productivity theory is an appropriate theory of fair or just shares, but whether there is some coherent notion of identifiable marginal product. It seems unlikely that Rawls' theory rests on the strong claim that there is no such reasonably serviceable notion. Anyway, once again we have a situation of a large number of bilateral exchanges: owners of resources reaching separate agreements with entrepreneurs about the use of their resources, entrepreneurs reaching agreements with individual workers, or groups of workers first reaching some joint agreement and then presenting a package to an entrepreneur, and so forth. People transfer their holdings or labor in free markets, with the exchange ratios (prices) determined in the usual manner. If marginal productivity theory is reasonably adequate, people will be receiving, in these voluntary transfers of holdings, roughly their marginal products.

But if the notion of marginal product were so ineffective that factors' marginal products in actual situations of joint production could not be identified by hirers or purchasers of the factors, then the resulting distribution to factors would not be patterned in accordance with marginal product. Someone who viewed marginal productivity theory, where it was applicable, *as a patterned theory of justice,* might think that such situations of joint production and indeterminate marginal product provided an opportunity for some theory of justice to enter to determine appropriate exchange ratios. But an entitlement theorist would find acceptable whatever distribution resulted from the party's voluntary exchanges. The questions about the workability of marginal productivity theory are intricate ones. Let us merely note here the strong personal incentive for owners of resources to converge to the marginal product, and the strong market pressures tending to produce this result. Employers of factors of productions are not all dolts who don't know what they're doing, transferring holdings they value to others on an irrational and arbitrary basis. Indeed, Rawls' position on inequalities requires that separate contributions to joint products be isolable, to some extent at least. For Rawls goes out of his way to argue that inequalities are justified if they serve to raise the position of the worst-off group in the society, if without the inequalities the worst-off group would be even more worse off. These serviceable inequalities stem, at least in part, from the necessity to provide incentives to certain people to perform various activities or fill various roles that not everyone can do equally well. (Rawls is *not* imagining that inequalities are needed to fill positions that everyone can do equally well, or that the most drudgery-filled positions that require the least skill will command the highest income.) But *to whom* are the incentives to be paid? To which performers of what activities?

When it is necessary to provide incentives to some to perform their productive activities, there is no talk of a joint social product from which no individual's contribution can be disentangled. If the product was all that inextricably joint, it couldn't be known that the extra incentives were going to the crucial persons; and it couldn't be known that the additional product produced by these now motivated people is greater than the expenditure to them in incentives. So it couldn't be known whether the provision of incentives was efficient or not, whether it involved a net gain or a net loss. But Rawls' discussion of justifiable inequalities presupposes that these things can be known. And so the claim we have imagined about the indivisible, nonpartitionable nature of the joint product is seen to dissolve, leaving the reasons for the view that social cooperation creates special problems of distributive justice otherwise not present, unclear if not mysterious.

Terms of Cooperation and the Difference Principle

Another entry into the issue of the connection of social cooperation with distributive shares brings us to grips with Rawls' actual discussion. Rawls imagines rational, mutually disinterested individuals meeting in a certain situation, or abstracted from their other features not provided for in this situation. In this hypothetical situation of choice, which Rawls calls "the original position," they choose the first principles of a conception of justice that is to regulate all subsequent criticism and reform of their institutions. While making this choice, no one knows his place in society, his class position or social status, or his natural assets and abilities, his strength, intelligence, and so forth.

> The principles of justice are chosen behind a veil of ignorance. This ensures that no one is advantaged or disadvantaged in the choice of principles by the outcome of natural chance or the contingency of social circumstances. Since all are similarly situated and no one is able to design principles to favor his particular condition, the principles of justice are the result of a fair agreement or bargain. [Rawls, 1971]

What would persons in the original position agree to?

> Persons in the initial situation would choose two . . . principles: the first requires equality in the assignment of basic rights and duties, while the second holds that social and economic inequalities, for example, inequalities of wealth and authority are just only if they result in compensating benefits for everyone, and in particular for the least advantaged members of society. These principles rule out justifying institutions on the grounds that the hardships of some are offset by a greater good in the aggregate. It may be expedient but it is not just that some should have less in order that others may prosper. But there is no injustice in the greater benefits earned by a few provided that the situation of persons not so fortunate is thereby improved. The intuitive idea is that since everyone's well-being depends upon a scheme of cooperation without which no one could have a satisfactory life, the division of advantages should be such as to draw forth the willing cooperation of everyone taking part in it, including those less well situated. Yet this can be expected only if reasonable terms are proposed. The two principles mentioned seem to be a fair agreement on the basis of which those better endowed, or more fortunate in their social position, neither of which we can be said to deserve, could expect the willing cooperation of others when some workable scheme is a necessary condition of the welfare of all. [Rawls, 1971]

This second principle, which Rawls specifies as the difference principle, holds that the institutional structure is to be so designed that the worst-off group under it is at least as well off as the worst-off group (not necessarily the same group) would be under any alternative institutional structure. If persons in the original position follow the minimax policy in making the significant choice of principles of justice, Rawls argues, they will choose the difference principle. Our concern here is not whether persons in the position Rawls describes actually would minimax and actually would choose the particular principles Rawls specifies. Still, we should question why individuals in the original position would choose a principle that focuses upon groups, rather than individuals. Won't application of the minimax principle lead each person in the original position to favor maximizing the position of the worst-off *individual?* To be sure, this principle would reduce questions of evaluating social institutions to the issue of how the unhappiest depressive fares. Yet avoiding this by moving the focus to groups (or representative individuals) seems *ad hoc,* and is inadequately motivated for those in the individual position. Nor is it clear which groups are appropriately considered; why exclude the group of depressives or alcoholics or the representative paraplegic?

If the difference principle is not satisfied by some institutional structure *J,* then under *J* some group *G* is worse off than it would be under another institutional structure *I* that satisfies the principle. If another group *F* is better off under *J* than it would be under the *I* favored by the difference principle, is this sufficient to say that under *J* "some . . . have less in order that others may prosper"? (Here one would have in mind that *G* has less in order that *F* prosper. Could one also make the same statement about *I?* Does *F* have less under *I* in order that *G* may prosper?) Suppose that in a society the following situation prevailed:

1. Group *G* has amount *A* and group *F* has amount *B,* with *B* greater than *A.* Also things could be arranged differently so that *G* would have more than *A,* and *F* would have less than *B.* (The different arrangement might involve a mechanism to transfer some holdings from *F* to *G.*)

Is this sufficient to say

2. *G* is badly off *because F* is well off; *G* is badly off *in order that F* be well off; *F*'s being well off makes *G* badly off; *G* is badly off *on account of F*'s being well off; *G* is not better off *because of* how well off *F* is.

If so, does the truth of statement 2 depend on *G*'s being in a worse position than *F?* There is yet another possible institutional structure *K* that transfers holdings from the worse-off group *G* to *F,* making *G* even more worse off. Does the possibility of *K* make it true to say that, under *J, F* is not (even) better off because of how well off *G* is?

We do not normally hold that the truth of a subjunctive (as in 1) is alone sufficient for the truth of some indicative causal statement (as in 2). It would improve my life in various ways if you were to choose to become my devoted slave, supposing I could get over the initial discomfort. Is the cause of my present state your not becoming my slave? Because your enslaving yourself to a poorer person would improve his lot and worsen yours, are we to say that the poor person is badly off because you are as well off as you are; has he less in order that you may prosper? From

3. If *P* were to do act *A* then *Q* would not be in situation *S.*

we will conclude

4. *P*'s not doing *A* is responsible for *Q*'s being in situation *S; P*'s not doing *A* causes *Q* to be in *S.*

only if we *also* believe that

5. *P* ought to do act *A,* or *P* has a duty to do act *A,* or *P* has an obligation to do act *A,* and so forth.

Thus the inference from 3 to 4, in this case, *presupposes* 5. One cannot argue from 3 to 4 as one step in order *to get to* 5. The statement that in a particular situation some have less in order that others may prosper is often based upon the very evaluation of a situation or an institutional framework that it is introduced to support. Since this evaluation does *not* follow merely from the subjunctive (for example, 1 or 3) an *independent* argument must be produced for it.

Rawls holds, as we have seen, that

> since everyone's well-being depends upon a scheme of cooperation without which no one could have a

> satisfactory life, the division of advantages should be such as to draw forth the willing cooperation of everyone taking part in it, including those less well situated. Yet this can be expected only if reasonable terms are proposed. The two principles mentioned seem to be a fair agreement on the basis of which those better endowed or more fortunate in their social position . . . could expect the willing cooperation of others when some workable scheme is a necessary condition of the welfare of all.

No doubt, the difference principle presents terms on the basis of which those less well endowed would be willing to cooperate. (What *better* terms could they propose for themselves?) But is this a fair agreement on the basis of which those *worse* endowed could expect the *willing* cooperation of others? With regard to the existence of gains from social cooperation, the situation is symmetrical. The better endowed gain by cooperating with the worse endowed, *and* the worse endowed gain by cooperating with the better endowed. Yet the difference principle is not neutral between the better and the worse endowed. Whence the asymmetry?

Perhaps the symmetry is upset if one asks *how much* each gains from the social cooperation. This question might be understood in two ways. How much do people benefit from social cooperation, as compared to their individual holdings in a *non*cooperative scheme? That is, how much is $T_i - S_i$, for each individual *i?* Or, alternatively, how much does each individual gain from general social cooperation, as compared, not with *no* cooperation, but with more limited cooperation? The latter is the more appropriate question with regard to general social cooperation. For failing general agreement on the principles to govern how the benefits of general social cooperation are to be held, not everyone will remain in a noncooperative situation if there is some other beneficial cooperative arrangement involving some, but not all, people, whose participants *can* agree. These people will participate in this more narrow cooperative arrangement. To focus upon the benefits of the better and the worse endowed cooperating together, we must try to imagine less extensive schemes of partitioned social cooperation in which the better endowed cooperate only among themselves and the worse endowed cooperate only among themselves, with no cross-cooperation. The members of both groups gain from the internal cooperation within their respective groups and have larger shares than they would if there were no social cooperation at all. An individual benefits from the wider system of extensive cooperation between the better and the worse endowed to the extent of his incremental gain from this wider cooperation; namely, the amount by which his share under a scheme of general cooperation is greater than it would be under one of limited intragroup (but not cross-group) cooperation. *General* cooperation will be of more benefit to the better or to the worse endowed if (to pick a simple criterion) the mean incremental gain from general cooperation (when compared with limited intragroup cooperation) is greater in one group than it is in the other.

One might speculate about whether there is an inequality between the groups' mean incremental gains and, if so, which way it goes. If the better-endowed group includes those who manage to accomplish something of great economic advantage to others, such as new inventions, new ideas about production or ways of doing things, skill at economic tasks, and so on, it is difficult to avoid concluding that the *less* well endowed gain *more* than the better endowed do from the scheme of general cooperation. What follows from this conclusion? I do *not* mean to imply that the better endowed should get even more than they get under the entitlement system of general social cooperation. What *does* follow from the conclusion is a deep suspicion of imposing, in the name of fairness, constraints upon voluntary social cooperation (and the set of holdings that arises from it) so that those already benefiting most from this general cooperation benefit even more!

Rawls would have us imagine the worse-endowed persons say something like the following: "Look, better endowed: you gain by cooperating with us. If you want our cooperation you'll have to accept reasonable terms. We suggest these terms: We'll cooperate with you only if we get *as much as possible.* That is, the terms of our cooperation should give us that maximal share such that, if it was tried to give us more, we'd end up with less." How generous these proposed terms are might be seen by imagining that the better endowed make the almost symmetrical opposite proposal: "Look, worse endowed: you gain by cooperating with *us*. If you want our cooperation you'll have to accept reasonable terms. We propose these terms: We'll cooperate with you so long as *we* get as much as possible. That is, the terms of our cooperation should give us the maximal share such that, if it was tried to give us more, we'd end up with less." If these terms seem outrageous, as they are, why don't the terms proposed by those worse endowed seem the same? Why shouldn't the better endowed treat this latter proposal as beneath consideration, supposing someone to have the nerve explicitly to state it?

Rawls devotes much attention to explaining why those less well favored should not complain at receiving less. His explanation, simply put, is that because the inequality works for his advantage, someone less well favored shouldn't complain about it; he receives *more* in the unequal system than he would in an equal one. (Though he might receive still more in another unequal system that placed someone else below him.) But Rawls discusses the question of whether those *more* favored will or should find the terms satisfactory *only* in the following passage, where *A* and *B* are any two representative men with *A* being the more favored:

> The difficulty is to show that *A* has no grounds for complaint. Perhaps he is required to have less than he might since his having more would result in some loss to *B*. Now what can be said to the more favored man? To begin with, it is clear that the well-being of each depends on a scheme of social cooperation without which no one could have a satisfactory life. Secondly, we can ask for the willing cooperation of everyone only if the terms of the scheme are reasonable. The difference principle, then, seems to be a fair basis on which those better endowed, or more fortunate in their social circumstances, could expect others to collaborate with them when some workable arrangement is a necessary condition of the good of all.

What Rawls imagines being said to the more favored men does *not* show that these men have no grounds for complaint, nor does it at all diminish the weight of whatever complaints they have. That the well-being of all depends on social cooperation without which no one could have a satisfactory life could also be said to the less well endowed by someone proposing any other principle, including that of maximizing the position of the best endowed. Similarly for the fact that we can ask for the willing cooperation of everyone only if the terms of the scheme are reasonable. The question is: What terms *would be* reasonable? What Rawls imagines being said thus far merely sets up his problem; it doesn't distinguish his proposed difference principle from the almost symmetrical counterproposal that we imagined the better endowed making, or from any other proposal. Thus, when Rawls continues, "The difference principle, then, seems to be a fair basis on which those best endowed, or more fortunate in their social circumstances, could expect others to collaborate with them when some workable arrangement is a necessary condition of the good of all," the presence of the "then" in his sentence is puzzling. Since the sentences which precede it are neutral between his proposal and any other proposal, the conclusion that the difference principle presents a fair basis for cooperation *cannot* follow from what precedes it in this passage. Rawls is merely repeating that it seems reasonable; hardly a convincing reply to anyone to whom it doesn't seem reasonable.

Rawls has not shown that the more favored man *A* has no grounds for complaint at being required to have less in order that another *B* might have more than he otherwise would. And he can't show this, since *A does* have grounds for complaint. Doesn't he?

The Original Position and End-Result Principles

How can it have been supposed that these terms offered by the less well-endowed are fair? Imagine a social pie somehow appearing so that *no one* has any claim at all on any portion of it, no one has any more of a claim than any other person; yet there must be unanimous agreement on how it is to be divided. Undoubtedly, apart from threats or holdouts in bargaining, an equal distribution would be suggested and found plausible as a solution. (It is, in Schelling's sense, a focal point solution.) If *somehow* the size of the pie wasn't fixed, and it was realized that pursuing an equal distribution somehow would lead to a smaller total pie than otherwise might occur, the people might well agree to an unequal distribution which raised the size of the least share. But in any actual situation, wouldn't this realization reveal something about differential claims on parts of the pie? Who is it that could make the pie larger, and would do it if given a larger share, but not if given an equal share under the scheme of equal distribution? To whom is an incentive to be provided to make this larger contribution? (There's no talk here of inextricably entangled joint product; it's known *to whom* incentives are to be offered, or at least to whom a bonus is to be paid after the fact.) Why doesn't this identifiable differential contribution lead to some differential entitlement?

If things fell from heaven like manna, and no one had any special entitlement to any portion of it, and no manna would fall unless all agreed to a particular distribution, and somehow the quantity varied depending on the distribution, then it is plausible to claim that persons placed so that they couldn't make threats, or hold out for specially large shares, would agree to the difference principle rule of distribution. But is *this* the appropriate model for thinking about how the things people produce are to be distributed? Why think the same results should obtain for situations where there *are* differential entitlements as for situations where there are not?

A procedure that founds principles of distributive justice on what rational persons who know nothing about themselves or their histories would agree to *guarantees that end-state principles of justice will be taken as fundamental.* Perhaps some historical principles of justice are derivable from end-state principles, as the utilitarian tries to derive individual rights, prohibitions on punishing the innocent, and so forth, from *his* end-state principle; perhaps such arguments can be constructed even for the entitlement principle. But no historical principle, it seems, could be agreed to in the first instance by the participants in Rawls' original position. For people meeting together behind a veil of ignorance to decide who gets what, knowing nothing about any special entitlements people may have, will treat anything to be distributed as manna from heaven.[3]

Suppose there were a group of students who have studied during a year, taken examinations, and received grades between 0 and 100 which they have not yet learned of. They are now gathered together, having no idea of the grade any one of them has received, and they are asked to allocate grades among themselves so that the grades total to a given sum (which is determined by the sum of the grades they actually have received from the teacher). First, let us suppose they are to decide jointly upon a particular distribution of grades; they are to give a particular grade to each identifiable one of them present at the meeting. Here, given sufficient restrictions on their ability to threaten each other, they probably would agree to each person receiving the same grade, to each person's grade being equal to the total divided by the number of people to be graded. Surely they would *not* chance upon the particular set of grades they already have received. Suppose next that there is posted on a bulletin board at their meeting a paper headed ENTITLEMENTS, which lists each person's name with a grade next to it, the listing being identical to the instructor's gradings. Still, this particular distribution will not be agreed to by those having done poorly. Even if they know what "entitlement" means (which perhaps we must suppose they don't, in order to match the absence of moral factors in the calculations of persons in Rawls' original position), why should they agree to the instructor's distribution? What self-interested reason to agree to it would they have?

Next suppose that they are unanimously to agree not to a *particular* distribution of grades, but rather to general principles to govern the distribution of grades. What principle would be selected? The equality principle, which gives each person the same grade, would have a prominent chance. And if it turned out that the total was variable depending upon how they divided it, depending on which of them got what grade, and a higher grade was desirable though they were not competing among each other (for example, each of them was competing for some position with the members of separate distinct groups), then the principle of distributing grades so as to maximize the lowest grades *might* seem a plausible one. Would these people agree to the non-end-state *historical* principle of distribution: give people grades according to how their examinations were evaluated by a qualified and impartial observer?[4] If all the people deciding knew the particular distribution that would be yielded by this historical principle, they wouldn't agree to it. For the situation then would be equivalent to the earlier one of their deciding upon a particular distribution, in which we already have seen they would not agree to the entitlement distribution. Suppose then that the people do not know the particular distribution actually yielded by this historical principle. They cannot be led to select this historical principle because it looks just, or fair, to them; for no such notions are allowed to be at work in the original position. (Otherwise people would argue there, like here, about what justice requires.) Each person engages in a calculation to decide whether it will be in his own interests to accept this historical principle of distribution. Grades, under the historical principle, depend upon nature and developed intelligence, how hard the people have worked, accident, and so on, factors about which people in the original position know almost nothing. (It would be risky for someone to think that since he is reasoning so well in thinking about the principles, he must be one of the intellectually better endowed. Who knows what dazzling argument the others are reasoning their way through, and perhaps keeping quiet about for strategic reasons.) Each person in the original position will do something like assigning probability distributions to his place along these various dimensions. It seems unlikely that each person's probability calculations would lead to the historical-entitlement principle, in preference to every other principle. Consider the principle we may call the reverse-entitlement principle. It recommends drawing up a list of the historical entitlements in order of magnitude, and giving the most anyone is entitled to, to the person entitled to the least; the second most to the person entitled to the second least, and so on. Any probability calculations of self-interested persons in Rawls' original position, or any probability calculations of the students we have considered, will lead them to view the entitlement and the reverse-entitlement principles as ranked equally insofar as their own self-interest is concerned! (What calculations could lead them to view one of the principles as superior to the other?) Their calculations will not lead them to select the entitlement principle.

The nature of the decision problem facing persons deciding upon principles in an original position behind a veil of ignorance limits them to end-state principles of distribution. The self-interested person evaluates any non-end-state principle on the basis of how it works out for him; his calculations about any principle focus on how he ends up under the principle. (These calculations include consideration of the labor he is yet to do, which does not appear in the grading example except as the sunk cost of the labor already done.) Thus for any principle, an occupant of the original position will focus on the distribution D of goods that it leads to, or a probability distribution over the distributions $D_1, \ldots, D_n$ it may lead to, and upon his probabilities of occupying each position in each D_i profile, supposing it to obtain. The point would remain the same if, rather than using personal probabilities, he uses some other decision rule of the sort discussed by decision theorists. In these calculations, the only role played by the principle is that of generating a distribution of goods (or whatever else they care about) or of generating a probability distribution over distributions of goods. Different principles are compared solely by comparing the alternative distributions they generate. Thus the principles drop out of the picture, and each self-interested person makes a choice among alternative end-state distributions. People in the original position either directly agree to an end-state distribution or they agree to a principle; if they agree to a principle, they do it solely on the basis of considerations about end-state distributions. The *fundamental* principles they agree to, the ones they can all converge in agreeing upon, *must* be end-state principles.

Rawls' construction is incapable of yielding an entitlement or historical conception of distributive justice. The end-state principles of justice yielded by his procedure might be used in an attempt to *derive,* when conjoined with factual information, historical-entitlement principles, as derivative principles falling under a nonentitlement conception of justice. It is difficult to see how such attempts could derive and account for the *particular* convolutions of historical-entitlement principles. And any derivations from end-state principles of approximations of the principles of acquisition, transfer, and rectification would strike one as similar to utilitarian contortions in trying to derive (approximations of) usual precepts of justice; they do not yield the particular result desired, and they produce the wrong reasons for the sort of result they try to get. If historical-entitlement principles are fundamental, then Rawls' construction will yield approximations of them at best; it will produce the wrong sorts of reasons for them, and its derived results sometimes will conflict with the precisely correct principles. The whole procedure of persons choosing principles in Rawls' original position presupposes that no historical-entitlement conception of justice is correct.

It might be objected to our argument that Rawls' procedure is designed to *establish* all facts about justice; there is no independent notion of entitlement, not provided by his theory, to stand on in criticizing his theory. But we do not need any *particular* developed historical-entitlement theory as a basis from which to criticize Rawls' construction. If *any* such fundamental historical-entitlement view is correct, then Rawls' theory is not. We are thus able to make this structural criticism of the type of theory Rawls presents and the type of principles it must yield, without first having formulated fully a particular historical-entitlement theory as an alternative to his. We would be ill advised to accept Rawls' theory and his construal of the problem as one of which principles would be chosen by rational self-interested individuals behind a veil of ignorance, unless we were sure that no adequate historical-entitlement theory was to be gotten.

Since Rawls' construction doesn't yield a historical or entitlement conception of justice, there will be some feature(s) of his construction in virtue of which it doesn't. Have we done anything other than focus upon the particular feature(s), and say that this makes Rawls' construction incapable in principle of yielding an entitlement or historical conception of justice? This would be a criticism without any force at all, for in this sense we would have to say that the construction is incapable in principle of yielding any conception other than the one it actually yields. It seems clear that our criticism goes deeper than this (and I hope it is clear to the reader); but it is difficult to formulate the requisite criterion of depth. Lest this appear lame, let us add that as Rawls states the root idea underlying the veil of ignorance, that feature which is the most prominent in excluding agreement to an entitlement conception, it is to prevent someone from tailoring principles to his own advantage, from designing principles to favor his particular condition. But not only does the veil of ignorance do this; it ensures that no shadow of entitlement considerations will enter the rational calculations of ignorant, nonmoral individuals constrained to decide in a situation reflecting some formal conditions of morality.[5] Perhaps, in a Rawls-*like* construction, some condition weaker than the veil of ignorance could serve to exclude the special tailoring of principles, or perhaps some other "structural-looking" feature of the choice situation could be formulated to mirror entitlement considerations. But as it stands there is no reflection of entitlement considerations in any form in the situation of those in the original position; these considerations do not enter even to be overridden or outweighed or otherwise put aside. Since no glimmer of entitlement principles is built into the structure of the situation of persons in the original position, there is no way these principles could be selected; and Rawls' construction is incapable in principle of yielding them. This is not to say, of course, that the entitlement principle (or "the principle of natural liberty") couldn't be *written* on the list of principles to be considered by those in the original position. Rawls doesn't do even this, perhaps because it is so transparently clear that there would be no point in including it to be considered *there*.

Collective Assets

Rawls' view seems to be that everyone has some entitlement or claim on the totality of natural assets (viewed as a pool), with no one having differential claims. The distribution of natural abilities is viewed as a "collective asset."

> We see then that the difference principle represents, in effect, an agreement to regard the distribution of natural talents as a common asset and to share in the benefits of this distribution whatever it turns out to be.

> Those who have been favored by nature, whoever they are, may gain from their good fortune only on terms that improve the situation of those who have lost out. . . . No one deserves his greater natural capacity nor merits a more favorable starting place in society. But it does not follow that one should eliminate these distinctions. There is another way to deal with them. The basic structure can be arranged so that these contingencies work for the good of the least fortunate. [Rawls, 1971]

People will differ in how they view regarding natural talents as a common asset. Some will complain, echoing Rawls against utilitarianism, that this "does not take seriously the distinction between persons"; and they will wonder whether any reconstruction of Kant that treats people's abilities and talents as resources for others can be adequate. "The two principles of justice . . . rule out even the tendency to regard men as means to one another's welfare." Only if one presses *very* hard on the distinction between men and their talents, assets, abilities, and special traits. Whether any coherent conception of a person remains when the distinction is so pressed is an open question. Why we, thick with particular traits, should be cheered that (only) the thus purified men within us are not regarded as means is also unclear.

People's talents and abilities *are* an asset to a free community; others in the community benefit from their presence and are better off because they are there rather than elsewhere or nowhere. (Otherwise they wouldn't choose to deal with them.) Life, over time, is not a constant-sum game, wherein if greater ability or effort leads to some getting more, that means that others must lose. In a free society, people's talents do benefit others, and not only themselves. Is it the extraction of even more benefit to others that is supposed to justify treating people's natural assets as a collective resource? What justifies this extraction?

No one deserves his greater natural capacity nor merits a more favorable starting place in society. But it does not follow that one should eliminate these distinctions. There is another way to deal with them. The basic structure can be arranged so that these contingencies work for the good of the least fortunate.

And if there weren't "another way to deal with them"? Would it then follow that one should eliminate these distinctions? What exactly would be contemplated in the case of natural assets? If people's assets and talents *couldn't* be harnessed to serve others, would something be done to remove these exceptional assets and talents, or to forbid them from being exercised for the person's own benefit or that of someone else he chose, even though this limitation wouldn't improve the absolute position of those somehow unable to harness the talents and abilities of others for their own benefit? Is it so implausible to claim that envy underlies this conception of justice, forming part of its root notion?

We have used our entitlement conception of justice in holdings to probe Rawls' theory, sharpening our understanding of what the entitlement conception involves by bringing it to bear upon an alternative conception of distributive justice, one that is deep and elegant. Also, I believe, we have probed deep-lying inadequacies in Rawls' theory. I am mindful of Rawls' reiterated point that a theory cannot be evaluated by focusing upon a single feature or part of it; instead the whole theory must be assessed (the reader will not know how whole a theory can be until he has read all of Rawls' book), and a perfect theory is not to be expected. However we have examined an important part of Rawls' theory, and its crucial underlying assumptions. I am as well aware as anyone of how sketchy my discussion of the entitlement conception of justice in holdings has been. But I no more believe we need to have formulated a complete alternative theory in order to reject Rawls' undeniably great advance over utilitarianism, than Rawls needed a complete alternative theory before he could reject utilitarianism. What more does one need or can one have, in order to begin progressing toward a better theory, than a sketch of a plausible alternative view, which from its very different perspective highlights the inadequacies of the best existing well-worked-out theory? Here, as in so many things, we learn from Rawls.

We began this chapter's investigation of distributive justice in order to consider the claim that a state more extensive than the minimal state could be justified on the grounds that it was necessary, or the most appropriate instrument, to achieve distributive justice. According to the entitlement conception of justice in holdings that we have presented, there is no argument based upon the first two principles of distributive justice, the principles of acquisition and of transfer, for such a more extensive state. If the set of holdings is properly generated, there is no argument for a more extensive state based upon distributive justice. (Nor, we have claimed, will the Lockean proviso actually provide occasion for a more extensive state.) If, however, these principles are violated, the principle of rectification comes into play. Perhaps it is best to view some patterned principles of distributive justice as rough rules of thumb meant to approximate the general results of applying the principle of rectification of injustice. For example, lacking much historical information, and assuming (1) that victims of injustice generally do worse than they otherwise would and (2) that those from the least well-off group in the society have the highest probabilities of being the (descendants of) victims of the most serious injustice who are owed compensation by those who benefited from the injustices (assumed to be those better off, though sometimes the perpetrators will be others in the worst-off group), then a *rough* rule of thumb for rectifying injustices might seem to be the following: organize society so as to maximize the position of whatever group ends up least well-off in the society. This particular example may well be implausible, but an important question for each society will be the following: given *its* particular history, what operable rule of thumb best approximates the results of a detailed application in that society of the principle of rectification? These issues are very complex and are best left to a full treatment of the principle of rectification. In the absence of such a treatment applied to a particular society, one *cannot* use the analysis and theory presented here to condemn any particular scheme of transfer payments, unless it is clear that no considerations of rectification of injustice could apply to justify it. Although to introduce socialism as the punishment for our sins would be to go too far, past injustices might be so great as to make necessary in the short run a more extensive state in order to rectify them.

NOTES

1. Might not a transfer have instrumental effects on a third party, changing his feasible options? (But what if the two parties to the transfer independently had used their holdings in this fashion?) I discuss this question below, but note here that this question concedes the point for distributions of ultimate intrinsic noninstrumental goods (pure utility experiences, so to speak) that are transferrable. It also might be objected that the transfer might make a third party more envious because it worsens his position relative to someone else. I find it incomprehensible how this can be thought to involve a claim of justice.

2. I am unsure as to whether the arguments I present below show that such taxation merely *is* forced labor; so that "is on a par with" means "is one kind of." Or alternatively, whether the arguments emphasize the great similarities between such taxation and forced labor, to show it is plausible and illuminating to view such taxation in the light of forced labor.

3. Do the people in the original position ever wonder whether *they* have the *right* to decide how everything is to be divided up? Perhaps they reason that since they are deciding this question, they must assume they are entitled to do so; and so particular people can't have particular entitlements to holdings (for then they wouldn't have the right to decide together on how all holdings are to be divided); and hence everything legitimately may be treated like manna from heaven.

4. I do not mean to assume that all teachers are such, nor even that learning in universities should be graded. All I need is some example of entitlement, the details of which the reader will have some familiarity with, to use to examine decision making in the original position. Grading is a simple example, though not a perfect one, entangled as it is with whatever ultimate social purposes the ongoing practice serves. We may ignore this complication, for their selecting the historical principle on the grounds that it effectively serves those purposes would illustrate our point below that their fundamental concerns and fundamental principles are end-state ones.

5. Someone might think entitlement principles count as specially tailored in a morally objectionable way, and so he might reject my claim that the veil of ignorance accomplishes more than its stated purpose. Since to specially tailor principles is to tailor them *unfairly* for one's own advantage, and since the question of the fairness of the entitlement principle is precisely the issue, it is difficult to decide which begs the question: my criticism of the strength of the veil of ignorance, or the defense against this criticism which I imagine in this note.

GERALD COHEN

Robert Nozick and Wilt Chamberlain: How Patterns Preserve Liberty

1977

According to Nozick

1. Whatever arises from a just situation by just steps is itself just. (p. 151)

Steps are just if they are free of injustice, and they are free of injustice if they are fully voluntary on the part of all legitimately concerned persons. Hence

2. Whatever arises from a just situation as a result of fully voluntary transactions on the part of all legitimately concerned persons is itself just.

So convinced is Nozick that (2) is true that he thinks it must be accepted by people attached to a doctrine of justice which in other respects differs from his own. That is why he feels able to employ (2) in the Chamberlain parable, despite having granted, for the sake of argument, the justice of an initial situation patterned by an egalitarian principle.

Even if (2) is true, it does not follow that pattern D1 can be maintained only at the price of injustice, for people might simply *fail* to use their liberty in a pattern-subverting manner. But that is not an interesting possibility. A more interesting one is that they deliberately *refuse* to use their liberty subversively. Reasons for refusing will be adduced shortly. But is (2) true? Does liberty always preserve justice?

A standard way of testing the claim would be to look for states of affairs which would be accounted unjust but which might be generated by the route (2) approves. Perhaps the strongest counterexample of this form would be slavery. We then say: voluntary self-enslavement is possible, slavery is unjust, therefore (2) is false. But whatever may be the merits of that argument, we know that Nozick is not moved by it. For he thinks there is no injustice in slavery to the extent that it arises out of the approved processes.

Though Nozick consistently endorses slavery of appropriate genesis, there is a restriction, derived from (2) itself, on the kind of slavery he accepts. (2) does not allow slave status to be inherited by offspring of the self-enslaved, for then a concerned party's situation would be decided for him, independently of his will. "Some things individuals may choose for themselves no one may choose for another" (p. 331). Let us remember this when we come to scrutinize the Wilt Chamberlain transaction, for widespread contracting of the kind which occurs in the parable might have the effect of seriously modifying, for the worse, the situation of members of future generations.

Should we say that in Nozick's conception of justice a slave society need be no less just than one where people are free? That would be a tendentious formulation. For Nozick can add to what was reported above that it is most unlikely that rational persons in an initially just situation will in full knowledge of what they are doing contract into slavery, except, indeed, where it would be wrong to forbid them to do so. This diminishes the danger that (2) can be used to stamp approval on morally repellent social arrangements.

I attribute some such response to Nozick on the basis, *inter alia* of this passage:

> [I]t must be granted that were people's reasons for transferring some of their holdings to others always irrational or arbitrary, we would find this disturbing. . . .

Gerald Cohen, pp. 7–14 of "Robert Nozick and Wilt Chamberlain." *Erkenntnis* 11 (1) (1977): 5–23. By permission of Springer.

> We feel more comfortable upholding the justice of an entitlement system if most of the transfers under it are done for reasons. This does not mean necessarily that all deserve what holdings they receive. It means only that there is a purpose or point to someone's transferring a holding to one person rather than to another; that usually we can see what the transferer *thinks* he's gaining, what cause he *thinks* he's serving, what goals he *thinks* he's helping to achieve, and so forth. Since in a capitalist society people often transfer holdings to others in accordance with how much they *perceive* these others benefiting them, the fabric constituted by the individual transactions and transfers is largely reasonable and intelligible (p. 159, my emphases).

Accordingly, Nozick emphasizes the motives people have when they pay to watch Chamberlain, instead of stipulating that they do so freely and leaving us to guess why. The example would be less impressive if Chamberlain or his agent had induced in the fans an inordinate taste for basketball, by means which fall short of what Nozick would consider coercive or fraudulent, but which remain unattractive. It is important to the persuasive allure of the example that we should think what the fans are doing not only voluntary but sensible.

So transactions are disturbing, even though they are just—Nozick does not quite say that what *disturbs* us undermines the *justice* of the transaction—when we cannot see what the (or some of the) contracting parties think they are gaining by them. But we should surely also be disturbed if though we can see what the agent *thinks* he's gaining, we know that what he *will* gain is not that, but something he thinks less valuable; or that what results is not only the gain he expects but also unforeseen consequences which render negative the net value, according to his preferences and standards, of the transaction. We should not be content if what he *thinks* he is getting is good, but what he actually gets is bad, by his own lights. I shall assume that Nozick would accept this plausible extension of his concession. If he would not, so much the worse for his position.

Hence if we can show that Chamberlain's fans get not only the pleasure of watching him minus twenty-five cents but also uncontemplated disbenefits of a high order, then even if for Nozick the outcome remains just, it should, even to Nozick, be rather disturbing. We shall need to ask whether we do not find irrationality in the Chamberlain transaction, when we think through, as Nozick's fans do not, the *full* consequences of what they are doing.

But now we can go further. For, in the light of the considerations just reviewed, (2) appears very probably false. Nozick says a transaction is free of injustice if every concerned party agrees to it. Perhaps that is so. But transactional justice, so characterized, is supposed—given an initially just situation—to confer justice on what results from it. (That is why (2) follows from (1)). And that is questionable. Of each person who agrees to a transaction we may ask: *would he have agreed to it had he known what its outcome was to be*? Since the answer may be negative, it is far from evident that transactional justice, as described, transmits justice to its results. Perhaps the effect obtains when the answer is positive. This leads us to revise (2), as follows:

(3) Whatever arises from a just situation as a result of fully voluntary transactions which all transagents would still have agreed to if they had known what the results of so transacting were to be is itself just.

(3) looks plausible, but its power to endorse market-generated states of affairs is, while not nil, very weak. Stronger principles may also be available, but (2), Nozick's principle, is certainly too strong.

Let us now apply this critique of Nozick's principles to the parable which is supposed to secure (or reveal) our allegiance to them.

Before describing the Chamberlain transaction, Nozick says: "It is not clear how those holding alternative conceptions of distributive justice can reject the entitlement conception of justice in holdings" (p. 160). There follows the Chamberlain story, where we assume that D1 is just, and are then, supposedly, constrained to admit that D2, into which it is converted, must also be just; an admission, according to Nozick, which is tantamount to accepting the entitlement conception. But how much of it must we accept if we endorse D2 as just? At most that there is *a* role for the entitlement principle. For what the transaction subverts is the original pattern, not the principle governing it, taken as a principle conjoinable with others to form a total theory of just or legitimate holdings. The example, even if successful, does not defeat the initial assumption that D1 is just. Rather, it exploits that assumption to argue that D2, though it breaks Dl's pattern, is also just. The story, if sound, impugns not the original distribution, but the *exclusive* rightness of the principle determining it.

Now Nozick is certainly right to this extent, even if we reject the Chamberlain story: there must be *a* role for entitlement in determining acceptable holdings. For unless the just society forbids gift, it must allow transfers which do not answer to a patterning principle. This is compatible with placing restraints on the scope of gift, and we shall shortly see why it may be justified in doing so. More generally, assigning a certain role to unregulated transactions in the determination of holdings is compatible with using an egalitarian principle to decide the major distribution of goods and to limit, for example by taxation, how much more or less than what he would get under that principle alone a person may come to have in virtue of transactions which escape its writ. I think socialists do well to concede that an egalitarian principle should not be the only guide to the justice of holdings, or, if it is, then justice should not be the only guide to the moral legitimacy of holdings.

Among the reasons for limiting how much an individual may hold, regardless of how he came to hold it, is to prevent him from acquiring, through his holdings, an unacceptable amount of *power* over others.

Is the Chamberlain transaction really beneficial (or at worst harmless) to everyone with an interest in it? I shall argue that it threatens to generate a situation in which some come to have unacceptable amounts of power over others.

The fans "are excited about seeing him play; it is worth the total admission price to them." The idea is that they see him play if and only if they pay, and seeing him play is worth more to them than anything else they can get for twenty-five cents. So it *may* be, but this fails to capture everything in the outcome which is relevant. For once Chamberlain has received the payments he is in a very special position of power in what was previously an egalitarian society. The fans' access to resources in future may be prejudiced by the disproportionate access Chamberlain's wealth gives him, and the consequent power over others he now has, *For all Nozick says,* the socialist may claim that this is not a bargain informed people in an egalitarian society will be apt to make: they will refrain from so contracting as to upset the equality they prize. They will be specially averse to doing so because the resulting changes would profoundly affect their children. (This may seem an hysterical projection of the effect of the Chamberlain transaction, but I take it we have to consider the upshot of general performance of transactions of that kind, and then the projection is, I submit, entirely realistic.)

It is easy to think carelessly about the example. How we feel about people like Chamberlain getting a lot of money *as things are* is a poor index of how people would feel in the imagined situation. Among us the ranks of the rich and the powerful exist, and it can be pleasing, given that they do, when a figure like Chamberlain joins them. Who better and more innocently deserves to be among them? But the case before us is a society of equality in danger of corruption. Reflective people would have to consider not only the joy of watching Chamberlain and its immediate money price but also the fact, which socialists say they would deplore, that their society would be set on the road to class division. In presenting the Chamberlain fable Nozick ignores the commitment people may have to living in a society of a particular kind, and the rhetorical power of the illustration depends on that omission. Later—see p. 14 below—Nozick takes up this point, but he says nothing interesting about it.

Nozick tacitly supposes that a person willing to pay twenty-five cents to watch Wilt play is *ipso facto* a person willing to pay *Wilt* twenty-five cents to watch him play. It is no doubt true that in our society people rarely care who gets the money they forgo to obtain goods, But the tacit supposition is false, and the common unconcern is irrational. Nozick exploits our familiarity with this unconcern. Yet a person might welcome a world in which he and a million others watch Wilt play, at a cost of twenty-five cents to each, and consistently disfavour one in which, in addition, Wilt receives a cool quarter million.

So if a citizen of the Dl society joins with others in paying twenty-five cents to Wilt to watch Wilt play, without thinking about the effect on Wilt's power, then the result may be deemed "disturbing" in the sense of p. 159. Of course a single person's paying a quarter will make no appreciable difference if the rest are already going to do so. But a convention might evolve not to make such payments, or, more simply, there could be a democratically authorized taxation system which maintains wealth differentials within acceptable limits. Whether Wilt would then still play is a further question on which I shall not comment, except to say that anyone who thinks it obvious he would not misunderstands human nature, or basketball, or both.

In defending the justice of the Chamberlain transaction, Nozick glances at the position of persons not directly party to it: "After someone transfers something to Wilt Chamberlain, third parties *still* have their legitimate shares; *their* shares are not changed." This is false, in one relevant sense. For a person's effective share depends on what he can do with what he has, and that depends not only on how much he has but on what others have and on how what others have is distributed. If it is distributed equally among them he will often be better placed than if some have especially large shares. Third parties, including the as yet unborn, therefore have an interest against the contract, which is not catered for. It is roughly the same interest as the fans have in not making it.

Nozick addresses this issue in a footnote:

> Might not a transfer have instrumental effects on a third party, changing his feasible options? (But what if the two parties to a transfer independently had used their holdings in this fashion?) (p. 162)

He promises further treatment of the problem later, and though he does not say where, he presumably means his section on "Voluntary Exchange," which we shall examine at the end of this paper. Here I respond to his parenthetical rhetorical question.

First, there are some upshots of transfers of holdings, some effects on the options of the other parties, which will not occur as effects of the unconcerted use of dispersed holdings by individuals, because they could not, or because they would not use them in that way. The Chamberlain fans, acting independently, would probably be unable to buy a set of houses and leave them unoccupied, with speculative intent, but Chamberlain can. So to begin with "this fashion" will sometimes not be one in which parties could or would use their holdings independently. And when the effect to which objection is made might indeed be realised by such independent action, then those concerned about the effect will naturally also be concerned about that action—the rhetorical question does not turn the attention of those who ask the first one to a parallel case where they have reason to agree with Nozick.

As an argument about *justice* the Chamberlain story is either question-begging or uncompelling. Nozick asks:

> If the people were entitled to dispose of the resources to which they were entitled (under D1), didn't this include their being entitled to give it to, or exchange it with, Wilt Chamberlain? (p. 161)

If this interrogative is intended as a vivid way of asserting the corresponding indicative, then Nozick is telling us that the rights in shares with which they were vested are violated unless they are allowed to contract as described. If so, he begs the question. For it will be clear that their rights are violated only if the entitlement they received was of the absolute Nozickian sort, and this cannot be assumed. Whatever principles underlie D1 will generate restrictions on the use of what is distributed in accordance with them.

The other way of taking the quoted question is not as an assertion but as an appeal. Nozick is then asking us whether we do not agree that any restrictions which would forbid the Chamberlain transaction must be unjustified. So construed the argument is not question-begging, but it is inconclusive. For considerations which might justify restrictions are not canvassed, such as the fact that the contract may generate inordinate power. It is easy to think that what happens afterwards is that Chamberlain eats lots of chocolate, sees lots of movies and buys lots of subscriptions to expensive socialist journals. But, as I have insisted, we must remember the considerable power he can now exercise over others. In general holdings are not only sources of enjoyment but in certain distributions sources of power. Transfers which look unexceptionable come to seem otherwise when we bring into relief the aspect neglected by bourgeois apologetic.

Turning from justice to *liberty,* is it true that a "socialist society would have to forbid capitalist acts between consenting adults" (p. 163)? Socialism perishes if there are too many such acts, but it does not follow that it must forbid them. In traditional socialist doctrine capitalist action wanes not primarily because it is illegal, but because the impulse behind it atrophies, or, less Utopianly, because other impulses become stronger, or because people believe that capitalistic exchange is unfair. *Such expectation rests on a conception of human nature, and so does its denial.* Nozick has a different conception, for which he does not argue, one that fits many 20th century Americans, which is no reason for concluding it is universally true. The people in his state of nature are intelligible only as well socialized products of a market society. In the contrary socialist conception human beings have and may develop further an unqualified (that is, non-"instrumental") desire for community, an unqualified relish of cooperation, and an unqualified aversion to being on either side of a master/servant relationship. No one should assume without argument, or take it on trust from the socialist tradition, that this conception is sound. But *if* it is sound, there will be no need for incessant invigilation against "capitalist acts," and Nozick does not *argue* that it is unsound. Hence he has not shown that socialism conflicts with freedom, even if his unargued premise that its citizens will want to perform capitalist acts attracts the assent of the majority of his readers.

8 Equality

The myth of Procrustes, who forced all people to fit the same bed, cutting off legs or stretching torsos as required, reveals an innate human disdain for the idea that perfect uniformity is desirable. There is nothing wrong with difference, taken on its own. Yet certain differences—those that arise from, or result in, injustice—are objectionable.

While economists often focus on economic inequality, it is worth noting that economic inequality does not seem objectionable in its own right. It is easy to imagine unequal holdings emerging as a result of voluntary exchanges among equals or as the result of social institutions designed for the benefit of all (say by allowing differential income as a reward for those who are socially productive). The morally important—and worrying—aspects of economic inequality show up only when we turn our attention to its sources and its effects, both of which may well be unjust. Economic inequality that results from slavery, exploitation, or force is obviously unjust. More controversially, many hold that economic inequalities due to large inequalities in opportunity are likewise unjust. Turning from the causes of inequality to its effects, many hold that unequal income is unjust, say, if it undermines equality of opportunity, or affects political power, or introduces a permanent underclass (to take just a few examples of the possible effects of economic inequality to which people have objected).

Harry Frankfurt concedes that economic equality seems superficially to be a desirable goal, but argues that it distracts us from what actually matters, which is having *enough*. According to Frankfurt, "To say that a person has enough money means that he is content, or that it is reasonable for him to be content, with having no more money than he has." Emphasizing economic equality is actually harmful, Frankfurt argues, in part because it leads people to place too much importance on comparing themselves with others, and in part because it keep them from focusing, as he thinks they should, on becoming the best person they can be. This is not to say that a person who has enough wouldn't be better off with even more money. But Frankfurt holds that neither maximizing the amount of money each has nor equalizing the income of all, are morally desirable goals.

Finally, Frankfurt criticizes the common belief that so-called "diminishing marginal utility of income" justifies moves toward economic equality. The justification goes something like this: If we take the last dollar earned by Bill Gates, and give it to a hobo, the loss to Gates is minimal, but the gain to the hobo is substantial. Therefore, total utility or social value is increased by redistributing from the very wealthy to the very poor. Frankfurt suggests that this approach, which seeks to reconcile the utilitarian concern with maximizing overall welfare and the egalitarian concern with equality, may be misguided. As utilitarians since Hume have observed, extensive redistribution can (1) have disincentive effects,

(2) increase corruption by giving policymakers power over income, and (3) may be based on profoundly false assumptions about how people convert resources into utility. David Schmidtz develops this argument further in *The Elements of Justice*.

Richard Arneson argues that we should harness social and political institutions to try to equalize *opportunities* for welfare. Arneson defines welfare as the satisfaction of suitably idealized preferences, by which he means preferences that are informed, and can survive reflective scrutiny (preferences differ from desires in that they rank different possible ends, rather than being directed at a single end). But rather than endorsing a view that maximizes the satisfaction of informed preferences, Arneson thinks we should allow inequalities in welfare when they arise from choices for which individuals can be held morally responsible. This does not include congenital handicaps, but it does include cases in which people are consigned to lower levels of welfare as a result of risky choices (assuming they were made with a full understanding of the consequences). In summarizing his view, Arneson says "[t]he argument for equal opportunity rather than straight equality is simply that it is morally fitting to hold individuals responsible for the foreseeable consequences of their voluntary choices, and in particular for that portion of these consequences that involves their own achievement of welfare or gain or loss of resources."

Given his entitlement theory of justice, Robert Nozick is skeptical of any redistribution (whether in the name of equality or not) except as required to redress past injustice. Indeed, Nozick questions the typical focus on outcomes (as measured by wealth, welfare, or opportunities for welfare), emphasizing that, from the point of view of justice, "life is not a race." Moreover, any attempt to redistribute resources in the service of egalitarian goals involves at least some coercive confiscation of resources from people who are entitled to those resources.

In his short story, "Harrison Bergeron," Kurt Vonnegut describes a dystopia in which the government has managed to equalize everything except native talents, and the advantages that flow from them. The Handicapper General is a government official whose job it is to lobotomize or distract smart people and cripple or encumber those with superior athletic talents. While sophisticated egalitarian theories can avoid the grim requirement of a Handicapper General, the story suggests that equality may require *decreasing the absolute capacities* of some to *increase the relative capacities* of others. To the extent that this is simply a new appearance of the Procrustean myth, focusing on capacities rather than stature, it becomes clear that using political institutions to promote such encompassing and intrusive forms of equality serve the vice of envy rather than the virtue of charity.

Amartya Sen surveys several dominant views about equality and finds many of them wanting. He criticizes utilitarianism (which treats people as equals in the sense of equally considering each person's welfare) because it does not take adequate account of undeserved sources of inequality, such as inherited disabilities. Because utilitarianism says that we ought to create a system in which resources are shifted to their highest valued use, it may very well justify distributive moves that remove resources from the disadvantaged and allocate them to the advantaged who can put them to greater use, which he takes to be manifestly unjust.

Rawlsians, in contrast with utilitarians, demand what Rawls calls fair equality of opportunity, which allows inequality only when it is to the advantage of those who are worst off (this is the so-called "difference principle"). Sen rejects Rawls's difference principle primarily on the grounds that he thinks welfare comes not from an absolute bundle of goods, but from the *relationships* between people and goods. For example, Sen emphasizes that a pregnant woman and a man with the same set of goods would have different amounts of freedom to pursue their ends. Finally, Sen agrees with Nozick that there is sometimes a conflict between individual liberty and social welfare, but he thinks Nozick puts too much weight on liberty.

Sen's ultimate goal is to defend equality as a moral and political goal, but also to demonstrate that it is only one of several desirable qualities of a just society. Sen argues that there are trade-offs between satisfying different conceptions of equality, as well as other competing moral goals.

FURTHER READING

Anderson, Elizabeth. 2012. "Equality." In *The Oxford Handbook of Political Philosophy*, edited by David Estlund. Oxford University Press.

Cohen, Gerald. 2011. *On the Currency of Egalitarian Justice, and Other Essays in Political Philosophy*, edited by Michael Otsuka. Princeton University Press.

Dworkin, Ronald. 1981. "What is Equality?" *Philosophy and Public Affairs* 10 (3): 185–246.

Gintis, Herbert and Samuel Bowles. 2002. "The Inheritance of Inequality." *Journal of Economic Perspectives*, 16(3): 3–30.

Hayek, Friedrich. 1978. "Equality, Value, and Merit." *The Constitution of Liberty*, chapter 6. University of Chicago Press.

Huemer, Michael. 2012. "Against Equality and Priority." *Utilitas* 24(4): 483–501.

Parfit, Derek. 1997. "Equality and Priority." *Ratio* 10 (3): 202–221.

Schmidtz, David. 2002. "Equal Respect and Equal Shares." *Social Philosophy and Policy* 19: 244–274.

Wolff, Jonathan. 2011. "Equality." *Oxford Handbook of the History of Political Philosophy*, edited by George Klosko. Oxford University Press.

HARRY FRANKFURT

Equality as a Moral Ideal

1987

I

Economic egalitarianism is, as I shall construe it, the doctrine that it is desirable for everyone to have the same amounts of income and of wealth (for short, "money").[1] Hardly anyone would deny that there are situations in which it makes sense to tolerate deviations from this standard. It goes without saying, after all, that preventing or correcting such deviations may involve costs which—whether measured in economic terms or in terms of noneconomic

Harry Frankfurt, "Equality as a Moral Ideal." *Ethics* 98 (1) (1987): 21–43. By permission of University of Chicago Press.

considerations—are by any reasonable measure unacceptable. Nonetheless, many people believe that economic equality has considerable moral value in itself. For this reason they often urge that efforts to approach the egalitarian ideal should be accorded—with all due consideration for the possible effects of such efforts in obstructing or in conducing to the achievement of other goods—a significant priority.[2]

In my opinion, this is a mistake. Economic equality is not, as such, of particular moral importance. With respect to the distribution of economic assets, what *is* important from the point of view of morality is not that everyone should have *the same* but that each should have *enough*. If everyone had enough, it would be of no moral consequence whether some had more than others. I shall refer to this alternative to egalitarianism—namely, that what is morally important with respect to money is for everyone to have enough—as "the doctrine of sufficiency."[3]

The fact that economic equality is not in its own right a morally compelling social ideal is in no way, of course, a reason for regarding it as undesirable. My claim that equality in itself lacks moral importance does not entail that equality is to be avoided. Indeed, there may well be good reasons for governments or for individuals to deal with problems of economic distribution in accordance with an egalitarian standard and to be concerned more with attempting to increase the extent to which people are economically equal than with efforts to regulate directly the extent to which the amounts of money people have are enough. Even if equality is not as such morally important, a commitment to an egalitarian social policy may be indispensable to promoting the enjoyment of significant goods besides equality or to avoiding their impairment. Moreover, it might turn out that the most feasible approach to the achievement of sufficiency would be the pursuit of equality.

But despite the fact that an egalitarian distribution would not necessarily be objectionable, the error of believing that there are powerful moral reasons for caring about equality is far from innocuous. In fact, this belief tends to do significant harm. It is often argued as an objection to egalitarianism that there is a dangerous conflict between equality and liberty: if people are left to themselves, inequalities of income and wealth inevitably arise, and therefore an egalitarian distribution of money can be achieved and maintained only at the cost of repression. Whatever may be the merit of this argument concerning the relationship between equality and liberty, economic egalitarianism engenders another conflict which is of even more fundamental moral significance.

To the extent that people are preoccupied with equality for its own sake, their readiness to be satisfied with any particular level of income or wealth is guided not by their own interests and needs but just by the magnitude of the economic benefits that are at the disposal of others. In this way egalitarianism distracts people from measuring the requirements to which their individual natures and their personal circumstances give rise. It encourages them instead to insist upon a level of economic support that is determined by a calculation in which the particular features of their own lives are irrelevant. How sizable the economic assets of others are has nothing much to do, after all, with what kind of person someone is. A concern for economic equality, construed as desirable in itself, tends to divert a person's attention away from endeavoring to discover—within his experience of himself and of his life—what he himself really cares about and what will actually satisfy him, although this is the most basic and the most decisive task upon which an intelligent selection of economic goals depends. Exaggerating the moral importance of economic equality is harmful, in other words, because it is alienating.[4]

To be sure, the circumstances of others may reveal interesting possibilities and provide data for useful judgments concerning what is normal or typical. Someone who is attempting to reach a confident and realistic appreciation of what to seek for himself may well find this helpful. It is not only in suggestive and preliminary ways like these, moreover, that the situations of other people may be pertinent to someone's efforts to decide what economic demands it is reasonable or important for him to make. The amount of money he needs may depend in a more direct way on the amounts others have. Money may bring power or prestige or other competitive advantages. A determination of how much money would be enough cannot intelligently be made by someone who is concerned with such things except on the basis of an estimate of the resources available to those with whose competition it may be necessary for him to contend. What is important from this point of view, however, is not the comparison of levels of affluence as such. The measurement of inequality is important only as it pertains contingently to other interests.

The mistaken belief that economic equality is important in itself leads people to detach the problem of formulating their economic ambitions from the problem of understanding what is most fundamentally significant to them. It influences them to take too seriously, as though it were a matter of great moral concern, a question that is inherently rather insignificant and not directly to the point, namely, how their economic status compares with the economic status of others. In this way the doctrine of equality contributes to the moral disorientation and shallowness of our time.

The prevalence of egalitarian thought is harmful in another respect as well. It not only tends to divert attention from considerations of greater moral importance than equality. It also diverts attention from the difficult but quite fundamental philosophical problems of understanding just what these considerations are and of elaborating, in appropriately comprehensive and perspicuous detail, a conceptual apparatus which would facilitate their exploration. Calculating the size of an equal share is plainly much easier than determining how much a person needs in order to have enough. In addition, the very concept of having an equal share is itself considerably more patent and accessible than the concept of having enough. It is far from self-evident, needless to say, precisely what the doctrine of sufficiency means and what applying it entails. But this is hardly a good reason for neglecting the doctrine or for adopting an incorrect doctrine in preference to it. Among my primary purposes in this essay is to suggest the importance of systematic inquiry into the analytical and theoretical issues raised by the concept of having enough, the importance of which egalitarianism has masked.

II

There are a number of ways of attempting to establish the thesis that economic equality is important. Sometimes it is urged that the prevalence of fraternal relationships among the members of a society is a desirable goal and that equality is indispensable to it. Or it may be maintained that inequalities in the distribution of economic benefits are to be avoided because they lead invariably to undesirable discrepancies of other kinds—for example, in social status, in political influence, or in the abilities of people to make effective use of their various opportunities and entitlements. In both of these arguments, economic equality is endorsed because of its supposed importance in creating or preserving certain noneconomic conditions. Such considerations may well provide convincing reasons for recommending equality as a desirable social good or even for preferring egalitarianism as a policy over the alternatives to it. But both arguments construe equality as valuable derivatively, in virtue of its contingent connections to other things. In neither argument is there an attribution to equality of any unequivocally inherent moral value.

A rather different kind of argument for economic equality, which comes closer to construing the value of equality as independent of contingencies, is based upon the principle of diminishing marginal utility. According to this argument, equality is desirable because an egalitarian distribution of economic assets maximizes their aggregate utility. The argument presupposes: (*a*) for each individual the utility of money invariably diminishes at the margin and (*b*) with respect to money, or with respect to the things money can buy, the utility functions of all individuals are the same. In other words, the utility provided by or derivable from an nth dollar is the same for everyone, and it is less than the utility for anyone of dollar $(n - 1)$. Unless *b* were true, a rich man might obtain greater utility than a poor man from an extra dollar. In that case an egalitarian distribution of economic goods would not maximize aggregate utility even if *a* were true. But given both *a* and *b*, it follows that a marginal dollar always brings less utility to a rich person than to one who is less rich. And this entails that total utility must increase when inequality is reduced by giving a dollar to someone poorer than the person from whom it is taken.

In fact, however, both *a* and *b* are false. Suppose it is conceded, for the sake of the argument, that the maximization of aggregate utility is in its own right a morally important social goal. Even so, it cannot legitimately be inferred that an egalitarian distribution of money must therefore have similar moral importance. For in virtue of the falsity of *a* and *b,* the argument linking economic equality to the maximization of aggregate utility is unsound.

So far as concerns *b,* it is evident that the utility functions for money of different individuals are not even approximately alike. Some people suffer from physical, mental, or emotional weaknesses or incapacities that limit the satisfactions they are able to obtain. Moreover, even apart from the effects of specific disabilities, some people simply enjoy things more than other people do. Everyone knows that there are, at any given level of expenditure, large differences in the quantities of utility that different spenders derive.

So far as concerns *a,* there are good reasons against expecting any consistent diminution in the marginal utility of money. The fact that the marginal utilities of certain goods do indeed tend to diminish is not a principle of reason. It is a psychological generalization, which is accounted for by such considerations as that people often tend after a time to become satiated with what they have been consuming and that the senses characteristically lose their freshness after repetitive stimulation. It is common knowledge that experiences of many kinds become increasingly routine and unrewarding as they are repeated.

It is questionable, however, whether this provides any reason at all for expecting a diminution in the marginal utility of *money*—that is, of anything that functions as a generic instrument of exchange. Even if the utility of everything money can buy were inevitably to diminish at the margin, the utility of money itself might nonetheless exhibit a different pattern. It is quite possible that money would be exempt from the phenomenon of unrelenting marginal decline because of its limitlessly protean versatility. As Blum and Kalven explain: "In . . . analysing the question whether money has a declining utility it is . . . important to put to one side all analogies to the observation that particular commodities have a declining utility to their users. There is no need here to enter into the debate whether it is useful or necessary, in economic theory, to assume that commodities have a declining utility. Money is infinitely versatile. And even if all the things money can buy are subject to a law of diminishing utility, it does not follow that money itself is."[5] From the supposition that a person tends to lose more and more interest in what he is consuming as his consumption of it increases, it plainly cannot be inferred that he must also tend to lose interest in consumption itself or in the money that makes consumption possible. For there may always remain for him, no matter how tired he has become of what he has been doing, untried goods to be bought and fresh new pleasures to be enjoyed.

There are in any event many things of which people do not, from the very outset, immediately begin to tire. From certain goods, they actually derive more utility after sustained consumption than they derive at first. This is the situation whenever appreciating or enjoying or otherwise benefiting from something depends upon repeated trials, which serve as a kind of "warming up" process: for instance, when relatively little significant gratification is obtained from the item or experience in question until the individual has acquired a special taste for it, has become addicted to it, or has begun in some other way to relate or respond to it profitably.

The capacity for obtaining gratification is then smaller at earlier points in the sequence of consumption than at later points. In such cases marginal utility does not decline; it increases. Perhaps it is true of everything, without exception, that a person will ultimately lose interest in it. But even if in every utility curve there is a point at which the curve begins a steady and irreversible decline, it cannot be assumed that every segment of the curve has a downward slope.[6]

III

When marginal utility diminishes, it does not do so on account of any deficiency in the marginal unit. It diminishes in virtue of the position of that unit as the latest in a sequence. The same is true when marginal utility increases: the marginal unit provides greater utility than its predecessors in virtue of the effect which the acquisition or consumption of those predecessors has brought about. Now when the sequence consists of units of money, what corresponds to the process of warming up—at least, in one pertinent and important feature—is *saving.* Accumulating money entails, as warming up does, generating a capacity to derive, at some subsequent point in a sequence, gratifications that cannot be derived earlier.

The fact that it may at times be especially worthwhile for a person to save money rather than to spend each dollar as it comes along is due in part to the incidence of what may be thought of as "utility thresholds." Consider an item with the following characteristics: it is nonfungible, it is the source of a fresh and otherwise unobtainable type of satisfaction, and it is too expensive to be acquired except by saving up for it. The utility of the dollar that finally completes a program of saving up for such an item may be greater than the utility of any dollar saved earlier in the program. That will be the case when the utility provided by the item is greater than the sum of the utilities that could be derived if the money saved were either spent as it came in or divided into parts and used to purchase other things. In a situation of this kind, the final dollar saved permits the crossing of a utility threshold.[7]

It is sometimes argued that, for anyone who is rational in the sense that he seeks to maximize the utility generated by his expenditures, the marginal utility of money must necessarily diminish. Abba Lerner presents this argument as follows:

> The principle of diminishing marginal utility of income can be derived from the assumption that consumers spend their income in the way that maximizes the satisfaction they can derive from the good obtained. With a given income, all the things bought give a greater satisfaction for the money spent on them than any of the other things that could have been bought in their place but were not bought for this very reason. From this it follows that if income were greater the additional things that would be bought with the increment of income would be things that are rejected when income is smaller because they give less satisfaction; and if income were greater still, even less satisfactory things would be bought. The greater the income the less satisfactory are the additional things that can be bought with equal increases of income. That is all that is meant by the principle of the diminishing marginal utility of income.[8]

Lerner invokes here a comparison between the utility of $G(n)$—the goods which the rational consumer actually buys with his income of n dollars—and "the other things that could have been bought in their place but were not." Given that he prefers to buy $G(n)$ rather than the other things, which by hypothesis cost no more, the rational consumer must regard $G(n)$ as offering greater satisfaction than the others can provide. From this Lerner infers that with an additional n dollars the consumer would be able to purchase only things with less utility than $G(n)$; and he concludes that, in general, "the greater the income the less satisfactory are the additional things that can be bought with equal increases of income." This conclusion, he maintains, is tantamount to the principle of the diminishing marginal utility of income.

It seems apparent that Lerner's attempt to derive the principle in this way fails. One reason is that the amount of satisfaction a person can derive from a certain good may vary considerably according to whether or not he also possesses certain other goods. The satisfaction obtainable from a certain expenditure may therefore be greater if some other expenditure has already been made. Suppose that the cost of a serving of popcorn is the same as the cost of enough butter to make it delectable, and suppose that some rational consumer who adores buttered popcorn gets very little satisfaction from unbuttered popcorn but that he nonetheless prefers it to butter alone. He will buy the popcorn in preference to the butter, accordingly, if he must buy one and cannot buy both. Suppose now that this person's income increases so that he can buy the butter too. Then he can have something he enjoys enormously: his incremental income makes it possible for him not merely to buy butter in addition to popcorn but also to enjoy buttered popcorn. The satisfaction he will derive by combining the popcorn and the butter may well be considerably greater than the sum of the satisfactions he can derive from the two goods taken separately. Here, again, is a threshold effect.

In a case of this sort, what the rational consumer buys with his incremental income is a good—$G(i)$—which, when his income was smaller, he had rejected in favor of $G(n)$ because having it alone would have been less satisfying than having only $G(n)$. Despite this, however, it is not true that the utility of the income he uses to buy $G(i)$ is less than the utility of the income he used to buy $G(n)$. When there is an opportunity to create a combination which is (like buttered popcorn) synergistic in the sense that adding one good to another increases the utility of each, the marginal utility of income may not decline even though the sequence of marginal items—taking each of these items by itself—does exhibit a pattern of declining utilities.

Lerner's argument is flawed in virtue of another consideration as well. Since he speaks of "the *additional* things that can be bought with equal increases of income," he evidently presumes that a rational consumer uses his first n dollars to purchase a certain good and that he uses any incremental income beyond that to buy something else. This leads Lerner to suppose that what the consumer buys when his income is increased by i dollars (where i is equal to or less than n) must be something which he could have bought and which he chose not to buy when his income was only n dollars. But this supposition is unwarranted. With an income of $(n + i)$ dollars, the consumer need not use his money to purchase both $G(n)$ and $G(i)$. He might use it to buy something which cost more than either of these goods—something which was too expensive to be available to him at all before his income increased. The point is that if a rational consumer with an income of n dollars defers purchasing a certain good until his income increases, this does not necessarily mean that he "rejected" purchasing it when his income was smaller. The good in question may have been out of his reach at that time because it cost more than n dollars. His reason for postponing the purchase may have had nothing to do with comparative expectations of satisfaction or with preferences or priorities at all.

There are two possibilities to consider. Suppose on the one hand that, instead of purchasing $G(n)$ when his income is n dollars, the rational consumer saves that money until he can add an additional i dollars to it and then purchases $G(n + i)$. In this case it is quite evident that his deferral of the purchase of $G(n + i)$ does not mean that he values it less than $G(n)$. On the other hand, suppose that the rational consumer declines to save up for $G(n + i)$ and that he spends all the money he has on $G(n)$. In this case too it would be a mistake to construe his behavior as indicating a preference for $G(n)$ over $G(n + i)$. For the explanation of his refusal to save for $G(n + i)$ may be merely that he regards doing so as pointless because he believes that he cannot reasonably expect to save enough to make a timely purchase of it.

The utility of $G(n + i)$ may not only be greater than the utility either of $G(n)$ or of $G(i)$. It may also be greater than the sum of their utilities. That is, in acquiring $G(n + i)$ the consumer may cross a utility threshold. The utility of the increment i to his income is then actually greater than the utility of the n dollars to which it is added, even though i equals or is less than n. In such a case, the income of the rational consumer does not exhibit diminishing marginal utility.

IV

The preceding discussion has established that an egalitarian distribution may fail to maximize aggregate utility. It can also easily be shown that, in virtue of the incidence of utility thresholds, there are conditions under which an egalitarian distribution actually minimizes aggregate utility. Thus, suppose that there is enough of a certain resource (e.g., food or medicine) to enable some but not all members of a population to survive. Let us say that the size of the population is ten, that a person needs at least five units of the resource in question to live, and that forty units are available. If any members of this population are to survive, some must have more than others. An equal distribution, which gives each person four units, leads to the worst possible outcome, namely, everyone dies. Surely in this case it would be morally grotesque to insist upon equality! Nor would it be reasonable to maintain that, under the conditions specified, it is justifiable for some to be better off only when this is in the interests of the worst off. If the available resources are used to save eight people, the justification for doing this is manifestly not that it somehow benefits the two members of the population who are left to die.

An egalitarian distribution will almost certainly produce a net loss of aggregate utility whenever it entails that fewer individuals than otherwise will have, with respect to some necessity, enough to sustain life—in other words, whenever it requires a larger number of individuals to be below the threshold of survival. Of course, a loss of utility may also occur even when the circumstances involve a threshold that does not separate life and death. Allocating resources equally will reduce aggregate utility whenever it requires a number of individuals to be kept below *any* utility threshold without ensuring a compensating move above some threshold by a suitable number of others.

Under conditions of scarcity, then, an egalitarian distribution may be morally unacceptable. Another response to scarcity is to distribute the available resources in such a way that as many people as possible have enough or, in other words, to maximize the incidence of sufficiency. This alternative is especially compelling when the amount of a scarce resource that constitutes enough coincides with the amount that is indispensable for avoiding some catastrophic harm—as in the example just considered, where falling below the threshold of enough food or enough medicine means death. But now suppose that there are available, in this example, not just forty units of the vital resource but forty-one. Then maximizing the incidence of sufficiency by providing enough for each of eight people leaves one unit unallocated. What should be done with this extra unit?

It has been shown above that it is a mistake to maintain that *where some people have less than enough, no one should have more than anyone else.* When resources are scarce, so that it is impossible for everyone to have enough, an egalitarian distribution may lead to disaster. Now there is another claim that might be made here, which may appear to be quite plausible but which is also mistaken: *where some people have less than enough, no one should have more than enough.* If this claim were correct, then—in the example at hand—the extra unit should go to one of the two people who have nothing. But one additional unit of the resource in question will not improve the condition of a person who has none. By hypothesis, that person will die even with the additional unit. What he needs is not one unit but five.[9] It cannot be taken for granted that a person who has a certain amount of a vital resource is necessarily better off than a person who has a lesser amount, for the larger amount may still be too small to serve any useful purpose. Having the larger amount may even make a person worse off. Thus it is conceivable that while a dose of five units of some medication is therapeutic, a dose of one unit is not better than none but actually toxic. And while a person with one unit of food may live a bit longer than someone with no food whatever, perhaps it is worse to prolong the process of starvation for a short time than to terminate quickly the agony of starving to death.

The claim that no one should have more than enough while anyone has less than enough derives its plausibility, in part, from a presumption that is itself plausible but that is nonetheless false: to wit, giving resources to people who have less of them than enough necessarily means giving resources to people who need them and, therefore, making those people better off. It is indeed reasonable to assign a higher priority to improving the condition of those who are in need than to improving the condition of those who are not in need. But giving additional resources to people who have less than enough of those resources, and who are accordingly in need, may not actually improve the condition of these people at all. Those below a utility threshold are not necessarily benefited by additional resources that move them closer to the threshold. What is crucial for them is to attain the threshold. Merely moving closer to it either may fail to help them or may be disadvantageous.

By no means do I wish to suggest, of course, that it is never or only rarely beneficial for those below a utility threshold to move closer to it. Certainly it may be beneficial, either because it increases the likelihood that the threshold ultimately will be attained or because, quite apart from the significance of the threshold, additional resources provide important increments of utility. After all, a collector may enjoy expanding his collection even if he knows that he has no chance of ever completing it. My point is only that additional resources do not necessarily benefit those who have less than enough. The additions may be too little to make any difference. It may be morally quite acceptable, accordingly, for some to have more than enough of a certain resource even while others have less than enough of it.

V

Quite often, advocacy of egalitarianism is based less upon an argument than upon a purported moral intuition: economic inequality, considered as such, just seems wrong. It strikes many people as unmistakably apparent that, taken simply in itself, the enjoyment by some of greater economic benefits than are enjoyed by others is morally offensive. I suspect, however, that in many cases those who profess to have this intuition concerning manifestations of inequality are actually responding not to the inequality but to another feature of the situations they are confronting. What I believe they find intuitively to be morally objectionable, in the types of situations characteristically cited as instances of economic inequality, is not the fact that some of the individuals in those situations have *less* money than others but the fact that those with less have *too little.*

When we consider people who are substantially worse off than ourselves, we do very commonly find that we are morally disturbed by their circumstances. What directly touches us in cases of this kind, however, is not a quantitative discrepancy but a qualitative condition—not the fact that the economic resources of those who are worse off are *smaller in magnitude* than ours but the different fact that these people are so *poor.* Mere differences in the amounts of money people have are not in themselves distressing. We tend to be quite unmoved, after all, by inequalities between the well-to-do and the rich; our awareness that the former are substantially worse off than the latter does not disturb us morally at all. And if we believe of some person that his life is richly fulfilling, that he himself is genuinely content with his economic situation, and that he suffers no resentments or sorrows which more money could assuage, we are not ordinarily much interested—from a moral point of view—in the question of how the amount of money he has compares with the amounts possessed by others. Economic discrepancies in cases of these sorts do not impress us in the least as matters of significant moral concern. The fact that some people have much less than others is morally undisturbing when it is clear that they have plenty.

It seems clear that egalitarianism and the doctrine of sufficiency are logically independent: considerations that support the one cannot be presumed to provide support also for the other. Yet proponents of egalitarianism frequently suppose that they have offered grounds for their position when in fact what they have offered is pertinent as support only for the doctrine of sufficiency. Thus they often, in attempting to gain acceptance for egalitarianism, call attention to disparities between the conditions of life characteristic of the rich and those characteristic of the poor. Now it is undeniable that contemplating such disparities does often elicit a conviction that it would be morally desirable to redistribute the available resources so as to improve the circumstances of the poor. And, of course, that would bring about a greater degree of economic equality. But the indisputability of the moral appeal of improving the condition of the poor by allocating to them resources taken from those who are well off does not even tend to show that egalitarianism is, as a moral ideal, similarly indisputable. To show of poverty that it is compellingly undesirable does nothing whatsoever to show the same of inequality. For what makes someone poor in the morally relevant sense—in which poverty is understood as a condition from which we naturally recoil—is not that his economic assets are simply of lesser magnitude than those of others.

A typical example of this confusion is provided by Ronald Dworkin. Dworkin characterizes the ideal of economic equality as requiring that "no citizen has less than an equal share of the community's resources just in order that others may have more of what he lacks."[10] But in support of his claim that the United States now falls short of this ideal, he refers to circumstances that are not primarily evidence of inequality but of poverty: "It is, I think, apparent that the United States falls far short now [of the ideal of equality]. A substantial minority of Americans are chronically unemployed or earn wages below any realistic 'poverty line' or are handicapped in various ways or burdened with special needs; and most of these people would do the work necessary to earn a decent living if they had the opportunity and capacity" (p. 208). What mainly concerns Dworkin—what he actually considers to be morally important—is manifestly not that our society permits a situation in which a substantial minority of Americans have *smaller shares* than others of the resources which he apparently presumes should be available for all. His concern is, rather, that the members of this minority *do not earn decent livings.*

The force of Dworkin's complaint does not derive from the allegation that our society fails to provide some individuals with as much as others but from a quite different allegation, namely, our society fails to provide each individual with "the opportunity to develop and lead a life he can regard as valuable both to himself and to [the community]" (p. 211). Dworkin is dismayed most fundamentally not by evidence that the United States permits economic inequality but by evidence that it fails to ensure that everyone has enough to lead "a life of choice and value" (p. 212)—in other words, that it fails to fulfill for all the ideal of sufficiency. What bothers him most immediately is not that certain quantitative relationships are widespread but that certain qualitative conditions prevail. He cares principally about the value of people's lives, but he mistakenly represents himself as caring principally about the relative magnitudes of their economic assets.

My suggestion that situations involving inequality are morally disturbing only to the extent that they violate the ideal of sufficiency is confirmed, it seems to me, by familiar discrepancies between the principles egalitarians profess and the way in which they commonly conduct their own lives. My point here is not that some egalitarians hypocritically accept high incomes and special opportunities for which, according to the moral theories they profess, there is no justification. It is that many egalitarians (including many academic proponents of the doctrine) are not truly concerned whether they are as well off economically as other people are. They believe that they themselves have roughly enough money for what is important to them, and they are therefore not terribly preoccupied with the fact that some people are considerably richer than they. Indeed, many egalitarians would consider it rather shabby or even reprehensible to care, with respect to their own lives, about economic comparisons of that sort. And, notwithstanding the implications of the doctrines to which they urge adherence, they would be appalled if their children grew up with such preoccupations.

VI

The fundamental error of egalitarianism lies in supposing that it is morally important whether one person has less than another regardless of how much either of them has. This error is due in part to the false assumption that someone who is economically worse off has more important unsatisfied needs than someone who is better off. In fact the morally significant needs of both individuals may be fully satisfied or equally unsatisfied. Whether one person has more money than another is a wholly extrinsic matter. It has to do with a relationship between the respective economic assets of the two people, which is not only independent of the amounts of their assets and of the amounts of satisfaction they can derive from them but also independent of the attitudes of these people toward those levels of assets and of satisfaction. The economic comparison implies nothing concerning whether either of the people compared has any morally important unsatisfied needs at all nor concerning whether either is content with what he has.

This defect in egalitarianism appears plainly in Thomas Nagel's development of the doctrine. According to Nagel: "The essential feature of an egalitarian priority system is that it counts improvements to the welfare of the worse off as more urgent than improvements to the welfare of the better off. . . . What makes a system egalitarian is the priority it gives to the claims of those . . . at the bottom. . . . Each individual with a more urgent claim has priority . . . over each individual with a less urgent claim."[11] And in discussing Rawls's Difference Principle, which he endorses, Nagel says: the Difference Principle "establishes an order of priority among needs and gives preference to the most urgent."[12] But the preference actually assigned by the Difference Principle is not in favor of those whose needs are most urgent; it is in favor of those who are identified as worst off. It is a mere assumption, which Nagel makes without providing any grounds for it whatever, that the worst off individuals have urgent needs. In most societies the people who are economically at the bottom are indeed extremely poor, and they do, as a matter of fact, have urgent needs. But this relationship between low economic status and urgent need is wholly contingent. It can be established only on the basis of empirical data. There is no necessary conceptual connection between a person's relative economic position and whether he has needs of any degree of urgency.[13]

It is possible for those who are worse off not to have more urgent needs or claims than those who are better off because it is possible for them to have no urgent needs or claims at all. The notion of "urgency" has to do with what is *important*. Trivial needs or interests, which have no significant bearing upon the quality of a person's life or upon his readiness to be content with it, cannot properly be construed as being urgent to any degree whatever or as supporting the sort of morally demanding claims to which genuine urgency gives rise. From the fact that a person is at the bottom of some economic order, moreover, it cannot even be inferred that he has *any* unsatisfied needs or claims. After all, it is possible for conditions at the bottom to be quite good; the fact that they are the worst does not in itself entail that they are bad or that they are in any way incompatible with richly fulfilling and enjoyable lives.

Nagel maintains that what underlies the appeal of equality is an "ideal of acceptability to each individual."[14] On his account, this ideal entails that a reasonable person should consider deviations from equality to be acceptable only if they are in his interest in the sense that he would be worse off without them. But a reasonable person might well regard an unequal distribution as entirely acceptable even though he did not presume that any other distribution would benefit him less. For he might believe that the unequal distribution provided him with quite enough, and he might reasonably be unequivocally content with that, with no concern for the possibility that some other arrangement would provide him with more. It is gratuitous to assume that every reasonable person must be seeking to maximize the benefits he can obtain, in a sense requiring that he be endlessly interested in or open to improving his life. A certain deviation from equality might not be *in* someone's interest because it might be that he would in fact be better off without it. But as long as it does not *conflict* with his interest, by obstructing his opportunity to lead the sort of life that it is important for him to lead, the deviation from equality may be quite acceptable. To be wholly satisfied with a certain state of affairs, a reasonable person need not suppose that there is no other available state of affairs in which he would be better off.[15]

Nagel illustrates his thesis concerning the moral appeal of equality by considering a family with two children, one of whom is "normal and quite happy" while the other "suffers from a painful handicap."[16] If this family were to move to the city the handicapped child would benefit from medical and educational opportunities that are unavailable in the suburbs, but the healthy child would have less fun. If the family were to move to the suburbs, on the other hand, the handicapped child would be deprived but the healthy child would enjoy himself more. Nagel stipulates that the gain to the healthy child in moving to the suburbs would be greater than the gain to the handicapped child in moving to the city: in the city the healthy child would find life positively disagreeable, while the handicapped child would not become happy "but only less miserable."

Given these conditions, the egalitarian decision is to move to the city; for "it is more urgent to benefit the [handicapped] child even though the benefit we can give him is less than the benefit we can give the [healthy] child." Nagel explains that this judgment concerning the greater urgency of benefiting the handicapped child "depends on the worse off position of the [handicapped] child. An improvement in his situation is more important than an equal or somewhat greater improvement in the situation of the [normal] child." But it seems to me that Nagel's analysis of this matter is flawed by an error similar to the one that I attributed above to Dworkin. The fact that it is preferable to help the handicapped child is not due, as Nagel asserts, to the fact that this child is worse off than the other. It is due to the fact that this child, and not the other, suffers from a painful handicap. The handicapped child's claim is important because his condition is *bad*—significantly undesirable—and not merely because he is *less well off* than his sibling.

This does not imply, of course, that Nagel's evaluation of what the family should do is wrong. Rejecting egalitarianism certainly does not mean maintaining that it is always mandatory simply to maximize benefits and that therefore the family should move to the suburbs because the normal child would gain more from that than the handicapped child would gain from a move to the city. However, the most cogent basis for Nagel's judgment in favor of the handicapped child has nothing to do with the alleged urgency of providing people with as much as others. It pertains rather to the urgency of the needs of people who do not have enough.[17]

VII

What does it mean, in the present context, for a person to have enough? One thing it might mean is that any more would be too much: a larger amount would make the person's life unpleasant, or it would be harmful or in some other way unwelcome. This is often what people have in mind when they say such things as "I've had enough!" or "Enough of that!" The idea conveyed by statements like these is that *a limit has been reached,* beyond which it is not desirable to proceed. On the other hand, the assertion that a person has enough may entail only that *a certain requirement or standard has been met,* with no implication that a larger quantity would be bad. This is often what a person intends when he says something like "That should be enough." Statements such as this one characterize the indicated amount as sufficient while leaving open the possibility that a larger amount might also be acceptable.

In the doctrine of sufficiency the use of the notion of "enough" pertains to *meeting a standard* rather than to *reaching a limit.* To say that a person has enough money means that he is content, or that it is reasonable for him to be content, with having no more money than he has. And to say this is, in turn, to say something like the following: the person does not (or cannot reasonably) regard whatever (if anything) is unsatisfying or distressing about his life as due to his having too little money. In other words, if a person is (or ought reasonably to be) content with the amount of money he has, then insofar as he is or has reason to be unhappy with the way his life is going, he does not (or cannot reasonably) suppose that money would—either as a sufficient or as a necessary condition—enable him to become (or to have reason to be) significantly less unhappy with it.[18]

It is essential to understand that having enough money differs from merely having enough to get along or enough to make life marginally tolerable. People are not generally content with living on the brink. The point of the doctrine of sufficiency is not that the only morally important distributional consideration with respect to money is whether people have enough to avoid economic misery. A person who might naturally and appropriately be said to have just barely enough does not, by the standard invoked in the doctrine of sufficiency, have enough at all.

There are two distinct kinds of circumstances in which the amount of money a person has is enough—that is, in which more money will not enable him to become significantly less unhappy. On the one hand, it may be that the person is suffering no substantial distress or dissatisfaction with his life. On the other hand, it may be that although the person is unhappy about how his life is going, the difficulties that account for his unhappiness would not be alleviated by more money. Circumstances of this second kind obtain when what is wrong with the person's life has to do with noneconomic goods such as love, a sense that life is meaningful, satisfaction with one's own character, and so on. These are goods that money cannot buy; moreover, they are goods for which none of the things money can buy are even approximately adequate substitutes. Sometimes, to be sure, noneconomic goods are obtainable or enjoyable only (or more easily) by someone who has a certain amount of money. But the person who is distressed with his life while content with his economic situation may already have that much money.

It is possible that someone who is content with the amount of money he has might also be content with an even larger amount of money. Since having enough money does not mean being at a limit beyond which more money would necessarily be undesirable, it would be a mistake to assume that for a person who already has enough the marginal utility of money must be either negative or zero. Although this person is by hypothesis not distressed about his life in virtue of any lack of things which more money would enable him to obtain, nonetheless it remains possible that he would enjoy having some of those things. They would not make him less unhappy, nor would they in any way alter his attitude toward his life or the degree of his contentment with it, but they might bring him pleasure. If that is so, then his life would in this respect be better with more money than without it. The marginal utility for him of money would accordingly remain positive.

To say that a person is content with the amount of money he has does not entail, then, that there would be no point whatever in his having more. Thus someone with enough money might be quite *willing* to accept incremental economic benefits. He might in fact be *pleased* to receive them. Indeed, from the supposition that a person is content with the amount of money he has it cannot even be inferred that he would not *prefer* to have more. And it is even possible that he would actually be prepared to *sacrifice* certain things that he values (e.g., a certain amount of leisure) for the sake of more money.

But how can all this be compatible with saying that the person is content with what he has? What *does* contentment with a given amount of money preclude, if it does not preclude being willing or being pleased or preferring to have more money or even being ready to make sacrifices for more? It precludes his having an *active interest* in getting more. A contented person regards having more money as *inessential* to his being satisfied with his life. The fact that he is content is quite consistent with his recognizing that his economic circumstances could be improved and that his life might as a consequence become better than it is. But this possibility is not important to him. He is simply not much interested in being better off, so far as money goes, than he is. His attention and interest are not vividly engaged by the benefits which would be available to him if he had more money. He is just not very responsive to their appeal. They do not arouse in him any particularly eager or restless concern, although he acknowledges that he would enjoy additional benefits if they were provided to him.

In any event, let us suppose that the level of satisfaction that his present economic circumstances enable him to attain is high enough to meet his expectations of life. This is not fundamentally a matter of how much utility or satisfaction his various activities and experiences provide. Rather, it is most decisively a matter of his attitude toward being provided with that much. The satisfying experiences a person has are one thing. Whether he is satisfied that his life includes just those satisfactions is another. Although it is possible that other feasible circumstances would provide him with greater amounts of satisfaction, it may be that he is wholly satisfied with the amounts of satisfaction that he now enjoys. Even if he knows that he could obtain a greater quantity of satisfaction overall, he does not experience the uneasiness or the ambition that would incline him to seek it. Some people feel that their lives are good enough, and it is not important to them whether their lives are as good as possible.

The fact that a person lacks an active interest in getting something does not mean, of course, that he prefers not to have it. This is why the contented person may without any incoherence accept or welcome improvements in his situation and why he may even be prepared to incur minor costs in order to improve it. The fact that he is contented means only that the possibility of improving his situation is not *important* to him. It only implies, in other words, that he does not resent his circumstances, that he is not anxious or determined to improve them, and that he does not go out of his way or take any significant initiatives to make them better.

It may seem that there can be no reasonable basis for accepting less satisfaction when one could have more, that therefore rationality itself entails maximizing, and, hence, that a person who refuses to maximize the quantity of satisfaction in his life is not being rational. Such a person cannot, of course, offer it as his reason for declining to pursue greater satisfaction that the costs of this pursuit are too high; for if that were his reason then, clearly, he would be attempting to maximize satisfaction after all. But what other good reason could he possibly have for passing up an opportunity for more satisfaction? In fact, he may have a very good reason for this: namely, *that he is satisfied with the amount of satisfaction he already has.* Being satisfied with the way things are is unmistakably an excellent reason for having no great interest in changing them. A person who is indeed satisfied with his life as it is can hardly be criticized, accordingly, on the grounds that he has no good reason for declining to make it better.

He might still be open to criticism on the grounds that he *should not* be satisfied—that it is somehow unreasonable, or unseemly, or in some other mode wrong for him to be satisfied with less satisfaction than he could have. On what basis, however, could *this* criticism be justified? Is there some decisive reason for insisting that a person ought to be so hard to satisfy? Suppose that a man deeply and happily loves a woman who is altogether worthy. We do not ordinarily criticize the man in such a case just because we think he might have done even better. Moreover, our sense that it would be inappropriate to criticize him for that reason need not be due simply to a belief that holding out for a more desirable or worthier woman might end up costing him more than it would be worth. Rather, it may reflect our recognition that the desire to be happy or content or satisfied with life is a desire for a satisfactory amount of satisfaction and is not inherently tantamount to a desire that the quantity of satisfaction be maximized.

Being satisfied with a certain state of affairs is not equivalent to preferring it to all others. If a person is faced with a choice between less and more of something desirable, then no doubt it would be irrational for him to prefer less to more. But a person may be satisfied without having made any such comparisons at all. Nor is it necessarily irrational or unreasonable for a person to omit or to decline to make comparisons between his own state of affairs and possible alternatives. This is not only because making comparisons may be too costly. It is also because if someone is satisfied with the way things are, he may have no motive to consider how else they might be.[19]

Contentment may be a function of excessive dullness or diffidence. The fact that a person is free both of resentment and of ambition may be due to his having a slavish character or to his vitality being muffled by a kind of negligent lassitude. It is possible for someone to be content merely, as it were, by default. But a person who is content with resources providing less utility than he could have may not be irresponsible or indolent or deficient in imagination. On the contrary, his decision to be content with those resources—in other words, to adopt an attitude of willing acceptance toward the fact that he has just that much—may be based upon a conscientiously intelligent and penetrating evaluation of the circumstances of his life.

It is not essential for such an evaluation to include an *extrinsic* comparison of the person's circumstances with alternatives to which he might plausibly aspire, as it would have to do if contentment were reasonable only when based upon a judgment that the enjoyment of possible benefits has been maximized. If someone is less interested in whether his circumstances enable him to live as well as possible than in whether they enable him to live satisfyingly, he may appropriately devote his evaluation entirely to an *intrinsic* appraisal of his life. Then he may recognize that his circumstances do not lead him to be resentful or regretful or drawn to change and that, on the basis of his understanding of himself and of what is important to him, he accedes approvingly to his actual readiness to be content with the way things are. The situation in that case is not so much that he rejects the possibility of improving his circumstances because he thinks there is nothing genuinely to be gained by attempting to improve them. It is rather that this possibility, however feasible it may be, fails as a matter of fact to excite his active attention or to command from him any lively interest.[20]

APPENDIX

Economic egalitarianism is a drily formalistic doctrine. The amounts of money its adherents want for themselves and for others are calculated without regard to anyone's personal characteristics or circumstances. In this formality, egalitarians resemble people who desire to be as rich as possible but who have no idea what they would do with their riches. In neither case are the individual's ambitions, so far as money is concerned, limited or measured according to an understanding of the goals that he intends his money to serve or of the importance of these goals to him.

The desire for unlimited wealth is fetishistic, insofar as it reflects with respect to a *means* an attitude—namely, desiring something for its own sake—that is appropriate only with respect to an *end*. It seems to me that the attitude taken by John Rawls toward what he refers to as "primary goods" ("rights and liberties, opportunities and powers, income and wealth")[21] tends toward fetishism in this sense. The primary goods are "all purpose means," Rawls explains, which people need no matter what other things they want: "Plans differ, since individual abilities, circumstances, and wants differ . . . ; but whatever one's system of ends, primary goods are a necessary means" (Rawls, p. 93). Despite the fact that he identifies the primary goods not as ends but as means, Rawls considers it rational for a person to want as much of them as possible. Thus, he says: "Regardless of what an individual's rational plans are in detail, it is assumed that there are various things which he would prefer more of rather than less. While the persons in the original position do not know their conception of the good, they do know, I assume, that they prefer more rather than less primary goods" (Rawls, pp. 92–93). The assumption that it must always be better to have more of the primary goods rather than less implies that the marginal utility of an additional quantity of a primary good is invariably greater than its cost. It implies, in other words, that the incremental advantage to an individual of possessing a larger quantity of primary goods is never outweighed by corresponding incremental liabilities, incapacities, or burdens.

But this seems quite implausible. Apart from any other consideration, possessing more of a primary good may well require of a responsible individual that he spend more time and effort in managing it and in making decisions concerning its use. These activities are for many people intrinsically unappealing; and they also characteristically involve both a certain amount of anxiety and a degree of distraction from other pursuits. Surely it must not be taken simply for granted that incremental costs of these kinds can never be greater than whatever increased benefits a corresponding additional amount of some primary good would provide.

Individuals in the original position are behind a veil of ignorance. They do not know their own conceptions of the good or their own life plans. Thus it may seem rational for them to choose to possess primary goods in unlimited quantities: since they do not know what to prepare for, perhaps it would be best for them to be prepared for anything. Even in the original position, however, it is possible for people to appreciate that at some point the cost of additional primary goods might exceed the benefits those goods provide. It is true that an individual behind the veil of ignorance cannot know at just what point he would find that an addition to his supply of primary goods costs more than it is worth. But his ignorance of the exact location of that point hardly warrants his acting as though no such point exists at all. Yet that is precisely how he does act if he chooses that the quantity of primary goods he possesses be unlimited.

Rawls acknowledges that additional quantities of primary goods may be, for some individuals, more expensive than they are worth. In his view, however, this does not invalidate the supposition that it is rational for everyone in the original position to want as much of these goods as they can get. Here is how he explains the matter:

> I postulate that they [i.e., the persons in the original position] assume that they would prefer more primary social goods rather than less. Of course, it may turn out, once the veil of ignorance is removed, that some of them for religious or other reasons may not, in fact, want more of these goods. But from the standpoint of the original position, it is rational for the parties to suppose that they do want a larger share, since in any case they are not compelled to accept more if they do not wish to, nor does a person suffer from a greater liberty. [Rawls, pp. 142–43]

I do not find this argument convincing. It neglects the fact that dispensing with or refusing to accept primary goods that have been made available is itself an action that may entail significant costs. Burdensome calculations and deliberations may be required in order for a person to determine whether an increment of some primary good is worth having, and making decisions of this sort may involve responsibilities and risks in virtue of which the person experiences considerable anxiety. What is the basis, moreover, for the claim that no one suffers from a greater liberty? Under a variety of circumstances, it would seem, people may reasonably prefer to have fewer alternatives from which to choose rather than more. Surely liberty, like all other things, has its costs. It is an error to suppose that a person's life is invariably improved, or that it cannot be made worse, when his options are increased.

NOTES

1. This version of economic egalitarianism (for short, simply "egalitarianism") might also be formulated as the doctrine that there should be no inequalities in the *distribution* of money. The two formulations are not unambiguously equivalent because the term "distribution" is equivocal. It may refer either to a pattern of possession or to an activity of allocation, and there are significant differences in the criteria for evaluating distributions in the two senses. Thus it is quite possible to maintain consistently both that it is acceptable for people to have unequal amounts of money and that it is objectionable to allocate money unequally.

2. Thus, Thomas Nagel writes: "The defense of economic equality on the ground that it is needed to protect political, legal and social equality . . . [is not] a defense of equality *per se*—equality in the possession of benefits in general. Yet the latter is a further moral idea of great importance. Its validity would provide an independent reason to favor economic equality as a good in its own right" ("Equality," in his *Mortal Questions* [Cambridge: Cambridge University Press, 1979], p. 107).

3. I focus attention here on the standard of equality in the distribution of money chiefly in order to facilitate my discussion of the standard of sufficiency. Many egalitarians, of course, consider economic equality to be morally less important than equality in certain other matters: e.g., welfare, opportunity, respect, satisfaction of needs. In fact, some of what I have to say about economic egalitarianism and sufficiency applies as well to these other benefits. But I shall not attempt in this essay to define the scope of its applicability, nor shall I attempt to relate my views to other recent criticism of egalitarianism (e.g., Larry S. Temkin, "Inequality," *Philosophy and Public Affairs* 15 [1986]: 99–121; Robert E. Goodin, "Epiphenomenal Egalitarianism," *Social Research* 52 [1985]: 99–117).

4. It might be argued (as some of the editors of *Ethics* have suggested to me) that pursuing equality as an important social ideal would not be so alienating as pursuing it as a personal goal. It is indeed possible that individuals devoted to the former pursuit would be less immediately or less intensely preoccupied with their own economic circumstances than those devoted to the latter. But they would hardly regard the achievement of economic equality as important for the society unless they had the false and alienating conviction that it was important for individuals to enjoy economic equality.

5. Blum and Kalven, pp. 57–58.

6. People tend to think that it is generally more important to avoid a certain degree of harm than to acquire a benefit of comparable magnitude. It may be that this is in part because they assume that utility diminishes at the margin, for in that case the additional benefit would have less utility than the corresponding loss. However, it should be noted that the tendency to place a lower value on

acquiring benefits than on avoiding harms is sometimes reversed: when people are so miserable that they regard themselves as "having nothing to lose," they may well place a higher value on improving things than on preventing them from becoming (to a comparable extent) even worse. In that case, what is diminishing at the margin is not the utility of benefits but the disutility of harms.

7. In virtue of these thresholds, a marginal or incremental dollar may have conspicuously greater utility than dollars that do not enable a threshold to be crossed. Thus, a person who uses his spare money during a certain period for some inconsequential improvement in his routine pattern of consumption—perhaps a slightly better quality of meat for dinner every night—may derive much less additional utility in this way than by saving up the extra money for a few weeks and going to see some marvelous play or opera. The threshold effect is particularly integral to the experience of collectors, who characteristically derive greater satisfaction from obtaining the item that finally completes a collection—whichever item it happens to be—than from obtaining any of the other items in the collection. Obtaining the final item entails crossing a utility threshold: a complete collection of twenty different items, each of which when considered individually has the same utility, is likely to have greater utility for a collector than an incomplete collection that is of the same size but that includes duplicates. The completeness of the collection itself possesses utility, in addition to the utility provided individually by the items of which the collection is constituted.

8. Lerner, pp. 26–27.

9. It might be correct to say that he does need one unit if there is a chance that he will get four more, since in that case the one unit can be regarded as potentially an integral constituent of the total of five that puts him across the threshold of survival. But if there is no possibility that he will acquire five, then acquiring the one does not contribute to the satisfaction of any need.

10. Ronald Dworkin, "Why Liberals Should Care about Equality," in his *A Matter of Principle* (Cambridge, Mass.: Harvard University Press, 1985), p. 206. Page numbers in parentheses in the text refer to this work.

11. Nagel, p. 118.

12. Ibid., p. 117.

13. What I oppose is the claim that when it comes to justifying attempts to improve the circumstances of those who are economically worst off, a good reason for making the attempt is that it is morally important for people to be as equal as possible with respect to money. The only morally compelling reason for trying to make the worse off better off is, in my judgment, that their lives are in some degree bad lives. The fact that some people have more than enough money suggests a way in which it might be arranged for those who have less than enough to get more, but it is not in itself a good reason for redistribution.

14. Nagel, p. 123.

15. For further discussion, see Sec. VII below.

16. Quotations from his discussion of this illustration are from Nagel, pp. 123–24.

17. The issue of equality or sufficiency that Nagel's illustration raises does not, of course, concern the distribution of *money*.

18. Within the limits of my discussion it makes no difference which view is taken concerning the very important question of whether what counts is *the attitude a person actually has* or *the attitude it would be reasonable for him to have*. For the sake of brevity, I shall henceforth omit referring to the latter alternative.

19. Compare the sensible adage: "If it's not broken, don't fix it."

20. People often adjust their desires to their circumstances. There is a danger that sheer discouragement, or an interest in avoiding frustration and conflict, may lead them to settle for too little. It surely cannot be presumed that someone's life is genuinely fulfilling, or that it is reasonable for the person to be satisfied with it, simply because he does not complain. On the other hand, it also cannot be presumed that when a person has accommodated his desires to his circumstances, this is itself evidence that something has gone wrong.

21. John Rawls, *A Theory of Justice* (Cambridge, Mass.: Harvard University Press, 1971), p. 92. Additional references to this book appear in parentheses in the text.

RICHARD ARNESON

Equality and Equal Opportunity for Welfare

1989

Insofar as we care for equality as a distributive ideal, what is it exactly that we prize? Many persons are troubled by the gap between the living standards of rich people and poor people in modern societies or by the gap between the average standard of living in rich societies and that prevalent in poor societies. To some extent at any rate it is the gap itself that is troublesome, not just the low absolute level of the standard of living of the poor. But it is not easy to decide what measure of the "standard of living" it is appropriate to employ to give content to the ideal of distributive equality. Recent discussions by John Rawls[1] and Ronald Dworkin[2] have debated the merits of versions of equality of welfare and equality of resources taken as interpretations of the egalitarian ideal. In this paper I shall argue that the idea of equal opportunity for welfare is the best interpretation of the ideal of distributive equality.

Consider a distributive agency that has at its disposal a stock of goods that individuals want to own and use. We need not assume that each good is useful for every person, just that each good is useful for someone. Each good is homogeneous in quality and can be divided as finely as you choose. The problem to be considered is: How to divide the goods in order to meet an appropriate standard of equality. This discussion assumes that some goods are legitimately available for distribution in this fashion, hence that the entitlements and deserts of individuals do not predetermine the proper ownership of all resources. No argument is provided for this assumption, so in this sense my article is addressed to egalitarians, not their opponents.

I. EQUALITY OF RESOURCES

The norm of equality of resources stipulates that to achieve equality the agency ought to give everybody a share of goods that is exactly identical to everyone else's and that exhausts all available resources to be distributed. A straightforward objection to equality of resources so understood is that if Smith and Jones have similar tastes and abilities except that Smith has a severe physical handicap remediable with the help of expensive crutches, then if the two are accorded equal resources, Smith must spend the bulk of his resources on crutches whereas Jones can use his resource share to fulfill his aims to a far greater extent. It seems forced to claim that any notion of equality of condition that is worth caring about prevails between Smith and Jones in this case.

At least two responses to this objection are worth noting. One, pursued by Dworkin,[3] is that in the example the cut between the individual and the resources at his disposal was made at the wrong place. Smith's defective legs and Jones's healthy legs should be considered among their resources, so that only if Smith is assigned a gadget that renders his legs fully serviceable in addition to a resource share that is otherwise identical with Jones's can we say that equality of resources prevails. The example then suggests that an equality of resources ethic should count personal talents among the resources to be distributed. This line of response swiftly encounters difficulties. It is impossible for a distributive agency to supply educational and technological aid that will offset inborn differences of talent so that all persons are blessed

Richard Arneson, "Equality and Equal Opportunity for Welfare." *Philosophical Studies* 56 (1) (1989): 77–93. By permission of Springer.

with the same talents. Nor is it obvious how much compensation is owed to those who are disadvantaged by low talent. The worth to individuals of their talents varies depending on the nature of their life plans. An heroic resolution of this difficulty is to assign every individual an equal share of ownership of everybody's talents in the distribution of resources.[4] Under this procedure each of the N persons in society begins adult life owning a tradeable 1/N share of everybody's talents. We can regard this share as amounting to ownership of a block of time during which the owner can dictate how the partially owned person is to deploy his talent. Dworkin himself has noticed a flaw in this proposal, which he has aptly named "the slavery of the talented."[5] The flaw is that under this equal distribution of talent scheme the person with high talent is put at a disadvantage relative to her low-talent fellows. If we assume that each person strongly wants liberty in the sense of ownership over his own time (that is, ownership over his own body for his entire lifetime), the high-talent person finds that his taste for liberty is very expensive, as his time is socially valuable and very much in demand, whereas the low-talent person finds that his taste for liberty is cheap, as his time is less valuable and less in demand. Under this version of equality of resources, if two persons are identical in all respects except that one is more talented than the other, the more talented will find she is far less able to achieve her life plan than her less talented counterpart. Again, once its implications are exhibited, equality of resources appears an unattractive interpretation of the ideal of equality.

A second response asserts that given an equal distribution of resources, persons should be held responsible for forming and perhaps reforming their own preferences, in the light of their resource share and their personal characteristics and likely circumstances.[6] The level of overall preference satisfaction that each person attains is then a matter of individual responsibility, not a social problem. That I have nil singing talent is a given, but that I have developed an aspiration to become a professional opera singer and have formed my life around this ambition is a further development that was to some extent within my control and for which I must bear responsibility.

The difficulty with this response is that even if it is accepted it falls short of defending equality of resources. Surely social and biological factors influence preference formation, so if we can properly be held responsible only for what lies within our control, then we can at most be held to be partially responsible for our preferences. For instance, it would be wildly implausible to claim that a person without the use of his legs should be held responsible for developing a full set of aims and values toward the satisfaction of which leglessness is no hindrance. Acceptance of the claim that we are sometimes to an extent responsible for our preferences leaves the initial objection against equality of resources fully intact. For if we are sometimes responsible we are sometimes not responsible.

The claim that "we are responsible for our preferences" is ambiguous. It could mean that our preferences have developed to their present state due to factors that lay entirely within our control. Alternatively, it could mean that our present preferences, even if they have arisen through processes largely beyond our power to control, are now within our control in the sense that we could now undertake actions, at greater or lesser cost, that would change our preferences in ways that we can foresee. If responsibility for preferences on the first construal held true, this would indeed defeat the presumption that our resource share should be augmented because it satisfies our preferences to a lesser extent than the resource shares of others permit them to satisfy their preferences. However, on the first construal, the claim that we are responsible for our preferences is certainly always false. But on the second, weaker construal, the claim that we are responsible for our preferences is compatible with the claim that an appropriate norm of equal distribution should compensate people for their hard-to-satisfy preferences at least up to the point at which by taking appropriate adaptive measures now, people could reach the same preference satisfaction level as others.

The defense of equality of resources by appeal to the claim that persons are responsible for their preferences admits of yet another interpretation. Without claiming that people have caused their preferences to become what they are or that people could cause their preferences to change, we might hold that people can take responsibility for their fundamental preferences in the sense of identifying with them and regarding these preferences as their own, not as alien intrusions on the self. T. M. Scanlon has suggested the example of religious preferences in this spirit.[7] That a person was raised in one religious tradition rather than another may predictably affect his lifetime expectation of preference satisfaction. Yet we would regard it as absurd to insist upon compensation in the name of distributive equality for having been raised fundamentalist Protestant rather than atheist or Catholic (a matter that of course does not lie within the individual's power to control). Provided that a fair (equal) distribution of the resources of religious liberty is maintained, the amount of utility that individuals can expect from their religious upbringings is "specifically not an object of public policy."[8]

The example of compensation for religious preferences is complex, and I will return to it in section II below. Here it suffices to note that even if in some cases we do deem it inappropriate to insist on such compensation in the name of equality, it does not follow that equality of resources is an adequate rendering of the egalitarian ideal. Differences among people including sometimes differences in their upbringing may render resource equality nugatory. For example, a person raised in a closed fundamentalist community such as the Amish who then loses his faith and moves to the city may feel at a loss as to how to satisfy ordinary secular preferences, so that equal treatment of this rube and city sophisticates may require extra compensation for the rube beyond resource equality. Had the person's fundamental values not altered, such compensation would not be in order. I am not proposing compensation as a feasible government policy, merely pointing out that the fact that people might in some cases regard it as crass to ask for indemnification of their satisfaction-reducing upbringing does not show that in principle it makes sense for people to assume responsibility (act as though they were responsible) for what does not lie within their control. Any policy that attempted to ameliorate these discrepancies would predictably inflict wounds on innocent parents and guardians far out of proportion to any gain that could be realized for the norm of distributive equality. So even if we all agree that in such cases a policy of compensation is inappropriate, all things considered, it does not follow that so far as distributive equality is concerned (one among the several values we cherish), compensation should not be forthcoming.

Finally, it is far from clear why assuming responsibility for one's preferences and values in the sense of affirming them and identifying them as essential to one's self precludes demanding or accepting compensation for these preferences in the name of distributive equality. Suppose the government has accepted an obligation to subsidize the members of two native tribes who are badly off, low in welfare. The two tribes happen to be identical except that one is strongly committed to traditional religious ceremonies involving a psychedelic made from the peyote cactus while the other tribe is similarly committed to its traditional rituals involving an alcoholic drink made from a different cactus. If the market price of the psychedelic should suddenly rise dramatically while the price of the cactus drink stays cheap, members of the first tribe might well claim that equity requires an increase in their subsidy to compensate for the greatly increased price of the wherewithal for their ceremonies. Advancing such a claim, so far as I can see, is fully compatible with continuing to affirm and identify with one's preferences and in this sense to take personal responsibility for them.

In practise, many laws and other public policies differentiate roughly between preferences that we think are deeply entrenched in people, alterable if at all only at great personal cost, and very widespread in the population, versus preferences that for most of us are alterable at moderate cost should we choose to try to change them and thinly and erratically spread throughout the population. Laws and public policies commonly take account of the former and ignore the latter. For example, the law caters to people's deeply felt aversion to public nudity but does not cater to people's aversion to the sight of tastelessly dressed strollers in public spaces. Of course, current American laws and policies are not designed to achieve any strongly egalitarian ideal, whether resource-based or not. But in appealing to common sense as embodied in current practises in order to determine what sort of equality we care about insofar as we do care about equality, one would go badly astray in claiming support in these practises for the contention that equality of resources captures the ideal of equality. We need to search further.

II. EQUALITY OF WELFARE

According to equality of welfare, goods are distributed equally among a group of persons to the degree that the distribution brings it about that each person enjoys the same welfare. (The norm thus presupposes the possibility of cardinal interpersonal welfare comparisons.) The considerations mentioned seven paragraphs back already dispose of the idea that the distributive equality worth caring about is equality of welfare. To bring this point home more must be said to clarify what "welfare" means in this context.

I take welfare to be preference satisfaction. The more an individual's preferences are satisfied, as weighted by their importance to that very individual, the higher her welfare. The preferences that figure in the calculation of a person's welfare are limited to self-interested preferences—what the individual prefers insofar as she seeks her own advantage. One may prefer something for its own sake or as a means to further ends; this discussion is confined to preferences of the former sort.

The preferences that most plausibly serve as the measure of the individual's welfare are hypothetical preferences. Consider this familiar account: The extent to which a person's life goes well is the degree to which his ideally considered preferences are satisfied.[9] My ideally considered preferences are those I would have if I were to engage in thoroughgoing deliberation about my preferences with full pertinent information, in a calm mood, while thinking clearly and making no reasoning errors. (We can also call these ideally considered preferences "rational preferences.")

To avoid a difficulty, we should think of the full information that is pertinent to ideally considered preferences as split into two stages corresponding to "first-best" and "second-best" rational preferences. At the first stage one is imagined to be considering full information relevant to choice on the assumption that the results of this ideal deliberation process can costlessly correct one's actual preferences. At the second stage one is imagined to be considering also information regarding (a) one's actual resistance to advice regarding the rationality of one's preferences, (b) the costs of an educational program that would break down this resistance, and (c) the likelihood that anything approaching this educational program will actually be implemented in one's lifetime. What it is reasonable to prefer is then refigured in the light of these costs. For example, suppose that low-life preferences for cheap thrills have a large place in my actual conception of the good, but no place in my first-best rational preferences. But suppose it is certain that these low-life preferences are firmly fixed in my character. Then my second-best preferences are those I would have if I were to deliberate in ideal fashion about my preferences in the light of full knowledge about my actual preferences and their resistance to change. If you are giving me a birthday present, and your sole goal is to advance my welfare as much as possible, you are probably advised to give me, say, a bottle of jug wine rather than a volume of Shelley's poetry even though it is the poetry experience that would satisfy my first-best rational preference.[10]

On this understanding of welfare, equality of welfare is a poor ideal. Individuals can arrive at different welfare levels due to choices they make for which they alone should be held responsible. A simple example would be to imagine two persons of identical tastes and abilities who are assigned equal resources by an agency charged to maintain distributive equality. The two then voluntarily engage in high-stakes gambling, from which one emerges rich (with high expectation of welfare) and the other poor (with low welfare expectation). For another example, consider two persons similarly situated, so they could attain identical welfare levels with the same effort, but one chooses to pursue personal welfare zealously while the other pursues an aspirational preference (e.g., saving the whales), and so attains lesser fulfillment of self-interested preferences. In a third example, one person may voluntarily cultivate an expensive preference (not cognitively superior to the preference it supplants), while another person does not. In all three examples it would be inappropriate to insist upon equality of welfare when welfare inequality arises through the voluntary choice of the person who gets lesser welfare. Notice that in all three examples as described, there need be no grounds for finding fault with any aims or actions of any of the individuals mentioned. No imperative of practical reason commands us to devote our lives to the maximal pursuit of (self-interested) preference satisfaction. Divergence from equality of welfare arising in these ways need not signal any fault imputable to individuals or to "society" understood as responsible for maintaining distributive equality.

This line of thought suggests taking equal opportunity for welfare to be the appropriate norm of distributive equality.

In the light of the foregoing discussion, consider again the example of compensation for one's religious upbringing regarded as affecting one's lifetime preference satisfaction expectation. This example is urged as a *reductio ad absurdum* of the norm of equality of welfare, which may seem to yield the counterintuitive implication that such differences do constitute legitimate grounds for redistributing people's resource shares, in the name of distributive equality. As I mentioned, the example is tricky; we should not allow it to stampede us toward resource-based construals of distributive equality. Two comments on the example indicate something of its trickiness.

First, if a person changes her values in the light of deliberation that bring her closer to the ideal of deliberative rationality, we should credit the person's conviction that satisfying the new values counts for more than satisfying the old ones, now discarded. The old values should be counted at a discount due to their presumed greater distance from deliberative rationality. So if I was a Buddhist, then become a Hindu, and correctly regard the new religious preference as cognitively superior to the old, it is not the case that a straight equality of welfare standard must register my welfare as declining even if my new religious values are less easily achievable than the ones they supplant.

Secondly, the example might motivate acceptance of equal opportunity for welfare over straight equality of welfare rather than rejection of subjectivist conceptions of equality altogether. If equal opportunity for welfare obtains between Smith and Jones, and Jones subsequently undergoes religious conversion that lowers his welfare prospects, it may be that we will take Jones's conversion either to be a voluntarily chosen act or a prudentially negligent act for which he should be held responsible. (Consider the norm: Other things equal, it is bad if some people are worse off than others through no voluntary choice or fault of their own.) This train of thought also motivates an examination of equal opportunity for welfare.

III. EQUAL OPPORTUNITY FOR WELFARE

An opportunity is a chance of getting a good if one seeks it. For equal opportunity for welfare to obtain among a number of persons, each must face an array of options that is equivalent to every other person's in terms of the prospects for preference satisfaction it offers. The preferences involved in this calculation are ideally considered second-best preferences (where these differ from first-best preferences). Think of two persons entering their majority and facing various life choices, each action one might choose being associated with its possible outcomes. In the simplest case, imagine that we know the probability of each outcome conditional on the agent's choice of an action that might lead to it. Given that one or another choice is made and one or another outcome realized, the agent would then face another array of choices, then another, and so on. We construct a decision tree that gives an individual's possible complete life-histories. We then add up the preference satisfaction expectation for each possible life history. In doing this we take into account the preferences that people have regarding being confronted with the particular range of options given at each decision point. Equal opportunity for welfare obtains among persons when all of them face equivalent decision trees—the expected value of each person's best (= most prudent[11]) choice of options, second-best, . . . *n*th-best is the same. The opportunities persons encounter are ranked by the prospects for welfare they afford.

The criterion for equal opportunity for welfare stated above is incomplete. People might face an equivalent array of options, as above, yet differ in their awareness of these options, their ability to choose reasonably among them, and the strength of character that enables a person to persist in carrying out a chosen option. Further conditions are needed. We can summarize these conditions by stipulating that a number of persons face *effectively* equivalent options just in case one of the following is true: (1) the options are equivalent and the persons are on a par in their ability to "negotiate" these options, or (2) the options are nonequivalent in such a way as to counterbalance exactly any inequalities in people's negotiating abilities, or (3) the options are equivalent and any inequalities in people's negotiating abilities are due to causes for which it is proper to hold the individuals themselves personally responsible. Equal opportunity for welfare obtains when all persons face effectively equivalent arrays of options.

Whether or not two persons enjoy equal opportunity for welfare at a time depends only on whether they face effectively equivalent arrays of options at that time. Suppose that Smith and Jones share equal opportunity for welfare on Monday, but on Tuesday Smith voluntarily chooses or negligently behaves so that from then on Jones has greater welfare opportunities. We may say that in an extended sense people share equal opportunity for welfare just in case there is some time at which their opportunities are equal and if any inequalities in their opportunities at later times are due to their voluntary choice or differentially negligent behavior for which they are rightly deemed personally responsible.

When persons enjoy equal opportunity for welfare in the extended sense, any actual inequality of welfare in the positions they reach is due to factors that lie within each individual's control. Thus, any such inequality will be non-problematic from the standpoint of distributive equality. The norm of equal opportunity for welfare is distinct from equality of welfare only if some version of soft determinism or indeterminism is correct. If hard determinism is true, the two interpretations of equality come to the same.

In actual political life under modern conditions, distributive agencies will be staggeringly ignorant of the facts that would have to be known in order to pinpoint what level of opportunity for welfare different persons have had. To some extent it is technically unfeasible or even physically impossible to collect the needed information, and to some extent we do not trust governments with the authority to collect the needed information, due to worries that such authority will be subject to abuse. Nonetheless, I suppose that the idea is clear in principle, and that in practise it is often feasible to make reliable rough-and-ready judgments to the effect that some people face very grim prospects for welfare compared to what others enjoy.

In comparing the merits of a Rawlsian conception of distributive equality as equal shares of primary goods and a Dworkinian conception of equality of resources with the norm of equality of opportunity for welfare, we run into the problem that in the real world, with imperfect information available to citizens and policymakers, and imperfect willingness on the part of citizens and officials to carry out conscientiously whatever norm is chosen, the practical implications of these conflicting principles may be hard to discern, and may not diverge much in practise. Familiar information-gathering and information-using problems will make us unwilling to authorize government agencies to determine people's distributive shares on the basis of their preference satisfaction prospects, which will often be unknowable for all practical purposes. We may insist that governments have regard to primary good share equality or resource equality as rough proxies for the welfarist equality that we are unable to calculate. To test our allegiance to the rival doctrines of equality we may need to consider real or hypothetical examples of situations in which we do have good information regarding welfare prospects and opportunities for welfare, and consider whether this information affects our judgments as to what counts as egalitarian policy. We also need to consider cases in which we gain new evidence that a particular resource-based standard is a much more inaccurate proxy for welfare equality than we might have thought, and much less accurate than another standard now available. Indifference to these considerations would mark allegiance to a resourcist interpretation of distributive equality in principle, not merely as a handy rough-and-ready approximation.

IV. STRAIGHT EQUALITY VERSUS EQUAL OPPORTUNITY; WELFARE VERSUS RESOURCES

The discussion to this point has explored two independent distinctions: (1) straight equality versus equal opportunity and (2) welfare versus resources as the appropriate basis for measuring distributive shares. Hence there are four positions to consider. On the issue of whether an egalitarian should regard welfare or resources as the appropriate standard of distributive equality, it is important to compare like with like, rather than, for instance, just to compare equal opportunity for resources with straight equality of welfare. (In my opinion Ronald Dworkin's otherwise magisterial treatment of the issue in his two-part discussion of "What Is Equality?" is marred by a failure to bring these four distinct positions clearly into focus.[12])

The argument for equal opportunity rather than straight equality is simply that it is morally fitting to hold individuals responsible for the foreseeable consequences of their voluntary choices, and in particular for that portion of these consequences that involves their own achievement of welfare or gain or loss of resources. If accepted, this argument leaves it entirely open whether we as egalitarians ought to support equal opportunity for welfare or equal opportunity for resources.

For equal opportunity for resources to obtain among a number of persons, the range of lotteries with resources as prizes available to each of them must be effectively the same. The range of lotteries available to two persons is effectively the same whenever it is the case that, for any lottery the first can gain access to, there is an identical lottery that the second person can gain access to by comparable effort. (So if Smith can gain access to a lucrative lottery by walking across the street, and Jones cannot gain a similar lottery except by a long hard trek across a desert, to this extent their opportunities for resources are unequal.) We may say that equal opportunity for resources in an extended sense obtains among a number of persons just in case there is a time at which their opportunities are equal and any later inequalities in the resource opportunities they face are due to voluntary choices or differentially negligent behavior on their part for which they are rightly deemed personally responsible.

I would not claim that the interpretation of equal opportunity for resources presented here is the only plausible construal of the concept. However, on any plausible construal, the norm of equal opportunity for resources is vulnerable to the "slavery of the talented" problem that proved troublesome for equality of resources. Supposing that personal talents should be included among the resources to be distributed (for reasons given in section I), we find that moving from a regime of equality of resources to a regime that enforces equal opportunity for resources does not change the fact that a resource-based approach causes the person of high talent to be predictably and (it would seem) unfairly worse off in welfare prospects than her counterpart with lesser talent.[13] If opportunities for resources are equally distributed among more and less talented persons, then each person regardless of her native talent endowment will have comparable access to identical lotteries for resources that include time slices of the labor power of all persons. Each person's expected ownership of talent, should he seek it, will be the same. Other things equal, if all persons strongly desire personal liberty or initial ownership of one's own lifetime labor power, this good will turn out to be a luxury commodity for the talented, and a cheap bargain for the untalented.

A possible objection to the foregoing reasoning is that it relies on a vaguely specified idea of how to measure resource shares that is shown to be dubious by the very fact that it leads back to the slavery of the talented problem. Perhaps by taking personal liberty as a separate resource this result can be avoided. But waiving any other difficulties with this objection, we note that the assumption that any measure of resource equality must be unacceptable if applying it leads to unacceptable results for the distribution of welfare amounts to smuggling in a welfarist standard by the back door.

Notice that the welfare distribution implications of equal opportunity for resources will count as intuitively unacceptable only on the assumption that people cannot be deemed to have chosen voluntarily the preferences that are frustrated or satisfied by the talent pooling that a resourcist interpretation of equal opportunity enforces. Of course it is strictly nonvoluntary that one is born with a particular body and cannot be separated from it, so if others hold ownership rights in one's labor power one's individual liberty is thereby curtailed. But in principle one's self-interested preferences could be concerned no more with what happens to one's own body than with what happens to the bodies of others. To the extent that you have strong self-interested hankerings that your neighbors try their hand at, say, farming, and less intense desires regarding the occupations you yourself pursue, to that extent the fact that under talent pooling your own labor power is a luxury commodity will not adversely affect your welfare. As an empirical matter, I submit that it is just false to hold that in modern society whether any given individual does or does not care about retaining her own personal liberty is due to that person's voluntarily choosing one or the other preference. The expensive preference of the talented person for personal liberty cannot be assimilated to the class of expensive preferences that people might voluntarily cultivate.[14] On plausible empirical assumptions, equal opportunity for welfare will often find tastes compensable, including the talented person's taste for the personal liberty to command her own labor power. Being born with high talent cannot then be a curse under equal opportunity for welfare (it cannot be a blessing either).

V. SEN'S CAPABILITIES APPROACH

The equal opportunity for welfare construal of equality that I am espousing is similar to a "capabilities" approach recently defended by Amartya Sen.[15] I shall now briefly sketch and endorse Sen's criticisms of Rawls's primary social goods standard and indicate a residual welfarist disagreement with Sen.

Rawls's primary social goods proposal recommends that society should be concerned with the distribution of certain basic social resources, so his position is a variant of a resource-based understanding of how to measure people's standard of living. Sen holds that the distribution of resources should be evaluated in terms of its contribution to individual capabilities to function in various ways deemed to be objectively important or valuable. That is, what counts is not the food one gets, but the contribution it can make to one's nutritional needs, not the educational expenditures lavished, but the contribution they make to one's knowledge and cognitive skills. Sen objects to taking primary social goods measurements to be fundamental on the ground that persons vary enormously from one another in the rates at which they transform primary social goods into capabilities to function in key ways. Surely we care about resource shares because we care what people are enabled to be and do with their resource shares, and insofar as we care about equality it is the latter that should be our concern.

So far, I agree. Moreover, Sen identifies a person's well-being with the doings and beings or "functionings" that he achieves, and distinguishes these functionings from the person's capabilities to function or "well-being freedom."[16] Equality of capability is then a notion within the family of equality of opportunity views, a family that also includes the idea of equal opportunity for welfare that I have been attempting to defend. So I agree with Sen to a large extent.

But given that there are indefinitely many kinds of things that persons can do or become, how are we supposed to sum an individual's various capability scores into an overall index? If we cannot construct such an index, then it would seem that equality of capability cannot qualify as a candidate conception of distributive equality. The indexing problem that is known to plague Rawls's primary goods proposal also afflicts Sen's capabilities approach.[17]

Sen is aware of the indexing problem and untroubled by it. The grand theme of his lectures on "Well-being, Agency and Freedom" is informational value pluralism: We should incorporate in our principles all moral information that is relevant to the choice of actions and policies even if that information complicates the articulation of principles and precludes attainment of a set of principles that completely rank-orders the available alternative actions in any possible set of circumstances. "Incompleteness is *not* an embarrassment," Sen declares.[18] I agree that principles of decision should not ignore morally pertinent matters but I doubt that the full set of my functioning capabilities does matter for the assessment of my position. Whether or not my capabilities include the capability to trek to the South Pole, eat a meal at the most expensive restaurant in Omsk, scratch my neighbor's dog at the precise moment of its daily maximal itch, matters not one bit to me, because I neither have nor have the slightest reason to anticipate I ever will have any desire to do any of these and myriad other things. Presumably only a small subset of my functioning capabilities matter for moral assessment, but which ones?

We may doubt whether there are any objectively decidable grounds by which the value of a person's capabilities can be judged apart from the person's (ideally considered) preferences regarding those capabilities. On what ground do we hold that it is valuable for a person to have a capability that she herself values at naught with full deliberative rationality? If a person's having a capability is deemed valuable on grounds independent of the person's own preferences in the matter, the excess valuation would seem to presuppose the adequacy of an as yet unspecified perfectionist doctrine the like of which has certainly not yet been defended and in my opinion is indefensible.[19] In the absence of such a defense of perfectionism, equal opportunity for welfare looks to be an attractive interpretation of distributive equality.

NOTES

1. John Rawls, "Social Unity and Primary Goods," in Amartya Sen and Bernard Williams, eds., *Utilitarianism and Beyond* (Cambridge: Cambridge University Press, 1982), pp. 159–185.

2. Ronald Dworkin, "What Is Equality? Part 1: Equality of Welfare," *Philosophy and Public Affairs* 10 (1981): 185–246; and "What Is Equality? Part 2: Equality of Resources," *Philosophy and Public Affairs* 10 (1981): 283–345. See Thomas Scanlon, "Preference and Urgency," *Journal of Philosophy* 72 (1975): 655–669.

3. Dworkin, "Equality of Resources."

4. Hal Varian discusses this mechanism of equal distribution, followed by trade to equilibrium, "Equity, Envy, and Efficiency," *Journal of Economic Theory* 9 (1974): 63–91. See also John Roemer, "Equality of Talent," *Economics and Philosophy* 1 (1985): 151–186; "Equality of Resources Implies Equality of Welfare," *Quarterly Journal of Economics* 101 (1986): 751–784.

5. Dworkin, "Equality of Resources," p. 312.

It should be noted that the defender of resource-based construals of distributive equality has a reply to the slavery of the talented problem that I do not consider in this paper. According to this reply, what the slavery of the talented problem reveals is not the imperative of distributing so as to equalize welfare but rather the moral inappropriateness of considering all resources as fully alienable. It may be that equality of resources should require that persons be compensated for their below-par talents, but such compensation should not take the form of assigning individuals full private ownership rights in other people's talents, which should be treated as at most partially alienable. Margaret Jane Radin, "Market-Inalienability," *Harvard Law Review* 100 (1987): 1849–1937.

6. Rawls, "Social Unity and Primary Goods," pp. 167–170.

7. Thomas Scanlon, "Equality of Resources and Equality of Welfare: A Forced Marriage?" *Ethics* 97 (1986): 111–118; see esp. pp. 115–117.

8. Scanlon, "Equality of Resources and Equality of Welfare," p. 116.

9. See, e.g., John Rawls, *A Theory of Justice* (Cambridge, MA: Harvard University Press, 1971), pp. 416–424; Richard Brandt, *A Theory of the Good and the Right* (Oxford: Oxford University Press, 1979), pp. 110–129; David Gauthier, *Morals by Agreement* (Oxford: Oxford University Press, 1986), pp. 29–38; and Derek Parfit, *Reasons and Persons* (Oxford: Oxford University Press, 1984), pp. 493–499.

10. In this paragraph I attempt to solve a difficulty noted by James Griffin in "Modern Utilitarianism," *Revue Internationale de Philosophie* 36 (1982): 331–375; esp. pp. 334–335. See also Amartya Sen and Bernard Williams, Introduction to *Utilitarianism and Beyond,* p. 10.

11. Here the most prudent choice cannot be identified with the choice that maximizes lifelong expected preference satisfaction, due to complications arising from the phenomenon of preference change. The prudent choice as

I conceive it is tied to one's actual preferences in ways I will not try to describe here.

12. See the articles cited in note 2. Dworkin's account of equality of resources is complex, but without entering into its detail I can observe that Dworkin is discussing a version of what I call "equal opportunity for resources." By itself, the name chosen matters not a bit. But confusion enters because Dworkin neglects altogether the rival doctrine of equal opportunity for welfare. For a criticism of Dworkin's objections against a welfarist conception of equality that do not depend on this confusion, see my "Liberalism, Distributive Subjectivism, and Equal Opportunity for Welfare."

13. Roemer notes that the person with high talent is cursed with an involuntary expensive preference for personal liberty. See Roemer, "Equality of Talent."

14. As Rawls writes, "those with less expensive tastes have presumably adjusted their likes and dislikes over the course of their lives to the income and wealth they could reasonably expect; and it is regarded as unfair that they now should have less in order to spare others from the consequences of their lack of foresight or self-discipline." See "Social Unity and Primary Goods," p. 169.

15. Amartya Sen, "Well-being, Agency and Freedom: The Dewey Lectures 1984," *Journal of Philosophy* 82 (1985): 169–221; esp. pp. 185–203. See also Sen, "Equality of What?" in his *Choice, Welfare and Measurement* (Oxford: Basil Blackwell, 1982), pp. 353–369.

16. Sen, "Well-being, Agency and Freedom," p. 201.

17. See Allan Gibbard, "Disparate Goods and Rawls' Difference Principle: A Social Choice Theoretic Treatment," *Theory and Decision* 11 (1979): 267–288; see esp. pp. 268–269.

18. Sen, "Well-being, Agency and Freedom," p. 200.

19. However, it should be noted that filling out a preference-satisfaction approach to distributive equality would seem to require a normative account of healthy preference formation that is not itself preference-based. A perfectionist component may thus be needed in a broadly welfarist egalitarianism. For this reason it would be misguided to foreclose too swiftly the question of the possible value of a capability that is valued at naught by the person who has it. The development and exercise of various capacities might be an important aspect of healthy preference formation, and have value in this way even though this value does not register at all in the person's preference satisfaction prospects.

AMARTYA SEN

Equality of What?

1992

1.1. WHY EQUALITY? WHAT EQUALITY?

Two central issues for ethical analysis of equality are: (1) Why equality? (2) Equality of what? The two questions are distinct but thoroughly interdependent. We cannot begin to defend or criticize equality without knowing what on earth we are talking about, i.e. equality of what features (e.g. incomes, wealths, opportunities, achievements, freedoms, rights)? We cannot possibly answer the first question without addressing the second. That seems obvious enough.

But if we *do* answer question (2), do we still *need* to address question (1)? If we have successfully argued in favour of equality of *x* (whatever that *x* is—some outcome, some right, some freedom, some respect, or some something else), then we have already

Amartya Sen, *Inequality Reexamined.* Oxford University Press, 1995. By permission of Oxford University Press.

argued for equality in *that* form, with x as the standard of comparison. Similarly, if we have rebutted the claim to equality of x, then we have already argued against equality in that form, with x as the standard of comparison. There is, in this view, no "further," no "deeper," question to be answered about why—or why not—"equality." Question (1), in this analysis, looks very much like the poor man's question (2).

There is some sense in seeing the matter in this way, but there is also a more interesting substantive issue here. It relates to the fact that every normative theory of social arrangement that has at all stood the test of time seems to demand equality of *something*—something that is regarded as particularly important in that theory. The theories involved are diverse and frequently at war with each other, but they still seem to have that common feature. In the contemporary disputes in political philosophy, equality does, of course, figure prominently in the contributions of John Rawls (equal liberty and equality in the distribution of primary goods"), Ronald Dworkin ("treatment as equals," "equality of resources"), Thomas Nagel ("economic equality"), Thomas Scanlon ("equality"), and others generally associated with a "pro equality" view. But equality in some space seems to be demanded even by those who are typically seen as having disputed the "case for equality" or for "distributive justice." For example, Robert Nozick may not demand equality of utility or equality of holdings of primary goods, but he does demand equality of libertarian rights—no one has any more right to liberty than anyone else. James Buchanan builds equal legal and political treatment—indeed a great deal more—into his view of a good society. In each theory, equality *is* sought in some space—a space that is seen as having a central role in that theory.

But what about utilitarianism? Surely, utilitarians do not, in general, want the equality of the total utilities enjoyed by different people. The utilitarian formula requires the maximization of the sum-total of the utilities of all people *taken together,* and that is, in an obvious sense, not particularly egalitarian. In fact, the equality that utilitarianism seeks takes the form of equal treatment of human beings in the space of *gains and losses of utilities.* There is an insistence on equal weights on everyone's utility gains in the utilitarian objective function.

This diagnosis of "hidden" egalitarianism in utilitarian philosophy might well be resisted on the ground that utilitarianism really involves a sum-total maximizing approach, and it might be thought that, as a result, any egalitarian feature of utilitarianism cannot be more than accidental. But this reasoning is deceptive. The utilitarian approach is undoubtedly a *maximizing* one, but the real question is what is the nature of the objective function it maximizes. That objective function could have been quite inegalitarian, e.g. giving much more weight to the utilities of some than to those of others. Instead, utilitarianism attaches exactly the same importance to the utilities of all people in the objective function, and that feature—coupled with the maximizing format—guarantees that everyone's utility gains get the same weight in the maximizing exercise. The egalitarian foundation is, thus, quite central to the entire utilitarian exercise. Indeed, it is precisely this egalitarian feature that relates to the foundational principle of utilitarianism of "giving equal weight to the equal interests of all the parties" (Hare 1981: 26), or to "always assign the same weight to all individuals' interests" (Harsanyi 1982: 47).

What do we conclude from this fact? One obvious conclusion is that being egalitarian (i.e. egalitarian in *some space or other* to which great importance is attached) is not really a "uniting" feature. Indeed, it is precisely because there are such substantive differences between the endorsement of different spaces in which equality is recommended by different authors that the basic similarity between them (in the form of wanting equality in *some* space that is seen as important) can be far from transparent. This is especially so when the term "equality" is defined—typically implicitly—as equality in a *particular* space.

For example, in his interesting essay, "The Case against Equality," Letwin (1983) argues against equal distribution of incomes (or commodities) thus: "Inasmuch as people are unequal, it is rational to presume that they ought to be treated unequally—which might mean larger shares for the needy or larger shares for the worthy" ("A Theoretical Weakness of

Egalitarianism," 8). But even the demand for equal satisfaction of "needs" is a requirement of equality (in a particular space), and it has indeed been championed as such for a long time. Even though the idea of individual "worth" is harder to characterize, the usual formulations of the demand for "larger shares for the worthy" tend to include equal treatment for equal worth, giving to each the same reward for worth as is given to another. Thus, these critiques of egalitarianism tend to take the form of being—instead—egalitarian in some *other* space. The problem again reduces to arguing, implicitly, for a different answer to the question "equality of what?"

Sometimes the question "equality of what?" gets *indirectly* addressed in apparently discussing "why equality?," with equality defined in a *specific* space. For example, Harry Frankfurt's (1987) well-reasoned paper attacking "equality as a moral ideal" is concerned mainly with disputing the claims of *economic* egalitarianism in the form of "the doctrine that it is desirable for everyone to have the same amounts of income and wealth (for short, "money")" (p. 21). Though the language of the presentation puts "egalitarianism" as such in the dock, this is primarily because Frankfurt uses that general term to refer specifically to a particular version of "economic egalitarianism": This version of economic egalitarianism (for short, simply "egalitarianism") might also be formulated as the doctrine that there should be no inequalities in the *distribution* of money" (p. 21).

The choice of space for equality is, thus, central to Frankfurt's main thesis. His arguments can be seen as disputing the specific demand for a common interpretation of economic egalitarianism by arguing (1) that such an equality is of no great intrinsic interest, *and* (2) that it leads to the violation of intrinsically important values—values that link closely to the need for paying equal attention to all in some other—more relevant—way.

Wanting equality of *something*—something seen as *important*—is undoubtedly a similarity of some kind, but that similarity does not put the warring camps on the same side. It only shows that the battle is not, in an important sense, about "why equality?," but about "equality of what?".

Since some spaces are traditionally associated with claims of "equality" in political or social or economic philosophy, it is equality in one of those spaces (e.g. incomes, wealths, utilities) that tend to go under the heading "egalitarianism." I am *not* arguing against the continued use of the term "egalitarianism" in one of those senses; there is no harm in that practice if it is understood to be a claim about equality in a specific space (and by implication, *against* equality in other spaces). But it is important to recognize the limited reach of that usage, and also the fact that demanding equality in one space—no matter how hallowed by tradition—can lead one to be anti-egalitarian in some other space, the comparative importance of which in the overall assessment has to be critically assessed.

1.2. IMPARTIALITY AND EQUALITY

The analysis in the last section pointed to the partisan character of the usual interpretations of the question "why equality?" That question, I have argued, has to be faced, just as much, even by those who are seen—by themselves and by others—as "anti-egalitarian," for they too are egalitarian in *some* space that is important in their theory. But it was not, of course, argued that the question "why equality?" was, in any sense, pointless. We may be persuaded that the basic disputations are likely to be about "equality of what?," but it might still be asked whether there *need be* a demand for equality in *some* important space or other. Even if it turns out that every substantive theory of social arrangements in vogue *is,* in fact, egalitarian in some space—a space seen as central in that theory—there is still the need to explain and defend that general characteristic in each case. The shared practice—even if it were universally shared—would still need some defence.

The issue to address is not so much whether there *must* be *for strictly formal reasons* (such as the discipline of "the language of morals"), equal consideration for all, at some level, in all ethical theories of social arrangement. That is an interesting and hard question, but one I need not address in the present context; the answer to it is, in my judgment, by no means clear. I am more concerned with the question whether ethical theories must have this basic feature of equality to have substantive plausibility in the world in which we live.

It may be useful to ask *why* it is that so many altogether different substantive theories of the ethics of social arrangements have the common feature of demanding equality of *something*—something important. It is, I believe, arguable that to have any kind of plausibility, ethical reasoning on social matters must involve elementary equal consideration for all at *some* level that is seen as critical. The absence of such equality would make a theory arbitrarily discriminating and hard to defend. A theory may accept—indeed demand—inequality in terms of many variables, but in defending those inequalities it would be hard to duck the need to relate them, ultimately, to equal consideration for all in some adequately substantial way.

Perhaps this feature relates to the requirement that ethical reasoning, especially about social arrangements, has to be, in some sense, credible from the viewpoint of others—potentially *all* others. The question "why this system?" has to be answered, as it were, for all the participants in that system. There are some Kantian elements in this line of reasoning, even though the equality demanded need not have a strictly Kantian structure.

Recently Thomas Scanlon (1982) has analysed the relevance and power of the requirement that one should "be able to justify one's actions to others on grounds that they could not reasonably reject." The requirement of "fairness" on which Rawls (1971) builds his theory of justice can be seen as providing a specific structure for determining what one can or cannot reasonably reject. Similarly, the demands of "impartiality"—and some substantively exacting forms of "universalizability"—invoked as general requirements have that feature of equal concern in some major way.

Reasoning of this general type certainly has much to do with the foundations of ethics, and has cropped up in different forms in the methodological underpinning of substantive ethical proposals.

The need to defend one's theories, judgments, and claims to others who may be—directly or indirectly—involved, makes equality of consideration at some level a hard requirement to avoid. There are interesting methodological questions regarding the status of this condition, in particular: whether it is a logical requirement or a substantive demand, and whether it is connected with the need for "objectivity" in ethics. I shall not pursue these questions further here, since the main concerns of this monograph do not turn on our answers to these questions.

What is of direct interest is the plausibility of claiming that equal consideration at some level—a level that is seen as important—is a demand that cannot be easily escaped in presenting a political or ethical theory of social arrangements. It is also of considerable pragmatic interest to note that impartiality and equal concern, in some form or other, provide a shared background to all the major ethical and political proposals in this field that continue to receive argued support and reasoned defence. One consequence of all this is the acceptance—often implicit—of the need to justify disparate advantages of different individuals in things that matter. That justification frequently takes the form of showing the integral connection of that inequality with equality in some *other* important—allegedly *more* important—space.

Indeed, it is equality in that more important space that may then be seen as contributing to the contingent demands for *inequality* in the other spaces. The justification of inequality in some features is made to rest on the equality of some other feature, taken to be more basic in that ethical system. Equality in what is seen as the "base" is invoked for a reasoned defence of the resulting inequalities in the far-flung "peripheries."

1.3. HUMAN DIVERSITY AND BASAL EQUALITY

Human beings differ from each other in many different ways. We have different external characteristics and circumstances. We begin life with different endowments of inherited wealth and liabilities. We live in different natural environments—some more hostile than others. The societies and the communities to which we belong offer very different opportunities as to what we can or cannot do. The epidemiological factors in the region in which we live can profoundly affect our health and well-being.

But in addition to these differences in natural and social environments and external characteristics, we also differ in our personal characteristics (e.g. age, sex, physical and mental abilities). And these are important for assessing inequality. For example, equal incomes can still leave much inequality in our ability to do what we would value doing. A disabled person cannot function in the way an able-bodied person can, even if both have exactly the same income. Thus, inequality in terms of one variable (e.g. income) may take us in a very different direction from inequality in the space of another variable (e.g. functioning ability or well-being).

The relative advantages and disadvantages that people have, compared with each other, can be judged in terms of many different variables, e.g. their respective incomes, wealths, utilities, resources, liberties, rights, quality of life, and so on. The plurality of variables on which we can possibly focus (the *focal variables*) to evaluate interpersonal inequality makes it necessary to face, at a very elementary level, a hard decision regarding the perspective to be adopted. This problem of the choice of the "evaluative space" (that is, the selection of the relevant focal variables) is crucial to analysing inequality.

The differences in focus are particularly important because of extensive human diversity. Had all people been exactly similar, equality in one space (e.g. incomes) would tend to be congruent with equalities in others (e.g. health, well-being, happiness). One of the consequences of "human diversity" is that equality in one space tends to go, in fact, with inequality in another.

For example, we may not be able to demand equality of welfare levels and other such "patterning"—to use Nozick's helpful description—once we demand the equality of libertarian rights as specified by Nozick (1974). If equal rights, in this form, are accepted, then so must be all their consequences, and this would include all the generated inequalities of incomes, utilities, well-being, and positive freedoms to do this or be that.

I am not examining, here, how convincing this defence is. The important issue in the present discussion is the nature of the strategy of justifying inequality through equality. Nozick's approach is a lucid and elegant example of this general strategy. If a claim that inequality in some significant space is right (or good, or acceptable, or tolerable) is to be defended by reason (not by, say, shooting the dissenters), the argument takes the form of showing this inequality to be a consequence of *equality* in some other—more centrally important—space. Given the broad agreement on the need to have equality in the "base," and also the connection of that broad agreement with this deep need for impartiality between individuals (discussed earlier), the crucial arguments have to be about the reasonableness of the "bases" chosen. Thus, the question: "equality of what?" is, in this context, not materially different from the enquiry: "what is the right space for basal equality?" The answer we give to "equality of what?" will not only endorse equality in that chosen space (the focal variable being related to the demands of basal equality), but will have far-reaching consequences on the distributional patterns (including necessary *inequalities*) in the other spaces. "Equality of what?" is indeed a momentous—and central —question.

1.4. EQUALITY VERSUS LIBERTY?

The importance of equality is often contrasted with that of liberty. Indeed, someone's position in the alleged conflict between equality and liberty has often been seen as a good indicator of his or her general outlook on political philosophy and political economy. For example, not only are libertarian thinkers (such as Nozick 1974) seen as anti-egalitarian, but they are diagnosed as anti-egalitarian *precisely because* of their overriding concern with liberty. Similarly, those diagnosed as egalitarian thinkers (e.g. Dalton 1920, Tawney 1931, or Meade 1976) may appear to be less concerned with liberty precisely because they are seen as being wedded to the demands of equality.

In the light of the discussion in the previous sections, we must argue that this way of seeing the relationship between equality and liberty is altogether faulty. Libertarians must think it important that people should have liberty. Given this, questions would immediately arise regarding: *who, how much, how distributed, how equal*? Thus the issue of equality immediately arises as a *supplement* to the assertion of the importance of liberty. The libertarian proposal has to be completed by going on to characterize the distribution of rights among the people involved. In fact, the libertarian demands for liberty typically include important features of "equal liberty," e.g. the insistence on equal immunity from interference by others. The belief that liberty is important cannot, thus, be in conflict with the view that it is important that the social arrangements be devised to promote equality of liberties that people have.

There can, of course, be a conflict between a person who argues for the equality of some variable *other than* liberty (such as income or wealth or well-being) and someone who wants only equal liberty. But that is a dispute over the question "equality of *what*?" Similarly, a distribution-independent general promotion of liberty (i.e. promoting it wherever possible without paying attention to the distributive pattern) could, of course, conflict with equality of some other variable, say, income, but that would be (1) partly a conflict between concentrating respectively on liberty and on incomes, and (2) partly one between a concern for distributive patterns (of incomes in this case) and non-distributive aggregative considerations (applied to liberty). It is neither accurate nor helpful to think of the difference in either case in terms of "liberty *versus* equality."

Indeed, strictly speaking, posing the problem in terms of this latter contrast reflects a "category mistake." They are not alternatives. Liberty is among the possible *fields of application* of equality, and equality is among the possible *patterns* of distribution of liberty.

As was discussed earlier, the need to face explicitly the choice of space is an inescapable part of the specification and reasoned evaluation of the demands of equality. There are, at one end, demands of equal libertarian rights only, and at the other end, various exacting demands of equality regarding an extensive list of *achievements* and also a corresponding list of *freedoms* to achieve. This study is much concerned with this plurality and its manifold consequences.

1.5. PLURALITY AND ALLEGED EMPTINESS

The recognition of plurality of spaces in which equality may be assessed can raise some doubts about the content of the idea of equality. Does it not make equality less powerful and imperative as a political idea? If equality can possibly speak with so many voices, can we take any of its demands seriously?

Indeed, the apparent pliability of the contents of equality has appeared to some analysts as a source of serious embarrassment for the idea of equality. As Douglas Rae (1981) has put it (in his meticulous and helpful exploration of the various contemporary notions of equality), "one idea that is more powerful than order or efficiency or freedom in resisting equality" is "equality itself" (p. 151).

While Rae argues that the idea of equality is, as it were, "overfull," others have argued, on similar grounds, that equality is "an empty idea"—it is "an empty form having no substantive content of its own." Since equality can be interpreted in so many different ways, the requirement of equality cannot, in this view, be taken to be a truly substantive demand.

It is certainly true that merely demanding equality without saying equality of what, cannot be seen as demanding anything specific. This gives some plausibility to the thesis of emptiness. But the thesis is, I believe, erroneous nevertheless. First, even before a specific space is chosen, the general requirement of the need to value equality in *some space that is seen to be particularly important* is not an empty demand. This relates to the discipline imposed by the need for some impartiality, some form of equal concern.

At the very least, it is a requirement of scrutiny of the basis of the proposed evaluative system. It can also have considerable cutting power, in questioning theories without a basal structure and in rejecting those that end up without a basal equality altogether. Even at this general level, equality is a substantive and substantial requirement.

Second, once the context is fixed, equality can be a particularly powerful and exacting demand. For example, when the space is fixed, demands for equality impose some ranking of patterns, even before any specific index of equality is endorsed. For example, in dealing with the inequality of incomes, the so-called "Dalton principle of transfer" demands that a small transfer of income from a richer person to a poorer one—keeping the total unchanged—must be seen to be a distributive improvement. In its context, this is a fairly persuasive rule in ranking distributions of the same total income by the general requirement of equality without invoking any specific index or measure.

In addition to such ordering of patterns in a *given* space, even the broader exercise of the choice of space itself may have clear links with the motivation underlying the demand for equality. For example, in evaluating justice, or social welfare, or living standards, or quality of life, the exercise of choice of space is no longer just *formal,* but one of substantive discrimination. As I shall try to show in the chapters that follow, the claims of many of these spaces can be forcefully disputed once the context is fixed. Though this need not lead us to *one* precise characterization of the demands of equality that is important in every context, this is far from a real embarrassment. In each context, the demands of equality may be both distinct and strong.

Third, the diversity of spaces in which equality may be demanded really reflects a deeper diversity, to wit, different diagnoses of objects of value—different views of the appropriate notions of individual advantage in the contexts in question. The problem of diversity is, thus, not unique to equality evaluation. The different demands of equality reflect divergent views as to what things are to be directly valued in that context. They indicate different ideas as to how the advantages of different people are to be assessed *vis-à-vis* each other in the exercise in question. Liberties, rights, utilities, incomes, resources, primary goods, need-fulfilments, etc., provide different ways of seeing the respective lives of different people, and each of the perspectives leads to a corresponding view of equality.

This plurality—that of assessing the advantages of different persons—reflects itself in different views not merely of equality, but also of any other social notion for which individual advantage substantially enters the informational base. For example, the notion of "efficiency" would have exactly the same plurality related to the choice of space. Efficiency is unambiguously increased if there is an enhancement of the advantage of each person (or, an advancement for at least one person, with no decline for any), but the content of that characterization depends on the way advantage is defined. When the *focal variable* is fixed, we get a specific definition of efficiency in this general structure.

Efficiency comparisons can be made in terms of different variables. If, for example, advantage is seen in terms of individual utility, then the notion of efficiency immediately becomes the concept of "Pareto optimality," much used in welfare economics. This demands that the situation is such that no one's utility can be increased without cutting down the utility of someone else. But efficiency can also be similarly defined in the spaces of liberties, rights, incomes, and so on. For example, corresponding to Pareto optimality in the space of utilities, efficiency in terms of liberty would demand that the situation is such that no one's liberty can be increased without cutting down the liberty of someone else. There is, formally, an exactly similar multiplicity of efficiency notions as we have already seen for equality, related to the plurality of spaces.

This fact is not surprising, since the plurality of spaces in which equality may be considered reflects a deeper issue, viz. plurality regarding the appropriate notion of individual advantage in social comparisons. The choice between these spaces is undoubtedly an integral part of the literature of inequality evaluation. But the plurality of spaces really reflects diversities in substantive approaches to individual advantage, and in the informational base of interpersonal comparisons.

Space plurality is not a unique problem—nor of course a source of special embarrassment—for the idea of equality as such.

1.6. MEANS AND FREEDOMS

It was suggested earlier that the class of normative theories of social arrangements with which we are concerned demand—for reasons that we discussed—equality in some space or other. This equality serves as the "basal equality" of the system and has implications on the distributive patterns in the other spaces. Indeed, basal equality may be directly responsible for inequalities in the other spaces.

It may be useful to discuss an example or two of the choice of space and its importance. In modern political philosophy and ethics, the most powerful voice in recent years has been that of John Rawls (1971). His theory of "justice as fairness" provides an interesting and important example of the choice of space and its consequences. In his "Difference Principle," the analysis of efficiency and equality are both related to the individual holdings of primary goods.

With that system, the diversity of inherited wealth and of talents would not generate income inequality in the same way as in Nozick's system, since the primary goods—on the distribution of which Rawls's Difference Principle imposes an egalitarian requirement—include incomes among their constitutive elements. Incomes are, thus, directly covered in the Rawlsian demands of basal equality. But the relationship between *primary goods* (including incomes), on the one hand, and *well-being,* on the other, may vary because of personal diversities in the possibility of converting primary goods (including incomes) into achievements of well-being. For example, a pregnant woman may have to overcome disadvantages in living comfortably and well that a man at the same age need not have, even when both have exactly the same income and other primary goods.

Similarly, the relationship between *primary goods* and the *freedom* to pursue one's objectives—well-being as well as other objectives—may also vary. We differ not only in our inherited wealths, but also in our personal characteristics. Aside from purely individual variations (e.g. abilities, predispositions, physical differences), there are also systematic contrasts between groups (for example between women and men in specific respects such as the possibility of pregnancy and neonatal care of infants). With the same bundle of primary goods, a pregnant woman or one with infants to look after has much less freedom to pursue her goals than a man not thus encumbered would be able to do. The relationship between *primary goods,* on the one hand, and *freedom* as well as *well-being,* on the other, can vary with interpersonal and intergroup variations of specific characteristics.

Inequalities in different "spaces" (e.g. incomes, primary goods, liberties, utilities, other achievements, other freedoms) can be very different from each other depending on interpersonal variations in the *relations* between these distinct—but interconnected—variables. One consequence of the basic fact of human diversity is to make it particularly important to be sure of the space in which inequality is to be evaluated. Person 1 can have more utility than 2 and 3, while 2 has more income than 1 and 3, and 3 is free to do many things that 1 and 2 cannot. And so on. Even when the rankings are the same, the relative distances (i.e. the extent of the superiority of one position over another) could be very diverse in the different spaces.

Some of the most central issues of egalitarianism arise precisely because of the contrast between equality in the different spaces. The ethics of equality has to take adequate note of our pervasive diversities that affect the relations between the different spaces. The *plurality* of focal variables can make a great difference precisely because of the *diversity* of human beings.

1.7. INCOME DISTRIBUTION, WELL-BEING AND FREEDOM

Our physical and social characteristics make us immensely diverse creatures. We differ in age, sex, physical and mental health, bodily prowess, intellectual abilities, climatic circumstances, epidemiological vulnerability, social surroundings, and in many other respects. Such diversities, however, can be hard to accommodate adequately in the usual evaluative framework of inequality assessment. As a consequence, this basic issue is often left substantially unaddressed in the evaluative literature.

An important and frequently encountered problem arises from concentrating on inequality of *incomes* as the primary focus of attention in the analysis of inequality. The extent of real inequality of opportunities that people face cannot be readily deduced from the magnitude of inequality of *incomes,* since what we can or cannot do, can or cannot achieve, do not depend just on our incomes but also on the variety of physical and social characteristics that affect our lives and make us what we are.

To take a simple illustration, the extent of comparative deprivation of a physically handicapped person *vis-à-vis* others cannot be adequately judged by looking at his or her income, since the person may be greatly disadvantaged in converting income into the achievements he or she would value. The problem does not arise only from the fact that income is just a means to our real ends, but (1) from the existence of *other* important means, and (2) from interpersonal variations in the *relation* between the means and our various ends.

These issues have on the whole tended to be neglected in the literature on the measurement of inequality in economics. For example, consider the approach to constructing "inequality indices" based on social loss of equivalent income pioneered by Atkinson (1970*b*). This approach has been, in many ways, remarkably influential and productive in *integrating* considerations of income-inequality with the overall evaluation of social welfare. The extent of inequality is assessed in this approach by using the same response function $u(y)$ for *all* individuals, defined over personal incomes. This strategy of inequality measurement, thus, incorporates the restrictive feature of treating everyone's incomes symmetrically no matter what difficulties some people have compared with others in converting income into well-being and freedom.

It is, of course, true that the object of this approach is to assess inequality specifically in the distribution of *incomes,* not in levels of well-being. But that assessment is done in the light of what is *achieved* from the respective person's income, and these achievements make up the aggregate "social welfare." Income inequality is assessed by Atkinson in terms of the loss of social welfare (in units of equivalent aggregate income) as a result of inequality in the distribution of aggregate income. Given this motivation, it will in general be necessary to bring in the effects of other influences on people's lives and well-being to assess *income* inequality itself. In general the measurement of inequality has to bring in information regarding other spaces—both (1) for the purpose of evaluating inequality in these spaces *themselves,* and (2) for that of assessing *income inequality* in a broader framework, taking note of the presence of other influences on the objective (in Atkinson's case, social welfare) in terms of which income inequality is to be ultimately assessed.

The tendency to assume away interpersonal diversities can originate not only from the pragmatic temptation to make the analytics simple and easy (as in the literature of inequality measurement), but also, as was discussed earlier, from the rhetoric of equality itself (e.g. "all men are created equal"). The warm glow of such rhetoric can push us in the direction of ignoring these differences, by taking "no note of them," or by "assuming them to be absent." This suggests an apparently easy transition between one space and another, e.g. from incomes to utilities, from primary goods to freedoms, from resources to well-being. They reduce—again only *apparently*—the tension between different approaches to equality.

But that comfort is purchased at a heavy price. As a result of that assumption, we are made to overlook the substantive inequalities in, say, well-being and freedom that may directly *result* from an equal distribution of incomes (given our variable needs and disparate personal and social circumstances). Both pragmatic shortcuts and grand rhetoric can be helpful for some purposes and altogether unhelpful and misleading for others.

Robert Nozick

Equality of Opportunity

1974

Equality of opportunity has seemed to many writers to be the minimal egalitarian goal, questionable (if at all) only for being too weak. (Many writers also have seen how the existence of the family prevents fully achieving this goal.) There are two ways to attempt to provide such equality: by directly worsening the situations of those more favored with opportunity, or by improving the situation of those less well-favored. The latter requires the use of resources, and so it too involves worsening the situation of some: those from whom holdings are taken in order to improve the situation of others. But holdings to which these people are entitled may not be seized, even to provide equality of opportunity for others. In the absence of magic wands, the remaining means toward equality of opportunity is convincing persons each to choose to devote some of their holdings to achieving it.

The model of a race for a prize is often used in discussions of equality of opportunity. A race where some started closer to the finish line than others would be unfair, as would a race where some were forced to carry heavy weights, or run with pebbles in their sneakers. But life is not a race in which we all compete for a prize which someone has established; there is no unified race, with some person judging swiftness. Instead, there are different persons separately giving other persons different things. Those who do the giving (each of us, at times) usually do not care about desert or about the handicaps labored under; they care simply about what they actually get. No centralized process judges people's use of the opportunities they had; that is not what the processes of social co-operation and exchange are *for.*

There is a reason why some inequality of opportunity might seem *unfair,* rather than merely unfortunate in that some do not have every opportunity (which would be true even if no one else had greater advantage). Often the person entitled to transfer a holding has no special desire to transfer it to a particular person; this contrasts with a bequest to a child or a gift to a particular person. He chooses to transfer to someone who satisfies a certain condition (for example, who can provide him with a certain good or service in exchange, who can do a certain job, who can pay a certain salary), and he would be equally willing to transfer to anyone else who satisfied that condition. Isn't it unfair for one party to receive the transfer, rather than another who had less opportunity to satisfy the condition the transferrer used? Since the giver doesn't care to whom he transfers, provided the recipient satisfies a certain general condition, equality of opportunity to be a recipient in such circumstances would violate no entitlement of the giver. Nor would it violate any entitlement of the person with the greater opportunity; while entitled to what he has, he has no entitlement that it be more than another has. Wouldn't it be *better* if the person with less opportunity had an equal opportunity? If one so could equip him without violating anyone else's entitlements (the magic wand?) shouldn't one do so? Wouldn't it be fairer? If it *would* be fairer, can such fairness also justify overriding some people's entitlements in order to acquire the resources to boost those having poorer opportunities into a more equal competitive position?

The process is competitive in the following way. If the person with greater opportunity didn't exist,

Robert Nozick, "Equality of Opportunity," from *Anarchy, State, and Utopia.* New York: Basic Books, 1974. By permission of Basic Books.

the transferer might deal with some person having lesser opportunity who then would be, under those circumstances, the best person available to deal with. This differs from a situation in which unconnected but similar beings living on different planets confront different difficulties and have different opportunities to realize various of their goals. There, the situation of one does *not* affect that of another; though it would be better if the worse planet were better endowed than it is (it also would be better if the better planet were better endowed than *it* is), it wouldn't be *fairer.* It also differs from a situation in which a person does not, though he could, choose to *improve* the situation of another. In the particular circumstances under discussion, a person having lesser opportunities would be better off if some particular person having better opportunities didn't exist. The person having better opportunities can be viewed not merely as someone better off, or as someone not choosing to aid, but as someone *blocking* or *impeding* the person having lesser opportunities from becoming better off. Impeding another by being a more alluring alternative partner in exchange is not to be compared to directly *worsening* the situation of another, as by stealing from him. But still, cannot the person with lesser opportunity justifiably complain at being so impeded by another who does not *deserve* his better opportunity to satisfy certain conditions? (Let us ignore any similar complaints another might make about *him.*)

While feeling the power of the questions of the previous two paragraphs (it is *I* who ask them), I do not believe they overturn a thoroughgoing entitlement conception. If the woman who later became my wife rejected another suitor (whom she otherwise would have married) for me, partially because (I leave aside my lovable nature) of my keen intelligence and good looks, neither of which did I earn, would the rejected less intelligent and less handsome suitor have a legitimate complaint about unfairness? Would my thus impeding the other suitor's winning the hand of fair lady justify taking some resources from others to pay for cosmetic surgery for him and special intellectual training, or to pay to develop in him some sterling trait that I lack in order to equalize our chances of being chosen? (I here take for granted the impermissibility of worsening the situation of the person having better opportunities so as to equalize opportunity; in this sort of case by disfiguring him or injecting drugs or playing noises which prevent him from fully using his intelligence.) *No such consequences follow.* (Against whom would the rejected suitor have a legitimate complaint? Against what?) Nor are things different if the differential opportunities arise from the accumulated effects of people's acting or transferring their entitlement as they choose. The case is even easier for consumption goods which cannot plausibly be claimed to have any such triadic impeding effect. *Is* it unfair chat a child be raised in a home with a swimming pool, using it daily even though he is no more *deserving* than another child whose home is without one? Should such a situation be prohibited? Why then should there be objection to the transfer of the swimming pool to an adult by bequest?

The major objection to speaking of everyone's having a right *to* various things such as equality of opportunity, life, and so on, and enforcing this right, is that these "rights" require a substructure of things and materials and actions; and *other* people may have rights and entitlements over these. No one has a right to something whose realization requires certain uses of things and activities that other people have rights and entitlements over. Other people's rights and entitlements to *particular things* (*that* pencil, *their* body, and so on) and how they choose to exercise these rights and entitlements fix the external environment of any given individual and the means that will be available to him. If his goal requires the use of means which others have rights over, he must enlist their voluntary cooperation. Even to *exercise* his right to determine how something he owns is to be used may require other means he must acquire a right to, for example, food to keep him alive; he must put together, with the cooperation of others, a feasible package.

There are particular rights over particular things held by particular persons, and particular rights to reach agreements with others, *if* you and they together can acquire the means to reach an agreement. (No one has to supply you with a telephone so that you may reach an agreement with another.) No rights exist in conflict with this substructure of particular rights. Since no neatly contoured right to achieve a goal will avoid incompatibility with this substructure, no such rights exist. The particular rights over things fill the space of rights, leaving no room for general rights to be in a certain material condition. The reverse theory would place only such universally held general "rights to" achieve goals or to be in a certain material condition into its substructure so as to determine all else; to my knowledge no serious attempt has been made to state this "reverse" theory.

KURT VONNEGUT

Harrison Bergeron

1968

The year was 2081, and everybody was finally equal. They weren't only equal before God and the law. They were equal every which way. Nobody was smarter than anybody else. Nobody was better looking than anybody else. Nobody was stronger or quicker than anybody else. All this equality was due to the 211th, 212th, and 213th Amendments to the Constitution, and to the unceasing vigilance of agents of the United States Handicapper General.

Some things about living still weren't quite right, though. April for instance, still drove people crazy by not being springtime. And it was in that clammy month that the H-G men took George and Hazel Bergeron's fourteen-year-old son, Harrison, away.

It was tragic, all right, but George and Hazel couldn't think about it very hard. Hazel had a perfectly average intelligence, which meant she couldn't think about anything except in short bursts. And George, while his intelligence was way above normal, had a little mental handicap radio in his ear. He was required by law to wear it at all times. It was tuned to a government transmitter. Every twenty seconds or so, the transmitter would send out some sharp noise to keep people like George from taking unfair advantage of their brains.

George and Hazel were watching television. There were tears on Hazel's cheeks, but she'd forgotten for the moment what they were about.

On the television screen were ballerinas.

A buzzer sounded in George's head. His thoughts fled in panic, like bandits from a burglar alarm.

"That was a real pretty dance, that dance they just did," said Hazel.

"Huh," said George.

"That dance—it was nice," said Hazel.

"Yup," said George. He tried to think a little about the ballerinas. They weren't really very good—no better than anybody else would have been, anyway. They were burdened with sashweights and bags of birdshot, and their faces were masked, so that no one, seeing a free and graceful gesture or a pretty face, would feel like something the cat drug in. George was toying with the vague notion that maybe dancers shouldn't be handicapped. But he didn't get very far with it before another noise in his ear radio scattered his thoughts.

George winced. So did two out of the eight ballerinas.

Hazel saw him wince. Having no mental handicap herself, she had to ask George what the latest sound had been.

"Sounded like somebody hitting a milk bottle with a ball peen hammer," said George.

"I'd think it would be real interesting, hearing all the different sounds," said Hazel a little envious. "All the things they think up."

"Um," said George.

"Only, if I was Handicapper General, you know what I would do?" said Hazel. Hazel, as a matter of fact, bore a strong resemblance to the Handicapper General, a woman named Diana Moon Glampers. "If I was Diana Moon Glampers," said Hazel, "I'd have chimes on Sunday—just chimes. Kind of in honor of religion."

"I could think, if it was just chimes," said George.

"Well-maybe make 'em real loud," said Hazel. "I think I'd make a good Handicapper General."

"Good as anybody else," said George.

"Who knows better than I do what normal is?" said Hazel.

"Right," said George. He began to think glimmeringly about his abnormal son who was now in jail, about Harrison, but a twenty-one-gun salute in his head stopped that.

"Boy!" said Hazel, "that was a doozy, wasn't it?"

It was such a doozy that George was white and trembling, and tears stood on the rims of his red eyes. Two of the eight ballerinas had collapsed to the studio floor, were holding their temples.

"All of a sudden you look so tired," said Hazel. "Why don't you stretch out on the sofa, so's you can rest your handicap bag on the pillows, honeybunch." She was referring to the forty-seven pounds of birdshot in a canvas bag, which was padlocked around George's neck. "Go on and rest the bag for a little while," she said. "I don't care if you're not equal to me for a while."

George weighed the bag with his hands. "I don't mind it," he said. "I don't notice it any more. It's just a part of me."

"You been so tired lately—kind of wore out," said Hazel. "If there was just some way we could make a little hole in the bottom of the bag, and just take out a few of them lead balls. Just a few."

"Two years in prison and two thousand dollars fine for every ball I took out," said George. "I don't call that a bargain."

"If you could just take a few out when you came home from work," said Hazel. "I mean—you don't compete with anybody around here. You just sit around."

"If I tried to get away with it," said George, "then other people'd get away with it—and pretty soon we'd be right back to the dark ages again, with everybody competing against everybody else. You wouldn't like that, would you?"

"I'd hate it," said Hazel.

"There you are," said George. The minute people start cheating on laws, what do you think happens to society?"

If Hazel hadn't been able to come up with an answer to this question, George couldn't have supplied one. A siren was going off in his head.

"Reckon it'd fall all apart," said Hazel.

"What would?" said George blankly.

"Society," said Hazel uncertainly. "Wasn't that what you just said?

"Who knows?" said George.

The television program was suddenly interrupted for a news bulletin. It wasn't clear at first as to what the bulletin was about, since the announcer, like all announcers, had a serious speech impediment. For about half a minute, and in a state of high excitement, the announcer tried to say, "Ladies and Gentlemen."

He finally gave up, handed the bulletin to a ballerina to read.

"That's all right—" Hazel said of the announcer, "he tried. That's the big thing. He tried to do the best he could with what God gave him. He should get a nice raise for trying so hard."

"Ladies and Gentlemen," said the ballerina, reading the bulletin. She must have been extraordinarily beautiful, because the mask she wore was hideous. And it was easy to see that she was the strongest and most graceful of all the dancers, for her handicap bags were as big as those worn by two-hundred pound men.

And she had to apologize at once for her voice, which was a very unfair voice for a woman to use.

Her voice was a warm, luminous, timeless melody. "Excuse me—" she said, and she began again, making her voice absolutely uncompetitive.

"Harrison Bergeron, age fourteen," she said in a grackle squawk, "has just escaped from jail, where he was held on suspicion of plotting to overthrow the government. He is a genius and an athlete, is under-handicapped, and should be regarded as extremely dangerous."

A police photograph of Harrison Bergeron was flashed on the screen—upside down, then sideways, upside down again, then right side up. The picture showed the full length of Harrison against a background calibrated in feet and inches. He was exactly seven feet tall.

The rest of Harrison's appearance was Halloween and hardware. Nobody had ever borne heavier handicaps. He had outgrown hindrances faster than the H-G men could think them up. Instead of a little ear radio for a mental handicap, he wore a tremendous pair of earphones, and spectacles with thick wavy lenses. The spectacles were intended to make him not only half blind, but to give him whanging headaches besides.

Scrap metal was hung all over him. Ordinarily, there was a certain symmetry, a military neatness to the handicaps issued to strong people, but Harrison looked like a walking junkyard. In the race of life, Harrison carried three hundred pounds.

And to offset his good looks, the H-G men required that he wear at all times a red rubber ball for a nose, keep his eyebrows shaved off, and cover his even white teeth with black caps at snaggle-tooth random.

"If you see this boy," said the ballerina, "do not—I repeat, do not—try to reason with him."

There was the shriek of a door being torn from its hinges.

Screams and barking cries of consternation came from the television set. The photograph of Harrison Bergeron on the screen jumped again and again, as though dancing to the tune of an earthquake.

George Bergeron correctly identified the earthquake, and well he might have—for many was the time his own home had danced to the same crashing tune. "My God—" said George, "that must be Harrison!"

The realization was blasted from his mind instantly by the sound of an automobile collision in his head.

When George could open his eyes again, the photograph of Harrison was gone. A living, breathing Harrison filled the screen.

Clanking, clownish, and huge, Harrison stood—in the center of the studio. The knob of the uprooted studio door was still in his hand. Ballerinas, technicians, musicians, and announcers cowered on their knees before him, expecting to die.

"I am the Emperor!" cried Harrison. "Do you hear? I am the Emperor! Everybody must do what I say at once!" He stamped his foot and the studio shook.

"Even as I stand here," he bellowed, "crippled, hobbled, sickened—I am a greater ruler than any man who ever lived! Now watch me become what I can become!"

Harrison tore the straps of his handicap harness like wet tissue paper, tore straps guaranteed to support five thousand pounds.

Harrison's scrap-iron handicaps crashed to the floor.

Harrison thrust his thumbs under the bar of the padlock that secured his head harness. The bar snapped like celery. Harrison smashed his headphones and spectacles against the wall.

He flung away his rubber-ball nose, revealed a man that would have awed Thor, the god of thunder.

"I shall now select my Empress!" he said, looking down on the cowering people. "Let the first woman who dares rise to her feet claim her mate and her throne!"

A moment passed, and then a ballerina arose, swaying like a willow.

Harrison plucked the mental handicap from her ear, snapped off her physical handicaps with marvelous delicacy. Last of all he removed her mask.

She was blindingly beautiful.

"Now—" said Harrison, taking her hand, "shall we show the people the meaning of the word dance? Music!" he commanded.

The musicians scrambled back into their chairs, and Harrison stripped them of their handicaps, too. "Play your best," he told them, "and I'll make you barons and dukes and earls."

The music began. It was normal at first—cheap, silly, false. But Harrison snatched two musicians from their chairs, waved them like batons as he sang the music as he wanted it played. He slammed them back into their chairs.

The music began again and was much improved.

Harrison and his Empress merely listened to the music for a while—listened gravely, as though synchronizing their heartbeats with it.

They shifted their weights to their toes.

Harrison placed his big hands on the girl's tiny waist, letting her sense the weightlessness that would soon be hers.

And then, in an explosion of joy and grace, into the air they sprang!

Not only were the laws of the land abandoned, but the law of gravity and the laws of motion as well.

They reeled, whirled, swiveled, flounced, capered, gamboled, and spun.

They leaped like deer on the moon.

The studio ceiling was thirty feet high, but each leap brought the dancers nearer to it.

It became their obvious intention to kiss the ceiling. They kissed it.

And then, neutraling gravity with love and pure will, they remained suspended in air inches below the ceiling, and they kissed each other for a long, long time.

It was then that Diana Moon Glampers, the Handicapper General, came into the studio with a double-barreled ten-gauge shotgun. She fired twice, and the Emperor and the Empress were dead before they hit the floor.

Diana Moon Glampers loaded the gun again. She aimed it at the musicians and told them they had ten seconds to get their handicaps back on.

It was then that the Bergerons' television tube burned out.

Hazel turned to comment about the blackout to George. But George had gone out into the kitchen for a can of beer.

George came back in with the beer, paused while a handicap signal shook him up. And then he sat down again. "You been crying," he said to Hazel.

"Yup," she said.

"What about?" he said.

"I forget," she said. "Something real sad on television."

"What was it?" he said.

"It's all kind of mixed up in my mind," said Hazel.

"Forget sad things," said George.

"I always do," said Hazel.

"That's my girl," said George. He winced. There was the sound of a rivetting gun in his head.

"Gee—I could tell that one was a doozy," said Hazel.

"You can say that again," said George.

"Gee—" said Hazel, "I could tell that one was a doozy."

9 Cost-Benefit Analysis

Oscar Wilde complained that a cynic "knows the price of everything and the value of nothing," while a sentimentalist "sees an absurd value in everything." Unreflective supporters of cost-benefit analysis seem cynical, while unreflective opponents seem sentimental.

Cost-benefit analysis (CBA) is a procedure that attaches aggregate monetary values to different possible outcomes. The results are often then used as if they set a standard in light of which options with a higher aggregate monetary value are to be preferred on moral grounds. Thus CBA is often appealed to as grounds for preferring one policy proposal over another. In general, CBA leaves out of account how various costs and benefits are distributed. As Stokey and Zeckhauser famously put it, "Make a change when total income increases; don't worry about how it is distributed." Individuals often, and perhaps appropriately, use some form of CBA in making personal investment decisions. But the question at the core of this chapter is whether policymakers should use CBA as the basis for public policy decisions.

Steven Kelman concedes that CBA can be useful, but construes it as a costly process that often delivers dubious results. For one thing, Kelman maintains that CBA is a form of applied utilitarianism, which is controversial as a moral theory. Moreover, Kelman highlights a number of ways in which CBA either fails to capture everything we care about or degrades the value of things like human health or environmental goods by attaching a price to them. For example, it is hard to attach a nonarbitrary price to our desire to save an endangered whale from extinction or to prevent the Grand Canyon from becoming an amusement park with roller coasters and soda stands. The very act of attaching prices here, Kelman argues, requires thinking of these things as mere commodities, like shoes or tires, that can be traded in a market.

Elizabeth Anderson shares some of Kelman's concerns, and adds a few others. For one thing, Anderson is skeptical of attempts by social scientists to infer people's preferences (and so corresponding prices) from observing their actions, as well as attempts to impute the value those people place on outcomes by how much they pay in markets to attain them. A common argument for CBA is that we can gauge the value people place on preserving a national park like Yosemite by seeing how much they will pay for entrance fees. But Anderson thinks the preferences revealed by these actions are not especially informative. Paying a fee to see a forest may fail to reflect how much we value the continued existence of the forest. In addition, even if we could determine how much a person happens to value something that she would pay to enjoy, her values may reflect rational ignorance about the instrumental benefits it provides or how much she or others would appreciate it if they experienced it.

More broadly, it is simply the nature of public goods and cultural tokens that the preferences and values of society cannot be inferred from the private consumption behavior of citizens as consumers. These are quite different spheres of human concern, and it is by no means obvious that values measured in this sphere can be imported unchanged into another sphere. In order to elicit accurate information about public goods and cultural symbols, Anderson thinks, a different approach is required. Analysts would need to ask people about their reasons for acting, and try to figure out what preferences they would have if they were (1) better informed and (2) considering the consequences for other people, including future generations. Since informed preferences only emerge through discussion and deliberation, Anderson proposes a democratic alternative to cost-benefit analysis. On Anderson's view, we should try to construct social and political institutions that better elicit the value that informed and reflective people place on shared goods like environmental quality and worker safety.

David Schmidtz argues, contra Kelman, that CBA does not commit us to utilitarianism. Instead, at its best, CBAs can clarify the relevant trade-offs by using a single commensurable currency to evaluate different kinds of gains and losses. Schmidtz thinks it is especially useful to run CBAs in two special cases where otherwise decisions are likely to be biased or based on poor information. The first is when one group pays the cost of a regulation or program while another group gets the benefit. The second is whenever decision makers have incentives—often because of the electoral process or personal interests—not to take full costs (or benefits) into account. He concedes that some goods do have intrinsic value, and are therefore hard to price accurately. But we often face trade-offs between different intrinsically valuable goods, and we have to make the trade-off whether we like it or not. For all its flaws, CBA at least offers an approach to decision-making in situations where scarce resources have to be allocated among preserving several goods, many of which we care about intrinsically.

Finally, Schmidtz emphasizes the importance of asking who has moral standing when it comes to who will pay the costs and who will enjoy the benefits of various decisions. He argues that a complete cost-benefit analysis should consider the welfare of nonhuman animals and future people (assuming other animals and future people have interests that deserve consideration). How *much* weight to put on animals or unborn people is a contested question, but Schimdtz argues that CBAs need not be anthropocentric or myopic. As a rule of thumb, Schmidtz proposes an asymmetric standard. If a policy fails a CBA we should probably reject it. But if a policy passes a CBA that is not sufficient to show that the policy is good. Any particular cost-benefit analysis may well have left out important values that are difficult or impossible to quantify.

FURTHER READING

Adler, Matthew and Eric Posner. 2001. *Cost-Benefit Analysis: Legal, Economic, and Philosophical Perspectives.* University of Chicago Press.

Diamond, Peter and Jerry Hausman. 1994. "Contingent Valuation: Is Some Number better than No Number?" *The Journal of Economic Perspectives* 8 (4): 45–64.

Frank, Robert. 2000. "Why is Cost-Benefit Analysis So Controversial?" *The Journal of Legal Studies* 29 (S2): 913–930.

Whittington, Dale and Duncan MacRae. 1986. "The Issue of Standing in Cost-Benefit Analysis." *Journal of Policy Analysis and Management* 5 (4): 665–682.

STEVEN KELMAN

An Ethical Critique of Cost-Benefit Analysis

1981

At the broadest and vaguest level, cost-benefit analysis may be regarded simply as systematic thinking about decision-making. Who can oppose, economists sometimes ask, efforts to think in a systematic way about the consequences of different courses of action? The alternative, it would appear, is unexamined decision-making. But defining cost-benefit analysis so simply leaves it with few implications for actual regulatory decision-making. Presumably, therefore, those who urge regulators to make greater use of the technique have a more extensive prescription in mind. I assume here that their prescription includes the following views:

1. There exists a strong presumption that an act should not be undertaken unless its benefits outweigh its costs.

2. In order to determine whether benefits outweigh costs, it is desirable to attempt to express all benefits and costs in a common scale or denominator, so that they can be compared with each other, even when some benefits and costs are not traded on markets and hence have no established dollar values.

3. Getting decision-makers to make more use of cost-benefit techniques is important enough to warrant both the expense required to gather the data for improved cost-benefit estimation and the political efforts needed to give the activity higher priority compared to other activities, also valuable in and of themselves.

My focus is on cost-benefit analysis as applied to environmental, safety, and health regulation. In that context, I examine each of the above propositions from the perspective of formal ethical theory, that is, the study of what actions it is morally right to undertake. My conclusions are:

1. In areas of environmental, safety, and health regulation, there may be many instances where a certain decision might be right even though its benefits do not outweigh its costs.

2. There are good reasons to oppose efforts to put dollar values on non-marketed benefits and costs.

3. Given the relative frequency of occasions in the areas of environmental, safety, and health regulation where one would not wish to use a benefits-outweigh-costs test as a decision rule, and given the reasons to oppose the monetizing of non-marketed benefits or costs that is a prerequisite for cost-benefit analysis, it is not justifiable to devote major resources to the generation of data for cost-benefit calculations or to undertake efforts to "spread the gospel" of cost-benefit analysis further.

I

How do we decide whether a given action is morally right or wrong and hence, assuming the desire to act morally, why it should be undertaken or refrained from? Like the Molière character who spoke prose without knowing it, economists who advocate use of cost-benefit analysis for public decisions are philosophers without knowing it: the answer given by cost-benefit analysis, that actions should be undertaken so as to maximize net benefits, represents one of the classic answers given by moral philosophers—that given by utilitarians. To determine whether an action is right or wrong, utilitarians tote up all the positive consequences of the action in terms of human satisfaction. The act that maximizes attainment of satisfaction under the circumstances is the right act.

Steven Kelman, "An Ethical Critique of Cost-Benefit Analysis." *Regulation* (1981): 33–40. By permission of *Regulation*.

That the economists' answer is also the answer of one school of philosophers should not be surprising. Early on, economics was a branch of moral philosophy, and only later did it become an independent discipline.

Before proceeding further, the subtlety of the utilitarian position should be noted. The positive and negative consequences of an act for satisfaction may go beyond the act's immediate consequences. A facile version of utilitarianism would give moral sanction to a lie, for instance, if the satisfaction of an individual attained by telling the lie was greater than the suffering imposed on the lie's victim. Few utilitarians would agree. Most of them would add to the list of negative consequences the effect of the one lie on the tendency of the person who lies to tell other lies, even in instances when the lying produced less satisfaction for him than dissatisfaction for others. They would also add the negative effects of the lie on the general level of social regard for truth-telling, which has many consequences for future utility. A further consequence may be added as well. It is sometimes said that we should include in a utilitarian calculation the feeling of dissatisfaction produced in the liar (and perhaps in others) because, by telling a lie, one has "done the wrong thing." Correspondingly, in this view, among the positive consequences to be weighed into a utilitarian calculation of truth-telling is satisfaction arising from "doing the right thing." This view rests on an error, however, because it *assumes* what it is the purpose of the calculation to *determine*—that telling the truth in the instance in question is indeed the right thing to do. Economists are likely to object to this point, arguing that no feeling ought "arbitrarily" to be excluded from a complete cost-benefit calculation, including a feeling of dissatisfaction at doing the wrong thing. Indeed, the economists' cost-benefit calculations would, at least ideally, include such feelings. Note the difference between the economist's and the philosopher's cost-benefit calculations, however. The economist may choose to include feelings of dissatisfaction in his cost-benefit calculation, but what happens if somebody asks the economist, "Why is it right to evaluate an action on the basis of a cost-benefit test?" If an answer is to be given to that question (which does not normally preoccupy economists but which does concern both philosophers and the rest of us who need to be persuaded that cost-benefit analysis is right), then the circularity problem reemerges. And there is also another difficulty with counting feelings of dissatisfaction at doing the wrong thing in a cost-benefit calculation. It leads to the perverse result that under certain circumstances a lie, for example, might be morally right if the individual contemplating the lie felt no compunction about lying and morally wrong only if the individual felt such a compunction!

This error is revealing, however, because it begins to suggest a critique of utilitarianism. Utilitarianism is an important and powerful moral doctrine. But it is probably a minority position among contemporary moral philosophers. It is amazing that economists can proceed in unanimous endorsement of cost-benefit analysis as if unaware that their conceptual framework is highly controversial in the discipline from which it arose—moral philosophy.

Let us explore the critique of utilitarianism. The logical error discussed before appears to suggest that we have a notion of certain things being right or wrong that *predates* our calculation of costs and benefits. Imagine the case of an old man in Nazi Germany who is hostile to the regime. He is wondering whether he should speak out against Hitler. If he speaks out, he will lose his pension. And his action will have done nothing to increase the chances that the Nazi regime will be overthrown: he is regarded as somewhat eccentric by those around him, and nobody has ever consulted his views on political questions. Recall that one cannot add to the benefits of speaking out any satisfaction from doing "the right thing," because the purpose of the exercise is to determine whether speaking out *is* the right thing. How would the utilitarian calculation go? The benefits of the old man's speaking out would, as the example is presented, be nil, while the costs would be his loss of his pension. So the costs of the action would outweigh the benefits. By the utilitarians' cost-benefit calculation, it would be *morally wrong* for the man to speak out.

Another example: two very close friends are on an Arctic expedition together. One of them falls very sick in the snow and bitter cold, and sinks quickly before anything can be done to help him. As he is dying, he asks his friend one thing, "Please, make me a solemn promise that ten years from today you will come back to this spot and place a lighted candle here to remember me." The friend solemnly promises to do so, but does not tell a soul. Now, ten years later, the friend must decide whether to keep his promise. It would be inconvenient for him to make the long trip. Since he told nobody, his failure to go will not affect the general social faith in promise-keeping. And the incident was unique enough so that it is safe to assume that his failure to go will not encourage him to break other promises. Again, the costs of the act outweigh the benefits. A utilitarian would need to believe that it would be *morally wrong* to travel to the Arctic to light the candle.

A third example: a wave of thefts has hit a city and the police are having trouble finding any of the thieves. But they believe, correctly, that punishing someone for theft will have some deterrent effect and will decrease the number of crimes. Unable to arrest any actual perpetrator, the police chief and the prosecutor arrest a person whom they know to be innocent and, in cahoots with each other, fabricate a convincing case against him. The police chief and the prosecutor are about to retire, so the act has no effect on any future actions of theirs. The fabrication is perfectly executed, so nobody finds out about it. Is the *only* question involved in judging the act of framing the innocent man that of whether his suffering from conviction and imprisonment will be greater than the suffering avoided among potential crime victims when some crimes are deterred? A utilitarian would need to believe that it is *morally right to punish the innocent man* as long as it can be demonstrated that the suffering prevented outweighs his suffering.

And a final example: imagine two worlds, each containing the same sum total of happiness. In the first world, this total of happiness came about from a series of acts that included a number of lies and injustices (that is, the total consisted of the immediate gross sum of happiness created by certain acts, minus any long-term unhappiness occasioned by the lies and injustices). In the second world the same amount of happiness was produced by a different series of acts, none of which involved lies or injustices. Do we have any reason to prefer the one world to the other? A utilitarian would need to believe that the choice between the two worlds is a *matter of indifference*.

To those who believe that it would not be morally wrong for the old man to speak out in Nazi Germany or for the explorer to return to the Arctic to light a candle for his deceased friend, that it would not be morally right to convict the innocent man, or that the choice between the two worlds is not a matter of indifference—to those of us who believe these things, utilitarianism is insufficient as a moral view. We believe that some acts whose costs are greater than their benefits may be morally right and, contrariwise, some acts whose benefits are greater than their costs may be morally wrong.

This does not mean that the question whether benefits are greater than costs is morally irrelevant. Few would claim such. Indeed, for a broad range of individual and social decisions, whether an act's benefits outweigh its costs is a sufficient question to ask. But not for all such decisions. These may involve situations where certain duties—duties not to lie, break promises, or kill, for example—make an act wrong, even if it would result in an excess of benefits over costs. Or they may involve instances where people's rights are at stake. We would not permit rape even if it could be demonstrated that the rapist derived enormous happiness from his act, while the victim experienced only minor displeasure. We do not do cost-benefit analyses of freedom of speech or trial by jury. As the United Steelworkers noted in a comment on the Occupational Safety and Health Administration's economic analysis of its proposed rule to reduce worker exposure to carcinogenic coke-oven emissions, the Emancipation Proclamation was not subjected to an inflationary impact statement. The notion of human rights involves the idea that people may make certain claims to be allowed to act in certain ways or to be treated in certain ways, even if the sum of benefits achieved thereby does not outweigh the sum of costs. It is this view that underlies the statement that "workers have a right to a safe and healthy work place" and the expectation that OSHA's decisions will reflect that judgment.

In the most convincing versions of non-utilitarian ethics, various duties or rights are not absolute. But each has a *prima facie* moral validity so that, if duties or rights do not conflict, the morally right act is the act that reflects a duty or respects a right. If duties or rights do conflict, a moral judgment, based on conscious deliberation, must be made. Since one of the duties non-utilitarian philosophers enumerate is the duty of beneficence (the duty to maximize happiness), which in effect incorporates all of utilitarianism by reference, a non-utilitarian who is faced with conflicts between the results of cost-benefit analysis and non-utility-based considerations will need to undertake such deliberation. But in that deliberation, additional elements, which cannot be reduced to a question of whether benefits outweigh costs, have been introduced. Indeed, depending on the moral importance we attach to the right or duty involved, cost-benefit questions may, within wide ranges, become irrelevant to the outcome of the moral judgment.

In addition to questions involving duties and rights, there is a final sort of question where, in my view, the issue of whether benefits outweigh costs should not govern moral judgment. I noted earlier that, for the common run of questions facing individuals and societies, it is possible to begin and end our judgment simply by finding out if the benefits of the contemplated act outweigh the costs. This very fact means that one way to show the great importance, or value, attached to an area is to say that decisions involving the area should not be determined by cost-benefit calculations. This applies, I think, to the view many environmentalists have of decisions involving our natural environment. When officials are deciding what level of pollution will harm certain vulnerable people—such as asthmatics or the elderly—while not harming others, one issue involved may be the right of those people not to be sacrificed on the altar of somewhat higher living standards for the rest of us. But more broadly than this, many environmentalists fear that subjecting decisions about clean air or water to the cost-benefit tests that determine the general run of decisions removes those matters from the realm of specially valued things.

II

In order for cost-benefit calculations to be performed the way they are supposed to be, all costs and benefits must be expressed in a common measure, typically dollars, including things not normally bought and sold on markets, and to which dollar prices are therefore not attached. The most dramatic example of such things is human life itself; but many of the other benefits achieved or preserved by environmental policy—such as peace and quiet, fresh-smelling air, swimmable rivers, spectacular vistas—are not traded on markets either.

Economists who do cost-benefit analysis regard the quest after dollar values for nonmarket things as a difficult challenge—but one to be met with relish. They have tried to develop methods for imputing a person's "willingness to pay" for such things, their approach generally involving a search for bundled goods that *are* traded on markets and that vary as to whether they include a feature that is, *by itself,* not marketed. Thus, fresh air is not marketed, but houses in different parts of Los Angeles that are similar except for the degree of smog are. Peace and quiet is not marketed, but similar houses inside and outside airport flight paths are. The risk of death is not marketed, but similar jobs that have different levels of risk are. Economists have produced many often ingenious efforts to impute dollar prices to non-marketed things by observing the premiums accorded homes in clean air areas over similar homes in dirty areas or the premiums paid for risky jobs over similar non-risky jobs.

These ingenious efforts are subject to criticism on a number of technical grounds. It may be difficult to control for all the dimensions of quality other than the presence or absence of the non-marketed thing. More important, in a world where people have different preferences and are subject to different constraints as they make their choices, the dollar value imputed to the non-market things that most people would wish to avoid will be lower than otherwise, because people with unusually weak aversion to those things or unusually strong constraints on their choices will be willing to take the bundled good in question at less of a discount than the average person. Thus, to use the property value discount of homes near airports as a measure of people's willingness to pay for quiet means to accept as a proxy for the rest of us the behavior of those least sensitive to noise, of airport employees (who value the convenience of a near-airport location) or of others who are susceptible to an agent's assurances that "it's not so bad." To use the wage premiums accorded hazardous work as a measure of the value of life means to accept as proxies for the rest of us the choices of people who do not have many choices or who are exceptional risk-seekers.

A second problem is that the attempts of economists to measure people's willingness to pay for nonmarketed things assume that there is no difference between the price a person would require for *giving up* something to which he has a preexisting right and the price he would pay to *gain* something to which he enjoys no right. Thus, the analysis assumes no difference between how much a homeowner would need to be paid in order to give up an unobstructed mountain view that he already enjoys and how much he would be willing to pay to get an obstruction moved once it is already in place. Available evidence suggests that most people would insist on being paid far more to assent to a worsening of their situation than they would be willing to pay to improve their situation. The difference arises from such factors as being accustomed to and psychologically attached to that which one believes one enjoys by right. But this creates a circularity problem for any attempt to use cost-benefit analysis to determine *whether* to assign to, say, the homeowner the right to an unobstructed mountain view. For willingness to pay will be different depending on whether the right is assigned initially or not. The value judgment about whether to assign the right must thus be made first. (In order to set an upper bound on the value of the benefit, one might hypothetically assign the right to the person and determine how much he would need to be paid to give it up.)

Third, the efforts of economists to impute willingness to pay invariably involve bundled goods exchanged in *private* transactions. Those who use figures garnered from such analysis to provide guidance for *public* decisions assume no difference between how people value certain things in private individual transactions and how they would wish those same things to be valued in public collective decisions. In making such assumptions, economists insidiously slip into their analysis an important and controversial value judgment, growing naturally out of the highly individualistic microeconomic tradition—namely, the view that there should be no difference between private behavior and the behavior we display in public social life. An alternative view—one that enjoys, I would suggest, wide resonance among citizens—would be that public, social decisions provide an opportunity to give certain things a higher valuation than we choose, for one reason or another, to give them in our private activities.

Thus, opponents of stricter regulation of health risks often argue that we show by our daily risk-taking behavior that we do not value life infinitely, and therefore our public decisions should not reflect the high value of life that proponents of strict regulation propose. However, an alternative view is equally plausible. Precisely because we fail, for whatever reasons, to give life-saving the value in everyday personal decisions that we in some general terms believe we should give it, we may wish our social decisions to provide us the occasion to display the reverence for life that we espouse but do not always show. By this view, people do not have fixed unambiguous "preferences" to which they give expression through private activities and which therefore should be given expression in public decisions. Rather, they may have what they themselves regard as "higher" and "lower" preferences. The latter may come to the fore in private decisions, but people may want the former to come to the fore in public decisions. They may sometimes display racial prejudice, but support antidiscrimination laws. They may buy a certain product after seeing a seductive ad, but be skeptical enough of advertising to want the government to keep a close eye on it. In such cases, the use of private behavior to impute the values that should be entered for public decisions, as is done by using willingness to pay in private transactions, commits grievous offense against a view of the behavior of the citizen that is deeply engrained in our democratic tradition. It is a view that denudes politics of any independent role in society, reducing it to a mechanistic, mimicking recalculation based on private behavior.

Finally, one may oppose the effort to place prices on a non-market thing and hence in effect incorporate it into the market system out of a fear that the very act of doing so will reduce the thing's perceived value. To place a price on the benefit may, in other words, reduce the value of that benefit. Cost-benefit analysis thus may be like the thermometer that, when placed in a liquid to be measured, itself changes the liquid's temperature.

Examples of the perceived cheapening of a thing's value by the very act of buying and selling it abound in everyday life and language. The disgust that accompanies the idea of buying and selling human beings is based on the sense that this would dramatically diminish human worth. Epithets such as "he prostituted himself," applied as linguistic analogies to people who have sold something, reflect the view that certain things should not be sold because doing so diminishes their value. Praise that is bought is worth little, even to the person buying it. A true anecdote is told of an economist who retired to another university community and complained that he was having difficulty making friends. The laconic response of a critical colleague—"If you want a friend why don't you buy yourself one"—illustrates in a pithy way the intuition that, for some things, the very act of placing a price on them reduces their perceived value.

The first reason that pricing something decreases its perceived value is that, in many circumstances, non-market exchange is associated with the production of certain values not associated with market exchange. These may include spontaneity and various other feelings that come from personal relationships. If a good becomes less associated with the production of positively valued feelings because of market exchange, the perceived value of the good declines to the extent that those feelings are valued. This can be seen clearly in instances where a thing may be transferred both by market and by non-market mechanisms. The willingness to pay for sex bought from a prostitute is less than the perceived value of the sex consummating love. (Imagine the reaction if a practitioner of cost-benefit analysis computed the benefits of sex based on the price of prostitute services.)

Furthermore, if one values in a general sense the existence of a non-market sector because of its connection with the production of certain valued feelings, then one ascribes added value to any nonmarketed good simply as a repository of values represented by the nonmarket sector one wishes to preserve. This seems certainly to be the case for things in nature, such as pristine streams or undisturbed forests: for many people who value them, part of their value comes from their position as repositories of values the non-market sector represents.

The second way in which placing a market price on a thing decreases its perceived value is by removing the possibility of proclaiming that the thing is "not for sale," since things on the market by definition are for sale. The very statement that something is not for sale affirms, enhances, and protects a thing's value in a number of ways. To begin with, the statement is a way of showing that a thing is valued for its own sake, whereas selling a thing for money demonstrates that it was valued only instrumentally. Furthermore, to say that something cannot be transferred in that way places it in the exceptional category—which requires the person interested in obtaining that thing to be able to offer something else that is exceptional, rather than allowing him the easier alternative of obtaining the thing for money that could have been obtained in an infinity of ways. This enhances its value. If I am willing to say "You're a really kind person" to whoever pays me to do so, my praise loses the value that attaches to it from being exchangeable only for an act of kindness.

In addition, if we have already decided we value something highly, one way of stamping it with a cachet affirming its high value is to announce that it is "not for sale." Such an announcement does more, however, than just reflect a preexisting high valuation. It signals a thing's distinctive value to others and helps us persuade them to value the thing more highly than they otherwise might. It also expresses our resolution to safeguard that distinctive value. To state that something is not for sale is thus also a source of value for that thing, since if a thing's value is easy to affirm or protect, it will be worth more than an otherwise similar thing without such attributes.

If we proclaim that something is not for sale, we make a once-and-for-all judgment of its special value. When something is priced, the issue of its perceived value is constantly coming up, as a standing invitation to reconsider that original judgment. Were people constantly faced with questions such as "how much money could get you to give up your freedom of speech?" or "how much would you sell your vote for if you could?", the perceived value of the freedom to speak or the right to vote would soon become devastated as, in moments of weakness, people started saying "maybe it's not worth *so much* after all." Better not to be faced with the constant questioning in the first place. Something similar did in fact occur when the slogan "better red than dead" was launched by some pacifists during the Cold War. Critics pointed out that the very posing of this stark choice—in effect, "would you *really* be willing to give up your life in exchange for not living under communism?"—reduced the value people attached to freedom and thus diminished resistance to attacks on freedom.

Finally, of some things valued very highly it is stated that they are "priceless" or that they have "infinite value." Such expressions are reserved for a subset of things not for sale, such as life or health. Economists tend to scoff at talk of pricelessness. For them, saying that something is priceless is to state a willingness to trade off an infinite quantity of all other goods for one unit of the priceless good, a situation that empirically appears highly unlikely. For most people, however, the word priceless is pregnant with meaning. Its value-affirming and value-protecting functions cannot be bestowed on expressions that merely denote a determinate, albeit high, valuation. John Kennedy in his inaugural address proclaimed that the nation was ready to "pay any price [and] bear any burden . . . to assure the survival and the success of liberty." Had he said instead that we were willing to "pay a high price" or "bear a large burden" for liberty, the statement would have rung hollow.

III

An objection that advocates of cost-benefit analysis might well make to the preceding argument should be considered. I noted earlier that, in cases where various non-utility-based duties or rights conflict with the maximization of utility, it is necessary to make a deliberative judgment about what act is finally right. I also argued earlier that the search for commensurability might not always be a desirable one, that the attempt to go beyond expressing benefits in terms of (say) lives saved and costs in terms of dollars is not something devoutly to be wished.

In situations involving things that are not expressed in a common measure, advocates of cost-benefit analysis argue that people making judgments "in effect" perform cost-benefit calculations anyway. If government regulators promulgate a regulation that saves 100 lives at a cost of $1 billion, they are "in effect" valuing a life at (a minimum of) $10 million, whether or not they say that they are willing to place a dollar value on a human life. Since, in this view, cost-benefit analysis "in effect" is inevitable, it might as well be made specific.

This argument misconstrues the real difference in the reasoning processes involved. In cost-benefit analysis, equivalencies are established *in advance* as one of the raw materials for the calculation. One determines costs and benefits, one determines equivalencies (to be able to put various costs and benefits into a common measure), and then one sets to toting things up—waiting, as it were, with bated breath for the results of the calculation to come out. The outcome is determined by the arithmetic; if the outcome is a close call or if one is not good at long division, one does not know how it will turn out until the calculation is finished. In the kind of deliberative judgment that is performed without a common measure, no establishment of equivalencies occurs in advance. Equivalencies are not aids to the decision process. In fact, the decision-maker might not even be aware of what the "in effect" equivalencies were, at least before they are revealed to him afterwards by someone pointing out what he had "in effect" done. The decision-maker would see himself as simply having made a deliberative judgment; the "in effect" equivalency number did not play a causal role in the decision but at most merely reflects it. Given this, the argument against making the process explicit is the one discussed earlier in the discussion of problems with putting specific quantified values on things that are not normally quantified—that the very act of doing so may serve to reduce the value of those things.

My own judgment is that modest efforts to assess levels of benefits and costs are justified, although I do not believe that government agencies ought to sponsor efforts to put dollar prices on non-market things. I also do not believe that the cry for more cost-benefit analysis in regulation is, on the whole, justified. If regulatory officials were so insensitive about regulatory costs that they did not provide acceptable raw material for deliberative judgments (even if not of a strictly cost-benefit nature), my conclusion might be different. But a good deal of research into costs and benefits already occurs—actually, far more in the U.S. regulatory process than in that of any other industrial society. The danger now would seem to come more from the other side.

ELIZABETH ANDERSON

Cost-Benefit Analysis, Safety, and Environmental Quality

1995

9.1 COST-BENEFIT ANALYSIS AS A FORM OF COMMODIFICATION

A good does not have to be traded on the market or privately owned to be treated as a commodity. Governments can treat public goods as commodities by regulating their protection according to market norms. Cost-benefit analysis, a technique for evaluating public policies which is widely promoted by economists, is one main way governments can do this. In this chapter I examine the application of cost-benefit analysis to public policies concerning the protection of human life and environmental quality. I will argue that these goods are not properly regarded as mere commodities. By regarding them only as commodity values, cost-benefit analysis fails to consider the proper roles they occupy in public life.

Cost-benefit analysis rests on two basic normative claims. First, it says that public policies ought to maximize efficiency. A state of affairs is Pareto efficient if and only if all opportunities for improving the welfare of any person without harming another have been exhausted. A policy makes a Pareto improvement if and only if it makes at least one person better off without making anyone worse off. A policy makes a potential Pareto improvement if and only if it produces gains that could be redistributed to make an actual Pareto improvement. Potential Pareto improvements make some people so much better off that they could fully compensate those made worse off and still come out ahead. Cost-benefit analysis recommends public policies that maximize potential Pareto improvements. This recommendation raises three questions. Why maximize efficiency rather than welfare? Economists answer that they have not yet found a satisfactory criterion for interpersonal

Elizabeth Anderson, "Cost-Benefit Analysis, Safety, and Environmental Quality," from Elizabeth Anderson, *Value in Ethics and Economics*. Cambridge, MA: Harvard University Press, 1995. By permission of Harvard University Press.

welfare comparisons. The only unambiguous welfare improvements are captured by the efficiency criteria. Why maximize potential rather than actual Pareto improvements? Every public policy inevitably makes at least one individual worse off than she was before, so the actual Pareto improvement criterion fails to discriminate among better and worse policies. But potential Pareto improvements still arguably increase net welfare, because they generate more wealth than would be needed to fully compensate the losers. Why ignore the distribution of gains from public policies? The potential Pareto improvement criterion is indifferent to distributional questions, for it neither considers the distributional effects of alternatives nor demands that compensation of losers actually take place. If distribution matters, the government can still use the potential Pareto improvement criterion and make lump-sum transfers to disadvantaged individuals from general revenues.

The second basic normative claim of cost-benefit analysis is that welfare be measured by an individual's "compensating variation." The compensating variation of an individual for a project is defined as the maximum sum of money she will pay to bring about the project, if she wants it to take place, or the minimum sum of money she will accept to put up with the project, if she does not want it to take place. I will call this measure of value the "willingness-to-pay" scale. Cost-benefit analysis claims that the best policy maximizes the sum of compensating variations of all affected individuals. Such a policy would maximize potential Pareto improvements if people are willing to accept that everything they value which is affected by the policy has a monetary equivalent.

Consider the implications of using cost-benefit analysis to choose policies regarding public health, safety, and environmental quality. The ideology of cost-benefit analysis regards these goods as commodity values at three levels of analysis. First, it claims that public policies for these goods are justified only because competitive markets for them cannot be established. Second, it claims that public policy should aim to mimic the outcomes competitive markets in these goods would achieve, were such markets possible. Public policies recommended by cost-benefit analysis are justified on grounds analogous to those that justify markets. Third, it measures the values of goods by inferring individuals' compensating variations in market interactions. By taking individuals' private market choices as normative for public policy, and by imputing a consumerist interpretation on how individuals view their choices, cost-benefit analysis accepts market norms for enjoying, distributing, and choosing goods as normative for public policy.

The theory of market failure provides the economic rationale for involving the state in protecting public, safety and environmental quality. Markets do not produce efficient outcomes when market transactions impose welfare changes or "externalities" on third parties. They also fail to produce or protect sufficient quantities of public goods—goods which can be provided to one person only on condition that others have access to them as well. No one in the affected area can be excluded from enjoying a reduction in air pollution or improved safety resulting from flood-control dams. Because access to these benefits cannot be restricted to those who pay for them, it will be unprofitable for individuals to try to provide them on a private market basis. And since no one has private property in the air, rivers, and oceans, individuals treat these goods as free resources, using them as dumping grounds for wastes and imposing negative externalities on the public. In the absence of government intervention, polluters will not be forced to pay the costs they impose on third parties and, consequently, will produce more than an "optimal" amount of pollution.

The theory of market failure is a theory not of what is wrong with markets, but of what goes wrong when markets are not available: it is a theory of what goes wrong when goods are not commodified. If cheaply enforceable private property rights and competitive markets with low transaction costs in public goods could be created, the theory recommends that this be done. It assumes that the optimal magnitudes and distributions of safety and environmental quality are those that would be produced by competitive markets, if markets in these goods were feasible. Because they aren't, governments should use cost-benefit analysis to generate the outcomes markets would produce if risks to life and environmental damage were private bads. Cost-benefit analysis is the state's way of mimicking the consequences of market transactions.

Economists argue that the outcomes produced by competitive markets are desirable for three reasons. First, such markets are Pareto efficient. Second, they are produced by voluntary exchanges. There is a strong moral presumption in favor of permitting outcomes to which the affected parties have consented. Third, the fact that these outcomes are voluntarily accepted is thought to show that the parties think they have received fair compensation for them. The state's use of cost-benefit analysis to mimic market outcomes has analogous virtues. The outcomes recommended by cost-benefit analysis are *potentially* Pareto efficient. Because these out-comes are efficient, they are thought to enjoy the *hypothetical* consent of everyone. Before knowing how the distribution of costs and benefits will affect individuals, everyone would consent to a scheme of costs and benefits that yields more net benefits than the alternatives. Finally, the consent of each person to such a scheme is thought to imply that she regards herself as compensated *ex ante* for the risks it imposes on herself (Posner 1980; Leonard and Zeckhauser 1985).

Cost-benefit analysis imitates the market by measuring the values of goods by individuals' willingness to pay for them. These figures are usually derived from studies of market transactions in which individuals trade off commodified versions of these goods against money. For example, the amount of money people pay for access to private parks, or the additional housing costs they pay for a scenic view from their windows, is used to measure the cash value of national parks and public vistas. The supposedly higher wages people accept for working at hazardous jobs are used to measure the cash value people are thought to implicitly place on their own lives. Cost-benefit analysis takes such market-determined prices for exclusively appropriated environmental goods and workplace safety and applies them to cases where the environmental goods in question are public or where the risks imposed on people are involuntarily imposed externalities. Use of the same prices in public and private contexts is justified on the grounds that people should exhibit consistent tradeoffs in all domains. Market choices are made normative for public choices because individuals' market choices are thought to reveal their authentic preferences better than the valuations they express in questionnaires or public debate.

Thus, cost-benefit analysis treats health, safety, and environmental quality as commodities in its procedures of justification and evaluation. A good is treated as a commodity if it is valued as an exclusively appropriated object of use and if market norms and relations govern its production, exchange, and distribution. Cost-benefit analysis assumes that people value safety and the environment as commodities in three ways. It measures people's valuations of these goods in market transactions and hence, only as they are valued as privately appropriated, exclusively enjoyed goods. This assumes that the public nature of some instances of these goods is merely a technical fact about them and not itself a valued quality. The possibility that national parks and public safety might be valued as shared goods does not enter into its evaluations. By accounting for the values of environmental quality and safety only through their cash "equivalents," cost-benefit analysis also assumes that these goods are substitutable with any alternative commodity bundles that can be purchased for the same price. This ignores the possibility that goods such as endangered species may be specially valued as unique and irreplaceable higher goods. The distinction between higher and lower goods, which supports norms that prohibit certain tradeoffs between them, plays no part in the analysis. Finally, cost-benefit analysis assumes that the preferences people express in private consumer choices should be normative for public choice, as if the valuations people make as consumers exhaust their concerns. Market failure can be analyzed as a failure to have markets only if all goods are mere commodities and different institutional mechanisms for producing and distributing these goods serve the same function of indiscriminate want-satisfaction that the market is supposed to serve. This assumes that people adequately express their valuations of goods only through satisfying their unexamined preferences.

By taking market prices and outcomes as the standard for public deliberation about safety and environmental quality, cost-benefit analysis allows market norms to govern decisions concerning safety and the environment. Markets are responsive only to given wants, without evaluating the reasons people have for wanting the goods in question, which may be based on ideals or principles. By using market valuations to guide public policies, cost-benefit analysis assumes that ideals, needs, and principles have no distinctive role to play with regard to safety and the environment. Markets respond to wants in proportion to individuals' willingness to pay for their satisfaction. By accepting market willingness-to-pay as a measure of value, cost-benefit analysis assumes that the influence of one's valuations should be determined by the money one is willing to pay to promote them, rather than by how well they stand up in public debate. This measure of value also weights the preferences of those with larger incomes more heavily than the preferences of those with smaller incomes. Because the power of an individual to promote her interests is a function of her financial resources and competitive position, cost-benefit analysis implicitly assumes that the state should reproduce in its public decisions the consequences of letting people with vastly unequal powers of self-protection fend for themselves. Markets generate prices for goods on the supposition that the parties to a market exchange have no pre-contractual obligations to provide them. By taking market-determined valuations as normative for public choice, cost-benefit analysis accepts this supposition. Finally, the market provides individuals with an avenue for expressing their valuations primarily through exit, not voice. Cost-benefit analysis ignores information about individuals' valuations discoverable only through voice and provides no integrated mechanism for enabling people to express valuations of goods that essentially require voice.

I reject all of the above assumptions that cost-benefit analysis makes about the modes of valuation and norms properly applicable to public safety and the environment. Critics of cost-benefit analysis have challenged these assumptions. I will show how such challenges can be persuasively grounded and integrated into a pluralist theory of value and rational choice that rejects universal commodification and poses substantial limits to the scope of markets. The arguments made here do not imply that cost-benefit analysis is an inappropriate tool for all public decisions. I object to the use of cost-benefit analysis in choices involving human lives and environmental quality because these goods are not properly regarded as commodities. But this tool may be appropriate for decisions involving goods that are properly regarded as mere commodities.

9.2 AUTONOMY, LABOR MARKETS, AND THE VALUE OF LIFE

Cost-benefit analysts claim to adequately represent the value of human life for public policy purposes by means of a cash equivalent. They argue that if we are to behave rationally, we must assign a cash value to risks to life. This argument is based on the assumption that the need to choose between two goods demands that we find some common measure of their values. Money offers the most practical common measure of the value of life in relation to other benefits. Of course no monetary value can be placed on the certain loss of one's life. Few people would accept any amount of money in return for certain death the next day. Rather, the willingness-to-pay criterion claims to measure the value of avoiding a determinate statistical probability of losing one's life.

An individual's willingness to pay for a marginal change in her risk of death may be discovered by her verbal responses or by inference from her market choices. Most economists and cost-benefit analysts distrust individuals' responses to questionnaires because people often either can't say what they would do when offered an abstract option of trading a small chance of death for money or give inconsistent answers. This problem is attributed to the fact that people generally can't handle very large or very small numbers. They may also have strategic reasons for misrepresenting the value they place on their lives. For example, if they suspect that their answers will be used to force a chemical firm to compensate its neighbors for the health risks it imposes through air pollution emissions, they might be tempted to overstate their compensating variations.

Economists prefer to infer individuals' willingness to pay for marginal risks to their lives from the tradeoffs between safety and money they actually make in their market choices. These figures are usually derived from an analysis of wage differentials between more and less hazardous jobs. Cost-benefit analysis assumes that people implicitly place a cash value on their lives when they trade off risks to them for money in choosing among jobs. If they did not believe their wages compensated them for their workplace risks, they could quit and find a less risky job. The pressure of exit from hazardous jobs forces firms to raise wages to attract enough workers. In competitive equilibrium with labor mobility and full information, wage differentials measure people's "revealed preferences" for safety and income—what they are willing to pay in reduced wages for avoiding job related hazards. Cost-benefit analysis takes such, market-determined prices of safety and applies them to contexts in which risks are not voluntarily accepted, on the presumption that one should pay the same amount to avoid a given risk wherever it occurs.

Attempts to estimate the monetary value individuals purportedly place on their lives have run into empirical difficulties. Different studies have produced inconsistent estimates of the value of life, ranging from a low of $15,000 to a high of $10,000,000 (Viscusi 1983; Mishan 1985). Economists have tried to explain these discrepancies by arguing that different industries attract individuals with different tastes for risk (Viscusi 1983). Furthermore, an individual's willingness to pay for a given quantum of risk reduction increases with the total magnitude of risk, but increases less than proportionally to the magnitude of the reduction. Individuals will pay much more to reduce the risk of death from 3/10 to 2/10 than from 2/10 to 1/10, but they will also pay for a risk reduction of 1/10,000 much more than one-tenth the amount they will pay to reduce a risk by 1/1,000 (Mishan 1985). As we shall see, these variables do not explain the most important differences in individuals' evaluations of risk reduction, which depend on the social context in which the risks are encountered.

Even if empirical studies yielded a consistent "value of life," the normative significance of this figure would remain in doubt. Such studies can at best tell us what workers actually pay in wage reductions for incremental reductions in workplace risks. But statistics about how much money people ("reveal" they are "willing" to) pay for safety have the normative significance claimed for them only if they reflect people's free, informed, autonomous consent to market-generated outcomes, based on the judgments that they have been fairly compensated for the costs imposed upon them and that the same risk/money tradeoff has the same value or acceptability, regardless of the social context in which it occurs. Willingness-to-pay statistics can support this interpretation only if the following assumptions are true.

First, workers must be free to choose without duress. This requires that workers are mobile and see themselves as having a significant range of worthwhile alternatives to the choice they actually make. Second, workers' choices must reflect deliberation upon full information about the risks they encounter. This requires not only that information be available to workers, but that they fulfill the internal conditions of autonomy necessary for them to make good use of this information. Third, workers' choices must express their own valuations, not the valuations others make of their lives. This requires that workers enjoy the external conditions for autonomy. Fourth, they must choose egoistically, with concern only for their own welfare, when they make wage/risk tradeoffs. This requires that workers' job choices not be motivated by any sense of moral obligation, personal responsibility, or benevolence, which moves them to sacrifice their own welfare for the sake of others. (If they are so motivated, then their wage premiums cannot be interpreted as fully compensating them for their personal sacrifices, and so will underestimate their welfare losses resulting from the risks they encounter.) Fifth, workers must care only about the relative magnitudes of risk/money tradeoffs in evaluating the acceptability of risks. This requires that they find the same risk/money tradeoffs in different social contexts equally acceptable.

Market norms and social relations do not supply an adequate context for people to autonomously express how they value their lives. Cost-benefit analysis therefore does not supply an adequate framework for evaluating public policies that involve risks to human life. This conclusion depends in part on the importance of securing the conditions for autonomy, which are often lacking in the context of workplace risk-taking. Can the case against cost-benefit analysis be expanded to cover goods where the autonomy of individuals' market choices over them is not as much in question? The next section provides distinct grounds for opposing the application of cost-benefit analysis to environmental goods.

9.3 CITIZENS, CONSUMERS, AND THE VALUE OF THE ENVIRONMENT

The case for using cost-benefit analysis to deal with environmental goods appears stronger than the case for using it to deal with matters of life and health. Whereas we neither have a market in human lives nor regard human beings primarily as economic resources, we do have markets in land, water, animals, and natural resources. Our dominant relations to these things are economic. The choices people make as consumers of environmental goods are arguably more autonomous than the choices people make as sellers of their labor power. Nevertheless, cost-benefit analysis does not adequately represent the ways people value environmental goods. It also fails to provide a suitable framework for deliberating about the conflicting ideals concerning our relationship to nature that inform the political and moral debates about preservation and development.

As it does with the value of life, cost-benefit analysis measures the value of environmental goods in terms of the amount of money individuals are willing to pay for them. Some goods of the environment, such as forests and mines, are economic goods with explicit market values. But so-called amenity values, such as scenic views, clear skies, national parks, endangered species, and diverse, stable ecosystems have no explicit market value because they are public goods. Economists claim that individuals' market choices give an indirect indication of the value they place on environmental amenities. The amenity may be a perfect substitute for a privately marketed good. The demand for the privately marketed good can then serve as a monetary measure of the value individuals place on the public good. For instance, opportunities for swimming, hiking, and camping are both publicly and privately available. A monetary measure of a decline in the quality of a public recreational area as a result of air, land, or water pollution can be inferred from the decline in demand for private recreational areas suffering from equivalent deterioration. Since environmental quality varies by region, the value individuals place on opportunities to consume clean air, the solitude afforded by surrounding wilderness, natural beauty, and so forth are also reflected in residential land prices and in the wages people are willing to sacrifice for living in areas with more attractive environments but fewer economic opportunities.

The crucial assumption behind this economic analysis of environmental goods is that the ways people value the environment when acting in their roles as consumers and producers exhaust the ways they care about it. Only if this is true is it proper to make their valuations of the environment on their market choices normative for public choice. If people have concerns about the environment that cannot be adequately expressed through market norms and commodity consumption, willingness-to-pay statistics will not capture them. Cost-benefit analysts make three assumptions about how consumers value commodities which they apply to their evaluation of environmental amenities. First, consumers seek to advance their personal welfare in purchasing commodities. Therefore, if environmental goods are just like commodities, their value is instrumental and consists in their uses for promoting human welfare. Second, commodities advance an individual's welfare best when she can privately appropriate them for her personal use. This follows from the fact that their value is a kind of use-value, realized in subordinating it to an individual's purposes, which are assumed to be definable and satisfiable independent of others' purposes. When access to a good is not limited, individuals tend to use it at cross-purposes. The market price of a good reflects how much people value it for exclusive use. If environmental goods are just commodities, then inferred market prices for them will effectively capture how much individuals value them. Third, as mere use-values, commodities are indifferently substitutable for any other bundle of goods with the same market price. If environmental goods are mere commodities, they should be comprehensively subject to tradeoffs against other commodities. This norm contrasts with norms for valuing higher goods, which prohibit some tradeoffs between higher and lower goods.

Cost-benefit analysts also make a crucial assumption about the regard public policy should have for individuals' values. Respect for an individual's values in the market sphere is expressed by satisfying her wants in proportion to the amount of money she is willing to put behind them, without questioning her reasons for having those wants. If people value the environment just as they value pure commodities, then this is also thought to be the way public bodies should express respect for individual concerns about the environment. Each of these assumptions about the ways people value the environment, and about how we should treat people's values in public policy formation, are subject to challenge.

Consider the claim that people value environmental goods only extrinsically, for their contribution to human welfare. Certainly, these goods contribute enormously to human welfare. But people value environmental goods in ways other than use: we admire many wild animals, feel wonder and awe at spectacular storms and volcanic eruptions, demand consideration for delicate ecosystems, appreciate mountains and seascapes for their beauty. These attitudes are intrinsic evaluative attitudes. It makes sense for us to take up these attitudes toward wild animals, ecosystems, natural wonders, and so forth independent of our caring about any other particular things or people. Many people dedicate themselves to preserving and protecting these goods for their own sakes, even at significant cost to their own welfare. And they care about preserving the pristine character of parts of the biosphere, such as the Antarctic, which few people will visit or use. The ways they care about these goods are independent of their concern for human welfare.

Some people strongly resist this conclusion. Most of the resistance is due to confusion in the theory of value. Some people hold that only things that care about other things are intrinsically valuable. The things they care about which don't care about other things are merely instrumentally valuable. This argument poses a false dichotomy between intrinsic and instrumental goods. One could choose to define intrinsic goods as the things that, in caring about other non-caring things, provide the conditions for the latter's being extrinsically valuable. This definition would make inanimate nature extrinsically good. But it would not follow that it is merely of instrumental value, since it can still make sense to care about it for its own sake. The condition of its being valuable, on this definition, is just that people sensibly care about it. People needn't care about it for the ways it serves human interests. We care about some things that are incapable of valuing anything independent of whether they serve our interests or purposes. Other theorists worry that to regard the environment as intrinsically valuable is to imply that human rights may be violated to protect it (McCloskey 1983). Some environmentalists, in their rush to protect goods such as forests and seals, have failed to take seriously the welfare and autonomy of indigenous peoples who depend on using these goods for their own survival. But valuing environmental goods intrinsically does not demand that we fail to respect human beings.

Consider the difficulties encountered in attempting to force all our valuations of environmental goods into the instrumental mold. People appreciate many environmental goods for their beauty. Appreciation is a mode of intrinsic valuation. It is immediately directed toward the object of beauty, not toward ourselves. But some economists deny that any tenable distinction can be drawn between economic (useful) and aesthetic values. This forces them to maintain that things of beauty are only of instrumental value for the enjoyment humans derive from beholding them. This view commits the crude hedonistic error of taking the object of intrinsic value to be a favorable response rather than the object of a favorable response. The hedonistic account of the value of beautiful natural objects mistakenly assimilates its value to the mere use-values of amusement park rides, or consciousness altering drugs. In the latter case the experience alone matters. Any alteration of these things that produces the same or better experiences improves them. But when we contemplate a beautiful natural scene, and are struck by its grandeur or peacefulness, we experience it as worthy of our appreciation, not just as good for kicks. In appreciating a thing of natural beauty, we acknowledge that it possesses an integrity not to be violated, a unity of characteristics not to be modified merely for our pleasure or for ends not tied to its preservation in a flourishing natural state. This is why people who intrinsically care about the environment object to practices that use natural wonders for mere spectacle-seeking, as when chemicals are poured into geysers to stimulate eruptions, or magnificent caves decked out in lurid colored lights. Appreciation, as a higher mode of valuation than use, demands constraints on the ways we may use its objects.

Economists object that the existence of markets in works of art and nature resorts shows that the value of aesthetic goods is no different from the value of pure commodities (Power 1980). The prices these goods command indicate how much people value them, just as with any other commodity. "The resources of the physical and social environment . . . and the services they provide contribute to human well-being in exactly the same way as marketable natural or human-made resources." But the fact that there are markets in aesthetic goods does not show that market prices comprehensively measure their values. Market prices measure only how much people value goods for exclusive appropriation and consumption. Many people care about protecting some environmental goods, such as the remote rain forests of Borneo or the California condor, even if they will never own or personally experience them. Many people care about having some environmental goods, such as national parks, open to the public and valued as shared parts of the national heritage, rather than privately developed as exclusive vacation resorts.

To claim that environmental goods have intrinsic worth is not to claim that they don't contribute to human welfare. Their preservation can contribute to human development in part because they have an intrinsic value which we acknowledge as independent of human self-interest. The natural environment inspires many evaluative responses in us: wonder, awe, delight, admiration, reverence, appreciation. So it provides us with a realm in which we can develop and maintain the capacity to respond in these ways to the natural world, to escape from the often tiresome burden of exercising our will over objects in the ceaseless cycle of production and consumption. To say this is to deny that all environmental goods "contribute to human well-being in exactly the same way as marketable natural or human-made resources." Some goods contribute to human well-being precisely in not being objects of private appropriation and use, as marketed goods are.

Advocates of cost-benefit analysis justify its methods as the best way public policy can be responsive to citizens' values. Taking their cue from market norms of "consumers' sovereignty," they hold that responsiveness to people's values is best achieved by treating them as uncriticized wants and interests, which public policy should satisfy in proportion to people's willingness to pay in the market domain. This view fails to capture the ways people value goods outside of market contexts, which in principle cannot be measured by a cash value. It also fails to be responsive to the ways citizens think their values should be reflected in public policy. Citizens do not regard their valuations of the environment as matters of mere self-interest or consumer demand. Since they value many environmental goods in higher ways than they value commodities, their valuations involve public ideals and principles. The respectful response to peoples' conflicting public ideals and principles is to take seriously the reasons offered in support of them in public deliberation. The norms of consumers' sovereignty amount to a tyranny over citizens when applied to the domain of public policy. They impose a narrow set of consumerist values on citizens and deprive them of vehicles for articulating and expressing their concerns, which in principle cannot be represented by market-based measures of bare preference intensity. Since cost-benefit analysis is justified as a way to enable public policy to respond to citizens' values, to the extent that its methods cannot capture these values or respond properly to them, it stands condemned by its own standards of justification. Cost-benefit analysis fails as a framework for deliberation about public policy toward environmental goods.

9.4 TOWARD DEMOCRATIC ALTERNATIVES TO COST-BENEFIT ANALYSIS

Advocates of cost-benefit analysis see its function as enabling political institutions to be more responsive to citizens' values. But it fails to serve this function with respect to non-commodity values. When matters of public health and environmental quality are at stake, this function would be better served by making our political institutions more democratic than by making them more like the market. For the goods in question are political goods. They can be adequately secured only through democratic institutions of voice, in which all citizens are entitled to participate on terms of equality. Such institutions are deliberative bodies that aim to reach decisions on the basis of principles, reasoning, and arguments that articulate the concerns of citizens in terms they reflectively endorse. The influence one's position should have in a democratic, deliberative institution is determined by the strength of one's reasons in favor of it, not by how much money one is willing to pay to make it prevail. Democratic respect for citizens' values is expressed by taking their reasons and principles seriously, not by blindly satisfying their unexamined wants, as these are interpreted by economistic technocrats.

Democratic institutions are necessary to respond to citizens' concerns about safety and the environment for two closely connected reasons. First, they provide the social conditions of autonomy people need to articulate, change, and promote their own values in ways they can reflectively endorse. In contrast, the hierarchical relations of the workplace deprive workers of the internal and external conditions of autonomy they need to effectively express their concerns. Cost-benefit analysis reproduces this heteronomy, by confusing employers' valuations of workers' lives for workers' self-evaluations. More generally, it tends to interpret citizens' values through an ideology of commodity fetishism, which supposes that people care only about privately appropriated goods and not about the social relations in which they are realized or the ideals and principles informing them. Institutions of voice allow people to articulate their concerns directly and thereby empower them to put new items on the agenda without depending on "experts" to speak for them. If they are fully democratic, they enable people to come to terms with their disagreements in relations of equality, where no one can claim authority over others or exercise disproportionate influence over outcomes in virtue of their command over wealth and property. Since relations of equality are necessary for objective dialogue, democratic institutions enable people to rationally deliberate about their ends. Politics is a domain for criticizing and changing desires through reasoned debate, not merely for aggregating given desires. This activity is partly constitutive of autonomy.

Second, democratic institutions are needed to enable people to express certain *kinds* of valuations that can be expressed only in non-market social relations. Some of the concerns people have as citizens cannot in principle be expressed in their roles as consumers, but must be expressed through their political relations with other citizens. Consumers act individually, taking the background social relations of their interactions for granted and generally assuming an instrumental attitude toward these relations. In their roles as consumers, they have little power over the social relations and norms governing their interactions, and hence little scope for expressing intrinsic concerns about their relations in market interactions. Citizens act collectively, taking their social relations as an immediate, intrinsic object of concern. Because these relations are constituted by shared legal, ethical, and social norms, people can reform them only through collective action. People care about the meanings embodied in the social relations in which risks are imposed and controlled, not just about the raw magnitudes and financial benefits of these risks. They also care about the character of their social life expressed by the ways they relate to the natural environment. For example, many U.S. citizens value the national parks as *shared* goods, whose nonexclusive provision to all citizens, explicitly based on shared ideals informing the national heritage, is constitutive of what makes them valuable. The ways we choose to protect them enable us to realize ourselves as trustees for the natural goods with which the country is endowed. To realize such goods as nationally shared, and ourselves as trustees for them, a democratic forum is needed to articulate their meaning, so that people can enjoy them on terms acknowledged by all, and enjoy them in part because they are shared. These examples offer just two kinds of concerns people express in the political sphere that they cannot effectively express as consumers. Since people rationally express different valuations in different social contexts, cost-benefit analysis deprives them of opportunities to express distinctively noneconomic concerns in taking consumer preferences as normative for democratic politics.

This view of the function of the state contrasts with the view advanced by welfare economics. On that view, the state and the market fulfill the same function of generic want-satisfaction and are evaluated by the same criteria of efficiency. The state fills in where markets fail to secure efficient outcomes, and it functions to mimic the results that competitive markets would achieve, if they could be constructed. This conception supposes that the state and the market are merely alternative means for securing the same sorts of outcomes and realizing the same sorts of goods according to the same (market) norms. Which institution we should use to govern outcomes concerning certain goods is strictly a question of efficiency. On the view defended here, the choice of institutions is conditioned by the kind of good at stake and the kinds of concerns people have with respect to it. Different sorts of institutions satisfy various sorts of concerns and enable people to express different ways of valuing goods. This is a basic implication of pluralism. That we express different valuations in different spheres is explained by the fact that various social contexts provide frameworks for distinct ways of valuing things.

The arguments presented here do not lead to a formula for institutional design. They only point in the direction we should be looking: toward making our political institutions more democratic, rather than more like the market. They call for experiments in expanding citizens' participation in formulating and implementing regulations concerning safety and environmental quality. This can be done either by devolving power from distant regulatory bureaucracies to local, self-managed institutions or citizen action groups, or, less radically, by opening up the regulatory process to more active inputs from ordinary citizens.

Consider one model of decentralizing authority, which may be called the worker management model. The worker management model is best applied to issues concerning workplace risks, where the costs of risk-taking activity are borne by those who impose it on themselves. In a democratically controlled worker-managed firm, workers collectively decide what risks they will assume, without having to obey orders from people who do not have their interests in mind. Because democratically run firms meet the internal and external conditions for workers' autonomy, the case for state regulation of workplace risks in such organizations is weakened. It would arise only if competing worker-managed firms faced collective action problems, in which case it would be in everyone's interest for all to stop a risky productive process, but none could do it individually without facing bankruptcy. Then the state might enter to facilitate collective self-restraint agreements among competing firms. Even judging from the welfare economists' narrow criteria of efficiency rather than from an autonomy perspective, worker self-management provides a superior solution to the problem of workplace risks than bureaucratic regulation, because it eliminates the agency problem (ensuring that regulators act in workers' interests) and is at least as efficient as capitalist-managed firms as long as the firm pays interest on workers' capital investments.

Since workers' cooperatives tend to attract workers motivated by progressive democratic ideals, they also present a more favorable record on environmental protection. The case of forest workers' cooperatives in the Pacific Northwest, which have pioneered forest conservation techniques and perform 25 percent of the reforestation work on public timberlands, is exemplary (Gunn 1984). Environmental protection tends to harmonize more with the interests as well as the ideals of worker-managed firms than with the interests of capitalist firms, since their capital assets, held mainly by workers, are not as mobile. Workers, unlike capitalist owners, have to live in the communities where they work and so must live with whatever pollution they create. This by no means eliminates the need for national environmental policies, but it does improve the prospects for cooperative rather than adversarial relations between business and environmental groups.

The worker-management model is unlikely to be fully generalizable in the United States in the near future. Nevertheless, democratic modifications of the management structure of traditional capitalist firms could begin to acknowledge the principle that people who are placed at risk should have the power to propose, debate, and vote on alternative health and safety projects, as well as to participate in the implementation of these projects. For example, people put at risk by a local power company could elect representatives to a committee, joined by elected representatives of workers and stockholders in the firm, which would be invested with the power to make health and safety decisions regarding the plant. The inclusion of representatives from all the interested groups in the decision-making process would provide reasonable assurance that the full range of costs and benefits would be articulated by the affected parties themselves, and there would be some likelihood that new perspectives, never noticed or anticipated by cost-benefit analysts, would emerge through dialogue.

Arnold (1990objects that such a proposal might incoherently divide management rights over firms between contending groups in an unsustainable manner. But divided sovereignty over firms is already more the rule than the exception in advanced capitalist economies, since local zoning boards exercise control over firm locations and the federal government already enforces regulatory rules on management that require it to invest in pollution-reducing technology, buildings accessible to the handicapped, and so forth. Other countries, such as Germany, have successfully institutionalized divided sovereignty on a comprehensive scale, with representatives from labor unions and major political parties routinely sitting on corporate boards of directors. The suggestion made here is well within the range of successful experiments that have already proven their feasibility. Indeed, there is considerable evidence that workers' productive efficiency increases when they gain real management power, even in firms still structured by a division between labor and management. Power enables workers to identify with the firm's goals and reduces the incentive to take an adversarial stance toward management, for it raises the likelihood that workers will share in the benefits of increased labor productivity (Gunn 1984). Theoretical work on labor management indicates that these improvements should not be surprising (Bowles and Gintis 1987).

Democracy is, of course, no panacea. Its participatory form has notable drawbacks. It doesn't work effectively for large groups. Many environmental problems, such as ozone depletion, are global problems that require international solutions. Participation can become burdensome and time-consuming. This means that decision-making power tends to concentrate in the hands of committed activists, who may not share the interests and ideals of less active members. Representative democracy helps to correct these defects but introduces agency problems of its own. Nevertheless, democratic forms of organization constitute the best models we have for the exercise of collective autonomy and rationality and provide indispensable vehicles for expressing certain kinds of concerns and realizing certain types of ideals of our relations to one another. There are certain aspirations that the market cannot fulfill at all.

Many advocates of cost-benefit analysis agree on the desirability of involving citizens more directly in the evaluative process (Leonard and Zeckhauser 1985). They argue that "process" values have a symbolic importance that is additional to the net benefits to be expected from policies that maximize efficiency. But they still insist that cost-benefit analysis provides the fundamental terms in which rival policies should be analyzed. After all, any rational evaluation of policies must take account of their costs and benefits. My argument does not deny this last point. Participants in the policy formation process will, of course, need to consult experts to gather facts about potential negative and positive consequences of alternative policy proposals. But these facts are best presented qualitatively, in terms deemed relevant by the participants. The willingness-to-pay measure of value must be rejected. In fact, no context-independent, global consequentialist formula for identifying and aggregating costs and benefits is generally valid. So facts about costs and benefits must be provided in disaggregated form. Because it depends on consequentialist and market norms, the form of cost-benefit analysis criticized here describes and takes account of the costs and benefits of health and safety projects in ways many people reject. Democratic participation in the decision-making process is needed to enable people to describe and take costs and benefits into account in their own ways.

One could conceive of a system of cost-benefit analysis that rejects the willingness-to-pay criterion and its attendant market norms. According to Allan Gibbard (1986), the normative appeal of cost-benefit analysis is based on its consequentialism, not on the ways its practitioners currently measure values. Cost-benefit analysis is valuable because it embodies a superior standard of rationality: the principle of maximizing expected intrinsic value. Only by regimenting our deliberations about risk to this "technocratic" standard can we avoid supposedly blatant irrationalities which infect ordinary opinions about acceptable risks. In light of the pluralist, expressive theory of value and rational choice defended in this book, we should be wary of consequentialist claims that ordinary people employing commonsense reasoning are irrational. Some of these claims presuppose the prior rationality of intrinsic value-maximization and count as irrational any preference structure that does not conform to this standard. I have argued that it is rational to reject this standard and that people's preferences in general do not conform to it, because they are structured by substantive non-consequentialist norms with their own expressive justification. Some of these claims depend on observations of individuals' difficulty in dealing with the mathematics of probability (Kahneman and Tversky 1979). But these observations are of individuals in socially impoverished environments, where they cannot engage in dialogue with others. There is no reason to think ordinary people are any less capable of correcting their mathematical errors after dialogue with others than are technocrats. If, after dialogue with others, ordinary people's judgments do not conform to consequentialist standards of rationality, this is evidence not that ordinary people are irrational but that consequentialism itself fails to do justice to the diversity of people's values. Our task is not to refine a technocratic standard of rationality alien to people's concerns, but to empower people to speak and act for themselves.

David Schmidtz

A Place for Cost Benefit Analysis

2001

What next? We are forever making decisions. Typically, when unsure, we try to identify, then compare, our options. We weigh pros and cons. Occasionally, we make the weighing explicit, listing pros and cons and assigning numerical weights. What could be wrong with that? In fact, things sometimes go terribly wrong. This paper considers what cost-benefit analysis can do, and also what it cannot.

David Schmidtz, "A Place for Cost-Benefit Analysis." *Philosophical Issues* 11 (2001): 148–171. By permission of *Philosophical Issues*.

1. WHAT IS CBA, AND WHAT IS IT FOR?

Here is an example of how things go wrong. Ontario Hydro is a Canadian government-owned utility company (a Crown Corporation, on a par with Canada Post). Ten years ago, Ontario Hydro was expecting to become a hugely profitable provider of electricity to consumers all over the continent. At that time, Ontario circulated a report explaining how it planned to meet projected demand. Of interest to us is the report's admission that, "The analysis conducted in the development of the Demand/Supply Plans includes those costs which are borne directly by Hydro. It is these costs which can properly be included in Hydro's rates. Costs and benefits for the Ontario community, beyond these direct costs, are not factored into the cost comparisons." Why not? Because "even if desirable, these costs are difficult to estimate in monetary terms given the diffuse nature of the impacts and wide variety of effects." The costs that Ontario Hydro proposed to take into account "include the social and environmental costs incurred by Hydro but do not include social and environmental costs external to Hydro. This reflects normal business practice. In Hydro's judgment, including additional costs and benefits on an equitable basis would be impracticable."[1]

It is amazing that people would defend such a patently unethical stance by describing it as "normal business practice." Sadly, though, appealing to "normal business practice" is itself normal business practice, and Ontario Hydro is not especially guilty in that regard. Indeed, it is notable that Ontario Hydro was not duplicitous, since it did, after all, express its policy bluntly and publicly. Those who wrote the report evidently had no idea that what they were saying was wrong.

Environmentalists have their own "normal business practices," though, and it is too easy to condemn organizations like Ontario Hydro without thinking things through. Many critics of cost-benefit analysis (henceforth CBA) seem driven by a gut feeling that CBA is heartless. They think that, in denouncing CBA, they are taking a stand against heartlessness. This is unfortunate. The fact is, weighing a proposal's costs and benefits does not make you a bad person. What makes you a bad person is *ignoring* costs— the costs you impose on others.

The problem with Ontario Hydro arose, not when Ontario Hydro took costs and benefits into account, but rather when it decided *not* to do so. The problem in general terms is a problem of *external* costs. External costs are costs that decision makers ignore, leaving them to be paid by someone else. Ontario Hydro makes a decision that has certain costs. Some of the costs will fall not on Ontario Hydro but on innocent bystanders; following normal business practice, Ontario Hydro seems to say, "That's not our problem."

Decision makers naturally are tempted to ignore external costs. It is only human. Almost everyone does the same sort of thing in one context or another. Every time you leave an empty popcorn box in a theater rather than dispose of it properly, you are doing the same sort of thing as the person who dumps industrial waste in the river rather than dispose of it properly. Every time you drive a car, you are risking other people's lives, and you probably have never wasted a minute feeling guilty about it. (And just like you, industrial polluters defend themselves by saying, "But everybody does it!") It is not only bad people who ignore the costs they impose on others. Part of the problem is simple laziness, when we think no one is watching. Another part of the problem is the normal human desire to conform, even when "normal practice" is unconscionable.

2. IS CBA ANTI-ENVIRONMENTALIST?

CBA comes in many variations, and there are many that no ethicist would defend. Needless to say, no ethicist would defend conventional CBA, that is, CBA in the narrowly focused way that Ontario Hydro used it at the end of the 1980s. All sides agree:

there can be no general justification for foisting external costs on innocent bystanders. Any controversy concerns whether there exists some other form of CBA that can, in general, be justified.

Those with expertise in accounting are trained to draw fine-grained distinctions between different variations on the basic theme of conventional CBA. Full Cost Accounting, for example, refers to an attempt to carry out CBA in such a way as to take *all* known costs, external as well as internal, into account.[2] From here on, except where otherwise noted, when I speak of CBA, I will be referring to cost-benefit analysis with Full Cost Accounting. As E. J. Mishan's influential text defines it, "in cost-benefit analysis we are concerned with the economy as a whole, with the welfare of a defined society, and not any smaller part of it."[3]

Understood in this way, CBA is not merely an accounting method. It is a commitment to take responsibility for the consequences of one's actions. That is why, historically, environmentalists were among the most vocal *advocates* of CBA as a vehicle for making industries and governments answerable for the full cost of their decisions. It can work. Indeed, there has been an interesting further development in the case of Ontario Hydro. Perhaps having learned something about environmental ethics, Ontario Hydro changed its stance in 1993 and now trumpets its use of Full Cost Accounting methods.[4]

Under what general circumstances, then, should we want policy makers to employ CBA? Two answers come to mind: first, when one group pays the cost of a piece of legislation while another group gets the benefit; second, and more generally, whenever decision makers have an incentive not to take full costs into account. Where benefits of political decisions are concentrated while costs are dispersed, special interest groups can push through favorable policies even when costs to the population at large outweigh benefits.[5] To contain the proliferation of such unconscionable policies, we might require that policies be justified by the lights of a proper CBA. Requiring decision makers to provide a CBA, which is then made available for public scrutiny, is one way of trying to teach decision makers to take environmental costs into account. We do not want upstream people ignoring costs they foist on downstream people.[6] We want social and cultural and legal arrangements that encourage people to be aware of the full environmental cost, and also the full human cost, of what they do.

The most fundamental argument in favor of CBA has to do with CBA's role as a means of introducing accountability into decisions that affect whole communities. Think about it. If a business pollutes, would it be wrong to insist that the business should be paying the true full cost of its operation? As a mechanism for holding decision makers publicly accountable for external costs, CBA has the potential to constrain activities that are not worthwhile when external costs are taken into account. Accordingly, the National Policy Act of 1969 required CBA of all environment-related federal projects. To that extent, CBA is a friend of the environment. Or at least, it seemed that way at one time.

The tables seemingly have been turning, though. Throughout the 1970s, the Council on Wage and Price Stability and the Office of Management and Budget pressured the Environmental Protection Agency to pay more attention to the costs of complying with standards the EPA was trying to impose on industry. Finally, in 1981, President Reagan issued an Executive Order requiring government agencies to justify new regulations by submitting a formal CBA (of which an environmental impact statement would be only one part) to the Office of Management and Budget. Why? Why force agencies to perform CBA of their regulatory proposals? The point, very generally, was to force agencies to take into account costs they otherwise would have preferred to ignore. The Reagan administration reputedly felt some regulations were being pushed through by environmental zealots who did not care what their proposals cost in human terms. Accordingly, the Executive Order mandating CBA was perceived as having an anti-environmental thrust. Perhaps partly because of that bit of recent history, current environmentalist opinion remains, on the whole, anti-CBA. The following sections consider some of the main reasons (some cogent, some not) for distrusting CBA.

3. IS CBA ANTHROPOCENTRIC?

Is it only the interests of human persons that can be taken into account in a CBA? If so, then isn't CBA essentially anthropocentric? The answer is no. CBA as construed here is partly an accounting procedure, and partly a way of organizing public debate. In no way is it a substitute for philosophical debate. Animal liberationists who think full costs must (by definition?) include pain suffered by animals, for example, must argue for that point in philosophical debate with those who think otherwise. If CBA presupposed one or the other position, thereby preempting philosophical debate, that would be a flaw.

4. DOES CBA PRESUPPOSE UTILITARIAN MORAL THEORY?

Utilitarian moral theory holds roughly that X is right if and only if X maximizes utility, where maximizing utility is a matter of producing the best possible balance of benefits over costs. It may seem obvious that CBA presupposes the truth of utilitarian moral theory. In fact, it does not. CBA is a way of organizing a public forum expressing respect for persons: persons present at the meeting and other persons as well, on whose behalf those present can speak (citizens of faraway countries, future generations, etc.). For that matter, those present at the forum will speak not only on behalf of other persons but on behalf of whatever they care about: animals, trees, canyons, historic sites, and so on.

The forum therefore is defensible on utilitarian grounds, but it does not depend on utilitarian moral theory, for this sort of CBA could and probably should be advocated by deontologists.[7] A conventional CBA that ignored external costs would be endorsed neither by deontologists nor utilitarians, but CBA with Full Cost Accounting, defended in a public forum, could be endorsed by either.[8]

5. DOES CBA TELL US TO SACRIFICE THE ONE FOR THE SAKE OF THE MANY?

We can imagine advocates of CBA jumping to the conclusion that policies are justified whenever benefits exceed costs. That would be a mistake. We need to be more circumspect than that. When benefits exceed costs, the conclusion should be that the policy has passed one crucial test and therefore further discussion is warranted. On the other hand, when a proposal *fails* the test of CBA, when costs exceed benefits, the implication is more decisive, namely that further discussion is not warranted. If enacting a certain proposal would help some people and hurt others, then showing that winners are gaining more than losers are losing counts for something, but it is not decisive. One must then argue that the gain is so great for some people that it justifies imposing a loss on other people. In contrast, to show that losers are losing more than winners are gaining should pretty much end the conversation. Failing CBA is a fairly reliable test of when something is wrong.[9] Passing CBA, however, is not a reliable test of when something is right.

Consider the following case.[10]

> HOSPITAL: Five patients lie on operating tables about to die for lack of suitable organ donors. A UPS delivery person just walked into the office. She is a suitable organ donor for all five patients. If you kidnap her and harvest her organs, you will be saving five and killing one.

Suppose we perform CBA in that case, and it yields the conclusion that, well, five is more than one. Would that imply that taking the delivery person's life is permissible? Required, even? No. Of course, we could quibble about how the calculation works out, but that would miss the fundamental point, which is that when we are talking about killing people, costs and benefits are not the only issue. CBA offers us guidance when our objective is to promote the best possible balance of costs and benefits, but not all situations call on us to maximize what is valuable. Promoting value is not always the best way of respecting it. There are times when morality calls on us not to maximize value but simply to respect it.

I argued that CBA does not presume the truth of utilitarian moral theory. Now it may seem that what I call CBA presumes that utilitarian moral theory is false! On the contrary, even from a broadly utilitarian perspective, we do not want ordinary citizens to have a license to kill whenever they think they can do a lot of good in the process. Some institutions have their utility precisely by *prohibiting* decisions based on utilitarian calculation. Hospitals, for example, cannot serve their purpose if they are a menace to innocent bystanders. Hospitals cannot serve their purpose unless people can trust hospitals to treat people as rights-bearers. Respecting people's rights is part of what helps make it safe to visit hospitals. And making it safe to visit the hospital is a prerequisite of hospitals functioning properly. Accordingly, we cannot justify cutting up one patient to save five simply by saying five is more than one. Sometimes, numbers do not count. It is good policy to forbid killing, requiring ordinary citizens to respect human rights, period.

Therefore, there are limits to the legitimate scope of CBA, and must be, even from a utilitarian perspective. Consider the case of *Peeveyhouse vs. Garland Coal.*[11] Having completed a strip-mining operation on the Peeveyhouse property, Garland Coal refused to honor its contractual promise to restore the land to its original condition. The restored land would have been worth only $300 and it would have cost $29,000 to restore it. Still, Peeveyhouse wanted the land restored and Garland Coal had promised to do it.

Incredibly, the Oklahoma court awarded Peeveyhouse only the $300, judging that Garland Coal could not be held financially liable for a restoration when such restoration would not be cost-effective. The Court's verdict generally is regarded as utterly mistaken, though, and one way of understanding the mistake is to see it as a case of failing to understand the limits of CBA's legitimate scope. We live in a society where hospitals cannot take organs without consent. We live in a society where Garland Coal normally would have to honor its contract with Peeveyhouse. Thus, we know where we stand. We need not be perpetually preparing to prove before a tribunal that strip-mining our land or harvesting our internal organs without consent is not cost-effective. Instead, we have a right simply to say no. In giving us moral space that we govern by right, our laws limit the energy we have to waste: trying to influence public regulators, fighting to keep what belongs to us, fighting to gain what belongs to others. In treating us as rights-bearers, our laws enable us simply to decline proposals that would benefit others at our expense.

Crucially, our being able to say no teaches people to search for ways of making progress that benefit everyone. CBA in its simplest form allows some to be sacrificed for the sake of the greater good of others, and therefore CBA in its simplest form is morally problematic. In contrast, CBA as a framework for public discussion, in a regime that treats people as rights-bearers, creates at least some pressure to craft proposals that promise benefits for all.[12]

Again, part of the message to take away from these discussions is that the proper purpose of CBA is not to show when a taking is permissible. If we see CBA as indicating when takings are permissible, we will have a problem, because breaking contracts, or taking things from people (including their lives) whenever the benefit is worth the cost is not a way of respecting people. But if we treat CBA as a *constraint* on takings, ruling out inefficient takings without licensing efficient takings, then it is not disrespectful.

Therefore, it would be a mistake to see CBA as an *alternative* to treating people as ends in themselves. On the contrary, when CBA is working properly, and in particular when treated not as a seal of approval for good proposals but rather as a means of filtering out bad proposals, CBA becomes a way of preventing people from treating each other as mere means. The point is to stop people from foisting the costs of their policies on innocent people without consent. In other words, requiring people to offer an accounting of the true costs and benefits of their operations is a way of holding them publicly accountable for failing to treat fellow citizens as ends in themselves. CBA will not filter out every proposal that ought to be filtered out, but it will help to filter out many of the most flagrantly disrespectful proposals, and that is its proper purpose.

6. MUST CBA TREAT ALL VALUES AS MERE COMMODITIES?

As Mark Sagoff nicely expresses the point, "There are some who believe on principle that worker safety and environmental quality ought to be protected only insofar as the benefits of protection balance the costs. On the other hand, people argue—also on principle—that neither worker safety nor environmental quality should be treated as a commodity to be traded at the margin for other commodities, but rather each should be valued for its own sake" (Sagoff 1981, pp. 1288–89). The second argument, though, presents a false dichotomy. CBA is perfectly compatible with the idea that worker safety and environmental quality ought to be valued for their own sake.

To see why, imagine a certain recycling process is risky to the workers involved. The process improves environmental quality, but inevitably workers risk getting their hands caught in the machines, and so on. Notice: although we treat both environmental quality and worker safety as ends in themselves, we still have to weigh the operation's costs and benefits. Is recycling's environmental benefit worth the risk? It is a good question, and we would be missing the point if we tried to answer it by saying environmental quality is valued for its own sake.

Nor must we imagine cases of different values (worker safety and environmental quality) coming into conflict. The need for CBA can arise even when environmental quality is the sole value at stake. For example, suppose the recycling process in question saves paper (and therefore trees), but saving trees comes at a cost of all the water and electricity used in the process; gasoline is used by trucks that collect the paper from recycling bins, and so on. Therefore, the very recycling process that reduces pollution and natural resource consumption in some respects also increases pollution and natural resource consumption in other respects. In this case, our reason to do CBA is precisely that we care about environmental quality. (If maintaining a politically correct environmentalist appearance were our only concern, we would not worry about it.)

Again, it would be beside the point to talk about environmental quality being valued for its own sake. In a nutshell, we sometimes find ourselves in situations of conflicting values, where the values at stake are really important. Critics of CBA sometimes seem to say, when values at stake are really important, that is when we should *not* think hard about the costs and benefits of resolving the conflict in one way rather than another. They seem to have things backwards.

Sagoff (1981, pp. 1290–91) asserts, "It is the characteristic of cost-benefit analysis that it treats all value judgments other than those made on its behalf as nothing but statements of preference, attitude, or emotion." There are several things going on in this passage. I will mention three. First, the words "other than those made on its behalf" are a jest at the pseudo-scientific posturing of radical subjectivists, and the jest is on target. Second, Sagoff is insinuating that it is a mistake simply to assume that all values are reducible to costs and benefits, and here too, Sagoff is on target. On the one hand, it is an economist's job to go as far as possible in treating values as preferences, and within economics narrowly construed, the reductionist bias serves a purpose. On the other hand, when we look at values in more philosophical terms, we cannot treat all values as mere preferences, as if attaching value to honesty were on a par with attaching value to chocolate. Accordingly, there is a problem with jumping from economic to philosophical discussions without stopping to remind ourselves that what is taken for granted in one kind of discussion cannot be taken for granted in the other.

The third thing Sagoff is saying is that CBA characteristically treats all values as mere preferences. Now, if Sagoff means to say CBA *typically* does so, he may be right. But if Sagoff were saying CBA *necessarily* does so, he would be mistaken. CBA is about weighing costs and benefits. It does not presume everything is either a cost or a benefit. We have to decide which values can be treated as mere preferences, costs, or benefits, and which have to be treated separately, as falling outside the scope of CBA. CBA itself does not make that decision for us. It is true by definition that to care about X is to have a preference regarding X, but we can care about X without thinking X is merely a preference. CBA assumes nothing about the nature of values, other than that they sometimes come into conflict and that no matter what we do, we will in effect be trading them off against each other.[13] It does not assume trading off values is unproblematic; it assumes only that we sometimes have no choice.

"Recycling" is a politically correct word, to be sure, but does that mean we should support any operation that uses the word in its title, even if the operation is environmentally catastrophic? Or should we instead stop to think about the operation's costs and benefits? Contra Sagoff, if we stop to think, that does not mean we are treating environmental quality as a mere "preference, attitude, or emotion." Stopping to think can be a way of showing respect.

7. CAN CBA HANDLE QUALITATIVE VALUES?

Steven Kelman (1981, p. 33) says CBA presupposes the desirability of being able to express all values as dollar values. However, as Kelman correctly notes, converting values to dollars can be a problem. It can distort the true nature of the values at stake. On the other hand, it would be a mistake to think CBA *requires* us to represent every value as a dollar value. For example, Kelman and Sagoff surely would agree that if we care about Atlantic Green Turtles and do a CBA of alternative ways of protecting them, nothing in that process even suggests we have reduced the value of turtles to dollars.

We can do CBA with respect to different values; we can accept conflicts of value that prevent definitive answers. Kelman is right that something is gained when we genuinely and fairly can reduce all values to dollar values, because if we can do that, then there will be a "bottom line." We can simply tally up values, and it will be clear what CBA recommends. Often, though, trying to force the process to yield an unambiguously numerical bottom line would be to chase a mirage. If the art museum is about to close and I have one last chance to see either my beloved Vermeer or my beloved Seurat, but there is no time to see both, then I must make a choice. The interesting point is, even when I know precisely what the costs and benefits will be of seeing the Vermeer versus seeing the Seurat, that does not entail that there will be an unambiguous bottom line. Normally, people do not attach numbers to their values. You never hear people saying, "Well, according to my calculations, the Vermeer experience is seven percent more valuable than the Seurat experience, so clearly Vermeer is the way to go." Nor do we hear, "Although I'm more in the mood for Seurat, the rational choice is the Vermeer, since appraisers say the Vermeer is worth more money." The latter thought would be irrelevant when the values at issue concern my own appreciation of the paintings' intrinsic merits as paintings rather than the paintings' value as instruments for raising cash. In cases like that, the bottom line will be qualitative rather than quantitative. No matter how accurately I appraise the intrinsic merits of the paintings, my appraisals will still be qualitative.

An object's *intrinsic* value is the value it has in and of itself, beyond any value it has as a means to further ends. Note that an object's having intrinsic value does not imply that the object is priceless. There is such a thing as limited intrinsic value. A painting can have an intrinsic value that is real without being infinite, or even particularly large. The value I would get from selling it is its instrumental value to me. The value it has to me in and of itself, simply because it is a beautiful painting, is its intrinsic value to me.[14] Both values are real, but one is instrumental and the other is intrinsic. Neither is necessarily large.

A related point: it would be better if Kelman (1981, p. 39) had not said, "selling a thing for money demonstrates that it was valued only instrumentally."[15] Suppose I sell a painting. The money I receive from the sale is the painting's instrumental value to me, but does my decision to sell imply that the painting had no intrinsic value? No. Suppose I love the painting, but I need to raise a large sum of money to save my life, so I sell the painting. What this implies is not that the painting has zero intrinsic value but rather that the instrumental value of selling it outweighs the intrinsic value of keeping it, in that circumstance.

More generally, we sometimes put dollar values on things even when their value to us is essentially different from the value of dollars. Incommensurability of different values is not generally an insurmountable obstacle to CBA. Still, there often is no point in trying to convert a qualitative balancing into something that *looks* like a precise quantitative calculation and thus *looks* scientific but in fact remains the same qualitative balancing, only now its qualitative nature is disguised by the attaching of made-up numbers.

Policy decisions can be like that. We can make up numbers when assessing the value of a public library we could build on land that otherwise will remain a public park. Maybe the numbers will mean something, maybe not. More often, even when we can accurately predict a policy's true costs and benefits, that does not entail that there will be any bottom line from which we simply read off what to do. When competing values cannot be reduced to a common measure without distortion, that makes it harder to know the bottom line. It may even mean there is no unitary bottom line to be known. Sometimes the bottom line is simply that one precious and irreplaceable thing is gained while another precious and irreplaceable thing is lost. Even so, that does not mean there is a problem with the very idea of taking costs and benefits into account. It just means we should not assume too much about what kind of bottom line we can expect to see.[16]

Ontario Hydro (since its reorganization), and the City of Vancouver Planning Department, to name two examples, say that in striving to provide a Full Cost Accounting, they try not to ignore vague nonmonetized costs, even though in practice such sensitivity means their bottom line will reflect not (or not only) numerical inputs so much as their version of informed common sense.[17] Consider an analogy. A computer program can play chess by algorithm. Human chess players cannot. Human chess players need creativity, experience, alertness to unintended consequences, and other skills and virtues that are not algorithmic. People who formulate policy need similar skills and virtues, and interpersonal skills as well. Employing CBA cannot change that.

8. SOME THINGS ARE PRICELESS. SO WHAT?

Critics of CBA think they capture the moral high ground when they say some things are beyond price. They miss the point. Even if Atlantic Green Turtles are a priceless world heritage, we still have to decide how to save them. We still need to look at costs and benefits of trying to protect them in one way rather than another, for two reasons. First, we need to know whether a certain approach will be effective, given available resources. Dollar for dollar, an effective way of protecting them is better than an ineffective way. Second, we need to know whether the cost of saving them involves sacrificing something else we consider equally priceless.

If baby Jessica has fallen into an abandoned well in Midland, Texas, and it will cost nine million dollars to rescue her, is it worth the cost? It seems somehow wrong even to ask the question; after all, it is only money. But it is not wrong. If it would cost nine million dollars to save Jessica's life, what would the nine million dollars otherwise have purchased? Could it have been sent to Africa where it might have saved nine thousand lives? Consider an even more expensive case. If a public utility company in Pennsylvania (in the wake of a frivolous lawsuit blaming its high-voltage power lines for a child's leukemia) calculates that burying its power lines underground will cost two billion dollars, in the process maybe preventing one or two deaths from leukemia, is it only money? If the two billion dollars could have been sent to Africa where it might have saved two million lives, is it obvious we should *not* stop to think about it?

Critics like to say not all values are economic values. They are right, but no values whatsoever are purely economic values in that sense. Even money itself is never only money. In a small town in Texas in 1987, a lot of money was spent to save a baby's life—money that took several lifetimes to produce. It was not only money. It did after all save a baby's life. It also gave a community a chance to show the world what it stands for. These are not trivial things. Neither are many of the other things on which nine million dollars could have been spent.

There are things so valuable to us that we think of them as beyond price. Some economists might disagree, but it is, after all, a fact. What does this fact imply? When we have no choice but to make tradeoffs, should we ignore items we consider priceless, or should we take them into account?[18] The hard fact is, priceless values sometimes come into conflict. When that happens, and when we try rationally to weigh our options, we are in effect putting a price on that which is priceless. In that case, CBA is not the problem. It is a response to the problem. The world has handed us a painful choice, and trying rationally to weigh our options is our way of trying to cope with it.

Note in passing that although critics often speak of incommensurable values, incommensurability is not quite the issue, strictly speaking. Consider the central dilemma of the novel, *Sophie's Choice* (Styron, 1979). Sophie's two children are about to be executed by a concentration camp commander. The commander says he will kill both children unless Sophie picks one to be killed, in which case the commander will spare the other one. Now, to Sophie, both children are beyond price. She does not value one more than the other. In some sense, she values each of them more than anything. Nevertheless, she does in the end pick one for execution, thereby saving the other one's life. The point is, although her values were incommensurate, she was still able to rank them in a situation where failing to rank them would have meant losing both. The values were incommensur*ate,* but not incommensur*able.* To Sophie, both children were beyond price, but when forced to put a price on them, she could.

Of course, the decision broke her heart. As the sadistic commander foresaw, the process of ranking her previously incommensurate values was psychologically devastating. At some level, commensuration is *always* possible, but there are times when something (our innocence, perhaps) is lost in the process of making values commensurate. Perhaps that explains why some critics want to reject CBA; they see it as a mechanism for ranking values that should not be ranked. Unfortunately, although we can hope people like Sophie will never need to rank their children and can instead go on thinking of each child as having infinite value, and although we can wish we never had to choose between worker safety and environmental quality, or between different aspects of environmental quality, the real world sometimes requires tradeoffs.

9. DOES CBA WORK?

When individuals engage in CBA, they typically are asking themselves how much they should be willing to pay. That is an obvious and legitimate question because they are, after all, constrained by their budget. In contrast, legislators ask themselves how much they are willing to make *other* people pay, and that is a problem. In that case, paying has become an external cost, and it is no surprise if legislators seem rather cavalier about how much they are making other people pay. I said earlier that if the analysis shows that losers are losing more than winners are gaining, that should pretty much end the conversation. Unfortunately, in the real world, the conversation does not always stop there. When a program's benefits are concentrated within influential constituencies, legislators conceal how costly the program is to taxpayers at large. Similarly, owners of dogs that bark all night ignore the costs they impose on neighbors. Again, it is not because people are evil. They are only human. Situations where we are not fully accountable—where we have the option of not paying the full cost of our decisions—tend not to bring out the best in us. CBA with Full Cost Accounting is one way of trying to introduce accountability.

In theory, then, CBA is a way of organizing agenda for public debates that respect all persons, and valuable nonpersons, too. How does it work in practice? An effective resolution to hold decision makers and policy makers accountable for all costs would, in theory, make for a cleaner, safer, more prosperous society. The prospect of a public accounting can make corporations and governments rethink what they owe to the environment, and in Ontario Hydro's case, it seems to have done exactly that. Still, there is much corruption in the world and nothing like CBA will ever put an end to it. As with any other accounting method, the quality of the output typically will be only as good as the quality of the inputs. The valuations we supply as inputs drive the results, so how to avoid biased valuations? Biased inputs generate biased outputs. CBA, then, has the potential to be a smokescreen for the real action that takes place before numbers get added.

Can anything guarantee that the process of CBA will not itself be subject to the same political piracy that CBA was supposed to limit? Probably not. As I said earlier, the verdict in *Peeveyhouse* generally is regarded as mistaken. What I did not mention is that, as Andrew Morriss (2000, p. 144) notes, "Shortly after the *Peeveyhouse* decision, a corruption investigation uncovered more than thirty years of routine bribery of several of the court's members." CBA per se does not correct for corrupted inputs. Neither does CBA stop people from applying CBA to cases in which CBA has no legitimate role. However, if the process is public, with affected parties having a chance to protest when their interests are ignored, public scrutiny will have some tendency to correct for biased inputs. It also will encourage planners to supply inputs that can survive scrutiny in the first place. If the process is public, people will step forward to scrutinize not only valuations, but also the list of options, suggesting possibilities that planners may have concealed or overlooked.

Even if we know the costs and benefits of any particular factor, that does not guarantee that we have considered everything. In the real world, we must acknowledge that for any actual calculation we perform, there could be some cost or benefit or risk we have overlooked. What can we do to avoid overlooking what in retrospect will become painfully obvious? Although it is no guarantee, the best thing I can think of is to open the process to public scrutiny.

Kelman (1981, p. 33) says CBA presumes we should spare no cost in enabling policy makers to make decisions in accordance with CBA. Kelman is right to be critical of such a presumption, for CBA is itself an activity with costs and benefits. The activity of analyzing costs and benefits is not always warranted on cost-benefit grounds. It can be a waste of time. Therefore, CBA on its own grounds ought to be able to recognize that there is a limit to CBA's legitimate scope. Decisions have to be made about what options are worth considering in cost-benefit terms. When we bring people together to scrutinize a proposal, we risk starting a fight over how to distribute costs and benefits. We take people who otherwise might peacefully mind their own business, and we teach them to think of each other as political adversaries. Not all problems can be solved by community policy. Often enough, neighbors are perfectly capable of quietly working things out among themselves, and often enough it is best simply to let them.

10. MUST CBA MEASURE VALUATIONS IN TERMS OF WILLINGNESS TO PAY?

Suppose we want to assess the costs and benefits of building a library on land that otherwise would remain a public park. How are we supposed to measure costs and benefits? Must we look into people's souls to see how much they really want the library? What alternative do we have? What if we asked people how much they are willing to pay to have the library, and compared that to what they say they are willing to pay to keep the park? Would that be a reasonable way of ascertaining how much they care?

CBA often is depicted as requiring us to measure a good's value by asking how much people would pay for it. Such a requirement is indeed problematic. One problem: willingness to pay is a function not only of perceived values but also of resources available for bidding on those values. Poorer people show up as less willing to pay even if, in some other sense, they value the good as much.

Is there anything we could do to make it legitimate to use willingness to pay as a surrogate for value in some other sense? Perhaps. Part of the problem, to judge from the literature, is that surveys designed to measure willingness to pay do not in fact take willingness to pay seriously. What they ask subjects to declare is not willingness to pay but *hypothetical* willingness to pay. The idea is, we justify building a waste treatment plant in a poorer neighborhood when we *judge* that poorer people would not pay as much as richer people would to have the plant built elsewhere. Critics call this environmental racism (because minorities tend to live in poorer neighborhoods). Whatever we call it, it looks preposterous.

Is there an alternative that would be more respectful of neighborhoods that provide the most likely building sites? Suppose we initially choose the site by random lottery, and suppose that by luck of the draw, Beverly Hills is selected as the site of the new waste treatment plant. Suppose we then ask Beverly Hills's rich residents what they are willing to pay to site the plant elsewhere. Suppose they say they jointly would pay ten million dollars to locate the plant elsewhere. Suppose we then announce that the people of Beverly Hills are actually, not just hypothetically, offering ten million to any neighborhood willing to make room for a waste treatment facility that otherwise will be built in Beverly Hills. Suppose one of the poorer neighborhoods votes to accept the bid. Would that be more respectful? Or instead, suppose no one accepts the Beverly Hills offer, and therefore the plant is built in Beverly Hills. Is there anything wrong with richer residents moving out, selling their houses to poorer people willing to live near the plant in order to live in better houses than they otherwise could afford? If siting a waste treatment plant drives down property values so that poorer people can afford to live in Beverly Hills, while rich people take their money elsewhere, is that a problem?

Note that even a random lottery will produce nonrandom results. No matter where the waste treatment facility is built, people who can afford to move away from waste treatment plants tend to be richer than the people who cannot. Home buyers who move in, accepting the nuisance in order to have a nicer house at a lower price, will tend to be poorer than buyers who opt to pay higher prices to live farther from the nuisance. One thing will never change: waste treatment facilities will tend to be found in poorer neighborhoods. Not even putting them all in Beverly Hills could ever change that.

Oddly, activists in effect are agitating for plants to be sited as far as possible from people who work in them, since siting waste treatment facilities within walking distance of the homes of people who might want the jobs they provide is classified as environmental racism. Perhaps the question of how far people have to commute is not important; normally, though, environmentalists urge us to pay more attention to such issues. In any case, if a waste treatment plant must be in a populated area, neighbors will be affected. Someone will have to pay, and no accounting tool is to blame for that.

Critics presume the process of siting waste treatment facilities will *not* be conducted in a respectful manner. They presume politicians will site waste treatment facilities not in response to actual negotiations with communities but rather in response to calculations about what will minimize adverse effects on campaign contributions and ultimately on reelection bids. The critics may be right.[19] If that is how it actually works, then politicians are asking the wrong question, morally speaking. In that case, no accounting method can yield the right answer. Under those circumstances, the point of subjecting the decision to public scrutiny is to lead (possibly racist) politicians not to recalculate answers so much as to start asking the right questions.

11. MUST FUTURE GENERATIONS BE DISCOUNTED?

In financial markets, a dollar acquired today is worth more than a dollar we will acquire in a year. The dollar acquired today can be put to work immediately. At worst, it can be put in the bank, and thus be worth perhaps $1.05 in a year. Therefore, if you ask me how much I would pay today to be given a dollar a year from now, I certainly would not pay as much as a dollar. I would pay something less, perhaps about ninety-five cents. Properly valued, then, the future dollar sells at a discount. Therefore, there is nothing irrational about borrowing against the future to get a profitable project off the ground, even though the cost of borrowing a thousand dollars now will be more than a thousand dollars later.

But here is the catch. There is nothing wrong with taking out a loan, so long as we *pay it back*. But there is something obviously wrong with taking out a loan we have no intention of repaying. In other words, discounting is one thing when the cost of raising capital is internalized; it is something else when we borrow against *someone else's* future rather than our own. We have no right to discount the price that *others* will have to pay for our projects. We have no right to discount externalities. *Redistributive* discounting is objectionable: morally, economically, and sometimes ecologically as well.

Some critics worry about the moral status of the discounting they think CBA presupposes. Thus, Peter Wenz (1989, p. 100) says, "Absurdities arise when the current worth of future human lives is discounted, as CBA requires of all values that will be realized only in the future." As an example of such an absurdity, Wenz (p. 100) goes on to calculate that at a five percent discount rate, "a human life today is worth four human lives that will not be realized for 28.8 years, eight lives that are 43.2 years in the future, and so on." Obviously, Wenz is right: that would be absurd.[20] So, why think CBA requires that life's value, or any other value, be discounted? Some economists say it does not, and few (none that I know) would discount the value of lives in the way Wenz says they must.[21] There are economists who go so far as to claim a proper analysis requires that values *not* be discounted.[22] In any case, if we undertake a CBA, we must decide whether to introduce a discount rate. CBA will not make the decision for us. We also must decide whether to discount all considerations or only some. For example, we must decide whether to discount a life in the same way we discount the financial cost of *saving* a life (say, by building safer highways). To philosophers, the decision appears clear-cut: human lives are not commodities, although things we use to save lives typically are.

The thing about affluent people, and the reason why environmentalists are correct (not merely politically correct) to worry about poverty, is that affluent people can afford to be more future-oriented, that is, to operate with lower discount rates. The task, then, is two-fold: first, to teach people to see their future as depending on resources they are in a position to preserve, conserve, or degrade, and, second, to put them in a position where they can afford to be future-oriented.

CONCLUSIONS

What can you do with a CBA? You can draw conclusions like this: "We conducted CBA, taking the following costs and benefits into account. The proposal before us appears to pass inspection by the lights of such analysis. We therefore recommend further discussion. Or where the proposal does not pass inspection, where the losers would lose more than the winners would gain, we recommend that the proposal be rejected. In either case, we could be wrong. First, there may be costs or benefits we have not anticipated. Second, even known costs and benefits are often impossible to quantify precisely; therefore, our numbers must be viewed with caution. Third, when used in support of a given proposal, CBA need not be decisive, for there are other grounds upon which policies can be prohibited, favorable CBA notwithstanding. Nevertheless, until someone either identifies additional costs or benefits for us to consider, or else informs us that the proposal violates a treaty (for example) that created rights and obligations that render costs and benefits moot, all we can do is go with our best understanding of the information before us. Barring new information, proceeding in accordance with the result of this CBA appears to be the best we can do."

I talked about doing CBA with Full Cost Accounting, but no mechanical procedure can be guaranteed to take all costs into account. For any mechanical procedure we devise, there will be situations where that procedure overlooks something important. This is not a reason to reject the very idea of CBA, though. Rather, it is a reason to be wary of the desire to make decisions in a mechanical way. We cannot wait for someone to devise the perfect procedure, guaranteed to give everything its proper weight. Whatever procedures we devise for making decisions as individuals or as a community, we need to exercise judgment. At some point we draw the line, make a decision, and get on with our lives, realizing that any real-world decision procedure inevitably will be of limited value. It will not be perfect. It never will be beyond question.

CBA with Full Cost Accounting is only one form of CBA. Many other forms of CBA are indefensible, and no ethicist would defend them. We do well not to conflate different forms of CBA, though, and we do well not to demonize the general idea of weighing costs and benefits. CBA is an important response to a real problem. However, it is not magic. There is a limit to what it can do. CBA is a way of organizing information. It can be a forum for eliciting further information. It can be a forum for correcting biased information. It can be a forum for giving affected parties a voice in community decision making, thereby leading to better understanding of, and greater acceptance of, the tradeoffs involved in running a community. CBA can be all of these good things, but it is not necessarily so. CBA can constrain a system's tendency to invite abuse, such as the environmental racism just discussed, but CBA is prone to the same abuse that infects the system as a whole. It is no panacea. It is an antidote to abuse that is itself subject to abuse.

CBA is not inherently biased, but if inputs are biased, then so will be the outputs, generally speaking. However, although the method does not inherently correct for biased inputs, if the process is conducted publicly, so that people can publicly challenge suppliers of biased inputs, there will be some tendency for the process to correct for biased inputs as well. We can hope there will be adequate opportunity for those with minority viewpoints to challenge mainstream biases, but we cannot guarantee it. The most we can say is that CBA done in public view helps to give democracies a fighting chance to operate as democracies are supposed to operate.

NOTES

1. Demand/Supply Report of the Ontario Hydro Commission, as quoted in McDonald, Stevenson, and Craig, (1992) pp. 33–34.

2. In speaking to different people, I find that the terms are not quite standardized. What I have in mind when I speak of Full Cost Accounting is what some people call Multiple Accounts Analysis or Life Cycle Analysis. They might reserve the term 'Full Cost Accounting' to refer to a kind of CBA that considers all costs, but only in terms of their impact on current stake-holders. Whatever term we use, though, suffice it to say I have in mind a kind of CBA that does not deliberately ignore any cost whatever, including costs imposed on future generations.

3. Mishan, (1976) p. 11.

4. I do not know whether Ontario Hydro's change of heart was partly in response to the 1992 *Ethical Assessment* of McDonald, Stevenson, and Craig, cited above.

5. And if everyone belongs to one interest group or another, that does not mean we all break even in the final accounting. It is as if a hundred of us sat in a circle, and the government went round the circle collecting a penny from each, then favoring one of us with a fifty cent windfall. After repeating the process a hundred times, we are each a dollar poorer, fifty cents richer, and happy. So Friedman (1989) describes the game.

6. This is the illuminating central metaphor used by Scherer (1990).

7. In modern moral theory, deontology often is thought of as the main theoretical alternative to utilitarianism. Generally and roughly, deontology is the theory that X is right if and only if X expresses respect for all persons as ends in themselves, and treats no one solely as a mere means.

8. Shrader-Frechette (1998) offers different arguments for a similar conclusion.

9. Kelman (1981, pp. 34–35) argues that there are cases in which an action is right even though its costs exceed its benefits. Kelman has in mind actions that involve keeping a promise or speaking out against injustice, cases in which there is something wrong with the very idea of asking about costs and benefits. In such cases, the balance of costs and benefits normally is not decisive because we should not have been asking about costs and benefits in the first place. All of that is compatible with my claim that, in cases where costs and benefits *should* be taken into account, determining that the losers are losing more than the winners are gaining should be considered a conversation stopper.

10. For a classic discussion of this case, see Thomson (1976).

11. 382 P.2d 109 Oklahoma, 1962. For a discussion of what the case shows about relative merits of statutory versus common law, see Morriss (2000, p. 144).

12. In the terminology of welfare economics, a move is a Pareto-improvement when it makes no one worse off and makes at least some people better off. In the most sophisticated critique of CBA of which I am aware, David Copp attributes to E. J. Mishan (citing an earlier work than the one cited above) the view that CBA's justification is linked

with the notion of Pareto-improvement because when benefits exceed costs, the move is *potentially* Pareto-improving. Copp (1985, p. 143) finds this puzzling, and so do I. As Mishan himself admits in his later work (1976, p. 15), "A Pareto improvement which positively requires that when some are made better off, no one is actually made worse off, is assured of fairly wide acceptance. . . . A *potential* Pareto improvement, which is consistent with a great many people actually being made worse off, has much less appeal."

13. Hubin (1994, p. 172n) says cost-benefit moral theories (admittedly a slightly different topic) are "absolutely agnostic on the question of what things are of intrinsic value."

14. There is also a debate over whether there is a kind of intrinsic value that does not presuppose the existence of a valuer. We often speak of persons as having a value as ends in themselves, independently of any value attributed to them by other valuers. The questions is whether trees, for example, also can in this sense be ends in themselves. The purpose of the "Last Man Argument" in environmental ethics is to set the stage for discussion of this latter question.

15. Kelman has authorized us to delete this phrase from the version of the paper to be reprinted in Schmidtz and Willott (2002).

16. See also Lindblom (1994).

17. As gleaned from case studies "Full Cost Accounting For Decision Making At Ontario Hydro" prepared by ICF Incorporated for the Environmental Protection Agency, and "Environmentally Sustainable Development Guidelines For Southeast False Creek," prepared by Sheltair Inc. For the City of Vancouver, 1998.

18. Hargrove (1989, p. 211) notes that quantitative analysis may be inappropriate when dealing with intrinsic values. Fair enough, but quantitative analysis often is inappropriate with purely instrumental values too. Not all instrumental values are reducible to monetary values. For example, seat belts are of purely instrumental value, yet when the car hits the ditch and begins to roll over, no amount of money would be a reasonable substitute for having our seat belts fastened.

19. Bullard (1990).

20. Actually, it looks economically problematic as well. If we suppose a zero inflation rate, then a dollar in the future is not worth less than a dollar today. It is worth exactly one dollar. That does not change when we introduce the possibility of earning interest. The possibility of interest means only that it is better to get the dollar earlier because we then can earn additional interest. If lives are like dollars in that respect, then the implication is not that a life later is worth less than a life now. Rather, the implication is very roughly that, just as it would be better to have an extra year's interest, it would be better to have an extra year of life. (That is, if I were going to be given a second life, and if I knew my second life would end in the year 2150, I would pay to have that life begin in 2110 rather than 2130. For analogous reasons, the dollar that began to collect interest in 2110 rather than 2130 would sell at a premium.)

21. For a typically circumspect discussion, see Stiglitz (1994).

22. See Cowen (1992); see also Cowen and Parfit (1992).

REFERENCES

Bullard, Robert. (1990) *Dumping In Dixie: Race, Class, and Environmental Quality,* Boulder: Westview Press.

Copp, David. (1985) "Morality, Reason, and Management Science: the Rationale of Cost-Benefit Analysis," *Social Philosophy and Policy* 2 (pp. 128–51).

Cowen, Tyler. (1992) "Consequentialism Implies a Zero Rate of Discount," *Philosophy, Politics, and Society,* sixth series, edited by Peter Laslett and James Fishkin, New Haven: Yale University Press (pp. 162–68).

Cowen, Tyler, and Derek Parfit. (1992) "Against the Social Discount Rate," *Philosophy, Politics, and Society,* sixth series, edited by Peter Laslett and James Fishkin, New Haven: Yale University Press (pp. 144–61).

Friedman, David. (1989) *The Machinery of Freedom,* LaSalle: Open Court Publishing.

Hargrove, Eugene C. (1989) *Foundations of Environmental Ethics,* Denton: Environmental Ethics Books.

Hubin, Donald C. (1994) "The Moral Justification of Benefit/Cost Analysis," *Economics and Philosophy* 10 (pp. 169–94).

Kelman, Steven. (1981) "Cost-Benefit Analysis: An Ethical Critique," *Regulation* (Jan./Feb., pp. 33–40).

Lindblom, Charles. (1994) "The Science of Muddling Through," *Foundations of Administrative Law,* edited by Peter Schuck, New York: Oxford University Press (pp. 104–10).

McDonald, Michael, J. T. Stevenson, and Wesley Craig. (1992) *Finding a Balance of Values: An Ethical Assessment of Ontario Hydro's Demand/Supply Plan,* Report to Aboriginal Research Coalition of Ontario.

Mishan, E. J. (1976) *Elements of Cost-Benefit Analysis,* 2nd ed., London: George Allen & Unwin.

Morriss, Andrew. (2000) "Lessons for Environmental Law from the American Codification Debate," *The Common Law and the Environment,* edited by Roger Meiners and Andrew Morriss, Lanham: Rowman & Littlefield (pp. 130–57).

Sagoff, Mark. (1981) "At the Shrine of Our Lady of Fatima, or Why Political Questions Are Not All Economic," *Arizona Law Review* 23 (pp. 1283–98).

Scherer, Donald. (1990) *Upstream/Downstream: Issues in Environmental Ethics,* Philadelphia: Temple University Press.

Schmidtz, David and Elizabeth Willott. (2002) *Environmental Ethics: What Really Matters. What Really Works,* New York: Oxford University Press.

Shrader-Frechette, Kristin. (1998) "A Defense of Risk-Cost-Benefit Analysis," *Environmental Ethics: Readings In Theory and Application,* edited by Louis Pojman, 2nd ed., Belmont: Wadsworth (pp. 507–14).

Stiglitz, J. E. (1994) "The Rate of Discount for Benefit-Cost Analysis and the Theory of the Second Best," *Cost-Benefit Analysis,* edited by Richard Layard and Stephen Glaister, Cambridge: Cambridge University Press (pp. 116–59).

Styron, William. (1979) *Sophie's Choice,* New York: Random House.

Thomson, Judith Jarvis. (1976) "Killing, Letting Die, and the Trolley Problem," *Monist* 59 (pp. 204–17).

Wenz, Peter. (1989) "Democracy and Environmental Change," *Ethics and Environmental Responsibility,* edited by Nigel Dower, Aldershot: Avebury (pp. 91–109).

10 Public Choice

In 1993, Alistair Cooke reported in the BBC program, *Letter from America*, that Public Choice theory rests on "the homely but important observation that politicians are, after all, no different than the rest of us." This is one important part of an approach founded at the University of Virginia in the early 1960s by James Buchanan and Gordon Tullock.

This approach, analyzing politics under the assumption that people are not angels, was seen as a commonsensical formalization of James Madison's use of exactly that logic, in *Federalist* 51:

> It may be a reflection on human nature, that such devices should be necessary to control the abuses of government. But what is government itself, but the greatest of all reflections on human nature? If men were angels, no government would be necessary. If angels were to govern men, neither external nor internal controls on government would be necessary. In framing a government which is to be administered by men over men, the great difficulty lies in this: you must first enable the government to control the governed; and in the next place oblige it to control itself.

But Public Choice also builds on a second assumption, another key premise of Madison's constitutional thought: politics can be thought of as a kind of mutually beneficial exchange, one that requires cooperation using nonmarket, collective institutions. Some institutions of collective choice are better than others; states, like markets, may fail to behave optimally, but there are conditions (externalities, public goods, etc.) where some form of collective choice mechanism is indispensable.

This second part of the Public Choice approach is all too often ignored, by both critics and proponents. Public Choice could not be *just* the application of economic motivational assumptions to the study of politics; it also requires an understanding that the institutional requirements for political exchange are profoundly different from market mechanisms.

Public Choice originated shortly after 1948, when James Buchanan came across a copy of Swedish economist Knut Wicksell's short book *A Theory of Just Taxation* (1898). Wicksell had argued that the only way to ensure Pareto optimality in public decisions was to require unanimity, since otherwise some could benefit at the expense of others. Buchanan recognized that Wicksell's notion of unanimity was crucial to understanding politics as a kind of exchange, analogous to, but different from, market exchange. But Buchanan quickly realized that requiring unanimity on decisions about political outcomes was simply unworkable.

Buchanan resolved to work out conditions under which unanimous consent (or something close to it) might be required at the level of choice of *rules*, with the outcomes selected under those rules then binding all citizens not because the outcomes received consent but because of prior consent to the rules that allowed them. This ability to voluntarily enter into contracts or agreements, with the explicit consent to suffer sanctions if terms of the contract are violated, is the essence of free markets. Buchanan sought to embed the same principle of contractarian consent in political exchange, first in his own writing and then most famously in the classic book *The Calculus of Consent* (1962), jointly authored by Buchanan and Tullock. These elements are all present in the first reading in this section, Buchanan's famous retrospective, "Politics without Romance."

Anthony Downs's contribution, "An Economic Theory of Political Action in a Democracy," is an examination of the incentives and problems created by incomplete information in voting processes. The key insight of this approach is not, as is often claimed by critics, that voters vote selfishly. Citizens can be assumed to have a wide variety of nonselfish motivations. The key problem of democracy, in Downs's view, is that voters have little incentive to acquire and process information about candidate platforms or the relation between various policies (means) and desired outcomes (the actual ends desired by voters).

1. Given the cost of gathering and processing information, voters will not invest in obtaining detailed information about candidates and their policies. Their "rational ignorance" will predictably lead voters to rely on intellectual shortcuts and general ideology to decide how to vote. A left-right ideological divide will stand in for the complex many-dimensioned space of actual policy.
2. Knowing that this is the essential grounds of political conflict, groups of political aspirants will organize themselves into teams, known as "parties," that seek to place candidates in office. These parties will take positions in the left-right ideological space, focusing on general statements of values rather than particular policy statements.
3. In a typical election, the party or candidate that locates nearer to the location of the preference of the median voter will have a better chance of winning. Knowing this, parties and candidates will move toward, and under some circumstances actually converge on, this median position, implying that observed party positions on many issues may be indistinguishable. However, when there is an issue or ideology that polarizes voters (one with multiple preference peaks rather than a single-peaked bell curve), politicians and parties will tend to diverge rather than converge on the same position in order to capture more votes (this is also true when there are more than two parties or candidates running against each other).

Michael Munger offers a short and whimsical view of rent-seeking, one of the central research areas in Public Choice. In standard economics, a "rent" is any return on an asset or activity above the competitive or opportunity cost rate of return. Public Choice scholars, beginning with Tullock (1967, who originated the concept) and Krueger (1974, who coined the name) define a "rent" as an artificially created return, a prize, resource transfer, property right or protected market. Rent *seeking* is then the resources dissipated in pursuit of ownership or *de facto* control of the rent, usually by manipulating the political system to obtain special favors for a particular industry.

The key difference between rent-seeking, which is a net loss of value, and profit-seeking, which can result in either an increase or decrease in value, is that rent-seeking typically involves the dissipation of some or most of the value of an artificially created transfer.[1] As Munger describes it, if one secures political protection from (for example) economic competition society lose twice. First, protection from competition restricts choices for consumers, raises prices, and throttles innovation. Second, and worse, the efforts by political actors to secure this protection distorts investment patterns and strategies, moving resources from the creative innovation of new products to investment in political assets (such as the plush lobbyist offices along K Street in Washington, DC), that help one secure the political protection in the first place.

The simple way to think of the difference between profit-seeking and rent-seeking is that the former encourages investment in engineers and sales people (in an attempt to attract customers) while the latter encourages investing in lobbyists and lawyers (in an attempt to attract politically powerful elected *officials* or appointed commissioners).

James Buchanan's "How Can Constitutions Be Designed . . .?" focuses on a constraint that would restrict many policies favored by politicians, out of concern for the unanimity principle described above. Buchanan's object is to ensure coercion or force can be used only with the consent of those being subjected to the coercion. In a way, this is simply the "equal protection" guarantee in portions of the U.S. Constitution, which guarantees that all citizens must enjoy equality before the law, so that none can be singled out or excluded.

The idea that individuals should rely on general rules because they lack the foresight to choose outcomes perfectly, combined with Wicksell's concern that unanimity or near-unanimity is required to ensure consent, gives rise to Buchanan's argument about the generality principle. For example, for a regulation on business to be legitimate, it must apply to all businesses, rather than singling some out for special treatment. If more taxes are needed, then taxes can be raised, but the increase must fall on everyone. This constraint might be seen as preventing some technically superior rules, rules that would discriminate "optimally" rather than treat everyone equally. But Buchanan makes two arguments in favor of keeping the restriction in place. First, no one and no group could have enough knowledge to be sure that waiving the rule is helpful rather than harmful. Second, people cannot be relied on to use waivers only to improve policy, even if they did have such knowledge. The temptation would be to use apparently innocuous restrictions to harm enemies and reward friends.

The final reading, by Michael Huemer, represents a counterweight to some of the more optimistic conclusions of Public Choice theory. As Huemer points out, and as was noted above, people are often ignorant—perhaps rationally so—of the complex considerations relevant to political choices. Yet that does not keep them from forming strong opinions, often on the basis of weak or biased information, opinions they take pleasure in forming and in acting on.[2] And their doing so is, in an important sense, irrational. Huemer's argument requires us to distinguish two kinds of rationality: instrumental rationality, which aims at utility; and epistemic rationality, which aims at truth. When Downs says "it is always rational to perform any act if its marginal return is larger than its marginal cost," he is clearly referring to instrumental rationality. But when Crick and Watson tell us that it is rational to believe that DNA has a helical structure, they are making a claim about what we have reason to believe the universe is like, whether or not the marginal benefits of knowing this fact exceed its marginal costs.

Anyone who has played competitive sports or fought a battle with cancer knows that beliefs can function as placebos, and that instrumental and epistemic rationality can come apart. In other words, we can be rationally irrational. Believing that you're better than your opponents (even if you're not), or that you can beat cancer (even if your prognosis is grim), may increase your chances of achieving your goals. In politics, especially, citizens have little incentive to correct poorly formed beliefs because doing so is unlikely to make a difference to electoral outcomes. Thus, Huemer thinks, democratic citizens are often rationally (in the instrumental sense) irrational (in the epistemic sense). Huemer thinks political irrationality is humanity's greatest problem since it impairs our ability to solve collective action problems through political institutions.

NOTES

1. We have followed conventional usage in characterizing rent-seeking as a negative sum interaction. But careful readers will notice that, given the technical definition of "rent" and the ordinary definition of "seeking," it is perfectly conceivable that sometimes *seeking rents* can be a positive sum game. The phrase "rent-seeking," then, can be misleading. For simplicity, we follow the classic account given by James Buchanan and Gordon Tullock (1980): "Rent-seeking involves social waste. Resources that could otherwise be devoted to value-producing activity are engaged in competitive effort that determines nothing other than the distributive results. Rent-seeking, as such, is totally without allocative value, although, of course, the institutional creation of an opportunity for rent-seeking ensures a net destruction of economic value."

2. It is worth emphasizing that rational ignorance and rational irrationality are not always morally excusable. Some philosophers, beginning with William Clifford in *The Ethics of Belief*, condemn people for forming beliefs that make themselves feel better but have pernicious social consequences. A variety of political and religious beliefs arguably fall under this category.

FURTHER READING

Brennan, Geoffrey and Loren Lomasky. 1993. *Democracy and Decision: The Pure Theory of Electoral Politics*. Cambridge University Press.

Brennan, Geoffrey and James Buchanan. 1988. "Is Public Choice Immoral?" *Virginia Law Review* 74 (2): 179–189.

Buchanan, James, and Roger Congleton. 1998. *Politics by Principle, Not Interest: Toward Nondiscriminatory Democracy*. Cambridge University Press.

Buchanan, James, and Gordon Tullock. 1962. *The Calculus of Consent*. University of Michigan Press.

Caplan, Bryan. 2001. "Rational Ignorance vs. Rational Irrationality." *Kyklos* 54 (1): 3–26.

Downs, Anthony. 1957. *An Economic Theory of Democracy*. Harper and Row.

Goodstein, Eban and Stephen Polasky. 2014. "The Political Economy of Environmental Regulation," in *Economics and the Environment*, 7th ed. Wiley-Blackwell.

Kelman, Steven. 1987. "Public Choice and Public Spirit." *Public Interest* 87: 80–94.

Krueger, Anne. 1974. "The Political Economy of the Rent-Seeking Society." *American Economic Review* 64 (3): 291–303.

List, Christian and Philip Pettit. 2002. "Aggregating Sets of Judgments: An Impossibility Result." *Economics and Philosophy*, 18: 89–110.

Mackie, Gerry. 2003. *Democracy Defended*. Cambridge University Press.

Munger, Michael and Kevin Munger. 2015. *Choosing in Groups: Analytical Politics Revisited*. Cambridge University Press.

Pennington, Mark. 2011. *Robust Political Economy*. Edward Elgar Publishers.

Pincione, Guido and Fernando Teson. 2011. *Rational Choice and Democratic Deliberation: A Theory of Discourse Failure*. Cambridge University Press.

Simmons, Randy. 2011. *Beyond Politics: The Roots of Government Failure*. Independent Institute Publishing.

Somin, Ilya. 2013. *Democracy and Political Ignorance: Why Smaller Government is Smarter*. Stanford University Press.

Yandle, Bruce. 1983. "Bootleggers and Baptists: The Education of a Regulatory Economist." *Regulation*, 7(3) 12–16.

JAMES BUCHANAN

Public Choice: Politics without Romance

2003

Public choice should be understood as a research programme rather than a discipline or even a sub-discipline of economics. Its origins date to the mid-20th century, and viewed retrospectively, the theoretical "gap" in political economy that it emerged to fill seems so large that its development seems to have been inevitable.

Nations emerging from World War II, including the Western democracies, were allocating between one-third and one-half of their total product through political institutions rather than through markets. Economists, however, were devoting their efforts almost exclusively to understanding and explaining the market sector. My own modest first entry into the subject matter, in 1949, was little more than a call for those economists who examined taxes and spending to pay some attention to empirical reality, and thus to politics.

Initially, the work of economists in this area raised serious doubts about the political process. Working simultaneously, but independently, Kenneth Arrow and Duncan Black proved that democracy, interpreted as majority rule, could not work to promote any general or public interest. The now-famous "impossibility theorem," as published in Arrow's book *Social Choice and Individual Values* (1951), stimulated an extended discussion. What Arrow and Black had in fact done was to discover or rediscover the phenomenon of "majority cycles," whereby election results rotate in continuous cycles with no equilibrium or stopping point. The suggestion of this analysis was that majoritarian democracy is inherently unstable.

I entered this discussion with a generalised critique of the analysis generated by the Arrow-Black approach. Aren't "majority cycles" the most desirable outcome of a democratic process? After all, any attainment of political equilibrium via majority rule would amount to the permanent imposition of the majority's will on the outvoted minority. Would not a guaranteed rotation of outcomes be preferable, enabling the members of the minority in one round of voting to come back in subsequent rounds and ascend to majority membership? My concern, then and later, was the prevention of discrimination against minorities rather than stability of political outcomes. The question, from an economist's perspective, was how to obtain a combination of efficiency and justice under majority rule.

WICKSELL'S INSIGHT

The great Swedish economist Knut Wicksell was the most important of all precursory figures in public choice. In his dissertation, published in 1896, he was concerned about both the injustice and the inefficiency resulting from unfettered majority rule in parliamentary assemblies. Majority rule seemed quite likely to impose net costs or damages on large segments of the citizen or taxpayer group. Why should members of such minorities, facing discrimination, lend their support to democratic political structures? Unless all groups can benefit from the ultimate exchange with government, how can overall stability be maintained?

These considerations led Wicksell to question the efficacy of majority rule itself. His solution to the problem was to propose that majority rule be modified in the direction of unanimity. If the agreement of all persons in the voting group is required to implement collective action, it would guarantee that all

James Buchanan, "Public Choice: Politics without Romance." *Policy* 19 (3) (2003): 13–18.

persons secure net gains and, further, that the approved actions would yield benefits in excess of costs. Of course, Wicksell recognised that, if applied in a literal voting setting, a requirement of unanimity would produce stalemate. To recognise this, however, does not diminish the value of the unanimity rule as a benchmark for comparative evaluation. In suggestions for practical constitutional reforms, Wicksell supported changes in voting rules from simple to qualified or super majorities, for example, a requirement of five-sixths approval for collective proposals.

In their analyses, Black and Arrow had assumed, more or less implicitly, that the choices to be voted on exist prior to, and outside of, the decision-making process itself. Wicksell understood the error in this assumption, although he did not recognise the importance of this insight. Neither did Gordon Tullock, who wrote a seminal paper in 1959 using the example of farmer voters, each of whom wants to have his local road repaired with costs borne by the whole community. Tullock showed that majority rule allows for coalitions of such farmers to generate election results that impose unjust costs on the whole community while producing inefficiently large outlays on local roads.

If majority rule produces unjust and inefficient outcomes, and if political stability is secured only by discrimination against minorities, how can democracy, as the organising principle for political structure, possibly claim normative legitimacy? Wicksell's criterion for achieving justice and efficiency in collective action—the shift from majority rule toward unanimity—seems institutionally impractical. But without some such reform, how could taxpayers be assured that their participation in the democracy would yield net benefits?

CONSTITUTIONAL ECONOMICS

In implicit response to these questions, Tullock and I commenced to work on what was to become *The Calculus of Consent,* published in 1962. The central contribution of this book was to identify a two-level structure of collective decision-making. We distinguished between "ordinary politics," consisting of decisions made in legislative assemblies, and "constitutional politics," consisting of decisions made about the rules for ordinary politics.

We were not, of course, inventing this distinction. Both in legal theory and in practice, constitutional law had long been distinguished from statute law. What we did was to bring this distinction into economic analysis. Doing so allowed us to answer the questions posed previously: From the perspective of both justice and efficiency, majority rule may safely be allowed to operate in the realm of ordinary politics provided that there is generalised consensus on the constitution, or on the rules that define and limit what can be done through ordinary politics. It is in arriving at this constitutional framework where Wicksell's idea of requiring unanimity—or at least super majorities—may be practically incorporated.

In a sense, the analysis in our book could have been interpreted as a formalisation of the structure that James Madison and his colleagues had in mind when they constructed the American Constitution. At the least, it offered a substantive criticism of the then-dominant elevation of unfettered majority rule to sacrosanct status in political science.

Our book was widely well received, which prompted Tullock and me, who were then at the University of Virginia, to initiate and organise a small research conference in April 1963. We brought together economists, political scientists, sociologists and scholars from other disciplines, all of whom were engaged in research outside the boundaries of their disciplines. The discussion was sufficiently stimulating to motivate the formation of an organisation which we first called the Committee on Non-Market Decision-Making, and to initiate plans for a journal to be called Papers on Non-Market Decision-Making.

We were unhappy with these awkward labels, and after several meetings there emerged the new name "public choice," both for the organisation and the journal. In this way the Public Choice Society and the journal *Public Choice* came into being. Both have proved to be quite successful as institutional embodiments of the research programme, and sister organisations and journals have since been set up in Europe and Asia.

Many sub-programmes have emerged from the umbrella of public choice. One in particular deserves mention—"rent seeking," a subprogramme initiated in a paper by Tullock in 1967, and christened with this title by Anne Krueger in 1974. Its central idea emerges from the natural mindset of the economist, whose understanding and explanation of human interaction depends critically on predictable responses to measurable incentives. In essence, it extends the idea of the profit motive from the economic sphere to the sphere of collective action. It presupposes that if there is value to be gained through politics, persons will invest resources in efforts to capture this value. It also demonstrates how this investment is wasteful in an aggregate-value sense.

Tullock's early treatment of rent seeking was concentrated on monopoly, tariffs and theft, but the list could be almost indefinitely expanded. If the government is empowered to grant monopoly rights or tariff protection to one group, at the expense of the general public or of designated losers, it follows that potential beneficiaries will compete for the prize. And since only one group can be rewarded, the resources invested by other groups—which could have been used to produce valued goods and services—are wasted. Given this basic insight, much of modern politics can be understood as rent-seeking activity. Pork-barrel politics is only the most obvious example. Much of the growth of the bureaucratic or regulatory sector of government can best be explained in terms of the competition between political agents for constituency support through the use of promises of discriminatory transfers of wealth.

As noted, the primary contribution of *The Calculus of Consent* was to distinguish two levels of collective action, ordinary or day-to-day politics and constitutional politics. Indeed, the subtitle of that book was "Logical Foundations of Constitutional Democracy." Clearly, political action takes place at two distinct levels, one within the existing set of rules or constitution, the other establishing the rules or constitution that impose limits on subsequent actions.

Only recently have economists broken away from the presumption that constraints on choices are always imposed from the outside. Recent research has involved the choice of constraints, even on the behavior of persons in non-collective settings, for instance, with regard to drug or gambling addiction. But even beyond that, what I have called the "constitutional way of thinking" shifts attention to the framework rules of political order—the rules that secure consensus among members of the body politic. It is at this level that individuals calculate their terms of exchange with the state or with political authority. They may well calculate that they are better off for their membership in the constitutional order, even while assessing the impact of ordinary political actions to be contrary to their interests.

A somewhat loose way of putting this is to say that in a constitutional democracy, persons owe loyalty to the constitution rather than to the government. I have long argued that on precisely this point, American public attitudes are quite different from those in Europe.

OBJECTIONS TO PUBLIC CHOICE

There is a familiar criticism of public choice theory to the effect that it is ideologically biased. In comparing and analysing alternative sets of constitutional rules, both those in existence and those that might be introduced prospectively, how does public choice theory, as such, remain neutral in the scientific sense?

Here it is necessary to appreciate the prevailing mindset of social scientists and philosophers at the midpoint of the 20th century when public choice arose. The socialist ideology was pervasive, and was supported by the allegedly neutral research programme called "theoretical welfare economics," which concentrated on identifying the failures of observed markets to meet idealised standards. In sum, this branch of inquiry offered theories of market failure. But failure in comparison with what? The implicit presumption was always that politicised corrections for market failures would work perfectly. In other words, market failures were set against an idealised politics.

Public choice then came along and provided analyses of the behavior of persons acting politically, whether voters, politicians or bureaucrats. These analyses exposed the essentially false comparisons that were then informing so much of both scientific and public opinion. In a very real sense, public choice became a set of theories of governmental failures, as an offset to the theories of market failures that had previously emerged from theoretical welfare economics. Or, as I put it in the title of a lecture in Vienna in 1978, public choice may be summarised by the three-word description, "politics without romance."

The public choice research programme is better seen as a correction of the scientific record than as the introduction of an anti-governmental ideology. Regardless of any ideological bias, exposure to public choice analysis necessarily brings a more critical attitude toward politicised nostrums to alleged socio-economic problems. Public choice almost literally forces the critic to be pragmatic in comparing alternative constitutional arrangements, disallowing any presumption that bureaucratic corrections for market failures will accomplish the desired objectives.

A more provocative criticism of public choice centres on the claim that it is immoral. The source of this charge lies in the application to politics of the assumption that individuals in the marketplace behave in a self-interested way. More specifically, economic models of behaviour include net wealth, an externally measurable variable, as an important "good" that individuals seek to maximise. The moral condemnation of public choice is centred on the presumed transference of this element of economic theory to political analysis. Critics argue that people acting politically—for example, as voters or as legislators—do not behave as they do in markets. Individuals are differently motivated when they are choosing "for the public" rather than for themselves in private choice capacities. Or so the criticism runs.

At base, this criticism stems from a misunderstanding that may have been fostered by the failure of economists to acknowledge the limits of their efforts. The economic model of behaviour, even if restricted to market activity, should never be taken to provide the be-all and end-all of scientific explanation. Persons act from many motives, and the economic model concentrates attention only on one of the many possible forces behind actions. Economists do, of course, presume that the "goods" they employ in their models for predicting behaviour are relatively important. And in fact, the hypothesis that promised shifts in net wealth modify political behaviour in predictable ways has not been readily falsifiable empirically.

Public choice, as an inclusive research programme, incorporates the presumption that persons do not readily become economic eunuchs as they shift from market to political participation. Those who respond predictably to ordinary incentives in the marketplace do not fail to respond at all when they act as citizens. The public choice theorist should, of course, acknowledge that the strength and predictive power of the strict economic model of behaviour is somewhat mitigated as the shift is made from private market to collective choice. Persons in political roles may, indeed, act to a degree in terms of what they consider to be the general interest. Such acknowledgment does not, however, in any way imply that the basic explanatory model loses all of its predictive potential, or that ordinary incentives no longer matter.

IMPACT OF PUBLIC CHOICE

Public choice theory has developed and matured over the course of a full half-century. It is useful to assess the impact and effects of this programme, both on thinking in the scientific community and in the formation of public attitudes. By simple comparison with the climate of opinion in 1950, both the punditry and the public are more critical of politics and politicians, more cynical about the motivations of political action, and less naive in thinking that political nostrums offer easy solutions to social problems. And this shift in attitudes extends well beyond the loss of belief in the efficacy of socialism, a loss of belief grounded both in historical regime failures and in the collapse of intellectually idealised structures.

As I noted earlier, when we look back at the scientific and public climates of discussion 50 years ago, the prevailing mindset was socialist in its underlying presupposition that government offered the solution to social problems. But there was a confusing amalgam of Marxism and ideal political theory involved: Governments, as observed, were modelled and condemned by Marxists as furthering class interests, but governments which might be installed "after the revolution," so to speak, would become both omniscient and benevolent.

In some of their implicit modelling of political behavior aimed at furthering special group or class interests, the Marxists seemed to be closet associates of public choice, even as they rejected methodological individualism. But how was the basic Marxist critique of politics, as observed, to be transformed into the idealised politics of the benevolent and omniscient superstate? This question was simply left glaringly unanswered. And the debates of the 1930s were considered by confused economists of the time to have been won by the socialists rather than by their opponents, Ludwig von Mises and Friedrich Hayek. Both sides, to an extent, neglected the relevance of incentives in motivating human action, including political action.

The structure of ideas that was adduced in support of the emerging Leviathan welfare state was logically flawed and could have been maintained only through long-continued illusion. But, interestingly, the failure, in whole or in part, of the socialist structure of ideas did not come from within the academy. Mises and Hayek were not successful in their early efforts, and classical liberalism seemed to be at its nadir at mid-century. Failure came, not from a collapse of an intellectually defunct structure of ideas, but from the cumulative record of non-performance in the implementation of extended collectivist schemes—non-performance measured against promised claims, something that could be observed directly. In other words, governments everywhere overreached. They tried to do more than the institutional framework would support. This record of failure, both in the socialist and welfare states, came to be recognised widely, commencing in the 1960s and accelerating in the 1970s.

Where is the influence of public choice in this history? I do not claim that it dislodged the prevailing socialist mindset in the academies, and that this intellectual shift then exerted feedback on political reality. What I do claim is that public choice exerted major influence in providing a coherent understanding and interpretation of what could be everywhere observed. The public directly sensed that collectivistic schemes were failing, that politicisation did not offer the promised correctives for any and all social ills, that governmental intrusions often made things worse rather than better. How could these direct observations be fitted into a satisfactory understanding?

Public choice came along and offered a foundation for such an understanding. Armed with nothing more than the rudimentary insights from public choice, persons could understand why, once established, bureaucracies tend to grow apparently without limit and without connection to initially promised functions. They could understand why pork-barrel politics dominated the attention of legislators; why there seems to be a direct relationship between the overall size of government and the investment in efforts to secure special concessions from government (rent seeking); why the tax system is described by the increasing number of special credits, exemptions, and loopholes; why balanced budgets are so hard to secure; and why strategically placed industries secure tariff protection.

A version of the old fable about the king's nakedness may be helpful here. Public choice is like the small boy who said that the king really has no clothes. Once he said this, everyone recognised that the king's nakedness had been recognised, but that no-one had really called attention to this fact.

Let us be careful not to claim too much, however. Public choice did not emerge from some profoundly new insight, some new discovery, some social science miracle. Public choice, in its basic insights into the workings of politics, incorporates an understanding of human nature that differs little, if at all, from that of James Madison and his colleagues at the time of the American Founding. The essential wisdom of the 18th century, of Adam Smith and classical political economy and of the American Founders, was lost through two centuries of intellectual folly. Public choice does little more than incorporate a rediscovery of this wisdom and its implications into economic analyses of modern politics.

ANTHONY DOWNS

An Economic Theory of Political Action in a Democracy[1]

1957

I

In spite of the tremendous importance of government decisions in every phase of economic life, economic theorists have never successfully integrated government with private decision-makers in a single general equilibrium theory. Instead they have treated government action as an exogenous variable, determined by political considerations that lie outside the purview of economics. This view is really a carry-over from the classical premise that the private sector is a self-regulating mechanism and that any government action beyond maintenance of law and order is "interference" with it rather than an intrinsic part of it.[2]

However, in at least two fields of economic theory, the centrality of government action has forced economists to formulate rules that indicate how government "should" make decisions. Thus in the field of public finance, Hugh Dalton states:

> As a result of [the] operations of public finance, changes take place in the amount and in the nature of the wealth which is produced, and in the distribution of that wealth among individuals and classes. Are these changes in their aggregate effects socially advantageous? If so the operations are justified; if not, not. The best system of public finance is that which secures the maximum social advantage from the operations which it conducts.[3]

A similar attempt to differentiate the operations "proper" to government from those "proper" to private agents has been made by Harvey W. Peck, who writes: "If public operation of an enterprise will produce a greater net social utility, the services rendered by this enterprise should belong in the category of public goods."[4] In addition, several welfare economists have posited general principles to guide government action in the economy. For example, Abba P. Lerner indirectly states such a rule when he says: "If it is desired to maximize the total satisfaction in a society, the rational procedure is to divide income on an equalitarian basis."[5]

Admittedly, this list of examples is not very long, primarily because overt statements of a decision rule to guide government action are extremely rare in economic theory. However, it does not unduly distort reality to state that most welfare economists and many public finance theorists implicitly assume that the "proper" function of government is to maximize social welfare. Insofar as they face the problem of government decision-making at all, they nearly all subscribe to some approximation of this normative rule.

The use of this rule has led to two major difficulties. First, it is not clear what is meant by "social welfare," nor is there any agreement about how to "maximize" it. In fact, a long controversy about the nature of social welfare in the "new welfare economics" led to Kenneth Arrow's conclusion that no rational method of maximizing social welfare can possibly be found unless strong restrictions are placed on the preference orderings of the individuals in society.[6]

The complexities of this problem have diverted attention from the second difficulty raised by the view

Anthony Downs, "An Economic Theory of Political Action in a Democracy." *The Journal of Political Economy* 65 (2) (1957): 135–150. By permission of University of Chicago Press.

that government's function is to maximize social welfare. Even if social welfare could be defined, and methods of maximizing it could be agreed upon, what reason is there to believe that the men who run the government would be motivated to maximize it? To state that they "should" do so does not mean that they will. As Schumpeter, one of the few economists who have faced this problem, has pointed out:

> It does not follow that the social meaning of a type of activity will necessarily provide the motive power, hence the explanation of the latter. If it does not, a theory that contents itself with an analysis of the social end or need to be served cannot be accepted as an adequate account of the activities that serve it.[7]

Schumpeter here illuminates a crucial objection to most attempts to deal with government in economic theory: they do not really treat the government as part of the division of labor. Every agent in the division of labor has both a private motive and a social function. For example, the social function of a coal-miner is removing coal from the ground, since this activity provides utility for others. But he is motivated to carry out this function by his desire to earn income, not by any desire to benefit others. Similarly, every other agent in the division of labor carries out his social function primarily as a means of attaining his own private ends: the enjoyment of income, prestige, or power. Much of economic theory consists in essence of proving that men thus pursuing their own ends may nevertheless carry out their social functions with great efficiency, at least under certain conditions.

In light of this reasoning, any attempt to construct a theory of government action without discussing the motives of those who run the government must be regarded as inconsistent with the main body of economic analysis. Every such attempt fails to face the fact that governments are concrete institutions run by men, because it deals with them on a purely normative level. As a result, these attempts can never lead to an integration of government with other decision-makers in a general equilibrium theory. Such integration demands a positive approach that explains how the governors are led to act by their own selfish motives. In the following sections, I present a model of government decision-making based on this approach.

II

In building this model, I shall use the following definitions:

1. *Government* is that agency in the division of labor which has the power to coerce all other agents in society; it is the locus of "ultimate" power in a given area.[8]
2. A *democracy* is a political system that exhibits the following characteristics:
    a. Two or more parties compete in periodic elections for control of the governing apparatus.
    b. The party (or coalition of parties) winning a majority of votes gains control of the governing apparatus until the next election.
    c. Losing parties never attempt to prevent the winners from taking office, nor do winners use the powers of office to vitiate the ability of losers to compete in the next election.
    d. All sane, law-abiding adults who are governed are citizens, and every citizen has one and only one vote in each election.

Though these definitions are both somewhat ambiguous, they will suffice for present purposes.

Next I set forth the following axioms:

1. Each political party is a team of men who seek office solely in order to enjoy the income, prestige, and power that go with running the governing apparatus.[9]
2. The winning party (or coalition) has complete control over the government's actions until the next election. There are no votes of confidence between elections either by a legislature or by the electorate, so the governing party cannot

be ousted before the next election. Nor are any of its orders resisted or sabotaged by an intransigent bureaucracy.

3. Government's economic powers are unlimited. It can nationalize everything, hand everything over to private interests, or strike any balance between these extremes.
4. The only limit on government's powers is that the incumbent party cannot in any way restrict the political freedom of opposition parties or of individual citizens, unless they seek to overthrow it by force.
5. Every agent in the model—whether an individual, a party or a private coalition—behaves rationally at all times; that is, it proceeds toward its goals with a minimal use of scarce resources and undertakes only those actions for which marginal return exceeds marginal cost.[10]

From these definitions and axioms springs my central hypothesis: political parties in a democracy formulate policy strictly as a means of gaining votes. They do not seek to gain office in order to carry out certain preconceived policies or to serve any particular interest groups; rather they formulate policies and serve interest groups in order to gain office. Thus their social function—which is to formulate and carry out policies when in power as the government—is accomplished as a by-product of their private motive—which is to attain the income, power, and prestige of being in office.

This hypothesis implies that, in a democracy, the government always acts so as to maximize the number of votes it will receive. In effect, it is an entrepreneur selling policies for votes instead of products for money. Furthermore, it must compete for votes with other parties, just as two or more oligopolists compete for sales in a market. Whether or not such a government maximizes social welfare (assuming this process can be defined) depends upon how the competitive struggle for power influences its behavior. We cannot assume a priori that this behavior is socially optimal any more than we can assume a priori that a given firm produces the socially optimal output.

I shall examine the nature of government decision-making in two contexts: (1) in a world in which there is perfect knowledge and information is costless and (2) in a world in which knowledge is imperfect and information is costly.

III

The analysis of government decision making in a perfectly-informed world is intended only to highlight the basic relationship between a democratic government and its citizens. This relationship can be stated in the following set of propositions:

1. The actions of the government are a function of the way it expects voters to vote and of the strategies of its opposition.
2. The government expects voters to vote according to (*a*) changes in their utility incomes from government activity and (*b*) the strategies of opposition parties.
3. Voters actually vote according to (*a*) changes in their utility incomes from government activity and (*b*) the alternatives offered by the opposition.[11]
4. Voters' utility incomes from government activity depend on the actions taken by government during the election period.
5. The strategies of opposition parties depend on their views of the voters' utility incomes from government activity and on the actions taken by the government in power.

These propositions actually form a set of five equations containing five unknowns: expected votes, actual votes, opposition strategies, government actions, and individual utility incomes from government activity. Thus the political structure of a democracy can be viewed in terms of a set of simultaneous equations similar to those often used to analyze an economic structure.

Because the citizens of our model democracy are rational, each of them views elections strictly as means of selecting the government most beneficial to him. Each citizen estimates the utility income from government action he expects each party would provide him if it were in power in the forthcoming election period, that is, he first estimates the utility income Party A would provide him, then the income Party B would provide, and so on. He votes for whatever party he believes would provide him with the highest utility income from government action. The primary factor influencing his estimate of each party's future performance is not its campaign promises about the future but its performance during the period just ending. Thus his voting decision is based on a comparison of the utility income he actually received during this period from the actions of the incumbent party and those he believes he would have received had each of the opposition parties been in power (I assume that each opposition party has taken a verbal stand on every issue dealt with concretely by the incumbents). This procedure allows him to found his decision on facts rather than on conjectures. Of course, since he is helping to choose a future government, he modifies his analysis of each party's past performance according to his estimate of probable changes in its behavior. Nevertheless, the current record of the incumbents remains the central item in his evaluation.

The government also makes decisions rationally, but its behavior is not so easy to analyze, because it is engaged in political warfare with its opponents. Each party resembles a player in an *N*-person game or an oligopolist engaged in cutthroat competition. However, the conjectural variation problem is somewhat simplified, because the incumbent party must always commit itself on each issue before the opposition parties do. Since it is in power, it must act whenever the occasion for a decision arises, if failure to respond is counted as a form of action. But the opposition, which is not responsible for the government, can wait until the pressure of events has forced the governing party to commit itself. Thus opposition parties have a strategic advantage—which incidentally makes the analysis of interparty warfare simpler than it would be if all parties revealed their strategies simultaneously.

However, I shall not explore party strategies in a perfectly informed world, because nearly all the conclusions that could be drawn are inapplicable to the imperfectly informed world in which we are primarily interested. Only one point should be stressed: in a world where perfect knowledge prevails, the government gives the preferences of each citizen exactly the same weight as those of every other citizen. This does not mean that its policies favor all citizens equally, since strategic considerations may lead it to ignore some citizens and to woo others ardently or to favor some with one policy and others with another. But it never deliberately eschews the vote of Citizen A to gain that of Citizen B. Since each citizen has one and only one vote, it cannot gain by trading A's vote for B's, *ceteris paribus*. In short, the equality of franchise is successful as a device for distributing political power equally among citizens.

IV

Lack of complete information on which to base decisions is a condition so basic to human life that it influences the structure of almost every social institution. In politics especially, its effects are profound. For this reason, I devote the rest of my analysis to the impact of imperfect knowledge upon political action in a democracy.

In this model, imperfect knowledge means (1) that parties do not always know exactly what citizens want: (2) that citizens do not always know what the government or its opposition has done, is doing, or should be doing to serve their interests; and (3) that the information needed to overcome both types of ignorance is costly—in other words, that scarce resources must be used to procure and assimilate it. Although these conditions have many effects upon the operation of government in the model, I concentrate on only three: persuasion, ideologies, and rational ignorance.

V

As long as we retain the assumption of perfect knowledge, no citizen can possibly influence another's vote. Each knows what would benefit him most, what the government is doing, and what other parties would do if they were in power. Therefore, the citizen's political taste structure, which I assume to be fixed, leads him directly to an unambiguous decision about how he should vote. If he remains rational, no persuasion can change his mind.

But, as soon as ignorance appears, the clear path from taste structure to voting decision becomes obscured by lack of knowledge. Though some voters want a specific party to win because its policies are clearly the most beneficial to them, others are highly uncertain about which party they prefer. They are not sure just what is happening to them or what would happen to them if another party were in power. They need more facts to establish a clear preference. By providing these facts, persuaders can become effective.

Persuaders are not interested per se in helping people who are uncertain become less so; they want to produce a decision that aids their cause. Therefore, they provide only those facts which are favorable to whatever group they are supporting. Thus, even if we assume that no erroneous or false data exist, some men are able to influence others by presenting them with a biased selection of facts.

This possibility has several extraordinarily important consequences for the operation of government. First, it means that some men are more important than others politically, because they can influence more votes than they themselves cast. Since it takes scarce resources to provide information to hesitant citizens, men who command such resources are able to wield more than proportional political influence, *ceteris paribus*. The government, being rational, cannot overlook this fact in designing policy. As a result, equality of franchise no longer assures net equality of influence over government action. In fact, it is irrational for a democratic government to treat its citizens with equal deference in a world in which knowledge is imperfect.

Second, the government is itself ignorant of what its citizens want it to do. Therefore it must send out representatives (1) to sound out the electorate and discover their desires and (2) to persuade them it should be re-elected. In other words, lack of information converts democratic government into representative government, because it forces the central planning board of the governing party to rely upon agents scattered throughout the electorate. Such reliance amounts to a decentralization of government power from the planning board to the agents.[12] The central board continues to decentralize its power until the marginal vote-gain from greater conformity to popular desires is equal to the marginal vote-loss caused by reduced ability to co-ordinate its actions.

This reasoning implies that a democratic government in a rational world will always be run on a quasi-representative, quasi-decentralized basis, no matter what its formal constitutional structure, as long as communication between the voters and the governors is less than perfect. Another powerful force working in the same direction is the division of labor. To be efficient, a nation must develop specialists in discovering, transmitting, and analyzing popular opinion, just as it develops specialists in everything else. These specialists are the representatives. They exercise more power, and the central planning board exercises less, the less efficient are communication facilities in society.

The third consequence of imperfect knowledge and the resulting need for persuasion is really a combination of the first two. Because some voters can be influenced, specialists in influencing them appear. And, because government needs intermediaries between it and the people, some of these influencers pose as "representatives" of the citizenry. On one hand, they attempt to convince the government that the policies they stand for—which are of direct benefit to themselves—are both good for and desired by a large portion of the electorate. On the other hand, they try to convince the electorate that these policies are in fact desirable. Thus one of their methods of getting government to believe that public opinion supports them is to create favorable opinion through persuasion. Though a rational government will discount their claims, it cannot ignore them altogether. It must give the influencers more than proportional weight in forming policy, because they may have succeeded in creating favorable opinions in the silent mass of voters and because their vociferousness indicates a high intensity of desire. Clearly, people with an intense interest in some policy are more likely to base their votes upon it alone than are those who count it as just another issue; hence government must pay more attention to the former than the latter. To do otherwise would be irrational.

Finally, imperfect knowledge makes the governing party susceptible to bribery. In order to persuade voters that its policies are good for them, it needs scarce resources, such as television time, money for propaganda, and pay for precinct captains. One way to get such resources is to sell policy favors to those who can pay for them, either by campaign contributions, favorable editorial policies, or direct influence over others. Such favor buyers need not even pose as representatives of the people. They merely exchange their political help for policy favors—a transaction eminently rational for both themselves and the government.

Essentially, inequality of political influence is a necessary result of imperfect information, given an unequal distribution of wealth and income in society. When knowledge is imperfect, effective political action requires the use of economic resources to meet the cost of information. Therefore, those who command such resources are able to swing more than their proportional weight politically. This outcome is not the result of irrationality or dishonesty. On the contrary, lobbying in a democracy is a highly rational response to the lack of perfect information, as is government's submission to the demands of lobbyists. To suppose otherwise is to ignore the existence of information costs—that is, to theorize about a mythical world instead of the real one. Imperfect knowledge allows the unequal distributions of income, position, and influence—which are all inevitable in any economy marked by an extensive division of labor—to share sovereignty in a realm where only the equal distribution of votes is supposed to reign.

VI

Since the parties in this model have no interest per se in creating any particular type of society, the universal prevalence of ideologies in democratic politics appears to contradict my hypothesis. But this appearance is false. In fact, not only the existence of ideologies, but also many of their particular characteristics, may be deduced from the premise that parties seek office solely for the income, power, and prestige that accompany it.[13] Again, imperfect knowledge is the key factor.

In a complex society the cost in time alone of comparing all the ways in which the policies of competing parties differ is staggering. Furthermore, citizens do not always have enough information to appraise the differences of which they are aware. Nor do they know in advance what problems the government is likely to face in the coming election period.

Under these conditions many a voter finds party ideologies useful because they remove the necessity for relating every issue to his own conception of "the good society." Ideologies help him focus attention on the differences between parties; therefore, they can be used as samples of all the differentiating stands. Furthermore, if the voter discovers a correlation between each party's ideology and its policies, he can rationally vote by comparing ideologies rather than policies. In both cases he can drastically reduce his outlay on political information by informing himself only about ideologies instead of about a wide range of issues.

Thus lack of information creates a demand for ideologies in the electorate. Since political parties are eager to seize any method of gaining votes available to them, they respond by creating a supply. Each party invents an ideology in order to attract the votes of those citizens who wish to cut costs by voting ideologically.[14]

This reasoning does not mean that parties can change ideologies as though they were disguises, putting on whatever costume suits the situation. Once a party has placed its ideology "on the market," it cannot suddenly abandon or radically alter that ideology without convincing the voters that it is unreliable. Since voters are rational, they refuse to support unreliable parties; hence no party can afford to acquire a reputation for dishonesty. Furthermore, there must be some persistent correlation between each party's ideology and its subsequent actions; otherwise voters will eventually eschew ideological voting as irrational. Finally, parties cannot adopt identical ideologies, because they must create enough product differentiation to make their output distinguishable from that of their rivals, so as to entice voters to the polls. However, just as in the product market, any markedly successful ideology is soon imitated, and differentiation takes place on more subtle levels.

Analysis of political ideologies can be carried even further by means of a spatial analogy for political action. To construct this analogy, I borrow and elaborate upon an apparatus first used by Harold Hotelling in his famous article "Stability in Competition."[15] My version of Hotelling's spatial market consists of a linear scale running from zero to one hundred in the usual left-to-right fashion. To render it politically meaningful, I make the following assumptions:

1. The political parties in any society can be ordered from left to right in a manner agreed upon by all voters.
2. Each voter's preferences arc single-peaked at some point on the scale and slope monotonically downward on either side of the peak (unless it lies at one extreme of the scale).
3. The frequency distribution of voters along the scale is variable from society to society but fixed in any one society.[16]
4. Once placed on the political scale, a party can move ideologically either to the left or to the right up to but not beyond the nearest party toward which it is moving.[17]
5. In a two-party system, if either party moves away from the extreme nearest it toward the other party, extremist voters at its end of the scale may abstain because they see no significant difference between the choices offered them.[18]

Under these conditions Hotelling's conclusion that the parties in a two-party system inevitably converge on the center does not necessarily hold true. If voters are distributed along the scale as shown in Figure 1, then Hotelling is right. Assuming that Party A starts at position 25 and Party B at 75, both move toward 50, since each can gain more votes in the center than it loses at the extremes because of abstention. But, if the distribution is like that shown

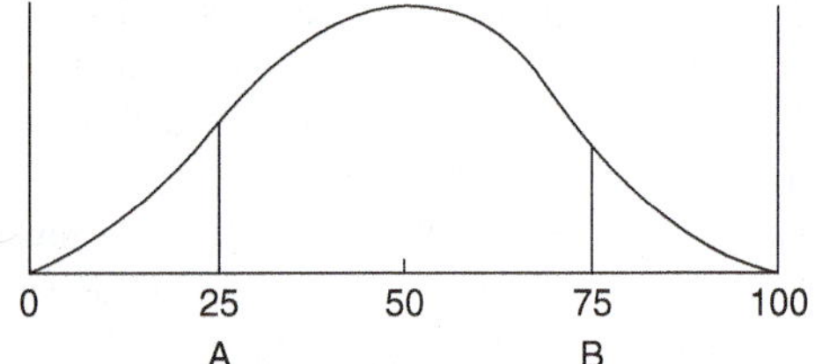

FIGURE 1

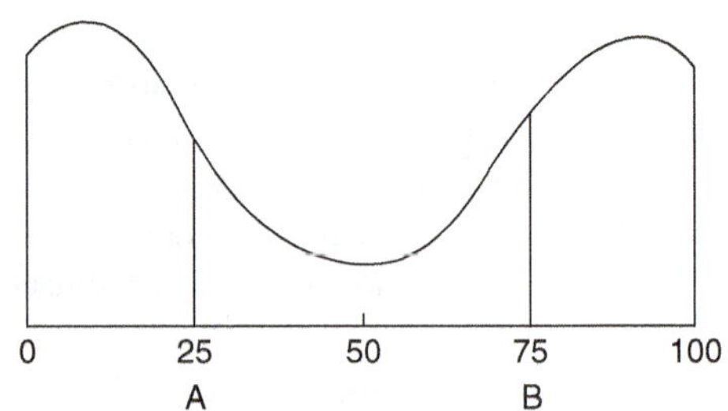

FIGURE 2

in Figure 2, the two parties diverge toward the extremes rather than converge on the center. Each gains more votes by moving toward a radical position than it loses in the center.

This reasoning implies that stable government in a two-party democracy requires a distribution of voters roughly approximating a normal curve. When such a distribution exists, the two parties come to resemble each other closely. Thus, when one replaces the other in office, no drastic policy changes occur, and most voters are located relatively close to the incumbent's position no matter which party is in power. But when the electorate is polarized, as in Figure 2, a change in parties causes a radical alteration in policy. And, regardless of which party is in office, half the electorate always feels that the other half is imposing policies upon it that are strongly repugnant to it. In this situation, if one party keeps getting re-elected, the disgruntled supporters of the other party will probably revolt; whereas if the two parties alternate in office, social chaos occurs, because government policy keeps changing from one extreme to the other. Thus democracy does not lead to effective, stable government when the electorate is polarized. Either the distribution must change or democracy will be

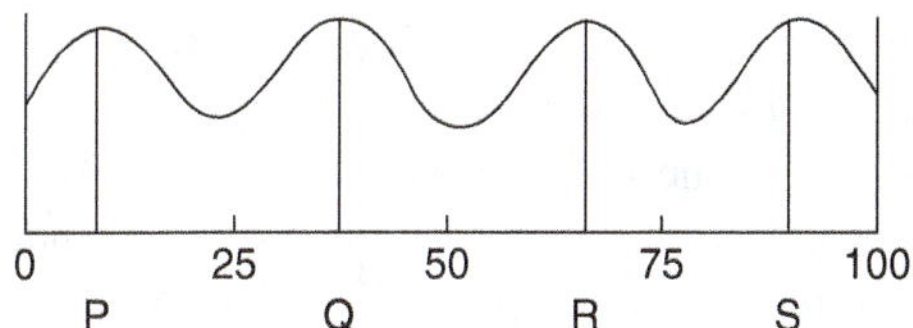

FIGURE 3

replaced by tyranny in which one extreme imposes its will upon the other.

Hotelling's original model was limited to the two-firm (or two-party) case, because, when three firms existed, the two outside ones converged on the middle one, which then leaped to the outside to avoid strangulation. Since this process repeated itself endlessly, no stable equilibrium emerged. But, in my model, such leaping is impossible, because each party has to maintain continuity in its ideology. Hence this model can be applied to multiparty systems without resulting in disequilibrium.

Multiparty systems are most likely to exist when the distribution of voters is multimodal, as shown in Figure 3. A separate party forms at each mode, and each party is motivated to stay at its mode and to differentiate itself as completely as possible from its neighbors. If it moves to the left so as to gain votes, it loses just as many votes to the party on its right (or loses them because of abstention if it is an extremist party at the right end of the scale), and vice versa. Thus its optimal course is to stay where it is and keep other parties from approaching it. In a multiparty system, therefore, we find conditions exactly opposite to those in a viable two-party system. Whereas in the former each party links itself to a definite ideological position and stresses its differences from other parties, in the latter both parties move toward the political center so as to resemble each other as closely as possible.

This conclusion implies that voters in multiparty systems have a wider range of choice than voters in two-party systems and that each choice in this range is more definitely linked to some ideological position. Thus it appears that the electorate exercises a more significant function in a multiparty system than in a two-party system, because only in the former does it make much difference which party gets elected.

However, appearances are deceiving in politics, because in fact the government in a multiparty system is likely to have a less definite, less coherent, and less integrated program than the government in a two-party system. This paradoxical outcome arises from the necessity in most multiparty systems of forming coalition governments. Since voters are scattered among several modes, only rarely does one party obtain the support of a majority of those voting. Yet, in most democracies, the government cannot function without at least the indirect support of a majority of voters. Even in systems in which the legislature selects the government, a majority of its members must support the coalition chosen to govern before the coalition can take office. If we assume that representation in the legislature is "fair"—that each member represents the same number of citizens—then even a coalition government must receive the indirect support of a majority in order to govern.

Such support can be maintained only if the government implements at least some policies that appeal to—are ideologically near—each cluster of voters whose support it needs. If a majority of voters are massed in one relatively narrow band on the left-right scale, then the government can choose all its policies from within this band. Hence its policies will form a fairly cohesive set embodying the ideological viewpoint associated with that area of the scale. This outcome is typical of a two-party system.

But in a multiparty system there are many modes scattered across the whole scale. Therefore, in order to appeal to a majority of voters, the government must be a coalition of parties and must include in its policy-set some policies espoused by each party in the coalition. In this manner it "pays off" voters at each cluster in return for their support. However, the result is that its program contains policies reflecting a wide variety of ideological viewpoints, so that no real cohesion or integration about any one Weltanschauung is possible. This outcome necessarily occurs whenever the distribution of voters along the scale is so scattered that only a very wide band can encompass a majority.

Consequently, a multiparty system offers voters an ostensible choice between definite, well-integrated policy-sets in each election, but only rarely does one of these sets actually govern. Usually a coalition governs, and its policies are likely to be less definite and less well integrated than those of the government in a two-party system. This is true even though voters in the latter are offered only two relatively unintegrated alternatives which closely resemble each other. No wonder politics often seems confusing.

Whether a political system has two or more parties depends on the distribution of voters along the scale and on the electoral rules governing the system. To demonstrate this dual dependence, I use the concept of "political equilibrium." A state of political equilibrium exists when no new parties can successfully be formed and when no existing party is motivated to move away from its present position.

The limit to the number of new parties that can be formed successfully springs from my definition of success as ability to gain the income, power, and prestige that go with office; that is, as ability to get elected. If the constitution calls for the election of a legislature by proportional representation and the subsequent formation of a government by the legislature, then many parties can be formed, because any given party can get at least some of its members elected by winning the support of only a small proportion of the citizens. Once elected, these members have a chance to share in the fruits of office by joining a coalition government. Hence it follows from my hypothesis about party motivation that many parties are likely to exist in a proportional representation system. Their number is limited only by the number of seats in the legislature and by the necessity of formulating ideologies sufficiently different from those of existing parties to attract votes away from them.[19] New parties continue to form until the distribution of voters is "saturated"—until there is not enough ideological "room" between existing parties to support others significantly different from them.

In an electoral system in which a plurality is necessary for victory, the limit on successful party formation is much more stringent. Since the only way to insure a plurality against all opponents is to win a majority of votes, small parties tend to combine until two giants are left, each of which has a reasonable chance of capturing a majority in any given election. Where these two parties are located on the ideological scale depends upon the distribution of voters, as explained before.

Actually, the policy position and stability of the government in a democracy are relatively independent of the number of parties; they follow primarily from the nature of the distribution of voters along the left-right scale.[20] If a majority of voters are massed within a narrow range of that scale, democratic government is likely to be stable and effective, no matter how many parties exist. As noted earlier, the government can formulate a policy-set which appeals to a majority of voters and yet does not contain policies embodying widely disparate points of view. But, if the government can win the support of a majority only by adopting a scattering of policies chosen from a broad range of viewpoints, these policies tend to cancel each other out, and the government's net ability to solve social problems is low. Thus the distribution of voters—which is itself a variable in the long run—determines whether or not democracy leads to effective government.

VII

When information is costly, no decision-maker can afford to know everything that might possibly bear on his decision before he makes it. He must select only a few data from the vast supply in existence and base his decision solely upon them. This is true even if he can procure data without paying for them, since merely assimilating them requires time and is therefore costly.

The amount of information it is rational for a decision-maker to acquire is determined by the following economic axiom: It is always rational to perform any act if its marginal return is larger than its marginal cost. The marginal cost of a "bit" of information is the return foregone by devoting scarce resources—particularly time—to getting and using it. The marginal return from a "bit" is the increase in utility income received because the information enabled the decision-maker to improve his decision. In an imperfectly informed world, neither the precise cost nor the precise return is usually known in advance; but decision makers can nevertheless employ the rule just stated by looking at expected costs and expected returns.

This reasoning is as applicable to politics as it is to economics. Insofar as the average citizen is concerned, there are two political decisions that require information. The first is deciding which party to vote for; the second is deciding on what policies to exercise direct influence on government policy formation (that is, how to lobby). Let us examine the voting decision first.

Before we do so, it is necessary to recognize that in every society a stream of "free" information is continuously disseminated to all citizens. Though such "free" data take time to assimilate, this time is not directly chargeable to any particular type of decision-making, since it is a necessary cost of living in society. For example, conversation with business associates, small talk with friends, reading the newspaper in a barber shop, and listening to the radio while driving to work are all sources of information which the average man encounters without any particular effort to do so. Therefore, we may consider them part of the "free" information stream and exclude them from the problem of how much information a decision-maker should obtain specifically to improve his decisions.

The marginal return on information acquired for voting purposes is measured by the expected gain from voting "correctly" instead of "incorrectly." In other words, it is the gain in utility a voter believes he will receive if he supports the party which would really provide him with the highest utility income instead of supporting some other party. However, unless his vote actually decides the election, it does not cause the "right" party to be elected instead of a "wrong" party; whether or not the "right" party wins does not depend on how he votes. Therefore, voting "correctly" produces no gain in utility whatsoever; he might as well have voted "incorrectly."

This situation results from the insignificance of any one voter in a large electorate. Since the cost of voting is very low, hundreds, thousands, or even millions of citizens can afford to vote. Therefore, the probability that any one citizen's vote will be decisive is very small indeed. It is not zero, and it can even be significant if he thinks the election will be very close; but, under most circumstances, it is so negligible that it renders the return from voting "correctly" infinitesimal. This is true no matter how tremendous a loss in utility income the voter would experience if the "wrong" party were elected. And if that loss is itself small—as it may be when parties resemble each other closely or in local elections—then the incentive to become well informed is practically nonexistent.

Therefore, we reach the startling conclusion that it is irrational for most citizens to acquire political information for purposes of voting. As long as each person considers the behavior of others as given, it is simply not worthwhile for him to acquire information so as to vote "correctly" himself. The probability that his vote will determine which party governs is so low that even a trivial cost of procuring information outweighs its return. Hence ignorance of politics is not a result of unpatriotic apathy; rather it is a highly rational response to the facts of political life in a large democracy.

This conclusion does not mean that every citizen who is well informed about politics is irrational. A rational man can become well informed for four reasons: (1) he may enjoy being well informed for its own sake, so that information as such provides him with utility; (2) he may believe the election is going to be so close that the probability of his casting the decisive vote is relatively high; (3) he may need information to influence the votes of others so that he can alter the outcome of the election or persuade government to assign his preferences more weight than those of others; or (4) he may need information to influence the formation of government policy as a lobbyist. Nevertheless, since the odds are that no election will be close enough to render decisive the vote of any one person, or the votes of all those he can persuade to agree with him, the rational course of action for most citizens is to remain politically uninformed. Insofar as voting is concerned, any attempt to acquire information beyond that furnished by the stream of "free" data is for them a sheer waste of resources.

The disparity between this conclusion and the traditional conception of good citizenship in a democracy is indeed striking. How can we explain it? The answer is that the benefits which a majority of citizens would derive from living in a society with a well-informed electorate are indivisible in nature. When most members of the electorate know what policies best serve their interests, the government is forced to follow those policies in order to avoid defeat (assuming that there is a consensus among the informed). This explains why the proponents of democracy think citizens should be well informed. But the benefits of these policies accrue to each member of the majority they serve, regardless of whether he has helped bring them about. In other words, the individual receives these benefits whether or not he is well informed, so long as most people are well informed and his interests are similar to those of the majority. On the other hand, when no one else is well informed, he cannot produce these benefits by becoming well informed himself, since a collective effort is necessary to achieve them.

Thus, when benefits are indivisible, each individual is always motivated to evade his share of the cost of producing them. If he assumes that the behavior of others is given, whether or not he receives any benefits does not depend on his own efforts. But the cost he pays does depend on his efforts; hence the most rational course for him is to minimize that cost—in this case, to remain politically ignorant. Since every individual reasons in the same way, no one bears any costs, and no benefits are produced.

The usual way of escaping this dilemma is for all individuals to agree to be coerced by a central agency. Then each is forced to pay his share of the costs, but he knows all others are likewise forced to pay. Thus everyone is better off than he would be if no costs were borne, because everyone receives benefits which (I here assume) more than offset his share of the costs. This is a basic rationale for using coercion to collect revenues for national defense and for many other government operations that yield indivisible benefits.[21]

But this solution is not feasible in the case of political information. The government cannot coerce everyone to be well informed, because "well-informedness" is hard to measure, because there is no agreed-upon rule for deciding how much information of what kinds each citizen "should" have, and because the resulting interference in personal affairs would cause a loss of utility that would probably outweigh the gains to be had from a well-informed electorate. The most any democratic government has done to remedy this situation is to compel young people in schools to take courses in civics, government, and history.

Consequently, it is rational for every individual to minimize his investment in political information, in spite of the fact that most citizens might benefit substantially if the whole electorate were well informed. As a result, democratic political systems are bound to operate at less than maximum efficiency. Government does not serve the interests of the majority as well as it would if they were well informed, but they never become well informed. It is collectively rational, but individually irrational, for them to do so; and, in the absence of any mechanism to insure collective action, individual rationality prevails.

VIII

When we apply the economic concept of rationality to the second political use of information, lobbying, the results are similarly incompatible with the traditional view of democracy. In order to be an effective lobbyist, a citizen must persuade the governing party that the policies he wants either are already desired by a large number of other citizens or are sufficiently beneficial to the rest of the electorate so that it will, at worst, not resent the enactment of these policies. To be persuasive, the would-be lobbyist must be extremely well informed about each policy area in which he wishes to exert influence. He must be able to design a policy that benefits him more than any other would, to counter any arguments advanced by opposing lobbyists, and to formulate or recognize compromises acceptable to him. Therefore, being a lobbyist requires much more information than voting, since even well-informed voters need only compare alternatives formulated by others.

For this reason, the cost of acquiring enough information to lobby effectively is relatively high. A lobbyist must be an expert in the policy areas in which he tries to exert influence. Since few men can afford the time or money necessary to become expert in more than one or two policy areas (or to hire those already expert), most citizens must specialize in a very few areas. Such behavior is rational even though policies in many areas affect them to some extent. Conversely, only a few specialists will actively exert pressure on the government in any one policy area. As a result, each need not heavily discount his own impact because of the large number of other persons influencing the decision, as he does in regard to voting. On the contrary, for those few lobbyists who specialize in any given area, the potential return from political information may be very high—precisely because they are so few.

The men who can best afford to become lobbyists in any policy area are those whose incomes stem from that area. This is true because nearly every citizen derives all his income from one or two sources; hence any government policy affecting those sources is of vital interest to him. In contrast, each man spends his income in a great many policy areas, so that a change in any one of them is not too significant to him. Therefore, men are much more likely to exert direct influence on government policy formation in their roles as producers than in their roles as consumers. In consequence, a democratic government is usually biased in favor of producer interests and against consumer interests, even though the consumers of any given product usually outnumber its producers. Tariff legislation provides a notorious example of this bias.

It should be stressed that such systematic exploitation of consumers by producers acting through government policy is not a result of foolish apathy on the part of consumers. In fact, just the opposite is true. Government's anti-consumer bias occurs because consumers rationally seek to acquire only that information which provides a return larger than its cost. The saving a consumer could make by becoming informed about how government policy affects any one product he purchases simply does not recompense him for the cost of informing himself—particularly since his personal influence on government policy would probably be slight. Since this is true of almost every product he buys, he adopts a course of rational ignorance, thereby exposing himself to extensive exploitation. Yet it would be irrational for him to act otherwise. In other words, lobbying is effective in a democracy *because* all the agents concerned—the exploiters, the exploited, and the government—behave rationally.

IX

Clearly, rational behavior in a democracy is not what most normative theorists assume it to be. Political theorists in particular have often created models of how the citizens of a democracy ought to behave without taking into account the economics of political action. Consequently, much of the evidence frequently cited to prove that democratic politics are dominated by irrational (non-logical) forces in fact demonstrates that citizens respond rationally (efficiently) to the exigencies of life in an imperfectly informed world.[22] Apathy among citizens toward elections, ignorance of the issues, the tendency of parties in a two-party system to resemble each other, and the anti-consumer bias of government action can all be explained logically as efficient reactions to imperfect information in a large democracy. Any normative theory that regards them as signs of unintelligent behavior in politics has failed to face the fact that information is costly in the real world. Thus political theory has suffered because it has not taken into account certain economic realities.

On the other hand, economic theory has suffered because it has not taken into account the political realities of government decision-making. Economists have been content to discuss government action as though governments were run by perfect altruists whose only motive was to maximize social welfare. As a result, economists have been unable to incorporate government into the rest of economic theory, which is based on the premise that all men act primarily out of self-interest. Furthermore, they have falsely concluded that government decision-making in all societies should follow identical principles, because its goal is always the maximization of social welfare. If my hypothesis is true, the goal of government is attaining the income, power, and prestige that go with office. Since methods of reaching this goal are vastly different in democratic, totalitarian, and aristocratic states, no single theory can be advanced to explain government decision-making in all societies. Nor can any theory of government decision-making be divorced from politics. The way every government actually makes decisions depends upon the nature of the fundamental power relation between the governors and the governed in its society; that is, upon the society's political constitution. Therefore, a different theory of political action must be formulated for each different type of constitution.

I conclude that a truly useful theory of government action in a democracy—or in any other type of society—must be both economic and political in nature. In this article I have attempted to outline such a theory. If nothing else, the attempt demonstrates how much economists and political scientists must depend on each other to analyze government decision-making, which is the most important economic and political force in the world today.

NOTES

1. The argument presented in this article is developed further in *An Economic Theory of Democracy,* 1957, Harper & Bros.

2. See Gerhard Colm, *Essays in Public Finance and Fiscal Policy* (New York: Oxford University Press. 1955). pp. 6–8.

3. *The Principles of Public Finance* (London: George Routledge & Sons, Ltd., 1932), pp. 9–10.

4. *Taxation and Welfare* (New York: Macmillan Co., 1925), pp. 30–36, as quoted in Harold M. Groves (ed.), *Viewpoints in Public Finance* (New York: Henry Holt & Co., 1948), p. 551.

5. *The Economics of Control* (New York: Macmillan Co., 1944), p. 32.

6. *Social Choice and Individual Values* (New York: John Wiley & Sons, 1951).

7. Joseph A. Schumpeter, *Capitalism, Socialism, and Democracy* (New York: Harper & Bros., 1950), p. 282.

8. This definition is taken from Robert A. Dahl and Charles E. Lindblom, *Politics, Economics, and Welfare* (New York: Harper & Bros., 1953), p. 42. However, throughout most of my analysis the word "government" refers to the governing party rather than the institution as here defined.

9. A "team" is a coalition whose members have identical goals. A "coalition" is a group of men who co-operate to achieve some common end. These definitions are taken from Jacob Marschak, "Towards an Economic Theory of Organization and Information," in *Decision Processes,* ed. R. M. Thrall, C. H. Coombs, and R. L. Davis (New York: John Wiley & Sons, 1954), pp. 188–89. I use "team" instead of "coalition" in my definition to eliminate intraparty power struggles from consideration, though in Marschak's terms parties are really coalitions, not teams.

10. The term "rational" in this article is synonymous with "efficient." This economic definition must not be confused with the logical definition (i.e., pertaining to logical propositions) or the psychological definition (i.e., calculating or unemotional).

11. In a perfectly informed world, voters always vote exactly the way government expects them to, so the relationships expressed in Nos. 2 and 3 are identical. But in an imperfectly informed world, the government does not always know what voters will do; hence Nos. 2 and 3 may differ.

12. Decentralization may be geographical or by social groups, depending upon the way society is divided into homogeneous parts.

13. I define "ideologies" as verbal images of "the good society" and of the chief policies to be used in creating it.

14. In reality, party ideologies probably stem originally from the interests of those persons who found each party. But, once a political party is created, it takes on an existence of its own and eventually becomes relatively independent of any particular interest group. When such autonomy prevails, my analysis of ideologies is fully applicable.

15. *Economic Journal,* XXXIX (1929), 41–57.

16. Actually, this distribution may vary in any one society even in the short run, but I assume it to be fixed in order to avoid discussing the complex of historical, sociological, psychological, and other factors which cause it to change.

17. It cannot go beyond the adjacent parties, because such "leaping" would indicate ideological unreliability and would cause its rejection by the electorate.

18. This is equivalent to assuming elastic demand along the scale, as Smithies did in his elaboration of the Hotelling model (see Arthur Smithies, "Optimum Location in Spatial Competition," *Journal of Political Economy,* XLIX [1941], 423–39).

19. The number of sufficiently different parties as system can support depends upon the shape of the distribution of voters along the scale.

20. However, because the preferences of rising generations are influenced by the alternatives offered them, the number of parties is one of the factors that determine the shape of the distribution of voters.

21. See Paul A. Samuelson, "The Pure Theory of Public Expenditures," *Review of Economics and Statistics,* XXXVI (November, 1954), 387–89.

22. In this sentence the word "irrational" is not the opposite of the word "rational," as the synonyms in parentheses show. Admittedly, such dual usage may cause confusion. However, I have employed the word "rational" instead of its synonym "efficient" throughout this article because I want to emphasize the fact that an intelligent citizen always carries out any act whose marginal return exceeds its marginal cost. In contrast, he does not always make use of logical thinking, because, under some conditions, the marginal return from thinking logically is smaller than its marginal cost. In other words, it is sometimes rational (efficient) to act irrationally (non-logically), in which case an intelligent man eschews rationality in the traditional sense so as to achieve it in the economic sense. This is really what is meant by the sentence in the text to which this footnote is attached.

MICHAEL MUNGER

Rent-Seek and You will Find

2006

"In politics you try to move money around and take credit for it. In markets you try to create value and make profits. I don't know if we should stay in this business." That city official was just being honest, but his framing of the problem surprised me. The "business" he was referring to was writing and winning grants from the Department of Housing and Urban Development (HUD), the federal agency charged with improving home ownership and low-income housing availability. Fifteen years ago, when I had this conversation, I didn't understand what he meant.

As director of the master of public administration program for UNC–Chapel Hill in the early 1990s my job was training city and county managers, sending them out to serve the public weal. Public grants were the mother's milk of city management; why would any city official think twice about getting free money to help citizens?

The answer is one of the paradoxes of public choice: free money isn't free. In fact, you have to pay for free money twice: first you have to collect the money, out of tax revenues. And then you have to pay for the money again, because the benefits are dissipated by what economists call "rent-seeking." Let me explain.

The technical definition of **rent** is any return to investment, or effort, that exceeds the opportunity cost rate of return. So, Alex Rodriguez of the New York Yankees earns a large rent, or premium, because of his scarce talents as a baseball player. He could earn a living as a banker, or a waiter, or something else. But it is unlikely that he could earn anything close to the $25 million per year he makes as a baseball player. Those rents encourage competition. And in most economic situations, that competition for profits produces benefits. But in politics, competition for those rents is often destructive.

The greater the rent, the greater the costs people are willing to incur to win it. When government hands out what appears to be free money, people are going to scramble to get some of it, incurring costs as long as those costs raise the chances of winning the "free" money sufficiently.

Michael Munger, "Rent-Seek and You Will Find." Online Library of Economics and Liberty, July 3, 2006. By permission of Liberty Fund.

Robert Tollison, one of America's premier students of public choice and government, defines **rent-seeking** this way: "Rent seeking is the expenditure of scarce resources to capture an artificially created transfer." Competition for government goodies—rent-seeking—is a wild goose chase, no matter how well-intentioned the goose or the chasers.

The city official told me that his office employed 15 people whose sole jobs were to identify and win federal grants. Their total salaries, and the staff and utilities required to support them, exceeded one quarter of the federal funds they had secured in grants the previous year. It seems like a pretty good deal to spend only 25 cents to win a dollar. But if you think about all the other cities doing the same thing, you realize that this system of distributing grants has some pretty perverse costs.

And the costs were climbing. Other cities around the nation, in the mid-1990s, had begun to get better at the HUD-grant game. At first, Charlotte had been able to win grants with a relatively short proposal, and some supporting documents. But as time passed, the amount of effort and resources required to win was increasing. Not only was Charlotte spending more and more city tax dollars just to win grants funded by federal tax dollars, but Charlotte was winning less and less often. It did sound like a dysfunctional system.

But I was stumped: this just seemed like competition. Isn't competition supposed to be good? How could the outcome seem so bad? It turns out that rent-seeking "competition" is a contest for a fixed price, a zero-sum problem that works like a transfer, at best. Competition in markets has no fixed price, and is robustly positive-sum. In politics you try to move money around and take credit for it. In markets you try to create value and make profits.

COMPETITION IN OTHER PLACES

My understanding of competition, after all, was that of the economist who studies markets. Lots of choices, lots of choosers, prices driven down toward the cost of production. New goods and services come constantly to the market, because producers' self-interest forces them to think of new and better ways to serve customer needs.

Can public policy work the same way? To put it in other terms, is competition always good? Is an increase in competition always the first solution we should think of, to any problem?

In political markets, there is good competition and bad competition. The fundamental human problem is to foster the good and block the bad. If the design of the institution fails to render the clash of self-interests beneficial to the community, then competition can make bad things happen to even the best people.

Not all political competition is bad. Madison, in *Federalist* #51,[1] famously argued that a government characterized by separation of powers among its branches would be more stable and more reliable than other forms. The reason? Competition! "Ambition must be made to counteract ambition. . . ." But, as we will see, not all political competition works this way.

TULLOCK LOTTERY

In my classes, I ask students to imagine an experiment that I call a Tullock lottery, after one of the inventors of the concept of rent-seeking, Gordon Tullock.

The lottery works as follows: I offer to auction off $100 to the student who bids the most. The catch is that each bidder must put the bid money in an envelope, and *I keep all of the bid money no matter who wins.*

So if you put $30 in an envelope and somebody else bids $31, you lose both the prize *and* the bid. When I run that game with students I can sometimes make $50 or more, even after paying off the prize. In politics, the secret to making money is to announce you are going to give money away.

Take a walk along K Street in Washington, DC. It is lined with tall buildings, full of fine offices and peopled by men and women with excellent educations and a real sense of ambition, a desire to make lots of money and achieve great things. What are those buildings, those people? They are nothing more than bids in the political version of a Tullock lottery. The cost of maintaining a DC office with a staff and lights and lobbying professionals is the offer to politicians. If someone else bids more and the firm doesn't get that tax provision or defense bid or road system contract, it doesn't get its bid back. The money is gone. It is thrown into the maw of bad political competition.

Who benefits from that system? Is it the contractors, all those companies and organizations with offices on K Street? Not really. Playing a rent-seeking game like that means those firms spend just about all they expect to win. It is true that some firms get large contracts and big checks, but all the players would be better off overall if they could avoid playing the game to begin with.

My students ask why anyone would play this sort of game. The answer is that the rules of our political system have created that destructive kind of political competition. When so much government money is available to the highest bidder, playing that lottery begins to look very enticing. The current Congress has, to say the least, failed to stem the rising tide of spending on domestic pork-barrel projects. Political competition run amok has increased spending nearly across the board. And sometimes, you have to bid just to keep from having money taken away from you through regulation.

In a well-functioning market system, competition rewards low price and high quality. Such optimal functioning requires either large numbers of producers or relatively low-cost entry and exit. Suppose that Coke and Pepsi not only had all the shelf space for drinks, but asked in addition if they could make their own rules outlawing the sale of any other drink. Adam Smith pointed this out in the *Wealth of Nations:*

> To widen the market and to narrow the competition is always the interest of the dealers. . . . The proposal of any new law or regulation of commerce which comes from this order, ought always to be listened to with great precaution, and ought never to be adopted, till after having been long and carefully examined, not only with the most scrupulous, but with the most suspicious attention. It comes from an order of men, whose interest is never exactly the same with that of the public, who have generally an interest to deceive and even to oppress the public, and who accordingly have, upon many occasions, both deceived and oppressed it (1776, Book 1, Chapter 11).

In the market system, we have safeguards set up, however imperfect they are. If nothing else, the Federal Trade Commission would not look favorably on the request, or the industry.

But in the American political system, we have an industry dominated by two firms, Republicans and Democrats. Together they have a 99 percent market share. They have undertaken actions at the state and national levels to make it practically impossible for any other party to enter. This system forecloses *good* competition, the kind that raises new ideas or asks embarrassing questions. We have been fooled into thinking the system is competitive, because we constantly see vigorous rent-seeking competition for access to the public purse. This bad competition is an expensive gladiatorial combat, where Congress keeps a lot of the ticket receipts. Some of the rest of the spending is simply wasted building those expensive office suites on K Street and using the time of those lobbyists who could be doing something more productive.

RENT-SEEKING: POLITICALLY, YOU CAN'T LOSE

When they set up a rent-seeking contest, politicians are gambling with house money. To simulate the real world of rent-seeking more closely, I would need to amend my classroom exercise. First, collect $10 from each student. Next, run the auction, giving the students a chance to buy their money back. I'm not sure what would happen, but this procedure would give you the "pay for it twice" aspect that real political rent-seeking games exhibit. And I wouldn't be surprised if some students just stayed home sick that day, as a way to avoid playing the game at all.

What did Charlotte decide? Did they drop out of the game? Of course not. True, spending city money to win pretty much the same amount of federal money makes little sense economically. But it makes a lot of sense politically. As long as politicians are able to claim credit for bringing new federal spending to their state, district, or city, it doesn't matter that each dollar "won" actually cost 30 cents, or even $1.20. On August 1, 2005, a story was published in the *Charlotte Observer*:

> WASHINGTON, DC—Senator Richard Burr today announced $8,329,494 in United States Department of Housing and Urban Development (HUD) grants for the City of Charlotte. The funds will expand affordable housing and emergency shelter to the and sick and extend home ownership opportunities to low-income and minority households.

Homeless, sick, low-income, and minority households? Who could object to that? Besides, it's free money! Isn't it?

NOTE

1. The full passage is this: "The great security against a gradual concentration of the several powers in the same department, consists in giving to those who administer each department the necessary constitutional means and personal motives to resist encroachments of the others. The provision for defense must in this, as in all other cases, be made commensurate to the danger of attack. Ambition must be made to counteract ambition. The interest of the man must be connected with the constitutional rights of the place. It may be a reflection on human nature, that such devices should be necessary to control the abuses of government. But what is government itself, but the greatest of all reflections on human nature? If men were angels, no government would be necessary. If angels were to govern men, neither external nor internal controls on government would be necessary. In framing a government which is to be administered by men over men, the great difficulty lies in this: you must first enable the government to control the governed; and in the next place oblige it to control itself. A dependence on the people is, no doubt, the primary control on the government; but experience has taught mankind the necessity of auxiliary precautions."

JAMES BUCHANAN

How Can Constitutions Be Designed So That Politicians Who Seek to Serve "Public Interest" Can Survive and Prosper?

1993

Distributional politics in modern democracy involves the exploitation of minorities by majorities, and as persons rotate membership, all parties in the "game" lose. This result emerges only because differences in treatment are permissible. If the principle of generality (analogous to that present in an idealized version of the rule of law) could, somehow, be introduced into politics, mutual exploitation could be avoided. The analysis offers support for such policies as (1) flat-rate taxes, (2) equal per head transfers

James Buchanan, "How Can Constitutions Be Designed So That Politicians Who Seek to Serve the "Public Interest" Can Survive and Prosper?" *Constitutional Political Economy* 4 (1) (1993): 1–6. By permission of Springer.

or demogrants and (3) uniform regulation of all industries.

In a short paper, "Public Choice after Socialism" (1993), I argued that the structure of modern democratic politics is such that the "players," the participants in the distributional game among competing constituency agents, are effectively forced to behave as if they are exclusively motivated by narrowly defined or differential special interests. Political players who might seek to further some conception of an all-encompassing general, or public, interest cannot survive. They tend to be eliminated from the political game in the evolution-like selection process.

In this note, I want to extend this argument further by asking the question: How could the structure (constitution) of modern politics be changed so that it would allow players who might try to further a more encompassing interest to survive and prosper? Or, in other terms, how could the constitutional framework be reformed so that players who advance generalized interests are rewarded rather than punished. As indicated in the other paper, the response is clear. The distributional elements in the inclusive political game must be eliminated, or at least very substantially reduced. But I want here, to the extent possible, to go beyond this generalized statement, even if the argument remains highly abstract.

I want first to ask, and to answer, the basic question: Why does the game of distributional politics guarantee that players (legislators as agents for constituencies) adopt strategies that reflect the promotion of narrowly defined differential interests rather than the interests of the all-encompassing membership of the polity?

Let me introduce the familiar two-person, two-strategy symmetrical matrix construction with the ordinal payoffs shown in figure 1. The interaction is assumed to occur in a state of nature, with each person having available only the two private or independent courses of action indicated. The outcome in Cell IV emerges from the separate and independent actions of players A and B, each of whom chooses to defect (*d*) due to the row or column dominance in the structure of payoffs. Each of the two players succeeds in avoiding the role of sucker; each player avoids being exploited by the other, while recognizing that a

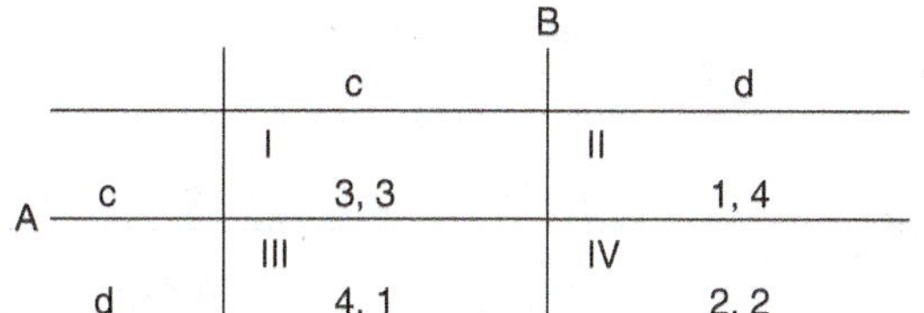

FIGURE 1 Classic PD

higher payoff might be secured through mutual cooperation. But so long as no explicit means of coordination is available, a single player cannot, independently, achieve the cooperative outcome (*c, c*).[1]

Collectivization of the activities described in the interaction may be recognized to be one means of securing the larger payoffs. The collective choice set includes the four possible outcomes: (*c, c*), (*c, d*), (*d, c*) and (*d, d*). And, while the mutually desirable outcome (*c, c*) may be attained, through collective action, an individual, independently, cannot protect against an exploitative result, (*c, d*) or (*d, c*), as is the case under autarchy. Unless collective choice operates under an effective rule of unanimity, the individual must be vulnerable to potential exploitation (Buchanan and Tullock 1962).

Consider a polity with many members, but with only two sets of orderings, such that any person can be represented by one or the other of the orderings shown ordinally in figure 1.[2] Collective action is assumed to be majoritarian, but no individual knows whether an effective majority coalition will be made up of persons with the A or B orderings. The outcome of the collective choice process will lie in either Cell II or Cell III, the off-diagonals in the matrix. Collective action is taken over a whole sequence of periods, and if we make the heroic assumption that membership is symmetrical among all participants, with each person holding equal prospects for membership in the majority and minority coalitions, the results will be "as if" the Cell IV payoffs are received, provided we make the assumption that distributional gains and losses are symmetrical in utilities. All persons will be dissatisfied with the distributional politics that they observe, and in which they are required to participate. Further, there may be a general recognition that any attempted escape

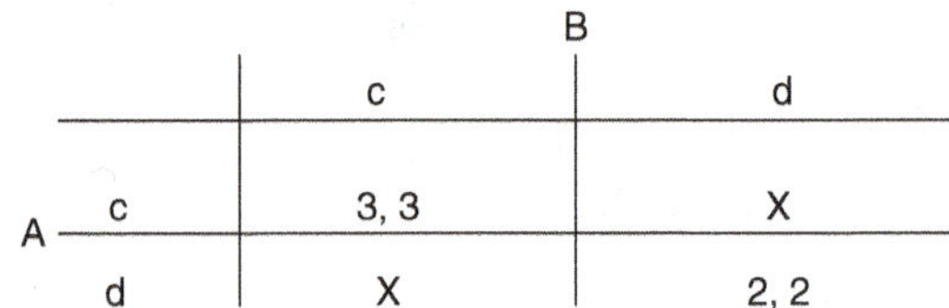

FIGURE 2 Diagonal Choices

from such politics by the emergence of a new ethics will be unlikely to succeed.

The direction of constitutional reform is obvious, even if we rule out the implementation of an effective unanimity rule. If, somehow, the off-diagonal solutions are simply made impossible to achieve by the introduction of some rule or norm that prevents participants from acting or being acted upon *differently*, one from the other, the off-diagonal attractors are eliminated and the players operate with the reduced matrix of figure 2. In this setting, each player, as a member of a political coalition, knows that any choice of an action or strategy must involve the *same* treatment of all players (constituencies). Differing treatments are not within the possible, given the constitutional constraints on the attainable set of possible outcomes.

The issues here are not, of course, nearly so simple as the analysis makes them appear. On the other hand, the directions for reform suggested by the extremely reduced abstract models should never be overlooked.

What the simple construction fails to suggest is that there may be many options that fall within the generalized ordinal solution in Cell I, and that there may be differential distributional consequences of these options. That is to say, the elimination of the off-diagonals may be less efficacious than the simple construction indicates. On the other hand, the normative thrust of the argument seems clear enough. To the extent that the political equivalents to the off-diagonal solutions to collective actions may be eliminated, the chances for the survival of encompassing interest as a political motive force are enhanced. The whole set of issues subsumed under the rent-seeking label can be viewed from this perspective as being generated by the potential for differential treatment. As such differential treatment—the availability of the off-diagonals—is reduced, so is the inducement to rent-seeking behavior.

Note that, in figure 2, with the off-diagonals eliminated, the motivation for the actors (or their agents) need not reflect self or own interest at all. Individual A may, instead, choose to further the interest of B, and/or vice versa, without in any way modifying the result. Or, if we treat the payoffs as cardinal utility indicators, the substitution of some aggregative magnitude for individual differential interest as the effective objective for strategy choice leaves the result unchanged.

As indicated, however, even if we limit political action to the choice among options that affect all parties *generally*, there may be widely differing evaluations placed on the options that qualify under this rubric. And these differing evaluations may be in part distributionally motivated. Consider a proposal to enact a general law requiring scrubbers on smokestacks in order to improve air quality. The law is general because it applies equally to all smoke generating plants, regardless of location or type of product. But the congressional district that contains relatively more of these plants will be adversely affected, relative to other districts, by the general law. It will be harder for the agent representing such a district to evaluate such a proposed law in terms of some consideration of the encompassing general interest than for the agent whose district contains relatively fewer such plants. But, also, note that it will indeed be much easier, even for the agent who represents the district with relatively more smoke generating plants, to act in accordance with an interpretation of the encompassing interest in this setting than it would be in one in which the proposal is one that allows for particularized territorial or product-category exemptions from the scrubbers-on-smokestacks requirement. Any move toward generality in treatment embodied in political action opens up the prospect for the consideration of the more general interest and thereby shifts the focus from distributional politics.

Without making any attempt to be comprehensive, I shall simply present below a two-column classification of familiar political proposals, or features

Table 1
Examples

Toward Generality	Toward Particularity
LAW	
—equality in treatment of all persons	—special treatment for any group for any reason
TAXATION	
—broad based taxes —uniform rates of tax —absence of exemption —inclusion of all persons in a tax structure	—exclusion of voters from tax rolls —shelters, exemptions, exclusions, special treatment of sources and uses of tax base —differential rates of tax, as among persons, forms of organization, professions, locations, products or other classificatory bases
EXPENDITURES	
—collective consumption goods, with benefits coincident with whole territory of polity —fiscal federalism, or subsidiarity, financing by political authority coincident in inclusivity with program benefits —demogrants as transfer payments	—local public goods centrally defined
REGULATION OF INDUSTRY	
—environmental controls over whole economy —uniform tariffs on all imports —uniform subsidy for all industry	—differential control, by territory, by industry, by product, etc. —differential tariff or quota protection product by product —differential subsidization by product, territory or other base

of proposals, with the distinction made in accordance with the generality criterion. To the extent that the center of gravity in democratic politics can be shifted leftward in the table, the potential efficacy of leadership exercised on behalf of some version of the all-encompassing interest of all members of the polity is increased.

There is nothing new or novel in the normative argument advanced here. Indeed, the argument is at least as old as Sir Henry Maine's reference to liberal progress as moving "from status to contract." One of the basic flaws of the welfare state as it has burgeoned in this century has been its implicit failure to understand the dependence of effective democracy upon the equality of persons and groups before the law, *and in politics.* As and to the extent that politics has come to be seen as the instrument for distributing the gains from collectivization *differentially,* the voices of those political leaders who would espouse the public or general interest are overwhelmed. Public choice theory models the behavior of those politicians who survive and prosper; public choice theory does not induce those politicians who might seek to do otherwise to behave sinfully or selfishly.

If a more wholesome ethics is to be introduced into the observed behavior of our politicians, and especially our legislators, it will be necessary to remake the constitutional structure. Distributional politics is viable and tends to become dominant to the extent that differential treatment is constitutionally permissible. Each and every step toward replacing differential treatment with equal treatment, or generality, must measure progress toward achievement of the general interest.

REFERENCES

Buchanan, J. M. (1993). "Public Choice After Socialism." *Public Choice* 77 (1): 67–74.

Buchanan, J. M. and G. Tullock (1962). *The Calculus of Consent.* Ann Arbor: University of Michigan Press.

NOTES

1. My interest here is not in the prospect for cooperative strategies that might emerge in an iterated game between two players in the state of nature setting. My interest lies exclusively with the implications of the basic structure for large number interaction.

2. The players may be identical in preferences, in which case the different ordering of outcomes simply reflects different distributional effects.

MICHAEL HUEMER

Why People Are Irrational about Politics

2015

1. INTRODUCTION: THE PROBLEM OF POLITICAL DISAGREEMENT

Perhaps the most striking feature of the subject of politics is how prone it is to disagreement—only religion and morality rival politics as a source of disagreement. There are three main features of political disagreements I want to point out: (i) They are very *widespread.* It isn't just a few people disagreeing about a few issues; rather, any two randomly-chosen people are likely to disagree about many political issues. (ii) They are *strong,* that is, the disagreeing parties are typically very convinced of their own positions, not at all tentative. (iii) They are *persistent,* that is, it is extremely difficult to resolve them. Several hours of argumentation typically fails to produce progress. Some disputes have persisted for decades (either with the same principals or with different parties over multiple generations).

This *should* strike us as very odd. Most other subjects—for instance, geology, or linguistics, or algebra—are not subject to disagreements at all like this; their disputes are far fewer in number and take place against a backdrop of substantial agreement in basic theory; and they tend to be more tentative and more easily resolved. Why is politics subject to such widespread, strong, and persistent disagreements? Consider four broad explanations for the prevalence of political disagreement:

A. *The Miscalculation Theory:* Political issues are subject to much dispute because they are very difficult issues; accordingly, many people simply make mistakes—analogous to miscalculations in working out difficult mathematical problems—leading them to disagree with others who have not made mistakes or have made different mistakes leading to different conclusions.
B. *The Ignorance Theory:* Rather than being inherently difficult (for instance, because of their

complexity or abstractness), political issues are difficult for us to resolve due to insufficient information, and/or because different people have *different* information available to them. If everyone had adequate factual knowledge, most political disputes would be resolved.

C. *The Divergent-Values Theory:* People disagree about political issues principally because political issues turn on moral/evaluative issues, and people have divergent fundamental values.
D. *The Irrationality Theory:* People disagree about political issues mainly because most people are irrational when it comes to politics.

Political disagreement undoubtedly has more than one contributing cause. Nevertheless, I contend that explanation (D), irrationality, is the most important factor, and that explanations (A) - (C), in the absence of irrationality, fail to explain almost any of the salient features of political disagreement.

2. POLITICAL DISPUTES ARE NOT EXPLAINED BY MISCALCULATION OR IGNORANCE

We begin with the two cognitive explanations—that is, theories that attempt to explain political disputes in terms of the normal functioning of our cognitive faculties. This is the most natural kind of explanation to look to, in the absence of specific evidence against a cognitive explanation.

Cognitive explanations, however, fail to explain the following salient features of political beliefs and political disputes:

a. The Strength of Political Beliefs

If political issues are merely very difficult, then we should expect most people to hold at most tentative opinions, or to suspend judgement altogether. This is what happens with other issues that are intrinsically difficult. If we have just worked out a very complicated mathematical problem, we tend to hold at most tentative belief in the answer arrived at. If another intelligent person reports having worked out the same problem and obtained a different answer, this shakes our confidence in our answer; we take this as strong evidence that we may be in error. But in political matters, people tend to hold their beliefs with great confidence, and to regard them as *not* very difficult to verify, that is, as *obvious.* Nor does the mere presence of another person with an opposing political belief typically shake our confidence.

The Ignorance Theory fares slightly better, since if people were ignorant, not only of the facts pertaining to the political issue, but also of their own level of ignorance, their confidence in their political beliefs would be understandable. However, it remains puzzling why people would be ignorant of their own level of ignorance—this itself calls for a further explanation. Moreover, the Ignorance Theory has difficulty explaining the following feature of political disputes.

b. The Persistence of Political Disputes

If political disputes had a purely cognitive explanation, we would expect them to be more easily resolvable. One party might point out to the other party where he had made an error in reasoning—a miscalculation—whereupon the latter person could correct his error. Or, in case the two parties have different information available to them, they could simply meet, share their information, and then come to an agreement. Although partisans of political disputes *do* commonly share their reasons and evidence with each other, the disputes persist.

c. The Correlations of Political Beliefs With Non-Cognitive Traits

People's political beliefs tend to correlate strongly with their race, sex, socioeconomic status, occupation, and personality traits. Members of minorities are more likely to support affirmative action than white men are. Members of the entertainment industry are much more likely to be liberal than conservative. People who like suits are more likely to be conservative than people who like tie-dye T-shirts. And so on. None of these correlations would be expected if political beliefs had a solely cognitive origin. These facts suggest that bias, rather than mere miscalculation, plays a key role in explaining political mistakes.

d. The Clustering of Political Beliefs

Two beliefs are "logically unrelated" if neither of them, even if true, would constitute evidence for or against the other. Many logically unrelated beliefs are correlated—that is, you can often predict someone's belief about one issue on the basis of his opinion about some other, completely unrelated issue. For example, people who support gun control are much more likely to support welfare programs and abortion rights. Since these issues are logically unrelated to each other, on a purely cognitive theory of people's political beliefs, we would expect there to be no correlation.

Sometimes the observed correlations are the *opposite* of what one would expect on the basis of reason alone—sometimes, that is, people who hold one belief are *less* likely to hold other beliefs that are supported by the first one. For instance, one would naively expect that those who support animal rights would be far more likely to oppose abortion than those who reject the notion of animal rights; conversely, those who oppose abortion should be much more likely to accept animal rights. This is because to accept animal rights (or fetus rights), one must have a more expansive conception of what sorts of beings have rights than those who reject animal rights (or fetus rights)—and because fetuses and animals seem to share most of the same morally relevant properties (e.g., they are both sentient, but neither are intelligent). I am not saying that the existence of animal rights *entails* that fetuses have rights, or vice versa (there are some differences between fetuses and animals); I am only saying that, if animals have rights, it is much more likely that fetuses do, and vice versa. Thus, if people's political beliefs generally have cognitive explanations, we should expect a positive statistical *correlation* between being pro-life and being pro-animal-rights. In fact, we observe precisely the opposite.

Some clustering of logically unrelated beliefs could be explained cognitively—for instance, by the hypothesis that some people tend to be good, in general, at getting to the truth (perhaps because they are intelligent, knowledgeable, etc.) So suppose that it is true both that affirmative action is just and that abortion is morally permissible. These issues are logically unrelated to each other; however, if some people are in general good at getting to the truth, then those who believe one of these propositions would be more likely to believe the other.

But note that, on this hypothesis, we would not expect the existence of an *opposite* cluster of beliefs. That is, suppose that liberal beliefs are, in general, true, and that this explains why there are many people who generally embrace this cluster of beliefs. (Thus, affirmative action is just, abortion is permissible, welfare programs are good, capital punishment is bad, human beings are seriously damaging the environment, etc.) Why would there be a significant number of people who tend to embrace the opposite beliefs on all these issues? It is not plausible to suppose that there are some people who are in general drawn toward falsity. Even if there are people who are not very good at getting to the truth (perhaps they are stupid, ignorant, etc.), their beliefs should be, at worst, *unrelated* to the truth; they should not be systematically directed *away* from the truth. Thus, while there could be a "true cluster" of political beliefs, the present consideration strongly suggests that neither the liberal nor the conservative belief-cluster is it.

3. POLITICAL DISPUTES ARE NOT EXPLAINED BY DIVERGENT VALUES

Political issues are normative; they concern what people *should* do: should abortion be permitted?, should we cut the military budget?, and so on.

Perhaps political disputes persist because people start from different fundamental values, and they correctly reason from those values to divergent political conclusions.

This hypothesis invites the further question, why do people have different fundamental values? If values are objective, then this question is just as puzzling as the initial question, "Why do people disagree about political issues?" But many people think that value questions have no objective answers, and that value is merely a matter of personal feelings and preferences. This would tend to explain, or at least render it none too surprising, that many people have divergent values and are unable to resolve these value-differences.

There are three reasons why I disagree with this explanation. The first is that value questions are objective, and moral anti-realism is completely unjustified. The second reason is that this hypothesis fails to explain the clustering of political beliefs described above. On the Divergent Fundamental Values theory, we should expect prevalent political belief clusters to correspond to different basic moral theories. Thus, there should be some core moral claim that unites all or most "liberal" political beliefs, and a different moral claim that unites all or most "conservative" political beliefs. What underlying moral thesis supports the views that (a) capitalism is unjust, (b) abortion is permissible, (c) capital punishment is bad, and (d) affirmative action is just? Here, I need not claim that those beliefs always go together, but merely that they are correlated (if a person holds one of them, he is more likely to hold another of them); the Divergent Values hypothesis fails to explain this. And the earlier example of abortion and animal rights (section 2d) shows that in some cases, the political belief clusters we find are the opposite of what we would expect from people who were correctly reasoning from fundamental moral theories.

The third and biggest problem with the Divergent Values theory is that political disputes involve all sorts of non-moral disputes. People who disagree about the justice of capital punishment also tend to disagree about the non-moral facts about capital punishment. Those who support capital punishment are much more likely to believe that it has a deterrent effect, and that few innocent people have been executed. Those who oppose capital punishment tend to believe that it does not have a deterrent effect, and that many innocent people have been executed. Those are factual questions, and my moral values should not have any effect on what I think about those factual questions. Whether capital punishment deters criminals is to be determined by examining statistical evidence and scientific studies on the subject—not by appealing to our beliefs about the nature of justice. Of course, it may be that my moral values affect my beliefs about those factual questions because I am irrational—that would be consistent with the theory put forward in this paper.

Similarly, people who support gun control generally believe that gun control laws significantly reduce violent crime. Those who oppose gun control generally believe that gun control laws do not significantly reduce violent crime, and even that they increase violent crime. This, too, is a factual question, and one cannot determine what effect gun control laws have on crime by appealing to one's moral beliefs.

As a final example, socialists tend to blame capitalism for the poverty of the Third World; but supporters of capitalism typically view capitalism as the *solution* to Third World poverty. Once again, this is a factual issue, which cannot be solved by appeal to moral beliefs.

Are there *some* differences of fundamental values? Probably. Are some political disagreements due to moral disagreements? Almost certainly (affirmative action and abortion are good candidates). Nevertheless, the point is that *many* political disagreements are factual disagreements and cannot be explained—without invoking a hypothesis of irrationality—by appeal to moral disagreements.

4. RATIONAL IGNORANCE AND RATIONAL IRRATIONALITY

The preceding considerations make a prima facie case for the importance of irrationality in explaining political disagreement—none of the other explanations seem to be very good. But we need to hear more about the Irrationality Theory—how and why are people irrational about politics?

First, a related theory. The theory of Rational Ignorance holds that people often choose—rationally—to remain ignorant because the costs of collecting information are greater than the expected value of the information. This is very often true of political information. To illustrate, on several occasions, I have given talks on the subject of this paper, and I always ask the audience if they know who their congressman is. Most do not. Among senior citizens, perhaps half raise their hands; among college students, perhaps a fifth. Then I ask if anyone knows what the last vote taken in Congress was. So far, of hundreds of people I have asked, not one has answered affirmatively. Why? It simply isn't worth their while to collect this information. If you tried to keep track of every politician and bureaucrat who is supposed to be representing (or serving) you, you'd probably spend your whole life on that. Even then, it wouldn't do you any good—perhaps you'd know which politician to vote for in the next election, but the other 400,000 voters in your district (or the 200,000 who are going to turn up to vote) are still going to vote for whomever they were going to vote for before you collected the information.

Contrast what happens when you buy a product on the market. If you take the time to read the *Consumer Reports* to determine which kind of car to buy, you then get that car. But if you take the time to research politicians' records to find out which politician to vote for, you do not thereby get that politician. You still get the politician that the majority of the other people voted for (unless the other voters are exactly tied, a negligible possibility). From the standpoint of self-interest, it is normally irrational to collect political information.

Similarly, the theory of Rational Irrationality holds that people often choose—rationally—to adopt irrational beliefs because the costs of rational beliefs exceed their benefits. To understand this, one has to distinguish two senses of the word "rational":

> *Instrumental rationality* (or "means-end rationality") consists in choosing the correct means to attain one's actual goals, given one's actual beliefs. This is the kind of rationality that economists generally assume in explaining human behavior.
>
> *Epistemic rationality* consists, roughly, in forming beliefs in truth-conducive ways—accepting beliefs that are well-supported by evidence, avoiding logical fallacies, avoiding contradictions, revising one's beliefs in the light of new evidence against them, and so on. This is the kind of rationality that books on logic and critical thinking aim to instill.

The theory of Rational Irrationality holds that it is often *instrumentally* rational to be *epistemically* irrational. In more colloquial (but less accurate) terms: people often think illogically because it is in their interests to do so. This is particularly common for political beliefs. Consider one of Caplan's examples. If I believe, irrationally, that trade between myself and other people is harmful, I bear the costs of this belief. But if I believe—also irrationally—that trade between my country and other countries is harmful, I bear virtually none of the costs of this belief. There is a tiny chance that my belief may have some effect on public policy; if so, the costs will be borne by society as a whole; only a negligible portion of it will be borne by me personally. For this reason, I have an incentive to be more rational about the individual-level effects of trade than I am about the general effects of trade between nations. In general, just as I receive virtually none of the benefit of my collecting of political information, so I receive virtually none of the benefit of my thinking rationally about political issues.

The theory of Rational Irrationality makes two main assumptions. First, individuals have *non-epistemic belief preferences* (otherwise known as "biases"). That is, there are certain things that people *want* to believe, for reasons independent of the truth of those propositions or of how well-supported they are by the evidence. Second, individuals can exercise some control over their beliefs. Given the first assumption, there is a "cost" to thinking rationally—namely, that one may not get to believe the things one wants to believe. Given the second assumption (and given that individuals are usually *instrumentally* rational), most people will accept this cost only if they receive greater benefits from thinking rationally.

But since individuals receive almost none of the benefit from being epistemically rational about political issues, we can predict that people will often choose to be epistemically irrational about political issues.

There may be some people for whom being *epistemically rational* is itself a sufficiently great value to outweigh any other preferences they may have with regard to their beliefs. Such people would continue to be epistemically rational, even about political issues. But there is no reason to expect that everyone would have this sort of preference structure. To explain why some would adopt irrational political beliefs, we need only suppose that some individuals' non-epistemic belief preferences are stronger than their desire (if any) to be epistemically rational.

In the next two sections, I discuss and defend the two main assumptions of the theory of Rational Irrationality just mentioned.

5. SOURCES OF BELIEF PREFERENCES

Why do people prefer to believe some things that are not true or not supported by the evidence? What kinds of non-epistemic belief preferences do we have?

A reasonably thorough answer to this would require extensive psychological study. Here I will just mention a few factors that seem to play a role in what people prefer to believe—no doubt these factors merit further study, and no doubt there are more factors to consider as well.

a. Self-Interested Bias

People tend to hold political beliefs that, if generally accepted, would benefit themselves *or the group they prefer to identify with*. Thus, those who stand to benefit from affirmative action programs are more likely to believe in their justice, public school teachers are more likely to support increases in budgets for public education, and existing doctors are more likely to support strict occupational licensing requirements that restrict the supply of new doctors.

The italicized phrase, "the group they prefer to identify with," is important for some cases. University professors, for instance, prefer to identify with the working class rather than businessmen; hence, they support policies they believe would benefit blue-collar workers. As this example illustrates, a group one identifies with need not be a group to which one actually belongs. (For this reason, "self-interested bias" is a slightly misleading term.)

b. Beliefs as Self-Image Constructors

People prefer to hold the political beliefs that best fit with the images of themselves that they want to adopt and to project. For example, a person may want to portray himself (both to himself and to others) as a compassionate, generous person. In this case, he will be motivated to endorse the desirability and justice of social welfare programs, and even to call for increases in their funding (regardless of what the current levels are), thereby portraying himself as *more* generous/compassionate than those who designed the present system. Another person may wish to portray himself as a tough guy, in which case he will be motivated to advocate increases in military spending (again, regardless of what the current levels are), thereby showing himself to be *more* tough than those who designed the present system.

It was presumably in recognition of this sort of bias that President Bush proclaimed his philosophy of "compassionate conservatism." The degree of compassion experienced by conservatives has no logical relevance to the merits of conservative policies, but Bush evidently recognized that some individuals gravitate towards liberalism from a desire to be (or be seen as) compassionate.

C. Beliefs as Tools of Social Bonding

People prefer to hold the political beliefs of other people they like and want to associate with. It is unlikely that a person who doesn't *like* most conservatives would ever convert to conservative beliefs. Relatedly, the physical attractiveness of people influences others' tendency to agree with them politically.

A study of Canadian federal elections found that attractive candidates received more than two and a half times as many votes as unattractive candidates—although most voters surveyed denied in the strongest possible terms that physical attractiveness had any influence on their votes.

The social role of political beliefs probably goes a long way towards explaining the clustering of logically unrelated beliefs. People with particular political orientations are more likely to spend time together than people with divergent political orientations. Quite a lot of evidence shows that people tend to conform to the beliefs and attitudes of those around them, particularly those they see as similar to themselves. Thus, people with a substantial degree of initial political agreement will tend to converge more over time—although what particular collection of beliefs they converge on may be largely a matter of historical accident (hence the difficulty of stating a general principle that unites either conservative or liberal beliefs).

d. Coherence Bias

People are biased towards beliefs that "fit well" with their existing beliefs. In one sense, of course, the tendency to prefer beliefs that fit well with an existing belief system is rational, rather than a bias. But this tendency can also function as a bias. For instance, there are many people who believe capital punishment deters crime and many who believe it doesn't; there are also many who believe that innocent people are frequently convicted and many who believe that they aren't. But there are relatively few people who think *both* that capital punishment deters crime, *and* that many innocent people are convicted. Likewise, few people think capital punishment fails to deter crime, but few innocent people are convicted. In other words, people will tend to either adopt both of the factual beliefs that would tend to support capital punishment, or adopt both of the factual beliefs that would tend to undermine capital punishment. On a similar note, relatively few people believe that drug use is extremely harmful to society *but* that laws against drugs are and will remain ineffective. Yet, a priori, there's no reason why those positions (i.e., positions in which a reason *for* a particular policy and a reason *against* that policy both have a sound factual basis) should be less probable than the positions we actually find to be prevalent (i.e., positions according to which the relevant considerations point in the same direction).

In one psychological study, subjects were exposed to evidence from studies of the deterrent effect of capital punishment. One study had concluded that capital punishment has a deterrent effect; another had concluded that it does not. All experimental subjects were provided with summaries of both studies, and then asked to assess which conclusion the evidence they had just looked at most supported overall. The result was that those who initially supported capital punishment claimed that the evidence they'd been shown, overall, supported that capital punishment has a deterrent effect. Those who initially opposed capital punishment thought that this same evidence, overall, supported that capital punishment had no deterrent effect. In each case, partisans came up with reasons (or rationalizations) for why the study whose conclusion they agreed with was methodologically superior to the other study. This points up one reason why people tend to become polarized about political issues: we tend to evaluate mixed evidence as supporting whichever belief we already incline towards—whereupon we increase our degree of belief.

6. MECHANISMS OF BELIEF FIXATION

The theory defended in the last two sections assumes that people have control over their beliefs; it explains people's beliefs in the same manner in which we often explain people's actions (by appeal to their desires). But many philosophers think that we can't control our beliefs—at least not directly. To show this, they often give examples of obviously false propositions, and then ask if you can believe them—for instance, can you, if you want to, believe that you are presently on the planet Venus?

Perhaps we cannot believe obviously false propositions at will. Still, we can exercise substantial control over our political beliefs. A "mechanism of belief fixation" is a way that we can get ourselves to believe the things we want to believe. Let's look at some of these mechanisms.

a. Biased Weighting of Evidence

One method is simply to attribute *slightly more* weight to each piece of evidence that supports the view one likes than it really deserves, and *slightly less* weight to each piece of evidence that undermines it. This requires only a slight departure from perfect rationality in each case, but it can have great effects when applied consistently to a great many pieces of evidence. The biased weighting need not be fully conscious; our desire to support a given conclusion just causes us to see each piece of favorable evidence as a little more significant. A related phenomenon is that we have an easier time *remembering* facts or experiences that support our beliefs than ones that fail to.

b. Selective Attention and Energy

Most of us spend more time thinking about arguments supporting our beliefs than we spend thinking about arguments supporting alternative beliefs. A natural result is that the arguments supporting our beliefs have more psychological impact on us, and we are less likely to be aware of reasons for doubting our beliefs. Most of us, when we hear an argument for a conclusion we disbelieve, immediately set about finding "what's wrong with the argument." But when we hear an argument for a conclusion we believe, we are much more likely to accept the argument at face value, thereby further solidifying our belief, than to look for things that might be wrong with it. This is illustrated by the capital punishment study mentioned above (section 5d): subjects scrutinized the study whose conclusion they disagreed with closely, seeking methodological flaws, but accepted at face value the study with whose conclusion they agreed. Almost all studies have some sort of epistemological imperfections, so this technique enables one to hold whichever factual beliefs about society one wants.

c. Selection of Evidence Sources

Similarly, people can select whom to listen to for information and arguments about political issues. Most people choose to listen mainly or solely to those they agree with. If you see someone sitting in the airport reading the *National Review,* you assume he's a conservative. The man reading the *New Republic* is presumably a liberal. Similarly, conservatives tend to have conservative friends, from whom they hear conservative arguments, whereas liberals have liberal friends. One reason is that it is unpleasant to listen to partisan (or as we sometimes say, "biased") assertions and arguments, unless one agrees with them. Another reason may be that we don't wish to be exposed to information that could undermine our desired beliefs. If I don't listen to the people I disagree with, it is virtually impossible that I will change my beliefs. (Rarely is one side to a debate so incompetent that they can't win if they get 95% of the speaking time.)

d. Subjective, Speculative, and Anecdotal Arguments

People often rely on anecdotal arguments—arguments appealing to particular examples, rather than statistics—to support generalizations. For example, in arguing that the American justice system is ineffective, I might cite the trials of O.J. Simpson and the Menendez brothers. Logically, the problem is that a single case, or even several cases, are insufficient evidence for drawing inductive generalizations. I cite this as a mechanism of belief fixation because, for most controversial social issues, there will be cases that support either of two contrary generalizations—certainly there would be cases one could cite, for instance, in which the justice system worked correctly. Thus, the method of anecdotes is usually capable of supporting whichever belief we want to hold.

A "subjective" statement, in the sense relevant here, is one that is difficult to verify or refute decisively, because it requires some kind of judgement call. There are degrees of subjectivity. For example, the statement, "American television programs are very violent" is relatively subjective. A *less* subjective statement would be, "The number of deaths portrayed in an average hour of American television programming is greater than the number of deaths portrayed in an average hour of British television programming." The second statement requires less exercise of judgement to evaluate. Scientists have come up with ways of reducing as much as possible their reliance on subjective statements in evaluating theories—a scientist arguing for a theory must use relatively objective statements as his evidence. But in the field of politics, subjective statements abound. Subjective statements are more easily influenced by bias; hence, the reliance on statements of this kind to evaluate theories makes it easier to believe what we want to believe.

A related phenomenon is the reliance on *speculative* judgements. These are judgements which may have clear truth-conditions, but we simply lack decisive evidence for or against them. For example, "The Civil War was primarily caused by economic motives" is speculative; "This table is about 5 feet long" is not. In the sciences, we rest our theories as much as possible on unspeculative claims like the latter. In politics, we often treat speculation as evidence for or against political theories. People with opposing initial political views will tend to find opposite speculations plausible, thus enabling each to support what they want to believe.

An interesting implication emerges from the consideration of the mechanisms of belief fixation. Normally, intelligence and education are aides to acquiring true beliefs. But when an individual has non-epistemic belief preferences, this need not be the case; high intelligence and extensive knowledge of a subject may even *worsen* an individual's prospects for obtaining a true belief (see chart below). The reason is that a biased person uses his intelligence and education as tools for rationalizing beliefs. Highly intelligent people can think of rationalizations for their beliefs in situations in which the less intelligent would be forced to give up and concede error, and highly educated people have larger stores of information from which to selectively search for information supporting a desired belief. Thus, it is nearly impossible to change an academic's mind about anything important, particularly in his own field of study. This is particularly true of philosophers (my own occupation), who are experts at argumentation.

Prospects for attaining truth with different intellectual traits

	Intelligence	Bias	
1.	+	–	(best)
2.	–	–	
3.	–	+	
4.	+	+	(worst)

7. WHAT TO DO

The problem of political irrationality is the greatest social problem humanity faces. It is a greater problem than crime, drug addiction, or even world poverty, because it is a problem that *prevents us from solving other problems.* Before we can solve the problem of poverty, we must first have correct beliefs about poverty, about what causes it, what reduces it, and what the side effects of alternative policies are. If our beliefs about those things are guided by the social group we want to fit into, the self-image we want to maintain, the desire to avoid admitting to having been wrong in the past, and so on, then it would be pure accident if enough of us were to actually form correct beliefs to solve the problem. An analogy: suppose you go to the doctor, complaining of an illness. The doctor picks a medical procedure to perform on you from a hat. You would be lucky if the procedure didn't *worsen* your condition.

What can we do about the problem?

First: Understanding the nature of political irrationality is itself a big step towards combating it. In particular, explicit awareness of the mechanisms discussed in section 6 should cause one to avoid using them. When learning about a political issue, for example, we should collect information from people on all sides of the issue. We should spend time thinking about objections to our own arguments. When we feel inclined to assert a political claim, we should pause to ask ourselves what reasons we have for believing it, and we should try to assess the subjective, speculative, and anecdotal character of those reasons—and perhaps downgrade our confidence in them accordingly.

Second: We should identify cases in which we are particularly likely to be biased, and in those cases hesitate to affirm the beliefs that we would be biased towards. (Aside: surveys indicate that most people consider themselves to be more intelligent, more fair-minded, and *less biased* than the average person—but most of these beliefs are themselves biases). These include: (a) Cases in which our own interests are involved. (b) Issues about which we feel strongly. If, for example, you get upset when talking about abortion, then your beliefs about that subject are probably unreliable. (c) If your beliefs tend to cluster in the traditional way (see section 2d), then many of them are probably the product of bias. (d) If your political beliefs are pretty much the ones that would be expected on the basis of your race, sex, occupation, and personality traits, then most of them are probably the product of bias. (e) If you have beliefs about an empirical question prior to gathering empirical data—or if your beliefs about some question *do not change* when you gather much more data—then you are probably biased about that question. As one particularly striking example, 41% of Americans believe that foreign aid is one of the two largest areas of federal government spending. This belief would be straightforward to check, and any effort to do so would show it to be laughably inaccurate; so it seems that this must be a belief held in the absence of evidence.

Third: We should take account of the irrationality of others, and adjust our confidence in reported information accordingly. We should recognize that much of the information that is presented to us in political arguments is probably (a) false, (b) highly misleading, and/or (c) incomplete. This is one reason why we need to hear from both sides before accepting any argument. Logically, the problem is that, by listening to an individual arguing for a specific position, we are *screening* evidence. The evidence that individual presents to us is not a random selection from the available evidence; all evidence *against* the conclusion being defended has been screened out. If we bear this in mind, we should be much less impressed by the arguments of political ideologues. Example: a proponent of gun control presents us with murder statistics from England (which has strict gun control) and the United States (which has less gun control). The numbers seem impressive. Then we remember that England and the United States were not randomly chosen from the countries for which we have data—they were most likely chosen because they were the cases most favorable to the position being defended, and any examples unfavorable to that position were excluded.

Fourth: Should you accuse other people of irrationality, if you suspect them of it? There's a dilemma here. On the one hand, recognizing one's irrationality may be necessary to combat it. Merely presenting evidence about the issue in dispute may not be enough, as this evidence will continue to be evaluated irrationally. The victim of bias may need to make a deliberate effort to combat it. On the other hand, people accused of irrationality may take the accusation as a personal attack, rather than as a point relevant to the political debate, and respond defensively. If that occurs, it is virtually impossible that they will change their political position.

I have witnessed few political conversions, so the most I can offer is speculation as to how one might occur. To begin with, if a person is to be reasoned into a change of position, he must not see the argument as a personal contest. For this reason, we must carefully avoid even slightly insulting remarks in the course of political discussions—whether directed at the individuals actually present or at others with whom they might identify.

A second suggestion is that one should first attempt to move an interlocutor to suspense of judgement, rather than to the position opposite to his own. One might try to accomplish this by first identifying empirical claims that his position depends upon. After securing agreement on what the relevant empirical issues are, one might attempt to secure agreement on what sort of evidence would be needed to resolve those issues. In most cases, one could then point out that neither party to the discussion actually has that sort of evidence. The rationale behind this procedure is that the question, "What sort of evidence is relevant to X?" is usually easier to answer than the question "Is X true?" For example: suppose you are arguing with someone about why America has a high rate of violent crime. He proposes that it is because of violence on television and movies. This is an empirical claim. How would we find out if it was true? Here are some suggestions: time series data about the amount of violence (for instance, the number of murders per hour of entertainment) portrayed on television over a period of many years; violent crime rates over the same time period; similar data for other countries; psychological studies of actual violent criminals that drew some conclusions about why they committed their crimes; data on the statistical correlation between owning a television set and crime; data on the statistical correlation between number of hours of television individuals watch and their risk of committing crimes. These are just a few examples. The important point is that, in most cases, neither party to the debate has any data of this kind. Upon realizing this, both parties should agree to suspend judgement on whether and how much television violence contributes to crime.

My third and final suggestion is to display fair-mindedness, which may induce an interlocutor to trust one and to attempt to display similar fair-mindedness. One displays fair-mindedness by (a) qualifying one's claims appropriately, i.e., acknowledging possible limitations of one's arguments and not making stronger claims than the evidence will warrant; (b) bringing forward evidence one knows of that goes against one's favored position; (c) acknowledging correct points made by the interlocutor.

I don't know whether these suggestions would be successful. They seem to conflict with accepted practice among those whom we might consider the experts in political debate; on the other hand, accepted practice seems to be highly unsuccessful at producing agreement (though it does appear successful at producing polarization, i.e., increasing the confidence of those who already hold a particular position).

8. SUMMARY

Based on the level of disagreement, human beings are highly unreliable at identifying correct political claims. This is extremely unfortunate, since it means that we have little chance of solving social problems and a good chance of creating or exacerbating them. The best explanation lies in the theory of Rational Irrationality: individuals derive psychological rewards from holding certain political beliefs, and since each individual suffers almost none of the harm caused by his own false political beliefs, it often makes sense (it gives him what he wants) to adopt those beliefs regardless of whether they are true or well-supported.

The beliefs that people want to hold are often determined by their self-interest, the social group they want to fit into, the self-image they want to maintain, and the desire to remain coherent with their past beliefs. People can deploy various mechanisms to enable them to adopt and maintain their preferred beliefs, including giving a biased weighting of evidence; focusing their attention and energy on the arguments supporting their favored beliefs; collecting evidence only from sources they already agree with; and relying on subjective, speculative, and anecdotal claims as evidence for political theories.

The irrationality hypothesis is superior to alternative explanations of political disagreement in its ability to account for several features of political beliefs and arguments: the fact that people hold their political beliefs with a high degree of confidence; the fact that discussion rarely changes political beliefs; the fact that political beliefs are correlated with race, sex, occupation, and other cognitively irrelevant traits; and the fact that numerous logically unrelated political beliefs—and even, in some cases, beliefs that rationally *undermine* each other—tend to go together. These features of political beliefs are not explained by the hypotheses that political issues are merely very difficult, that we just haven't yet collected enough information regarding them, or that political disputes are primarily caused by people's differing fundamental value systems.

It may be possible to combat political irrationality, first, by recognizing one's own susceptibility to bias. One should recognize the cases in which one is most likely to be biased (such as issues about which one feels strongly), and one should consciously try to avoid using the mechanisms discussed above for maintaining irrational beliefs. In the light of widespread biases, one should also take a skeptical attitude towards evidence presented to one by others, recognizing that the evidence has probably been screened and otherwise distorted. Lastly, one may be able to combat others' irrationality by identifying the sort of empirical evidence that would be required to test their claims, and by taking a fair-minded and cooperative, rather than combative, approach towards discussion. It remains a matter of speculation whether these measures will significantly alleviate the problem of political irrationality.

REFERENCES

Caplan, Bryan. 2003. "The Logic of Collective Belief," *Rationality and Society* 15: 218–42.

Caplan, Bryan. 2007. *The Myth of the Rational Voter.* Princeton, N.J.: Princeton University Press.

Cialdini, Robert B. 1993. *Influence: The Psychology of Persuasion.* New York: William Morrow & Company.

Downs, Anthony. 1957. *An Economic Theory of Democracy.* New York: Harper.

Feynman, Richard. 1974. "Cargo Cult Science," commencement address at Caltech. Reprinted in Richard Feynman, *Surely You're Joking, Mr. Feynman* (New York: Bantam Books, 1989).

Friedman, David. 1989. *The Machinery of Freedom.* LaSalle, Ill.: Open Court.

Gilovich, Thomas. 1991. *How We Know What Isn't So.* New York: Free Press.

Hanson, Robin and Tyler Cowen. 2003. "Are Disagreements Honest?" Unpublished ms., http://hanson.gmu.edu/deceive.pdf.

Huemer, Michael. 2005. *Ethical Intuitionism.* New York: Palgrave Macmillan.

Hume, David. 1975. *An Enquiry Concerning Human Understanding* in *Enquiries Concerning Human Understanding and Concerning the Principles of Morals,* edited by L.A. Selby-Bigge. Oxford: Clarendon.

Kornblith, Hilary. 1999. "Distrusting Reason," *Midwest Studies in Philosophy* 23: 181–96.

Owens, David. 2000. *Reason without Freedom: The Problem of Epistemic Normativity.* London: Routledge.

11 Reasons to Vote

It is widely believed that citizens in democratic nations have a duty to vote. But since voting is a public good, and voting is often costly (for many it involves taking time off work, in addition to gathering and processing information for the purposes of voting), standard models of rational choice predict widespread free riding and rational ignorance on the part of voters. Given how unlikely it is that one's vote will actually change an electoral outcome, it remains a difficult question whether there are good reasons (including moral reasons) to vote.

Geoff Brennan and Loren Lomasky examine the popular belief in a duty to vote and find it hard to justify. They concede that people may have good reasons to vote if they are likely to affect the outcome, or if they have incurred special obligations to vote—for example, because of their role on a corporate board, or a promise they have made to a friend. But they conclude that in standard cases of large elections belief in a duty to vote is mistaken.

Consequentialist arguments for a duty to vote ask us to assess the expected impact of voting on the welfare of everyone, including future people. Since the stakes are so high, we might think even a small probability of casting the winning vote can change the expected payoff so that voting becomes obligatory from a consequentialist standpoint. Yet even if we are considering the welfare of other people, Brennan and Lomasky argue, we should still assess our ability to get the answer right. Consequentialists care about good consequences, not good intentions, and voters are often unable to accurately assess the relevant alternatives with any precision. Even when the candidates appear to be offering very different packages of goods (a rare situation if the median voter theorem is right),[1] prospective voters must be able to assign proper weights to competing goods (education, environmental goods, national defense, etc); assess the efficacy of different proposals for providing different goods; overcome bias; and predict the likelihood that candidates will stick to their platforms once elected. At best, Lomasky and Brennan conclude, consequentialists would support a duty to vote *well.*

Kantians, by contrast, might think a duty to vote derives from the fact that we cannot accept as a universal principle one that allows people not to vote within an effective democracy whenever voting involves a relatively slight cost to them. More generally, we might argue that fairness requires everyone to vote, since the benefits of democracy would evaporate if too few people voted. In response, Brennan and Lomasky argue that effective democracy doesn't require everyone to vote, and that people who are uninformed, biased, or malevolent, may actually be providing a public service by staying home rather than casting ballots for inept politicians.

Moving from moral to prudential considerations, Brennan and Lomasky argue that prudential reasons to vote are usually weak, in light of the cost of voting (and of gathering political information), and the fact that voting will almost surely make no difference to the outcome. Indeed, they suggest that the argument from prudence will often imply that one should stay home and read a book or go to the movies rather than slogging to the polls.

We may wonder why people vote at all if there is little causal connection between an individual act of voting and a candidate's election. Brennan and Lomasky propose that voting is less like buying a car than rooting for a sports team. When we hand over cash for a car, we get the car, and when we *play* sports we can help determine the outcome. But when we *watch* sports on television we play no such role. Cheering for the Duke Blue Devils or Carolina Tar Heels to win a basketball game on television is perfectly rational behavior, but not because it helps Blue Devils or Tar Heels win games. *Instrumental* action involves selecting means to our ends. *Expressive* action involves acting in ways that express our commitments (to Blue Devils or Tar Heels, or to Democrats or Republicans). On Brennan and Lomasky's account, voting makes perfect sense as expressive behavior, but it is not always morally obligatory.

Jason Brennan takes the argument a step further and compares bad voting with polluting the environment. Because we share the costs and benefits of public policy, bad votes create negative externalities and good votes produce positive externalities. Because of the harm that can come from voting, Brennan argues that bad voters—those who are poorly informed or biased or malevolent—have a moral obligation to refrain from polluting the polls. Brennan thinks this is just one instance of a more general moral duty to refrain from collectively harmful actions when the cost is low.

Geoff Brennan and Geoff Sayre-McCord explore two ways of thinking about the impact of a particular vote. On the classical account, what matters in assessing whether one has reason to vote is the probability that one's vote will decide the outcome. This probability will be extremely small in most large scale elections. On a much less standard account, defended by Alvin Goldman and Richard Tuck, what matters is the probability that one will be a member of the minimally sufficient set of voters needed to produce an electoral outcome. This probability will often be reasonably large even in large scale elections. When it is, Goldman and Tuck argue, one has an instrumental reason to vote, since one has a good chance of being causally (and morally) responsible for the outcome.

Brennan and Sayre-McCord suggest that the Goldman and Tuck account still leaves the amount of causal responsibility a particular voter might reasonably be assigned for bringing about an outcome even in very close elections quite small—even when the probability that they would be a part of the set that brought about the outcome is quite large. It is even smaller in a landslide victory, they argue, since in those elections other votes were in place to ensure the outcome whether one voted or not. And this is one reason Brennan and Sayre-McCord doubt that the Goldman and Tuck approach can provide us with strong reasons to vote, or that it implies that we should receive significant moral praise if we end up being part of a set of voters that produces the best outcome. Instead of focusing on causal efficacy, Brennan and Sayre-McCord suggest we should look to the reasons there are for praising or blaming people for voting (or not) as they do, in order to discover the reasons we take people to have. As they note, we condemn people who admire Hitler, think worse of people who publicly praise him, and think even worse of those who vote for him (regardless of whether he wins), and we do this not on the grounds that they played a role in his taking power. The causal role individual voters play (or not) in securing Hitler's election does not govern the strength of the reasons we take people to have not to support Hitler. Turning to candidates and outcomes that deserve support, Brennan and Sayre-McCord maintain that the causal role individuals play (or not) in securing their victory does not govern the strength of the reasons we take people to have to support them.

Some are surprised by how low voter turnout is in large democracies like the US and UK. Others are surprised by how high it is, given the insignificance of a particular person's vote. Perhaps voting is no less puzzling than recycling or throwing litter in garbage cans rather than rose gardens: individuals internalize the costs of these actions, while the benefits are diffuse and uncertain. But these are precisely the kinds of collective action problems our sense of fairness evolved to solve, albeit imperfectly.

FURTHER READING

Brennan, Geoff and Philip Pettit. 1990. "Unveiling the Vote." *British Journal of Political Science* 20 (3): 311–333.

Goldman, Alvin. 1999. "Why Citizens Should Vote: A Causal Responsibility Approach." *Social Philosophy and Policy* 16 (2): 201–217.

Riker, William and Peter Ordeshook. 1968. "A Theory of the Calculus of Voting." *American Political Science Review* 62 (1): 25–42.

Tuck, Richard. 2008. *Free Riding*. Harvard University Press.

Meehl, Paul. 1977. "The Selfish Voter Paradox and the Thrown-Away Vote Argument." *The American Political Science Review* 71 (1): 11–30.

NOTE

1. See Anthony Downs and the chapter on public choice theory for more on this.

GEOFFREY BRENNAN AND LOREN LOMASKY

Is There a Duty to Vote?

2000

I. INTRODUCTION

The genre of public service advertisements that appear with two- and four-year cyclical regularity is familiar. Cameras pan across scenes of marines hoisting the flag on Iwo Jima, a bald eagle soaring in splendid flight, rows of grave markers at Arlington. The somber-voiced announcer remonstrates: "*They* did their part; now *you* do yours." Once again it is the season to fulfill one's civic duty, to vote.

Good citizenship in the final decade of the twentieth century does not seem to require much of the individual beyond simple law-abidingness. We have traveled

Geoffrey Brennan and Loren Lomasky, "Is There a Duty to Vote?" *Social Philosophy and Policy* 17 (1) (2000): 62–86. By permission of *Social Philosophy and Policy*.

a far distance from the Athenian agora. However, there exists a remarkable degree of consensus that voting is requisite, that one who fails to exercise the franchise is thereby derelict. Candidates for the nation's highest office publicly proclaim that duty; so do one's neighbors and associates—perhaps with some asperity in their voices—when informed that you chose to absent yourself from the polls that they took the trouble to visit. We call that consensus remarkable because, as will become evident, it is exceedingly difficult to develop a persuasive rationale for the existence of a duty to vote. Often that duty is simply taken for granted. Where arguments are given, they typically invoke either fallacious reasoning or dubious empirical premises. A cautious surmise is that the assurance with which the duty to vote is affirmed is not matched by equivalent cogency of justification. But we wish to advance a bolder conclusion: There is no satisfactory rationale for a duty to vote. Contra the popular wisdom, an individual who chooses not to exercise the franchise does not thereby fall short with regard to any responsibility entailed by citizenship.

The argument that follows does not trade on any ambiguity or delicate nuance in the term "duty." Thus, some may concede that there is, in the strict sense, no *duty* to vote, yet affirm that omitting to vote is nonetheless morally subpar.[1] Our claim is stronger. We argue that, under standard circumstances, voting is not morally superior to abstention. One does not do morally better to vote than, say, to spend the time playing golf instead. That is not to maintain that individuals have no reason to vote. Some do, some don't. The same is true for golfing: if voting/golfing affords one enjoyment or otherwise contributes to leading one's preferred mode of life,[2] then one has reason to vote/play golf; otherwise one does not.

We know of no way to generate a general nonexistence proof of the duty to vote. Instead, this essay follows a strategy of enumeration. Section II specifies the range of voting scenarios over which the discussion is meant to apply. The succeeding four sections take up, in turn, various families of arguments that have been offered in support of the existence of a citizen's duty to vote. Section III examines the prudential case for a duty to vote. It is most often encountered in public service propaganda: "Your vote matters!" "Only by voting can *you* be heard!" But these hardly amount to even an embryonic justificatory argument. Indeed, we are unaware of any important *normative* theory of democracy that locates the duty to vote in the enlightened pursuit of self-interest. Mainstream *positive* theories of voting behavior do, however, routinely hypothesize that individuals decide both whether to vote and how to vote as a prudentially motivated investment in political outcomes. By explaining why voting cannot reasonably be construed as that sort of straightforward advancement of self-interest, we sharpen the difficulties that will be faced by the other normative theories to be investigated. Section IV examines the act-consequentialist case for a duty to vote; Section V examines that duty's putative derivation as the conclusion of a generalization argument. Section VI addresses the case for voting grounded on an "expressive ethics," one we have elsewhere developed at some length and found to supply the most persuasive rationale for the moral superiority of voting over abstention.[3] Each of these, even the last, ultimately fails to support a general duty to vote. We therefore conclude that no such case can be made. There remains the puzzle of why, given the insufficiencies of the supporting arguments, there obtains a strong and widely held intuition that voting is meritorious. Section VII offers some speculations concerning why this might be so.

II. THE ARGUMENT DELIMITED

Sometimes one does wrong not to vote. An impanceled juror who declines to cast a ballot concerning the guilt or innocence of the defendant fails to fulfill one of the duties attached to that office. Similarly, a university faculty member who absents herself from a departmental decision concerning a junior colleague's tenure and promotion case is, exceptional considerations aside, derelict. In both instances the duty to vote is consequent on the individual's occupying a special office or role, the satisfactory performance of which requires, but is not confined to, casting a vote. (It is also part of the officeholder's duty that the vote be well-considered, based on admissible evidence, and so on.) To infer from these special cases a citizen's duty to vote in general elections would, of course, be invalid.

One may, in virtue of special circumstances, be morally obligated to vote in a general election. If, for example, Jones has promised her spouse that she will cast a ballot in the upcoming presidential election, then she stands under an obligation to do so as an entailment of the duty to keep promises one has made. If Smith is an active member of a political party who has aligned himself with others in the task of securing its victory at the polls, then he may be guilty of bad faith, of letting the side down, if he chooses to spend election day sharpening his short iron play. The former explicitly, and the latter implicitly, voluntarily took on a commitment that created an obligation to vote which, in the absence of that undertaking, would not have obtained.

A further qualification concerns the nature of the venue in which the general elections take place. Abercrombie lives in a small community in which all adult residents routinely enlist themselves in public business. Among its traditions are that individuals serve on various committees, attend town meetings, publicly announce their views, and periodically make themselves available to hold down the community's elective offices. It is plausible to maintain that Abercrombie and all his co-residents have a duty to vote. They are the beneficiaries of practices of widespread political involvement in which each citizen plays a roughly equal and complementary part with all others. One who declines to vote or in some other manner opts out can be seen as free-riding on the exertions of others.[4] If Abercrombie has chosen to live in the community in order to secure advantages arising from patterns of citizen involvement, then the existence of the duty seems manifest; if Abercrombie is the inadvertent recipient of benefits not deliberately sought, the existence of a strict duty derived from considerations of fairness is more questionable.[5] Even in the latter case, however, voting would seem to be more morally meritorious than abstention.

In Australia it is a legal requirement, backed up by a $50 fine, that all adult citizens vote. That law may or may not be well-conceived. But if there is a moral duty to obey the laws of a reasonably just society, then Australians have a moral duty to vote. The latter duty is entirely derivative from the former.

The subsequent discussion of the duty to vote is not meant to apply to cases like these. We explicitly restrict our discussion to voting in general elections by people who are under no special obligation to exercise the franchise and who are not required by law to do so. We further confine our attention to the kinds of elections that characteristically occur in modern nation-states and their substantial political subunits in which populations number in the hundreds of thousands or millions and in which, for most individuals, political activity is only an occasional, part-time pursuit. When there is reference in what follows to a *citizen's duty to vote,* that is the context we have in mind.

III. THE ARGUMENT FROM PRUDENCE

How things go with a person can be substantially affected by collective determinations. "Your vote makes a difference," the pre-election propaganda intones. If that is so, then prudent individuals will vote in order to augment the probability that electoral outcomes will favor their interests. If prudence is a duty (or, if not a duty in the strict sense, then a virtue), then one ought to vote.

Whether individuals owe duties to themselves, including a duty of prudence, is debatable. That question can, though, be set to one side here, because the key premise of the prudential argument is defective. In any election with a large number of voters, the chance that my vote will make a difference to the outcome is small. On most electoral occasions it will be infinitesimal. Therefore, one aiming to maximize her own utility may have many alternative paths for doing so, but almost surely one of the least efficacious will be to bestir herself to cast a ballot in order to influence electoral outcomes. That will be so even if much hangs on the results of the election.[6]

Consider an election between candidates/policies A and B in which there are 2n other voters (in addition to Voter *I*).[7] Voter *I* will bring about the victory of A if the other voters array themselves such that there are exactly *n* ballots cast for A and *n* for B. In such a circumstance we describe the *i*th voter (Voter *I*) as being *decisive*. Otherwise, a vote for A will not affect the electoral outcome. Thus, we can represent the expected return to a vote for A insofar as it bears on electoral outcomes as:

$$(1)\ U_i = p[V_i(A) - V_i(B)]$$

where

U_i = Utility to a vote for A by Voter *I*

p = Probability of being decisive

$V_i(A)$ = Return to Voter *I* of A's being victorious

$V_i(B)$ = Return to Voter *I* of B's being victorious

We can, in turn, represent the likelihood of being decisive as:

$$(2)\ p = f(E, m)$$

where

E = Total number of those casting votes

m = Anticipated proportional majority

More explicitly, holding other factors constant, the larger the number of voters, the lower the probability of being decisive. Among these other factors, the most significant for purposes of this analysis is the expected closeness of the result. Closeness here is usually conceived in terms of the probability that an individual voter selected at random casts a ballot for A rather than B; the nearer that probability is to .5, the smaller m will be.

The direction of these relationships is intuitive. Less so are the relative magnitudes. It can be demonstrated that p is a slowly decreasing function of E but a very quickly decreasing function of m. To pass quickly over calculational complications which we address at length elsewhere,[8] in a large-number electorate the size of a U.S. congressional district, a voter who would benefit a great deal from the victory of A over B (measuring the benefit in monetary terms, suppose the voter would gain $1,000) has an expected return to a vote for A of a few pennies if m is zero. If, though, the anticipated proportional majority is as small as .01 (i.e., the probability that a randomly selected voter will vote for A is 50.5 percent), then for U_i to be valued as high as one cent, the *i*th voter must value A's victory in excess of $1 million. But an anticipated majority of .01 represents what we would normally think of as an exceedingly close election, one the pollsters dub "too close to call." The formal model generates a conclusion in accord with most people's intuitions: the chance that one's vote will be decisive in a national or large subnational election ranges between vanishingly small and infinitesimal.

Voting is costly in the opportunity sense. The time and effort and perhaps other resources that go into casting a ballot have alternative employments. These costs will vary from individual to individual, but for virtually everyone these will be orders of magnitude greater than the expected return to a vote as expressed in (1). Therefore, a rationally self-interested individual will vote neither for A nor for B, but will instead refrain from voting. At least that will be so if voting is exclusively an investment in electoral outcomes. If, however, there are direct returns to a vote—avoiding a fine if one is an Australian, securing a pleasant warm glow if one simply enjoys the act of voting, and so on—then self-interest may indeed prompt one to vote. We can restate the individual's utility calculation as:

$$(3)\ U_i = p[V_i(A) - V_i(B)] + S - C$$

where

S = Direct return to *I* of a vote for A

C = Cost to *I* of voting

For reasons adduced above, in virtually all large-number elections the probabilistic impact on electoral outcomes is nil, and thus the *i*th voter's utility is approximated very closely by:

$$(4)\ U_i = S - C$$

In other words, a prudent individual votes if and only if the direct return to casting a ballot exceeds the cost. Note that voting so understood is a consumption good among other consumption goods, rather than an investment in political outcomes. I may indeed have self-interested reasons to vote, but these reasons have virtually nothing to do with the advantages that would accrue to me from the victory of the more favored candidate. Casting a ballot, then, is similar to bowling or tending petunias or listening to a "Metallica's Greatest Hits" tape: if one appreciates that sort of activity, then one has reason to engage in it; otherwise one does not. From the perspective of prudence there is nothing intrinsically commendable or inadvisable about any of these activities.

IV. THE ARGUMENT FROM ACT-CONSEQUENTIALISM

The result of the preceding section is not likely to prove upsetting to many exponents of a citizen's duty to vote. Few will have conceived it to be primarily a self-regarding duty. To the contrary: even if the act of voting involves some measure of personal sacrifice it is meritorious because of the benefits thereby conferred on the population at large. That is precisely the point of speaking of it as a *citizen's* duty.

Nonetheless, a shift of perspective from prudence to the well-being of the entire community does not remove the sting of the preceding section's analysis. If the inconsequentiality of voting renders it unimportant with regard to one's own self-interest whether one bothers to cast a ballot, then that inconsequentiality also infects the claim that one is producing some public good through exercising the franchise. It seems on first blush, then, that only a slightly modified version of the argument from prudence is needed to dispose of the argument from act-consequentialism. Why should minute probabilities draw one to the polls in the latter case if they do not in the former?

The answer the consequentialist will give is: because the stakes are disproportionate. When appraising voting prudentially, only *one's own* utility enters into the picture, but when thinking about how a vote can bear on the political community's well-being, *everyone's* utility counts. Moving from the micro to the macro dimension effects a change in degree which, because it is so great, becomes a difference in kind as well. Derek Parfit offers an analogy:

> It may be objected that it is *irrational* to consider very tiny chances. When our acts cannot affect more than a few people, this may be so. But this is because the stakes are here comparatively low. Consider the risks of causing accidental death. It may be irrational to give any thought to a one-in-a million chance of killing one person. But if I was a nuclear engineer, would I be irrational to give any thought to the same chance of killing a million people? This is what most of us believe. When the stakes are very high, no chance, however small, should be ignored.[9]

Some hyperbole in the concluding sentence aside, Parfit's point seems undeniable: even very small probabilities that bear heavily on the wellbeing of a multitude ought to be incorporated in the deliberations preceding one's decision on how to act. Brian Barry interprets this as a generally applicable utilitarian rationale for voting:

> If an act-utilitarian really gives full weight to the consequences for *everyone* that he expects will be affected, this will normally provide an adequate reason for voting. If I think that one party will increase the GNP by 1/4 per cent over five years more than the other party, that for a utilitarian is a big aggregate difference. Are there *really* so many more beneficial things one could do with fifteen minutes?[10]

Do these observations indicate, then, that if we extend the scope of our concern from one solitary individual to many, there is a directly consequentialist rationale for a duty to vote despite the minuscule likelihood of altering the outcome? In a word, no. We have no quarrel with the other sides of the respective analogies: it is, indeed, for almost all people almost all of the time, a worthwhile moral bargain to expend fifteen minutes to avert a one-in-a-million chance of a nuclear power plant meltdown or to bring about a one-quarter percent increase in GNP over five years. What we deny is the relevance of these analogies to voting.

There is no question that a nuclear accident costing a million lives is a terrifically bad outcome. Somewhat less spectacularly, it is also uncontroversial that, all else equal, an increase in the national wealth amounting to several billions of dollars is welcome news indeed.[11] A terrible disaster or its nonoccurrence; a noteworthy augmentation of the citizenry's wealth or its absence—who doubts where the balance of good lies or whether it is large enough to make a valid claim on one's attention and effort? But alternatives faced in electoral competitions are not of that sort. We do not see Party B campaigning on the platform, "We commit ourselves to doing everything that Party A promises and in exactly the way that Party A promises to do it—except that in addition we propose to sabotage a nuclear power plant at the expected cost of a million lives"; or "We pledge to run the economy much as Party A does—but one-quarter percent less efficiently." In hotly contested elections there is never anything approaching consensus concerning which candidates or which set of policies will best secure the common good. Each side identifies some ends as valuable and proposes various political means to secure them. The competing sides typically will concur to a considerable extent concerning which items are to be valued and which disvalued (both are pro-liberty; both favor prosperity) but will assign different weights to the various goods and bads, thereby differing in the trade-offs that they will countenance (for example: "Shall the liberty of workers to strike be limited so as to secure greater prosperity?"). Or they will differ concerning factual propositions ("We are/are not in the midst of a period of global warming"). Or they will advance opposed judgments concerning the instrumental merits of different policies advocated to secure the ends they value ("Capital punishment will/will not decrease the homicide rate"). Or they will dispute the competence or commitment of would-be executors of policy, or enter into subtle semantic debates (Is affirmative action best described as setting "goals" or "quotas"?). And so on. When each side has its fervent partisans, its roster of so-called experts, its loquacious evangelists, assurance concerning where the common good lies is apt to be elusive.

This is not to deny that during the course of an election campaign there will be numerous affirmations of unshakeable conviction concerning the manifest merits of Party A and the gross deficiencies of the candidates and policies put forward by Party B. It is, though, to note that their epistemic clout is tainted by outpourings of equally confident testimony issuing from the other side. There is, of course, nothing surprising in the existence of this phenomenon. Political operatives are in the business of winning adherents to their cause, the more zealous and unshakeable the better. To the extent that a candidate or party succeeds in persuading citizens—for most of whom political involvement is a very occasional avocation—that momentous matters are indeed at stake and that here is the side of Truth and Goodness, the opponent's side that of Disaster and Despair, citizens are thereby provided with an incentive to make their way to the polls on election day and to cast a ballot in the desired direction. Ratcheting up emotional fever makes for loyal party supporters in the political arena, much as it makes for loyal fans in sporting arenas. An important difference between the two brands of enthusiasm is that probably not even the die-hard fans themselves are inclined to correlate the lustiness of the cheers that ring around them with epistemic warrant. Citizens embroiled in political campaigns do, however, mistake their own depth of conviction for evidentiary weight. They should not set an example for theorists who conduct their analyses from a safe emotional distance.

By way of contrast to the Parfit/Barry analogies, a more recognizable (although still greatly simplified) rendering of the voter's scenario might go something like this. Party A proposes a set of economic policies that have some hard-to-quantify but non-negligible likelihood of generating a higher national product over the next five years than those of Party B: a best rough estimate is something on the order of one-quarter percent per year. Party B's economic program, however, seems likely to yield somewhat less inflation over the course of those five years. Complicating matters further are conflicting estimates concerning the economic policies' respective merits with regard to effects on capital investment, unemployment, the trade balance, and measures of economic equality. All that one can be reasonably confident of is that A's policies will do better with regard to some of these, and B's policies will do better with regard to others. And beyond the parties' economic programs there are another two dozen or so major areas of dispute—over defense, civil rights, education, housing, environmental policy, etc. With regard to each, a greater or lesser degree of murkiness obtains; different trade-offs are on offer; both sides swear fealty to the common good. What is the conscientious act-utilitarian now to do? Does it still seem so apparent that spending fifteen minutes to cast a ballot is one of the most socially beneficial things one can do with one's time—especially if one has not previously invested for each of those minutes several dozen hours devoted to securing and assessing relevant political information?

The utilitarian rationale for voting can be expressed by a variant of expression (1):

$$(1') \; U = p[V(A) - V(B)]$$

In this variant, relativization to the self-interest of the individual voter is replaced by a representation of overall effects on well-being. When the affected population is large, U may be substantial even for very small p values. But what the preceding discussion suggests is that (1′) stands in need of modification. It would be adequate as it stands if we could estimate with assurance the [V(A) − V(B)] term. Since we cannot, however, the value of U must be discounted not only by the probability of being decisive but, additionally, by the probability that one has overestimated or even reversed the respective merits of A and B. Call this the *epistemic discount rate.*

Although the appropriate rate of epistemic discounting will vary from election to election and, of course, from voter to voter, in virtually all real-world election scenarios and for the vast majority of voters, it will be large enough to bring the U term very close to zero. That is because political uncertainties are not all of one species but several, and they compound each other. First, as suggested above, one has to discount for mistakes in assigning comparative weights to the various competing goods (or, more rarely, for having identified as a good something that is a bad, or vice versa). Second, one has to discount for the fallibility inherent in empirical assessments concerning matters of fact and causal judgments concerning the instrumental effects of alternative policy options.

Third, one must then discount by the likelihood that the platform on which the party is running is indicative of the actions that it will indeed undertake should it gain office. That is, even if one knew with certainty that giving effect to the A platform would be superior to realizing the B platform, the return to a vote for A has to be discounted by the probability that A will defect from its own standard. It is not only inordinate cynicism about politicians and their campaign promises that might induce one to attach substantial weight to this factor; political history is full of spectacular and momentous turnarounds. To take just twentieth-century United States presidential elections as examples, in 1916 Woodrow Wilson ran for reelection on the slogan "He kept us out of war!" He was duly reelected and then didn't. In 1964, Lyndon Johnson alleged that if the wrong candidate was elected the U.S. would find itself mired in an unwinnable land war in Asia. So it proved. And of course there is the whimsically delightful insouciance of George Bush's "Read my lips; no new taxes!"

Fourth, one must discount for historical accidents and inadvertencies. Unpredictable wars, assassinations, stock market crashes, famine, or incapacity of the officeholder might turn what had *ex ante* seemed to be a good bet into an *ex post* loser. Fifth and finally, one must discount all of the above by a measure of one's own judiciousness or lack of same as a political evaluator, asking: How well-attested is the data on which I rely? How adequate are my technical capabilities in economics, international affairs, defense studies, social policy, etc. for supporting the instrumental analyses I bring to competing policy proposals? Is my judgment liable to be affected by any hidden biases or blind spots? How successfully have I managed to detach myself from evanescent enthusiasms so as to preserve a cool objectivity? And the like.

If, after all the discounts are appropriately assigned, it still seems manifest that A is the better party/candidate, then one may have some utilitarian reason to cast a ballot for A. But even then, perhaps not. If knowledge of the superiority of A is not confined to some esoteric coterie but rather is possessed by me because it is readily available to the citizenry at large, and if members of that citizenry for the most part will vote against a palpably inferior candidate should they bother to vote at all, then employing one's fifteen minutes to vote may, on utilitarian grounds, be inadvisable. Recall that the value of p is a rapidly diminishing function of m, the expected proportional majority. If, say, for any representative voter in an electorate in which one million individuals cast ballots, it is .6 likely that she will recognize B to be inferior and thus vote in opposition, then the likelihood of one's own vote being decisive is so indescribably small as to be entirely negligible. (If the question is, "Should we bestir ourselves to avert nuclear meltdowns?," how likely is it that my vote will be needed to tip the balance?) To oversimplify a bit, on those occasions when one's vote is most likely to make the sort of difference that stirs the hearts of act-consequentialists, there will rarely be any firm indication concerning for whom it ought to be cast; and when there is unmistakable evidence concerning which is the better candidate or policy, it is almost inconceivable that one's vote will be needed.

Suppose, for the sake of argument, that all the preceding cautions could be met by an exceptional public-spirited citizen confident of her ability to evaluate the issues, judge the fitness of the candidates, and cast a well-directed ballot. That would still not support a general duty to vote. Rather, it would at most show that there are consequentialist reasons for *someone who is good at voting* to do so—and consequentialist reasons for someone who is bad at voting to abstain. If, for example, despite my best efforts I am more likely than not to be a sucker for an inferior candidate (this is my track record; past attempts to mend my ways have met with no success; etc.), then I confer on the citizenry a benefit by staying at home on election day. It follows that there cannot be a completely general citizen's duty to vote, because *I* am a citizen and it does not include me.

One does not, however, need so strong an assumption of political ineptitude to support a rationale for not voting. That is because the relevant measure of facility as a voter is comparative. To see that this is so, consider a radically simplified electorate of three individuals, voters X, Y, and Z. X and Y have demonstrated an aptitude of .6 for identifying which of two candidates is the better one. Z is yet more skilled, with a success rate of 90 percent. When they all vote in an election contested by candidates A and B, they select the better candidate—let us assume it is A—whenever either X and Y, X and Z, Y and Z, or all three of them vote for A. That sums to a success rate of 79 percent. But if X and Y should abstain, the likelihood of selecting the better candidate soars to 90 percent.

Whether those with lower voter-facility scores increase the likelihood of a favorable electoral determination by abstaining will depend on the actual distribution of scores. So, for example, if X and Y each had a .8 aptitude, the expected value of the outcome would be diminished rather than enhanced by their abstention. But although no universal generalization is at hand, over a wide range of distributions it will be the case that those who are considerably below the median level of voter facility will improve electoral outcomes by abstaining. That will raise the median level of the remaining voter population, thereby making it incumbent on those citizens in the new bottom group to abstain. Again the median has been raised, and again a new crop of abstainers sprouts, the process iterating until only a small number of extraordinarily acute political evaluators remains in the voting pool. Something has gone awry, but piquantly so. For on the way to providing a utilitarian argument for a citizen's duty to vote, Parfit and Barry have (re)invented—the regime of Philosopher-Kings!

It could be argued in response that not everyone is a utilitarian. There will be lots of people casting ballots predicated on some incentive other than concern for the greatest happiness of the greatest number. Predictably, many will vote self-interestedly; others will cast ballots expressive of malice; some will just grab the lever closest to their dominant hand. Some always vote for the Democrat, some never do, and others are as irregular as a quantum particle dance. In virtue of such diverse political phenomena, it is by no means out of the question that the consequentialist stakes are indeed large and that your estimate of their size and direction is substantially better than average. Under such circumstances, the utilitarian objects, there may well be a morally compelling reason for you to vote.

We need not look too deeply into the particulars of the sort of case hereby envisioned to observe that all such scenarios are intrinsically incapable of supporting a generalized duty to vote. If they carry any moral entailments, it is not to a duty to vote *simpliciter* but rather to a citizen's duty to *vote right.* That is, assuming that A is the better of the two candidates,

$$V_A > \text{Not voting} > V_B$$

where V_A represents voting for candidate A and V_B represents voting for candidate B. But this is not how a duty to vote is supposed to work. Rather, when it is said that voting is morally meritorious, what normally is meant is that the goodness of rousing oneself to visit the polls is independent of the subsequent choice of which candidate will receive one's vote. (There may be additional moral merit in ascertaining who is the best candidate and then voting for that person, but this is in addition to that which attaches to the voting act as such.) On an act-consequentialist analysis, however, it is the direction of the vote that is crucial; any of those B voters would have done better with regard to his duty as a citizen had he instead spent his fifteen minutes in the pub.[12]

There is a further reason why the consequentialist case for a duty to vote is strained. The argument hinges on there being matters of huge moment at stake so as to offset the tiny likelihood of one's own vote tipping the balance. However, there are good reasons in general to think that this will not often be the case—at least if democracy is working tolerably well. It is a well-established proposition in the formal literature on electoral competition that parties/candidates will be constrained to offer policy platforms that lie not too far from that which the median voter prefers. In two-party electoral races of the familiar kind, political equilibrium, if it exists, will be characterized by the parties/candidates locating themselves in near-proximity to each other, and this co-location result is quite robust to assumptions about voter motivation. One does not have to take these formal models too literally to recognize the force of the simple reasoning at stake—namely, that competition tends to restrict the policies that parties will offer, to the extent that those parties are interested in maximizing their chances of being elected. Such centripetal forces depend on the threat that voters will vote against things they do not like—but if that threat has been effective, then it is not necessary for citizens actually to exercise the franchise! In the limit, when rival candidates offer virtually identical policies, it seems inordinately precious to insist that we should all turn out because of some putative democratic duty. At least that is so within an act-consequentialist scheme.

We conclude that on every front the argument from act-consequentialism fails. It cannot support a duty to vote except when the stakes are very high, a circumstance which we have given reason to believe is rarer than is commonly made out. Even then, act-consequentialism does not support a duty to vote but rather a duty to vote *right.* Thus, it is not a duty of the citizenry at large, but only of the political cognoscenti. Even for political junkies, a healthy dose of confidence that one is in fact voting right is rarely justified; and the more likely it is that such confidence is justified, the less likely it is that one's vote will be needed to tip the balance. Conclusion: On any list of the top thousand or so ways an ordinary citizen can usefully augment social well-being, casting a ballot on election day will either rank low or not be present at all.

V. THE ARGUMENT FROM GENERALIZATION

> But what if everyone were to stay home and not vote? The results would be disastrous! Therefore, I (you/she) should vote.

Some version of the preceding is, by our casual tally, the most commonly adduced justification for a duty to vote. It can be presented as a reflection on the utility ramifications of a general practice of nonvoting, or it can take on a more Kantian wrapping in which willing the universalized form of the maxim "Vote only if it involves no sacrifice of one's own interests" is shown to embody an inconsistency. Often, of course, it is neither, but merely the inchoate apprehension on the part of the thoroughly nontheoretical man that he is doing wrong by abstaining from an activity that he would not wish most of his compatriots to omit. Although there are significant differences among various generalization strategies, the following analysis abstracts from those differences. Instead, we attempt to identify certain features that regularly separate persuasive from less persuasive generalization arguments. We then show that the generalization argument for a duty to vote falls among the latter.

To begin, we note in passing that the claim that it would be disastrous if no one voted is far from evident.[13] That is because the scenario under which abstention becomes universal has not been specified. There are an indefinite number of possible worlds in which no one votes. In some there is no voting because there are no elections; in others there is no voting because there are no people. For purposes of a generalization argument, some of these possible worlds are more relevant than others. Presumably, what is intended is a scenario in which there are eligible voters, there are contested elections in which they are at liberty to cast ballots, but all refrain from doing so in order to pursue their various private ends. That is a possible world sufficiently close to the actual world to have some purchase.

Even so, the indicated conclusion is ambiguous. To limn the details of this possible world, we might suppose that people abstain from voting because political determinations are largely irrelevant to their interests: Collective action beyond that in which people voluntarily engage is almost never required to secure any appreciable good, and when it is required, one candidate for office is as likely as any other to do a creditable job in orchestrating it. So no one bothers to vote. Is this a woeful world in which to find oneself? To our eyes it has more the aspects of a paradise! Alternatively, for the sake of theological balance we may speculate that no one bothers to vote in Hell because the totals invariably are corrupted. Splitting the difference leaves one agnostic concerning the putative badness of universal abstention.

Such qualms duly noted, let it be granted for the sake of argument that generalized nonvoting would indeed be undesirable. Still, the indicated conclusion ("Therefore I/you/she ought to vote") does not automatically follow. It is notoriously easy to produce arguments that display the same surface form as the generalized-failure-to-vote argument, yet yield preposterous conclusions. For example, suppose that Dalrymple is considering leaving the farm to pursue a career as a dentist. The question is put to her, "What if no one grew fruits and vegetables?" The result, Dalrymple admits, would be disastrous. Therefore, it is urged, she would do wrong to abandon farming for dentistry. Against this suffices the retort, "But *not everyone will* give up farming!"

By way of contrast, Throckmorton is about to take a shortcut across the newly seeded lawn and is brought up by the reproof, "Well, what if everyone were to walk across the lawn? All the grass would be killed!" The reply, "But not everyone will cut across the lawn; most people take more heed of signs than I do," carries distinctly less conviction. The two cases display the same surface form, yet one intuitively is weak and the other strong. What accounts for the difference?

We cannot here attempt to offer a comprehensive theory of soundness in generalization arguments, especially as we are abstracting from different underlying approaches to generalization. There are, though, certain more or less readily identifiable features which attach to those generalization arguments that intuitively persuade and which are notably absent from those that do not.

Sometimes by doing or refraining from some action one thereby perpetrates an *unfairness.* This will be so when one benefits from or otherwise assigns positive value to the opposite type of performance on the part of others. By not doing as others do, one takes a free ride on their compliance. When Throckmorton ignores the "Keep Off the Grass!" sign and cuts across the newly seeded lawn, he thereby secures a quicker route to his destination; when others comply with the directive, they get to enjoy a flourishing green lawn—but so too does Throckmorton. The individual who picks out an apple from the orchard saying, "One won't be missed," may be entirely correct, but he is thereby presuming that the disappearance of this particular apple will not be followed by the like disappearance of bushels more; that is, he is presuming that others are more firmly bound than he is himself by norms of property ownership.[14] And similarly for the casual litterer, the tax evader, the illicit occupier of "Handicapped Only" parking spots, and their numerous kin.

In many though not all cases of such free-riding behavior, initial defection by one or a small number of persons tends to promote further defections. In the extreme case the equilibrium outcome is universal defection. Suppose that one individual backs out of paying her share of the cost required to produce some public good. That single act of defection increases the per-person cost of the good to the remainder of the group, which may, in turn, induce others to back out, and so on, until production is no longer sustainable and the free-riding behavior becomes self-annihilating. This is one (not very Kantian) way of reconstructing Kant's demonstration in the *Grundlegung* of the inconsistency generated by application of the Categorical Imperative to a practice of borrowing money in the expectation that one will not be able to pay back the loan when it comes due.

In cases such as these, generalization is useful, if only as a heuristic device. It simultaneously levels the playing field and puts the tendency of an individual's action under a moral microscope through which the wrongness of the conduct is rendered evident. Free-riding, when generalized, is shown to be no more viable than the village in which everyone made a living by taking in others' washing. Strictly speaking, what makes an ungeneralizable action wrong is not that it fails the generalization test. Rather, it fails the generalization test because of underlying unfairness, and it is the unfairness that accounts for the action's wrongness. Passing a generalization test is secondary; fairness or the lack of same is what is primary.

That is why some arguments that exhibit disastrous results of a certain generalized practice fail to persuade. They are examples in which the universal practice of S would indeed be unfortunate, but not because of any unfairness embedded in an individual instance of S. Such is the case with the decision to abandon farming in order to take up dentistry. When Dalrymple ceases to farm she does not thereby perpetrate any unfairness on those who remain in farming. Rather, each remaining farmer is, all else equal, rendered better off at the margin in virtue of the lower level of competition. In a large economy the effect may be so small as to be entirely unnoticeable, but the key point is its direction, not the magnitude. Moreover, as one person or several people leave farming, there is no tendency to set up a spiral of further departures; just the reverse. The process is self-stabilizing, with inducements to remain (or, once having left, to return) growing progressively greater the more who withdraw. The equilibrium that emerges is morally satisfactory; there will be both dentists and farmers, and neither reaps unfair advantage at the expense of the other.

Abstaining from voting is more like choosing a profession of dentistry than it is like cutting across a newly seeded lawn or failing to pay one's share of taxes. Individuals who choose to vote do so because, as modeled in expression (3), the benefits they secure from voting exceed the costs. Those benefits are the sum of direct returns to a vote—for example, "having my say!"[15]—and the return constituted by raising the probability of the desired electoral outcome taking place. When an eligible voter abstains, thereby lowering E, the total size of the electorate, the probability p of one's own vote proving decisive increases. That is, each remaining voter is rendered better off by the lower level of electoral competition. In a large electorate, as with a large economy, the effect of one person's withdrawal may be so small as to be entirely unnoticeable, but the key point is its direction, not the magnitude. Therefore, as in the preceding example, the process tends to be self-stabilizing. An equilibrium emerges that does not have any evident morally unsatisfactory properties.

Some will respond by objecting that this equilibrium may be substantially less than full citizen participation, perhaps well under 50 percent of the eligible population,[16] and therefore is objectionable for being less democratic than full participation. We are unmoved by this response because we are unsure what it means to be "more/less democratic" and why in this context being more democratic should be deemed better than being less democratic. If "more democratic" simply *means* displaying greater levels of citizen participation, then of course it is true that high rates of voting are more democratic than lower ones, but it would be begging the question to take that definitional circumstance as a reason for preferring greater participation. If what is meant is that democratic institutions do better with greater levels of participation, then we would need to have a specification of the normative criteria for "doing better" and empirical grounds for maintaining that these criteria are more fully realized with increased participation. It is not obvious to us that democratic ideals would be better served if, instead of two major parties, there were twenty, or if the size of Congress were enlarged by a factor of a hundred, or if elections were held on a fortnightly basis. Against each of these envisioned "reforms," the status quo does not seem obviously inferior. Similarly, we do not find it obvious that election outcomes would be "better" or political institutions more "legitimate" (in whatever nontrivial senses of these words might be supplied) if voting were to take place at 90 percent rather than 50 percent or even 5 percent participation levels. And even if more did mean better, it would still require further argument to show that this establishes a duty to vote. Wishing not to prejudge such complex questions, we conclude this section by observing that no such duty emerges straightforwardly from a generalization argument.[17]

VI. EXPRESSIVE ETHICS AND VOTING

Not all that uncommonly during classroom discussions of the ethics of democratic participation which we have superintended over the years, some student would rouse himself to a greater than customary pitch of moral seriousness and exclaim, "If you don't bother to vote, then you don't have any right to complain afterwards about what the government does!" Often this rebuke elicits a buzz of approval from the other students.

It is not difficult to find any number of reasons to dismiss this declaration as more passionate than cogent. In no actually legislated bill of rights or credible theory of free expression is a right to complain about the activities of government contingent on one's prior electoral participation. And if there were such a theory, what would it look like? Would someone who has voted for A over B have no right to complain about anything the government subsequently does should A in fact defeat B? If one wished to be sure of retaining the right to complain, would it not be prudent to vote for some obscure third-party candidate in order to assure that one is not muffled by one's prior electoral support? Doesn't the plausibility of this entire series of speculations presume that one had—and then, by abstaining, irresponsibly squandered—some realistic opportunity through one's vote to make a difference with regard to political outcomes, a proposition examined and rejected in Section III? If no voter or no nonvoter is individually responsible for the outcome that emerged, why should one more than the other be consigned by shame or compunction or opprobrium to silence? It may seem appropriate, in short, to conclude that this line of thought is the sort of sophomoric effusion not uncommon in a classroom of sophomores.

The dismissal is too quick. (Take the preceding paragraph as a pedagogical confession.) The student's response is, to be sure, naive, but it conceals a promising insight that has largely been banished from more sophisticated ethical theories. Interpreted charitably, the response maintains that alongside, and to a considerable extent independent of, direct or indirect consequential considerations there exist *norms of expression*. Through one's spoken utterances and other expressive activity, one aligns oneself with certain values and opposes others. To the extent that it is inherently and not simply instrumentally good to identify—and to identify oneself with—that which is good (and evil to align oneself with that which is evil), an ethics of expression is not reducible to even a sophisticated consequentialism.[18]

The universe of value is enormous, and no one can stand for everything that is intrinsically worthy. Each of us, though, is situated by circumstance or by our own prior choices in proximity to certain morally trenchant items. One's stance with regard to them goes a long way toward defining one's character as an acting being. That stance incorporates both consequentialist and nonconsequentialist aspects. No more than the passionate sophomore are we able to offer an in-depth account of their interworkings, but we would be surprised if most readers do not acknowledge in their own moral lives expressive as well as outcome-directed imperatives. In particular, we expect considerable concurrence with the assessment that one is obliged on suitable occasions to express support for certain practices and institutions if one is to be entitled to play any significant part within them. Some examples:

To be a fan of the New York Yankees is more than to have a "pro" attitude toward the Yankees' winning ball games and pennants. It additionally involves a disposition to engage in activity that expresses support of the team. A true-blue fan may never actually attend a game, but if she does she will cheer as the Yankees load the bases, and will commiserate with other fans as the rally is snuffed out by a double play. Fans will scream and contort themselves even in front of unresponsive TV screens. To observe that these antics do no good with regard to the team's win-loss statistics is to miss the point; the practice of being a fan has very little to do with undertaking consequentially fruitful activity on behalf of the object of one's passions and very much to do with expressing support.

Friendship is in some ways similar, in some ways different. Friends do act to procure goods for each other. One not only expresses a wish that the friend's life go well but endeavors to make that be so. Sometimes, however, there is nothing one can do for one's friend. He is gravely ill; the doctors will either find some way to save him or they will not; it is entirely out of one's own hands. But one who can do nothing for the recovery will nonetheless expressively support that eventuality.[19] To do otherwise is literally to render oneself a "fair-weather friend"—that is, not a genuine friend at all. The practice of friendship carries both consequential and expressive elements, with neither reducible to the other.

Numerous related instances can be adduced. The momentousness of particular items of our experience is regularly underscored via symbolic acts that express our respect, regret, appreciation, devotion, implacable opposition, or other intentional stances. One who insists on representing all rational activity as directed toward the production of consequences will be unable satisfactorily to account for the retrospective dimension of our activity. For example, sacramental or commemorative activities will be systematically misunderstood as essentially forward-looking—that is, as other than they represent themselves as being—if not indeed as embodying some harebrained confusion about the temporal direction of causality.

Not only in private life do expressive considerations come to the fore. It is in the nature of democratic politics that matters presented and widely acknowledged as items of momentous concern to all members of the polity are held up to examination, debated, and eventually put to popular determination through elections. Even in the age of the professionally packaged candidate and the ten-second sound bite, a certain measure of pomp and ceremony still attaches to the electoral process, thereby emphasizing that it is indeed serious business. The individual in her capacity as *citizen* has an assigned role in this process. Outsiders may be affected by the polity's electoral determinations, but the citizen is, additionally, an *agent* of those determinations. Through appearing at the polls and casting a ballot, she expresses her engagement with the concerns and undertakings of her compatriots and displays her assent to the legitimacy of the public enterprise through which she and they are bound together as partners within civil society.

Conversely, it can be argued, someone who chooses to be absent from the polls thereby expresses detachment from the enterprise, if not indeed active disdain. The doings of the polity are not his affair, he proclaims through his absence. It can go on without him—and he very well without it. That which is a matter of profound significance to his neighbors does not merit the allocation of even a few minutes of token symbolic support. It is for this reason that one who fails to vote imperils any right sub-sequently to complain about the government—not in the technical sense of being legally barred from doing so, but as an implication of common decency. One ought not bother others by raising matters that are none of one's business, and insofar as one who is eligible to vote declines to do so, one is expressing a disinclination to acknowledge the business of the *res publica* as one's own. To complain after the fact may be within the law, but it is base. It is like fulsomely bemoaning at the end of the season the also-ran finish of the Yankees after making no prior effort to take in a game, to apprise oneself of the team's fortunes, or even to cheer from a distance. It is anomalous in the same way as gnashing one's teeth and weeping bitter tears at the passing of someone of whom, in life, one was oblivious. It is, we might say, an exercise of bad faith and is to be condemned as such. That is the fleshed-out rendering of the student's exclamation.

Abstention by itself is not bad faith. It is, though, arguably discreditable. The office of citizen is no mean one, and to fail to display adequate regard for the station can be categorized as inherently condemnable. Not voting, so construed, is akin to declining to stand at the playing of the national anthem or trampling on the flag. Each is an expressively laden action that aligns one with certain political values and against others. Therefore, they are properly subject to praise or blame in virtue of what they *mean,* not simply because of what they *bring about.* The expressive argument for a duty to vote maintains that one evinces a minimally decent level of regard for the political weal by periodic appearances at the polls; to do less is to do too little.

Of all the rationales for a duty to vote, we find the expressive account strongest, if only by default. At one time we pronounced ourselves half-persuaded that the case it makes is sound,[20] but that now seems to be an overestimation. The chief inadequacies of the expressive case for a duty to vote are internal: the mere act of showing up at the polls every several years and grabbing some levers is palpably inadequate to qualify as a significant act of political expression.

Is exercise of the franchise to be construed as the expression of fidelity to the country's democratic institutions? Day-by-day residence within its borders and adherence to its laws and customs attests more explicitly and continuously to one's allegiance. Should the act of voting instead be construed as expressing some appreciation of the significance to the polity of the particular issues and debates that are spotlighted by the current election campaign? That is to read rather a lot into the act of voting. As exponents of a duty to vote often remark, for most people voting is a low-cost activity. No political literacy test must be passed before one is allowed to matriculate at the polls. Because the ballot is secret, the direction of one's vote is not subject to scrutiny and thus lacks the expressive dimensions of a genuinely public performance.[21] A vote cast from habitual allegiance to one party or TV-ad-induced prejudice or whimsy counts as much as one that is the product of diligent pre-election scrutiny of the candidates and issues. To presume that the act of voting expresses significant psychic involvement in the political affairs of the nation is like inferring from someone's sporadic church attendance an abiding concern with the theological ramifications of the Augsburg Confession.

This is not to deny the expressive salience of political activity. We are among the millions of people worldwide who were transfixed by the televised image of the anonymous man in Tiananmen Square who time and again defiantly interposed his body before the advancing tanks. We admired his heroism for reasons quite apart from any speculations concerning its likely effect on the decision making of the autocratic Beijing gerontocracy. Similarly, we acknowledge the expressive richness that was inherent in political participation by free citizens of the Greek *polis,* Roman republic, or Renaissance city-states. For them, political involvement gave shape to large swatches of a life in its public aspect. For some people today, it still does. But no such elevated status can be claimed for a desultory visit to the polls every few years. We do not deny that the rush of events can sometimes impose on citizens certain expressive obligations; it may be culpably shameless during times of great civic unrest or national mourning to present oneself to one's compatriots as uninvolved and unconcerned. And we acknowledge the coherence, if not the persuasiveness, of a republicanism that promotes vigorous citizen involvement in public affairs. There is, however, no sense in attaching to a perfunctory political performance more expressive weight than it can bear.[22]

Finally, there is the simple point that refraining from voting can be no less expressive than voting. One may wish to record one's total contempt for all the candidates, or one's conscientious objection to some policy that is a feature of all the major candidates' platforms, or one's belief that the entire enterprise is a fraud and a delusion. Turning one's back on the entire business, refusing to be implicated—these may not be the most extreme forms of civic rebellion, but they are ones that the democratic form characteristically admits. And compared to rushing to the barricades or joining the Michigan Militia, they have the added merit of civic gentleness. We might disagree in particular cases concerning the moral advisability of expressive abstention, but it is certainly not an incoherent practice.

VII. BELIEF IN A DUTY TO VOTE

One question raised by the foregoing is why, if grounding for a duty to vote is so distinctly shaky, belief in its existence should be widespread and insistent. Although popular sentiment is not decisive in these matters, one might reasonably locate the onus of proof on those who would call into question a venerable piece of folk wisdom. We believe that this onus has been successfully borne in the earlier sections. Since the argument has proceeded by enumeration, however, suspicion may remain that popular sentiment rests on some significant line of support that has been left unexamined. There is no way to put such a suspicion entirely to rest, but it is rendered less acute if the prevalence of the belief can be explained by factors other than those that would constitute its justification. Three factors suggest themselves.

First, in some political environments ancestral to that of contemporary representative liberal democracy, the persona of the activist citizen was central in a way it need not and cannot be today. In republics where free adult males possessing affluence sufficient to allow attention to affairs of state were a small minority of a small population, the demand that all who were entitled to participate should do so enjoyed considerable cogency. We are heirs to the political tradition of Aristotle's *Politics,* Renaissance humanism, the *Federalist Papers.* It is not surprising that we remain partially in thrall to ideals that were informed by very different conditions.[23] Civic republicanism is an ideology crafted by and for political elites. Its classical formulations have nothing to say about vast mega-states, universal enfranchisement, widely shared economic affluence, far-advanced division of political labor with concomitant specialization of function, neutral public bureaucracies, moderated party competition, and a host of other shifts in circumstance that separate us from our republican forebears. It is no longer possible, let alone desirable, that all free citizens devote themselves intensively to public concerns. Insofar, though, as traces of that superannuated republicanism linger, they support an ethos of universal participation, the lowest common denominator of which is periodic appearance at the polls.

Second, belief in a duty to vote promotes the self-esteem of voters. The public rhetoric of democracies is redolent with invocations of the dignity of active citizenship; it is fully one-third of government of the people, by the people, and for the people. Yet most individuals find themselves, in their daily affairs, distant from the precincts in which governance is exercised. The gulf of separation between one's democratic faith and predominant patterns of private activity can engender a sort of cognitive dissonance. That dissonance will be eased if one can establish for oneself solid lines of association with "the people" who are supposed to be sovereign within a democracy. The act of voting constitutes such a connection. One who votes can say, "Well, I did *something.*" If that something can, additionally, be characterized as the discharge of a solemn civic trust, there is comfort to be taken in its fulfillment, no matter how meager the demands thereby placed on one's wit and energies, the irrelevance of one's vote to the emergence of political outcomes, and the paucity of expressive potential in casting a ballot. Cheap grace is, after all, still grace.

Third, we ask, *Cui bono*? Who are the major beneficiaries of the myth of a duty to vote? Well, we can begin with those who do vote, since they can bask in the satisfaction of duty done. However, since the logical foundations of that supposed duty are rickety, its survival stands in need of some external nurturing. The opening sentence of this essay observed that such nurturing is periodically provided by public service announcements in the media; it is also provided by earnest declarations from political plenipotentiaries that yes, each citizen's vote is heard—that they, the people, are the true masters and candidates for office only their would-be servants. These sonorous harmonies are, to be sure, balm for democratic anxieties, but we might speculate that the benefits accruing to those who hum the tune are yet more substantial. Unlike the general run of citizens for whom political activity is an occasional thing, for a minority it is the primary business. Its rewards include position, prominence, power, and financial prosperity, and the fact that there is never a shortage of aspirants willing to enter the fray is some evidence that the magnitude of those rewards is substantial.

For the circle that thrives on the practice of politics it is, therefore, a matter of no small significance that those who foot the bill remain, if not eager to do so, then at least complaisant. If citizens come to believe that their abbreviated appearances at the polls suffice to render them crucial contributors to democratic affairs, respected and heeded by those who bid for their votes, then they are more likely to feel satisfied with the rules of the game as it is actually played rather than grump about the shortness of their end of the stick. From the perspective of political elites, widespread belief in a duty to vote passes the Goldilocks test: it is not too small, it is not too big; it is just right. If citizens were to believe that political activity had no moral claim on them at all, then they might feel alienated from its practice, especially as the costs they must bear to sustain democratic forms are not negligible. If, on the other hand, citizens believed that they were morally obligated to understand the issues, scrutinize carefully the performances of officeholders, investigate gaps between promised benefits and realized outcomes, and organize independent campaigns whenever they determined that the current political establishment was lax in its attention to the public weal, they would make terrible pests of themselves. The mean between these defective states is just enough participation to make ordinary citizens feel importantly implicated in the process and no more. Belief that voting is necessary and sufficient to enjoy the status *good citizen* is the perfect moral underpinning for that mean. No wonder, then, that it receives such enthusiastic support from political elites. Belief in a duty to vote is the opiate of democratic masses.

VIII. CONCLUSION

We have argued that a duty to vote cannot be sustained on prudential grounds, nor can it be justified through act-consequentialistic, generalization, or expressive reasoning. There are, though, several plausible explanations of why such a belief, though groundless, can be expected to enjoy wide currency among citizens of contemporary democracies.

That is not, of course, to argue that voting by citizens is morally wrong. Nor is it to call into question the supreme importance of the right to vote enjoyed by citizens of a democracy; on that matter we chant in unison with the civics textbooks and profess ourselves well-pleased to live in jurisdictions in which suffrage is universal and elections vigorously contested rather than, say, Burma or Cuba.[24] It is not even to argue against legally compulsory voting.[25] This much should be clear. But we know based on responses to prior versions of this essay that some people will take us to be saying that voting is irrational, "a waste of time." Not so. There are numerous good and sufficient reasons why someone might decide to vote. The point is merely that the belief that there is a general citizen's duty to do so is not among them. Through voting I can "get it off my chest"; I can evince solidarity with some cause or candidate; I can occupy a walk-on role within the ongoing kaleidoscopic civil drama; or I can simply take comfort from being in step with my neighbors.[26] In short, voting is like playing golf or being a member of a choral group or piecing together patchwork quilts: if it is the sort of thing in which one enjoys participating then there is a reason to do so, but morality does not nudge, one way or the other, except in special cases. And special cases do not make for a general duty.

NOTES

1. We are in sympathy with this distinction, believing that the Kantian equation of moral worth with adherence to duty is seriously deficient. That theme will not, however, be pressed in what follows.

2. For example, one may establish valuable business contacts while on the links; one can appease querulous folk who do believe in the existence of a duty to vote by putting in an appearance at the polls.

3. See Geoffrey Brennan and Loren E. Lomasky, *Democracy and Decision: The Pure Theory of Electoral Preference* (New York: Cambridge University Press, 1993), ch. 7.

4. Why this does not generalize to more usual democratic polities is discussed in Section V.

5. See Robert Nozick's discussion in his *Anarchy, State, and Utopia* (New York: Basic Books, 1974), 90–95.

6. We argue below that political rhetoric routinely overstates the magnitude of the electoral stakes.

7. The assumption of an odd-number electorate simplifies the analysis by allowing us to ignore the possibility of ties and rules for handling them. It does not modify the conclusion regarding the relative inconsequentiality of an individual vote.

8. See Brennan and Lomasky, *Democracy and Decision,* esp. ch. 4, "The Analytics of Decisiveness," 54–73.

9. Derek Parfit, *Reasons and Persons* (Oxford: Oxford University Press, 1984), 74–75 (emphasis in the original).

10. Brian Barry, "Comment," in *Political Participation,* ed. Stanley Benn (Canberra: Australian National University Press, 1978), 39 (emphases in the original).

11. But all else is quite certainly not equal; see below.

12. We omit here complications arising from the voter's *beliefs* concerning the merits of the candidates, the *intentions* that inform the act of voting, and the *motivation* for exercising the franchise rather than abstaining. Different consequentialists attach different moral implications to these, and their resolution is, in any event, peripheral to an alleged duty to vote.

13. Compare Anthony Downs in his classic *An Economic Theory of Democracy* (New York: Harper and Row, 1957), 269: "Since the consequences of universal failure to vote are both obvious and disastrous, and since the cost of voting is small, at least some men can rationally be motivated to vote even when their personal gains in the short run are outweighed by their personal costs."

14. Here the benefit secured by others' compliance extends primarily to the orchard owner but can be understood derivatively as a public good, the obtaining of a higher level of obedience to law, enjoyed equally by those who contribute to the production of that good and those who do not.

15. For a model of voting behavior that takes electoral activity to be primarily motivated by expressive concerns, see Brennan and Lomasky, *Democracy and Decision,* especially ch. 3, "The Nature of Expressive Returns," 32–53.

16. During recent decades, turnout for American presidential elections has tended to be near the 50 percent mark of the eligible population, turnout for off-year elections well under 50 percent. For example, in 1996 and 1992 (presidential election years), voters constituted 49.1 percent and 55.1 percent respectively, while the figures for 1994 and 1990 were 38.8 percent and 36.5 percent respectively. Note that approximately one-quarter of the eligible population is not registered to vote. Statistics on voter turnout are available on the Infoplease.com website (http://www.infoplease.com/ipa/A0763629.html).

17. Sometimes the case for a duty to vote is offered as a quasi-generalization argument based on the observation that, in real-world politics, abstention is not uniform across groups or classes. We might, for example, observe that the frequency of voting by poor black single mothers is less than that of well-to-do white male retirees. Then, on the assumption of reasonably systematic interest-based voting, the results that can be predicted to emerge if everyone votes can be compared with those that actually prevail; the difference becomes a measure of the *democratic deficit* which one might be thought to have a duty to overcome. But even if this constitutes a rationale for voting by the electorally underrepresented, it just as strongly argues for abstention by the overrepresented. (And since all of us are members of an indefinitely large number of classes—single mothers, left-handed philatelists, Albanian Buick-owning Rosicrucians—it will be hard to come up with an unambiguous criterion for determining whether one's proper home is among the under- or overrepresented.) Unsurprisingly, if a generalization argument is directed at specific groups, it cannot really function as a generalization argument.

18. Nor is it in any obvious way a corollary of Kantian ethics, but this is a matter that could bear further examination.

19. It is a piece of conspicuous consequentialist obtuseness to attempt to find the rationale for all such expressive activity in the effects that such messages of support will have on the stricken individual's medical prognosis or emotional state. Is it necessary to explain to anyone who is not deep in the caverns of utilitarianism that, for example, one does not automatically score high marks as a friend if, instead of displaying a long face before the bedridden individual, thereby adding misery to misery, one eschews the hospital visit in favor of an evening's carousing at the pub?

20. See Brennan and Lomasky, *Democracy and Decision,* 186–89.

21. See Geoffrey Brennan and Philip Pettit, "Unveiling the Vote," *British Journal of Political Science* 20 (1990): 311–33.

22. In the mid-1970s, when soaring inflation was ravaging the economy, President Gerald Ford commandeered

the nation's television screens to display to the American people WIN ("Whip Inflation Now") buttons that they were bidden to wear as a signal of their determination to overcome the blight. At the time, some critics lampooned the buttons as an ineffective instrument for combating ratcheting price levels. That was unfair. What rendered the WIN button ludicrous was not lack of causal efficacy but rather its bathetic expressive quality. It was of a piece with Ford's errant golf shots and occasional airport tarmac pratfalls.

Much contemporary passion directed toward collecting newspapers and bottles in recycling bins has about as much effect on the level of depletion of natural resources as WIN buttons did on the level of inflation. However, recycling activity has an inner complexity adequate to render it expressively articulate with regard to the ends thereby endorsed. Recycling's wisdom may be disputed, but the practice is not inherently laughable.

23. Compare the transition from eighteenth-century ideals of a citizen's militia to the variety of contemporary enthusiasms for a right to keep and bear arms.

24. Nonvoting no more undermines the foundations of the right to vote than does remaining a bachelor undermine a right to marry.

25. Consider a parallel case: A law requiring two witnesses for a will to be valid is not shown to be undesirable by a proof that there is no antecedent moral duty in the state of nature to have one's testament doubly witnessed.

26. Some of these reasons might explain why some people choose to bear modest tariffs by dialing a special number that constitutes a vote in a telephone poll that elects nobody and brings about no outcome.

JASON BRENNAN

Polluting the Polls: When Citizens Should Not Vote

2009

Just because one has the right to vote does not mean just any vote is right. Citizens should not vote badly. This duty to avoid voting badly is grounded in a general duty not to engage in collectively harmful activities when the personal cost of restraint is low. Good governance is a public good. Bad governance is a public bad. We should not be contributing to public bads when the benefit to ourselves is low. Many democratic theorists agree that we shouldn't vote badly, but that's because they think we should vote well. This demands too much of citizens.

I. INTRODUCTION

The typical citizen of a Western democracy has a political right to vote, founded on justice. By "political right," I mean a right that ought to be legally protected. Yet the right to vote does not imply the rightness of voting.[1] For instance, I have the political right of free association to participate in neo-Nazi rallies. A society that failed to allow me to do this would be to that extent unjust. No one should coerce

Jason Brennan, "Polluting the Polls: When Citizens Should Not Vote." *Australasian Journal of Philosophy* 87 (4): 535–549. 2009.

me to prevent me from participating. Still, my participation would be morally wrong. I also have the political right of free speech to write pamphlets advocating slavery, but it would be morally wrong for me to do so. This paper discusses some conditions under which voting might be morally wrong. I argue that one has a moral obligation not to vote badly, even though one has the political right to do so.

An outline of my argument is:

1. One has an obligation not to engage in collectively harmful activities when refraining from such activities does not impose significant personal costs.
2. Voting badly is to engage in a collectively harmful activity, while abstaining imposes low personal costs.
3. Therefore, one should not vote badly.

Below I will make the argument in a more complete manner and consider various objections.

My goal in this paper is to argue for the position that one ought not to vote badly. I will assume for the sake of argument that there is no general duty to vote well.[2] In a later section, I will explain why the reasons underlying the duty to refrain from voting badly are not also reasons to vote well, but I will not attempt to show that there are no independent reasons for a duty to vote well. (See, however, Lomasky and Brennan [2000].)

Irresponsible individual voters ought to abstain rather than vote badly. This thesis may seem antidemocratic. Yet it is really a claim about voter responsibility and how voters can fail to meet this responsibility. On my view, voters are not obligated to vote, but if they do vote, they owe it to others and themselves to be adequately rational, unbiased, just, and informed about their political beliefs. Similarly, most of us think we are not obligated to become parents, but if we are to be parents, we ought to be responsible, good parents. We are not obligated to become surgeons, but if we do become surgeons, we ought to be responsible, good surgeons. We are not obligated to drive, but if we do drive, we ought to be responsible drivers. The same goes for voting. My view contrasts with those that think 1) we have no obligations regarding voting, 2) we are obligated to vote, but any or nearly any vote is acceptable, 3) we must vote well, and 4) (the comparatively rare view that) we ought not to vote.

II. WHAT IS BAD VOTING?

As a first pass, we could characterize bad voting as occurring when citizens vote for harmful or unjust policies or for candidates likely to enact harmful or unjust policies.[3] However, this seems too strong of a characterization. One might vote for what is in fact a harmful policy but be justified in doing so. For instance, imagine that the past two hundred years of work by thousands of independent political scientists, each of whom exhibits all the characteristic epistemic virtues, points towards a particular policy's being good. The policy might still end up being harmful, though everyone was justified in thinking it would not be. We shouldn't characterize people who vote on the basis of strong evidence as having voted badly.[4]

So, as a second pass, let us say that bad voting occurs when a citizen votes *without sufficient reason* for harmful or unjust policies or for candidates that are likely to enact harmful or unjust policies. Note that this characterization of bad voting does not make it tautologous that one should not vote badly. Even if one accepts this characterization, one might hold that there is no duty to refrain from bad voting so defined.

Note that this characterization allows that one might sometimes be justified in voting for the lesser of two (or more) evils. Putting Mussolini in power is harmful, but not as harmful as putting Hitler in power. We can construct scenarios under which voting for the equivalent of Mussolini is the better alternative as compared to abstaining from voting or voting for the equivalent of Hitler. Note that this characterization also allows that one might be justified in voting for a policy or candidate whose probable degree of harmfulness is unknown, provided this helps prevent a known-to-be dangerous policy or candidate from winning. So, if I had to choose between Stalin and a random unknown person, I could be justified in voting for the unknown person as opposed to abstaining or voting for Stalin. This characterization also allows that a good voter can sometimes vote for otherwise unknown candidates because of party affiliation, provided the voter really has sufficient reason to believe that most members of that party do not promote bad policies.

The "without sufficient reason" clause is important because one might vote for a harmful policy but not be negligent in doing so. I have compared voters to surgeons: not everyone has to be a surgeon or a voter, but if a person is a surgeon or a voter, she should be a good one. Surgeons make mistakes. Some mistakes are excusable. We don't typically blame clinicians when they misdiagnose an unknown, extremely rare disease that has all the symptoms of a common disease. We don't hold it against a surgeon today that she isn't using better techniques that won't be invented until the next century. Since she has performed properly by a reasonable standard of care appropriate to the current level of knowledge, she is not culpable. On the other hand, some mistakes result from negligence, from falling below a reasonable standard of care.

In medicine and other professions, standards of care are usually defined as what a normal, prudent practitioner would do in similar circumstances. However, note that quality of care from a surgeon 1000 years ago was so low that one might reasonably claim that all surgeons at that time were culpable for doing surgery. Accordingly, this definition of a standard of care in medicine presupposes that average levels of competence are generally high. Thus, we shouldn't use this definition of standard of care for voting—it might be that normal, prudent voters have been voting badly.

Instead, voters can be said to have voted well, despite having voted for what turned out to be bad policies, provided they have a sufficient moral or epistemic justification for their votes. Otherwise, they vote badly when they vote without sufficient reason for harmful policies or candidates that are likely to enact harmful policies. However, I won't try to settle the standards for justified belief here. Instead, I leave that to be determined by the best epistemological theories. My argument then rests upon there being such a thing as unjustified political beliefs, but it need not be committed to any particular epistemology. On any reasonable epistemological view, there will be such a thing as unjustified beliefs about political matters.[5]

In some elections, it will be difficult even for highly educated experts to judge the expected consequences of electing one candidate over another. Judging candidates' comparative merits is often, but not always, difficult even for experts. Provided that the evidence shows that each candidate is likely to be on the whole good rather than harmful, then well-informed, adequately rational, just voters can be said to vote well regardless of which candidate they select. The claim that voters ought not to vote badly does not imply the stronger claim that they must vote only for the most optimal candidate.

The most common forms of bad voting are voting 1) from immoral beliefs, 2) from ignorance, or 3) from epistemic irrationality and bias. This is not to give a new formula for bad voting. Sometimes, as per the characterization of bad voting above, voting on the basis of 1–3 won't count as bad voting.

For an instance of 1: Suppose Alex believes that blacks are inferior and should be treated as second-class citizens. This is an immoral belief. If Alex votes for policies because he wishes to see blacks treated as inferiors, he votes badly.

As an instance of 2: Suppose Bob is *completely* ignorant about a series of propositions on a ballot. While he desires to promote the common good, he has no idea which policy would in fact promote the common good. In this case, if he votes either way, he votes badly.[6]

As an instance of 3: Candice might vote with the goal of increasing the nation's material prosperity. However, she might have formed her beliefs about what stimulates economic growth via an unreliable, biased process. She might find a candidate espousing a regressive neo-mercantilist (i.e., imperialist, protectionist) platform emotionally appealing, and vote for that candidate despite the evidence showing that the candidate's platform is inimical to the goal of creating prosperity. In this case, Candice has false means-ends beliefs on the basis of irrational belief formation processes.[7] If she votes on these beliefs, she votes badly.

III. THE DUTY TO REFRAIN FROM COLLECTIVE HARMS

I will argue that one has the duty not to vote badly because this violates a more general duty not to engage in collectively harmful activities. A collectively harmful activity is an activity that is harmful when many people engage in it, though it might not be harmful (or is negligibly harmful) when only a few individuals engage in it. My argument relies on the empirical premise that politicians generally attempt to give people what they ask for. I will not examine this point at length in this paper [Caplan 2007: 166–81; Less, Moretti, and Butler 2004].

The duty to refrain from voting badly is not generally grounded in the harmfulness of individual votes. In most elections, individual bad votes are unlikely to have significant expected disutility. Suppose electing candidate P over candidate Q will cost the economy 33 billion dollars next year, and this comparative loss will not be offset by any other value P provides. At the time of the election, P commands an anticipated proportional majority of 50.5% of the voters (i.e., there is a 50.5% chance a random voter will vote for P), and there is a turn out of 122,293,332 voters (the number of voters in the 2004 U.S. presidential election). In this case, if I also vote for P, the objectively worse candidate, my individual vote has an expected disutility of a mere $\$4.77 \times 10^{-2650}$, thousands of orders of magnitude below a penny.[8]

Bad voting is collectively, not individually, harmful. The harm is not caused by individual voters, but by voters together. (In this respect, voting is unlike surgery or driving.) When I refrain from voting badly, this does not fix the problem. Still, it is plausible that I am obligated to refrain from collectively harmful activities, even when my contribution has negligible expected cost, provided I do not incur significant personal costs from my restraint. I will argue that this is the reason I ought not to vote badly.

What does morality require of us in a collective action problem, especially in cases where we are acting in collectively harmful ways? Suppose the problem can be solved only if everyone or the vast majority of people acts differently. Morality does not require me, as an individual, to solve the problem. It can't require me to solve the problem, in part, because I can't solve it. If, e.g., I am in a prisoner's dilemma or a tragic commons, restraining myself from contributing to the problem fails to solve the problem. Rather, my restraint exposes me to exploitation as a sucker and can exacerbate the problem.

In some cases, I might be able to solve the problem through extraordinary personal effort. Suppose I live in a small village where everyone except me litters. If I spend ninety hours a week picking up litter, the town will be clean. Here I can solve the problem as an individual, but it is implausible to think morality requires me to do so. It's too much of a burden, and it's unfair that I have to clean up after everyone else.

It's more plausible that morality requires something weaker. When there is a collective action problem, I don't have to solve the problem, but I should not be part of the problem, provided I can avoid being part of the problem at a low personal cost. In classic prisoner's dilemmas, I can't avoid being part of the problem. My attempt to avoid causing the problem opens me up to exploitation. Also, in cases of tragic commons, I often cannot avoid being part of the problem without incurring a high personal cost. If the only way I can feed my children is to join in exploiting a common resource others are already turning to dust, arguably I am permitted to do so.

Bad voting is a collective action problem. But it is not generally like a prisoner's dilemma or a tragic commons. In the prisoner's dilemma or tragic commons, it's individually rational for me to engage in collectively harmful behaviour. *A fortiori,* it's often downright necessary for me to engage in the behaviour. If I don't contribute to the problem, I suffer a personal disaster. But bad voting is not like that. Refraining from bad voting has little personal cost. That's not to say it has no cost. Voting makes people feel good about themselves or makes them feel like they've done their duty as citizens, even if they have no such duty.

Why does morality require me not to be part of the problem, at least in cases where there is little personal cost in not being part of the problem? The principle that one should not engage in collectively harmful activities (when the cost of restraint is low) needn't be grounded in any particular moral theory. It is a freestanding idea that coheres with a variety of plausible background theories. For example, consider Brad Hooker's sophisticated "rule consequentialism." In its basic form, his rule consequentialism holds that an action is wrong if it violates the code of norms whose internalization by the overwhelming majority of people would lead to the best consequences [2000: 32]. A *pro tanto* norm against engaging in collectively harmful activity would almost certainly form part of this code [2000: 159–74]. Or a Kantian might argue that engaging in collectively harmful behaviour is not universalizable. Imagine a maxim of the form, "I shall feel free to engage in collectively harmful behaviour when there is little personal benefit doing so." If everyone followed this maxim, it would be harmful to almost everyone. The maxim would thus fail the "contradiction in the will" test, because no rational agent would will that everyone behave according to that maxim [Timmons 2002: 169–70]. Or a eudaimonist might claim the type of person who contributes to certain kinds of collective harms is vicious. And so on.

For illustrative purposes, I will discuss at greater length how a duty to avoid engaging in collective harms could be grounded in plausible views about fairness. Consider that the problem of bad voting is analogous in many respects to the problem of air pollution. Rita Manning asks:

> Why then does it sound odd to suggest that each driver is morally obligated to control air pollution? Presumably because air pollution is not caused by any one driver and cannot be ended by the single actions of any one driver. If I were the owner of the only car in America, I could drive to my heart's content and not cause any air pollution.
>
> [1984: 217]

(Manning recognizes that one will cause some pollution, but she means that this pollution will be negligible.) Of course, polluting and bad voting are not completely analogous. (The surgery and driving analogies are not perfect either.) If I am the only small-scale polluter, my pollution makes no significant difference. However, if I am the only voter, my vote makes all the difference. Still, when I am one of many bad voters or many polluters, my individual contribution is negligible, but I am nonetheless part of the problem. Yet, if I stop voting badly or polluting, the problem does not go away.

Individual drivers are part of the group causing the problem. Individual obligations derive from finding fair ways to solve the problem. Suppose pollution would be at acceptable levels if cut in half. One way to achieve this is could be to require half the population not to drive, while the other half may continue to drive at their current levels with their current highly polluting cars. One is assigned driver/non-driver status by lottery. This solution is unfair because it burdens some but not all who cause the problem. The default moral position is that everyone causing the problem should bear at least some of the burden of correcting it. More controversially, one might claim either that people should bear this burden equally, or in proportion to how much they contribute to the problem, at least in the absence of countervailing conditions.

Fairness is one way to bridge the gap between collectively harmful behaviour and individual action. *We* should pollute less because pollution harms us all, but *I* should pollute less because, all things equal, it is unfair for me to benefit from polluting as I please while others suffer the burden of polluting less. *Ceteris paribus,* we should share the burdens of not polluting. The duty not to vote badly could follow this pattern. *We* bad voters should not vote because it is harmful to everyone, but *I,* the individual bad voter, should not vote because it is unfair that I benefit from polluting democracy as I please while others suffer the burden of polluting democracy less. *Ceteris paribus,* we should share the burdens of not polluting the polls.

If restraining oneself from voting caused significant personal harm, then individuals might be permitted to vote badly. In fact, such restraint does have costs. Individual bad voters receive various psychological payoffs from voting—it makes them feel good about themselves for a short time. If they were prohibited (by morality) from voting, they lose this payoff. However, elections decided by bad voters mean that citizens have to live with racist and sexist laws, unnecessary wars, lower economic opportunities, lower levels of welfare, etc. The type of harm or loss of pleasure suffered by the bad voter from abstention seems relatively trivial compared to the type of harm suffered by the citizen who bears the burden of bad policy. The bad voter's pleasure in voting is not sufficient to counterbalance a potential duty to refrain from polluting the polls. By voting, bad voters consume psychological goods at our collective expense.

In parallel, an individual might drive a gas-guzzling Hummer to promote his self-image, getting real pleasure from this activity. I do not take his pleasure to be sufficient to counterbalance the harms imposed on all by smog and global warming. This is not to say that one must never drive, or even that one may not pollute in the pursuit of pleasure. We all have reason to favour principles that allow us to lead happy lives. Rather, it is to say that at some point, the pursuit of individual pleasure is outweighed by the need to preserve the healthy environment that makes pleasurable lives possible.

There are also collective costs from bad voters staying home. Widespread voting helps produce more social cohesion. It's at least empirically possible that when bad voters vote, this tends to make them care about voting more, and this may inspire them to reform and become better voters. I think these opportunity costs are likely to be outweighed by the benefits of reducing bad voting, but it's hard to say without something like an empirical study of the indirect positive effects of bad voting. Another complaint is that it's hard to take democracy seriously when most voters abstain from voting. I agree, but in response, it's also hard to take democracy seriously when a large percentage of bad voters vote. Regardless, democracy performs better, even with low voter participation, than its competitors (oligarchy, etc.) do. So, at worst, low voter participation means we are not able to take democracy as seriously as some people would like to, but this doesn't mean we must replace democracy with something else.

IV. DOING ONE'S PART IN MODERN DEMOCRACY

Citizens of modern democracies are not obligated to vote, but if they do vote, they are obligated not to vote badly. They should abstain rather than impose bad governance on everyone.

Since I describe good governance as a public good (like roads or police protection), one might object that instead of there being a duty not to vote badly (a duty that can be performed by abstaining), there is instead a duty for all to vote well. If good governance is valuable, shouldn't people do their part to help produce it, rather than simply refraining from producing bad governance? I agree that we have an obligation not to free ride on the provision of good governance, so doesn't that commit me to holding that everyone ought to vote well? While I don't intend to refute all possible arguments that there is a duty to vote well, I will explain here why the reasons I've articulated not to vote badly are not also sufficient reasons to vote well.

Consider how difficult it is to have justified beliefs, e.g., about good economic policy. As anyone who has taught basic economics knows, overcoming basic economic fallacies takes significant effort. Most people find it painful to contemplate how their (emotionally-charged ideological) beliefs could be false. Our biases make economics counterintuitive. Thus, understanding basic economics is difficult. Consider what else is needed to form good policy preferences. One might need some political philosophy to assist one in developing a well-grounded conception of justice. Even if we agree that government ought to provide for the equal welfare of citizens, it is an empirical, social scientific question what type of institutional response best achieves that goal. What strategies actually can be expected to succeed is an empirical question and cannot be determined by looking at the intentions or values of people advocating different policies. One will need some knowledge of statistics, political science, sociology, international relations, and the other social sciences to grasp the expected effectiveness of various policies. While political science, economics, and philosophy are all worthwhile endeavours, studying them to develop even a basic level of comprehension requires serious investment.

This investment has major opportunity costs. Time is scarce. Time spent overcoming economic bias is not spent learning the violin, becoming a medical doctor, playing football, or watching grass grow. There are myriad worthwhile life goals, which, owing to time scarcity, are incompatible with becoming a level-headed amateur social scientist.

One might say that people should vote well so that they can contribute to social welfare. However, besides voting, debating, rallying, supporting causes, writing to senators, writing letters to editors, and so on, there are countless other ways of contributing to society and the common good. One contributes one's share of the social surplus just by working at a productive job that provides goods and services others want. One makes the world a better place to live in by participating in culture and counterculture. One makes the world safer by fighting in just wars.

Though good governance is a public good, it doesn't follow that every member of society that benefits from that good must directly contribute to it. Instead, even if people have debts to pay to society for the goods they receive, there are many ways of paying those debts. Some people will pay by providing good governance, others by providing good culture, and others by providing good economic opportunity. One reason to favour this model of paying debts—where the debts can be paid with multiple currencies—is that it's more compatible with the pluralism liberals want to protect.

To live in a well-functioning liberal democracy is a great gift and something citizens should be thankful for. Yet one reason liberal democracy is such a great gift is that it does not require us to be political animals. It makes space for many ways of life, including avowedly non-political lives. In parallel, we might say that a good feature of well-functioning markets is that they make people rich enough to afford to engage in non-market activities and even in some cases to avoid the market altogether. A good liberal democracy would make people safe enough in their status as free and equal citizens that they could freely choose to avoid politics.

Liberal democracy is an important public good. We should all do our part to maintain it. One way a person can do his part is by bowing out. A bad vote cancels a good vote. If a good vote is a gift to society, avoiding a bad vote is also a kind of gift. In fact, using Lomasky and Brennan's formulae, we can construct scenarios under which avoiding a bad vote has the same expected value as a making a good vote.[9]

If the survival of a well-functioning democracy depended on more people voting well, this might impose a duty to do so. For example, though John Rawls rejected civic humanism (which claims that active political participation is part of a fully human life), he claimed that justice as fairness is compatible with classical republicanism. Classic republicanism holds that we ought to participate in politics, not because it is constitutive of the good life, but because it is a necessary instrument to maintaining a constitutional regime [2001: 144]. However, Rawls stressed, and I agree, that the extent and type of participation needed from citizens on classical republican grounds is largely an empirical question. It seems that reasonably just constitutional democracies survive despite less than full participation and despite serious shortcomings in citizens' civic virtue. Given the extent of bad voting and its effects on policy, some of these democracies might function better with even *less* participation than is now seen. What contemporary democracies need most to preserve equality and liberty is not full, informed participation, but an electorate that retains a constitutional culture and remains vigilant enough that it will rise against any leader that tries to abuse their liberties.

V. DOES ABSTENTION IMPLY EPISTOCRACY?

My position is elitist. Some forms of elitism are bad. Yet claiming that only competent people should undertake certain activities is not obviously a bad sort of elitism. It's elitist to claim that a person with an unsteady grasp of comparative advantage should not vote on trade policy and immigration reform, but it's also elitist to claim that a person with an unsteady hand should not perform surgery.

David Estlund defines "the epistocracy of the educated thesis" (a view he rejects) as the view that when "some are well educated and others are not, the polity would (other things equal) be better ruled by the giving the well educated more votes" [2007: 212]. This seems to be a bad form of elitism. I hold that all adult citizens have an equal political right to vote, one vote per person. (I will not defend this position here.) My view is that some citizens should not exercise their right. "I have the political right to X" does not imply "It is morally right for me to X." However, since I claim that some people should not vote, perhaps Estlund's arguments against epistocracy would count against my position.

Estlund says to the potential epistocrat, "You might be correct, but who made you boss?" [2007: 40]. Good voters have no more right to rule than bad voters. Estlund argues that universal suffrage is a default because any other system invites "invidious comparisons." Making political wisdom a condition of the right to vote would not be generally acceptable to the people under the government's authority [2007: 36]. I agree. My position is not that the good voters should rule by right, or that the bad voters are by right forbidden from ruling. Rather, bad voters should exercise their equal right to rule in the way that is most advantageous to themselves and others: by abstaining from politics. I advocate morally compulsory but politically voluntary abstention by potential bad voters. That is, people should not vote badly, but no one should force them not to vote badly.

Estlund's main worry is about people having unequal voting power. I hold that people should *have* equal voting power, but many should not *exercise* the power they have. Still, one might object that not exercising power is equivalent to not having power. Thomas Christiano worries that when citizens allow others to make decisions, this results in a society in which the few rule and the many obey [1996: 6].

This needn't be so. In committees, clubs, and at the polls, I have been asked to vote on issues I did not understand, have much knowledge about, or about which I was biased. My concern was to do the right thing and help make sure the best policy goes through. If I do not know what I am talking about, or if I know that I am prone to error and bad judgment about a given issue, one way of respecting my fellow citizens/committee members/etc. is to abstain. The times I have abstained were not losses of power. While I permitted other people to make the decisions, they did not rule me. After all, *I* permitted them to make the decision.

Abstention is not like relinquishing one's right to rule. *A fortiori,* abstention can be a way of voting indirectly. Suppose we are deciding on a restaurant. I am not indifferent to the outcome; I prefer that we eat at the best place. However, I know that you know more than I about which restaurants are good. Despite your greater knowledge, a concern for fair procedure entails that we should each get an equal vote. You do not have the right to tell me where to eat. You know better, but no one made you boss. Yet, since I want to pick the best restaurant, I can choose to abstain. I could vote directly for a specific restaurant. But, since I don't know which is best, I could also say, "I vote for the best restaurant, but I do not know which one that is. Since the rest of you know better, I vote that my vote reflects your collective wisdom." I then abstain, but in effect vote indirectly.

Some might see abstention as a violation of autonomy, perhaps even slave-like, but this seems mistaken. So long as I have an equal right to vote, choosing not to vote can be an autonomous act, a way of expressing my will that the best outcome be achieved. Since I retain a right to vote, I am an equal citizen and the democratic decision-making procedure remains generally acceptable.

VI. VOTING FOR CHARACTER, NOT POLICIES

One objection to my position is that voters tend to vote for character, not for policies. They might be quite good at judging the character of candidates, even if they are bad at judging the efficacy of different proposed policies for achieving different ends. If so, the objection goes, then most voters do not act wrongly when they vote.

First, this paper does not take a position regarding how well or badly actual voters vote. Taking such a position would require significant surveying of voting behaviour and why voters choose the policies they do.[10] My goal is to establish a normative conclusion—one should not vote badly—not to show how frequently people violate this norm. Even if we fortuitously lived in a world where everyone voted well, it would still be true that people should not vote badly. Even if it turned out that people were good judges of character, voted as such, and that voting for virtuous candidates meant good policies would be enacted, it would still be true that people should not vote badly. Thankfully, this would just mean that citizens act well.

However, character-based voting might actually be the most common form of bad voting, because (to a significant degree) voting for character is voting for the wrong reasons. Politicians tend to take votes as mandates even when they shouldn't. They tend to try to enact the policies they favour. Except at the extremes, character is not a reliable guide to political leadership. A virtuous politician with a powerful sense of justice might still be deeply misguided and committed to all sorts of counterproductive, harmful policies. Having the right values is not sufficient for making good policy, because it requires social scientific knowledge to know whether any given set of policies is likely to achieve those values. Just as an incompetent surgeon can be still be a virtuous person, so an incompetent politician can be a virtuous person. If there is good evidence that a politician is likely to enact harmful policies, one should not vote for her (without sufficient reason) even if she is a good person. Voting on the moral virtue of a candidate counts as good voting only when the candidate's moral virtue is evidence that she will not enact harmful policies.

The objection might be recast in terms of political skill rather than moral virtue. Politicians extol their years of experience and ability to work across party lines in generating outcomes. Still, even if voters are good judges of such political skills and vote accordingly, it's possible that such skill means bad policies will be enacted. Senator P might be excellent at getting bills passed, but perhaps all of the bills have been harmful. Just as voting on moral character is not obviously a reliable way of generating good policy outcomes, neither is voting on this kind of political skill.

Perhaps, though, voters are good at judging which candidates are likely to produce good policy, even if the voters don't themselves know what the good policies are. One might think that just as the average person can pick a good surgeon or plumber without much knowledge of medicine or plumbing, so she can pick a good candidate without knowing economics. To some extent this is true—voters rarely vote in completely disastrous candidates. However, there are more resources for a non-expert to judge surgeons or plumbers than political candidates. When a surgeon or plumber makes a mistake, the mistake is often obvious to the clients. Not so with politicians. It's hard to determine what harms they've caused. Bad surgeons are easily sued; bad politicians are not. Medical and plumbing standards are more uniform. That a surgeon went to Harvard Medical School is a count in his favour. It's less obvious that a candidate's having gone to Yale as an undergraduate shows he will enact good policy.

VII. SELF-EFFACINGNESS

I think people who would vote badly should not vote. However, the people I describe as bad voters are not likely to recognize that they are among those obligated not to vote. To confirm this in at least one instance, as an unscientific experiment, I discussed my thesis with a person who I believe exemplifies bad voting. He agreed that *other* people should not vote. Even worse, if good voters were to hear that bad voters shouldn't vote, they might stop voting out of fear of doing wrong.

Thus, my position in this paper might be self-effacing. However, even if this were so, my thesis is simply that people should not vote badly. It is not that advertising this thesis to the general public would make the world better. Whether telling the truth about morality makes the world a better place depends on many contingencies. It's possible that people are corrupt enough that hearing the truth inspires bad behaviour.

A self-effacing position need not be false. For instance, suppose certain critics of utilitarianism are correct when they claim that if people accepted utilitarianism, this would make the world worse by utilitarian standards, simply because most people are not good at employing such standards. If so, this does not show that utilitarian standards are false. Rather, it just shows that we should not advertise them. As David Brink notes, there is a difference between a *criterion of right* and a *method for making decisions* [1986]. The former is about what makes actions right or wrong, but the latter is about figuring out how to do what's right or wrong. A good method for Alex might be different from what's good for Bob because they have different cognitive abilities. Alex is good at making calculations while Bob isn't. But the standard of right action is the same for both. The point of the decision-making method is to help them get to the right action.[11]

More simply: this paper is a piece of moral philosophy, not a manual for civic education. The point of the paper is to identify that there is a problem, but it would take much more work to determine how to solve the problem. I argue that people should not vote badly, but I do not explain how to prevent them from voting badly.

Despite this, one might still argue that self-effacingness harms my position because ought implies can. People have a duty only if they can follow the duty. One might pose the following dilemma. Either people can't recognize they're bad voters, in which case they can't obey the principle and thus are not subject to it. Or, if they do recognize they are bad voters, this will turn them into good voters, and so they are no longer subject to the duty.

This appears to be a false dilemma. In moments of clarity we sometimes recognize that we have bad character or tend to act badly in certain ways. But realizing our errors doesn't fix them—we easily slip back into old behaviour. For instance, one might notice that one has been repeatedly dating people with the same flaws, but this rarely fixes the problem.

Still, the view that bad voters shouldn't vote does have a practical upshot. We sometimes can minimize the effects of some vices even when we cannot rid ourselves of them. For example, overeaters sometimes realize that in future moments of temptation, they will rationalize eating any junk food in easy reach. Thus, some overeaters do not keep junk food in their homes and take alternative routes to work to avoid passing fast food restaurants. If a person could recognize that she tends to be a bad voter, she might take action to improve her voting behaviour, or at least choose to abstain, just as I have in cases where I was not in a position to vote well.

VIII. CONCLUSION

I see myself as a defender of democracy. I wish to keep the voting process free of pollution, and what defender of democracy wishes to see her favoured system polluted? Many democrats are concerned both with democratic procedures and democratic outcomes [Christiano 2004; Brettschneider 2007]. Not just any outcome produced by democratic procedure is acceptable, nor is every outcome aligning with democratic values acceptable regardless of what procedure produced it. Universal voting by bad voters might make procedures more democratic than massive abstention by people who would vote badly. Yet, this does not mean the outcome of this procedure will align better with democratic values, and thus does not mean that opposing universal voting is inherently undemocratic.

When people call for universal or extended participation, we have to ask what would be the point of the institution of universal participation. If we are passionate lovers of democracy, we might celebrate what universal participation would symbolize. Yet, in the real world, we have to ask how institutions would function. Institutions are not people. They are not ends in themselves. They are not paintings, either, to be judged by their beauty, by what they symbolize, or who made them. Institutions are more like hammers—they are judged by how well they work.

Good institutions get us good results; bad institutions get us bad results.

REFERENCES

Brennan, Geoffrey and Loren Lomasky 1993. *Democracy and Decision,* Cambridge: Cambridge University Press.

Brennan, Jason 2008. Beyond the Bottom Line: The Theoretical Goals of Moral Theorizing, *Oxford Journal of Legal Studies* 28/2: 277–96.

Brettschneider, Corey 2007. *Democratic Rights,* Princeton: Princeton University Press.

Brink, David O. 1986. Utilitarian Morality and the Personal Point of View, *The Journal of Philosophy* 83/8: 417–38.

Caplan, Bryan 2007. *The Myth of the Rational Voter,* Princeton: Princeton University Press.

Christiano, Thomas 1996. *The Rule of the Many,* Boulder: Westview Press.

Christiano, Thomas 2004. The Authority of Democracy, *The Journal of Political Philosophy* 12/3: 266–90.

Estlund, David 1997. Beyond Fairness and Deliberation: The Epistemic Dimension of Democratic Authority, in *Deliberative Democracy: Essays on Reason and Policies,* ed. James Bowman and William Rehg, Cambridge, MA: MIT Press: 173–204.

Estlund, David 2007. *Democratic Authority,* Princeton: Princeton University Press.

Fischer, A. J. 1999. The Probability of Being Decisive, *Public Choice* 101/3–4: 263–7.

Funk, Carolyn 2000. The Dual Influence of Self-Interest and Societal Interest in Public Opinion, *Political Research Quarterly* 53/1: 37–62.

Funk, Carolyn and Patricia Garcia-Monet 1997. The Relationship Between Personal and National Concerns in Public Perceptions of the Economy, *Political Research Quarterly* 50/2: 317–42.

Gaus, Gerald F. 2003. *Contemporary Theories of Liberalism,* London: Sage Publications.

Hooker, Brad 2000. *Ideal Code, Real World,* Oxford: Oxford University Press.

Less, David, Enrico Moretti, and Matthew Butler 2004. Do Voters Affect or Elect Policies? Evidence from the U.S. House, *Quarterly Journal of Economics* 119/3: 807–59.

Lomasky, Loren and Geoffrey Brennan 2000. Is There a Duty to Vote?, *Social Philosophy and Policy* 17/1: 62–86.

Manning, Rita C. 1984. Air Pollution: Group and Individual Obligations, *Environmental Ethics* 6/3: 211–25.

Melden, A. I. 1959. *Rights and Right Conduct,* Oxford: Oxford University Press.

Miller, Dale 1999. The Norm of Self-Interest, *American Psychologist* 54/12: 1053–60.

Mutz, Diana and Jeffrey Mondak 1997. Dimensions of Sociotropic Behavior: Group-Based Judgments of Fairness and Well-Being, *American Journal of Political Science* 41/1: 284–308.

Rawls, John 2001. *Justice as Fairness: A Restatement,* Cambridge, MA: Harvard University Press.

Timmons, Mark 2002. *Moral Theory,* Lanham, MD: Rowman and Littlefield.

Waldron, Jeremy 1981. A Right to Do Wrong, *Ethics* 92/1: 21–39.

Westen, Drew, Pavel S. Blagov, Keith Harenski, Clint Kilts, and Stephan Hamann 2006. The Neural Basis of Motivated Reasoning: An fMRI Study of Emotional Constraints on Political Judgment During the U.S. Presidential Election of 2004, *The Journal of Cognitive Neuroscience* 18/11: 1947–58.

NOTES

1. In general, the political right to X does not imply that X-ing is right. See Waldron [1981] and Melden [1959].

2. Some countries, such as Australia and Belgium, have compulsory voting. (In Australia and many others with such laws, citizens are required to show up at the polls, but nothing stops them from leaving the ballot blank or scribbling on the ballot. So, it is more accurate to say Australia has compulsory ballot casting rather than compulsory voting.) Compulsory voting introduces a number of complications I will not examine at length here, though this paper bears on the justice of compulsory voting laws. (If, empirically, compulsory voting laws lead to widespread bad voting, this is a reason to dispense with such laws.) Some questions: Do compulsory voting laws tend to induce better voting from citizens? Are compulsory voting laws unjust, for example, on grounds that they violate liberty? Even if such laws are unjust, might citizens have an obligation to obey them once they have been enacted? If citizens should obey such laws (and are literally required to vote, rather than to cast a possibly blank or spoiled ballot), is this obligation stronger than the obligation not to vote badly that I describe in this paper? Even if the obligation not to vote badly is stronger than any obligation to obey compulsory voting laws, might citizens be excused from the obligation not to vote badly if they are punished when they abstain?

3. I won't settle on a particular account of harmfulness or injustice here. In particular, I won't settle whether

voters should consider the interests merely of fellow citizens (as per extreme nationalism), of everyone worldwide equally (as per extreme cosmopolitanism), or some view in between. The argument of this paper is compatible with whatever position on that debate turns out to be correct. Also, this paper does not take a position on the descriptive question of what voters are trying to do with their votes. Voters vote for a variety of reasons. Some vote for character, some vote to express their values, some vote to enact good policies for all, and some vote to enact good policies for themselves. While I argue here that citizens should not vote for candidates who are likely to enact bad policies, this does not mean that I believe most voters actually vote out of consideration for candidates' policies. I argue voters should be concerned with policy, but this is compatible with the claim that few are.

4. Alternatively, one might want to say that one votes badly but is not blameworthy for voting badly. If one prefers this way of talking, then one can modify my thesis to be that citizens have a duty not to vote badly when they are blameworthy for voting badly.

5. Certain defenders of epistemic democracy use Condorcet's Jury Theorem to argue that democracies will tend to make good policy choices. Such defenders might claim that one is justified in voting provided one is more likely than not to be right. For two critiques of this misuse of Condorcet, see Gaus [2003: 158–65] and Estlund [1997: 185–6].

6. Thanks to the so-called "miracle of aggregation," ignorant voting may tend to be the least dangerous kind of bad voting. If ignorant voters' positions are essentially random, then it is preferable to have an *infinite* number of ignorant voters to just a few, as their random votes will tend to cancel the others out, leaving only the informed voters votes to carry the day. I find this lacking as a defence of ignorant voting. First, and most importantly, it is unclear that even purely ignorant voters will vote randomly. For instance, there have been many studies confirming *position bias*—where early answers in multiple-choice tests tend to be favoured over later answers. Ballots approximate such multiple-choice tests, and we can expect position bias to influence ignorant voters votes away from random. Random orderings in ballots may overcome this, but then, there are other similar behaviours that could prevent ignorant voters from voting in random and therefore harmless ways. The miracle of aggregation excuses ignorant voting only if ignorant voters vote randomly. Second, with any finite number of votes from ignorant voters, there is some probability that the votes will deviate from a random distribution and upset or outweigh the contribution from informed voters. So, while at best an ignorant voter adds noise that might be cancelled by a different ignorant voter, at worst, the ignorant voter corrupts the outcome. This gives her some reason to stay home. Third, there might be systematic dangers from people seeing that so many ignorant voters are voting. This could tend to dissuade them from making the effort to vote well. Note that Lucio Gutiérrez did a terrible job as president of Ecuador. He may have come to power because of compulsory voting. Many Ecuadorians were illiterate and uneducated, and there is evidence that they voted for Gutiérrez simply because his name was most familiar. So, one last problem with ignorant voting is that ignorant citizens are often not ignorant enough to vote randomly—they choose familiar names, and familiar names are not necessarily good ones. (However, even if all of these criticisms are overcome, this says nothing about voting from irrational or immoral beliefs.)

7. Bryan Caplan [2007] claims that citizens quite frequently have epistemically irrational beliefs about economic policy, i.e., their beliefs about economics result from biases. Caplan also claims that voters tend to be less biased than non-voters [2007: 198]. Some independent work on political bias and irrationality in political belief formation can be found in Westen et al. [2006].

8. This calculation uses the formula for the expected utility of votes given in Brennan and Lomasky [1993: 56–7, 119] and Lomasky and Brennan [2000: 86]. For a criticism of this and related formulae, see Fischer [1999].

9. Here is a cartoon case. Suppose there is an election between two candidates. One candidate is a disaster but appeals to irrational people. The other is excellent and appeals to rational people. Each candidate votes for herself. There are two other voters, one well-informed rational person and one ignorant and irrational person. In this case, if the irrational voter abstains, there is a 100% chance of the good candidate winning. If she becomes rational and votes, there is a 100% chance of the good candidate winning. The expected utilities of abstaining and of voting well are thus equal.

10. Political scientists generally agree that voters tend to vote in what they *perceive* to be the national interest, though of course this does not mean they vote well (since their perceptions could be unjustified). See Funk and Garcia-Monet [1997], Funk [2000], Miller [1999], Mutz and Mondak [1997]. Caplan lists twelve other references for this position [2007: 229].

11. Brennan [2008] argues that moral theory's primary task is not to produce a method of making decisions but to identify criteria of right as well as answer other theoretical questions about morality.

GEOFFREY BRENNAN AND GEOFFREY SAYRE-MCCORD

Voting and Causal Responsibility

2015

I. INTRODUCTION

In the standard Rational Choice Theory account of voting behavior (RCV henceforth), the idea of a vote being "pivotal" plays a central role. Votes are pivotal when an electoral option wins by one vote. In "pivotal" cases, the voters who vote for the winning option (J) are both jointly sufficient and individually necessary for J's victory. Each voter composing that set can, on this basis, be described as having "brought about" the victory of J. Each is causally efficacious in the sense that if she had voted for a different candidate (and everything else had remained the same), J would not have won. In all cases where the outcome is non-pivotal, any individual voter, had she voted differently, would not have altered the electoral outcome. Her vote would have been consequentially irrelevant (in this sense) in all but the non-pivotal case.[1]

For this reason, the *ex ante* probability of being pivotal is taken by RCV to be a crucial parameter in each individual voter's deliberations. It is this *ex ante* probability (denoted h henceforth) that influences:

how much information about alternative candidates it will be rational for the voter to acquire;
the extent to which decisions about which candidate to vote for will be influenced by the voter's individual self-interest;
and whether it will be rational to vote at all, given the stakes involved in the election for the individual as she perceives them, and the expected closeness of the race and the alternative actions to voting available.[2]

In most large elections, clearly, h (even capaciously defined in the sense of footnote 1) will be miniscule. Given this fact[3], rationality considerations (as RCV understands them) can explain:

1. why individual voters do not expend much effort in acquiring relevant information about candidates and their policies. After all, their votes are very unlikely to make a difference to the outcome. (This is the basis of Downs' [1957] claims about electoral "rational ignorance." For a more recent treatment see Caplan [2007].)
2. why considerations of individual interest as opposed to public interest are likely to play a smaller role in decisions about how to vote than in those same agents' market decisions. After all, since the chance that one's voting decision will have an impact on the outcome is far lower than in market contexts, where one's choice is usually decisive, the chance that it will have an impact on one's individual interest is correspondingly small. (This is the central upshot of the "expressive" account of voting behavior—as analyzed for example by Brennan and Lomasky [1993].)
3. why certain factors, and not others, are likely to influence aggregate levels of voter turnout.[4] After all, if the chance that one's vote will make a difference to the outcome is exceedingly small, the incentive provided by the thought that one's vote will make a difference will be small as well.

An implication of RCV is that any voter who votes in standard large-number democratic settings,

Geoff Sayre-McCord and Geoffrey Brennan, "Voting and Causal Responsibility" *Oxford Studies in Political Philosophy*, edited by David Sobel, Peter Vallentyne, and Steven Wall (Oxford University Press, in press).

thinking that her vote is likely to be causally efficacious in determining the electoral outcome, is making a mistake. Causal efficacy is possible: but its probability is so low that a rational voter will not include that prospect as being a major, let alone a predominant, "reason for voting."[5]

In one sense, such conclusions could be seen as showing the power of RCV logic. Means-ends thinking can indicate settings in which certain things are unlikely to work as a means to an end because the connection between the end (in this case the electoral *outcome*) and the means (the individual's vote) is too tenuous. Where there is reason to think one's vote won't serve as an effective means to securing a particular electoral outcome, the quest would then be for ends that *could* be appropriately cast as "rational reasons" for voting. And, predictably, people have suggested ends other than the electoral outcome that might provide people with reasons to vote (e.g. a concern to do their duty, or to avoid substantial regret, or to serve as an example to others). In each case, of course, the question will arise as to whether voting is actually an effective means to the suggested end, but assuming it is, one will have found reasons to vote that do not depend on thinking that voting is an effective means to bringing about one's preferred outcome.

The RCV's position, which is now standard in both economics and political science, hinges on h (the ex ante probability that one's vote will be pivotal) being the appropriate parameter for assessing an individual's causal efficacy when it comes to voting.

Alvin Goldman (1999), and more recently, with some variation[6], Richard Tuck (2008), have challenged this idea. They grant that it matters whether one's vote might be the cause of victory. Yet they maintain that the account of causal efficacy accepted by RCV is wrong. On the RCV view, one's vote counts as causing the outcome if, but only if, one's vote is pivotal—only if, one were to vote differently, the outcome would be different. Against this, Goldman and Tuck argue that what matters in thinking about whether one's vote might be the cause of victory is not whether it is necessary for the outcome, but whether it is a part of what is, in the appropriate way, sufficient for it.[7] To take an example from Tuck, a police officer will have killed a robber—will be the cause of the robber's death—even if some other officer would have shot the robber had the first missed. So the first's accurate shooting was not necessary in order for the robber to die. And a lifeguard saves your live—is the cause of you not drowning—even if, had she not saved you, another lifeguard standing by would have: so the first lifeguard's action was the cause of your being saved even though her saving you was not necessary for you to survive. Similarly, on their view, one's vote can be a cause of an electoral outcome even in cases where there are more than enough votes for victory, so even when one's voting is not necessary for the outcome (although Goldman and Tuck differ concerning just when one's vote is properly seen as a cause in such cases). As a result, they argue, h is not the probability that deserves attention in thinking about whether one's vote will be causally efficacious; rather, what is important is the *ex ante* probability that one's vote will be among those that are, in the appropriate way, sufficient for electoral victory. (In what follows we refer to this at the "Goldman/Tuck account.")

So while RCV and Goldman/Tuck agree that in thinking about whether to vote a central question is whether in voting one will bring about, or cause, the desired outcome, they differ concerning their understanding of what it takes to be a cause. On the RCV view, the relevant test is counterfactual: would the outcome have been the same even if you had voted differently. If yes, then your vote is not pivotal, and so not (on this view) causally efficacious. On the Goldman/Tuck account, even if your vote is not pivotal, it will be causally efficacious if it is among the votes that are, in the appropriate way, sufficient for the outcome.

There are some important differences between Goldman and Tuck concerning just which sufficient set of votes matters in the context of voting.

In particular, on Tuck's view, it is whichever minimally sufficient set actually settled the election. The idea shows up nicely, as Tuck emphasizes, in a roll call vote, where at a certain point victory is secured by someone's vote, together with those before, even if those following in the roll call would have voted in the same way.[8] The same idea shows up, although with complications due to the electoral college, in thinking about the causal efficacy of votes cast on the West Coast or in Hawaii in US Presidential elections. Often the outcome is settled, by the votes cast earlier, farther East, in a way that makes the later votes immaterial to the actual outcome.[9] For other votes as well, Tuck maintains, there is some subset of the votes cast for the victor—a minimally sufficient set—that will have been causally efficacious, because actually sufficient for the outcome.[10] On Tuck's reckoning the *ex ante* probability that one's vote for a victorious candidate will be causally efficacious—the probability that it will be in the minimally sufficient set—is normally much higher than *h*, even in large landslide elections. For instance, in an election with a million voters, where the victor is expected to win with 60% of the vote, the probability that one will be in the minimally sufficient set, *g*, is .66 (whereas *h* is vanishingly small). And this is true even though, as is often the case, we cannot know which subset of the votes actually proved to be the sufficient set.

Suppose in a two candidate race, J emerges as victor, receiving N votes out of the total voting population of M. Now, since (M − N) voters voted for the alternative (K), the minimal set of voters J required for victory was in fact (M − N + 1). We do not know which particular voters compose that minimal set. But Tuck supposes, for this example, that the votes were counted in a particular order and there is indeed a determinate set of voters who compose that minimal set. So there is a fact of the matter about which voters these were. A, who voted for J, can reasonably ask what the probability is that she (A) herself was a member of that minimally sufficient set. And that probability is just the number of voters required for the minimal majority divided by the actual number of J-voters—or (M − N + 1)/N. Denote this probability, *g*. Tuck sees *g* as the appropriate measure of the probability that a voter is in the relevant minimally sufficient set, and thus a cause of the victory.

To take a simple arithmetic example, J gets 6000 votes out of a total of 9999 voters. So 3999 individuals voted for K. For J to win, J would have needed 4000 votes: this is the minimal set of voters required to bring about J's victory. So each of the 6000 actual J voters has a 2/3rds chance of being in that set –and should on this basis be seen as having a 2/3rds chance of being causally responsible for J's victory.

Goldman, in contrast, holds that in normal elections a vote is a "partial" or a "contributory" cause as long as it is a member of *any* minimally sufficient set, privileging no particular set as the one that, in the event, was sufficient. This means that *every* vote cast for a victor, even in a landslide, counts as causally efficacious, not just those that are in some privileged minimally sufficient set.[11] As a result, the *ex ante* probability that one's vote for a victorious candidate will be causally efficacious, as Goldman thinks of things, is 1. (Of course, when one does not know for certain which candidate will win, the *ex ante* probability that one's vote will be causally efficacious in bringing about victory will be less than 1, reflecting the probability, whatever it is, that another candidate will win, but in any case, still much higher than *h*). Importantly, in developing his view, Goldman focuses on cases of what might be called simultaneous over-determination, where the sets of sufficient conditions are all in place at the same time. In these cases it is hard, to say the least, to make sense of the idea (important to Tuck) that one of the minimally sufficient conditions takes precedence over all of the others. Yet Goldman recognizes the challenge posed by cases of non-simultaneous over-determination (e.g. the roll call vote and our national elections), where the order of the votes, or the order in which they are counted, suggest that, as a matter of fact, one sufficient condition pre-empts all the others. In response, Goldman argues that in many elections we have a conventional system in place that "abstracts from this actual or "natural" order and considers all the votes on an equal basis" turning an apparent case of pre-emption into one of simultaneous over-determination.[12]

We are unsure as to whether the difference just noted is simply due to Tuck's focusing on cases of non-simultaneous over-determination, where one sufficient set of voters is reasonably seen as pre-empting the others, and Goldman focusing on cases of simultaneous over-determination, where there seems to be no grounds for privileging one set of sufficient conditions over others. It may be that each would accept the views of the other for the relevant cases. What is important for us here is that Goldman and Tuck both reject RCV, along with its emphasis on *h*, and recommend thinking of causation in terms of the sufficient, rather than necessary, conditions for an outcome. For the most part, differences between Goldman and Tuck (to the extent there are differences) won't matter to what follows, though where it does we will default to Tuck, using *g* (interpreted as his view, rather than Goldman's, would recommend). This is for two reasons. The first is that we think that in many cases (in elections and otherwise) the kind of convention Goldman relies on in forestalling worries about pre-emption is not in place. And we take it that when it is not we should be thinking in terms of preemption (as per Tuck) rather than simultaneous over-determination. The second is that the interpretation Tuck's account gives to *g* makes that probability more directly comparable to RCV's *h* than is the interpretation provided by Goldman's account (which would set the probability at 1 in cases where one is certain which candidate will win).

The contrast between *g* and *h* is striking. For a start, *g* is very much larger in all democratically relevant cases. As noted in footnote 3, the probability of an exact tie (*h*) between candidates in a US presidential election too close to call is estimated at around 1/12500. But for just such an election, *g* will be quite close to 1. Even if the margin turned out to be 4 million voters out of 120 million (perhaps not so very close after all) then *g* is 58/62 or roughly .94. On Tuck's view, this probability measures the probability that one will be a cause of J's victory.

Note too that *g* and *h* vary in different ways. As electorate size increases, the probability of an exact tie declines roughly with the square root of size: so when M doubles, *h* declines by about 40%. By contrast, *g* is a matter of relevant *proportion,* increasing as the size of the minimally sufficient set increases.

It is worth emphasizing that *g* can be thought of as an *ex post* probability—to be calculated after the election is settled—whereas *h* cannot be. After the election, you will know whether you were pivotal or not. But the decision as to whether to vote or not depends on the probability that one will be a cause of the outcome in question; and so *g* should properly be thought of here in *ex ante,* expected terms. The *ex ante* expected value of *g* will be based on the *expected* size of the majority. The voter properly expects *h* to be tiny; but *g* is likely to be substantial.

In developing their accounts of how it is our votes might be causes of an electoral victory without be required for it, Goldman and Tuck are especially interested in why voters "should vote." They want to identify reasons people have to vote even in cases in which one candidate will predictably beat others, with or without their vote. Goldman explicitly recognizes that the reasons in play might be either prudential or moral; and though his own account focuses on the moral aspect, he thinks his reasoning has clear implications for the prudential dimension as well. Specifically, Goldman claims that:

> the account [of causal responsibility] presented here . . . can explain why people *should* vote (after obtaining sufficient information) and it can explain why people *do* vote (in fairly substantial numbers) [p. 216]

Taken in context, the idea, as we understand it, is that, once voters reckon properly the probability of their vote being causally efficacious, they will see that their vote is likely to have a causal impact on the outcome and will be able to take some moral satisfaction, after the fact, in having been part of the cause of their favored candidate's victory. Furthermore, the prospect of such moral satisfaction (and/or any social esteem that might attach to recognition of their role as members of the group that brought about that candidate's victory) is a significant incentive.

Interestingly, Goldman and Tuck both talk not just in terms of casual *efficacy* but also in terms of causal *responsibility.* And we shall have something to say later about the significance of this choice of terms. But we think the account draws much of its intuitive force from its use of "responsibility" language, since, with them, we do think that in elections all those who voted for the victor—not just one pivotal voter—are responsible for the outcome. So consider, for example, an individual who voted for Hitler in the German elections of July 1932. This individual, one might think, and *all* the others who voted with her, must bear some responsibility for Hitler's successes in that election. Any such voter should properly be held in some contempt; and she ought to feel guilty for having voted in this way.

Suppose in her defense, she were to point out that her own *individual* vote almost surely made no difference to the electoral outcome. Hitler, she observes, would have been every bit as successful whether she had voted for him or not. Would we be—should we be—moved by this observation? Almost certainly not! Horribly bad moral consequences are associated with her actions and she has moral responsibility for them.[13] And she ought to do so specifically despite the fact that her individual vote almost surely made no difference to the electoral outcome.

As will become clear below, we think Goldman and Tuck are right that there is an important sense in which in elections a group of voters, not just one, is causally responsible for the outcome. Our concern is with how thinking about what one might cause figures in justifying and explaining how people vote. In particular we want to focus on two questions:

1. What exactly is each J-voter responsible *for*?
2. And does such responsibility that arises by virtue of being *causally* efficacious (or *causally* responsible) exhaust electoral responsibility more generally? For example, what account of voter responsibility can RCV, as we have conceived it, put in play against the Goldman/Tuck account—and does the best RCV account serve to satisfy our intuitions in cases like the Hitler-success case?

We shall address those questions in turn in what follows.

The upshots of our discussion are twofold. The first is that there are serious reasons to doubt whether the Goldman/Tuck account of why people should vote succeeds in giving the right action-guiding advice. In that sense, the *normative* strand of the Goldman/Tuck account is suspect.

Our second claim is that the explanatory version of the account depends on assumptions that the circumstances of voting make rather dubious; and that under plausible conditions, the effect of the "Goldman/Tuck account of causal responsibility" on anyone convinced by it may well lead them to be less likely rather than more likely to vote. In that sense, the *explanatory* strand of the Goldman/Tuck argument is suspect.

Both RCV and the rival Goldman/Tuck account are about choices: the choices individuals do make; and the choices they ought to make. In the choice context, the proper *weight* of various considerations bears; and, in this context, we think two questions loom: "What value is to be placed on being the cause of some outcome?" and "What probability is to be assigned to that value?"

The stakes for RCV orthodoxy are considerable. Given that g can be close to 100% for close elections (and far from negligible for even not so close ones):

1. We should expect, contra RCV, that the high probability that one's vote will be causally efficacious will motivate many people to expend time and energy in voting. This is, of course, precisely the point that Goldman and Tuck seek to make.
2. We should correspondingly expect voters to expend significant effort in acquiring relevant information about candidates and their policies, contra Downs and Caplan. (Unless, of course, they, perhaps mistakenly, think that they already have the relevant information.)
3. We should expect that considerations of individual self-interest are likely to play nearly as large a role in electoral settings as in those same agents' market decisions. After all, the probability that one will be causally efficacious (on the Goldman/Tuck account) will often be nearly the same in both contexts.

One crucial question is whether g or h is the way that people *actually* think about the probability that their vote will be causally efficacious.[14] The difference will have a significant impact when it comes to *explaining* voting behavior. Another crucial question is whether g or h is the *appropriate* way to think about the probability that one's vote will be causally efficacious. The difference will have a significant impact when it comes to justifying voting behavior.

II. RESPONSIBILITY FOR WHAT?

Goldman and Tuck tie their account of moral *responsibility* to the notion of *causal efficacy*. We think that this elision is misleading. We think a proper account of moral responsibility is often usefully kept apart from any particular account of causation, and, indeed, in many cases, apart from causation altogether; and that this is true in the electoral case. Several considerations incline us to this view.

For one thing, we think that the Goldman/Tuck formulation, by grounding the idea of moral responsibility in its causal effects on the electoral *outcome*, fixes the idea of moral responsibility in electoral behavior too narrowly. It is not that we think that bringing about an electoral outcome is totally irrelevant to the ethics of voting behavior, but as we shall argue, it is not the *only* relevant aspect.

More generally, though both responsibility and causality are notions whose application turns on context and convention, the relevant contexts and conventions are significantly different in the two cases.

Take causation. It seems clear that in most (perhaps almost all) possible descriptions of what caused some "outcome" X, there are a number of factors that might be isolated all of which were present—and necessarily—for X to come about. But what counts as a *cause* of that outcome—and what in particular as "*the*" cause, or a *primary* cause—can be highly contextual. As Goldman puts it, "*causal upshots*" can be "*defined or stipulated by social convention*."

Nevertheless, causation does not seem to be as permissive in this respect as is responsibility. Take the linguistic indicators. Common parlance allows variously: "holding responsible"; "feeling responsible"; "taking responsibility"; "being responsible"; "acting responsibly"; and related expressions. All these states of feeling/holding/taking etc. refer to social and psychological facts of an impressively wide variety. When people talk of their "taking responsibility for X," they seem to do so not so much because they believe that they have caused X but rather in face of the conviction that they have not. Equally, when people take the trouble to declare that they are holding A responsible for X, it is often enough in a setting where the causal connection between A's actions and X is either unclear—or seen as irrelevant. The analogous linguistic indicators and practices with respect to causation seem different and much more constrained. People do not talk so readily of "accepting causation"—except perhaps in the rather loose sense in which causation might be connected to responsibility. We might invite others to treat us *as if* we were causally efficacious but only as a maneuver in getting them to assign responsibility to us: causal efficacy remains "as if"—while the responsibility we take on, we do indeed treat as ours.

It is, we think, unexceptionable that when A votes for a winning option J, people at large *are* disposed to "hold A partially responsible for J's victory" in a way that they would not hold B, who abstained, responsible; and in turn more than C who voted for K. But this is a weak claim—entirely consistent with the thought that A's voting for J rather than for K (or abstaining) almost surely made no difference to whether J would win. A's responsibility might derive from the fact of A's *supporting* some outcome, even if, as we think, it is not restricted to A's being causally efficacious in bringing the outcome about.

Consider for example citizen A. Suppose that J and K are rivals in an electoral race. Suppose that it would be desirable from a moral point of view if J were to win; and that A recognizes this fact. So, A thinks, in any case where the chances that J will win are pretty high, that fact is a good thing (better than if J were likely to lose). A has, as we might put it, a morally grounded "pro-attitude" towards J's victory. In that attitudinal sense, A supports J.

However, A could support J in another way—by bending her own agency to the project of J's election by voting for her. In that way, so the thought goes, A might well turn out to be a *cause* of J's victory in a way that A wouldn't be if she failed to vote.[15] And when J is duly elected, A could properly feel moral satisfaction for her own part in supporting this desirable outcome. Now, it is important to emphasize that A's contribution here does *not* collapse to the difference A's vote made to whether the good outcome would come about. *That* effect is fully captured by the *h* factor—which by hypothesis here is very small; J's chances of winning without A's "contribution" in the postulated example are already high. Perhaps A's "responsibility" lies, as the Goldman/Tuck account would have it, in A being, as they think about it, a cause of the victory. But we think that does not capture all that is in play, and, in fact, we suspect it misses the most important part: That what A is doing when he votes for J is *exercising agency* in support of the relevant outcome. And that seems to us to be the appropriate turn of phrase. Accordingly, we want to say a little more about what is at stake in this "agency" thought.

As the Goldman/Tuck view in effect emphasizes, in lots of situations, individuals want not just that something good comes about but also that it is *they* who bring it about. A wants his partner to enjoy pleasure: but it is likely that A wants that pleasure to be at *A's* hands. We ourselves desire intellectual progress in understanding "reasons to vote"—but we also want that progress to come about partly as a result of *our* work—not just that some paper be written and make its contribution, but that it be *our* paper. In a similar way, it is a familiar experience that a newly appointed CEO (or new Dean in the University setting) wants to make changes in the way things are done, or in the personnel who are her underlings—not just because those changes are good in themselves (though she may well think so) but also because she wants to leave her mark. She has the power to make changes for the better and she relishes the exercise of that power.[16]

In the case of the new CEO/Dean (and perhaps the others as well), this motivation can appear to include an "ego trip" element: she may be making the changes simply because she can, and largely independent of whether the changes represent genuine improvements. But this (limiting) case reminds us that the exercise of agency can come apart from approval of the changes in the outcome qua outcome. And once we recognize that the exercise of agency can be desired for its own sake, we can see that changes might be made even when the agent does not know or much care whether such changes would be desirable were they to come about in some other way. A person may think: "These are *my* changes and I am making *my* mark upon the world." And that exercise of agency may well be the source of her satisfaction.

Note that, since on the Goldman/Tuck account the reason to vote relates to being causally responsible for the outcome, the desire to be a cause provides individuals with incentives to vote for the candidate most likely to win. This is so because on the Goldman/Tuck account, you cannot be causally responsible for something that doesn't happen: voting for a losing candidate deprives you of anything to be responsible for.[17] So if you want to be causally responsible for an event in political history, just for the sake of leaving your mark, you need to vote for the winner.[18]

It is worth noting too in passing that the notion of agency at stake here is distinct from that implicit in most rational actor theory, because in RCT any and all rational action is seen as the outcome of *choice*. So *any* choice is an example of the individual exercising "agency." In particular, the choice to abstain rather than to vote is a *choice*—and hence abstaining becomes an action, an instance of agency. By contrast, the notion of "agency" we see as being brought to the fore in the Goldman/Tuck account of voting has a more common sense quality: to play tennis or go jogging is to exercise agency in a way that choosing to do nothing would not be; to choose to intervene in the world is to exercise agency where to choose to let things take their course would not be. And specifically, to vote is to be active in a process, in a manner that abstaining would be passive. Both voting and abstaining involve choices; but only one of those choices involves one's full political agency. Or at least, so the thought goes. And it is by no means an unfamiliar thought. The distinction between killing and letting die depends precisely on a notion of agency in this "common sense" sense. The decision as to what to do in familiar trolley problems involves a choice; but "agency" is involved only when you pull levers or push fat men.

Of course, in the CEO/Dean cases, and many others, the agent is fully causally efficacious in bringing about the outcomes that represent her mark upon the world. That is not so in the voting case. Nevertheless, there *can be* an agency effect—something for the voter to be responsible for, over and above that voter's (usually very small) impact on the likelihood of J's victory. A has chosen to be causally involved by bending her agency in the furtherance of J's election;

and the spirit of the Goldman/Tuck account seems to be that there is a level of causal responsibility associated with the fact of "being a cause"—distinct from her individual contribution to likelihoods. Further, this agency effect can both: a) motivate individuals to vote; and b) provide a moral justification for A's voting.

The a) aspect we find perfectly plausible. Individuals might well be induced to vote for candidates because they want *themselves* to be a cause of that candidate's victory. In what follows we grant this point.[19] At the same time, we note that where people do have this concern, their voting has a very high probability of being pivotal to their success in pursuing *that* end.

However the b) aspect requires more argument. We think there is at least a range of cases in which including the agency effect will secure a worse outcome than if no such effect were present. In that sense, the Goldman/Tuck account of causal efficacy seems to give the wrong action-guiding advice. To show this is the aim of the ensuing section.

III. ACTION-GUIDING ADVICE

Begin with a simple example. There is a community of voters and an election in which the moral stakes are seriously large. The expected outcome is that 60% of voters will vote for J. This means that the probability is quite high that in voting of J one will be (in the Goldman/Tuck sense) a cause of J's victory, and so able properly to see oneself as having brought it about (along with others).

Now consider, in this setting, a specific voter A, who has an opportunity to bring a real, but not especially large, benefit, of E, to the community. There is however a difficulty—namely, that securing this benefit requires A to be out of town on voting day and hence unable to cast a vote. Should A remain in town and vote; or secure the benefit of E? On the stipulated assumptions, we think it is clear: A should go out of town and secure the benefit, even if the value of J's victory is *much* greater than the value of E.[20] This is because it is virtually certain that J will win (since 60% of the electorate is expected to vote for J): A's vote will almost surely not make a difference to the outcome. That is, *h* is very small. At the same time, *g* is substantial and the Goldman/Tuck emphasis on whether one will be a cause (in their sense) of a valuable outcome misdirects attention to the possibility of being a cause of that outcome, ignoring the crucial fact that one is close to decisive over E. Absent there being an independent (and substantial) value to *being* a cause (again, in the Goldman/Tuck sense) of some outcome, a concern for the value of outcomes ought to lead one to be both indifferent to *g* and attentive to *h* in determining what one should do.

Now, Goldman and Tuck may dispute that A can know with total certainty that J will win. We of course concede that point. Suppose we allow that A's absence does reduce the probability that J will win by a certain fraction. So the expected cost of A going out of town is not zero after all. That does not bring the Goldman/Tuck account of causal responsibility in line with reasonable action guiding advice, unless the probability that J might lose is extremely high (given the assumed values at stake). And to insist that it matters that the probability is not zero is, in effect, to concede what is at stake—namely that what is relevant for determining what A should do is not the share of so-called "causal responsibility" (as Goldman/Tuck would have it)—not the probability that A, if she votes, would have been one of the people that counted to make up the minimal majority—but rather the likelihood that J will lose *because* A doesn't vote. In short, *h*.[21]

The example could be set out, not in terms of voting, but in other terms where the same issues are in play. Suppose the Coast Guard has two boats—a small one and a large one. The small one requires only a one-person crew; the large one requires a six-person crew. There are seven people on call at the station and two distress calls come in from different points along the coast. One involves a ship with 140 people; the other involves a boat that has just one person. All seven could attend to the ship with 140. Or six could crew the larger boat, while the seventh takes the smaller boat out to save one more. The best outcome is achieved, we assume, if both boats go out and 141 are saved. We take it that under these circumstances the right action guiding advice is that someone take the small boat out.

But it is far from clear that this outcome is what the Goldman/Tuck approach would recommend. Consider the calculus of each of the Coast Guards. Each can go with the larger ship and take moral credit for saving 140. (Just how much credit redounds to each is unclear.) One reasonable suggestion is that the credit should be divided equally among all who participate in the rescue, or among the six in the minimally sufficient set; alternatively, though, it might be (as Tuck argues) that each rescuer in the minimally sufficient set can take full credit for saving all 140,[22] still another is that the credit to be shared equally is determined by the size of the minimally sufficient crew.) Or one could crew the smaller rescue-vessel (receiving full moral credit for saving just one person) and allow her colleagues to crew the larger ship.

Suppose for the example that, out of gratitude, each person saved provides a reward of $N to the crew that saves her, and let's tentatively use that reward as a proxy either for the moral credit, or for the value, of saving them. Then the crew of the larger boat will collectively receive $140N (to be shared in some way by those who are causally efficacious), whereas crewing the smaller boat promises only $N. Absent side payments—and irrespective of whether each in the larger group divides the money, credit, or utility, evenly, or each can claim the total amount of what they cause (as understood by Goldman and Tuck)—each reasonably prefers to crew the larger boat. And this remains the case whether the reward comes as money, or social esteem, or moral satisfaction.[23]

Of course, there *is* a reward/credit-sharing scheme that will create incentives to produce the best outcome (which, in this case, we take to involve maximizing lives saved). That scheme will require that the total amount of reward to be distributed across all seven in a way that is insensitive to who saves whom. This will secure the best outcome because, when the seventh goes with the larger boat rather than the smaller, her participation serves to reduce *pari passu* the reward each of the six would otherwise receive. The total reward (monetary, social, or moral) across all who crew would be maximized when all 141 are saved. And one can certainly imagine a "reward-sharing" scheme that would secure this result. But note that that "best-outcome" reward-sharing scheme is more difficult to imagine operating in the case where the reward comes in the form of esteem or moral satisfaction. Monetary rewards are readily transferable between persons: esteem and moral satisfaction are not. That is, it seems plausible to suppose that public esteem and even "moral self-satisfaction" associated with worthy acts (like saving people in distress) accrues to those actors who are "causally responsible" whether in whole or in part. Securing the "incentive-compatible" reward-sharing would require a separation of *reward* from *agency* that seems entirely alien to the spirit of the Goldman/Tuck treatment.[24]

The divergence between what action serves to secure the best outcome and what action serves (on the Goldman/Tuck account) to maximize the individual actor's moral credit is troubling. It is troubling not least because, for Goldman and Tuck, the analysis is supposed to explain why individuals will have incentives to behave in particular ways—and if moral credit is indeed allocated according to the Goldman/Tuck scheme, then it is clear that the outcomes secured will often not be best.

There are really two issues here, as we see it. One concerns which scheme would provide incentives that would predictably provide better outcomes. The other concerns which way of thinking about what one might cause by acting provides the right account of what one has reason to do. (We here take no stand on how tightly connected these two concerns are, though we think they are connected.) Our main point is that the weight the Goldman/Tuck account gives to being (in their sense) a cause of an outcome gives the wrong action guiding advice, if what matters is the moral (or other) value of the outcome.

We recognize that these examples may not be decisive. There may be other examples where the Goldman/Tuck approach might produce better outcomes than the RCV equivalent. Furthermore, we concede that quality of outcomes qua outcomes may not exhaust the moral domain. Nevertheless, it seems to us that failure to provide the right action-guiding advice in the case we describe (and the many others that have the same structure) is a significant count against the Goldman/Tuck account. To meet this charge defenders of the Goldman/Tuck account need arguments for thinking either that each person should indeed join the larger boat or that their account does not make that recommendation. As far as we can see, Goldman and Tuck provide no such arguments. Nor do we see how those might go.

IV. ELECTORAL RESPONSIBILITY WITHIN EXPRESSIVE THEORY

Nothing that we have said so far denies that when A votes for J, A is in fact supporting J's victory, nor is it to deny that A might have a high probability of being (in the Goldman/Tuck sense) a cause of J's victory. What we deny is that that probability (*g*) provides much by way of a reason to vote. But that doesn't mean that J has no substantial reason to vote. Indeed, we think people find, and are right to find, significant value in exercising their agency, in no small part as a way of expressing their political commitments. And we think people are rightly seen as responsible for exercising their agency in this way (as in others). Yet the importance of exercising agency is in play regardless of whether one votes for the victor or not. What matters in elections, we are thinking, is both the outcome and the exercise of agency, but not that in exercising that agency one happens to be among those who (in the Goldman/Tuck sense) cause the outcome.

When A votes for J, she does three things: first, she reveals certain things about her *attitudes* and *beliefs;* second she reveals her preparedness to *express* those attitudes and beliefs; and third, she expresses those beliefs specifically at the ballot box. All of these attributes/actions are ones for which A can properly be held responsible (and are proper grounds for pride or guilt). The moral responsibility for those attitudes and expressions applies, over and above any causal influence on J's election and, indeed, independently of whether J wins.

Consider attitudes first. People can be, and typically are, held responsible for their political attitudes, whether or not those attitudes actually bring about the states of affairs that are the content of those attitudes. Someone who holds the view that Hitler's eugenics policies were admirable surely does deserve our contempt on that account, even if she never does anything in relation to those policies other than to admire them. If A's moral judgments are defective then A is morally defective to that extent.

But *expression* of such attitudes involves a further step. Sometimes, when people have odious views, it is best that those people keep such views to themselves. They ought to be silent at dinner parties when certain topics come up; they ought to refrain from writing op-ed pages; or calling in to live radio shows. It is one thing to *hold* the views in question, another to *express* them. If A gives expression to the attitudes in question—if he declares them—he is endorsing them, giving them a public life that they do not deserve.

We are drawn to the Goldman/Tuck idea (as we interpret it) that when A expresses his attitudes at the ballot box he is expressing them in a distinctive way—in a way that may have causal upshots, however small. For given the effects on the probability of success of his favored candidate are positive, A can be thought of as "bending his agency" to the cause of that candidate's victory, whether or not he is a cause of that victory. Voting falls under the description of "agency-bending" because the consequential effects are strictly non-zero. But it would be a mistake to think that because the agency effect depends on *h* being non-zero, the agency value is a direct function of the degree of causal impact. A's bending his agency towards the cause of J's victory has to be sharply distinguished from the causal impact of A's vote on the likelihood of J's victory.

So when A votes he can be held morally responsible for the *political attitude* that vote reveals, for *expressing* the attitude, and for the mobilization of his agency in a given direction. Note that these are all things that depend not at all on what any other voter does, nor on what the outcome of the election ends up being, nor on whether one is among those in the set of votes that were minimally sufficient for victory.

But here is one (further) sense in which this "expressive" version differs from the Goldman/Tuck account. A central feature of the Goldman/Tuck account is that what individual voters are (partially) responsible for is the electoral *outcome,* and hence that only those voters who vote for the actual outcome can bear this responsibility: voters who vote for the unsuccessful candidate have no outcome to be responsible *for.* But on our view, those who vote for a bad, but happily unsuccessful, candidate do not avoid responsibility just because their candidate was unsuccessful. Bad but unsuccessful voters bear the responsibility for their odious attitudes, for their expressions of those attitudes, for bending their agency in a bad cause, and for the risky behavior they undertook in promoting the chances of a seriously bad outcome. And these components of moral responsibility remain, whether the candidate won or not. Of course, Goldman and Tuck need not deny this. They do not claim that their account of causal responsibility exhausts all that might be said about electoral responsibility. However, when these other aspects of responsibility are included—elements that the RCV account can in principle include—it is not so clear that the Goldman/Tuck account of specifically *causal* responsibility adds much.[25]

In summary, a plausible account of what one is morally responsible *for* in voting provides a notion of *responsibility* captures what lends the Goldman/Tuck view most of its intuitive force. Such an account suggests that a voters' causal *efficacy* in relation to electoral outcomes is rather less important than Goldman and Tuck seem to imply. Certainly, on the account of responsibility we've highlighted, individuals will systematically be morally responsible for their beliefs and attitudes, and their expressions of them, and how they cast their votes, and will remain so whether they vote for the winner or the loser. At the same time, we are inclined to think having bent one's agency in support of an outcome that is realized one is as responsible for it if one failed to be causally efficacious (in the Goldman/Tuck sense) as if one succeeded.

V. THE NORMATIVE VS. THE EXPLANATORY

The Goldman/Tuck account purports to show not only why agents *ought* (or at least have moral or prudential reason) to vote; but also to explain why significant numbers of them actually *do.* We have already indicated why the normative aspect of the argument is questionable. But as we indicated at the close of section II, the explanatory and the normative aspects of the account are less closely linked than Goldman and Tuck suppose. And indeed, as we indicated there, the desire to exercise agency in and of itself might well provide a plausible motive for voting. So insofar as that desire is what Goldman and Tuck have in mind by "causal responsibility," the explanatory part of the argument seems to proceed intact.

To be sure, that explanatory story requires certain assumptions about the role of moral factors in agent motivation—the idea specifically that agents are motivated in part by the prospect of moral satisfaction and social esteem. These motivational assumptions might be controversial in some RCV circles but they are ones we broadly endorse, and so we shall not discuss them further here.

Nevertheless, to the extent that these motivational matters are in play, it is not entirely clear that they do indeed give rise to higher turnout than would arise if agents based their voting decisions on the standard RCV calculus—or some other calculus in which perceived causal efficacy in producing the electoral outcome to be lower.

To give a sense of our misgivings here, return to the example of agency effects involving the new Dean/CEO, exercising her agency largely for its own sake. She may well receive satisfaction from "leaving her mark" and she may do so somewhat independently of whether the mark so left is actually desirable or not. Perhaps she thinks her innovations probably *are* consequentially desirable; but it may well be that her epistemic warrant for this belief is somewhat tenuous. But now she reads Goldman and/or Tuck and realizes that she is more accountable for her actions than she had previously realized. She now sees that the moral and reputational stakes are higher than she had thought: her "sense of responsibility" increases. Accordingly, if there is a serious possibility that the changes she intended to make may be changes for the worse, then she may well be inhibited in making them. In the same way, if there is a serious chance that J will turn out to be an inferior candidate, any increase in perceived responsibility may well inhibit A from voting. The Goldman/Tuck examples take it as given that J's election is independently morally desirable.[26] But that assumption occludes real life uncertainty about the moral qualities of candidates and their policies.

Recall that by hypothesis there is a significant vote for K as well as J. Of course, motives for voting can be various; but in the Goldman/Tuck spirit, it seems reasonable to think that many of those K voters actually believe that K, not J, is the morally superior candidate. In the absence of any contrary argument, this fact should give the J-voter pause. Confidence in the proposition that J is indeed superior ought to be somewhat shaken.

And in the face of increased uncertainty about the moral qualities of options, A's voting calculus takes on a different hue. After all, we take it that it is a worse thing to bend your agency to the cause of the worse candidate than it is to abstain. So the effect of increased uncertainty about whether J is indeed the superior candidate to K seems bound to *reduce* turnout. And the effect of increased responsibility, in the face of a given level of such uncertainty, seems likely to have a similar effect. Greater probability that one will cause an outcome—a greater chance of being causally responsible for the outcome—will encourage individuals to acquire more information about candidates given that they intend to vote. But whether, given the cost of information acquisition and the risk of making an error, the greater probability of responsibility will also induce more individuals to vote seems at best an open question.[27]

It is worth noting that increased perceived probability of responsibility may lead A to abstain even when A is *certain* that J is the superior candidate. If what morally commends J is not that J is good but rather that K is even worse, A may have to wear a certain social and moral opprobrium just for voting for a bad candidate. In such a case, increased perceived probability of responsibility for the outcome may leave A wanting to keep her hands clean—abstention may here too emerge as the preferred option.[28]

What greater perceived responsibility *will* do is to increase the proportion of voters who are morally confident or who are ignorant as to how ignorant they actually are. Voting is left not only to those who properly see themselves to be relatively well-informed, but also to the opinionated, the self-deceptive and those who vote for non-morally grounded reasons. A heightened sense of responsibility, as Goldman and Tuck think a more proper view of causal efficacy would generate, will not necessarily lead to higher turnout. But it probably will lead to a voting body that is more morally confident, whether because voters have gathered more information or because of independent psychological factors (whose normative status seems rather more dubious).

VI. CONCLUSION

The "causal responsibility" account of voting behavior, advanced by Goldman (1999) and endorsed with some variation by Tuck (2008), purports to show why individuals *should* vote, and why they *will* vote in larger numbers than they would if they were informed by the standard rational choice account of voting behavior. According to the latter account, the *ex ante* probability of influencing the electoral outcome is the probability of a pivotal result—one in which voters for the successful candidate are individually necessary and jointly sufficient for the electoral outcome.

In our assessment of the Goldman/Tuck account, we have wanted to attend to three issues:

1. What is the distinction (if Goldman and Tuck see one) between causal *efficacy* and causal *responsibility?*
2. When an individual causes, or is a "part of the cause," of a candidate's success, what is she responsible *for*? Is she responsible (at least in

part) for the electoral *outcome,* or for being (in the Goldman/Tuck sense) a cause of her favored candidate's success? If the latter, is there a material difference between being a cause of the candidate's success and "bending one's agency towards (the cause of) that candidate's success" (which is our own preferred way of thinking about such cases)?

To the extent that the issue does revolve around agency effects so understood, two further questions arise:

a. Does the inclusion of agency effects give rise to the correct "action-guiding" advice in electoral contexts?
b. Is it plausible that including such effects will encourage increased turnout in the circumstances of normal elections?

Our answers to these two questions are negative.

Perhaps a negative response in relation to the first should occasion no surprise. Agency effects invoke factors that seem more at home in a "virtue" account of electoral behavior than a standard consequentialist one; and it ought to be expected that adding normative requirements of this voter-virtue kind might "cost" something in terms of the quality of outcomes qua outcomes. To be sure, Goldman and Tuck do not cast their "causal responsibility" story in virtue language; but we suspect that that is where their account properly belongs.

As to the second, explanatory question, the issue hangs on whether seeing oneself as more rather than less likely to be responsible for the outcomes of one's voting behavior increases the incentive to vote. Much depends on the weight of guilt/shame when one votes for the "wrong" candidate vis-à-vis moral satisfaction/pride when one votes the right one. If the latter is less weighty than the former (as we think most likely) then the best course, in the face of uncertainty about which *is* the better candidate, may well be to abstain. Goldman and Tuck steer clear of such uncertainty in their examples—but it is difficult to ignore the prospect of this kind of error in fact, or indeed to account for the patterns of voting behavior that Goldman and Tuck assume in their examples (and especially for anything other than landslide victories) without risk of voter error being part of the story. Of course, having voters abstain when they would otherwise have voted for the worse candidate is presumably a good thing. But the expected value of that effect is properly measured by relying on the parameter that RCV theorists have long insisted *is* the proper parameter—namely, *h*.

BIBLIOGRAPHY

Brennan, G. and L. Lomasky (1993). *Democracy and Decision*, New York: Cambridge University Press.

Brennan, G. and P. Pettit (1990). "Unveiling the Vote," *British Journal of Political Science,* 20: 311–333.

Caplan, B. (2007). *The Myth of the Rational Voter*, Princeton: Princeton University Press.

Downs, A. (1957). *An Economic Theory of Democracy*, New York: Harper.

Goldman, A. (1999). "Why Citizens Should Vote: A Causal Responsibility Approach," *Social Philosophy and Policy* 16: 201–217.

Riker, W. and Ordeshook, P. (1968). "A Theory of the Calculus of Voting," *American Political Science Review* 62: 25–42.

Schuessler, A. (2000). *A Logic of Expressive Choice*, Princeton: Princeton University Press.

Tullock, G. (1967) *Toward a Mathematics of Politics*, Ann Arbor: University of Michigan Press.

Tuck, R. (2008). *Free Riding*, Cambridge, Mass.: Harvard University Press.

NOTES

1. There is a second-order complication that we should dispose of at the outset: J might win the election following an exact tie among all voters. The decision over who wins in the event of a tie might be determined by tossing a coin; and J, rather than K, might win that coin toss. Each voter, in these cases, is such that had she abstained, or voted differently, she would have brought about the victory of K. And in the case where J wins by exactly one vote, if a voter had abstained, she *might* have brought about the victory of K via a tie-breaking mechanism. So if voter A abstains rather than votes for J, in the first case, she would cause K to win by a majority of 1; or, in the second case, she would give rise to a situation in which K might win via a tie-breaking procedure. What this means is that the idea of being pivotal is slightly different depending on whether the option under consideration is voting for an alternative

candidate or abstaining, and on whether the number of voters is odd or even. Here, we shall treat the idea of being pivotal capaciously—allowing it to cover all cases in which A's voting behavior could influence which candidate wins.

2. It is perhaps worth emphasizing that the question of whether it is rational to vote or not involves a deployment of the logic of rationality that is somewhat at odds with its use in "rational choice theory." Charges of irrationality involve argument from presumed desires and beliefs on the one hand to actions that are inconsistent with those desires and beliefs on the other. The rational choice theory approach involves argument from observed behavior "backwards" to the beliefs and desires that are thought to motivate that behavior. Here, rationality works as an analytic assumption rather than an issue to be determined in any specific case. So, the presumption in RCV is (or ought to be) that both voters and abstainers are rational: the question then becomes—what differences in beliefs and desires of the two sets of agents would explain these behavioral differences? The notion that one of these groups might be "rational" while the other group is not is alien from the spirit of the RCV enterprise—a fact which did not prevent some early RCV theorists from speculating as to whether voting is "rational" or not. See for example, Tullock (1967).

3. For example, in US Presidential elections, at most of the order of 1/12500 and almost certainly rather smaller than this. See Brennan and Lomasky (1993) chapter 4.

4. The classic treatment is Riker and Ordershook (1968).

5. Of course, expected benefit might be a reason for voting if the stakes for the voter are huge—but then it is the size of the stakes rather than the probability of making a difference to the outcome that is the primary "reason" to vote.

6. The variations are far from minor, but they share enough, we think, for it to make sense to consider them together, not least their rejection of the idea that what matters is that one's vote will be pivotal.

7. We write of being sufficient "in the appropriate way" because Goldman and Tuck differ when it comes to identifying which votes are a part of what is sufficient for the outcome. We highlight the difference below.

8. Tuck.

9. Tuck's account faces complications, of course, in cases where votes are cast simultaneously, since the roll call voting method of isolating which set of votes was, in fact, sufficient, depends on temporal order. This fact plays an important role in motivating Goldman's account, which takes simultaneous voting as the normal case (on the grounds that our voting conventions treat the timing of ballots, and of their being counted, as irrelevant (p. 213).

10. Writing about British parliamentary elections, Tuck notes that "at some point in the course of the evening one candidate's piles of ballot papers add up to the precise figure necessary for a majority, and those ballot papers have therefore by themselves accomplished the task of electing him." And he goes on to note that in the event of a recount, the original count proves not to have settled the election and "the set which first reaches the majority in the second count will then do so, or in the third count, or in however many counts are necessary to satisfy the satisfy the returning officer and the candidates that a proper count has been made" (p. 43).

11. Goldman advances this idea as a way of understanding Mackie's INUS account of causation in light of which something is a partial or contributory cause if and only if it is "an *insufficient* but *necessary* part of a condition that is itself *unnecessary* but *sufficient* for the result" (p. 206).

12. Goldman points out that "In the United States House or Senate, for example, a roll-call vote is completed even if the outcome is clear long before the last vote has been voiced. This is because, officially, votes are not counted or 'registered' until all have been voiced. Because of this conventional feature, the causal impact of a late vote is not really preempted by a collection of early votes. From the official, conventional perspective, they are all simultaneous; hence, their causal statuses are perfectly symmetric" (p. 213).

13. We leave to one side the important question of just how to think of the relative degree to which she, as compared to others, is responsible for those consequences. We also leave to one side questions concerning the responsibility she bears for her vote, regardless of the consequences associated with it. (Here we are being careful to talk of the consequences *associated with* her vote, rather than of the consequences *of* her vote, since the latter assumes her vote had the consequences in questions—that it was causally efficacious, and it is that assumption that we are exploring.

14. We believe it is likely that many people do think that as long as they voted for the winner of an election, they helped to cause the victory, as Goldman's (but not Tuck's) version of g would have it. Yet we suspect that thought does not depend on ideas concerning their being in a minimally sufficient set. In any case, it does seem

plausible that many people recognize that they cannot claim credit for a victory without voting and suppose that as long as they do vote (for they winner) they can claim credit. And we think that is likely a real incentive to many people.

15. Whether she is a part of the cause depends, of course, on whether J wins and also, on the Goldman/Tuck account, on whether her vote was part of (on Tuck's version) *the* minimal set of votes that was sufficient for J's victory or (on Goldman's version) *a* minimal set of votes sufficient for J's victory.

16. As Tuck notes acknowledging a concern with agency, and with being oneself the cause of an outcome, is perfectly compatible with a holding that RCV offers the right account of when a prospective outcome provides instrumental reason to act. See pp. 54–57.

"On my account," Tuck writes, "it is rational to vote (all other things being equal) only if I believe that there are likely to be enough votes for my candidate for my vote to be part of a causally efficacious set. . . . In other words, I think that it is precisely in the situation where it looks on the standard modern view [RCV] as if my vote is unnecessary that I have a good reason to vote" (p. 60).

17. For an account of voting behavior based on the related, but importantly different, conjecture that voters want to be on the winning side for its own sake (at least over some range) see Schuessler (2000).

18. Though we will have cause to revisit that issue briefly in section IV.

19. Of course, there is some difference in the relative values of J's victory and of E that would recommend staying and voting. But for a broad range, the fact that J's victory is more valuable will in effect be irrelevant to what A has reason to do, given the expected votes of others.

20. Tuck acknowledges that "it might obviously be a good reason for doing something that I am probably the only person able to do it" (p. 59), so it may be that our disagreement is more a matter of emphasis, than principle. But we are struck by the extent to which Tuck (and Goldman) think the relevant consideration in contexts of voting is whether one will likely be part of a relevant set of votes that is minimally sufficient for victory, and not whether one's vote is likely to be necessary.

21. Tuck focuses on the allocation of utility, not moral credit, arguing that in an election that has an outcome with a utility of 200, each vote that is part of the causally sufficient set, "represents" a utility of 200. But he cautions that we shouldn't conclude "that it possesses such utility, precisely because the notion of representation implies that the thing represented is different from its representative" (pp. 42–43).

22. The difference between *h* and *g* makes all the difference here, since however the credit or utility is to be apportioned, the much higher value of *g*, compared to *h*, makes the expected utility of joining the crew of the larger boat much greater than the value of crewing the smaller boat.

23. One might seek to block the force of the Coast Guard example in a number of ways. One might be to insist that the seventh is likely not a cause because she adds nothing to whether the project of saving will be successful, assuming the other six are in place. This is a point defenders of RCV would make (even as they allow that there is a small chance that the seventh would prove necessary to success since, for instance, one of the others might become sick or fall overboard). But clearly, since only six are needed, and so only six are in the minimally sufficient set, *g*, for each, will still be extremely high on Tuck's interpretation (and one on Goldman's, since each of the seven is a member of some set of sailors that is sufficient).

24. And we are concerned that taking *g*, rather than *h*, as the probability relevant in making choices obscures, rather than clarifies, what is at stake. When it is important to an agent to exercise her agency, as we recognize it might well be, we think it appropriate to use *h*, not *g*, in thinking about the expected value of the options (in these cases not just the agency-independent value of the potential outcome of that exercise, but also the value of exercising agency). Of course, choosing to exercise one's agency is, normally, both necessary and sufficient for doing so, so *h*, in such cases, will be 1.

25. Goldman considers cases in which someone's preferred candidate is objectively worse and argues that when that is true the person does not have (an objective) reason to vote. (He notes that she may still have a subjective reason, depending on the evidence she has concerning which candidate is better.) But he does not consider, as we do in what follows, the impact recognition of the possibility might have on voter behavior, in light of the more expansive account of causal responsibility he and Tuck defend (pp. 209–210).

26. What is at stake here is how the moral payoffs to the three prospects —voting for the better candidate, abstaining and voting for the worse candidate — each respond to changes in the perceived likelihood of responsibility.

27. We are grateful to Emma Johnson for this observation.

28. See Anthony Downs and the chapter on public choice theory for more on this.

12 Liberty and Paternalism

"Paternalism" provokes powerful visceral reactions, and for good reason. States have a sordid history of overriding their citizens' judgments about how to live their lives. There are at least two different problems with paternalism, and it is useful to distinguish them.

The first is that government paternalism can undermine autonomy by limiting individual liberty. Yet personal autonomy is a precondition for independent judgment and action, which are required for human flourishing, and for effective democracy.

Second, there are serious "public choice" questions about the practical capacity of the state to reach superior judgments about what is good for people. It cannot simply be assumed that experts have better information than individuals about what individuals should want; neither can it be assumed that political authorities will act on the advice of experts, even if that advice were correct.

The most famous defense of individual liberty remains John Stuart Mill's essay, *On Liberty*. Although a major part of Mill's project is to defend free speech and thought, the excerpt reprinted here focuses on liberty of *action*. Mill suggests at the outset that his support for individual liberty rests mainly on the instrumental benefits of liberty, rather than its intrinsic value. One implication of this view is that those who lack psychological stability or enough foresight to make effective use of their liberty may—in theory, at least, and assuming the public choice problems can be overcome—benefit from paternalistic interference. Mill's arguments against paternalism only apply to "human beings in the maturity of their faculties."

Mill appeals to a panoply of arguments to support his case for liberty and against paternalism. One of the more important considerations is that when people are free to make—and learn from—mistakes, they develop their moral, creative, and intellectual powers. Mill worries about blind conformity to custom and law, and suggests that the best society is one in which people are not only legally free to pursue their own ends but one in which they are actively encouraged to try out different "experiments in living."

Gerald Dworkin is sympathetic to Mill, but highlights the defeasibility of Mill's presumption that individuals know their interests, and understand how best to promote them. Mill concedes that children and mentally unstable adults often fail to make effective use of their freedom, and can rightly have their liberty restricted if they tend to use it in ways that make them worse off. Dworkin extends this reasoning to otherwise competent adults who consistently act contrary to their own interests. For example, some people fail to wear a seatbelt because of bad habits rather than thoughtful consideration of the consequences; others may be tempted to commit suicide after a traumatic experience like a failed relationship or financial difficulties, but they may prefer not to commit suicide once they escape the grip of depression.

In cases like this, Dworkin thinks paternalistic restrictions like a mandatory cooling off period in which suicide is prohibited, by force if necessary, *might* be justified. The justification turns on the thought that the same adult, if fully rational, free from bias, better informed, and free from momentary despondency, would agree to the coercion. But Dworkin is skeptical of moving from a *moral* justification for paternalism to the actual imposition of paternalistic *laws*. To justify a paternalistic law Dworkin says the state must show that nearly everyone really would agree to it if they were in an idealized epistemic environment. Even then, the paternalistic law could only apply to decisions that are "far-reaching, potentially dangerous, and irreversible." And Dworkin imposes one additional precautionary rule: "If there is an alternative way of accomplishing the desired end without restricting liberty, even though it may involve great expense, inconvenience, etc., the society must adopt it." According to Dworkin, it is impossible to infer from the content of an action or law whether it is paternalistic. Paternalism is one justification for limiting liberty, but not every limitation of liberty is paternalistic. There are many other justifications or explanations for why a law or regulation exists. One legislator might endorse a restriction as a favor to another legislator (in exchange for a vote on some other bill), or as a way to curry favor with interest groups as a means of attracting campaign contributions. Another legislator might endorse a rule because she believes the restriction will prevent externalities, or harm to others, requiring state action to "internalize" the costs of action so that an individual takes full account of those costs in choosing how to act. Popular use of the term "paternalism" often conflates these reasons, as when people misleadingly claim that occupational licensing, vaccination programs, or mandatory food labeling are paternalistic. On Dworkin's view, if a policy serves as a coordination mechanism to solve a collective action problem or produce a public good for which there is widespread demand, it is not paternalistic.

Cass Sunstein and Richard Thaler outline a framework that builds upon Dworkin's rationale for paternalism. Libertarian paternalists like Sunstein and Thaler exploit specific insights from behavioral economics—the psychology of decision-making—to support their case for paternalism. The theory is *libertarian* in the sense that Sunstein and Thaler wish to preserve freedom of choice within a specified range of options, but *paternalistic* because they think governments should sometimes design the "choice architecture" within which people choose in order to "nudge" them to make choices that are likely to increase their welfare. For example, libertarian paternalists often advocate changing the default option from "opt out" to "opt in" for retirement annuities, noticing that many people want to save for retirement but will fail to opt in to retirement savings plans unless this is the default option. Alternatively, libertarian paternalists might notice that gamblers often fail to think through the probability of winning, and thus wish to make it less attractive by relegating casinos to operating in a seedy part of town, or forcing gaming companies to publish the objective probability of winning at roulette or slots, and to operate only during certain hours of the day. Gamblers are still free to play, but planners make the harmful option a little less attractive. In some ways, this is consistent with Mill's view since it assumes that liberty is only instrumentally valuable, and that limiting liberty *might* be worthwhile if the authorities really are better judges of harm, and if the public choice objections can be overcome. Libertarian paternalists seem to have more confidence than Mill and public choice theorists that government agents have the correct information and the right incentives to improve people's ability to act in ways that advance their interests.

Sunstein and Thaler attempt to justify paternalism by appealing to the infirmities that plague our choices—our lack of information, or short-sightedness, our tendency to stick with the status quo, whatever it is. But even if individuals sometimes fail to know their own interests, or how to advance them effectively, we should still ask whether paternalistic planners are likely to know how to promote other people's interests better than those people themselves and whether, even if they do, the laws passed will actually promote those interests well (without serious unintended consequences). The question is not just one of static interests. Since people's preferences change over time as they learn from experience, Mill worries that paternalistic policies limit people's development as mature citizens. This can be true quite apart from the possibility that actual, fallible real-world planners will make citizens worse off in the short run by nudging them in different directions. The alternative of allowing individual firms to order products in a way that maximizes expected profit may be preferable in a world in which people with diverse and changing interests want firms to respond to their desires by supplying products that are conveniently arranged.

FURTHER READING

Camerer, Colin *et al.* 2003. "Regulation for Conservatives: Behavioral Economics and the Case for 'Asymmetric Paternalism,'" *University of Pennsylvania Law Review* 151: 1211–1254.

DeMarneffe, Peter. 2006. "Avoiding Paternalism," *Philosophy and Public Affairs* 34 (1): 68–94.

Husak, Douglas. 2003. "Legal Paternalism." In Hugh LaFollette (ed.), *The Oxford Handbook of Practical Ethics.* Oxford University Press.

Rizzo, Mario and Douglas Whitman. 2009. "The Knowledge Problem of New Paternalism." *Brigham Young University Law Review* 4: 103–161.

Sugden, Robert. 2008. "Why Incoherent Preferences Do Not Justify Paternalism." *Constitutional Political Economy* 19: 226–248.

Sunstein, Cass and Richard Thaler. 2009. *Nudge: Improving Decisions about Health, Wealth, and Happiness*, revised and expanded edition. Penguin Books.

White, Mark. 2013. *The Manipulation of Choice: Ethics and Libertarian Paternalism.* Palgrave MacMillan.

JOHN STUART MILL

On Liberty

1859

The object of this Essay is to assert one very simple principle, as entitled to govern absolutely the dealings of society with the individual in the way of compulsion and control, whether the means used be physical force in the form of legal penalties, or the moral coercion of public opinion. That principle is, that the sole end for which mankind are warranted, individually or collectively in interfering with the

From John Stuart Mill, *On Liberty*, 4th ed. London: Longmans, Green, Reader and Dyer, 1869.

liberty of action of any of their number, is self-protection. That the only purpose for which power can be rightfully exercised over any member of a civilized community, against his will, is to prevent harm to others. His own good, either physical or moral, is not a sufficient warrant. He cannot rightfully be compelled to do or forbear because it will be better for him to do so, because it will make him happier, because, in the opinions of others, to do so would be wise, or even right. These are good reasons for remonstrating with him, or reasoning with him, or persuading him, or entreating him, but not for compelling him, or visiting him with any evil, in case he do otherwise. To justify that, the conduct from which it is desired to deter him must be calculated to produce evil to someone else. The only part of the conduct of any one, for which he is amenable to society, is that which concerns others. In the part which merely concerns himself, his independence is, of right, absolute. Over himself, over his own body and mind, the individual is sovereign.

It is, perhaps, hardly necessary to say that this doctrine is meant to apply only to human beings in the maturity of their faculties. We are not speaking of children, or of young persons below the age which the law may fix as that of manhood or womanhood. Those who are still in a state to require being taken care of by others, must be protected against their own actions as well as against external injury. For the same reason, we may leave out of consideration those backward states of society in which the race itself may be considered as in its nonage. The early difficulties in the way of spontaneous progress are so great, that there is seldom any choice of means for overcoming them; and a ruler full of the spirit of improvement is warranted in the use of any expedients that will attain an end, perhaps otherwise unattainable. Despotism is a legitimate mode of government in dealing with barbarians, provided the end be their improvement, and the means justified by actually effecting that end. Liberty, as a principle, has no application to any state of things anterior to the time when mankind have become capable of being improved by free and equal discussion. Until then, there is nothing for them but implicit obedience to an Akbar or a Charlemagne, if they are so fortunate as to find one. But as soon as mankind have attained the capacity of being guided to their own improvement by conviction or persuasion (a period long since reached in all nations with whom we need here concern ourselves), compulsion, either in the direct form or in that of pains and penalties for non-compliance, is no longer admissible as a means to their own good, and justifiable only for the security of others.

It is proper to state that I forego any advantage which could be derived to my argument from the idea of abstract right as a thing independent of utility. I regard utility as the ultimate appeal on all ethical questions; but it must be utility in the largest sense, grounded on the permanent interests of man as a progressive being. Those interests, I contend, authorize the subjection of individual spontaneity to external control, only in respect to those actions of each, which concern the interest of other people. If any one does an act hurtful to others, there is a prima facie case for punishing him, by law, or, where legal penalties are not safely applicable, by general disapprobation. There are also many positive acts for the benefit of others, which he may rightfully be compelled to perform; such as, to give evidence in a court of justice; to bear his fair share in the common defence, or in any other joint work necessary to the interest of the society of which he enjoys the protection; and to perform certain acts of individual beneficence, such as saving a fellow creature's life, or interposing to protect the defenceless against ill-usage, things which whenever it is obviously a man's duty to do, he may rightfully be made responsible to society for not doing. A person may cause evil to others not only by his actions but by his inaction, and in either case he is justly accountable to them for the injury. The latter case, it is true, requires a much more cautious exercise of compulsion than the former. To make any one answerable for doing evil to others, is the rule; to make him answerable for not preventing evil, is, comparatively speaking, the exception. Yet there are many cases clear enough and grave enough to justify that exception. In all things which regard the external relations of the individual, he is de jure amenable to those whose interests are concerned, and if need be, to society as their protector. There are often good reasons for not holding him to the responsibility; but these reasons must arise from the special expediencies of the case: either because it is a kind of case in which he is on the whole likely to act better, when left to his own discretion, than when controlled in any way in which society have it in their power to control him; or because the attempt to exercise control would produce other evils, greater than those which it would prevent. When such reasons as these preclude the enforcement of responsibility, the conscience of the agent himself should step into the vacant judgment-seat, and protect those interests of others which have no external protection; judging himself all the more rigidly, because the case does not admit of his being made accountable to the judgment of his fellow-creatures.

But there is a sphere of action in which society, as distinguished from the individual, has, if any, only an indirect interest; comprehending all that portion of a person's life and conduct which affects only himself, or, if it also affects others, only with their free, voluntary, and undeceived consent and participation. When I say only himself, I mean directly, and in the first instance: for whatever affects himself, may affect others through himself; and the objection which may be grounded on this contingency, will receive consideration in the sequel. This, then, is the appropriate region of human liberty. It comprises, first, the inward domain of consciousness; demanding liberty of conscience, in the most comprehensive sense; liberty of thought and feeling; absolute freedom of opinion and sentiment on all subjects, practical or speculative, scientific, moral, or theological. The liberty of expressing and publishing opinions may seem to fall under a different principle, since it belongs to that part of the conduct of an individual which concerns other people; but, being almost of as much importance as the liberty of thought itself, and resting in great part on the same reasons, is practically inseparable from it. Secondly, the principle requires liberty of tastes and pursuits; of framing the plan of our life to suit our own character; of doing as we like, subject to such consequences as may follow; without impediment from our fellow-creatures, so long as what we do does not harm them even though they should think our conduct foolish, perverse, or wrong. Thirdly, from this liberty of each individual, follows the liberty, within the same limits, of combination among individuals; freedom to unite, for any purpose not involving harm to others: the persons combining being supposed to be of full age, and not forced or deceived.

No society in which these liberties are not, on the whole, respected, is free, whatever may be its form of government; and none is completely free in which they do not exist absolute and unqualified. The only freedom which deserves the name, is that of pursuing our own good in our own way, so long as we do not attempt to deprive others of theirs, or impede their efforts to obtain it. Each is the proper guardian of his own health, whether bodily, or mental or spiritual. Mankind are greater gainers by suffering each other to live as seems good to themselves, than by compelling each to live as seems good to the rest. . . .

OF INDIVIDUALITY, AS ONE OF THE ELEMENTS OF WELLBEING

. . . Acts of whatever kind, which, without justifiable cause, do harm to others, may be, and in the more important cases absolutely require to be, controlled by the unfavorable sentiments, and, when needful, by the active interference of mankind. The liberty of the individual must be thus far limited; he must not make himself a nuisance to other people. But if he refrains from molesting others in what concerns them, and merely acts according to his own inclination and judgment in things which concern himself, the same reasons which show that opinion should be free, prove also that he should be allowed, without molestation, to carry his opinions into practice at his own cost. That mankind are not infallible; that their truths, for the most part, are only half-truths; that unity of opinion, unless resulting from the fullest and freest comparison of opposite opinions, is not desirable, and diversity not an evil, but a good, until mankind are much more capable than at present of recognizing all sides of the truth, are principles applicable to men's modes of action, not less than to their opinions. As it is useful that while mankind are imperfect there should be different opinions, so is it that there should be different experiments of living; that free scope should be given to varieties of character, short of injury to others; and that the worth of different modes of life should be proved practically, when anyone thinks fit to try them. It is desirable, in short, that in things which do not primarily concern others, individuality should assert itself. Where, not the person's own character, but the traditions of customs of other people are the rule of conduct, there is wanting one of the principal ingredients of human happiness, and quite the chief ingredient of individual and social progress.

In maintaining this principle, the greatest difficulty to be encountered does not lie in the appreciation of means towards an acknowledged end, but in the indifference of persons in general to the end itself. If it were felt that the free development of individuality is one of the leading essentials of well-being; that it is not only a coordinate element with all that is designated by the terms civilization, instruction, education, culture, but is itself a necessary part and condition of all those things; there would be no danger that liberty should be undervalued, and the adjustment of the boundaries between it and social control would present no extraordinary difficulty. But the evil is, that individual spontaneity is hardly recognized by the common modes of thinking as having any intrinsic worth, or deserving any regard on its own account. The majority, being satisfied with the ways of mankind as they now are (for it is they who make them what they are), cannot comprehend why those ways should not be good enough for everybody; and what is more, spontaneity forms no part of the ideal of the majority of moral and social reformers, but is rather looked on with jealousy, as a troublesome and perhaps rebellious obstruction to the general acceptance of what these reformers, in their own judgment, think would be best for mankind. . . .

He who lets the world, or his own portion of it, choose his plan of life for him, has no need of any other faculty than the ape-like one of imitation. He who chooses his plan for himself, employs all his faculties. He must use observation to see, reasoning and judgment to foresee, activity to gather materials for decision, discrimination to decide, and when he has decided, firmness and self-control to hold to his deliberate decision. And these qualities he requires and exercises exactly in proportion as the part of his conduct which he determines according to his own judgment and feelings is a large one. It is possible that he might be guided in some good path, and kept out of harm's way, without any of these things. But what will be his comparative worth as a human being? It really is of importance, not only what men do, but also what manner of men they are that do it. Among the works of man, which human life is rightly employed in perfecting and beautifying, the first in importance surely is man himself. Supposing it were possible to get houses built, corn grown, battles fought, causes tried, and even churches erected and prayers said, by machinery—by automatons in human form—it would be a considerable loss to exchange for these automatons even the men and women who at present inhabit the more civilized parts of the world, and who assuredly are but starved specimens of what nature can and will produce. Human nature is not a machine to be built after a model, and set to do exactly the work prescribed for it, but a tree, which requires to grow and develop itself on all sides, according to the tendency of the inward forces which make it a living thing. . . .

Having said that individuality is the same thing with development, and that it is only the cultivation of individuality which produces, or can produce, well-developed human beings, I might here close the argument: for what more or better can be said of any condition of human affairs, than that it brings human beings themselves nearer to the best thing they can be? or what worse can be said of any obstruction to good, than that it prevents this? Doubtless, however, these considerations will not suffice to convince those who most need convincing; and it is necessary further to show, that these developed human beings are of some use to the undeveloped—to point out to those who do not desire liberty, and would not avail themselves of it, that they may be in some intelligible manner rewarded for allowing other people to make use of it without hindrance.

In the first place, then, I would suggest that they might possibly learn something from them. It will not be denied by anybody, that originality is a valuable element in human affairs. There is always need of persons not only to discover new truths, and point out when what were once truths are true no longer, but also to commence new practices, and set the example of more enlightened conduct, and better taste and sense in human life. This cannot well be gainsaid by anybody who does not believe that the world has already attained perfection in all its ways and practices. It is true that this benefit is not capable of being rendered by everybody alike: there are but few persons, in comparison with the whole of mankind, whose experiments, if adopted by others, would be likely to be any improvement on established practice. But these few are the salt of the earth; without them, human life would become a stagnant pool. Not only is it they who introduce good things which did not before exist; it is they who keep the life in those which already existed. If there were nothing new to be done, would human intellect cease to be necessary? Would it be a reason why those who do the old things should forget why they are done, and do them like cattle, not like human beings? There is only too great a tendency in the best beliefs and practices to degenerate into the mechanical; and unless there were a succession of persons whose ever-recurring originality prevents the grounds of those beliefs and practices from becoming merely traditional, such dead matter would not resist the smallest shock from anything really alive, and there would be no reason why civilization should not die out, as in the Byzantine Empire. Persons of genius, it is true, are, and are always likely to be, a small minority; but in order to have them, it is necessary to preserve the soil in which they grow. Genius can only breathe freely in an atmosphere of freedom. . . .

Originality is the one thing which unoriginal minds cannot feel the use of. They cannot see what it is to do for them: how should they? If they could see what it would do for them, it would not be originality. The first service which originality has to render them, is that of opening their eyes: which being once fully done, they would have a chance of being themselves original. Meanwhile, recollecting that nothing was ever yet done which someone was not the first to do, and that all good things which exist are the fruits of originality, let them be modest enough to believe that there is something still left for it to accomplish, and assure themselves that they are more in need of originality, the less they are conscious of the want.

In sober truth, whatever homage may be professed, or even paid, to real or supposed mental superiority, the general tendency of things throughout the world is to render mediocrity the ascendant power among mankind. In ancient history, in the Middle Ages, and in a diminishing degree through the long transition from feudality to the present time, the individual was a power in himself; and if he had either great talents or a high social position, he was a considerable power. At present individuals are lost in the crowd. In politics it is almost a triviality to say that public opinion now rules the world. The only power deserving the name is that of masses, and of governments while they make themselves the organ of the tendencies and instincts of masses. This is as true in the moral and social relations of private life as in public transactions. Those whose opinions go by the name of public opinion, are not always the same sort of public: in America, they are the whole white population; in England, chiefly the middle class. But they are always a mass, that is to say, collective mediocrity. And what is still greater novelty, the mass do not now take their opinions from dignitaries in Church or State, from ostensible leaders, or from books. Their thinking is done for them by men much like themselves, addressing them or speaking in their name, on the spur of the moment, through the newspapers. I am not complaining of all this. I do not assert that anything better is compatible, as a general rule, with the present low state of the human mind. But that does not hinder the government of mediocrity from being mediocre government. No government by a democracy or a numerous aristocracy, either in its political acts or in the opinions, qualities, and tone of mind which it fosters, ever did or could rise above mediocrity, except in so far as the sovereign Many have let themselves be guided (which in their best times they always have done) by the counsels and influence of a more highly gifted and instructed One or Few. The initiation of all wise or noble things, comes and must come from individuals; generally at first from some one individual. The honor and glory of the average man is that he is capable of following that initiative; that he can respond internally to wise and noble things, and be led to them with his eyes open. I am not countenancing the sort of "hero-worship" which applauds the strong man of genius for forcibly seizing on the government of the world and making it do his bidding in spite of itself. All he can claim is, freedom to point out the way. The power of compelling others into it, is not only inconsistent with the freedom and development of all the rest, but corrupting to the strong man himself. It does seem, however, that when the opinions of masses of merely average men are everywhere become or becoming the dominant power, the counterpoise and corrective to that tendency would be, the more and more pronounced individuality of those who stand on the higher eminences of thought. It is in these circumstances most especially, that exceptional individuals, instead of being deterred, should be encouraged in acting differently from the mass. In other times there was no advantage in their doing so, unless they acted not only differently, but better. In this age the mere example of non-conformity, the mere refusal to bend the knee to custom, is itself a service. Precisely because the tyranny of opinion is such as to make eccentricity a reproach, it is desirable, in order to break through that tyranny, that people should be eccentric. Eccentricity has always abounded when and where strength of character has abounded; and the amount of eccentricity in a society has generally been proportional to the amount of genius, mental vigor, and moral courage which it contained. That so few now dare to be eccentric, marks the chief danger of the time. . . .

OF THE LIMITS TO THE AUTHORITY OF SOCIETY OVER THE INDIVIDUAL

WHAT, then, is the rightful limit to the sovereignty of the individual over himself? Where does the authority of society begin? How much of human life should be assigned to individuality, and how much to society?

Each will receive its proper share, if each has that which more particularly concerns it. To individuality should belong the part of life in which it is chiefly the individual that is interested; to society, the part which chiefly interests society.

Though society is not founded on a contract, and though no good purpose is answered by inventing a contract in order to deduce social obligations from it, everyone who receives the protection of society owes a return for the benefit, and the fact of living in society renders it indispensable that each should be bound to observe a certain line of conduct towards the rest. This conduct consists, first, in not injuring the interests of one another; or rather certain interests, which, either by express legal provision or by tacit understanding, ought to be considered as rights; and secondly, in each person's bearing his share (to be fixed on some equitable principle) of the labors and sacrifices incurred for defending the society or its members from injury and molestation. These conditions society is justified in enforcing, at all costs to those who endeavor to withhold fulfilment. Nor is this all that society may do. The acts of an individual may be hurtful to others, or wanting in due consideration for their welfare, without going the length of violating any of their constituted rights. The offender may then be justly punished by opinion, though not by law. As soon as any part of a person's conduct affects prejudicially the interests of others, society has jurisdiction over it, and the question whether the general welfare will or will not be promoted by interfering with it, becomes open to discussion. But there is no room for entertaining any such question when a person's conduct affects the interests of no persons besides himself, or needs not affect them unless they like (all the persons concerned being of full age, and the ordinary amount of understanding). In all such cases there should be perfect freedom, legal and social, to do the action and stand the consequences.

It would be a great misunderstanding of this doctrine, to suppose that it is one of selfish indifference, which pretends that human beings have no business with each other's conduct in life, and that they should not concern themselves about the well-doing or well-being of one another, unless their own interest is involved. Instead of any diminution, there is need of a great increase of disinterested exertion to promote the good of others. But disinterested benevolence can find other instruments to persuade people to their good, than whips and scourges, either of the literal or the metaphorical sort. I am the last person to undervalue the self-regarding virtues; they are only second in importance, if even second, to the social. It is equally the business of education to cultivate both. But even education works by conviction and persuasion as well as by compulsion, and it is by the former only that, when the period of education is past, the self-regarding virtues should be inculcated. Human beings owe to each other help to distinguish the better from the worse, and encouragement to choose the former and avoid the latter. They should be forever stimulating each other to increased exercise of their higher faculties, and increased direction of their feelings and aims towards wise instead of foolish, elevating instead of degrading, objects and contemplations. But neither one person, nor any number of persons, is warranted in saying to another human creature of ripe years, that he shall not do with his life for his own benefit what he chooses to do with it. He is the person most interested in his own well-being, the interest which any other person, except in cases of strong personal attachment, can have in it, is trifling, compared with that which he himself has; the interest which society has in him individually (except as to his conduct to others) is fractional, and altogether indirect: while, with respect to his own feelings and circumstances, the most ordinary man or woman has means of knowledge immeasurably surpassing those that can be possessed by any one else. The interference of society to overrule his judgment and purposes in what only regards himself, must be grounded on general presumptions; which may be altogether wrong, and even if right, are as likely as not to be misapplied to individual cases, by persons no better acquainted with the circumstances of such cases than those are who look at them merely from without. In this department, therefore, of human affairs, Individuality has its proper field of action. In the conduct of human beings towards one another, it is necessary that general rules should for the most part be observed, in order that people may know what they have to expect; but in each person's own concerns, his individual spontaneity is entitled to free exercise. Considerations to aid his judgment, exhortations to strengthen his will, may be offered to him, even obtruded on him, by others; but he, himself, is the final judge. All errors which he is likely to commit against advice and warning, are far outweighed by the evil of allowing others to constrain him to what they deem his good.

I do not mean that the feelings with which a person is regarded by others, ought not to be in any way affected by his self-regarding qualities or deficiencies. This is neither possible nor desirable. If he is eminent in any of the qualities which conduce to his own good, he is, so far, a proper object of admiration. He is so much the nearer to the ideal perfection of human nature. If he is grossly deficient in those qualities, a sentiment the opposite of admiration will follow. There is a degree of folly, and a degree of what may be called (though the phrase is not unobjectionable) lowness or depravation of taste, which, though it cannot justify doing harm to the person who manifests it, renders him necessarily and properly a subject of distaste, or, in extreme cases, even of contempt: a person could not have the opposite qualities in due strength without entertaining these feelings. Though doing no wrong to any one, a person may so act as to compel us to judge him, and feel to him, as a fool, or as a being of an inferior order: and since this judgment and feeling are a fact which he would prefer to avoid, it is doing him a service to warn him of it beforehand, as of any other disagreeable consequence to which he exposes himself. It would be well, indeed, if this good office were much more freely rendered than the common notions of politeness at present permit, and if one person could honestly point out to another that he thinks him in fault, without being considered unmannerly or presuming. We have a right, also, in various ways, to act upon our unfavorable opinion of any one, not to the oppression of his individuality, but in the exercise of ours. We are not bound, for example, to seek his society; we have a right to avoid it (though not to parade the avoidance), for we have a right to choose the society most acceptable to us. We have a right, and it may be our duty, to caution others against him, if we think his example or conversation likely to have a pernicious effect on those with whom he associates. We may give others a preference over him in optional good offices, except those which tend to his improvement. In these various modes a person may suffer very severe penalties at the hands of others, for faults which directly concern only himself; but he suffers these penalties only in so far as they are the natural, and, as it were, the spontaneous consequences of the faults themselves, not because they are purposely inflicted on him for the sake of punishment. A person who shows rashness, obstinacy, self-conceit—who cannot live within moderate means—who cannot restrain himself from hurtful indulgences—who pursues animal pleasures at the expense of those of feeling and intellect—must expect to be lowered in the opinion of others, and to have a less share of their favorable sentiments, but of this he has no right to complain, unless he has merited their favor by special excellence in his social relations, and has thus established a title to their good offices, which is not affected by his demerits towards himself.

What I contend for is, that the inconveniences which are strictly inseparable from the unfavorable judgment of others, are the only ones to which a person should ever be subjected for that portion of his conduct and character which concerns his own good, but which does not affect the interests of others in their relations with him. Acts injurious to others require a totally different treatment. Encroachment on their rights; infliction on them of any loss or damage not justified by his own rights; falsehood or duplicity in dealing with them; unfair or ungenerous use of advantages over them; even selfish abstinence from defending them against injury—these are fit objects of moral reprobation, and, in grave cases, of moral retribution and punishment. And not only these acts, but the dispositions which lead to them, are properly immoral, and fit subjects of disapprobation which may rise to abhorrence. Cruelty of disposition; malice and ill-nature; that most anti-social and odious of all passions, envy; dissimulation and insincerity, irascibility on insufficient cause, and resentment disproportioned to the provocation; the love of domineering over others; the desire to engross more than one's share of advantages; the pride which derives gratification from the abasement of others; the egotism which thinks self and its concerns more important than everything else, and decides all doubtful questions in his own favor;—these are moral vices, and constitute a bad and odious moral character: unlike the self-regarding faults previously mentioned, which are not properly immoralities, and to whatever pitch they may be carried, do not constitute wickedness. They may be proofs of any amount of folly, or want of personal dignity and self-respect; but they are only a subject of moral reprobation when they involve a breach of duty to others, for whose sake the individual is bound to have care for himself. What are called duties to ourselves are not socially obligatory, unless circumstances render them at the same time duties to others. The term duty to oneself, when it means anything more than prudence, means self-respect or self-development; and for none of these is any one accountable to his fellow-creatures, because for none of them is it for the good of mankind that he be held accountable to them.

The distinction between the loss of consideration which a person may rightly incur by defect of prudence or of personal dignity, and the reprobation which is due to him for an offence against the rights of others, is not a merely nominal distinction. It makes a vast difference both in our feelings and in our conduct towards him, whether he displeases us in things in which we think we have a right to control him, or in things in which we know that we have not. If he displeases us, we may express our distaste, and we may stand aloof from a person as well as from a thing that displeases us; but we shall not therefore feel called on to make his life uncomfortable. We shall reflect that he already bears, or will bear, the whole penalty of his error; if he spoils his life by mismanagement, we shall not, for that reason, desire to spoil it still further: instead of wishing to punish him, we shall rather endeavor to alleviate his punishment, by showing him how he may avoid or cure the evils his conduct tends to bring upon him. He may be to us an object of pity, perhaps of dislike, but not of anger or resentment; we shall not treat him like an enemy of society: the worst we shall think ourselves justified in doing is leaving him to himself, If we do not interfere benevolently by showing interest or concern for him. It is far otherwise if he has infringed the rules necessary for the protection of his fellow-creatures, individually or collectively. The evil consequences of his acts do not then fall on himself, but on others; and society, as the protector of all its members, must retaliate on him; must inflict pain on him for the express purpose of punishment, and must take care that it be sufficiently severe. In the one case, he is an offender at our bar, and we are called on not only to sit in judgment on him, but, in one shape or another, to execute our own sentence: in the other case, it is not our part to inflict any suffering on him, except what may incidentally follow from our using the same liberty in the regulation of our own affairs, which we allow to him in his.

The distinction here pointed out between the part of a person's life which concerns only himself, and that which concerns others, many persons will refuse to admit. How (it may be asked) can any part of the conduct of a member of society be a matter of indifference to the other members? No person is an entirely isolated being; it is impossible for a person to do anything seriously or permanently hurtful to himself, without mischief reaching at least to his near connections, and often far beyond them. If he injures his property, he does harm to those who directly or indirectly derived support from it, and usually diminishes, by a greater or less amount, the general resources of the community. If he deteriorates his bodily or mental faculties, he not only brings evil upon all who depended on him for any portion of their happiness, but disqualifies himself for rendering the services which he owes to his fellow-creatures generally; perhaps becomes a burden on their affection or benevolence; and if such conduct were very frequent, hardly any offence that is committed would detract more from the general sum of good. Finally, if by his vices or follies a person does no direct harm to others, he is nevertheless (it may be said) injurious by his example; and ought to be compelled to control himself, for the sake of those whom the sight or knowledge of his conduct might corrupt or mislead.

And even (it will be added) if the consequences of misconduct could be confined to the vicious or thoughtless individual, ought society to abandon to their own guidance those who are manifestly unfit for it? If protection against themselves is confessedly due to children and persons under age, is not society equally bound to afford it to persons of mature years who are equally incapable of self-government? If gambling, or drunkenness, or incontinence, or idleness, or uncleanliness, are as injurious to happiness, and as great a hindrance to improvement, as many or most of the acts prohibited by law, why (it may be asked) should not law, so far as is consistent with practicability and social convenience, endeavor to repress these also? And as a supplement to the unavoidable imperfections of law, ought not opinion at least to organize a powerful police against these vices, and visit rigidly with social penalties those who are known to practise them? There is no question here (it may be said) about restricting individuality, or impeding the trial of new and original experiments in living. The only things it is sought to prevent are things which have been tried and condemned from the beginning of the world until now; things which experience has shown not to be useful or suitable to any person's individuality. There must be some length of time and amount of experience, after which a moral or prudential truth may be regarded as established, and it is merely desired to prevent generation after generation from falling over the same precipice which has been fatal to their predecessors.

I fully admit that the mischief which a person does to himself, may seriously affect, both through their sympathies and their interests, those nearly connected with him, and in a minor degree, society at large. When, by conduct of this sort, a person is led to violate a distinct and assignable obligation to any other person or persons, the case is taken out of the self-regarding class, and becomes amenable to moral disapprobation in the proper sense of the term. If, for example, a man, through intemperance or extravagance, becomes unable to pay his debts, or, having undertaken the moral responsibility of a family, becomes from the same cause incapable of supporting or educating them, he is deservedly reprobated, and might be justly punished; but it is for the breach of duty to his family or creditors, not for the extravagance. If the resources which ought to have been devoted to them, had been diverted from them for the most prudent investment, the moral culpability would have been the same. George Barnwell murdered his uncle to get money for his mistress, but if he had done it to set himself up in business, he would equally have been hanged. Again, in the frequent case of a man who causes grief to his family by addiction to bad habits, he deserves reproach for his unkindness or ingratitude; but so he may for cultivating habits not in themselves vicious, if they are painful to those with whom he passes his life, or who from personal ties are dependent on him for their comfort. Whoever fails in the consideration generally due to the interests and feelings of others, not being compelled by some more imperative duty, or justified by allowable self-preference, is a subject of moral disapprobation for that failure, but not for the cause of it, nor for the errors, merely personal to himself, which may have remotely led to it. In like manner, when a person disables himself, by conduct purely self-regarding, from the performance of some definite duty incumbent on him to the public, he is guilty of a social offence. No person ought to be punished simply for being drunk; but a soldier or a policeman should be punished for being drunk on duty. Whenever, in short, there is a definite damage, or a definite risk of damage, either to an individual or to the public, the case is taken out of the province of liberty, and placed in that of morality or law.

But with regard to the merely contingent or, as it may be called, constructive injury which a person causes to society, by conduct which neither violates any specific duty to the public, nor occasions perceptible hurt to any assignable individual except himself; the inconvenience is one which society can afford to bear, for the sake of the greater good of human freedom. If grown persons are to be punished for not taking proper care of themselves, I would rather it were for their own sake, than under pretence of preventing them from impairing their capacity of rendering to society benefits which society does not pretend it has a right to exact. But I cannot consent to argue the point as if society had no means of bringing its weaker members up to its ordinary standard of rational conduct, except waiting till they do something irrational, and then punishing them, legally or morally, for it. Society has had absolute power over them during all the early portion of their existence: it has had the whole period of childhood and nonage in which to try whether it could make them capable of rational conduct in life. The existing generation is master both of the training and the entire circumstances of the generation to come; it cannot indeed make them perfectly wise and good, because it is itself so lamentably deficient in goodness and wisdom; and its best efforts are not always, in individual cases, its most successful ones; but it is perfectly well able to make the rising generation, as a whole, as good as, and a little better than, itself. If society lets any considerable number of its members grow up mere children, incapable of being acted on by rational consideration of distant motives, society has itself to blame for the consequences. . . .

But the strongest of all the arguments against the interference of the public with purely personal conduct, is that when it does interfere, the odds are that it interferes wrongly, and in the wrong place. On questions of social morality, of duty to others, the opinion of the public, that is, of an overruling majority, though often wrong, is likely to be still oftener right; because on such questions they are only required to judge of their own interests; of the manner in which some mode of conduct, if allowed to be practised, would affect themselves. But the opinion of a similar majority, imposed as a law on the minority, on questions of self-regarding conduct, is quite as likely to be wrong as right; for in these cases public opinion means, at the best, some people's opinion of what is good or bad for other people; while very often it does not even mean that; the public, with the most perfect indifference, passing over the pleasure or convenience of those whose conduct they censure, and considering only their own preference. There are many who consider as an injury to themselves any conduct which they have a distaste for, and resent it as an outrage to their feelings; as a religious bigot, when charged with disregarding the religious feelings of others, has been known to retort that they disregard his feelings, by persisting in their abominable worship or creed. But there is no parity between the feeling of a person for his own opinion, and the feeling of another who is offended at his holding it; no more than between the desire of a thief to take a purse, and the desire of the right owner to keep it. . . .

Gerald Dworkin

Paternalism

1972

I take as my starting point the "one very simple principle" proclaimed by Mill in *On Liberty* . . . "That principle is, that the sole end for which mankind are warranted, individually or collectively, in interfering with the liberty of action of any of their number, is self-protection. That the only purpose for which power can be rightfully exercised over any member of a civilized community, against his will, is to prevent harm to others. He cannot rightfully be compelled to do or forbear because it will be better for him to do so, because it will make him happier, because, in the opinion of others, to do so would be wise, or even right."[1]

This principle is neither "one" nor "very simple." It is at least two principles; one asserting that self-protection or the prevention of harm to others is sometimes a sufficient warrant and the other claiming that the individual's own good is *never* a sufficient warrant for the exercise of compulsion either by the society as a whole or by its individual members. I assume that no one with the possible exception of extreme pacifists or anarchists questions the correctness of the first half of the principle. This essay is an examination of the negative claim embodied in Mill's principle—the objection to paternalistic interferences with a man's liberty.

I

By paternalism I shall understand roughly the interference with a person's liberty of action justified by reasons referring exclusively to the welfare, good, happiness, needs, interests or values of the person being coerced. One is always well-advised to illustrate one's definitions by examples but it is not easy to find "pure" examples of paternalistic interferences. For almost any piece of legislation is justified by several different kinds of reasons and even if historically a piece of legislation can be shown to have been introduced for purely paternalistic motives, it may be that advocates of the legislation with an anti-paternalistic outlook can find sufficient reasons justifying the legislation without appealing to the reasons which were originally adduced to support it. Thus, for example, it may be that the original legislation requiring motorcyclists to wear safety helmets was introduced for purely paternalistic reasons. But the Rhode Island Supreme Court recently upheld such legislation on the grounds that it was "not persuaded that the legislature is powerless to prohibit individuals from pursuing a course of conduct which could conceivably result in their becoming public charges," thus clearly introducing reasons of a quite different kind. Now I regard this decision as being based on reasoning of a very dubious nature but it illustrates the kind of problem one has in finding examples. The following is a list of the kinds of interferences I have in mind as being paternalistic.

II

1. Laws requiring motorcyclists to wear safety helmets when operating their machines.
2. Laws forbidding persons from swimming at a public beach when lifeguards are not on duty.
3. Laws making suicide a criminal offense.

Gerald Dworkin, "Paternalism." *The Monist* 56 (1) (1972): 64–84. By permission of *The Monist*.

4. Laws making it illegal for women and children to work at certain types of jobs.
5. Laws regulating certain kinds of sexual conduct, e.g. homosexuality among consenting adults in private.
6. Laws regulating the use of certain drugs which may have harmful consequences to the user but do not lead to anti-social conduct.
7. Laws requiring a license to engage in certain professions with those not receiving a license subject to fine or jail sentence if they do engage in the practice.
8. Laws compelling people to spend a specified fraction of their income on the purchase of retirement annuities (Social Security).
9. Laws forbidding various forms of gambling (often justified on the grounds that the poor are more likely to throw away their money on such activities than the rich who can afford to).
10. Laws regulating the maximum rates of interest for loans.
11. Laws against duelling.

In addition to laws which attach criminal or civil penalties to certain kinds of action there are laws, rules, regulations, decrees, which make it either difficult or impossible for people to carry out their plans and which are also justified on paternalistic grounds. Examples of this are:

1. Laws regulating the types of contracts which will be upheld as valid by the courts, e.g. (an example of Mill's to which I shall return) no man may make a valid contract for perpetual involuntary servitude.
2. Not allowing as a defense to a charge of murder or assault the consent of the victim.
3. Requiring members of certain religious sects to have compulsory blood transfusions. This is made possible by not allowing the patient to have recourse to civil suits for assault and battery and by means of injunctions.
4. Civil commitment procedures when these are specifically justified on the basis of preventing the person being committed from harming himself. (The D.C. Hospitalization of the Mentally Ill Act provides for involuntary hospitalization of a person who "is mentally ill, and because of that illness, is likely to injure *himself* or others if allowed to remain at liberty." The term injure in this context applies to unintentional as well as intentional injuries.)
5. Putting fluorides in the community water supply.

All of my examples are of existing restrictions on the liberty of individuals. Obviously one can think of interferences which have not yet been imposed. Thus one might ban the sale of cigarettes, or require that people wear safety-belts in automobiles (as opposed to merely having them installed) enforcing this by not allowing motorists to sue for injuries even when caused by other drivers if the motorist was not wearing a seat-belt at the time of the accident.

I shall not be concerned with activities which though defended on paternalistic grounds are not interferences with the liberty of persons, e.g. the giving of subsidies in kind rather than in cash on the grounds that the recipients would not spend the money on the goods which they really need, or not including a $1000 deductible provision in a basic protection automobile insurance plan on the ground that the people who would elect it could least afford it. Nor shall I be concerned with measures such as "truth-in-advertising" acts and the Pure Food and Drug legislation which are often attacked as paternalistic but which should not be considered so. In these cases all that is provided—it is true by the use of compulsion—is information which it is presumed that rational persons are interested in having in order to make wise decisions. There is no interference with the liberty of the consumer unless one wants to stretch a point beyond good sense and say that his liberty to apply for a loan without knowing the true rate of interest is diminished. It is true that sometimes there is sentiment for going further than providing information, for example when laws against usurious interest are passed preventing those who might wish to contract loans at high rates of interest from doing so, and these measures may correctly be considered paternalistic.

III

Bearing these examples in mind let me return to a characterization of paternalism. I said earlier that I meant by the term, roughly, interference with a person's liberty for his own good. But as some of the examples show the class of persons whose good is involved is not always identical with the class of person's whose freedom is restricted. Thus in the case of professional licensing it is the practitioner who is directly interfered with and it is the would-be patient whose interests are presumably being served. Not allowing the consent of the victim to be a defense to certain types of crime primarily affects the would-be aggressor but it is the interests of the willing victim that we are trying to protect. Sometimes a person may fall into both classes as would be the case if we banned the manufacture and sale of cigarettes and a given manufacturer happened to be a smoker as well.

Thus we may first divide paternalistic interferences into "pure" and "impure" cases. In "pure" paternalism the class of persons whose freedom is restricted is identical with the class of persons whose benefit is intended to be promoted by such restrictions. Examples: the making of suicide a crime, requiring passengers in automobiles to wear seat-belts, requiring a Christian Scientist to receive a blood transfusion. In the case of "impure" paternalism in trying to protect the welfare of a class of persons we find that the only way to do so will involve restricting the freedom of other persons besides those who are benefitted. Now it might be thought that there are no cases of "impure" paternalism since any such case could always be justified on non-paternalistic grounds, i.e. in terms of preventing harms to others. Thus we might ban cigarette manufacturers from continuing to manufacture their product on the grounds that we are preventing them from causing illness to others in the same way that we prevent other manufacturers from releasing pollutants into the atmosphere, thereby causing danger to the members of the community. The difference is, however, that in the former but not the latter case the harm is of such a nature that it could be avoided by those individuals affected if they so chose. The incurring of the harm requires, so to speak, the active co-operation of the victim. It would be mistaken theoretically and hypocritical in practice to assert that our interference in such cases is just like our interference in standard cases of protecting others from harm. At the very least someone interfered with in this way can reply that no one is complaining about his activities. It may be that impure paternalism requires arguments or reasons of a stronger kind in order to be justified since there are persons who are losing a portion of their liberty and they do not even have the solace of having it be done "in their own interest." Of course in some sense, if paternalistic justifications are ever correct then we are protecting others, we are preventing some from injuring others, but it is important to see the differences between this and the standard case.

Paternalism then will always involve limitations on the liberty of some individuals in their own interest but it may also extend to interferences with the liberty of parties whose interests are not in question.

IV

Finally, by way of some more preliminary analysis, I want to distinguish paternalistic interferences with liberty from a related type with which it is often confused. Consider, for example, legislation which forbids employees to work more than, say, 40 hours per week. It is sometimes argued that such legislation is paternalistic for if employees desired such a restriction on their hours of work they could agree among themselves to impose it voluntarily. But because they do not the society imposes its own conception of their best interests upon them by the use of coercion. Hence this is paternalism.

Now it may be that some legislation of this nature is, in fact, paternalistically motivated. I am not denying that. All I want to point out is that there is another possible way of justifying such measures which is not paternalistic in nature. It is not paternalistic because as Mill puts it in a similar context such measures are "required not to overrule the judgment of individuals respecting their own interest, but to give effect to that judgment: they being unable to give effect to it except by concert, which concert again cannot be effectual unless it receives validity and sanction from the law."[2]

The line of reasoning here is a familiar one first found in Hobbes and developed with great sophistication by contemporary economists in the last decade or so. There are restrictions which are in the interests of a class of persons taken collectively but are such that the immediate interest of each individual is furthered by his violating the rule when others adhere to it. In such cases the individuals involved may need the use of compulsion to give effect to their collective judgment of their own interest by guaranteeing each individual compliance by the others. In these cases compulsion is not used to achieve some benefit which is not recognized to be a benefit by those concerned, but rather because it is the only feasible means of achieving some benefit which *is* recognized as such by all concerned. This way of viewing matters provides us with another characterization of paternalism in general. Paternalism might be thought of as the use of coercion to achieve a good which is not recognized as such by those persons for whom the good is intended. Again while this formulation captures the heart of the matter—it is surely what Mill is objecting to in *On Liberty*—the matter is not always quite like that. For example when we force motorcyclists to wear helmets we are trying to promote a good—the protection of the person from injury—which is surely recognized by most of the individuals concerned. It is not that a cyclist doesn't value his bodily integrity; rather, as a supporter of such legislation would put it, he either places, perhaps irrationally, another value or good (freedom from wearing a helmet) above that of physical well-being or, perhaps, while recognizing the danger in the abstract, he either does not fully appreciate it or he underestimates the likelihood of its occurring. But now we are approaching the question of possible justifications of paternalistic measures and the rest of this essay will be devoted to that question.

V

I shall begin for dialectical purposes by discussing Mill's objections to paternalism and then go on to discuss more positive proposals.

An initial feature that strikes one is the absolute nature of Mill's prohibitions against paternalism. It is so unlike the carefully qualified admonitions of Mill and his fellow Utilitarians on other moral issues. He speaks of self-protection as the *sole* end warranting coercion, of the individual's own goals as *never* being a sufficient warrant. Contrast this with his discussion of the prohibition against lying in *Util.*

> Yet that even this, rule, sacred as it is, admits of possible exception, is acknowledged by all moralists, the chief of which is where the with-holding of some fact . . . would save an individual . . . from great and unmerited evil.[3]

The same tentativeness is present when he deals with justice.

> It is confessedly unjust to break faith with any one: to violate an engagement, either express or implied, or disappoint expectations raised by our own conduct, at least if we have raised these expectations knowingly and voluntarily. Like all the other obligations of justice already spoken of, this one is not regarded as absolute, but as capable of being overruled by a stronger obligation of justice on the other side.[4]

This anomaly calls for some explanation. The structure of Mill's argument is as follows:

1. Since restraint is an evil the burden of proof is on those who propose such restraint.
2. Since the conduct which is being considered is purely self-regarding, the normal appeal to the protection of the interests of others is not available.
3. Therefore we have to consider whether reasons involving reference to the individual's own good, happiness, welfare, or interests are sufficient to overcome the burden of justification.
4. We either cannot advance the interests of the individual by compulsion, or the attempt to do so involves evil which outweigh the good done.

5. Hence the promotion of the individual's own interests does not provide a sufficient warrant for the use of compulsion.

Clearly the operative premise here is (4) and it is bolstered by claims about the status of the individual as judge and appraiser of his welfare, interests, needs, etc.

> With respect to his own feelings and circumstances, the most ordinary man or woman has means of knowledge immeasurably surpassing those that can be possessed by any one else.[5]

> He is the man most interested in his own well-being: the interest which any other person, except in cases of strong personal attachment, can have in it, is trifling, compared to that which he himself has.[6]

These claims are used to support the following generalizations concerning the utility of compulsion for paternalistic purposes.

> The interferences of society to overrule his judgment and purposes in what only regards himself must be grounded on general presumptions; which may be altogether wrong, and even if right, are as likely as not to be misapplied to individual cases.[7]

> But the strongest of all the arguments against the interference of the public with purely personal conduct is that when it does interfere, the odds are that it interferes wrongly and in the wrong place.[8]

> All errors which the individual is likely to commit against advice and warning are far outweighed by the evil of allowing others to constrain him to what they deem his good.[9]

Performing the utilitarian calculation by balancing the advantages and disadvantages we find that:

> Mankind are greater gainers by suffering each other to live as seems good to themselves, than by compelling each other to live as seems good to the rest.[10]

From which follows the operative premise (4).

This classical case of a utilitarian argument with all the premises spelled out is not the only line of reasoning present in Mill's discussion. There are asides, and more than asides, which look quite different and I shall deal with them later. But this is clearly the main channel of Mill's thought and it is one which has been subjected to vigorous attack from the moment it appeared—most often by fellow Utilitarians. The link that they have usually seized on is, as Fitzjames Stephen put it, the absence of proof that the "mass of adults are so well acquainted with their own interests and so much disposed to pursue them that no compulsion or restraint put upon them by any others for the purpose of promoting their interest can really promote them."[11] Even so sympathetic a critic as Hart is forced to the conclusion that:

> In Chapter 5 of his essay Mill carried his protests against paternalism to lengths that may now appear to us as fantastic. . . . No doubt if we no longer sympathise with this criticism this is due, in part, to a general decline in the belief that individuals know their own interest best.[12]

> Mill endows the average individual with "too much of the psychology of a middle-aged man whose desires are relatively fixed, not liable to be artificially stimulated by external influences; who knows what he wants and what gives him satisfaction of happiness; and who pursues these things when he can."[13]

Now it is interesting to note that Mill himself was aware of some of the limitations on the doctrine that the individual is the best judge of his own interests. In his discussion of government intervention in general (even where the intervention does not interfere with liberty but provides alternative institutions to those of the market) after making claims which are parallel to those just discussed, e.g.

> People understand their own business and their own interests better, and care for them more, than the government does, or can be expected to do.[14]

He goes on to an intelligent discussion of the "very large and conspicuous exceptions" to the maxim that:

> Most persons take a juster and more intelligent view of their own interest, and of the means of promoting it than can either be prescribed to them by a general enactment of the legislature, or pointed out in the particular case by a public functionary.[15]

Thus there are things

> of which the utility does not consist in ministering to inclinations, nor in serving the daily uses of life, and the want of which is least felt where the need is greatest.

This is peculiarly true of those things which are chiefly useful as tending to raise the character of human beings. The uncultivated cannot be competent judges of cultivation. Those who most need to be made wiser and better, usually desire it least, and, if they desired it, would be incapable of finding the way to it by their own lights.

. . . A second exception to the doctrine that individuals are the best judges of their own interest, is when an individual attempts to decide irrevocably now what will be best for his interest at some future and distant time. The presumption in favor of individual judgment is only legitimate, where the judgment is grounded on actual, and especially on present, personal experience; not where it is formed antecedently to experience, and not suffered to be reversed even after experience has condemned it.[16]

The upshot of these exceptions is that Mill does not declare that there should never be government interference with the economy but rather that

in every instance, the burden of making out a strong case should be thrown not on those who resist but on those who recommend government interference. Letting alone, in short, should be the general practice: every departure from it, unless required by some great good, is a certain evil.[17]

In short, we get a presumption not an absolute prohibition. The question is why doesn't the argument against paternalism go the same way?

I suggest that the answer lies in seeing that in addition to a purely utilitarian argument Mill uses another as well. As a Utilitarian Mill has to show, in Fitzjames Stephen's words, that:

Self-protection apart, no good object can be attained by any compulsion which is not in itself a greater evil than the absence of the object which the compulsion obtains.[18]

To show this is impossible; one reason being that it isn't true. Preventing a man from selling himself into slavery (a paternalistic measure which Mill himself accepts as legitimate), or from taking heroin, or from driving a car without wearing seat-belts may constitute a lesser evil than allowing him to do any of these things. A consistent Utilitarian can only argue against paternalism on the grounds that it (as a matter of fact) does not maximize the good. It is always a contingent question that may be refuted by the evidence. But there is also a non-contingent argument which runs through *On Liberty.* When Mill states that "there is a part of the life of every person who has come to years of discretion, within which the individuality of that person ought to reign uncontrolled either by any other person or by the public collectively" he is saying something about what it means to be a person, an autonomous agent. It is because coercing a person for his own good denies this status as an independent entity that Mill objects to it so strongly and in such absolute terms. To be able to choose is a good that is independent of the wisdom of what is chosen. A man's "mode of laying out his existence is the best, not because it is the best in itself, but because it is his own mode."[19]

It is the privilege and proper condition of a human being, arrived at the maturity of his faculties, to use and interpret experience in his own way.[20]

As further evidence of this line of reasoning in Mill consider the one exception to his prohibition against paternalism.

In this and most civilised countries, for example, an engagement by which a person should sell himself, or allow himself to be sold, as a slave, would be null and void; neither enforced by law nor by opinion. The ground for thus limiting his power of voluntarily disposing of his own lot in life, is apparent, and is very clearly seen in this extreme case. The reason for not interfering, unless for the sake of others, with a person's voluntary acts, is consideration for his liberty. His voluntary choice is evidence that what he so chooses is desirable, or at least endurable, to him, and his good is on the whole best provided for by allowing him to take his own means of pursuing it. But by selling himself for a slave, he abdicates his liberty; he foregoes any future use of it beyond that single act.

He therefore defeats, in his own case, the very purpose which is the justification of allowing him to dispose of himself. He is no longer free; but is thenceforth in a position which has no longer the presumption in its favour, that would be afforded by his voluntarily remaining in it. The principle of freedom cannot require that he should be free not to be free. It is not freedom to be allowed to alienate his freedom.[21]

Now leaving aside the fudging on the meaning of freedom in the last line it is clear that part of this argument is incorrect. While it is true that *future* choices of the slave are not reasons for thinking that what he chooses then is desirable for him, what is at issue is limiting his immediate choice; and since this choice is made freely, the individual may be correct in thinking that his interests are best provided for by entering such a contract. But the main consideration for not allowing such a contract is the need to preserve the liberty of the person to make future choices. This gives us a principle—a very narrow one—by which to justify some paternalistic interferences. Paternalism is justified only to preserve a wider range of freedom for the individual in question. How far this principle could be extended, whether it can justify all the cases in which we are inclined upon reflection to think paternalistic measures justified remains to be discussed. What I have tried to show so far is that there are two strains of argument in Mill—one a straight-forward Utilitarian mode of reasoning and one which relies not on the goods which free choice leads to but on the absolute value of the choice itself. The first cannot establish any absolute prohibition but at most a presumption and indeed a fairly weak one given some fairly plausible assumptions about human psychology; the second while a stronger line of argument seems to me to allow on its own grounds a wider range of paternalism then might be suspected. I turn now to a consideration of these matters.

VI

We might begin looking for principles governing the acceptable use of paternalistic power in cases where it is generally agreed that it is legitimate. Even Mill intends his principles to be applicable only to mature individuals, not those in what he calls "non-age." What is it that justifies us in interfering with children? The fact that they lack some of the emotional and cognitive capacities required in order to make fully rational decisions. It is an empirical question to just what extent children have an adequate conception of their own present and future interests but there is not much doubt that there are many deficiencies. For example it is very difficult for a child to defer gratification for any considerable period of time. Given these deficiencies and given the very real and permanent dangers that may befall the child it becomes not only permissible but even a duty of the parent to restrict the child's freedom in various ways. There is however an important moral limitation on the exercise of such parental power which is provided by the notion of the child eventually coming to see the correctness of his parent's interventions. Parental paternalism may be thought of as a wager by the parent on the child's subsequent recognition of the wisdom of the restrictions. There is an emphasis on what could be called future-oriented consent—on what the child will come to welcome, rather than on what he does welcome.

The essence of this idea has been incorporated by idealist philosophers into various types of "real-will" theory as applied to fully adult persons. Extensions of paternalism are argued for by claiming that in various respects, chronologically mature individuals share the same deficiencies in knowledge, capacity to think rationally, and the ability to carry out decisions that children possess. Hence in interfering with such people we are in effect doing what they would do if they were fully rational. Hence we are not really opposing their will, hence we are not really interfering with their freedom. The dangers of this move have been sufficiently exposed by Berlin in his *Two Concepts of Liberty*. I see no gain in theoretical clarity nor in practical advantage in trying to pass over the real nature of the interferences with liberty that we impose on others. Still the basic notion of consent is important and seems to me the only acceptable way of trying to delimit an area of justified paternalism.

Let me start by considering a case where the consent is not hypothetical in nature. Under certain conditions it is rational for an individual to agree that others should force him to act in ways in which, at the time of action, the individual may not see as desirable. If, for example, a man knows that he is subject to breaking his resolves when temptation is present, he may ask a friend to refuse to entertain his requests at some later stage.

A classical example is given in the Odyssey when Odysseus commands his men to tie him to the mast and refuse all future orders to be set free, because he knows the power of the Sirens to enchant men with their songs. Here we are on relatively sound ground in later refusing Odysseus' request to be set free. He may even claim to have changed his mind but since it is just such changes that he wished to guard against we are entitled to ignore them.

A process analogous to this may take place on a social rather than individual basis. An electorate may mandate its representatives to pass legislation which when it comes time to "pay the price" may be unpalatable. I may believe that a tax increase is necessary to halt inflation though I may resent the lower pay check each month. However in both this case and that of Odysseus the measure to be enforced is specifically requested by the party involved and at some point in time there is genuine consent and agreement on the part of those persons whose liberty is infringed. Such is not the case for the paternalistic measures we have been speaking about. What must be involved here is not consent to specific measures but rather consent to a system of government, run by elected representatives, with an understanding that they may act to safeguard our interests in certain limited ways.

I suggest that since we are all aware of our irrational propensities, deficiencies in cognitive and emotional capacities and avoidable and unavoidable ignorance it is rational and prudent for us to in effect take out "social insurance policies." We may argue for and against proposed paternalistic measures in terms of what fully rational individuals would accept as forms of protection. Now, clearly since the initial agreement is not about specific measures we are dealing with a more-or-less blank check and therefore there have to be carefully defined limits. What I am looking for are certain kinds of conditions which make it plausible to suppose that rational men could reach agreement to limit their liberty even when other men's interests are not affected.

Of course as in any kind of agreement schema there are great difficulties in deciding what rational individuals would or would not accept. Particularly in sensitive areas of personal liberty, there is always a danger of the dispute over agreement and rationality being a disguised version of evaluative and normative disagreement.

Let me suggest types of situations in which it seems plausible to suppose that fully rational individuals would agree to having paternalistic restrictions imposed upon them. It is reasonable to suppose that there are "goods" such as health which any person would want to have in order to pursue his own good—no matter how that good is conceived. This is an argument that is used in connection with compulsory education for children but it seems to me that it can be extended to other goods which have this character. Then one could agree that the attainment of such goods should be promoted even when not recognized to be such, at the moment, by the individuals concerned.

An immediate difficulty that arises stems from the fact that men are always faced with competing goods and that there may be reasons why even a value such as health—or indeed life—may be overridden by competing values. Thus the problem with the Christian Scientist and blood transfusions. It may be more important for him to reject "impure substances" than to go on living. The difficult problem that must be faced is whether one can give sense to the notion of a person irrationally attaching weights to competing values.

Consider a person who knows the statistical data on the probability of being injured when not wearing seat belts in an automobile and knows the types and gravity of the various injuries. He also insists that the inconvenience attached to fastening the belt every time he gets in and out of the car outweighs for him the possible risks to himself. I am inclined in this case to think that such a weighing is irrational. Given his life-plans which we are assuming are those of the average person, his interests and commitments already undertaken, I think it is safe to predict that we can find inconsistencies in his calculations at some point. I am assuming that this is not a man who for some conscious or unconscious reasons is trying to injure himself nor is he a man who just likes to "live dangerously." I am assuming that he is like us in all the relevant respects but just puts an enormously high negative value on inconvenience—one which does not seem comprehensible or reasonable.

It is always possible, of course to assimilate this person to creatures like myself. I, also, neglect to fasten my seat belt and I concede such behavior is not rational but not because I weigh the inconvenience differently from those who fasten the belts. It is just that having made (roughly) the same calculation as everybody else I ignore it in my actions. [Note: a much better case of weakness of the will than those usually given in ethics texts.] A plausible explanation for this deplorable habit is that although I know in some intellectual sense what the probabilities and risks are I do not fully appreciate them in an emotionally genuine manner.

We have two distinct types of situation in which a man acts in a non-rational fashion. In one case he attaches incorrect weights to some of his values; in the other he neglects to act in accordance with his actual preferences and desires. Clearly there is a stronger and more persuasive argument for paternalism in the latter situation. Here we are really not—by assumption—imposing a good on another person. But why may we not extend our interference to what we might call evaluative delusions? After all in the case of cognitive delusions we are prepared, often, to act against the expressed will of the person involved. If a man believes that when he jumps out the window he will float upwards—Robert Nozick's example—would not we detain him, forcibly if necessary? The reply will be that this man doesn't wish to be injured and if we could convince him that he is mistaken as to the consequences of his action he would not wish to perform the action. But part of what is involved in claiming that a man who doesn't fasten his seat-belts is attaching an irrational weight to the inconvenience of fastening them is that if he were to be involved in an accident and severely injured he would look back and admit that the inconvenience wasn't as bad as all that. So there is a sense in which if I could convince him of the consequences of his action he also would not wish to continue his present course of action. Now the notion of consequences being used here is covering a lot of ground. In one case it's being used to indicate what will or can happen as a result of a course of action and in the other it's making a prediction about the future evaluation of the consequences—in the first sense—of a course of action. And whatever the difference between facts and values—whether it be hard and fast or soft and slow—we are genuinely more reluctant to consent to interferences where evaluative differences are the issue. Let me now consider another factor which comes into play in some of these situations which may make an important difference in our willingness to consent to paternalistic restrictions.

Some of the decisions we make are of such a character that they produce changes which are in one or another way irreversible. Situations are created in which it is difficult or impossible to return to anything like the initial stage at which the decision was made. In particular some of these changes will make it impossible to continue to make reasoned choices in the future. I am thinking specifically of decisions which involve taking drugs that are physically or psychologically addictive and those which are destructive of one's mental and physical capacities.

I suggest we think of the imposition of paternalistic interferences in situations of this kind as being a kind of insurance policy which we take out against making decisions which are far-reaching, potentially dangerous and irreversible. Each of these factors is important. Clearly there are many decisions we make that are relatively irreversible. In deciding to learn to play chess I could predict in view of my general interest in games that some portion of my free-time was going to be pre-empted and that it would not be easy to give up the game once I acquired a certain competence. But my whole life-style was not going to be jeopardized in an extreme manner. Further it might be argued that even with addictive drugs such as heroin one's normal life plans would not be seriously interfered with if an inexpensive and adequate supply were readily available. So this type of argument might have a much narrower scope than appears to be the case at first.

A second class of cases concerns decisions which are made under extreme psychological and sociological pressures. I am not thinking here of the making of the decision as being something one is pressured into—e.g. a good reason for making duelling illegal is that unless this is done many people might have to manifest their courage and integrity in ways in which they would rather not do so—but rather of decisions such as that to commit suicide which are usually made at a point where the individual is not thinking clearly and calmly about the nature of his decision. In addition, of course, this comes under the previous heading of all-too-irrevocable decision. Now there are practical steps which a society could take if it wanted to decrease the possibility of suicide—for example not paying social security benefits to the survivors or as religious institutions do, not allowing such persons to be buried with the same status as natural deaths. I think we may count these as interferences with the liberty of persons to attempt suicide and the question is whether they are justifiable.

Using my argument schema the question is whether rational individuals would consent to such limitations. I see no reason for them to consent to an absolute prohibition but I do think it is reasonable for them to agree to some kind of enforced waiting period. Since we are all aware of the possibility of temporary states, such as great fear or depression, that are inimical to the making of well-informed and rational decisions, it would be prudent for all of us if there were some kind of institutional arrangement whereby we were restrained from making a decision which is (all too) irreversible. What this would be like in practice is difficult to envisage and it may be that if no practical arrangements were feasible then we would have to conclude that there should be no restriction at all on this kind of action. But we might have a "cooling off" period, in much the same way that we now require couples who file for divorce to go through a waiting period. Or, more far-fetched, we might imagine a Suicide Board composed of a psychologist and another member picked by the applicant. The Board would be required to meet and talk with the person proposing to take his life, though its approval would not be required.

A third class of decisions—these classes are not supposed to be disjoint—involves dangers which are either not sufficiently understood or appreciated correctly by the persons involved. Let me illustrate, using the example of cigarette smoking, a number of possible cases.

1. A man may not know the facts—e.g. smoking between 1 and 2 packs a day shortens life expectancy 6.2 years, the costs and pain of the illness caused by smoking, etc.
2. A man may know the facts, wish to stop smoking, but not have the requisite will-power.
3. A man may know the facts but not have them play the correct role in his calculation because, say, he discounts the danger psychologically because it is remote in time and/or inflates the attractiveness of other consequences of his decision which he regards as beneficial.

In case 1 what is called for is education, the posting of warnings, etc. In case 2 there is no theoretical problem. We are not imposing a good on someone who rejects it. We are simply using coercion to enable people to carry out their own goals. (Note: There obviously is a difficulty in that only a subclass of the individuals affected wish to be prevented from doing what they are doing.) In case 3 there is a sense in which we are imposing a good on someone since given his current appraisal of the facts he doesn't wish to be restricted. But in another sense we are not imposing a good since what is being claimed—and what must be shown or at least argued for—is that an accurate accounting on his part would lead him to reject his current course of action. Now we all know that such cases exist, that we are prone to disregard dangers that are only possibilities, that immediate pleasures are often magnified and distorted.

If in addition the dangers are severe and far-reaching we could agree to allowing the state a certain degree of power to intervene in such situations. The difficulty is in specifying in advance, even vaguely, the class of cases in which intervention will be legitimate.

A related difficulty is that of drawing a line so that it is not the case that all ultra-hazardous activities are ruled out, e.g. mountain-climbing, bull-fighting, sports-car racing, etc. There are some risks—even very great ones—which a person is entitled to take with his life.

A good deal depends on the nature of the deprivation—e.g. does it prevent the person from engaging in the activity completely or merely limit his participation—and how important to the nature of the activity is the absence of restriction when this is weighed against the role that the activity plays in the life of the person. In the case of automobile seat belts, for example, the restriction is trivial in nature, interferes not at all with the use or enjoyment of the activity, and does, I am assuming, considerably reduce a high risk of serious injury. Whereas, for example, making mountain climbing illegal prevents completely a person engaging in an activity which may play an important role in his life and his conception of the person he is.

In general the easiest cases to handle are those which can be argued about in the terms which Mill thought to be so important—a concern not just for the happiness or welfare, in some broad sense, of the individual but rather a concern for the autonomy and freedom of the person. I suggest that we would be most likely to consent to paternalism in those instances in which it preserves and enhances for the individual his ability to rationally consider and carry out his own decisions.

I have suggested in this essay a number of types of situations in which it seems plausible that rational men would agree to granting the legislative powers of a society the right to impose restrictions on what Mill calls "self-regarding" conduct. However, rational men knowing something about the resources of ignorance, ill-will and stupidity available to the lawmakers of a society—a good case in point is the history of drug legislation in the United States—will be concerned to limit such intervention to a minimum. I suggest in closing two principles designed to achieve this end.

In all cases of paternalistic legislation there must be a heavy and clear burden of proof placed on the authorities to demonstrate the exact nature of the harmful effects (or beneficial consequences) to be avoided (or achieved) and the probability of their occurrence. The burden of proof here is twofold—what lawyers distinguish as the burden of going forward and the burden of persuasion. That the authorities have the burden of going forward means that it is up to them to raise the question and bring forward evidence of the evils to be avoided. Unlike the case of new drugs where the manufacturer must produce some evidence that the drug has been tested and found not harmful, no citizen has to show with respect to self-regarding conduct that it is not harmful or promotes his best interests. In addition the nature and cogency of the evidence for the harmfulness of the course of action must be set at a high level. To paraphrase a formulation of the burden of proof for criminal proceedings—better 10 men ruin themselves than one man be unjustly deprived of liberty.

Finally I suggest a principle of the least restrictive alternative. If there is an alternative way of accomplishing the desired end without restricting liberty then although it may involve great expense, inconvenience, etc. the society must adopt it.

NOTES

1. J. S. Mill, *Utilitarianism* and *On Liberty* (Fontana Library Edition, ed. by Mary Warnock, London, 1962), p. 135. All further quotes from Mill are from this edition unless otherwise noted.
2. J. S. Mill, *Principles of Political Economy* (New York: P. F. Collier and Sons, 1900), p. 442.
3. Mill, *Utilitarianism* and *On Liberty,* p. 174.
4. *Ibid.,* p. 299.
5. *Ibid.,* p. 207.
6. *Ibid.,* p. 206.
7. *Ibid.,* p. 207.
8. *Ibid.,* p. 214.
9. *Ibid.,* p. 207.
10. *Ibid.,* p. 138.
11. J. F. Stephens, *Liberty, Equality, Fraternity* (New York: Henry Holt & Co., n.d.), p. 24.
12. H. L. A. Hart, *Law, Liberty and Morality* (Stanford: Stanford University Press, 1963), p. 32.
13. *Ibid.,* p. 33.
14. Mill, *Principles,* II, 448.
15. *Ibid.,* II, 458.
16. *Ibid.,* II, 459.
17. *Ibid.,* II, 451.
18. Stephen, p. 49.
19. Mill, *Utilitarianism* and *On Liberty,* p. 197.
20. *Ibid.,* p. 186.
21. *Ibid.,* pp. 235–236.

Richard Thaler and Cass Sunstein

Libertarian Paternalism Is Not an Oxymoron

2003

INTRODUCTION

Consider two studies of savings behavior:

- Hoping to increase savings by workers, several employers have adopted a simple strategy. Instead of asking workers to elect to participate in a 401(k) plan, workers will be assumed to want to participate in such a plan, and hence they will be enrolled automatically unless they specifically choose otherwise. This simple change in the default rule has produced dramatic increases in enrollment.[1]
- Rather than changing the default rule, some employers have provided their employees with a novel option: *Allocate a portion of future wage increases to savings.* Employees who choose this plan are free to opt out at any time. A large number of employees have agreed to try the plan, and only a few have opted out. The result has been significant increases in savings rates.[2]

Libertarians embrace freedom of choice, and so they deplore paternalism.[3] Paternalists are thought to be skeptical of unfettered freedom of choice and to deplore libertarianism.[4] According to the conventional wisdom, libertarians cannot possibly embrace paternalism, and paternalists abhor libertarianism. The idea of libertarian paternalism seems to be a contradiction in terms.

Generalizing from the two studies just described, we intend to unsettle the conventional wisdom here. We propose a form of paternalism, libertarian in spirit, that should be acceptable to those who are firmly committed to freedom of choice on grounds of either autonomy or welfare.[5] Indeed, we urge that libertarian paternalism provides a basis for both understanding and rethinking a number of areas of contemporary law, including those aspects that deal with worker welfare, consumer protection, and the family.[6] In the process of defending these claims, we intend to make some objections to widely held beliefs about both freedom of choice and paternalism.[7] Our emphasis is on the fact that in many domains, people lack clear, stable, or well-ordered preferences. What they choose is strongly influenced by details of the context in which they make their choice, for example default rules, framing effects (that is, the wording of possible options), and starting points. These contextual influences render the very meaning of the term "preferences" unclear.

Consider the question whether to undergo a risky medical procedure. When people are told, "Of those who undergo this procedure, 90 percent are still alive after five years," they are far more likely to agree to the procedure than when they are told, "Of those who undergo this procedure, 10 percent are dead after five years."[8] What, then, are the patient's "preferences" with respect to this procedure? Repeated experiences with such problems might be expected to eliminate this framing effect, but doctors too are vulnerable to it.[9] Or return to the question of savings for retirement. It is now clear that if an employer requires employees to make an affirmative election in favor of savings, with the default rule devoting 100 percent of wages to current income, the level of savings will be far lower than if the employer adopts an automatic enrollment program from which employees are

Richard Thaler and Cass Sunstein, "Libertarian Paternalism Is Not an Oxymoron." *University of Chicago Law Review* 70 (4) (2003): 1195–1202. By permission of University of Chicago.

freely permitted to opt out.[10] Can workers then be said to have well-defined preferences about how much to save? This simple example can be extended to many situations involving the behavior of workers and consumers.

As the savings problem illustrates, the design features of both legal and organizational rules have surprisingly powerful influences on people's choices. We urge that such rules should be chosen with the explicit goal of improving the welfare of the people affected by them. The libertarian aspect of our strategies lies in the straightforward insistence that, in general, people should be free to opt out of specified arrangements if they choose to do so. To borrow a phrase, libertarian paternalists urge that people should be "free to choose."[11] Hence we do not aim to defend any approach that blocks individual choices.

The paternalistic aspect consists in the claim that it is legitimate for private and public institutions to attempt to influence people's behavior even when third-party effects are absent. In other words, we argue for self-conscious efforts, by private and public institutions, to steer people's choices in directions that will improve the choosers' own welfare. In our understanding, a policy therefore counts as "paternalistic" if it attempts to influence the choices of affected parties in a way that will make choosers better off.[12] Drawing on some well-established findings in behavioral economics and cognitive psychology, we emphasize the possibility that in some cases individuals make inferior decisions in terms of their own welfare—decisions that they would change if they had complete information, unlimited cognitive abilities, and no lack of self-control.[13] In addition, the notion of libertarian paternalism can be complemented by that of libertarian benevolence, by which plan design features such as default rules, framing effects, and starting points are enlisted in the interest of vulnerable third parties. We shall devote some discussion to this possibility.

Libertarian paternalism is a relatively weak and nonintrusive type of paternalism, because choices are not blocked or fenced off. In its most cautious forms, libertarian paternalism imposes trivial costs on those who seek to depart from the planner's preferred option. But the approach we recommend nonetheless counts as paternalistic, because private and public planners[14] are not trying to track people's anticipated choices, but are self-consciously attempting to move people in welfare-promoting directions. Some libertarians are likely to have little or no trouble with our endorsement of paternalism for private institutions; their chief objection is to paternalistic law and government. But as we shall show, the same points that support welfare-promoting private paternalism apply to government as well. It follows that one of our principal targets is the dogmatic anti-paternalism of numerous analysts of law, including many economists and economically oriented lawyers.[15] We believe that this dogmatism is based on a combination of a false assumption and two misconceptions.[16]

The false assumption is that almost all people, almost all of the time, make choices that are in their best interest or at the very least are better, by their own lights, than the choices that would be made by third parties. This claim is either tautological, and therefore uninteresting, or testable. We claim that it is testable and false, indeed obviously false. In fact, we do not think that anyone believes it on reflection. Suppose that a chess novice were to play against an experienced player. Predictably the novice would lose precisely because he made inferior choices—choices that could easily be improved by some helpful hints. More generally, how well people choose is an empirical question, one whose answer is likely to vary across domains.[17] As a first approximation, it seems reasonable to say that people make better choices in contexts in which they have experience and good information (say, choosing ice cream flavors) than in contexts in which they are inexperienced and poorly informed (say, choosing among medical treatments or investment options). So long as people are not choosing perfectly, it is at least possible that some policy could make them better off by improving their decisions.

The first misconception is that there are viable alternatives to paternalism, In many situations, some organization or agent *must* make a choice that will affect the behavior of some other people. There is, in those situations, no alternative to a kind of paternalism—at least in the form of an intervention that affects what people choose. We are emphasizing, then, the possibility that people's preferences, in certain domains and across a certain range, are influenced by the choices made by planners.[18] The point applies to both private and public actors, and hence to those who design legal rules as well as to those who serve consumers. As a simple example, consider the cafeteria at some organization. The cafeteria must make a multitude of decisions, including which foods to serve, which ingredients to use, and in what order to arrange the choices. Suppose that the director of the cafeteria notices that customers have a tendency to choose more of the items that are presented earlier in the line. How should the director decide in what order to present the items? To simplify, consider some alternative strategies that the director might adopt in deciding which items to place early in the line:

1. She could make choices that she thinks would make the customers best off, all things considered.
2. She could make choices at random.
3. She could choose those items that she thinks would make the customers as obese as possible.
4. She could give customers what she thinks they would choose on their own.

Option 1 appears to be paternalistic, but would anyone advocate options 2 or 3? Option 4 is what many anti-paternalists would favor, but it is much harder to implement than it might seem. Across a certain domain of possibilities, consumers will often lack well-formed preferences, in the sense of preferences that are firmly held and preexist the director's own choices about how to order the relevant items. If the arrangement of the alternatives has a significant effect on the selections the customers make, then their true "preferences" do not formally exist.

Of course, market pressures will impose a discipline on the self-interested choices of those cafeteria directors who face competition. To that extent, those directors must indeed provide people with options they are willing to buy. A cafeteria that faces competition and offers healthy but terrible-tasting food is unlikely to do well. Market-oriented libertarians might urge that the cafeteria should attempt to maximize profits, selecting menus in a way that will increase net revenues. But profit maximization is not the appropriate goal for cafeterias granted a degree of monopoly power—for example, those in schools, dormitories, or some companies. Furthermore, even those cafeterias that face competition will find that some of the time, market success will come not from tracking people's ex ante preferences, but from providing goods and services that turn out, in practice, to promote their welfare, all things considered. Consumers might be surprised by what they end up liking; indeed, their preferences might change as a result of consumption.[19] And in some cases, the discipline imposed by market pressures will nonetheless allow the director a great deal of room to maneuver, because people's preferences are not well-formed across the relevant domains.

While some libertarians will happily accept this point for private institutions, they will object to government efforts to influence choice in the name of welfare. Skepticism about government might be based on the fact that governments are disciplined less or perhaps not at all by market pressures. Or such skepticism might be based on the fear that parochial interests will drive government planners in their own preferred directions (the public choice problem).[20] We agree that for government, the risks of mistake and overreaching are real and sometimes serious. But governments, no less than cafeterias (which governments frequently run), have to provide starting points of one or another kind; this is not avoidable. As we shall emphasize, they do so every day through the rules of contract and tort, in a way that inevitably affects some preferences and choices.[21] In this respect, the anti-paternalist position is unhelpful—a literal nonstarter.

The second misconception is that paternalism always involves coercion. As the cafeteria example illustrates, the choice of the order in which to present food items does not coerce anyone to do anything, yet one might prefer some orders to others on grounds that are paternalistic in the sense that we use the term. Would anyone object to putting the fruit and salad before the desserts at an elementary school cafeteria if the result were to increase the consumption ratio of apples to Twinkies? Is this question fundamentally different if the customers are adults? Since no coercion is involved, we think that some types of paternalism should be acceptable to even the most ardent libertarian. In the important domain of savings behavior, we shall offer a number of illustrations. To those anti-libertarians who are suspicious of freedom of choice and would prefer to embrace welfare instead, we urge that it is often possible for paternalistic planners to make common cause with their libertarian adversaries by adopting policies that promise to promote welfare but that also make room for freedom of choice. To confident planners, we suggest that the risks of confused or ill-motivated plans are reduced if people are given the opportunity to reject the planner's preferred solutions.

The thrust of our argument is that the term "paternalistic" should not be considered pejorative, just descriptive. Once it is understood that some organizational decisions are inevitable, that a form of paternalism cannot be avoided, and that the alternatives to paternalism (such as choosing options to make people worse off) are unattractive, we can abandon the less interesting question of whether to be paternalistic or not, and turn to the more constructive question of how to choose among the possible choice-influencing options. To this end we make two general suggestions. First, programs should be designed using a type of welfare analysis, one in which a serious attempt is made to measure the costs and benefits of outcomes (rather than relying on estimates of willingness to pay). Choosers should be given more choices if the welfare benefits exceed the welfare costs. Second, some results from the psychology of decision-making should be used to provide ex ante guidelines to support reasonable judgments about when consumers and workers will gain most by increasing options. We argue that those who are generally inclined to oppose paternalism should consider these suggestions uncontroversial.

The remainder of this reading is organized as follows. In Part I, we briefly support the claim that people's choices might not promote their own welfare. We suggest that because of the likely effects of default rules, framing effects, and starting points on choices and preferences, paternalism, at least in a weak sense, is impossible to avoid. To be sure, planners can try to avoid paternalism by requiring people to make active choices, but sometimes people will resist any such requirement (which is along one dimension paternalistic too, simply because people sometimes do not want to choose).[22] Part III investigates how a libertarian paternalist might select among the major options, including minimal paternalism, required active choices, procedural constraints, and substantive constraints. We identify a set of questions that must be answered in order to know whether people's welfare is likely to be promoted or undermined by a large option set. Part V explores objections.

I. THE RATIONALITY OF CHOICES

The presumption that individual choices should be respected is usually based on the claim that people do an excellent job of making choices, or at least that they do a far better job than third parties could possibly do.[23] As far as we can tell, there is little empirical support for this claim, at least if it is offered in this general form. Consider the issue of obesity. Rates of obesity in the United States are now approaching 20 percent, and over 60 percent of Americans are considered either obese or overweight.[24] There is overwhelming evidence that obesity causes serious health risks, frequently leading to premature death.[25] It is quite fantastic to suggest that everyone is choosing the optimal diet, or a diet that is preferable to what might be produced with third-party guidance. Of course, rational people care about the taste of food, not simply about health, and we do not claim that everyone who is overweight is necessarily failing to act rationally. It is the strong claim that all or almost all Americans are choosing their diet *optimally* that we reject as untenable. What is true for diets is true as well for much other risk-related behavior, including smoking and drinking, which produce over 500,000 premature deaths each year.[26] In these circumstances, people's choices cannot reasonably be thought, in all domains, to be the best means of promoting their well-being. Indeed, many smokers, drinkers, and overeaters are willing to pay for third parties to help them choose better consumption sets.

On a more scientific level, research by psychologists and economists over the past three decades has raised questions about the rationality of many judgments and decisions that individuals make. People fail to make forecasts that are consistent with Bayes's rule,[27] use heuristics that can lead them to make systematic blunders,[28] exhibit preference reversals (that is, they prefer A to B *and* B to A),[29] suffer from problems of self-control,[30] and make different choices depending on the framing of the problem.[31] It is possible to raise questions about some of these findings and to think that people may do a better job of choosing in the real world than they do in the laboratory.[32] But studies of actual choices reveal many of the same problems, even when the stakes are high.[33]

We do not intend to outline all of the relevant evidence here, but consider an illustration from the domain of savings behavior. Benartzi and Thaler have investigated how much investors like the portfolios they have selected in their defined contribution savings plans.[34] Employees volunteered to share their portfolio choices with the investigators by bringing a copy of their most recent statement to the lab. They were then shown the probability distributions of expected retirement income for three investment portfolios simply labeled A, B, and C. Unbeknownst to the subjects, the three portfolios were their own and portfolios mimicking the average and median choices of their fellow employees. The distributions of expected returns were computed using the software of Financial Engines, the financial information company founded by William Sharpe. On average, the subjects rated the average portfolio equally with their own portfolio, and judged the median portfolio to be significantly more attractive than their own.[35] Indeed, only 20 percent of the subjects preferred their own portfolio to the median portfolio.[36] Apparently, people do not gain much, by their own lights, from choosing investment portfolios for themselves.

Or consider people's willingness to take precautions. In general, the decision to buy insurance for natural disasters is a product not of a systematic inquiry into either costs or benefits, but of recent events.[37] If floods have not occurred in the immediate past, people who live on flood plains are far less likely to purchase insurance.[38] In the aftermath of an earthquake, the level of insurance coverage for earthquakes rises sharply—but it declines steadily from that point, as vivid memories recede.[39] Findings of this kind do not establish that people's choices are usually bad or that third parties can usually do better. But they do show that some of the time, people do not choose optimally even when the stakes are high.

It is true that people sometimes respond to their own bounded rationality by, for example, hiring agents or delegating decisions to others.[40] It is also true that learning frequently enables people to overcome their own limitations. But many of the most important decisions (for example, buying a home or choosing a spouse) are made infrequently and typically without the aid of impartial experts. The possibilities of delegation and learning are insufficient to ensure that people's choices always promote their welfare or that they always choose better than third parties would.

In any event, our emphasis here is not on blocking choices, but on strategies that move people in welfare-promoting directions while also allowing freedom of choice. Evidence of bounded rationality and problems of self-control is sufficient to suggest that such strategies are worth exploring. Of course many people value freedom of choice as an end in itself, but they should not object to approaches that preserve that freedom while also promising to improve people's lives.[41]

III. HOW TO CHOOSE: THE TOOLBOX OF THE LIBERTARIAN PATERNALIST

How should sensible planners choose among possible systems, given that some choice is necessary? We suggest two approaches to this problem. If feasible, a comparison of possible rules should be done using a form of cost-benefit analysis, one that pays serious attention to welfare effects. In many cases, however, such analyses will be both difficult and expensive. As an alternative, we offer some rules of thumb that might be adopted to choose among various options. In general, it makes sense to experiment with possible approaches to identify their results for both choices and outcomes. We have emphasized automatic enrollment plans and Save More Tomorrow because studies have suggested that both of these have a great deal of potential. In other domains, plans are likely to be proposed in the face of highly imperfect information; more data will reveal a great deal. Large-scale programs are most justified if repeated experiments have shown that they actually work.

A. Costs and Benefits

The goal of a cost-benefit study would be to measure the full ramifications of any design choice. In the context at hand, the cost-benefit study cannot be based on willingness to pay (WTP), because WTP will be a function of the default rule.[42] It must be a more open-ended (and inevitably somewhat subjective) assessment of the welfare consequences. To illustrate, take the example of automatic enrollment. Under automatic enrollment, some employees, who otherwise would not join the plan, will now do so. Presumably, some are made better off (especially if there is an employer match), but some may be made worse off (for example, those who are highly liquidity-constrained and do not exercise their right to opt out). A cost-benefit analysis would attempt to evaluate these gains and losses.

If the issue were only enrollment, we think it highly likely that the gains would exceed the losses. Because of the right to opt out, those who need the money immediately are able to have it. In principle one could also compare the costs of foregone current consumption and the benefits of increased consumption during retirement, though this is, admittedly, difficult to do in practice. It is also possible to make inferences from actual choices about welfare. For example, most employees do join the plan eventually, and very few drop out if automatically enrolled.[43] These facts suggest that, at least on average, defaulting people into the plan will mostly hasten the rate at which people join the plan, and that the vast majority of those who are so nudged will be grateful.

Some readers might think that our reliance on behavior as an indication of welfare is inconsistent with one of the central claims of this Article—that choices do not necessarily coincide with welfare. But in fact, there is no inconsistency. Compare rules calling for mandatory cooling-off periods. The premise of such rules is that people are more likely to make good choices when they have had time to think carefully and without a salesperson present. Similarly, it is reasonable to think that if, on reflection, workers realized that they had been "tricked" into saving too much, they might take the effort to opt out. The fact that very few participants choose to opt out supports (though it does not prove) the claim that they are helped by a system that makes joining easy.

Once the other effects of automatic enrollment are included, the analysis becomes cloudier. Any plan for automatic enrollment must include a specified default savings rate. Some of those automatically enrolled at a 3 percent savings rate—a typical default in automatic enrollment—would have chosen a higher rate if left to their own devices.[44] If automatic enrollment leads some or many people to save at a lower rate than they would choose, the plan might be objectionable for that reason. Hence we are less confident that this more complete cost-benefit analysis would support the particular opt-out system, though a higher savings rate might well do so. A more sophisticated plan, avoiding some of these pitfalls, is discussed below.

Similar tradeoffs are involved with another important issue: the appropriate default rule for organ donations. In many nations—Austria, Belgium, Denmark, Finland, France, Italy, Luxembourg, Norway, Singapore, Slovenia, and Spain—people are presumed to consent to allow their organs to be used, after death, for the benefit of others; but they are permitted to rebut the presumption, usually through an explicit notation to that effect on their drivers' licenses.[45] In the United States, by contrast, those who want their organs to be available for others must affirmatively say so, also through an explicit notation on their drivers' licenses. The result is that in "presumed consent" nations over 90 percent of people consent to make their organs available for donation, whereas in the United States, where people have to take some action to make their organs available, only 28 percent elect to do so.[46] We hypothesize that this dramatic difference is not a product of deep cultural differences, but of the massive effect of the default rule. Hence we would predict that a European-style opt-out rule in the United States would produce donation rates similar to those observed in the European countries that use this rule. Note in this regard that by one report, over 85 percent of Americans support organ donation—a statistic that suggests opt-outs would be relatively rare.[47]

A recent study strongly supports this prediction.[48] Suggesting that preferences are constructed by social frames, Johnson and Goldstein urge that with respect to organ donation, people lack stable preferences and that their decisions are very much influenced by the default rule.[49] A controlled online experiment showed a substantial effect from the default rule: The opt-in system created a 42 percent consent rate, about half of the 82 percent rate for an opt-out system.[50] The real-world evidence is even more dramatic. Presumed consent nations show consent rates ranging from a low of 85.9 percent (Sweden) to a high of 100 percent (Austria), with a median of 99 percent.[51] The default also produces a significant, though less dramatic, increase in actual donations, meaning that many people are saved as a result of the presumed consent system.[52] There is reason to believe that in the United States, a switch in the default rule could save thousands of lives.

The default rules for organ donation do not fit the usual definition of paternalism. The issue is the welfare of third parties, not of choosers. Here we are speaking not of libertarian paternalism, but of libertarian benevolence: an approach that attempts to promote benevolence, and to assist vulnerable people, without mandating behavior in any way. We suggest that changes in default rules, or a system of Give More Tomorrow, could produce large increases in public assistance—and that such approaches could do so in a way that avoids coercion. With respect to behavior, the analysis of libertarian benevolence is quite similar to that of libertarian paternalism. One of the advantages of that analysis is the demonstration that when third-party interests are at stake, the default rule will matter a great deal. It follows that planners can often deliver significant benefits to third parties simply by switching the default rule. In the case of organ donation, this is what we observe.

Does one or another default rule promote welfare? At first glance, the opt-out rule common in Europe seems better, simply because it should save a large number of lives without compromising any other important value. The most that can be said against the opt-out rule is that through inertia, perceived social pressure, or confusion, some people might end up donating their organs when they would not, all things considered, prefer to do so ex ante. (Their ex post preferences are difficult to infer!) If this objection (or some other[53]) seems forceful, an alternative would be to require active choices—for example, to mandate, at the time of applying for a driver's license, that applicants indicate whether they want to allow their organs to be used for the benefit of others. We make only two claims about this example. First, the evaluative question turns in large part on empirical issues of the sort that it would be both possible and useful to investigate. Second, the opt-in approach is unlikely to be best.[54]

B. Rules of Thumb

In many cases, the planner will be unable to make a direct inquiry into welfare, either because too little information is available or because the costs of conducting the analysis are not warranted. The committed anti-paternalist might say, in such cases, that people should simply be permitted to choose as they see fit. We hope that we have said enough to show why this response is unhelpful. What people choose often depends on the starting point, and hence the starting point cannot be selected by asking what people choose. In these circumstances, the libertarian paternalist would seek indirect proxies for welfare—methods that test whether one or another approach promotes welfare without relying on guesswork about that question. We suggest three possible methods.

First, the libertarian paternalist might select the approach *that the majority would choose if explicit choices were required and revealed.* In the context of contract law, this is the most familiar inquiry in the selection of default rules[55]—provisions that govern contractual arrangements in the absence of express decisions by the parties. Useful though it is, this market-mimicking approach raises its own problems. Perhaps the majority's choices would be insufficiently informed, or a reflection of bounded rationality or bounded self-control. Perhaps those choices would not, in fact, promote the majority's welfare. At least as a presumption, however, it makes sense to follow those choices if the planner knows what they would be. A deeper problem is that the majority's choices might themselves be a function of the starting point or the default rule. If so, the problem of circularity dooms the market-mimicking approach. But in some cases, at least, the majority might go one way or the other regardless of the starting point; and to that extent, the market-mimicking strategy is workable. Note that in the cafeteria example, some options would not fit with the majority's ex ante choices (healthy but terrible-tasting food, for example), and that for savings, some allocations would certainly violate the choices of ordinary workers (say, an allocation of 30 percent or more to savings). In fact a clear understanding of majority choices might well support a default rule that respects those choices even if the planner thinks that an inquiry into welfare would support another rule. At the very least, planners should be required to have real confidence in their judgment if they seek to do something other than what a suitably informed majority would find to be in its interest.

Second, the libertarian paternalist might select the approach that we have called required active choices, one *that would force people to make their choices explicit*. This approach might be chosen if the market-mimicking strategy fails, either because of the circularity problem or because the planner does not know which approach would in fact be chosen by the majority. We have seen the possibility of requiring active choices in the context of retirement plans and organ donations; it would be easy to multiply examples. In the law of contract, courts sometimes choose "penalty defaults"—default rules that penalize the party in the best position to obtain a clear statement on the question at hand, and hence create an incentive for clarity for the person who is in the best position to produce clarity.[56] Libertarian paternalists might go along the same track; in fact penalty defaults can be seen as a form of libertarian paternalism.

Here too, however, there is a risk that the choices that are actually elicited will be inadequately informed or will not promote welfare. In the case of retirement plans, for example, forced choices have been found to produce higher participation rates than requiring opt-ins, but lower rates than requiring opt-outs.[57] If it is likely that automatic enrollment promotes people's welfare, perhaps automatic enrollment should be preferred over requiring active choices. The only suggestion is that where social planners are unsure how to handle the welfare question, they might devise a strategy that requires people to choose.

Third, the libertarian paternalist might select the approach *that minimizes the number of opt-outs*. Suppose, for example, that when drivers are presumed to want to donate their organs to others, only 10 percent opt out, but that when drivers are required to signal their willingness to donate their organs to others, 30 percent opt in. This is an ex post inquiry into people's preferences, in contrast to the ex ante approach favored by the market-mimicking strategy. With those numbers, there is reason to think that the presumption in favor of organ donation is better, if only because more people are sufficiently satisfied to leave it in place.

V. OBJECTIONS

The argument for libertarian paternalism seems compelling to us, even obvious, but we suspect that hard-line anti-paternalists, and possibly others, will have objections. We respond to three possible objections here.

The first objection is that by advocating libertarian paternalism, we are starting down a very slippery slope. Once one grants the possibility that default rules for savings or cafeteria lines should be designed paternalistically, it might seem impossible to resist highly non-libertarian interventions. Critics might envisage an onslaught of what seem, to them, to be unacceptably intrusive forms of paternalism, from requiring motorcycle riders to wear helmets, to mandatory waiting periods before consumer purchases, to bans on cigarette smoking, to intrusive health care reforms of many imaginable kinds. In the face of the risk of overreaching, might it not be better to avoid starting down the slope at all?

There are three responses. First, in many cases there is simply no viable alternative to paternalism in the weak sense, and hence planners are forced to take at least a few tiny steps down that slope. Recall that paternalism, in the form of effects on behavior, is frequently inevitable. In such cases, the slope cannot be avoided. Second, the libertarian condition, requiring opt-out rights, sharply limits the steepness of the slope. So long as paternalistic interventions can be easily avoided by those who seek to adopt a course of their own, the risks emphasized by anti-paternalists are minimal. Third, those who make the slippery slope argument are acknowledging the existence of a self-control problem, at least for planners. But if planners, including bureaucrats and human resource managers, suffer from self-control problems, then it is highly likely that other people do too.[58]

A second and different sort of objection is based on a deep mistrust of the ability of the planner (especially the planner working for the government) to make sensible choices. Even those who normally believe that everyone chooses rationally treat with deep skepticism any proposal that seems to hinge on rational choices by bureaucrats. Part of the skepticism is based on a belief that bureaucrats lack the discipline imposed by market pressures; part of it is rooted in the fact that individuals have the welfare-promoting incentives that are thought to come from self-interest; part of it is rooted in the fear that well-organized private groups will move bureaucrats in their preferred directions. We happily grant that planners are human, and thus are both boundedly rational and subject to the influence of objectionable pressures.[59] Nevertheless, as we have stressed, these human planners are sometimes forced to make choices, and it is surely better to have them trying to improve people's welfare rather than the opposite. In emphasizing the important effect of plan design on choice (a point underappreciated by economists, lawyers, and planners), we hope to encourage plan designers to become more informed. And by arguing for a libertarian check on bad plans, we hope to create a strong safeguard against ill-considered or ill-motivated plans. To the extent that individual self-interest is a healthy check on planners, freedom of choice is an important corrective.

A third objection would come from the opposite direction. Enthusiastic paternalists, emboldened by evidence of bounded rationality and self-control problems, might urge that in many domains, the instruction to engage in only libertarian paternalism is too limiting. At least if the focus is entirely or mostly on welfare, it might seem clear that in certain circumstances, people should not be given freedom of choice for the simple reason that they will choose poorly. In those circumstances, why should anyone insist on libertarian paternalism, as opposed to unqualified or non-libertarian paternalism?

This objection raises complex issues of both value and fact, and we do not intend to venture into difficult philosophical territory here.[60] Our basic response is threefold. First, we reiterate our understanding that planners are human, and so the real comparison is between boundedly rational choosers with self-control problems and boundedly rational planners facing self-control problems of their own.[61] It is doubtful that the comparison can sensibly be made in the abstract. Second, an opt-out right operates as a safeguard against confused or improperly motivated planners, and in many contexts, that safeguard is crucial even if it potentially creates harm as well. Third, nothing we have said denies the possibility that in some circumstances it can be advisable to impose significant costs on those who reject the proposed course of action, or even to deny freedom of choice altogether. Our only qualification is that when third-party effects are not present, the general presumption should be in favor of freedom of choice, and that presumption should be rebutted only when individual choice is demonstrably inconsistent with individual welfare.[62]

CONCLUSION

Our goal here has been to describe and to advocate libertarian paternalism—an approach that preserves freedom of choice but that encourages both private and public institutions to steer people in directions that will promote their own welfare. Some kind of paternalism is likely whenever such institutions set out default plans or options. Our central empirical claim has been that in many domains, people's preferences are labile and ill-formed, and hence starting points and default rules are likely to be quite sticky. In these circumstances, the goal should be to avoid random, inadvertent, arbitrary, or harmful effects and to produce a situation that is likely to promote people's welfare, suitably defined. Indeed, many current social outcomes are, we believe, both random and inadvertent, in the sense that they are a product of default rules whose behavior-shaping effects have never been a product of serious reflection.

When the direct welfare inquiry is too hard to handle, libertarian paternalists have a range of alternatives. They might, for example, select an approach that would be sought by the majority, that requires or promotes explicit choices, or that minimizes opt-outs. We have also identified the factors that make it most sensible to increase the range of options, in an effort to show that the relationship between choice and welfare presents tractable empirical questions, and should not be resolved by dogmas, a priori arguments, and definitions.

In our view, libertarian paternalism is not only a conceptual possibility; it also provides a foundation for rethinking many areas of private and public law. We believe that policies rooted in libertarian paternalism will often be a big improvement on the most likely alternative: inept neglect.

NOTES

1. See James J. Choi, et al, *Defined Contribution Pensions: Plan Rules, Participant Choices, and the Path of Least Resistance,* in James M. Poterba, ed, 16 *Tax Policy and the Economy* 67, 70 (MIT 2002); Brigitte C. Madrian and Dennis F. Shea, *The Power of Suggestion: Inertia in 401(k) Participation and Savings Behavior,* 116 Q J Econ 1149, 1149–50 (2001).

2. See Richard H. Thaler and Shlomo Benartzi, *Save More Tomorrow: Using Behavioral Economics to Increase Employee Saving,* J Polit Econ (forthcoming), online at http://gsbwww.uchicago.edu/fac/richard.thaler/research/SMarT14.pdf (visited May 10, 2003).

3. See, for example, David Boaz, *Libertarianism: A Primer* 16–19 (Free Press 1997).

4. See, for example, Robert E. Goodin, *Permissible Paternalism: In Defense of the Nanny State,* 1 Responsive Community 42, 44 (Summer 1991) (justifying traditional paternalism on the grounds that "public officials might better respect your own preferences than you would have done through your own actions").

5. A very brief companion essay, intended for an economic audience and not dealing with law, investigates some of the issues explored here. See Richard H. Thaler and Cass R. Sunstein. *Libertarian Paternalism,* 93 Am Econ Rev 175 (May 2003).

6. Our defense of libertarian paternalism is closely related to the arguments for "asymmetric paternalism," illuminatingly discussed in Colin Camerer, et al, *Regulation for Conservatives: Behavioral Economics and the Case for "Asymmetric Paternalism,"* 151 U Pa L Rev 1211 (2003). Camerer, et al, urge that governments should consider a weak form of paternalism—a form that attempts to help those who make mistakes, while imposing minimal costs on those who are fully rational. Id at 1212. Our Article, written in parallel, has similar motivations, though libertarian paternalism may or may not be asymmetric in the sense identified by Camerer and his coauthors.

7. See, for example, Dennis F. Thompson, *Political Ethics and Public Office* 154–55 (Harvard 1987), which lists three criteria for justified paternalism: impaired judgment, temporary and reversible intervention, and prevention of serious and irreversible harm. We think that this account points in many sensible directions, but it neglects the inevitable effects of default rules, framing effects, and starting points on choices.

8. See Donald A. Redelmeier, Paul Rozin, and Daniel Kahneman, *Understanding Patients' Decisions: Cognitive and Emotional Perspectives,* 270 JAMA 72, 73 (1993).

9. See id ("The framing effect was just as large with physicians as with lay people.").

10. See note 1 and accompanying text.

11. See Milton Friedman and Rose Friedman, *Free to Choose: A Personal Statement* (Harcourt Brace Jovanovich 1980). To be sure, it would be possible to imagine a more robust understanding of libertarianism, one that attempts to

minimize influences on free choice, or to maximize unfettered liberty of choice. We suggest below that influences on freedom of choice are often impossible to avoid. We also offer reasons to believe that more choices are not always better than fewer. A policy of requiring active choices, we shall show, does promote a form of choice, but it has problems of its own. We hope not to have any real quarrels with libertarians here, simply because our approach allows people to opt out of any specified arrangements.

12. For a similar definition, see Donald VanDeVeer. *Paternalistic Intervention: The Moral Bounds on Benevolence* 22 (Princeton 1986).

13. Bounded rationality and bounded self-control are described in Christine Jolts, Cass R. Sunstein, and Richard Thaler. *A Behavioral Approach to Law and Economics,* 50 Stan L Rev 1471, 1477–79 (1998).

14. When we use the word "planner" in this Article, we mean anyone who faces the job of designing institutional features such as rules, procedures, information packages, and the like. A large firm will typically have many employees who are serving as "planners" in this sense, from the human resources manager who chooses the set of health insurance options to the CEO who decides whether to pay the match in the 401(k) plan in shares of company stock. For most of our examples, planners are not government officials, though the arguments apply to this class of planners as well.

15. See, for example, Richard A. Epstein, *In Defense of the Contract at Will,* 51 U Chi L Rev 947 (1984).

16. For a complaint similar to ours, see Ted O'Donoghue and Matthew Rabin, *Studying Optimal Paternalism, Illustrated by a Model of Sin Taxes,* 93 Am Econ Rev 186 (May 2003):

> [B]y explicitly addressing when and how people do and do not pursue their own best interests, economists will be better able to contribute to policy debates. To contribute to debates over regulating private financial decisions, we must study whether financial decisions are based on fallacious statistical reasoning and whether self-control problems lead people to borrow too heavily; to contribute to debates over teenage smoking, we must study whether teenagers become smokers against their long-run best interest. Economists will and should be ignored if we continue to insist that it is axiomatic that constantly trading stocks or accumulating consumer debt or becoming a heroin addict must be optimal for the people doing these things merely because they have chosen to do it.

17. In some areas, of course, it will be difficult to reach uncontroversial conclusions on the basis of empirical study alone, because contested judgments of value are in the background. Do people choose well if they choose to marry young, or do they choose better if they cohabit for a long time before marrying? Do young, unmarried women choose well if they choose abortion? Empirical issues are highly relevant here, but they will hardly resolve all social disputes on these questions. We are not attempting to say anything controversial about welfare, or to take sides in reasonable disputes about how to understand that term. For discussion of these normative issues, see Amartya Sen, *Development as Freedom* 74–76 (Knopf 1999) (maintaining that welfare should be seen in terms of the substantive freedoms of people to choose a life that they have reason to value); Daniel Kahneman, Ed Diener, and Norbert Schwarz, *Preface,* in Daniel Kahneman, Ed Diener, and Norbert Schwarz, eds, *Well-Being: The Foundations of Hedonic Psychology* ix, xi–xii (Russell Sage 1999) (urging a view of human welfare that extends beyond traditional economic indicators to include "desirable goods such as love, mental challenge, and stress").

18. For claims to this effect, see Russell Korobkin, *The Status Quo Bias and Contract Default Rules,* 83 Cornell L Rev 608, 675 (1998) (asserting that "the preference exogeneity assumption, implicit in all law-and-economics theories of efficient contract default rule selection, is probably false"); Cass R. Sunstein, *Endogenous Preferences, Environmental Law,* 22 J Leg Stud 217, 224 (1993) (arguing that the demand for environmental regulation is affected by the initial allocation of rights by government planners). Important qualifications come from Robert C. Ellickson, *Order without Law: How Neighbors Settle Disputes* (Harvard 1991) (discussing settings in which people organize their affairs without reference to law). But even with those qualifications, there is no objection to libertarian paternalism; in the contexts explored by Ellickson, the default rule is irrelevant, not harmful.

19. See generally Gary S. Becker, *Accounting for Tastes* (Harvard 1996).

20. For a classic illustration, see Bruce A. Ackerman and William T. Hassler, *Clean Coal/Dirty Air: Or How the Clean Air Act Became a Multibillion-Dollar Bail-Out for High-Sulfur Coal Producers and What Should Be Done about It* (Yale 1981).

21. See Korobkin, 83 Cornell L Rev at 611 (cited in note 18) (suggesting that "when lawmakers anoint a contract term the default, the substantive preferences of contracting parties shift—that term becomes more desirable, and other competing terms becom[e] less desirable").

22. We've omitted Parts II and IV of the reading.

23. It is usually, but not always, based on this claim. Some of the standard arguments against paternalism rest

not on consequences but on autonomy—on a belief that people are entitled to make their own choices even if they err. Thus John Stuart Mill, *On Liberty* (1859), reprinted in *Utilitarianism, On Liberty, Considerations on Representative Government* 69 (Dent 1972) (H.B. Acton, ed), is a mix of autonomy-based and consequentialist claims. Our principal concern here is with welfare and consequences, though as we suggest below, freedom of choice is sometimes an ingredient in welfare. We do not disagree with the view that autonomy has claims of its own, but we believe that it would be fanatical, in the settings that we discuss, to treat autonomy, in the form of freedom of choice, as a kind of trump not to be overridden on consequentialist grounds. In any case, the autonomy argument is undermined by the fact, discussed in Part I, that sometimes preferences and choices are a function of given arrangements. Most importantly, we think that respect for autonomy is adequately accommodated by the libertarian aspect of libertarian paternalism, as discussed below.

We note as well that the complex relationship among preferences, choices, and autonomy is a large theme in the liberal tradition. See Don Herzog, *Happy Slaves: A Critique of Consent Theory* 229 (Chicago 1989) (challenging consent theory on the ground that some individuals may not really be capable of choice, or that the preexisting social roles people occupy do not provide them with real choice); Jon Elster, *Sour Grapes: Studies in the Subversion of Rationality* 109 (Cambridge 1983) (discussing adaptation of preferences to existing opportunities). Sometimes it is emphasized that preferences and choices are a product of unjust background conditions, jeopardizing autonomy, and that when choices are a product of background injustice, respect for those choices may not promote autonomy. See Amartya Sen, *Commodities and Capabilities* (North-Holland 1985). Our discussion does not engage these issues, but there is a clear connection between such arguments and claims about "adaptive preferences," see Elster, *Sour Grapes* at 109–10, and our emphasis on status quo bias and the endowment effect in Part II.C.

24. See Centers for Disease Control. This represents a 61 percent increase in obesity between 1991 and 2000; 38.8 million Americans qualify as obese. See id. See also Ali H. Mokdad, et al, *The Continuing Epidemics of Obesity and Diabetes in the United States,* 286 JAMA 1195 (2001).

25. See, for example, Eugenia E. Calle, et al, *Body-Mass Index and Mortality in a Prospective Cohort of U.S. Adults,* 341 New Eng J Med 1097 (1999) (discussing increased risk of death from all causes among the obese). See also National Institute of Diabetes & Digestive & Kidney Diseases, *Understanding Adult Obesity,* NIH Pub No 01-3680 (Oct 2001),

26. See Cass R. Sunstein, *Risk and Reason: Safety, Law, and the Environment* 8–9 (Cambridge 2002), relying on J. Michael McGinnis and William H. Foege, *Actual Causes of Death in the United States,* 270 JAMA 2207 (1993). For an interesting discussion, see Jonathan Gruber, *Smoking's 'Internalities,'* 25 Regulation 52, 54–55 (Winter 2002/2003) (finding a disconnect between smokers' short-term desire for self-gratification and their long-term desire for good health, and suggesting that cigarette taxation can help smokers exercise the self-control needed to act on behalf of their long-term interests).

27. See David M. Grether, *Bayes Rule as a Descriptive Model: The Representativeness Heuristic,* 95 Q J Econ 537 (1980). Bayes's rule explains how to change existing beliefs as to the probability of a particular hypothesis in the light of new evidence. See Jonathan Baron, *Thinking and Deciding* 109–15 (Cambridge 3d ed 2000) (giving a mathematical explanation and examples of the rule's application).

28. See, for example, Daniel Kahneman and Shane Frederick, *Representativeness Revisited: Attribute Substitution in Intuitive Judgment,* in Thomas Gilovich, Dale Griffin, and Daniel Kahneman, eds, *Heuristics and Biases: The Psychology of Intuitive Judgment* 49, 53 (Cambridge 2002); Amos Tversky and Daniel Kahneman, *Judgment under Uncertainty: Heuristics and Biases,* 185 Science 1124 (1974); Amos Tversky and Daniel Kahneman, *Availability: A Heuristic for Judging Frequency and Probability,* 5 Cognitive Psych 207 (1973).

29. See Richard H. Thaler, *The Winner's Curse: Paradoxes and Anomalies of Economic Life* 79–91 (Free Press 1992). In the legal context, see Cass R. Sunstein, et al. *Predictably Incoherent Judgments,* 54 Stan L Rev 1153 (2002).

30. See Shane Frederick, George Loewenstein, and Ted O'Donoghue, *Time Discounting and Time Preference: A Critical Review,* 40 J Econ Lit 351, 367–68 (2002).

31. See Colin F. Camerer, *Prospect Theory in the Wild: Evidence from the Field,* in Daniel Kahneman and Amos Tversky, eds, *Choices, Values, and Frames* 288, 294–95 (Cambridge 2000); Eric J. Johnson, et al, *Framing, Probability Distortions, and Insurance Decisions,* in id at 224, 238.

Note also the emerging literature on people's inability to predict their own emotional reactions to events, a literature that might well bear on the uses of libertarian paternalism. See Timothy D. Wilson and Daniel T. Gilbert,

Affective Forecasting, 35 Advances in Experimental Soc Psych 345 (2003).

32. For some evidence in favor of consumer sovereignty, see Joel Waldfogel, *Does Consumer Irrationality Trump Consumer Sovereignty?: Evidence from Gifts and Own Purchases* (Feb 2003), online at http://papers.ssrn.com/abstractid=337261 (visited May 10, 2003). Waldfogel finds that people value their own purchases more highly than they value gifts from third parties—a finding that, in his view, provides support for the idea that consumers are the best judges of what goods will promote their welfare. We do not doubt the finding. Note, however, that Waldfogel is studying the context of ordinary consumer purchases, in which people are in an especially good position to know what they like. We are focusing on less familiar situations, which present special puzzles.

33. For evidence that heuristics and biases operate in the real world, even when dollars are involved, see Werner F. M. De Bondt and Richard H. Thaler, *Do Security Analysts Overreact?,* 80 Am Econ Rev 52 (1990) (demonstrating that security analysts overreact to market data and produce forecasts that are either too optimistic or too pessimistic); Robert J. Shiller, *Irrational Exuberance* 135–47 (Princeton 2000) (discussing anchoring and overconfidence in market behavior); Colin F. Camerer and Robin M. Hogarth, *The Effects of Financial Incentives in Experiments: A Review and Capital-Labor-Production Framework,* 19 J Risk & Uncertainty 7 (1999) (finding that financial incentives have *never* eliminated anomalies or persistent irrationalities). See also Colin F. Camerer, *Behavioral Game Theory: Experiments in Strategic Interaction* 60–62 (Princeton 2003) (finding little effect from increased stakes in ultimatum games designed to test the hypothesis that people are self-interested, and adding, "If I had a dollar for every time an economist claimed that raising the stakes would drive ultimatum behavior toward self-interest, I'd have a private jet on standby all day").

34. See Shlomo Benartzi and Richard H. Thaler, *How Much Is Investor Autonomy Worth?,* 57 J Fin 1593 (2002).

35. Id at 1598.

36. Id.

37. See Paul Slovic, Howard Kunreuther, and Gilbert F. White, *Decision Processes, Rationality and Adjustment to Natural Hazards* (1974), reprinted in Paul Slovic. *The Perception of Risk* 1, 14 (Earthscan 2000) (explaining that the availability heuristic "is potentially one of the most important ideas for helping us understand the distortions likely to occur in our perceptions of natural hazards"). See also Howard Kunreuther, *Mitigating Disaster Losses through Insurance,* 12 J Risk & Uncertainty 171, 174–78 (1996) (explaining why individuals fail to take cost-effective preventative measures or voluntarily insure against natural disasters).

38. See Kunreuther, 12 J Risk & Uncertainty at 176–77 (cited in note 36) (concluding, based in part on in-person interviews of homeowners in flood-prone areas, that "[t]he occurrence of a disaster causing damage to one's home is likely to have a significant impact on the demand for insurance").

39. See id; Slovic, Kunreuther, and White, *Decision Processes* at 14 (cited in note 36).

40. See Cass R. Sunstein and Edna Ullmann-Margalit, *Second-Order Decisions,* 110 Ethics 5 (1999).

41. See note 22. Some people will favor uninfluenced choice, and object to any effort to move people's choices in certain directions. But as Part II explains, it is often impossible to avoid influences on choice.

42. See Kahneman, Knetsch. and Thaler, 5 J Econ Persp at 202–03 (cited in note 43). See also Korobkin, 83 Cornell L Rev at 636–41 (cited in note 18). For a discussion of the variation of potential employees' WTP for vacation days based on default rules, see text accompanying notes 57–59.

43. See Choi, et al, *Defined Contribution Pensions* at 78 (cited in note 1); Madrian and Shea, 116 Q J Econ at 1158–61 (cited in note 1).

44. See Choi, et al, *Defined Contribution Pensions* at 78–79 (cited in note 1).

45. See http://www.presumedconsent.org/solutions.htm (visited Sept 6, 2003).

46. Id (reporting opt-out rates in presumed consent nations); Jean Kadooka Mardfin, *Heart and Soul: Anatomical Gifts for Hawaii's Transplant Community* 5, Hawaii Legislative Reference Bureau Report No 3 (1998), online at http://www.state.hi.us/lrb/rpts98/sout.pdf (visited Nov 20, 2003) (reporting results of a 1993 Gallup poll that asked Americans whether they had "granted permission for organ donation on [their] driver's license or on a signed donor card").

47. See http://www.presumedconsent.org/issues.htm (visited Sept 6, 2003).

48. See Eric J. Johnson and Daniel Goldstein, *Do Defaults Save Lives?* (unpublished working paper, Center for Decision Sciences, Columbia University, 2003).

49. Id at 2.

50. Id at 6–7.

51. Id at 7, Figure 2.

52. Id at 8–9. Many factors determine how many organs are actually made available and used for transplants. The transplant infrastructure is certainly important, and fewer

organs will be available if family members and heirs can veto transplants, even under a presumed consent regime. Johnson and Goldstein estimate that switching to an opt-out system increases organs actually used by 16 percent, holding everything else constant.

53. It is conceivable that the care of fatally ill patients might be sacrificed in order to harvest their organs, but no evidence suggests that this is a serious risk.

54. It follows from this example that if private or public planners would like to increase charitable donations, they could easily do that simply by creating automatic deductions for charity. Even if workers are allowed to opt out, clever planners should easily be able to ensure a much higher level of donations.

55. See, for example, Ayres and Gertner, 99 Yale L J at 90–91.

56. See id at 101–06 (providing examples of judicial use of penalty defaults).

57. See note 48 and accompanying text.

58. We acknowledge that bureaucrats might be subject to distinctive pressures that aggravate self-control problems.

59. See Jolls, Sunstein, and Thaler, 50 Stan L Rev at 1543–45 (cited in note 13).

60. For a discussion of that territory, see Dworkin, *Theory and Practice of Autonomy* at 78–81.

61. See the discussion of behavioral bureaucrats in Jolls, Sunstein, and Thaler, 50 Stan L Rev at 1543–45 (cited in note 13).

62. This is a necessary condition, not a sufficient one; believers in autonomy will not agree that welfarist concerns override freedom of choice. We do not attempt to speak to the underlying debates here; libertarian paternalists need not take a stand on the competing positions. For relevant discussion, see Dworkin, *Theory and Practice of Autonomy* at 78–81.

13 Markets on the Margin

In the first half of the twentieth century welfare economists developed the theory of *market failure*, comparing actual market performance to a benchmark of fully efficient, competitive market process. The justification for government intervention rested on the claim that markets sometimes fail to achieve an efficient outcome, meaning that it was possible in theory to reallocate productive resources in ways that could make some better off without leaving others worse off. To reallocate in this way is what is called a weak Pareto improvement, and to achieve a distribution that leaves no room for further Pareto improvements is to achieve Pareto optimality. A common thought has been that whenever Pareto improvements are possible through legislation or other forms of government action they should be made.

Against this thought, public choice economists appeal to the risk of *government failure* to argue that even when charged with making Pareto improvements governments will often fail to achieve the desired results and will make things worse than they would have been with "uncorrected" market failure. Importantly, the public choice argument extends beyond just the narrow focus on Pareto optimality, and raises questions about the efficacy of government action to achieve broader goals like fairness or justice. Public choice theorists challenge us to ask the comparative, and empirical, question: when real-world markets fail to allocate resources according to a normative benchmark—efficiency, fairness, justice, or anything else—are real-world political interventions actually likely to improve the outcome, rather than making it even worse?

Markets on the margin provide case studies that require us to think through the topics discussed in earlier sections of this book. "Marginal" markets encourage us to ask whether governments have the right, or even the ability, to block or alter voluntary transactions in which both parties consider themselves better off. They also show us that while markets can produce outcomes that some consider odious—such as the exchange of sex for money—government intervention may well make the outcome worse.

For example, markets for sex make many people uncomfortable. Further, some people's choice to engage in sex work is less than fully voluntary, especially workers who are very young or in desperate poverty. The case could be made that such markets unjustly exploit women and commodify something that should not be bought or sold. But Martha Nussbaum argues that even when a transaction has some pernicious consequences, attempts to ban the transaction can make conditions even worse for people who are already desperate.

For example, Nussbaum notes that when prostitution is legal, the associated contracts are legally binding, so women can prosecute those who abuse them or who violate the contract, and can minimize harassment. Legal sex workers can also force customers to wear condoms or get tested for sexually transmitted infections, and can seek payment directly rather than going through an abusive intermediary (or "pimp") whose job is to provide enforcement services unavailable through the police when contracts are illegal. When prostitution is illegal, the pimp's threat of violence is just as likely to be directed at the prostitute he has agreed to protect.

On Nussbaum's view, legalizing prostitution for adults makes it safer and reduces the social costs of exchanging sex for money. Of course, it is possible to argue that commodifying sex by selling sexual services is intrinsically immoral. But Nussbaum counters that the underlying activity is not obviously immoral, and that such criticism may simply be disguised sexism. Indeed, according to Nussbaum, we should stop casting aspersions on the (mostly female) labor force that comprise the sex work industry.

Friedman uses economic reasoning to explain how a variety of conventions surrounding sex, marriage and procreation evolved. Among the many fascinating facts he tries to explain is the phenomenon of men buying engagement rings for women. Why did this once rare convention catch on in the twentieth century? Friedman cites Margaret Brinig's argument that once judges stopped upholding the right of women to sue when a man breached his promise to marry after having sex with his fiancé, women needed a "performance bond" that was fungible, both to ensure performance of the agreement and to give the woman some source of independent wealth if the contract was broken. A portable solution emerged in the form of a diamond ring that could be readily redeemed for cash by a jilted bride-to-be. This is just one of several possible explanations for the increasing popularity of engagement rings in the twentieth century. Rings clearly serve many functions—among other things, they send signals to unwanted suitors, and symbolize sacrifice and commitment. But economic analysis can help explain why social conventions surrounding sex and marriage change in ways that otherwise appear mysterious.

Friedman also uses economic analysis to explain the shortage of babies available for adoption in relatively wealthy countries. We don't normally think of adoption as a market for babies, but Friedman suggests that thinking along these lines can help explain why it is easier to adopt some babies rather than others (parents have preferences about the characteristics of children), and why price controls (currently set at zero) lead to longer waiting times for parents who would like to adopt. Friedman challenges us to think about whether it would be better if people were legally allowed to pay for children to adopt, so that babies go to those willing to pay the most rather than those willing to wait the longest in line. The idea of removing price controls for adopting babies (or allowing people to pay women to have children so they can be adopted) strikes many as outrageous, but Friedman suggests that it is worth asking what the actual consequences would be if babies were allowed to be bought and sold (subject, of course, to background restrictions on how parents can treat children they buy or sell).

Our second topic, markets for recreational drugs such as heroin and cocaine, has come under increasing scrutiny as governments spend enormous sums trying to reduce the use and sale of illegal drugs. Michael Huemer argues for the legalization of all recreational drugs. He invokes the moral intuition that if people have any rights at all, these rights must begin with the right to do with their body what they see fit, provided they don't harm others in relevant ways in the process. Huemer points out that there are many ways we can waste our time or destroy our lives that are (rightly) not legally forbidden. People are allowed to play video games for days, to read gossip magazines, max out credit cards on luxuries, stay in abusive relationships, fail to exercise, eat junk food, and so on. If these clearly harmful activities are not illegal, Huemer concludes, the use of drugs should not be either.

Peter deMarneffe argues that we should decriminalize but not legalize recreational drugs that cause significant harm. *Decriminalization* means that drug users (but not necessarily drug sellers) would be exempt from criminal penalties. *Legalization*, as deMarneffe defines it, is the further step of exempting those who manufacture and sell drugs from criminal punishment, and even extending legal protection for contracts to buy and sell drugs. Two of the main claims deMarneffe uses to support his view favoring decriminalization but not legalization are these: (1) Parents who regularly use harmful drugs are more likely to abuse or neglect their children. (2) If all drugs were legal, it is likely that people who are unable to make wise decisions would have ready access to, and would be more likely to try, even the most addictive drugs. The first argument appeals to a "harm to others" principle, while the second is a form of soft paternalism that appeals to considerations about how most drug users (especially non-adults and addicts) would act if they were thinking more clearly.

Whatever one thinks of the moral status of drugs, the costs and consequences of prosecuting drug use are astonishing. For example, between 2006 and 2012, 60,000 people were killed in Mexico alone as the Mexican government has cracked down on drug trafficking. These deaths result not from any inherent dangers of trafficking, but as a predictable consequence of turning those who buy, sell, or use drugs into enemies of the state. During the same period in Mexico the number of deaths associated with the alcohol trade was approximately zero.

Jeffrey Miron argues that although drug use can cause harm, especially to drug users, we should compare the harm to individuals and the harm to others that arises from *drug use* with the harms created by *laws against drug use*. Drug laws do not enforce themselves: they are only effective, to the extent that they are, when enormous resources are directed toward finding and prosecuting traffickers. This, of course, drives up the price of drugs by creating short run supply shortages, though increased prices also encourage competitors to enter the market, and incentivizes the creation of new substitutes (consider the shift in demand from cocaine to crack during the 1980s, and from crack to methamphetamine in the 1990s, as drug laws increased the relative price of pure cocaine, and then crack cocaine). Somewhat surprisingly, Miron suggests—and most evidence confirms—that even harsh penalties for drug use do not work very well. This is partly because users often switch to even more dangerous substitutes, but also because demand for certain drugs is relatively inelastic, meaning that it doesn't decrease sharply in response to price increases. Miron also distinguishes between rational and irrational drug use, and dismisses the moralistic claim that all users of illegal drugs are irrational maniacs frothing at the mouth. Many who study drug policy look to Portugal, which decriminalized the use and sale of all recreational drugs in the year 2000. Portugal has seen increases in the use of some drugs, and decreases in others, but overall the level of drug use has been fairly stable rather than, as some predicted, rising precipitously. Meanwhile, drug addiction and drug-related crime have decreased in Portugal.

Organs are another commodity that many people think should not be bought or sold. Markets for kidneys have existed in Iran for over three decades, though nearly all other countries have made organ markets illegal. In most countries, it is legal—even encouraged—to donate, or to exchange, body parts, provided the price is zero. It is also (in many countries) legal to buy someone an expensive gift as thanks for their donated kidney. But it is not legal if the transaction is a sale rather than an exchange of gifts. One consequence is that there is a massive worldwide organ shortage. A related consequence is that there is a flourishing black market for organs, especially in countries like India. Indeed, the shortage of organs has driven the price up so high that some gangs have taken to kidnapping living "donors" and then either anesthetizing or euthanizing them and removing their kidneys.

Arthur Caplan argues that governments might increase the supply of organs by presuming that all people are willing to be organ donors upon death, but allowing them to opt out. This is quite different from the current presumption (in many countries) that people are not donors, unless they opt in. Still, he thinks, we should not allow a market for organs since it would incentivize doctors to violate the Hippocratic Oath, which says we should "do no harm" to patients. Unless there are compensating benefits for patients themselves, Caplan argues, doctors should not harm them. Of course, in the case of a kidney donation by a living person, there is harm without compensating benefit, whereas if people can sell one of their kidneys, there may be a compensating benefit that makes them better off. Along the way, Caplan argues as well that while donations of a kidney can be voluntary, the incentives at play within a market undermine voluntary choice.

Gerald Dworkin considers a mixture of arguments against organ markets and finds problems with all of them. He concludes that if it is both individually and socially beneficial to permit legal organ markets, we should legalize such transactions. In particular, he thinks, if people fear the distributive consequences of a full free market for organs, we could make it legal to *sell* organs, but then manage the allocation of organs to recipients on the basis of fairness principles set by governments or hospitals, rather than fully deregulating purchases so that organs go to the highest bidder.

Sweatshop labor is another market that many people think should be made illegal (and it has been in many countries, including the United States and United Kingdom). Benjamin Powell and Matt Zwolinski, though, offer a defense of sweatshop labor, albeit a tentative one. They suggest, among other things, that even if the set of options available to low skilled workers is small, we should still respect their right to choose the best option among a bad set. According to Zwolinski and Powell, some workers are likely to be harmed if the state imposes regulations like mandatory wage and safety increases. The harms result from the fact that, in the face of additional costs imposed by regulators, employers will often shut down factories, move to other countries where labor costs are cheaper, or replace workers with machinery.

While Zwolinski and Powell focus on the harms to workers that result from imposing regulations on sweatshops, Mathew Coakley and Michael Kates argue that we should recognize the potentially significant benefits of regulations. They agree that precipitous wage or regulation increases can lead to more unemployment among workers, but argue that a lot depends on the magnitude of changes. It is plausible to suppose that defenders and opponents of sweatshop labor agree on the underlying moral principles (that exploitation is wrong, that workers should be allowed to make choices that benefit themselves, and that unemployment is bad), but disagree about things like *how much* unemployment would result from, say, doubling the minimum wage, or imposing new worker safety requirements. Much of the empirical literature on such matters is tainted by ideological commitments, so readers should always be skeptical of findings that reinforce their pre-existing beliefs.

Our final topic, price gouging, occurs when a disaster such as an earthquake, war, or famine causes massive price increases in essential goods. Price gouging happens when sellers exploit short-run shortages in a good for which there is significant demand, and charge abnormally high prices. Michael Munger introduces the issue with an example from North Carolina, after a hurricane hit Raleigh and knocked out electrical power for several weeks. People came to Raleigh from other cities to sell ice at very high prices. Hurricane victims wanted to preserve frozen food or to cool medicine or drinks, and so needed ice desperately.

People lined up to pay very high prices for ice, which would seem to indicate they preferred the ice to the cash (under the circumstances). Yet when police came to prosecute the ice sellers for violating anti-price-gouging laws, some of the people in line clapped. They seemed happy to see the arrest, even though it meant they would go home without any ice. This may seem irrational, though perhaps a better explanation is that clappers considered the behavior of sellers immoral but nevertheless mutually beneficial. They clapped for justice but lamented the fact that their unrefrigerated food would go bad. These two considerations, a desire for material benefit and a desire to see justice enforced, may often be in conflict. The desire to see justice enforced may explain why anti-gouging laws are so popular in state legislatures.

Whether charging abnormally high prices is unjust, though, is open to question. Indeed, Matt Zwolinski defends the moral and legal permissibility of charging unusually high prices during disasters, primarily because of the socially beneficial consequences of market allocation. After all, if laws that prohibit price gouging are vigorously enforced, they prevent anyone but the richest and most powerful members of a community from getting what they want. Moreover, enforcement of price gouging laws makes scarcity worse, not better, by removing incentives for potential suppliers to enter the market. The result is that those with the least ability to pay are absolutely precluded from accessing whatever goods are especially prized.

Jeremy Snyder tentatively defends anti-price gouging laws by appealing to the fact that they support fair access. He claims that states should step in to provide access rather than relying on markets to solve shortages created by natural disasters. Snyder concedes that the price mechanism is crucial in sending signals to sellers that they should bring products to places where shortages exist, but he thinks laws should sometimes attempt to counteract precipitous price increases for essential goods during states of emergency, especially when the supply response is less important than fair access to the limited quantity of goods already available.

FURTHER READING

General

Jaworski, Peter and Jason Brennan. 2015. *Markets without Limits*. Routledge Press.

Satz, Debra. 2010. *Why Some Things Should not be for Sale*. Oxford University Press.

Sex

Posner, Richard. 1994. *Sex and Reason*. Harvard University Press.

Spector, Jessica. 2006. *Prostitution and Pornography: Philosophical Debate about the Sex Industry*. Stanford University Press.

Drugs

Anomaly, Jonathan. 2013. "Collective Action and Individual Choice: Rethinking How We Regulate Narcotics and Antibiotics." *Journal of Medical Ethics* 39 (12): 752–756.

Hughes, Caitlin and Alex Stevens. 2010. "What Can We Learn from the Portugese Decriminalization of Illicit Drugs?" *British Journal of Criminology* 50 (6): 999–1022.

Husak, Doug and Peter deMarneffe. 2005. *The Legalization of Drugs: For and Against.* Cambridge University Press.

Okrent, Daniel. 2011. *Last Call: The Rise and Fall of Prohibition.* Scribner Publishing.

Organs

Carney, Scott. 2014. *The Red Market: On the Trail of the World's Organ Brokers.* William Morrow & Co.

Epstein, Richard. 2008. "The Human and Economic Dimensions of Altruism: The Case of Organ Transplantation." *The Journal of Legal Studies* 37 (2): 459–501.

Sweatshops

Arnold, Denis and Norman Bowie. 2003. "Sweatshops and Respect for Persons." *Business Ethics Quarterly* 13 (2), 221–242.

Powell, Benjamin. 2014. Out of Poverty: *Sweatshops in the Global Economy.* Cambridge University Press.

Sex

Martha Nussbaum

Whether from Reason or Prejudice: Taking Money for Bodily Services

1998

I. BODY SELLERS

All of us, with the exception of the independently wealthy and the unemployed, take money for the use of our body. Professors, factory workers, lawyers, opera singers, prostitutes, doctors, legislators–we all do things with parts of our bodies, for which we receive a wage in return.[1] Some people get good wages and some do not; some have a relatively high degree of control over their working conditions and some have little control; some have many employment options and some have very few. And, some are socially stigmatized and some are not.

The stigmatization of certain occupations may be well founded, based on convincing, well-reasoned

Martha Nussbaum, "Whether from Reason or Prejudice: Taking Money for Bodily Services." *The Journal of Legal Studies* 27 (2) (1998): 693–724. By permission of *The Journal of Legal Studies.*

arguments. But it may also be based on class prejudice, or stereotypes of race or gender. Stigma may also change rapidly, as these background beliefs and prejudices change. Adam Smith, in *The Wealth of Nations,* tells us that there are "some very agreeable and beautiful talents" that are admirable as long as no pay is taken for them, "but of which the exercise for the sake of gain is considered, whether from reason or prejudice, as a sort of publick prostitution." For this reason, he continues, opera singers, actors, and dancers must be paid an "exorbitant" wage, to compensate them for them for the stigma involved in using their talents "as the means of subsistence." "Should the publick opinion or prejudice ever alter with regard to such occupations," he concludes, "their pecuniary recompense would quickly diminish."[2] Smith was not altogether right about the opera market,[3] but his discussion is revealing for what it shows us about stigma. Today few professions are more honored than that of opera singer, and yet only two hundred years ago, that public use of one's body for pay was taken to be a kind of prostitution. Looking back at that time, we now think that the judgments and emotions underlying the stigmatization of singers were irrational and objectionable, like prejudices against members of different classes and races. (I shall shortly be saying more about what I think those reasons were.) Nor do we see the slightest reason to suppose that the unpaid artist is a purer and truer artist than the paid artist. We think it entirely right and reasonable that high art should receive a high salary. If a producer of opera should take the position that singers should not be paid, on the grounds that receiving money for the use of their talents involves an illegitimate form of commodification and even market alienation of those talents, we would think that this producer was a slick exploiter, out to make a profit from the ill treatment of vulnerable and impressionable artists.[4] On the whole we think that far from cheapening or ruining talents, the presence of a contract guarantees conditions within which the artist can develop her art with sufficient leisure and confidence to reach the highest level of artistic production.[5]

It is widely believed, however, that taking money or entering into contracts in connection with the use of one's sexual and/or reproductive capacities is genuinely bad. Feminist arguments about prostitution, surrogate motherhood, and even marriage contracts standardly portray financial transactions in the area of female sexuality as demeaning to women and as involving a damaging commodification and market alienation of women's sexual and reproductive capacities.[6] The social meaning of these transactions is said to be both that these capacities are turned into objects for the use and control of men and also that the activities themselves are being turned into commodities, and thereby robbed of the type of value they have at their best.

One question we shall have to face is whether these descriptions of our current judgments and intuitions are correct. But even if they are, what does this tell us? Many things and people have been stigmatized in our nation's history, often for very bad reasons. An account of the actual social meaning of a practice is therefore just a door that opens onto the large arena of moral and legal evaluation. It invites us to raise Adam Smith's question: Are these current beliefs the result of reason or prejudice? Can they be defended by compelling moral arguments? And, even if they can, are these the type of moral argument that can properly be a basis for a legal restriction? Smith, like his Greek and Roman Stoic forebears, understood that the evaluations that ground emotional responses and ascriptions of social meaning in a society are frequently corrupt—deformed by self-interest, resentment, and mere unthinking habit. The task he undertook, in *The Theory of Moral Sentiments,* was to devise procedures and strategies of argument through which one might separate the rationally defensible emotions from the irrational and prejudiced. In so proceeding, Smith and the Stoics were correct. Social meaning does no work on its own. It offers an invitation to normative moral and political philosophy.

My aim in this essay will be to investigate the question of sexual "commodification" by focusing on the example of prostitution.[7] I argue that a fruitful debate about the morality and legality of prostitution should begin from a twofold starting point; from a broader analysis of our beliefs and practices with regard to taking pay for the use of the body, and from a broader awareness of the options and choices available to poor working women. The former inquiry suggests that at least some of our beliefs about prostitution are as irrational as the beliefs Smith reports about singers; it will therefore help us to identify the elements in prostitution that are genuinely problematic. Most, though not all, of the genuinely problematic elements turn out to be common to a wide range of activities engaged in by poor working women, and the second inquiry suggests that many of women's employment choices are so heavily constrained by poor options that they are hardly choices at all. I think that this should bother us—and that the fact that a woman with plenty of choices becomes a prostitute should not bother us provided there are sufficient safeguards against abuse and disease, safeguards of a type that legalization would make possible.

It is therefore my conclusion that the most urgent issue raised by prostitution is that of employment opportunities for working women and their control over the conditions of their employment. The legalization of prostitution, far from promoting the demise of love, is likely to make things a little better for women who have too few options to begin with.[8] The really helpful thing for feminists to ponder, if they deplore the nature of these options, will be how to promote expansion in the option set, through education, skills training, and job creation. These unsexy topics are not common themes in U.S. feminist philosophy, but they are inevitable in any practical project dealing with prostitutes and their female children.[9] This suggests that at least some of our feminist theory may be insufficiently grounded in the reality of working-class lives and too focused on sexuality as an issue in its own right, as if it could be extricated from the fabric of poor people's attempts to survive.

II. STIGMA AND WAGE LABOR

Why were opera singers stigmatized? If we begin with this question, we can move on to prostitution with expanded insight. Although we can hardly provide more than a sketch of the background here, we can confidently say that two common cultural beliefs played a role. First, throughout much of the history of modern Europe—as, indeed, in ancient Greece—there was a common aristocratic prejudice against earning wages. The ancient Greek gentleman was characterized by "leisure"—meaning that he did not have to work for a living. Aristotle reproved the Athenian democracy for allowing such base types as farmers and craftsmen to vote, because, in his view, the unleisured character of their daily activities and their inevitable preoccupation with gain would pervert their political judgment, making them grasping and small-minded.[10] The fact that the Sophists typically took money for their rhetorical and philosophical teaching made them deeply suspect in the eyes of such aristocrats.[11] Much the same view played a role in the medieval Church, where it was controversial whether one ought to offer philosophical instruction for pay.[12] Bernard of Clairvaux, for example, held that taking fees for education is a "base occupation" (*turpis quaestus*). (Apparently he did not think this true of all wage labor but only where it involved deep spiritual things.)

Such views about wage labor remained closely linked to class privilege in modern Europe and exercised great power well into the twentieth century. Any reader of English novels will be able to produce many examples of the view that a gentleman does not earn wages, and that someone who does is too preoccupied with the baser things in life, and therefore base himself. Such views were a prominent source of prejudice against Jews, who, not having the same land rights as Christians, had no choice but to earn their living. Even in this century, in the United States, Edith Wharton shows that these attitudes were still firmly entrenched. Lily Bart, impoverished heroine of *The House of Mirth* (1905), is discussing her situation with her friend Gus Trenor. He praises the investment tips he has gotten from Rosedale, a Jewish Wall Street investments expert, whose wealth has given him entry into the world of impoverished aristocrats who both use and despise him. Trenor urges Lily to encourage Rosedale's advances: "The man is mad to know the people who don't want to know him, and when a fellow's in that state, there is nothing he won't do for the first woman who takes him up." Lily dismisses the idea, calling Rosedale "impossible" and thinking silently of his "intrusive personality." Trenor replies: "Oh, hang it—because he's fat and shiny and has a shoppy manner! A few years from now he'll be in it whether we want him or not, and then he won't be giving away a half-a-million tip for a dinner!" In the telling phrase "a shoppy manner," we see the age-old aristocratic prejudice against wage work, so deeply implicated in stereotypes of Jews as pushy, intrusive, and lacking in grace.

To this example we may add a moment in the film *Chariots of Fire* when the Jewish sprinter hires a professional coach to help him win. This introduction of money into the gentlemanly domain of sport shocks the head of his college, who suggests to him that as a Jew he does not understand the true spirit of English athletics. Genteel amateurism is the mark of the gentleman, and amateurism demands, above all, not earning or dealing in money. It may also imply not trying too hard, as if it were really one's main concern in life, but this attitude appears to be closely related to the idea that the gentleman does not *need* the activity because he has his living provided already; so the rejection of hard work is a corollary of the rejection of the tradesman. (Even today in Britain, such attitudes have not totally disappeared; people from aristocratic backgrounds frequently frown on working too hard at one's scholarly or athletic pursuits, as if this betrays a kind of base tradesmanly mentality.)

What is worth noting about these prejudices is that they do not attach to activities themselves, as such, but, rather, to the use of these activities to make money. To be a scholar, to be a musician, to be a fine athlete, to be an actor even, is fine—so long as one does it as an amateur. But what does this mean? It means that those with inherited wealth[13] can perform these activities without stigma and others cannot. In England in the nineteenth century, it meant that the gentry could perform those activities, and Jews could not. This informs us that we need to scrutinize all our social views about money making and alleged commodification with extra care, for they are likely to embed class prejudices that are unjust to working people.

Intersecting with this belief, in the opera singer example, is another: that is shameful to display one's body to strangers in public, especially in the expression of passionate emotion. The anxiety about actors, dancers, and singers reported by Smith is surely of a piece with the more general anxiety about the body, especially the female body, that has been a large part of the history of quite a few cultures. Thus, in much of India until very recently (and in some parts, still), it is considered inappropriate for a woman of good family to dance in public; when Rabindranath Tagore included middle-class women in his theatrical productions early in this century, it was a surprising and somewhat shocking move. Similarly in the West: The female body should be covered and not displayed, although in some respects these conditions could be relaxed among friends and acquaintances. Female singers were considered unacceptable during the early history of opera; indeed, they were just displacing the *castrati* during Smith's lifetime, and they were widely perceived as immoral women.[14] Male actors, singers, and dancers suffered too; and clearly Smith means to include both sexes. Until very recently such performers were considered to be a kind of gypsy, too fleshy and physical, unsuited for polite company. The distaste was compounded by a distaste for, or at least a profound ambivalence about, the emotions that it was, and is, the business of these performers to portray. In short, such attitudes betray an anxiety about the body, and about strong passion, that we are now likely to think irrational, even though we may continue to share them at times; certainly we are not likely to think them a good basis for public policy.

When we consider our views about sexual and reproductive services, then, we must be on our guard against two types of irrationality: aristocratic class prejudice and fear of the body and its passions.

IV. SEX AND STIGMA

Prostitution, we now see, has many features that link it with other forms of bodily service. It differs from these other activities in many subtle ways, but the biggest difference consists in the fact that it is, today, more widely stigmatized. Professors no longer get told that selling their teaching is a *turpis quaestus.* Opera singers no longer get told that they are unacceptable in polite society. Even the masseuse has won respect as a skilled professional. What is different about prostitution? Two factors stand out as sources of stigma. One is that prostitution is widely held to be immoral; the other is that prostitution (frequently at least) is bound up with gender hierarchy, with ideas that women and their sexuality are in need of male domination and control, and the related idea that women should be available to men to provide an outlet for their sexual desires. The immorality view would be hard to defend today as a justification for the legal regulation of prostitution, and perhaps even for its moral denunciation. People thought prostitution was immoral because they thought nonreproductive and especially extramarital sex was immoral; the prostitute was seen, typically, as a dangerous figure whose whole career was given over to lust. But female lust was (and still often is) commonly seen as bad and dangerous, so prostitution was seen as bad and dangerous. Some people would still defend these views today, but it seems inconsistent to do so if one is not prepared to repudiate other forms of nonmarital sexual activity on an equal basis. We have to grant, I think, that the most common reason for the stigma attaching to prostitution is a weak reason, at least as a public reason: a moralistic view about female sexuality that is rarely consistently applied (to premarital sex, for example), and that seems unable to justify restriction on the activities of citizens who have different views of what is good and proper. At any rate, it seems hard to use the stigma so incurred to justify perpetuating stigma through criminalization unless one is prepared to accept a wide range of morals laws that interfere with chosen consensual activities, something that most feminist attackers of prostitution rarely wish to do.

More promising as a source of good moral arguments might be the stigma incurred by the connection of prostitution with gender hierarchy. But what is the connection, and how exactly does gender hierarchy explain pervasive stigma? It is only a small minority of people for whom prostitution is viewed in a negative light because of its collaboration with male supremacy; for only a small minority of people at any time have been reflective feminists, concerned with the eradication of inequality. Such people will view the prostitute as they view veiled women, or women in *purdah*; with sympathetic anger, as victims of an unjust system. This reflective feminist critique, then, does not explain why prostitutes are actually stigmatized and held in disdain—both because it is not pervasive enough and because it leads to sympathy rather than to disdain.

The way that gender hierarchy actually explains stigma is a very different way, a way that turns out in the end to be just another form of the immorality charge. People committed to gender hierarchy, and determined to ensure that the dangerous sexuality of women is controlled by men, frequently have viewed the prostitute as a sexually active woman, as a threat to male control of women. They therefore become determined either to repress the occupation itself by criminalization or, if they also think that male sexuality needs such an outlet and that this outlet ultimately defends marriage by giving male desire a safely debased outlet, to keep it within bounds by close regulation. (Criminalization and regulation are not straightforwardly opposed; they can be closely related strategies. Similarly, prostitution is generally conceived as not the enemy but the ally of marriage: The two are complementary ways of controlling women's sexuality.) The result is that social meaning is deployed in order that female sexuality will be kept in bounds carefully set by men. The stigma attached to the prostitute is an integral part of such bounding.

A valuable illustration of this thesis is given by Alain Corbin's valuable and careful study of prostitutes in France in the late nineteenth century.[15] Corbin shows that the interest in legal regulation of prostitution was justified by the alleged public interest in reining in and making submissive a dangerous female sexuality that was always potentially dangerous to marriage and social order. Kept in carefully supervised houses known as *maisons de tolérance,* prostitutes were known by the revealing name of *filles soumises,* a phrase that most obviously designated them as registered, "subjugated" to the law, but that also connoted their controlled and confined status. What this meant was that they were controlled and confined so that they themselves could provide a safe outlet for desires that threatened to disrupt the social order. The underlying aim of the regulationist project, argues Corbin (with ample documentation), was "the total repression of sexuality."[16] Regulationists tirelessly cited St. Augustine's dictum: "Abolish the prostitutes and the passions will overthrow the world; give them the rank of honest women and infamy and dishonor will blacken the universe" (*De ordine* 2.4.12). In other words, stigma has to be attached to prostitutes because of the necessary hierarchy that requires morality to subjugate vice, and the male the female, seen as an occasion and cause of vice. Bounding the prostitute off from the "good woman," the wife whose sexuality is monogamous and aimed at reproduction, creates a system that maintains male control over female desire.[17]

This attitude to prostitution has modern parallels. One instructive example is from Thailand in the 1950s, when Field Marshal Sarit Thanarat began a campaign of social purification, holding that "uncleanliness and social impropriety led to the erosion of social orderliness."[18] In theory, Thanarat's aim was to criminalize prostitution by the imposition of prison terms and stiff fines; in practice, the result was a system of medical examination and "moral rehabilitation" that shifted the focus of public blame from the procurers and traffickers to prostitutes themselves. Unlike the French system, the Thai system did not encourage registered prostitution, but it was similar in its public message that the problem of prostitution is a problem of "bad" women, and in its reinforcement of the message that female sexuality is a cause of social disruption unless tightly controlled.

In short, sex hierarchy causes stigma, commonly, not through feminist critique but through a far more questionable set of social meanings, meanings that anyone concerned with justice for women should call into question. For it is these same meanings that are also used to justify the seclusion of women, the veiling of women, the genital mutilation of women. The view boils down to the view that women are essentially immoral and dangerous and will be kept in control by men only if men carefully engineer things so that they do not get out of bounds. The prostitute, being seen as the uncontrolled and sexually free woman, is in this picture seen as particularly dangerous, both necessary to society and in need of constant subjugation. As an honest woman, a woman of dignity, she will wreck society. As a *fille soumise,* her reputation in the dirt, she may be tolerated for the service she provides (or, in the Thai case, she may provide an engrossing public spectacle of "moral rehabilitation").

All this diverts attention from some very serious crimes, such as the use of kidnapping, coercion, and fraud to entice women into prostitution. For these reasons, international human rights organizations, such as Human Rights Watch and Amnesty International, have avoided taking a stand against prostitution as such and have focused their energies on the issue of trafficking and financial coercion.[19]

It appears, then, that the stigma associated with prostitution has an origin that feminists have good reason to connect with unjust background conditions and to decry as both unequal and irrational, based on a hysterical fear of women's unfettered sexuality. There may be other good arguments against the legality of prostitution, but the existence of widespread stigma all by itself does not appear to be among them. As long as prostitution is stigmatized, people are injured by that stigmatization, and it is a real injury to a person not to have dignity add self-respect in her own society. But that real injury (as with the comparable real injury to the dignity and self-respect of interracial couples, or of lesbians and gay men) is not best handled by continued legal strictures against the prostitute and can be better dealt with in other ways (e.g., by fighting discrimination against these people and taking measures to promote their dignity). As the Supreme Court said in a mixed-race custody case, "Private biases may be outside the reach of the law, but the law cannot, directly or indirectly, give them effect."[20]

V. CRIMINALIZATION: SEVEN ARGUMENTS

Pervasive stigma itself, then, does not appear to provide a good reason for the continued criminalization of prostitution, any more than it does for the illegality of interracial marriage. Nor does the stigma in question even appear to ground a sound *moral* argument against prostitution. This is not, however, the end of the issue. There are a number of other significant arguments that have been made to support criminalization. With our six related cases in mind, let us now turn to those arguments.

1. *Prostitution involves health risks and risks of violence.* To this we can make two replies. First, insofar as this is true, as it clearly is, the problem is made much worse by the illegality of prostitution, which prevents adequate supervision, encourages the control of pimps, and discourages health checking. As Corbin shows, regimes of legal but regulated prostitution have not always done well by women: The health checkups of the *filles soumises* were ludicrously brief and inadequate.[21] But there is no reason why one cannot focus on the goal of adequate health checks, and some European nations have done reasonably well in this area.[22] The legal brothels in Nevada have had no reported cases of AIDS.[23] Certainly risks of violence can be far better controlled when the police are the prostitute's ally rather than her oppressor.

To the extent to which risks remain an inevitable part of the way of life, we must now ask what general view of the legality of risky undertakings we wish to defend. Do we ever want to rule out risky bargains simply because they harm the agent? Or do we require a showing of harm to others (as might be possible in the case of gambling, for example)?

Whatever position we take on this complicated question, we will almost certainly be led to conclude that prostitution lies well within the domain of the legally acceptable, for it is certainly far less risky than boxing, another activity in which working-class people try to survive and flourish by subjecting their bodies to some risk of harm. There is a stronger case for paternalistic regulation of boxing than of prostitution, and externalities (the glorification of violence as example to the young) make boxing at least as morally problematic and probably more so. And yet I would not defend the criminalization of boxing, and I doubt that very many Americans would either. Sensible regulation of both prostitution and boxing, by contrast, seems reasonable and compatible with personal liberty.

In the international arena, many problems of this type stem from the use of force and fraud to induce women to enter prostitution, frequently at a very young age and in a strange country where they have no civil rights. An especially common destination, for example, is Thailand, and an especially common source is Burma, where the devastation of the rural economy has left many young women an easy mark for promises of domestic service elsewhere. Driven by customers' fears of HIV, the trade has focused on increasingly young girls from increasingly remote regions. Human rights interviewers have concluded that large numbers of these women were unaware of what they would be doing when they left their country and are kept there through both economic and physical coercion. (In many cases, family members have received payments, which then become a "debt" that the girl has to pay off.)[24] These circumstances, terrible in themselves, set the stage for other forms of risk and/or violence. Fifty to seventy percent of the women and girls interviewed by Human Rights Watch were HIV positive; discriminatory arrests and deportations are frequently accompanied by abuse in police custody. All these problems are magnified by the punitive attitude of the police and government toward these women as prostitutes or illegal aliens or both, although under both national and international law trafficking victims are exempt from legal penalty and are guaranteed safe repatriation to their country of origin. This situation clearly deserves both moral condemnation and international legal pressure, but it is made worse by the illegality of prostitution itself.

2. *The prostitute has no autonomy; her activities are controlled by others.* This argument[25] does not distinguish prostitution from very many types of bodily service performed by working-class women. The factory worker does far worse on the scale of autonomy, and the domestic servant no better. I think this point expresses a legitimate moral concern: A person's life seems deficient in flourishing if it consists only of a form of work that is totally out of the control and direction of the person herself. Marx rightly associated that kind of labor with a deficient realization of full humanity and (invoking Aristotle) persuasively argued that a flourishing human life probably requires some kind of use of one's own

reasoning in the planning and execution of one's own work.[26] But that is a pervasive problem of labor in the modern world, not a problem peculiar to prostitution as such. It certainly does not help the problem to criminalize prostitution—any more than it would be to criminalize factory work or domestic service. A woman will not exactly achieve more, control and "truly human functioning" by becoming unemployed. What we should instead think about are ways to promote more control over choice of activities, more variety, and more general humanity in the types of work that are actually available to people with little education and few options. That would be a lot more helpful than removing one of the options they actually have.

3. *Prostitution involves the invasion of one's intimate bodily space.* This argument[27] does not seem to support legal regulation of prostitution, provided that as the invasion in question is consensual; that is, that the prostitute is not kidnapped, or fraudulently enticed, or a child beneath the age of consent, or under duress against leaving if she should choose to leave. In this sense prostitution is quite unlike sexual harassment and rape, and far more like the activity of the colonoscopy artist—not to everyone's taste, and involving a surrender of bodily privacy that some will find repellant—but not for that reason necessarily bad, either for self or others. The argument does not even appear to support a moral criticism of prostitution unless one is prepared to make a moral criticism of all sexual contact that does not involve love or marriage.

4. *Prostitution makes it harder for people to form relationships of intimacy.* This argument is prominently made by Elizabeth Anderson, in defense of the criminalization of prostitution.[28] The first question we should ask is, Is this true? People still appear to fall in love in the Netherlands and Germany and Sweden; they also fell in love in ancient Athens, where prostitution was not only legal but also, probably, publicly subsidized.[29] One type of relationship does not, in fact, appear to remove the need for the other—any more than a Jackie Collins novel removes the desire to read Proust. Proust has a specific type of value that is by no means found in Jackie Collins, so people who want that value will continue to seek out Proust, and there is no reason to think that the presence of Jackie Collins on the bookstand will confuse Proust lovers and make them think that Proust is really like Jackie Collins. So, too, one supposes, with love in the Netherlands: People who want relationships of intimacy and commitment continue to seek them out for the special value they provide, and they do not have much trouble telling the difference between one sort of relationship and another, despite the availability of both.

Second, one should ask which women Anderson has in mind. Is she saying that the criminalization of prostitution would facilitate the formation of love relationships on the part of the women who were (or would have been) prostitutes? Or, is she saying that the unavailability of prostitution as an option for working-class women would make it easier for romantic middle-class women to have the relationships they desire? The former claim is implausible, because it has hard to see how reinforcing the stigma against prostitutes, preventing some poor women from taking one of the few employment options they might have, would be likely to improve their human relations.[30] The latter claim might possibly be true (though it is hardly obvious), but it seems a repugnant idea, which I am sure Anderson would not endorse, that we should make poor women poorer so that middle-class women can find love. Third, one should ask Anderson whether she is prepared to endorse the large number of arguments of this form that might plausibly be made in the realm of popular culture—and, if not, whether she has any way of showing how she could reject those as involving an unacceptable infringement of liberty and yet allowing the argument about prostitution that she endorses. For it seems plausible that making rock music illegal would increase the likelihood that people would listen to Mozart and Beethoven; that making Jackie Collins illegal would make it more likely that people would turn to Joyce Carol Oates; that making commercial advertising illegal would make it more likely that we would appraise products with high-minded ideas of value in our minds; that making television illegal would improve children's reading skills. What is certain, however, is that we would and do utterly reject those ideas (we do not even seriously entertain them) because we do not want to live in Plato's *Republic,* with our cultural options dictated by a group of wise guardians, however genuinely sound their judgments may be.[31]

5. *The prostitute alienates her sexuality on the market; she turns her sexual organs and acts into commodities.*[32] Is this true? It seems implausible to claim that the prostitute alienates her sexuality just on the grounds that she provides sexual services to a client for a fee. Does the singer alienate her voice, or the professor her mind? The prostitute still has her sexuality; she can use it on her own, apart from the relationship with the client, just as the domestic servant may cook for her family and clean her own house.[33] She can also cease to be a prostitute, and her sexuality will still be with her, and hers, if she does. So she has not even given anyone a monopoly on those services, far less given them over into someone else's hands. The real issue that separates her from the professor and the singer seems to be the degree of choice she exercises over the acts she performs. But is even this a special issue for the prostitute, any more than it is for the factory worker or the domestic servant or the colonoscopy artist—all of whom choose to enter trades in which they will not have a great deal of say over what they do or (within limits) how they do it? Freedom to choose how one works is a luxury, highly desirable indeed, but a feature of few jobs that nonaffluent people perform.

As for the claim that the prostitute turns her sexuality into a commodity, we must ask what that means. If it means only that she accepts a fee for sexual services, then that is obvious, but nothing further has been said that would show us why this is a bad thing. The professor, the singer, the symphony musician—all accept a fee, and it seems plausible that this is a good state of affairs, creating spheres of freedom. Professors are more free to pursue their own thoughts now, as money makers, than they were in the days when they were supported by monastic orders; symphony musicians playing under the contract secured by the musicians' union have more free time than nonunionized musicians, and more opportunities to engage in experimental and solo work that will enhance their art. In neither case should we conclude that the existence of a contract has converted the abilities into things to be exchanged and traded separately from the body of the producer; they remain human creative abilities, securely housed in their possessor. So, if to "commodify" means merely to accept a fee, we have been given no reason to think that this is bad.

If, on the other hand, we try to interpret the claim of "commodification" using the narrow technical definition of "commodity" used by the Uniform Commercial Code,[34] the claim is plainly false. For that definition stresses the "fungible" nature of the goods in question, and "fungible" goods are, in turn, defined as goods "of which any unit is, by nature or usage of trade, the equivalent of any other like unit." Although we may not think that the soul or inner world of a prostitute is of deep concern to the customer, she is usually not regarded as simply a set of units fully interchangeable with other units.[35] Prostitutes are probably somewhat more fungible than bassoon players but not totally so. (Corbin reports that all *maisons de tolérance* standardly had a repertory of different types of women, to suit different tastes, and this should not surprise us.) What seems to be the real issue is that the woman is not attended to as an individual, not considered a special, unique being. But that is true of many ways people treat one another in many areas of life, and it seems implausible that we should use that kind of disregard as a basis for criminalization. It may not even be immoral, for surely we cannot deeply know all the people with whom we have dealings in life, and many of those dealings are just fine without deep knowledge. So our moral question boils down to the question: Is sex without deep personal knowledge always immoral? It seems to me officious and presuming to use one's own experience to give an affirmative answer to this question, given that people have such varied experiences of sexuality.

In general, then, there appears to be nothing baneful or value debasing about taking money for a service, even when that service expresses something intimate about the self. Professors take a salary, artists work on commission under contract—frequently producing works of high intellectual and spiritual value. To take money for a production does not turn either the activity or the product (e.g., the article or the painting) into a commodity in the baneful sense in which that implies fungibility. If this is so, there is no reason to think that a prostitute's acceptance of money for her services necessarily involves a baneful conversion of an intimate act into a commodity in that sense. If the prostitute's acts are, as they are, less intimate than many other sexual acts people perform, that does not seem to have a great deal to do with the fact that she receives money, given that people engage in many intimate activities (painting, singing, writing) for money all the time without loss of expressive value. Her activity is less intimate because that is its whole point; it is problematic, to the extent that it is, neither because of the money involved nor because of the nonintimacy (which, as I have said, it seems officious to declare bad in all cases) but because of features of her working conditions and the way she is treated by others.

Here we are left with an interesting puzzle. My argument about professors and painters certainly seems to imply that there is no reason, in principle, why the most committed and intimate sex cannot involve a contract and a financial exchange. So why doesn't it, in our culture? One reply is that it quite frequently does, when people form committed relationships that include an element of economic dependence, whether one-sided or mutual; marriage has frequently had that feature, not always for the worse. But to the extent that we do not exchange money for sex, why don't we? In a number of other cultures, courtesans, both male and female, have been somewhat more common as primary sexual partners than they are here. Unlike quite a few cultures, we do not tend to view sex in intimate personal relationships the way we view an artist's creation of a painting, namely, as an intimate act that can nonetheless be deliberately undertaken as the result of an antecedent contract-like agreement. Why not? I think there is a mystery here, but we can begin to grapple with it by mentioning two features. First, there is the fact that sex, however prolonged, still takes up much less time than writing an article or producing a painting. Furthermore, it also cannot be done too often; its natural structure is that it will not very often fill up the entire day. One may therefore conduct an intimate sexual relationship in the way one would wish, not feeling that one is slighting it, while pursuing another line of work as one's way of making a living. Artists and scholars sometimes have to pursue another line of work, but they prefer not to. They characteristically feel that to do their work in the way they would wish, they ought to spend the whole day doing it. So they naturally gravitate to the view that their characteristic mode of creative production fits very well with contract and a regular wage.

This, however, still fails to explain cultural differences. To begin to grapple with these we need to mention the influence of our heritage of romanticism, which makes us feel that sex is not authentic if not spontaneous, "natural," and to some degree unplanned. Romanticism has exercised a far greater sway over our ideas of sex than over our ideas of artistic or intellectual production, making us think that any deal or antecedent arrangement somehow diminishes that characteristic form of expression.

Are our romantic ideas about the difference between sex and art good, or are they bad? Some of each, I suspect. They are problematic to the extent that they make people think that sex happens naturally, does not require complicated adjustment and skill, and flares up (and down) uncontrollably.[36] Insofar as they make us think that sex fits badly with reliability, promise keeping, and so forth, these ideas are certainly subversive of Anderson's goals of "intimacy and commitment," which would be better served, probably, by an attitude that moves sex in intimate personal relationships (and especially marriages) closer to the activity of the artist or the professor. On the other hand, romantic views also promote Anderson's goals to some degree, insofar as they lead people to connect sex with self-revelation and self-expression rather than prudent concealment of self. Many current dilemmas concerning marriage in our culture stem from an uneasy struggle to preserve the good in romanticism while avoiding the dangers it poses to commitment. As we know, the struggle is not always successful. There is much more to be said about this fascinating topic. But since (as I've argued) it leads us quite far from the topic of prostitution, we must now return to our primary line of argument.

6. *The prostitute's activity is shaped by, and in turn perpetuates, male dominance of women.*[37] The

institution of prostitution as it has most existed is certainly shaped by aspects of male domination of women. As I have argued, it is shaped, by the perception that female sexuality is dangerous and needs careful regulation; that male sexuality is rapacious and needs a "safe" outlet; that sex is dirty and degrading, and that only a degraded woman is an appropriate sexual object.[38] Nor have prostitutes standardly been treated with respect, or given the dignity one might think proper to a fellow human being. They share this with working-class people of many, types in many ages, but there is no doubt that there are particular features of the disrespect that derive from male supremacy and the desire to lord it over women, as well as a tendency to link sex to (female) defilement that is common in the history of Western European culture. The physical abuse of prostitutes and the control of their earnings by pimps—as well as the pervasive use of force and fraud in international markets—are features of male dominance that are extremely harmful and do not have direct parallels in other types of low-paid work. Some of these forms of conduct may be largely an outgrowth of the illegality of the industry and closely comparable to the threatening behavior of drug wholesalers to their—usually male—retailers. So there remains a question how far male dominance as such explains the violence involved. But in the international arena where regulations against these forms of misconduct are usually treated as a joke, illegality is not a sufficient explanation for them.

Prostitution is hardly alone in being shaped by, and reinforcing, male dominance. Systems of patrilineal property and exogamous marriage, for example, almost certainly do more to perpetuate not only male dominance but also female mistreatment and even death. There probably is a strong case for making the giving of dowry illegal, as has been done since 1961 in India and since 1980 in Bangladesh[39] (though with little success), for it can be convincingly shown that the institution of dowry is directly linked with extortion and threats of bodily harm, and ultimately with the deaths of large numbers of women.[40] It is also obvious that the dowry system pervasively conditions the perception of the worth of girl children: They are a big expense, and they will not be around to protect one in one's old age. This structure is directly linked with female malnutrition, neglect, noneducation, even infanticide, harms that have caused the deaths of many millions of women in the world.[41] It is perfectly understandable that the governments of India, Bangladesh, and Pakistan are very concerned about the dowry system, because it seems very difficult to improve the very bad economic and physical condition of women without some structural changes. (Pakistan has recently adopted a somewhat quixotic remedy, making it illegal to serve food at weddings—thus driving many caterers into poverty.) Dowry is an institution affecting millions of women, determining the course of almost all girl children's lives pervasively and from the start. Prostitution as such usually does not have either such dire or such widespread implication: (Indeed, it is frequently the product of the dowry system, when parents take payment for prostituting a female child for whom they would otherwise have to pay dowry.) The case for making it illegal on grounds of subordination seems weaker than the case for making dowry, or even wedding feasts, illegal, and yet these laws are themselves of dubious merit and would probably be rightly regarded as involving undue infringement of liberty under our constitutional tradition. (It is significant that Human Rights Watch, which has so aggressively pursued the issue of forced prostitution, takes no stand one way or the other on the legality of prostitution itself.)

More generally, one might argue that the institution of marriage as most frequently practiced both expresses and reinforces male dominance. It would be right to use law to change the most inequitable features of that institution—protecting women from domestic violence and marital rape, giving women equal property and custody rights and improving their exit options by intelligent shaping of the divorce law. But to rule that marriage as such should be illegal on the grounds that it reinforces male dominance would be an excessive intrusion upon liberty, even if one should believe marriage irredeemably unequal. So, too, I think, with prostitution: What seems right is to use law to protect the bodily safety of prostitutes from assault, to protect their rights to their incomes against the extortionate behavior of pimps, to protect poor women in developing countries from forced trafficking and fraudulent offers, and to guarantee their full civil rights in the countries where they end up—to make them, in general, equals under the law, both civil and criminal. But the criminalization of prostitution seems to pose a major obstacle to that equality.

Efforts on behalf of the dignity and self-respect of prostitutes have tended to push in exactly the opposite direction. In the United States, prostitutes have long been organized to demand greater respect, though their efforts, are hampered by prostitution's continued illegality. In India, the National Federation of Women has adopted various strategies to give prostitutes more dignity in the public eye. For example, on National Women's Day, they selected a prostitute to put a garland on the head of the prime minister. Similarly, UNICEF in India's Andhra Pradesh has been fighting to get prostitutes officially classified as "working women" so that they can enjoy the child-care benefits local government extends to that class. As with domestic service, so here: Giving workers greater dignity and control can gradually change both the perception and the fact of dominance.

7. *Prostitution is a trade that people do not enter by choice; therefore the bargains people make within it should not be regarded as real bargains.* Here we must distinguish three cases. First is the case in which the woman's entry into prostitution is caused by some type of conduct that would otherwise be criminal: kidnapping, assault, drugging, rape, statutory rape, blackmail, a fraudulent offer. Here we may certainly judge that the woman's choice is not a real choice, and that the law should take a hand in punishing her coercer. This is a terrible problem currently in developing countries; international human rights organizations are right to make it a major focus.[42]

Closely related is the case of child prostitution. Child prostitution is frequently accompanied by kidnapping and forcible detention; even when children are not stolen from home, their parents have frequently sold them without their own consent. But even where they have not, we should judge that there is an impermissible infringement of autonomy and liberty. A child (and, because of clients' fears of HIV, brothels now often focus on girls as young as ten[43]) cannot give consent to a life in prostitution; not only lack of information and of economic options (if parents collude in the deal) but also absence of adult political rights, makes such a "choice" no choice at all.

Different is the case of an adult woman who enters prostitution because of bad economic options: because it seems a better alternative than the chicken factory, because there is no other employment available to her, and so on. This too, we should insist, is a case in which autonomy has been infringed but in a different way. Consider Joseph Raz's vivid example of "the hounded woman," a woman on a desert island who is constantly pursued by a man-eating animal.[44] In one sense, this woman is free to go anywhere on the island and do anything she likes. In another sense, of course, she is quite unfree. If she wants not to be eaten, she has to spend all her time and calculate all her movements in order to avoid the beast. Raz's point is that many poor people's lives are non-autonomous in just this way. They may fulfill internal conditions of autonomy, being capable of making bargains, reflecting about what to do, and so on. But none of this counts for a great deal, if in fact the struggle for survival gives them just one unpleasant option, or a small set of (in various ways) unpleasant options.

This seems to me the truly important issue raised by prostitution. Like work in the chicken factory, it is not an option many women choose with alacrity, when many other options are on their plate.[45] This might not be so in some hypothetical culture, in which prostitutes have legal protection, dignity and respect, and the status of skilled practitioner, rather like the masseuse.[46] But it is true now in most societies, given the reality of the (albeit irrational) stigma attaching to prostitution. But the important thing to realize is that this is not an issue that permits us to focus on prostitution in isolation from the economic situation of women in a society generally. Certainly it will not be ameliorated by the criminalization of prostitution, which reduces poor women's options still further. We may grant that poor women do not have enough options, and that society has been unjust to them in not extending more options while nonetheless respecting and honoring the choices they actually make in reduced circumstances.

How could it possibly be ameliorated? Here are some things that have actually been done in India, where prostitution is a common last-ditch option for women who lack other employment opportunities. First, both government and private groups have focused on the provision of education to women, to equip them with skills that will enhance their options. One group I recently visited in Bombay focuses in particular on skills training for the children of prostitutes, who are at especially high risk of becoming prostitutes themselves unless some action increases their option. Second, nongovernmental organizations have increasingly focused on the provision of credit to women, in order to enhance their employment options and give them a chance to "upgrade" in the domain of their employment. One such project that has justly won international renown is the Self-Employed Women's Association (SEWA), centered in Ahmedabad in Gujerat, which provides loans to women pursuing a variety of informal-sector occupations,[47] from tailoring to hawking and vending to cigarette rolling to agricultural labor.[48] With these loans, they can get wholesale rather than retail supplies, upgrade their animals or equipment, and so forth. They also get skills training and, frequently, the chance to move into leadership roles in the organization itself. Such women are far less likely to need to turn to prostitution to supplement their income. Third, they can form labor organizations to protect women employed in low-income jobs and to bargain for better working conditions—once again making this work a better source of income and diminishing the likelihood that prostitution will need to be selected. (This is the other primary objective of SEWA, which is now organizing hawkers and vendors internationally.) Fourth, they can form groups to diminish the isolation and enhance the self-respect of working women in low-paying jobs; this was a ubiquitous feature of both government and nongovernment programs I visited in India, and a crucial element of helping women deliberate about their options if they wish to avoid prostitution for themselves or their daughters.

These four steps are the real issue, I think, in addressing the problem of prostitution. Feminist philosophers in the United States do not write many articles about credit and employment;[49] they should do so far more. Indeed, it seems a dead end to consider prostitution in isolation from the other realities of working life of which it is a part, and one suspects that this has happened because prostitution is a sexy issue and getting a loan for a sewing machine appears not to be. But feminists had better talk more about getting loans, learning to read, and so forth if they want to be relevant to the choices that are actually faced by working women, and to the programs that are actually doing a lot to improve such women's options.

VI. TRULY HUMAN FUNCTIONING

The stigma traditionally attached to prostitution is based on a collage of beliefs most of which are not rationally defensible, and which should be especially vehemently rejected by feminists: beliefs about the evil character of female sexuality, the rapacious character of male sexuality, and the essentially marital and reproductive character of "good" women and "good" sex. Worries about subordination more recently raised by feminists are much more serious concerns, but they apply to many types of work poor women do. Concerns about force and fraud should be extremely urgent concerns of the international women's movement. Where these conditions do not obtain, feminists should view prostitutes as (usually) poor working women with few options, not as threats to the intimacy and commitment that many women and men (including, no doubt, many prostitutes) seek. This does not mean that we should not be concerned about ways in which prostitution as currently practiced, even in the absence of force and fraud, undermines the dignity of women; just as domestic service in the past undermined the dignity of members of a given race or class. But the correct response to this problem seems to be to work to enhance the economic autonomy and the personal dignity of members of that class, not to rule off limits an option that may be the only livelihood for many poor women and to further stigmatize women who already make their living this way.

In grappling further with these issues, we should begin from the realization there is nothing per se wrong with taking money for the use of one's body. That's the way most of us live, and formal recognition of that fact through contract is usually a good thing for people, protecting their security and their employment conditions. What seems wrong is that relatively few people in the world have the option to use their body, in their work, in what Marx would call a "truly human" manner of functioning, by which he meant (among other things) having some choices about the work to be performed, some reasonable measure of control over its conditions and outcome, and also the chance to use thought and skill rather than just to function as a cog in a machine. Women in many parts of the world are especially likely to be stuck at a low level of mechanical functioning, whether as agricultural laborers or as factory workers or as prostitutes. The real question to be faced is how to expand the options and opportunities such workers face, how to increase the humanity inherent in their work, and how to guarantee that workers of all sorts are treated with dignity. In the further pursuit of these questions, we need, on balance, more studies of women's credit unions and fewer studies of prostitution.

NOTES

1. Even if one is a Cartesian dualist, as I am not, one must grant that the human exercise of mental abilities standardly requires the deployment of bodily skills. Most traditional Christian positions on the soul go still further: Aquinas, for example, holds that souls separated from the body have only a confused cognition and cannot recognize particulars. So my statements about professors can be accepted even by believers in the separable soul.

2. Smith, The *Nature and Causes of the Wealth of Nations,* I.x.b.25. Elsewhere, Smith points out that in ancient Greece acting was "as creditable . . . as it is discreditable now" (LRBL ii.230).

3. He expresses the view that the relevant talents are not so rare, and that when stigma is removed, many more people will compete for the jobs, driving down wages; this is certainly true today of acting, but far less so of opera, where "the rarity and beauty of the talents" remains at least one dominant factor.

4. Such arguments have often been used in the theater; they were used, for example, in one acting company of which I was a member, in order to persuade actors to kick back their (union-mandatory) salaries to the owners. This is fairly common in theater, where the union is weak and actors are so eager for employment that they are vulnerable to such arguments.

5. The typical contract between major U.S. symphony orchestras and the musicians' union, for example, guarantees year-round employment to symphony musicians, even though they do not play all year; this enables them to use summer months to play in low-paying or experimental settings in which they can perform contemporary music and chamber music, do solo and concerto work, and so forth. It also restricts hours of both rehearsal and performance during the performing season, leaving musicians free to teach students, attend classes, work on chamber music with friends, and in other ways to enrich their work. It also mandates blind auditions (i.e., players play behind a curtain)—with the result that the employment of female musicians has risen dramatically over the past twenty or so years since the practice was instituted.

6. See Elizabeth Anderson, *Value in Ethics and Economics* (Cambridge, MA: Harvard University Press, 1993), and Anderson, "Is Women's Labor a Commodity?" *Philosophy and Public Affairs* 19 (1990), 71–92; Margaret Jane Radin, *Contested Commodities: The Trouble with the Trade in Sex, Children, Bodily Parts, and Other Things* (Cambridge, MA: Harvard University Press, 1996); and Radin, "Market-Inalienability," *Harvard Law Review* 100 (1987), 1849–1937; Cass R. Sunstein, "Neutrality in Constitutional Law (With Special Reference to Pornography, Abortion, and Surrogacy)," *Columbia Law Review* 92 (1992), 1–52; and Sunstein, *The Partial Constitution* (Cambridge, MA: Harvard University Press, 1993), 257–90. For contrasting feminist perspectives on the general issue of contract, see Jean Hampton, "Feminist Contractarianism," in *A Mind of One's Own: Feminist Essay on Reason and Objectivity* (Boulder, CO: Westview, 1993), 227–55; Susan Moller Okin, *Justice, Gender, and the Family* (New York: Basic Books, 1989).

7. I use this term throughout because of its familiarity, although a number of international women's organizations now avoid it for reasons connected to those in this essay, preferring the term "commercial sex worker" instead. For one recent example, see Report of the Panel on Reproductive Health, National Research Council, *Reproductive Health in Developing Countries: Expanding Dimensions, Building Solutions,* ed. Amy O. Tsui, Judith N. Wasserheit, and John G. Haaga (Washington, DC: National Academy Press, 1997), 30, stressing the wide variety of practices

denoted by the term "commercial sex" and arguing that some studies show economic hardship as a major factor but some do not.

8. Among feminist discussions of prostitution, my approach is close to that of Sibyl Schwarzenbach, "Contractarians and Feminists Debate Prostitution," *New York University Review of Law and Social Change* 18 (1990–1), 103–29, and to Laurie Shrage, "Prostitution and the Case for Decriminalization," *Dissent* (Spring 1996), 41–5 (in which Shrage criticizes her earlier view expressed in "Should Feminists Oppose Prostitution?," *Ethics 99* [1989]: 347–61).

9. To give just one example, the Annapurna Mahila Mandel project in Bombay offers job training and education to the daughters of prostitutes, in a residential school setting; they report that in five years they have managed to arrange reputable marriages for 1,000 such girls.

10. Aristotle, *Politics,* III.5 and VII.9–10.

11. See Plato, *Apology* 19D–20C, *Protagoras* passim, Gorgias passim.

12. I have profited here from reading an unpublished paper by Dan Klerman, "Slavery, Simony and Sex: An Intellectual History of the Limits of Monetary Relations."

13. Or those supported by religious orders.

14. Mrs. Elizabeth Billington, who sang in Arne's *Artaxerxes* in London in 1762, was forced to leave England because of criticisms of her morals; she ended her career in Italy. Another early *diva* was Maria Catalani, who sang for Handel (d. 1759), for example, in *Samson.* By the time of the publication of *The Wealth of Nations,* female singers had made great headway in displacing the *castrati,* who ceased to be produced shortly thereafter. For Smith's own attitudes to the female body, see *The Theory of Moral Sentiments* I.ii.1.3, where he states that as soon as sexual passion is gratified it gives rise to "disgust," and leads us to wish to get rid of the person who is their object, unless some higher moral sentiment preserves our regard for (certain aspects of) this person. "When we have dined, we order the covers to be removed; and we should treat in the same manner the objects of the most ardent and passionate desires, if they were the objects of no other passions but those which take their origin from the body." Smith was a bachelor who lived much of his life with his mother and did not have any lasting relationships with women.

15. *Women for Hire: Prostitution and Sexuality in France After 1850,* trans. Alan Sheridan (Cambridge, MA: Harvard University Press, 1990).

16. Ibid., 29. Representative views of the authors of regulationism include the view that "[d]ebauchery is a fever of the senses carried to the point of delirium; it leads to prostitution (or to early death). . ." and that "[t]here are two natural sisters in the world: prostitution and riot." Ibid., 373.

17. For a more general discussion of the relationship between prostitution and various forms of marriage, see Richard Posner, *Sex and Reason* (Cambridge, MA: Harvard University Press, 1992), 130–3.

18. Sukanya Hantrakul, "Thai Women: Male Chauvinism à la Thai," *The Nation,* November 16, 1992, cited with further discussion in Asia Watch Women's Rights Project, *A Modern Form of Slavery: Trafficking of Burmese Women and Girls into Brothels in Thailand* (New York: Human Rights Watch, 1993).

19. See *A Modern Form of Slavery; the Human Rights Watch Global Report on Women's Human Rights* (New York: Human Rights Watch, 1995), 196–273, esp. 270–3. The pertinent international human rights instruments take the same approach, including the International Covenant on Civil and Political Rights, the Convention on the Elimination of All forms of Discrimination against Women, and the Convention for the Suppression of Traffic in Persons and the Exploitation of the Prostitution of Others.

20. *Palmore v. Sidoti,* 466 U.S. 429 (1984).

21. See Corbin, 90: In Paris, Dr. Clerc boasted that he could examine a woman every thirty seconds, and estimated that a single practitioner saw 400 women in a single twenty-four-hour period. Another practitioner estimated that the average number of patients per hour was fifty-two.

22. For a more pessimistic view of health checks, see Posner, *Sex and Reason,* 209, pointing out that they frequently have had the effect of driving prostitutes into the illegal market.

23. See Richard Posner, *Private Choices and Public Health: The AIDS Epidemic in an Economic Perspective* (Cambridge, MA: Harvard University Press, 1993), 149, with references.

24. See *Human Rights Watch Global Report,* 1–7.

25. See Anderson, *Value in Ethics and Economics,* 156: "Her actions under contract express not her own valuations but the will of her customer."

26. This is crucial in the thinking behind the "capabilities approach" to which I have contributed in *Women, Culture, and Development* and other publications. For the connection between this approach and Marx's use of Aristotle, see Martha C. Nussbaum, "Aristotle on Human Nature and the Foundations of Ethics," in *World, Mind, and Ethics: Essays on the Philosophy of Bernard Williams,* ed. J. E. J. Altham and R. Harrison (Cambridge: Cambridge University Press, 1993).

27. Made frequently by my students, not necessarily to support criminalization.

28. *Value in Ethics and Economics,* 150–8; Anderson pulls back from an outright call for criminalization, concluding that her arguments "establish the legitimacy of a state interest in prohibiting prostitution, but not a conclusive case for prohibition," given the paucity of opportunities for working women.

29. See K. J. Dover, *Greek Homosexuality,* 2nd ed. (Cambridge, MA: Harvard University Press, 1978); and David Halperin, "The Democratic Body," in *One Hundred Years of Homosexuality and Other Essays on Greek Love* (New York: Routledge, 1990). Customers were all males, but prostitutes were both male and female. The evidence that prostitution was publicly funded is uncertain because it derives from comic drama, but it is clear that both male and female prostitution enjoyed broad public support and approval.

30. For a similar point, see M. J. Radin, "Market-Inalienability," 1921–25; and *Contested Commodities,* 132–6; Anderson refers to this claim of Radin's, apparently as the source of her reluctance to call outright for criminalization.

31. I would not go quite as far as John Rawls, however, in the direction of letting the market determine our cultural options. He opposes any state subsidy to opera companies, symphony orchestras, museums, and so on, on the grounds that this would back a particular conception, of the good against others. I think, however, that we could defend such subsidies, within limits, as valuable because they preserve a cultural option that is among the valuable ones, and that might otherwise cease to exist. Obviously much more argument is needed on this entire question.

32. See Radin, "Market-Inalienability"; and Anderson, 156: "The prostitute, in selling her sexuality to a man, alienates a good necessarily embodied in her person to him and thereby subjects herself to his commands."

33. On this point, see also Schwarzenbach, with discussion of Marx's account of alienation.

34. See Richard Epstein, "Surrogacy: The Case for Full Contractual Enforcement," *Virginia Law Review* 81 (1995), 2327.

35. Moreover, the UCC does not cover the sale of services, and prostitution should be classified as a service rather than a good.

36. It is well-known that these ideas are heavily implicated in the difficulty of getting young people, especially young women, to use contraception.

37. See Shrage's earlier article; Andrea Dworkin, "Prostitution and Male Supremacy," *Life and Death* (New York: The Free Press, 1997).

38. An eloquent examination of the last view, with reference to Freud's account (which endorses it) is in William Miller, *The Anatomy of Disgust* (Cambridge, MA: Harvard University Press, 1997), chap. 6.

39. The Dowry Prohibition Act of 1961 both makes both taking and giving of dowry illegal; in Bangladesh, demanding, taking, and giving dowry are all criminal offenses.

40. It is extremely difficult to estimate how many women are damaged and killed as a result of this practice; it is certainly clear that criminal offenses are vastly underreported, as is domestic violence in India generally, but that very problem makes it difficult to form any reliable idea of the numbers involved. See Indira Jaising, *Justice for Women* (Bombay: The Lawyers' Collective, 1996).

41. See Amartya Sen and Jean Drèze, *Hunger and Public Action* (Oxford: Clarendon Press, 1989), 52; and chapter 1 (in this volume). Kerala, the only Indian state to have a matrilineal property tradition, also has an equal number of men and women (contrasted with a 94/100 sex ratio elsewhere), and 97 percent both male and female literacy, as contrasted with 32 percent female literacy elsewhere.

42. See, for example, *A Modern Form of Slavery: Trafficking of Burmese Women; Human Rights Watch Global Report,* 1296–373; Amnesty International, *Human Rights Are Women's Right* (London: Amnesty International, 1995), 53–6.

43. See *Human Rights Watch Global Report,* 197, on Thailand.

44. Joseph Raz, *The Morality of Freedom* (Oxford: Clarendon Press, 1986), 374.

45. See Posner. *Sex and Reason,* 132 n. 43 on the low incidence of prostitution in Sweden, even though it is not illegal; his explanation is that "women's opportunities in the job market are probably better there than in any other country."

46. See Schwarzenbach.

47. An extremely high proportion of the labor force in India is in the informal sector.

48. SEWA was first directed by Ela Bhatt, who is now involved in international work to improve the employment options of informal-sector workers. For a valuable description of the movement, see Kalima Rose, *Where Women Are Leaders: The SEWA Movement in India* (Delhi: Sage Publications, 1995).

49. But see, here, Schwarzenbach and Shrage (op. cit.). I have also been very much influenced by the work of Martha Chen, *A Quiet Revolution: Women in Transition in Rural Bangladesh* (Cambridge, MA: Schenkman, 1983); Chen, "A Matter of Survival: Women's Right to Work in India and Bangladesh," in *Women, Culture, and*

Development, ed. M. Nussbaum and J. Glover (Oxford: Clarendon Press, 1995); and Bina Agarwal, *A Field of One's Own: Gender and Land Rights in South Asia* (Cambridge: Cambridge University Press, 1994); and also "'Bargaining' and Gender Relations: Within and Beyond the Household," FCND Discussion Paper No. 27, Food Consumption and Nutrition Division, International Food Policy Research Institute, Washington, DC.

DAVID FRIEDMAN

Marriage, Sex, and Babies

1999

In most past societies that we know of, most people got married, most marriages lasted until the death of one of the partners, and most babies were born, although not necessarily conceived, in wedlock. None of these statements is true of the United States at present.

This raises a set of interesting questions. One is whether there is a plausible economic explanation for these changes. Another is what part legal rules have played, either as cause or effect, in the process.

The first step to the answer is another question: Why, in most societies, are childbearing and household production undertaken primarily by couples who have committed themselves to the long-term, often lifetime, partnership called marriage?

WHY PEOPLE GET MARRIED

Many years ago I accepted a position in the UCLA economics department. Doing so required me to move across the country, find a place to live, develop relationships with a new set of friends and colleagues—costly activities that produced a return only if I remained at or near UCLA.

Suppose that when I came I received a salary of forty thousand dollars. A year or two later the department chairman, who is of course an economist, makes the following calculation: "If Friedman was willing to come for forty thousand dollars, despite all of the transitional costs he had to pay, he would be willing to stay for thirty. After all, if he leaves he has no way of getting back his moving costs, or taking his new friends with him, or . . ." The chairman calls me into his office to discuss the tight state of the department's budget.

I am happy to talk to the chairman. I too am an economist and have made my own analysis of sunk costs. I knew, and the chairman presumably knew, that for my first year or two I would not be a very productive member of the faculty, since I would be distracted by the costs of learning a new environment, finding out what colleagues I could usefully interact with, and the like. Now that I have finished that process I am more useful as teacher, researcher, and colleague. If he was willing to pay me forty thousand dollars to come, he should be willing to pay me fifty to stay. After all, there is no way he can get back the money he lost during my first year.

This stylized fiction demonstrates a real and important point: A fundamental reason for long-term contracts, in marriage or business, is the existence of relation-specific sunk costs. Before I came to UCLA both they and I were bargaining on a competitive market; there are other universities and other economists. Once I had been hired and both they and I had adapted to our relationship, we were stuck in a bilateral monopoly with potential bargaining costs. One way of reducing those costs is through long-term contracts—explicit, as in the tenure system, or implicit, as in the general custom of not cutting an employee's salary save under special circumstances.

Marriage is an extreme example. While many of us like to believe that our husbands or wives are uniquely suited to that role, it is not true; if it were, the chance of finding them would be remote. At one time I did some rough calculations on the subject and concluded that my present wife is about a one in two hundred thousand catch. That seems reasonably consistent with the fact that I found her, given the mechanisms our society provides for the early stages of the search process, such as sorting people socially by interests and educational status. I was lucky, but not unreasonably lucky. It is also consistent with the fact that in the years since finding her I have met one or two other women who might have been as well suited to me.

They might have been as well suited to me, but it would have been foolish to investigate the matter. Once a couple has been married for a while, they have made a lot of relationship-specific investments, borne costs that will produce a return only if they remain together. Each has become, at considerable cost, an expert on how to get along with the other. Both have invested, materially and emotionally, in their joint children. Although they started out on a competitive market, they are now locked into a bilateral monopoly with associated bargaining costs.

One way of reducing those costs is a long-term contract, till death do us part. There remains room for bargaining within the marriage, but the threat of walking out is removed. And bargaining within the marriage can be reduced by well-defined social roles, laws and customs prescribing each party's obligations, as well as by the knowledge that when the bargaining is over the two parties will still have to live with each other.

There are costs to that solution. The most obvious is that people who make the wrong choice are stuck with it. That problem that can be reduced by more careful search, but not eliminated. Clearly defined sexual roles may result in an inefficient division of labor, a husband who is good with children working while a wife who is good at earning money stays home. And even within the prescribed pattern, each partner still has available the threat of adhering to the letter but not the spirit of the contract. So far as I know, nobody has ever been divorced for cooking, or making love, badly.

My favorite evidence of the limits to contract enforcement in a traditional system of marriage is provided by al-Tanukhi, a ninth-century Arab judge who produced a volume of anecdotes for the entertainment of his contemporaries:

> A woman stood waiting on the road for the Vizier Hāmīd ibn 'Abbas and complained to him of poverty, asking alms. When he had taken his seat, he gave her an order for two hundred dinars. The paymaster, unwilling to pay such a sum to a woman of her class, consulted the vizier, who said that he had only meant to give her two hundred dirhems. But as God had caused him to write dinar for dirhem, gold for silver, so the sum should be paid out as it was written.
>
> Some days later, a man put a petition into his hand, wherein he said that the vizier had given his wife two hundred dinars, in consequence whereof she was giving herself airs and trying to force him to divorce her. Would the vizier be so good as to give orders to someone to restrain her? Hāmīd laughed and ordered the man to be given two hundred dinars.

In traditional Islamic society men could divorce their wives, but women could not divorce their husbands. Yet the vizier, and presumably al-Tanukhi, took it for granted that as a practical matter the wife could force a divorce, and not even the vizier could prevent it.

If traditional marriage provides a solution to the problems of relationship-specific sunk costs, why have we abandoned it? One answer is that in traditional societies child rearing was something close to a full-time job, and child rearing plus household management at least a full-time job. One profession, housewife, absorbed almost half the labor force. Most individual women were specialized to the job of being the wife of a particular man.

Two things changed that. One was the enormous drop in infant mortality over the past two centuries. It used to be the case that in order to be reasonably sure of ending up with two or three children, a woman had to produce children practically nonstop during her fertile years. Today a family that wants two children has two children.

The second change was the shift of production out of the home. Clothes are now made in factories by machines, bacon is cured by professionals. Clothes may be washed in the home, but most of the work is done by the washing machine. The job of housewife has, for most families, gone from a full-time to a part-time job. The result is that women are less specialized to a particular job and a particular man. There are still substantial costs to breaking up a marriage, but they are considerably lower than two hundred years ago, and, as a result, more marriages break up. Our legal institutions have changed accordingly, shifting away from indissoluble marriage to something close to divorce on demand.

I GAVE HIM THE BEST YEARS OF MY LIFE: THE PROBLEM OF OPPORTUNISTIC BREACH

Two firms agree on a long-term joint project. One will research and design a new product; the other will produce and market it. The first, having done its part of the job, hands over the designs—and, in a world without enforceable contracts, the second firm dissolves the agreement, produces and markets the product, and keeps the money. This is the problem of opportunistic breach.

A couple marries. For the next fifteen years the wife is bearing and rearing children—a more than full-time job, as those who have tried it can attest. The husband supports the couple, but not very well, since he is still in the early stages of his career.

Finally the children are old enough to be only a part-time job, and the wife can start living the life of leisure that she has earned. The husband gets promoted to vice president. He divorces his wife and marries a younger woman.

It makes a better soap opera than my first story, but the economics are the same. In a traditional marriage the wife performs her part of the joint project early, the husband late. That timing, combined with easy divorce, creates the potential for opportunistic breach—encouraged by the fact that most men find women more attractive at twenty-five than at forty.

Once women recognize that problem, as by now they have, they adjust their behavior accordingly. One way is to become less specialized to the job of housewife, to have a career and hire someone else to clean the house and watch the kids. Another is to postpone or spread out childbearing, so as to make the pattern of performance by the two partners more nearly the same. Both adjustments fit, and may help explain, changes in recent decades, including the increase in both age at first marriage and age at first child.

Another solution is to make the contract more nearly enforceable by imposing substantial damage payments on the breaching spouse. While that happens to some extent, there are a number of practical problems. One is the difficulty of enforcing such rules. Human capital is mobile, and a man ordered to pay alimony or child support may move to another jurisdiction, making collection hard. A second is the problem of monitoring quality, discussed earlier. If a husband who asks for a divorce must pay large damages, he has the alternative of trying to make his wife's life so miserable that she is willing to give him a divorce without being asked. And if we try to prevent that with a legal rule that automatically gives the wife a large compensation whenever a marriage breaks up, we create a risk of opportunistic breach in the opposite direction. The net result at present appears to be that, although husbands are sometimes required to pay money to their wives when there is a divorce, the ex-wife ends up, on average, worse off, and the ex-husband better off, after the divorce.

So far I have mostly been concerned with one oddity of modern society: the historically extreme ease and high frequency of divorce. The same arguments help explain a less striking oddity: the substantial number of people who never get married. We are left with a third puzzle: the large and perhaps historically unprecedented number of people who don't get married but do have children.

OUT-OF-WEDLOCK BIRTHS

One popular explanation for the sharp increase in the illegitimacy rate over the past few decades is that it is a consequence of welfare laws. Poor women are, in effect, paid to have children—perhaps not enough to make having children profitable in an accounting sense, but enough to make it profitable for some in the more relevant economic sense, which includes nonpecuniary benefits as well as pecuniary ones. A woman who is not quite willing to have a child if she knows she must support it herself may be just barely willing if she knows that the state will pay part of the cost.

The problem with this explanation is that although the highest illegitimacy rates occur in low-income populations, illegitimacy rates in parts of the population to which welfare is almost irrelevant have also risen. So although welfare might be one cause of the changes, it cannot be the only cause. A second piece of evidence in the same direction is that, despite recent decreases in the real subsidy to childbirth, the illegitimacy rate continues to rise.

A second explanation, proposed by my friend James Woodhill, is that the illegitimacy rate, like the divorce rate, has increased as an indirect consequence of reduced mortality—this time not infant mortality but mortality in childbirth. Until recent times the single most dangerous thing that an ordinary person could do was to have a baby. He argues that the result was a world where, in the age groups relevant to marriage, men outnumbered women. Women were thus in a sufficiently strong market position to be able to demand support for their offspring as a condition for sleeping with a man and bearing his children. As medicine improved and the numbers shifted, women's market position became weaker, with the result that some who wanted children were unable to find a man willing to support them.

To make the story more vivid, add in one more factor. Women typically marry men a few years older than they are. In the mid-sixties, as the children of the baby boom reached marriageable age, women born in 1947 were looking for men born in 1945—and there weren't very many of them. Some, unable to find a husband, accepted a lover instead. And so the sexual revolution was born.

A different and more elaborate explanation has been offered by two economists, George Akerlof and Janet Yellin, who argue that the increase in illegitimacy was an indirect consequence of the widespread availability of abortion and contraception. On the face of it, that seems backwards: Abortion and contraception prevent unwanted children, and we would expect that, on average, people who are not married are less likely to want children than people who are. Their argument, in my words, not theirs, goes as follows:

In a world without contraception or abortion, sex and childbearing are linked; they are, in the jargon of economics, *joint products*. Each act of intercourse produces both sexual pleasure and, with some probability, a baby. Both women and men enjoy children, but not equally; women have a higher demand for children than men do.

Here as elsewhere in economics, "demand is higher" means that the quantity demanded is higher at any given price. In a world where men father children but women raise them at their own expense, men may well want more children than women since, in that world, having children is expensive for women and inexpensive for men. But in a world where the costs were evenly divided, women would choose more children. That, at least, is the underlying conjecture.

As long as sex and childbearing are linked, someone who wants sex can only get it combined with a possibility of children. That is a good reason for women to refuse to consent to sex unless the man guarantees support for any children that result, either by marrying her or by committing himself to do so if she gets pregnant. She can expect to get those terms because other women face the same risk and thus make the same demand.

We now add in legal abortion and widely available contraception, breaking the link between sex and childbearing. Women who don't want children are willing to provide sex on much less demanding terms, since they enjoy it too. Women who want both sex and children must compete for men with women who want only the former. They end up getting them, on average, on less favorable terms. Some women who want children must have them without husbands.

There is an empirical problem with this explanation. Both reliable contraception and safe illegal abortions were available to middle- and upper-class women before they were available to poorer women. If the Akerlof-Yellin explanation is correct, high illegitimacy rates should have appeared first near the top of the income scale and then worked their way down. What actually happened was the reverse. To explain that one must combine their explanation with something else, perhaps the role of welfare payments in encouraging illegitimacy at the bottom of the ladder.

Before closing, I should add one more possible explanation: rising incomes. The richer people are, the easier it is for a woman to support children by herself. Some women may regard a husband as a net cost and so prefer, if possible, to do without one.

EXPLAINING SEX LAW

Many societies, including ours, forbid prostitution. Many societies, until recently including ours, forbid fornication and adultery. The arguments in favor of permitting people to engage in transactions in their mutual benefit seem to apply to sex as to anything else, so why do these laws exist?

The easiest to explain is the law against adultery—especially, although not exclusively, female adultery, which in most societies is more severely sanctioned than male adultery. The terms of a traditional marriage include sexual exclusivity. From the standpoint of the husband, one reason is that he wants to be sure the children he is supporting are his own. The wife does not have that problem, but she would like to be sure that her husband is not spending money that should go to her and her children on another woman and other children instead. For both there is also a link between sexual fidelity and emotional commitment—and emotional commitment, or if you prefer mutual altruism, helps reduce the problems of a bilateral monopoly bargaining game, which is one of the things a marriage is.

The Akerlof-Yellin argument provides a possible explanation for laws against fornication and prostitution. Even in a world without reliable birth control, it was still sometimes possible to get sex without marriage, and that fact weakened the bargaining position of women who wanted sex, babies, and husbands. Laws making sex outside of marriage illegal improve the bargaining position of women who want to get married, or stay married, or to maintain a strong bargaining position within marriage. Hence it is rational for such women to support such laws.

It may also be rational for at least some men to support them. If the argument is right, a longer-term result of access to sex without marriage may be a partial breakdown of the institution of marriage. If, as seems to be the case, children brought up by two parents end up on average as better people, more valuable trading partners and fellow citizens, than children brought up by one, preserving the institution of marriage may be desirable for men as well as for women.

GLITTERING BONDS

Premarital sex is not, popular opinion to the contrary, a new discovery. In most societies we know of, however, men prefer to marry women who have never slept with anyone else. This creates a problem. Unmarried women are reluctant to have sex for fear that it will lower their ability to find a suitable husband, and as a result unmarried men have difficulty finding women to sleep with.

One traditional solution to this problem is for unmarried couples to sleep together on the understanding that if the woman gets pregnant the man will marry her. This practice was sufficiently common in a number of societies for which we have data that between a quarter and half of all brides went to the altar pregnant.

One problem with this practice is that it creates an opportunity for opportunistic breach by the man, the strategy of seduce and abandon familiar in folk songs, romantic literature, and real life. That problem can be reduced by converting the understanding into an enforceable contract. Under traditional common law a jilted bride could sue for breach of promise to marry. The damages she could collect reflected the reduction in her future marital prospects. They were in fact, although not in form, damages for loss of virginity.

Starting in the 1930s U.S. courts became increasingly reluctant to recognize the action for breach of promise to marry, with the result that between 1935 and 1945 it was abolished in states containing about half the population. This created a problem for women who wanted to engage in premarital sex but did not want to end up as single mothers in a society in which that status was both economically difficult and heavily stigmatized.

The solution they found was described in "Rings and Promises," an ingenious article by Margaret Brinig. The practice of a man giving his intended a valuable diamond engagement ring is not, De Beers' ads to the contrary, an ancient custom. Data for diamond imports in the early part of the century are not very good, but Brinig's conclusion from such information as she was able to find was that the practice became common only in the 1930s, peaked in the 1950s, and has since declined.

Her explanation was that the engagement ring served as a performance bond for the promise to marry. Instead of suing, the jilted bride could simply keep the ring, confiscating the posted bond. The practice eventually declined not because of further legal changes—at present no states recognize the action for breach of promise to marry—but as a result of social changes. As premarital sex became more common, contraception more reliable, and virginity of less importance on the marriage market, the risk of opportunistic breach, and thus the need for a bonding mechanism, declined.

BYWAYS OF SEDUCTION LAW

A few years back, while investigating the history of punitive damages, I stumbled across an odd and interesting bit of nineteenth-century law. In both England and America, when a man discovered that his daughter had been seduced he could sue the seducer—even if the daughter was an adult. The grounds on which he sued were that he, the father, had been deprived of the daughter's services. Suits for seduction were thus treated as a special case of the doctrine under which a master could sue for injuries to his servant.

In one case a judge held that it was sufficient basis for the action if the daughter occasionally acted as hostess at her father's tea parties. Once the father had standing to sue as a master deprived of his servant's services, he could then base his claim, not on the actual value of the services, but on the reputational injuries suffered by the family as a result of the seduction.

The obvious question is why, given that seduction was considered a wrongful act, the law took such a roundabout approach to dealing with it. The explanation I found in the legal literature was that one party to an illegal act cannot sue another for damages associated with the act. If you and I rob a bank and you drop the loot on the way out, I am not entitled to collect damages for your negligence. Fornication was illegal, hence a seduced woman was party to an illegal act, hence she could not sue for damages. So the law substituted the legal fiction of the father suing as a master deprived of his daughter's services.

It occurred to me at the time that there was another, and perhaps more plausible, explanation of what was going on. In traditional societies, including eighteenth- and nineteenth-century England, fathers attempt to control whom their daughters marry. One tactic available to a daughter who disagrees with her father's choice is to allow herself to be "seduced" by the man she wants to marry, in the expectation that her father, faced with a fait accompli and possibly a pregnancy, will give his consent. That tactic appears explicitly in Casanova's *Memoires,* which provide a vivid and detailed firsthand account of life in eighteenth-century Europe.

A legal doctrine that gave the daughter the right to sue would lower the risk of the daughter's tactic for evading parental control by making it possible for her to punish a seducer who refused to marry her, and would thus weaken paternal authority. A legal doctrine that gave the father control over the action gave him a threat that could be used to discourage enterprising, and unacceptable, suitors.

The economic analysis of law involves three different projects: predicting the effect of legal rules, explaining legal rules, and choosing legal rules. In discussing the second project I offered as an example the Posner conjecture that common law rules tend to be economically efficient.

I have just provided a different example. My explanation for why common law treated seduction in the peculiar way it did depends on the assumption that the people shaping the law wanted fathers to be able to control whom their daughters married. I do not assume that such control was efficient.

BUYING BABIES

Some years ago I came across an article in the *Wall Street Journal* that astonished me for the degree of economic ignorance displayed by a publication whose writers I expected better of. Its subject was the adoption market. The writers discussed how that market has swung between shortage and surplus, between periods when infants were unable to find adoptive parents and periods when potential parents were unable to find suitable infants to adopt. They concluded that it demonstrated a failure of the free market.

There was one small point that the article omitted. Under U.S. law it is illegal for prospective adoptive parents to pay a mother for permission to adopt her infant. The adoption market is thus a "free market" on which the price is set, by law, at zero. The observation that price control leads to shortages when the controlled price is below the market price and surpluses when it is above is neither surprising nor a failure of the free market.

There are at least three ways in which shortages produced by price control can be dealt with. The simplest is queuing. When the United States experimented with gasoline price control under President Nixon, one result was long lines at gas stations. Waiting in lines is a cost, so when the lines get long enough the sum of the money cost of gasoline plus the time cost becomes large enough to drive quantity demanded down to quantity supplied. In the adoption market at present prospective parents must often wait years to adopt an infant.

A second way of dealing with the problem is rationing. Some authority decides which prospective buyers are given how much of the limited supply. In the case of the adoption market, the rationing is done by adoption agencies that are authorized to arrange legal adoptions. They impose their own criteria in order to eliminate enough prospective parents so that they can provide adoptions for the remainder. Some of the criteria they have used may be defensible as attempts to select the applicants best suited to be parents. Others, such as the requirement that the adoptive parents be of the same religion as the infant's natural mother, seem to make sense mainly as a way of reducing the number of applicants.

The third possibility under price control is a black market. It is legal for adoptive parents to make payments to lawyers to arrange adoptions and to the infant's biological mother to cover her medical costs. Currently, the cost of arranging a private adoption of a healthy white infant is in the tens of thousands of dollars, which is quite a lot more than the pecuniary costs usually associated with childbirth. Presumably some of that ends up as an illegal payment to the mother for her consent, disguised as something else, and some goes to the lawyers who arrange the transaction.

On this market as on others, the problem could be eliminated by eliminating price control, permitting adoptive parents to negotiate mutually acceptable terms with the natural mother. That solution has been proposed by, among others, Judge Posner. It is widely believed among his fellow legal academics that that fact alone makes it almost certain he will never be on the Supreme Court, despite being one of the most distinguished jurists and legal scholars of his generation. What senator would vote for the confirmation of a candidate who had openly advocated selling babies?

Why does the proposal produce such a strong negative reaction? The obvious answer is that it involves selling human beings, and human beings should not be owned. But what an adoptive parent gets is not ownership of a baby but parental rights (and obligations) with regard to a baby. If "owning" a child in that sense is objectionable, why is it not equally objectionable when the owner is a natural or adoptive parent under current law?

A better argument against a free market in adoptions is that, while it will maximize the joint benefit to the parties to the transaction—adoptive parents and natural mother—it may ignore costs and benefits to the child. But it is hard to see why that should be more true than under current institutions; in neither case do the infants get a vote. People willing to pay money to adopt a child are typically people who very much want to be parents—which is, after all, one of the chief qualifications for the job. Why is the willingness to wait three years and fill out lots of forms, or the ability to find and willingness to pay a lawyer with the right connections, better evidence? Adoption agencies claim to impose their restrictions with the welfare of the child as their chief objective—but why should we expect them to be more concerned with the welfare of a particular infant than either its natural mother or the couple that wants to adopt it? Infants have considerable influence over their parents, natural or adoptive, and very little over the running of adoption agencies.

A more interesting argument, and one with a much broader range of applications, goes under the name of "commodification." The idea is that a transaction between two parties affects others, not in the direct ways economists normally include in their analysis of externalities but in a more subtle fashion—by changing how people think. If we permit payments of money in exchange for babies—even for parental rights with regard to babies—we will start thinking of babies as things like automobiles and jewelry, commodities, not people. If we permit cash payments between a prostitute and her customer, we will start thinking of sex as a service that women sell rather than part of a loving relationship. Thus, argued Margaret Radin in a widely cited law review article, even if permitting prostitution makes both prostitutes and their customers better off, it might still be proper to prohibit it on the grounds that permitting it commodifies sex and so makes men and women in general worse off. On similar grounds it might be proper to prohibit a free market in adoptions.

I find the argument ingenious but unconvincing. Even where prostitution is common, very few people—prostitutes, customers, or others—regard it as a model for what sex is supposed to be. Men sleep with prostitutes not because they would not prefer to sleep with women who love them but because there are no suitable women who love them and are willing to sleep with them.

Also implicit in the argument is the assumption that what matters is what the law says rather than what people do. Prostitution, as Radin recognizes, exists at present throughout the United States, even though it is legal only in two rural counties in Nevada. Adoptive parents pay money at present to get an infant, probably more than they would pay if direct payments were legal, since the real cost of price-controlled goods, including waiting time, covert payments, and the like, is usually higher than the cost of the same goods on legal markets without price control.

To argue that legalizing such transactions will also make people see them as legitimate requires two assumptions, both implausible. The first is that if anything is not illegal it must be good, which suggests a view of society along the general lines of T. H. White's ant nest, where everything was either forbidden or compulsory. In a nation where private gambling is illegal but many states conduct lotteries, it is hard to believe that many of us make a close identification between good/bad and legal/illegal.

The second necessary assumption is that people view government as a source of moral authority. Current polling results put government fairly far down on the scale of public approval. As William

Godwin put it almost two hundred years ago, in his response to the argument that we need government-run schooling in order to teach people morality, one should hope "that mankind will never have to learn so important a lesson through so corrupt a channel."

Commodification is an ingenious argument, but less novel than it appears. It is simply a new version of the traditional social conservative argument against both immoral behavior and free speech: that ideas matter, that preaching, or demonstrating, bad principles leads to bad behavior.

Seen from this standpoint, Radin's argument for why laws against prostitution might be justified fits oddly with the jurisprudence of the First Amendment. Courts routinely hold that acts that might properly be banned as acts, such as burning the American flag, are also speech, and because they are speech are legally protected. The commodification argument holds that some acts that ought not to be banned as acts, such as the transaction between a prostitute and her client, are also speech, and because they are bad speech ought to be banned. There is nothing logically indefensible in the claim, but once it has been accepted it becomes hard to see why one should not accept broader arguments in favor of government censorship of bad ideas.

I have devoted so much time to this set of arguments not only because they are interesting but also because they relate to an important set of legal issues raised by new reproductive technology. One such technology, in vitro fertilization, has now become both common and widely accepted. A second and technologically simpler practice, the use of surrogate mothers, is still controversial, with courts generally reluctant to enforce a contract by which a woman agrees to be artificially inseminated with sperm from a man whose wife is infertile and to turn over the resulting infant to the couple for adoption. A third, producing an infant by cloning a cell from an adult human, has not, so far as we know, happened yet but is almost certainly possible now. Coming up in the near future is the possibility of giving parents some control over which of the children they could produce they do produce, and perhaps, in the somewhat further future, giving their children characteristics that no child naturally produced by those parents would have. Other technologies, some of which have already been implemented in mice and could be in humans, could permit a lesbian couple to produce a child genetically related to both of them.

All of these practices have been or will be criticized in ways similar to current criticisms of legalizing the adoption market. Arguments will include claims that even though the transactions are voluntary, some participants are being taken advantage of. They will include arguments based on the presumed interest of children, with the implicit assumption that parents who employ new technologies will be less committed to their children than parents who produced them the old-fashioned way. They will get much of their force from a deep-seated belief that these things are contrary to nature, that they treat human life in ways it ought not to be treated. New things are frightening:

> What this new technique, and so many others like it, tell us is that there is nothing special about human reproduction, nor any other aspect of human biology, save one. The specialness of humanity is found only between our ears; if you go looking for it anywhere else, you'll be disappointed. (Mouse geneticist Lee Silver, responding to a bioethicist concerned that a technique that might make it possible to produce human sperm by implanting human cells in the testes of an animal challenged "the specialness of humanity")

While arguments against the transactions associated with new reproductive technologies will probably prevail in many courts, that may have very little effect on how widely such technologies are used. Consider the case of host mother contracts. Such contracts are criminal in at least one state and to varying degrees unenforceable in most. But that has very little effect on what actually happens, because people who want to make such contracts can choose where to do so—and, of course, choose states with favorable legal rules. Even where the contract is not entirely enforceable, that fact has become relatively unimportant as firms in the business of arranging host mother transactions have learned to identify and avoid potential host mothers who are likely to try to renege on their agreement after the fact.

RATIONING SURPLUS KITTENS: A FELINE DIGRESSION

Some time back my children decided that they wanted kittens, so we took a trip to the local humane society. It was an interesting experience. We ended up spending several hours waiting in line to receive one of a small number of permissions to "adopt" a pet, filling out forms, and then being interviewed by a humane society employee to make sure we were suitable adopters.

What was puzzling about the experience is that kittens are a good in excess supply. The humane society has more of them (and of cats, puppies, and dogs) than it can find homes for and, although it does not like to say so, routinely kills surplus animals. Rationing goods in excess supply is not usually a problem. Yet the humane society was deliberately making it costly, in time and effort, to adopt a kitten and trying to select which lucky people got to do so, despite their knowledge that the alternative to being adopted was not another adoption but death. Why?

Part of the answer was that they gave out only seven adoption permits in each two-hour interval because that was as many as they could process, given a limited staff and the requirement that each adopter be suitably checked and instructed. But that raises a second question. Since they did not have enough staff to process everyone who came, why insist on extensive interviews? Better owners are no doubt superior, from the standpoint of a kitten, to worse owners, but almost any owner is better than being killed, which was the alternative.

So far as I could tell, the only real function of the process was to make the employees feel important and powerful, handing out instructions and boons to humble petitioners. That suspicion was reinforced when the woman interviewing us insisted very strongly that cats should never be permitted outdoors, stopping just short of implying that if we would not promise to keep our new pets indoors, she would not let us have them. On further questioning it turned out that she did not apply that policy to her own cat.

We left the center petless, obtained two kittens from a friend (and very fine cats they have become), and I wrote an unhappy letter to the local newspaper with a copy to the humane society. The result was a long phone conversation with one of the women running the shelter. She explained that there were two models for such shelters: one in which animals were given out on a more or less no-questions-asked basis and one involving the sort of "adoption procedures" I had observed. When pressed on the fact that the real effect of her shelter's policy was to discourage adoptions and thus kill animals that might otherwise have lived, she responded that if they followed the alternative policy, nobody would be willing to work for the shelter, since employees would feel they were treating the animals irresponsibly. That struck me as a kinder version of the explanation I had already come up with.

When the decision of what baby goes to what parent is made by an adoption agency, there is no good reason to expect the people making it to prefer the baby's welfare to their own. When the equivalent decisions are made for pets, there is no good reason to expect the people making them to put the animal's welfare—or life—above their own feelings.

ARE BABIES A GOOD THING?

In recent decades it has been widely argued that babies are a bad thing, that when I decide to have one more child the predictable result is that other people are worse off and the world a less pleasant place. This belief, which has led to a variety of proposals for laws and policies designed to reduce the birth rate, is based in part on bad economics and in part on possible, but contestable, empirical claims.

The argument starts with the idea that more people mean less resources for each—less land, water, minerals, petroleum, and the like. The statement may be true, but the conclusion that by having a child I make yours worse off does not follow. Children are not born clutching deeds to a per capita share of the world's land and oil. In order for my child to acquire land he must buy it, which means that he must produce, or I must provide him, enough valuable resources to compensate the previous owner for giving up his land. The same is true for any other owned resource.

By buying land my child may (very slightly) bid up its price. But while that is a bad thing for those who are buying, it is a good thing for those who are selling. The externality is only pecuniary.

A better argument looks to real externalities associated with childbearing. My child may use the public schools. He may pollute. He may become a criminal. He may go on welfare. In these and other ways he may impose net costs on other people.

The list of externalities is too selective. My child may find the cure for cancer, and so save your child from an agonizing death. He will pay taxes, some of which will go to help pay fixed expenses such as the national debt or veterans' pensions that your child would otherwise have to pay. More people means a bigger market, more competition, more customers to share in the fixed costs of designing goods or writing books. An additional child generates positive as well as negative externalities. In order to argue for policies designed to reduce the birth rate, one must show not merely that there are some negative effects but that the net effect is negative.

As it happens, my first piece of economic research dealt with just this question. In it I attempted to estimate the size of the relevant externalities in order to calculate whether the net effect was positive or negative, whether someone having one more child makes the rest of us, on average, better or worse off. I concluded that the numbers were too uncertain to permit me to calculate with any confidence the sign of the result.

The point is not limited to this particular issue. Any time you are involved in a political controversy and somebody argues for taxing or banning something because it produces negative externalities, or for subsidizing something because it produces positive externalities, it is worth trying to draw up your own list of externalities—of both signs. It is only too easy to generate an apparently objective argument for either conclusion by suitable selection.

TWO ROUTES TO EFFICIENCY

Perceptive readers may have noticed that in this chapter I have invoked two different sorts of arguments for the efficiency of law and custom. One derives efficiency from standard economic arguments. The use of engagement rings as bonds, for example, is a rational response by individuals to the problem of making possible sex before marriage while controlling the risk of opportunistic breach by the male partner. The increased instability of marriage over the past century would have happened in a world where marriage contracts were explicitly negotiated as couples rationally adapted the terms of their agreement in response to a decrease in the sunk costs associated with it. The same individualistic approach can sometimes also be used to derive from rational behavior the existence of inefficient outcomes, such as opportunistic breach due to women performing early in marriage and men late.

The same cannot be said of arguments that interpret laws against adultery or prostitution, or legal rules designed to protect children, as efficient adjustments to the corresponding problems. It cannot even be said of changes in marriage law as they actually happened, since in our society terms of marriage are not individually negotiated; contractual agreements on terms such as easy divorce would almost certainly be held unenforceable as contrary to public policy. Such arguments require some more general mechanism to push legal rules toward efficiency. It is not obvious, *pace* Posner, that such a mechanism exists. It is particularly puzzling if we wish to explain legal rules designed to protect children. Children, after all, neither vote, lobby, nor litigate, which ought to eliminate their welfare from influencing the mechanisms that most obviously determine law.

Altruistic parents care about the welfare of their own children—but not, or not very much, about the welfare of other people's children. If I care about the welfare of my children, I have no need to lobby for laws against abuse, or to make divorce more difficult; I know I am not going to abuse my children and that I will take due account of their welfare when deciding whether to get a divorce.

The distinction between arguments for efficiency based directly on individual rationality and those that require some more elaborate mechanism runs through the analysis of the law. The efficiency of the terms of a negotiated contract follows directly from the rationality of the parties. The efficiency of the law of contracts—supposing that it is efficient—is harder to explain.

FURTHER READING

The anecdote of the poor woman and the two hundred dinar is slightly condensed from *The Table-Talk of a Mesopotamian Judge,* by al-Muhassin ibn Ali al-Tanukhi, trans. D. S. Margoliouth.

Both the idea and the title of one section of this chapter are borrowed from Lloyd Cohen, "Marriage, Divorce, and Quasi Rents; or, 'I Gave Him the Best Years of My Life,'" *Journal of Legal Studies* 16 (1987).

The classic presentation of the commodification argument is Margaret Radin, "Market-Inalienability," *Harvard Law Review* 100 (1987) 1849; you may find it more convincing than I did.

Lee Silver, *Remaking Eden,* provides an entertaining and informative account of reproductive technology, current and forthcoming.

Drugs

Michael Huemer

America's Unjust Drug War

2004

Should the recreational use of drugs such as marijuana, cocaine, heroin, and LSD, be prohibited by law? *Prohibitionists* answer yes. They usually argue that drug use is extremely harmful both to drug users and to society in general, and possibly even immoral, and they believe that these facts provide sufficient reasons for prohibition. *Legalizers* answer no. They usually give one or more of three arguments: First, some argue that drug use is not as harmful as prohibitionists believe, and even that it is sometimes beneficial. Second, some argue that drug prohibition "does not work", i.e., is not very successful in preventing drug use and/or has a number of very bad consequences. Lastly, some argue that drug prohibition is unjust or violates rights.

I won't attempt to discuss all these arguments here. Instead, I will focus on what seem to me the three most prominent arguments in the drug legalization debate: first, the argument that drugs should be outlawed because of the harm they cause to drug users; second, the argument that they should be outlawed because they harm people other than the user; and third, the argument that drugs should be legalized because drug prohibition violates rights. I shall focus on the moral/philosophical issues that these arguments raise, rather than medical or sociological

Michael Huemer, "America's Unjust Drug War." In *The New Prohibition*, ed. Bill Masters (St. Louis, MO: Accurate Press, 2004), pp. 133–44. By permission of Accurate Press.

issues. I shall show that the two arguments for prohibition fail, while the third argument, for legalization, succeeds.

I. DRUGS AND HARM TO USERS

The first major argument for prohibition holds that drugs should be prohibited because drug use is extremely harmful to the users themselves, and prohibition decreases the rate of drug abuse. This argument assumes that the proper function of government includes preventing people from harming themselves. Thus, the argument is something like this:

1. Drug use is very harmful to users.
2. The government should prohibit people from doing things that harm themselves.
3. Therefore, the government should prohibit drug use.

Obviously, the second premise is essential to the argument; if I believed that drug use was very harmful, but I did *not* think that the government should prohibit people from harming themselves, then I would not take this as a reason for prohibiting drug use. Furthermore, premise (2), if taken without qualification, is extremely implausible. Consider some examples of things people do that are harmful (or entail a risk of harm) to themselves: smoking tobacco, drinking alcohol, eating too much, riding motorcycles, having unprotected or promiscuous sex, maintaining relationships with inconsiderate or abusive boyfriends and girlfriends, maxing out their credit cards, working in dead-end jobs, dropping out of college, moving to New Jersey, and being rude to their bosses. Should the government prohibit all of these things?[1] Most of us would agree that the government should not prohibit *any* of these things, let alone all of them. And this is not merely for logistical or practical reasons; rather, we think that controlling those activities is not the business of government.

Perhaps the prohibitionist will argue, not that the government should prohibit *all* activities that are harmful to oneself, but that it should prohibit activities that harm oneself in a certain way, or to a certain degree, or that also have some other characteristic. It would then be up to the prohibitionist to explain how the harm of drug use (to users) differs from the harms (to those who engage in them) of the other activities mentioned above. Let's consider three possibilities.

1. One suggestion would be that drug use also harms people other than the user; we will discuss this harm to others in section II below. If, as I will contend, neither the harm to drug users nor the harm to others justifies prohibition, then there will be little plausibility in the suggestion that the combination of harms justifies prohibition. Of course, one could hold that a certain threshold level of total harm must be reached before prohibition of an activity is justified, and that the combination of the harm of drugs to users and their harm to others passes that threshold even though neither kind of harm does so by itself. But if, as I will contend, the "harm to users" and "harm to others" arguments both fail for the reason that it is not the government's business to apply criminal sanctions to prevent the kinds of harms in question, *then* the combination of the two harms will not make a convincing case for prohibition.

2. A second suggestion is that drug use is generally *more* harmful than the other activities listed above. But there seems to be no reason to believe this. As one (admittedly limited) measure of harmfulness, consider the mortality statistics. The Office of National Drug Control Policy claims that drugs kill 18,000 Americans per year.[2] By contrast, tobacco causes an estimated 440,000 deaths per year.[3] Of course, more people use tobacco than use illegal drugs,[4] so let us divide by the number of users: tobacco kills 15 people per 1000 users per year; illegal drugs kill 2.6 people per 1000 users per year.[5] Yet almost no one favors outlawing tobacco and putting smokers in prison. On a similar note, obesity may cause 420,000 deaths per year (due to increased incidence of heart disease, strokes, and so on), or 11 per 1000 at-risk persons.[6] Health professionals have warned about the pandemic of obesity, but no one has yet called for imprisoning fat people.

There are less tangible harms of drug use—harms to one's general quality of life. These are difficult to quantify. But compare the magnitude of the harm to one's quality of life that one can bring about by, say, dropping out of high school, working in a dead-end job for several years, or marrying a jerk—these things can cause extreme and lasting detriment to one's well-being. And yet no one proposes jailing those who drop out, work in bad jobs, or make poor marriage decisions. The idea of doing so would seem ridiculous, clearly beyond the state's prerogatives.

3. Another suggestion is that drug use harms users *in a different way* than the other listed activities. Well, what sorts of harms do drugs cause? First, illicit drugs may worsen users' health and, in some cases, entail a risk of death. But many other activities—including the consumption of alcohol, tobacco, and fatty foods; sex; and (on a broad construal of "health") automobiles—entail health risks, and yet almost no one believes those activities should be criminalized.

Second, drugs may damage users' relationships with others—particularly family, friends, and lovers—and prevent one from developing more satisfying personal relationships.[7] Being rude to others can also have this effect; yet no one believes you should be put in jail for being rude. Moreover, it is very implausible to suppose that people should be subject to criminal sanctions for ruining their personal relationships. I don't have a general theory of what sort of things people should be punished for, but consider the following example: Suppose that I decide to break up with my girlfriend, stop calling my family, and push away all my friends. I do this for no good reason—I just feel like it. This would damage my personal relationships as much as anything could. Should the police now come and arrest me, and put me in jail? If not, then why should they arrest me for doing something that only has a *chance* of indirectly bringing about a similar result? The following seems like a reasonable political principle: If it would be wrong (because not part of the government's legitimate functions) to punish people for *directly bringing about* some result, then it would also be wrong to punish people for doing some other action on the grounds that the action has a *chance* of bringing about that result indirectly. If the state may not prohibit me from directly cutting off my relationships with others, then the fact that my drug use might have the result of damaging those relationships does not provide a good reason to prohibit me from using drugs.

Third, drugs may harm users' financial lives, costing them money, causing them to lose their jobs or not find jobs, and preventing them from getting promotions. The same principle applies here: if it would be an abuse of government power to prohibit me from directly bringing about those sorts of negative financial consequences, then surely the fact that drug use might indirectly bring them about is not a good reason to prohibit drug use. Suppose that I decide to quit my job and throw all my money out the window, for no reason. Should the police come and arrest me, and put me in prison?

Fourth and finally, drugs may damage users' moral character, as James Q. Wilson believes:

> [I]f we believe—as I do—that dependency on certain mind-altering drugs *is* a moral issue and that their illegality rests in part on their immorality, then legalizing them undercuts, if it does not eliminate altogether, the moral message. That message is at the root of the distinction between nicotine and cocaine. Both are highly addictive; both have harmful physical effects. But we treat the two drugs differently not simply because nicotine is so widely used as to be beyond the reach of effective prohibition, but because its use does not destroy the user's essential humanity. Tobacco shortens one's life, cocaine debases it. Nicotine alters one's habits, cocaine alters one's soul. The heavy use of crack, unlike the heavy use of tobacco, corrodes those natural sentiments of sympathy and duty that constitute our human nature and make possible our social life.[8]

In this passage, Wilson claims that the use of cocaine: (a) is immoral, (b) destroys one's humanity, (c) alters one's soul, and (d) corrodes one's sense of sympathy and duty. One problem with Wilson's argument is the lack of evidence supporting claims (a)–(d). Before we put people in prison for corrupting their souls, we should require some objective evidence that their souls are in fact being corrupted. Before we put people in prison for being immoral, we should require some argument showing that their actions are in fact immoral. Perhaps Wilson's charges of immorality and corruption all come down to the charge that drug users lose their sense of sympathy and duty—that is, claims (a)–(c) all rest upon claim (d). It is plausible that *heavy* drug users experience a decreased sense of sympathy with others and a decreased sense of duty and responsibility. Does this provide a good reason to prohibit drug use?

Again, it seems that one should not prohibit an activity on the grounds that it may indirectly cause some result, unless it would be appropriate to prohibit the direct bringing about of that result. Would it be appropriate, and within the legitimate functions of the state, to punish people for being unsympathetic and undutiful, or for behaving in an unsympathetic and undutiful way? Suppose that Howard—though not a drug user—doesn't sympathize with others. When people try to tell Howard their problems, he just tells them to quit whining. Friends and coworkers who ask Howard for favors are rudely rebuffed. Furthermore—though he does not harm others in ways that would be against our current laws—Howard has a poor sense of duty. He doesn't bother to show up for work on time, nor does he take any pride in his work; he doesn't donate to charity; he doesn't try to improve his community. All around, Howard is an ignoble and unpleasant individual. Should he be put in jail?

If not, then why should someone be put in jail merely for doing something that would have a *chance* of causing them to become like Howard? If it would be an abuse of governmental power to punish people for being jerks, then the fact that drug use may cause one to become a jerk is not a good reason to prohibit drug use.

II. DRUGS AND HARM TO OTHERS

Some argue that drug use must be outlawed because drug use harms the user's family, friends, and coworkers, and/or society in general. A report produced by the Office of National Drug Control Policy states:

> Democracies can flourish only when their citizens value their freedom and embrace personal responsibility. Drug use erodes the individual's capacity to pursue both ideals. It diminishes the individual's capacity to operate effectively in many of life's spheres—as a student, a parent, a spouse, an employee—even as a coworker or fellow motorist. And, while some claim it represents an expression of individual autonomy, drug use is in fact inimical to personal freedom, producing a reduced capacity to participate in the life of the community and the promise of America.[9]

At least one of these alleged harms—dangerous driving—*is* clearly the business of the state. For this reason, I entirely agree that people should be prohibited from driving while under the influence of drugs. But what about the rest of the alleged harms?

Return to our hypothetical citizen Howard. Imagine that Howard—again, for reasons having nothing to do with drugs—does not value freedom, nor does he embrace personal responsibility. It is unclear exactly what this means, but, for good measure, let us suppose that Howard embraces a totalitarian political ideology and denies the existence of free will. He constantly blames other people for his problems and tries to avoid making decisions. Howard is a college student with a part-time job. However, he is a terrible student and worker. He hardly ever studies and frequently misses assignments, as a result of which he gets poor grades. As we mentioned earlier, Howard comes to work late and takes no pride in his work. Though he does nothing against our current laws, he is an inattentive and inconsiderate spouse and parent. Nor does he make any effort to participate in the life of his community, or the promise of America. He would rather lie around the house, watching television and cursing the rest of the world for his problems. In short, Howard does all the bad things to his family, friends, coworkers, and society that the ONDCP says *may* result from drug use. And most of this is voluntary.

Should Congress pass laws against what Howard is doing? Should the police then arrest him, and the district attorney prosecute him, for being a loser?

Once again, it seems absurd to suppose that we would arrest and jail someone for behaving in these ways, undesirable as they may be. Since drug use only has a *chance* of causing one to behave in each of these ways, it is even more absurd to suppose that we should arrest and jail people for drug use on the grounds that drug use has these potential effects.

III. THE INJUSTICE OF DRUG PROHIBITION

Philosopher Douglas Husak has characterized drug prohibition as the greatest injustice perpetrated in the United States since slavery.[10] This is no hyperbole. If the drug laws are unjust, then we have 450,000 people unjustly imprisoned at any given time.[11]

Why think the drug laws are *unjust*? Husak's argument invokes a principle with which few could disagree: it is unjust for the state to punish people without having a good reason for doing so.[12] We have seen the failure of the most common proposed rationales for drug prohibition. If nothing better is forthcoming, then we must conclude that prohibitionists have no rational justification for punishing drug users. We have deprived hundreds of thousands of people of basic liberties and subjected them to severe hardship conditions, for no good reason.

This is bad enough. But I want to say something stronger: it is not just that we are punishing people for no good reason. We are punishing people for exercising their natural rights. Individuals have a right to use drugs. This right is neither absolute nor exceptionless; suppose, for example, that there existed a drug which, once ingested, caused a significant proportion of users, without any further free choices on their part, to attack other people without provocation. I would think that stopping the use of this drug would be the business of the government. But no existing drug satisfies this description. Indeed, though I cannot take time to delve into the matter here, I think it is clear that the drug *laws* cause far more crime than drugs themselves do.

The idea of a right to use drugs derives from the idea that individuals own their own bodies. That is, a person has the right to exercise control over his own body—including the right to decide how it should be used, and to exclude others from using it—in a manner similar to the way one may exercise control over one's (other) property. This statement is somewhat vague; nevertheless, we can see the general idea embodied in common sense morality. Indeed, it seems that if there is *anything* one would have rights to, it would be one's own body. This explains why we think others may not physically attack you or kidnap you. It explains why we do not accept the use of unwilling human subjects for medical experiments, even if the experiments are beneficial to society—the rest of society may not decide to use your body for its own purposes without your permission. It explains why some believe that women have a right to an abortion—and why some others do not. The former believe that a woman has the right to do what she wants with her own body; the latter believe that the fetus is a distinct person, and a woman does not have the right to harm *its* body. Virtually no one disputes that, *if* a fetus is merely a part of the woman's body, *then* a woman has a right to choose whether to have an abortion; just as virtually no one disputes that, *if* a fetus is a distinct person, then a woman lacks the right to destroy it. Almost no one disputes that persons have rights over their own bodies, but not over other people's bodies.

The right to control one's body cannot be interpreted as implying a right to use one's body in *every* conceivable way, any more than we have the right to use our property in every conceivable way. Most importantly, we may not use our bodies to harm others in certain ways, just as we may not use our property to harm others. But drug use seems to be a paradigm case of a legitimate exercise of the right to control one's own body. Drug consumption takes place in and immediately around the user's own body; the salient effects occur *inside* the user's body. If we consider drug use merely as altering the user's own body and mind, it is hard to see how anyone who believes in rights at all could deny that it is protected by a right, for: (a) it is hard to see how anyone who believes in rights could deny that individuals have rights over their own bodies and minds, and (b) it is hard to see how anyone who believes in such rights could deny that drug use, considered merely as altering the user's body and mind, is an example of the exercise of one's rights over one's own body and mind.

Consider two ways a prohibitionist might object to this argument. First, a prohibitionist might argue that drug use does not *merely* alter the user's own body and mind, but also harms the user's family, friends, co-workers, and society. I responded to this sort of argument in section II. Not just *any* way in which an action might be said to "harm" other people makes the action worthy of criminal sanctions. Here we need not try to state a general criterion for what sorts of harms make an action worthy of criminalization; it is enough to note that there are some kinds of "harms" that virtually no one would take to warrant criminal sanctions, and that these include the "harms" I cause to others by being a poor student, an incompetent worker, or an apathetic citizen.[13] That said, I agree with the prohibitionists at least this far: no one should be permitted to drive or operate heavy machinery while under the influence of drugs that impair their ability to do those things; nor should pregnant mothers be permitted to ingest drugs, if it can be proven that those drugs cause substantial risks to their babies (I leave aside the issue of what the threshold level of risk should be, as well as the empirical questions concerning the actual level of risk created by illegal drugs—I don't know those things). But, in the great majority of cases, drug use does not harm anyone in any *relevant* ways—that is, ways that we normally take to merit criminal penalties—and should not be outlawed.

Second, a prohibitionist might argue that drug use fails to qualify as an exercise of the user's rights over his own body, because the individual is not truly acting freely in deciding to use drugs. Perhaps individuals only use drugs because they have fallen prey to some sort of psychological compulsion, because drugs exercise a siren-like allure that distorts users' perceptions, because users don't realize how bad drugs are, or something of that sort. The exact form of this objection doesn't matter; in any case, the prohibitionist faces a dilemma. If users do not freely choose to use drugs, then it is unjust to *punish* them for using drugs. For if users do not choose freely, then they are not morally responsible for their decision, and it is unjust to punish a person for something he is not responsible for. But if users *do* choose freely in deciding to use drugs, then this choice is an exercise of their rights over their own bodies.

I have tried to think of the best arguments prohibitionists could give, but in fact prohibitionists have remained puzzlingly silent on this issue. When a country goes to war, it tends to focus on how to win, sparing little thought for the rights of the victims in the enemy country. Similarly, one effect of America's declaring "war" on drug users seems to have been that prohibitionists have given almost no thought to the rights of drug users. Most either ignore the issue or mention it briefly only to dismiss it without argument.[14] In an effort to discredit legalizers, the Office of National Drug Control Policy produced the following caricature—

> The easy cynicism that has grown up around the drug issue is no accident. Sowing it has been the deliberate aim of a decades-long campaign by proponents of legalization, critics whose mantra is "nothing works," and whose central insight appears to be that they can avoid having to propose the unmentionable—a world where drugs are ubiquitous and where use and addiction would skyrocket—if they can hide behind the bland management critique that drug control efforts are "unworkable."[15]

—apparently denying the existence of the central issues I have discussed in this essay. It seems reasonable to assume that an account of the state's right to forcibly interfere with individuals' decisions regarding their own bodies is not forthcoming from these prohibitionists.

IV. CONCLUSION

Undoubtedly, the drug war has been disastrous in many ways that others can more ably describe—in terms of its effects on crime, on police corruption, and on other civil liberties, to name a few. But more than that, the drug war is morally outrageous in its very conception. If we are to retain some sort of respect for human rights, we cannot deploy force to deprive people of their liberty and property for whimsical reasons. The exercise of such coercion requires a powerful and clearly-stated rationale. Most of the reasons that have actually been proposed in the case of drug prohibition would be considered feeble if advanced in other contexts. Few would take seriously the suggestion that people should be imprisoned for harming their own health, being poor students, or failing to share in the American dream. It is still less credible that we should imprison people for an activity that only *may* lead to those consequences. Yet these and other, similarly weak arguments form the core of prohibition's defense.

Prohibitionists are likewise unable to answer the argument that individuals have a right to use drugs. Any such answer would have to deny either that persons have rights of control over their own bodies, or that consuming drugs constituted an exercise of those rights. We have seen that the sort of harms drug use allegedly causes to society do not make a case against its being an exercise of the user's rights over his own body. And the claim that drug users can't control their behavior or don't know what they are doing renders it even more mysterious why one would believe drug users deserve to be punished for what they are doing.

I will close by responding to a query posed by prohibition-advocate James Inciardi:

> The government of the United States is not going to legalize drugs anytime soon, if ever, and certainly not in this [the 20th] century. So why spend so much time, expense, and intellectual and emotional effort on a quixotic undertaking? . . . [W]e should know by now that neither politicians nor the polity respond positively to abrupt and drastic strategy alterations.[16]

The United States presently has 450,000 people unjustly imprisoned. Inciardi may—tragically—be correct that our government has no intention of stopping its massive violations of the rights of its people any time soon. Nevertheless, it remains the duty of citizens and of political and social theorists to identify the injustice, and not to tacitly assent to it. Imagine a slavery advocate, decades before the Civil War, arguing that abolitionists were wasting their breath and should move on to more productive activities—such as arguing for incremental changes in the way slaves are treated—since the southern states had no intention of ending slavery any time soon. The institution of slavery is a black mark on our nation's history, but it would be even more shameful if no one at the time had spoken against it.

Is this comparison overdrawn? I don't think so. The harm of being unjustly imprisoned is qualitatively comparable (though it usually ends sooner) to the harm of being enslaved. The increasingly popular scapegoating and stereotyping of drug users and sellers on the part of our nation's leaders is comparable to the racial prejudices of previous generations. Yet very few seem willing to speak on behalf of drug users. Perhaps the unwillingness of those in public life to defend drug users' rights stems from the negative image we have of drug users and the fear of being associated with them. Yet these attitudes remain baffling. I have used illegal drugs myself. I know many decent and successful individuals, both in and out of my profession, who have used illegal drugs. One United States president, one vice-president, a Speaker of the House, and a Supreme Court justice have all admitted to having used illegal drugs.[17] More than a third of all Americans over the age of 11 have used illegal drugs.[18] But now leave aside the absurdity of recommending criminal sanctions for all these people. My point is this: if we are convinced of the injustice of drug prohibition, then—even if our protests should fall on deaf ears—we can not remain silent in the face of such a large-scale injustice in our own country. And, fortunately, radical social reforms *have* occurred, more than once in our history, in response to moral arguments.

REFERENCES

Allison, David B., et al. "Annual Deaths Attributable to Obesity in the United States." *Journal of the American Medical Association* 282 no. 16 (1999): 1530–38.

Centers for Disease Control (CDC) [a]. "Annual Smoking-Attributable Mortality, Years of Potential Life Lost, and Economic Costs—United States, 1995–1999." *Morbidity and Mortality Weekly Report* 51 (2002): 300–303. http://www.cdc.gov/mmwr/PDF/wk/mm5114.pdf

CDC [b]. "Prevalence of Obesity Among U.S. Adults, by Characteristics."

CDC [c]. "Overweight and Obesity: Frequently Asked Questions."

Husak, Douglas [a]. *Drugs and Rights* (Cambridge University Press, 1992).

Husak, Douglas [b]. *Legalize This! The Case for Decriminalizing Drugs* (London: Verso, 2002).

Inciardi, James A. "Against Legalization of Drugs" in Arnold Trebach and James Inciardi, *Legalize It? Debating American Drug Policy* (Washington, D.C.: American University Press, 1993).

Lungren, Daniel. "Legalization Would Be a Mistake" in Timothy Lynch, ed., *After Prohibition* (Washington, D.C.: Cato Institute, 2000).

Office of National Drug Control Policy (ONDCP) [a]. *National Drug Control Strategy 2002* (Washington, D.C.: Government Printing Office). http://www.whitehouse drugpolicy.gov/publications/policy/03ndcs/

ONDCP [b]. "Drug Use Consequences." http://www .whitehousedrugpolicy.gov/publications/policy/03ndcs/ table19.html

Phinney, David. "Dodging the Drug Question." ABCNews.com, Aug. 19, 1999.

Trebach, Arnold S. "For Legalization of Drugs" in Arnold Trebach and James Inciardi, *Legalize It? Debating American Drug Policy* (Washington, D.C.: American University Press, 1993).

U.S. Census Bureau [a]. *Statistical Abstract of the United States* 2001 (Washington, D.C.: Government Printing Office).

U.S. Census Bureau [b]. "Resident Population Estimates of the United States by Sex, Race, and Hispanic Origin." (2001) http://www.census.gov/population/estimates/nation/ intfile3-1.txt

Wilson, James Q. "Against the Legalization of Drugs." *Commentary* 89 (1990): 21–8.

U.S. Department of Justice (DOJ) [a]. "Profile of Jail Inmates 1996." (Washington, D.C.: Government Printing Office, 1998).

U.S. DOJ [b]. "Prisoners in 2001." (Washington, D.C.: Government Printing Office, 2002).

NOTES

1. Husak ([b], pp. 7, 101–3) makes this sort of argument (I have added my own examples of harmful activities to his list).

2. ONDCP [b]. The statistic includes both legal (prescription) and illegal drugs.

3. CDC [a], p. 300.

4. Inciardi (1993, pp. 161, 165) makes this point, accusing drug legalizers of "sophism." He does not go on to calculate the number of deaths per user, however.

5. Based on the assumption of 29.7 million smokers in 1999 and 7.0 million users of illicit drugs (U.S. Census Bureau [a], p. 122). However, these figures maybe off by quite a bit; CDC ([a], p. 303) reports 46.5 million smokers in the same year, based on a different survey.

6. Based on the assumptions of 240,000 premature deaths caused by obesity in 1991 (Allison, et al.), a 61% increase in the prevalence of obesity between 1991 and 2000 (CDC [b]), a 9% increase in population between 1991 and 2000 (U.S. Census Bureau [b], p. 8), and 38.8 million obese Americans in 2000 (CDC [c]).These figures may also be off—different sources give different estimates for each of these quantities.

7. See Inciardi, pp. 167, 172.

8. Wilson, p. 26.

9. ONDCP [a], pp. 1–2.

10. Husak [b], p. 2.

11. Based on 73,389 drug inmates in federal prison in 2000 (U.S. DOJ [b], p. 14), 251,000 drug inmates in state prisons in 2000 (U.S. DOJ [b], p. 13), and 137,000 drug inmates in local jails. The last statistic is based on the 2000 jail population of 621,149 (U.S. DOJ [b], p. 2) and the 1996 rate of 22% drug offenders in local jails (U.S. DOJ [a], p. 1). The numbers have probably increased in the last 3 years.

12. Husak [b], p. 15. See his chapter 2 for an extended discussion of various proposed rationales for drug prohibition, including many issues that I lack space to discuss here.

13. Husak ([a], pp. 166–8), similarly, argues that no one has a *right* that I be a good neighbor, proficient student, and so on, and that only "harms" that *violate rights* can justify criminal sanctions.

14. See Inciardi for an instance of ignoring and Lungren (p. 180) for an instance of dismissal without argument. Wilson (p. 24) addresses the issue, if at all, by arguing that drug use makes users worse parents, spouses, employers, and co-workers. This fails to refute the contention that individuals have a right to use drugs.

15. ONDCP [a], p. 3.

16. Inciardi, p. 205.

17. Bill Clinton, Al Gore, Newt Gingrich and Clarence Thomas (reported by Phinney). George W. Bush has refused to state whether he has ever used illegal drugs.

18. U.S. Census Bureau [a], p. 122.

PETER DE MARNEFFE

Against the Legalization of Drugs

2013

INTRODUCTION

By the *legalization of drugs* I mean the removal of criminal penalties for the manufacture, sale, and possession of large quantities of recreational drugs, such as marijuana, cocaine, heroin, and methamphetamine. In this chapter, I present an argument against drug legalization in this sense. But I do not argue against *drug decriminalization,* by which I mean the removal of criminal penalties for recreational drug use and the possession of small quantities of recreational drugs. Although I am against drug legalization, I am for drug decriminalization. So one of my goals here is to explain why this position makes sense as a matter of principle.

The argument against drug legalization is simple. If drugs are legalized, they will be less expensive and more available. If drugs are less expensive and more available, drug use will increase, and with it, proportionately, drug abuse. So if drugs are legalized, there will be more drug abuse. By *drug abuse* I mean drug use that is likely to cause harm.

INEFFECTIVENESS OBJECTION

A common objection is that drug laws do not work. The imagined proof is that people still use drugs even though they are illegal. But this is a bad argument. People are still murdered even though murder is illegal, and we do not conclude that murder laws do not work or that they ought to be repealed. This is because we think these laws work well enough in reducing murder rates to justify the various costs of enforcing them. So even if drug laws do not eliminate drug abuse, they might likewise reduce it by enough to justify their costs.

Why should we think that drug laws reduce drug abuse? For one thing, our general knowledge of human psychology and economic behavior provides a good basis for predicting that drug use will increase if drugs are legalized. People use drugs because they enjoy them. If it is easier and less expensive to do something enjoyable, more people will do it and those who do it already will do it more often. Laws against the manufacture and sale of drugs make drugs less available, because they prohibit their sale in convenient locations, such as the local drug or liquor or grocery store, and more expensive, because the retail price of illegal drugs reflects the risk to manufacturers and sellers of being arrested and having their goods confiscated. So if drugs are legalized, the price will fall and they will be easier to get. "Hey honey, feel like some heroin tonight?" "Sure, why not stop at Walgreens on the way home from picking up the kids?"

The claim that drug laws reduce drug abuse is also supported by the available empirical evidence. During Prohibition it was illegal to manufacture, sell, and transport "intoxicating liquors" (but not illegal to drink alcoholic beverages or to make them at home for one's own use). During this same period, deaths from cirrhosis of the liver and admissions to state hospitals for alcoholic psychosis declined dramatically compared to the previous decade (Warburton, 1932, pp. 86, 89). Because cirrhosis and alcoholic psychosis

Peter de Marneffe, "Against the Legalization of Drugs." From Andrew I. Cohen and Christopher Heath Wellman, eds., *Contemporary Debates in Applied Ethics*. Malden, MA: Blackwell Pub., 2013. By permission of Blackwell Publishing.

are highly correlated with heavy drinking, this is good evidence that Prohibition reduced heavy drinking substantially (Miron and Zwiebel, 1991). Recent studies of alcohol consumption also conclude that heavy drinking declines with increases in price and decreases in availability (Edwards *et al.*, 1994; Cook, 2007). Further evidence that drug use is correlated with availability is that the use of controlled psychoactive drugs is significantly higher among physicians and other health care professionals (who have much greater access to these drugs) than it is among the general population (Goode, 2012, pp. 454–455), and that veterans who reported using heroin in Vietnam, where it was legal, reported not using it on returning to the USA, where it was illegal (Robins *et al.*, 1974).

For all these reasons it is a safe bet that drug abuse would increase if drugs were legalized, and it is hard to find an expert on drug policy who denies this. This alone, however, does not settle whether laws against drugs are a good policy because we do not know by how much drug abuse would increase if drugs were legalized and we do not know how much harm would result from this increase in drug abuse. It is important to recognize, too, that drug laws also cause harm by creating a black market, which fosters violence and government corruption, and by sending people to prison. It is possible that the harms created by drug laws outweigh their benefits in reducing drug abuse. I will say more about this possibility below, but first I address some philosophical objections to drug laws.

PATERNALISM OBJECTION

One objection is that drug laws are paternalistic: they limit people's liberty for their own good. A related objection is that drug laws are moralistic: they impose the view that drug use is wrong on everyone, including those who think it is good. It is true that drug use can be harmful, but most people who use drugs do not use them in a way that harms someone or that creates a significant risk of harm. This is true even of so-called "hard drugs" such as heroin and cocaine. Is it not wrong for the government to prohibit us from doing something we enjoy if it causes no harm?

To oppose drug legalization, however, is to oppose the removal of penalties for the *commercial manufacture* and *sale* and *possession of large quantities* of drugs; it is not to support criminal penalties for the use or possession of small quantities of drugs. To oppose drug legalization is therefore not to hold that anyone should be prohibited from doing something they enjoy for their own good, or that the government should impose the controversial view that drug use is wrong on everyone.

VIOLATION OF RIGHTS OBJECTION

A more fundamental objection to drug laws is that they violate our rights. I believe there is some truth to this. So I want to explain why it makes sense to oppose drug legalization even though some drug laws do violate our rights.

Each of us has a right of self-sovereignty: a moral right to control our own minds and bodies. Laws that prohibit people from using drugs or from possessing small quantities of them violate this right because the choice to use drugs involves an important form of control over our minds and bodies, and recreational drug use does not usually harm anyone or pose a serious risk of harm. The choice to use drugs involves an important form of control over our minds partly because recreational drug use is a form of mood control, which is an important aspect of controlling our minds. There are also perceptual experiences that we can have only as the result of using certain drugs, such as LSD, and certain kinds of euphoria that we can experience only as the result of using certain drugs, such as heroin. The choice to put a drug into one's body—to snort it, smoke it, inject it, or ingest it—is also an important form of control over one's body. Because we have a right to control our own minds and bodies, the government is justified in prohibiting us from using a drug only if the choice to use this drug is likely to harm someone, which is not true of most recreational drug use. Laws that prohibit us from using recreational drugs therefore violate our right of self-sovereignty and for this reason should be repealed.

The choice to manufacture or sell drugs, in contrast, does not involve an important form of control over one's own mind or body—no more than the choice to manufacture or sell any commercial product does. These are choices to engage in a commercial enterprise for profit, and may therefore be regulated or restricted for reasons of public welfare, just as any other commercial enterprise may be. One might think that there is something "hypocritical" or "inconsistent" about prohibiting the manufacture and sale of drugs and not prohibiting their possession and use, but this is confused. If one opposes drug legalization on the ground that the government should do whatever it can to reduce drug abuse, regardless of whether it violates anyone's rights, then it would be inconsistent to oppose drug criminalization. But it is not inconsistent to oppose drug criminalization if one opposes drug legalization on the ground that the government should do whatever it can to reduce drug abuse consistent with respect for individual rights. This is because it makes sense to hold that whereas drug criminalization violates the right of self-sovereignty, non-legalization does not (de Marneffe, 2013).

Some might argue that non-legalization violates the right of self-sovereignty too, because it is not possible to use drugs if no one is legally permitted to sell them. But this is obviously false because people still use drugs even though selling them is illegal. Although this fact is sometimes cited to demonstrate the futility of drug control, ironically it makes drug control easier to justify. If drug non-legalization really did make it impossible to use drugs, and so to have the unique experiences they provide, this policy would arguably violate the right of self-sovereignty on this ground. But drug control laws do not make drug use impossible; they only increase the price and reduce the availability of drugs. This is no more a violation of self-sovereignty than a decision by the local supermarket not to carry a certain food or to double its price.

HIGH COSTS OF THE DRUG WAR OBJECTION

Laws against the manufacture and sale of drugs might of course still be a bad policy even if they do not violate the right of self-sovereignty. This is because these laws have costs, and these costs might outweigh the benefits of these laws in reducing drug abuse. Laws against the manufacture and sale of drugs create a black market, which fosters violence, because when disputes arise in an illegal trade the disputants cannot go to the legal system for resolution. The black market also fosters government corruption, because those in an illegal trade must pay government officials for protection from arrest and confiscation. Drug laws also cost money to enforce, which might be better spent in other ways. Finally, drug laws result in some people being arrested and imprisoned and being left with criminal records. It is certainly possible that these costs outweigh the benefits of drug control in reducing drug abuse.

It is important to understand, though, that drug control policy need not be as costly as the so-called War on Drugs, which is current US policy. So even if the War on Drugs is too costly, as critics maintain, it does not follow that drugs should be legalized. The case against drug legalization rests on the assumption that the benefits of drug control in reducing drug abuse are sufficient to justify the costs of drug control *once these costs are reduced as much as possible consistent with effective drug control.* By *effective* drug control, I mean a policy that reduces drug abuse substantially compared to the amount of drug abuse that would exist if drugs were legalized. I do not mean a policy that eliminates drug abuse altogether. It is no more possible to eliminate drug abuse than it is to eliminate crime. But just as effective crime control is still possible, effective drug control is possible too. And if it is possible to have effective drug control without the high costs of the War on Drugs, then the benefits of prohibiting the manufacture and sale of drugs are more likely to justify the costs.

One compelling objection to the War on Drugs is to the sentencing rules for drug law violations, which require judges to impose long prison terms for drug trafficking offenses. Critics rightly argue that mandatory sentences and long prison terms for selling drugs are morally indefensible. These are not, however, necessary features of effective drug control policy. They are not features of European drug control policy, for example. So it makes sense to oppose harsh mandatory penalties while also opposing drug legalization.

Drug control works primarily by increasing price and reducing availability, which can be accomplished by reliably enforcing laws against the manufacture and sale of drugs with moderate penalties. Where it is illegal to manufacture and sell drugs, most business persons avoid the drug trade because they do not want to be arrested and have their goods confiscated. This reduces supply, which increases price. Where it is illegal to sell drugs, stores that aim to retain their licenses also do not sell them, which reduces availability. Heavy penalties no doubt drive the price up even higher and decrease availability even more by increasing the risks of drug trafficking—but the biggest increases in price and the biggest reductions in availability come simply from the illegality of the trade itself together with reliable enforcement of laws against manufacture and sale (Kleiman *et al.*, 2011, pp. 48–50). If effective drug control does not require harsh mandatory penalties, then the fact that such penalties are unjustifiable is not a good argument for drug legalization.

EFFECT ON IMPRISONED YOUTHS OBJECTION

Another objection to US drug control policy is that it results in many young people being arrested, imprisoned, and left with criminal records, who would otherwise not suffer these misfortunes. Some might retort that if a person chooses to deal drugs illegally, he cannot legitimately complain about the foreseeable consequences of his choice. But this response is inadequate because by making drugs illegal the government creates a hazard that otherwise would not exist. By making the manufacture and sale of drugs illegal, the government creates a lucrative illegal market, and the money-making opportunities that this market creates are attractive, especially to young people who lack a college education or special training, because they can make much more money by dealing drugs than by doing anything else. When the government creates a system of penalties for manufacturing and selling drugs it therefore creates a hazard; it creates a tempting opportunity to make money and then imposes penalties for making money in this way.

In general, the government has an obligation to reduce the risk to individuals of being harmed by the hazards it creates. When the government tests weapons, for example, it must take care that people do not wander into the testing areas. Bright signs are not enough; it must also build fences and monitor against trespass. The government also has an obligation to help young people avoid the worst consequences of their willingness to take unwise risks. It has an obligation to require teenagers to wear helmets when they ride a motorcycle, for example. So when the government creates the hazard of imprisonment by making the manufacture and sale of drugs illegal, it must guard against the likelihood of imprisonment, and it must take special care to reduce this likelihood for young people who commonly lack a proper appreciation of the negative impact that conviction and imprisonment will have on their lives. For all these reasons, the government must structure drug laws so that young people have an adequate opportunity to avoid being imprisoned for drug offenses, and to avoid acquiring a criminal record. This means, among other things, that no one should be arrested for a drug offense prior to receiving an official warning; no penalty for a first conviction should involve prison time; initial jail or prison sentences should be short and subject to judicial discretion; and imprisonment for subsequent convictions should increase in length only gradually and also be subject to judicial discretion.

RACIAL DISCRIMINATION OBJECTION

A related objection to the War on Drugs is that those imprisoned for drug offenses in the USA are disproportionately black inner city males (Alexander, 2012). This objection would be addressed to some degree by the changes in sentencing policy just proposed, but one might predict that any effective drug control policy would result in the same sort of disproportionality, which some might see as an argument for drug legalization. However, it also is important to consider the potential negative impact of drug legalization on inner city communities. Drug legalization will result in a substantial increase in drug abuse. Drug abuse commonly leads parents to neglect their children, and to neglect their own health and jobs, which harms their children indirectly. Drug abuse also distracts teenagers from their schoolwork, interferes with the development of a sense of responsibility, and makes young people less likely to develop the skills necessary for acquiring good jobs as adults. If drugs are legalized, there will therefore be more child neglect as a result and more truancy by teenagers. This is likely to have an even more devastating impact on the life prospects of young people in non-affluent inner city communities than it has on the life prospects of young people in affluent suburbs. I suspect this is the primary reason why many inner city community leaders oppose drug legalization.

It is true that incarcerating large numbers of inner city youths for drug offenses also has a negative impact on inner city communities. A man who is in jail cannot be present as a parent or make money to support his children, and a person with a criminal record has a harder time finding a decent job. These consequences alone would warrant drug legalization if there were no downside. If we assume, however, that drug legalization would result in a substantial increase in child neglect and adolescent truancy, then legalization does not seem like a good way to improve the life prospects of inner city youth overall. It seems better to maintain laws against the manufacture and sale of drugs, and reduce the number of those who are convicted and imprisoned for drug offenses. This would be consistent with effective drug control because the number of dealers in prison could be reduced dramatically without making drugs noticeably cheaper or easier to get (Kleiman *et al.*, 2011, p. 203).

INCREASE IN VIOLENCE OBJECTION

Another objection to US drug control policy is that it has increased violence in other countries, particularly Mexico. Americans enjoy using drugs and are willing to pay for them. Because it is illegal to manufacture and sell drugs in the USA, American drug control policy creates opportunities for people south of the border to get rich by making drugs and selling them wholesale to retailers north of the border. Because those in the drug trade use violence to control market share and to intimidate law enforcement, US drug laws result in violence. If drugs were legalized in the USA, the recreational drug market would presumably be taken over by large US drug, liquor, and food companies and it would not be possible for anyone in Mexico to get rich by selling illegal drugs to Americans, which would eliminate the associated violence there.

Drug legalization, however, is not the only way to reduce drug-related violence abroad. Here are some alternative strategies:

- The USA might legalize the private production of marijuana for personal use (the way it was legal during Prohibition to make alcoholic beverages at home). Because much of the Mexican drug trade is in marijuana, this would reduce its profitability, and so presumably the associated violence.
- The USA might also concentrate its drug enforcement efforts in Mexico on the most violent drug trafficking organizations, as opposed to concentrating on the biggest and most profitable organizations, which would create incentives for those in the Mexican drug trade to be less violent.
- The USA might also ease border control at entry points not on the US-Mexico border. The violence in Mexico is created partly by the fact that

it is the primary conduit of cocaine from South and Central America to North America. If the USA were to loosen border control in Florida, fewer drugs would travel through Mexico. Because the USA imports so many goods, it is not possible to stop drugs from coming into this country. Some would cite this as proof that drug control is futile, but this conclusion is unwarranted because border controls still raise the retail price of drugs substantially, which results in less drug abuse (Kleiman *et al.,* 2011, pp. 162–163). The suggestion here is that a general policy of border control is consistent with US law enforcement experimenting with different border control policies with an eye to reducing violence abroad (Kleiman *et al.,* 2011, p. 170).

None of these proposals would eliminate drug-related violence in Mexico, but it is unrealistic to think that criminal violence in Mexico would be eliminated by drug legalization in the USA. After all, what will career criminals in Mexico do once they cannot make money via the drug trade? Presumably they will turn to other criminal activities, such as kidnapping, extortion, and human trafficking, which also involve violence.

CORRUPTION OF FOREIGN GOVERNMENTS OBJECTION

Another objection to US drug control policy is that it fosters the corruption of foreign governments. Because those in the foreign drug trade need protection from arrest, prosecution, and confiscation of assets, because they are willing to pay government officials to look the other way, and because some government officials are willing to accept this payment, the drug trade increases government corruption. If drugs were legalized in the USA, this would destroy the illegal market abroad, which would remove an important contributing factor in government corruption.

It is naive, though, to think that US drug control policy is the primary cause of government corruption abroad. Although we associate police corruption with drug trafficking, the latter tends to flourish where government officials are already corrupt (Kleiman *et al.,* 2011, p. 177). Although it provides a good plot line for movies and television shows, drug trafficking has not in fact resulted in the widespread financial corruption of US police. One explanation for this is the existence of multiple US enforcement agencies—federal, state, municipal—which have overlapping jurisdictions (Kleiman *et al.,* 2011, p. 65). This arrangement reduces bribery, because in paying protection money to one government agency, a criminal organization does not gain protection from the others, which makes bribery less cost-effective. Overlapping jurisdictions also increases interagency monitoring, which functions as a check on corruption within any one agency. A skeptic might observe that there were also overlapping jurisdictions during Prohibition when US police were notoriously corrupt. But US police departments are now far more professionalized than they were in the 1920s, when positions on municipal police forces were commonly doled out as political spoils by political bosses. A police officer must now receive specialized training and pass the kinds of tests that are required of all civil service employees, and the internal affairs divisions of police departments are now much more effective at monitoring the illegal activities of their members. In any case, the fact that there has been relatively little drug-related financial corruption of US law enforcement shows that a fully professionalized police force with overlapping jurisdictions and strong internal affairs divisions can effectively resist financial corruption even where drugs are illegal. In contrast, a foreign police force that is not fully professionalized will be susceptible to financial corruption regardless of whether the USA legalizes drugs.

THE INCONSISTENCY OBJECTION

Another argument against drug laws is that it is hypocritical or inconsistent for our government to prohibit the manufacture and sale of heroin, cocaine, and methamphetamine while permitting the manufacture and sale of alcohol and cigarettes. Drinking and smoking cause far more harm than other kinds of recreational drug use. This is partly because there is so much more drinking and smoking, which is partly because the manufacture and sale of alcohol and cigarettes are legal. But drinking and smoking are also inherently more harmful than other forms of drug use. Drinking alcohol is correlated much more highly with violence, property crime, and accidental injury than the use of heroin is, and a regular user of heroin who uses it safely—in moderate doses with clean equipment—does not face any significant health risk as a result, whereas cigarette smoking is known to cause heart and lung disease. So it can seem that if the government is justified in prohibiting the manufacture and sale of heroin, it must also be justified in prohibiting the manufacture and sale of alcohol and cigarettes.

This would be a good objection to drug laws if laws against the manufacture and sale of alcoholic beverages and cigarettes were wrong in principle, but it is hard to see why they would be. After all, drinking and smoking cause a lot of harm and neither policy would violate the right of self-sovereignty discussed above, because a law that prohibits only the manufacture and sale of a drug does not prohibit its possession or make its use impossible. Of course, the suggestion that alcohol prohibition might be justified is commonly dismissed with the incantation that Prohibition was a disastrous failure, but historians agree that Prohibition succeeded in substantially reducing heavy drinking, and it would have been even more effective had its enforcement been adequately funded and had it been administered from the outset by law enforcement professionals instead of by political appointees (Okrent, 2010, pp. 134–145, 254–261). Prohibition did fail politically, but so did Reconstruction and the Equal Rights Amendment. The fact that a policy is rejected or abandoned does not show that it was wrong in principle. Finally, it is worth noting that alcohol prohibition still exists in some parts of this country, on Indian reservations, for example, and that these policies make sense as part of an effort to reduce alcoholism and the harms associated with it.

It is not necessary, though, to advocate alcohol prohibition in order to defend other drug laws, because there are relevant differences between them. For one thing, the institution of alcohol prohibition now is likely not to reduce heavy drinking by as much as drug non-legalization reduces drug abuse. Drinking is widely accepted and a part of normal social rituals, in a way that heroin, cocaine, and methamphetamine use is not. This means that alcohol prohibition now would not work in tandem with a strong social stigma, which would presumably reduce its effectiveness in reducing alcohol abuse. It is possible, too, that in an environment of social acceptance, sharply increasing the excise taxes on alcoholic beverages would achieve almost as much as prohibition in reducing the harms caused by heavy drinking with none of the costs of prohibition (though it is worth noting here that liquor industry lobbying has been more effective in preventing excise tax increases than it was in preventing Prohibition). There are also important ways in which instituting alcohol prohibition now would be more burdensome than continuing with drug non-legalization. Many people have built their lives around the alcoholic beverage industry. If alcohol were now prohibited, many of these people would lose their jobs, and many companies, restaurants and bars would go out of business, which would be a serious hardship for owners and employees. In contrast, people who go into the drug trade do so knowing that it is illegal. So the burden on them of maintaining drug laws is not as great as the burden that alcohol prohibition would impose on those who have built their lives around the liquor trade on the assumption that the manufacture and sale of alcohol will remain legal. Ironically, it is drug *legalization* that would burden those in the illegal drug trade, in much the same way as Prohibition burdened those in the legal liquor trade: by depriving them of their livelihood.

There are also important differences between illicit drugs and cigarettes. Drug legalization, I assume, would result in a substantial increase in drug abuse, which, I assume, would also result in a substantial increase in child neglect and adolescent truancy, which would have a substantial negative impact on the life prospects of many young people. Cigarette smoking, in contrast, does not make someone a worse parent or a worse student or employee. Furthermore, because heavy smoking typically has a negative impact on a person's life only toward the end when he or she is older, smoking as a young person is less likely than adolescent drug abuse to have a negative impact on the *kind* of life a person has. Finally, although psychologically challenging, it is quite possible to quit smoking as an adult and so to reduce the long-term health consequences of starting to smoke as a teenager—much easier than it is to reverse the long-term negative consequences of having had inadequate parenting or having failed out of high school as the result of drug abuse. Given these differences between the consequences of smoking and drug abuse, one can consistently oppose the legalization of drugs for the reasons I have given here without advocating prohibiting the manufacture and sale of cigarettes.

In explaining above how one might consistently oppose the legalization of drugs without advocating alcohol prohibition, I observed that drinking is so widespread and socially accepted that alcohol prohibition is likely to reduce heavy drinking by less than drug abuse is reduced by laws against the manufacture and sale of illicit drugs. This same point might now be given as an argument for legalizing marijuana: marijuana use is so widespread and socially accepted that laws against the manufacture and sale of marijuana do not do very much to reduce it. It might also be argued that legalizing marijuana would not result in a dramatic increase in drug abuse because marijuana is less subject to abuse than other drugs (including alcohol). Finally, legalizing marijuana in the USA would dramatically reduce the drug trade in Mexico, which would result in a corresponding reduction in violence and government corruption there. Should not marijuana be legalized, then, even if other drugs should not be?

In this chapter I am arguing against the view that the manufacture and sale of *all* drugs should be legalized; I am not arguing that there is *no* drug that should be legalized. Suppose that marijuana legalization would not result in a substantial increase in drug abuse. Suppose that most of those who would use marijuana if it were legalized are already using it and using it almost as much as they want to. Or suppose that marijuana use itself is harmless and does not lead to the use of more harmful drugs. If either of these things is true, then marijuana should be legalized. It is also possible, though, that, as a result of legalization, many more young people would use marijuana than do now, and that a sizable fraction of them would use it in ways that interfere with their education or employment, and that a sizable fraction of them would go on to abuse more harmful drugs who would otherwise never have tried them. Because I am not sure that these things would not happen, I do not support legalizing marijuana. With more information, though, I might change my mind. So it is important to make clear that whether a drug should be legalized depends on the consequences of legalizing it, and not on whether any *other* drug should be legalized. Hence, even if marijuana should be legalized, it would not follow that heroin, cocaine, and methamphetamine should be legalized too.

UNHEALTHY FOODS OBJECTION

Another argument against drug laws is that if the government is justified in prohibiting us from putting a drug into our bodies for our own good, then it is also justified in prohibiting us from putting unhealthy foods into our bodies for our own good. The suggestion that the government is entitled to control what we eat strikes many of us as outrageous. Why is it not likewise outrageous for the government to prohibit us from using recreational drugs?

For the reasons given above, I think it is. Laws that prohibit us from using drugs—or drinking alcohol or smoking cigarettes—violate our right of self-sovereignty in the same way that laws that prohibit us from eating high fat or high sugar foods would. However, just as laws that prohibit the manufacture and sale of drugs do not violate our self-sovereignty, laws that regulate the sale of fatty or sugary foods do not either. So if the government prohibits fast food restaurants from selling humongous hamburgers, or prohibits convenience stores from selling sugary soda in giant cups, or prohibits vending machines in schools from stocking items with high fat or sugar content, no one's right of self-sovereignty is violated.

Whether these policies are a good idea is a separate question, but if they are a bad idea, it is not because they violate anyone's rights.

NO SCIENTIFIC PROOF OBJECTION

In arguing against drug legalization, I assume that drug abuse would increase substantially if drugs were legalized. Some might now object that there is no proof of this, and this is true, but there is also no proof that murder rates will rise if murder is decriminalized. That is, this assumption is not warranted by any set of controlled laboratory experiments or randomized field trials. Should murder therefore be decriminalized? Obviously not. Some might say that the freedom to murder is not a very important liberty, so the standard of proof need not be so high. But most of us also support on the basis of assumptions for which there is no scientific proof policies that do impinge on important liberties. For example, many of us support restrictions on campaign contributions on the assumption that unrestricted contributions would result in more political corruption. But there is no scientific proof of this, and restrictions on campaign contributions impinge on the important freedom of political speech. Many of us also support immigration laws on the assumption that unrestricted immigration would lower our quality of life. But there is also no scientific proof of this, and freedom of movement is also an important liberty. Should we withdraw our support for these policies just because we support them on the basis of scientifically unproven assumptions? I think not. In general we are justified in supporting a legal restriction for a reason if two conditions are met: (a) this reason would justify this restriction if it was based on true assumptions, and (b) we are warranted by the available evidence in believing that the relevant assumptions are true. So if we are warranted by the available evidence in believing that drug abuse will increase if drugs are legalized, then we are justified in making this assumption for the purpose of evaluating drug control policy. And we are warranted in making this assumption—by what we know about patterns of alcohol and drug consumption and more generally about human psychology and economic behavior.

CONCLUSION

If drug abuse would increase substantially if drugs were legalized, and laws that prohibit the manufacture and sale of drugs do not violate our right of self-sovereignty, and effective drug control requires only moderate penalties reliably and conscientiously enforced, then it makes sense to oppose drug legalization. This, in essence, is the argument I have made here. In evaluating drug policy, it is important, too, to consider how public policy would be shaped if drugs were legalized. Beer, liquor, and cigarette companies already do as much as they can to prevent the government from adopting policies that would reduce drinking and smoking and so their associated harms. They do as much as they can to prevent increases in excise taxes, which increase the price of alcohol and cigarettes, and so reduce their sales, and so smoking and drinking. They do as much as they can to prevent restrictions on the hours and locations of the sale of alcohol and cigarettes. They do as much as they can to prevent licensing and rationing policies, which would reduce the amount of alcohol consumed by problem drinkers. And they do as much as they can to make their products attractive through advertising, particularly to young people. We should expect that if drugs are legalized, drug companies will behave in the same way: that they will do everything they can to prevent the enactment of laws that restrict the marketing and sale of heroin, cocaine, and methamphetamine, and that they will do everything they can to market these drugs successfully, particularly to young people, who will be their most profitable market. Because drug use is currently stigmatized, drug companies are unlikely to be as successful as liquor companies in preventing sound public policy, at least initially. But if we envision a world in which legal drug companies are legally trying to persuade consumers to buy recreational drugs from legal vendors and legally trying to prevent any socially responsible legislation that reduces their legal sales, it is hard to envision a world that does not have much more drug abuse.

REFERENCES

Alexander, M. (2012) *The New Jim Crow: Mass Incarceration in the Age of Colorblindness.* New York: New Press.

Cook, P.J. (2007) *Paying the Tab: The Economics of Alcohol Policy.* Princeton, NJ: Princeton University Press.

de Marneffe, P. (2013) Vice laws and self-sovereignty. *Criminal Law and Philosophy* 7: 29–41.

Edwards, G., Anderson, P., Babor, T.F. *et al.* (1994) *Alcohol Policy and the Public Good.* New York: Oxford University Press.

Goode, E. (2012) *Drugs in American Society,* 8th ed. New York: McGraw-Hill.

Kleiman, M.A.R. *et al.* (2011) *Drugs and Drug Policy: What Everyone Needs to Know.* New York: Oxford University Press.

Miron, J.A. and Zwiebel. J. (1991) Alcohol consumption during prohibition. *American Economic Review* 81: 242–247.

Okrent, D. (2010) *Last Call: The Rise and Fall of Prohibition.* New York: Scribner.

Robins, L.N. *et al.* (1974) Drug use by U.S. army in Vietnam: a follow-up on their return home. *American Journal of Epidemiology* 99: 235–249.

Warburton, C. (1932) *The Economic Results of Prohibition.* New York: Columbia University Press.

JEFFREY MIRON

The Economics of Drug Prohibition and Drug Legalization

2001

I. INTRODUCTION

Around the world, the legal status of commodities such as marijuana, cocaine, and heroin differs dramatically from that of nearly all other goods. Most commodities are subject to substantial regulation and taxation, but the production, distribution, sale, and possession of illegal drugs are prohibited outright. Violation of these prohibitions is punishable by lengthy jail terms, and many governments devote enormous resources to enforcing these prohibition regimes.

The presumed justification for the special legal treatment of drugs is that drug use causes substantial harm both to drug users and to society generally. According to conventional wisdom, drug use diminishes the productivity of the drug user, encourages violent and nonviolent crime, contributes to moral degradation, damages the public purse, harms unborn children, etc. The prohibition of drugs is assumed necessary to reduce the consumption of drugs and thereby reduce the ills caused by drug consumption.

This paper explains that many of the harms typically attributed to drug use are instead due to drug prohibition. This is not to deny that drugs can have powerful effects on the user, nor to deny that drugs differ in some respects from other commodities. But a wide range of outcomes typically thought to result

Jeffrey A. Miron. "The Economics of Drug Prohibition and Drug Legalization." *Social Research* 68 (3) (2001): 835–855.

from drug use is far more accurately attributed to the current legal treatment of drugs.

To make this case, the paper first presents an economic analysis of drug prohibition and demonstrates how drug markets under prohibition compare to drug markets under legalization. The analysis shows that many negative outcomes typically attributed to drugs are the result of prohibition, and it explains why these outcomes would be reduced or eliminated under legalization. This analysis does not by itself imply that legalization is preferable to prohibition; the analysis suggests that one effect of prohibition is reduced consumption of drugs, and under some views this is a desirable outcome. The analysis simply makes clear that some features of drug markets and drug use are the result of drug prohibition—independent of the physical or pharmacological properties of drugs—and it provides a framework for thinking about the consequences of alternative policies.

The second part of the paper discusses the conditions under which drug prohibition is likely to be the right public policy response to the negative outcomes that can accompany drug use. Since most effects of prohibition are undesirable, the main potential benefit of prohibition is any reduction in drug consumption relative to what would occur under legalization. I discuss different perspectives on drug consumption and how these relate to the virtues, or not, of prohibition. The discussion explains that standard arguments used to justify policies to reduce drug consumption are less compelling than commonly asserted, even though drug use causes substantial harm in some cases. The discussion also explains that, even if reducing drug use is an appropriate public policy goal, other methods for reducing drug consumption are available that potentially achieve a better balance between the harms of drug use and the harms of drug policy.

The paper's third section discusses alternatives to prohibition and legalization, such as sin taxation, subsidized treatment, medical provision of drugs, needle exchanges, and public health campaigns. Many of these policies can and do coexist with prohibition or legalization, but they are distinct policies that require separate analysis. I show that each policy has positive and negative aspects, and that evaluation of each depends on views about drug consumption and on relevant evidence.

II. THE POSITIVE ANALYSIS OF DRUG PROHIBITION

In this section I present what economists refer to as a "positive" analysis of prohibition, meaning one that describes the effects of prohibition without addressing whether those effects are good or bad. To conduct such an analysis, one must compare prohibition to a particular alternative; here I assume the alternative is the policy currently applied to most goods, namely, legalization. Under legalization, drug markets would be subject to standard tax and regulatory policies, but these would be no different than those for coffee or ice cream. There are many alternatives to prohibition besides legalization, such as sin taxation and subsidized treatment; I abstract from these here for simplicity but discuss them explicitly in section IV.

The Demand and Supply of Drugs under Prohibition and Legalization

The starting point for analyzing drug prohibition is the observation that drugs continue to be supplied and demanded despite prohibition. This point might seem obvious, but it bears repeating because so many policies, statements by politicians, and even scientific analyses assume that what happens under a law is whatever that law directs. Yet abundant evidence from prohibitions of drugs, alcohol, gambling, prostitution, and other commodities demonstrates that a sizeable fraction of the population continues to supply and demand commodities that are prohibited. Thus, drug prohibition creates a black market in drugs rather than eliminating drugs.

Even though prohibition does not eliminate drugs, it is likely to have important effects on the operation of the market. In particular, prohibition might affect the demand for drugs as well as the supply. I address each of these in turn.

Prohibition potentially affects the demand for drugs through one of several mechanisms. First, the mere existence of prohibition might reduce demand if some consumers exhibit respect for the law. This mechanism does not appear to be quantitatively important since abundant evidence suggests that many people disregard laws that are weakly enforced. Second, prohibition might encourage demand for the good through a "forbidden fruit" effect. There is little concrete evidence to support this effect, although anecdotally it appears plausible for some groups (for example, teenagers). Third, prohibition might reduce demand directly by punishing purchase or possession of the good.

The degree to which drug prohibition imposes penalties for purchase and possession is arguably lax. Although more than 1 million arrests are recorded each year for possession of drugs, there are more than 20 million drug users, and most of these users have purchased drugs on many occasions. Thus, the most obvious calculation—the number of arrests divided by the number of drug purchases—suggests very low probabilities of being arrested for mere purchase or possession. Moreover, many of the arrests for possession occur because the arrestee violated some other law—against prostitution, theft, speeding, loitering, disorderly conduct, and so on—and was also found to possess drugs. The arrest was recorded as possession partly because of FBI data-keeping practices (which suggest recording each incident under the most serious category) and partly because possession is easy to prove. Thus, otherwise law-abiding citizens who wish to purchase and consume drugs face minimal risks of arrest or other sanction.

In addition to possibly affecting the demand for drugs, prohibition is likely to have an effect on the supply. Prohibition increases the costs of manufacturing, transporting, and distributing drugs, since suppliers must take steps to avoid detection by law enforcement authorities. There is also an indirect effect of prohibition on costs; conditional on operating in secret, black market suppliers face low marginal costs of evading tax laws and regulatory policies, and this gives them a cost-advantage relative to legal suppliers. This provides a partial offset to the direct effects of prohibition on costs; moreover, other mechanisms (such as differences in advertising incentives, differences in enforcement, differences in market power) might also offset the direct effects of prohibition. The existing evidence suggests that net costs for drugs are higher under prohibition—substantially higher in some cases (Miron, 2000).

The net implication of this analysis for the effect of prohibition on drug use is therefore more nuanced than usually assumed. The presumption is probably that prohibition reduces the quantity consumed, since the direct effects on supply and demand go in this direction. But these are not necessarily large, and there are indirect effects that go in the other direction.

The evidence on whether drug prohibition significantly reduces drug consumption is incomplete. There is no question that many people continue to consume drugs under prohibition, but this fact alone does not determine whether the quantity is different from what it would be under legalization. A substantial social science literature exists that attempts to estimate this effect, in some cases using evidence on prohibitions of other commodities such as alcohol (for example, Dills and Miron, 2001). Overall, this literature suggests that drug prohibition has modest but not dramatic negative effects on consumption (see Miron, 1998).

The first-order effects of prohibition are therefore as follows: prohibition probably raises the costs of supplying drugs, which implies higher prices and lower consumption; and prohibition may reduce the demand for drugs, implying lower prices and reduced consumption. Whether these effects are large or small is not yet resolved.

Prohibitions and Crime

In addition to affecting the supply of and possibly the demand for drugs, prohibition has numerous other effects. Probably the most important of these is increased crime.

Prohibition increases violent crime by preventing drug market participants from resolving their differences through standard nonviolent mechanisms. In all markets, disputes arise between buyer and seller, supplier and purchaser, employer and employee. In a legal market participants use courts and related nonviolent mechanisms to resolve these disputes. In a black market participants do not have this option because they would reveal their identity and illegal activities to the authorities by using the courts, and courts do not enforce contracts involving illegal goods. Suppliers in legal markets can also use advertising to compete with rivals; this is difficult in a black market, where violent turf battles are one possible substitute.

This simple prediction of economic reasoning is consistent with a substantial body of evidence. The use of violence to resolve disputes is common in drug markets and prostitution markets, and it was common in gambling markets before the introduction of state lotteries and expanded legal gambling combined to eliminate the black market. Similarly, the use of violence to resolve commercial disputes in the alcohol trade was widespread during Alcohol Prohibition (1920–1933), but rare both before and after (Friedman, 1991). And the overall incidence of violence has increased and decreased systematically over the past 100 years with enforcement of drug and alcohol prohibition (Miron, 1999).

Prohibitions also encourage crime through several other mechanisms. By raising the price of drugs, prohibition encourages income-generating crime such as theft or prostitution, since users need additional income to purchase drugs. And enforcement of prohibition diverts criminal justice resources from deterrence of all kinds of crime (Benson and Rasmussen, 1991; Benson et al., 1992).

The conclusion that prohibition causes crime contrasts starkly with the usual claim that drug use itself causes crime. There is little evidence, however, that drug use per se promotes violence or other criminal behavior (Duke and Gross, 1993; U.S. Department of Justice, 1992). Considerable evidence that purports to show such an effect merely indicates a correlation between drug use and crime; the same methodology would suggest that wearing blue jeans or eating fast food is criminogenic.

Other Effects of Prohibitions

Product Quality: A different effect of prohibition is decreased product quality. In a legal market, consumers who purchase faulty goods can attempt to punish suppliers with liability claims, by causing bad publicity, by avoiding repeat purchases, or by reporting such events to private or government groups. In a black market, most of these mechanisms are unavailable, and the remaining ones (such as avoiding repeat purchases) are likely to work less effectively. United States experience with alcohol prohibition provides a classic example of this effect; deaths from adulterated alcohol soared (Miron and Zwiebel, 1991; Morgan, 1982). In drug markets, this effect potentially explains many accidental overdoses and poisonings.

Corruption: In legal markets participants have little incentive to bribe the police, and they have legal mechanisms such as lobbying or campaign contributions by which to influence politicians. In black markets participants must either evade law enforcement authorities or pay them to look the other way, so the scope for corruption is substantial. Similarly, standard lobbying techniques are more difficult for a black market supplier, and campaign contributions are automatically illegal bribes. Thus, prohibition increases corruption of law enforcement authorities and politicians.

Redistributions to Criminals: In a legal market the income generated by production and sale of drugs is subject to taxation, and these tax revenues accrue to the government. In a black market, suppliers capture these revenues as profits. Thus prohibition enriches the segment of society willing to evade the law. The revenue involved is substantial; estimates suggest the black market has revenues of tens of billions of dollars, so at standard tax rates the government would collect at least several billion dollars in additional revenues.

Complications of Policymaking in Other Areas: Because drug crimes involve voluntary exchange, enforcement relies on asset seizures, aggressive search tactics, and racial profiling, tactics that strain accepted notions of civil liberty (see, for example, Schlosser, 1994a, 1994b). Because of prohibition, many states prohibit the sale of syringes, which increases sharing of dirty needles and thus promotes the spread of HIV. Because of prohibition, marijuana is even more tightly controlled than morphine or cocaine and cannot be used for medical purposes (Grinspoon and Bakalar, 1993). Because of prohibition, foreign policy decisions and free trade negotiations are intertwined with decisions about drug policy (see, for example, Barro, 1992).

Respect for the Law: All experience to date indicates that, even with draconian enforcement, prohibitions fail to deter a great many people from supplying and consuming drugs. This fact signals users and nonusers that laws are for suckers; it undermines a spirit of voluntary compliance essential to law enforcement in a free society.

Direct Costs of Enforcement: Expenditure across all levels of government for enforcement of drug prohibition is currently at least $20 billion per year and plausibly in excess of $30 billion (Miron, 2001a). This estimate includes only those expenditures directly attributable to drug policy, not auxiliary expenditures related to prohibition-induced crime.

Summary

Drug prohibition probably reduces drug consumption relative to what would occur under legalization, but existing evidence suggests this reduction is modest. But whether the effect is large or small, prohibition has many other effects compared to legalization.

III. THE NORMATIVE ANALYSIS OF DRUG PROHIBITION

I now present what economists call a normative analysis of drug prohibition, meaning one that asks whether prohibition is preferable to legalization. As a starting point, I note that most effects of prohibition are, in and of themselves, negative (for example, increased crime, redistributions to criminals, greater corruption, diminished civil liberties). The most important exception is prohibition's effect on drug consumption. This effect might not be large, and it might even be perverse (because of the forbidden fruit effect, for example). But there is little dispute that this is the key issue: if prohibition fails to reduce consumption, it is unambiguously inferior to legalization. If prohibition reduces consumption, the bottom line depends on how one views this effect and on the magnitude of prohibition's negative consequences.

In this section I discuss four different perspectives on how public policy might view drug consumption. I emphasize the distinction between two questions: first, whether policy should attempt to reduce such consumption; and second, whether prohibition is the right policy by which to achieve this objective if the objective is sensible in the first place.

Rational Consumption

One view of drug consumption—the one assumed in the standard economic paradigm—is that people consume drugs because they think it makes them better off. According to this view, it does not matter whether people consume drugs because they enjoy the psychopharmacological effects, because they believe drugs have medicinal properties, or because they think drugs are cool; all that matters is that they voluntarily choose to consume drugs. Similarly, under this view, it does not matter whether drugs are addictive or if consumption negatively affects health or productivity; if rational people choose to accept these risks, they must think the benefits are worth the costs.

The rational model of consumption was long believed to be inconsistent with many observed behaviors related to drug consumption, such as addiction, withdrawal, and relapse. Theoretical work by Becker and Murphy (1988) shows that the rational model is potentially consistent with these phenomena, and a growing body of empirical work has had some success in fitting the model to data (see the discussion in Miron, 1998). This empirical work does not prove the rational model is correct with respect to all drug consumption, but it undermines the presumption that all drug use (or other addictive consumption) is necessarily irrational.

If one adopts the rational model, then the normative analysis of drug prohibition is simple: any policy that reduces drug use is a cost, not a benefit. Thus, all of prohibition's effects are negative. If drug consumption is not rational, the conclusion that policy-induced reductions in consumption are a cost does not necessarily hold.

There are numerous reasons why the rational model of drug consumption strikes many as inaccurate. No doubt there are some individuals for whom this description is not even close. But it is hard to deny that at least some drug use fits the rational model. Many people claim to enjoy the high associated with marijuana consumption; others value the pain relief or mental calm produced by opiates; still others appreciate the stimulation of cocaine. An objective evaluation of prohibition, therefore, should include as one cost any reduction in rational drug consumption.

Externalities

A second perspective on drug consumption holds that even if drug consumption is rational and thus a benefit to the person who consumes drugs, such consumption might harm innocent third parties (in the vocabulary of economics, cause externalities) and thus be excessive from society's perspective. Although conventional accounts often exaggerate the magnitude of drug-consumption-induced externalities (see Miron and Zwiebel, 1995; Miron, 1998), it cannot be disputed that these are significant in some cases. For example, drug consumption can impair one's ability to drive or operate machinery safely; it can have negative health effects on the fetus; or it can cause additional use of publicly funded health care.

The mere existence of externalities, however, does not by itself justify policies to reduce drug consumption; one must compare the magnitude of externalities to the costs of the policy, including any unintended consequences. The analysis in section II, for example, shows that prohibition itself generates externalities, including increased crime and corruption, the spread of HIV, and reduced civil liberties. Even if the externalities from drug consumption are substantial, they might be smaller than the externalities from policy. This is especially true if the policy in question has only modest effects on drug consumption.

In addition, the ability of policy to reduce drug-related externalities is limited by the fact that reduced drug use might translate into increased use of other substances that have similar if not greater externalities. For example, marijuana appears to impair driving ability substantially less than alcohol (U.S. Department of Transportation, 1993; Crancer et al. 1969), and there is evidence of substitution between the two in response to changes in the relative price of the two commodities (DiNardo and Lemieux, 1992; Chaloupka and Laixuthai, 1994).

In addition, the net effect of any particular externality is often difficult to calculate or even perverse. The classic example is the effect of smoking on the use of publicly funded health care (Viscusi, 1994). The standard argument in favor of smoking-reduction policies is that smoking causes decreased health and increased use of Medicaid, Medicare, or other subsidized health care. But any action that tends to shorten life means decreased use of publicly funded Social Security and Medicare, thereby positively affecting the nation's fiscal balance. In some cases calculations of this type suggest that the "positive" effects are similar in magnitude to the negative ones.

Finally, even if drug use does cause externalities, and even if these are sufficiently great to justify a public policy response, there are policies other than prohibition that can reduce drug consumption without the negative effects of prohibition. And the existence of externalities does not imply that the optimum level of consumption is zero, assuming consumers get benefits from drug consumption. Rather, the standard externality argument suggests reducing consumption relative to legalization, but not all the way to zero.

Irrational Consumption

A different perspective on drug use, independent of externalities, is that some consumers are not rational; they harm themselves by using or abusing drugs because they fail to account for the negative consequences. According to this view, policy-induced reductions in drug consumption benefit such people by preventing them from harming themselves. It is undeniable that some people make bad decisions about drugs, although, as with externalities, the harms from drug consumption are often exaggerated (Miron and Zwiebel, 1995; Miron, 1998).

The mere fact that irrationality exists, however, does not mean attempts to reduce drug consumption are desirable policy; the benefits of reducing irrational consumption must be weighed against the costs of any policy used to achieve that reduction, and they must be balanced against the costs of reducing rational consumption. Further, as with externalities, policy-induced reductions in irrational drug consumption might induce substitution toward goods that have similar or more harmful effects.

Even if attempts to reduce drug consumption are warranted by irrationality, prohibition is not necessarily the right policy, given the negative effects of prohibition. Indeed, prohibition might exacerbate the effects of irrationality to a greater degree than alternative approaches. Prohibition potentially glamorizes drug use in the eyes of those too young, naive, foolish, or myopic to consider the long-term consequences. Also, prohibition alters the reward structure in the illegal drug trade in ways that entice the myopic into that trade. Under prohibition, the monetary rewards for working in the trade are high, but this is merely compensation for the elevated risk of injury, death, and imprisonment. Rational people understand this and work in this trade only if the total compensation equals that available in other sectors. Myopic teenagers, on the other hand, likely focus on the cash and thus expose themselves excessively to substantial risk of death or prison.

Immoral Consumption

A final perspective on drug consumption and public policy is that drug use is evil or immoral, and thus policy should discourage drug use to demonstrate society's disapproval.

Economic analysis does not address the morality argument per se. But unless one puts infinite weight on taking a moral stand against drugs, the benefits of making a moral statement must be weighed against the costs of any policy that makes this statement. Similarly, prohibition is not the only policy that can send a message about society's disapproval of drug consumption, which means that the costs of using prohibition to make a moral statement must be weighed against the costs of using other policies to this end.

The previous analysis also suggests that, from a moral perspective, prohibition has many undesirable effects. Prohibition causes increased violence, some of which affects innocent bystanders caught in drive-by shootings carried out by rival drug gangs or in guerrilla bombings, for example, in Colombia. Prohibition-induced restrictions on clean needles mean that more children are born HIV-infected. Prohibition means that peasants in Latin America, including some who do not grow coca, have their crops destroyed by aerial spraying of pesticides. And prohibition means that criminals get rich at the expense of society generally.

Summary

The normative analysis of drug prohibition suggests three key conclusions. First, virtually all the effects of prohibition are undesirable, with the possible exception of reduced consumption. Second, reduced drug consumption is not necessarily desirable; in particular, any reduction in rational drug consumption is a cost, not a benefit, of policies that reduce drug consumption; the right objective is eliminating externality generating or irrational drug consumption. Third, even if policy should attempt to reduce drug consumption, prohibition is not the only possible approach.

IV. ALTERNATIVE POLICIES

The preceding analysis suggests that prohibition has many undesirable consequences relative to prohibition, but it does not by itself imply that legalization is preferable. The choice between these two approaches depends in part on one's moral stance with respect to drug consumption but more importantly on evidence about the degree of rational versus irrational consumption and about the magnitude of various drug-related externalities.

In addition, prohibition and legalization are not the only policies available by which to address the harms of drug use. In this section I discuss other possible drug policies and explain how they compare with prohibition or legalization.

Sin Taxation

A policy that is "between" prohibition and legalization is sin taxation: a tax on drugs in excess of that on other goods. Sin taxes raise drug prices relative to those of other goods, thereby discouraging their consumption. Most economies impose sin taxes on various commodities, including tobacco, alcohol, and gasoline.

The use of sin taxes to discourage drug consumption faces an important constraint: the tax must not be so high that it itself generates a black market because suppliers can profitably evade the tax, even given reasonable enforcement. Existing evidence confirms that tax rates beyond a certain point indeed force markets underground; but existing evidence also indicates that sin taxes can be substantial without so doing. For example, cigarette taxes in some European countries account for 75 to 85 percent of the price.

Assuming sin taxation does not drive the market underground, it will not generate the negative effects of prohibition-induced black markets, and it will decrease consumption of drugs to the extent that demand is responsive to price. Evidence suggests that demand is indeed responsive, contrary to earlier characterization of drug use as being price insensitive because of the addictive properties of some drugs. Whether this responsiveness is large or small is harder to pin down (see Miron, 1998 for a discussion of the evidence). Sin taxation also means that the drug trade occurs "aboveground," so standard policies such as minimum wage laws, environmental laws, and product liability laws can still be enforced. Assuming these policies are beneficial, this represents a plus for sin taxation relative to prohibition.

The standard objection to sin taxation relative to prohibition is the presumption that prohibition can reduce drug use more effectively than can sin taxation. This presumption is not necessarily valid, however. The reason for the presumption is the view that prohibition reduces demand because of respect for the law or because it establishes a social norm that drug use is wrong. This is possible, but prohibition might also glamorize drug use in ways that sin taxation would not, and sin taxation can also send a signal that society disapproves of drug consumption.

Setting aside the possibility that prohibition reduces demand more effectively than sin taxation, there is no guarantee that prohibition reduces consumption more effectively than sin taxation. As shown explicitly in Miron (2001b), sin taxation can always raise costs and thus price to exactly the same degree as prohibition, holding enforcement constant. And the efficacy of enforcement under sin taxation might exceed that under prohibition.

Whether sin taxation is superior to legalization depends in part on the magnitude of externalities relative to irrational consumption. If drug users impose significant externalities, then sin taxes discourage these externalities and generate revenue that can mitigate the effects. If drug users mainly harm themselves, and if their demands are relatively inelastic, then sin taxes are less appealing since they force drug users to pay higher prices without reducing consumption, leaving users with less income for food, shelter, and clothing, and also possibly encouraging crime. In addition, sin taxation raises political economy issues; political pressures, rather than economics, might determine which commodities are considered sinful. Further, there is a danger under sin taxation that the tax may be raised sufficiently to generate a black market.

Subsidized Treatment

A different policy toward illegal drugs, which can and does coexist with prohibition or legalization, is government-subsidized drug abuse treatment. The desired effect of subsidies is to increase the number of people receiving such treatment, thereby reducing the overall quantity of drug use.

A policy of subsidizing drug treatment raises a number of issues. Although it is easy to advocate such policies out of compassion for drug abusers, the question for society is whether the benefits (such as increased earnings for drug users, lower crime committed by users) exceed the costs. Answering this question is difficult, mainly because assignment to treatment is not random. The available evidence does not make a strong case for subsidized treatment (Apsler and Harding, 1991).

An additional issue is that subsidizing drug treatment, by lowering the price of such treatment to drug users, might encourage drug use. Further, even the perception that this could occur—or a feeling by some that it "rewards" drug use—is a problematic consequence of this policy.

None of these caveats is meant to disparage treatment. The point is that subsidizing treatment is a separate question from whether treatment is beneficial, and it is a separate question from whether prohibition is preferable to legalization. Many critics of prohibition take as given that reduced expenditures for prohibition should translate into increased expenditures for subsidized treatment. It might be desirable to legalize drugs and subsidize treatment, but subsidized treatment has its own costs and benefits that require independent analysis.

Medicalization

An alternative to prohibition, which might be termed medicalization, is to put control over drugs in the hands of physicians, with little or no oversight from law enforcement. Under current United States policy, doctors can prescribe cocaine, and most opiates, amphetamines, and depressants under certain conditions. But their ability to prescribe is strictly limited, and drugs such as heroin, marijuana, and LSD cannot legally be prescribed under any circumstance. More broadly, even when doctors can legally prescribe various controlled substances, they avoid doing so because of concern about legal monitoring of their prescription practices. Under a more liberal, medical approach, which exists to some degree in Europe, doctors would face minimal legal restraint on the prescribing of controlled substances. In particular, they might be allowed to "maintain" addicts, meaning the ability to prescribe continued supplies of opiates as the "treatment" for addiction.

The critical effect of such a policy change would be to provide many drug users with a legal source of drugs, thereby reducing the size of the black market relative to prohibition. If the restraints were minimal, some physicians would prescribe freely, potentially reducing the black market to insignificance. Thus, from the perspective of eliminating the negative effects of a prohibition-induced black market, medicalization is certainly beneficial. It is not obvious, however, that this approach is better than simple legalization. Medicalization also implies increased consumption of drugs, so to the extent there are externalities and irrationality related to consumption, this is a negative.

Needle Exchanges

A policy that has received significant attention in recent years is needle exchanges. Under this system, private or government groups provide clean needles to addicts who might otherwise share dirty needles and thereby spread HIV and other diseases. These programs exist in substantial part because of government restrictions on the sale of clean needles, which in turn reflects prohibition. If drugs were legal there would be far fewer restrictions on non-prescription needle sales.

This approach differs from those discussed earlier because the main objective is to reduce the harms of drug use rather than drug use itself, although many needle exchanges do provide counseling and guidance into drug treatment. Under prohibition, needle exchanges are an awkward activity for the government, since this policy appears to accept drug use at the same time that prohibition seeks to punish drug use. Government could reduce the controversy surrounding the issue by repealing the prohibitions on the sale of clean needles; this would allow private groups greater freedom to run needle exchanges. There is some evidence that these programs reduce the sharing of needles and little evidence that they encourage drug use (Gostin, 1991).

Public Education Campaigns

Under legalization or prohibition, public health campaigns that provide information about the consequences of drug use are also an element of drug policy. More information is generally better, and persuading people not to use drugs would circumvent most other issues. But this is probably not the right benchmark for gauging government anti-drug campaigns. In many cases these exaggerate the dangers of drug use to such a degree that the audience ignores the message entirely. And available evidence fails to show that anti-drug campaigns such as DARE significantly reduce drug use (Rosenbaum and Hanson, 1998).

Summary

The main point of this section is not to endorse or criticize the policies discussed earlier; as with the choice between prohibition and legalization, a full evaluation depends partly on personal values and even more on the evidence, which I have not attempted to evaluate systematically here. Instead, the objective has been to clarify the effects of different policies and to show how they relate to prohibition and legalization. The key message is that each of these policies has its own costs and benefits; each requires its own evaluation.

V. CONCLUSIONS

This paper does not attempt to make the case for or against prohibition or legalization; likewise, it does not claim to be a complete or systematic evaluation of the evidence. The goal has been to show how the legal status of drugs affects the market for drugs and to demonstrate that many outcomes commonly attributed to drugs are instead due to drug prohibition.

It is worth noting that much of the analysis made no reference to any specific property of drugs, such as addictiveness. The basic analysis applies to any commodity for which there is substantial demand and relatively imperfect substitutes. So the key message is that the legal treatment of drugs plays a huge role in explaining how drug markets operate, not the physical or psychopharmacological properties of drugs.

REFERENCES

Apsler, Robert, and Wayne M. Harding. "Cost-Effectiveness Analysis of Drug Abuse Treatment: Current Status and Recommendations for Future Research." "Drug Abuse Services Research: Background Papers on Drug Abuse Financing and Services Research." Washington, D.C.: National Institute on Drug Abuse, 1991.

Barro, Robert J. "To Avoid Repeats of Peru, Legalize Drugs." *Wall Street Journal* 27 April 1992.

Becker, Gary S., and Kevin M. Murphy. "A Theory of Rational Addiction." *Journal of Political Economy* 96 (1988): 675–700.

Benson, Bruce L., and David W. Rasmussen. "Relationship between Illicit Drug Enforcement Policy and Property Crimes." *Contemporary Policy Issues* IX (October 1991): 106–115.

Benson, Bruce L., et al. "Is Property Crime Caused by Drug Use or by Drug Enforcement Policy?" *Applied Economics* 24 (1992): 679–692.

Chaloupka, Frank J., and Adit Laixuthai. "Do Youths Substitute Alcohol and Marijuana? Some Econometric Evidence." National Bureau of Economic Research. Working Paper No. 4662 (1994).

Crancer, Alfred, et al. "Comparison of the Effects of Marihuana and Alcohol on Simulated Driving Performance." *Science* 164 (1969): 851–854.

Dills, Angela, and Jeffrey A. Miron. "Alcohol Prohibition, Alcohol Consumption, and Cirrhosis." Manuscript. Boston University, 2001.

DiNardo, John, and Thomas Lemieux. "Are Marijuana and Alcohol Substitutes? The Effect of State Drinking Age Laws on the Marijuana Consumption of High School Seniors." National Bureau of Economic Research. Working Paper No. 4212 (1992).

Duke, Steven B., and Albert C. Gross. *America's Longest War: Rethinking Our Tragic Crusade against Drugs.* New York: Putnam, 1993.

Friedman, Milton. "The War We Are Losing." *Searching for Alternatives: Drug-Control Policy in the United States.* Eds. Melvyn B. Krauss and Edward P. Lazear. Stanford: Hoover Institution Press, 1991: 53–67.

Gostin, Larry. "The Interconnected Epidemic of Drug Dependency and AIDS." *Harvard Civil Rights-Civil Liberties Law Review* 26 (1991): 113–184.

Grinspoon, Lester, and James B. Bakalar. *Marihuana: The Forbidden Medicine.* New Haven: Yale University Press, 1993.

Miron, Jeffrey A. "Drug Prohibition." *The New Palgrave Dictionary of Economics and the Law.* Ed. Peter Newman. London: Macmillan, 1998: 648–652.

———. "Violence and the U.S. Prohibitions of Drugs and Alcohol." *American Law and Economics Review* 1:1–2 (Fall 1999): 78–114.

———. "Prohibition versus Legalization: An Economic Analysis." Manuscript. Boston University, 2001a.

———. "Prohibitions Raise Prices? Evidence from the Markets for Cocaine and Heroin." Manuscript, 2001b.

Miron, Jeffrey A., and Jeffrey Zwiebel. "Alcohol Consumption During Prohibition." *American Economic Review* 81 (1991): 242–247.

———. "The Economic Case against Drug Prohibition." *Journal of Economic Perspectives* 9:4 (Fall 1995): 175–192.

Morgan, John P. "The Jamaica Ginger Paralysis." *Journal of the American Medical Association* 245:15 (15 October 1982): 1864–1867.

Morgan, John P. "Prohibition Is Perverse Policy: What Was True in 1933 Is True Now." *Searching for Alternatives: Drug-Control Policy in the United States.* Eds. Melvyn B. Krauss and Edward P. Lazear. Stanford: Hoover Institution Press, 1991: 405–423.

Rosenbaum, Dennis P., and Gordon S. Hanson. "Assessing the Effects of School-Based Drug Education: A Six-Year Multilevel Analysis of Project D.A.R.E." *Journal of Research in Crime and Delinquency* 35:4 (November 1998): 381–412.

Schlosser, Eric. "Reefer Madness." *Atlantic Monthly* (August 1994a): 45–63.

———. "Marijuana and the Law." *Atlantic Monthly* (September 1994b): 84–94.

U.S. Department of Justice. *Drugs, Crime and the Justice System: A National Report for the Bureau of Justice Statistics.* Washington, D.C., 1992.

U.S. Department of Transportation. *Marijuana and Actual Driving Performance.* Washington, D.C., 1993.

Viscusi, W. Kip. "Cigarette Taxes and the Social Consequences of Smoking." National Bureau of Economic Research. Working Paper No. 4891 (1994).

Organs

ARTHUR CAPLAN

Organ Transplantation

2008

FRAMING THE ISSUE

Every day about a dozen people in the United States die waiting for organ transplants. The deaths are especially tragic since many might be prevented if more organs were available. Every day very hard choices have to be made about who will live and who will die. With close to 100,000 people on waiting lists for kidneys, hearts, livers, lungs, and intestines, the pressure to distribute scarce organs fairly and to find ways to increase their supply is enormous.

Arthur Caplan, "Organ Transplantation," from Hastings Center, *From Birth to Death and Bench to Clinic: The Hastings Center Bioethics Briefing Book for Journalists, Policymakers, and Campaigns.* Garrison, NY: The Hastings Center, 2008. By permission of the Hastings Center.

The pressure is getting worse because waiting lists are growing faster than the supply of organs. And if transplant centers were to relax their standards to include more people—such as the those who lack insurance, have severe intellectual disabilities, older persons, prisoners, illegal aliens, and foreigners who cannot get transplants in their own countries—then the lists of those waiting could easily triple or quadruple.

To close this gap, policymakers will have to consider new options for inducing people to donate organs, and organ transplant centers may have to rethink their criteria for determining who is allowed on their waiting lists and who has priority. These decisions involve many ethical and legal issues, including:

- Who on the waiting lists should get transplants first: patients in the greatest need or those most likely to benefit?
- Should certain people, like illegal aliens, foreigners, and people with a history of addiction or a criminal record, be denied a place on waiting lists?
- Should people be paid to donate their organs?
- Should federal law be changed to permit people to buy and sell organs?

DISTRIBUTING ORGANS: WHAT IS JUST AND FAIR?

Rationing is unavoidable in organ transplantation, but the system for allocating organs must be just and fair. Justice requires some rule or policy that insures that the supply of donated organs is used wisely and consistently with what donors and their families would wish, such as giving priority to saving children's lives, or to American citizens. Fairness demands that like cases be treated alike and that the allocation system be transparent, so that all who wait know why some are selected and some are not.

There are valid questions about the justice and fairness of the current system. Transplant centers are the gatekeepers who decide whom they will and will not admit as transplant candidates. Their policies vary. Many nonmedical values shape their decisions, and it can be argued that some centers invoke these values in ways that are not truly just. Among these considerations:

- Many transplant centers will not accept people without insurance.
- Transplant teams rarely consider anyone over 75 years of age.
- Some centers exclude patients with moderate mental retardation, HIV, a history of addiction, or a long criminal record.
- Though American transplant centers can list foreigners, they can make up no more than 5% of any center's list. Most of non–U.S. citizens listed have substantial financial resources and pay in cash.
- Some transplant programs will admit illegal aliens, but most are children. Some transplant centers have caused controversy by refusing to retransplant illegal aliens whose initial organs, received at the same hospital during childhood, have failed.

Value judgments may also influence the process of matching cadaver organs with patients on the waiting lists. The United Network for Organ Sharing (UNOS), a national network based in Richmond, Virginia, bears this responsibility. At present, its driving considerations are matching a donor and a recipient by blood type, tissue type, and organ size. Some weight is also given to the urgency or need for a transplant as reflected by time on the waiting list and the person's physical condition. There has been some push in recent years to steer organs toward those who are not seriously ill so as to maximize the chances for successful transplantation. UNOS used to have to allocate organs locally, but recently it has moved to a more regional distribution, as organ preservation techniques and other aspects of organ transplantation have improved.

Debates are growing louder about the criteria that should be used to dominate UNOS's distribution process—should it be the urgency of a patient's medical need? Or should it be efficacy? In recent years, there has been a shift toward efficacy. UNOS proposed new regulations, available to the public on its Web site, in an effort to improve the fairness of the allocation process.

Furthermore, patients can increase their chances of getting a transplant by enrolling at more then one transplant center—a practice known as multiple listing. About 10% of the current waiting list consists of persons who are listed at more than one center. Critics of multiple listing say that it is unjust because it gives an advantage to people with the resources to pay for more than one evaluation and listing. Each evaluation can cost tens of thousands of dollars.

INCREASING THE SUPPLY

A number of steps have been taken over the years to try to increase the supply of organs. The first attempt was from state laws permitting the use of organ donor cards or family consent to donate a deceased relative's organs. Then, states began requiring hospitals to ask all patients' families about organ donation. Most recently, state laws required hospitals to honor a patient's donor card even when the family opposed donation.

None of these policies has significantly increased the supply of organs. Therefore, some people now argue for a shift away from a reliance on voluntary altruism in organ donation toward either a paid market or presumed consent.

ORGAN MARKETS

Two basic strategies have been proposed to provide incentives for people to sell their organs upon their death. One strategy is simply to permit organ sale by changing the National Organ Transplant Act (NOTA), the federal law that bans organ sales. Then, individuals would be free to broker contracts with persons interested in selling at prices mutually agreed upon by both parties. Markets already exist on the Internet between potential live donors and people in need of organs, but these transactions are illegal. The other strategy is a regulated market in which the government would act as the purchaser of organs—setting a fixed price and enforcing conditions of sale. Both proposals have drawn heated ethical criticism.

One criticism is that only the poor and desperate will want to sell their body parts. If you need money, you might sell your kidney to try and feed your family or to pay back a debt. This may be a "rational" decision, but that does not make it a matter of free choice. Watching your child go hungry when you have no job and a wealthy person waves a wad of bills in your face is not exactly a scenario that inspires confidence in the fairness of a market for body parts. Talk of individual rights and autonomy is hollow if those with no options must "choose" to sell their organs to purchase life's necessities. Choice requires information, options, and some degree of freedom, as well as the ability to reason.

It is hard to imagine many people in wealthy countries eager to sell their organs upon their death. In fact, even if compensation is relatively high, few will agree to sell. That has been the experience with markets in human eggs for research purposes and with paid surrogacy in the United States—prices have escalated, but there are still relatively few sellers. Selling organs, even in a tightly regulated market, violates the ethics of medicine.

Should the Definition of Death be Changed?

Most donated organs now come from people declared dead on the basis of neurological criteria—the absence of brain activity. Brain death typically occurs after cardiopulmonary death, the cessation of a heartbeat and breathing. One way to expand to pool of deceased donors is to include those declared dead by cardiopulmonary criteria. This recommendation was made in 2006 by a panel of the Institute of Medicine chaired by Hastings Center Fellow James F. Childress and including Hastings Scholar Mary Ann Baily.

Donation after circulatory determination of death (DCDD) has become more common around the world, but the practice is controversial. For one thing, it is medically more complex than donation after brain death because of the risk of organs being harmed by oxygen deprivation. In addition, there is ethical concern that DCDD will lead to substandard health care at the end of life—for example, inadequate morphine in the effort to avoid harming the organs. The Institute of Medicine report recommends ethical guidelines already used in Europe, such as preventing the organ recovery team from being the ones to decide when to discontinue cardiopulmonary resuscitation.

The core ethical norm of the medical profession is the principle, "Do no harm." The only way that removing an organ from someone seems morally defensible is if the donor chooses to undergo the harm of surgery solely to help another, and if there is sufficient medical benefit to the recipient.

The creation of a market puts medicine in the position of removing body parts from people solely to abet those people's interest in securing compensation. A market in human organs has a model in the existing market for human eggs for assisted reproduction and research purposes, but that practice is highly controversial. Is this a role that the health professions can ethically countenance? In a market—even a regulated one—doctors and nurses still would be using their skills to help people harm themselves solely for money. The resulting distrust and loss of professional standards is too a high price to pay to gamble on the hope that a market may secure more organs for those in need.

PRESUMED CONSENT

There is another option for increasing the organ supply that has not been tried in the United States but is practiced abroad. Spain, Italy, Austria, Belgium, and some other European countries have enacted laws that create presumed consent, or what I prefer to call "default to donation." In such a system, the presumption is that you want to be an organ donor upon your death—the default to donation. People who don't want to be organ donors have to say so by registering this wish on a computer, carrying a card, or telling their loved ones. With default to donation, no one's rights are taken away—voluntary altruism remains the moral foundation for making organs available, and, therefore, procuring organs is consistent with medical ethics. Based on the European experience, there is a good chance America could get a significant jump in the supply of organs by shifting to a default-to-donation policy. Donation rates in European countries with presumed consent are about 25% higher than in other European nations.

Default to donation proposals have been submitted in several states. The United Kingdom is also considering implementing presumed consent, and if it does—and if the policy is successful—that may provide more momentum for trying it in the United States. The main ethical objection to presumed consent is the perceived loss of patient autonomy–that it is wrong to take someone's organs without that person's explicit consent. In addition, some people believe that presumed consent violates the 5th Amendment prohibition against taking private property without due process and compensation. Critics are also concerned about mistakes in which there is the presumption that someone consented when, in fact, either the individual had failed to indicate opposition or the record of that opposition was lost.

ON THE HORIZON

The need for organ transplantation may eventually be reduced by stem cell therapies. Scientists hope to repair or even replace damaged organs with new cells grown from adult or embryonic stem cells. Earlier this year, researchers at the University of Minnesota reported that they had built a beating heart in a laboratory with stem cells from neonatal and fetal rats. And British scientists are undertaking pioneering clinical trials that attempt to repair the hearts of heart attack patients by injecting them with stem cells.

GERALD DWORKIN

Markets and Morals: The Case for Organ Sales

1993

Arthur Caplan has said that "perhaps the most pressing policy issue facing those within and outside of the field [of organ transplantation] concerns the shortage of organs available for transplantation to those with end-stage organ failure" (1). The options available to increase the supply of scarce goods are basically three—donation, conscription, or sale. A good deal of attention has been focused on the first two methods (I take presumed consent to be basically conscription with an option to opt out before death), but the sale of organs has been little discussed.

I focus on the issue of whether there are good arguments of an ethical nature which rule out a market in organs. I leave to one side discussion of whether such markets would in fact increase the supply of organs, whether there are practical difficulties in the implementation of such a scheme, whether political considerations (in the broad sense) would make it difficult to gain support for such a system. My only task today is to assess the moral arguments.

The first distinction we must make is between a futures market and a current market—that is, between the decision of an individual to sell the right to his organs after his death, and the decision to sell organs while he is alive. I assume, for the sake of this discussion, that if there are moral objections to the sale of organs they will take their strongest form against the sale of organs from living donors. Hence if one can show that there are no conclusive arguments against such sales, one will have shown, ipso facto, that there are no conclusive objections against the sale of cadaver organs.

I first briefly consider the arguments in favor of a market in organs and claim that in the absence of moral objections, there is no reason for not having such markets. I then want to consider all the plausible arguments against the sale of organs and show that they are not legitimate objections. My conclusion will be that, in the absence of further arguments which survive critical scrutiny, there are good reasons for favoring a market in organs.

ARGUMENTS FOR A MARKET

We currently accept the legitimacy of noncommercial solid-organ donations. We also accept the legitimacy of the sale of blood, semen, ova, hair, and tissue. By doing so we accept the idea that individuals have the right to dispose of their organs and other bodily parts if they so choose. By recognizing such a right we respect the bodily autonomy of individuals, that is, their capacity to make choices about how their body is to be treated by others. By recognizing such a right we also produce good consequences for others, that is, save lives, allow infertile couples to have children, further medical research, and so on. But the primary good achieved by such a right is the recognition of the individual as sovereign over his own body. A market transaction is one species of the larger class of voluntary transactions. Allowing people to sell things is one way of recognizing their sphere of control.

Finally, by allowing individuals to either barter or sell something, we increase their level of well-being. Since such transactions are voluntary, they are presumably only engaged in when the individual believes himself or herself better off without the

Gerald Dworkin, "Markets and Morals: The Case for Organ Sales," from Gerald Dworkin, *Morality, Harm and the Law*. Westview Press, 1994. By permission of Westview Press.

good and with the cash (or an alternative good in the case of barter) than without the cash and with the good.

So markets can increase both autonomy and well-being.

ARGUMENTS AGAINST A MARKET

There are often compelling reasons why we should not allow individuals to sell what they could give. We do not allow markets in votes, in babies, in judicial decisions, in college grades. In these cases we recognize countervailing considerations which are sufficient to overrule the considerations in favor of markets. So the question before us is whether there are such counterarguments in the case of markets for human organs. I propose to consider the arguments that have been adduced and show that they are not compelling.

Exploitation of the Poor

One of the most powerful arguments against a market in organs is the element of exploitation of the poor. Clearly, those who are most likely to wish to sell their organs are those whose financial situation is most desperate. Those who have alternative sources of income are not likely to choose an option which entails some health risk, some disfigurement, some pain and discomfort. The risks of such sales will certainly fall disproportionately by income class.

But what exactly is supposed to follow from these facts? Is it that, because of this, the choices of the poor are not, in fact, fully voluntary? This seems to me false. Or if it is true, it has a much wider implication than that organs should not be sold. It suggests that poor people should not be allowed to enter the army, to engage in hazardous occupations such as high-steel construction, to become paid subjects for medical experimentation. There are certainly objections of justice to the current highly unequal income distribution. But it seems to me paternalistic in the extreme, given that injustice, to deny poor people choices which they perceive as increasing their well-being.

Here it is important to have some idea of the size of the risk we are talking about. One study has estimated that the increased risk of death to a 35-year-old from giving up one kidney is roughly the same as that associated with driving a car to work 16 miles a day (2). Imagine saying to a poor person either that her choice to commute such a distance is not voluntary, or that if it is, she still ought not to be allowed to commute such a distance, although we will allow middle-class persons to do so.

To make this point more vivid, what would your reaction be to the following proposal made by one author in response to this objection? Prohibit purchases from individuals whose average income is less than 80% of median family income. This has the effect of removing persons in the lower 40% of the income distribution from the market (3). Would you now be more, or less, inclined to favor organ sales?

Note also in the context of arguments about justice that the poor are disproportionately represented among those who need transplants. Thus, assuming—as is currently the case—that the government subsidizes most organ transplants, they stand to gain as a class more than the rich.

Another objection based on the fact of income inequality is that because of unequal bargaining power the price paid to the poor will not be a fair one. They will not get the full market value of their organs. If there were evidence that this was true, the solution would be to regulate the market, not forbid the sale. One could establish minimum prices analogous to minimum wage laws.

Distributional Consequences

If organs are for sale to the highest bidder, the rich will get them and the poor will not.

First, this seems an objection not to the sale of organs but to the general system of medical care based on ability to pay. There are currently at least 50 different types of artificial body parts which are distributed according to ability to pay. Why is it better for the rich to have better access to artificial than to human kidneys?

Second, currently, few individuals pay for transplants out of their own funds. Most transplants are paid for by public and private insurance. So the issue again is access to health insurance, not access to organs.

Note also that the main costs associated with transplants are likely to remain the fees of doctors and hospitals and the costs of drugs, all determined by markets. Why is it legitimate for these to be the results of markets and not the organs themselves?

But if one finds that the distributional implications are unsatisfactory, regulations or restriction on sales are called for. We could adopt a scheme, for example, in which it would be illegal for private individuals to sell organs to other private individuals. They could only sell them to the state. The state then could adopt whatever scheme of distribution would ensure justice in transfer—perhaps a lottery among the equally medically needy, or a first-come, first-served principle.

Irreversibility

One objection to the sale of organs, as opposed to renewable tissues such as blood or semen, is that the decision is irreversible. Individuals may come to regret the fact that they have sold a kidney—particularly if they develop kidney problems with the remaining organ. But we currently allow individuals to make many permanent changes in their body, including breast diminishment and sterilization. If we feel the problem is more severe we can establish waiting periods, counseling, and so forth.

More Choices Not Always Better

The argument that more choices are not always better says that allowing new options does not leave the old options unaltered. Applied to the sale of organs, the claim is that once a market price is established for organs, individuals who choose not to sell do so in the knowledge that they have made a choice which leaves their family worse off economically than they might have been. Individuals are choosing to decline an option which they formerly did not have. They may be psychically worse off than if they never had such a choice. I agree that this is a cost. I do not see, however, that it is anywhere near the psychic costs that are incurred by individuals and their families who face blindness and death as a result of an inadequate supply of organs.

Another psychic cost is more significant, as Hansman argues (3). If one assumes that because of tissue matches, the most efficient donations are from family members, it is likely that introducing markets is liable to strain family relations. Family members are likely to be resentful of being asked to contribute without compensation when a stranger would receive substantial payment. It seems, however, that the rapid development of immunosuppressive drugs may considerably weaken the first premise of this argument.

Commodification

Finally we come to a large class of arguments which object to the commodification of organs. These arguments are rather diverse in character—many are discussed by Radin (4)—and one has to examine them carefully to see how they differ and whether any of them have sufficient force to overcome the presumption in favor of allowing sales of organs.

Altered Nature of the Transaction

Peter Singer, in a well-known argument against the sale of blood which would carry over to the sale of organs, claims that the nature of giving changes when blood is allowed to be sold as well as donated:

> If blood is a commodity with a price, to give blood means merely to save someone money. Blood has a cash value of a certain number of dollars, and the importance of the gift will vary with the wealth of the recipient. If blood cannot be bought, however, the gift's value depends upon the need of the recipient (5).

There are actually two arguments here. The first is that the sale of blood means that the significance of the transfer will vary with the wealth rather than the need of the recipient. Unfortunately this argument is much too powerful, since it is an argument against the sale of anything. Why distinguish blood from food?

The second argument has more weight. It is that if one adds to the existing practice of donation the use of a market, the situation for donors is altered. Whereas before they were able to give something that could not also be purchased, now they can only give something that has a price as well. The nature of their gift is changed. Although I concede that this is true, I do not see it as a compelling objection to allowing such sales. Donors do not have the right to have their gift retain its special character, and if the price of so doing is that potential recipients of life-saving resources are excluded from receiving them (because the supply of donations is limited), the consequences alone would argue for not forbidding such sales.

Alienation

Charles Fried argues that:

> When a man sells his body he does not sell what is his, he sells himself. What is disturbing, therefore, about selling human tissue is that the seller treats his body as a foreign object . . . the shame of selling one's body is just that one splits apart an entity one knows should not be so split (6).

Notice first that this argument (similar to one given by Kant) applies to the sale of blood and semen as well as organs. So if this argument is good, it shows that our current policies are illegitimate. (Although Fried seems to take it back in a footnote [6, p. 143] saying that the selling of blood is "personally bad . . . though not in any sense wrong.")

But the main objection to this argument is that it implies not only that the sale of blood or hair is bad, but also that the donation of such bodily parts is bad as well. For if selling organs splits apart an entity one knows should not be so split, so does donating it. One treats one's body just as much as a foreign object if one gives away a kidney as if one sells it.

The danger we want to avoid at almost all cost is that people start to be treated as property by others. But this is avoided by leaving all decisions about their organs, tissues, and so on to the persons themselves, and insuring that their decisions are voluntary.

Driving Out Altruism

The argument about driving out altruism is that allowing a market in some item will make it less likely that those who were inclined to give on altruistic grounds will continue to do so. The data on blood are ambiguous on this point—some tending to show such an effect, some not. It is clear, however, that the presence of markets does not generally drive out altruistic motives. Most hospital workers are paid, but there are still volunteer workers. There are markets for used clothing, but many people give their used clothing to the needy. Lawyers are paid for their services, but many contribute a portion of their time pro bono. Finally, even if it were true that a market in organs would somewhat reduce the number of people who donate organs, if the total supply is increased, one has to weigh the loss of altruism against the gain in human lives. I see no reason to suppose that the balance will be negative. After all, we allow a commercial market for caregivers for our elderly parents—surely an arena in which not only generalized altruism but debts of gratitude play an important role.

CONCLUSIONS

It seems to me that if we take into account all the welfare losses that will accrue because of the introduction of markets for organs, it will still be the case that if the supply of such organs is significantly increased, the two major gains in welfare (improved health and decreased mortality, and increased income for sellers) will significantly outweigh the losses. If there are no non-consequentialist considerations (such as denials of rights or considerations of justice) which might trump such consequentialist considerations, the consequences ought to be determining.

My conclusion is that, absent other and stronger arguments than those considered, given that both rights and welfare argue in favor of a market for living organ donations, there is no reason not to allow them. In addition, whatever the force of these objections, most of them are considerably weaker when applied to the sale of future rights in cadaver organs. So such a scheme is, I believe, certainly warranted.

REFERENCES

Caplan A. Beg, borrow, or steal: the ethics of solid organ procurement. In: Mathieu D, ed. *Organ Substitution Technology*. Boulder: Westview Press, 1989, 60.

Hamburger J, Crosnier J. Moral and ethical problems in transplantation. In: Johnson D, ed. *Blood Policy: Issues and Alternatives*. Washington: American Enterprise Institute, 1968.

Hansmann H. The economics and ethics of markets for human organs. J Health Politics Policy Law 1989; 14(1):74.

Radin M. Market-inalienability. Harvard Law Rev 1987; 100.

Singer P. Altruism and commerce: a defense of titmuss against arrow. Phil Publ Affairs 1973; 2:314.

Fried C. *Right and Wrong*. Cambridge: Harvard University Press, 1978, 142.

Sweatshops

BENJAMIN POWELL AND MATT ZWOLINSKI

The Ethical and Economic Case Against Sweatshop Labor: A Critical Assessment

2012

INTRODUCTION

Over the last decade the academic debate over sweatshops has grown increasingly sophisticated. Critics of sweatshops now defend their position with nuanced arguments drawn from a variety of moral theories. And the economists' early rejoinder to critics has, at least superficially, been taken to heart. All sides to the debate now recognize that sweatshop labor often represents the best option available for desperately poor workers to improve their lives and the lives of their families, and that any attempt to reform sweatshops must proceed

Benjamin Powell and Matt Zwolinski. "The Ethical and Economic Case Against Sweatshop Labor: A Critical Reassessment." Journal of Business Ethics, 107 (2012): 449–472.

with caution lest the incentives that produce this benefit be destroyed.

Still, this concession has only modified, not softened, the form in which sweatshops are criticized. Scholars such as Dennis Arnold, Norman Bowie, Laura Hartman, Jeremy Snyder, Robert Pollin, and John Miller have raised a variety of new objections to sweatshops, and to the arguments of those who have sought to defend them. They argue that the textbook economic models economists use do not apply to the situation in sweatshops for a variety of reasons and they attempt to articulate the economic mechanisms that undermine standard predictions. They condemn sweatshops for violating the laws of the countries in which they operate. And they charge that sweatshop labor, even if mutually beneficial, is nevertheless often or necessarily coercive or exploitative.

We focus on the arguments made by these scholars because they have wide relevance for the anti-sweatshop movement. Many of the policies advocated by individuals and groups within the anti-sweatshop movement, such as living wages and OSHA-style safety regulations, would be predicted by economic theory to generate adverse consequences for workers. The scholars listed above, and particularly Arnold and his co-authors, have carved out a distinctive position for themselves in that they have given a defense for these policies while largely embracing much of standard neoclassical economic theory. What distinguishes their conclusions from those of standard economic theory is their belief in the existence of special moral principles or economic mechanisms that make sweatshops unique. In short, they offer the most rigorous arguments for policies advocated by many organizations in the anti-sweatshop movement. If the arguments developed by Arnold et al. are incorrect, then much of the activity of the anti-sweatshop movement will have to be questioned and refocused.

Before proceeding, it is worth taking some time to set out the general character of the economic and moral perspective that informs the argument of this paper. Economically, we start from the basic economic defense of sweatshops. One sweatshop critic succinctly summarized that the basic defense was, "as simple as this: 'Either you believe labor demand curves are downward sloping, or you don't' . . . Of course, not to believe that demand curves are negatively sloped would be tantamount to declaring yourself an economic illiterate."[1] In other words, if economic agents demand less of a good the more that good costs, then any policies that raise the cost of sweatshop labor will result in less labor being demanded, i.e. unemployment. Many of the arguments we counter below begin from this framework and attempt to offer economic theories that describe why the sweatshop labor demand curve might be positively sloped or flat. As such, both our arguments and those of our critics fall within neoclassical economic price theory. The dispute between us lies in determining the correct understanding and implications of that framework. However, while we believe that neoclassic economic price theory provides a useful framework for analyzing debates over sweatshop labor, it is important to stress that we do not believe that markets are always in equilibrium and that all information has been discovered. Rather, markets are a discovery procedure thus we do not believe that every advance that could improve worker welfare without harming firms or other workers has been discovered.[2] This belief will play an important role in our argument below.

Morally, it might seem to some readers that a vast gulf separates the perspective of those who criticize sweatshops and those who defend them. But we do not believe this is the case, with respect to either or own argument or indeed to most significant defenses of sweatshops in the academic and popular literature.[3] The argument in this paper, like those other defenses, does not seek to refute the case against sweatshops from the perspective of a single narrow and controversial moral theory. Instead, it seeks to show that anti-sweatshop arguments fail in one of two ways: either they fail *internally,* by running afoul of the moral criteria to which they themselves proclaim allegiance, or that they fail in a way that is *external but uncontroversial,* by succumbing to objections that any reasonable moral theory ought to view as legitimate concerns.

Our moral approach in this paper is a pluralistic one. Objections to sweatshops grounded in concepts of coercion and exploitation are perhaps most at home within a deontological system of ethics, but in the final analysis these are concerns that any plausible moral theory must take seriously. We will therefore attempt to meet these objections on their own terms.

Still, our primary moral focus in this paper will be welfarist in nature. That is to say, the main question on which our moral evaluation of sweatshop labor will turn will be a question about how sweatshops and the various proposed regulations of sweatshops affect the welfare of actual and potential sweatshop workers. We have two reasons for adopting this focus. First, to the extent that there is something morally objectionable with the low wages, dangerous working conditions, long hours, and degrading treatment typically associated with sweatshop labor, the most natural explanation for this is that these conditions are *bad for the persons who suffer them.* Considerations of welfare thus play a major role in standard moral objections to sweatshops. Second, many of the persons affected by sweatshops and anti-sweatshop regulations live in conditions of desperate poverty, in which small gains (or losses) to their objective material conditions can make a tremendous difference in their well-being. Morally, we have very strong reason to take these effects seriously. This is so whether we are utilitarians motivated by considerations of diminishing marginal utility, prioritarians who hold that the interests of the least-advantaged should have a disproportionately great weight in our moral calculus, sufficientarians who believe that the needs of those who do not have *enough* in some non-relative sense have a special moral claim on us, Catholics who believe in a preferential option for the poor, or believers in some principle of social justice for a host of other reasons.

Our concern for the welfare of persons affected by sweatshops includes, of course, sweatshop workers themselves. But it also includes—and this is a point we feel our opponents too often neglect—individuals who do not work in sweatshops. It includes individuals who work elsewhere in the developing world, often in worse conditions and for less pay, and who perhaps would *like* to work in a sweatshop if there were more jobs available there. It includes individuals who have no jobs at all. And it includes future generations—individuals who do not yet exist but will one day benefit or suffer as a result of the economic development that has or has not taken place in the time prior to their birth.

Let us be perfectly explicit about this point: our objection to bans of or regulations on sweatshop labor is not based on the claim that such bans or regulations are economically inefficient. A regulation that imposed a small cost on the very wealthy for the sake of significant gains to the working poor might not be efficient in the sense of wealth maximization or Kaldor-Hicks terms, but nothing in the argument of this paper or most other defenses of sweatshops of which we are aware is committed to opposing such a regulation. This is not, however, how our opponents seem to have interpreted our position. Our opponents seem to believe that defenders of sweatshops are willing to sacrifice the welfare of the working poor for the sake of some overarching, impersonal aggregate measure of wealth or well-being in the economy as a whole. They seem to believe that we oppose regulations on sweatshops because they decrease GDP, or because they are bad for economic growth.

There is a grain of truth to this argument. To the extent that sweatshop regulations do, in fact, hinder economic growth, this really is a strong (though perhaps not overriding) reason to oppose them. But not because economic growth is an end in itself. Rather because economic growth is one of the most stable and effective ways of lifting the poor out of their poverty.[4] Economic growth is a means to an end. And the end, for us, is the welfare of the least advantaged—sweatshop workers, potential sweatshop workers, and future generations of workers and potential workers who will deal with the economic aftermath of today's economic and political decisions.

One can imagine a public policy that would hinder economic growth while nevertheless making the least advantaged better off. But most anti-sweatshop activity, according to our argument, is not like this. Such activity may be inefficient and at odds with economic growth, but these are not the fundamental moral reasons to oppose it. The fundamental moral reason to oppose it is that it hurts those who can least afford to be hurt.

COERCION AND EXPLOITATION

Apart from economic considerations about the connection between labor laws, wage floors, and employment, there still remain two concerns that lead many to doubt the moral defensibility of sweatshop labor. The first is that sweatshop workers are *coerced*—either in their decision to accept sweatshop labor in the first place, or in certain of the demands that are placed on them once they are on the job. The second is that sweatshop workers are *exploited*—either by managers of sweatshops themselves or by the MNEs with which those sweatshops contract. This section will explore, and ultimately reject, the claim that these two considerations support the anti-sweatshop position.

Coercion

Coercion is a philosophically contested concept, and we will not try to settle any grand debates about its precise meaning in this section.[5] Rather, our goal is to assess the role that the concept of coercion has played in anti-sweatshop arguments from a perspective that makes as few assumptions as possible about controversial normative and conceptual issues.

Before proceeding to examine the controversial issues regarding sweatshops and coercion, however, it is worth pausing to take stock of what is *not* controversial. First, no one—not even the most ardent defender of sweatshops—condones the use of physical coercion to force individuals to work in sweatshops, or to prevent them from quitting once they have begun work. Forced labor is a serious moral wrong, and its status as such has been explicitly affirmed by almost every participant in the debate over sweatshops.[6]

Second, no participant in the current debate holds that typical workers are coerced into *taking* sweatshop jobs. That is, all of us reject the claim that individuals are "forced" to work in sweatshops by "the coercion of poverty."[7] Even Arnold and Bowie, ardent critics of sweatshops though they may be, grant that typical sweatshop workers take their jobs because "they believe they can earn more money there than they can in alternative employment."[8] They might wish that they had even better employment options available, but "having to make a choice among undesirable options is not sufficient for coercion" according to their analysis.[9] If there is a moral wrong in transactions such as this, it is better described as "exploitation" than as "coercion." We shall have more to say about the concept of exploitation below.

Still, there remain important disagreements about whether certain activities of sweatshops are properly analyzed as coercive. Arnold and Bowie, for instance, hold that coercion is "widespread" in the demands that are made of sweatshop workers *after* they have taken the job.[10] This coercion is used to force workers to work long hours of overtime, to meet production quotas in spite of physical injuries, to remain working while in need of medical care, and so on.[11] The coercion involved, however, is not physical but "psychological" coercion. Psychological coercion, as understood by Arnold and Bowie, occurs when three conditions are met: (i) the coercer has a "desire about the will of his or her victim," (ii) the coercer has an effective desire to compel his or her victim to act in a manner which makes efficacious the coercer's other-regarding desire," (iii) the coercer is "successful in getting his or her victim to conform to his or her other-regarding desire."[12] So, for example, "when a worker is threatened with being fired by the supervisor unless she agrees to work overtime, and when the supervisor's intention in making the threat is to ensure compliance, then the supervisor's actions are properly understood as coercive."[13]

This account of coercion has been subjected to criticism elsewhere.[14] And while the account plays no role in Arnold's most recent writing on the topic of sweatshops,[15] Arnold and Bowie have attempted to defend their account against some of the criticisms that have been leveled against it.[16] We therefore believe it is worthwhile to subject the theory to one more round of scrutiny.

First, it is not at all helpful to define "coercion" in terms of "compulsion," as this account does, since the latter concept is just as unclear, and raises almost precisely the same sort of philosophic questions, as the former. Essentially, Arnold and Bowie's account says that if I desire that you give me your car, and if I intentionally attempt, and succeed, in compelling you to give it to me, then I have coerced you. But what kinds of activity on my part count as "compelling you"? Arnold and Bowie make clear that they want to distinguish coercion from "rational persuasion," so presumably my trying to convince you that you have overwhelmingly good reason to give me the car would not count as compulsion of the relevant sort. And, presumably, my threatening to beat you severely unless you gave it to me would count as a paradigm case of compulsion. But what if I were to offer to give you a million dollars for your car? We should hardly want to describe such an offer as "coercive," and yet in an earlier article on the subject Arnold identifies a category of compulsion which he describes as "rational compulsion," and which occurs "when an agent is forced to choose between two actions, one of which is plainly superior."[17] Unless your car is very nice indeed, the prospect of a million dollars is likely to be plainly superior to keeping it. But if my offer is really a form of compulsion, and hence coercion, then it is difficult to see how we could maintain the common-sense idea, which Arnold explicitly embraces, that coercion is as a conceptual matter *prima facie* wrong.[18] On the other hand, if we rule out rational compulsion as a genuine form of compulsion, then all that we are left with, on Arnold's account, are "psychological compulsion" and "physical compulsion." The former occurs when *A* acts in a way so as to create an "irresistible desire" in *B* to act in a certain way, and the latter occurs when *A* forcefully moves *B*'s body. But genuinely "irresistible" desires are almost certainly either nonexistent or so rare as to provide scarce basis for Arnold's claim that psychological coercion is "widespread" in sweatshops.[19] This leaves only physical compulsion, and this means that psychological coercion simply reduces to threatening to physically coerce someone, a phenomenon that Arnold and Bowie themselves admit is "comparatively rare," and which we have already noted is universally condemned by all sides of the sweatshop debate.[20] One serious problem with Arnold and Bowie's account, then, is that it fails to provide an analysis of psychological coercion that distinguishes it from physical coercion, on the one side, and rational persuasion, on the other.

A second and third problem can be seen by examining Gordon Sollars and Fred Englander's criticism of Arnold and Bowie's claims regarding psychological coercion in sweatshops. These authors find Arnold and Bowie's example of a worker being threatened with termination unless she agrees to work overtime unconvincing as an instance of coercion. Of course, workers might not like to work overtime, and we can safely assume that they would prefer to keep their jobs without having to comply with their bosses' demands. But Sollars and Englander interpret these requests, so long as they are routine and known about in advance by workers, as simply part of the conditions of employment.[21] If Arnold and Bowie describe them as coercive, it suggests that their view really does just collapse to one in which being forced to choose between bad alternatives counts as coercion, something which, as we saw earlier, they had previously denied.[22]

In response, Arnold and Bowie object that Sollars and Englander focused their critique on only one of their three examples of coercion. Their second example involved a hypothetical account of a supervisor threatening a worker who was ill or injured with termination unless she meets a production quota that is either impossible for her to meet or impossible for her to meet without sustaining further injury, and their third involved an actual account of a pregnant worker in El Salvador who began hemorrhaging on the job and was not allowed to leave the factory to seek medical attention.[23]

These examples are indeed shocking. But what renders them shocking, we will argue, has to do with the perceived unreasonableness of the *substance* of what is being demanded of workers, and not with a belief that the workers are being *coerced* into complying with the substance of the demand. After all, if the demands above indeed qualify as coercive on Arnold and Bowie's account,[24] then so too does almost *any* instance of an employer demanding her employee to *X* or else be fired—even the demand that the employee show up regularly to work at the scheduled time. If these are genuine examples of coercion, then coercion is everywhere in the workplace. And an account of coercion that has this implication seems too over-inclusive to be much use in moral theorizing. Nor does Arnold and Bowie's reassurance that coercion is only *prima facie* wrong do much to help. For starters, this places all the weight of determining which instances of coercion are *really* wrong, and which are acceptable, on further moral theorizing which they have not so far explained in any detail, let alone defended. But moreover, many of the actions that would qualify as coercive on their account do not seem wrong even in a *prima facie* sense. Telling a worker that she will be fired unless she performs the basic functions of her job is not something that should appear to us as wrong until we investigate further and find some other features of the situation that might justify it. It is just not wrong at all.

In conclusion, Arnold and Bowie have provided us with some examples of shocking behavior on the part of sweatshops, but they have not yet given us a satisfactory argument for why we should conclusively regard such behavior as wrong, nor have they given us a satisfactory theoretical account of what this wrongness is supposed to consist of. Our own view is that there is probably not wrong for sweatshops to demand long overtime hours, that it might or might not be wrong to demand that injured workers meet production quotas or be fired, depending on the circumstances, and that it is almost certainly wrong to refuse permission for a worker to seek urgently needed medical care. But the permissibility or impermissibility of each of these actions is not something that can be explained by appeals to the wrongfulness of coercion. The burden of proof thus remains on the critics of sweatshops to provide a compelling argument and explanation for the alleged wrongness.

Exploitation

The charge that sweatshop labor is coercive is, as we have seen, difficult to sustain in the face of rigorous philosophical analysis. And, perhaps for this reason, most current academic criticisms of sweatshops are not based primarily on this charge. Far more common is the charge that sweatshop labor is wrongfully *exploitative*.[25]

What it is for a person to be exploited is a matter of some philosophical dispute, and again the purpose of this section is not to try to resolve that dispute.[26] Most accounts, however, hold that wrongful exploitation consists in taking advantage of another person in a way that is either unfair or that fails to manifest sufficient respect for that person's dignity. Understood in this way, an interaction can be exploitative without being coercive. Indeed, an interaction can be both voluntary and beneficial to both parties (relative to how they would have fared in the absence of any interaction), while still being wrongfully exploitative. Suppose, for example, that *A* offers to rescue *B* from drowning by selling *B* a spot on *A*'s boat for $10,000. Assuming we reject the "hard choices" account of coercion, and thus the claim that *B* is coerced into accepting *A*'s offer, we can hold *B*'s choice to be voluntary. And while the deal is clearly beneficial to *A*—we can stipulate that *A* values the $10,000 much more highly than the time and effort he must sacrifice—it is no less clearly beneficial to *B*. *B* surely values her life more highly than the $10,000 she had to give up to save it. If she did not, why would she have accepted *A*'s offer? Still, most people (including us) would judge that *A* has clearly acted wrongly in making his rescue contingent upon *B*'s paying such an exorbitant sum. In doing so, *A* seems to be taking wrongful advantage of his monopoly on the means of rescue, and failing to treat *B* with the respect she deserves.

Can we analyze sweatshop labor in a similar way? Perhaps potential sweatshop workers are like people drowning in ponds, and the MNEs (Multi-National Enterprises) that ultimately finance their employment are like the man in the boat. The potential workers are in a desperate situation, "drowning" in poverty and perhaps unable to adequately provide for themselves and their families. MNEs have power in the form of wealth to rescue these individuals. But rather than providing that rescue out of common kindness or a sense of moral obligation, they make it contingent on an onerous payment. The MNE will provide the worker with just enough money to make the employment offer attractive, and will demand in exchange the worker to toil for long hours in dangerous and unpleasant conditions. Such an offer might present the worker with a better alternative than anything else she has available. But so does the boatman's offer, and this does not make it any less unfair, demeaning, or objectionable.

Still, there are good reasons for thinking that the standard cases of sweatshop labor—even those involving low wages and very bad working conditions—are not wrongfully exploitative. First, it is not clear that the distribution of burdens and benefits between sweatshop workers and MNEs is *unfair,* and hence not clear that MNEs are taking unfair advantage of sweatshop workers. Part of the problem in credibly establishing the charge of unfairness stems from the immense difficulty in specifying a general principle of fair distribution, something no critic of sweatshops has yet managed to do. Even without such a principle, of course, critics of sweatshops might hold that the division is unfair in some obvious and intuitive way—perhaps because MNEs are clearly getting more than they ought to out of the transaction, or because workers are clearly getting less. But neither of the factual claims on which this "obvious and intuitive" account of unfairness rests are accurate. The rate of profit in MNEs that outsource is generally no higher than it is in other industries with a similar level of risk. The often cited fact that a sweatshop worker who produces, say, a pair of Reebok shoes, is paid only one US dollar to make a shoe that sells for around $100 does not mean that Reebok is walking away from the exchange with $99 and the worker with only $1.[27] Most of the $100 goes to paying for advertising, retailer markup, raw materials, transportation costs, and so on. The amount that actually accrues to Reebok as profit is generally no greater as a percentage of their investment than the profits in any other competitive industry. So MNEs are not earning unusually high profits off the backs of sweatshop workers. Nor is it obvious that sweatshop workers are receiving less than they ought to earn in wages. Such a claim might be credible if MNEs were, as some critics have charged, utilizing their monopsonistic power to pay workers less than the market rate for their labor. But as we have argued earlier in this paper, there is no reason to think that workers' wages are not determined, by and large, by their productivity—just as the wages of non-sweatshop workers are.

The charge of unfairness, and hence of exploitation, derives some traction in the comparison drawn between sweatshops and the rescue case described above. But on closer examination, these cases are dissimilar in ways that seem morally significant. First, part of what pulls our intuition in the rescue case is the belief that the boat owner will not be made (significantly) worse off by having to perform the rescue *gratis.* As we have tried to argue in this paper, though, increases in sweatshop wages or improvements in their working conditions will usually come at a cost to someone—if not to the employer then to customers, or to potential workers. Moreover, the rescue in the example we have provided is entirely fortuitous. The boat owner *just happened* to be there when the victim needed rescuing. Our intuitions might be different if the boat owner were there *precisely because* he anticipated that people might need rescued, especially if his being there required significant investment of time and capital. With this contrast in mind, sweatshops look less like cases of fortuitous rescue and more like cases of professional salvage operations, and it is noteworthy that admiralty law has traditionally recognized that the latter are entitled to claim significantly higher awards than the former.[28]

It is important to recognize, however, that even if sweatshops are not guilty of providing their workers with less compensation than they should, it is still possible that workers' income is lower than it morally ought to be. The claim that MNEs do not exploit sweatshop workers is entirely compatible with the claim that sweatshop workers are suffering grievous injustice, and with the claim that the income of sweatshop workers is lower than it morally ought to be as a result of this injustice.

The explanation for this paradoxical claim lies in the fact that the labor agreements between sweatshops and their employees are a product of a wide variety of factors, many of which fall well outside the responsibility of MNEs. The background political and economic institutions of the host country, for instance, shape and constrain the opportunities available to potential sweatshop workers. To the extent that those institutions erect barriers to entry to new businesses, deny workers the freedom to organize collectively, or fail to ensure that citizens have reasonable access to food, shelter, and education, workers' opportunities to advance their interests and the interests of their families will be severely limited.[29] Workers' opportunities are almost certainly further restricted by injustices in the global economic order, including the unjust seizure of land and natural resources by states and other entities,[30] and the unjust restriction of free access to Western markets by various forms of protectionism.[31] And the more limited their opportunities are, the more likely it is that an offer of sweatshop labor will be workers' most attractive option.

Sometimes, MNEs themselves will bear partial responsibility for the unjust background conditions against which labor agreements are formed. Because of the benefits that MNEs can bring to host countries, especially in the form of increased tax revenue, they are often well-positioned to influence the behavior of the host country government. MNEs can make their economic investment in a country contingent upon the government's willingness to use its power to secure special benefits for the MNE—benefits that will often come at the cost of the MNEs competitors, the country's workers, and its citizens. To the extent that MNEs influence governments to act unjustly in a way that constrains workers' options, MNEs *do* bear moral responsibility for the background conditions against which labor agreements are made. In this case, however, the real wrong of which MNEs are guilty would seem to be a form of joint-coercion with the government, rather than exploitation per se.[32]

Very often, however, limiting background conditions will not be the result of any injustice assignable to MNEs. Sometimes, the main constraint on workers' options will be a poverty that is due not to any positive evil but rather to the absence of the delicate combination of social, political, geographic, and other factors needed for the production of wealth and economic development. At other times, it will be an injustice perpetrated by their own government without the collusion of foreign business interests. When workers' options are constrained by factors such as these, and where the labor agreements between workers and sweatshops are not plagued by any form of procedural wrongdoing such as deception or coercion, it is difficult to see how the claim that sweatshops are taking *unfair* advantage of workers could be maintained. They are taking advantage, to be sure. But they are doing so by entering into an agreement with workers that is mutually beneficial relative to their antecedent circumstances. And while sweatshop workers might reasonably wish that their antecedent circumstances were better, and hence that their bargaining power with sweatshops were stronger, it is far from obvious that they have any grounds for complaint *against sweatshops* in circumstances such as those that we have described here.

Such a complaint could only be grounded in the claim that sweatshops, or more plausibly the MNEs with which they contract, have some kind of moral obligation to rectify the injustice of the background conditions against which labor contracts are formed. Or, at least, to try to "correct" for this background injustice in some way when forming labor agreements with workers—perhaps by entering into only those agreements of the sort that would have been formed had background conditions *not* been unjust. But as Alan Wertheimer has noted, this way of understanding what a non-exploitative transaction requires seems to place an unduly heavy burden on those interacting with the victims of background injustice.[33] Why should MNEs bear special responsibility for rectifying injustices for which they were not responsible?

Jeremy Snyder has argued that MNEs' special obligation has its origin in a Kantian duty of beneficence.[34] Part of what it means to respect other persons as ends in themselves, according to this line of reasoning, is to not merely refrain from interfering with their actions, but take positive steps to promote their autonomy. As a general matter, this duty of beneficence has an imperfect form, meaning that individuals have "considerable leeway in determining when and where to direct their resources toward supporting" the autonomy of others.[35] But Snyder's key move is to argue that when we enter into certain forms of special relationships with others, this general duty takes on a "perfect, strict form."[36] MNEs, then, that enter into relationships with particular sweatshop employees have a special obligation of beneficence toward *those* employees. Because they are in a direct relationship with other human beings in desperate need, they no longer have the leeway they once had in determining how to discharge their duty of beneficence. Rather, "they are required to cede as much of their benefit from the interaction to their employees as is reasonably possible toward the end of their employees achieving a decent minimum standard of living."[37]

But there is something puzzling about Snyder's position. As we have seen, sweatshop labor generally represents a more attractive option than any other option available to workers—often a *significantly* better option. By making such labor opportunities available, then, MNEs thereby confer considerable benefit upon their workers. But why should the very act of providing such a benefit impose upon MNEs a moral obligation to confer an even *greater* benefit? Why does providing *some* help to workers in the developing world confer an obligation to help *more*, especially when those who provide *no* help are (on Snyder's account) guilty of no moral wrongdoing?[38] Consider the following two companies:

Company A—This company, based in the United States, outsources production to a developing country. The wages it pays are considerably higher than the wages paid elsewhere in that country, and workers' lives are greatly improved by the benefits those wages confer. Moreover, the company uses a portion of the profits it earns to fund various charitable causes in its home country. It does not, however, give to its workers as much "as is reasonably possible."

Company B—This company, based in the United States, does not outsource production at all. It does, however, use a portion of its profits to fund various charitable causes in its home country.

Let us stipulate that both Company A and Company B give enough to charity to satisfy an imperfect duty of beneficence. Snyder's account nevertheless implies that Company A is acting wrongly, whereas Company B is not.[39] This implication would seem to hold even if workers in the developing country to which Company A outsources stand in greater need of aid than the beneficiaries of the charitable causes that Companies A and B fund, since according to Snyder the perfect nature of Company A's obligations toward its employees is not a function of their need, but rather of their interaction with Company A. This seems implausible.

But suppose we agreed with Snyder that a company's entering into an employment relationship with a needy individual was sufficient to generate a strict, perfect duty of beneficence on the part of the company toward that employee.[40] Compliance with such a duty, let us stipulate, would require the company to provide a benefit to its employee of amount Y. But let us suppose that the employer is only willing to provide its employees with a benefit of amount X, where $X < Y$. Would it be permissible, on Snyder's account, for the employer to make its offer of employment contingent upon its workers' willingness to waive their right to benefits of amount Y? Prior to entering into a relationship with employees, the employer has only an imperfect duty of beneficence. No prospective employee has any valid moral claim upon its assistance. Thus, the company would not be acting wrongly if it refused to hire or assist the prospective employee at all. But if it is permissible for the employer not to hire prospective workers, and if hiring prospective workers at benefit level X is better for both the employer and the worker than not hiring the prospective workers at all, then how could doing so be wrong? If employees' claim to benefits at level Y is waivable, then employers are not necessarily acting wrongly in providing their employees with benefits at level X. If, on the other hand, employees' claim to benefits at level Y is not waivable, then Snyder's account is committed to holding that failing to benefit needy workers at all is better than benefiting them at a level which is (significantly) greater than zero but less than the morally required amount—even if workers themselves would strongly prefer and would like to choose the latter over the former.

This strikes us as a deeply implausible conclusion. The structure of our argument, of course, draws on many of the same intuitions as those invoked in Zwolinski's presentation of the "non-worseness claim."[41] And Snyder has attempted to argue that this claim is false, and hence not a threat to his theory.[42] But we are not convinced that his response succeeds. The first point he makes, that "by choosing to enter into a relationship with another person, we can take on new duties or specify existing duties beyond the duty not to harm others," is true as far as it goes but does not save him from the problem posed by the argument above.[43] For we do not deny that entering into a relationship can create new obligations. We simply hold that it is implausible to hold that those new obligations are not waivable, even when one party regards the other's waiving of the obligation to be a necessary precondition for entering into the relationship, and the other party strongly prefers the relationship without the obligation to no relationship at all. Snyder has given us no reason to think otherwise.

Snyder's second point is an appeal to intuition: he borrows an example from Alan Wertheimer in which *A* proposes to marry *B* only if *B* agrees to "an unfair distribution of financial arrangements, childcare, and household labor."[44] Even if we agree that *A* has a moral right not to marry *B* at all, Snyder says, and even if we grant that an unfair marriage is better for both *A* and *B* than no marriage at all, *A*'s proposal still seems morally objectionable, despite the fact that NWC says that it should not be.

Similar cases might be multiplied. What if sweatshops offer jobs that are better than workers' best alternatives, but that involve shocking and degrading treatment? What if workers are required to perform sexual acts as a condition of employment? Or to work 18-hour days behind locked doors with no fire extinguishers?[45]

We share Snyder's intuitive discomfort with *A*'s behavior in this case. As Snyder himself notes, however, it is difficult to know what to make of our intuitive responses to cases like this without some kind of underlying theoretical account. One possibility worth considering, however, is that our intuition in this case is a product of some contingent feature of the way in which the case is described, rather than a reflection of some deep truth about the situation itself. As Wertheimer describes the exploitative marriage case, for instance, and as we have presented it here, the only details we are given concern the unsavory aspects of the exploitative marriage. Regarding the situation of *B* in the absence of the exploitative marriage, we are told only that it is worse for her, without any correspondingly detailed account of what this worseness consists of. It is possible that because the non-marriage situation is not described in any detail, it does not play as a great a role in shaping our intuition as does the exploitative-marriage situation. In effect, our intuitions may be "discounting" the badness of the alternative. There is some experimental evidence which suggests that the level of concreteness with which a situation is described has a significant impact on our moral intuitions, and it does not seem unreasonable to suppose that something like this may be at work in the present case.[46]

At the end of the day, however, we are prepared to bite the bullet with respect to the possibly counter-intuitive implications of NWC. After all, we hope to have shown that the rejection of NWC entails strongly counter-intuitive implications as well. Moreover, we hope to have shown that the rejection of NWC is at odds with two core moral values that both consequentialists and Kantians must recognize: welfare and autonomy. It is clear enough that the rejection of NWC cannot be based on concern for sweatshop workers' welfare, since rejecting NWC entails rejecting transactions that are Pareto-superior. But our discussion of non-waivability above shows that the rejection of NWC cannot be grounded in concern for workers' autonomy either. After all, if workers' autonomy was a central value, then why would we not allow them to waive certain of their rights when they themselves judged that the benefits they could gain by doing so are worth the cost? Not only is the rejection of NWC counterintuitive, then, it also seems to involve a kind of paternalistic substitution of the moral theorist's own values for those of the workers themselves. Until such time as the critics of sweatshops can provide a theoretical account for their intuitions, and/or show that the balance of counterintuitiveness tilts more in their favor than it has appeared from our presentation, we are not prepared to abandon this principle.

CONCLUSION

We have carefully considered the arguments in a body of scholarship critical of sweatshops and found that, while going beyond the superficial objections to sweatshops raised by activists in the 1990s, the more sophisticated arguments still fail to undermine the basic economic and ethical defense of sweatshops. No economic mechanisms have been identified which would allow higher wages or better working conditions to be legally mandated without harming workers. The only meaningful type of coercion in sweatshops is the threat of physical violence if a worker refuses a job or attempts to leave. This form of coercion is relatively rare and defenders and critics of sweatshops alike condemn this type of coercion. And while the claim that sweatshop workers are often the victims of gross injustice is plausible, the claim that it is sweatshops or the MNEs with which they contract that perpetrate this injustice through wrongful exploitation is difficult to sustain.

We have answered the major critiques of the standard defense of sweatshops. We hope that if scholars continue to be critical of sweatshops they will address the arguments we raised here. Specifically we challenge them to demonstrate what economic mechanisms would allow for universal adoption of higher wages and better working conditions. Until they can persuasively argue for such mechanisms we call on them to join us in denouncing all legal mandates for higher wages and better working conditions and to advocate only for voluntarily adopted company policies. We call on them to explicitly state under what, if any, conditions they would advocate violating local labor laws. We have argued that since they have not identified any universal economic mechanisms, opposing legal mandates for wages and working conditions, and violating them when they already exist, will often be in the best interest of the workers and thus should be advocated if worker welfare or autonomy is their goal. We challenge them to demonstrate that there is meaningful widespread coercion in sweatshops. We've argued that only the threat of physical violence counts as meaningful coercion and that our critics admit that this is relatively rare. Finally we ask if they think that mutually beneficial exploitation (sweatshop labor that provides a benefit to workers and yet falls short of meeting the labor rights Arnold et al. want to see enforced) is worse than failing to outsource at all, and to provide a compelling theoretical explanation for the rejection of NWC. Until these challenges are met, the economic and ethical case for sweatshops has been reclaimed.

NOTES

1. Miller, John, "Why Economists Are Wrong About Sweatshops and the Anti-Sweatshop Movement." *Challenge* 46 (2003): 93–122.

2. See Friedrich A. Hayek, "Competition as a Discovery Procedure," *New Studies in Philosophy, Politics, Economics, and the History of Ideas*, ed. Friedrich A. Hayek (Chicago: University of Chicago Press, 1968).

3. In the business ethics literature, the most significant defenses have been presented in Ian Maitland, "The Great Non-Debate over International Sweatshops," *Ethical Theory and Business*, 6th ed., eds. Tom L. Beauchamp and Norman E. Bowie (Engelwood Cliffs, NJ: Prentince Hall, 1996). and Matt Zwolinski, "Sweatshops, Choice, and Exploitation," *Business Ethics Quarterly* 17.4 (2007). In the popular media, Paul Krugman's 1997 defense ("In Praise of Cheap Labor," *Slate*, March 21, 1997) is still frequently cited, as are several articles by Nicholas Kristof (Nicholas D. Kristof and Sheryl Wudunn, "Two Cheers for Sweatshops," *The New York Times*, September 24, 2000, and Nicholas D. Kristof, "Where Sweatshops Are a Dream," *New York Times*, January 14, 2009).

4. See, for instance, Peter Singer's discussion of the living standards of the world's poor today compared to twenty years ago. Peter Singer, *The Life You Can Save: Acting Now to End World Poverty* (New York: Random House, 2009).

5. See, for an overview, Scott Anderson, *Coercion*, 2006, Available: http://plato.stanford.edu/entries/coercion/, October 1, 2010.

6. See Arnold and Hartman, "Beyond Sweatshops: Positive Deviancy and Global Labour Practices," 679, n. 5 ("No one in this debate advocates forced labor"), Sollars and Englander, "Sweatshops: Kant and Consequences," 122 ("We agree . . . that workers should not be physically coerced"), Zwolinski, "Sweatshops, Choice, and Exploitation," 696 ("The truth of premise 1 [in the argument for the moral impermissibility of interfering with sweatshop labor]

hinges on whether people *do* in fact choose to work in sweatshops, and fails in cases of genuinely forced labor.")

7. The only person of whom we are aware who does make this claim is John Miller, in "Why Economists Are Wrong About Sweatshops and the Antisweatshop Movement," *Challenge*, (January/February 2003): 97. But he does not defend the claim at any length, and has not (as far as we are aware) repeated it since.

8. Arnold and Bowie, "Sweatshops and Respect for Persons," 229.

9. Arnold and Bowie, "Sweatshops and Respect for Persons," 229.

10. Arnold and Bowie, "Sweatshops and Respect for Persons," 229. See also Denis G. Arnold and Norman E. Bowie, "Respect for Workers in Global Supply Chains: Advancing the Debate over Sweatshops," *Business Ethics Quarterly* 17.1 (2007).

11. Arnold and Bowie, "Sweatshops and Respect for Persons," 229–31.

12. Arnold and Bowie, "Sweatshops and Respect for Persons," 229.

13. Arnold and Bowie, "Sweatshops and Respect for Persons," 230.

14. See Sollars and Englander, "Sweatshops: Kant and Consequences," 122–23, and Zwolinski, "Sweatshops, Choice, and Exploitation."

15. Arnold, "Working Conditions: Safety and Sweatshops."

16. Arnold and Bowie, "Respect for Workers in Global Supply Chains: Advancing the Debate over Sweatshops," 140–42.

17. Denis Arnold, "Coercion and Moral Responsibility," *American Philosophical Quarterly* 38.1 (2001): 56.

18. Arnold, "Coercion and Moral Responsibility," 54.

19. See Stephen J. Morse, "Uncontrollable Urges and Irrational People," *Virginia Law Review* 88 (2000): 1054–63.

20. Arnold and Bowie, "Sweatshops and Respect for Persons," 229.

21. Sollars and Englander, "Sweatshops: Kant and Consequences," 123. We are not convinced that the distinction between "conditions of employment" and "informal practices" suggested by Sollars and Englander (p. 123), and picked up explicitly by Arnold and Bowie in "Respect for Workers in Global Supply Chains: Advancing the Debate over Sweatshops," 141, is a helpful one. For, in the standard case, one of the conditions of employment will simply be that one comply with the informal practices of the workplace and the occasional job-related special requests of one's supervisor.

22. Sollars and Englander, "Sweatshops: Kant and Consequences," 123, and Arnold and Bowie, "Sweatshops and Respect for Persons," 229.

23. These examples were originally presented in Arnold and Bowie, "Sweatshops and Respect for Persons," but are reproduced in their entirety in Arnold and Bowie, "Respect for Workers in Global Supply Chains: Advancing the Debate over Sweatshops," 140–41.

24. We leave this as an open question, since it is not clear from Arnold and Bowie's presentation which of the three possible types of "compulsion" are supposed to be at work in them. Threatening to fire an employee might qualify as "rational compulsion," but it is doubtful that it could be interpreted as either psychological or physical compulsion.

25. See, for instance, Arnold and Bowie, "Sweatshops and Respect for Persons"; Robert Mayer, "Sweatshops, Exploitation, and Moral Responsibility," *Journal of Social Philosophy* 38.4 (2007); Chris Meyers, "Wrongful Beneficence: Exploitation and Third World Sweatshops," *Journal of Social Philosophy* 35.3 (2004); Jeremy C. Snyder, "Exploitation and Sweatshop Labor: Perspectives and Issues," *Business Ethics Quarterly* 20.2 (2010); and Iris Marion Young, "Responsibility and Global Justice: A Social Connection Model," *Social Philosophy and Policy* 23.01 (2006).

26. Some of the most influential accounts include Robert E. Goodin, "Exploiting a Situation and Exploiting a Person," *Modern Theories of Exploitation*, ed. Andrew Reeve (London: Sage, 1987); Allen W. Wood, "Exploitation," *Social Philosophy and Policy* 12.2 (1995); Alan Wertheimer, *Exploitation* (Princeton, NJ: Princeton University Press, 1996); Ruth Sample, *Exploitation: What It Is and Why It's Wrong* (New York: Rowman and Littlefield, 2003); Snyder, "Needs Exploitation"; Robert Mayer, "What's Wrong with Exploitation?," *Journal of Applied Philosophy* 24.2 (2007); Mikhail Valdman, "Exploitation and Injustice," *Social Theory and Practice: An International and Interdisciplinary Journal of Social Philosophy* 34.4 (2008); and Mikhail Valdman, "A Theory of Wrongful Exploitation," *Philosophers' Imprint* 9.6 (2009). Alan Wertheimer, *Exploitation*, 2008, available: http://plato.stanford.edu/archives/fall2008/entries/exploitation/, January 12 2010, provides an overview of most of the main philosophical accounts. Snyder, "Exploitation and Sweatshop Labor: Perspectives and Issues," provides another overview with specific focus on the application of such accounts to the issue of sweatshop labor.

27. This particular version of the claim is taken from Meyers, "Wrongful Beneficence: Exploitation and Third World Sweatshops," 331.

28. Melvin Eisenberg, "The Principle of Unconscionability," *Law and Economics Workshop* (Berkeley, CA: Berkeley Law School, 2009), 15–16.

29. We defend workers' freedom to organize collectively voluntarily which is distinct from laws that allow labor unions to organize workers where a subset of all workers has the legal right to collectively bargain for all workers even when some workers would rather bargain individually.

30. See Thomas W. Pogge, "World Poverty and Human Rights," *Ethics and International Affairs* 19.1 (2005): 7.

31. Pogge, "World Poverty and Human Rights," 6.

32. See Zimmerman, "Coercive Wage Offers."

33. Wertheimer, *Exploitation* 234.

34. See Snyder, "Needs Exploitation," and Snyder, "Exploitation and Sweatshop Labor: Perspectives and Issues."

35. Snyder, "Needs Exploitation," 396.

36. Snyder, "Needs Exploitation," 390.

37. Snyder, "Needs Exploitation," 396.

38. So long as they discharge their imperfect duty of beneficence in some other way. The point here is really a specific application of what has been called, in the literature on exploitation, the "non-worseness claim," which holds that it cannot be morally worse for A to interact with B than it is for A not to interact with B when the interaction is mutually beneficial, consensual, and free from negative externalities. See, for a discussion, Zwolinski, "Sweatshops, Choice, and Exploitation," 708–10; Matt Zwolinski, "The Ethics of Price Gouging," *Business Ethics Quarterly* 18.3 (2008): 357–60; Matt Zwolinski, "Price Gouging, Non-Worseness, and Distributive Justice," *Business Ethics Quarterly* 19.2 (2009); Jeremy C. Snyder, "Efficiency, Equality, and Price Gouging: A Response to Zwolinski," *Business Ethics Quarterly* 19.2 (2009); and Alan Wertheimer, *Widening the Lens: Philosophical Essays on Research with Human Subjects* (New York: Oxford University Press, 2011), chapter 6. It is beyond this article to set out a full defense of the non-worseness claim (though see Matt Zwolinski, "Exploitation and Neglect," San Diego: University of San Diego, Department of Philosophy, for an attempt to do this). Instead, the discussion that follows attempts to press the intuitive force of the non-worseness claim in this specific context, without fully defending it as a general principle.

39. Alternatively, Snyder could hold that Company A is guilty of exploitation, while Company B is not, but that Company B is guilty of some other and perhaps more serious form of moral offense. This would save Snyder's account from having to embrace the counterintuitive claim that Company A is acting in a worse way than Company B, but only at the price of reducing the moral significance of exploitation.

40. Actually, Snyder does not quite hold that it is "sufficient." Several other conditions must be met for the employer to have this duty, but as they do not affect the present argument these need not concern us here.

41. Zwolinski, "Sweatshops, Choice, and Exploitation"; Matt Zwolinski, "The Ethics of Price Gouging," *Business Ethics Quarterly* 18.3 (2008); Matt Zwolinski, "Price Gouging, Non-Worseness, and Distributive Justice," *Business Ethics Quarterly* 19.2 (2009).

42. Jeremy C. Snyder, "Efficiency, Equality, and Price Gouging: A Response to Zwolinski," *Business Ethics Quarterly* 19.2 (2009).

43. Snyder, "Efficiency, Equality, and Price Gouging: A Response to Zwolinski," 305.

44. Snyder, "Efficiency, Equality, and Price Gouging: A Response to Zwolinski," 305.

45. We thank an anonymous referee for raising these questions.

46. In one extremely interesting experiment, Christopher Freiman and Shaun Nichols presented subjects with either an abstract or a concrete description of a situation involving a distribution of resources. The abstract version asks subjects to "suppose that some people make more money than others solely because they have genetic advantages," while the concrete version asks them to "suppose Amy and Beth both want to be professional jazz singers. They both practice singing equally hard. Although jazz singing is the greatest natural talent of both Amy and Beth, Beth's vocal range and articulation is naturally better than Amy's because of differences in their genetics. Solely as a result of this genetic advantage, Beth's singing is much more impressive. As a result, Beth attracts bigger audiences and hence gets more money than Amy." Subjects were then asked whether the fact that the genetically advantaged individuals make more money is fair. Surprisingly, subjects who were given the concrete version of the case were significantly more likely to say that it *is* fair for the genetically advantaged individuals to make more money than those who were given the abstract version of the case. See Christopher Freiman and Shaun Nichols, "Is Desert in the Details?," *Philosophy and Phenomenological Research* 81(1): 121–133.

Mathew Coakley and Michael Kates

The Ethical and Economic Case for Sweatshop Regulation

2013

INTRODUCTION

Three types of objections have been raised against sweatshops. According to their critics, sweatshops are (1) exploitative, (2) coercive, and (3) harmful to workers. In "The Ethical and Economic Case Against Sweatshop Labor: A Critical Assessment," Powell and Zwolinski critique all three objections and thereby offer what is arguably the most powerful defense of sweatshops in the philosophical literature to date.[1] Our aim in this article is to demonstrate that, whether or not unregulated sweatshops are exploitative or coercive, they are, pace Powell and Zwolinski, harmful to workers.

We focus here exclusively on the objection that sweatshops are harmful to workers because not only does this form the core of Powell and Zwolinski's argument against sweatshop regulation but it also seems the most obvious place for moral inquiry on this subject to start. Since even an exploitative transaction can be mutually beneficial, and since even a coerced choice can be better than no choice at all, the case for or against sweatshops has typically begun with the question of whether or not they are harmful to workers. Or, as Powell and Zwolinski put it, "to the extent that there is something morally objectionable with the low wages, dangerous working conditions, long hours, and degrading treatment typically associated with sweatshop labor, the most natural explanation for this is that these conditions are bad for the persons who suffer them" (p. 451).

Unlike other critics, however, our argument does not proceed from "special" (p. 450) economic or moral principles. To the contrary, our strategy will be to demonstrate that even if we grant the truth of Powell and Zwolinski's economic and moral assumptions for the sake of argument, it nevertheless still does not follow that regulating sweatshops will be harmful to workers. Powell and Zwolinski's defense of sweatshops thus fails on its own terms.

THE CASE AGAINST SWEATSHOP REGULATION

Powell and Zwolinski's argument against regulating sweatshop labor can be reformulated as follows.

1. Sweatshops are better for workers than the available alternatives.
2. Regulating sweatshop labor will lead to a decrease in sweatshop employment.
3. Therefore, regulating sweatshop labor will be harmful to workers.

Now there are two initial points to emphasize about this argument. The first is that the justification of premises (1) and (2) hinge on contested economic and moral assumptions. Indeed, it is here that much of the debate in the literature has focused. Premise (2), for example, assumes that increasing the price of sweatshop labor via minimum wage laws or other

Mathew Coakley and Michael Kates. "The Ethical and Economic Case for Sweatshop Regulation." *Journal of Business Ethics* 117 (2013): 553–558.

worker benefits will predictably lead to a decrease in sweatshop employment as a result. The evidence for this assumption is, however, mixed. Some critics of sweatshops have argued that due to market imperfections (Arnold and Hartman 2005) or productivity gains from improved workplace conditions or remuneration (Pollin et al. 2004), regulating sweatshop labor will not in fact lead to a decrease in sweatshop employment overall.[2] Premise (1), moreover, assumes that "workers' voluntary choice to accept sweatshop employment demonstrates that sweatshops were the best alternative available to them" (p. 451). But there are grounds for being skeptical of this assumption as well. One might deny that such a choice was genuinely voluntary (Cohen 1983, 1987). Or one might reject the moral force of economic exchanges made in conditions of extreme desperation (Walzer 1983).

As stated above, however, we will not challenge either one of these assumptions here. Nor will we invoke any novel ones of our own. Instead, our strategy in what follows will be to grant the truth of both of Powell and Zwolinski's economic and moral assumptions for the sake of argument and demonstrate that regulating sweatshop labor is morally desirable nevertheless.

The second point to emphasize is that, as it currently stands, this argument is invalid. From the premise that (1) sweatshops are better for workers than the available alternatives and that (2) regulating sweatshop labor will lead to a decrease in sweatshop employment, it does not follow that (3) regulating sweatshop labor will be harmful to workers. In order for this argument to be valid, at least one additional premise is required: (2') regulating sweatshop labor will lead to greater overall harm to workers than not regulating sweatshops. Once (2') is made explicit, however, the argument against regulating sweatshop labor is far more difficult to sustain. For not only must Powell and Zwolinski demonstrate that regulating sweatshop labor will harm some workers by decreasing sweatshop employment, but they must also demonstrate that not regulating sweatshop labor will lead to less overall harm than regulating it will.

Unfortunately, however, Powell and Zwolinski do not defend this comparative judgment at all. To the contrary, they simply argue that increasing the price of sweatshop labor via minimum wage laws or other worker benefits will lead to a decrease in sweatshop employment. No attempt is made, however, to compare this expected harm with the expected harms that result from not regulating sweatshop labor. But, as we demonstrate below, there are very strong grounds for believing that premise (2') is false. The upshot is that Powell and Zwolinski's argument against the regulation of sweatshop labor is unsound.[3]

THE CASE FOR SWEATSHOP REGULATION

To see why premise (2') is false, consider a proposal to regulate sweatshop labor by increasing the minimum wage paid to workers. How ought such a proposal to be evaluated? Here we simply follow Powell and Zwolinski, for whom the "primary moral focus in this article will be welfarist in nature. That is to say, the main question on which our moral evaluation of sweatshop labor will turn will be a question about how sweatshops and the various proposed regulations of sweatshops affect the welfare of actual and potential sweatshop workers" (pp. 450–451). In order to assess the moral desirability of this proposal, therefore, we ought to compare its expected costs and benefits in terms of human welfare.

Now, the certain and primary consequence of increasing sweatshop worker wages is, of course, that sweatshop workers will have more income. There is a range of potential secondary consequences too. First, depending on both efficiency effects and its share of the total cost, the price of the goods that these workers produce might thereby increase.[4] Second, profits for sweatshop owners might decrease. Third, given that sweatshop workers spend their additional income on local goods and services, the employment of developing world non-sweatshop workers might increase as a result.[5] Fourth, and what Powell and Zwolinski attempt to establish, if the price of the produced goods increases, and if consumers reduce consumption accordingly, then employment in developing world sweatshops might decrease as well.

Overall, then, increasing the minimum wage paid to workers has a number of consequences, both good and bad. The first certain effect—additional worker income—is a large welfare gain. The secondary consequences contain three potential costs—higher prices paid by developed world consumers (or substitution to inferior goods), lower profits for sweatshop owners, and decreased sweatshop employment—and one potential benefit—increased non-sweatshop employment. A basic welfare analysis of this proposal must, therefore, estimate the magnitude of each one of these consequences and determine whether the gains—primary and secondary—are expected to outweigh the losses.

For that reason, demonstrating that one of the secondary consequences—a decrease in the level of sweatshop employment—is potentially negative establishes nothing about the overall moral desirability of the proposal on welfarist grounds. Every social and economic practice has costs as well as benefits. What matters is which is greater overall. Thus even if Powell and Zwolinski are correct in assuming that "any nationwide law or regulation that mandates higher wages . . . will raise the cost of labor and thus end up unemploying some workers and moving them to less desirable alternatives" (p. 457), it nevertheless still does not follow that such a proposal will be harmful to workers.

In passing, Powell and Zwolinski do touch upon the fact that increasing the minimum wage paid to workers has a number of potential consequences and that these might matter morally as well. As they briefly note: "It is theoretically possible that a large mandated wage increase might be met with laying off only 1% of workers, whereas the other 99% were made better off. Depending on one's normative framework, it would then be at least possible to deem the unemployment effects a tolerable cost" (p. 456). But this is very odd. According to the normative framework that they explicitly adopt—welfarism—this is exactly the kind of change that ought to be regarded as highly morally desirable (even more so once the potential increase in employment arising from additional worker spending on local goods and services is factored in as well).

Consider, for example, the study of Pollin et al. (2004, discussed by Powell and Zwolinski) which found that a 100% increase in garment worker wages in US and Mexican firms would result in a price increase of between 2 and 6% for the garments they produced. In order to estimate the welfare effects of doubling working wages, we need to determine what would happen to demand if prices rose by 2–6%. Assume, for example, that the median increase of 4% were to occur and that this would lead to a decrease in consumer spending of *x*%. Whereas Pollin et al. are confident that the decrease would be close to or at zero, Powell and Zwolinski hold that it would in fact be greater.

Let us assume for the sake of argument, however, that Powell and Zwolinski are correct and that there would be, say, a 4% decrease in consumer spending. The primary consequence of such a change will thus be that 96% of sweatshop workers have their income doubled and that 4% of them lose their jobs.[6] An estimate of the multiplier effect is, however, needed as well. If 96% of workers in a sweatshop have their income doubled, then some of their additional income will be spent in the local economy; this has the potential to increase wages or employment there. It is, therefore, unclear whether the overall level of unemployment in the developing world would either rise or fall. The upshot is that even if Powell and Zwolinski are correct about the sweatshop employment effects, it nevertheless still does not follow that there are negative employment effects overall. More importantly, however, it does not follow that in those cases where there are negative employment effects, a basic welfarist analysis would judge them as outweighing the gains from workers having massively higher incomes.

The only other study of the developing world employment effects of minimum wage laws that Powell and Zwolinski cite is that of Harrison and Scorse (2010). They estimate that in Indonesia a "100 percentage point increase in the real minimum wage would be accompanied by employment declines between 12 and 36%" (2010, p. 263). But, from the point of view of welfarism, not only is the 100% increase in workers' income morally significant but so too is the question of whether the factories simply relocated to other countries and thereby increased employment there. For although Harrison and Scorse are explicit that they are only studying the effects of a 100% minimum wage increase on employment in Indonesia, if the increased worker costs forced some factory owners to relocate production (or to set up new factories elsewhere), then that need not have a negative effect on developing world employment overall; such a decision might instead be accompanied by a net increase in worker remuneration in those factories that remain.

In order to determine the overall employment effects, therefore, we would need once again to estimate the price elasticity of consumers. If Nike shoes became 2% more expensive because worker wages were raised by 50%, then will the sale of those shoes decline?[7] If so, by how much? Were Powell and Zwolinski to include such estimates, the reader would at least have a sense of why they were opposed to such laws on welfarist grounds and/or why they believed that a 50% increase in worker wages and a potentially large increase in non-sweatshop employment was morally outweighed by a 2% drop in sweatshop employment instead. Powell and Zwolinski do not, therefore, demonstrate that increasing sweatshop wages will result in a decrease in welfare overall. Nor do the specific studies they cite demonstrate this conclusion either.

Furthermore, there are strong grounds for believing that raising sweatshop worker wages would normally be expected to lead to a large welfare gain. The reasons are twofold. First, the beneficiaries of this change would all be extremely poor whereas the cost-bearers would primarily (but not necessarily exclusively) be drawn from the global rich. That is, if we assume that a minimum wage increase would lead to higher worker wages at the expense of consumers and owners, then the first key factor in estimating the magnitude of the welfare change of the income shift from consumers and owners to workers is their relative wealth.[8] The greater the difference in their income, the greater the expected welfare gain overall.[9]

The second factor to consider for any worker wage increase is the effect that this will have on employment in both the industry affected and the local economy as a whole. This would, once again, partly depend on the level of expected consumer price elasticity. Would a 5% increase in price cause consumers to buy, say, 2% less of the good or more? But it would also depend crucially on the percentage of the goods' total price that can be attributable to worker wages. If the percentage is small—and with sweatshops it most likely would be—then both the increase in price and the concomitant decrease in the good's consumption are likely to be small as well.

Thus, aside from the general product price elasticity, there are two fundamental factors to consider in determining whether an increase in the minimum wage paid to workers is likely to lead to an expected welfare gain overall. First, how poor are the workers compared to owners and consumers? Second, how much of the product price is attributable to worker wages? This in turn yields two predictions: that the poorer the workers compared to owners and consumers, the larger the welfare gain from the income transfer effects; and that the smaller the proportion of the cost attributable to worker wages, the smaller the welfare loss from direct employment effects. The upshot is that welfare gains from an increase in the minimum wage paid to workers are expected to be the highest in the following set of circumstances: where consumers and owners are much more wealthy than workers and where worker compensation is a small part of the product price overall. These are precisely the dominant characteristics of developing world export-oriented sweatshops.

OBJECTIONS

Our argument thus far has been that even if Powell and Zwolinski are correct that large mandated increases in sweatshop worker wages will be expected to lead to a decrease in sweatshop employment, it nevertheless still does not follow that such a change would be morally undesirable on welfarist grounds. To the contrary, there are strong grounds for believing that such regulation would lead to a large increase in human welfare overall.

There are, however, two natural objections to this argument: (A) that the end—overall human welfare—is too broad; and (B) that the means—"regulation"—is under-specified. Let us consider each of these objections in turn.

(A) Ends

We have argued that regulating sweatshop labor can be expected to lead to an increase in human welfare overall. But, as Powell and Zwolinski maintain, "the main question on which [their] moral evaluation of sweatshop labor will turn will be a question about how sweatshops and the various proposed regulations of sweatshops affect the welfare of actual and potential sweatshop workers" (pp. 450–451). For that reason, one might object that our argument misses the mark. In order to determine the moral desirability of sweatshop regulation, we ought not to compare its costs and benefits in terms of human welfare overall but rather in terms of its impact on sweatshop workers alone.

There are two points in response. First, from a welfarist point of view, the restriction to sweatshop workers alone is unwarranted. Any proposed regulation must instead be evaluated on the basis of the expected costs and benefits for all those who are affected by them. For if increased sweatshop worker income leads to increased consumption of non-sweatshop labor, then that too must be included in the moral calculus. As we have demonstrated, however, Powell and Zwolinski simply argue for the existence of one particular cost—a decrease in sweatshop employment. This is, of course, an important factor to consider. But no welfare analysis of the effects of regulating sweatshop labor is at all complete without taking into account both the direct and indirect welfare effects of increasing the minimum wage paid to workers.

Second, even if we were to grant for the sake of argument that it is indeed justified to focus on sweatshop workers alone, it nevertheless still does not follow that this objection is correct. For it is not at all clear why a large increase in worker welfare (via an increase in the minimum wage) is outweighed by a decrease in sweatshop employment. Or, to return to our previous example, why a 50% increase in worker wages is outweighed by a 2% decrease in sweatshop employment (assuming, unrealistically, no related increase in non-sweatshop employment). The pattern of moral concern that establishes this conclusion does not appear to have any obvious logic or justification. Thus whether we focus on sweatshop workers alone, individuals in the developing world in general, or all those affected by our actions, there are good reasons for expecting sweatshop regulation to be morally desirable on welfarist grounds.

At this point, however, it might be argued that the justification for the above pattern of moral concern is in fact priority for the worst off and, in particular, priority for the welfare of the society's least advantaged workers, i.e., those who as a result of the proposed increase in wages may subsequently be unemployed.[10] A revised version of Powell and Zwolinski's argument against sweatshop regulation could accordingly be reformulated as follows:

1*. Sweatshops are better for the society's least advantaged workers than the available alternatives.
2*. Regulating sweatshop labor will lead to a decrease in sweatshop employment.
3*. Therefore, regulating sweatshop labor will be harmful to the society's least advantaged workers.

If this argument can be sustained, then it would indeed constitute a coherent critique of sweatshop regulation. For this construal of Powell and Zwolinski's argument would entail that a policy is morally undesirable just in case it causes any deterioration in the situation of the worst off and thus irrespective of whether or not it represents a large gain in human welfare overall.

We do not think that this is the moral position that Powell and Zwolinski are advancing; nor is it one that we would defend ourselves. For the sake of argument, however, let us assume that it is correct.[11] Is this an argument against sweatshop regulation that we should be willing to accept? No. There are in fact two reasons for thinking that just the opposite is the case.

First, as noted above, there is a strong prima facie reason for believing that increasing worker wages will lead to an overall increase in employment in the developing world since both the share of the product price from wages is small and the local employment multiplier from increased worker spending is likely to be large (due to significant underutilization in the local economy). Sweatshop regulation that dramatically boosts worker wages is thus likely to increase employment in the developing world overall even if it decreases sweatshop employment at the margin.

Second, and perhaps more importantly, if the correct pattern of moral concern holds that a policy is morally desirable to the extent that it reduces unemployment for workers in the developing world, then this is actually not an argument against sweatshop regulation but for it: specifically, it is a very strong argument for massively reducing the average working hours of individual sweatshop workers. For such regulation would be expected to reliably produce a large increase in overall sweatshop employment levels. Instead of having three people do a particular process full-time, for example, we might end up with six people being employed part-time. One might, of course, oppose such a policy on welfarist grounds—the productive efficiency loss might mean that a general increase in worker wages with working hours determined on a local basis was a better policy for increasing welfare overall. But if one is primarily concerned with the welfare of the very worst off, and, in particular, those workers who as a result of a proposed increase in wages may subsequently be unemployed, then one should strongly support the regulation and reduction of average sweatshop working hours as a way to boost sweatshop employment.

(B) Means

But even if there are strong grounds for believing that regulating sweatshop labor is morally desirable in principle, that does not mean that the same is true in practice. For there are a number of means by which such regulation can be undertaken—individual-based activism, host-country labor laws, consumer country pressure, intergovernmental standards, or unilateral or industry-wide international company policies—and it might be the case that implementing them has unintended consequences or otherwise does more harm than good.

This is a very important objection. But it is not inconsistent with our argument at all. To the contrary, such an objection presupposes an analysis exactly like our own. For it is only by setting out in principle the different possible effects of sweatshop regulation and the accompanying impact in terms of human welfare that we thereby gain a moral framework for both assessing the costs and benefits of different mechanisms and integrating any empirical evidence we can gather to that end. Because of the secondary employment effects from sweatshop workers spending their increased income in the local economy, for example, there is a prima facie case for preferring worker wage increases over other benefits that have no such multiplier (such as safety gains). Or perhaps it is the latter that can be more effectively and efficiently enforced. This is, of course, an empirical question. Our claim is simply that it is in virtue of two prominent features of sweatshops—the relatively small percentage of product price attributable to worker wages, and the large disparity in income between workers on the one hand and consumers and owners on the other—that sweatshop regulation is likely to lead to large welfare gains overall. It thus does not undermine the basic logic of our argument that the form of regulation most likely to be effective in this regard will ultimately depend on the circumstances at hand.

CONCLUSION

In "The Ethical and Economic Case Against Sweatshop Labor: A Critical Assessment," Powell and Zwolinski conclude by stating that "no economic mechanisms have been identified that would allow higher wages or better working conditions to be legally mandated without harming workers" (p. 470). But the converse is also true as well. No economic mechanisms have been identified that would allow higher wages or better working conditions to be legally mandated without benefiting workers either. The reason is clear. Any legal change has costs and benefits. A basic welfare analysis will identify which of the different costs and benefits are morally significant and how they are to be compared. Simply demonstrating that there is one cost, namely, a decrease in sweatshop employment, does nothing to establish that the change is morally undesirable overall. Of course, that is not to deny the moral significance of the question of whether increasing the minimum wage paid to workers will thereby decrease employment in sweatshops as a result. But the debate over sweatshops cannot hinge entirely on this factor alone. The moral case against sweatshops remains strong. The regulation of sweatshop labor has the potential to greatly increase overall human welfare in general, and the welfare of the globally worst off in particular. Powell and Zwolinksi provide no reason to think otherwise.

REFERENCES

Arnold, D., & Hartman, L. (2005). Beyond sweatshops: Positive deviancy and global labour practices. *Business Ethics: A European Review, 14(3),* 206–222.

Bell, L. (1997). The impact of minimum wages in Mexico and Columbia. *Journal of Labor Economics, 15(3),* 102–135.

Card, D., & Krueger, A. (1994). Minimum wages and employment: A case study of the fast-food industry in New Jersey and Pennsylvania. *American Economic Review, 84(4),* 772–793.

Card, D., & Krueger, A. (1997). *Myth and measurement: The new economics of the minimum wage.* Princeton, NJ: Princeton University Press.

Cohen, G. A. (1983). The structure of proletarian unfreedom. *Philosophy and Public Affairs, 12(1),* 3–33.

Cohen, G. A. (1987). Are disadvantaged workers who take hazardous jobs forced to take hazardous jobs? In G. Ezorsky (Ed.), *Moral rights in the workplace.* Albany, NY: State University of New York Press.

Feinberg, J. (1987). *The moral limits of the criminal law,* vol. 1, harm to others. New York: Oxford University Press.

Harrison, A., & Scorse, J. (2010). Multinationals and anti-sweatshop activism. *American Economic Review, 100(1),* 247–273.

Maloney, W., & Nunez, J. (2001). Measuring the impact of minimum wages: Evidence from Latin America. World Bank Policy Research Working Paper 2597.

Parker, J. A. (2011). On measuring the effects of fiscal policy in recessions. *Journal of Economic Literature,49(3),* 703–718.

Pollin, R., Burns, J., & Heintz, J. (2004). Global apparel production and sweatshop labour: Can raising retail prices finance living wages? *Cambridge Journal of Economics, 28,* 153–171.

Powell, B., & Zwolinski, M. (2012). The ethical and economic case against sweatshop labor: A critical assessment. *Journal of Business Ethics,107,* 449–472.

Rama, M. (1996). The consequences of doubling the minimum wage: The case of Indonesia. World Bank Policy Research Working Paper 1643.

Strobl, E., & Walsh, F. (2000). Minimum wages and compliance: The case of Trinidad and Tobago. *Economic Development and Cultural Change, 51(2),* 427–450.

Walzer, M. (1983). *Spheres of justice: A defense of pluralism and equality.* New York: Basic Books.

NOTES

1. Powell and Zwolinski (2012). All subsequent parenthetical references are to this article.

2. For the general debate over the relationship between minimum wage increases and employment levels, see, e.g., Card and Krueger (1994, 1997); for a range of developing world studies looking at actual regulatory compliance and the associated wage and employment effects, see Strobl and Walsh (2000), Bell (1997), Maloney and Nunez (2001), and Rama (1996).

3. For the purposes of this paper, we follow Feinberg (1987) in understanding harm as behavior that causes someone to be worse off than they would otherwise have been. Hence if what we are doing will not be worse for someone, or will even be better for them, then we are not, properly speaking, harming them.

4. Whether this will occur in practice is, of course, disputed. But we will, once again, grant the truth of this assumption for the purposes of our argument here.

5. Note that, as these are societies characterized by large resource under-utilization in the form of un- and under-employment, the multiplier effect here might be quite large. For a recent summary of the vast literature on the link between multipliers and idle resources, see Parker (2011).

6. Indeed, this might actually overestimate the loss of employment to the developing world in general since consumers might substitute into other goods produced there. If the price of garments made in Mexico goes up 4%, then

those consumers who no longer buy them might buy from other countries in the developing world, thereby partly offsetting the Mexican sweatshop employment loss. A 4% decrease in sweatshop employment thus represents the upper bound of the overall potential developing world sweatshop employment effect given the price elasticity assumed.

7. These illustrative figures are taken from Harrison and Scorse (2010, p. 270), who note that Nike estimated in 1998 that developing world factory labor costs accounted for about 4% of the overall product price on a typical $90 shoe.

8. For the sake of argument, we are once again accepting Powell and Zwolinski's claim that efficiency wages will not render this a mutually beneficial change for all three groups.

9. Note that Powell and Zwolinski are quite rightly not using money as a welfare proxy undifferentiated by income. Hence their welfare analysis correctly focuses on the effects on those in the developing world.

10. We are grateful to an anonymous reviewer for suggesting this possibility.

11. To see why there are very strong grounds for believing this moral position to be false, consider the fact that it would imply, absurdly, that no amount of welfare increases to the vast majority of all sweatshop workers, however high, can ever justify any amount of welfare decreases to a tiny minority of them, however low. A 100-fold increase in wages to 99% of all sweatshops workers would, for example, be outweighed by the loss of employment to only 1% of them. On its face, however, this seems fundamentally implausible.

Price Gouging

MICHAEL MUNGER

They Clapped: Can Price Gouging Laws Prohibit Scarcity?

2007

"There were no generators, ice, or chain saws to be had, none. But that means that anyone who brought these commodities into the crippled city, and charged less than infinity, would be doing us a service." Here's the thing: They clapped. I can't for the life of me understand why the people would clap. But I'm starting in the middle. Here is what happened:

Hurricane "Fran" smashed into the North Carolina coastline at Cape Fear at about 8:30 pm, 5 September 1996. It was a category 3, with 120 mph winds, and enormous rain bands. It ran nearly due north, hitting the state capital of Raleigh about 3 am, and moving north and east out of the state by morning. The storm also dropped as much as ten inches of

Michael Munger, "They Clapped: Can Price Gouging Laws Prohibit Scarcity?" January, 8, 2007. Online Library of Economics and Liberty. By permission of Liberty Fund.

rain. In some counties, nearly every building was damaged; total reconstruction cost and damages were later calculated at $5 billion (2006 $).

In the Triangle (Raleigh, Durham, and Chapel Hill), more than a million people were without power the next morning. Humidity made everything sticky. Hundreds of homes had roofs damaged by falling pines and powerful winds. Few residences had any kind of back-up power. Many roads were blocked by large fallen trees. Within hours, food in refrigerators and freezers started to go bad. Insulin, baby formula, and other necessities immediately became susceptible to spoilage in the 92+ degree heat.

The damage was so widespread, and communication so sketchy, that no one had any firm idea of when power would be restored. More than a million people needed ice. And they needed it now.

One might think that thousands of entrepreneurs in the surrounding areas, little touched by the storm, would load trucks and head to the disaster area. After all, they owned, or could obtain, all the things that the residents of central North Carolina needed so desperately. Ice, chain saws, generators, lumber, tarps for covering gaping holes in roofs . . . we needed it all. I say "we" because my family lived in North Raleigh. No power, and 36 large pine trees smashed down like God's own pick-up-stix. We couldn't get out of our immediate neighborhood, and my underpowered chain saw burned out on the first tree I tried to cut.

But no such mass movement of resources to their highest valued use took place. North Carolina had an "anti-gouging law," which made it illegal to sell anything useful at a price that was "unreasonably excessive under the circumstances." This had been widely interpreted to limit price increases to around 5% or less. Each instance of violation of this law could result in a fine of up to $5,000. So, ice that happened in Charlotte, *stayed* in Charlotte. Why drive three hours to Raleigh when you can only charge the Charlotte price, plus just enough for gas money to break even?

The problem for Raleigh residents was all about price, at that point. The prices of all the necessities that I wanted to use to "preserve, protect, or sustain" my own life shot up to infinity. Within a day after the storm, there were no generators, ice, or chain saws to be had, none. *But that means that anyone who brought these commodities into the crippled city, and charged* less than infinity, *would be doing us a service.*

Some service was, in fact, on the way. Four young men in the town of Goldsboro, an hour east of Raleigh and largely untouched by the storm, noticed that the freezers at the Circle P's, the Stop Marts, and the Handee Sluggos were brimming with ice. Convenience stores had stocked up, expecting a more easterly course for the storm. Now, there was an ice surplus in Goldsboro, and a shortage in Raleigh. These young men rented two small freezer trucks, paid $1.70 each for 500 bags of ice for each truck and set off, filled with a sense of charity and the public good.

Okay, I made that last part up. They were filled with a sense of greed. They may have been bad human beings, real jerks. But who cares? If there had been a benevolent, omniscient social planner, she would have been yelling: *(1) Raleigh is desperate for ice. (2) If you have ice, take it to Raleigh.* Of course, there could never be a social planner with that level of information and authority, as Hayek (1945) argued so persuasively. But these yahoos acted *as if* they heard one anyway, speaking through the price system: cheap ice in Goldsboro was expensive ice in Raleigh, so they could make money.

Our icemen came to the outskirts of Raleigh, and headed for the interior, where the citizens waited, icelessly. The path was blocked by fallen trees, but these were yahoos, not idiots. Yahoos have chain saws, big ones. They rolled the cut logs off the road so their trucks (and, by the way, other cars and emergency vehicles) could pass.

One truck apparently parked in Five Points, near downtown, and another parked a bit west, near wealthy St. Mary's Street, and opened for business. I have not been able to find a definitive claim about price, but it was more than $8. (All three of my personal "sources" knew someone who saw events, but . . . I'd love to be able to ask the sellers if they knew of the anti-gouging law, but we'll never know, I guess.)

On reaching the front of the line, some customers were angry that the price was so high, but almost no one refused to pay for the ice. I have also been told that the sellers limited purchases to 4, or 6, bags per customer, but I'm not sure. If it is true, it reflects the altruism of the native North Carolinian, even ones who are just trying to make a buck.

But the police are charged with upholding the law, even the dumb ones (laws, not police). Someone must have made a call, because two Raleigh police cars and an unmarked car pulled up to the Five Points truck after about an hour. The officers talked to the sellers, talked to some buyers, still holding their ice, and confirmed that the price was much higher than the "correct" price of $1.75 (the cost of a bag of ice before the storm). The officers did their duty, and arrested the yahoos.

Apparently the truck was then driven to the police impoundment lot in downtown Raleigh, as evidence. The ice may or may not have melted (accounts vary), but it certainly was not given out to citizens.

And now we are back to where I started: the citizens, the prospective buyers being denied a chance to buy ice . . . *they clapped.* Clapped, cheered, and hooted, as the vicious ice sellers were handcuffed and arrested. Some of those buyers had been standing in line for five minutes or more, and had been ready to pay 4 times as much as the maximum price the state would allow. And they clapped as the police, at gunpoint, took that opportunity away from them.

WHAT WERE THEY THINKING?

From Roy Cordato, North Carolina's Price Control Laws:

From the perspective of economic science, and particularly the subdiscipline known as "price theory," the concept of "price gouging" or "extreme pricing" or "unreasonable pricing" has no meaning. In fact, none of these terms appear in the index of any of the five most widely adopted principles of economics textbooks used in college classes in the United States. The extent to which this price control law ignores economic analysis cannot be overstated. It has no grounding in the role of prices discussed above. As noted, while the law specifies several factors that should be used to determine whether prices are illegally high, including facts that are completely irrelevant (such as the average price over the previous 60 days), there is no mention of whether the prices are consistent with actual conditions of supply and demand—which, from an economic perspective, is all that matters.

I am completely stumped by the clapping. But then I'm stumped on why people support anti-gouging laws. I strongly suspect the two things are related.

Consider some quotes from the Raleigh paper, the News and Observer, in the days following the hurricane. First, on September 10, 1996, less than a week after the storm, in two different page one stories, we were told:

> "Ice shortages are becoming severe in some places—so much so that local counties are asking the federal government to send as much ice as it can." (Eisley, 1996)

> And:

> "At the cabinet meeting, Richard Moore, Hunt's secretary for crime control and public safety, said . . . he was . . . deploying the state's Alcohol Law Enforcement officers to investigate reports of price-gouging of products in short supply. Hunt said both Florida Gov. Lawton Chiles and South Carolina Gov. David Beasley had agreed to send truckloads of ice and other supplies to North Carolina." (Wagner and Whitlock, 1996)

When I read these two articles, I started sputtering like a crazy person to my poor wife. And I am still sputtering about it. These articles told me two things: #1—Police and other government officials were being sent out to arrest anyone selling ice at a profit. #2—There was a terrible ice shortage. We were so desperate for ice that the only option is to beg the federal government, or other state governments, for supplies from their ice hoards, because there was no other way to get it.

I'm pretty sure I have a solution: stop doing #1, and #2 will go away like . . . well, like ice on a steamy September day in Raleigh. Ice is easy to make; just freeze some water. It's hard to make ice without electricity, but most of east, and all of west, North Carolina had plenty of electricity. And, in fact, they had plenty of ice. The problem is that the only real omniscient social planner we have is the market, and she speaks to people through prices. Do this, stop doing that, build something here, move to this city. When the state made it a crime to sell ice at a profit, the price mechanism was struck dumb. Only a few people could hear it. And we threw *them* in jail, ensuring that even fewer would heed the desperate call in the next crisis of deprivation.

TALE OF TWO PRICES

Consider two prices. First, the price of ice before the storm, which most people know, or have a feel for. Second, the price of ice after the storm, which is unknown and highly variable. People who favor price-gouging laws think that the first price, the price *before* the storm, is the fair price, and that is the price they want to pay. The market price *after* the storm reflects both the difficulty of getting ice from stores, because the store has no electricity, and the huge bump in demand for ice as thousands try to buy it. Clearly, the relative scarcity of ice after the storm is much higher.

The market price rises rapidly to reflect this increased scarcity. This makes people who would have used ice at the old price economize, and use something else. They can drink their bottled water, or their Carolina Ale, warm if they don't want to pay $12 for a bag of ice. So ice only goes to people who really value it. And the higher price also signals yahoos, wahoos, and all sorts of regular folks that one can make boxloads of money by taking truckloads of ice to Raleigh. The price system is automatically doing its job, signaling to buyers that they should cut back, and signaling to sellers (even potential sellers, those who have to enter the market from Goldboro) that they should sell more.

If enough people bring ice to Raleigh, of course, the price won't be $12, or $8, for very long. Ice is easy to make and transport, so without market restrictions price *after* the storm will quickly be driven down near the price *before* the storm, because there is so much more ice available. That's what the clapping people *must have wanted.* Even the supporters of price-gouging laws want low prices and large supplies. But they can't get those things from a price-gouging law. Precisely the opposite happens, as the supply of ice disappears and the effective price, what people would be *willing* to pay, goes higher and higher. I admit that it's not intuitive, until you think about it. The only way to ensure *low* prices, and large supply, to buyers is to allow sellers to charge *high* prices, the highest they can get.

Well, but what if you seek a political solution, rather than trusting markets? What if you pass an anti-gouging law, to symbolize your opposition to scarcity? Scarcity hurts; it means that I can't have everything I want. Let's abolish scarcity; what then? As I have tried to argue, all a state accomplishes by passing an anti-gouging law is to ensure that there is no ice. I can't get it for $100, or $1,000. And too many citizens say, "Help: the market has failed! Let's call on government to rescue us!"

But they are wrong. Markets didn't fail. All that happened was that the price mechanism was bound and gagged, held hostage in the attic of the legislature.

JEREMY SNYDER

What's the Matter with Price Gouging?

2009

Prices for essential goods are likely to increase when a disaster strikes, should that event decrease available supplies of these goods, increase demand, or both.[1] Sometimes these price increases are condemned as "price gouging" or "profiteering." Such labels are not intended as simply descriptions of price increases; rather, they carry a strong negative moral valence. In many cases, the moral wrong of these price increases is identified as wrongfully gaining from another's misfortune. Consider the common view that "[t]hings like selling generators for four and five times their cost is not free enterprise, that's taking advantage of other people's misery" (Rushing 2004, A-1). In other cases, price gouging is condemned as unfairly taking advantage of others' needs, language that is often associated with exploitation.[2]

But it isn't clear from these kinds of sentiments when a price increase amounts to price gouging or why, if at all, certain price increases following disasters are morally worrisome. Moreover, there are many reasons to think that price increases can create a net benefit for a community following a disaster. As one critic of anti-price gouging legislation puts it:

> Price to the left of the intersection of the supply-and-demand curve and you are guaranteed to vaporize whatever you are attempting to keep inexpensive. . . . The reason that gasoline is disappearing from service stations across the nation is because station owners aren't gouging with sufficient gusto. Whether out of a misguided sense of kindness, concern about what politicians might think, fear of bad press, or the desire to keep customers happy, they are pricing below what the market would otherwise bear and, as a result, their inventory has disappeared. Now, how are the poor being helped by service stations closing down for lack of fuel? Gas at $6 a gallon, after all, is better than gas unavailable at any price. (Taylor 2005)

Price increases lead to rationing by consumers and encourage increased production of scarce goods. If the aim of anti-gouging legislation is to prevent vendors from profiting too much from a supply disruption, then achieving this aim may come at the cost of a swift return to normal market conditions.

In this paper, I discuss what moral wrongs, if any, are most reasonably ascribed to accusations of price gouging. This discussion keeps in mind both practical and moral defenses of price gouging following disasters.[3] In the first section of this paper, I examine existing anti-gouging legislation for commonalities in their definitions of gouging. I then present arguments in favor of the permissibility of gouging, focusing on the economic benefits of price increases following disasters. In the third section I present a critique of gouging based on specific forms of a failure of respect for others. This critique is followed by a discussion of means for avoiding gouging in practice and responses to objections to my view. As I will argue, even when morally defensible anti-gouging legislation is not in place, individual vendors will have a duty not to gouge their customers.

Before proceeding, I should note very clearly what I do *not* mean to be covered by the potential wrongness of price gouging. Sometimes price gouging is accompanied by other factors that overdetermine the wrongness of the action. A hotel might advertise a normal price for rooms but then demand

Jeremy Snyder, "What's the Matter with Price Gouging?" *Business Ethics Quarterly* 19 (2) (April 2009): 275–293. By permission of *Business Ethics Quarterly*.

that potential customers pay much more in person. Workers might arrive in a disaster area, demand a higher than normal deposit for repairs, then leave without doing any of the contracted work.[4] A disaster can make deception and fraud more likely and easier to get away with, and these wrongs will sometimes accompany price gouging. However, the wrongs of deception and fraud are distinct from the wrongs of price gouging. Therefore, I will assume that neither deception nor fraud are present in my subsequent discussion in order to focus on the specific wrongs associated with price gouging.

PRICE GOUGING IN THE LAW

At present, thirty-two states and the District of Columbia have passed some form of anti-gouging legislation. Although there is no federal anti-gouging law in the US, a bill targeting fuel price increases passed the House of Representatives in 2007. In order to develop a better sense of what actions raise worries about price gouging, I will briefly examine this body of legislation.

Anti-gouging legislation is typically triggered by the declaration of a state of emergency or disaster. This declaration may be made by the state governor, local officials, or even the president. In substantially fewer cases, anti-gouging legislation requires a declaration by public officials in addition to a declaration of emergency. The duration of the activation of anti-gouging controls can vary from the length of the declaration of a disaster to a fixed length of time or some mix of the two.[5]

Laws against price gouging limit price increases for goods during their period of activation. For the most part, price increases are allowed when they reflect increases in the cost of doing business following the disaster and, to some extent, changes in the market. For example, the Federal Trade Commission defined price gouging as occurring when "a firm's average monthly sales price for gasoline in a particular area is higher than for a previous month, *and* where such higher prices are not substantially attributable to *either* (1) increased costs, or (2) national or international market trends" (Federal Trade Commission 2006, 137). In many cases, these caps seek to factor in changes in the market and costs by allowing the price of goods to increase a certain percentage above the pre-disaster price. Otherwise, vague language prohibiting "unconscionable" or "gross" increases in prices is used.[6] At their most extreme, anti-gouging legislation may forbid *any* increase in the prices of goods beyond those justified by higher business costs. These more extreme restrictions are unusual and at present limited to Georgia, Louisiana, Mississippi, and Connecticut.[7]

Anti-gouging laws can be tied to all goods and services following activation of anti-gouging statutes[8] or limited to specific, essential goods. What counts as an essential good is often left undefined but can explicitly include dwelling units, gasoline, food, water, supplies for home repair, and pharmaceuticals.[9] Florida Statute 501.160, for example, states that following a state of emergency, it is unlawful "for a person or her or his agent or employee to rent or sell or offer to rent or sell at an unconscionable price within the area for which the state of emergency is declared, any essential commodity including, but not limited to, supplies, services, provisions, or equipment that is necessary for consumption or use as a direct result of the emergency."

Despite many broad commonalities in state anti-gouging legislation, this overview reveals four key areas of disagreement and vagueness in determining what constitutes price gouging. First, there is disagreement as to how much of a price increase, particularly beyond what can be justified by increases in business costs, is allowable. Second, state legislatures disagree as to whether prohibitions of price increases should be extended to all goods and services or limited only to certain exchanges, although most favor the latter. Third, when legislation is limited to certain exchanges, there is disagreement as to what goods and services should be covered. Fourth, and most importantly from the perspective of this paper, when anti-gouging legislation uses moral language to justify itself, this language tends to be vague.[10]

IN DEFENSE OF PRICE INCREASES

Anti-gouging legislation and charges of price gouging are common. While the precise nature of the moral wrong associated with gouging is unclear, there is widespread agreement that *something* is wrong about these price increases. Yet, there are many reasons to think that price increases condemned as gouging are morally innocent at worst and, more often, create a positive and morally praiseworthy benefit for all concerned.

In a gouging situation following a disaster, both vendor and customer understand the exchange to be to their advantage. Since the good being exchanged is likely to be something essential to the well-being of the customer (e.g., food, water, shelter), the exchange is actually likely to provide proportionally greater utility to the customer than the vendor even at the higher than usual price. While the vendor may stand to clear a larger than normal profit as a result of the disaster, the essential nature of the goods mean that they will be of enormous, possibly even life saving, benefit to the consumer. Despite the harms to the consumer and possibly vendor as a result of the disaster, the high price exchange does no harm in itself when compared to the welfare of each person following the disaster. Rather, the exchange will provide the customer with essential goods that increase her welfare.

While disasters create a temporary increase in the pricing power of vendors, this shift can easily be explained and justified by the rules of the market. A disaster is likely to cause a reduction in essential supplies. For example, fuel may no longer be able pass through ruptured pipes or closed roads. These disasters—or even the threat of one—may also create an increase in demand for essential goods, such as plywood for protecting homes. The resulting shift in the equilibrium point between supply and demand predictably creates an increase in prices for goods, especially for essential goods that have inelastic demand, without any untoward manipulation of the market. From the standpoint of the dynamic functioning of the market, these higher prices should be allowed and the market can be trusted to maintain itself (Jacoby 2004).

Not only are price increases explainable as a result of the natural functioning of the market, it is argued, they serve a beneficial purpose. High prices for essential goods have the effect of helping the market to return to pre-disaster prices. These prices achieve a signaling effect for both vendors and consumers (Hayek 1945). The high prices charged by vendors will lure other suppliers into the market, quickly increasing supplies of essential goods. An increase in supplies will meet increased demand and help move prices toward pre-disaster levels. Without these price increases, vendors may lack both the information and motivation necessary to enter the post-disaster market and increase supplies.

Defenders of price gouging argue that higher prices also aid in the conservation of scarce goods by making it more likely that they will be purchased by those who place the greatest value on them. These high prices also tend to ensure that scarce essential goods will be used sparingly. While ice might be valuable to those seeking to keep their beer cold following a hurricane, higher prices will tend to ensure that those purchasing ice put it to more highly valued uses such as preserving medicine and scarce food. This efficiency of allocation is coupled with a rationing effect created by higher prices. When fuel prices spike, generators that might have been used to power the air conditioning in an entire house will instead be limited to cooling a single room. As a result, fuel supplies that would have been exhausted quickly at pre-disaster prices are now prolonged (Wall Street Journal 2005).

The promise of price increases following a disaster can also help increase supplies of essential goods prior to the event. If the disaster is foreseeable (as in the case of a hurricane), suppliers can pre-position goods in the area likely to be affected. The prospect of higher prices encourages such preemptive actions and acts in the long run to keep prices relatively low, meeting the needs of far more people than otherwise would have been the case.

Some extra profit following a disaster can also serve as a fair reward for the efforts and risks undertaken by vendors. Vendors of scarce goods may go to extraordinary lengths to get goods to the market following a disaster. A vendor might pre-position goods in a likely disaster area at considerable cost to himself and at considerable risk if the disaster destroys these stocks or strikes too far away for the supplies to be of use. Vendors in the affected area might act to protect existing stocks of supplies from damage at great expense to themselves and perhaps at some sacrifice to their own safety. If some of these supplies are lost, the local vendor, too, will be a victim of the disaster. Those who bring needed goods into the affected area after the event may also forgo opportunities for profit at home, face high costs in transporting the goods to the affected area, and may be subjected to bodily danger if the disaster is still ongoing or law and order have broken down.

Given these positive economic effects, price increases following a disaster need not be morally troubling. In fact, it could be argued, given that the needs of the affected population are especially strong, the so-called gouger might even deserve special praise for her efforts. At the very least, her self-interested motives in the post-disaster market are not obviously different from those typically judged to be morally innocent in a normal market.

PRICE GOUGING AND RESPECT FOR OTHERS

If there is something morally wrong with price gouging, it is not that gouging causes direct harms or economic inefficiency. In fact, a critique of price gouging will need to confront the positive moral value of the efficiencies and rationing effect created by price increases.

As I have noted, many anti-gouging laws are limited to price increases on certain goods that are tied to basic human needs. I believe that this characteristic of anti-gouging legislation offers an important insight regarding what is morally objectionable about price gouging. As not all types of price increases trigger the worry about gouging, it is not price increases themselves that motivate this concern. Rather, I would like to argue, it is price increases that undermine equitable access to certain, essential goods that motivate the worry about price gouging.

Put another way, worries about price gouging are engaged when price increases cut off poor consumers from necessary goods, not when price increases are unfair. We might think that price increases following a disaster are unfair in the sense that they allow for a large shift in the social surplus of the interaction in the favor of the vendor. If the normally functioning market serves as a benchmark for a fair transaction and fair distribution of the social surplus generated by that transaction, then the disaster shifts the equilibrium point between supply and demand in such a way that the vendor can now charge unfair prices for her products (Wertheimer 1996).

To see that it is not fairness, *per se,* that motivates concerns over price gouging, consider an example. An avalanche outside of an exclusive ski resort blocks the only road to the resort on New Year's eve. Because this road is blocked, a group of wealthy revelers at the resort no longer have access to a resupply of champagne that was to be used to celebrate the new year. While there is food, drink, and shelter to meet everyone's essential needs until the road is cleared, there is far too little champagne on hand to ensure that everyone will be able to make a toast at midnight. Because of the high value placed on participating in the midnight toast by the resort's wealthy patrons, the owners of the limited remaining supply of champagne are able to clear unusually high profits by selling their supplies.

The actions of these vendors could certainly be considered unfair by the lights of the normally functioning market. But to label these actions as a case of price gouging strains the normal use of the term.[11] Consider that the language surrounding gouging typically focuses on the vulnerability created by the disaster and the desperation of consumers to meet their basic needs. As the Attorney General of Texas put it, following gouging accusations in the wake of hurricane Ike, "They took advantage of the fear and the needs of people who were evacuating the Gulf Coast region, and they jacked up prices" (Elliott 2008). Price hikes for gasoline following that same hurricane again focus on the absolute needs of consumers: "It's sad to think that merchants would take advantage of people who are already struggling to fill their gas tanks just to get from home to work or from home to church and back" (*Jackson Sun* 2008). While the would-be champagne drinkers may be desperate to participate in the New Year's toast and willing to pay unusually high prices to do so, their desperation is of an entirely different kind than that which normally motivates the charge of gouging. It is the desperation of individuals for essential goods, rather than simply the unfairness of the transaction, that motivates accusations of price gouging following a disaster.

Having located the wrongness of price gouging in access to essential goods, we can now say more about the duty that price gouging violates. To be specific, I would like to argue that price increases following a disaster can undermine equitable access to the goods essential to minimal human functioning. When price increases do so, they violate the norm of equal respect for persons. Respect for persons is often understood in terms of a duty to treat others as ends in themselves. More specifically, this respect is expressed both through recognizing that human animals are capable of forming and acting on a conception of the good life but need material support in order to do so (Hill 1991).[12]

Proponents of various ethical theories can agree that basic respect for human persons will entail two components: Negatively, we should not interfere with others as they live out their conception of the good life given reciprocal respect and non-interference. Positively, we should aid others in forming and living out their conception of the good life, particularly by ensuring that they have the minimal means of developing such a conception. An attitude of respect for others will be expressed through our actions, including non-interference, positive support, and other expressions of the equal value of all human persons (Anderson 1993).

At first glance, it would seem that placing limits on the functioning of the market through anti-gouging legislation would run counter to the goal of respecting others' freedom to pursue their conception of the good life. In the first place, I have discussed how price increases efficiently bring new supplies of essential goods into the market and help ration existing supplies. In this way, free markets serve as a means of supplying the goods essential to forming and acting on a conception of the good life.

Secondly, in their ideal form, markets carry their own value as institutions that protect and enlarge human freedom.[13] By offering a space in which consumers can freely negotiate, consummate, and exit exchanges, markets ensure that consumers are not beholden to any particular vendor in their pursuit of the good life.[14] Adam Smith specifically defends markets in terms of their historical role in undermining the oppressive feudal system of production (Satz 2007). Under a feudal system, serfs are tied to single masters and denied the freedoms of movement and exit created by a well-functioning market. Without the freedom to exit from the feudal relationship, the serf is condemned to take whatever terms of exchange are offered by her master. In a market, on the other hand, the "tradesman or artificer derives his subsistence from the employment, not of one, but of a hundred or thousand different customers. Though in some measure obliged to them all, therefore, he is not absolutely dependent on any one of them" (Smith 1976, 420). Markets guarantee legal protections for persons so that the equal right to make exchanges is enshrined as an entitlement, creating political equality between richer and poorer (Anderson 2004). The moral concern that justifies the idealized institution of the market, then, is an interest in providing the material means to and institutional protection of individual freedom.

Conditions following a disaster can be highly non-ideal for a market, however, at least from the perspective of a stable balance between supply and demand. A disaster potentially results in a reduction of supply and spike in demand for some or all essential goods. While price increases reflect a new, post-disaster balance between supply and demand, over the short-term this new equilibrium point can be particularly disruptive to the lives of the poorest members of a community. Until the pricing signals created by the new equilibrium increase supplies of essential goods, prices will remain high and supplies may be insufficient to meet demand. This gap between supply and demand is morally troubling because the goods in question are essential to minimal human functioning and may be out of reach for the poorest members of the affected community. While price increases in a free market represent one means of restoring supplies and rationing existing stocks of essential goods, anti-gouging legislation offers an alternative approach to this problem.

There are many good reasons to think that, following a disaster, an unfettered free market does not best serve the freedom-enhancing purpose by which it is morally justified. While unfettered price increases work toward *efficiently* promoting increases in the supply of essential goods following a disaster, the concern that motivates price gouging laws is that an unfettered market in these goods runs counter to the goal of *equity,* a key component of respect for persons. This failure of equity takes place in terms of the distribution of scarce essential goods within the affected community.[15]

While price increases can decrease consumption rates of essential goods, they do so at the cost of giving the wealthiest members of a community the greatest access to limited supplies. This access is created in two ways. First, and most obviously, wealthy persons will have greater financial means with which to bid on scarce resources when they have been located (Ramasastry 2005).[16] Second, these persons will likely have greater access to the information and transport needed to locate and reach scarce resources. In an idealized market, free competition lowers prices in order to put essential goods into the hands of all but the poorest members of a community. Following a disaster, free competition gives greater access to these goods to those who have the greatest resources within a community.

Under these conditions, the market does not act as the great equalizer and vehicle of individual freedom praised by Smith. Instead, for the period of time between the occurrence of the disaster and when the market again becomes competitive and prices normalize, the market serves to distribute scarce and essential goods on the basis of pre-existing privilege within a community.

While the wealthiest within a community certainly have many advantages over the poor in a market under normal conditions, the market can be defended as creating greater supplies of essential goods at lower prices than would be available within a restricted market. This defense of unfettered markets becomes stronger when a social safety net is included for the poorest members of a society in order to ensure access to essential goods for all. These defenses of the market break down, however, following a disaster. During the period between the disaster and the point where price signaling delivers sufficient supplies of essential goods to the affected community, unfettered price increases do little good for the neediest within a community. These prices may have a long-term beneficial effect of increasing supplies of essential goods and lowering prices, but over the short-term they create a rationing scheme that favors the wealthy over the poor. Because these goods are essential to basic human functioning, rationing of goods such as food, medicine, and shelter in a way that disadvantages the poorest members of a community creates a disfavored class during the period immediately following the disaster. Members of this class are not merely inconvenienced but, because the goods in question are considered essential, face a threat to their basic well-being.

The message sent by a rationing scheme that favors the wealthy is that greater value is given to those members of a community who have the good fortune of being members of the most well-off class. Members of disadvantaged classes are sent to the end of the line for the distribution of scarce essential goods and forced to bear a disproportionate share of the burden created by the disaster. A system that gives all persons roughly equal access to essential goods, on the other hand, reaffirms the equal value of all persons through the equal right of all to the goods essential to minimal human functioning. Anti-gouging legislation can be designed to limit price increases, thus fulfilling the egalitarian goal of giving all persons roughly equal access to essential goods following a disaster. Communities that fail to protect all persons through such legislation will fail to express equal respect for their members by instead allowing their wealthiest members unequal access to essential goods.

In the absence of anti-gouging legislation, we can also assess the behavior of individual vendors who have legally sanctioned opportunities to raise their prices on essential goods following a disaster. While legal, this behavior can be morally impermissible. All of us share a general duty to further the goal of access to essential goods for all persons. This duty is a form of a general duty of beneficence, where we are granted latitude in determining which needy persons to aid in this regard. Our relationships with others, however, can help specify this general duty (Reader 2003) (Kittay 1999) (Waldron 2003) (Snyder 2008). Following a disaster, a vendor's general duty to ensure others' access to essential goods can become more focused, targeting the members of her community who will vie for access to her supplies. The vendor's decision as to how to ration her limited supplies—whether by ability to pay for the goods or through some other, more equitable means—will have a direct impact on her customers' access to these goods. Should she choose to ration her goods according to ability to pay, then she will fail to discharge her duty of beneficence toward all those in her community in need of essential goods or, rather, privileging the wealthiest members of her community.

Of course, merchants normally set their prices at the highest point the market will bear with little moral condemnation. Why, then, would it be impermissible to do so following a disaster? In an idealized market, competition is established through hard bargaining—that is, seeking out the best terms of exchange for oneself. This bargaining takes place between people in roughly equal positions, where the consumer has the option to exit the exchange in search of better terms. Even when the exchange involves an essential good, the ability to select from multiple vendors and flexibility as to when the good is purchased preserves the consumer's option of exit from any given exchange. When functioning in this way, the institution of the market transforms the self-interested nature of hard-bargaining into a vehicle for generating efficiencies in the production and distribution of goods. At the same time, the market remains a venue in which to pursue one's own conception of the good life through the consumption and exchange of goods.

But these institutional protections are undermined when normal competition is disrupted by a disaster. When this happens, hard-bargaining has different implications. Competition, adequate supplies of essential goods, and flexibility as to when these goods are purchased all expand access to essential goods for all members of the community. When these conditions are disrupted, the self-interested motivation of hard bargaining is no longer limited by the institutional protections of a well-functioning market such as consumers' power of exit from the exchange. Instead, self-interest unconstrained by a well-functioning market fails to protect the access of the poorest members of the communities to the goods essential to minimal human functioning.

Following a disaster, then, a vendor who increases her prices in the face of inelastic demand and diminished supply will undercut access by the poorest members of her community to essential goods. In doing so, she will fail to demonstrate the value of equitable access to these goods for all members of her community. If the vendor's own livelihood has not been threatened by the disaster—through, for example, the destruction of supplies or damage to buildings—then these price increases serve merely as an opportunity for the vendor to reap unusual profits. Instead of discharging a specified duty of beneficence to all members of her community, with whom she now stands in a special relationship of dependence, the vendor merely looks to her own good. These profits can be compared to those accrued under a well-functioning market, where they are conjoined with efficiencies that are spread more evenly across the community through decreased prices and increased supplies.

In short, the market disruption brought on by a disaster can have two important effects from the perspective of price gouging. First, the loss of access to essential goods can create a pool of persons to whom the vendor is connected in a relationship of dependence and to whom the vendor has a special responsibility. Second, the institutional protections of an ideally functioning market can become undermined. If so, a vendor who chooses to charge the highest prices the market will bear and thereby distributes her goods according to ability to pay will fail to demonstrate equal respect for all members of her community. Taken together, these effects create the opportunity for price gouging by the vendor, even when anti-gouging legislation has not been enacted in her community.

A vendor, facing this criticism, can appeal to the rationing effect of her price increases. How can she be accused of undermining equitable access to essential goods when her actions serve to ration those very same goods? When compared to a rationing scheme where prices are capped at pre-disaster levels, her choice of rationing mechanism meets the needs of the community taken as a whole better than would be the case if prices were capped. In fact, it seems that true disregard for the needs of others takes place through price gouging legislation that would force caps on essential goods, distributing them on a first come, first served basis. Granted that a random distribution might seem more fair than distribution according to ability to pay, price caps do not limit consumption. Price increases by the vendor, on the other hand, serve to ration her goods.

This response must be judged on the basis of the range of alternatives available to the vendor. If alternative rationing schemes are available to the vendor and consistent with equal respect for all persons, then this response becomes less convincing. In the next section I will discuss forms of price gouging legislation and conduct by vendors that can avoid the moral wrongs discussed in this section. I conclude that more equitable means of distribution are available that still encourage new supplies to enter the market and preserve a rationing effect.

AVOIDING PRICE GOUGING IN PRACTICE

A vendor concerned about the effects of unconstrained price increases on equitable access to essential goods might respond by retaining pre-disaster prices for his poorest customers while allowing price increases for the remainder. That is, instead of allowing price increases according to the market, a vendor might adjust prices according to each consumer's ability to pay. This response would have the benefit of protecting the vendor against committing the moral wrongs I have described while preserving some of the price signaling and rationing effects of price increases.

In practice, vendors will face a range of difficulties should they attempt to price goods according to consumers' ability to pay. A great deal of information will often not be available to the merchant, particularly the means available to customers for purchasing essential goods. While some vendors in smaller communities will be intimately familiar with the needs and vulnerabilities of their customers, typically this will not be the case, particularly if the vendor enters the market from outside of the community in response to a disaster.

Given this problem, legislators and vendors can take two steps in order to avoid the moral wrong that I have argued is associated with price gouging. First, legislators can adopt a typical strategy found in existing state price gouging legislation and limit price increases to the going market rate prior to the disaster, plus increases for additional costs and risks to the vendor. When legislation of this kind has not been enacted within a community, individual vendors should still take it upon themselves to moderate their price increases. The aim of this moderation is to prevent vendors from receiving windfall profits in the face of the desperate need of their individual customers. By raising prices only to reflect changes in costs and risks in the post-disaster market, vendors maintain their own access to essential goods without unduly worsening others' access.

This strategy presumes that the going fair market price enabled members of the community generally to meet their essential needs prior to the disaster. Of course, this is an imperfect strategy since some persons will be priced out of competitive markets for essential goods even under normal conditions. If the local market prior to the disaster does not provide access to essential goods for a large portion of the community prior to the disaster, then this benchmark for setting prices should be discarded. This problem demonstrates that pre-disaster prices can serve as a useful shortcut under conditions of uncertainty only;

these prices do not carry normative weight of their own. Nonetheless, a competitive market, in conjunction with a social safety net to make up for those priced out of the market, will serve as a useful mechanism for distributing goods essential to basic functioning.

Because the exchanges under discussion are mutually advantageous, there is good reason to allow for prices to exceed slightly the pre-disaster rate. As I have noted, price increases following a disaster have the positive effect of increasing supplies, encouraging rationing, and discouraging waste. Insofar as the prices charged by merchants aim at these goals, they can also serve the goal of equitable access to essential goods. Therefore, limited price increases even beyond those justified by increased costs and risks can be justified. Otherwise, price increases merely promote the vendor's self-interest at the cost of the basic needs of those around her.

While even limited price increases achieve a rationing effect, they will typically need to be supplemented with non-price rationing mechanisms, such as caps on purchases. As a second step, legislators should impose caps on the purchase of essential goods in order to ration these goods without distributing them according to ability to pay. When these caps are not mandated by law, individual vendors should impose caps on the sale of their own stocks of essential goods. The limits placed by these caps should depend on supplies and demand for essential goods following a disaster and the needs of the local population. For example, rationing of generators will not be necessary in a post-disaster setting where ample electricity remains available. Therefore, attention to the context in which the disaster takes place will be essential to the proper execution of this step.

Caps on purchases retain some of the rationing effect of unlimited price increases without rationing according to ability to pay. Instead of distributing scarce goods to those with the greatest financial resources in a community, caps on purchases mimic a lottery for essential goods, treating all persons as equally deserving of the goods essential to basic human functioning. In practice, those individuals with the greatest resources within a community will retain some advantage in obtaining scarce goods under a system of purchasing caps. Well-off members of a community may be better able to obtain information about the location of scarce goods, to travel to the location of these goods, and to have the time to wait in line to obtain these goods compared to less well-off persons.

A coordinated, community-wide cap on purchases of essential goods would seemingly reduce this problem. A central authority could distribute equal numbers of vouchers for essential goods to each member of the community, and vendors would be required to sell essential goods only to those customers holding a voucher. Moreover, these vouchers could be accepted in lieu of payment, with the local government repaying vendors at a later time for their goods. This policy would limit all members of the community to the same numbers of essential goods with the added benefit of ensuring that even very poor persons would have an equal opportunity to access essential goods.

However, the level of coordination between vendors required for a communitywide cap is likely to be impractical given the disruption created by the disaster, at least over the short-term.[17] A system of caps on purchases enforced by individual vendors represents a compromise between achieving a rationing effect that is to the benefit of all persons within a community and ensuring that this benefit is spread evenly throughout the community. Insofar as the state and federal government are able to distribute supplies, those supplies should be distributed on a lottery basis.

Both of the steps I have recommended are restricted to essential goods. Since the moral concerns facing price increases are triggered by the capacity of customers to engage in minimal human functioning, those goods not necessary to this purpose may be given whatever price the post-disaster market will bear. Following a disaster, for example, an individual might desperately wish to replace a damaged wide screen, high definition television. If many other persons in the local community share this desire and supplies of the product have been disrupted by the disaster, we can expect that the market price of high-end televisions will rise substantially. But, because this product is non-essential, television vendors can ethically charge whatever price the market will bear for their products.[18] While would-be customers might resent this situation, by the standards of price gouging the merchant does not act unethically.

Recall that state price gouging legislation is divided on what price increases were acceptable following a disaster and on what goods should be covered by the legislation. My account suggests that, for the vendor operating under conditions of uncertainty, equal respect for all members of a community will require: 1) Limited price increases beyond those justified by increases in costs and risk; and 2) Caps on purchases of essential goods in order to ration supplies of these goods. Neither of these restrictions should apply to persons selling non-essential goods. These guidelines will be most relevant when the pre-disaster market is reasonably successful at meeting the basic needs of all members of the community. Therefore, contextual factors make these guidelines defeasible.

OBJECTIONS

Matt Zwolinski (2008) argues against both the effectiveness of price gouging legislation and the immorality of price increases that are typically condemned as gouging. His positive argument hinges largely on the benefits created by price increases, which I have largely granted in this paper.[19] In order to strengthen my argument as to the immorality of these price increases, I will respond to two of Zwolinski's central arguments. First, I will address the "non-worseness claim" (NWC) that it cannot be morally worse to engage in a voluntary and mutually beneficial exchange than no exchange at all. Second, I will consider Zwolinski's argument that price increases do not exhibit a failure of respect for consumers.

Zwolinski asks how we can criticize vendors who engage in voluntary and mutually beneficial exchanges while we ignore those who do nothing to help the needy in disaster areas:

> On the one hand, to the extent that we hold that price gougers are guilty of mutually beneficial exploitation, we hold that they are acting wrongly even though their actions bring *some* benefit to disaster victims. On the other hand, many of *us* do *nothing* to relieve the suffering of most disaster victims, and we generally do not view ourselves as acting wrongly in failing to provide this benefit—or, at least, we do not view ourselves as acting *as* wrongly as price gougers. (Zwolinski 2008, 356–57)

This "non-worseness claim" asks why we should condemn those who help bring needed supplies into disaster areas as "gougers" when we do not condemn those who stay home, helping no one.[20] That is, how can it be morally worse to engage in a voluntary and mutually beneficial interaction than to do nothing at all?[21]

In response, I believe that we must take the long view when assessing the moral principles underlying our actions. Individual actions, such as charging high prices for essential goods or sitting on one's couch in response to a disaster, may not tell the full story as to one's responsiveness toward the basic needs of others. One is not required to respond to every disaster nor every needy person in order to live a morally praiseworthy life. However, a *pattern* of failure to respond to the needs of others can exhibit a greater level of indifference toward the basic needs of others than is exhibited through a single instance of price gouging.

Zwolinski is right to note that some of those who charge market clearing prices following a disaster might be motivated both by self-interest and the benefits created for some consumers (Zwolinski 2008, 337–68). These motives may be morally superior to those of the person motivated to enter the disaster zone purely by self-interest. My point is that the person who chooses not to enter the disaster zone may be motivated purely by self-interest or have other, morally laudable responses toward the basic needs of her fellow humans. As the non-gouger's duty of beneficence has not been specified in the way that, as I have argued, the gouger's duty has been specified, she retains leeway as to how she will discharge this duty.

In order to assess a non-gouger's underlying moral motivation, we must consider her responsiveness to others who lack access to essential goods. For example, does the non-gouger rise from her couch to help some other persons in situations of desperate need? Or is she solely moved to maximize her own welfare? In the latter case, the non-gouger can be accurately assessed as being guided by more morally problematic principles than those that guide a gouger who is motivated both by self-interest and the needs of others. The NWC, then, is false when motivations are assessed through sets of actions rather than single, morally ambiguous actions.

A second concern raised by Zwolinski also hinges on the positive consequences created by price gouging. Given that the exchanges I have been discussing are mutually beneficial and voluntary, Zwolinski questions whether placing limits on these exchanges is in keeping with respect for others:

> Exploitation might plausibly be argued to manifest a lack of respect for the personhood of the exploitee. But laws against price gouging both manifest and encourage similar or greater lack of respect. They manifest a lack of respect for both merchants and customers by preventing them from making the autonomous choice to enter into economic exchanges at the market-clearing price. They send the signal, in effect, that *your* decision that this exchange is in your best interest is unimportant, and that the law will decide for you what sorts of transactions you are allowed to enter into. (Zwolinski 2008, 352–53)

That is, if consumers are not forced into these exchanges—and in fact they desperately seek them out—how can it be consistent with respect for others' choices to rule them out of bounds?

I have argued that proper respect for the needs of others demands that vendors moderate their price increases and engage in non-price rationing. This argument does not hold that agreements between vendors and consumers at market clearing prices are coercive. Rather, vendors ought to limit their price increases and legislators ought to pass laws requiring vendors to do so. These restrictions aim to aid the entire post-disaster community while distributing essential goods more equitably. My claim is not that individual freedom is unimportant, but that the market may not support freedom equitably following a disaster.

Zwolinski defends his position by noting, "Price gougers treat their fellow human beings as traders, rather than as brothers and sisters in the Kingdom of Ends. But to treat someone as a trader is still a far cry more respectful than treating him as an object" (Zwolinski 2008, 359). Perhaps so, but I have argued that a disaster disrupts the market in a way that makes it *inappropriate* to treat one's fellow human beings as traders. When the market is functioning under normal conditions, it can be appropriate to treat one's fellow humans as traders in market transactions, especially in the presence of an adequate social safety net. This is so because the institution of the market creates a space in which self-interest and hard bargaining enhances the freedom of all persons. Following a disaster, however, the market fails to behave in this way over the short-term, pricing the poorest members of the community out of the market for essential goods.

Treating one's fellow humans as traders is appropriate under conditions where trading in the market enables efficient and reasonably equitable access to essential goods. The justification for treating others as traders, however, is not that persons are appropriately understood as purely self-interested actors who are disinterested as to others' capacity to obtain essential goods. Rather, treating others as traders is one way, in the setting of a well-functioning market, to help others to efficiently and reasonably equitably obtain those essential goods. The conditions where it is appropriate to treat others as traders can break down because trading is merely instrumentally valuable toward respecting others as vulnerable persons in need of support in order to engage in minimal human functioning. When market conditions change so that trading no longer serves to support reasonably equitable access to these goods and where other, more equitable options are available, then treating others as traders is inconsistent with respect for persons as rational but vulnerable agents.

A choice between market clearing and pre-disaster prices represents a false dichotomy. Instead, I have argued, price increases following a disaster should be limited to reflect changes in risks and business costs to the vendor and perhaps a small premium as well. These price increases should also be coupled with caps on purchases of essential goods by consumers. I have provided an argument for why we should attempt to adopt legislation that protects consumers in a post-disaster market and am optimistic that creative solutions to the shortcomings of existing legislation can be found.[22] However, I also grant the possibility that these policies cannot be reflected in price gouging legislation without being so detailed as to restrict efficient increases in supplies of essential goods or so flexible as to be capricious in their application, as Zwolinski charges.

But, if not, my argument still stands as a guide for the behavior of individual vendors whose actions can be more sensitive to local context. Raising prices on essential goods can fail to express appropriate respect for others. Even if it is not illegal to raise prices on essential goods following a disaster, I have argued that it can be immoral to do so. While on the macro level price gouging legislation might undermine the price signaling effect needed to address the needs of the community affected by the disaster, individual vendors can, and should, choose to constrain their prices to reasonable levels out of an interest in the basic needs of all those around them.

CONCLUSIONS

If my account of the wrongness of price gouging is correct, it supports three major conclusions. First, the moral wrongs associated with price gouging should be understood generally as failures of respect for others. Vendors who ration scarce essential goods according to ability to pay undercut the goal of equitable access to essential goods within their community. This failure of respect takes place in a setting where the vendor owes a specified duty of beneficence to her customers and alternative means of achieving price signaling (through modest price increases) and rationing (through purchasing caps) are available.

Second, price gouging is only possible in transactions involving some good essential to living a distinctly human life. Price increases for diamonds, for example, are not instances of price gouging under my account. Moral wrongs, such as unfairness, may accompany price increases for non-essential goods. These wrongs, however, are distinct from the wrongs I have ascribed to price gouging.

Finally, the potential for price gouging will depend on the extent and strength of non-market social institutions for distributing essential goods. If these institutions are in place prior to a disaster and survive that event, price gouging is unlikely to occur even if vendors freely raise their prices in the post-disaster market. Individuals are more highly susceptible to price gouging in communities where entitlements to essential goods are weak or non-existent. Therefore, the moral wrong of price gouging cannot be reduced merely to price increases for essential goods following a disaster, even if these prices cannot be justified by increased costs.

The general shape of anti-gouging legislation gives a good rule of thumb for avoiding gouging. Price gouging legislation should allow for price increases justified by changes in the costs and risks of doing business. Otherwise, price increases should be limited and vendors should be required to ration their goods by placing caps on the number of purchases of essential goods. These limits on the market should be triggered by declarations of a state of emergency and limited to essential goods. Price controls should be restricted to the area affected by the disaster rather than entire states (Rapp 2005/2006). If price gouging legislation along these lines should prove to be deeply impractical or has not been enacted in a community, vendors should still constrain their market transactions along these lines.

Many cases of what are sometimes popularly called gouging are not morally problematic under my account nor considered cases of gouging. We should expect price increases on many goods following a disaster and many, if not most, of these increases will be justified by increases in cost, supply disruptions, and increased risk. However, in the most egregious cases, price increases cannot be justified in these ways, giving justification to the charge of price gouging as representing a kind of moral wrong.

These observations depend on an account of price gouging as a kind of failure of respect for others, but I hope to have shown that this account tracks well with widespread intuitions as to when and why certain price increases are morally problematic while revealing where those intuitions are unjustified. In practice, determining whether gouging has taken place will require great attention to local context, as shaped by the goal of equitable access to goods that meet the essential needs of consumers.

NOTES

1. I am grateful to Robert Leider, Maggie Little, Daniel Levine, Leigh Anne Palmer, David Skarbek, Justin Weinberg, and Matt Zwolinski for their extensive comments on earlier versions of this paper. I am also thankful to the participants in a presentation of an earlier version of this paper at the 2008 APA Pacific Division Annual Meeting.

2. For example, a proposed federal anti-gouging law bans "taking unfair advantage of the circumstances related to an energy emergency to increase prices unreasonably." See http://thomas.loc.gov/cgi-bin/bdquery/z?d110:h.r.01252: (accessed May 28, 2008). New York's anti-gouging law (NY GEN BUS S 396-r) is justified by the need to prevent vendors "from taking unfair advantage of consumers during abnormal disruptions of the market." In broader terms, *USA Today* condemns gougers as "Vultures" (McCarthy 2004). Similarly, Florida governor Charlie Crist complained that "It is astounding to me, the level of greed that someone must have in their soul to be willing to take advantage of someone suffering in the wake of a hurricane" (Jacoby 2004, F11).

3. I will use the term "disasters" to include any event that creates physical damage to a discrete area, disrupting the normal functioning of the market. These events include both natural disasters such as hurricanes and man-made disasters such as terrorist attacks.

4. See, for example, Joseph Treaster (2004).

5. For a helpful summary of US anti-gouging laws, see Skarbek & Skarbek 2008.

6. See, for example, Michigan (Mich. Stat. Ann. §445.903(z)), Missouri (15 CSR §60-8.030), and Texas (Tex. Bus & Com. Code §17.46(b)(27)).

7. See Geoffrey Rapp (2005/2006).

8. For example, California, Connecticut, the District of Columbia, Hawaii, and Mississippi make general prohibitions against price increases. California prohibits price increases generally for consumer goods and services (Cal. Pen. Code §396), Connecticut includes any item (Conn. Gen. Stat. §42-230), DC any merchandise or service (D.C. Code §28.4101 to 4102), Hawaii any commodity (Haw. Rev. Stat. §209-9), and Mississippi all goods and services (Miss. Code Ann. §75-24-25).

9. See generally the American Bar Association's summary of state legislation.

10. When explicit justification for anti-gouging legislation is given, references to "unfair" prices is most common. The language of unconscionable and gross price increases, drawn from the common law tradition, are frequent as well (Rapp 2005/2006).

11. If one feels that "price gouging" can appropriately apply to the champagne example, we can discriminate between two senses of price gouging. "Fairness gouging" can apply to price increases on all goods following a disaster or other market disruption while "needs gouging" will be limited to price increases on essential goods. As I argue, "needs gouging" is at the heart of the moral wrong that is typically associated with gouging.

12. The goods essential to minimal human functioning are supported through various non-essential goods. For this reason, I will also discuss non-essential goods like electrical generators, gasoline, and ice that are, in many communities, instrumental to the durability of essential goods such as food, water, and adequate shelter. Insofar as the essential goods are relevant to the wrongness of gouging, these non-essential goods will be relevant as well.

13. Of course, disagreement will take place as to what corresponding regulatory environment best supports this freedom-enhancing function.

14. This point has been made by authors as diverse as Milton Friedman (1962) and Amartya Sen (1999).

15. There is a long history within Judeo-Christian and Islamic thought condemning excessive price increases against vulnerable populations. These restrictions are motivated by concerns about oppression of the weak. Consider, for example, Leviticus 25:14: "And if thou sell ought unto thy neighbor, or buyest ought of thy neighbor's hand, ye shall not oppress one another." More generally, see Brewer 2007, 1104–06.

16. In some cases, even wealthy persons following a disaster may not have the immediately available resources to afford price increases on essential goods. When referencing "the wealthy" I intend those with the resources available to afford price increases rather than those with the greatest savings and assets within a community. My thanks to an anonymous reviewer for pointing out this ambiguity.

17. Moreover, such a system, even if it could be established, would likely create or exacerbate a black market in

essential goods (Rockoff 2002). See also Abhi Raghunathan (2005).

18. By the standards of fairness, the price *might* be morally problematic. At the least, however, the vendor does not gouge his customer by the standard I am proposing.

19. There is some disagreement on this point, however. Geoffrey Rapp (2005/2006, 553–59) argues that anti-gouging laws are economically justified in two ways. First, they help preserve hard currency reserves when a disaster or terrorist attack disrupts electronic payment systems such as ATMs. Second, they counteract the effects of pricing irrationality that prevent efficient pricing during market disruptions.

20. Zwolinski discusses price increases among vendors who bring goods into the post-disaster market whereas I have focused my discussion on vendors with goods already in the market. The risks and opportunity costs faced by outsiders may be different from those of locals, meaning that outsiders and locals may be justified in offering different prices for their goods based on different levels of risk and cost. I discuss the relevance of vendors' risks and costs to post-disaster prices in the previous section. The source of these goods, however, is not relevant to the basic moral wrong of price gouging.

21. Alan Wertheimer (1996, 289–93) describes the non-worseness claim as holding that an interaction Y between A and B cannot be morally worse than no interaction at all if Y makes both A and B better off when compared to a baseline of no interaction. In other words, the NWC denies the possibility that a mutually beneficial exploitative interaction can be morally worse than no interaction at all.

22. Reforms and standardization of existing legislation have been suggested. Anita Ramasastry (2005) argues that anti-gouging legislation should give clear guidance as which price increases are impermissible while allowing increases that reflect changes in costs and risks for vendors. See also, Page & Cho 2006.

BIBLIOGRAPHY

Anderson, Elizabeth. 1993. *Value in Ethics and Economics.* Cambridge, MA: Harvard University Press.

———. 2004. Ethical assumptions in economic theory: Some lessons from the history of credit and bankruptcy. *Ethical Theory and Moral Practice,* 7: 347–60.

Brewer, Michael. 2007. Planning disaster: Price gouging statutes and the shortages they create. *Brooklyn Law Review,* 72: 1101–37.

Elliott, Janet. 2008. Two hotels face lawsuits for raising rates. *The Houston Chronicle* (October 3).

Federal Trade Commission. 2006. *Investigation of Gasoline Price Manipulation and Post-Katrina Gasoline Price Increases.* http://www.ftc.gov/reports/060518PublicGasolinePricesInvestigationReportFinal.pdf.

Friedman, Milton. 1962. *Capitalism and Freedom.* Chicago: University of Chicago Press.

Hayek, Friedrich. 1945. The use of knowledge in society. *American Economic Review,* 35(4): 519–30.

Hill, Thomas. 1991. *Autonomy and Self-Respect.* New York: Cambridge University Press.

Jackson Sun. 2008. Go after those who may be price gouging. *The Jackson Sun* (September 17).

Jacoby, Jeff. 2004. Bring on the "price gougers." *The Boston Globe* (August 22): F11.

Kittay, Eva. 1999. *Love's Labor: Essays on Women, Equality, and Dependency.* New York: Routledge.

McCarthy, Michael. 2004. After the storm come the vultures. *USA Today* (August 20): 6B.

Nussbaum, Martha. 2000. *Women and Human Development.* New York: Cambridge University Press.

Page, Edward, & Cho, Min. 2006. Price gouging 101: A call to Florida lawmakers to perfect Florida's price gouging law, *Florida Bar Journal,* 80: 49–52.

Raghunathan, Abhi. 2005. South Florida shortages fuel black market. *St. Petersburg Times* (October 29): 1B.

Ramasastry, Anita. 2005. Assessing anti-price-gouging statutes in the wake of hurricane Katrina: Why they're necessary in emergencies, but need to be rewritten. *Findlaw* (September 15). Available at http://writ.news.findlaw.com/ramasastry/20050916.html.

Rapp, Geoffrey. 2005/2006. Gouging: Terrorist attacks, hurricanes, and the legal and economic aspects of post-disaster price regulation. *Kentucky Law Journal,* 94: 535–60.

Reader, Soran. 2003. Distance, relationship and moral obligation. *The Monist,* 86: 367–81.

Rockoff, Hugh. 2002. Price controls. In David R. Henderson (Ed.), *The Concise Encyclopedia of Economics.* Indianapolis: Liberty Fund, Inc. Available at http://www.econlib.org/library/Enc/PriceControls.html.

Rushing, J. Taylor. 2004. Storms stir up price gouging. *Florida Times-Union* (September 18): A-1.

Satz, Debra. 2007. Liberalism, economic freedom, and the limits of markets. *Social Philosophy and Policy,* 24: 120–40.

Sen, Amartya. 1992. *Inequality Reexamined.* Cambridge, MA: Harvard University Press.

———. 1999. *Development as Freedom.* New York: Knopf.

Skarbek, Brian R., & Skarbek, David B. 2008. The price is right: Regulation, reputation, and recovery. *Dartmouth Law Journal,* 6(2): 235–76.

Smith, Adam. 1976 (1776). *An Inquiry into the Nature and Causes of the Wealth of Nations.* Ed. R. H. Campbell, Andrew Skinner, and W. B. Todd. Oxford: Oxford University Press.

Snyder, Jeremy. 2008. Needs exploitation. *Ethical Theory and Moral Practice,* 11: 389–405.

Taylor, Jerry. 2005. Gouge on. *National Review Online* (September 2).

Treaster, Joseph. 2004. With storm gone, Floridians are hit with price gouging. *New York Times* (August 18): A1.

Waldron, Jeremy. 2003. Who is my neighbor?: Humanity and proximity. *The Monist,* 86: 333–54.

Wall Street Journal. 2005. In praise of "gouging." *Wall Street Journal* (September 7): A16.

Wertheimer, Alan. 1996. *Exploitation.* Princeton, NJ: Princeton University Press.

Zwolinski, Matt. 2008. The ethics of price gouging. *Business Ethics Quarterly,* 18: 347–78.

MATT ZWOLINSKI

Price Gouging, Non-Worseness, and Distributive Justice

2009

Price gouging tends to evoke from humane and decent people an immediate and overwhelming sense of repugnance.[1] Most people have a strong sense that price gouging involves a kind of predatory behavior—a ruthless satisfaction of individual greed at the expense of the vulnerable—and that it must therefore constitute a serious moral wrong. Indeed, recent research in moral psychology suggests that this kind of "gut" reaction against price gouging might be very deeply rooted in us indeed. Instinctive and powerful reactions against the exploitation of the vulnerable may have served our early ancestors well by promoting the cohesion and survival of the small groups in which they lived.[2] But while reliance on automatic emotional reactions might have worked well for our primitive ancestors, such reactions are of little help in coming to a sophisticated and subtle understanding of the many and varied questions bearing on the morality of price gouging.[3] For such an understanding requires us to do more than simply decide whether "price gouging" is "good" or "bad." It requires us to discriminate among the many forms price gouging can take—between, for instance, an established merchant's raising prices to cover increased costs of supplies and risk, and a low-level entrepreneur who is drawn by the lure of high profits to begin selling items for the first time in the wake of a disaster. And it requires us to discriminate between

Matt Zwolinski, "Price Gouging, Non-Worseness, and Distributive Justice." *Business Ethics Quarterly* 19 (2) (April 2009): 295–306. By permission of *Business Ethics Quarterly.*

the many different kinds of moral evaluations we can make of price gouging—whether it ought to be morally permissible or impermissible; whether it is morally praiseworthy, morally blameworthy, or merely morally tolerable; whether we have good moral reasons to prohibit it by law or by social pressure; and so forth. Each of these questions in turn raises a host of differing and difficult subsidiary questions that require both careful empirical research and thoughtful philosophical analysis to fully address.

Fortunately, Jeremy Snyder's paper on the subject contains no shortage of precisely this sort of thoughtful analysis.[4] Although his conclusions differ in some ways from my own,[5] he nevertheless provides a carefully argued case for the immorality of price gouging, while at the same time demonstrating an admirable sensitivity to the many morally attractive features of a free-market price system. Still, in spite of its many strengths, there are some points at which Snyder's position is less clear or less well-defended than it might be. Rather than continuing to sing the praises of what is generally a very fine piece of work, then, I shall focus my comments on what I take to be two problematic areas of his paper—first, Snyder's rejection of the non-worseness claim appears to be based on a misunderstanding of the kind of moral objects to which that principle is meant to apply; and second, Snyder's appeal to considerations of distributive justice and equal respect for persons is flawed insofar as it rests on two false assumptions—that price gouging undermines equitable access to vital goods, and that a regime in which price gouging is banned promotes equitable access. I will conclude with some brief comments on how Snyder's evaluation of price gouging compares with my own.

1. THE NON-WORSENESS CLAIM

One of Snyder's major objections to my argument stems from my use of the "nonworseness claim" (NWC) to defend price gouging against the charge that it is wrongfully exploitative. NWC, as I described it, holds that "in cases where *A* has a right not to transact with *B*, and where transacting with *B* is not worse for *B* than not transacting with *B* at all, then it cannot be seriously wrong for *A* to engage in this transaction, even if its terms are judged to be unfair by some external standard" (Zwolinski 2008: 357). If the NWC is true, then it is hard to see how standard cases of price gouging can be serious moral wrongs. After all, most of us would think that an individual who could sell generators to victims of a disaster but chose not to do so would be acting within his rights (even if we also believe that she would be acting less than fully virtuously), and it also seems clear (Snyder himself concedes this [Snyder 2009: 277–78]) that those who buy from price gougers at inflated prices are nevertheless better off as a result than they would have been had the transaction not taken place at all. So, since gouging someone is better for them than neglecting them, and we have a moral right to neglect them, must we not therefore have a moral right to gouge them as well? How could gouging possibly be worse than neglect?

Snyder takes issue with this argument by holding that it fails when "motivations are assessed through sets of actions rather than single, morally ambiguous actions" (Snyder 2009: 288). Price gougers might indeed be acting in ways that help their customers, Snyder concedes, but they might be doing so only out of the vicious motive to extract as much profit as possible out of people in desperate need. Of course, they *might* be doing it out of a sense of morally virtuous beneficence as well. We can't tell just by looking at one action in isolation. To determine whether a person is properly motivated by a responsiveness to the needs of others, we need to look at their pattern of action as a whole, and not just one isolated instance.

This reasoning seems correct, as far as it goes. But it is not clear what lesson Snyder thinks he can draw from it. At times, Snyder writes as though he is making a point about the *moral character* of the price gouger and what it takes to lead a "morally praiseworthy life" (Snyder 2009: 287). With this point I am in full agreement. One's moral character is a matter of one's general disposition to see the needs of others as reason-giving and to respond appropriately to those reasons. And the act of price gouging is too morally ambiguous for us to read this disposition (or its absence) off of it. But NWC is not a thesis about moral character, it is a thesis about the wrongness of moral *acts*. And this is importantly different. Vicious people can perform morally permissible actions. Think, for instance, of Kant's shopkeeper who returns the correct change to a naive customer *only* out of a selfish concern for his own reputation and long-term profit. If he could be sure he could steal a penny from a child's change and get away with it, he would, but prudence dictates restraint. Such a person has a bad moral character. But the act he is performing—giving the child back her correct change—is perfectly innocent. The distinction between these two moral assessments becomes clear, and especially important to recognize, when we think about their respective implications for third parties. If we see a person—vicious or innocent—performing a morally *impermissible* action then, all else being equal, we should try to stop him, either as individuals or perhaps through the collective institutions of the state. But there is no comparable reason for us to try to stop someone from doing that which it is morally permissible for her to do, even if the person doing it is morally vicious. Her moral viciousness might give us *other* kinds of reason for action. We might have reason to censure her and get her to see the intrinsic value of all persons. And, in the case of Kant's shopkeeper, we might be very hesitant to patronize her store for fear that circumstances in the future will *not* always tip the scales of self-interest toward the side of honesty. But we do not have reason to interfere with her performance of a morally permissible act, or even to morally condemn the act, though we might have reason to morally condemn the agent.

Thus, Snyder's concerns about NWC do not give us reason to prohibit price gouging, or even condemn it. For all his arguments show (correctly, I think) is that price gouging can sometimes be done by morally vicious people. They do not show that the act of price gouging itself is morally impermissible. And that is all that my use of NWC was ever meant to deny.

2. DISTRIBUTIVE JUSTICE

One of the most common criticisms of price gouging, and one which is central to Snyder's argument as I understand it, is that it leads to vital resources being distributed in a morally objectionable way. Because price gouging involves charging a higher than normal price for goods, it disadvantages those who are poor relative to those who are well off. According to Snyder, price gouging thus undermines equitable access to essential goods, and thereby manifests a lack of equal respect for persons (Snyder 2009: 280).

However, the claim that price gouging undermines equitable access to goods is problematic for two reasons. First, it is the *emergency* that undermines equitable access, not whatever price gouging may occur in response to that disaster. Prior to the emergency, there is generally a well-functioning market in food, water, and other vital goods that generally ensures that all who need these goods will be able to purchase them. Emergencies lead to either a sharp increase in the demand for, or a sharp decrease in the supply of, these goods, and it is *this fact* that undermines equitable access. When supply and demand are radically altered so that there are not enough goods to go around, *no* method of distribution will produce equitable access—at least not at levels sufficient to meet people's needs.[6] Some people will get the goods, and others will not.

This is true of all methods of distribution, including Snyder's proposed method involving legislatively imposed caps on both the price of essential goods and on the amount of those goods that any consumer can purchase. Such a method of distribution, Snyder says, "mimic[s] a lottery for essential goods, treating all persons as equally deserving of the goods essential to basic human functioning" (Snyder 2009: 285). But the lottery metaphor, while apt in its characterization of a system of this sort, is puzzling as a way of highlighting the alleged distributive justice of such a system. For a lottery has seemed to many—most memorably to John Rawls—the paradigm case of moral arbitrariness (Rawls 1971: 74). In a lottery, some will obtain goods, some will not, and the difference between the two is nothing more than brute luck. In Snyder's lottery-like system, people will likewise be divided into "Haves" and "Have-Nots," and the difference between them will be based on who manages to get in line before supplies run out. This may not be *entirely* a matter of luck—perhaps it gives an edge to the perceptive, or those with a lot of time on their hands to stand in line. But it can hardly be said to be a system that distributes in accordance with any characteristic of great moral significance.

Furthermore, the sense in which it can be said to be a system that treats people as "equals" is at best a highly attenuated one. Because the context in which such a system operates is one where demand greatly exceeds supply, it is highly unlikely that the result of such a system will be equal units of vital goods being distributed to each person. For non-divisible goods like generators and radios, there will simply be no alternative to some people getting the good while others go away empty-handed. Other goods like ice could theoretically be divided into equally sized units for each person. But such a proposal is rife with practical difficulties. What if the portions of the good, once equally divided, are too small to be of any practical use? A bag of 300 ice cubes equally divided among 300 people is almost infinitely less useful than the same bag of ice in one person's hands. How is the relevant "community" among which equal distribution is to take place to be defined? How are shopkeepers to determine what an equal unit of the good should be? And, most significantly, what sort of restrictions are to be put on the use to which people's shares of the good may be put? Will people be allowed to sell their goods to others—even though this would be certain to undermine equitable access?[7] Or will such secondary markets be prohibited?

The only kind of equality that Snyder's system can hope to achieve, then, is equality of *opportunity* to access vital goods. But this too, on closer examination, turns out to be less satisfying from a moral perspective than we might have hoped for. For in reality, opportunity under Snyder's proposed system will *not* be equal. Even if the system runs perfectly, those who show up first to a vendor will have a better opportunity than those who show up later. And in reality, rationing systems like the one proposed are often subject to corruption that favors "insiders"—those with a personal, religious, ethnic, or other connection to those with resources or the power to affect their distribution.[8] It is true that nothing in Snyder's proposed system directly makes access to vital goods contingent on wealth, so with respect to *that* variable opportunity may be said to be equal. But in reality, and with respect to other equally if not more arbitrary variables, opportunity will not be equal.

Finally, it is worth noting that while Snyder's proposed distributive mechanism seeks to mimic while improving upon the *allocative* function of prices, it makes *no* effort to mimic their equally if not more important *signaling* function.[9] Prices that increase and decline in response to changes in supply and demand are important not only to allocate scarce resources among competing uses, but to signal when too much or too little social resources are being invested in a particular activity. In particular, the high prices that vital goods like water, sandbags, and hotel rooms command in the wake of a disaster signal to entrepreneurs to provide *more* of these goods, and indicate that larger-than-normal profits can be made by doing so. Post-disaster high prices thus convey both the *information* that increased supply is needed, and the *incentive* to provide that additional supply. But in so doing, high prices provide their own best corrective—as profit-seeking entrepreneurs rush to reap the windfall profits that the radically altered balance of supply and demand makes possible, they increase supply and in doing so drive the price down to something approximating its pre-disaster equilibrium. This means that the window of opportunity during which price gouging can occur is narrow, *but only if individuals are free to set prices as they see fit.*

This point is crucial. No one, not even those of us who argue that price gouging is morally permissible, thinks that price gouging is unqualifiedly *good* in the sense of being something that would occur in an ideal world. Cases of price gouging occur in circumstances of desperate need and terrible suffering. And in the short run, price gouging is just one more allocative mechanism among others, with the result that some people's needs—often the needs of the poorest and most vulnerable—will go unmet. But policies and moral injunctions that prevent prices from rising freely in the wake of a disaster do not diminish the desperation of the short run; they simply make it harder to move past that short run into a period of recovery. This might not be the case if we could rely on all people to act on the principles of beneficence that Snyder enjoins. And indeed, one of the most heartening aspects of some of the recent natural disasters in the United States has been the extent to which beneficence *has* been effective in delivering vital goods and services to those who so desperately need them. But it is probably a permanent feature of the human condition that there will always be less beneficence to go around than is needed. And in such a condition we would do well to take as much advantage as we can of the market's ability to channel individual self-interest toward socially desirable ends. In some cases, as is demonstrated in the response of Wal-Mart and Home Depot to Hurricane Katrina, even narrow self-interest will not lead to price gouging, and this is a happy result.[10] But where it does, we should recognize that gouging ought to be tolerated not as an end in itself, but merely as a method of making a very bad short-run situation less bad (by conserving scarce resources and allocating them effectively) and also of making that short run as short as possible (by providing incentives to increase supply).

3. CONCLUSION

Despite the concerns raised above, Snyder's ultimate position on the morality of price gouging does not seem to be too distant from my own. We both believe that price increases in the wake of a disaster can, in some circumstances, be not only morally permissible but positively morally desirable insofar as they serve to promote the interests of those suffering in the wake of a disaster. And we both believe that under other circumstances, price gouging can be wrongfully exploitative. The main differences between our views seem to be two: we differ regarding the precise conditions under which price gouging becomes wrongfully exploitative, and we differ regarding the desirability of the legal regulation of price gouging.

On the first of these differences, Snyder's position is somewhat unclear. He states that some "price increases condemned as gouging are morally innocent at worst and, more often, create a positive and morally praiseworthy benefit for all concerned" (Snyder 2009: 277). They do this, he notes, in many of the ways I discussed in my own paper: they aid "in the conservation of scarce goods by making it more likely that they will be purchased by those who place the greatest value on them" (Snyder 2009: 278), they send signals which lead "other suppliers into the market, quickly increasing supplies of essential goods" (Snyder 2009: 278), they provide an incentive to merchants to "increase supplies of essential goods prior to the [disaster]" (Snyder 2009: 278), and they serve as a "fair reward for the efforts and risks undertaken by vendors" (Snyder 2009: 278). And Snyder seems to indicate that insofar as price increases are necessary to serve these morally praiseworthy goals, they are morally permissible, as when he writes that "price increases even beyond those justified by increased costs and risks can be justified" insofar as they increase supplies, encourage rationing, and discourage waste (Snyder 2009: 285).

The question this raises, then, is under what conditions price gouging *will not* be morally acceptable on Snyder's account. The only clue Snyder provides to an answer is that price increases will be unacceptable when they "undermine equitable access to certain, essential goods" (Snyder 2009: 279). But this is puzzling, since price increases can presumably serve the morally praiseworthy goals described above (e.g. increasing rationing, discouraging waste) while *at the same time* undermining the equitable access of individuals to those goods. Indeed, it seems likely that the only way that price increases *can* promote goals like allocative efficiency and signaling new supply is by undermining equitable access, since these price increases will operate in a context in which individuals will face dramatically different budget constraints. This suggests that we cannot hope for both equitable access and the morally attractive benefits of price increases, and it is not clear which of these Snyder's account counsels us to choose in the (possibly ubiquitous) cases of conflict.

The second difference between Snyder's account and my own is that I favor the repeal of all laws prohibiting or regulating price gouging, whereas Snyder thinks some regulation is appropriate. Here, again, it is easy to overstate the differences between our accounts. We both think, as far as I can tell, that current laws are a bad idea insofar as they prohibit many mutually beneficial exchanges that would not be objectionably exploitative. But Snyder does seem to suggest that there is some role for the legal regulation of price gouging, and that it will involve limiting permissible price increases to those necessary to promote allocative efficiency, signal new supply, and compensate for increased risk and costs to merchants (Snyder 2009: 285). Now, I actually think that Snyder provides a fairly exhaustive list of the morally praiseworthy aspects of price increases, such that somebody who knowingly increased her price beyond this level could properly be described as satisfying her individual greed with no morally redeeming side-effects. So as an account of the conditions under which price increases are *morally praiseworthy,* I don't have much to disagree with in Snyder's proposal. But as a proposal for the *legal regulation* of price gouging (or even the social regulation of price gouging in the forms of boycotts/social pressure), I have a serious problem with it. The problem is that by Snyder's standard, it is virtually impossible to know whether any given price increase is moral or immoral.[11] What percentage price increase is necessary to encourage the optimal level of rationing among one's consumers? In trying to answer this question, the merchant at least has the advantage of observing the behavior of her customers and seeing who responds in what way to a certain rate of price increase. But how will the merchant know who *should* be buying less, and who *should* be buying more? How would legislators now this? And what hope does a merchant or a legislator have—even if she is lucky enough to have a PhD in econometrics—of predicting the level of price increase necessary to attract sufficient supply to where it is needed?[12]

Thus, even if Snyder's list of morally relevant criteria is complete, it is useless as a standard of regulation because we cannot ever know if we are satisfying it. My contention is that the best hope we have of finding a price that approximates the satisfaction of these criteria is to let that price emerge through the free choices of numerous individuals in the market. This, too, is an imperfect mechanism, since actual prices do not always and necessarily reflect a proper balance of supply and demand, nor do they even purport to approximate "fair rewards" for risk and effort. Market prices, in other words, are not a perfect measure of moral significance. My claim, though, is that given the constraints in knowledge faced by those who would be charged with regulating prices, reliance on market prices in post-disaster contexts does a better job at promoting our moral values than any feasible alternative mechanism.

NOTES

1. For a discussion of the role of repugnance as a reaction to price gouging and other forms of market exchange, see Roth 2007: 43–44.

2. For an overview of the possible evolutionary origins of "deontic" moral intuitions, such as those which tend to be invoked against the permissibility of mutually beneficial exploitation, see Greene 2007; Haidt 2001; Prinz 2008.

3. They may also be less helpful in a world in which distant, impersonal relationships have replaced close-knit societies as the locus of interpersonal interaction, and in which the distant indirect and non-obvious effects of our actions have an increasingly great relative causal significance on human well-being as the direct and visible ones. On this point, see Hayek's discussion of the extended order in Hayek and Bartley 1988: chap. 1, but also the concluding sections of Greene 2007.

4. Snyder 2009.

5. See Zwolinski 2008. See also Zwolinski forthcoming.

6. Of course, one could guarantee equity of a sort with a policy that bans distribution of the good altogether. Such a policy, if effectively enforced, could result in each person getting an equitable share of nothing.

7. Here we face a problem similar to that illustrated by Robert Nozick's famous Wilt Chamberlain example (Nozick 1974: 160–64). The maintenance of an initially equal distribution will require either a prohibition on trades or continual redistribution. And since Snyder's

proposal is not to initially distribute *all* resources equally, but only to provide equal access to certain vital resources, the difficulty of maintaining equality will be even greater.

8. See, for a discussion, Alchian and Allen 1968: 95–99.

9. On this distinction, see Zwolinski 2008: 360–64.

10. Steven Horowitz has documented the response of the private sector to Hurricane Katrina, noting that in the two weeks following the disaster Wal-Mart shipped over 2500 truckloads of needed goods to Louisiana, a substantial portion of which was given away free. This quick response time was made possible by Wal-Mart's elaborate mechanisms for tracking storms before they hit in order to ensure that its stores are well stocked prior to the time that demand increases. Neither Home Depot nor Wal-Mart engaged in price gouging in the aftermath of Katrina. And while it is possible that this restraint was at least partly motivated by altruistic concerns, no doubt a large part of it was motivated by the recognition that their behavior during this highly public and emotionally charged disaster situation would affect consumers' future willingness to give them their business. For established retailers, post-disaster deals are but one move in a long series of iterated prisoners' dilemmas with customers, and in such contexts mutual cooperation is often the strategy best in accord with individual self-interest (Axelrod 1984). Or, as one Home Depot executive put it, "I can't think of a quicker way to lose customers than price gouging." See Horowitz 2008; Horowitz forthcoming.

11. The problem is that no individual or group of individuals has sufficient information to know what price would be necessary to satisfy the criteria Snyder sets out. This problem is essentially just a specific instance of the more general knowledge problem discussed by Friedrich Hayek in Hayek 1937, 1945, and elsewhere.

12. There is strong evidence that even well-trained economists are severely limited in their ability to predict how actual markets will respond to events like a change in the general price level, much less a change in the price charged by one particular merchant. See, for a discussion, Gaus forthcoming; Gaus 2007.

BIBLIOGRAPHY

Alchian, A., and W. Allen. 1968. *University Economics,* 2nd ed. New York: Wadsworth.

Axelrod, R. 1984. *The Evolution of Cooperation.* New York: Basic Books.

Gaus, G. F. 2007. "Social Complexity and Evolved Moral Principles," in *Liberalism, Conservatism, and Hayek's Idea of Spontaneous Order,* ed. P. McNamara. London: Palgrave Macmillan.

———. 2008. "Is the Public Incompetent? Compared to Whom? About What?" *Critical Review* 20(3): 291–311.

Greene, J. 2007. "The Secret Joke in Kant's Soul," in *Moral Psychology, Vol. 3: The Neuroscience of Morality: Emotion, Disease, and Development,* ed. W. Sinnott-Armstrong. Cambridge, Mass.: MIT Press.

Haidt, J. 2001. "The Emotional Dog and its Rational Tail: A Social Intuitionist Approach to Moral Judgment," *Psychological Review* 108: 814–34.

Hayek, F. A. 1937. "Economics and Knowledge," *Economica* 4: 33–54.

———. 1945. "The Use of Knowledge in Society," *American Economic Review* 35(4): 519–30.

Hayek, F. A., and W. W. Bartley III. 1988. *The Fatal Conceit: The Errors of Socialism.* Chicago: University of Chicago Press.

Horowitz, S. 2008. *Making Hurricane Response More Effective: Lessons from the Private Sector and the Coast Guard During Katrina.* Washington, D.C.: Mercatus Center.

———. 2009. "Wal-Mart to the Rescue: Private Enterprise's Response to Hurricane Katrina," *The Independent Review* 13(4): 511–528.

Nozick, R. 1974. *Anarchy, State, and Utopia.* New York: Basic Books.

Prinz, J. 2008. *The Emotional Construction of Morals.* Oxford: Oxford University Press.

Rawls, J. 1971. *A Theory of Justice,* 1st ed. Cambridge: Belknap Press.

Roth, A. 2007. "Repugnance as a Constraint on Markets," *Journal of Economic Perspectives* 21(3): 37–58.

Snyder, J. 2009. "What's the Matter with Price Gouging?" *Business Ethics Quarterly.* 19(2) (April): 275–93.

Zwolinski, M. 2008. "The Ethics of Price Gouging," *Business Ethics Quarterly* 18(3): 347–78.

———. 2010. "Price Gouging and Market Failure," in *New Essays on Philosophy, Politics & Economics: Integration and Common Research Projects,* ed. G. Gaus, J. Lamont, and C. Favor. Stanford, Calif.: Stanford University Press.